Lecture Notes in Computer Science　3414

Commenced Publication in 1973
Founding and Former Series Editors:
Gerhard Goos, Juris Hartmanis, and Jan van Leeuwen

Manfred Morari Lothar Thiele (Eds.)

Hybrid Systems: Computation and Control

8th International Workshop, HSCC 2005
Zurich, Switzerland, March 9-11, 2005
Proceedings

 Springer

Volume Editors

Manfred Morari
Swiss Federal Institute of Technology (ETH)
Automatic Control Laboratory
8092 Zurich, Switzerland
E-mail: morari@control.ee.ethz.ch

Lothar Thiele
Swiss Federal Institute of Technology (ETH)
Computer Engineering and Networks Laboratory
8092 Zurich, Switzerland
E-mail: thiele@tik.ee.ethz.ch

Library of Congress Control Number: 2005921209

CR Subject Classification (1998): C.3, C.1.m, F.3, D.2, F.1.2, J.2, I.6

ISSN 0302-9743
ISBN 3-540-25108-1 Springer Berlin Heidelberg New York

Springer is a part of Springer Science+Business Media

springeronline.com

© Springer-Verlag Berlin Heidelberg 2005
Printed in Germany

Typesetting: Camera-ready by author, data conversion by Scientific Publishing Services, Chennai, India
Printed on acid-free paper   SPIN: 11400745   06/3142   5 4 3 2 1 0

Preface

This volume contains the proceedings of the 8th Workshop on *Hybrid Systems: Computation and Control* (HSCC 2005) held in Zurich, Switzerland during March 9–11, 2005. The annual workshop on hybrid systems attracts researchers from academia and industry interested in modeling, analysis, and implementation of dynamic and reactive systems involving both discrete and continuous behaviors. The previous workshops in the HSCC series were held in Berkeley, USA (1998), Nijmegen, The Netherlands (1999), Pittsburgh, USA (2000), Rome, Italy (2001), Palo Alto, USA (2002), Prague, Czech Republic (2003), and Philadelphia, USA (2004). This year's HSCC was technically co-sponsored by the IEEE Control Systems Society.

The program consisted of 3 invited talks and 40 regular papers selected from 91 regular submissions. The program covered topics such as tools for analysis and verification, control and optimization, modeling, engineering applications, and emerging directions in programming language support and implementation.

We would like to thank the Program Committee members and reviewers for an excellent job of evaluating the submissions and participating in the online Program Committee discussions. Special thanks go to Markus P.J. Fromherz (Palo Alto Research Center, USA), Edward A. Lee (University of California, Berkeley, USA), and Pablo A. Parrilo (Massachusetts Institute of Technology, USA) for their participation as invited speakers. We are also grateful to the Steering Committee for helpful guidance and support. Many other people worked hard to make the HSCC 2005 a success. We would like to thank Frank J. Christophersen and Ernesto Wandeler, the Publicity Chairs (with the help of Urban Mäder); Martine D'Emma and Monica Fricker for local arrangements, and Frank J. Christophersen for putting together the proceedings. We would like to express our gratitude to HYCON and ARTIST, Networks of Excellence of the Sixth Framework Programme of the European Commission, for their financial support.

January 2005   Manfred Morari and Lothar Thiele

Organization

Organizing Committee

Program Co-chairs   Manfred Morari (ETH Zurich, Switzerland)
                               Lothar Thiele (ETH Zurich, Switzerland)

Local Chairs   Frank J. Christophersen (ETH Zurich, Switzerland)
                               Ernesto Wandeler (ETH Zurich, Switzerland)

Program Committee

Alberto Bemporad (University of Siena, Italy)
Albert Benveniste (IRISA/INRIA, France)
Antonio Bicchi (University of Pisa, Italy)
Vincent Blondel (Université catholique de Louvain, Belgium)
Ed Brinksma (University of Twente, The Netherlands)
Paul Caspi (VERIMAG, France)
Jennifer Davoren (University of Melbourne, Australia)
Magnus Egerstedt (Georgia Institute of Technology, USA)
Giancarlo Ferrari-Trecate (INRIA, France)
Maurice Heemels (Embedded Systems Institute, The Netherlands)
Tom Henzinger (University of California, Berkeley, USA)
João P. Hespanha (University of California, Santa Barbara, USA)
Bengt Jonsson (Uppsala University, Sweden)
Stefan Kowalewski (RWTH Aachen University, Germany)
Kim Larsen (Aalborg University, Denmark)
Edward A. Lee (University of California, Berkeley, USA)
Insup Lee (University of Pennsylvania, USA)
John Lygeros (University of Patras, Greece)
Ian M. Mitchell (University of British Columbia, Canada)
George J. Pappas (University of Pennsylvania, USA)
Ashish Tiwari (SRI, USA)
Claire J. Tomlin (Stanford University, USA)
Arjan van der Schaft (University of Twente, The Netherlands)
Jan H. van Schuppen (CWI, The Netherlands)
Long Wang (Peking University, China)

Steering Committee

Rajeev Alur (University of Pennsylvania, USA)
Bruce H. Krogh (Carnegie Mellon University, USA)
Oded Maler (VERIMAG, France)
Manfred Morari (ETH Zurich, Switzerland)
George J. Pappas (University of Pennsylvania, USA)
Anders P. Ravn (Aalborg University, Denmark)

Sponsors

HYCON, a Network of Excellence of the Sixth Framework Programme
ARTIST, a Network of Excellence of the Sixth Framework Programme

Additional Referees

Parosh Abdulla	Mehdi Gati	Oded Maler
Alessandro Alessio	Ronojoy Ghosh	Alexander Medvedev
Madhukar Anand	Nicolo Giorgetti	David Muñoz de la Peña
Ahmed Attia	Antoine Girard	Meeko Oishi
Mohamed Babaali	Luca Greco	Lucia Pallottino
Eric Badouel	Esfandiar Haghverdi	Simone Paoletti
Andrea Balluchi	Gabe Hoffmann	Mihály Petreczky
Giorgio Battistelli	Andras Horvath	Bruno Picasso
Alexandre Bayen	Jianghai Hu	Benedetto Piccoli
Pierre-Alexandre Bliman	Yerang Hur	Luis Pina
Francesco Borrelli	Inseok Hwang	Vinayak Prabhu
Peter Brende	R. Izadi-Zamanabad	Stephen Prajna
Bernard Brogliato	Pieter J.L. Cuijpers	Robin Raffard
Manuela Bujorianu	Zhijian Ji	E. Rodríguez-Carbonell
Kanat Camlibel	A. Agung Julius	Lorenzo Sella
Frank J. Christophersen	Aleksandar Lj. Juloski	Sriram Shankaran
Pieter Collins	Jorge Julvez	Oleg Sokolsky
Thao Dang	R. Kakumani	Marielle Stoelinga
Gregory Davrazos	Eric Kerrigan	Paulo Tabuada
Alexandre Donze	Gaurav Khanna	Herbert Tanner
Hidde de Jong	Jesung Kim	Nathan van der Wouw
Stefano Di Cairano	Ioannis Kitsios	Björn Victor
Dimos Dimarogonas	Tomas Krilavicius	René Vidal
Alexandre Donze	Rom Langerak	Yi Wang
Arvind Easwaran	Mircea Lazar	Steven Waslander
Aaron Evans	Andrea Lecchini	Rafael Wisniewski
Emmanuel Fleury	Didier Lime	Guangming Xie
Daniele Fontanelli	Pritha Mahata	Chenggui Yuan

Table of Contents

Coordinated Control for Highly Reconfigurable Systems

(Invited Paper)

Markus P.J. Fromherz, Lara S. Crawford, and Haitham A. Hindi

Palo Alto Research Center, 3333 Coyote Hill Road, Palo Alto, CA 94304, USA
{fromherz, lcrawford, hhindi}@parc.com
http://www.parc.com/era

Abstract. The remarkable drop in the cost of embedded computing, sensing, and actuation is creating an explosion in applications for embedded software. As manufacturers make use of these technologies, they attempt to reduce complexity and contain cost by modularizing their systems and building reconfigurable products from simpler but smarter components. Of particular interest have recently been highly reconfigurable systems, i.e., systems that can be customized, repaired, and upgraded at a fine level of granularity throughout their lifetime.

High reconfigurability is putting new demands on the software that is dynamically calibrating, controlling, and coordinating the operations of the system's modules. There is much promise in existing software approaches, in particular in model-based approaches; however, current techniques face a number of new challenges before they can be embedded in the kind of real-time, distributed, and dynamic environment found in highly reconfigurable systems. Here, we discuss challenges, solutions, and lessons learned in the context of a long-term project at PARC to bring such techniques to a highly reconfigurable paper path system.

1 Introduction

The remarkable drop in the cost of embedded computing as well as sensing and actuation hardware is creating an explosion in applications for embedded software. Yet while manufacturers are able to add ever more functionality and safety features to their products, they also struggle with the resulting complexity. Increasingly, companies attempt to reduce this complexity, decrease development time, and contain cost by modularizing their systems and building *reconfigurable products* from simpler but smarter networked components. This in turn requires new capabilities from the software that is controlling and coordinating these modules in order to provide an integrated system that is flexible, effective, robust, and safe.

As an example, consider modern high-end printers. One such product comes with about one hundred embedded processors, controlling everything from individual motors in the paper transport to image processing functions to high-level

M. Morari and L. Thiele (Eds.): HSCC 2005, LNCS 3414, pp. 1–24, 2005.

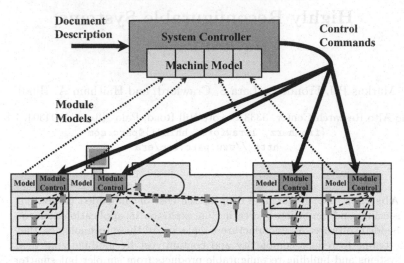

Fig. 1. A modular printing system (feeder, marking engine, and finishers) with model-based auto-configuration and control at three levels

coordination of the entire system to the interaction with the operator. Figure 1 sketches such a system, together with controllers at three different levels (system, module, and component). In this prototypical system, each of the four modules comes with a model, a declarative description of its capabilities, which is passed to the system controller at boot time. This system controller accepts a stream of document descriptions (print jobs) and, using the models, plans and schedules the necessary operations. This results in a stream of control commands to the modules, which in turn control their individual components, many of which have their own low-level controllers. The many controllers in such a system together enable the totally automated operation of a highly complex system that can be considered one of the most sophisticated robots today. These distributed controllers monitor, coordinate, calibrate, optimize, and compensate hundreds of processes with virtually no human involvement.

Today, such high-end print systems are put together from about ten to twenty feeder, marking, and finishing modules. Given the trends and motivations indicated above, it is conceivable that these numbers will increase by an order of magnitude with a corresponding reduction in module size, leading to highly reconfigurable (or hyper-modular) systems. We define a highly reconfigurable system as a modular system that can be reconfigured both in the factory and in the field, often dynamically and at a fine level of granularity. Consequently, there is no final configuration, and both hardware and software modules have to be designed without knowledge of future configurations and other modules that form the context in which a module will operate. Where so far most of a system's behaviors were confined to individual modules, with little regard to concurrent activities in other modules, now most of the behavior comes from the interaction and collaboration of networked, tightly coupled modules.

We believe that highly reconfigurable systems with coordinated control will appear in a number of domains. In some high-end cars, for example, a braking operation already involves the coordinated execution of subsystems such as engine and suspension control, in addition to the coordinated control of the brakes in all four wheels. Today, though, these controllers require careful tuning, and subsystems cannot be upgraded easily. Similarly, in the domain of assembly lines and production systems, retooling and reprogramming the robot stations for new product models sometimes takes days, if not weeks or even months, as much of the equipment works without awareness of the environment. Adding coordinating controllers that can reasons about the capabilities and coupled actions of multiple robots will allow the overall system to adapt automatically when robots are added, upgraded, or replaced over time. In other domains, there are strong incentives to modularize systems from current monolithic designs. In the space exploration domain, for example, weight is a dominant cost factor in the deployment of robots and material. Sustainable planetary missions will only be possible with modular robots and reconfigurable structures that allow for local reuse and reduced material transport across space. Overall, modular architectures promise to lower production, deployment, and maintenance costs and at the same time improve flexibility, performance, and safety. As a consequence, more emphasis will be on the coordinated control of the diverse functions of modular systems.

There is much promise in existing software approaches to address the challenges of highly reconfigurable systems. In particular, *reasoning techniques* such as model-predictive control, model-based planning and scheduling, knowledge-based diagnosis, and intelligent configuration [21] promise powerful solutions to the problems of embedded control and coordination. However, current techniques face a number of challenges that revolve around the *location and communication of knowledge* in a distributed control system, namely knowledge about the system's capabilities, its states, and its goals. In designing architectures and algorithms for such systems, we have to consider where this knowledge is generated, where it will be applied, how it is to be communicated, and how it has to be transformed in order to provide fully integrated system behavior without losing the advantages of high reconfigurability. This leads to the fundamental tension between *module autonomy* and *integrated behavior*: module controllers need to be able to make valid and efficient local decisions that are consistent and even optimal with respect to decisions of other relevant controllers.

This paper discusses challenges, solutions, and lessons learned in the context of a long-term project to embed reasoning techniques in a highly reconfigurable system. We provide a first description of our domain in Section 2. In Sections 3 and 4, we describe the top control design challenges we experienced so far, and we present a set of principles for compositional control that we found useful in addressing these challenges. In Section 5, the approach to our concrete control coordination problem is presented and discussed. We note that the discussion of design challenges and principles will necessarily be somewhat abstract. We invite the reader to jump from Section 2 to Section 5 for a concrete embodiment. We end with conclusions and thoughts about future work.

2   A Simple Domain Example

As a simple model domain, consider a linear sequence of rollers that together are transporting an object, such as a sheet of paper (Figure 2). Each roller is powered by its own independent motor, and each motor is controlled by its dedicated controller. The rollers are spaced such that a typical object will be moved by several rollers at a time, e.g., between two and six consecutive rollers depending on the object's size. For our purposes, we treat each roller with associated motor and controller as a separate transport module. We assume exactly one roller per module and call its controller the module controller. Each module further has associated sensors to detect the presence of the object. In general, all modules do not have to be identical, but instead may differ in their elements (e.g., the number of sensors) and in their behavior characteristics (e.g., velocity and acceleration limits). When used in a production line, there will be multiple parallel and interconnected material paths, with special branching modules for splitting and merging these material paths. We disregard these capabilities in this paper.

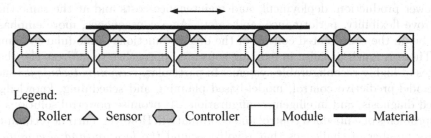

Legend:

⬤ Roller   △ Sensor   ⬡ Controller   ▢ Module   ━ Material

Fig. 2. Modular material path

At the top level of this system, a centralized planner (and scheduler) receives a series of job requests and determines the overall flow of material to produce these jobs [6, 20]. In the following, we provide a short overview of the planning level. The remainder of this paper will focus on the problem of implementing the planner's output, in particular on controlling the transport of objects along modular reconfigurable material paths.

A typical job description is a set of literals that describe an initial state and a desired output, as in the following example.

Job-23	
initial:	goal:
Location(Job-23, Source)	Location(Job-23, Destination)
Blank(Job-23)	Image(Job-23, Black)
Color(Job-23, White)	Color(Job-23, White)
Size(Job-23, A4)	Size(Job-23, A4)
¬Aligned(Job-23)	

In this example, Source and Destination are virtual locations where all sources or destinations are placed. All other literals describe initial or desired attributes of the job.

The movement of material by transports and the transformation of material by machine actions can be directly translated from the plant model into traditional logical preconditions and effects that test and modify attributes of the material. A simple example is as follows.

Print(?object)
_____
preconditions: Location(?object, Machine-2-Input)
Blank(?object)
Aligned(?object)
CanPrintSize(Machine-2, ?size)
effects: Location(?object, Machine-2-Output)
¬Location(?object, Machine-2-Input)
Size(?object,?size)
¬Blank(?object)
Image(?object, Black)
duration: 13.2 secs
allocations: M-2-Printer at ?start + 5.9 for 3.7 secs

This action model describes preconditions before the action, such as its location, and the effects of the action, such as a new location and an image. The model also specifies a duration, with the intended semantics that the logical effects become true exactly when the action's duration has elapsed. Actions can specify the exclusive use of unit-capacity resources for time intervals specified relative to the action's start or end times. For example, the Print action in the example above specifies exclusive use of the M-2-Printer from 5.9 seconds after the start of the action until 3.7 seconds later.

There may be several different sequences of actions and thus different paths that can produce a given job. A typical system may have anywhere from a few to a few hundred transport modules moving objects between the manufacturing stations. The setting is on-line in the sense that additional jobs arrive asynchronously, perhaps several per second, while plans for previous jobs are being executed.

We have implemented various temporal planners adapted to this on-line domain [6, 20]. The overall objective is to minimize the end time of the known jobs. The latest planner [20] uses state-space regression to plan each job. Temporal constraints are used to represent the order and durations of actions and to resolve resource contention. A* search is used to find the optimal plan for the job, in the context of all previous jobs [21].

We assume that each transport module runs its roller at one of several predetermined velocities that are known to the planner through their action models. For each job, the planner produces a plan that states where each object will be at what time as it is transported along its path, taking into account the capabilities of the modules as well as the plans for other objects in the material paths. The necessary control commands are then sent to the selected modules for execution at the selected times. In addition to being physically connected, module actions are further coupled through the object. In our domain, with typical velocities of 0.5 to 3 m/s and roller spacing of no more than 15 cm, the set of modules acting on the sheet is changing rapidly. Sheets are typically packed tightly in the material path, and sheet collisions are not allowed, so the tolerance for deviations from the scheduled plan is very tight. Also, even minor velocity discrepancies between the modules acting on the sheet may tear the paper. Thus, tight control and coordination of the transport modules is required.

3   Control Challenges in Highly Reconfigurable Systems

In this section, we will reflect on control challenges that we have found in building a prototype of such a highly reconfigurable system. We will focus on the issues arising out of the reconfigurability of the system. We present these challenges in three categories: compositional knowledge, hierarchical control, and distributed coordination.

3.1   Compositional Knowledge

In a compositional system, the capabilities of the system arise out of the capabilities of its constituent modules. In conventional control systems, knowledge about these capabilities is often not available on-line. Even as many components, from stepper motors to anti-lock braking systems, come with increasingly sophisticated built-in controllers, these controllers are typically closed to the outside. For reconfigurable systems, we believe that all factors relevant for interaction should be captured in *formal models* and made available in open modules in order to enable system auto-configuration. It can be surprisingly difficult, though, to describe module features and constraints in a decomposable manner.

A suggested solution from the model-based reasoning community has been the "no function in structure" principle [5], which requires that the laws of the parts of a system may not presume the functioning of the whole. Such laws may include forces on jointly controlled objects, the use of shared resources, and the timing of operations. For example, behavior constraints often restrict the interaction of different actions in the system: "if action A happens, action B cannot happen at the same time." This constraint on the second operation is expressed directly with respect to the first operation, which may or may not occur in a given configuration. A composable alternative is to express such interactions as constraints on common resources which can then be resolved by a separate coordinator: "action A (B) will require resource R", where R is a shared resource, with a resource coordinator that requires that any two actions using this resource must be sequentialized.

In a compositional system, knowledge about module capabilities often needs to be *integrated* at multiple levels of abstraction to plan, schedule, control, and coordinate the actions that will achieve the goals. A first challenge is *model composition*, i.e., integrating the module models into subsystem and system models. It is particularly difficult to integrate information about exceptions and exception handling, i.e., to capture and reason about abnormal behavior. A related challenge is the reuse of lower-level models to generate higher-level models. This *model abstraction* could start, for instance, from the detailed models of the individual modules (perhaps even their electromechanical drawings) and automatically generate the higher-level, coarser-grained models for the controllers at supervisory or coordinating levels.

Model abstraction is further complicated by its integration with the *control abstraction* at each level. For example, one abstraction from transport modules to the planning level in our domain is to assume piecewise linear trajectories, where the modules run at constant velocities, and velocities change discontinuously from one module to another when slowing down or speeding up. In reality, of course, the transport modules will likely change the velocity more gradually. While this abstraction makes the planning problem significantly more tractable, it has consequences for the interface and protocol between planner and module controller. Even if all models are written "by hand" ahead of time, these challenges in model granularity, composition semantics, and interface protocols have to be addressed.

3.2   Hierarchical Control

Compositional systems generally call for a *hierarchical control* approach, where the system's actions are monitored and directed at multiple levels of abstraction in time and space. Designing a clean architecture that integrates pre-existing module controllers and allocates the remaining control responsibilities remains a difficult and often domain-specific challenge.

One particular issue where reconfigurable systems pose both a challenge and an opportunity is reconciling the *logical* and *physical architectures* of the control system. The logical architecture specifies the roles and connections of different controllers in the system. The physical architecture specifies where those controllers are executed and what interfaces and protocols are used internally and to interface with the environment. The two architectures are typically conflated in conventional systems. In reconfigurable systems, which often have a certain redundancy in both computing and physical capabilities, the designer has the opportunity to keep the two architectures separate. In fact, with open modules, sensors and actuators may be the only elements whose roles are fixed, and controllers may be assigned their processors based on computation and communication needs. As a consequence, the control system may also become more robust, since control roles can be moved flexibly from failing to healthy components when necessary.

We found the most challenging aspect of hierarchical control to be in *exception handling*. When a transport module in our domain fails to move an object as expected, it is usually not able to correct the problem by itself. Worse, if one object is delayed, other objects may have to be delayed as well in order to avoid collisions, all while the modules try to get the objects back on track. In conventional systems with larger modules, all exception handling can be delegated to individual modules. Internal compensation is not possible with the kind of fine-grained modularity of our domain, as the object is never completely inside just one module. Instead, a module must be able to cooperate with other modules to correct problems, e.g., to try to speed up or slow down the object. In other words, any unplanned operation has to be understood immediately in context in order to take appropriate action to correct or contain the behavior.

Thus, the challenge in exception handling is how to coordinate compensation and when to escalate recovery when things go wrong. To further illustrate this point, consider some available options in our domain. Using a traffic metaphor, it could be argued that each module controller, or an "object controller", should decide how to direct objects in case of an exception, akin to a car driver who may decide to exit a highway and take an alternative route if she has been told of a traffic jam ahead. However, this would not only require endowing the controller with the full capabilities of the planner, but it would also require coordination with every object in the path. In contrast to traffic, there is often little slack in the system. Conversely, all deviations could be escalated immediately to the planner, which would require tight supervisory control of all module controllers as well as potentially constant replanning. Neither of these options is attractive (or even feasible).

3.3   Distributed Coordination

We have repeatedly emphasized the challenge of coordination among multiple controllers in what is inherently a highly distributed system. While the previous subsection primarily addressed the coordination of different control roles in a control hierarchy, the control of many tightly coupled modules also requires significant lateral coordination. This is the issue that posed the most challenges for us from a control theory point of view. One of these challenges is *observer coordination*. Since both sensors and controllers are distributed, the controllers acting on the same object ideally receive and act on the same sensor data. This requires that sensor updates are shared among all relevant controllers in a uniform fashion. For example, as an object in our model domain moves through multiple transport modules, sensors in different modules will pick up the edge transitions at different times, and this information must be communicated to all other modules in such a way that all module controllers can act on the same information. Solutions need to take into account communication issues such as protocol limitations, network delays, and bandwidth constraints. In some domains, sensor data from multiple sensors may have to be aggregated before it can be sent to the controllers. While sensor fusion is not a new issue per se, reconfigurable systems require that the algorithms are independent of the configuration and potentially compensate for differences in the available modules.

A related challenge is *controller synchronization*. In our domain, it is easiest to guarantee tight tolerances if all module controllers intrinsically behave in the same way (e.g., implement the same control approach). Such controllers will act in synchrony when presented with the same sensor data. Even this simplification of a homogeneous system, however, requires that all the controllers cooperating on the same task are synchronized. In particular, as module controllers join the coordinated action, they need to be brought up to speed, so to speak, before they can be relied upon to help control the joint process. More generally, as multiple controllers cooperate temporarily on the control of a coupled process, both their control processes and the membership process need to be coordinated. This problem becomes even more complex in a heterogeneous system, with different types of controllers, potentially acting at different time scales, where new controllers cannot learn from existing controllers as easily as in a homogeneous system.

4   Design Principles for Compositional Control

In the process of designing and implementing a control system for our domain, we have identified a number of principles as guidelines for the system's design.

Multi-scale Control. A basic principle is to decompose or aggregate control roles horizontally and vertically guided by the locality and timeliness of knowledge required for the control tasks. This suggests, for example, to separate the control of a module's actuators from the coordination of multiple modules, and it forced us to think deeply about each controller's model and interface.

Closed Loop. Another basic principle is to allow for feedback throughout the system and between all levels. This may be obvious, but it appears that many existing control systems still have a significant amount of open-loop control in both supervisory and low-level controllers. This is often acceptable for well-engineered systems where assumptions about the behavior of subsystems can be built into the controllers. Open-loop control is less suitable for highly reconfigurable systems, with its need for tight synchronization and behavior coordination among multiple modules.

Control Coordination. Where multiple modules interact in an immediate sense and require integrated feedback of their actions, new, "floating" controllers can facilitate the coordination of these modules. Such controllers are associated with a task or a process that is determined by multiple controllers and are logically "between" or "above" the modules. They may be either installed permanently or exist only temporarily and expressly to facilitate a particular task. The use of coordinating controllers was not immediately obvious to us at first. Alternatives would be to assign this role to a single supervisory controller (e.g., the planner) or to apply one of the decentralized coordination techniques commonly used in multi-agent systems (e.g., an auction mechanism). Our analysis suggested, however, that it is more efficient and more powerful to create a temporary task controller that facilitates the coordination of the individual controllers. In our domain, the result is an object controller that coordinates all aspects, from membership to synchronization, of those modules currently acting on an object. In a sense, coordination is adding a wider awareness to the self-awareness of an individual module controller, but restricts it to the task at hand.

Encapsulation. Whenever possible, we try to encapsulate knowledge about module or system behavior together with the algorithms acting on it; in other words, to keep knowledge together, to act where the knowledge is, and not to replicate the same control role at multiple levels in the control hierarchy. This means, for example, that all models for planning and scheduling in our domain are located in (or moved to) the planner, and therefore all decisions about plans, rerouting, and plan exception handling have to be made by the planner. A downside is that many deviations and changes in an execution may have to be escalated to supervisory controllers. This leads to the need for delegation.

Delegation. Delegation of control responsibility may sound like a straightforward hierarchical decomposition of goals or commands to lower and lower levels. However, with the responsibility to control we also want to delegate the responsibility to correct and compensate, within bounds. This is only practically feasible if we also give the lower-level controller sufficient insight into the context within which it will be working. For instance, the planner can give each module controller information about the current state and imminent plans for the rest of the system. To make this efficiently possible, this context information can be summarized and only contain what is relevant to the module, e.g., in form of a safe envelope around the commanded behavior. This tells the module controller how much it can deviate from the plan without violating any constraints (e.g., leading to collisions with other objects). This general principle, to communicate both goals and constraints between controllers, can be applied at all levels in the control hierarchy. Delegation can be quite demanding, since it may require substantial computation at the supervisory or coordinating control levels.

Autonomy. The goal of delegation is to allow individual controllers to monitor and determine their behavior without constant external monitoring and synchronization. Delegation, in other words, asks controllers to control their behaviors with respect to both goals and constraints, and it gives them the autonomy to act locally, and to keep changes local, while their behavior is within bounds.

Escalation. The corollary principle to delegation is escalation. This simply means that controllers report feedback when their behavior is out of bounds as defined by the constraints given by the higher-level controller. The exception is then to be handled by the level that has the necessary information and time horizon to consider all effects of the exception. Delegation, autonomy, and escalation determine a trade-off between locally fast and globally appropriate action.

Explicit Contracts. In a reconfigurable system, the joint principles of control coordination, delegation, autonomy, and escalation are best implemented through explicit representation of capability models, goals, and contexts. In our domain, module models form the contracts from module controllers to the planner of what behaviors can be executed. Conversely, goal constraints used in delegation are the contracts from the planner to the module controllers about what they are allowed to change during execution and what not.

These principles together yield a "compositionally aware" system in which knowledge about states and capabilities is shared and control is coordinated as appropriate and no more, in turn leading to a system that is efficient in its

separation of concerns and still robust in the face of real-time distributed actions
of tightly coupled modules.

5   Coordinated Control for Tightly Coupled, Reconfigurable Modules

This section describes a concrete approach to a specific application, highly modular printing systems. In these systems, as discussed above, there is a strong need
for coordinating multi-module behavior. A given sheet of paper is typically in
multiple modules at once, so in order to process the sheet correctly without damaging it, the actuators in different modules must cooperate. This coordination
is particularly important because of the fast, real-time nature of the system.

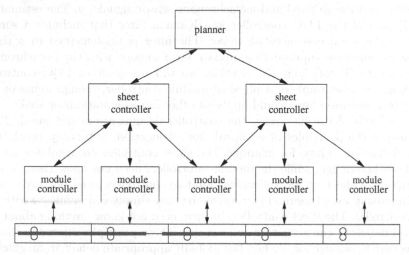

Fig. 3. Control hierarchy. The bottom portion of the diagram shows two sheets inside a
sequence of modules controlled by module controllers. Each sheet controller communicates with the module controllers acting on or about to act on its sheet (a dynamically
changing set). There is one sheet controller per sheet; a sheet controller is created when
each new sheet enters the system. At the top, the planner communicates with all the
sheet controllers

5.1   Hierarchical System Architecture

In our hierarchical approach, shown in Figure 3, the coordination task is assigned
to an entity called a *sheet controller*. There is one sheet controller per sheet; a
new controller is activated for each new sheet in the system. From the point of
view of the planner, the sheet controller serves as a proxy for the sheet control
task. The sheet controller communicates over a network with all the module
controllers currently interacting with its sheet as well as those about to interact
with it (see Figure 3). The sheet controller has three main roles:

- Interpreting the plan for the sheet, translating it into trajectories for the actuators to track, and distributing these trajectories, ensuring that the trajectories of different modules are synchronized
- Serving as a conduit of feedback information between the module controllers
- Monitoring the progress of the sheet through the system and reporting to the planner if necessary

The *module controllers*, in turn, are responsible for tracking the trajectories provided by the sheet controller and thus moving the sheet appropriately. They also have direct access to sensor information. In order to perform tracking, each module controller must maintain a model of the local (single-module) dynamics. As an example of a concrete implementation of a module controller, consider a 2-degree-of-freedom LQG controller [1]. This controller takes as input a reference signal, r, computed from the trajectory supplied by the sheet controller, and the delayed and asynchronous sensor signals, y. The estimation (model) part of the LQG controller is a Kalman filter that includes a simple model of the worst-case network delay. The filter is implemented in a time-varying measurement-update/time-update form to cope with the asynchronous measurements. Throughout this section, we will use such an LQG controller as an illustrative example of a physical module controller, though many of the approaches described here would apply to other implementations as well.

At all levels of the hierarchy, the controller designs are model-based. They make use of the principles of encapsulation, delegation, autonomy, escalation, and coordination. Thus, for example, the sheet controller encapsulates all the sheet-level knowledge, while the module controllers need not know there is such an entity as a sheet at all. Individual module controllers need not even know anything about any other module controllers; they simply communicate with the sheet controller. The sheet controller, in turn, need not know anything about the low-level details of the actuators and sensors. These principles allow the control architecture to achieve locally fast but globally appropriate behavior, an efficient separation of concerns, and robustness under tightly coupled distributed actions.

The next several sections will discuss various elements of our control and coordination approach. We will first describe the sheet controller and its roles in the system in more detail. Then, our mechanism for coordinating feedback among the modules, using the sheet controller, will be further delineated. Next, we will discuss our method for synchronizing the distributed module controllers when they first join a control action (module-module coordination). Then we will describe a method for implementing self-awareness at the module control level. Finally, we will discuss various implementation issues.

There are other control challenges in the domain of high performance copiers that we will not cover here. These include image registration, color consistency control, banding artifact reduction, and also alternative approaches to (centralized) paper path control. These are covered in the survey paper by Hamby and Gross [7] and in more detail in the references [13, 19, 4, 11].

5.2   Coordinating Control

The sheet controller is responsible for sheet-level concerns. It takes the plan received (delegated) from the planner, which is in terms of tuples of modules, operations, and times, and translates it into positions and times. It divides this trajectory into segments for the individual actuators to follow. To fulfill this responsibility, it must be aware of the machine configuration and the capabilities of the various modules and their actuators. In order for the trajectories to be trackable, the sheet controller may need to smooth the piecewise linear trajectory implied by the plan's waypoints. Since the sheet will be in multiple modules at once, the trajectories generated for different actuators will overlap in time (Figure 4). Trajectories for different actuators must be identical during the overlapping portions in order to avoid damaging the sheet. Should anything go wrong in the system that requires the sheet to be rerouted, the sheet controller must accept updated plans from the planner, create updated trajectories accordingly, and communicate the changes to the module controllers.

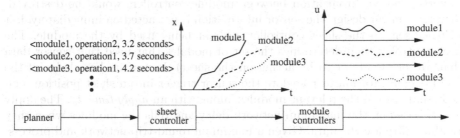

Fig. 4. Plan translation and distribution by the sheet controller. The planner sends a plan in the form of a list of tuples to the sheet controller, which converts it into trajectories for the modules to track. During times of overlap, the trajectories are identical up to positional translation. The module controllers track the identical trajectories, producing synchronized actuator outputs

The sheet controller also monitors the progress of the sheet. It receives sensor messages from the control modules and uses these to maintain an internal model of the sheet's progress. If something goes wrong, this kind of self-awareness allows it to anticipate unacceptable errors and notify the planner. The definition of an "unacceptable" error can be supplied by the planner based on the separation between neighboring sheets; this knowledge provides a level of context awareness and is important for successful delegation and autonomy. Additionally, since the sheet controller is monitoring the sheet progress in the context of the system configuration, it can identify where in the system (in which module) the error has occurred. It could then use its sensor information to distinguish between some different types of problems (e.g., a paper jam vs. a simple delay). This information may be useful for escalation, particularly should the system need to reconfigure to avoid blocked or damaged modules.

Finally, the sheet controller serves as a clearinghouse for sensor information from the modules. Each module has edge sensors that detect when the leading or trailing edge of the sheet crosses them. Since multiple modules are acting on the sheet at once, they all need access to this sensor information in order to accurately track the desired sheet trajectories given them by the sheet controller. In order to preserve the encapsulation of knowledge, so that the module controllers need not know about each other, the modules send their sensor data to the sheet controller, which then distributes it appropriately.

5.3   Distributed Feedback

In a tightly coupled system sharing sensor information over a network, timing is crucial in coordinating the distributed feedback. When a sheet sensor is tripped, for example, the module local to that sensor has access to the information immediately. If the module were to use the sensor data right away, it would update its internal model (observer), and its controller would respond well before the other modules could do so, as they must receive the sensor information over the network. The synchronization between module controllers would be destroyed. Therefore, in our design the sensor information is not acted on immediately, but is rather sent to the sheet controller without being used by the module. The sheet controller then determines the set of modules that need that sensor data (that are or are about to be acting on the sheet). It uses its knowledge of the machine configuration to translate the sensor trigger into a sheet position, and sends that data to the relevant modules, along with an *apply time*, t_a. The apply time is based on the maximum network delay and tells the modules when they are allowed to use the data. Given a maximum round-trip network and processing delay (module controller to sheet controller to module controller) d and a sensor trigger time t_s, $t_a = t_s + d$. The modules, including the one that originated the sensor message, wait until t_a to use the sensor data, at which time they all update their internal models simultaneously, preserving their coordination (see Figure 5). This approach assumes that the modules and the sheet controller all have synchronized clocks, so that t_a is the same globally for all modules.

Because the sensor data is not used until the apply time, it is delayed when it is incorporated into the module controllers' observers or other models. The module controllers must therefore save a history of their local state and control values for an amount of time d, so that they can roll back to the appropriate time to apply the sensor data. Thus, at time t_a, the module controller must perform the following steps:

1. Access the saved state from time $t_a - d = t_s$, $x(t_s)$, and update it with the new sensor data. In our example LQG controller, this update consists of performing the measurement update portion of the Kalman filter.
2. Evolve the state forward from time t_s until time t_a to obtain $x(t_a)$, using the control history, and update the state history accordingly. This step means performing multiple time updates in the Kalman filter setting.

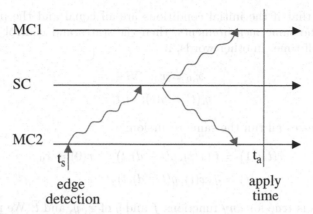

Fig. 5. Diagram illustrating apply time. An edge detection occurs at a sensor in module 2, whose module controller sends that information over the network to the sheet controller. The sheet controller translates the edge detection event into a sheet position and sends the data back to all module controllers involved with the sheet. The module controllers wait until the apply time to make use of the sheet position data

5.4   Distributed Control Synchronization

Feedback coordination, as just described, keeps the module controllers synchronized once they are running. In our system, however, new controllers are constantly being added to (and leaving) the coordinated control action as the sheet passes through the system. Thus, there is also the issue of bringing each new controller into the control action appropriately; new controllers must synchronize with the ones already in the control action. Our approach has been to synchronize the internal controller state directly. The challenge is in obtaining the current state in the presence of network delays. Here, we briefly outline the mechanism from Hindi, et al. [9]. Similar work has recently appeared in other areas, notably networked computer games [14, 17].

Consider a set of control processes $\{p_0, \dots, p_{n-1}\}$, where each process p_i runs the following state based iterations over time $t = 0, 1, 2, \dots$

$$x_i(t+1) = f\left(x_i(t), y_i(t-d), t\right); \quad x_i(0) = x_{i0}$$
$$u_i(t) = g\left(x_i(t), y_i(t-d), t\right)$$

where x_i is the state, u_i is the control output, y_i is measurement input, d is some nonnegative fixed integer delay (e.g., the worst-case network delay), and f and g are some functions of state, measurement, and time. Note that we make no assumptions about the spaces over which x, u, or y are defined: they could be numbers, symbols, discrete, or continuous. (For $t < d$, we assume that f and g are functions of only x and t, and that they do not depend explicitly on y. Hence, we can take $y_i(t) = \emptyset$ (undefined) for $t < d$).

It is clear that if the initial conditions are all equal and the processes are driven with the same measurements, then the states and control outputs are *identical* for all time. In other words, if

$$x_{i0} = x_0; \quad \forall i$$
$$y_i(t) = y(t); \forall i, t,$$

then the processes all run the same recursion:

$$x(t+1) = f\left(x(t), y(t-d), t\right); \quad x(0) = x_0$$
$$u(t) = g\left(x(t), y(t-d), t\right).$$

(1)

Note that this is true for *any* functions f and g of x, y, and t. We refer to such a set of processes, with $x(t)$ and $u(t)$ identical for all time, as *synchronized*.

We are concerned with the following synchronization problem: We seek a method for synchronizing a new process p_n, which starts at some time $t' \geq d$, to the existing processes $\{p_0, \ldots, p_{n-1}\}$, for all time $t \geq t'$. We assume p_n knows f and g, but not x_0. We would like this method to work for *any* choice of functions f and g of x, y, and t.

Synchronization with Delayed Measurements. For any $t' \geq 0$, it follows immediately from (1) that p_n would be synchronized with $\{p_0, \ldots, p_{n-1}\}$ for all time $t \geq t'$, and for any functions f and g of x, y and t, if we set

$$x_n(t') = x(t') \qquad ; \text{at time } t'$$
$$y_n(t-d) \equiv y(t-d) ; \forall t \geq t'$$

(2)

Now suppose that, because of the delay, at the desired synchronization time t', we can receive only $x(t'-d)$ but not the current state $x(t')$. In this case, provided that $t' \geq d$, synchronization proceeds in two phases. First, starting d time steps prior to t', the process p_n must collect a delayed history that is *d time steps deep*, namely $x(t'-d)$ and $\{y(t'-2d), \ldots, y(t'-d-1)\}$. Then, at time t', $x(t')$ is immediately computed by *forward propagating* the state from $x(t'-d)$ to $x(t')$ by performing d iterations of the state recursion in (1) in one time step:

$$x(t'-d+1) = f\left(x(t'-d), y(t'-2d), t'-d\right)$$
$$x(t'-d+2) = f\left(x(t'-d+1), y(t'-2d+1), t'-d+1\right)$$
$$\vdots$$
$$x(t') = f\left(x(t'-d+(d-1)), y(t'-2d+(d-1)), t'-d+(d-1)\right)$$
$$\equiv f\left(x(t'-1), y(t'-d-1), t'-1\right).$$

(3)

Thus, p_n is synchronized from t' onwards.

Essentially the same technique can handle the case of asynchronous measurements, where at certain times some of the elements of the measurement sequence $\{y(t-d) \mid t \geq 0\}$ could be missing, but the ones that arrive do so in the right order. This scenario can still be modeled by (1) as follows: at each time t, define $y(t - d)$ as:

$$y(t - d) = \begin{cases} y_m(t - d) \; ; \text{if measurement arrives} \\ \emptyset \qquad\quad \; ; \text{otherwise} \end{cases}$$

where $\{y_m(t - d) \mid t \geq 0\}$ is some uncorrupted sequence of measurements, and the symbol $\emptyset$ denotes missing measurements. The functions f and g should also be properly defined for values of $\emptyset$. Additionally, in the asynchronous case, synchronization using forward propagation is only possible at times t' when delayed state $x(t' - d)$ is not missing. Otherwise it is necessary to wait until a time at which the delayed state is available [9].

This synchronization mechanism enables distributed module controllers to synchronize with an existing control action. The sheet controller is used as a conduit for sending the state information (as well as the sensor information) to each new controller.

State Machine Implementation. This section gives an example of how the synchronization mechanism can be implemented in practice. The goal in this example is to synchronize p_n to $\{p_0, \ldots, p_{n-1}\}$ from time tDrive until a time tOff. This will be accomplished by *embedding the process in a finite state machine* (FSM), which is shown in Figure 5.4, drawn using Statechart notation [9, 8, 22].

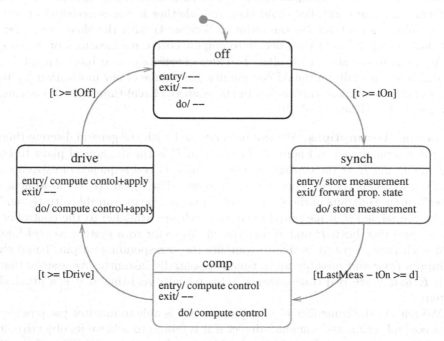

Fig. 6. Simplified finite state machine implementation of synchronization mechanism

The FSM has four states: off, synch, compute, and drive. In the off-state, the FSM waits until a time tOn, at which point it transitions to the synch-state. The time tOn is chosen to be sufficiently in advance of tDrive, such that there is enough time and enough measurements arrive before tDrive so that synchronization can be completed. The synch-state collects measurements, until a time when it has a delayed measurement history that is d time steps deep *and* a state measurement arrives. At that point it exits the synch-state, initializing the control process by forward propagation. Then it transitions to the compute-state, and executes the entry action, namely performing the first iteration of (1). It then continues to perform the control computation (1), as shown in the do-statement, until a time tDrive, at which point it transitions to the drive-state. The drive-state is very similar to the compute-state, except that the control is actually applied to the target system. Then, at a time tOff, the FSM turns itself off. By embedding the process p_n in an FSM, the desired synchronization can be accomplished in a practical manner.

5.5   Real-time Self-aware Paradigm

Once the module controllers are synchronized, they can track the trajectories supplied by the sheet controller. Though each controller can measure its track-ing error through its internal observer, it cannot tell whether this error is con-sidered "large," except possibly through external context cues provided by the sheet controller. It is useful, therefore, to think about adding an extra level of self-awareness to the module controller, to enable it to better monitor its own performance. The controller could then tell whether it was succeeding or fail-ing to fulfill its contract (in the sense of Section 4) with the sheet controller. If it was failing, it could then decide to employ corrective measures or escalate the problem to the sheet controller. The idea of self-awareness has been gaining recognition, especially in the AI community, the source of our motivation [2]. In this section, we explore this notion in the context of real-time control systems, as presented in Hindi, *et al.* [10].

Modeling Assumptions. We will be concerned with the general discrete time control system shown in Figure 7. The system P is the dynamical plant to be controlled, and K is the controller. The signal $w(t)$ is a sequence of exogenous inputs, and $u(t)$ is the sequence of control inputs. The signal $z(t)$ is the sequence of performance outputs of the system which may not be measurable directly, and $y(t)$ is the sequence of measured outputs which are available to the controller. We assume that both P and K are causal. We refer to a system as *real-time* if, at each time step t, it is able to compute its corresponding output, based on all inputs prior and possibly up to time t, essentially instantly. We assume that both K and P are real-time systems. (P is trivially real-time if it is a physical system).

We refer to the controller K as *self-aware* if it is able to monitor the progress of its control action and somehow detect if it is failing to achieve its objective; it is *real-time* self-aware if it is able to do this at each point in time. This abstract definition will be made more concrete below.

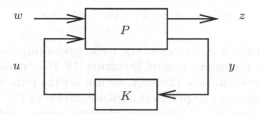

Fig. 7. Generic control system

The following conditions on the system, labeled M, I, and K, are generally assumed to be true:

(M) The plant P is a member of some model set $\mathcal{M}$
(I) The exogenous inputs w are in some input set $\mathcal{I}$
(K) The controller K really is being implemented correctly

The controller is also generally designed to solve some optimization problem with some criterion J, which is usually a function of the performance variable z. We remark that although the condition (K) may seem unnecessary or awkward, experience has shown that getting the software and hardware to implement the controller correctly without bugs or artifacts can be quite nontrivial in practice.

Adding Self-awareness. Self-awareness can easily be added to the controller using ideas from the model validation literature [18, 15]. Suppose that in a situation in which conditions M, I, and K hold, it is also possible to derive certain conditions that the control and the measured output must satisfy, respectively, U and Y[1]. This would be equivalent to the following:

$$(M \wedge I \wedge K) \quad \Rightarrow \quad (U \wedge Y) \tag{4}$$

For example, we could have

(U) The control input u lies in some set $\mathcal{U}$
(Y) The measured output y lies in some set $\mathcal{Y}$

In general, it is not possible to check that U (or Y) is true until the entire sequence $u(t)$ (or $y(t)$) has been observed. However, it is often possible to check for the *violation* of U and Y, at each point in time, i.e., in real-time. For example, suppose that U imposes conditions on the signal $u(t)$ that must be true at each point in time:

$$(u \in \mathcal{U}) \quad \Leftrightarrow \quad (u(t) \in \mathcal{U}(t); \; \forall \, t)$$

and similarly for Y. Then violation can be detected by checking that those conditions hold at each time step. Hence, the negation of (4) is more useful for real-time applications:

---

[1] The conditions could be also be joint in u and y, such as $(u, y) \in \mathcal{Z}$. For simplicity we keep them distinct here, but coupling would not change our results.

$$\neg M \vee \neg I \vee \neg K \quad \Leftarrow \quad \neg U \vee \neg Y \tag{5}$$

which is simply a logical statement of the basic model (in)validation paradigm. We remark that in the robust control literature [18, 15], "model (in)validation" has a very specific connotation. However, we will use the term more loosely here, namely, as a reference to any practical implementation of (5).

Equation (5) states that, as long as our physical system satisfies our modeling, input and control assumptions, M, I, and K, then both the measured output and control input will remain in their prescribed sets. However, if the measured output or control input violate conditions U or Y, then we know that at least one of the assumptions on the model, input, or controller is incorrect[2].

The above development shows that real-time self-awareness can be implemented via the augmentation of the controller with *on-line model (in)validation*. Hence, additional machinery would be added to K, which monitors the signals y and u at each time step, and checks that they are consistent with M, I, and K, by checking that U and Y are not violated.

In practice, it might not be possible to perform all the computations associated with Y, U, and the invalidation exactly. This could be either because the computation is too expensive to do in real-time, or simply because we do not even know how theoretically. Thus we will be content with reasonable approximations to these various steps below.

Self-aware LQG Control. As a concrete application of the abstract ideas above, consider the familiar formulation of LQG control [3, 1]:

(M) The plant P is a linear system, with Gaussian initial condition with zero mean and known covariance
(I) The input w is made up of Gaussian i.i.d. processes and sensor noises, which are zero mean, are uncorrelated with each other and the initial condition, and have known covariance
(K) The controller K is a linear LQG optimal controller

An important fact about the LQG scenario, which can be used easily in practice, is that all the resulting closed loop states, control signals, and outputs will also be zero mean Gaussian random variables, whose covariances can also be computed explicitly. Thus we can take

(U) $u(t) \sim \mathcal{N}(0, \Lambda_u(t))$
(Y) $y(t) \sim \mathcal{N}(0, \Lambda_y(t))$

---

[2] Note that the reverse implication does not hold; specifically, it could happen that one of M, I, or K is not true, but Y and U are still true. This could be viewed as a fortuitous situation, where our controller seems to work, even though our original assumptions are false. From a very pragmatic point of view, there should be no objection to this situation, assuming that the variables y and u are able to capture all system parameters and signals of interest.

where $\mathcal{N}(\mu, \Lambda)$ denotes the normal distribution with mean μ and covariance Λ. Hence an LQG controller can easily implement a very basic level of self-awareness by checking, at each time step, that u and y are within their "5σ" values; otherwise it can flag an error or warning. This can be viewed as a form of (very crude) on-line model validation, in the sense of (5).

Of course, many other more complex options for U and Y are possible, with calculation requirements ranging from solving optimization problems at each time step to maintaining sophisticated real-time statistical estimators of different quantities such as the performance variable z and the objective J. Similar arguments apply to other common control design approaches such as l_1 and $\mathcal{H}_\infty$.

5.6   Implementation

Some of the more painful issues to resolve in developing a prototype often center around integration and implementation. Our first choices for implementation were motivated by the need for rapid prototyping. The module and sheet controllers were developed using C, Matlab, Simulink, and the MathWorks xPC rapid prototyping environment. The xPC environment allows development of code within the Matlab environment that can then be compiled for a target embedded platform. There are, of course, other possible choices for modeling and development environments for real-time embedded systems, such as CORBA [16] or Ptolemy [12].

Within this development framework, the module controllers use a Statechart implementation in C based on Samek's formulation [22] to perform synchronization, as described earlier. The system models and control were developed using linear techniques.

The module controllers in this implementation run on GENE-4310 single-board computers (SBC). Each has a National Semiconductor 300MHz Geode processor (Intel-compatible) and uses less than 16 MB of memory. The controllers use a PC104 interface to two Diamond I/O cards. The SBCs use these I/O boards to link to custom circuitry for the actuators and the sensors. This configuration clearly has more processor power and memory than would be feasible in a real product, but it does allow for freedom of experimentation in the prototyping stage, and is compatible with the xPC environment and operating system. The sheet controllers all run on a single central PC. One could imagine that the sheet controllers could be located on distributed processors as well, and could even travel with their respective sheets; our choice of centralized sheet controllers was made largely for simplicity in early prototyping. The module controllers, sheet controller PC, and planner communicate with each other over Ethernet, using the UDP protocol. (The xPC environment does not support TCP.) Ethernet and UDP allowed for easy monitoring and debugging of the communications, as well as high bandwidth.

Although our hardware and software environment was useful for rapid prototyping, there were several drawbacks that became apparent throughout the system development and integration process. For example, the xPC environment does allow users to ignore many platform-specific and embedded coding concerns, but it introduces significant overhead into the controllers. Additionally, xPC, Matlab, and Simulink are usable but not all that well suited to developing highly distributed systems with many concurrent components using asynchronous messaging.

6   Conclusion

We have discussed here some of the challenges inherent in the control of highly reconfigurable systems and the design principles we have developed for meeting these challenges. Knowledge modeling, how to formulate what a system knows about itself, others, and the environment, comes to the fore in a distributed, compositional, reconfigurable setting. One aspect of the modeling problem is the question of where knowledge should be located in the system. This issue ties in with that of hierarchical control design, or how to divide up and compose control responsibilities, as control of a system requires knowledge about that system. Finally, a hierarchical, reconfigurable system requires special care in synchronizing control actions and feedback; this is the challenge of distributed coordination. The themes of self-awareness and context awareness run throughout all of these challenges.

We have also described a particular application of these principles to a modular printing system. This implementation makes use of sheet controllers for coordination. Module controllers use state machines to perform synchronization when joining a sheet control action. This synchronization is preserved through distributed feedback using apply times.

The module controllers described here are based on LQG control techniques. They thus do not reason about an explicit on-line model. One direction of future work is to investigate this type of more model-based approach at the module control level. Such an approach could enable further explorations, such as synchronization for heterogeneous module controllers. A model-based reasoning approach would clearly be useful in expanding the self-awareness of the module controllers, enabling them to perform more extensive self-diagnostics and some level of exception handling. Additionally, it would enable them to better interpret some level of context awareness provided by the sheet controller. More detailed modeling of this type might also help in enhancing the sheet controller; for example, the sheet controller could precisely take into account a module's capabilities when smoothing a trajectory for it to track.

There are also a number of larger research issues, three of which we describe here.

One unresolved set of issues centers on control and computing *architectures*. Our system is highly distributed, which gives some benefits in terms of modularity and reconfigurability, but may have a cost in terms of control complexity. A centralized controller becomes infeasible in larger systems with more and more sensors and actuators. Sometimes there may be a happy medium between fully distributed and fully centralized control, but there usually is no single answer. What is missing today is an ability to compare different architectures analytically in terms of control quality, robustness, and reconfigurability, as well as communication and processing requirements.

The architecture question also ties in with the problem of *verification*. With complex, compositional systems, it is increasingly difficult to verify or sometimes even understand their behavior. This complexity is exacerbated when automated optimization or search-based solution methods are used. In these cases, it is not only important to verify correct behavior but also, when a control choice is made, to be able to explain the reasoning behind that choice to external entities, including humans.

Complex, compositional systems also present the issue of *model abstraction*. With each new composition in a model-based system comes the need for a new model at a new granularity, perhaps with a different focus and aimed at a different type of reasoning engine. It would be useful for both development and verification if this model abstraction could be done automatically. Such abstraction, if done properly, would assist both in designing hierarchical architectures and in explaining and verifying compositional behavior.

In closing, highly reconfigurable systems allow designers to make the most of the recent explosions in embedded computing, sensing, and actuator capabilities. Reconfigurable systems can be made up of relatively simple components and rapidly customized for particular needs, thus reducing product complexity and development costs. On-line reconfigurability also enables a high level of system flexibility and robustness. It is now up to software and control engineers to meet the challenges imposed by these new systems and fully realize their potential.

References

1. Astrom, K.J., and Wittenmark, B.: Computer Controlled Systems. Prentice Hall, 1997
2. Bobrow, D., and Fromherz, M.P.J.: Compositional Self-Awareness. DARPA Workshop on Self-aware Computer Systems, Position Statement, May 2004
3. Bryson, A.E., and Ho, Y.-C.: Applied Optimal Control. Academic Press, 1975
4. Chen, C.-L. and Chiu, G.: Incorporating Human Visual Model and Spatial Sampling in Banding Artifact Reduction. American Control Conference, Boston, June 2004
5. de Kleer, J. and Brown, J.S.: A Framework for Qualitative Physics. Proc. of the Sixth Annual Conference of the Cognitive Science Society, 1984, pp. 11–18
6. Fromherz, M.P.J. , Bobrow, D.G., and de Kleer, J.: Model-based Computing for Design and Control of Reconfigurable Systems. AI Magazine, Special Issue on Qualitative Reasoning, vol. 24, no. 4, Winter 2003, pp. 120–130
7. Hamby, E. and Gross, E.: A Control-Oriented Survey of Xerographic Systems: Basic Concepts to New Frontiers. American Control Conference, Boston, June 2004
8. Harel, D.: Statecharts: A Visual Formalism for Complex Systems. Science of Computer Programming, vol. 8, 1987, pp. 231–274
9. Hindi, H.A., and Crawford, L.S.: Method and State Machine Implementation of Synchronization of State Based Control Processes with Delayed and Asynchronous Measurements. Palo Alto Research Center (PARC), Internal Report, September, 2004

10. Hindi, H.A., Crawford, L.S., and Fromherz, M.P.J.: Toward Self-aware Real-time Controllers Using Online Approximate Model Validation. Palo Alto Research Center (PARC), Internal Report, December, 2004
11. Krucinski, M., Cloet, C., Horowitz, R., and Tomizuka, M.: A Mechatronics Approach to Copier Paperpath Control. First IFAC Conference on Mechatronic Systems, Darmstadt, Germany, September 2000
12. Lee, E.: Overview of the Ptolemy Project. Technical Memorandum UCB/ERL M03/25, July 2, 2003, University of California, Berkeley, CA, 94720, USA
13. Li, P., Sim, T. and Lee, D.: Time Sequential Sampling and Reconstruction of Tone and Color Reproduction Functions for Xerographic Printing. American Control Conference, Boston, June 2004
14. Mauve, M.: Consistency in Continuous Distributed Interactive Media. ACM CSCW, 2000, pp. 181–190
15. Newlin, M., and Smith, R.S.: A Generalization of the Structured Singular Value and its Application to Model Validation. IEEE Transactions on Automatic Control, 1998, pp. 901-907
16. Object Management Group. http://www.omg.org/
17. Owada, Y., and Asahara, S.: Distributed Processing System, Distributed Processing Method and Client Terminal Capable of Using the Method. US Patent Application Publication US 2002/0194269 A1, December 2002
18. Poolla, K., Khargonekar, P., Tikku, A., Krause, J., and Nagpal, K.: A Time-Domain Approach to Model Validation. IEEE Transactions on Automatic Control, 1994, pp. 951–959
19. Rotea, M. and Lana, C.: A Robust Estimation Algorithm for Printer Modeling. American Control Conference, Boston, June 2004
20. Ruml, W. and Fromherz, M.P.J.: On-line Planning and Scheduling in a High-speed Manufacturing Domain. ICAPS 2004 Workshop on Integrating Planning into Scheduling, Whistler, BC, Canada, June 2004 (updated version submitted to ICAPS 2005)
21. Russell, S. and Norvig, P.: Artificial Intelligence: A Modern Approach, 2nd Ed. Prentice Hall, 2003
22. Samek, M.: Practical Statecharts in C/C++. CMP Books, 2002

Operational Semantics of Hybrid Systems

(Invited Paper)

Edward A. Lee and Haiyang Zheng*

Center for Hybrid and Embedded Software Systems (CHESS)
University of California, Berkeley, 94720, USA
{eal, hyzheng}@eecs.berkeley.edu

Abstract. This paper discusses an interpretation of hybrid systems as executable models. A specification of a hybrid system for this purpose can be viewed as a program in a domain-specific programming language. We describe the semantics of HyVisual, which is such a domain-specific programming language. The semantic properties of such a language affect our ability to understand, execute, and analyze a model. We discuss several semantic issues that come in defining such a programming language, such as the interpretation of discontinuities in continuous-time signals, and the interpretation of discrete-event signals in hybrid systems, and the consequences of numerical ODE solver techniques. We describe the solution in HyVisual by giving its operational semantics.

1 Introduction

Hybrid systems are heterogeneous systems that include continuous-time subsystems interacting with discrete events. They are effective models for physical systems interacting with software or undergoing discrete mode changes. Typically, the continuous subsystem is modeled by differential equations, while the discrete events are modeled by finite state machines. Transitions between states represent either discrete mode changes or actions taken by software subsystems. Most of the major contributions in hybrid systems have been in the construction of a systems theory, theories of control, and analysis and verification tools (see for example [1, 2, 3, 4, 5, 6]). A few software tools have been built to support such analytical methods, such as Charon [7], CheckMate [8], d/dt [9], HyTech [10], Kronos [11], Uppaal [12], and a toolkit for level-set methods [13]. In addition, some software tools provide simulation of hybrid systems, including Charon [7], Hysdel [14], HyVisual [15], Modelica [16], Scicos [17], Shift [18], and Simulink/Stateflow (from The MathWorks). An excellent analysis and comparison of these tools is given by Carloni, et al. [19].

---

* This paper describes work that is part of the Ptolemy project, which is supported by the National Science Foundation (NSF award number CCR-00225610), and Chess (the Center for Hybrid and Embedded Software Systems), which receives support from NSF and the following companies: Infineon, Hewlett-Packard, Honeywell, General Motors, and Toyota.

M. Morari and L. Thiele (Eds.): HSCC 2005, LNCS 3414, pp. 25–53, 2005.
© Springer-Verlag Berlin Heidelberg 2005

In this paper, we focus on the simulation tools, but take the perspective that hybrid systems are not so much "simulated" as "executed." We view the semantics of hybrid systems as a concurrent model of computation, and the "simulation" tools as compilers and/or interpreters for programming languages that happen to have a hybrid systems semantics. Although many of the issues are closely related to those that arise in the design of simulators (see for example [20]), the emphasis becomes one of modularity and predictable and understandable behavior, rather than one of accurate approximation of unachievable behavior. Of the above tools, Shift and Modelica probably come closest to reflecting this philosophy, since they are consistently presented as programming languages more than as simulation tools.

The view of hybrid systems as executable computational artifacts was stimulated by the DARPA MoBIES project (model-based integration of embedded software), which undertook the challenging task of establishing an interchange format for hybrid systems. The goal was to facilitate exchange of models and techniques between tools. The effort was led by the key proponents of model-integrated computing [21], the developers of Charon, CheckMate, and HyVisual, and users of Simulink/Stateflow. The result of this work was a formalism called HSIF (hybrid system interchange format) [22]. A proposal for the next generation of interchange format can be found in [19].

One of the key objectives of HSIF, that of model exchange among diverse tools, was at odds with another of its key objectives, that of defining an executable and complete hybrid systems semantics. The diverse tools represented by the HSIF community have significant differences in their semantics, often reflecting their differing objectives (e.g. verification vs. simulation). In this paper, we set aside the concern for interchange of models, and focus instead on defining a clean and complete hybrid systems semantics. The objective is to define behaviors, including subtle corner cases, by giving a complete semantics for a programming language. We have implemented the semantics in HyVisual [15] in a version scheduled to be released (in open-source form, as usual) concurrently with the publication of this paper.

2   Example Model

We start by considering a fairly typical hybrid system example shown in figure 1 that we can use to frame the discussion. The model is deliberately small and simple, making it easier to discuss semantic issues without the distracting complexity of a more "real-world" example. The figure shows the visual syntax of HyVisual [15], which is implemented within the Ptolemy II software framework [23]. The reader should not be misled by the visual syntax. While visual syntaxes are commonly used for models that approximate real systems, they can also be used as a programming language syntax, in which case the model *is* the real system (the program), in the same sense that the text of a C program is the program. We nonetheless call a visual program like that in figure 1 a "model" because calling it a "program" would confuse too many readers who assume that programs must have textual syntaxes.

The model in figure 1 is of a physical system consisting of two masses on springs that oscillate.[1] When the masses collide, they stick together with an exponentially decaying stickiness. When the differential force of the springs exceeds the stickiness, the masses come apart. The three-dimensional rendition of the physical system shown in the figure is a snapshot of an animation created using the Ptolemy II graphics infrastructure [26]. The top-level of the hierarchy in the figure shows a continuous-time model, where boxes represent actors and connections between them represent continuous-time signals. The Masses block encapsulates the spring-masses model. The other three blocks are plotters.

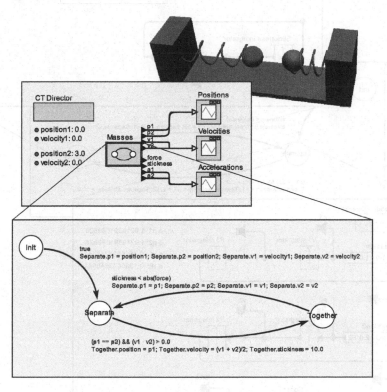

Fig. 1. A hybrid system of two masses on springs

The next level of the hierarchy shows a finite-state machine with an (unimportant) initial state and two states representing the two modes of operation. Since states of this state machine represent modes of operation, we use the terms "state" and "mode" interchangeably for them. In the "Separate" mode, the masses are separately oscillating, and in the "Together" mode, they are stuck together. The behavior in each of these modes is specified at the third level of the

---

[1] This model was studied by Liu [24] and was inspired by microelectromechanical accelerometers [25].

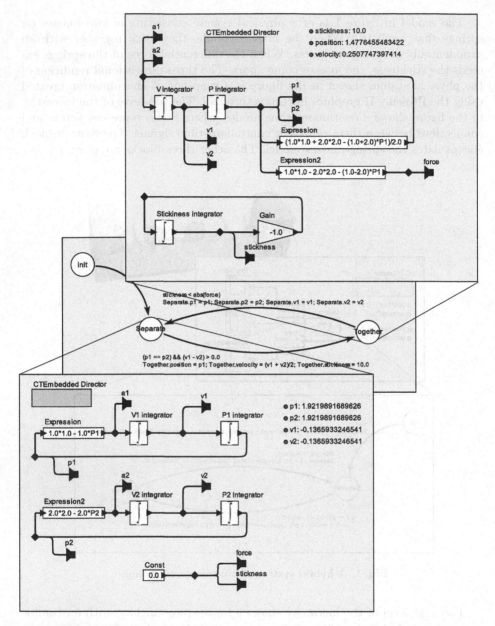

Fig. 2. The refinements of the modes of the hybrid system in figure 1

hierarchy shown in figure 2. Each mode is given by a signal-flow block diagram representing the ordinary differential equations that model the dynamics.

The traces of an execution are shown in figure 3, where it can be seen that the masses start with separated positions, come together and collide, oscillate together for a short time, come apart, then again collide and come apart. The three plots, produced by the three plotter blocks at the top level in figure 1, represent the positions, velocities, and accelerations of the two masses as a function of time. The Masses block in figure 1 produces as outputs the positions of the

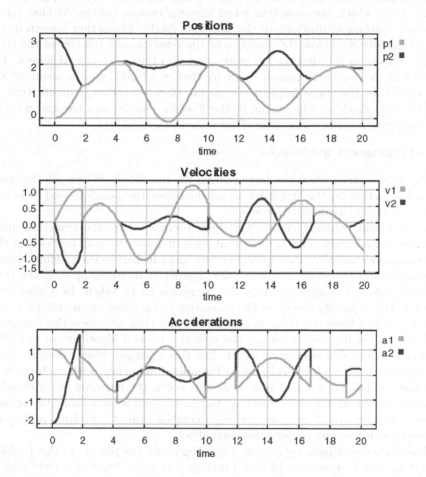

Fig. 3. The plots resulting from executing the hybrid systems model in figure 1

two masses (*p1* and *p2*), their velocities (*v1* and *v2*), and their accelerations (*a1* and *a2*). The state machine diagram at the bottom of figure 1 shows the mode logic. The state machine starts in the *Init* state, which has a single outgoing transition with guard expression true.[2] This guard expression evaluates to true, so the transition is taken immediately, and the action expression (immediately

---

[2] In the HyVisual syntax, each mode transition is annotated with two lines of text, where the first line is the *guard*, a predicate that determines when the transition is taken, and the second line is the *action*, a set of statements executed when the transition is taken.

below the guard expression) is executed. This action expression initializes the positions and velocities in the destination mode, *Separate*.

The state machine remains in the *Separate* mode until the guard on its outgoing transition becomes true. The guard expression is "(p1 == p2) && (v1 - v2) > 0", which becomes true when the two masses collide. At that point, the state machine transitions to the *Together* mode. The action (shown in the figure immediately below the guard) sets the position and velocity of the (now joined) masses in the destination mode, and also initializes the stickiness. The velocity in the destination mode is set to "(v1 + v2)/2", which, assuming the two masses are the same, implements the law of conservation of momentum.

The state machine will remain in the *Together* mode until the guard on its outgoing transition becomes true. That guard expression is

```
stickiness < abs(force)
```

which becomes true when the force pulling the masses apart exceeds the stickiness. The action on the transition again initializes the positions and velocities of the masses in the destination mode.

In HyVisual, when a guard expression becomes true, the transition must be taken immediately. This is consistent with the physics being modeled in this spring-masses example. Many hybrid system formalisms, however, define a guard expression on a transition as an enabler. Rather than requiring that the transition be taken, it simply permits the transition to be taken. In a simulator, however, this typically results in the transition to be taken at an arbitrary time after the guard becomes true. In simulation, the time at which the transition is taken is typically dependent on the step-size control algorithm of the ODE (ordinary differential equation) solver. For this example, that behavior would be inappropriate. Such hybrid system formalisms associate with each state an *invariant*, which like a guard is a predicate. When the invariant becomes false, a transition out of the state must be taken. In such a formalism, the spring-masses example would be expressed by a combination of invariants and guard expressions that would achieve the same effect.

The system is depicted schematically in figure 4. The physics of this problem is quite simple if we assume idealized springs. Let $p_1(t)$ denote the right edge of the left mass at time t, and $p_2(t)$ denote the left edge of the right mass at time

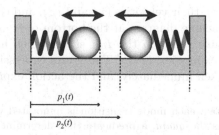

Fig. 4. A schematic illustration of the system that is modeled in figure 1

t, as shown in figure 4. Let n_1 and n_2 denote the neutral positions of the two masses, i.e. when the springs are neither extended nor compressed, so the force is zero. For an ideal spring, the force at time t on the mass is proportional to $n_1 - p_1(t)$ (for the left mass) and $n_2 - p_2(t)$ (for the right mass). The force is positive to the right and negative to the left.

Let the spring constants be k_1 and k_2, respectively. Then the force on the left spring is $k_1(n_1 - p_1(t))$, and the force on the right spring is $k_2(n_2 - p_2(t))$. Let the masses be m_1 and m_2 respectively. Now we can use Newton's law, which relates force, mass, and acceleration, $f = ma$. The acceleration is the second derivative of the position with respect to time, which we write $\ddot{p}_1(t)$ and $\ddot{p}_2(t)$ respectively. Thus, as long as the masses are separate, their dynamics are given by

$$\ddot{p}_1(t) = k_1(n_1 - p_1(t))/m_1 \tag{1}$$
$$\ddot{p}_2(t) = k_2(n_2 - p_2(t))/m_2. \tag{2}$$

If we integrate both sides twice, we get

$$p_1(t) = \int_{t_0}^{t} \left(\int_{t_0}^{\alpha} \frac{k_1}{m_1}(n_1 - p_1(\tau))d\tau + v_1(t_0) \right) d\alpha + p_1(t_0) \tag{3}$$

$$p_2(t) = \int_{t_0}^{t} \left(\int_{t_0}^{\alpha} \frac{k_2}{m_2}(n_2 - p_2(\tau))d\tau + v_2(t_0) \right) d\alpha + p_2(t_0) \tag{4}$$

Figure 2 shows the hierarchical models contained by the two modes, Separate and Together. These models are called *refinements* of the modes. They give the behavior of the modal component when the component is in the corresponding mode. The two equations above are depicted by the state refinements in figure 2, where it is assumed that $k_1 = 1$, $m_1 = 1$, $n_1 = 1$, and $k_2 = 2$, $m_2 = 1$, $n_2 = 2$. The initial values $p_1(t_0)$, $p_2(t_0)$, $v_1(t_0)$ and $v_2(t_0)$ are the initial states of the integrators in the figures, which are set by the actions upon entering the mode.

When the masses collide, the situation changes. With the masses stuck together, they behave as a single object with mass $m_1 + m_2$ and positions $p_1(t) = p_2(t)$. This single object is pulled in opposite directions by two springs. Let

$$p(t) = p_1(t) = p_2(t).$$

The dynamics are then given by

$$\ddot{p}(t) = \frac{k_1 n_1 + k_2 n_2 - (k_1 + k_2)p(t)}{m_1 + m_2}. \tag{5}$$

Again we can integrate both sides twice to get the relation represented by the mode refinement at the top of figure 2.

3   Discussion of the Example

The most notable feature of our example, and the one which distinguishes it most from other "programs," is the continuous-time evolution of its "variables."

In the visual syntax of HyVisual, the lines connecting blocks (sometimes called "wires" in analogy with circuit diagrams) represent variables of the program. In a corresponding textual syntax, these variables would be given names and referred to by name. In a visual syntax, however, there is usually no need to name them, since their users can simply connect to them. Whereas in a textual syntax "scoping rules" would limit the visibility of such variables, in a visual syntax like HyVisual, visibility is limited by the constraints on wiring in the diagram, for example that the wires cannot cross levels of the hierarchy. In HyVisual, to make variables visible across levels of the hierarchy, we use named "ports." In figure 2, the ports labeled p1, p2, v1, v2, a1, a2, force, and stickiness are the inside view of the same ports with the same names in figure 1. These ports represent the continuously evolving variables representing position, velocity, and acceleration of the masses, plus the force pulling them apart and the stickiness holding them together.[3]

The continuous evolution of the values of such variables, of course, is what presents the greatest challenge to a programming language designer, since continuous evolution of variables is outside the domain of discourse of today's computers. Thus, while a denotational semantics for a hybrid systems language might embrace continuous evolution of the variable values, an operational semantics can only define values at discrete points in time. It is the relationship between such a denotational semantics and operational semantics that is the principal topic of this paper.

One solution to this conundrum is to simply disallow continuous evolution. We can invoke sampling theory to assert that any continuously evolving signal (with finite bandwidth) can be sampled uniformly at a sufficiently high rate without loss of information. Indeed, some of the tools mentioned above (notably Hysdel [14] and Shift [18]) operate only on models that have been discretized by sampling by the programmer. This greatly simplifies the programming language semantics, since now the semantics of the model easily matches well-known techniques for synchronous concurrent programming languages such as the synchronous/reactive languages [27]. The problem is that even an example as simple as our spring masses violates the finite bandwidth assumption. As shown in figure 3, the velocities and accelerations both have discontinuities that imply infinite bandwidth. In hybrid system modeling, these discontinuities are the principle subject of study, so a failure to properly represent them is a serious omission.

We can do better than uniform sampling with non-uniform sampling, where we include the points of discontinuity in the samples. However, this is not quite enough. Non-uniform sampling, by itself, is not sufficient to unambiguously represent discontinuities. We examine this issue next.

---

[3] We use the term "continuously evolving" for signals whose values evolve continuously rather than in discrete steps. We do not require continuously evolving signals to be continuous. We will make this more precise below.

4 Discontinuities in Continuously Evolving Signals

Continuous signals exhibit an intrinsic robustness under discretization. Mathematically, the continuously evolving variables of figure 3 are typically represented as functions of the form

$$x: T \rightarrow \mathcal{R}^n,$$

where T (called the *time line*) is a connected subset of the reals, $\mathcal{R}$, and $\mathcal{R}^n$ is a normed vector space consisting of n-tuples of real numbers with some norm. This function is continuous at $t \in T$ if for all $\epsilon > 0$, there exists a $\delta > 0$ such that for all τ in the open neighborhood $(t - \delta, t + \delta) \subset \mathcal{R}$

$$||x(t) - x(\tau)|| < \epsilon.$$

This means that if we examine the value of the signal at a point in time, if the signal is continuous at that point in time, then small errors in the time at which we examine it result in small errors in the value.

In a computational setting, signal values may have data types significantly different from $\mathcal{R}^n$, in which case, if the set of data values form a topological space, then the topological form of continuity provides similar robustness.

However, signals in hybrid systems are not typically continuous at all points in time. Specifically, let $D \subset T$ be a discrete subset[4] of T. A signal is piecewise continuous if it is continuous at all points in $T \backslash D$, where D is some discrete subset of T, and where the backslash represents set subtraction. However, this leaves open the question in an operational semantics about how to represent the signal at or near points in D.

A typical approach in mathematical modeling of hybrid systems is to define signals to be *continuous on the right* at points in D. A function $x: T \rightarrow \mathcal{R}^n$ is continuous on the right at $t \in T$ if for all $\epsilon > 0$, there exists a $\delta > 0$ such that for all τ in the interval $[t, t + \delta)$

$$||x(t) - x(\tau)|| < \epsilon.$$

This makes explicit the non-robustness of piecewise continuous signals. It is straightforward to generalize this to topological spaces rather than normed vector spaces, so that the same argument may be applied to other data types than $\mathcal{R}^n$.

An operational semantics must somehow represent that a signal value infinitesimally before some $t \in D$ is significantly different from the value at t. Unfortunately, no discretized rendition can properly represent this.

To make this concrete, assume that we seek an operational semantics for an execution of a hybrid system on a computer. This semantics can represent continuously evolving signals only on a discrete subset of real-valued times. Let $D' \subset T$ be the discrete subset of the reals where it will explicitly represent signal values. We can require that the points of discontinuity D be in this set, or

---

[4] A discrete subset is a subset for which there exists an order embedding to the integers [28]. Note that "discrete" is a stronger condition than "countable."

$D \subset D'$. However, how can we choose D' to represent the discontinuity? Suppose $t \in D$. Then, since D' is discrete,[5] there is a $t' \in D'$ where $t' < t$ and there is no $\tau \in D'$ such that $t' < \tau < t$. We say that t' *immediately precedes* t. Since $t' < t$, there is a non-zero interval between the samples that span the discontinuity. Given only the discrete samples, therefore, the discontinuous signal is fundamentally indistinguishable from a continuous signal that simply changes sufficiently rapidly. This is not splitting hairs. It means that an operational semantics based on discrete samples cannot unambiguously represent discontinuities. In addition to semantic difficulties, this ambiguity creates practical problems for numerical ODE solvers. Variable step solvers typically adjust the spacing between sample points to be smaller where signals are varying rapidly and larger where they are varying more smoothly. With this ambiguity, such solvers must be made explicitly aware of the discontinuities or they will be forced to reduce step sizes down to resolution tolerances before giving up and deciding that the variability represents a discontinuity.

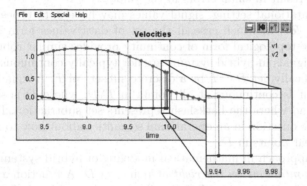

Fig. 5. A portion of the plot of velocities in figure 3, showing multiple values at one time

The key problem here is the form of the function

$$x \colon T \to \mathcal{R}^n.$$

Whereas this form works well in a mathematics that embraces the continuum of $\mathcal{R}$, it fails in the formal framework of computing, where continuums are not directly manageable. Figure 5 shows a portion of the velocities plot from figure 3 where at time approximately 9.965 the masses collide. The plot shows a dot for each computed value of the velocities, showing the discretization that is not evident in figure 3. At time 9.965, the two velocity signals have more than one value. They have both the value just prior to the collision and the value just after the collision. Having two values at one time is semantically unambiguously distinct from having two distinct values closely spaced in time. But it requires augmenting the mathematical model for signals. We do that next.

---

[5] The existence of an order embedding to the integers is essential to this argument [28]. Countable sets would not be sufficient.

5   The Semantics of Signals

To unambiguously represent discontinuities, we define a *continuously evolving signal* to be a function

$$x: T \times \mathcal{N} \to V, \tag{6}$$

where $T \subset \mathcal{R}$ is a connected subset (the time line), $\mathcal{N}$ is the non-negative integers, and V is some set of values (the data type of the signal, such as $\mathcal{R}^n$ for signals whose values are n-tuples of reals). In the terminology of the tagged signal model [29], $T \times \mathcal{N}$ is the *tag set*. A particular tag is a member of $T \times \mathcal{N}$, a tuple with a time value and an *index*. This models that at each time $t \in T$, the signal x can have finitely many values. To ensure that the number of values at a time is finite, we require that for all $t \in T$, there exist an $m \in \mathcal{N}$ such that

$$\forall n > m, \quad x(t, n) = x(t, m). \tag{7}$$

This constraint prevents what is sometimes called *chattering Zeno* conditions, where a signal takes on infinitely many values at a particular time. Such conditions would prevent an execution from progressing beyond that point in time, assuming the execution is constrained to produce values in chronological order.

Assuming x has no chattering Zeno condition, then there is a least m satisfying (7). We call this least value of m the *final index* and $x(t, m)$ the *final value* of x at t. We call $x(t, 0)$ the *initial value* at time t. If $m = 0$, then we say that x has only one value at time t. Note that the values at time t are well ordered using the ordinary ordering of integers.

Define the *initial value function* $x_i: T \to V$ by

$$\forall t \in T, \quad x_i(t) = x(t, 0).$$

Define the *final value function* $x_f: T \to V$ by

$$\forall t \in T, \quad x_f(t) = x(t, m),$$

where m is final index. Note that x_i and x_f are conventional continuous-time functions.

A *piecewise continuous signal* is a function x of the above form satisfying three conditions:

1. the initial value function x_i is continuous on the left;
2. the final value function x_f is continuous on the right; and
3. x has only one value at all $t \in T \backslash D$, where D is a discrete subset of T.

It is easy to see that if $D = \emptyset$, then $x_i = x_f$ is a continuous function. Otherwise each of these functions is piecewise continuous.

6   Ideal Solver Semantics

In this section, we consider the semantics of a discrete representation of a hybrid system under a simple idealization, which is that over time intervals that are sufficiently small, the differential equations giving the dynamics can be solved exactly. This finesses the issue of approximate executions based on numerical solutions, which we will address below. This *ideal solver semantics* was introduced in [30]. Note that it is not as far-fetched as it might sound. Many of the differential equations in hybrid systems can be solved exactly (including those for the spring masses example) by finding a closed form expression for the solution over the intervals of continuous behavior. Even when we don't have closed form solutions, for many special cases numerical solutions yield exact answers (using appropriate solvers). But even in cases where the solution must be approximated, we would like to separate the issue of approximate ODE solutions from the other semantic issues in hybrid systems. Hence, the idealization remains useful.

$$x : T \to R^n \qquad T = [t_0, \infty) \subset R$$

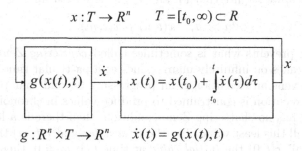

$$g : R^n \times T \to R^n \qquad \dot{x}(t) = g(x(t), t)$$

Fig. 6. Schematic of the ODE solver problem

In general, a hybrid systems model is a set of piecewise continuous signals and a set of actors that establish relations between these signals. Examining figures 1 and 2 we see that while the state machine is in any state, the actors relating signals are integrators and **Expression** actors. For **Expression** actors, the output is a memoryless function of the inputs. More general actors are allowable, as we will discuss below, but for now, let's assume that the actors are either integrators or memoryless functions. In this case, a hybrid system can be restructured to have the form shown in figure 6, which has two components: a vector integrator and a function g giving the input to the integrator as a function of its output and the current time.

The function g encapsulates the effects of all actors that are not integrators in the model. Notice that in order for this abstraction to work, every directed cycle in the model must have at least one integrator. The abstraction also requires that data precedences be satisfied. That is, the two paths shown in figure 7 must be semantically equivalent. This requires that the run-time execution engine analyze the data dependencies and invoke actors in the order implied by those data dependencies. Specifically, at each tag $(t, n) \in T \times \mathcal{N}$, actor **Expression1** must be invoked before actor **Expression2**. This point might seem obvious, but some hybrid systems simulators have assumed the order of invocation of these actors to be nondeterministic at a particular time.

The framework in figure 6 ignores the index portion of the tag. Indeed, this conceptual framework is only valid over time intervals where signals have only one value. Over these regions of the time line, x is differentiable, so the framework in the figure is equivalent to the vector differential equation

$$\dot{x}(t) = g(x(t), t), \tag{8}$$

with some initial condition $x(t_0)$.

Let $D \subset T$ be a discrete set that includes the times at which signals have more than one value. Let D' be a superset that includes D and the initial time, t_0. A *discrete trace* of the hybrid system is the set

$$\{x(t, n) \mid t \in D', \text{ and } n \in \mathcal{N}\}. \tag{9}$$

The discrete trace includes the values at each discontinuity plus the values at the initial time and (possibly) some additional values. To be a valid trace, we require that for each interval between times in D', that (8) have a unique and continuous solution, and that the endpoints of the solution in this interval be in the trace. Notice that as long as there is no chattering Zeno condition, a trace can be fully represented by a discrete subset of (9).

Specifically, consider the interval $[t_i, t_{i+1})$ where $t_i, t_{i+1} \in D$ and t_i immediately precedes t_{i+1}. Assume $x_f(t_i)$ is known (our induction starts, obviously, with $x_f(t_0)$, which we assume we can obtain). We take this to be the initial condition for x in figure 6, and we require that (8) have a unique solution over the interval $[t_i, t_{i+1})$. Such a unique solution is assured if the interval is "sufficiently small" and the function the function $g \colon \mathcal{R}^n \times T \to \mathcal{R}^n$ is continuous in the interval and satisfies a *local Lipschitz condition* (see [31] or [32], for example). The details of these conditions are not important for our purposes here. It is sufficient to know that there are such conditions and that the conditions are checkable. The value at the end of the interval will be taken to be the initial value $x(t_{i+1}, 0)$ at time t_{i+1}.

We now can begin to give an operational semantics under the ideal solver assumption. Begin with the initial condition $x(t_0, 0)$, which we assume is given (in figure 2 it is a parameter of the integrators). We then execute the model until the final index at t_0 (we discuss the semantics of this execution, which we call the *discrete phase* of execution, below in section 8.3). The final value of $x_f(t_0)$ is the initial value $x(t_0)$ for the differential equation (8). We identify a t_1 such that the continuity and local Lipschitz condition of g is satisfied over $[t_0, t_1)$ (this is assured of not traversing a discontinuity, and therefore will not miss any points in time where the signal has multiple values). We then solve the differential equation to determine $x_i(t_1) = x(t_1, 0)$. We then perform a discrete phase execution at t_1 to get $x_f(t_1)$ and repeat the process.

In this description of the ideal solver semantics, there are two key issues that we have not fully resolved. The first is the semantics of the discrete phase execution. The second is how to determine the *step size*, which takes us from one time $t_i \in D'$ to the next time $t_{i+1} \in D'$. We address these issues next, in turn.

7   Discrete Events

Hybrid systems mix continuous and discrete phenomena. The discontinuities in the spring-masses example are the result of discrete mode transitions in system that evolves in the time continuum. At these mode transitions, the behavior of a system may be considerably more complex than in the spring-masses example. In systems that mix software with physical systems, sequences of mode transitions can be used to model the software. The events in such sequences are ordered but not timed. This fits the realities of software, where timing is not part of the semantics, and is consistent with abstractions for software that are increasingly used for embedded software such as synchronous languages [27] and time-triggered languages [33]. Then we take a step further, and introduce intrinsically discrete signals within the semantics.

7.1   Transient States

The piecewise continuous signals in our semantics are continuous at all points on the time line T except for a discrete subset D. At these discontinuities, a signal may take on a finite sequence of values. An operational semantics needs to define the construction of these sequences of values.

The first mechanism we will consider is *transient states*. Consider the modification of the spring-masses example that is shown in figure 8. In that example, an additional state has been added (called "Time") that has a refinement that produces on one of the output ports the current time. The transition coming out of the Time state has a guard expression "**true**", which of course is always true. Since in HyVisual semantics, when guard is true the transition must be taken, the time spent in the state is zero. Such a state is called a *transient state*.[6]

A plot of the signal $v1$ with the additional output is shown in figure 9. At any time t that the masses collide, there are three distinct values of the signal $v1$, each in a well-defined order. Moreover, since this value is held for zero time, it has no impact on the signal $p1$, which is the integral of $v1$. The zero-width pulse integrates to zero.

Although the example in figure 8 has no particular usefulness, it is easy to imagine using this capability to model a sequence of software-based actions, which could, for example, be used to model software-based controllers.

7.2   Discrete Signals

So far, we have considered only continuously-evolving signals, which have a value for all $(t, n) \in T \times \mathcal{N}$. In mixed hardware/software systems, however, some signals

---

[6] Many hybrid system simulators will remain in a transient state for at least one time step of the ODE solver. This effectively results in nondeterministic behavior, since the programmer is typically unaware of the mechanisms that is used to define the time steps. In our semantics, this would be incorrect behavior. Moreover, it is a poor model for the behavior of software, since it neither models the actual time taken by software nor provides a usable abstraction, such as the synchrony hypothesis [27].

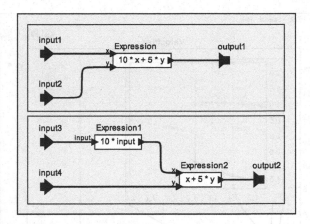

Fig. 7. The abstraction of figure 6 requires that these two paths be semantically equivalent

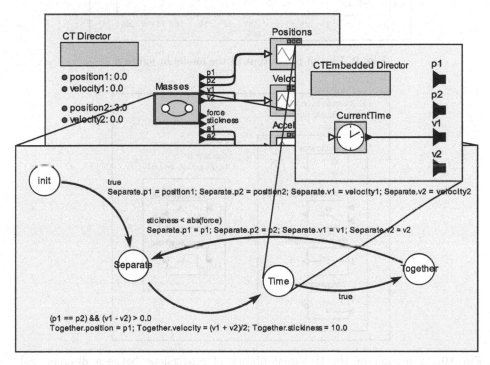

Fig. 8. Variation of the model in figure 1 that has a transient state

are intrinsically discrete, and it makes little sense to talk about their values at all points in time. HyVisual semantics supports such signals by augmenting the set of possible values to

$$V_d = V \cup \{\varepsilon\},$$

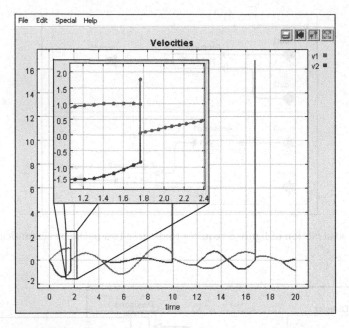

Fig. 9. Plot of the output of the model in figure 8

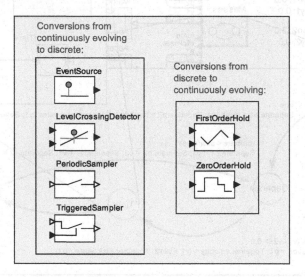

Fig. 10. A portion of the HyVisual library of conversions between discrete and continuously-evolving signals

where ε represents "absent" (equivalently, we could define signals to be partial functions from $T \times \mathcal{N}$ to V).

A *discrete signal* is a function $x \colon T \times \mathcal{N} \to V_d$, where $x(t, n) = \varepsilon$ for all $n \in \mathcal{N}$ and $t \notin D$, where $D \subset T$ is a discrete set. Moreover, as with continuously-evolving signals, discrete signals are constrained to have no chattering Zeno condition, but in this case, the final value is required to be ε. Hence, the tags where a discrete signal is not absent are a discrete subset of $T \times \mathcal{N}$.

In HyVisual, a discrete signal is indicated by annotating a port that produces or consumes it with an attribute named DISCRETE. HyVisual performs a simple consistency check to ensure that ports that produce discrete signals are connected only to ports that consume discrete signals. A port that requires a continuously-evolving signal (such the integrator input or output) is annotated with an attribute named CONTINUOUS. If there is no annotation, then HyVisual assumes the port is *agnostic*, in which case HyVisual will infer whether it is operating on a discrete or continuous signal. The ports of the Expression actor used in figure 2, for example, are agnostic.

In the operational semantics, discrete signals are involved only in the discrete phases of execution. If all the ports of an actor are discrete, then the actor itself is called discrete. Discrete actors are invoked only in the discrete phases of execution. Of course, as with continuous actors, we require that data precedences be satisfied. As discussed in section 6, the actors in figure 7, if provided with discrete inputs, must react to those inputs in data-precedence order. Again, some hybrid systems simulators assume this order to be nondeterministic.

It is possible in HyVisual to create models that have directed cycles that consist entirely of discrete signals. Such cycles are required to have a delay. The delay is detected by a dependence analysis. Each actor that introduces delay declares as part of its interface definition that the value at a particular output port does not depend on the value at a particular input port at a particular tag. The scheduler uses this dependence information to determine the data precedences, and hence determine the order in which actors must be invoked.

Recall from section 6 that directed cycles with continuous signals require at least one integrator. We can now state the overall requirement on a model precisely. Every directed cycle must have either a delay on a discrete signal or an integrator on a continuous signal. Thus, mixed signal cycles are supported.

Note that we have left unsaid how an execution engine decides when a discrete phase is complete. Recall that each signal can have any number of values at a particular time, but it is required to have a final value after some finite number of values. We will explain this below in section 8.3.

HyVisual provides a small library of actors to create discrete signals from continuously-evolving ones, and vice versa. Some of these are shown in figure 10. The EventSource actor produces one or more discrete events at specified (possibly periodic) times. The LevelCrossingDetector produces a discrete event on the output when the continuous-evolving input crosses a specified threshold. The PeriodicSampler produces discrete events whose values are the initial values of the continuously-evolving input signal at multiples of a specified sampling period. Note that the HyVisual semantics give this actor an unambiguous semantics even for samples at discontinuities. The TriggeredSampler actor uses a discrete input signal to specify when to take samples of a continuously-evolving input

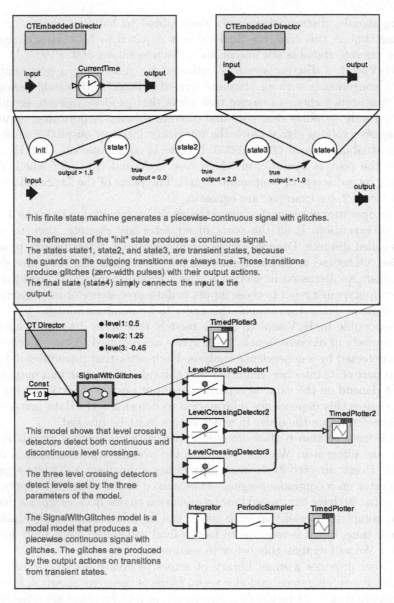

Fig. 11. A simple model that illustrates discrete signals

signal. Whereas the `PeriodicSampler` uses the initial value of the input, the `TriggeredSampler` uses whatever value has the same tag as the trigger event.

The example in figure 11 illustrates the use of a `LevelCrossingDetector` actor combined with transient states. The result of an execution is shown in figure 12. Note that although outputs produced by transient states integrate to nothing, they nonetheless trigger level-crossing detectors. This predictable and understandable behavior is a result of the clean semantics.

The `FirstOrderHold` and `ZeroOrderHold` actor take discrete input signals and produce continuously-evolving output signals. In the case of `ZeroOrderHold`, the output signal value in the interval $t \in [t_i, t_{i+1})$ is equal to the final value of the input signal at t_i, where t_i and t_{i+1} are discrete times when the input is not absent and t_i immediately precedes t_{i+1}. The `FirstOrderHold` actor linearly extrapolates from the final value $x_f(t_i)$ given its derivative $\dot{x}_f(t_i)$.

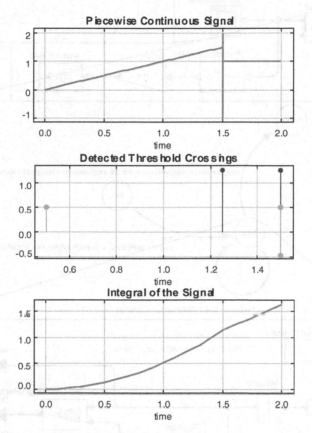

Fig. 12. A simple model that illustrates discrete signals

Notice that the tagged signal model semantics of HyVisual, which unambiguously defines initial and final values, makes it easy to give predictable and understandable behaviors for these actors.

Note that some hybrid system simulators, such as Simulink/Stateflow, do not have discrete signals. Instead, discrete signals are approximated as piecewise-constant signals. This is adequate for many purposes, but we believe that genuinely discrete signals are a better model for the externally visible actions of software.

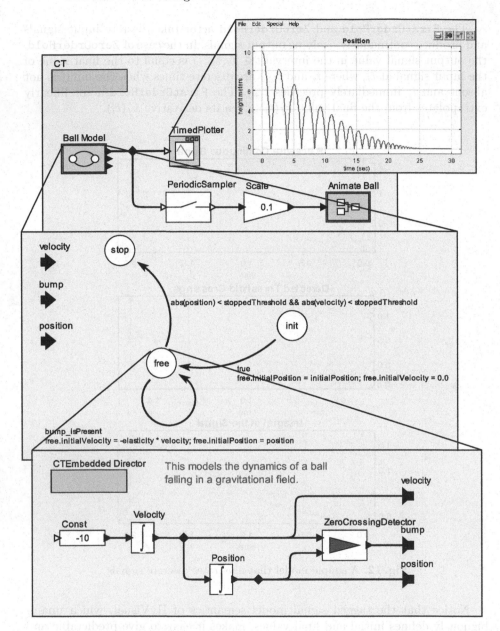

Fig. 13. A classic example of a Zeno system, the bouncing ball

7.3   Zeno Conditions

We have already discussed chattering Zeno conditions, where a signal fails to
reach a final value at some $t \in T$. It is also possible to get Zeno conditions where
a discrete signal has infinitely many events at distinct times within a finite time
interval. A classic example is the bouncing ball model, shown in figure 13.

In the idealized bouncing ball example, there are infinitely many events in a finite amount of time. An event is a collision of the ball with the surface on which it bounces. Let $D \subset T$ be the times at which the ball collides with the surface. Notice that even though this is a Zeno system, the set D is discrete. That is, there is an order embedding from D to the integers.

However, "discreteness" of sets is not a compositional property. In particular, let $D' = \mathcal{N}$, the non-negative integers. Then $D \cup D'$ is not a discrete set. We say that a model is *non-Zeno* if it is free of chattering Zeno conditions and if $D \cup D'$ is discrete, where $D \subset T$ is the times at which the model has discrete events.

A sufficient condition for a model to be non-Zeno is that there is a lower bound $\delta > 0$ on the time between events, and that there be no chattering Zeno conditions. Although this statement is rather obvious, the classical approach to proving it leverages some fairly sophisticated mathematics, constructing a metric space of signals using the so-called Cantor metric, and then invoking the Banach fixed point theorem [28].

8   Actor Semantics

So far, our examples have included a limited library of actors consisting of integrators, state machines to represent modal behavior, Expression actors, and a library of actors for converting between discrete and continuously-evolving signals. In principle one could define a primitive library set that is sufficiently expressive to represent many useful hybrid systems. But this would not be sufficient. Modern software systems require both (1) *user-defined components* and (2) *compositionality*. To support user-defined components, we need to define exactly what is required of an actor for it to be usable in a hybrid system model. To support compositionality, we need to define how a hybrid system model itself can become an actor within another hybrid system model. We address both of these problems by defining what we call an *abstract semantics* for actors. It is abstract in that it omits details of execution that are not relevant, such as how the actor actually performs computation. It strives for maximal "information hiding," imposing just enough constraints on actor designers to enable our two objectives, and no more.

First, we leverage our ideal-solver semantics to observe that actors in model will be required to react to inputs only at a discrete subset D' of the time line T. The memoryless actors (like the Expression actor), need only to provide a function that can be evaluated where, given the values of the inputs and the current time, the actor asserts the values of the outputs.

Some actors, however, need to be able to affect what times are present in D'. The LevelCrossingDetector and PeriodicSampler in figure 10 are two examples. So is the modal actor Masses in figure 1, and in fact any modal model constructed hierarchically in HyVisual.

Discrete events are either *predictable* or *unpredictable*. For predictable events, the time of the event is known before the execution has advanced to that time. To support both of these, HyVisual uses the mechanism developed by Liu [24]. First, an actor provides a function that, given the state of the actor and the current time, returns a "suggested" step size. The step size taken by the execution engine is guaranteed to not exceed this suggestion. So an actor with predictable events simply has to implement this function return appropriate suggestions. Second, an actor provides a predicate that given the state of the actor and the current time, returns true if the step taken to reach this current time was sufficiently small. Actors with unpredictable events will return false if the execution has missed an event. The execution engine is then required to backtrack and re-execute the model with a smaller step size. Note that exactly the same mechanism is used to implement variable step-size ODE solvers.

There are two consequences to this strategy. First, events may be missed. Consider for example a guard on a mode transition that fails to become true only because the step size was too large. Second, every actor must be able to backtrack. We deal with these two issues next, in turn.

8.1 Event Detection

Considering the first consequence, the event detection problem for differential-algebraic models (of which hybrid systems are examples) is studied in [34]. Methods specifically for hybrid systems are considered in [35], where a method is proposed that under certain assumptions that are often satisfied, an event is guaranteed to be detected. Moreover, the method guarantees that the boundary is not crossed in the process of detecting it (which could result in attempting to evaluate the function g in a region where it is undefined). This method is implemented in Charon [7]. However, this mechanism requires that the solver be able to identify and support the mechanisms that create the events. For example, when guards on mode transitions are threshold checks on linear functions of the continuously-evolving variables, the methods work well. At a minimum, the technique requires that the guard expressions have a finite Taylor series expansion, or that they be closely approximated by a finite Taylor series expansion. This makes it more difficult to support user-defined actors that detect events. It also makes compositionality more difficult, and the computational cost is high.

The method for event detection used in HyVisual allows for implementation of such techniques because components can provide constraints on step sizes. As discussed above, every actor can implement a function that suggests the next step size, and that step size will not be exceeded by the solver. Note that this mechanism would be implemented by an actor, not by the core infrastructure, so its expensive computation would only be incurred when the model designer chooses to use an actor that implements it. Although we agree that such methods could be useful, we have not implemented the mechanism suggested in [35] in any actor in HyVisual, and most particularly we have not implemented it in the modal model actor, which defines the semantics of the state machines like that shown in figure 1. The mechanism we have implemented for event detection in the state machines is more computationally lightweight, but it does not offer any assurance that the model will not be evaluated in regions where the guard has been crossed. However, it is adequate for many applications.

8.2   Backtracking

Since any actor can implement a predicate that rejects the last executed step size, all actors must be able to backtrack after having provided outputs at a specified time. To accomplish this, we require that actors follow a *stateful abstract semantics*, which we now define.

An actor with a stateful abstract semantics provides two functions f and g, where f is an output function and g is a state update function. For an actor with n input ports and m output ports, these functions have the form

$$f : V_d^n \times T \times \Sigma \to V_d^m \qquad (10)$$
$$g : V_d^n \times T \times \Sigma \to \Sigma, \qquad (11)$$

where V_d is the set of possible values at the input ports (including, possibly, the absent value ε), T is the time line, and Σ is the state space of the actor. Given these two functions, the execution engine controls the state of the actor, and does not commit an actor to a new state until all actors have "approved" the step size. In the Ptolemy II infrastructure, on which HyVisual is based, this mechanism is implemented by actor by providing two distinct methods, `fire()` and `postfire()`, the first of which reacts to inputs by providing outputs, and the second of which commits the state changes (if any) of the actor. However, as we will see below in section 10, this mechanism is not rich enough to fully support compositionality.

8.3   Fixed Point Iteration

Making the state of an actor explicit also helps us solve the problem raised in section 7.2, which is to determine when signals have reached their final value at a time stamp. Suppose that an actor is defined by functions f and g of the forms given by (10) and (11). Let the input be $x: T \times \mathcal{N} \to V_d^n$ and the output be $y: T \times \mathcal{N} \to V_d^m$. Let the state of the actor at each tag be given by a function $\sigma: T \times \mathcal{N} \to \Sigma$. Then at time $t \in T$, execution proceeds as follows:

$$y(t, 0) = f(\sigma(t, 0), t, x(t, 0))$$
$$\sigma(t, 1) = g(\sigma(t, 0), t, x(t, 0))$$
$$y(t, 1) = f(\sigma(t, 1), t, x(t, 1))$$
$$\sigma(t, 2) = g(\sigma(t, 1), t, x(t, 1))$$
$$\cdots$$

When all actors in the model have reached a point where their state no longer changes, then the final values have been reached for all signals and the execution at the time t is complete.

9 ODE Solvers

So far, we have assumed an ideal ODE solver. Fortunately, the semantic framework we have developed under this assumption accomodates, with some care, practical numerical ODE solvers. These solvers typically include algorithms for dynamically adjusting the step sizes. These step size adjustments typically require backtracking because they try a step size and then estimate the error. If the error is too large, they reduce the step size and redo the calculation. The abstract semantics for actors given in the previous section supports such backtracking. The key desired properties of an ODE solver are *consistency* (the error divided by the integration step size goes to zero as the step size goes to zero) and *stability* (errors do not accumulate as integration steps increase).

We consider two popular classes of ODE solvers, *linear multistep methods* (LMS) and *Runge-Kutta methods* (RK). Assume a model of the form given by figure 6, where again we ignore the index, assuming that the solver is applied over regions of time where the signals involved have only one value. LMS methods require solving the following equation at each time step t_n,

$$\sum_{i=0}^{k-1} \alpha_i x(t_{n-i}) + h_n \sum_{i=0}^{k-1} \beta_i \dot{x}(t_{n-i}) = 0, \tag{12}$$

where $h_n = t_n - t_{n-1}$, and k, α_i, and β_i are parameters of the particular LMS method being used. For example, the well-known *trapezoidal rule* is a two-step $(k = 2)$ LMS method with the form

$$x(t_n) - x(t_{n-1}) - \frac{h_n}{2}(\dot{x}(t_n) + \dot{x}(t_{n-1})) = 0. \tag{13}$$

This method has been proved stable and the most accurate among two-step LMS methods.

Notice that in order to compute the output of an integrator at time t_n, an LMS method generally needs to have access to the input of the integrator $\dot{x}(t_n)$ at that same time. In a model with no directed cycles, this poses no difficulty. However, in a model of the form given in figure 6, the input to the integrator cannot generally be known until its output is known. Such methods are called *implicit methods* because the solution depends on itself. One possible solution to this self-referential conundrum is to use iterative solution techniques like the Newton-Raphson method [36]. A second problem with LMS methods is that when there are more than two steps, past values of the signal x and its derivative must be known. At the start time of a model and after any discontinuity, these values are not known in any useful way.

Another common solution is to use an RK method. RK methods perform interpolation at each integration step to approximate the derivative. An explicit k stage RK method has the form

$$x(t_n) = x(t_{n-1}) + \sum_{i=0}^{k-1} c_i K_i, \tag{14}$$

where

$$K_0 = h_n g(x(t_{n-1}), t_{n-1}),$$

$$K_i = h_n g(x(t_{n-1}) + \sum_{j=0}^{i-1} A_{i,j} K_j, t_{n-1} + h b_i), \quad i \in \{1, \cdots, k-1\}$$

and $A_{i,j}$, b_i and c_i are algorithm parameters calculated by comparing the form of a Taylor expansion of x with (14). The first order RK method, also called the *forward Euler* method, has the (much simpler) form

$$x(t_n) = x(t_{n-1}) + h_n \dot{x}(t_{n-1}). \tag{15}$$

Notice that there is no difficulty with self referentiality here, and the only past information required is $\dot{x}(t_{n-1})$, which can always be computed from $x(t_{n-1})$, which is known, even at the execution start time and after a discontinuity.

The so-called RK2-3 ODE solver is a $k = 3$ step method used by default in HyVisual and given by

$$x(t_n) = x(t_{n-1}) + \frac{2}{9} K_0 + \frac{3}{9} K_1 + \frac{4}{9} K_2, \tag{16}$$

where

$$K_0 = h_n g(x(t_{n-1}), t_{n-1})$$
$$K_1 = h_n g(x(t_{n-1}) + 0.5 h_n K_0, t_{n-1} + 0.5 h_n)$$
$$K_2 = h_n g(x(t_{n-1}) + 0.75 h_n K_1, t_{n-1} + 0.75 h_n).$$

Notice that this method requires evaluation of the function g in figure 6 at intermediate times $t_{n-1} + 0.5 h_n$ and $t_{n-1} + 0.75 h_n$, in addition to the times t_{n-1}. This fact has significant consequences for compositionality of this method, considered below in section 10.

In summary, the RK2-3 ODE solver performs the following steps:

1. Evaluate $g(x(t_{n-1}), t_{n-1})$ to get $\dot{x}(t_{n-1})$.
2. Evaluate g again to get an estimate of $\dot{x}(t_{n-1} + 0.5 h_n)$.
3. Evaluate g a third time to get an estimate of $\dot{x}(t_{n-1} + 0.75 h_n)$.
4. Combine these estimates to get an estimate of $x(t_n)$.

In addition, after these steps are complete, the RK2-3 method estimates the local truncation error as follows,

$$K_3 = g(x(t_n), t_n)$$
$$\varepsilon = h_n \frac{-5}{72} K_0 + \frac{1}{12} K_1 + \frac{1}{9} K_2 + \frac{-1}{8} K_3.$$

This estimate will be larger when the derivative of the signal varies more over the interval $[t_{n-1}, t_n)$. If the error estimate exceeds some specified threshold, then the whole process needs to be repeated with a smaller step size.

A key consequence is that since g in figure 6 is a function representing the combined effect of a composition of actors, it is necessary to be able to repeatedly execute these actors without altering the state of the actors. The abstract actor semantics in section 8.2 supports this. However, this has unfortunate consequences for compositionality, discussed next.

10   Compositionality

Compositionality is property of programming languages where compositions of language primitives can themselves be treated as a language primitive. Given a composition of actors, if that composition conforms with the abstract semantics that we have outlined, then the composition itself is an actor, and can be used in a model like any other actor. The hierarchy we have seen in the various HyVisual examples exploits this fact.

However, when considering ODE solvers, there is a more subtle issue. Notice in figures 1 and 2 that each level of the hierarchy has its own director (the director is not shown explicitly in the FSM levels, but it is there). A director implements the ODE solver, so this fact means that we can use diverse ODE solvers at different levels of the hierarchy. This can be very useful, since different solvers are better for different models.

The subtle issue, however, is that intuition dictates that if we use the same solver, then the behavior of a model should be the same whether we use hierarchy or not. So, for example, in figures 1 and 2, if we eliminated the FSM level and constructed a flat model (no hierarchy) that only included the behavior of the masses when they are separate, then an execution should yield exactly the same result as the hierarchical model during the times that the masses are separate. In other words, hierarchy alone should not change behavior.

This seeming simple objective turns out to be hard to achieve. In particular, the RK2-3 solver described in the previous section requires that actors be evaluated not just at the discrete times in the trace, but also at intermediate times that play a role in the approximation. With hierarchical solvers, when we ask for an evaluation at time $t_{n-1} + 0.5h$, for example, the inner solver will treat this as the desired step, and will therefore evaluate the inner model at additional intermediate times $t_{n-1} + 0.5 \cdot 0.5h$ and $t_{n-1} + 0.5 \cdot 0.75h$. In a flat model, these evaluations will not occur. As a consequence, the numerical results of the hierarchical model will differ from the results of the flat model. This is neither expected nor desirable.

The solution that we have come up with violates information hiding across levels of the hierarchy, but only in a disciplined way. When the same kind of solver is being used across levels of the hierarchy, the solvers coordinate their actions to behave as if the hierarchy were flat. This yields the invariant that hierarchy does not change behavior *as long as the same kind of solver is used*. But it leaves open the possibility of using multiple solvers.

11   Nondeterminism

All the examples here are all determinate systems. A key design objective in HyVisual is to give deterministic execution to determinate models. We have achieved that. Sometimes, however, useful models are nondeterministic.

One possible form of nondeterminsm is when a state machine has two or more enabled transitions at some time. A key question, however, is how to assign an execution to such a model. It is incorrect to choose an arbitrary enabled transition because this could result in a model producing misleading traces. They appear determinate, but are in fact nondeterminate.

A better solution is Monte Carlo execution, where probabilities are assigned to the outcomes and the execution uses random numbers to make the choices. However, this requires that the probabilities be assigned as part of the modeling process. In fact, HyVisual fully supports Monte Carlo execution of nondeterminate models, where the probabilities are explicitly included in the model.

An intriguing possibility, not yet implemented in HyVisual, is to use model checking to simultaneously explore all traces of a nondeterministic model. As with many applications of model checking, scalability will be a key issue.

12 Conclusions

We have approached hybrid systems as a model of computation, and have presented HyVisual as a domain-specific programming language with hybrid systems semantics. We have introduced a tagged signal model for hybrid systems that embraces discontinuities and discrete events along with the usual piecewise continuous signals, and we have given a clear and simple executable semantics. The semantics separates concerns for the accuracy of numerical approximation techniques from other semantic issues. The result is a predictable, understandable, and composable semantics for executable models of hybrid systems.

References

1. Deshpande, A., Varaiya, P.: Information structures for control and verification of hybrid systems. In: American Control Conference (ACC). (1995)
2. Henzinger, T.A.: The theory of hybrid automata. In Inan, M., Kurshan, R., eds.: Verification of Digital and Hybrid Systems. Volume 170 of NATO ASI Series F: Computer and Systems Sciences. Springer-Verlag (2000) 265–292
3. Kopke, P., Henzinger, T., Puri, A., Varaiya, P.: What's decidable about hybrid automata? In: 27th Annual ACM Symposioum on Theory of Computing (STOCS). (1995) 372–382
4. Lygeros, J., Tomlin, C., Sastry, S.: Controllers for reachability specifications for hybrid systems. Automatica (1999)
5. Puri, A., Varaiya, P.: Verification of hybrid systems using abstractions. In: Hybrid Systems Workshop. Volume Hybrid Systems II, LNCS 999., Springer-Verlag (1994) 359–369
6. Lynch, N., Segala, R., Vaandrager, F., Weinberg, H.: Hybrid I/O automata. In Alur, R., Henzinger, T., Sontag, E., eds.: Hybrid Systems III. Volume LNCS 1066. Springer-Verlag (1996) 496–510
7. Alur, R., Dang, T., Esposito, J., Hur, Y., Ivancic, F., Kumar, V., Lee, I., Mishra, P., Pappas, G.J., Sokolsky, O.: Hierarchical modeling and analysis of embedded systems. Proceedings of the IEEE 91 (2003) 11–28
8. Silva, B.I., Richeson, K., Krogh, B., Chutinan, A.: Modeling and verifying hybrid dynamic systems using checkmate. In: Automation of Mixed Processes : Dynamic Hybrid Systems (ADPM), Dortmund Germany, Shaker Verlag, Aachen (2000)

9. Asarin, E., Bournez, O., Dang, T., Maler, O.: Approximate reachability analysis of piecewise-linear dynamical systems. In: Hybrid Systems: Computation and Control (HSCC). Volume LNCS 1790., Springer-Verlag (2000) 2131

10. Henzinger, T.A., Ho, P.H., Wong-Toi, H.: (hytech): A model checker for hybrid systems. International Journal on Software Tools for Technology Transfer 1 (1997) 110–122

11. Daws, C., Olivero, A., Tripakis, S., Yovine, S.: The tool kronos. In: Hybrid Systems III: Verification and Control. Volume LNCS 1066., Springer-Verlag (1996) 208219

12. Larsen, K., Pettersson, P., Yi, W.: Uppaal in a nutshell. International Journal on Software Tools for Technology Transfer 1 (1997)

13. Mitchell, I., Tomlin, C.: Level set methods for computation in hybrid systems. In: Hybrid Systems: Computation and Control (HSCC). Volume LNCS 1790., Springer-Verlag (2000) 310323

14. Torrisi, F.D., Bemporad, A., Bertini, G., Hertach, P., Jost, D., Mignone, D.: Hysdel 2.0.5 - user manual. Technical report, ETH (2002)

15. Cataldo, A., Hylands, C., Lee, E.A., Liu, J., Liu, X., Neuendorffer, S., Zheng, H.: Hyvisual: A hybrid system visual modeler. Technical Report Technical Memorandum UCB/ERL M03/30, University of California, Berkeley (2003)

16. Tiller, M.M.: Introduction to Physical Modeling with Modelica. Kluwer Academic Publishers (2001)

17. Djenidi, R., Lavarenne, C., Nikoukhah, R., Sorel, Y., Steer, S.: From hybrid simulation to real-time implementation. In: 11th European Simulation Symposium and Exhibition (ESS99). (1999) 7478

18. Deshpande, A., Gollu, A., Varaiya, P.: The shift programming language for dynamic networks of hybrid automata. IEEE Trans. on Automatic Control 43 (1998)

19. Carloni, L.P., DiBenedetto, M.D., Pinto, A., Sangiovanni-Vincentelli, A.: Modeling techniques, programming languages, and design toolsets for hybrid systems. Technical Report IST-2001-38314 WPHS, Columbus Project (2004)

20. Mosterman, P.: An overview of hybrid simulation phenomena and their support by simulation packages. In Varager, F., Schuppen, J.H.v., eds.: Hybrid Systems: Computation and Control (HSCC). Volume LNCS 1569., Springer-Verlag (1999) 165177

21. Sztipanovits, J., Karsai, G.: Model-integrated computing. IEEE Computer (1997) 110112

22. University of Pennsylvania MoBIES team: HSIF semantics (version 3, synchronous edition). Technical Report Report, University of Pennsylvania (2002)

23. Lee, E.A.: Overview of the ptolemy project. Technical Report Technical Memorandum UCB/ERL M03/25, University of California, Berkeley (2003)

24. Liu, J.: Continuous Time and Mixed-Signal Simulation in Ptolemy II. M.s. thesis, University of California, Berkeley (1998)

25. Lemkin, M.A.: Micro Accelerometer Design with Digital Feedback Control. Ph.d., University of California, Berkeley (1997)

26. Fong, C.: Discrete-Time Dataflow Models for Visual Simulation in Ptolemy II. Master's report, University of California, Berkeley (2001)

27. Benveniste, A., Berry, G.: The synchronous approach to reactive and real-time systems. Proceedings of the IEEE 79 (1991) 1270–1282

28. Lee, E.A.: Modeling concurrent real-time processes using discrete events. Annals of Software Engineering 7 (1999) 25–45

29. Lee, E.A., Sangiovanni-Vincentelli, A.: A framework for comparing models of computation. IEEE Transactions on CAD 17 (1998)

30. Liu, J., Lee, E.A.: On the causality of mixed-signal and hybrid models. In: 6th International Workshop on Hybrid Systems: Computation and Control (HSCC '03), Prague, Czech Republic (2003)
31. Sastry, S.: Nonlinear Systems: Analysis, Stability, and Control. Springer (1999)
32. Callier, F.M., Desoer, C.A.: Linear System Theory. Springer-Verlag (1991)
33. Henzinger, T.A., Horowitz, B., Kirsch, C.M.: Giotto: A time-triggered language for embedded programming. In: EMSOFT 2001. Volume LNCS 2211., Tahoe City, CA, Springer-Verlag (2001)
34. Park, T., Barton, P.I.: State event location in differential-algebraic models. ACM Transactions on Modeling and Computer Simulation (TOMACS) **6** (1996) 137–165
35. Esposito, J., Kumar, V., Pappas, G.J.: Accurate event detection for simulating hybrid systems. In: Hybrid Systems: Computation and Control (HSCC). Volume LNCS 2034., Springer-Verlag (2001) 204217
36. Press, W.H., Teukolsky, S., Vetterling, W.T., Flannery, B.P.: Numerical Recipes in C: the Art of Scientific Computing. Cambridge University Press (1992)

SOS Methods for Semi-algebraic Games and Optimization

(Invited Paper)

Pablo A. Parrilo

Laboratory for Information and Decision Systems,
Massachusetts Institute of Technology (MIT), Cambridge,
MA 02139-4307, USA
parrilo@mit.edu

Abstract. Semialgebraic computations, i.e., the manipulation of sets and logical conditions defined by polynomial inequalities in real variables, are an essential "primitive" in the analysis and design of hybrid dynamical systems. Fundamental tasks such as reachability analysis, abstraction verification, and the computation of stability and performance certificates, all use these operations extensively, and can quickly become the computational bottleneck in the design process. Although there is a well-developed body of both basic theory and algorithms for these tasks, the practical performance of most available methods is still far from being satisfactory on real-world problems. While there are several possible causes for this (besides the NP-hardness of the task), a sensible explanation lies in the purely algebraic nature of the usual methods, as well as the insistence on exact (as opposed to approximate or "relaxed") solutions. For these reasons, there is a strong interest in the development of efficient techniques for (perhaps restricted) classes of semialgebraic problems. In this talk we review the basic elements and present several new results on the SOS approach to semialgebraic computations, that combines symbolic and numerical techniques from real algebra and convex optimization. Its main defining feature is the use and computation of sum of squares (SOS) decompositions for multivariate polynomials via semidefinite programming. These are extended, using the Positivstellensatz, to structured infeasibility certificates for polynomial equations and inequalities. The developed techniques unify and generalize many well-known existing methods.

In particular, we will discuss semialgebraic problems with at most two quantifier alternations (i.e., classical polynomial optimization problems as well as the related games and minimax problems). As an example, we will solve in detail a class of zero-sum two-person games with an infinite number of pure strategies, where the payoff function is a polynomial expression of the actions of the players.

Although particular emphasis will be given to the hybrid systems viewpoint, the basic ideas and algorithms, as well as these recent extensions, will be illustrated with examples drawn from a broad range of related domains, including dynamical systems and geometric theorem proving.

M. Morari and L. Thiele (Eds.): HSCC 2005, LNCS 3414, p. 54, 2005.
© Springer-Verlag Berlin Heidelberg 2005

The Discrete Time Behavior of Lazy Linear Hybrid Automata

Manindra Agrawal and P.S. Thiagarajan

School of Computing,
National University of Singapore
{agarwal, thiagu}@comp.nus.edu.sg

Abstract. We study the class of *lazy linear hybrid automata with finite precision*. The key features of this class are:

- The observation of the continuous state and the rate changes associated with mode switchings take place with bounded delays.
- The values of the continuous variables can be observed with only finite precision.
- The guards controlling the transitions of the automaton are finite conjunctions of arbitrary linear constraints.

We show that the discrete time dynamics of this class of automata can be effectively analyzed without requiring resetting of the continuous variables during mode changes. In fact, our result holds for guard languages that go well beyond linear constraints.

1 Introduction

We present a class of linear hybrid automata and show that their discrete time behavior can be effectively computed and represented as finite state automata. A hybrid automaton of the kind we study is meant to be a model of a closed loop system consisting of a digital controller interacting with a plant whose state variables evolve in a continuous manner. The controller will sample the state of the plant at periodic *discrete time instances*. Typically, these time instances will be determined by the system clock of the processor implementing the controller. This state information will consist of the current values of the relevant plant variables as observed by the sensors. These values will be digitized with *finite precision* and reported to the controller. Using this information, the controller may decide to switch the mode of the plant by generating suitable output signals that will be transmitted to the actuators, which in turn will effect the desired mode change.

An important feature in this setting -and this will be reflected in our automata- is that the sensors will report the current values of the variables and the actuators will effect changes in the rates of evolution of the variables with *bounded delays*. More specifically, the state observed at the instant T_k is a state that held at some time in a bounded interval contained in (T_{k-1}, T_k). Further, if an instantaneous mode change has taken place at T_k from the standpoint of the digital controller,

M. Morari and L. Thiele (Eds.): HSCC 2005, LNCS 3414, pp. 55–69, 2005.
© Springer-Verlag Berlin Heidelberg 2005

then any necessary change in the rate of a variable will not kick in immediately. Rather, it will do so at some time in a bounded interval contained in (T_k, T_{k+1}).

A restriction we impose is that each variable's allowed range of values is bounded. In addition, we focus, for simplicity, on the case where there is a single rate vector associated with each mode instead of a bounded (rectangular) region of flows as is often done [1]. Our automata are a variant of *linear* hybrid automata [2] in that the guards controlling the mode switches are assumed to be conjunctions of *linear inequalities*.

Our main result is that the discrete time behavior of such an automaton is regular and moreover, this behavior can be effectively computed and represented as a finite state automaton. Indeed, any reasonable language of constraints can be used to form the guards (for instance, conjunctions of polynomial inequalities) and the main result will continue to hold.

As is well known, hybrid automata have a great deal of expressive power. In a variety of settings, the control state reachability problem is undecidable, as reported for instance in [3, 4]. A number of undecidability results in a discrete time setting have also been reported in the literature but these results are mainly for piecewise-affine (and not, as considered here, piecewise constant) systems with infinite precision; see for instance [5, 6]. A sharp delineation of the boundary between decidable and undecidable features of hybrid automata is drawn in [7] as well as [1].

These results, as also the positive results reported for example in [8, 9, 10, 11] suggest that except under very restrictive settings, one can not expect to get decidability if the continuous variables don't get reset during mode changes (in case their rates change as a result of the mode change). Viewed as a model of digital controllers that interact with plants through sensors and actuators, the resetting requirement severely restricts the modelling power of the automaton. Our results show that by focusing on the discrete time behavior *and* requiring finite precision, we can allow the continuous variables to retain their values during mode changes. Furthermore, we can allow a rich class of guards and cope with lazy sensors and actuators that have bounded delays associated with them.

Our work here is in a sense a generalization and in another sense specialization of the work reported in [12]. Finite precision was not demanded in [12] but the guards were required to be *rectangular*. In contrast we permit here the guards to be far more general. We do not know at present whether the finite precision assumption can be dropped for our linear hybrid automata though it is a natural one in the setting that we are considering. A closely related earlier work is [13] where the discrete time behavior of rectangular hybrid automata is studied but with the requirement that all instantaneous transitions should take place only at integer-valued instances of time. In our terms, [13] assumes that the sensors and actuators function with zero delays which considerably simplifies the analysis. On the other hand, [13] does not assume finite precision and yet establishes a decidability result for automata with triangular guards (i.e. conjunctions of constraints of the form $x - y \sim c$ where $\sim \in \{<, \leq, >, \geq\}$) and rectangular initial regions. It turns out that, as we observe in a later section, without finite precision but with zero delays sensors and actuators and *linear constraints* we can show a corresponding decidability result. As its title suggests, [13] is concerned with controller synthesis problems too. By viewing our automata as suitable open systems, we can also tackle controller synthesis problems using standard techniques.

Though not directly related to our work here, there have been a number of previous attempts to reduce the expressive power of timed and rectangular automata by taking away their ability to define trajectories with infinite precision [14, 15, 16]. Typically one demands, the set of admitted trajectories to be "fuzzy"; if a trajectory is admitted by the automaton then it should also admit trajectories that are sufficiently close to the trajectory where "closeness" is captured using a natural topology over the trajectories. This does not lead to more tractability as shown in [15] and [16]. The key difference between our work and these previous works is that in our automata, the fuzziness lies in the gap between the observed continuous state based on which a mode change takes place and the actual continuous state that holds at that instant. Further, the actual rate at which a variable may be evolving at an instant may be different from the rate demanded by the current mode of the automaton.

In the next section, we formulate the model of lazy linear hybrid automata with finite precision. In section 3 we prove our main result, namely, the language of state sequences and action sequences generated by our automaton are regular and that finite state automata representing these languages can be effectively computed. In section 4 we discuss the restrictions placed on our automata and point out that many of them can be easily relaxed. We also point how our main result can be easily extended to a much richer class of guards. In the concluding section we discuss the prospects for extending the results reported here.

2   Lazy Linear Hybrid Automata

Fix a positive integer n and one function symbol x_i for each i in $\{1, 2, \ldots, n\}$. We view each x_i as a function $x_i : \mathbb{R}_{\geq 0} \mapsto \mathbb{R}$ with $\mathbb{R}$ being the set of reals and $\mathbb{R}_{\geq 0}$, the set of non-negative reals. We let $\mathbb{Q}$ denote the set of rationals.

A *linear constraint* is an inequality of the form $a_1 \cdot x_1 + a_2 \cdot x_2 + \ldots + a_n \cdot x_n \sim c$ where $a_1, a_2, \ldots a_n$ as well as c are rational numbers and $\sim \in \{<, \leq, >, \geq\}$. A *guard* is a finite conjunction of linear constraints. We let Grd denote the set of guards.

A *valuation* is just a member of $\mathbb{R}^n$. The valuation V will be viewed as prescribing the value $V(i)$ to each variable x_i. The notion of a valuation satisfying a guard is defined in the obvious way.

A *lazy linear hybrid automaton* is a structure $\mathcal{A} = (Q, Act, q_{in}, V_{in}, D, \epsilon, \{\rho_q\}_{q \in Q}, \mathrm{B}, \longrightarrow)$ where:

- Q is a finite set of *control states*.
- Act is a finite set of *actions*.
- $q_{in} \in Q$ is the initial control state.

- $V_{in} \in \mathbb{Q}^n$ is the initial valuation.
- $D = \{g, \delta_g, h, \delta_h\} \subseteq \mathbb{Q}$ is the *set of delay parameters* such that $0 < g < g + \delta_g < h < h + \delta_h < 1$.
- ϵ is the *precision of measurement*, $\epsilon \in \mathbb{Q}$.
- $\rho_q \in \mathbb{Q}^n$ is a rate vector which specifies the rate $\rho_q(i)$ at which each x_i evolves when the system is in the control state q.
- $B = \{v \mid B_{min} \leq v \leq B_{max}, B_{min}, B_{max} \in \mathbb{Q}\}$ is the *allowed range*.
- $\longrightarrow \subseteq Q \times Act \times Grd \times Q$ is a transition relation such that $q \neq q'$ for every (q, a, φ, q') in $\longrightarrow$.

We shall study the discrete time behavior of our automata. At each time instant T_k, the automaton receives a measurement regarding the current values of the x_i's. However, the value of x_i that is observed at T_k is the value that held at some $t \in [T_{k-1} + h, T_{k-1} + h + \delta_h]$. Further, the value is observed with a precision of ϵ. More precisely, any value of x_i in the half-open interval $[(l - 1/2)\epsilon, (l + 1/2)\epsilon)$ is reported as $l\epsilon$ where l is an integer. For any real number v, we will denote this rounded-off value relative to ϵ as $\langle v \rangle$.

If at T_k, the automaton is in control state q and the observed n-tuple of values $(\langle v_1 \rangle, \langle v_2 \rangle, \ldots, \langle v_n \rangle)$ satisfies the guard φ with (q, a, φ, q') being a transition, then the automaton may perform this transition instantaneously by executing the action a and move to the control state q'. As a result, as usual, the x_i's will cease to evolve at the rates ρ_q and instead start evolving at the rates $\rho_{q'}$. However, this change in the rate of evolution will not kick in at T_k but at some time $t \in [T_k + g, T_k + g + \delta_g]$. In this sense, both the sensing of the values of the x_i's and the rate changes associated with mode switching take place in a lazy fashion but with bounded delays. We expect g to be close to 0, h to be close to 1 and both δ_g and δ_h to be small compared to 1.

Thus in the idealized setting, which we shall consider briefly later, the change in rates due mode switching would kick in immediately ($g = 0 = \delta_g$) and the value observed at T_k is the value that holds at exactly T_k ($h = 1$ and $\delta_h = 0$). In addition, assuming perfect precision would boil down to setting $\langle v \rangle = v$ for every real number v.

B specifies the range of values within which the automaton's dynamics are valid. The automaton gets stuck if any of the x_i's ever assume a value outside the allowed range $[B_{min}, B_{max}]$. A number of the restrictions that we have imposed are mainly for ease of presentation. Later, we will discuss how these restrictions can be relaxed.

Our main result is that the control state and action sequence languages generated by a lazy linear hybrid automaton are both regular. Furthermore, these languages can be computed effectively.

2.1   The Transition System Semantics

Through the rest of this section we fix a lazy linear hybrid automaton $\mathcal{A}$ as defined above and assume its associated notations and terminology. We shall often say "automaton" to mean "lazy linear hybrid automaton". The behavior of $\mathcal{A}$ will be defined in terms of an associated transition system.

A *configuration* is a triple (q, V, q') where q, q' are control states and V is a valuation. q is the control state holding at the current time instant and q' is the control state that held at the previous time instant. V captures the *actual* values of the variables at the current instance. The configuration (q, V, q') is *feasible* iff $V(i) \in [B_{min}, B_{max}]$ for every i. The initial configuration is, by convention, the triple (q_{in}, V_{in}, q_{in}). We assume without loss of generality that the initial configuration is feasible. We let $C_{\mathcal{A}}$ denote the set of configurations. Since $\mathcal{A}$ will be clear from the context, we will often write C instead of $C_{\mathcal{A}}$.

As in the case of timed automata [17], a convenient way to understand the dynamics is to break up each move of the automaton into a time-passage move followed by an instantaneous transition. At T_0, the automaton will be in its initial configuration.

We assume that the unit of time has been fixed at some suitable level of granularity and that the rate vectors $\{\rho_q\}$ have been scaled accordingly. Suppose the automaton is in the configuration (q_k, V_k, q'_k) at T_k. Then one unit of time will pass and at time instant T_{k+1}, the automaton will make an instantaneous move by performing an action a or the silent action τ and move to a configuration $(q_{k+1}, V_{k+1}, q'_{k+1})$. The silent action will be used to record that no mode change has taken place during this move. Again, as often done in the case of timed automata, we will collapse these two sub-steps of a move (unit-time-passage followed by an instantaneous transition) into one "time-abstract" transition labelled by a member of Act or by τ.

With this scheme in mind, we now define the transition relation $\Longrightarrow \subseteq C \times (Act \cup \{\tau\}) \times C$ as follows.

- Let (q, V, q') and $(q1, V1, q1')$ be configurations and $a \in Act$. Then $(q, V, q') \overset{a}{\Longrightarrow} (q1, V1, q1')$ iff $q1' = q$ and there exists in $\mathcal{A}$ a transition of the form $q \overset{a,\varphi}{\longrightarrow} q1$ and there exist $\widehat{t1} \in [g, g + \delta_g]^n$ and $\widehat{t2} \in [h, h + \delta_h]^n$ such that the following conditions are satisfied.
  (1) Let $v_i = V(i) + \rho_{q'}(i) \cdot \widehat{t1}(i) + \rho_q(i) \cdot (\widehat{t2}(i) - \widehat{t1}(i))$ for each i. Then $(\langle v_1 \rangle, \langle v_2 \rangle, \ldots, \langle v_n \rangle)$ satisfies φ.
  (2) $V1(i) = V(i) + \rho_{q'}(i) \cdot \widehat{t1}(i) + \rho_q(i) \cdot (1 - \widehat{t1}(i))$ for each i.
- Let (q, V, q') and $(q1, V1, q1')$ be configurations. Then

$$(q, V, q') \overset{\tau}{\Longrightarrow} (q1, V1, q1') \quad \text{iff} \quad q1 = q1' = q$$

and there exists $\widehat{t1} \in [g, g + \delta_g]^n$ such that

$$V1(i) = V(i) + \rho_{q'}(i) \cdot \widehat{t1}(i) + \rho_q(i) \cdot (1 - \widehat{t1}(i)) \quad \text{for each } i.$$

Basically there are four possible transition types depending on whether $q = q'$ and $\alpha \in Act$. Suppose $(q, V, q') \overset{a}{\Longrightarrow} (q1, V1, q1')$ with $a \in Act$. Assume that $q \overset{a,\varphi}{\longrightarrow} q1$ in $\mathcal{A}$ and $\widehat{t1} \in [g, g + \delta_g]^n$ and $\widehat{t2} \in [h, h + \delta_h]^n$ are as specified above. We first note that $q1 \neq q$ by the definition of the transition relation of $\mathcal{A}$. The requirement $q1' = q$ follows from our convention that $q1'$ is the control state that held in the previous instant and we know this was q.

First consider the case $q \neq q'$ and let us suppose that the configuration (q, V, q') holds at T_k. We take $q \neq q'$ to mean that a change of mode from q' to q has just taken place (instantaneously) at T_k based on the observations that were made available at T_k. However, at T_k, the automaton will continue to evolve at the rate dictated by $\rho_{q'}$. Indeed, each x_i will, starting from T_k, evolve at rate $\rho_{q'}(i)$ until some $T_k + t_1$ with $t_1 \in [g, g + \delta_g]$. It will then start to evolve at rate $\rho_q(i)$ until T_{k+1}. Consequently, at T_{k+1}, the value of x_i will be $V1(i) = V(i) + \rho_{q'}(i) \cdot t_1 + \rho_q(i) \cdot (1 - t_1)$. On the other hand, $q1 \neq q$ implies that another instantaneous mode change has taken place at T_{k+1} based on the measurements made in the interval $[T_k + h, T_k + h + \delta_h]$. Suppose x_i was measured at $T_k + t_2$ with $t_2 \in [T_k + h, T_k + h + \delta_h]$. Then in order for the transition $q \xrightarrow{a, \varphi} q1$ of $\mathcal{A}$ to be enabled at T_{k+1}, it must be the case that the observed values of x_i's at $T_k + t_2$ satisfy the guard φ. But then these values are $\langle v_i \rangle$ with $v_i = V(i) + \rho_{q'}(i) \cdot t_1 + \rho_q(i) \cdot (t_2 - t_1)$. This explains the demands placed on the transition $(q, V, q') \xRightarrow{a} (q1, V1, q1')$. It is worth noting that if $q = q'$ (i.e. no mode change has taken place at T_k) then $V1(i) = V(i) + \rho_q(i) \cdot t_1 + \rho_q(i) \cdot (1 - t_1) = V(i) + \rho_q(i)$ as it should be. Furthermore, $V(i) + \rho_q(i) \cdot t_1 + \rho_q(i) \cdot (t_2 - t_1) = V(i) + \rho_q(i) \cdot t_2$.

Similar (and simpler) considerations motivate the demands placed on transitions of the form $(q, V, q') \xRightarrow{\tau} (q1, V1, q1')$. Here again, it is worth noting that, in case $q = q'$, $V1(i)$ is determined uniquely, namely, $V1(i) = V(i) + \rho_q(i)$.

We now define the transition system
$TS_{\mathcal{A}} = (RC_{\mathcal{A}}, (q_{in}, V_{in}, q_{in}), Act \cup \{\tau\}, \Longrightarrow_{\mathcal{A}})$ via:

- $RC_{\mathcal{A}}$, the set of *reachable configurations* of $\mathcal{A}$ is the least subset of C that contains the initial configuration (q_{in}, V_{in}, q_{in}) and satisfies:
  Suppose (q, V, q') is in $RC_{\mathcal{A}}$ and is a feasible configuration. Suppose further, $(q, V, q') \xRightarrow{\alpha} (q1, V1, q)$ for some $\alpha \in Act \cup \{\tau\}$. Then $(q1, V1, q) \in RC_{\mathcal{A}}$.
- $\Longrightarrow_{\mathcal{A}}$ is $\Longrightarrow$ restricted to $RC_{\mathcal{A}} \times (Act \cup \{\tau\}) \times RC_{\mathcal{A}}$.

We will often write RC instead of $RC_{\mathcal{A}}$ and write $\Longrightarrow$ instead of $\Longrightarrow_{\mathcal{A}}$. We note that a reachable configuration can be the source of a transition in $TS_{\mathcal{A}}$ only if it is feasible. Thus infeasible reachable configurations will be deadlocked in $TS_{\mathcal{A}}$.

A *run* of $TS_{\mathcal{A}}$ is a finite sequence of the form
$\sigma = (q_0, V_0, q_0') \alpha_0 (q_1, V_1, q_1') \alpha_1 (q_2, V_2, q_2') \ldots (q_k, V_k, q_k')$ where (q_0, V_0, q_0') is the initial configuration and $(q_m, V_m, q_m') \xRightarrow{\alpha_m} (q_{m+1}, V_{m+1}, q_{m+1}')$ for $0 \leq m < k$. The *st-sequence (state sequence)* induced by the run σ above is denoted as $st(\sigma)$ and it is the sequence $q_0 q_1 \ldots q_k$. On the other hand, the *act-sequence* induced by σ is denoted as $act(\sigma)$ and it is the sequence $\alpha_0 \alpha_1 \ldots \alpha_k$. We now define the languages $\mathcal{L}_{st}(\mathcal{A})$ and $\mathcal{L}_{act}(\mathcal{A})$ as :

- $\mathcal{L}_{st}(\mathcal{A}) = \{st(\sigma) \mid \sigma \text{ is a run of } \mathcal{A}\}$.
- $\mathcal{L}_{act}(\mathcal{A}) = \{act(\sigma) \mid \sigma \text{ is a run of } \mathcal{A}\}$.

Our main result is that $\mathcal{L}_{st}(\mathcal{A})$ is a regular subset of $Q^\star$ while $\mathcal{L}_{act}(\mathcal{A})$ is a regular subset of $(Act \cup \{\tau\})^\star$. Moreover, we can effectively construct finite state automata representing these languages. As a consequence, a variety of verification problems and controller synthesis problems for our automata can be effectively solved.

3   Proof of the Main Result

The transition guards in [12] were of the form $x_i = c$ for some constant c. This fact was critical for the finite division of B^n resulting in a finite automata. If the guards are more general then quantization of the continuous state space as done in [12] is not possible. We shall address this point again in the next section.

However the extra structure provided by the finite precision of observations comes to the rescue. As we show below, it enables us to generalize the proof idea of [12].

Let $\mathcal{A} = (Q, Act, q_{in}, V_{in}, D, \epsilon, \{\rho_q\}_{q \in Q}, B, F, \longrightarrow)$ be a lazy automaton. We assume for $\mathcal{A}$, the terminology and notations defined in the previous section.

We shall generalize the proof strategy of [12]. Define Δ to be the largest positive rational number that *integrally* divides every number in the finite set of rational numbers $\{g, \delta_g, h, \delta_h, 1\}$. We next define Γ to be the largest positive rational number that *integrally* divides each number in the finite set of rational numbers $\{\rho_q(i) \cdot \Delta \mid q \in Q, 1 \le i \le n\} \cup \{B_{min}, B_{max}\} \cup \{V_{in}(i) \mid 1 \le i \le n\} \cup \{\frac{\epsilon}{2}\}$.

Let $\mathbb{Z}$ denote the set of integers. We now define the map $\|\cdot\| : \mathbb{R} \to \mathbb{Z} \times \{I, S, \perp\}$ as follows.

- If $v \in (-\infty, B_{min})$, then $\|v\| = (k_{min} - 1, \perp)$ where $k_{min} \cdot \Gamma = B_{min}$.
- If $v \in (B_{max}, \infty)$, then $\|v\| = (k_{max}, \perp)$ where $k_{max} \cdot \Gamma = B_{max}$.
- Suppose $v \in [B_{min}, B_{max}]$ and $v = k\Gamma + \hat{v}$ with $k \in \mathbb{Z}$ and $\hat{v} \in [0, \Gamma)$. Then $\|v\| = (k, S)$ if $\hat{v} = 0$, and $\|v\| = (k, I)$ if $\hat{v} \ne 0$.

This map is extended in the obvious way to points in $\mathbb{R}^n$: $\|(v_1, v_2, \ldots, v_n)\| = (\|v_1\|, \|v_2\|, \ldots, \|v_n\|)$.

The map $\|\cdot\|$ can also be extended in a natural way to configurations. Denoting this extension also as $\|\cdot\|$, we define $\|(q, v, q')\|$ to be $(q, \|v\|, q')$. Let $\mathcal{D}_{\mathcal{A}} = \{\|c\| \mid c \in C_{\mathcal{A}}\}$. Clearly $\mathcal{D}_{\mathcal{A}}$ is a finite set and we will often write $\mathcal{D}$ instead of $\mathcal{D}_{\mathcal{A}}$. Our goal is to show that the equivalence relation over the reachable configurations RC of $\mathcal{A}$ induced by the map $\|\cdot\|$ in turn induces a right congruence of finite index over $Q^\star$.

We are now ready to tackle the main part of the proof.

Theorem 1. *Let $c1$ and $c2$ be two reachable configurations such that $\|c1\| = \|c2\|$. Suppose $\alpha \in Act \cup \{\tau\}$ and $c1'$ is a reachable configuration such that $c1 \overset{\alpha}{\Longrightarrow}_{\mathcal{A}} c1'$. Then there exists a reachable configuration $c2'$ such that $c2 \overset{\alpha}{\Longrightarrow}_{\mathcal{A}} c2'$ and $\|c1'\| = \|c2'\|$.*

Proof. Clearly $c1$ is feasible and since $\|c1\| = \|c2\|$, it follows that $c2$ is also feasible.

Let $c1$ and $c2$ be configurations at time instant t. Let us split the unit time interval in which $c1$ moves to $c1'$ into intervals of size Δ. We refer to these smaller intervals as *basic* intervals. By the choice of Δ, there will be an integral number, say m, of basic intervals in the unit time interval. Let $c1_0 = c1, c1_1, \ldots,$ $c1_m$ be the configurations that hold at the end of each of these basic intervals when the starting configuration is $c1$. Configuration $c1'$ is obtained by making an instantaneous state transition from $c1_m$. Let $[t + u\Delta, t + (u+1)\Delta]$ be one such basic interval. In this interval, assuming that $[u\Delta, (u+1)\Delta]$ lies in the range of $[g, g + \delta_g]$ or $[h, h + \delta_h]$, one of the two types of events may occur:

Rate Change: For some $J \subseteq \{1, 2, \ldots, n\}$ and $\{t_j\}_{j \in J}$ with $t_j \in [0, \Delta]$, the rate of variable x_j changes at $t + u\Delta + t_j$ for each $j \in J$.

Valuation: For some $J \subseteq \{1, 2, \ldots, n\}$ and $\{t_j\}_{j \in J}$ with $t_j \in [0, \Delta]$, the value of the variable x_j is recorded at time $t + u\Delta + t_j$ for each $j \in J$.

While the first event affects the current configuration immediately (by making the variables change at different rates), the affect of the second event is at the end of unit interval when an instantaneous state transition is made based on the values recorded by the event. We now prove a lemma about the behavior across basic intervals that will be crucial in proof of the theorem.

Lemma 1. *Let $c1_u$ and $c2_u$ be two configurations with $\|c1_u\| = \|c2_u\|$ at the beginning of basic interval $[t + u\Delta, t + (u+1)\Delta]$. For every $i \in \{1, 2, \ldots, n\}$ and for every time instant $t1_i \in [0, \Delta]$, there exists another time instant $t2_i \in [0, \Delta]$ such that the following holds:*

- *Suppose, starting from $c1_u$, a rate change is affected for x_i at time $t + u\Delta + t1_i$ and the valuation of x_i at the end of interval is $V1_{u+1}(i)$. Suppose, starting from $c2_u$, a rate change is affected for x_i at time $t + u\Delta + t2_i$ and the valuation of x_i at the end of the interval is $V2_{u+1}(i)$. Then $\|V1_{u+1}(i)\| = \|V2_{u+1}(i)\|$.*
- *Suppose, starting from $c1_u$, valuation $V1(i)$ is made for variable x_i at time $t + u\Delta + t1_i$ and its valuation at the end of the interval is $V1_{u+1}(i)$. Suppose, starting from $c2_u$, valuation $V2(i)$ is made for variable x_i at time $t + u\Delta + t2_i$, and its valuation at the end of the interval is $V2_{u+1}(i)$. Then, $\|V1_{u+1}(i)\| = \|V2_{u+1}(i)\|$ and $\|V1(i)\| = \|V2(i)\|$.*

Proof. Let $c1_u = (q_t, V1_u, q'_t)$ and $c2_u = (q_t, V2_u, q'_t)$ with $\|V1_u\| = \|V2_u\|$. Let $V1_u(i) = k\Gamma + \alpha_1$ with $k \in \mathbb{Z}$ and $0 \le \alpha_1 < \Gamma$.

We first handle a simple case: If $\|V1_u(i)\| = (k, S)$ then $V1_u(i) = V2_u(i) = k\Gamma$. So setting $t2_i = t1_i$ will do the trick.

Suppose that $\|V1_u(i)\| = \|V2_u(i)\| = (k, I)$. We first handle the case when rate changes. Let (the initial rate of x_i) $\rho_{q_t}(i) = \frac{\ell}{\Delta}\Gamma$ with $\ell \in \mathbb{Z}$ and the changed rate be $\frac{\ell'}{\Delta}\Gamma$ with $\ell' \in \mathbb{Z}$. We get the following value of x_i at the end of basic interval when starting from configuration $c1_u$:

$$V1_{u+1}(i) = V1_u(i) + \frac{\ell}{\Delta}\Gamma \cdot t1_i + \frac{\ell'}{\Delta}\Gamma \cdot (\Delta - t1_i)$$

$$= k\Gamma + \alpha_1 + \ell'\Gamma + \frac{(\ell - \ell')}{\Delta}\Gamma \cdot t1_i.$$

Thus, $\|V1_{u+1}(i)\|$ lies in the range $[k + \ell, k + \ell']$. Suppose we change the rate of x_i, when starting from configuration $c2_u$ after time t_i. Then,

$$V2_{u+1}(i) = k\Gamma + \alpha_2 + \ell'\Gamma + \frac{(\ell - \ell')}{\Delta}\Gamma \cdot t_i$$

where $\alpha_2 \in [0, \Gamma)$ since $\|V1_u(i)\| = \|V2_u(i)\|$. Therefore, $\|V2_{u+1}(i)\|$ also lies in the range $[k + \ell, k + \ell']$. Also, by appropriately choosing the value of t_i, we can make $\|V2_{u+1}(i)\|$ take any value in its range. It therefore follows that there always exists a t_i such that $\|V2_{u+1}(i)\| = \|V1_{u+1}(i)\|$.

Now suppose that a valuation is made instead of rate change. It is clear that $\|V2_{u+1}(i)\| = \|V1_{u+1}(i)\|$ as this situation is same as rate changing to itself above. Moreover, as configuration $c1_u$ moves to $c1_{u+1}$, the norm of the value of x_i varies smoothly between $\|V1_u(i)\|$ and $\|V1_{u+1}(i)\|$. The same holds as $c2_u$ moves to $c2_{u+1}$. Since $\|V1_u(i)\| = \|V2_u(i)\|$ and $\|V1_{u+1}(i)\| = \|V2_{u+1}(i)\|$, it follows that there will always be a time period in the basic interval during which the norm of the value of x_i, when started on configuration $c2_u$ will be equal to $\|V1(i)\|$. Fix any such time for valuation $V2(i)$ and we get $\|V2(i)\| = \|V1(i)\|$.
□

The proof of the theorem now proceeds as follows: We have that starting from $c1_0 = c1$, the configuration sequence at the end of basic intervals is $c1_1, c1_2, \ldots,$ $c1_m$ and there is an instantaneous transition from $c1_m$ to $c1'$. The above lemma shows that, starting from $c2_0 = c2$ with $\|c2\| = \|c1\|$, there exist configurations $c1_1, c2_2, \ldots, c2_m$ at the end of basic intervals such that $\|c1_j\| = \|c2_j\|$ for each j. Further, if a rate change is made during the transition from $c1$ to $c1'$, the same change is also made during the transition from $c2$ to $c2'$ (for different variables the rate may change in different basic intervals). Also, if a valuation $V1$ is made during transition from $c1$ to $c1'$ then a valuation $V2$ is made during transition from $c2$ to $c2'$ such that $\|V1\| = \|V2\|$. Finally, note that there is complete freedom to choose a time instant to make a rate change or valuation for each variable within the specified range and that time instants of different variables can be chosen independently. Hence it is acceptable that for different variables the rate change or valuation may occur in different basic intervals.

Now consider the instantaneous transition from $c1_m$ to $c1'$. This transition depends on the current state q_t, the valuation $V1$ and some constraint φ. By our assumption about finite precision of the observations, the observed values of variable x_i from the valuations $V1$ and $V2$ are $\langle V1(i) \rangle$ and $\langle V2(i) \rangle$ respectively. We now note:

Lemma 2. *For any v, $v' \in \mathbb{R}$, If $\|v\| = \|v'\|$ then $\langle v \rangle = \langle v' \rangle$.*

Proof. Let $v = k\Gamma + v_0$ and $v' = k'\Gamma + v_0'$ for $v_0, v_0' \in [0, \Gamma)$. Since $\|v\| = \|v'\|$, $k' = k$. Since Γ divides $\frac{\epsilon}{2}$, let $\epsilon = 2\ell\Gamma$ and $k = k_1 \cdot 2\ell + k_0$ with $k_0 \in \{0, 1, \ldots, 2\ell - 1\}$. So, $v = k_1\epsilon + k_0\Gamma + v_0$ and $v' = k_1\epsilon + k_0\Gamma + v_0'$. We have: $k_0\Gamma + v_0 < \frac{\epsilon}{2} = \ell\Gamma$ iff $k_0\Gamma < \ell\Gamma$ (since $v_0 \in [0, \Gamma)$) iff $k_0\Gamma + v_0' < \ell\Gamma$ (since $v_0' \in [0, \Gamma)$). Therefore, $\langle v \rangle = \langle v' \rangle$.
□

Since we know that $\|V1(i)\| = \|V2(i)\|$, the above lemma gives that $\langle V1(i)\rangle = \langle V2(i)\rangle$. Therefore, $(\langle V1(1)\rangle, \ldots, \langle V1(n)\rangle)$ satisfies φ iff $(\langle V2(1)\rangle, \ldots, \langle V2(n)\rangle)$ does. This implies that if $c2'$ is the resulting configuration after making an instantaneous transition from $c2_m$, then $\|c2'\| = \|c1'\|$. $\quad\square$

We now define the finite state automaton
$\mathcal{Z}_A = (\mathcal{D}, (q_{in}, \|V_{in}\|, q_{in}), Act \cup \{\tau\}, \leadsto)$ where:

- $\mathcal{D} \subseteq Q \times (\mathbb{Z} \times \{\perp, S, I\})^n \times Q$, and
- the transition relation $\leadsto \subseteq \mathcal{D} \times (Act \cup \{\tau\}) \times \mathcal{D}$ is given by: $(q, \widehat{v}, q1) \overset{\alpha}{\leadsto} (q', \widehat{v'}, q1')$ iff there exist configurations $(q, V, q1)$ and $(q', V', q1')$ such that $(q, V, q1) \overset{\alpha}{\Longrightarrow} (q', V', q1')$ and $\|V\| = \widehat{v}$ and $\|V'\| = \widehat{v'}$.

In what follows, we will often write $\mathcal{Z}_A$ as just $\mathcal{Z}$. Note that, we are setting all the states of $\mathcal{Z}$ to be its final states.

We define $\mathcal{L}_{st}(\mathcal{Z})$ to be the subset of $Q^\star$ as follows. A *run* of $\mathcal{Z}$ is a sequence of the form $(q_0, \widehat{v_0}, q_0')\, \alpha_0\, (q_1, \widehat{v_1}, q_1')\, \alpha_1 \ldots (q_m, \widehat{v_m}, q_m')$ where $(q_0, \widehat{v_0}, q_0') = (q_{in}, \|V_{in}\|, q_{in})$ and $(q_j, \widehat{v_j}, q_j') \overset{\alpha_j}{\leadsto} (q_{j+1}, \widehat{v_{j+1}}, q_{j+1}')$ for $0 \le j < m$. Next we define $q_0 q_1 \ldots q_m \in \mathcal{L}_{st}(\mathcal{Z})$ iff there exists a run of $\mathcal{Z}$ of the form $(q_0, \widehat{v_0}, q_0')\, \alpha_0\, (q_1, \widehat{v_1}, q_1')\, \alpha_1 \ldots (q_m, \widehat{v_m}, q_m')$. Clearly $\mathcal{L}_{st}(\mathcal{Z})$ is a regular subset of $Q^\star$ and it does not involve any loss of generality to view $\mathcal{Z}_A$ itself as a representation of this regular language.

Theorem 2. $\mathcal{L}_{st}(\mathcal{A}) = \mathcal{L}_{st}(\mathcal{Z}_A)$ and $\mathcal{L}_{act}(\mathcal{A}) = \mathcal{L}(\mathcal{Z}_A)$ where $\mathcal{L}(\mathcal{Z}_A)$ is the regular subset of $(Act \cup \{\tau\})^\star$ accepted by $\mathcal{Z}_A$ in the usual sense. (Note that all the states of $\mathcal{Z}_A$ are final states.) Further, the automaton $\mathcal{Z}_A$ can be computed in time $O(|Q|^4 \cdot 2^{2n} \cdot K^{3n} \cdot |Act|)$ where $K = \frac{(B_{max} - B_{min})}{\Gamma}$.

Proof. To see that $\mathcal{L}_{st}(\mathcal{A}) = \mathcal{L}_{st}(\mathcal{Z})$ we first note that $\mathcal{L}_{st}(\mathcal{A}) \subseteq \mathcal{L}_{st}(\mathcal{Z})$ follows from the definition of $\mathcal{Z}_A$. To conclude inclusion in the other direction, we will argue that for each run $(q_0, \widehat{v_0} = \|V_{in}\|, q_0')\, \alpha_0\, (q_1, \widehat{v_1}, q_1')\, \alpha_1 \ldots (q_m, \widehat{v_m}, q_m')$ of $\mathcal{Z}$ there exist $V_0, V_1 \ldots V_m \in \mathbb{R}^n$ such that

$(q_0, V_0, q_0')\, \alpha_0\, (q_1, V_1, q_1')\, \alpha_1 \ldots (q_m, V_m, q_m')$ is a run of TS_A. And furthermore, $\|V_j\| = \widehat{v_j}$ for $0 \le j \le m$. The required inclusion will then follow at once. For $m = 1$, it is clear from the definitions and so suppose that $(q_0, \widehat{v_0}, q_0')\, \alpha_0\, (q_1, \widehat{v_1}, q_1')\, \alpha_1 \ldots (q_m, \widehat{v_m}, q_m')\, \alpha_m\, (q_{m+1}, \widehat{v_{m+1}}, q_{m+1}')$ is a run of $\mathcal{Z}$. By the induction hypothesis, there exists a run $(q_0, V_0, q_0')\, \alpha_0\, (q_1, V_1, q_1')\, \alpha_1 \ldots (q_m, V_m, q_m')$ of TS_A with the property, $\|V_j\| = \widehat{v_j}$ for $0 \le j \le m$.

Now $(q_m, \widehat{v_m}, q_m') \overset{\alpha_m}{\leadsto} (q_{m+1}, \widehat{v_{m+1}}, q_{m+1}')$ implies that there exist V_m' and V_{m+1}' such that $(q_m, V_m', q_m') \overset{\alpha_m}{\leadsto} (q_{m+1}, V_{m+1}', q_{m+1}')$ and $\|V_m'\| = \widehat{v_m}$ and $\|V_{m+1}'\| = \widehat{v_{m+1}}$. But this implies that $\|V_m'\| = \|V_m\|$. Hence by Theorem 1, there exists V_{m+1} such that $(q_m, V_m, q_m') \overset{\alpha_m}{\leadsto} (q_{m+1}, V_{m+1}, q_{m+1}')$ and moreover $\|V_{m+1}'\| = \|V_{m+1}\|$. Thus $\mathcal{L}_{st}(\mathcal{A}) = \mathcal{L}_{st}(\mathcal{Z}_A)$. It now also follows easily that $\mathcal{L}_{act}(\mathcal{A}) = \mathcal{L}(\mathcal{Z}_A)$.

Let us now analyze the complexity of constructing the automata $\mathcal{Z}_A$. We first estimate the size of the automaton. Each state of the automata is of the form

$(q, \widehat{v}, q')$ with $q, q' \in Q$ and $\widehat{v} \in (\{k_{min}, \ldots, k_{max}\} \times \{I, S\} \cup \{k_{min} - 1, k_{max}\} \times \{\perp\})^n$. Therefore, The number of states is $O(m^2 \cdot 2^n \cdot K^n)$ where $m = |Q|$ and $K = k_{max} - k_{min}$. For constructing the transitions, we need to check if there is a transition from $(q, \widehat{v}, q')$ to $(q1, \widehat{v1}, q)$ labeled with the action α. It is clear that the most complex case is when $\alpha \in Act$ and $q \neq q'$ and we need to check for the existence of at most $O(m^4 \cdot 2^{2n} \cdot K^{2n} \cdot |Act|)$ such possible transitions.

To decide if such a transition exists from $(q, \widehat{v}, q')$ to $(q1, \widehat{v1}, q)$ with $\widehat{v} = ((k_1, d_1), (k_2, d_2), \ldots, (k_n, d_n))$, $\widehat{v1} = ((k1_1, d1_1), (k1_2, d1_2), \ldots, (k1_n, d1_n))$, and a given symbolic transition in the lazy automaton of the form $(q, a, \varphi, q1)$ we need to check if there exists $\widehat{V}$ and $\widehat{t1}$ and $\widehat{t2}$ such that:

- For each i, $1 \leq i \leq n$:
$$k_i \cdot \Gamma < V(i) < (k_i + 1) \cdot \Gamma,$$

- For each i, $1 \leq i \leq n$:
$$g \leq \widehat{t1}(i) \leq g + \delta_g,$$

- For each i, $1 \leq i \leq n$:
$$k1_i \cdot \Gamma < V(i) + \rho_{q'}(i) \cdot \widehat{t1}(i) + \rho_q(i) \cdot (1 - \widehat{t1}(i)) < (k1_i + 1) \cdot \Gamma,$$

- For each i, $1 \leq i \leq n$:
$$h \leq \widehat{t2}(i) \leq h + \delta_h,$$

- For each i, $1 < i < n$, letting:
$$u_i = V(i) + \rho_{q'}(i) \cdot \widehat{t1}(i) + \rho_q(i) \cdot (\widehat{t2}(i) - \widehat{t1}(i)),$$

$(\langle u_1 \rangle, \langle u_2 \rangle, \ldots, \langle u_n \rangle)$ satisfies φ.

The above are $10n$ linear inequalities in $4n$ variables along with one constraint satisfaction check. The constraints themselves are linear inequalities and so one can use linear programming to check if there exists a feasible solution. However, the constraints require a "grid point" as a solution and to check if a grid point lies inside a convex region is NP-hard. So we need to spend exponential time $(= O(K^n))$ in checking if a grid point satisfies all the inequalities.

Therefore, the time complexity of the algorithm to construct the automata is $O(m^4 \cdot 2^{2n} \cdot K^{3n} \cdot |Act|)$.   □

4 Limitations and Generalizations

Our construction also works for several generalizations of the problem. On the other hand, finite precision is really required in a number of settings.

4.1   The Need for Finite Precision

The finite division of B^n in the presence of guards defined by general hyperplanes critically depends on the finite precision of the observation. For infinite precision, such a division is not possible. We defer the proof to the full version of the paper. We wish to emphasize that we *do not claim* that there is no finite state automaton recognizing the set of state-sequences in the presence of infinite precision. The only claim we make is that our way of constructing such an automaton will fail.

4.2   Infinite Precision When $\delta_g = \delta_h = 0$

There is one important case when infinite precision can be allowed: when we do not allow any uncertainty in the time at which rate change and valuation are made. In other words, when $\delta_g = \delta_h = 0$. (Note that g and h may be non-zero and so these events may still occur with non-zero delays). We sketch an argument to prove this below.

Compute Δ and Γ as before and split the space B^n into n-cubes of side length Γ. Call the vertices of these cubes *grid points*. It is now easy to see that the starting valuation of the system is at a grid point as well as valuation after each basic interval (of length Δ) remains at a grid point irrespective of the transitions that may occur. Therefore, there are only finitely many valuations possible and this immediately leads to a finite automaton. Notice that guards can be very general here, e.g., arbitrary polynomial surfaces.

In fact, even if the initial valuation is a rectangular region instead of a point in $\mathbb{R}^n$, the construction goes through after a slight modification. Now, instead of only grid points, we get a region around each grip point that may be a possible valuation. All these regions are identical to the initial region. However, we cannot always put points in a region into one equivalence class since a guard surface might intersect the region. We handle this in the following way.

Take a region around a grid point and suppose that the guards split it into k k disjoint pieces. Mirror this split into the copy of the region around every grid point. This increases the number of regions, however, note that now the guards do not intersect any region around the chosen grid point. Repeating this for all the grid points one-by-one splits the space into many more, but still finite, number of regions such that no region is intersected by any guard. After each basic interval, points in a single such region will evolve to points in another region of *identical* shape. So we can collect points in each region in one equivalence class and the automaton can be now be constructed as before. In fact, this argument will go through even for more complex regions.

4.3   Initial Valuation Region

We have assumed that the initial valuation is a point in $\mathbb{Q}^n$. A more general case is when initial valuation can be any point in an effectively presented (say, as a conjunction of linear constraints) convex region of $\mathbb{R}^n$. This is handled easily. Calculate the Γ as before (ignoring V_{in} now as there is none). The n-cubes of size length Γ will form an equivalence class as before. The initial region intersects some of these cubes. Let these be $\|V_1\|$, $\|V_2\|$, ..., $\|V_m\|$. Introduce a new initial state for $\mathcal{Z}_A$ from which make a non-deterministic transition to each of $(q_{in}, \|V_i\|, q_{in})$. The rest of the automata remains as before. Actually we can permit the initial regions to be more complicated but what we have dealt with should do for now.

4.4   Generalizing Guards

We have assumed the guards to consist of finite conjunctions of linear inequalities. However, at no point in the proof we actually made use of this property except when calculating the time taken to construct the automata $\mathcal{Z}_A$. In fact, we can allow *any reasonable computable function* (polynomials for example) as guards and the construction goes through without any changes. The only difference is that construction of the automata $\mathcal{Z}_A$ may take more time since one needs to check if a specific grid point satisfies a guard. Let T be the upper bound on the time needed to evaluate any guard. Then the time complexity of the construction will be $O(|Q|^4 \cdot 2^{2n} \cdot K^{3n} \cdot |Act| \cdot T)$.

4.5   Uncertainty in Rounding Off

We have assumed no uncertainty in rounding off valuations. In other words, we assumed that every number in the interval $[(k - \frac{1}{2})\epsilon, (k + \frac{1}{2})\epsilon)$ is observed as $k\epsilon$. A more realistic situation would be to assume some uncertainty even here. For example, every number in $((k - \frac{1}{2})\epsilon, (k + \frac{1}{2})\epsilon)$ is observed as $k\epsilon$ while $(k + \frac{1}{2})\epsilon$ can be observed as either $k\epsilon$ or $(k + 1)\epsilon$.

This can be handled with no change in the construction. The crucial observation is that numbers of the form $(k + \frac{1}{2})\epsilon$ have norm $(2k\ell + \ell, I)$ (assuming $\epsilon = 2\ell l'$) since l' integrally divides $\frac{\ell}{2}$. And as observed in the proof of Theorem 1, if $\|V1(i)\| = (k', I) = \|V2(i)\|$ for any two valuations $V1$ and $V2$, then $V1(i) = V2(i)$. Therefore, if there is uncertainty in rounding off $V1(i)$, there will be uncertainty in rounding off $V2(i)$ as well.

In fact, we can handle the more general case when there is a whole interval of uncertainty. Specifically, let η with $0 < \eta \le \frac{1}{2}$ be such that any number in $((k - \eta)\epsilon, (k + \eta)\epsilon)$ is observed as $k\epsilon$ while any number in $[(k + \eta)\epsilon, (k + 1 - \eta)\epsilon]$ can be observed to be either $k\epsilon$ or $(k + 1)\epsilon$. For this case, we choose Γ such that it divides both ϵ and $\eta\epsilon$. Now if $\|V1(i)\| = \|V2(i)\|$ then either $V1(i) = V2(i) = (k \pm \eta)\epsilon$ (both uncertain), or $V1(i), V2(i) \in ((k + \eta)\epsilon, (k + 1 - \eta)\epsilon)$ (both uncertain), or $V1(i), V2(i) \in ((k - \eta)\epsilon, (k + \eta)\epsilon)$ (both certain). In each of the cases, the required equivalence holds.

4.6   Additional Relaxations

We can also permit the rates of evolution at a control location to range over a *rectangular region* instead of associating a single rate vector with each location. The proof of the main result will go through with minor modifications. We have not studied carefully the effect of more complex flow constraints while being mindful of the undecidability result presented in [13] for triangular flow constraints. We can easily handle state invariants formulated using linear constraints and the delay parameters can be permitted to spill across more than one unit time interval. Finally, our construction will extend to a network of automata that synchronize on common actions.

5   Conclusion

We have formulated here a class of lazy linear automata. These are basically linear hybrid automata but where each automaton is accompanied by the delay parameters $\{g, \delta_g, h, \delta_h\}$ and a finite precision of measurement parameter ϵ. Our main result is that the discrete time behavior of these automata can be effectively computed if the allowed ranges of values for the variables are bounded.

We have not detailed the verification problems that can be settled effectively for these automata. It is however clear that we can model-check the discrete time behavior of our automata against a variety of linear time and branching time temporal logic specifications. We can also view (a subset of) the transitions of the automaton to be controllable and solve the problem of devising a switching strategy that can win against a given specification; again, these specifications can be a variety of linear time and branching time specifications.

We believe that associating non-zero bounded delays with the sensors and actuators and demanding that the values of the plant variables be observed with only finite precision are natural requirements. We also believe that it is useful to focus on the discrete time behavior of hybrid automata. As our results show, the pay-off is the ability to effectively solve a host of verification and controller synthesis problems for a rich class of hybrid automata.

Finally, based on the results reported here, there is some hope that a even larger class of lazy hybrid automata will turn out to be tractable in terms of their discrete time behaviors. We have in mind automata in which the dynamics of each mode is given by a simultaneous system of linear differential equations.

A related interesting problem which is open is to determine the border between the decidable and undecidable in the context of laziness, finite precision and discrete time semantics. Here the undecidability results reported in [5, 6] may provide the required technical tools.

References

1. Alur, R., Henzinger, T., Lafferriere, G., Pappas, G.: Discrete abstractions of hybrid systems. Proc. of the IEEE **88** (2000) 971–984
2. Henzinger, T.: The theory of hybrid automata. In: 11th LICS, IEEE Press (1996) 278–292
3. Asarin, E., Maler, O.: Achilles and the tortoise climbing up the arithmetical hierarchy. J. of Comp. and Sys. Sci. **57** (1998) 389–398
4. Asarin, E., Maler, O., Pnueli, A.: Reachability analysis of dynamical systems having piecewise-constant derivatives. Theoretical Comp. Sci. **138** (1995) 35–65
5. Blondel, V., Tsitsiklis, J.: Complexity of stability and controllability of elementary hybrid systems. Automatica **35** (1999) 479–489

6. Blondel, V., Bournez, O., Koiran, P. Papdamitrou, C., Tsitsiklis, J.: Deciding stability and mortality of piecewise affine dynamical systems. Theoretical Comp. Sci. **255** (2001) 687–696
7. Henzinger, T., Kopke, P., Puri, A., Varaiya, P.: What's decidable about hybrid automata? J. of Comp. and Sys. Sci. **57** (1998) 94–124
8. Henzinger, T.: Hybrid automata with finite bisimulations. In: 22nd ICALP, LNCS 944, Springer (1995) 324–335
9. Kesten, Y., Pnueli, A., Sifakis, J., Yovine, S.: Integration graphs: A class of decidable hybrid systems. In: Hybrid Systems, LNCS 736, Springer (1993) 179–208
10. McManis, J., Varaiya, P.: Suspension automata: A decidable class of hybrid automata. In: 6th CAV, LNCS 818, Springer (1994) 105–117
11. Puri, A., Varaiya, P.: Decidability of hybrid systems with rectangular differential inclusions. In: 6th CAV, LNCS 818, Springer (1994) 95–104
12. Agrawal, M., Thiagarajan, P.: Lazy rectangular hybrid automat. In: 7th HSCC, LNCS 2993, Springer (2003) 1–15
13. Henzinger, T., Kopke, P.: Discrete-time control for rectangular hybrid automata. Theoretical Comp. Sci. **221** (1999) 369–392
14. Gupta, V., Henzinger, T., Jagadeesan, R.: Robust timed automata. In: HART '97, LNCS 1201, Springer (1997) 331–345
15. Henzinger, T., Raskin, J.F.: Robust undecidability of timed and hybrid systems. In: HSCC '00, LNCS 1790, Springer (2000) 145–159
16. Ouaknine, J., Worrell, J.: Revisiting digitization, robustness and decidability for timed automata. In: 25th LICS, IEEE Press (2003) 198–207
17. Alur, R., Dill, D.: A theory of timed automata. Theoretical Comp. Sci. **126** (1994) 183–235

Perturbed Timed Automata*

Rajeev Alur[1], Salvatore La Torre[2], and P. Madhusudan[3]

[1] University of Pennsylvania
[2] Università degli Studi di Salerno
[3] University of Illinois at Urbana-Champaign

Abstract. We consider timed automata whose clocks are imperfect. For a given perturbation error $0 < \varepsilon < 1$, the *perturbed language* of a timed automaton is obtained by letting its clocks change at a rate within the interval $[1 - \varepsilon, 1 + \varepsilon]$. We show that the perturbed language of a timed automaton with a single clock can be captured by a *deterministic* timed automaton. This leads to a decision procedure for the language inclusion problem for systems modeled as products of 1-clock automata with imperfect clocks. We also prove that determinization and decidability of language inclusion are not possible for multi-clock automata, even with perturbation.

1 Introduction

Traditional automata do not admit an explicit modeling of time and consequently *timed automata* [1] were introduced as a formal notation to model the behavior of real-time systems. Timed automata are finite automata extended with real-valued variables called *clocks*, whose vertices and edges are annotated with clock constraints that allow specification of constant bounds on delays among events. Timed automata accept *timed languages* consisting of sequences of events tagged with their occurrence times. Over the years, the formalism has been extensively studied leading to many results establishing connections to circuits and logic, and much progress has been made in developing verification algorithms, heuristics, and tools (see [2] for a recent survey and [3, 4, 5] for sample tools). The class of timed regular languages —languages definable by timed automata— is closed under union, intersection and projection, but not under complementation, and while language emptiness can be decided by symbolic algorithms manipulating clock constraints, decision problems such as universality and language inclusion are undecidable for timed automata [1].

The undecidability of language inclusion and nonclosure under complementation has motivated many researchers to search for ways to limit the expressiveness of timed automata (see for example [1, 6, 7, 8, 9, 10, 11, 12]). A canonical

* This research was partially supported by the US National Science Foundation under grants ITR/SY0121431 and CCR0410662. The second author was also supported by the MIUR grant ex-60% 2003 Università degli Studi di Salerno.

M. Morari and L. Thiele (Eds.): HSCC 2005, LNCS 3414, pp. 70–85, 2005.

example of a timed regular language whose complement is not timed regular, is the language L^1 of timed words containing *some* two symbols separated *exactly* by 1 time unit. In fact, a single clock suffices to express L^1. Typical proofs of undecidability of language inclusion crucially use the language L^1. One way to avoid L^1 is to require that the automaton be *deterministic*: since there can be unboundedly many symbols in an interval of 1 time unit, nondeterminism is *necessary* to accept L^1. The class of deterministic timed automata is closed under union, intersection, and complementation, and problems such as universality and inclusion are decidable for deterministic timed automata [1]. An alternative way to rule out L^1 is inspired by the observation that L^1 relies on the (infinite) precision of the timing constraints. In *robust timed automata* fuzziness is introduced in the language of an automaton semantically using a *metric* over the timed words, and considering a word to be accepted/rejected only if a *dense* subset around the word is accepted/rejected [13]. Unfortunately, language inclusion remains undecidable under the robust semantics also, and robust languages are not closed under complementation [14].

In this paper, we propose and study an alternative way of introducing imprecision in timed automata by introducing *errors in the rates of clocks*. Given a timed automaton A and a rational constant $0 \leq \varepsilon < 1$, let $L_\varepsilon(A)$ be the language of the automaton in the *perturbed* semantics, where each clock increases at a rate within the interval $[1 - \varepsilon, 1 + \varepsilon]$. If we add a perturbation ε to the standard timed automaton accepting L^1, then the resulting language consists of timed words with some two symbols separated by a distance d such that $1 - \varepsilon \leq d \leq 1 + \varepsilon$. Perturbed timed automata can be seen to be special kinds of (initialized) *rectangular automata* [15]. It follows that a perturbed timed automaton can be translated to a timed automaton preserving the timed language, and emptiness of perturbed languages is decidable.

Our main result is that if A has one clock, then the language $L_\varepsilon(A)$, $\varepsilon > 0$, can be accepted by a *deterministic* timed automaton. Intuitively, when the clock has a drift, then instead of guessing the event on which the clock gets reset, it suffices to remember the *first* and the *last* possible times when the reset may occur in every interval of length ε. More precisely, given a 1-clock automaton A with m locations and c as the largest (integer) constant in its clock constraints, and an error $\varepsilon = 1/n$, we show how to construct a deterministic timed automaton B with $O(cmn)$ clocks that accepts the language $L_\varepsilon(A)$. We also prove the construction to be essentially tight via lower bounds on the number of clocks in any equivalent deterministic automaton. This construction, however, does not generalize when A has multiple clocks: we show that for every $\varepsilon > 0$, there exists a timed automaton A with two clocks such that $L_\varepsilon(A)$ is not definable using deterministic timed automata.

Our result leads to a decision procedure for checking inclusion for systems expressed as products of 1-clock automata with perturbation. That is, consider a system A expressed as a product of 1-clock components A_i, and a system B expressed as a product of 1-clock components B_j. Then, given a perturbation error $\varepsilon > 0$, we can test whether the language of the product of $L(A_i)$ is included in the language of the product of $L_\varepsilon(B_j)$, using our translation from 1-clock perturbed automata to deterministic ones. This procedure requires space that is linearly proportional to $1/\varepsilon$, linearly proportional to the maximum constant c mentioned in the component automata, and polynomial in the size of the automata.

Systems expressed as products of 1-clock nondeterministic timed automata are common. For example, an asynchronous circuit with timing assumptions can be expressed as a product of 1-clock automata modeling individual gates, where the clock measures the time elapsed since the switch to the excited state, and nondeterminism is used to model the unpredictable effect of an input in the excited state (see for example [16, 17, 18, 19]). As we explain in the paper, the results on perturbed timed automata can be used for checking inclusion $L(I) \subseteq L(S)$, where I and S are asynchronous circuits with I being a refinement of S, and where they are modeled using products of 1-clock automata. For establishing decidability of this problem, it is crucial that we take product *after* perturbing the components, rather than perturbing the standard product that allows precise synchronization.

Related Work. There have been many attempts to introduce errors in timed automata. As mentioned earlier, robust timed automata have been introduced and studied by changing the notion of acceptance using a metric over timed words that allows perturbation of occurrence times of events [13]. The impact of introducing drifts in clocks on reachability is studied by Puri in [20]: a location of a timed automaton A is defined to be *limit-reachable* if, for every $\varepsilon \geq 0$, it is reachable if we let the clocks change at a rate within the interval $[1-\varepsilon, 1+\varepsilon]$, and the paper shows that while limit reachability is different from standard reachability, it can be decided by modifying the search in the region graph. Instead of perturbing the clock rates, if we perturb the guards, and ask if a location is reachable for every perturbation ε of the guards, then the problem is solvable by similar techniques [21]. The benefits of disallowing precise timing constraints have been observed in other contexts also. For example, the model checking problem for real-time linear temporal logics with modalities bounded by intervals becomes decidable if the intervals are required to be non-singular [22], and the requirement for decidability of language emptiness of rectangular automata that all clocks be initialized, can be relaxed if the guards are perturbed [23].

Among the numerous results pertaining to language inclusion for timed automata, the most relevant result for this paper is that checking whether the language of a timed automaton A is contained in that of B is decidable if B has a single clock [12]. This result, in conjunction with translation from initialized rectangular automata to timed automata, however, does not imply decidability of language inclusion problem for single-clock perturbed automata, since the translation doubles the number of clocks. Furthermore, the algorithm in [12] has high complexity and some recent work shows that it must require space that is not even primitive-recursive in the input [24]. Our results hence show that introducing perturbation leads to a sharp drop in complexity for the decision procedures.

2   Perturbed Timed Automata

Let C be a finite set of clocks. The set of clock constraints $\Phi(C)$ is the smallest set that contains:

- $x \leq y + c$, $x \geq y + c$, $x = y + c$, $x \leq c$, $x \geq c$ and $x = c$ for every $x, y \in C$ and rational number c; we call such constraints *atomic* clock constraints;
- $\neg \delta$ and $\delta_1 \wedge \delta_2$ where $\delta, \delta_1, \delta_2 \in \Phi(C)$.

A *clock interpretation* is a mapping $\nu : C \longrightarrow \mathbb{R}_+$, where $\mathbb{R}_+$ is the set of nonnegative real numbers. If ν is a clock interpretation and d is a real number, let $(\nu + d)$ denote the clock interpretation that maps each clock x to $\nu(x) + d$. If $\lambda \subseteq C$, let $[\lambda \to 0](\nu)$ be the clock interpretation that maps each clock $x \in \lambda$ to 0 and maps each clock $x \notin \lambda$ to $\nu(x)$.

A *timed automaton* A is a tuple $(\Sigma, Q, Q_0, C, \Delta, F)$ where:

- Σ is a finite set of symbols (alphabet);
- Q is a finite set of locations;
- $Q_0 \subseteq Q$ is a set of initial locations;
- C is a finite set of clock variables;
- Δ is a finite subset of $Q \times \Sigma \times \Phi(C) \times 2^C \times Q$ (edges);
- $F \subseteq Q$ is a set of final locations.

A timed automaton is *deterministic* if $|Q_0| = 1$ and for each pair of distinct edges $(q, \sigma, \delta_1, \lambda_1, q_1), (q, \sigma, \delta_2, \lambda_2, q_2) \in \Delta$, $\delta_1 \wedge \delta_2$ is not satisfiable.

A *state* of a timed automaton A is a pair (q, ν) where $q \in Q$ and ν is a clock interpretation. An *initial state* is a state (q_0, ν_0) where $q_0 \in Q_0$ and $\nu_0(x) = 0$ for every $x \in C$. A *final state* is a state (q, ν) where $q \in F$. The semantics of a timed automaton is given by a transition system over the set of its states. The transitions of this system are divided into *discrete steps* and *time steps*. A discrete step is of the form $(q, \nu) \xrightarrow{\sigma} (q', \nu')$ where there is an edge $(q, \sigma, \delta, \lambda, q') \in \Delta$ such that ν satisfies δ and $\nu' = [\lambda \leftarrow 0]\nu$. A time step is of the form $(q, \nu) \xrightarrow{d} (q, \nu')$ where $\nu' = \nu + d$, $d \in \mathbb{R}_+$. A *step* is $(q, \nu) \xrightarrow{\sigma, d} (q', \nu')$ where $(q, \nu) \xrightarrow{d} (q, \nu'')$ and $(q, \nu'') \xrightarrow{\sigma} (q', \nu')$, for some clock interpretation ν''.

A *timed word* (σ, τ) over the alphabet Σ is such that $\sigma \in \Sigma^*$, $\tau \in \mathbb{R}_+^*$, $|\sigma| = |\tau|$, and if $\tau = \tau_1 \ldots \tau_k$, then for each $i < k$, $\tau_i \leq \tau_{i+1}$.

Let (σ, τ) be a timed word with $\sigma = \sigma_1 \ldots \sigma_k$ and $\tau = \tau_1 \ldots \tau_k$. A run r of a timed automaton A on (σ, τ) is a sequence $(q_0, \nu_0) \xrightarrow{\sigma_1, \tau_1} (q_1, \nu_1) \xrightarrow{\sigma_2, \tau_2 - \tau_1} \ldots \xrightarrow{\sigma_k, \tau_k - \tau_{k-1}} (q_k, \nu_k)$.

The timed word (σ, τ) is *accepted* by a timed automaton A if there is a run r of A on (σ, τ) starting from an initial state and ending in a final state. The (timed) language accepted by A, denoted $L(A)$, is defined as the set $\{(\sigma, \tau) \mid (\sigma, \tau)$ is accepted by $A\}$.

Nondeterministic timed automata are more powerful than their deterministic counterparts. For example, consider the language L^1 of timed words over the single symbol a such that there are two occurrences of a one unit apart. A timed

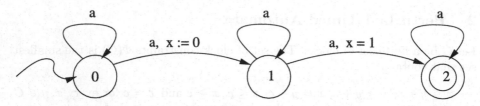

Fig. 1. Timed automaton accepting words with two occurrences of a one unit apart

automaton accepting L^1 is shown in Figure 1. This automaton nondeterministi-
cally guesses an occurrence of a on which it resets the clock x and then checks
that there is a following occurrence of a when $x = 1$.

Any deterministic strategy to check a pair of occurrences of a with the above
property would need to reset a clock on each occurrence of a. Intuitively, since a
clock cannot be reused until time 1 has elapsed and there could be an arbitrary
number of a occurrences in a time interval of length 1, in a deterministic automaton we would need to use an unbounded number of clocks, and thus there
is no deterministic timed automaton accepting this language (see [2] for a formal
proof).

Perturbed Semantics for Timed Automata

The clocks of a timed automaton are assumed to be perfect, and all clocks
increase at the exact rate 1 with respect to time. We proceed to introduce errors
in clock rates to model imprecision.

Let A be a timed automaton $(\Sigma, Q, Q_0, \Delta, C, F)$ and let $0 \le \varepsilon < 1$ be a
rational number. An ε-*perturbed time step* of A is $(q, \nu) \xrightarrow{d}_\varepsilon (q, \nu')$ where $\nu(x) +
d(1-\varepsilon) \le \nu'(x) \le \nu(x) + d(1+\varepsilon)$. An ε-*perturbed step* of A is $(q, \nu) \xrightarrow{\sigma, d}_\varepsilon (q', \nu')$
where $(q, \nu) \xrightarrow{d}_\varepsilon (q, \nu'')$ and $(q, \nu'') \xrightarrow{\sigma} (q', \nu')$, for some clock interpretation
ν''.

An ε-*perturbed run* r of A on a timed word (σ, τ), where $\sigma = \sigma_1 \ldots \sigma_k$ and
$\tau = \tau_1 \ldots \tau_k$, is a sequence $(q_0, \nu_0) \xrightarrow{\sigma_1, \tau_1}_\varepsilon (q_1, \nu_1) \xrightarrow{\sigma_2, \tau_2 - \tau_1}_\varepsilon \ldots \xrightarrow{\sigma_k, \tau_k - \tau_{k-1}}_\varepsilon (q_k, \nu_k)$.
The ε-perturbed language accepted by A, denoted $L_\varepsilon(A)$, is the language of all
the timed words (σ, τ) such that there is an ε-perturbed run r of A on (σ, τ)
starting from an initial state and ending in a final state.

As an example of an ε-perturbed language, consider again the timed automaton in Figure 1. For a given ε, the language $L_\varepsilon(A)$ contains all the timed
words over the symbol a such that some two a's occur at a distance d, for some
$d \in [1 - \varepsilon, 1 + \varepsilon]$.

Note that according to the definitions, $L_0(A) = L(A)$ for any timed automaton A. Also, note that during a perturbed time step, the drifts in the clocks
are independent. Perturbation in the language of a timed automaton can also
be expressed by transforming a timed automaton into an initialized rectangular
automaton where the rate of change of each clock x is modeled by the differential
inclusion $\dot{x} \in [1 - \varepsilon, 1 + \varepsilon]$. From the results on rectangular automata, it follows

that the timed language of the transformed automaton can be captured by a (nondeterministic) timed automaton [15].

Proposition 1. *For every timed automaton A and a rational constant* $0 \leq \varepsilon < 1$, *the perturbed language* $L_\varepsilon(A)$ *is a timed regular language.*

3   Determinization

For the automaton A of Figure 1, while, as observed before, $L(A)$ is not accepted by any deterministic timed automaton, for each $0 < \varepsilon < 1$ it is possible to construct a deterministic timed automaton B that accepts $L_\varepsilon(A)$.

Let us say that two a events, or their occurrence times, are *matching* if they are separated by a distance $d \in [1 - \varepsilon, 1 + \varepsilon]$. A timed word is in $L_\varepsilon(A)$ if it contains a matching pair. Consider any three events within a time interval of length 2ε occurring respectively at time t_1, t_2 and t_3 with $t_1 < t_2 < t_3$. If an event a occurs at a time $t \in [t_2 + 1 - \varepsilon, t_2 + 1 + \varepsilon]$, then also $t \in [t_1 + 1 - \varepsilon, t_1 + 1 + \varepsilon] \cup [t_3 + 1 - \varepsilon, t_3 + 1 + \varepsilon]$ holds. In other words, if the events at occurrence times t_2 and t are matching, then either the occurrences at t_1 and t are matching, or the occurrences at times t_3 and t are matching. This property is easily shown by observing that since $t_3 - t_1 \leq 2\varepsilon$, we have that $t_3 + 1 - \varepsilon \leq t_1 + 1 + \varepsilon$ and thus the interval $[t_2 + 1 - \varepsilon, t_2 + 1 + \varepsilon]$ is contained in the union of the intervals $[t_1 + 1 - \varepsilon, t_1 + 1 + \varepsilon]$ and $[t_3 + 1 - \varepsilon, t_3 + 1 + \varepsilon]$. This implies that to search for matching pairs, the event at time t_2, and in fact, at any time between t_1 and t_3, is not needed.

This property suggests to split any timed word into intervals such that each interval has length at least 2ε and any two occurrences of a in it are at most 2ε apart from each other. This can be achieved by resetting a clock x^ε every time it exceeds 2ε. A reset of this clock corresponds to the beginning of a new interval. Note that the total length of any $\lceil \frac{1}{2\varepsilon} \rceil + 1$ consecutive intervals is at least $1 + \varepsilon$.

Then, we can use separate clocks to remember the time elapsed since the first and the last occurrences of a in each such interval. A clock can be reused once it exceeds $1 + \varepsilon$ (recall that the only time constraint in the timed automaton A is $x = 1$). By a simple counting we just need $\lceil \frac{1}{2\varepsilon} \rceil + 1$ pairs of clocks to handle the sampling. Since we need a clock for splitting the timed word into intervals, the deterministic timed automaton B has exactly $2\left(\lceil \frac{1}{2\varepsilon} \rceil + 1\right) + 1$ clocks. The role of the guard $x = 1$ in A is played in B by guards of the form $1 - \varepsilon \leq y \leq 1 + \varepsilon$, where y is one of the clocks assigned to a 2ε interval.

3.1   Determinization Construction for Perturbed One-Clock Automata

In this section, we outline the determinization for the perturbed languages of 1-clock timed automata.

Theorem 1. *Let A be a timed automaton with one clock, c be the largest constant used in A, and Q be the set of A locations. For a rational number* $0 < \varepsilon < 1$, *the language* $L_\varepsilon(A)$ *is accepted by a deterministic timed automaton with* $O(\lceil \frac{1}{\varepsilon} \rceil |Q| c)$ *clocks and* $2^{O(\lceil \frac{1}{\varepsilon} \rceil |Q| c)}$ *locations.*

Proof. Consider a timed automaton $A = (\Sigma, Q^A, Q_0^A, \{x\}, \Delta^A, F^A)$ with a single clock variable x. For the ease of presentation, we consider here the case when the only constants used in the clock constraints of A are 0 and 1, and the atomic clock constraints using constant 1 are of the form $x \leq 1$, $x < 1$ or $x = 1$. The general case reduces to this case simply constructing an equivalent automaton that keeps track of the integral part of the clock value in the location. (This automaton also needs to reset the clock every time it reaches 1. To trigger the resets, we require that the input words contain a dummy event at each integral time. Note that this does not add to the recognizing power of timed automata [2].)

Fix $n = \lceil \frac{1}{2\varepsilon} \rceil + 1$. Let $Q^A = \{q_1, \ldots, q_m\}$. In the following, we describe the construction of a deterministic automaton $B = (\Sigma, Q^B, \{q_0\}, C^B, \Delta^B, F^B)$ such that $L(B) = L_\varepsilon(A)$.

The set of clocks C^B contains a clock x^ε and clocks y_i^α and z_i^α for all $q_i \in Q^A$ and $\alpha \in \{0, 1, \ldots, n\}$. Clock x^ε is used, as in the example discussed above, to split the input word in intervals such that each interval has length at least 2ε and any two symbols in it are at most 2ε apart from each other.

Let us number modulo $(n + 1)$ these intervals in the order they appear, starting from 0 for the first interval and so on. In the following, we refer to an interval numbered with α also as an α-*interval*.

For a given timed word w as input, consider all the ε-perturbed runs of A on w ending at q_i such that the last reset of x is in the last α-interval. Clock y_i^α is used to store the *maximum* value of x that is reached at the end of the above runs, i.e., this clock is reset in correspondence to the earliest among the last resets of x in the above runs. Similarly, clock z_i^α is used to store the *minimum* value of x that is reached at the end of the above runs, i.e., this clock is reset in correspondence to the latest reset of x in the above runs. Since these two events are at most 2ε time apart from each other, after 1 unit of time has elapsed, any possible value of x that can be reached on an ε-perturbed run of A resetting x at any point in between these events can be reached by resetting x at one of these two extreme points. Thus, sampling these events for each α-interval and for each location q_i suffices to capture all the ε-perturbed runs of A that end in q_i. Also, since the largest constant in the clock constraints of A is 1, the largest value that needs to be compared with y_i^α and z_i^α is $1 + \varepsilon$. Recall that the total length of any n consecutive intervals in the considered splitting is at least $1 + \varepsilon$. Thus, after $n + 1$ intervals these clocks can be reused since they have exceeded the value $1 + \varepsilon$. At this point, in case there are edges of A from q_i on which x is not reset, then when reusing y_i^α (resp. z_i^α), we need to remember in the location of B the fact that the value of the clock is larger than the maximum constant. For this purpose, we just use a bit for each $q_i \in Q^A$.

More precisely, the set of locations of B contains locations of the form $\langle Q, \boldsymbol{a}, \boldsymbol{b}, \alpha \rangle$, where $\alpha \in \{0, 1, \ldots, n\}$ and:

$$Q \subseteq Q^A, \qquad \boldsymbol{a} = \begin{pmatrix} a_1^0 & \ldots & a_m^0 \\ \cdots & \cdots & \cdots \\ \cdots & \cdots & \cdots \\ a_1^n & \ldots & a_m^n \end{pmatrix}, \qquad \boldsymbol{b} = (b_1, \ldots, b_m)$$

Each component b_i is either 0 or 1. Value 1 denotes that from q_i we can take edges as if there is a clock z_i^β whose value is larger than $1 + \varepsilon$. Note that this implies that also the value of y_i^β is larger than $1 + \varepsilon$. Each component a_i^β is 1 if the pair of clocks y_i^β and y_i^β are used, and is 0 otherwise. The set Q is a set of locations of A. In this construction, the component Q is used as in the usual subset construction for determinizing finite automata. In particular, after reading a timed word w, B will reach a location $\langle Q, a, b, \alpha \rangle$ where Q contains all the locations q such that there is an ε-perturbed run of A over w ending at (q, ν) for some clock valuation ν. Component α simply implements a modulo $(n + 1)$ counter that stores the number of the current interval and gets incremented whenever clock x^ε is reset.

The construction of B aims at maintaining the following invariant:

P1. For a timed word w, the run of the automaton B on w ends at a state $(\langle Q, a, b, \alpha \rangle, \nu)$ such that
  - Q is exactly the set of A locations q_i such that there is an ε-perturbed run of A over w ending at a state (q_i, ν_i);
  - $a_i^\beta = 1$ iff there is an ε-perturbed run of A on w ending at a state (q_i, ν_i) such that the last reset of x happened in the last β interval;
  - for each $a_i^\beta = 1$, $\nu(y_i^\beta)$ and $\nu(z_i^\beta)$ are the (upper and lower) bounds on the values of x in the A states that can be reached by an ε-perturbed run on w ending at location q_i and such that the last reset of x happened in the last β interval;
  - $b_i = 1$ iff there is an ε-perturbed run of A on w ending at a state (q_i, ν_i) such that $\nu_i(x) > 1$.

The initial state q_0 is $\langle Q_0^A, a_0, b_0, 0 \rangle$, where:

$$a_0 = \begin{pmatrix} a_1^0 \cdots a_m^0 \\ 0 \cdots 0 \\ \cdots\cdots\cdots \\ 0 \cdots 0 \end{pmatrix}, \qquad b_0 = (0, \ldots, 0).$$

and $a_i^0 = 1$ if and only if $q_i \in Q_0^A$ (the active clocks are those of the first interval that correspond to the initial locations of A).

The set of final locations F^B is the set of all locations $\langle Q, a, b, \alpha \rangle$ such that $Q \cap F^A \neq \emptyset$.

For describing the edges of B we need to introduce first some notation. We also assume that the guards of A edges are conjunctions of atomic constraints. This is without loss of generality since the automaton A is nondeterministic and top level disjunction can be modelled with nondeterminism. Let $I_\varepsilon(\delta, y)$ be a mapping that transforms every clock constraint δ involving only x into a clock constraint involving a clock y, as follows:

  - if δ is $x \approx c$ with $\approx \in \{<, \leq\}$, then $I_\varepsilon(\delta, y)$ is $y \approx c(1 + \varepsilon)$;
  - if δ is $x \approx c$ with $\approx \in \{>, \geq\}$, then $I_\varepsilon(\delta, y)$ is $y \approx c(1 - \varepsilon)$;
  - if $\delta = \delta_1 \wedge \delta_2$, then $I_\varepsilon(\delta, y) = I_\varepsilon(\delta_1, y) \wedge I_\varepsilon(\delta_2, y)$.

For a guard δ and clocks y, z, we denote by $g(\delta, y, z)$ the clock constraint $I_\varepsilon(\delta, y) \vee I_\varepsilon(\delta, z)$. For a B location $s = \langle Q, \boldsymbol{a}, \boldsymbol{b}, \alpha \rangle$, a clock constraint δ over x and a location $q_i \in Q$, let $h(\delta, i, s) = \delta$ if $b_i = 0$ and otherwise, let $h(\delta, i, s)$ be δ with every term $x > 1$ in it replaced by TRUE. For a location $q_i \in Q^A$, we denote by Δ_i the set of all edges contained in Δ^A from q_i. Given an edge e, we denote by δ_e its guard and $d(e) = i$ if the location entered when e is taken is q_i. Given a set X, we denote by $P(X)$ the set of partitions of X into two sets. A two-set partition is denoted by a pair of sets.

Consider a location $s = \langle Q, \boldsymbol{a}, \boldsymbol{b}, \alpha \rangle$. For each $q_i \in Q$ fix a partition (Δ_i', Δ_i'') of Δ_i. For each of such choice of partitions, we insert in Δ_B an edge such that:

- the guard is the conjunction of $x^\varepsilon < 2\varepsilon$ and
$$\bigwedge_{q_i \in Q} \bigwedge_{e \in \Delta_i'} \left(\bigvee_{\beta=0}^n (a_i^\beta = 1) \wedge g(h(\delta_e, i, s), y_i^\beta, z_i^\beta) \right) \wedge$$
$$\bigwedge_{e \in \Delta_i''} \left(\bigwedge_{\beta=0}^n (a_i^\beta = 1) \rightarrow \neg g(h(\delta_e, i, s), y_i^\beta, z_i^\beta) \right);$$
- the destination location is $\langle Q', \boldsymbol{a}', \boldsymbol{b}', \alpha' \rangle$ where:
  - Q' is the set of all q_j such that $j = d(e)$ for some $e \in \Delta_i'$ and $q_i \in Q$;
  - $a_i'^\beta = 1$ if and only if either:
    * $\beta = \alpha$ and there is an edge in Δ_i' on which x is reset, or
    * $a_i^\beta = 1$ and there is an edge in Δ_i' on which x is not reset;
    (clocks y_j^β and z_j^β are in use in the new location either if they refer to the current interval and x is reset on a possible edge from the current state, or they inherit the values of previously used clocks that still need to be considered)
  - $\boldsymbol{b}' = \boldsymbol{b}$ (these bits can change only when entering the next interval in the splitting of the input word);
  - $\alpha' = \alpha$;
- clocks are updated according to the following rules:
  - for each edge $e \in \Delta_i'$ from q_i to q_j on which x is reset: if $a_j^\alpha = 0$ then both y_j^α and z_j^α are reset, otherwise only z_j^α is reset; (recall that by y_j^α and z_j^α we wish to capture the time elapsed respectively from the earliest among the last resets and the latest reset of x over all the runs ending at q_j for which the reset happens in the last α-interval. Thus, if the clocks are already in use, we only have to reset the z-clock since the earliest reset is captured when the y-clock starts being used.)
  - let $\bar{\Delta}_j$ be the set of edges e in $\cup_i \Delta_i'$ on which x is not reset and such that $d(e) = j$. Also, for an edge e from a location q_i denote $o(e) = i$. In case there is an edge in $\bar{\Delta}_j$ whose guard contains only atomic constraints using constant 0 (that is, they are of the form $x \geq 0$ or $x > 0$), then for $\beta \neq \alpha$, clock y_j^β is assigned with the maximum of y_h^β over $h = d(e)$ for $e \in \bar{\Delta}_j$ and clock z_j^β is assigned with the minimum of z_h^β over $h = d(e)$ for $e \in \bar{\Delta}_j$ (we aim to keep the largest possible interval of x-values). In the other cases, we compute for each edge $e \in \Delta_i'$:

* y_e^β as the minimum between $1 + \varepsilon$ and the value of y_h^β for $h = d(e)$, and
* z_e^β as the maximum between $1 - \varepsilon$ and the value of z_h^β for $h = d(e)$, if there is a conjunct of δ_e (the guard of e) of the form $x = 1$, and as the value of z_h^β for $h = d(e)$, otherwise.

The choice of the values y_e^β and z_e^β aims to rule out all runs that cannot be continued with $\bar{\Delta}_j$ edges. Then, for $\beta \neq \alpha$, y_j^β is assigned with the maximum of y_e^β over $\bar{\Delta}_j$ and z_j^β is assigned with the minimum of z_e^β over $\bar{\Delta}_j$. If $x < 1$ is a conjunct of the guards of all the $\bar{\Delta}_j$ edges and the value assigned to a y-clock is $1 + \varepsilon$, we also need to remember that for this clock, its value is actually the supremum of the actual values of x in the represented runs (this can be handled with an additional bit).

With respect to the same partition we also insert in Δ^B edges that differ from the ones described above for the conjunct $x^\varepsilon \geq 2\varepsilon$ instead of $x^\varepsilon < 2\varepsilon$ in their guards, the clock x^ε is reset, and $\alpha' = (\alpha + 1)\,(mod(n + 1))$. Moreover, b_j' is set to 1 if there is an i such that there is an edge $e \in \Delta_i'$ from q_i to q_j that does not reset x, and either $a_i^{\alpha'} = 1$ or $b_i = 1$ (i.e., clock $y_i^{\alpha'}$ is active or its value is larger than $1 + \varepsilon$). In fact, in both cases, there is a run of A that reaches q_j with the value of x larger than 1. Also, $a'_j^{\alpha'}$ is set to 1 if and only if there is a edge $e \in \Delta_i'$ from q_i to q_j that resets x.

The automaton B so defined is clearly deterministic (we use disjoint guards on edges from a given location and symbol) but does not respect the definition of a timed automaton. In fact, we use updates (that compute minimum and maximum over clock values) instead of resets. To determine the minimum/maximum over clock values on an edge we can split an edge into several edges each corresponding in turn to a variable being the minimum/maximum. For this purpose, we can just add on each such edge an appropriate conjunct and then rename the clock corresponding to the minimum/maximum with y_j^α. Thus, we are done since clock renaming does not add expressiveness to timed automata (see [25] for example).

It is possible to prove by induction on the number of steps that the above construction preserves the invariant **P1**. Thus, by the definition of F^B, we can conclude that $L(B) = L_\varepsilon(A)$. ∎

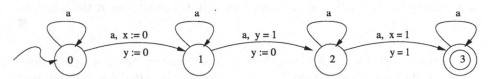

Fig. 2. Automata $\frac{1}{3}$-accepting timed words with two occurrences of a at distance $\frac{3}{2}$

3.2   Lower Bounds

The determinization was based on "forgetting" events by covering them with extreme events. This idea fails when there are 2 or more clocks in an automaton. To see this consider the automaton A given in Figure 2. For $\varepsilon = \frac{1}{3}$, the language $L_\varepsilon(A)$ contains all the timed words over the symbol a such that there is a subsequence aaa where both pairs of events are distance $\frac{3}{4}$ apart. In fact, the only way to fulfill the constraints $x = 1$ and $y = 1$ on the edge from location 2 to location 3 is to let clock y increase at the fastest possible rate (i.e., $\frac{4}{3}$) and clock x increase at the slowest possible rate (i.e., $\frac{2}{3}$). This timed language is basically the same as language L^1 except for the fact that we require that the two occurrences of a are $\frac{3}{2}$ (instead of 1) time apart. Thus, using the same argument as in [2], the complement of the language $L_{\frac{1}{3}}(A)$ cannot be accepted by any timed automaton. Therefore, $L_{\frac{1}{3}}(A)$ cannot be accepted by any deterministic timed automaton as deterministic timed automata are complementable. For any choice of a rational number $\varepsilon \in [0, 1[$, we can generalize the intuition behind the above example and construct a timed automaton that is not complementable. Thus, we have the following:

Proposition 2. *For each perturbation $0 \leq \varepsilon < 1$, there is a timed automaton A with two clocks such that the complement of $L_\varepsilon(A)$ is not accepted by any timed automaton.*

We proceed to show that our construction of determinization for perturbed 1-clock automata is essentially tight. Recall that for a perturbed timed automaton A with locations Q, we built a deterministic timed automaton with $O(\lceil 1/\varepsilon \rceil |Q|)$ clocks. We can show that both these factors are unavoidable:

Theorem 2. *Let $n \in \mathbb{N}$ and let $\varepsilon = 1/n$. Then there exists a 1-clock timed automaton A_n with a constant number of locations such that any deterministic timed automaton B accepting $L_\varepsilon(A_n)$ has at least $n/4$ clocks.*

Proof. Consider the language L^1 consisting of timed words over $\{a\}$ where there are two events a that are one unit apart. It is accepted by the 1-clock nondeterministic timed automaton A shown in Figure 1. Now let $n \in \mathbb{N}$ and $\varepsilon = 1/n$. Let B be a deterministic timed automaton accepting $L_\varepsilon(A)$. Consider an input where there are $n/4$ a events at times $t_1, \ldots t_{n/4}$ where $t_1 = d_1$ and each $t_i = t_{i-1} + 2\varepsilon + d_i$, where each $d_i < \varepsilon$. In order to accept an extension of this word, it is easy to see that an a-event is required in the range $[1, 2]$ in subranges defined by the set of all the values $d_1, \ldots d_{n/4}$. If B uses less than $n/4$ clocks, then there must be some a-event on which a clock was not reset. By making small changes to the values d_i, we can show that B cannot accept the language $L_\varepsilon(A)$. ∎

Theorem 3. *Let $0 < \varepsilon < 1$ be any fixed rational number. For any $n \in \mathbb{N}$, there exists a 1-clock timed automaton A_n with $O(n)$ states such that any deterministic timed automaton B accepting $L_\varepsilon(A_n)$ has at least n clocks.*

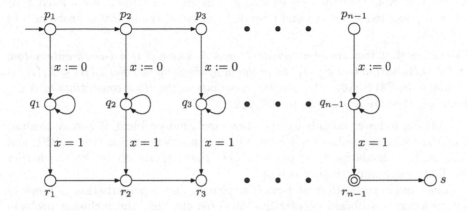

Fig. 3. Automaton used in the lower bound proof of Theorem 3

Proof. For any n, consider the language over $\Sigma = \{a\}$, consisting all timed words $(a^k, \tau_1, \tau_2, \dots \tau_k)$ such that there exist $1 \le i < j \le k$ with $i + k - j = n$ and $\tau_j - \tau_i = 1$. In other words, there are two events separated by exactly one unit such that the length of the prefix till the first event and the length of the suffix from the latter event add up to n. Figure 3 illustrates a 1-clock timed automaton with $O(n)$ states that guesses these events and accepts the language.

Now consider any deterministic automaton B accepting $L_\varepsilon(A_n)$. Consider a word where n events all before time ε are fed to B. If B had less than n clocks, then there must be some event where a clock was not reset; let this be the i'th event. By suitably extending the word using $n - i$ events after time unit 1 and by timing the first such event after time 1, one can show that B either rejects a word that is in $L_\varepsilon(A_n)$ or accepts a word that is not in $L_\varepsilon(A_n)$. ∎

4   Language Inclusion

Let us now consider the inclusion problem for timed automata, which is the problem of deciding whether $L(B) \subseteq L(A)$, for two given timed automata B and A. This question is relevant in the verification context where B can model a timed system and A the safety specification. This problem however turns out to be undecidable; in fact, checking whether $L(A)$ is universal, which is a simpler problem, is itself undecidable [1].

However, if A is a 1-clock timed automaton, then since we can build a deterministic timed automaton A' that accepts the perturbed language of A, it follows that we can decide the language inclusion $L(B) \subseteq L_\varepsilon(A)$ by complementing A', taking its product with B and solving for emptiness. From the results in the previous section, A' has $O(\lceil 1/\varepsilon \rceil |Q| c)$ clocks, if A has locations Q and c is the maximum constant in its guards. Since the emptiness problem for timed automata is in PSPACE, it follows that the inclusion problem can be solved in

EXPSPACE. Note that the only exponential factor is in ε and c. For a fixed ε (or if ε was presented in unary) and bounded constants, the inclusion problem is in PSPACE:

Theorem 4. *Given timed automata B and A, where A is a 1-clock automaton, and a perturbation $0 < \varepsilon < 1$, the problem of checking whether $L(B) \subseteq L_\varepsilon(A)$ is decidable in* EXPSPACE. *If ε and the constants in the clock constraints of A are bounded, then the problem is in* PSPACE.

Turning to lower bounds for the above inclusion problem, it is easy to show that the inclusion problem is PSPACE-hard (using a reduction from QBF), and this hardness holds for any fixed ε as well. However, we do not know whether the EXPSPACE upper bound is tight.

The double restriction to 1-clock automata and ε-perturbation is however not necessary to obtain decidability. It turns out that the inclusion problem $L(B) \subseteq L(A)$ is solvable even when A is a 1-clock automaton [12]. However, the decision procedure for this is extremely involved and uses techniques similar to those used in solving questions on (unbounded) Petri nets, and no upper bounds on the complexity are reported. In fact, recent results suggest that the universality problem for 1-clock automata requires non-primitive-recursive space complexity [24]. We note here that the problem is at least EXPSPACE-hard:

Theorem 5. *The universality problem for 1-clock timed automata is* EXPSPACE-*hard.*

Proof. The proof proceeds by a reduction from the membership problem for any EXPSPACE Turing machine. Given an input of length n to such a Turing machine M, we construct a 1-clock timed automaton that accepts the set of all timed words that do *not* correspond to accepting runs of M on that word. Each configuration of M is encoded as a string $c_1 a_1 c_2 a_2 \ldots c_m a_m$ where $a_1 \ldots a_m$ is the contents of the tape cell, m is the space required by M (m is exponential in n) and each c_i is a word of $\log m$-bits that encodes the cell number i in binary. A sequence of configurations is then encoded using strings of such sequences. In addition, we require that an encoding of a sequence of configurations be timed correctly, where the distance between a particular bit of c_i in a configuration is encoded exactly one unit from the corresponding bit of c_i in the previous configuration. A timed automaton with $O(n)$ states and 1-clock can easily check if the c_i's in each configuration are encoded correctly, and also check whether the corresponding cells in successive configurations match using the fact that they are exactly one unit of time apart. It follows that this automaton is universal iff M does not accept the input word. ∎

Perturbing 1-clock automata with bounded constants by a fixed ε however results in a simpler determinization construction (non-perturbed 1-clock automata are not determinizable) and a reduction in complexity for the inclusion problem to PSPACE.

The restriction to 1-clock automata is crucial. Recall Proposition 2 which states that there exist automata (in fact with two clocks) such that the complement of its perturbed language is not timed regular. Using the property that using two perturbed clocks one can require two events to be some precise distance apart, we can encode computations of Turing machines to show that:

Theorem 6. *Given timed automata B and A, and a perturbation $\varepsilon > 0$, the problem of deciding whether $L(B) \subseteq L_\varepsilon(A)$ is undecidable.*

4.1   Checking Refinement

An application of our results on perturbed timed automata is to check refinement for systems modeled as products of 1-clock automata. Systems such as asynchronous circuits can be modeled using *products of nondeterministic 1-clock automata*: each gate in the circuit is modeled as a timed automaton where the upper and lower bounds on the delay between the excitation of the gate and the triggering of its output is captured using a single clock [16, 17, 18, 19]. It is common to model the uncertainty of switching of gates (gates can miss unstable signals, switching of gates can be after varying delays, etc.) using nondeterminism. The asynchronous circuit itself is then a product of 1-clock automata, where the automata synchronize on input-output signals of the respective gates, capturing the design of the circuit.

Consider two systems I and S, each modeled as a product of 1-clock automata, where S is a specification and I is a refinement of S, where some components in S have been implemented using lower level components. We are interested in checking whether all behaviors of I are behaviors of S as well. Let X be the set of events present in the higher level specification S and let I contain events over the set $X \cup Y$, where Y is the new set of events introduced in the implementation.

The problem of checking whether the timed behaviors of I are included in that of S translates into checking if $L(A_I) \subseteq L(A_S)$, where A_I models the behaviors of I and A_S models the behaviors of S in which the new events Y can occur at any time and are ignored. Our results suggest a new way to answer this question. If $A_S = A_1 \| A_2 \| \dots A_k$, where each A_i is a 1-clock timed automaton, then we can perturb each component A_i of S and then take the product. Such a perturbation is natural in the setting of asynchronous circuits as they anyway model unpredictable perturbation of their signals. We can hence proceed to check whether $L(A_I) \subseteq L_\varepsilon(A_1) \| L_\varepsilon(A_2) \| \dots L_\varepsilon(A_k)$, which we know is decidable using the results of the previous sections. Notice that in the above expression, we first compute the ε-perturbed languages corresponding to each component and then take the product, which ensures that synchronization is "fudged". This fudging of synchronization is crucial: if we consider $L_\varepsilon(A_1 \| \dots A_k)$, then since the automata can synchronize precisely on events, they can accept languages that check whether two events are precisely one unit apart, and the perturbed language of the products of 1-clock automata are not determinizable.

5   Conclusions

Motivated by the gap in the expressiveness in the nondeterministic and deterministic timed automata, and undecidability of the language inclusion problem for nondeterministic timed automata, we initiated the study of timed automata with perturbation in the clock rates. We have proved that one-clock automata are determinizable in presence of perturbation. For systems expressed as products of one-clock automata, this leads to a decidable language inclusion if we perturb individual components. However, if we allow perfect synchronization, and perturb the product, we lose determinization and complementability. The complexity of the inclusion test is exponential in the number of locations as well as the magnitudes of the constants. It remains open whether exponential dependence on the constants, including the perturbation error, can be avoided. There is an alternative way of introducing errors by perturbing the guards of the automaton instead of the clock rates: replace each atomic constraint $x \leq c$ by $x \leq c + \varepsilon$, and $x \geq d$ by $x \geq d - \varepsilon$. The resulting class of perturbed languages has similar properties as the class studied in the paper. Finally, perturbed languages are not closed under projection, and thus, checking language inclusion $L(I) \subseteq L(S)$, when the specification S has internal events not mentioned in the implementation I, is not possible by our techniques even when S is a product of perturbed one-clock components. Thus, checking equivalence of timed circuits composed of components with imperfect clocks, in terms of timed languages over inputs and outputs, remains an interesting open problem.

Acknowledgments. We thank Radha Jagadeesan for helpful discussions.

References

1. Alur, R., Dill, D.: A theory of timed automata. Theoretical Computer Science **126** (1994) 183–235.
2. Alur, R., Madhusudan, P.: Decision problems for timed automata: a survey. In: Formal Methods for the Design of Real-Time Systems. LNCS 3185, Springer (2004) 1–24.
3. Larsen, K., Pettersson, P., Yi, W.: UPPAAL in a nutshell. Springer International Journal of Software Tools for Technology Transfer **1** (1997).
4. Daws, C., Olivero, A., Tripakis, S., Yovine, S.: The tool KRONOS. In: Hybrid Systems III: Verification and Control. LNCS 1066, Springer-Verlag (1996) 208–219.
5. Wang, F.: Efficient data structures for fully symbolic verification of real-time software systems. In: TACAS '00: Sixth Intl Conf on Tools and Algorithms for the Construction and Analysis of Software. LNCS 1785 (2000) 157–171.
6. Henzinger, T., Manna, Z., Pnueli, A.: What good are digital clocks? In: ICALP 92: Automata, Languages, and Programming. LNCS 623. Springer-Verlag (1992) 545–558.
7. Alur, R., Fix, L., Henzinger, T.: Event-clock automata: a determinizable class of timed automata. Theoretical Computer Science **211** (1999) 253–273 A preliminary version appears in *Proc. CAV'94*, LNCS 818, pp. 1–13.
8. Alur, R., Courcoubetis, C., Henzinger, T.: The observational power of clocks. In: CONCUR '94: Fifth International Conference on Concurrency Theory. LNCS 836. Springer-Verlag (1994) 162–177.

9. Alur, R., Henzinger, T.: Back to the future: Towards a theory of timed regular languages. In: Proceedings of the 33rd IEEE Symposium on Foundations of Computer Science. (1992) 177–186.
10. Henzinger, T., Raskin, J., Schobbens, P.: The regular real-time languages. In: ICALP'98: Automata, Languages, and Programming. LNCS 1443. Springer (1998) 580–593.
11. Ouaknine, J., Worrell, J.: Revisiting digitization, robustness, and decidability for timed automata. In: Proc. of the 18th IEEE Symp. on Logic in Comp. Sc. (2003).
12. Ouaknine, J., Worrell, J.: On the language inclusion problem for timed automata: Closing a decidability gap. In: Proceedings of the 19th IEEE Symposium on Logic in Computer Science. (2004).
13. Gupta, V., Henzinger, T., Jagadeesan, R.: Robust timed automata. In: Hybrid and Real Time Systems: International Workshop (HART'97). LNCS 1201, Springer (1997) 48–62.
14. Henzinger, T., Raskin, J.: Robust undecidability of timed and hybrid systems. In: Hybrid Systems: Computation and Control, Third International Workshop. LNCS 1790 (2000) 145–159.
15. Henzinger, T., Kopke, P., Puri, A., Varaiya, P.: What's decidable about hybrid automata. Journal of Computer and System Sciences 57 (1998) 94–124.
16. Brzozowski, J., Seger, C.: Advances in asynchronous circuit theory, Part II: Bounded inertial delay models, MOS circuit design techniques. In: Bulletin of the European Assoc. for Theoretical Comp. Sc. Volume 43. (1991) 199–263.
17. Rokicki, T.: Representing and modeling digital circuits. PhD thesis, Stanford University (1993).
18. Maler, O., Pnueli, A.: Timing analysis of asynchronous circuits using timed automata. In: Proc. of CHARME'95. LNCS 987, Springer (1995) 189–205.
19. Tasiran, S., Brayton, R.: STARI: a case study in compositional and hierarchical timing verification. In: Proceedings of the Ninth International Conference on Computer Aided Verification. LNCS 1254, Springer-Verlag (1997) 191–201.
20. Puri, A.: Dynamical properties of timed automata. In: Proceedings of the 5th International Symposium on Formal Techniques in Real Time and Fault Tolerant Systems. LNCS 1486 (1998) 210–227.
21. De Wulf, M., Doyen, L., Markey, N., Raskin, J.: Robustness and implementability of timed automata. In: Proc. FORMATS. (2004).
22. Alur, R., Feder, T., Henzinger, T.: The benefits of relaxing punctuality. Journal of the ACM 43 (1996) 116–146.
23. Agrawal, M., Thiagarajan, P.S.: Lazy rectangular hybrid automata. In: Hybrid Systems: Computation and Control, Proc. of 7th Intl. Workshop. LNCS 2993, Springer (2004) 1–15.
24. Ouaknine, J.: Personal communication. (2004).
25. Bouyer, P.: Forward analysis of updatable timed automata. Formal Methods in System Design 24 (2004) 281–320.

A Homology Theory for Hybrid Systems: Hybrid Homology

Aaron D. Ames and Shankar Sastry

Department of Electrical Engineering and Computer Science,
University of California at Berkeley,
Berkeley, CA 94720
{adames, sastry}@eecs.berkeley.edu

Abstract. By transferring the theory of hybrid systems to a categorical framework, it is possible to develop a homology theory for hybrid systems: *hybrid homology*. This is achieved by considering the underlying "space" of a hybrid system—its *hybrid space* or *H-space*. The homotopy colimit can be applied to this H-space to obtain a single topological space; the hybrid homology of an H-space is the homology of this space. The result is a spectral sequence converging to the hybrid homology of an H-space, providing a concrete way to compute this homology. Moreover, the hybrid homology of the H-space underlying a hybrid system gives useful information about the behavior of this system: the vanishing of the first hybrid homology of this H-space—when it is contractible and finite—implies that this hybrid system is not Zeno.

1 Introduction

In this paper we develop a homology theory for hybrid systems: hybrid homology. Up to this point, the limited mathematical understanding of hybrid systems has precluded the development of such a theory. In this paper, a categorical definition of a hybrid system is given; a hybrid system is essentially a small category $\mathfrak{H}$ of a specific form, called an *H-small category*, together with a functor from this small category to the category of dynamical systems: $\mathbf{S}_{\mathscr{H}} : \mathfrak{H} \to \mathfrak{Dyn}$. This definition establishes a strong connection between the area of hybrid systems and the areas of algebraic topology and category theory. Preexisting mathematical constructions in these areas can be applied to hybrid systems when they are viewed from a categorical perspective.

The categorical approach to hybrid systems gives rise to the idea of the underlying "space" of a hybrid system: its hybrid space or H-space, $\mathbb{H}$. An H-space is given by an H-small category $\mathfrak{H}$ and a functor, $\mathbf{S}_{\mathbb{H}} : \mathfrak{H} \to \mathfrak{Top}$, from this small category to the category of topological spaces. Pairs of this form—small categories together with functors to the category of topological spaces—have been well studied (cf. [1],[2],[3]); important preexisting constructions can be applied to hybrid systems by exploiting this connection. A construction of special interest is the homotopy colimit which associates to an H-space, $\mathbb{H} = (\mathfrak{H}, \mathbf{S}_{\mathbb{H}})$, a

M. Morari and L. Thiele (Eds.): HSCC 2005, LNCS 3414, pp. 86–102, 2005.

single topological space, $\mathrm{Top}(\mathbb{H}) := \mathrm{hocolim}^{\mathfrak{H}}(\mathbf{S}_{\mathbb{H}})$, referred to as the *underlying topological space* of the H-space $\mathbb{H}$.

The underlying topological space of an H-space allows us to define a homology theory of H-spaces simply by considering the homology of this space. This homology theory is termed *hybrid homology* and is denoted by $HH_n(\mathbb{H}, A) := H_n(\mathrm{Top}(\mathbb{H}), A)$; here A is an abelian group. One of the main impétuses for considering the homotopy colimit is that there is a spectral sequence converging to the homology of this space (cf. [1]). In the case of hybrid homology, this implies the existence of the *hybrid homology* spectral sequence

$$E^2_{p,q} = H_p(\mathfrak{H}, H_q(\mathbf{S}_{\mathbb{H}}, A)) \Rightarrow HH_{p+q}(\mathbb{H}, A),$$

where $H_q(\mathbf{S}_{\mathbb{H}}, A)$ is the functor from the small category $\mathfrak{H}$ to the category of abelian groups given by composing the homology functor with the functor $\mathbf{S}_{\mathbb{H}}$, and $H_p(\mathfrak{H}, H_q(\mathbf{S}_{\mathbb{H}}, A))$ is the homology of the small category $\mathfrak{H}$ with coefficients in the functor $H_q(\mathbf{S}_{\mathbb{H}}, A)$. In this paper it will be seen that this spectral sequence gives very concrete ways to compute the hybrid homology of an H-space. Specifically, because of the particular structure of an H-small category, this spectral sequence reduces to a series of short exact sequences

$$0 \longrightarrow H_1(\mathfrak{H}, H_{n-1}(\mathbf{S}_{\mathbb{H}}, A)) \longrightarrow HH_n(\mathbb{H}, A) \longrightarrow H_0(\mathfrak{H}, H_n(\mathbf{S}_{\mathbb{H}}, A)) \longrightarrow 0.$$

In the case when the H-space $\mathbb{H}$ is *contractible*, i.e., when each domain of the H-space is contractible, the spectral sequences collapses to yield isomorphisms

$$HH_n(\mathbb{H}, A) \cong H_n(\mathfrak{H}, A),$$

where $H_n(\mathfrak{H}, A)$ is the homology of the small category $\mathfrak{H}$ with coefficients in an abelian group A. The startling point is that these facts can be used to show that the hybrid homology of an H-space dictates the type of behavior that a hybrid system on this H-space can have, especially with regard to Zeno.

Given a (categorical) hybrid system $\mathscr{H}$ we can associate to it its *underlying H-space* $\mathbb{H}^{\mathscr{H}}$, and we are able to show that this space gives useful information about the hybrid system. By considering the forgetful functor $\mathbf{U} : \mathfrak{H}\mathfrak{cat} \to \mathfrak{Grph}$ from that category of H-small categories to the category of small graphs, we are able to show that in the case when $\mathbb{H}$ is contractible and *finite* there is an isomorphism

$$HH_n(\mathbb{H}, \mathbb{R}) \cong H_n(\mathbf{U}(\mathfrak{H}), \mathbb{R}),$$

where $H_n(\mathbf{U}(\mathfrak{H}), \mathbb{R})$ is the graph homology of the graph $\mathbf{U}(\mathfrak{H})$. By considering the underlying H-space $\mathbb{H}^{\mathscr{H}}$ of a hybrid system $\mathscr{H}$, this result together with the results of [4] allows us to show that when $\mathbb{H}^{\mathscr{H}}$ is contractible and finite

$$\dim_{\mathbb{R}} HH_1(\mathbb{H}^{\mathscr{H}}, \mathbb{R}) = \dim_{\mathbb{R}} \mathcal{N}(K_{\mathbf{U}(\mathfrak{H})}) = 0 \quad \Rightarrow \quad \mathscr{H} \text{ is not Zeno}$$

where $\mathcal{N}(K_{\mathbf{U}(\mathfrak{H})})$ is the null space of the incidence matrix $K_{\mathbf{U}(\mathfrak{H})}$ of the graph $\mathbf{U}(\mathfrak{H})$. This final statement seems to imply that the definition of hybrid homology is the right one because it gives useful information about the hybrid system. The statement also supports the claim that the theory developed here has useful and practical implications.

2   Categorical Hybrid Systems

Up to this point, a hybrid system has been defined to be a tuple which is a collection of spaces subject to certain relations given by maps between these spaces. A set of vector fields or flows is also included in the definition. To better understand hybrid systems, we consider this collection of spaces and this collection of flows separately; the former is referred to as a hybrid space or H-space and the latter is a "flow" on this H-space. The motivation for this is derived from dynamical system theory where there is a clear distinction between the "underlying topological space" of a dynamical system and a flow on that space. Paralleling dynamical systems, a hybrid system is obtained by adding a collection of flows to an H-space.

In this section, we give the classical definition of an H-space and then proceed to give a categorical definition of an H-space in terms of a small category and a functor; the advantage of the categorical definition of an H-space is that it is not only more general but also more concise. We then proceed to give the definition of a hybrid system utilizing the categorical framework developed—a hybrid system is also defined by a small category and a functor. These constructions will be essential in developing a homology theory for hybrid systems, although this seems to be only the first step in exploring their power.

H-Space. Define a *classical H-space* (short for *classical hybrid space*) as a tuple

$$\mathbb{H}_{\text{class}} = (Q, E, D, G, R)$$

where

- $Q = \{1, ..., m\} \subset \mathbb{Z}$ is a set of *discrete states*.
- $E \subset Q \times Q$ is a set of *edges* which define relations between the domains. For $e = (i, j) \in E$, we denote the source of e by $\mathfrak{s}(e) = i$ and the target of e by $\mathfrak{t}(e) = j$.
- $D = \{D_i\}_{i \in Q}$ is a set of *domains* where D_i is a topological space.
- $G = \{G_e\}_{e \in E}$ is a set of *guards*, where $G_e \subseteq D_{\mathfrak{s}(e)}$ is also a topological space.
- $R = \{R_e\}_{e \in E}$ is a set of *reset maps* or *transition maps*; these are continuous maps from $G_e \subseteq D_{\mathfrak{s}(e)}$ to $R_e(G_e) \subseteq D_{\mathfrak{t}(e)}$.

The subscript "class" indicates that this is a "classical" definition, meaning that this definition is one of the most commonly used ones (cf. [5]). For a classical H-space the pair (Q, E) is an oriented graph (technically a pseudograph), so we can write a classical H-space as a tuple $\mathbb{H}_{\text{class}} = (\Gamma, D, G, R)$. The graph $\Gamma = (Q, E)$ is referred to as the *underlying graph* of the H-space.

We can demand that the collection of topological spaces D be a collection of manifolds $M = \{M_i\}_{i \in Q}$, that the maps R be a collection of smooth embeddings R^S, and that the set of guards be a set of smooth manifolds, G^M, such that G_e^M is an embedded submanifold of $M_{\mathfrak{s}(e)}$. In this case we call the H-space $\mathbb{G}_{\text{class}} = (Q, E, M, G^M, R^S)$ a *smooth classical hybrid space* or a *smooth classical H-space* or a *classical G-space*. This more restrictive definition is the starting point for much of the literature on hybrid systems.

Example 1. The hybrid system modeling a water tank system (cf. [5] for a complete explanation, although we assume the reader is familiar with this example) is a classical example of a hybrid system that displays Zeno behavior. Beyond this observation, we will not discuss the dynamics of this hybrid system as in this paper we are more interested in its underlying "space". The hybrid space for the water tank will be denoted by $\mathbb{H}^W_{\text{class}} = (\Gamma^W, D^W, G^W, R^W)$. It has as its underlying graph Γ_W given by the diagram

$$1 \underset{e_2}{\overset{e_1}{\rightleftarrows}} 2$$

The other elements of the hybrid system are defined as: $D_1^W = D_2^W = \{(x_1, x_2) : x_1, x_2 \geq 0\}$, $G^W_{e_1} = \{(x_1, 0) : x_1 \geq 0\}$, $G^W_{e_2} = \{(0, x_2) : x_2 \geq 0\}$, and $R^W_{e_1}(x_1, x_2) = R^W_{e_2}(x_1, x_2) = (x_1, x_2)$. We will refer back to this example throughout this paper in order to illustrate the concepts being introduced.

H-Small Categories. An *H-small category* is a small category $\mathfrak{H}$ (cf. [6] for more information on small categories and category theory in general) satisfying the following conditions:

1. Every object in $\mathfrak{H}$ is either the source of a non-identity morphism in $\mathfrak{H}$ or the target of a non-identity morphism but never both, i.e., for every diagram

$$a_0 \xrightarrow{\alpha_1} a_1 \xrightarrow{\alpha_2} \cdots \xrightarrow{\alpha_n} a_n$$

   in $\mathfrak{H}$, all but one morphism must be the identity (the longest chain of composable non-identity morphisms is of length one).
2. If an object in $\mathfrak{H}$ is the source of a non-identity morphism, then it is the source of exactly two non-identity morphisms, i.e., for every diagram in $\mathfrak{H}$ of the form

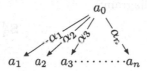

   either all of the morphisms are the identity or two and only two morphisms are not the identity.

Important Objects in H-Small Categories. Let $\mathfrak{H}$ be an H-small category. We use $\mathfrak{Ob}(\mathfrak{H})$ to denote the objects of $\mathfrak{H}$ and $\mathfrak{Mor}_{i\mathfrak{d}}(\mathfrak{H})$ to denote the *non-identity* morphisms of $\mathfrak{H}$; all of the morphisms in $\mathfrak{H}$ are the union of these morphisms with the identity morphism from each object to itself. For a morphism $\alpha : a \to b$ in $\mathfrak{H}$, its source is denoted by $\mathfrak{s}(\alpha) = a$ and its target is denoted by $\mathfrak{t}(\alpha) = b$. For H-small categories, there are two sets of objects that are of particular interest; these are subsets of the set $\mathfrak{Ob}(\mathfrak{H})$. The first of these is called the *wedge set*, denoted by $\wedge(\mathfrak{H})$, and defined to be

$$\wedge(\mathfrak{H}) := \{a \in \mathfrak{Ob}(\mathfrak{H}) : a = \mathfrak{s}(\alpha), \ a = \mathfrak{s}(\beta), \ \alpha, \beta \in \mathfrak{Mor}_{i\mathfrak{d}}(\mathfrak{H}), \ \alpha \neq \beta\}.$$

For all $a \in \wedge(\mathfrak{H})$ there are two and only two morphisms (which are not the identity) $\alpha, \beta \in \mathfrak{Mor}_{i\mathfrak{A}}(\mathfrak{H})$ such that $a = \mathfrak{s}(\alpha)$ and $a = \mathfrak{s}(\beta)$, so we denote these morphisms by α_a and β_a. Conversely, given a morphism $\gamma \in \mathfrak{H}$ (which is not the identity), there exists a unique $a \in \wedge(\mathfrak{H})$ such that $\gamma = \alpha_a$ or $\gamma = \beta_a$. The symbol $\wedge$ is used because every object $a \in \wedge(\mathfrak{H})$ sits in a diagram of the form:

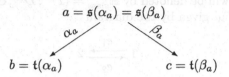

$$a = \mathfrak{s}(\alpha_a) = \mathfrak{s}(\beta_a)$$

$$b = \mathfrak{t}(\alpha_a) \qquad\qquad c = \mathfrak{t}(\beta_a)$$

Note that giving all diagrams of this form (of which there is one for each $a \in \wedge(\mathfrak{H})$) gives all the objects in $\mathfrak{H}$, i.e., every object of $\mathfrak{H}$ is the target of α_a or β_a, or their source, for some $a \in \wedge(\mathfrak{H})$. In particular, we can define $\vee(\mathfrak{H}) = (\wedge(\mathfrak{H}))^c$ where $(\wedge(\mathfrak{H}))^c$ is the complement of $\wedge(\mathfrak{H})$ in the set $\mathfrak{Ob}(\mathfrak{H})$.

Definition 1. *A categorical H-space is a pair* $\mathbb{H}_{\mathrm{cat}} = (\mathfrak{H}, \mathbf{S}_{\mathbb{H}})$ *where* $\mathfrak{H}$ *is an H-small category and* $\mathbf{S}_{\mathbb{H}} : \mathfrak{H} \to \mathfrak{Top}$ *is a functor such that for every diagram of the form*

$$A \xleftarrow{\ \alpha\ } E \xrightarrow{\ \beta\ } B$$

in $\mathfrak{H}$ *in which* α *and* β *are not the identity, either* $\mathbf{S}_{\mathbb{H}}(\alpha)$ *or* $\mathbf{S}_{\mathbb{H}}(\beta)$ *is an inclusion.*

Theorem 1. *There is an injective correspondence*

$$\{\text{Classical H} - \text{spaces, } \mathbb{H}_{\mathrm{class}}\} \longrightarrow \{\text{Categorical H} - \text{spaces, } \mathbb{H}_{\mathrm{cat}}\}$$

This is a bijective correspondence if $\mathfrak{H}$ *has a finite number of objects.*

Example 2. The categorical hybrid space for the water tank, $\mathbb{H}_{\mathrm{cat}}^W = (\mathfrak{H}^W, \mathbf{S}_{\mathbb{H}}^W)$ is defined by the following diagram:

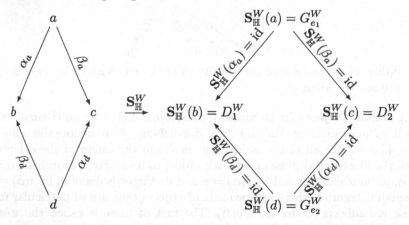

Note that the H-small category $\mathfrak{H}^W$ is defined by the diagram on the left together with the identity morphism on each object, while the functor $\mathbf{S}_{\mathbb{H}}^W$ is defined by the diagram of topological spaces on the right. To complete the description of the functor $\mathbf{S}_{\mathrm{H}}^{W}$, on identity morphisms $\mathbf{S}_{\mathrm{H}}^{W}$ is defined to be the identity map.

Smooth Categorical Hybrid Spaces. We can define a *categorical G-space* in a way analogous to the definition of a categorical H-space, i.e., it is a pair $\mathbb{G}_{\mathrm{cat}} = (\mathfrak{H}, \mathbf{T}_{\mathbf{G}})$, where $\mathfrak{H}$ is an H-small category and $\mathbf{T}_{\mathbf{G}}$ is a functor $\mathbf{T}_{\mathbf{G}} : \mathfrak{H} \to \mathfrak{Man}$ from $\mathfrak{H}$ to the category of manifolds, such that the pair $(\mathfrak{H}, \mathbf{I} \circ \mathbf{T}_{\mathbf{G}})$ is also a categorical H-space; here $\mathbf{I} : \mathfrak{Man} \to \mathfrak{Top}$ is the inclusion functor. With this definition, Theorem 1 yields the following corollary.

Corollary 1. *There is an injective correspondence*

$$\{\text{Classical G} - \text{spaces}, \ \mathbb{G}_{\mathrm{class}}\} \longrightarrow \{\text{Categorical G} - \text{spaces}, \ \mathbb{G}_{\mathrm{cat}}\}$$

The Category of Dynamical Systems. We can consider both the category of dynamical systems and the category of smooth dynamical systems. The category of dynamical systems, denoted by $\mathfrak{Dyn}$, has as objects dynamical systems and dynamical subsystems. A dynamical system is a pair (X, φ) where X is a topological space and φ is a flow on that topological space—more precisely, this is a local flow (cf. [7]). A morphism of two dynamical systems $\alpha : (X, \varphi) \to (Y, \psi)$ in this category is defined by a pair $\alpha = (h, r)$ of continuous maps, $h : X \to Y$ and $r : \mathbb{R} \to \mathbb{R}$, such that the following diagram

$$\begin{array}{ccc} \widetilde{X}_{\varphi} \subset X \times \mathbb{R} & \xrightarrow{\ h \times r\ } & \widetilde{Y}_{\psi} \subset Y \times \mathbb{R} \\ {\scriptstyle \varphi}\Big\downarrow & & \Big\downarrow{\scriptstyle \psi} \\ X & \xrightarrow{\quad h \quad} & Y \end{array}$$

commutes, i.e., $h(\varphi_t(x)) = \psi_{r(t)}(h(x))$; here $\widetilde{X}_{\varphi}$ is the maximal flow domain of the flow φ (as defined in [7]). Clearly, from this definition it follows that two dynamical systems are isomorphic (in the categorical sense) if and only if they are topologically orbital equivalent. A dynamical subsystem is a pair $(U \subsetneq X, \varphi|_U)$ where U is a topological space contained in X and $\varphi|_U$ is the restriction of a flow φ on X to U; we say that this dynamical subsystem is a subsystem of (X, φ). Morphisms of dynamical subsystems are defined in a way analogous to the definition of morphisms of dynamical systems (cf. [8] for a definition).

Similarly, we can define the category $\mathfrak{SDyn}$ of smooth dynamical systems whose objects are smooth dynamical systems and smooth dynamical subsystems.[1] A smooth dynamical system is a pair (M, V) where M is a manifold and V is a vector field on that manifold (both of which are smooth). A morphism between smooth dynamical systems $\alpha = (f, F) : (M, V) \to (N, W)$ is given by smooth maps, $f : M \to N$ and $F : TM \to TN$, such that the diagram

---

[1] This definition is a generalization of the one given in [9], although there it was defined as the category of dynamical systems and not smooth dynamical systems.

$$M \xrightarrow{f} N$$
$$V \downarrow \qquad \downarrow W$$
$$TM \xrightarrow{F} TN$$

commutes, and for each $p \in M$ the restriction of F to the fiber T_pM, $F|_{T_pM} :$ $T_pM \to T_{f(p)}N$, is linear. In the case when F is the pushforward of f, i.e., $F = f_*$, this definition implies that V and W are f-related (cf. [7]). A smooth dynamical subsystem is a pair $(S \subseteq M, V|_S)$ where S is an embedded sub-manifold of M and $V|_S$ is the restriction of a vector field V on M to S, and hence a vector field *along* S. As in the case of dynamical systems, morphisms of smooth dynamical subsystems are given in a way analogous to the definition of morphisms of dynamical systems (cf. [8] for a definition).

Note that there is a projection functor $\mathbf{P}_{\mathfrak{Top}} : \mathfrak{Dyn} \to \mathfrak{Top}$ from the category of dynamical systems to the category of topological spaces given by $\mathbf{P}_{\mathfrak{Top}}(X, \varphi) = X$ on objects and $\mathbf{P}_{\mathfrak{Top}}(h, r) = h$ on morphisms. Similarly, we have a projection functor from the category $\mathfrak{SDyn}$ to the category $\mathfrak{Man}$, $\mathbf{P}_{\mathfrak{Man}} : \mathfrak{SDyn} \to \mathfrak{Man}$ defined in an analogous way.

Hybrid Systems. With the definitions of dynamical systems and smooth dynamical systems in hand, we can define hybrid systems. A *classical hybrid system* is a tuple $\mathscr{H}_{\mathrm{class}} = (\mathbb{H}_{\mathrm{class}}, \Phi) = (Q, E, D, G, R, \Phi)$ where $\mathbb{H}_{\mathrm{class}}$ is a classical H-space and $\Phi = \{\varphi_i\}_{i \in Q}$ where φ_i is a flow on the topological space D_i, i.e., (D_i, φ_i) is a dynamical system for each $i \in Q$.

Similarly, we can define *smooth classical hybrid systems* as pairs $\mathscr{G}_{\mathrm{class}} = (\mathbb{G}_{\mathrm{class}}, V) = (Q, E, M, G^M, R^S, V)$ where $\mathbb{G}_{\mathrm{class}}$ is a classical G-space and $V = \{V_i\}_{i \in Q}$ where V_i is a smooth vector field on the manifold M_i, i.e., (M_i, V_i) is a smooth dynamical system for each $i \in Q$.

Definition 2. *A categorical hybrid system is a pair* $\mathscr{H}_{\mathrm{cat}} = (\mathfrak{H}, \mathbf{S}_{\mathscr{H}})$ *where* $\mathfrak{H}$ *is an H-small category and* $\mathbf{S}_{\mathscr{H}} : \mathfrak{H} \to \mathfrak{Dyn}$ *is a functor such that the pair* $(\mathfrak{H}, \mathbf{P}_{\mathfrak{Top}} \circ \mathbf{S}_{\mathscr{H}})$ *is a categorical H-space. The H-space*

$$\mathbb{H}^{\mathscr{H}} = (\mathfrak{H}, \mathbf{P}_{\mathfrak{Top}} \circ \mathbf{S}_{\mathscr{H}}) := (\mathfrak{H}, \mathbf{S}_{\mathbb{H}}^{\mathscr{H}})$$

is referred to as the underlying H-space *of the hybrid system* $\mathscr{H}_{\mathrm{cat}}$.

Theorem 2. *If for each* $e \in E$ *there exists a morphism of dynamical sub-systems*

$$\alpha_e : (G_e \subseteq D_{\mathfrak{s}(e)}, \varphi_{\mathfrak{s}(e)}|_{G_e}) \to (R_e(G_e) \subseteq D_{\mathfrak{t}(e)}, \varphi_{\mathfrak{t}(e)}|_{R_e(G_e)}),$$

then there is an injective correspondence

$$\{\text{Classical Hybrid Systems}, \mathscr{H}_{\mathrm{class}}\} \longrightarrow \{\text{Categorical Hybrid Systems}, \mathscr{H}_{\mathrm{cat}}\}.$$

Smooth Categorical Hybrid Systems. As in the case of categorical hybrid systems, we can define a smooth categorical hybrid system. A *smooth categorical hybrid system* is a pair $\mathscr{G}_{\mathrm{cat}} = (\mathfrak{H}, \mathbf{T}_{\mathscr{G}})$ where $\mathfrak{H}$ is an H-small category and $\mathbf{T}_{\mathscr{G}} : \mathfrak{H} \to \mathfrak{Sdyn}$ is a functor such that the pair $(\mathfrak{H}, \mathbf{P}_{\mathfrak{Man}} \circ \mathbf{T}_{\mathscr{G}})$ is a categorical G-space. As before, the *underlying G-space* of a smooth hybrid system $\mathscr{G}_{\mathrm{cat}}$ is given by

$$\mathbb{G}^{\mathscr{G}} = (\mathfrak{H}, \mathbf{P}_{\mathfrak{Man}} \circ \mathbf{T}_{\mathscr{G}}) := (\mathfrak{H}, \mathbf{T}_{\mathbb{G}}^{\mathscr{G}}).$$

With this notation there is the following corollary of Theorem 2.

Corollary 2. *If for each edge $e \in E$ there exists a morphism of smooth dynamical subsystems*

$$\alpha_e : (G_e \subseteq M_{s(e)}, V_{s(e)}|_{G_e}) \to (R_e(G_e) \subseteq M_{t(e)}, V_{t(e)}|_{R_e(G_e)}),$$

then there is an injective correspondence

$$\{\text{Smooth Classical Hybrid Systems, } \mathscr{G}_{\mathrm{class}}\}$$
$$\downarrow$$
$$\{\text{Smooth Categorical Hybrid Systems, } \mathscr{G}_{\mathrm{cat}}\}.$$

Remark 1. Because of Theorem 1 and 2, we use $\mathbb{H}$ and $\mathscr{H}$ to denote categorical hybrid spaces and hybrid systems, respectively, and simply refer to them as hybrid spaces and hybrid systems. Similarly, because of Corollary 1 and 2 we use $\mathbb{G}$ and $\mathscr{G}$ to denote smooth categorical hybrid spaces and systems; we simply refer to them as smooth hybrid spaces and systems.

The Categorical Framework for Hybrid Systems. To conclude this section, we note that the categorical framework introduced here gives a unifying framework for all of the definitions introduced here. More specifically, fixing an H-small category $\mathfrak{H}$, an H-space, G-space, hybrid system or smooth hybrid system is just given by the following functors

$$\mathfrak{H} \overset{\mathbf{S}_{\mathbb{H}}}{\to} \mathfrak{Top}, \qquad \mathfrak{H} \overset{\mathbf{T}_{\mathbb{G}}}{\to} \mathfrak{Man}, \qquad \mathfrak{H} \overset{\mathbf{S}_{\mathscr{H}}}{\to} \mathfrak{Dyn}, \qquad \mathfrak{H} \overset{\mathbf{T}_{\mathscr{G}}}{\to} \mathfrak{Sdyn},$$

respectively. Namely, all that changes is the functor and the target category. Here the H-small category can be thought of as the "discrete" component of the hybrid system and the functor can be thought of as the "continuous" component. This general framework indicates that in studying hybrid systems, one need only consider functors from small categories to other categories. Note that this categorical notion of hybrid systems, hybrid spaces, *et cetera*, makes easy work of defining the category of hybrid systems and hybrid spaces. Studying the properties of these categories would seem to be a promising area of future research in hybrid systems.

3   Hybrid Homology

In this section, a homology theory for hybrid systems is developed. Recall from Section 2 that every hybrid system has an underlying "space," termed an H-space. With every H-space, we can associate a single topological space through the use of the homotopy colimit; the homology of this space is defined to be the hybrid homology of an H-space. Fortunately, there is a spectral sequence converging to the hybrid homology of an H-space. It will be seen that this spectral sequence implies a series of short exact sequences computing the hybrid homology in terms of the homology of a small category with coefficients in a certain functor. In the case when the H-space is contractible, the hybrid homology of this H-space is just the homology of a certain small category with coefficients in an abelian group.

The Homotopy Colimit. Let $\mathfrak{C}$ be a small category and $\mathbf{F} : \mathfrak{C} \to \mathfrak{Top}$ a functor from this category to the category of topological spaces. There are two well known ways to associate to such a pair a single topological space. The first, and more obvious way, is through a construction known as the colimit. This is defined as

$$\mathrm{colim}^{\mathfrak{C}}(\mathbf{F}) = \frac{\coprod_{a \in \mathfrak{Ob}(\mathfrak{C})} \mathbf{F}(a)}{x \sim \mathbf{F}(\alpha)(x)}, \qquad \alpha \in \mathfrak{Mor}_{i,\mathfrak{U}}(\mathfrak{C}).$$

This construction has been used in the past in hybrid systems, namely in [5], although it was not recognized that this was actually the colimit as the categorical definition of hybrid systems was not available in that paper; the hybrifold was defined as $\mathrm{colim}^{\mathfrak{H}}(\mathbf{S})$ for an H-space $\mathbb{H} = (\mathfrak{H}, \mathbf{S})$ (for the rest of the paper we drop the "$\mathbb{H}$" subscript, i.e., we take $\mathbf{S} = \mathbf{S}_{\mathbb{H}}$). The key point is that although this construction is the obvious way of associating a single space to a hybrid system, it does not seem to be the "correct" one. There are many ways to justify this statement. In the context of algebraic topology, it has been known for a long time that the colimit does not possess desirable properties with respect to homotopies of spaces. A more subtle argument follows by considering the homology of these spaces; the colimit does not seem to encode the correct information about the behavior of hybrid systems—namely, with respect to Zeno. This problem is rooted in the fact that the colimit "forgets" about the information encoded in the edges of a hybrid system.

     There is another, albeit more complicated, way of associating a single topological space to a hybrid system—through the homotopy colimit. This construction seems to encode the correct information about the hybrid system, both with respect to homotopies (cf. [1],[3]) and with respect to homology. For this reason we focus on the homotopy colimit. For simplicity, we will not introduce the definition of the homotopy colimit but refer the interested reader to [1] for a complete tutorial on homotopy colimits. The pertinent point regarding homotopy colimits is the simple form that they take when considering H-spaces.

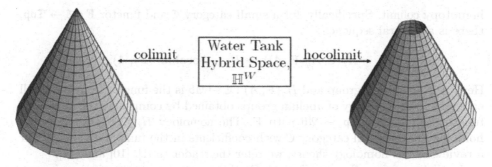

Fig. 1. The colimit and homotopy colimit of the water tank hybrid space

Theorem 3. *For an H-space* $\mathbb{H} = (\mathfrak{H}, \mathbf{S})$,

$$\mathrm{hocolim}^{\mathfrak{H}}(\mathbf{S}) = \frac{\left(\coprod_{b \in V(\mathfrak{H})} \mathbf{S}(b)\right) \amalg \left(\coprod_{a \in \wedge(\mathfrak{H})} (\mathbf{S}(a) \times I)\right)}{(x,0) \sim \mathbf{S}(\alpha_a)(x), \ (x,1) \sim \mathbf{S}(\beta_a)(x)}.$$

Example 3. For the water tank hybrid space $\mathbb{H}^W = (\mathfrak{H}^W, \mathbf{S}^W)$, the colimit is homotopic to the (2-dimensional) cone, while the homotopy colimit is homotopic to the punctured cone (see Figure 1). It will be seen that the "hole" in this cone is a warning that the hybrid system may be Zeno, i.e., if the hole was not present, the hybrid system could not be Zeno—the topology of this space dictates the types of behavior this hybrid system can display.

The Underlying Topological Space of an H-Space. Since the homotopy colimit is a single topological space, we can define the *underlying topological space* of an H-space as

$$\mathrm{Top}(\mathbb{H}) := \mathrm{hocolim}^{\mathfrak{H}}(\mathbf{S})$$

and we can consider the homology of this space. More explicitly, this gives a definition of hybrid homology—the homology of an H-space. The authors believe that this space will prove useful for other constructions on hybrid systems.

Definition 3. *The homology of an H-space* $\mathbb{H} = (\mathfrak{H}, \mathbf{S})$, *denoted by* $HH_i(\mathbb{H}, A)$ *and termed the hybrid homology of* $\mathbb{H}$ *with coefficients in an abelian group* A, *is defined to be*

$$HH_i(\mathbb{H}, A) := H_i(\mathrm{Top}(\mathbb{H}), A) = H_i(\mathrm{hocolim}^{\mathfrak{H}}(\mathbf{S}), A).$$

The Homotopy Colimit Spectral Sequence. One of the important benefits of considering homotopy colimits is the *homotopy colimit spectral sequence* (cf. [1]) that relates the homology of the homotopy colimit to that of the homology of the underlying small category with coefficients in a functor. Note that there is not a similar spectral sequence for the colimit; this alone motivates the use of the homotopy colimit. Specifically, for a small category $\mathfrak{C}$ and functor $\mathbf{F} : \mathfrak{C} \to \mathfrak{Top}$, there is a spectral sequence

$$E^2_{p,q} = H_p(\mathfrak{C}, H_q(\mathbf{F}, A)) \Rightarrow H_{p+q}(\mathrm{hocolim}^{\mathfrak{C}}(\mathbf{F}), A).$$

Here A is an abelian group and $H_q(\mathbf{F}, A) : \mathfrak{C} \to \mathfrak{Ab}$ is the functor from the small category to the category of abelian groups obtained by composing the homology functor $H_q(-, A) : \mathfrak{Top} \to \mathfrak{Ab}$ with $\mathbf{F}$. The homology $H_p(\mathfrak{C}, H_q(\mathbf{F}, A))$ is the homology of the small category $\mathfrak{C}$ with coefficients in the functor $H_q(\mathbf{F}, A)$. For a review of this homology theory, we refer the reader to [1], [10] and [11].

In the case of an H-space $\mathbb{H} = (\mathfrak{H}, \mathbf{S})$ this spectral sequence gives us important information about the underlying topological space of the hybrid system, $\mathrm{Top}(\mathbb{H})$. In this case the spectral sequence becomes

$$E^2_{p,q} = H_p(\mathfrak{H}, H_q(\mathbf{S}, A)) \Rightarrow HH_{p+q}(\mathbb{H}, A),$$

and we refer to this spectral sequence as the *hybrid homology spectral sequence*. Because $\mathfrak{H}$ is an H-small category, and by definition the longest chain of composable non-identity morphisms is of length one, for any functor $\mathbf{L} : \mathfrak{H} \to \mathfrak{Ab}$,

$$H_n(\mathfrak{H}, \mathbf{L}) = 0,$$

for $n \geq 2$. This implies that the spectral sequence will simplify even further into a set of short exact sequences.

Short Exact Sequences from a Spectral Sequence. Suppose that there is a spectral sequence $E^2_{p,q} \Rightarrow H_{p+q}$. If $E^2_{p,q} = 0$ except when $p = 0, 1$ then there are short exact sequences

$$0 \longrightarrow E^2_{1,n-1} \longrightarrow H_n \longrightarrow E^2_{0,n} \longrightarrow 0$$

for all $n \geq 0$ (cf. [12]). Because $H_n(\mathfrak{H}, \mathbf{L}) = 0$ for $n \geq 2$ and any functor $\mathbf{L} : \mathfrak{H} \to \mathfrak{Ab}$, for the hybrid homology spectral sequence $E^2_{p,q} = H_p(\mathfrak{H}, H_q(\mathbf{S}, A)) = 0$ for $p \neq 0, 1$. Therefore, we have established the following important theorem.

Theorem 4. *For an H-space $\mathbb{H} = (\mathfrak{H}, \mathbf{S})$ and an abelian group A, there are short exact sequences*

$$0 \longrightarrow H_1(\mathfrak{H}, H_{n-1}(\mathbf{S}, A)) \longrightarrow HH_n(\mathbb{H}, A) \longrightarrow H_0(\mathfrak{H}, H_n(\mathbf{S}, A)) \longrightarrow 0.$$

Collapsing Spectral Sequences. For a spectral sequence $E^2_{p,q} \Rightarrow H_{p+q}$, if $E^2_{p,q} = 0$ except when $q = 0$, then the spectral sequence is said to *collapse*. In this case there is an isomorphism $H_n \cong E^2_{n,0}$. This isomorphism will yield the theorem shown below, which will be used in the following section to establish a very concrete method for computing the hybrid homology of an H-space in the case when the hybrid homology spectral sequence collapses. This will happen for a special class of hybrid systems, as given in the following definition.

Definition 4. *The H-space* $\mathbb{H} = (\mathfrak{H}, \mathbf{S})$ *is contractible if* $\mathbf{S}(a)$ *is contractible for every* $a \in \mathfrak{Ob}(\mathfrak{H})$ *and* $\mathbf{S}(\alpha) \sim$ id *for every* $\alpha \in \mathfrak{Mor}_{i_{\mathcal{A}}}(\mathfrak{H})$ *(here* $\sim$ *denotes homotopic). We say that* $\mathbb{H}$ *is finite if* $\mathfrak{H}$ *has a finite number of objects and hence a finite number of morphisms. The H-space* $\mathbb{H}$ *is* connected *if* $\mathrm{Top}(\mathbb{H})$ *is connected.*

Theorem 5. *If the H-space* $\mathbb{H} = (\mathfrak{H}, \mathbf{S})$ *is contractible, then*

$$HH_i(\mathbb{H}, A) \cong H_i(\mathfrak{H}, A)$$

for an abelian group A. *It follows that* $HH_n(\mathbb{H}, A) = 0$ *for* $n \geq 2$.

4 Morse Theory and the Euler Characteristic of H

It is interesting to note that we can define the Euler characteristic for an H-space $\mathbb{H}$. Moreover, it will be seen that the Euler characteristic of an H-space can be expressed as a combination of the Euler characteristics of individual topological spaces in the hybrid space. As an application, a Morse theory type of theorem can be established for hybrid systems in a very special case.

The Euler Characteristic. Let $\mathbb{F}$ be a field. Since $\mathrm{Top}(\mathbb{H})$ is a topological space, we can define the Euler characteristic of the hybrid homology of an H-space in the usual fashion. If $\dim_{\mathbb{F}} HH_i(\mathbb{H}, \mathbb{F})$ is finite and nonzero for only a finite number of $i's$ (here the dimension of $HH_i(\mathbb{H}, \mathbb{F})$ is its dimension as a vector space over $\mathbb{F}$), then the Euler characteristic of $\mathbb{H}$ with coefficients in a field $\mathbb{F}$ is given by

$$\chi(\mathbb{H}, \mathbb{F}) = \sum_{i=0}^{\infty} (-1)^i \dim_{\mathbb{F}} HH_i(\mathbb{H}, \mathbb{F}).$$

The Euler characteristic also can be defined when considering $HH_i(\mathbb{H})$; since this is not a vector space, the Euler characteristic is defined using the *rank of an abelian group*. For an abelian group A, define its rank (over $\mathbb{Z}$) by $\mathrm{rank}_{\mathbb{Z}}(A) = \dim_{\mathbb{Q}} (A \otimes_{\mathbb{Z}} \mathbb{Q})$. In this case the Euler characteristic is defined to be

$$\chi(\mathbb{H}) = \sum_{i=0}^{\infty} (-1)^i \mathrm{rank}_{\mathbb{Z}} HH_i(\mathbb{H}) = \sum_{i=0}^{\infty} (-1)^i \dim_{\mathbb{Q}} HH_i(\mathbb{H}) \otimes_{\mathbb{Z}} \mathbb{Q},$$

where, again, for this to be well–defined, $HH_i(\mathbb{H}) \otimes_{\mathbb{Z}} \mathbb{Q}$ must be a finite dimensional vector space and nonzero for only a finite number of $i's$.

The main theorem of this section is that the Euler characteristic of an arbitrary H-space can be computed in terms of the Euler characteristic of the topological spaces that determine the H-space, i.e., the topological space $\mathbf{S}(a)$ for $a \in \mathfrak{Ob}(\mathfrak{H})$. This theorem yields a corollary that allows for the easy computation of the Euler characteristic in a special case.

Theorem 6. *For an H-space* $\mathbb{H} = (\mathfrak{H}, \mathbf{S})$,

$$\chi(\mathbb{H}, \mathbb{F}) = \sum_{a \in \mathfrak{Ob}(\mathfrak{H})} \chi(\mathbf{S}(a), \mathbb{F}) - \sum_{\alpha \in \mathfrak{Mor}_{\mathrm{id}}(\mathfrak{H})} \chi(\mathbf{S}(\mathfrak{s}(\alpha)), \mathbb{F}).$$

Corollary 3. *For an H-space* $\mathbb{H} = (\mathfrak{H}, \mathbf{S})$,

$$\chi(\mathbb{H}) = \sum_{a \in \mathfrak{Ob}(\mathfrak{H})} \chi(\mathbf{S}(a)) - \sum_{\alpha \in \mathfrak{Mor}_{\mathrm{id}}(\mathfrak{H})} \chi(\mathbf{S}(\mathfrak{s}(\alpha))).$$

If $\mathbb{H}$ *is contractible and finite then for an arbitrary field* $\mathbb{F}$

$$\chi(\mathbb{H}) = \chi(\mathbb{H}, \mathbb{F}) = |\mathfrak{Ob}(\mathfrak{H})| - |\mathfrak{Mor}_{\mathrm{id}}(\mathfrak{H})|$$

where $|\mathfrak{Ob}(\mathfrak{H})|$ *is the number of objects of* $\mathfrak{H}$ *and* $|\mathfrak{Mor}_{\mathrm{id}}(\mathfrak{H})|$ *is the number of (non-identity) morphisms.*

Morse Theory. The Euler characteristic is important because it relates the homology of a space with the behavior of flows on that space. It is possible to give a "Morse type theorem" for hybrid homology by considering the Morse theory of a smooth dynamical system.

Let (M, V) be a smooth dynamical system as defined in Section 2. Assume that M is a boundaryless compact n-dimensional manifold and that V has only isolated singularities (equilibrium points). If $\mathrm{Index}(V)$ is the index of V, then the Poincaré-Hopf theorem states that

$$\mathrm{Index}(V) = \chi(M).$$

Similarly, if f is a *Morse function* on M, and $C(f)_k$ is the number of critical points of index k, then the Morse theorem says that

$$\chi(M) = \sum_{k=0}^{n} (-1)^k \, C(f)_k.$$

We will not review these definitions and constructions in this paper (for a complete review, the reader is referred to [13] and [14]). The important point is that it is possible to relate these results in smooth manifold theory to hybrid systems.

Now consider a smooth hybrid system $\mathscr{G} = (\mathfrak{H}, \mathbf{T}_{\mathscr{G}})$ where $\mathbf{T}_{\mathscr{G}} : \mathfrak{H} \to \mathfrak{Sdyn}$ and its corresponding underlying G-space $\mathbb{G}^{\mathscr{G}} = (\mathfrak{H}, \mathbf{P} \circ \mathbf{T}_{\mathscr{G}}) := (\mathfrak{H}, \mathbf{T}_{\mathbb{G}}^{\mathscr{G}})$. Assume that for each object $a \in \mathfrak{Ob}(\mathfrak{H})$, $\mathbf{T}_{\mathscr{G}}(a) = (M(a), X_a)$ where $M(a)$ is a smooth manifold and X_a is a vector field *on* that manifold (this functor sends objects in $\mathfrak{H}$ to the subcategory of $\mathfrak{Sdyn}$ whose objects are smooth dynamical systems), and that $M(a)$ is compact and boundaryless for every $a \in \mathfrak{Ob}(\mathfrak{H})$. In this case call $\mathscr{G}$ a *smooth compact boundaryless hybrid system*.

Note that there is an embedding $\mathbf{E} : \mathfrak{Gspc} \to \mathfrak{Hspc}$ from the category of G-spaces, $\mathfrak{Gspc}$, to the category of H-spaces, $\mathfrak{Hspc}$ (cf. [8]). The *underlying topological space* of a smooth hybrid system is defined by $\mathrm{Top}(\mathbb{G}) := \mathrm{Top}(\mathbf{E}(\mathbb{G}))$, and

we can consider the homology of these spaces, i.e., $HH_i(\mathbb{G}, A) := HH_i(\mathbf{E}(\mathbb{G}), A)$.
Note that in general $\mathrm{Top}(\mathbb{G})$ is *not* a smooth manifold, or even a manifold at
all. The amazing thing is that, regardless of this, it still is possible to obtain a
Morse type theorem for hybrid systems of this form, i.e., we have the following
corollary of Theorem 6.

Corollary 4. *Let $\mathscr{G}$ be a smooth compact boundaryless hybrid system and $\mathbb{G}^\mathscr{G}$
its underlying G-space. If $n(a) = \dim(M(a))$, then*

$$\chi(\mathbb{G}^\mathscr{G}) = \sum_{a \in \mathfrak{Db}(\mathfrak{H})} \mathrm{Index}(X_a) - \sum_{\alpha \in \mathfrak{Mor}_{\mathrm{id}}(\mathfrak{H})} \mathrm{Index}(X_{s(\alpha)})$$

$$= \sum_{a \in \mathfrak{Db}(\mathfrak{H})} \sum_{k=0}^{n(a)} (-1)^k C(f_a)_k - \sum_{\alpha \in \mathfrak{Mor}_{\mathrm{id}}(\mathfrak{H})} \sum_{k=0}^{n(s(\alpha))} (-1)^k C(f_{s(\alpha)})_k$$

where f_a is a Morse function of $M(a)$ for each $a \in \mathfrak{Db}(\mathfrak{H})$.

Remark 2. It would be desirable to determine a Morse type theorem involving
only the topological space $\mathrm{Top}(\mathbb{G})$, but this does not seem possible (at least in
any generality) because, as mentioned before, $\mathrm{Top}(\mathbb{G})$ is not a smooth manifold
and will almost never be one—or even ... neomorphic to one. Generalizations of
this theorem seem most promising in the context of Conley index theory since
those results are based on topological spaces and flows on those spaces.

5   Characterization of Zeno Behavior Through Hybrid Homology

In this section we show that the hybrid homology of an H-space in some ways
dictates the type of behavior that a hybrid system can have on this H-space. This
result also will be related to the homology of the graph Γ that a hybrid system
has as its basic indexing set. Namely, we will show that in the case when the
H-space underlying a hybrid system is contractible, the vanishing of the hybrid
homology in nonzero degrees implies that there are no Zeno executions. We will
not review the definition of a hybrid system, or executions of hybrid systems;
for a review of these definitions in the context of homology we refer the reader
to [4]. Note that examples can also be found in this paper.

The Homology of a Graph. Recall that it is possible to define the homology of
an oriented graph $\Gamma = (Q, E)$ with coefficients in the real numbers: $H_i(\Gamma, \mathbb{R})$. The
important point about the homology of a graph is that it is easy to compute—
one need only compute the null space of the *incidence matrix* of the graph. For
the graph Γ, the incidence matrix, denoted by K_Γ, is a $|Q| \times |E|$ matrix given
by

$$K_\Gamma = \left(\lambda_{t(e_1)} - \lambda_{s(e_1)} \quad \cdots \quad \lambda_{t(e_{|E|})} - \lambda_{s(e_{|E|})} \right)$$

where $E = \{e_1, \ldots, e_{|E|}\}$ and λ_i is the ith standard basis vector for $\mathbb{R}^{|Q|}$.

It is easy to show (for a proof see [4]) that, if $\mathcal{N}(K_\Gamma)$ is the null space of K_Γ, then

$$H_0(\Gamma, \mathbb{R}) \cong \mathbb{R}^{|Q|-|E|+\dim_\mathbb{R} \mathcal{N}(K_\Gamma)}, \qquad H_1(\Gamma, \mathbb{R}) \cong \mathbb{R}^{\dim_\mathbb{R} \mathcal{N}(K_\Gamma)}$$

and $H_n(\Gamma, \mathbb{R}) = 0$ for $n \geq 2$. This implies that the Euler characteristic of Γ is given by

$$\chi(\Gamma) = \dim_\mathbb{R}(H_0(\Gamma, \mathbb{R})) - \dim_\mathbb{R}(H_1(\Gamma, \mathbb{R})) = |Q| - |E|.$$

A Forgetful Functor. Given a small category $\mathfrak{C}$, we can "forget" about some of its structure in order to obtain a graph; in other words, there is a *forgetful functor* $\mathbf{U} : \mathfrak{Cat} \to \mathfrak{Grph}$ where $\mathfrak{Cat}$ is the category of small categories and $\mathfrak{Grph}$ is the category of small graphs. If $\mathfrak{C}$ is a small category, then the graph $\mathbf{U}(\mathfrak{C})$ is obtained by forgetting about which arrows are composites and which are identities; every functor $\mathbf{F} : \mathfrak{C} \to \mathfrak{C}'$ is also a morphism $\mathbf{U}(\mathbf{F}) : \mathbf{U}(\mathfrak{C}) \to \mathbf{U}(\mathfrak{C}')$ of graphs. For more details see [6].

It easily can be seen that the category $\mathfrak{Hcat}$ of all H-small categories is a full subcategory of the category $\mathfrak{Cat}$ (cf. [8]). If $\mathbf{I} : \mathfrak{Hcat} \to \mathfrak{Cat}$ is the inclusion functor, then we have a functor from $\mathfrak{Hcat}$ to $\mathfrak{Grph}$ given by the composition

$$\mathfrak{Hcat} \xrightarrow{\ \mathbf{I}\ } \mathfrak{Cat} \xrightarrow{\ \mathbf{U}\ } \mathfrak{Grph}.$$

By abuse of notation, we will denote the composition of these two functors by $\mathbf{U}$ as well, i.e., $\mathbf{U} : \mathfrak{Hcat} \to \mathfrak{Grph}$. This functor is important in that it relates the hybrid homology of an H-space to the homology of a graph.

Theorem 7. *Let* $\mathbb{H} = (\mathfrak{H}, \mathbf{S})$ *be a finite and contractible H-space, then*

$$HH_n(\mathbb{H}, \mathbb{R}) \cong H_n(\mathbf{U}(\mathfrak{H}), \mathbb{R})$$

where $H_n(\mathbf{U}(\mathfrak{H}), \mathbb{R})$ *is the graph homology of the graph* $\mathbf{U}(\mathfrak{H})$.

An important corollary of this theorem is that it gives a very easy and concrete way to compute the hybrid homology of a contractible and finite H-space.

Corollary 5. *Let* $K_{\mathbf{U}(\mathfrak{H})}$ *be the incidence matrix of the graph* $\mathbf{U}(\mathfrak{H})$, *then if* $\mathbb{H}$ *is contractible and finite*

$$HH_0(\mathbb{H}, \mathbb{R}) \cong \mathbb{R}^{|\mathfrak{Ob}(\mathfrak{H})|-|\mathfrak{Mor}_{\mathfrak{id}}(\mathfrak{H})|+\dim_\mathbb{R} \mathcal{N}(K_{\mathbf{U}(\mathfrak{H})})}, \quad HH_1(\mathbb{H}, \mathbb{R}) \cong \mathbb{R}^{\dim_\mathbb{R} \mathcal{N}(K_{\mathbf{U}(\mathfrak{H})})}$$

and $HH_n(\mathbb{H}, \mathbb{R}) = 0$ *for* $n \geq 2$.

Homological Relationships with Classical H-Spaces. If $\mathbb{H} = (\mathfrak{H}, \mathbf{S})$ is the (categorical) H-space, obtained from the classical H-space $\mathbb{H}_{\text{class}} = (\Gamma, D, G, R)$ via the correspondence given in Theorem 1, or vise versa, then we can relate these two "spaces" via homology—at least in the case when $\mathbb{H}$ is contractible and finite. This relationship is given in the following proposition. This proposition supports the claim that the definition of a categorical H-space is the right one because it says that when the domains of the hybrid system are contractible the hybrid homology of an H-space is isomorphic to the graph homology.

A Homology Theory for Hybrid Systems: Hybrid Homology 101

Proposition 1. *Let* $\mathbb{H} = (\mathfrak{H}, \mathbf{S})$ *be the finite H-space obtained from the classical H-space* $\mathbb{H}_{\text{class}} = (\Gamma, D, G, R)$. *If* $\mathbb{H}$ *is contractible, then*

$$HH_n(\mathbb{H}, \mathbb{R}) \cong H_n(\Gamma, \mathbb{R})$$

and it follows that $\chi(\mathbb{H}) = \chi(\Gamma)$.

A rather startling point is that the underlying H-space of a hybrid system—more specifically its homology—in some way dictates the behavior that this hybrid system can display (for a complete discussion on this, as well examples and a review of Zeno behavior, see [4]). Even more importantly, the type of behavior that the homology of an H-space "notices" is exactly the behavior that is central, and unique, to hybrid systems: Zeno behavior. This point is made more clear in the following theorem:

Theorem 8. *Let* $\mathbb{H}^{\mathscr{H}} = (\mathfrak{H}, \mathbf{S}^{\mathscr{H}}) := (\mathfrak{H}, \mathbf{P}_{\mathfrak{Top}} \circ \mathbf{S}_{\mathscr{H}})$ *be the underlying H-space of the hybrid system* $\mathscr{H} = (\mathfrak{H}, \mathbf{S}_{\mathscr{H}})$. *If* $\mathbb{H}^{\mathscr{H}}$ *is contractible and finite, then*

$$\dim_{\mathbb{R}} HH_1(\mathbb{H}^{\mathscr{H}}, \mathbb{R}) = \dim_{\mathbb{R}} \mathcal{N}(K_{\mathbf{U}(\mathfrak{H})}) = 0 \quad \Rightarrow \quad \mathscr{H} \text{ is not Zeno.}$$

If $\mathbb{H}^{\mathscr{H}}$ is connected, it implies that $\dim_{\mathbb{R}} HH_0(\mathbb{H}^{\mathscr{H}}, \mathbb{R}) = 1$, and so we have the following corollary to this theorem which is in a form more reminiscent of "Morse-type" theorems.

Corollary 6. *If* $\mathbb{H}^{\mathscr{H}}$ *is connected, contractible and finite, then*

$$\chi(\mathbb{H}^{\mathscr{H}}) = |\mathfrak{Ob}(\mathfrak{H})| - |\mathfrak{Mor}_{i\mathfrak{d}}(\mathfrak{H})| = 1 \quad \Rightarrow \quad \mathscr{H} \text{ is not Zeno.}$$

In many ways, this theorem (and its corollary) is more of a "Morse-type" theorem than Theorem 4. The hope is, through the use of the categorical framework for hybrid systems introduced here, to incorporate the dynamics of a hybrid system into the above theorems in order to obtain tighter algebraic theorems on the nonexistence of Zeno.

Example 4. For the water tank hybrid space $\mathbb{H}^W$, using Proposition 1, it is easy to see that $HH_1(\mathbb{H}^W, \mathbb{R}) \cong HH_0(\mathbb{H}^W, \mathbb{R}) \cong \mathbb{R}$. So we cannot say that the water tank is not Zeno, which is good because it is Zeno.

References

1. Bousfield, A.K., Kan, D.M.: Homotopy Limits, Completions and Localizations. Volume 304 of Lecture Notes in Mathematics. Springer-Verlag (1972)
2. Thomason, R.W.: First quadrant spectral sequences in algebraic K-theory. In Dupont, J.L., Madsen, I.H., eds.: Algebraic Topology. Volume 763 of Lecture Notes in Mathematics. Springer-Verlag (1978) 332–355
3. Vogt, R.M.: Homotopy limits and colimits. Mathematische Zeitschrift **134** (1973) 11–52
4. Ames, A.D., Sastry, S.: Characterization of Zeno behavior in hybrid systems using homological methods. Submitted to ACC (2005)

5. Simic, S., Johansson, K.H., Sastry, S., Lygeros, J.: Towards a geometric theory of hybrid systems. In Krogh, B., Lynch, N., eds.: HSCC. Volume 1790 of LNCS., Springer Verlag (2000) 421–436
6. Lane, S.M.: Categories for the Working Mathematician. second edn. Volume 5 of Graduate Texts in Mathematics. Springer (1998)
7. Lee, J.M.: Introduction to Smooth Manifolds. Volume 218 of Graduate Texts in Mathematics. Springer (2003)
8. Ames, A.D., Sastry, S.: A categorical theory of hybrid systems. Technical Report (2004)
9. Haghverdi, E., Tabuada, P., Pappas, G.J.: Bisimulation relations for dynamical, control, and hybrid systems. Submitted to Theoretical Computer Science (2003)
10. Gabriel, P., Zisman, M.: Calculus of Fractions and Homotopy Theory. Volume 35 of Ergenbnisse der Mathematik und Ihrer Grenzgebiete. Springer-Verlag (1967)
11. Thomason, R.W.: First quadrant spectral sequences in algebraic K-theory via homotopy colimits. Communications in Algebra **10** (1982) 1589–1668
12. Weibel, C.A.: An Introduction to Homological Algebra. Cambridge University Press (1994)
13. Milnor, J.: Morse Theory. Princeton University (1963)
14. Madsen, I., Tornehave, J.: From Calculus to Cohomology: De Rahm Cohomology and Characteristic Classes. Cambridge University (1997)

Observability of Switched Linear Systems in Continuous Time*

Mohamed Babaali and George J. Pappas

Electrical and Systems Engineering,
University of Pennsylvania,
Philadelphia, PA USA
{babaali, pappasg}@grasp.cis.upenn.edu

Abstract. We study continuous-time switched linear systems with unobserved and exogenous mode signals. We analyze the observability of the initial state and initial mode under arbitrary switching, and characterize both properties in both the autonomous and non-autonomous cases.

1 Introduction

The general model being considered here is[1]

$$\dot{x}_t = A(r_t)x_t + B(r_t)u_t$$
$$y_t = C(r_t)x_t + D(r_t)u_t \tag{1}$$

where $x_t \in \mathbb{R}^n$, $u_t \in \mathbb{R}^m$ and $y_t \in \mathbb{R}^p$, and where $A(\cdot)$, $B(\cdot)$ and $C(\cdot)$ are real matrices of compatible dimensions. The input signals $u : [0, \infty) \to \mathbb{R}^m$ are assumed to be analytic. The exogenous, yet unobserved, mode (or switching) signal

$$r : [0, \infty) \to Q \triangleq \{1, \ldots, s\} \tag{2}$$

is furthermore assumed to be right-continuous and to assume only a finite number of jumps in any finite interval of $[0, \infty)$, so that all trajectories of vector-valued variables are well defined and infinitely right-differentiable over $[0, \infty)$. Note that Zeno behaviors can thus not occur, even though no minimum separation between consecutive switches (or minimum dwell time) is imposed.

While observability is well understood in classical linear system theory [14], it becomes more complex in the switched case. One reason is that the switching gives rise to a richer set of problems. First, the discrete modes may or may not be observed, giving rise to two sets of problems. Second, in the latter case,

---

* This work was supported by NSF CAREER Grant 0132716.

[1] For notational convenience, we have chosen to subscript time: We will denote the value of some signal x at time t by x_t instead of the standard $x(t)$, while x and $x_{[t,t']}$ will denote the whole signal and its restriction to $[t, t']$, respectively.

M. Morari and L. Thiele (Eds.): HSCC 2005, LNCS 3414, pp. 103–117, 2005.
© Springer-Verlag Berlin Heidelberg 2005

since one may also want to recover the modes, a distinction must be made between recovering the modes and recovering the states. Moreover, one can no longer decouple observation from control, which makes for the need to distinguish between the autonomous and non-autonomous cases, creating the problem of existence of controls allowing observation. Finally, two sets of problems arise from the fact that one may want the observability properties to hold for either all possible mode signals (i.e. *universal problems*) or for some mode signal (i.e. *existential problems*), in which case a characterization of the class of signals may be desired. In this paper, we assume that the mode signals are unobserved (i.e. unknown), and study the mode and state observability properties under arbitrary switching.

Observability of hybrid systems has recently been the center of a great deal of attention. However, most of the resulting literature is not related to the problems under consideration here. For instance, while the work in [6, 11, 12, 15, 23] was carried out in a stochastic setting, the papers [3, 5, 9, 18, 13] studied observability of hybrid linear systems, where the modes depend on the state trajectory, and deterministic discrete-time switched linear systems were considered in [1, 21]. However, in contrast to classical linear systems, there are differences between the discrete and continuous time cases in switched linear systems, which require them to be studied independently. For example, in continuous-time, taking successive time derivatives of the output allows the current mode to fully express itself in infinitesimal time, i.e. provide all the information it can provide about the current state. It is thus possible to decouple the modes in the known modes case, as we will see later in this paper. However, arbitrary switching removes such a luxury in discrete-time (see, e.g., [1]).

Returning to continuous-time switched linear systems, we first report the results for observed switching. First, observability under arbitrary switching has long been known to be equivalent to standard observability of every pair $(A(q), C(q))$ (see, e.g., [8]). However, the existence of a mode signal making the initial state observable, which has proven to be a challenging problem, has only recently been characterized, and shown to be decidable, in [10, 19]. It was shown to be equivalent to $\mathcal{V} = \mathbb{R}^n$, $\mathcal{V}$ being the minimal subspace of $\mathbb{R}^n$ invariant with respect to each $A(q)^T$, $q \in Q$, and containing $\sum_{q \in Q} \mathrm{Im} C(q)^T$. Furthermore, a constructive procedure for designing the mode signal r was given in [19], along with an upper bound on the minimum number of switches necessary to achieve observability.

It appears that the unobserved switching case has only been analyzed in [2, 7, 22]. In [22], the problem of recovering, simultaneously, the initial mode and state was considered along with the switch detection problem, but for autonomous systems. In [2], sufficient conditions were given for *generic final state determinability*, which we do not consider here. Finally, in [7], notions of observability and detectability were proposed in the framework of *linear switching systems*, of which our model is a special case. The authors considered the problem of recovering both the initial state and initial mode for some input, again simultaneously, and the problem of detecting the switches, generalizing the results of [22] to the non-autonomous case.

In this paper, we give linear-algebraic characterizations of mode observability and state observability under arbitrary and unobserved switching. The fact that we analyze them separately not only provides criteria for simultaneous state/mode observability (since such a property is characterized by the intersection of both sets of criteria), but provides some additional insight into the specific problems. In particular, by showing that mode and state observability are not necessary for each other, we relax some of the conditions previously given in the literature.

The outline of this paper is as follows. In Section 2, we establish some notation in order to simplify the subsequent exposition. In Section 3, we study the initial mode and initial state observability problems for autonomous systems. The same treatment is then repeated in the non-autonomous case in Section 4.

2   Notation

Letting w denote a trajectory (or execution) of some system comprising all signals of interest, including inputs, outputs and states, we decompose w into three collections of signals or portions of signals over time segments as $w = (w_d, w_o, w_r)$, and we say a system $\Sigma = \{w_i\}_{i \in I}$ is

$$(w_d/w_o) - \text{observable} \tag{3}$$

if w_d, the "desired" set of quantities, can be uniquely recovered when w_o is "observed", while w_r, i.e. the 'rest", is neither observed nor desired. In other words, it means that

$$\forall w, w' \in \Sigma, \ (w_o = w'_o \Rightarrow w_d = w'_d). \tag{4}$$

By default, the domains of all variables are the full spaces of definition, which is often too restrictive since one may find systems that are not (w_d/w_o)-observable, and yet exhibit trajectories for which w_d can be observed from w_o. Of course the "golden" solution to the observation problem is to actually determine all such trajectories, i.e., find $\Sigma_0 \triangleq \{w \in \Sigma \mid \forall w' \in \Sigma, \ w_o = w'_o \Rightarrow w_d = w'_d\}$, the "observable" subset of trajectories. However, we will take a different approach in this paper, and will instead isolate some components of interest (typically inputs, known or unknown) and either restrict them a priori or ask whether the system is observable for some value or for generic values of those components.

We thus define $(w_d \in W_d/w_o \in W_o/w_r \in W_r)$-observability as

$$\forall w, w' \in \Sigma, \ (w_d \in W_d, \ w_o \in W_o, \ w_r \in W_r, \ w_o = w'_o \Rightarrow w_d = w'_d). \tag{5}$$

Note that w' in (5) ranges over Σ: Indeed, for any execution w to determine w_d, one needs to rule out $w'_d \neq w_d \wedge w'_0 = w_0$ for all $w' \in \Sigma$. In particular, restricting, say w_r, to $\{0\}$ will be denoted "$\underline{w_r}$" instead of "$w_r \in \{0\}$." Moreover, since, any two restricting sets being fixed (say W_o and W_d), one can compute the largest possible third one (i.e., W_r) such that the system remains $(w_d \in W_d/w_o \in W_o/w_r \in W_r)$-observable, we will set to compute it, and we will then say the system is

$$(w_d \in W_d/w_o \in W_o/w_r^*) - \text{observable or} \tag{6}$$
$$(w_d \in W_d/w_o \in W_o/\overline{w_r}) - \text{observable} \tag{7}$$

according as W_r is nonempty or generic[2] (when w_r lies in a vector space). Informally, (6) reads "is w_d observable from w_o for *some* w_r?", while (7) reads "is w_d observable from w_o for *generic* w_r?", and are natural questions to ask when w_r is some input to the system. Finally, extending the previous conventions to the case where the three components of w themselves have components, we can summarize what has been studied in the following table.

Table 1. Observability Concepts

Property	Paper
$(r_0, x_0 \neq 0/y, \underline{u})$-observability	[22]
$(r_0, x_0/y, u^*)$-observability	[7]
$(r_0/y, \underline{u}/\overline{x_0})$-observability $(x_0/y, \underline{u})$-observability $(r_0/y, u^*)$-observability $(x_0/y, u^*)$-observability	This paper

Finally, we establish the following notational conventions to ease the discussion. First, let $y(r, x_0, u)$ be the output signal y of (1) when the initial state is x_0, the input signal is u and the mode signal is r. For any vector-valued signal z, let $z^{(N)}$ denote its Nth right-derivative with respect to time, and let

$$z^{[N]} \triangleq \begin{pmatrix} z \\ z' \\ \vdots \\ z^{(N-1)} \end{pmatrix}. \tag{8}$$

Now, let the *N-step observability matrix* of a mode $q \in Q$ be

$$\mathcal{O}_N(q) \triangleq \begin{pmatrix} C(q) \\ \vdots \\ C(q)A(q)^{N-1} \end{pmatrix}, \tag{9}$$

the *N-step behavior (Toeplitz) matrix* of a mode q be

---

[2] We define a generic subset of a finite-dimensional vector space as a set containing an open and dense subset (here, all such subsets will be complements of finite unions of proper subspaces), and a generic subset of the space S of analytic signals from $[0, \infty)$ to $\mathbb{R}^m$ as a set containing a set of signals that can be written $\{s \in S \mid s_t^{[N]} \in G\}$ for some integer N, some time t, and some generic subset G of $\mathbb{R}^{Nm}$.

$$\Gamma_N(q) \triangleq \begin{pmatrix} D(q) & \cdots & 0 & 0 \\ C(q)B(q) & \cdots & 0 & 0 \\ C(q)A(q)B(q) & \cdots & \vdots & 0 \\ \vdots & & \cdots & D(q) & \vdots \\ C(q)A(q)^{N-1}B(q) & \cdots & C(q)B(q) & D(q) \end{pmatrix}, \tag{10}$$

and define the following mapping as

$$Y_N(q, x, U) \triangleq \mathcal{O}_N(q)x + \Gamma_N(q)U, \tag{11}$$

where $U \in \mathbb{R}^{mN}$, so that

$$y_t^{[N]}(r, x_0, u) = Y_N(r_t, x_t, u_t^{[N]}). \tag{12}$$

In words, $Y_N(q, x, U)$ is the stack of the first N derivatives of the output y_t when $r_t = q$, $x_t = x$, and $u_t^{[N]} = U$.

For further reference, we define the following coupled system parameters

$$\begin{aligned} A(q, q') &\triangleq \begin{pmatrix} A(q) & 0 \\ 0 & A(q') \end{pmatrix} & B(q, q') &\triangleq \begin{pmatrix} B(q) \\ -B(q') \end{pmatrix} \\ C(q, q') &\triangleq (C(q) \ C(q')) & D(q, q') &\triangleq D(q) - D(q'), \end{aligned} \tag{13}$$

and we note that the N-step Kalman observability matrix of the pair $(A(q, q')$, $C(q, q'))$ is $(\mathcal{O}_N(q) \ \mathcal{O}_N(q'))$ and that the behavior matrix of the tuple $(A(q, q')$, $B(q, q'), C(q, q'), D(q, q'))$ is simply $\Gamma_N(q) - \Gamma_N(q')$.

Furthermore, we let $\rho(M)$, $\mathfrak{R}(M)$ and $M^{\{1\}}$ denote the rank, the column range space, and a (generalized) $\{1\}$-inverse of any real matrix M (see [4]). A matrix N is a $\{1\}$-inverse of M if $MNM = M$. The pseudo-inverse is thus always a $\{1\}$-inverse, and whenever M is of full column rank, any $\{1\}$-inverse N of M is also a left inverse of M in the sense that $M^{\{1\}}M$ equals the identity matrix. Moreover, x is a solution to the equation $Y = Mx$ if and only if $x = M^{\{1\}}Y$ for some $\{1\}$-inverse $M^{\{1\}}$ of M. Given a subspace V of $\mathbb{R}^n$, we let P_V denote the matrix of the orthogonal projection on V. Finally, let $\mathcal{A}$ denote the set of analytic signals from $[0, \infty)$ to $\mathbb{R}^m$.

3 Autonomous Systems

In this section we assume that $u = 0$, hence the autonomous case. We start with the important observation that the SLS (1) cannot be $(r_0/y, \underline{u})$-observable. Indeed, if $x_0 = 0$, then $y = 0$ identically for all r, and so the measurements give no information about r_0. We therefore need to lower our expectation on the observability of the initial mode, and relax the previous requirements. We thus consider observability of the initial mode for *generic* initial states, and define *discernibility* as follows.

Definition 1. *The mode q is* discernible *from another mode q' if for all $T > 0$, whenever $r_{[0,T]} \equiv q$ and $r'_{[0,T]} \equiv q'$, the set*

$$\{x_0 \in \mathbb{R}^n \mid \forall x'_0 \in \mathbb{R}^n, \ y_{[0,T]}(r, x_0, 0) \neq y_{[0,T]}(r', x'_0, 0)\}. \tag{14}$$

is generic in $\mathbb{R}^n$.

In words, q is discernible from q' if, for generic initial states x_0, one can rule out q' when observing $y(r, x_0, 0)$ over $[0, T]$. Before giving a characterization of discernibility, let us establish the following straightforward lemma:

Lemma 1. *Let M and M' be two real $N \times n$ matrices, and define $V \triangleq \Re(M) \cap \Re(M')$. Then*

$$\dim M^{-1}(V) = n - \rho((M\ M')) + \rho(M'), \tag{15}$$

where M^{-1} denotes the set-valued inverse of M.

Proof. The Grassmann relation gives $\dim(V) = \rho(M) + \rho(M') - \rho((M\ M'))$, the Rank Plus Nullity Theorem $\dim(M^{-1}(V)) = \dim(V) + \dim \ker(M)$ and $n = \rho(M) + \dim \ker(M)$, and the lemma follows. $\qquad\square$

We have:

Proposition 1. *A mode q is discernible from q' if and only if*

$$\rho((\mathcal{O}_{2n}(q)\ \mathcal{O}_{2n}(q'))) > \rho(\mathcal{O}_{2n}(q')). \tag{16}$$

Proof. Fix $T > 0$. We need to show that

$$\{x_0 \in \mathbb{R}^n \mid \forall x'_0 \in \mathbb{R}^n, \ y_{[0,T]}(r, x_0, 0) = y_{[0,T]}(r', x'_0, 0)\} \tag{17}$$

is a generic set if and only if (16) holds. Recalling that $(\mathcal{O}_{2n}(q)\ \mathcal{O}_{2n}(q'))$ is the Kalman observability matrix of the pair $(A(q, q'), C(q, q'))$ and that $y_{[0,T]}(r, x_0, 0)$ $-y_{[0,T]}(r', x'_0, 0)$ is its output in free evolution with initial state $\begin{pmatrix} x_0 \\ -x'_0 \end{pmatrix}$, we have

$$y_{[0,T]}(r, x_0, 0) = y_{[0,T]}(r', x'_0, 0) \Leftrightarrow (\mathcal{O}_{2n}(q)\ \mathcal{O}_{2n}(q')) \begin{pmatrix} x_0 \\ -x'_0 \end{pmatrix} = 0 \tag{18}$$

since $\ker((\mathcal{O}_{2n}(q)\ \mathcal{O}_{2n}(q')))$ is $A(q, q')$-invariant. We can therefore shift our attention to showing that the complement of

$$v(q, q') \triangleq \left\{ x_0 \in \mathbb{R}^n \mid \exists x'_0 \in \mathbb{R}^n, (\mathcal{O}_{2n}(q)\ \mathcal{O}_{2n}(q')) \begin{pmatrix} x_0 \\ x'_0 \end{pmatrix} = 0 \right\} \tag{19}$$

in $\mathbb{R}^n$ is generic if and only if (16) holds. Defining $V(q, q') \triangleq \Re(\mathcal{O}_{2n}(q)) \cap \Re(\mathcal{O}_{2n}(q'))$, noting that $v(q, q') = \mathcal{O}_{2n}(q)^{-1}(V(q, q'))$, and then using Lemma 1, we get

$$\dim v(q, q') = n - \rho((\mathcal{O}_{2n}(q)\ \mathcal{O}_{2n}(q'))) + \rho(\mathcal{O}_{2n}(q')). \tag{20}$$

Therefore, we see that $\dim(v(q, q')) < n$, thus that its complement is generic, if and only if (16) holds, which completes the proof. $\qquad\square$

Theorem 1. *The SLS (1) is $(r_0/y, \underline{u}/\overline{x_0})$-observable if and only if every pair of different modes is mutually discernible.*

Proof. $(r_0/y, \underline{u}/\overline{x_0})$-observability means that the set

$$P \triangleq \{x_0 \in \mathbb{R}^n \mid \forall r, r', \ \forall x_0', \ r_0' \neq r_0 \Rightarrow y(r, x_0, 0) \neq y(r', x_0', 0)\}. \tag{21}$$

is generic in $\mathbb{R}^n$. Letting

$$Q(q, q') \triangleq \{x_0 \in \mathbb{R}^n \mid \exists r, r', \ r_0 = q, \ r_0' = q', \ \exists x_0', \ y(r, x_0, 0) \neq y(r', x_0', 0)\}, \tag{22}$$

we get

$$P = \mathbb{R}^n \setminus \cup_{q \neq q'} Q(q, q'). \tag{23}$$

Now, by right-continuity of the mode signals, for every pair r, r', there exists $0 < T \leq \infty$ such that $r_{[0,T]} \equiv q$, $r'_{[0,T]} \equiv q'$, and so $v(q, q') \subset Q(q, q')$ (see Proposition 1). On the other hand, $Q(q, q') \subset v(q, q')$ follows by considering $r \equiv q$ and $r' \equiv q'$. Consequently,

$$P = \mathbb{R}^n \setminus \cup_{q \neq q'} v(q, q'), \tag{24}$$

and is generic if and only if each $v(q, q')$ is a proper subspace of $\mathbb{R}^n$, and thus if and only if every pair of modes is mutually discernible. $\qquad\square$

Example 1. Consider (1), where $s = 2$, $B(1) = B(2) = 0$, $D(1) = D(2) = 0$, and where

$$A(1) = \begin{pmatrix} 1 & 1 \\ 0 & 1 \end{pmatrix} \ A(2) = \begin{pmatrix} 1 & 2 \\ 0 & 3 \end{pmatrix}$$
$$C(1) = \begin{pmatrix} 1 & 0 \end{pmatrix} \ C(2) = \begin{pmatrix} 1 & 0 \end{pmatrix}. \tag{25}$$

Then

$$(\mathcal{O}_4(1) \ \mathcal{O}_4(2)) = \begin{pmatrix} 1 & 0 & 1 & 0 \\ 1 & 1 & 1 & 2 \\ 1 & 2 & 1 & 8 \\ 1 & 3 & 1 & 26 \end{pmatrix}, \tag{26}$$

and has rank 3, while $\rho(\mathcal{O}_4(1)) = \rho(\mathcal{O}_4(2)) = 2$. Therefore, it is possible to recover the initial mode for generic initial states. For instance,

$$y_0^{[4]}(r_0, x, o) = \begin{pmatrix} 1 \\ 2 \\ 3 \\ 4 \end{pmatrix} \tag{27}$$

could only have been produced by $r_0 = 1$ (with $x_0 = (1, 1)$). It is actually possible to recover r_0 uniquely whenever the second entry of x_0 is not zero, which constitutes a generic subset of $\mathbb{R}^2$.

We now turn to the study of the ability to recover the initial state x_0 of the system, based only on the output signal y. A first route for that is, first, to recover the initial mode r_0, and, then, to invert the Gramian to get x_0. Noting that this can only be done for generic x_0, we state the following corollary to Theorem 1.

Corollary 1. *The SLS (1) is $(\overline{x_0}/y, \underline{u})$-observable if every mode is observable and every pair of modes is mutually discernible.*

Even though this route may seem to be the natural way to proceed, we will now show that it is neither necessary nor sufficient for $(x_0/y, \underline{u})$-observability, which is in fact possible. In other words, it is possible to determine the initial state from the output *globally*, for *all* mode signals, and *without* necessarily recovering the modes. To this end, we define *joint observability* as follows:

Definition 2. *Two different modes q and q' are jointly observable if for all $T > 0$, whenever $r_{[0,T]} \equiv q$ and $r'_{[0,T]} \equiv q'$,*

$$\forall x_0, \ \forall x'_0, \ x_0 \neq x'_0 \Rightarrow y_{[0,T]}(r, x_0, 0) \neq y_{[0,T]}(r', x'_0, 0). \tag{28}$$

Note that, in contrast to discernibility, joint observability is symmetric. That two modes are jointly observable means that one can recover the initial state from the output without knowledge of the initial mode. We have:

Proposition 2. *q and q' are jointly observable if and only if they are both observable (i.e., $\rho(\mathcal{O}_n(q)) = \rho(\mathcal{O}_n(q')) = n$) and the left inverses of their 2n-step observability matrices agree on $V(q, q')$, i.e.*

$$(\mathcal{O}_{2n}(q)^{\{1\}} - \mathcal{O}_{2n}(q')^{\{1\}})P_{V(q,q')} = 0. \tag{29}$$

Proof. Assume that q and q' are both observable and satisfy (29), and suppose that $y_{[0,T]}(r, x_0, 0) = y_{[0,T]}(r', x'_0, 0)$ (with $T > 0$ and $r_{[0,T]} \equiv q$ and $r'_{[0,T]} \equiv q'$). Then, recalling (18), we get

$$\mathcal{O}_{2n}(q)x_0 = \mathcal{O}_{2n}(q')x'_0. \tag{30}$$

Furthermore, q and q' being observable, (29) implies that $v(q, q') = v(q', q)$ and that $(\mathcal{O}_{2n}(q) - \mathcal{O}_{2n}(q'))P_{v(q,q')} = 0$, which, in turn, implies that

$$\mathcal{O}_{2n}(q)x_0 = \mathcal{O}_{2n}(q')x_0, \tag{31}$$

since $x_0 \in v(q, q')$. Combining (30) and (31), we get

$$\mathcal{O}_{2n}(q')(x_0 - x'_0) = 0, \tag{32}$$

hence that $x_0 = x'_0$ since q' is observable.

Conversely, assume that, say q, is not observable. Then taking $x_0 \in \ker(\mathcal{O}_n(q))$ \\$\{0\}$, we get $y_{[0,T]}(r, x_0, 0) = y_{[0,T]}(r', 0, 0) = 0$ while $x_0 \neq 0$, hence that q and q' are not jointly observable. Finally, assuming q and q' are both observable but that (29) does not hold, we have the existence of $Y \in V(q, q')$ such that $(\mathcal{O}_{2n}(q)^{\{1\}} - \mathcal{O}_{2n}(q')^{\{1\}})Y \neq 0$. Letting $x_0 = \mathcal{O}_{2n}(q)^{\{1\}}Y$ and $x'_0 = \mathcal{O}_{2n}(q')^{\{1\}}Y$, we have $x_0 \neq x'_0$ but $\mathcal{O}_{2n}(q)x_0 = \mathcal{O}_{2n}(q')x'_0 = Y$, and thus $y_{[0,T]}(r, x_0, 0) = y_{[0,T]}(r', x'_0, 0)$ and q and q' are not jointly observable. $\qquad\square$

A characterization of $(x_0/y, \underline{u})$-observability follows.

Theorem 2. *The SLS (1) is $(x_0/y, \underline{u})$-observable if and only if every mode is observable and any two different modes are jointly observable.*

Proof. $(x_0/y, \underline{u})$-observability means that

$$\forall r, \ \forall r', \ \forall x_0, \ \forall x_0', \ x_0' \neq x_0 \Rightarrow y(r, x_0, 0) \neq y(r', x_0', 0). \tag{33}$$

Assume that every mode is observable, that any pair is jointly observable, and that $y(r, x_0, 0) = y(r', x_0', 0)$. First, by right-continuity of both mode signals, there exist $0 < T \leq \infty$ and two modes q, q' such that $r_{[0,T]} \equiv q$, $r'_{[0,T]} \equiv q'$. Then $x_0 = x_0'$ is implied by observability of each mode or joint observability of each pair of modes according as $q = q'$ or $q \neq q'$, by definition.

Conversely, assume that, say q, is not observable. Then letting $r = r' \equiv q$, and choosing $x_0 \in \ker(\mathcal{O}_n(q)) \setminus \{0\}$, we have $y(r, x_0, 0) \neq y(r', 0, 0)$ even though $x_0 \neq 0$. On the other hand, assuming the existence of a jointly unobservable pair q, q', letting $r \equiv q$ and $r' \equiv q'$, there must exist $x_0 \neq x_0'$ such that $y(r, x_0, 0) \neq y(r', x_0', 0)$, by definition of joint observability. $\qquad\square$

Remark 1. In [22], it was established that $(r_0, x_0 \neq 0/y, \underline{u})$-observability was equivalent to the *rank-$2n$* condition

$$\forall q, q' \in Q, \ q \neq q' \Rightarrow \rho((\mathcal{O}_{2n}(q)\mathcal{O}_{2n}(q'))) = 2n. \tag{34}$$

Since $\rho([\mathcal{O}_{2n}(j)]) \leq n$ for both $j = q$ and $j = q'$, (34) is sufficient for mutual discernibility of q and q', and therefore for $(r_0/y, \underline{u}/\overline{x_0})$-observability. In fact, by (20), it is equivalent to

$$\forall q, q', \ q \neq q' \to v(q, q') - \{0\}, \tag{35}$$

which is the least-dimensional possible subspace of conflict, and hence to $(r_0/y, \underline{u}/x_0 \neq 0)$-observability. What we have thus shown is that it is possible to recover r_0 even if $v(q, q') \neq \{0\}$, and we have relaxed (34) into (16) to account for such cases.

As for state observability, it turns out that (34) is not necessary for $(x_0/y, \underline{u})$-observability, simply because it is not necessary to recover the initial mode in order to infer the initial state when the initial state is not trivial. For instance, the system in Example 1 is $(x_0/y, \underline{u})$-observable, but does not satisfy (34). Recall that

$$v(1, 2) = \left\{ \begin{pmatrix} \alpha \\ 0 \end{pmatrix} \Big| \alpha \in \mathbb{R} \right\}. \tag{36}$$

If $x_0 \notin v(1, 2)$, then one can uniquely infer r_0 and recover x_0, since every mode is observable. However, if $x_0 \in v(1, 2)$, then

$$y_0^{[2]}(r, x_0, 0) = \begin{pmatrix} \alpha \\ \alpha \end{pmatrix} \Rightarrow x_0 = \begin{pmatrix} \alpha \\ 0 \end{pmatrix} \tag{37}$$

for all r, hence the claim.

4   Non-autonomous Systems

We now turn to the non-autonomous case, and study both existence and generic problems in u. We will show that existence and generic properties will be equivalent for the initial mode observability properties, and that the genericity requirement on x_0 can actually be waived. We will need the following definition and lemma.

Definition 3. *Two different modes q and q' are controlled-discernible if for all $T > 0$, whenever $r_{[0,T]} \equiv q$ and $r'_{[0,T]} \equiv q'$, there exists an input u such that*

$$\forall x_0, \ \forall x'_0, \ y_{[0,T]}(r, x_0, u) \neq y_{[0,T]}(r', x'_0, u). \tag{38}$$

In other words, q and q' are controlled-discernible if there exists a control making it possible to distinguish them by their outputs.

Lemma 2. *The two modes q and q' are controlled-discernible if and only if there exists a positive integer N such that*

$$(I - P_N(q, q'))(\Gamma_N(q) - \Gamma_N(q')) \neq 0, \tag{39}$$

where $P_N(q, q')$ is the matrix of the orthogonal projection on $\Re(\mathcal{O}_N(q)) \cap \Re(\mathcal{O}_N(q'))$. Moreover, (38) then holds if and only if $(I - P_N(q, q'))(\Gamma_N(q) - \Gamma_N(q'))u_0^{[N]} \neq 0$.

Proof. First, note that since the inputs u are analytic, we have

$$y_{[0,T]}(r, x_0, u) = y_{[0,T]}(r', x'_0, u) \tag{40}$$

$$\Longleftrightarrow \forall N, \ y_0^{[N]}(r, x_0, u) = y_0^{[N]}(r', x'_0, u) \tag{41}$$

$$\Longleftrightarrow \forall N, \ Y_N(q, x_0, u_0^{[N]}) = Y_N(q', x'_0, u_0^{[N]}). \tag{42}$$

Therefore, q and q' are controlled-discernible if and only if there exists u such that

$$\forall x_0, \ \forall x'_0, \ \exists N, \ \mathcal{O}_N(q)x_0 + \Gamma_N(q)u_0^{[N]} \neq \mathcal{O}_N(q')x'_0 + \Gamma_N(q')u_0^{[N]} \tag{43}$$

$$\Longleftrightarrow \exists N, \ \forall x_0, \ \forall x'_0, \ \mathcal{O}_N(q)x_0 + \Gamma_N(q)u_0^{[N]} \neq \mathcal{O}_N(q')x'_0 + \Gamma_N(q')u_0^{[N]} \tag{44}$$

$$\Longleftrightarrow \left(\Re(\mathcal{O}_N(q)) + \Gamma_N(q)u_0^{[N]}\right) \cap \left(\Re(\mathcal{O}_N(q')) + \Gamma_N(q')u_0^{[N]}\right) = \emptyset \tag{45}$$

$$\Longleftrightarrow (I - P_N(q, q'))(\Gamma_N(q) - \Gamma_N(q'))u_0^{[N]} \neq 0. \tag{46}$$

Equivalence of (44) and (43) follows from the fact that the sets

$$S_N \triangleq \left\{ \begin{pmatrix} x_0 \\ -x'_0 \end{pmatrix} \in \mathbb{R}^{2n} \ \middle| \ (\mathcal{O}_N(q) \ \mathcal{O}_N(q')) \begin{pmatrix} x_0 \\ -x'_0 \end{pmatrix} + (\Gamma_N(q) - \Gamma_N(q'))u_0^{[N]} = 0 \right\} \tag{47}$$

are affine subspaces of $\mathbb{R}^{2n}$ satisfying $S_N \subset S_{N'}$ if $N > N'$, and so $\cap_{N=1}^{\infty} S_N = \emptyset$ if and only if S_N eventually stabilizes at $\emptyset$.

Therefore, there exists an input u such that (38) holds if and only if there exists N such that (39) holds, and the set of such inputs then contains the set

$$\left\{ u \in \mathcal{A} \mid u_0^{[N]} \in \mathbb{R}^{mN} \setminus \ker \left((I - P_N(q, q'))(\Gamma_N(q) - \Gamma_N(q')) u_0^{[N]} \right) \right\}, \qquad (48)$$

which is generic.   □

The next result establishes the decidability of the condition given in the previous lemma.

Proposition 3. *The two modes q and q' are controlled-discernible if and only if*

$$\Gamma_{2n}(q) - \Gamma_{2n}(q') \neq 0, \qquad (49)$$

and, equivalently, if (39) is satisfied with $N = 4n$.

Proof. First, let us show that

$$\exists N, \; (I - P_N(q, q'))(\Gamma_N(q) - \Gamma_N(q')) \neq 0 \qquad (50)$$
$$\Longleftrightarrow \exists N', \; \Gamma_{N'}(q) - \Gamma_{N'}(q') \neq 0, \qquad (51)$$

To see this, note that

$$(I - P_N(q, q'))(\Gamma_N(q) - \Gamma_N(q')) \neq 0 \qquad (52)$$
$$\Longleftrightarrow \rho\left((\Gamma_N(q) - \Gamma_N(q') \; \mathcal{O}_N(q) \; \mathcal{O}_N(q')) \right) > \rho\left((\mathcal{O}_N(q) \; \mathcal{O}_N(q')) \right), \qquad (53)$$

which clearly proves the implication in (51). On the other hand, necessity in (51) stems from the fact that if $\Gamma_N(q) - \Gamma_N(q') \neq 0$, then the rank of $\Gamma_N(q) - \Gamma_N(q')$, thus that of $(\Gamma_N(q) - \Gamma_N(q') \; \mathcal{O}_N(q) \; \mathcal{O}_N(q'))$, grows unbounded in N. Therefore, since the rank of $(\mathcal{O}_N(q) \; \mathcal{O}_N(q'))$ is bounded by $2n$,

$$\rho\left((\Gamma_N(q) - \Gamma_N(q') \; \mathcal{O}_N(q) \; \mathcal{O}_N(q')) \right) - \rho\left((\mathcal{O}_N(q) \; \mathcal{O}_N(q')) \right) \qquad (54)$$

is unbounded.

Now, a straightforward consequence of the Cayley-Hamilton Theorem is that $\Gamma_N(q) \neq 0$ for some N if and only if $\Gamma_n(q) \neq 0$. Therefore, recalling that $\Gamma_N(q) - \Gamma_N(q')$ is exactly the N-step behavior matrix of the tuple $(A(q, q'), B(q, q'), C(q, q'), D(q, q'))$, we get that (51) holds if and only if $\Gamma_{2n}(q) - \Gamma_{2n}(q') \neq 0$. Moreover, in that case, it is easy to see that $\rho(\Gamma_{4n}(q) - \Gamma_{4n}(q')) > 2n$, and therefore that the integer expressed in (54) is positive, and thus that $(I - P_{4n}(q, q'))(\Gamma_{4n}(q) - \Gamma_{4n}(q')) \neq 0$.   □

Remark 2. An interesting question is whether the smallest N' in (51) could be strictly smaller than the smallest N. Equivalently, can the degree of a polynomial input u' of smallest degree satisfying

$$y(r, 0, u) \neq y(r', 0, u), \tag{55}$$

where $r \equiv q$ and $r' \equiv q'$, be strictly smaller then the degree of a polynomial input u of smallest degree satisfying (38)? The answer is yes, and as an example, take $q = 1$ and $q' = 2$, with $A(1) = B(1) = (1)$, $A(2) = B(2) = (2)$, $C(1) = C(2) = (1)$, and $D(1) = D(2) = 0$, and let $u \equiv -1$. Then

$$y_0^{[4]}(r, 0, u) = \begin{pmatrix} 0 \\ -1 \\ -1 \\ -1 \end{pmatrix} \neq y_0^{[4]}(r', 0, u) = \begin{pmatrix} 0 \\ -2 \\ -4 \\ -8 \end{pmatrix}, \tag{56}$$

hence (55). However, if $u \equiv \alpha$, then whenever $x_0 = x_0' = -\alpha$, we get

$$y(r, x_0, u) = y(r', x_0', u). \tag{57}$$

In fact, it can be verified that the minimum degree of a polynomial u for (38) to hold is 1, as opposed, obviously, to 0 for (55).

We can now establish the following characterization of $(r_0/y, u^*)$-observability and $(r_0/y, \bar{u})$-observability.

Theorem 3. *The following are equivalent.*

1. *The SLS (1) is $(r_0/y, u^*)$-observable.*
2. *The SLS (1) is $(r_0/y, \bar{u})$-observable.*
3. *Every pair of different modes is controlled-discernible.*

Proof. 2 ⇒ 1 is obvious.

1 ⇒ 3: Assume some pair of modes (q, q') is not controlled-discernible. Then, by definition, there exists no input u such that $y(r, x_0, u) \neq y(r', x_0', u)$ for all x_0, x_0' when $r \equiv q$ and $r' \equiv q'$.

3 ⇒ 2: We need to show that the set of controls

$$\mathcal{U} \triangleq \{ u \in \mathcal{A} \mid \forall r, \ \forall r', \ \forall x_0, \ \forall x_0', \ r_0' \neq r_0 \Rightarrow y(r, x_0, u) \neq y(r', x_0', u) \} \tag{58}$$

is generic if condition 3. holds. Let us show that it in fact contains

$$\mathcal{U}_{4n} \triangleq \left\{ u \in \mathcal{A} \mid u_0^{[4n]} \in \mathbb{R}^{4mn} \setminus \bigcup_{q \neq q'} \ker \left((I - P_{4n}(q, q'))(\Gamma_{4n}(q) - \Gamma_{4n}(q')) \right) \right\}, \tag{59}$$

which is indeed generic if ever pair of modes is controlled-discernible, by Proposition 3. That $\mathcal{U}_{4n} \subset \mathcal{U}$ follows from Lemma 2 and from the fact that, since the mode signals are right-continuous, there exists for any r and r' a time $T > 0$ such that $r_{[0,T]} \equiv q$ and $r'_{[0,T]} \equiv q'$. □

As for state observability, we have:

Theorem 4. *The following are equivalent.*

1. *The SLS (1) is $(x_0/y, u^*)$-observable.*
2. *The SLS (1) is $(x_0/y, \overline{u})$-observable.*
3. *Every mode is observable and every pair of modes is either controlled-discernible or jointly observable.*

Proof. $2 \Rightarrow 1$ is obvious.

$1 \Rightarrow 3$: If some mode q is not observable, then whenever $x_0 \in \ker(\mathcal{O}_n(q)) \backslash \{0\}$, we have $y(r, x_0, u) = y(r, 0, u)$ for any u when $r \equiv q$. Assume now that q and q' are neither controlled-discernible nor jointly observable. Then $\Gamma_N(q) - \Gamma_N(q') = 0$ for all N and, letting $r \equiv q$ and $r' \equiv q'$, we get

$$y(r, x_0, u) - y(r', x_0', u) = y(r, x_0, 0) - y(r', x_0', 0), \tag{60}$$

and so, by definition of joint observability, there exist two initial states x_0 and x_0' such that $y(r, x_0, 0) \neq y(r', x_0', 0)$, and by (60), such that $y(r, x_0, u) \neq y(r', x_0', u)$ for all controls u.

$3 \Rightarrow 2$: We need to show that the set of controls

$$\mathcal{U} \triangleq \{u \in \mathcal{A} \mid \forall r, \, \forall r', \, \forall x_0, \, \forall x_0', \, x_0' \neq x_0 \Rightarrow y(r, x_0, u) \neq y(r', x_0', u)\} \tag{61}$$

is generic if condition 3. holds. Let us show that it in fact contains

$$\mathcal{U}_{4n} \triangleq \left\{ u \in \mathcal{A} \mid u_0^{[4n]} \in \mathbb{R}^{4mn} \backslash \bigcup_{(q,q') \in S} \ker\left((I - P_{4n}(q, q'))(\Gamma_{4n}(q) - \Gamma_{4n}(q'))\right) \right\}, \tag{62}$$

where S is the set of controlled-discernible pairs of modes. By proposition 3, $\mathcal{U}_{4n}$ is of course generic. Now, take $x_0 \neq x_0'$, r, r' and $T > 0$ such that $r_{[1,T]} \equiv q$ and $r'[0,T] \equiv q'$. If $q = q'$, then of course $y(r, x_0, u) \neq y(r', x_0', u)$ for all $u \in \mathcal{A}$ since q is observable. If $q \neq q'$ and they are controlled-discernible, then by Lemma 2 and Proposition 3, $y_{[0,T]}(r, x_0, u) \neq y_{[0,T]}(r', x_0', u)$ if $u \in \mathcal{U}_{4n}$. If they are not controlled-discernible, then they are jointly observable and so $y_{[0,T]}(r, x_0, u) \neq y_{[0,T]}(r', x_0', u)$ for all $u \in \mathcal{A}$ since $y_{[0,T]}(r, x_0, u) - y_{[0,T]}(r', x_0', u) = y_{[0,T]}(r, x_0, 0) - y_{[0,T]}(r', x_0', 0)$. $\square$

Remark 3. What we have just shown is that for switched linear systems with arbitrary and unknown mode signals, *single-experiment observability* and *generic single-experiment observability*, as defined in [17], are equivalent, whether one wishes to *observe* the initial mode or the initial state.

Remark 4. In [7], recall that a necessary and sufficient condition for $(r_0, x_0/y, u^*)$-observability was established as the combination of controlled-discernibility of each pair of modes and observability of each mode. While controlled-discernibility of every pair of modes is indeed necessary and sufficient for $(r_0/y, u^*)$-observability, we have established that it is not necessary for $(x_0/y, u^*)$-observability. Indeed, as noted in Remark 1, the system given in Example 1 is $(x_0/y, u^*)$-observable even though $\Gamma_N(q) = 0$ for any mode, making controlled-discernibility an impossibility. Informally, it shows that it is not necessary to recover the initial mode in order to figure out the initial state.

5   Conclusion

We have characterized several observability notions for continuous-time switched linear systems. The analysis is of course still incomplete, and several problems still need to be solved. For instance, mode and state observability properties under fully or partially unknown inputs still have not been investigated in the switched setting. Furthermore, we will be investigating the *existential* counterparts of our current results, i.e. conditions for existence of mode signals allowing the initial or current mode or state to be inferred. It turns out that, in contrast with the universal problems that reduce to instantaneous inversions, such problems will involve observing the outputs *over a period of time*, and will involve the design of switching signals (as pointed out, e.g., in [22], and as is the case in the known modes case [19]). In future work, we will furthermore explore the connection between observability and bisimulation theory for discrete event and hybrid systems [16, 20].

Acknowledgements

The authors wish to thank the anonymous reviewers for their careful reviews and insightful comments, as well as Hakan Yazarel for valuable discussions.

References

1. M. Babaali and M. Egerstedt, "Observability of switched linear systems." in *Hybrid Systems: Computation and Control (R. Alur and G. Pappas, eds.)*. Springer, 2004, pp. 48–63.
2. A. Balluchi, L. Benvenuti, M. D. Di Benedetto, and A. L. Sangiovanni-Vincentelli, "Observability for hybrid systems," in *Proceedings of the 42nd IEEE Conference on Decision and Control*, Maui, HW, December 2003.
3. A. Bemporad, G. Ferrari-Trecate, and M. Morari, "Observability and controllability of piecewise affine and hybrid systems," *IEEE Transactions on Automatic Control*, vol. 45, no. 10, pp. 1864–1876, October 2000.
4. S. L. Campbell and C. D. J. Meyer, *Generalized Inverses of Linear Transformations*. New York, NY: Dover, 1991.
5. P. Collins and J. H. van Schuppen, "Observability of piecewise-affine hybrid systems," ser. Hybrid Systems: Computation and Control. Springer-Verlag, 2004.
6. E. F. Costa and J. B. R. do Val, "On the detectability and observability of discrete-time Markov jump linear systems," in *Proceedings of the 39th IEEE Conference on Decision and Control*, Sydney, Australia, December 2000, pp. 2355–2360.

7. E. De Santis, M. D. Di Benedetto, and G. Pola, "On observability and detectability of continuous-time linear switching systems," in *Proceedings of the 42nd IEEE Conference on Decision and Control*, Maui, HW, December 2003.
8. J. Ezzine and A. H. Haddad, "Controllability and observability of hybrid systems," *International Journal of Control*, vol. 49, no. 6, pp. 2045–2055, 1989.
9. G. Ferrari-Trecate and M. Gati, "Computation of observability regions for discrete-time hybrid systems," in *Proceedings of the 42nd IEEE Conference on Decision and Control*, Maui, HW, December 2003.
10. L. Gurvits, "Stabilities and controllabilities of switched systems (with applications to the quantum systems)," in *Proceedings of the Fifteenth International Symposium on Mathematical Theory of Networks and Systems*, Univ. Notre Dame, August 2002.
11. I. Hwang, H. Balakrishnan, and C. Tomlin, "Observability criteria and estimator design for stochastic linear hybrid systems," in *Proceedings of the IEE European Control Conference*, Cambridge, UK, September 2003.
12. Y. Ji and H. Chizeck, "Controllability, observability and discrete-time jump linear quadratic control," *International Journal of Control*, vol. 48, no. 2, pp. 481–498, 1988.
13. A. Juloski, M. Heemels, and S. Weiland, "Observer design for a class of piecewise affine systems," in *Proceedings of the 41st IEEE Conference on Decision and Control*, Las Vegas, NV, December 2002.
14. T. Kailath, *Linear Systems.* Englewood Cliffs, NJ: Prentice Hall, 1980.
15. M. Mariton, "Stochastic observability of linear systems with markovian jumps," in *Proceedings of the 25th IEEE Conference on Decision and Control*, Athens, Greece, December 1986, pp. 2208–2209.
16. G. J. Pappas, "Bisimilar linear systems," *Automatica*, vol. 39, no. 12, pp. 2035–2047, December 2003.
17. E. D. Sontag, "On the observability of polynomial systems, I: Finite-time problems," *SIAM Journal on Control and Optimization*, vol. 17, no. 1, pp. 139–151, 1979.
18. ——, "Nonlinear regulation: The piecewise linear approach," *IEEE Transactions on Automatic Control*, vol. 26, no. 2, pp. 346–358, April 1981.
19. Z. Sun, S. S. Ge, and T. H. Lee, "Controllability and reachability criteria for switched linear systems," *Automatica*, May 2002.
20. P. Tabuada and G. J. Pappas, "Bisimilar control affine systems," *Systems & Control Letters*, vol. 52, no. 1, pp. 49–58, May 2004.
21. R. Vidal, A. Chiuso, and S. Soatto, "Observability and identifiability of jump linear systems," in *Proceedings of the 41st IEEE Conference on Decision and Control*, Las Vegas, NV, December 2002, pp. 3614–3619.
22. R. Vidal, A. Chiuso, S. Soatto, and S. Sastry, "Observability of linear hybrid systems," ser. Hybrid Systems: Computation and Control. Springer-Verlag, 2003.
23. P. D. West and A. H. Haddad, "On the observability of linear stochastic switching systems," in *Proceedings of the 1994 American Control Conference*, Baltimore, MD, June 1994, pp. 1846–1847.

Controller Synthesis on Non-uniform and Uncertain Discrete–Time Domains[*]

Andrea Balluchi[1], Pierpaolo Murrieri[1],
and Alberto L. Sangiovanni-Vincentelli[1,2]

[1] PARADES GEIE, Via di S. Pantaleo, 66, 00186 Roma, Italy
{balluchi, murrieri, alberto}@parades.rm.cnr.it
http://www.parades.rm.cnr.it
[2] Dept. of EECS, University of California at Berkeley, CA 94720, USA
alberto@eecs.berkeley.edu
http://www.eecs.berkeley.edu/alberto

Abstract. The problem of synthesizing feedback controllers that perform sensing and actuation actions on non–uniform and uncertain discrete time domains is considered. This class of problems is relevant to many application domains. For instance, in engine control a heterogenous and, to some extent, uncertain event–driven time domain is due to the behavior of the 4-stroke internal combustion engine, with which the controller has to synchronize to operate the engine properly. Similar problems arise also in standard discrete–time control systems when considering the behavior of the system with controller implementation and communication effects. The design problem is formalized in a hybrid system framework; synthesis and verification methods, based on robust stability and robust performance results, are presented. The effectiveness of the proposed methods is demonstrated in an engine control application.

1 Introduction

This paper considers the problem of synthesizing feedback controllers that perform sensing and actuation actions on non–uniform and uncertain discrete–time domains. The approach was initially motivated by control problems in the automotive industry, but it is certainly extensible to other application domains.

In engine control applications the existence of non–uniform and, to some extent, uncertain time–domains is a characteristic of the plant behavior itself and the controller implementation. Heterogeneity in time domains arises in engine control from nested control-loops of both:

---

[*] This research has been partially supported by the E.C. grant *Control and Computation* IST-2001-33520. The authors are members of the *HyCon* Network of Excellence, E.C. grant IST-511368.

M. Morari and L. Thiele (Eds.): HSCC 2005, LNCS 3414, pp. 118–133, 2005.
© Springer-Verlag Berlin Heidelberg 2005

- *discrete–time domain* control loops with fixed sampling rate, e.g. cruise control (with sampling time of the order of dsec) and throttle valve control (with sampling time of the order of msec);
- *event–driven control* actions synchronized with the evolution of the engine cycle[1], such as control of the engine torque (delivered by each cylinder during the power stroke), fuel injection (during the exhaust stroke in multi–point injection engines) and spark ignition (either at the end of the compression stroke or at the beginning of the power stroke).

In particular, event–driven control actions are synchronized with the engine cycle and issued on a non–uniform discrete–time domain, characterized by drifts of the activation times and frequency, which is synchronous with the crankshaft revolution speed.

Moreover, similar problems arise also in standard discrete–time control systems when considering

- the effects of the implementation of control algorithms in embedded systems, which range from uncertain and time–varying delays introduced in the loop (e.g. latency due to scheduling of the algorithms on time–shared CPUs) to the intermittent dropping of some executions of the control algorithm, due to either computation overload of the CPU or communications errors with sensors and actuators;
- sporadic failures on sensors, actuators, embedded controllers or communication.

The Lee-Sangiovanni Vincentelli (LSV) tagged-signal model (TSM) [1] is a formalism for describing aspects of models of computation that very naturally allows the representation of signals defined on non–uniform time–domains. Benveniste *et al.* [2] used the TSM to describe interacting synchronous and asynchronous models of computation and communication. Controller design taking into account implementation constraints was investigated by Bicchi *et al.* [3, 4], who considered input signals quantization, and Palopoli et al. [5], who proposed an optimal trade-off between closed–loop performances and scheduling for a multi–rate control system that is in charge of controlling a number of independent plants.

In this paper we address the problem of synthesizing and verifying control algorithms that are executed at discrete times with phase drifts of the activation event sequence and uncertainties in the activation times. Today, the best practice in industry for dynamic compensators design for this class of control problems is gain scheduling with possibly some on–line adaptation to the varying sampling time. However, the correctness of the controller in terms of stability and closed–loop performance under drifting of the sampling times is not formally guaranteed.

---

[1] An interesting topic is the design of efficient interfaces between multi–rate feedback loops characterized by phase and frequency drifts of the activation times. This topic will be the subject of a future paper.

The synthesis and verification problems can be properly formalized and solved using hybrid systems techniques. We show that fundamental results on robust stability and robust performance can be successfully used and reformulated in a hybrid system framework to obtain both:

- synthesis procedures that take into account time–domain uncertainties and produce controllers with guaranteed performances, and
- formal verification techniques that guarantee the correctness of controllers designed either abstracting or partially compensating time–domain uncertainties.

We consider the design of dynamic compensators for continuous–time uncertain plants with non–uniform and uncertain activation times. In particular, the final aim is to design linear time–invariant dynamic controllers for sampled–data systems, derived from a non–uniform sampling of the plant model, which guarantee stability and achieve desired rate of convergence despite sampling time variance.

The paper is organized as follows. In Section 2, the motivating automotive application, namely the synthesis of an algorithm for idle speed control, is described. In Section 3, fundamental results on robust stability and robust performance are reviewed. In Section 4, the problem of the design of dynamic compensators under non–uniform and uncertain activation times is formalized. In addition, synthesis and verification methods obtained from the results presented in Section 3 are described. Finally, in Section 5, the proposed techniques are applied to the idle speed control problem showing the degree of robustness of a controller designed without taking into account time–domain uncertainties and a synthesis procedure that, by considering them, produces a controller with improved closed–loop stability. Some concluding remarks are presented in Section 6.

2   Idle Speed Control Problem Formulation

The motivating application for the work presented in this paper is the synthesis of an algorithm for idle speed control. The objective is to keep the speed of the crankshaft within a specified range despite the actions of unpredictable but bounded load torques acting on the crankshaft, when the engine is idle.

In Figure 1, a hybrid model describing the behavior of a 4–stroke 4–cylinder spark ignition engine at idle is depicted (more details on the model are given in [6, 7, 8]). The hybrid model has a urgent semantic, some nonlinear continuous dynamics and some continuous variables with piece-wise constant evolutions. Engine control inputs are:

- The throttle valve command u_α, used to control the engine air charge[2] m;
- The spark advance angle[3] u_φ, which defines ignition timing.

---

[2] Fuel injection is set according to the evolution of the air charge m so to have stoichiometric mixtures, as requested for tailpipe emission control.

[3] It denotes the angle performed by the crankshaft from the time at which the spark is ignited to the time at which the piston reaches the next top dead center. It is negative if the spark is given after the top dead center.

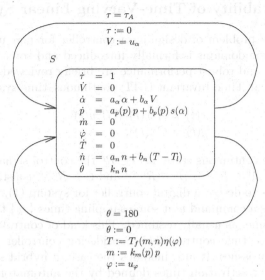

$$\tau = \tau_A$$
$$\tau := 0$$
$$V := u_\alpha$$

S

$$\begin{aligned}
\dot{\tau} &= 1 \\
\dot{V} &= 0 \\
\dot{\alpha} &= a_\alpha\,\alpha + b_\alpha\,V \\
\dot{p} &= a_p(p)\,p + b_p(p)\,s(\alpha) \\
\dot{m} &= 0 \\
\dot{\varphi} &= 0 \\
\dot{T} &= 0 \\
\dot{n} &= a_n\,n + b_n\,(T - T_l) \\
\dot{\theta} &= k_n\,n
\end{aligned}$$

$$\theta = 180$$

$$\theta := 0$$
$$T := T_f(m,n)\eta(\varphi)$$
$$m := k_m(p)\,p$$
$$\varphi := u_\varphi$$

Fig. 1. Hybrid model of the cylinders

The command u_α to the throttle valve motor is a discrete–time signal produced with a constant sampling period τ_A. The timer τ, the piece–wise constant variable V, and the self-loop transition with guard condition $\tau = \tau_A$ model the uniform sampling of the discrete–time throttle valve control. To take into account the actuation delay, the desired spark advance u_φ has to be set for each cylinder at the bottom dead center at the end of the intake stroke, so that the ignition subsystem can be programmed to ignite the spark at the proper time. Dead center events are modelled by the self-loop transition with guard condition $\theta = 180$ and reset $\theta := 0$, where θ denotes the crankshaft angle.

The continuous state variables with no trivial dynamics are: the throttle valve angle α; the intake manifold pressure p; the crankshaft revolution speed n and the crankshaft angle θ. The evolution of the intake manifold pressure p depends on the throttle valve angle α, which is controlled by the input u_α. The crankshaft speed n depends on the engine torque T and defines the evolution of the crankshaft angle θ. At each dead–center, i.e. when θ reaches 180, the crankshaft angle θ is reset and the engine torque T is set according to the applied spark advance φ and the air charge m. Moreover, the air charge m and the desired spark advance φ for the next expansion cycle are initialized according to the current value of the intake manifold pressure p and the input u_φ, respectively.

The design of the spark advance control algorithm is particularly challenging since it is defined on a non–uniform discrete–time domain, with sampling period varying according to the evolution of the crankshaft revolution speed.

3   Robust Stability of Time-Varying Linear Systems

In this section, the problem of designing a controller for non–uniform and uncertain discrete–time domains is formally introduced and some relevant results
on robust stability and robust performance are briefly reviewed.

Consider a Linear Time Invariant (LTI) continuous–time system

$$\dot{x}(t) = A^c x(t) + B^c u(t)$$
$$y(t) = C x(t) \,, \tag{1}$$

with $x(t) \in R^n$ the continuous state, $u(t) \in R^p$ the control signal, $y(t) \in R^o$ the
output signal, and $A^c \in R^{n \times n}$, $B^c \in R^{n \times p}$ and $C \in R^{o \times n}$ constant matrices.

The objective is to design a digital controller for system (1), which reads the
output y and issues a command u at some sampling times $\{\tau_k\}$ that are not uniformly spaced in time, as usually assumed. This kind of control problems arises
in standard discrete–time control when considering controller implementation
and communication issues. It also includes the case of hybrid systems with no
resets and controller activation times defined by the automaton transitions. In
this case, the non–uniformity of the time domain is given by the hybrid behavior
of the plant itself[4].

By sampling the continuous–time dynamics (1) on a non–uniform time domain $\{\tau_k\}$, the following Linear Time Variant (LTV) discrete–time system is
obtained:

$$x(k+1) = A(k)x(k) + B(k)u(k)$$
$$y(k) \quad = Cx(k) \,, \tag{2}$$

where $x(k) = x(\tau_k)$, $u(k) = u(\tau_k) = u(t) \; \forall t \in [\tau_k, \tau_{k+1})$, and $y(k) = y(\tau_k)$ are
samples of the corresponding continuous signals, and the system matrices are
obtained by integration of (1) over the interval $[\tau_k, \tau_{k+1}]$, i.e.

$$A(k) = e^{A^c(\tau_{k+1} - \tau_k)}$$
$$B(k) = \int_0^{\tau_{k+1} - \tau_k} e^{A^c(\tau_{k+1} - \tau_k - \tau)} d\tau \; B^c \,. \tag{3}$$

Let the time domain $\{\tau_k\}$ be such that the sampling intervals $\tau_{k+1} - \tau_k$ satisfy

$$\tau_{k+1} - \tau_k = \tau^0 + \delta(k) \qquad \text{with } |\delta(k)| \le \Delta \text{ and } \Delta > 0 \,, \tag{4}$$

where τ^0 is a nominal constant sampling period and $\delta(k)$ is a bounded perturbation. Then, in (2),

$$A(k) = \bar{A} + \Delta_A(k)$$
$$B(k) = \bar{B} + \Delta_B(k) \,, \tag{5}$$

where $\bar{A} = e^{A^c \tau^0}$ and $\bar{B} = \int_0^{\tau^0} e^{A^c(\tau^0 - \tau)} d\tau B^c$ are the contributions associated
to the nominal sampling period τ^0 and $\Delta_A(k) = A(k) - \bar{A}$, $\Delta_B(k) = B(k) - \bar{B}$
take into account sampling time variations.

---

[4] For instance, in the idle speed control problem, activation times are triggered by
dead–center events that are produced when the crankshaft angle θ reaches 180.

Perturbations $\Delta_A(k)$ and $\Delta_B(k)$ in (5) are bounded[5]as follows:

– If $A^c = 0$, then $\Delta_A(k) = 0$ and

$$\|\Delta_B(k)\| \le \|B^c\| \Delta ; \tag{6}$$

– If $A^c \ne 0$ and if the geometric multiplicity of the eigenvalues of A^c is equal to their algebraic multiplicity, then

$$\|\Delta_A(k)\| = \sigma_{max}(\Delta_A(k))$$
$$\le \left\| e^{-A^c \tau^0} \right\| \left\| e^{A^c \delta(k)} - I \right\|$$
$$\le \left\| \bar{A}^{-1} \right\| \|A^c\| \, k\,(A^c) \, \frac{e^{\bar{\alpha}(A^c)\Delta} - 1}{\bar{\alpha}(A^c)} , \tag{7}$$

$$\|\Delta_B(k)\| = \sigma_{max}(\Delta_B(k))$$
$$\le \left\| \bar{A} \right\| \|B^c\| \, k\,(A^c) \, \frac{e^{\bar{\alpha}(A^c)\Delta} - 1}{\bar{\alpha}(A^c)} , \tag{8}$$

where $k(A) = \|T\| \|T^{-1}\|$ denotes the condition number with respect to inversion of the matrix T such that $T^{-1}AT$ is in the Jordan normal form[6]and $\bar{\alpha}(A) = \max\{\alpha(A), \alpha(-A)\}$, with $\alpha(A) = \max\{\mathrm{Re}(\lambda)|\lambda \in \lambda(A)\}$ the spectral abscissa of A. Note that, since $\lim_{\Delta \to 0} \frac{e^{\bar{\alpha}(A^c)\Delta}-1}{\bar{\alpha}(A^c)} \approx \lim_{\Delta \to 0} \Delta$, then the upper bounds (7–8) converge to zero with Δ.

Upper bounds similar to (7–8) can be obtained when the geometric multiplicity of the eigenvalues of A^c is lower than their algebraic multiplicity, in which case the Jordan normal form has blocks of order greater than 1 (details on the approximation of the norm of the exponential matrix can be found in [9]).

The design problem on non–uniform discrete–time domains can be successfully approached by exploiting interesting results on robust stability (see [10, 11, 12, 13, 14, 15, 16, 17, 18, 19, 20, 21, 22, 23, 24, 25]) for perturbed systems of type

$$x(k+1) = [A + \Delta A(k)]x(k) . \tag{9}$$

To the best of our knowledge, the work of Bauer *et al.* [10], along with [16, 17, 18], gives the tightest stability conditions for parametric uncertainties of type

$$\Delta A(k) = \sum_{j=0}^{r} a_j(k)A_j , \tag{10}$$

---

[5] Unless differently specified, we consider the Euclidean norm of matrices and vectors defined as $\|z\| = \sqrt{\sum_{i=1}^{n} z_i^2}$ for $z \in R^n$ and $\|M\| = \sigma_{max}(M) = \max\{\lambda|\lambda^2 \in \lambda(M^T M)\}$, for $M \in R^{n \times n}$, with $\sigma_{max}(M)$ the maximum singular value of M and $\lambda(M)$ the set of eigenvalues of M.

[6] It is well known that the matrix T is not unique; in what follows, less conservative conditions will be obtained for T such that $k(A)$ is minimized.

with $A_j \in R^{n \times n}$ and $a_j(k) \in [\underline{a}_j, \overline{a}_j]$, for $j = 1, \cdots, r$. Introduce the set $\tilde{\mathcal{A}}$ of extremal matrices

$$\tilde{\mathcal{A}} = \{\tilde{A} = A + \sum_{j=0}^{r} a_j A_j \mid a_j = \underline{a}_j \text{ or } a_j = \overline{a}_j, \text{ for all } j = 1, \cdots, r \} . \quad (11)$$

The set $\tilde{\mathcal{A}}$ in (10) defines a polytope $\mathcal{P}_{\tilde{A}}$ whose vertices coincide with extremal matrices. In [10], the following result was presented:

Proposition 1. *System (9) with time–varying dynamical matrix inside the polytope $\mathcal{P}_{\tilde{A}}$ is asymptotically stable[7] in norm-1 (norm-∞) if and only if there exists a $\bar{k} > 0$ such that, for any sequence of $\bar{k}$ matrices $\tilde{A}_j \in \tilde{\mathcal{A}}$,*

$$[\text{C1}] \qquad \|\prod_{j=1}^{\bar{k}} \tilde{A}_j\|_1 < 1 \qquad (\|\prod_{j=1}^{\bar{k}} \tilde{A}_j\|_\infty < 1, \text{respectively}) . \quad (12)$$

Molchanov *et al.* [16] extended the previous result by proving that condition [C1] can be formulated for any norm. Condition [C1] is strong since robust stability for a dynamic matrix varying inside the polytope $\mathcal{P}_{\tilde{A}}$ can be tested by checking combinations of the extremal matrices in $\tilde{\mathcal{A}}$ only. However, it could require many computations if the number r of elements in the linear combination (10) is large. Indeed, the cardinality of $\tilde{\mathcal{A}}$ is 2^r and the stability test on k steps requires 2^{rk} matrix multiplications. In [17, 18], simplified stability tests had been proposed for specific classes of systems.

In [26], Blanchini compares stabilizability via gain scheduling (with measurement of time–varying parameters) and robust state feedback for perturbed systems of type (9–10) and shows that the two approaches are equivalent.

Sufficient conditions for robust stability, based on the Lyapunov approach, had been proposed in [11, 12, 13, 14]. Given a positive-definite function $V(X)$, system (9) asymptotically converges[8] to the equilibrium with convergence rate $\mu > 0$ if the difference $V(X(k+1)) - \mu V(X(k))$ is negative for any $k \geq 0$. By slightly extending the work in [11], the following sufficient condition can be obtained:

Proposition 2. *System (9) is globally asymptotically stable with rate of convergence $0 < \mu < 1$ if*

$$[\text{C2}] \qquad \sigma_{max}(\Delta A(k)) < -\sigma_{max}(A) + \sqrt{\sigma_{max}^2(A) + \frac{\sigma_{min}(Q)}{\sigma_{max}(P)}} , \quad (13)$$

where $P = P^T > 0$ is the solution of the discrete-time Lyapunov equation

---

[7] Given $z \in R^n$, $\|z\|_1 = \sum_{i=1}^{n} |z_i|$ and $\|z\|_\infty = \max_{i=1}^{n} |z_i|$. Given $M \in R^{n \times n}$, $\|M\|_1 = \max_{j=1}^{n} \sum_{i=1}^{n} |m_{ij}|$ and $\|M\|_\infty = \max_{i=1}^{n} \sum_{j=1}^{n} |m_{ij}|$. A system is asymptotically stable in norm-1 (norm-∞) if $\lim_{k \to \infty} \|x(k)\|_1 = 0$ ($\lim_{k \to \infty} \|x(k)\|_\infty = 0$).

[8] The stability of the autonomous system coincide with BIBO stability if $B_C(k)$ is bounded in norm.

$$A^T P A - \mu P = -Q, \quad for \ Q = Q^T > 0 \ . \tag{14}$$

Finally, if the nominal matrix A in (9) verifies $\|A\|_p < 1$, for some norm $\| \cdot \|_p$, then a further condition that ensures robust stability is given by

$$[\textbf{C3}] \quad \|\Delta A(k)\|_p < 1 - \|A\|_p \ . \tag{15}$$

A simple proof is obtained by noting that, since

$$\|A + \Delta A(k)\|_p \leq \|A\|_p + \|\Delta A(k)\|_p < 1$$

then the next–state map is a contraction in the chosen p–norm.

Further robust stability conditions have been obtained using LMI techniques (see [20, 22, 23, 25]) and H_1 and H_∞ formulations (see [19, 21, 24]). Such approaches will be evaluated in future work.

4   Dynamic Compensators Design Under Non-uniform and Uncertain Activation Times

Standard design techniques based on frequency domain representations cannot be applied to design control algorithms for system (2), since such system is not time-invariant. However, often linear time–invariant controllers are adopted even for time–varying plants. This is the case for instance when the design is subject to very limiting constraints on the implementation platform. Consider the LTI compensator

$$\begin{aligned} w(k+1) &= Fw(k) + Ge(k) \\ u(k) &= Hw(k) + Le(k) \end{aligned} \tag{16}$$

where $e(k) = r(k) - y(k) \in R^o$ is the error between the controlled output and the reference signal $r(k)$, $w \in R^m$ is the state of the controller, $F \in R^{m \times m}$, $G \in R^{m \times o}$, $H \in R^{p \times m}$ and $L \in R^{p \times o}$ are constant matrices.

By (2) and (16), the closed–loop system is described in the extended state space $X = [x, w]^T$ as follows

$$\begin{bmatrix} x \\ w \end{bmatrix}(k+1) = \begin{pmatrix} A(k) - B(k)LC & B(k)H \\ -GC & F \end{pmatrix} \begin{bmatrix} x \\ w \end{bmatrix}(k) + \begin{pmatrix} B(k)L & I_{n \times n} \\ G & 0_{m \times n} \end{pmatrix} \begin{bmatrix} r \\ d \end{bmatrix}(k) \tag{17}$$

or equivalently, by (5),

$$X(k+1) = [\bar{A}_C + \Delta A_C(k)] X(k) + [\bar{B}_C + \Delta B_C(k)] U(k) \ , \tag{18}$$

where $U = [r, d]^T$ and

$$\bar{A}_C = \begin{pmatrix} \bar{A} - \bar{B}LC & \bar{B}H \\ -GC & F \end{pmatrix}, \quad \Delta A_C(k) = \begin{pmatrix} \Delta_A(k) - \Delta_B(k)LC & \Delta_B(k)H \\ 0_{n\times n} & 0_{m\times m} \end{pmatrix},$$

$$\bar{B}_C = \begin{pmatrix} \bar{B}L & I_{n\times n} \\ G & 0_{m\times n} \end{pmatrix}, \quad \Delta B_C(k) = \begin{pmatrix} \Delta_B(k)L & 0_{m\times n} \\ 0_{m\times 1} & 0_{m\times n} \end{pmatrix}.$$

$$(19)$$

The closed–loop system (18) is both time–varying, due to the sampling time variations, and parameterized in the controller matrices (16). Upper bounds for the closed–loop perturbation matrices $\Delta A_C(k)$ and $\Delta B_C(k)$ are obtained from (6),(7) and (8), including additional terms p_A and p_B that model parameters uncertainties on $A(k)$ and $B(k)$ in (2). We have:

- If $A^c = 0$, then from (6)

$$\|\Delta A_C(k)\| \le (\|B^c\|\Delta + p_A + p_B)\gamma_C \quad \text{with} \quad \gamma_C = \left\| \begin{pmatrix} I & 0 \\ -LC & H \end{pmatrix} \right\|$$

$$\|\Delta B_C(k)\| \le (\|B^c\|\Delta + p_B)\|L\|$$

- If $A^c \ne 0$ and if the geometric multiplicity of the eigenvalues of A^c is equal to their algebraic multiplicity, then

$$\|\Delta A_C(k)\| \le \left[\left(\|\bar{A}^{-1}\|\,\|A^c\| + \|\bar{A}\|\,\|B^c\| \right) k(A^c) \frac{e^{\bar{\alpha}(A^c)\Delta} - 1}{\bar{\alpha}(A^c)} + p_A + p_B \right] \gamma_C$$

$$\|\Delta B_C(k)\| \le \left[\|\bar{A}\|\,\|B^c\| k(A^c) \frac{e^{\bar{\alpha}(A^c)\Delta} - 1}{\bar{\alpha}(A^c)} + p_B \right] \|L\|$$

Conditions [C1], [C2] and [C3] – as formulated – can be applied for the verification of the correctness of a given dynamic compensator (16), in presence of time–domain and plant parameter uncertainties. On the other hand, they can also be used for controller synthesis if included in an exploration algorithm of the controller parameters space.

Among them, [C1] is the least conservative. However, for synthesis purposes [C1] could be numerically unfeasible, due to the dependency of the extremal matrices in (11) on the controller parameters: $2^{(2m+n)\bar{k}}$ multiplications between extremal matrices are necessary to perform the test on a given set of controller parameters. Then, [C1] is more suitable for verification of a given controller, possibly obtained using either [C2] or [C3].

The Lyapunov approach employed in [C2] allows the designer to set a desired convergence rate in (14) and handle separately in (13) the robustness with respect to time–domain and plant parameter uncertainties.

This approach can be specialized to the case of the design of dead–beat controllers, obtained when the nominal closed–loop system has all poles in the origin of the complex plane and having finite impulse response.

Proposition 3. *If the nominal closed–loop matrix $\bar{A}_C$ has all eigenvalues in 0, then the closed–loop uncertain time-varying system is asymptotically stable, with convergence rate $\mu \in (0,1)$, provided that*

[C4] $\sigma_{max}(\Delta A_C(k)) <$

$$-\sigma_{max}(\bar{A}_C) + \sqrt{\sigma_{max}^2(\bar{A}_C) + \mu \frac{\sigma_{min}(Q)}{\sigma_{max}(Q)} \frac{1 - \frac{\sigma_{max}^2(\bar{A}_C)}{\mu}}{1 - \left(\frac{\sigma_{max}^2(\bar{A}_C)}{\mu}\right)^{n+m}}} \quad (20)$$

for some symmetric positive–definite matrix Q.

Proof. The solution to the Lyapunov equation (14) for a given symmetric positive definite matrix Q and convergence rate μ, can be written as

$$P = \frac{1}{\mu} \sum_{k=0}^{\infty} \frac{(\bar{A}_C^T)^k Q \bar{A}_C^k}{\mu^k}.$$

If all eigenvalues of $\bar{A}_C$ are in 0, then $\bar{A}_C$ is nilpotent of order $n + m$ and

$$P = \frac{1}{\mu} \sum_{k=0}^{n+m-1} \frac{(\bar{A}_C^T)^k Q \bar{A}_C^k}{\mu^k}. \quad (21)$$

Then,

$$\sigma_{max}(P) = \|P\| \leq \frac{1}{\mu} \sum_{k=0}^{n+m-1} \frac{\|(\bar{A}_C^T)^k Q \bar{A}_C^k\|}{\mu^k} \leq \frac{\sigma_{max}(Q)}{\mu} \frac{1 - \left(\frac{\sigma_{max}^2(\bar{A}_C)}{\mu}\right)^{n+m}}{1 - \frac{\sigma_{max}^2(\bar{A}_C)}{\mu}}.$$

$$(22)$$

Inequality (22) gives a lower bound for $\frac{\sigma_{max}(Q)}{\sigma_{max}(P)}$, which substituted in (13) gives condition [C4].   Q.E.D.

Notice that condition [C4] is much easier to test than [C2], since the Lyapunov equation is explicitly solved. Moreover, it is important to observe that the time-varying closed–loop system does not preserve the dead–beat response due to the time–domain and plant parameters uncertainties.

5   Idle Speed Control Application

In this section, the design methodology proposed in Section 4 is applied to the idle speed control problem described in Section 2. In particular, the design and verification of spark advance control algorithms are illustrated. Spark advance control is activated on the non–uniform discrete–time domain given by the dead-center times $\{\tau_k\}$. Since in idle speed control the engine speed is constrained by specification, then the dead-center times sequence $\{\tau_k\}$ satisfies condition (4) on bounded sampling time variation.

According to the model depicted in Figure 1, the torque generated by the engine during the k–th power stroke depends on: the spark advance command $u_\varphi(\tau_{k-1})$ (set at the beginning of the compression stroke), the mass of loaded air $m(\tau_{k-1})$, and the engine speed at the beginning of the power stroke $n(\tau_k)$. The engine torque, $T(t)$, is modeled as a piece–wise constant signal, with discontinuity points at dead-center times τ_k, i.e.

$$T(t) = T_f(m(\tau_{k-1}), n(\tau_k)) \, \eta(u_\varphi(\tau_{k-1})) \qquad \text{for } t \in [\tau_k, \tau_{k+1}) \ . \tag{23}$$

The crankshaft dynamics, discretized on dead–center times $\{\tau_k\}$, is

$$n(k+1) = A(k) \, n(k) + B(k) \, u(k) \ , \tag{24}$$

where the input $u(k)$ comprises both the load disturbance T_l and the engine torque T, i.e.

$$u(k) = T_l(k) + T(k) \ .$$

To control the engine speed n to a given reference value n_r, the engine torque T is modulated, using the spark advance command, so to implement the LTI compensator (16), where $e = n - n_r$ and $u = T$. That is

$$T(k) = c(k) \otimes [n(k) - n_r(k)]$$

with

$$C(z) = H(zI - F)^{-1}G + L = \frac{p_m z^m + p_{m-1} z^{m-1} + \cdots + p_0}{q_m z^m + q_{m-1} z^{m-1} + \cdots + q_0} \ . \tag{25}$$

The one–step delay between spark advance control and engine torque in (23) is attributed to the controller by fixing $q_0 = 0$.

The results presented in Section 4 are applied to the closed–loop system given by the plant (24) and the controller (25). The parameters of the compensator (25) are chosen so as to obtain a dead–beat controller for the nominal LTI system. The characteristic polynomial of the closed–loop system is

$$p(\lambda) = \lambda^{m+1} + \frac{q_{m-1} + \bar{b} p_m - \bar{a} q_m}{q_m} \lambda^m + \cdots + \frac{q_0 + \bar{b} p_1 - \bar{a} q_1}{q_m} \lambda + \frac{\bar{b} p_0 - \bar{a} q_0}{q_m} \ .$$

The nominal closed–loop system has all poles in zero, provided that the controller parameters verify

$$\begin{aligned} l_{m+1} &= q_m \\ 0 &= q_{m-1} + \bar{b} p_m - \bar{a} q_m \\ &\ \ \vdots \\ 0 &= \bar{b} p_0 - \bar{a} q_0 \ . \end{aligned} \tag{26}$$

Condition [C4] can be applied to verify the correctness of the proposed spark advance dead–beat controller. Since the open–loop dynamics is scalar, then $\Delta A_C(k)$ has rank one for any realization (16) of (25), hence $\Delta A_C(k)^T \Delta A_C(k)$ has an eigenvalue equal to the trace of $\Delta A(k)^T \Delta A(k)$ and $(n + m - 1)$ zero eigenvalues. In particular, for the canonical reachable–form realization of (25), the maximum singular value of the closed–loop perturbed matrix ΔA_C is upper bounded as follows

$$\sigma_{max}(\Delta A_C) \leq (\|\Delta_A(k)\| + \|\Delta_B(k)\| \left| \frac{p_m}{q_m} \right|)^2 + \|\Delta_B(k)\|^2 \sum_{i=0}^{m-1} (p_i - \frac{q_i p_m}{q_m})^2 \ . \tag{27}$$

In engine control, the drift term $A(k)n(k)$ in (24) is usually compensated by an inner control loop. In this case, (27) simplifies to

$$\sigma_{max}(\Delta A_C) \leq \left[\left(\frac{p_m}{q_m}\right)^2 + \sum_{i=0}^{m-1}\left(p_i - \frac{q_i p_m}{q_m}\right)^2\right] \|B^c\|^2 \, \delta^2(k) \ . \qquad (28)$$

The robustness of dead-beat controllers with respect to the time–domain uncertainty given by the variability of dead–centers events is evaluated using condition $[C4]$. For given values of desired convergence rates in the continuous–time domain[9] for the closed–loop time–varying system, the controller parameters that maximize the admissible variation Δ of the sampling time and verify condition $[C4]$ are computed. The result is depicted in Figure 2. As expected, the bigger the desired convergence rate, the smaller the admissible variation on the sampling period.

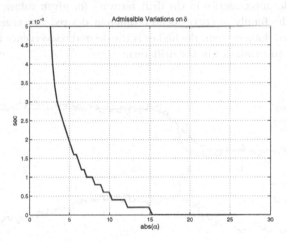

Fig. 2. Maximum variation of the sampling period for given convergence rate

Condition $[C4]$ can also be used to obtain the largest time–domain uncertainty Δ for which a desired convergence rate is guaranteed for the time-varying closed–loop system, when there are some uncertainties in the plant model. In particular, bounded uncertainties for the drift term of the crankshaft dynamics are considered. The controller parameters that maximize the time–domain uncertainty bound Δ are computed according to condition $[C4]$. Figure 3 reports the result: the higher the desired convergence rate and plant model uncertainties, the smaller the allowed time–domain variation will be.

Finally, a dead–beat idle speed controller developed by Magneti Marelli Powertrain is considered. Some experimental results obtained with the controlled engine are reported in Figure 4. Table 1 reports the admissible uncertainties

---

[9] The continuous–time convergence rate is computed as $1/\tau^0 \ln(\mu)$.

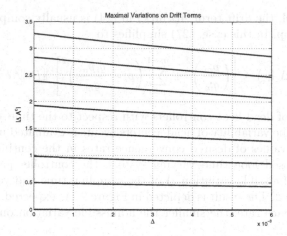

Fig. 3. Admissible uncertainties in the drift term p_A for given values of time–domain uncertainty Δ. The family of curves denote different desired convergence rate for the time-varying closed–loop system: the higher is the desired convergence rate, the smaller is the admissible uncertainties in the drift term

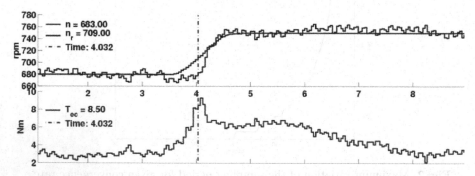

Fig. 4. Experimental results on idle speed control provided by Magneti Marelli Powertrain, for a reference idle speed n_r

in terms of upper bounds on $\|\Delta_A\|$ and $\|\Delta_B\|$, for which closed–loop stability is guaranteed, according to conditions [C1], [C2], and [C4]. It is worthwhile to note that checking the condition [C1] is feasible in this case since controller parameters are fixed (the stability test converged at the 6–th step). Condition [C3] could not be used since the proposed controller does not satisfies the assumption of having nominal matrices with either norm-1, norm-2 or norm-∞ smaller than 1. From the upper bounds on $\|\Delta_A\|$ and $\|\Delta_B\|$, the corresponding maximum time–domain perturbations Δ are obtained. Since the non–uniformity of the dead–centers time domain depends on the crankshaft speed, then the bounds on sampling period Δ are converted into corresponding intervals for the crankshaft speed. Since [C1] is more accurate then [C2] and [C4], then it gives much larger bounds. The range $450 - 1050$ rpm covers typical operating inter-

Table 1. Maximum time–domain variations for idle speed dead–beat controller tuned by Magneti Marelli Powertrain

bounds	[C1]	[C2]	[C4]
$\|\Delta_A\|/\|A\|$	34%	8%	1%
$\|\Delta_B\|/\|B\|$	42%	11%	1.3%
Δ [sec]	0.03	0.008	0.001
n [rpm])	450 − 1050	670 − 830	740 − 760

vals of crankshaft speeds for idle engines, considering nominal idle speed equal to 750 rpm. According to the analysis, the proposed dead-beat controller has no guaranteed stability outside the range 450 − 1050 rpm. The results given by [C2] and [C4] are quite conservative and the corresponding ranges of crankshaft speed are not satisfactory.

6   Conclusions

This paper addressed the problem of robustly controlling non–periodically sampled dynamics. The motivating application is the design and verification of an idle speed controller for automotive applications. By sampling the continuous–time crankshaft dynamics at dead–center times, an event–based nonlinear time–variant model is obtained. Robust techniques developed in the last two decades for linear–time variant discrete systems are revised with the aim of proposing a design methodology that takes into account time–domain uncertainties. The proposed methodology has been applied to the design and verification of a dead–beat algorithm for idle speed control of an automotive engine. The largest acceptable perturbations due to non–uniform sampling and plant uncertainties for which a desired rate of convergence is guaranteed were evaluated.

References

1. Lee, E., Sangiovanni-Vincentelli, A.: A unified framework for comparing models of computation. IEEE Trans. on Computer Aided Design of Integrated Circuits and Systems **17** (1998) 1217–1229
2. Benveniste, A., Caillaud, B., Carloni, L.P., Caspi, P., Sangiovanni-Vincentelli, A.L.: Heterogeneous reactive systems modelling: Capturing casuality and the correctness of loosely time–triggered architectures (ltta). In: Procedeeings of Forth ACM International Conference on Embedded Systems, Pisa, Italy (2004) 220–229
3. Picasso, B., Bicchi, A.: Stabilization of LTI Systems with Quantized State-Quantized Input Static Feedback. LNCS. In: HSCC 2003. Springer Verlag (2003) 405–416
4. Bicchi, A., Marigo, A., Piccoli, B.: On the reachability of quantized control systems. IEEE Trans. on Automatic Control **47** (2002) 546–563

5. Palopoli, L., Bicchi, A., Sangiovanni-Vincentelli, A.L.: Numerically efficient control of systems with communication constraints. In: Proceedings of the 41st IEEE Conference on Decision and Control 2002. Volume 2. (2002) 1626–1631

6. Balluchi, A., Benvenuti, L., Di-Benedetto, M.D., Pinello, C., Sangiovanni-Vincentelli, A.L.: Automotive engine and power-train control: a comprehensive hybrid model. In: Proc. 8th Mediterranean Conference on Control and Automation, MED2000, Patras, Greece (2000)

7. Balluchi, A., Benvenuti, L., Di-Benedetto, M.D., Villa, T., Wong-Toi, H., Sangiovanni-Vincentelli, A.L.: Hybrid controller synthesis for idle speed management of an automotive engine. In: Proc. 2000 IEEE American Control Conference. Volume 2., ACC, Chicago, USA (2000) 1181–1185

8. Balluchi, A., Benvenuti, L., Di-Benedetto, M.D., Pinello, C., Sangiovanni-Vincentelli, A.L.: Automotive engine control and hybrid systems: Challenges and opportunities. In: Proceedings of the IEEE, 88, "Special Issue on Hybrid Systems". Volume 7. (2000) 888–912

9. Loan, C.V.: The sensitivity of the matrix exponential. SIAM Journal of Number Analysis **14** (1977) 971–981

10. Bauer, P., Premaratne, K., Duran, J.: A necessary and sufficient condition for robust asymptotic stability of time-variant discrete systems. IEEE Transactions on Automatic Control **38** (1993) 1427–1430

11. Farison, J., Kolla, S.: Relationship of sigular value stability robustness bounds to spectral radius for discrete systems with application to digital filters. In: Proc. IEEE. Volume 138. (1991)

12. Kolla, S., Yedavalli, R., Farison, J.: Robust stability bounds on time-varying perturbations for state space model of linear discrete time systems. International Journal of Control **50** (1989) 151–159

13. Yaz, E., Xiaoru, N.: New robustness bounds for dyscrete systems with random perturbations. IEEE Transaction on Automatic Control **38** (1993) 1866–1870

14. Xiaoru, N., Abreu-Garcia, J.D., Yaz, E.: Improved bounds for linear discrete-time systems with structured perturbations. IEEE Transaction on Automatic Control **37** (1992) 1170–1173

15. Gajić, Z., Qureschi, M.: Lyapunov Matrix Equation in System Stability and Control, San Diago, CA. (1995) Academic.

16. Molchanov, A.P., Liu, D.: Robust absolute stability of time-varying nonlinear discrete-time systems. IEEE Transactions on Circuits and Systems **49** (2002) 1129–1137

17. Premaratne, K., Mansour, M.: Robust stability of time-variant discrete-time system with bounded parameter perturbations. IEEE Transactions on Circuits and Systems **42** (1995) 40–45

18. Mandic, D.P., Chambers, J.: On robust stability of time-varying discrete-time nonlinear systems with bounded parameter perturbations. IEEE Transactions on Circuits and Systems **47** (2000) 185–188

19. De-Souza, C.E., Fu, M., Xie, L.: h_∞ analysis and synthesis of discrete-time systems with time-varying uncertainty. IEEE Transactions on Automatic Control **38** (1993) 459–462

20. Karan, M., Sezer, M.E., Ocali, O.: Robust stability of discrete-time systems under parametric perturbations. IEEE Transactions on Automatic Control **39** (1994) 991–995

21. Johansson, M., Rantzer, A., Arzen, K.E.: Piecewise quadratic stability of fuzzy systems. IEEE Transactions on Fuzzy Systems **7** (1999) 713–722

22. De-Oliveira, P.J., Oliveira, R.C.L.F., Peres, P.L.D.: A new lmi condition for robust stability of polynomial matrix polytopes. IEEE Transactions on Automatic Control **47** (2002) 1775–1779
23. Schinkel, M., Chen, W., Rantzer, A.: Optimal control for systems with varying sampling rate. In: Proc. of the American Control Conference, Anchorage, AK (2002)
24. Yuan, L., Achenie, L.E.K., Jiang, W.: Robust H_∞ Control for Linear Discrete-Time Systems with Norm-Bounded Time-Varying Uncertainty. In: Systems and Control Letters. Volume 27. (1996) 199–208
25. Hu, L.S., Lam, J., Cao, Y.Y., Shao, H.H.: A linear matrix inequality (lmi) approach to robust h_2 sampled-data control for linear uncertain systems. IEEE Transactions on Systems, Man., and Cybernetics **33** (2003) 149–155
26. Blanchini, F.: The gain scheduling and the robust state feedback stabilization proplems. IEEE Transaction on Automatic Control **AC–45** (2000) 2061–2070

Qualitative Analysis and Verification of Hybrid Models of Genetic Regulatory Networks: Nutritional Stress Response in *Escherichia coli*

Grégory Batt[1,2], Delphine Ropers[1], Hidde de Jong[1], Johannes Geiselmann[3], Michel Page[1,4], and Dominique Schneider[3]

[1] INRIA Rhône-Alpes, 655 avenue de l'Europe, Montbonnot,
38334 Saint Ismier Cedex, France
{Gregory.Batt, Delphine.Ropers, Hidde.de-Jong, Michel.Page}@inrialpes.fr
[2] Université Joseph Fourier, Grenoble, France
[3] Laboratoire Adaptation et Pathogénie des Microorganismes,
CNRS UMR 5163, Université Joseph Fourier, Grenoble, France
{Hans.Geiselmann, Dominique.Schneider}@ujf-grenoble.fr
[4] Université Pierre Mendès France, Grenoble, France

Abstract. The switch-like character of the dynamics of genetic regulatory networks has attracted much attention from mathematical biologists and researchers on hybrid systems alike. We extend our previous work on a method for the qualitative analysis of hybrid models of genetic regulatory networks, based on a class of piecewise-affine differential equation (PADE) models, in two directions. First, we present a refinement of the method using a discrete or qualitative abstraction that preserves stronger properties of the dynamics of the PA systems, in particular the sign patterns of the derivatives of the concentration variables. The discrete transition system resulting from the abstraction is a conservative approximation of the dynamics of the PA system and can be computed symbolically. Second, we apply the refined method to a regulatory system whose functioning is not yet well-understood by biologists, the nutritional stress response in the bacterium *Escherichia coli*.

1 Introduction

The functioning and development of living organisms is controlled on the molecular level by networks of genes, proteins, small molecules, and their mutual interactions, so-called *genetic regulatory networks*. The dynamics of these networks is hybrid in nature, in the sense that the continuous evolution of the concentration of proteins and other molecules is punctuated by discrete changes in the activity of genes coding for the proteins. The switch-like character of the dynamics of genetic regulatory networks has attracted much attention from mathematical biologists and researchers on hybrid systems alike (*e.g.*, [1, 2, 3, 4, 5, 6, 7]).

While powerful techniques for the analysis, verification, and control of hybrid systems have been developed (see [8, 9] for reviews), the specificities of the

M. Morari and L. Thiele (Eds.): HSCC 2005, LNCS 3414, pp. 134–150, 2005.
© Springer-Verlag Berlin Heidelberg 2005

biological application domain pose a number of challenges [10]. First, most genetic regulatory networks of interest consist of a large number of genes that are involved in complex, interlocked feedback loops. Second, the data available on both the structure and the dynamics of the systems is currently essentially qualitative in nature, meaning that numerical values for concentration variables and interaction parameters are generally absent. The above characteristics require hybrid-system methods and tools to be upscalable and capable of dealing with qualitative information.

In previous work [4, 11], we have developed a method for the *qualitative analysis of hybrid models of genetic regulatory networks*, using a class of piecewise-affine differential equation (PADE) models that has been well-studied in mathematical biology [1, 2] (see also [5]). The method is based on a qualitative abstraction of the dynamics of the PA systems and exploits favorable mathematical properties of the models to symbolically compute reachability properties. The method has been implemented in the publicly-available computer tool *Genetic Network Analysis (GNA)* [12] and validated on a well-understood network, the initiation of sporulation in *B. subtilis* [13].

The present paper extends our previous work in two directions. First, we present a refinement of the method using a qualitative abstraction that preserves stronger properties of the dynamics of the PA systems, in particular the sign patterns of the derivatives of the concentration variables. This information is critical for the experimental validation of models of genetic regulatory networks, since experimental measurements of the system dynamics by means of quantitative RT-PCR, reporter genes, and DNA microarrays usually result in observations of changes in the sign of derivatives. The refinement of the method, which has required us to deal with non-trivial technical difficulties arising from discontinuities in the righthand-side of the PADE models, has resulted in a new prototype version of the computer tool GNA. Second, we have applied the refined method to a biological system whose functioning is not yet well-understood by biologists, the nutritional stress response in the bacterium *E. coli*. This has led to new insights into how the adaptation of cell growth to nutritional stress emerges from the molecular interactions. Moreover, it has given rise to predictions of the behavior of the system after a nutrient upshift, which are currently being tested in our laboratory.

In Sections 2 and 3 of the paper, we review PADE models and their mathematical properties, with a special emphasis on a partition of the phase space preserving the sign of the derivatives of the concentration variables. This partition forms the basis for the definition, in Section 4, of a qualitative abstraction, transforming the continuous transition system associated with a PADE model into a discrete transition system. The discrete transition system is a simulation of the continuous transition system, thus providing a conservative approximation of the network dynamics. Moreover, the discrete transition system can be easily computed in a symbolic manner from inequality constraints on the parameters. In Section 5, we describe the application of the method to the qualitative analysis of the nutritional stress response in *E. coli*. The final section of the paper discusses the results in the context of related work on hybrid systems.[1]

2   PADE Models of Genetic Regulatory Networks

The dynamics of genetic regulatory networks can be modeled by a class of piecewise-affine differential equations (PADE) of the following general form [1, 2]:

$$\dot{x} = h(x) = f(x) - g(x)\,x, \tag{1}$$

where $x = (x_1, \ldots, x_n)' \in \Omega$ is a vector of cellular protein concentrations, $f = (f_1, \ldots, f_n)'$, $g = \mathrm{diag}(g_1, \ldots, g_n)$, and $\Omega \subset \mathbb{R}_{\geq 0}^n$ is a bounded n-dimensional phase space box. The rate of change of each protein concentration x_i, $1 \leq i \leq n$, is thus defined as the difference of the rate of synthesis $f_i(x)$ and the rate of degradation $g_i(x)\,x_i$ of the protein.

The function $f_i : \Omega \to \mathbb{R}_{\geq 0}$ expresses how the rate of synthesis of the protein encoded by gene i depends on the concentrations x of the proteins in the cell. More specifically, the function f_i is defined as

$$f_i(x) = \sum_{l \in L_i} \kappa_i^l\, b_i^l(x), \tag{2}$$

where $\kappa_i^l > 0$ is a rate parameter, $b_i^l : \Omega \to \{0,1\}$ a piecewise-continuous *regulation function*, and L_i a possibly empty set of indices of regulation functions. The function g_i expresses the regulation of protein degradation. It is defined analogously to f_i, except that we demand that g_i is strictly positive. In addition, in order to formally distinguish degradation rate parameters from synthesis rate parameters, we will denote the former by γ instead of κ. Notice that with the above definitions, h is a *piecewise-affine (PA)* vector-valued function.

A regulation function b_i^l describes the conditions under which the protein encoded by gene i is synthesized (degraded) at a rate κ_i^l $(\gamma_i^l\, x_i)$. It is defined in terms of step functions and is the arithmetic equivalent of a Boolean function expressing the logic of gene regulation [1, 2]. More precisely, the conditions for synthesis or degradation are expressed using the step functions s^+, s^-:

$$s^+(x_j, \theta_j) = \begin{cases} 1, & \text{if } x_j > \theta_j, \\ 0, & \text{if } x_j < \theta_j, \end{cases} \text{ and } s^-(x_j, \theta_j) = 1 - s^+(x_j, \theta_j). \tag{3}$$

where x_j is an element of the state vector x and θ_j a constant denoting a threshold concentration.

Figure 1(a) gives an example of a simple genetic regulatory network consisting of two genes, a and b. When a gene (a or b) is expressed, the corresponding protein (A or B) is synthesized at a specified rate (κ_a or κ_b). Proteins A and B

---

[1] A detailed description of the method and the proofs of the propositions can be found in [14].

regulate the expression of genes a and b. More specifically, protein B inhibits the expression of gene a, above a certain threshold concentration θ_b, while protein A inhibits the expression of gene b above a threshold concentration θ_a^1, and the expression of its own gene above a second, higher threshold concentration θ_a^2. The degradation of the proteins is not regulated and therefore proportional to the concentration of the proteins (with degradation parameters γ_a or γ_b).

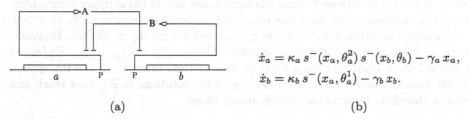

$$\dot{x}_a = \kappa_a\, s^-(x_a, \theta_a^2)\, s^-(x_b, \theta_b) - \gamma_a\, x_a,$$
$$\dot{x}_b = \kappa_b\, s^-(x_a, \theta_a^1) - \gamma_b\, x_b.$$

(a)   (b)

Fig. 1. (a) Example of a genetic regulatory network of two genes (a and b), each coding for a regulatory protein (A and B). For legend, see Figure 4. (b) PADE model corresponding to the network in (a)

The use of step functions $s^\pm(x_j, \theta_j)$ in (1) gives rise to complications, because the step functions are discontinuous at $x_j = \theta_j$, and therefore h is discontinuous on $\Theta = \bigcup_{i\in[1..n], l_i\in[1..p_i]}\{x \in \Omega \mid x_i = \theta_i^{l_i}\}$, the union of the threshold hyperplanes (where the protein encoded by gene i is assumed to have p_i threshold concentrations). In order to deal with this problem, we can follow an approach widely used in control theory, originally proposed by Filippov [15]. It consists in extending the differential *equation* $\dot{x} = h(x)$, $x \in \Omega \setminus \Theta$, to the differential *inclusion*

$$\dot{x} \in K(x), \text{ with } K(x) = \overline{co}(\{\lim_{y\to x, y\notin\Theta} h(y)\}), \ x \in \Omega, \tag{4}$$

where $\overline{co}(P)$ denotes the smallest closed convex set containing the set P and $\{\lim_{y\to x, y\notin\Theta} h(y)\}$, the set of all limit values of $h(y)$, for $y \notin \Theta$ and $y \to x$. This approach has been applied in the context of genetic regulatory network modeling by Gouzé and Sari [16].

In practice, $K(x)$ may be difficult to compute because the smallest closed convex set can be a complex polyhedron in Ω. We therefore employ an alternative extension of the differential equation:

$$\dot{x} \in H(x), \text{ with } H(x) = \overline{rect}(\{\lim_{y\to x, y\notin\Theta} h(y)\}), \ x \in \Omega, \tag{5}$$

where $\overline{rect}(P)$ denotes the smallest closed *hyperrectangular* set containing the set P [11, 14]. The advantage of using $\overline{rect}$ is that we can rewrite $H(x)$ as a system of differential inclusions $\dot{x}_i \in H_i(x)$, $i \in [1..n]$. Notice that $H(x)$ is an overapproximation of $K(x)$, for all $x \in \Omega$.

Formally, we define the *PA system* Σ as the triple (Ω, Θ, H), that is, the set-valued function H given by (5), defined on the n-dimensional phase space

Ω, with Θ the union of the threshold hyperplanes. A *solution* of the PA system Σ on a time interval I is a solution of the differential inclusion (5) on I, that is, an absolutely-continuous vector-valued function $\xi(t)$ such that $\dot{\xi}(t) \in H(\xi(t))$ almost everywhere on I. In particular, $\dot{\xi}(t) \in H(\xi(t))$ may not hold, if ξ reaches or leaves Ω at t.

For all $x_0 \in \Omega$ and $\tau \in \mathbb{R}_{>0} \cup \{\infty\}$, $\Xi_\Sigma^\omega(x_0, \tau)$ will denote the set of solutions $\xi(t)$ of the PA system Σ, for the initial condition $\xi(0) = x_0$, and $t \in [0, \tau]$, if τ is finite, or $[0, \infty)$, otherwise.[2] Since the right-hand side of (5) is upper semicontinuous, the existence of at least one solution ξ on some time interval $[0, \tau]$, $\tau > 0$, with initial condition $\xi(0) = x_0$ is guaranteed for all x_0 in Ω [15]. However, there is, in general, not a unique solution. The set $\Xi_\Sigma^\omega = \bigcup_{x_0 \in \Omega, \tau > 0} \Xi_\Sigma^\omega(x_0, \tau)$ is the set of all solutions, on a finite or infinite time interval, of the PA system Σ. We restrict our analysis to the set Ξ_Σ of the solutions in Ξ_Σ^ω that reach and leave a threshold hyperplane finitely-many times.

3   Mathematical Analysis of PA Systems

The dynamical properties of the solutions of Σ can be analyzed in the n-dimensional phase space box $\Omega = \Omega_1 \times \ldots \times \Omega_n$, where $\Omega_i = \{x_i \in \mathbb{R} \mid 0 \le x_i \le max_i\}$ and max_i denotes a maximum concentration of each protein, $1 \le i \le n$. The $(n-1)$-dimensional threshold hyperplanes $\{x \in \Omega \mid x_i = \theta_i^{l_i}\}$, $1 \le l_i \le p_i$, $1 \le i \le n$, partition Ω into (hyper)rectangular regions. Since the regulation of gene expression is identical everywhere in such a region (see below), it corresponds to a regulatory *mode*. Consequently, the regions are called *mode domains*. The set of mode domains of Ω is referred to as $\mathcal{M}$.

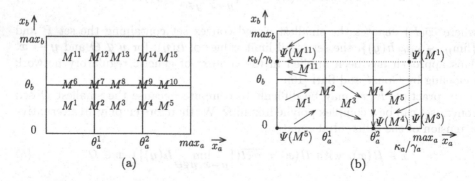

Fig. 2. (a) Partition by mode domains of the phase space corresponding to the model of Figure 1(b). (b) Focal sets and dynamics of the mode domains M^1 to M^5, and M^{11}

---

[2] In the sequel, we say, by abuse of terminology, that ξ is a solution of Σ on $[0, \tau]$, $\tau \in \mathbb{R}_{>0} \cup \{\infty\}$.

Figure 2(a) shows the partitioning into mode domains of the two-dimensional phase space of the example network. We distinguish between mode domains like M^7 and M^2, which are located on (intersections of) threshold hyperplanes, and mode domains like M^1, which are not. The former domains are called *singular* mode domains and the latter *regular* mode domains. We denote by $\mathcal{M}_r$ and $\mathcal{M}_s$ the sets of regular and singular mode domains, respectively.

We introduce some simple topological concepts. For every hyperrectangular region, $R \subseteq \Omega$, of dimension k, $0 \le k \le n$, we define the supporting hyperplane of R, $supp(R) \subseteq \Omega$, as the k-dimensional hyperplane containing R. The boundary of R in $supp(R)$ is denoted by ∂R. Suppose that M is a singular mode domain, *i.e.* $M \in \mathcal{M}_s$. Then $R(M)$ is defined as the set of regular mode domains M' having M in their boundary, *i.e.* $R(M) = \{M' \in \mathcal{M}_r \mid M \subseteq \partial M'\}$.

Using the definition of the differential inclusion (5), it can be easily shown that in a regular mode domain M, $H(\boldsymbol{x})$ reduces to the singleton set $\{\boldsymbol{\mu}^M - \boldsymbol{\nu}^M \boldsymbol{x}\}$, for all $\boldsymbol{x} \in M$, where $\boldsymbol{\mu}^M$ is a vector of (sums of) synthesis rate constants and $\boldsymbol{\nu}^M$ a diagonal matrix of (sums of) degradation rate constants. This yields the classical result that all solutions $\boldsymbol{\xi}$ in M monotonically converge towards the *focal set* $\Psi(M) = \{\psi(M)\}$, where $\psi(M) = (\boldsymbol{\nu}^M)^{-1}\boldsymbol{\mu}^M$ [1]. We will make the generic assumption that the focal sets $\Psi(M)$, for all $M \in \mathcal{M}_r$, are not located in the threshold hyperplanes Θ. Figure 2(b) shows the focal sets of four regular mode domains (M^1, M^3, M^5 and M^{11}). In the case of M^{11}, we see that $\Psi(M^{11}) \subseteq M^{11}$, so that $\psi(M^{11})$ is an asymptotically stable equilibrium point of Σ.

In a singular mode domain, the right-hand side of the differential inclusion (5) reduces to $H(\boldsymbol{x}) = \overline{rect}(\{\boldsymbol{\mu}^{M'} - \boldsymbol{\nu}^{M'}\boldsymbol{x} \mid M' \in R(M)\})$, for all $\boldsymbol{x} \in M$ [11, 16]. The focal set associated with the domain now becomes $\Psi(M) = supp(M) \cap \overline{rect}(\{\psi(M') \mid M' \in R(M)\})$, which is generally not a single point in higher dimensional domains [11, 16]. Two different cases can be distinguished. If $\Psi(M)$ is empty, then every solution passes through M instantaneously [16] and M is called an *instantaneous* mode domain. If not, then some (but not necessarily all) solutions arriving at M will remain in M for some time, sliding along the threshold planes containing M [16]. M is then called *persistent*. If $\Psi(M)$ is a single point, then all solutions in M monotonically converge towards this point. In the case that $\Psi(M)$ is not a single point, a weaker monotonicity property holds [11, 16]. Figure 2(b) shows two singular mode domains, M^2 and M^4. M^2 is an instantaneous mode domain ($\Psi(M^2) = \emptyset$), whereas M^4 is a persistent mode domain in which solutions slide along the threshold plane. In this simple example, it is intuitively clear how to define the flow in M^4, given the dynamics in M^3 and M^5. The use of differential inclusions as described above makes it possible to define the flow in singular domains in a systematic and mathematically proper way.

The fact that every mode domain is associated with a unique focal set has provided the basis for the abstraction criterion employed in our previous work [4, 11]. However, this criterion disregards that the system does not always exhibit the same qualitative dynamics in different parts of a mode domain, in the sense that the sign pattern of the derivatives of the solutions ξ may not be unique. Consider the case of M^{11} in Figure 2(b): depending on whether $\xi_b(t)$ is above, on, or below the focal concentration κ_b/γ_b in M^{11}, ξ_b will be decreasing, steady, or increasing. As a consequence, if we abstract the domain M^{11} away in a single discrete state, we will not be able to unambiguously infer that solutions entering this domain from M^6 are increasing in the x_b-dimension. This may lead to problems when comparing predictions from the model with gene expression data, for instance the observed variation of the sign of x_b. Today's experimental techniques, such as quantitative RT-PCR, reporter genes, and DNA microarrays, usually produce information on changes in the sign of the derivatives of the concentration variables.

The mismatch between the abstraction levels of the mathematical analysis and the experimental data calls for a finer partitioning of the phase space, which can then provide the basis for a more adequate abstraction criterion. Along these lines, the regular and singular mode domains distinguished above are repartitioned into (hyper)rectangular regions called *flow domains*. In the case that a mode domain M is regular, it is split by the $(n-1)$-dimensional hyperplanes $\{x \in \Omega \mid x_i = \psi_i(M)\}$, $i \in [1..n]$, that intersect with M. Under the same condition, singular mode domains M are repartitioned by the $(n-1)$-dimensional hyperplanes $\{x \in \Omega \mid x_i = \psi_i(M')\}$, $M' \in R(M)$, $i \in [1..n]$. The resulting set of flow domains is denoted by $\mathcal{D}$ [14]. The partitioning of the phase space into 27 flow domains is illustrated for the example system in Figure 3(a). Every flow domain is included in a single mode domain, a relation captured by the surjective function *mode*: $\mathcal{D} \to \mathcal{M}$, defined as $mode(D) = M$, iff $D \subseteq M$. Similarly, the function *flow*: $\Omega \to \mathcal{D}$ denotes the surjective mapping that associates a point in the phase space to its flow domain: $flow(x) = D$, iff $x \in D$.

The repartitioning of mode domain M^{11} leads to six flow domains (Figure 3(a)). The finer partition guarantees that in every flow domain of M^{11}, the derivatives have a unique sign pattern. In $D^{11.2}$, for instance, the x_a-derivative is negative and the x_b-derivative is positive, whereas in $D^{11.3}$ both derivatives equal zero (in fact, $D^{11.3}$ coincides with $\psi(M^{11})$ and is an equilibrium point of the system). The above property is true more generally. Consider a point x in a flow domain $D \in \mathcal{D}$. We denote by $S(x) \in 2^{\{-1,0,1\}^n}$ the set of derivative sign vectors of the solutions in D passing through x, that is, $S(x) = \{sign(\dot{\xi}(t_x)) \mid \xi \in \Xi_\Sigma \text{ in } D, \, \xi(t_x) = x, \text{ and } \dot{\xi}(t_x) \in H(\xi(t_x))\}$. Notice that the definition of S as a set is a direct consequence of the use of differential inclusions. Theorem 1 states that $S(x)$ is the same for every $x \in D$.

Theorem 1 (Qualitatively-identical dynamics in flow domain). For all $D \in \mathcal{D}$, for all $x, x' \in D$, $S(x) = S(x')$.

The theorem suggests that the partition of the phase space introduced in this section can be used as an abstraction criterion better-adapted to the available experimental data on gene expression. This idea will be further developed in the next section.

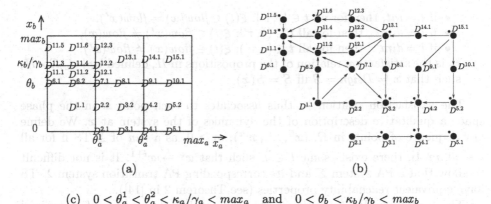

(a)   (b)

(c) $0 < \theta_a^1 < \theta_a^2 < \kappa_a/\gamma_a < max_a$ and $0 < \theta_b < \kappa_b/\gamma_b < max_b$

Fig. 3. (a) Partition by flow domains of the phase space of the model in Figure 1(b). (b) State transition graph of the corresponding qualitative transition system. For the sake of clarity, self-transitions are represented by dots and transition labels are omitted. (c) Inequality constraints on parameters for which the graph in (b) is obtained

4   Qualitative Abstraction of the Dynamics of PA Systems

As a preparatory step, we define a *continuous transition system* having the same reachability properties as the original PA system Σ. Consider $x \in D$ and $x' \in D'$, where $D, D' \in \mathcal{D}$ are flow domains. If there exists a solution ξ of Σ passing through x at time $\tau \in \mathbb{R}_{\geq 0}$ and reaching x' at time $\tau' \in \mathbb{R}_{>0} \cup \{\infty\}$, without leaving $D \cup D'$ in the time interval $[\tau, \tau']$, then the absolute continuity of ξ implies that D and D' are either equal or contiguous. More precisely, one of the three following cases holds: $D = D'$, $D \in \partial D'$, or $D' \in \partial D$. We consequently distinguish three types of continuous transition that correspond to these three cases: *internal*, denoted by $x \xrightarrow{int} x'$, *dimension increasing*, denoted by $x \xrightarrow{dim^+} x'$, and *dimension decreasing*, denoted by $x \xrightarrow{dim^-} x'$. The latter two terms refer to the increase or decrease in dimension when going from D to D'. This leads to the following definition:

Definition 1 (PA transition system). Σ-TS = $(\Omega, L, \Pi, \rightarrow, \models)$ is the transition sytem corresponding to the PA system $\Sigma = (\Omega, \Theta, H)$, where:

- Ω is the state space;
- $L = \{int, dim^+, dim^-\}$ is a set of labels denoting the three different types of transitions;
- $\Pi = \{Dsign = S \mid S \in 2^{\{-1,0,1\}^n}\}$ is a set of propositions describing the signs of the derivatives of the concentration variables;
- $\rightarrow$ is the transition relation describing the continuous evolution of the system, defined by $\rightarrow \subseteq \Omega \times L \times \Omega$, such that $x \xrightarrow{l} x'$ iff there exists $\xi \in \Xi_\Sigma$ and τ, τ', such that $0 \leq \tau < \tau'$, $\xi(\tau) = x$, $\xi(\tau') = x'$, and

- if $l = int$, then for all $t \in [\tau, \tau']$: $\boldsymbol{\xi}(t) \in flow(\boldsymbol{x}) = flow(\boldsymbol{x}')$,
- if $l = dim^+$, then for all $t \in (\tau, \tau']$: $\boldsymbol{\xi}(t) \in flow(\boldsymbol{x}') \neq flow(\boldsymbol{x})$,
- if $l = dim^-$, then for all $t \in [\tau, \tau')$: $\boldsymbol{\xi}(t) \in flow(\boldsymbol{x}) \neq flow(\boldsymbol{x}')$;
- $\models$ is the satisfaction relation of the propositions in Π, defined by $\models \subseteq \Omega \times \Pi$, such that $\boldsymbol{x} \models Dsign = S$ iff $S = S(\boldsymbol{x})$.

The satisfaction relation $\models$ thus associates to each point $\boldsymbol{x}$ in the phase space a qualitative description of the dynamics of the system at $\boldsymbol{x}$. We define any sequence of points in Ω, $(\boldsymbol{x}^0, \ldots, \boldsymbol{x}^m)$, $m \geq 0$, as a *run* of Σ-TS if for all $i \in [0..m-1]$, there exists some $l \in L$ such that $\boldsymbol{x}^i \xrightarrow{l} \boldsymbol{x}^{i+1}$. It is not difficult to show that a PA system Σ and its corresponding PA transition system Σ-TS have equivalent reachability properties (see Theorem 2 in [14]).

The continuous PA transition system has an infinite number of states and transitions, as a consequence of which conventional tools for model checking cannot be used to verify properties of the system. However, we can define a discrete transition system, with a finite number of states and transitions, that preserves important properties of the qualitative dynamics of the system. In order to achieve this, we introduce the equivalence relation $\sim_\Omega \subseteq \Omega \times \Omega$ induced by the partition $\mathcal{D}$ of the phase space: $\boldsymbol{x} \sim_\Omega \boldsymbol{x}'$ iff $flow(\boldsymbol{x}) = flow(\boldsymbol{x}')$. From Theorem 1 it follows that $\sim_\Omega$ is *proposition-preserving* [17, 18], in the sense that for all $\boldsymbol{x}, \boldsymbol{x}' \in D$ and for all $\pi \in \Pi$, $\boldsymbol{x} \models \pi$ iff $\boldsymbol{x}' \models \pi$.

The discrete or *qualitative abstraction* of a PA transition system Σ-TS, called *qualitative PA transition system*, is now defined as the quotient transition system of Σ-TS, given the equivalence relation $\sim_\Omega$ [17, 18].

Definition 2 (Qualitative PA transition system). The qualitative PA transition system corresponding to the PA transition system Σ-TS $= (\Omega, L, \Pi, \rightarrow, \models)$ is Σ-QTS $= (\Omega/_{\sim_\Omega}, L, \Pi, \rightarrow_{\sim_\Omega}, \models_{\sim_\Omega})$.

Proposition 1 (Qualitative PA transition system). Let Σ-QTS $= (\Omega/_{\sim_\Omega}, L, \Pi, \rightarrow_{\sim_\Omega}, \models_{\sim_\Omega})$ be the qualitative PA transition system corresponding to the PA transition system Σ-TS $= (\Omega, L, \Pi, \rightarrow, \models)$. Then

- $\Omega/_{\sim_\Omega} = \mathcal{D}$;
- $\rightarrow_{\sim_\Omega} \subseteq \mathcal{D} \times L \times \mathcal{D}$, such that $D \xrightarrow{l}_{\sim_\Omega} D'$ iff $\exists \boldsymbol{\xi} \in \Xi_\Sigma, \exists \tau, \tau', 0 \leq \tau < \tau'$ such that $\boldsymbol{\xi}(\tau) \in D$, $\boldsymbol{\xi}(\tau') \in D'$, and
  - if $l = int$, then for all $t \in [\tau, \tau']$: $\boldsymbol{\xi}(t) \in D = D'$,
  - if $l = dim^+$, then for all $t \in (\tau, \tau']$: $\boldsymbol{\xi}(t) \in D' \neq D$,
  - if $l = dim^-$, then for all $t \in [\tau, \tau')$: $\boldsymbol{\xi}(t) \in D \neq D'$;
- $\models_{\sim_\Omega} \subseteq \mathcal{D} \times \Pi$, such that $D \models Dsign = S$ iff $\forall \boldsymbol{x} \in D$: $S(\boldsymbol{x}) = S$.

Notice that the transitions labeled by dim^+ or dim^- connect two different flow domains, since in Proposition 1 we require that $D \neq D'$. This corresponds to a continuous evolution of the system along which it switches from one flow domain to another. On the contrary, the transitions labeled by int correspond to the continuous evolution of the system in a single flow domain. Notice also that qualitative PA transition systems are non-deterministic.

As for Σ-TS, we define any sequence of flow domains $(D^0, \ldots, D^m)$, $m \geq 0$, as a *run* of Σ-QTS iff for all $i \in [0..m-1]$, there exists $l \in L$ such that $D^i \xrightarrow{l}_{\sim_\Omega} D^{i+1}$. The satisfaction relation $\models_{\sim_\Omega}$ associates to every run a qualitative description of the evolution of the derivatives over time. Σ-QTS can be represented by a directed graph $G = (\mathcal{D}, \to_{\sim_\Omega})$, called the *state transition graph*. The paths in G represent the runs of the system. The state transition graph corresponding to the two-gene example is represented in Figure 3(b), and $(D^{1.1}, D^{2.2}, D^{3.2}, D^{4.2}, D^{4.1})$ is an example of a run.

It directly follows from the definitions of quotient transition system and simulation of transition systems [17, 18] that Σ-QTS is a *simulation* of Σ-TS. The converse is not true in general, so that Σ-QTS and Σ-TS are not bisimilar.

Proposition 2. Σ-QTS is a simulation of Σ-TS.

As a consequence of Proposition 2, if there exists a run $(x^0, \ldots, x^m)$ of Σ-TS, then there also exists a run $(D^0, \ldots, D^m)$ of Σ-QTS such that $x^i \in D^i$, for all $i \in [0..m]$. In other words, Σ-QTS is a *conservative approximation* of Σ-TS.

In [14] we introduce a second equivalence relation $\sim_\Gamma \subseteq \Gamma \times \Gamma$, defined on the parameter space Γ of the PA system. Two parameter vectors p and p' are equivalent, if their corresponding qualitative PA transition systems, and hence the state transition graphs, are isomorphic. We show that a certain class of parameter inequality constraints define regions $P \subseteq \Gamma$, such that for every $p, p' \in P$, it holds that $p \sim_\Gamma p'$. More precisely, there exists some $Q \in \Gamma/_{\sim_\Gamma}$, such that $P \subseteq Q$ (Theorem 3 in [14]). As a consequence, for all vectors of parameter values satisfying the inequality constraints, the system has the same qualitative dynamics. Whereas exact numerical values for the parameters are usually not available, the weaker information required for the formulation of the inequality constraints can often be obtained from the experimental literature, as illustrated in Section 5. Figure 3(c) shows the inequality constraints for which the state transition graph of our example is obtained.

The inequality constraints also play a key role in the actual computation of the qualitative PA transition system Σ-QTS [14]. The computation of Σ-QTS is greatly simplified by the fact that the domains D and the focal sets $\Psi(M)$ are hyperrectangular sets, which allows them to be expressed as product sets, i.e. $D = D_1 \times \ldots \times D_n$ and $\Psi(M) = \Psi_1(M) \times \ldots \times \Psi_n(M)$. As a consequence, the computation can be carried out for each dimension separately. For instance, the repartitioning of mode domain D^{11} into flow domains (Figure 3(a)) is based on the fact that the x_a-component $[0, \theta_a^1)$ is partitioned into two subsets by the segment $x_a = 0$, and the x_b-component $(\theta_b, max_b]$ into three subsets by the segment $x_b = \kappa_b/\gamma_b$. The product of these subsets yields the six flow domains shown in the figure. Notice also that, in order to derive this result, we only need to know the ordering of θ_a^1 and κ_a/γ_a in the x_a-dimension, and that of θ_b and κ_b/γ_b in the x_b-dimension, which are fixed by the inequality constraints in Figure 3(c). This result is true more generally and also applies to the transition relation $\to_{\sim_\Omega}$ and the satisfaction relation $\models_{\sim_\Omega}$. That is, the domains, the transitions, and the sign pattern of the derivatives can be straightforwardly derived by means of symbolic computation using the inequality constraints. The algorithms are described in more detail in [14] and have been implemented in a new prototype version of the computer tool *GNA* [12]. The state transition graph generated by GNA can be exported to standard model-checking tools like NuSMV and CADP [22].

5   Application: Qualitative Analysis of Nutritional Stress Response in *E. coli*

In case of nutritional stress, an *Escherichia coli* population abandons exponential growth and enters a non-growth state called *stationary phase*. This growth-phase transition is accompanied by numerous physiological changes in the bacteria, concerning among other things the morphology and the metabolism of the cell, as well as gene expression [19]. On the molecular level, the transition from exponential phase to stationary phase is controlled by a complex genetic regulatory network integrating various environmental signals. The molecular basis of the adaptation of the growth of *E. coli* to nutritional stress conditions has been the focus of extensive studies for decades [20]. However, notwithstanding the enormous amount of information accumulated on the genes, proteins, and other molecules known to be involved in the stress adaptation process, there is currently no global understanding of how the response of the cell emerges from the network of molecular interactions. Moreover, with some exceptions, numerical values for the parameters characterizing the interactions and the molecular concentrations are absent, which makes it difficult to apply traditional methods for the dynamical modeling of genetic regulatory networks.

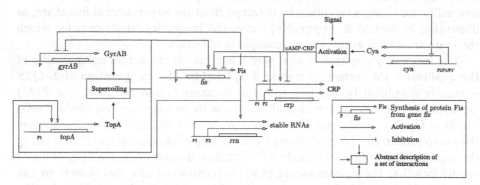

Fig. 4. Network of key genes, proteins, and regulatory interactions involved in the nutritional stress network in *E. coli*. The contents of the boxes labelled 'Activation' and 'Supercoiling' are detailed in [21]

The above circumstances have motivated the qualitative analysis of the nutritional stress response network in *E. coli* by means of the method presented in this paper [21]. On the basis of literature data, we have decided to focus, as a first step, on a network of six genes that are believed to play a key role in the nutritional stress response (Figure 4). The network includes genes involved in the transduction of the nutritional stress signal (the global regulator *crp* and the adenylate cyclase *cya*), metabolism (the global regulator *fis*), cellular growth (the *rrn* genes coding for stable RNAs), and DNA supercoiling, an important modulator of gene expression (the topoisomerase *topA* and the gyrase *gyrAB*).

Based on this information, a PADE model of seven variables has been constructed, one protein concentration variable for each of the six genes and one input variable (u_{signal}) representing the presence or absence of a nutritional stress signal [21]. As an illustration, the piecewise-affine differential equation and the parameter inequality constraints for the state variable x_{topA} are given below.

$$\dot{x}_{topA} = \kappa^1_{topA} + \kappa^2_{topA}\, s^+(x_{gyrAB}, \theta^3_{gyrAB})\, s^-(x_{topA}, \theta^1_{topA})\, s^+(x_{fis}, \theta^4_{fis}) - \gamma_{topA}\, x_{topA}$$

$$0 < \kappa^1_{topA}/\gamma_{topA} < \theta^1_{topA} < \theta^2_{topA} < \theta^3_{topA} < (\kappa^1_{topA} + \kappa^2_{topA})/\gamma_{topA} < max_{topA}$$

The above equation and inequalities state that the basal expression of *topA* is low ($\kappa^1_{topA}/\gamma_{topA} < \theta^1_{topA}$), whereas in the presence of a high concentration of Fis ($s^+(x_{fis}, \theta^4_{fis}) = 1$), and of a low level of DNA supercoiling ($s^+(x_{gyrAB}, \theta^3_{gyrAB})$ $s^-(x_{topA}, \theta^1_{topA}) = 1$), the concentration of TopA increases, converging towards a high value ($(\kappa^1_{topA} + \kappa^2_{topA})/\gamma_{topA} > \theta^3_{topA}$).

Using the computer tool GNA, we have performed reachability analyses on the qualitative PA transition system associated with the PADE model. The simulation of the entry into stationary phase has given rise to a state transition graph of 712 states, computed in 5.0 s on a PC (800 MHz, 256 Mb). Figure 5 represents the temporal evolution of two of the protein concentrations in a run. The evolutions are consistent with the observations [21]. The coupling of GNA with model-checking tools [22] has allowed a more systematic verification of observed dynamical properties.

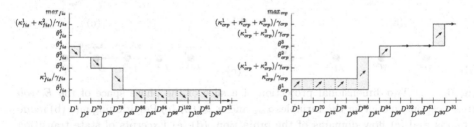

Fig. 5. Temporal evolution of Fis and CRP concentrations in the run ($D^1, \ldots, D^{31}$). Arrows indicate the sign of the derivative for persistent states

The application of the method has led to new insights into how the nutritional stress signal results in the slowing-down of bacterial growth characteristic for the stationary phase [21]. In summary, the analysis has brought to the fore the role of the mutual inhibition of Fis and CRP, which in the presence of a nutritional stress signal results in the inhibition of *fis* and in the activation of *crp*. This causes a decrease of the expression of the *rrn* genes, which code for stable RNAs and are a reliable indicator of cellular growth. In addition to this increased understanding of the transition from exponential to stationary phase, the model has yielded predictions on the occurrence of oscillations in some of the protein concentrations after a nutrient upshift, predictions that are currently being tested in our laboratory. The scope of our study is now being enlarged to more complex nutritional stress response networks.

The analysis of the nutritional stress response in *E. coli* has confirmed the utility of the refined qualitative abstraction presented in this paper. Repartitioning the mode domains, such that the sign patterns of the derivatives of the concentration variables in the states of the qualitative PA transition system are unique, avoids verification of dynamical properties to be over-conservative. Consider Figure 6, which compares two-dimensional projections of a phase-space slice of the stress response model. Depending on whether mode domains or flow domains are used as the abstraction criterion, the state transition graph will be different (compare (d) and (e) of Figure 6). Whereas the CTL formula $EF(\dot{x}_{crp} > 0 \wedge EF\,(\dot{x}_{crp} < 0))$ holds for the graph in (d), this is not true in (e), thus revealing that the coarse-grained abstraction may cause models to escape refutation by available experimental data.

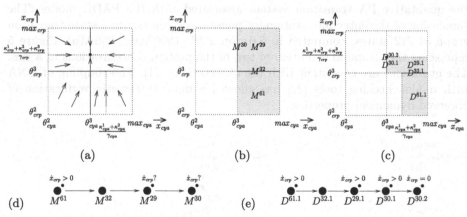

Fig. 6. (a) Two-dimensional projection of a slice of the phase space of the *E. coli* stress response model for the variables x_{crp} and x_{cya}. (b)-(c) Partitioning into (b) mode domains and (c) flow domains of the projection. (d)-(e) Excerpts of state transition graph resulting from the qualitative abstraction based on (d) mode domains and (e) flow domains

The application of the fine-grained qualitative abstraction to the nutritional stress response system has also revealed that it is not much more computationally-expensive than the coarse-grained abstraction used in our previous work. In fact, when analyzing the transition from exponential to stationary phase, the refined abstraction generates 712 persistent states, whereas the original qualitative PA transition system has 39 persistent states. However, when defining a single initial state, corresponding to the biologically most plausible flow domain after repartitioning of the mode domain, the refined abstraction yields only 40 persistent states. A more systematic study of a PADE model with nine state and two input variables, describing the initiation of sporulation in *B. subtilis* for the wild-type and a dozen of mutant strains, confirms this result. On average, the refined abstraction generates only twice as much states, under the condition that the reachability analysis is carried out from a single flow domain.

6   Discussion and Conclusions

We have presented a method for the qualitative analysis and verification of hybrid models of genetic regulatory networks. The method is based on a class of piecewise-affine differential equation models that has been well-studied in mathematical biology. By defining a qualitative abstraction preserving the sign pattern of the derivatives of concentration variables, the continuous PA transition system associated with a PADE model is transformed into a discrete or qualitative PA transition system whose properties can be analyzed by means of classical model-checking tools. The qualitative PA transition is a simulation of the underlying continuous PA transition system and can be easily computed in a symbolic manner by exploiting inequality constraints on the parameters.

The results of this paper extend our previous work [4, 11] in two directions. In the first place, we have defined a refined partitioning of the phase space which underlies a qualitative abstraction preserving stronger properties of the qualitative dynamics of the system, *i.e.* the derivative sign pattern. The resulting qualitative PA transition system is better adapted to the abstraction level of the experimental data, in the sense that it avoids verification of dynamical properties to be over-conservative. In the second place, we have applied the implementation of the method to the analysis of a system whose functioning is not well-understood by biologists today, the nutritional stress response in the bacterium *E. coli*. The application has led to biologically interesting results and has confirmed the importance of the refined qualitative abstraction.

The hybrid character of the dynamics of genetic regulatory networks has stimulated the interest in the application of hybrid-systems methods and tools over the past few years [3, 4, 5, 6, 7]. Our approach differs from this related work on several counts. Whereas we use piecewise-affine deterministic models, other groups have employed multi-affine deterministic models [3, 7] or stochastic models [6]. Without denying the interest of the latter approaches, we note that the class of models underlying our approach allows the qualitative analysis of high-dimensional systems, and is therefore well-adapted to state-of-the-art measurement techniques in molecular biology. The PADE models (1) in this paper have been well-studied in mathematical biology [1, 2], and have also formed the basis for other work in the field of hybrid systems [5]. However, the latter approach does not take into account the dynamics of the system on threshold hyper-planes, where equilibrium points and other phenomena of interest may occur [16]. In addition, we use a tailored method for the computation of a qualitative PA transition system, instead of the generic quantifier elimination method used in [5]. This allows us to fully exploit the favorable mathematical properties of the PADE models (1), and thus promote the upscalability of the method to large and complex networks (Section 5), even when using a fine-grained partitioning of the phase space.

From a more general perspective, our approach can be seen as an applica-tion of the notion of discrete abstraction, introduced to study the dynamics of systems with an infinite number of states [17,18]. Much work has focused on the identification of classes of continuous and discrete dynamical systems for which bisimulation relations with finite transition systems are guaranteed to ex-ist. The results of this paper can be seen as showing that the weaker simulation relation may also be of considerable practical interest, especially for classes of systems for which the existence of a finite bisimulation cannot be guaranteed. Discrete abstraction criteria similar to the one used in this paper, based on the sign of the (higher) derivatives of continuous variables, have also been proposed by other authors in the fields of hybrids systems [23] and qualitative reasoning [24]. In comparison with these approaches, our work deals with a less general class of models. However, this allows the development and implementation of efficient, tailored algorithms for the practical computation of the qualitative dy-namics of the system, even on (intersections of) threshold hyperplanes, where discontinuities may occur.

The possibility to use efficient algorithms for the computation of the quali-tative PA transition system rests, to a large extent, on the approximation of the set $K(x)$ in (4) by the set $H(x)$ in (5). Because the latter set is hyperrectangu-lar, the computation of domains, transitions, and sign patterns can be carried out seperately in every dimension, using the ordering of parameter values fixed by inequality constraints. Because $H(x)$ is an overapproximation of $K(x)$, the state transition graph may contain sequences of states that would not occur in the graph obtained by using $K(x)$. As a consequence, a PADE model may fail to be rejected by an observed time-series of measurements of the concentration variables. However, due to the fact that the approximation of $H(x)$ by $K(x)$ is conservative, a PADE model will never be falsely rejected. An obvious direc-tion for further research would be to see whether finer approximations of $H(x)$ can be found that still allow tailored symbolic algorithms to be used that do not compromise the upscalability of the method to large and complex genetic regulatory networks.

References

1. Glass, L., Kauffman, S.: The logical analysis of continuous non-linear biochemical control networks. J. Theor. Biol. **39** (1973) 103–129
2. Thomas, R., d'Ari, R.: Biological Feedback. CRC Press (1990)

3. Belta, C., Finin, P., Habets, L., Halász, A., Imielinski, M., Kumar, V., Rubin, H.: Understanding the bacterial stringent response using reachability analysis of hybrid systems. In Alur, R., Pappas, G., eds.: Proc. HSCC 2004. LNCS 2993, Springer (2004) 111–125
4. de Jong, H., Gouzé, J.L., Hernandez, C., Page, M., Sari, T., Geiselmann, J.: Hybrid modeling and simulation of genetic regulatory networks: A qualitative approach. In Pnueli, A., Maler, O., eds.: Proc. HSCC 2003. LNCS 2623, Springer (2003) 267–282
5. Ghosh, R., Tomlin, C.: Symbolic reachable set computation of piecewise affine hybrid automata and its application to biological modeling: Delta-Notch protein signalling. Syst. Biol. 1 (2004) 170–183
6. Hu, J., Wu, W.C., Sastry, S.: Modeling subtilin production in *B. subtilis* using stochastic hybrid systems. In Alur, R., Pappas, G., eds.: Proc. HSCC 2004. LNCS 2993, Springer (2004) 417–431
7. Asarin, E., Dang, T.: Abstraction by projection and application to multi-affine systems. In Alur, R., Pappas, G., eds.: Proc. HSCC 2004. LNCS 2993, Springer (2004) 32–47
8. Lygeros, J., Pappas, G., Sastry, S.: An introduction to hybrid system modeling, analysis, and control. Preprints of 1st Nonlinear Control Network Pedagogical School, Greece (1999)
9. Antsaklis, P., Koutsoukos, X.: Hybrid dynamical systems: review and recent progress. In Samad, T., Balas, G., eds.: Software-enabled Control: Information Technologies for Dynamical Systems. Wiley-IEEE Press (2003)
10. de Jong, H.: Modeling and simulation of genetic regulatory systems: A literature review. J. Comput. Biol. 9 (2002) 69–105
11. de Jong, H., Gouzé, J.L., Hernandez, C., Page, M., Sari, T., Geiselmann, J.: Qualitative simulation of genetic regulatory networks using piecewise-linear models. Bull. Math. Biol. 66 (2004) 301–340
12. de Jong, H., Geiselmann, J., Hernandez, C., Page, M.: Genetic Network Analyzer: Qualitative simulation of genetic regulatory networks. Bioinformatics 19 (2003) 336–344
13. de Jong, H., Geiselmann, J., Batt, G., Hernandez, C., Page, M.: Qualitative simulation of the initiation of sporulation in *B. subtilis*. Bull. Math. Biol. 66 (2004) 261–300
14. Batt, G., de Jong, H., Geiselmann, J., Page, M., Ropers, D., Schneider, D.: Symbolic reachability analysis of genetic regulatory networks using qualitative abstraction. Technical report RR-5362 INRIA (2004)
15. Filippov, A.: Differential Equations with Discontinuous Righthand Sides. Kluwer Academic Publishers (1988)
16. Gouzé, J.L., Sari, T.: A class of piecewise linear differential equations arising in biological models. Dyn. Syst. 17 (2002) 299–316
17. Alur, R., Henzinger, T., Lafferriere, G., Pappas, G.: Discrete abstractions of hybrid systems. Proc. IEEE 88 (2000) 971–984
18. Chutinan, A., Krogh, B.: Verification of infinite-state dynamic systems using approximate quotient transition systems. IEEE Trans. Automat. Contr. 46 (2001) 1401–1410
19. Huisman, G., Siegele, D., Zambrano, M., Kolter, R.: Morphological and physiological changes during stationary phase. In Neidhardt *et al.* eds.: *E. coli* and *Salmonella*: Cellular and Molecular Biology. ASM Press (1996) 1672–1682.
20. Hengge-Aronis, R.: The general stress response in *E. coli*. In Storz, G., Hengge-Aronis, R., eds.: Bacterial Stress Responses. ASM Press (2000) 161–177

21. Ropers, D., de Jong, H., Page, M., Schneider, D., Geiselmann, H.: Qualitative simulation of nutritional stress response in *E. coli*. Technical Report RR-5412 (2004), submitted for publication
22. Batt, G., Bergamini, D., de Jong, H., Gavarel, H., Mateescu, R.: Model checking genetic regulatory networks using GNA and CADP. In Graf, S., Mounier, L., eds.: Proc. SPIN 2004. LNCS 2989, Springer (2004) 158–163
23. Tiwari, A., Khanna, G.: Series abstractions for hybrid automata. In Tomlin, C., Greenstreet, M., eds.: Proc. HSCC 2002. LNCS 2289, Springer (2002) 465–478
24. Kuipers, B.: Qualitative Reasoning: Modeling and Simulation with Incomplete Knowledge. MIT Press (1994)

Optimal Control of Discrete Hybrid Stochastic Automata

Alberto Bemporad and Stefano Di Cairano

Dip. Ing. Informazione, Università di Siena, via Roma 56, 53100 Siena, Italy
{bemporad, dicairano}@dii.unisi.it
http://www.dii.unisi.it

Abstract. This paper focuses on hybrid systems whose discrete state transitions depend on both deterministic and stochastic events. For such systems, after introducing a suitable hybrid model called Discrete Hybrid Stochastic Automaton (DHSA), different finite-time optimal control approaches are examined: (1) Stochastic Hybrid Optimal Control (SHOC), that "optimistically" determines the trajectory providing the best trade off between the tracking performance and the probability that stochastic events realize as expected, under specified chance constraints; (2) Robust Hybrid Optimal Control (RHOC) that, in addition, less optimistically, ensures that the system remains within a specified safety region for all possible realizations of stochastic events. Sufficient conditions for the asymptotic convergence of the state vector are given for receding-horizon implementations of the above schemes. The proposed approaches are exemplified on a simple benchmark problem in production system management.

1 Introduction

Hybrid systems were proved to be a powerful framework for the analysis and synthesis of embedded systems, as they provide a model in which continuous and discrete behaviors coexist [1]. Several mathematical models were proposed in the last years for *deterministic* hybrid systems, for the analysis of their structural properties, and for controller synthesis. However, there are relatively few studies regarding *stochastic* hybrid systems, except the remarkable results presented in [2, 3] regarding modeling aspects, the ones in [4, 5, 6] regarding structural properties, and important results in applications, such as air traffic control [7], manufacturing systems [8], and communication networks [9].

In this paper we introduce a discrete-time model and suitable control algorithms based on optimization techniques for a class of stochastic hybrid systems, denoted as Discrete Hybrid Stochastic Automata (DHSA), in which the uncertainty appears on the discrete component of the hybrid dynamics, in the form of stochastic events that, together with their deterministic counterparts, determine the transition of the discrete state. As a consequence, mode switches of the continuous dynamics become non-deterministic and uncertainty propagates also to the continuous states.

M. Morari and L. Thiele (Eds.): HSCC 2005, LNCS 3414, pp. 151–167, 2005.
© Springer-Verlag Berlin Heidelberg 2005

Unpredictable behaviors such as delays or faults in digital components and discrete approximations of continuous input disturbances can be both modeled by DHSA. The main advantage of DHSA is that the number of possible values that the overall system state can have at each time instant is finite (although it may be large), so that the problem of controlling DHSA can be conveniently treated by numerical optimization.

The paper is organized as follows. Section 2 is concerned with modeling aspects. In Section 3 we present a control approach that uses stochastic information about the uncertainty to obtain an optimal trajectory whose probability of realization is known and in Section 4 we extend the approach to ensure also robust safety properties. Finally, after presenting an application example in Section 5, in Section 6 we provide sufficient conditions for the asymptotic convergence of the state in case of receding-horizon implementations of the proposed optimal control schemes.

2   Discrete Hybrid Stochastic Automaton

A model for deterministic hybrid systems called Discrete Hybrid Automaton (DHA) was introduced in [10]. We introduce here the Discrete Hybrid Stochastic Automaton (DHSA), that in addition takes into account possible stochastic discrete state transitions.

2.1   Model Formulation

A DHSA is composed by four components: a Switched Affine System (SAS), an Event Generator (EG), a stochastic (non-deterministic) Finite State Machine (sFSM) and a Mode Selector (MS). The switched affine system satisfies the equations

$$
\begin{aligned}
x_r(k+1) &= A_{i(k)}x_r(k) + B_{i(k)}u_r(k) + f_{i(k)}, \\
y_r(k) &= C_{i(k)}x_r(k) + D_{i(k)}u_r(k) + g_{i(k)},
\end{aligned} \tag{1}
$$

in which $k \in \mathbb{K} = \{0, 1, \dots, \}$ is the time index, $i \in \mathcal{I} = \{1, 2, \dots, s\}$ is the current mode of the system, $x_r \in \mathcal{X}_r \subseteq \mathbb{R}^n$ is the continuous component of the state, $u_r \in \mathcal{U}_r \subseteq \mathbb{R}^m$ is the continuous input vector, $y_r \in \mathcal{Y}_r \subseteq \mathbb{R}^p$ is the output vector and $\{A_i, B_i, f_i, C_i, D_i, g_i\}_{i\in\mathcal{I}}$, are matrices of suitable dimensions. The EG produces event signals $\delta_e(k) \in \{0, 1\}^{n_e}$, that we consider as the *endogenous* discrete input signals, defined as

$$
\delta_e(k) = f_{\mathrm{H}}(x_r(k), u_r(k), k), \tag{2}
$$

where $f_{\mathrm{H}} : \mathcal{X}_r \times \mathcal{U}_r \times \mathbb{K} \to \{0, 1\}^{n_e}$ is the event generator function [10]. The mode selector is defined by a discrete function $f_{\mathrm{M}} : \{0, 1\}^{n_b} \times \{0, 1\}^{m_b} \times \{0, 1\}^{n_e} \to \mathcal{I}$

$$
i(k) = f_{\mathrm{M}}(x_b(k), u_b(k), \delta_e(k)), \tag{3}
$$

where $x_b \in \{0, 1\}^{n_b}$ is the discrete state and $u_b \in \{0, 1\}^{m_b}$ is the discrete *exogenous* input.

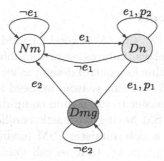

Fig. 1. Stochastic Finite State Machine: 3 states, 2 events and 2 stochastic transitions

The above three building elements are the same as presented in [10] for DHA. The difference between DHA and DHSA[1] is in the element defining the discrete state dynamics: a Finite State Machine (FSM) in DHA, a stochastic FSM (sFSM) in DHSA. While a FSM is defined by the purely discrete difference equation

$$x_b(k+1) = f_B(x_b(k), u_b(k), \delta_e(k)), \qquad (4)$$

where $f_B : \{0,1\}^{n_b} \times \{0,1\}^{m_b} \times \{0,1\}^{n_e} \to \{0,1\}^{n_b}$, a sFSM is defined by the probability that the discrete state will take a given value at the next step, given the actual state and inputs:

$$P[x_b(k+1) = \bar{x}_b] = f_b(x_b(k), u_b(k), \delta_e(k), \bar{x}_b), \qquad (5)$$

where $f_b : \{0,1\}^{n_b} \times \{0,1\}^{m_b} \times \{0,1\}^{n_e} \times \{0,1\}^{n_b} \to [0,1]$. The information contained in the stochastic finite state machine is the following: Given the state value at step k and the inputs $\delta_e(k), u_b(k)$, the probability that the next discrete state takes a certain value is known. An example of sFSM is reported in Figure 1.

Definition 1. *Given a binary state* $x_b(k) = \bar{x}_b$, *an exogenous binary input* $u_b(k) = \bar{u}_b$, *an endogenous vector of events* $\delta_e(k) = \bar{\delta}_e$, *we say that a discrete transition* $\bar{x}_b \to \hat{x}_b$ *to the successor state* $x_b(k+1) = \hat{x}_b$ *is enabled for* $(\bar{x}_b, \bar{u}_b, \bar{\delta}_e)$, *if the probability* $P_{\bar{x}_b \to \hat{x}_b} = f_b(\bar{x}_b, \bar{u}_b, \bar{\delta}_e, \hat{x}_b) > 0$. *An enabled transition is said stochastic if* $P_{\bar{x}_b \to \hat{x}_b} < 1$.

Definition 2. *Given a triple* $(\bar{x}_b, \bar{u}_b, \bar{\delta}_e)$, *two or more enabled transitions are called* conflicting *on* $(\bar{x}_b, \bar{u}_b, \bar{\delta}_e)$.

A more formal definition of conflicting transitions is given in [11], we just note here that for a correctly defined sFSM the sum of the probabilities of conflicting transitions at every given $(\bar{x}_b, \bar{u}_b, \bar{\delta}_e)$ must be 1.

---

[1] The resets maps introduced in [10] can be straightforwardly included also in DHSA, so they are not explicitly considered in this paper.

2.2   Computational Model

The DHSA formulation (1), (2), (3), (5) is good for modeling stochastic discrete effects (such as stochastic delays, failures, unpredictable or external decisions), but not conveniently exploitable for control design, as we will more clearly justify in the beginning of Section 3. For this reason, we need rephrase the DHSA into an equivalent model that is easier to manage in computations.

The key idea is that a sFSM having stochastic conflicting transitions can be equivalently represented by a deterministic FSM having additional exogenous random binary inputs $w_1, w_2, \ldots, w_l$, that we call *uncontrollable events*, where if $w_i = 1$ the corresponding stochastic transition, if enabled, is taken. Given a system with l stochastic transitions, we denote by $W \subseteq \{0,1\}^l$ the set of vectors $w = [w_1(k) \ \ldots \ w_l(k)]^T$ that satisfy the conditions

$$\left[(x_b = \bar{x}_b) \wedge (u_b = \bar{u}_b) \wedge (\delta_e = \bar{\delta}_e)\right] \rightarrow \left[\sum_{i \in I(\bar{x}_b, \bar{u}_b, \bar{\delta}_e)} w_i = 1\right], \tag{6}$$
$$\forall(\bar{x}_b, \bar{u}_b, \bar{\delta}_e) \in \{0,1\}^{n_b} \times \{0,1\}^{m_b} \times \{0,1\}^{n_e} : |I(\bar{x}_b, \bar{u}_b, \bar{\delta}_e)| > 1$$

where $I(\bar{x}_b, \bar{u}_b, \bar{\delta}_e) \subseteq \{1, \ldots, l\}$ is the subset of indices of the uncontrollable events associated with the conflicting transitions on $(\bar{x}_b, \bar{u}_b, \bar{\delta}_e)$ and $|\cdot|$ denotes cardinality.

As an example, the sFSM represented in Figure 1 can be associated with a FSM having additional uncontrollable events $w_1, w_2 \in \{0,1\}$ that affect the stochastic transitions: transition $Dn \rightarrow Dn$ happens when $e_1 \wedge w_2{}^2$ is true, while transition $Dn \rightarrow Dmg$ when $e_1 \wedge w_1$ is true, w_1 and w_2 are mutually exclusive, and $\mathbf{P}[w_1 = 1] = p_1$ and $\mathbf{P}[w_2 = 1] = p_2$. More generally, a sFSM having l stochastic transitions can be transformed into a deterministic automaton, denoted as uncontrollable-events FSM (ueFSM), defined by the state-update function:

$$x_b(k+1) = f_B(x_b(k), u_b(k), \delta_e(k), w(k)), \tag{7}$$

where $w(k) = [w_1(k) \ \ldots \ w_l(k)]^T \in W$ is the random vector of uncontrollable events at time k and $f_B : \{0,1\}^{n_b} \times \{0,1\}^{m_b} \times \{0,1\}^{n_e} \times W \rightarrow \{0,1\}^{n_b}$.

An uncontrollable-events Discrete Hybrid Automaton (ueDHA) is obtained from a DHSA by substituting the sFSM with its corresponding ueFSM (7), leaving the switched affine system, the mode selector and the event generator unchanged.

An ueDHA obtained from a DHSA is equivalent to the DHSA itself when the additional exogenous variables w are produced by a random binary number generator under the conditions

$$\mathbf{P}[w_i = 1] = p_i, \quad i = 1, \ldots, l, \qquad w \in W, \tag{8}$$

that ensure that the uncontrollable events take value 1 with probability equal to the one associated with the corresponding stochastic transition.

---

^{2} "$\wedge$" denote logic "and".

The advantages of transforming a DHSA into the related ueDHA are three:

1. Uncertainty is now associated with binary signals $w(k)$.
2. The ueDHA is an extended DHA model, thus it can be converted into equivalent hybrid models, and in particular into Mixed Logical Dynamical (MLD) systems [12] for solving optimization problems.
3. The probability of a given discrete state trajectory can be obtained as a function of the uncontrollable event vector $\{w(k)\}_{k=0}^{N-1}$, as explained in the following paragraphs.

The uncontrollable events contain the whole information about stochastic transitions, thus, when vectors $\{w(k)\}_{k=0}^{N-1}$ are known, the probability of the state trajectory $\{x(k)\}_{k=0}^{N}$ can be computed once $\{u(k)\}_{k=0}^{N-1}$ and $x(0)$ are also given. Consider a system with l uncontrollable events and let $w(k) = [w_1(k) \ldots w_l(k)]^T$ be the uncontrollable event vector at step k. Consider an additional $w_{l+1}(k)$ taking value 1 when the transition taken by the DHSA at step k is deterministic and extend conditions (6) with this. Consider the vector $p = [p_1 \ldots p_l \, 1]^T$ containing the probability coefficients of the stochastic transitions. Then, consider the products

$$\begin{bmatrix} \pi(0) \\ \vdots \\ \pi(N-1) \end{bmatrix} = \begin{bmatrix} w^T(0) \\ \vdots \\ w^T(N-1) \end{bmatrix} \cdot p, \quad \pi = \pi(w(0), \ldots, w(N-1)) = \prod_{k=0}^{N-1} \pi(k). \quad (9)$$

The coefficient $\pi(k)$ contains the probability of transition at step k, π the probability of the complete trajectory. In this way it is possible to know the probability to have a certain trajectory given the initial condition and input signals.

Finally we mention that the well posedness of a DHSA is ensured if its related ueDHA is a well posed DHA [10], if conditions (6) hold, and if the probability coefficients of stochastic transitions are correctly defined as proven in [11], where it is also shown the existing relations between DHSA, Markov Chains and Piecewise Deterministic Markov Processes [2, 13].

Thanks to the uncontrollable events, the whole statistical information about transitions is removed from the system structure and associated to the stochastic properties of the binary signals. In the following sections we will show how the ueDHA can be used to formulate optimization problems that consider the information regarding trajectory probability in the objective function and in the constraints.

3   Stochastic Hybrid Optimal Control

In [11] we showed that it is not possible to obtain average state optimal control of DHSA by exploiting similarities with Markov Chains average state optimal control [14], as some of the control signals of the discrete dynamics are not exogenous and they depend on the continuous dynamics. The only way to optimally control the average state is to use a "scenario enumeration" approach [15], which however generates a numerically intractable problem as the optimal control horizon N gets large. In this paper we take a different approach and consider the problem of choosing the input profile that optimizes the most favorable situation, under penalties and hard constraints on the probability of the disturbance realization that determines such a situation. Given a DHSA, by exploiting the equivalent ueDHA and the probability computed in (2), we can formulate such an optimal control problem as an MIP.

3.1   Problem Setup

Consider the convex *performance index*

$$C_d = \sum_{k=0}^{N-1} \ell_k(x(k+1) - r_x(k+1), u(k) - r_u(k)), \tag{10}$$

which is a function of $x(k)$, $u(k)$, $k = 0, \ldots, N-1$. Typically $\ell_k(x, u) = \|Q(x - r_x)\|_\infty + \|R(u - r_u)\|_\infty$ where Q, R full rank or $\ell_k(x, u) = (x - r_x)^T Q(x - r_x) + (u - r_u)^T R(u - r_u)$ where $Q \geq 0$, $R > 0$, in which r_x and r_u are given references on the state and on the input, respectively.

Next, consider the *probability cost*

$$C_p = \ln \frac{1}{\pi(w(0), \ldots, w(N-1))} = -\ln\left(\pi(w(0), \ldots, w(N-1))\right), \tag{11}$$

which is a function of $w(k)$, $k = 0, \ldots, N-1$. The smaller is the probability of a trajectory, the larger is the probability cost, so that the trajectories that realize rarely are penalized. The most desirable situation is to obtain a trajectory with good performance and high probability. For this reason, we define as the *objective function* the cost

$$C = C_d + q_p C_p, \tag{12}$$

in which $q_p \in (0, +\infty)$ is a trade off coefficient called *probability coefficient*.

In order to hardly eliminate trajectories that realize rarely, we also wish to impose the *chance constraint*

$$\pi(w(0), \ldots, w(N-1)) \geq \tilde{p}, \tag{13}$$

where the coefficient $\tilde{p} \in (0, 1]$ is called *probability limit*.

The chance constraint (13) ensures that when the chosen input profile $\{u(k)\}_{k=0}^{N-1}$ is applied to the system, the corresponding trajectory $\{x(k)\}_{k=0}^{N}$ realizes with probability greater or equal to $\tilde{p}$. Other constraints on probabilities may be imposed, such as constraints defining the minimum allowed probability at every single step.

The problem of optimally control a DHSA in respect to the cost function (12), considering (13) as additional constraint is then formulated as:

Problem 1 (Stochastic Hybrid Optimal Control, SHOC).

$$\min_{\{w(k),u(k)\}_{k=0}^{N-1}} \quad \mathcal{C}_d + q_p\mathcal{C}_p \tag{14a}$$

$$\text{s.t.} \quad \text{DHSA dynamics } (1), (2), (3), (7), (6) \tag{14b}$$

$$\text{chance constraint } (13). \tag{14c}$$

3.2   Optimization Problem

In order to cast problem (14) as a mixed-integer linear or quadratic problem, we need to transform (11) and (13) into linear functions of the uncontrollable event values w. The performance index in (10) can be dealt with as described in [16] for deterministic hybrid systems.

Consider a DHSA with l stochastic transitions whose probabilities are collected in vector $p = [p_1 \ldots p_l]^T$, and consider the equivalent ueDHA with uncontrollable events $w = [w_1 \ldots w_l]^{T\,3}$. The probability of a trajectory depends only on the transitions, thus it can be computed as a function of the uncontrollable events as $\pi(w(0), \ldots, w(N-1)) = \prod_{k=0}^{N-1} \prod_{i=1}^{l} \pi_i(k)$ where $\pi_i(k)$ represents the contribution of the stochastic transition i at step k on the trajectory probability,

$$\pi_i(k) = \begin{cases} 1 & \text{if } w_i(k) = 0 \\ p_i & \text{if } w_i(k) = 1. \end{cases} \tag{15}$$

Equivalently, $\pi_i(k) = 1 + (p_i - 1)\,w_i(k)$, $w_i(k) \in \{0, 1\}$. The probability cost (11) is equal to

$$-\sum_{k=0}^{N-1}\sum_{i=1}^{l} \ln \pi_i(k). \tag{16}$$

With an exp-log transformation, provided that $\pi(w(0), \ldots, w(N-1)) > 0$, $\pi(w(0), \ldots, w(N-1)) = \exp(\ln \prod_{i,k} \pi_i(k))$, thus $\ln \pi(w(0), \ldots, w(N-1)) = \ln \prod_{i,k} \pi_i(k) = \sum_{i,k} \ln \pi_i(k) = \sum_{i,k} \ln(1 + (p_i - 1)\,w_i(k))$. Although this expression is still nonlinear in $w_i(k)$ because of the logarithms, we note that $\ln \pi_i(k) = w_i(k) \ln(p_i)$ for $w_i(k) \in \{0, 1\}$. Hence, the logarithm of the trajectory probability $\ln \pi(w(0), \ldots, w(N-1)) = \sum_{k=0}^{N-1} \sum_{i=1}^{l} w_i(k) \ln(p_i)$, and therefore the probability cost (16) can be expressed as a linear function of the uncontrollable events $w_i(k) \in \{0, 1\}$, so that the chance constraint (13) becomes a linear constraint on $w_i(k) \in \{0, 1\}$.

By converting the ueDHA into MLD form [10], the optimal control problem (14) can be solved by standard mixed integer programming solvers [17].

The solution of (14) is a couple (u^*, w^*), where u^* is the optimal control sequence and w^* is the desired uncontrollable events sequence. Only u^* is actuated, thus the actual trajectory may be different from the expected one. However, if the realization of the stochastic events is equal to w^* the actual trajectory is

---

[3] This can be extended by considering the fictitious event for deterministic transitions having $p_d = 1$. As explained below its contribution will disappear because $\log p_d = 0$.

equal to the one obtained from (14). The largest q_p is, the most likely the actual w will coincide with w^*, and the most cautious will be the control action.

In [11] it is shown that several DHA can be extracted from a single DHSA by fixing a nominal behavior for the uncertain transitions, that is, by fixing $w = \bar{w} \in W$ in the equivalent ueDHA. The Stochastic Hybrid Optimal Control problem solved on the DHSA will always give a better solution than the optimal control problem formulated on an extracted DHA having C_d as cost function: the solution of the SHOC has either higher probability or better performance.

4 Robust Hybrid Optimal Control of DHSA

The approach of Section 3 does not ensure that the behavior of the system is correct when the actual w is different from w^*, as some constraints may be violated for particular realizations. Therefore, this approach can be used only if possible deviations from the desired trajectory are not critical. However, considering those situations in which constraint violation is critical, we define another control approach that considers not only the desired trajectory, but also the possible deviations from it, due to unexpected stochastic transitions.

Definition 3. *Given a stochastic system $x(k+1) = f(x(k), u(k), \phi(k))$ in which $\phi(k) \in \Phi$ is a stochastic disturbance, the constraint $h(x(k), u(k), \phi(k)) < 0$ is robustly satisfied at time k if $h(x(k), u(k), \phi(k)) < 0, \forall \phi(k) \in \Phi$.*

Problem 2 (Robust Hybrid Optimal Control, RHOC).

$$\min_{\{w(k),u(k)\}_{k=0}^{N-1}} \quad C_d + q_p C_p \tag{17a}$$

$$\text{s.t.} \quad \text{DHSA dynamics } (1), (2), (3), (7), (6) \tag{17b}$$

$$\text{chance constraint } (13) \tag{17c}$$

$$\text{constraint } h(\cdot) \le 0 \text{ is robustly satisfied, } \forall k \in [0, N-1]. \tag{17d}$$

Compared to Problem 1, Problem 2 (RHOC) also requires that the optimal input u^* is such that a set of constraints $h(\cdot) \le 0$ is always satisfied for all the admissible values of stochastic events w that may realize.

By exploiting the techniques developed in Section 3 and in [12], problem (17) can be rephrased as:

$$\min_{u,w,\xi} \quad f(u, w, \xi) \tag{18a}$$

$$\text{s.t.} \quad A_u\, u + A_w\, w + A_\xi\, \xi \le b \tag{18b}$$

$$\mathbf{P}[w] \ge \tilde{p} \tag{18c}$$

$$h(u, w, \xi) \le 0, \forall w \in W \text{ such that } \mathbf{P}[w] > p_s, \tag{18d}$$

where u is the vector of deterministic decision variables, w is the vector of uncontrollable events, ξ is the vector of auxiliary variables (z, δ) obtained by translating the ueDHA into MLD form[4] and $\mathbf{P}[\cdot]$ denotes the probability of its argument. Cost function (18a), system dynamics/operation constraints (18b), and chance constraint (18c) are the same of the SHOC problem (14). The quantified constraints (18d) are safety constraints that must be robustly enforced with respect to stochastic events having at least probability $p_s \geq 0$: (18d) is the implicit expression extended along the whole control horizon $k \in [0, N-1]$ on ueDHA of $h(x, u, \phi) \leq 0$ in Definition 3, where the role of ϕ is taken by w. If $p_s = 0$, safety with respect to all trajectories having finite probability is ensured, hence obtaining a complete robustness. Robustness in probability is otherwise enforced.

4.1   Robust Optimal Control Algorithm

Because of the quantified constraints (18d), problem (18) cannot be directly formulated as an MIP. As the feasible values of (w, ξ) are finite, in principle it is possible to explode the quantified constraints in several groups of constraints, one for each realization of stochastic events, according to the so called "scenario enumeration" approach of stochastic optimization [15]. However, the number of scenarios is combinatorial with respect to the number of stochastic events and control horizon, so that the numerical problem is intractable in most practical cases.

On the other hand, one only needs to ensure robust safety of the *optimal* sequence u^*, thus only the stochastic event sequences potentially unsafe and enabled by u^* must be considered. Following this consideration we can apply a strategy based on the interaction between a "partially" robustly safe control problem and a reachability analysis problem, described in Algorithm 4.1.

The algorithm is based on the iterative solution of an optimal control problem, whose dimension increases at each iteration of step 3.3.1., and that looks for a candidate solution $\tilde{u}_i$, and a verification problem, whose dimension remains constant, and that looks for an unsafe[5] stochastic event sequence for $u = \tilde{u}_i$. Both problems can be solved via MIP. The dimension of the control problem keeps increasing as long as an unsafe stochastic sequence $\tilde{w}_i$ is found. The ξ variables and the constraints are duplicated to explicitly enforce safety with respect to the trajectory generated by $\tilde{w}_i$ while optimizing a different trajectory: in this way we request that the trajectory generated by $\tilde{w}_i$ satisfies $h(x(k), u(k), \tilde{w}_i(k)) \leq 0, \forall k \in [0, N-1]$. Algorithm 4.1 terminates in finite time because the number of admissible stochastic event sequences w is finite.

Let $\mathcal{V}$ be the set of input sequences that fulfils constraints (18b), (18c) and (18d) without quantification, and $\mathcal{S}$ be the set of input sequences that fulfils (18b), (18c), (18d). $\mathcal{V}$ is the feasible input set for the SHOC problem, $\mathcal{S}$ is the feasible input set for the RHOC problem, and $\mathcal{S} \subseteq \mathcal{V}$. The behavior of Algorithm 4.1 is the following. At the beginning $\mathcal{V}$ is known, since it is defined by the constraints of the optimal control problem, while $\mathcal{S}$ is not. The information

---

[4] Possibly ξ also includes slack variables required to optimize infinity norms, unless 2-norms are used.

[5] In case a set of robust constraints is considered, it is sufficient that one is violated.

1. Let the control problem be (18) after removing quantification from (18d);
2. Set $i = 0$;
3. do
      3.1. $i \leftarrow i + 1$
      3.2. Solve the control problem and get a candidate solution $\widetilde{u}_i$;
      3.3. if $\widetilde{u}_i \neq \varnothing$
           Solve a reachability problem for $\widetilde{u}_i$ and find $\widetilde{w}_i : \exists k : h(x(k), \widetilde{u}_i(k), \widetilde{w}_i(k)) > 0$
          3.3.1. if $\widetilde{w}_i \neq \varnothing$
              Add to the control problem variables ξ_i and constraints $A_u u + A_w \widetilde{w}_i + A_\xi \xi_i \leq b$ and $h(u, \widetilde{w}_i, \xi_i) \leq 0$ that enforce safety with respect to $\widetilde{w}_i$;
   while $\widetilde{u}_i \neq \varnothing$ and $\widetilde{w}_i \neq \varnothing$
4. if $\widetilde{u}_i = \varnothing$
      4.1. Problem (18) is unfeasible.
      else
      4.2. Set $u^* = \widetilde{u}_i$.

Algorithm 4.1: Robust hybrid optimal control algorithm

obtained from the verification problem is used to cut a part of $\mathcal{V}$ while maintaining $\mathcal{S} \subseteq \mathcal{V}$. This procedure continues until the optimal point computed at step 3.2 belongs to $\mathcal{S}$, and therefore the RHOC problem is solved, without in most cases explicitly characterizing $\mathcal{S}$.

Usually, only a small fraction of stochastic events affects the evolution of the system when a particular control sequence is chosen, and an even smaller fraction brings the system to the unsafe region. The iterative approach aims at considering only these stochastic event sequences among all the possible ones, thus solving many smaller problems rather than one large MIP in which all possible realizations of stochastic events are enumerated. Nevertheless, it must be noted that in the worst case Algorithm 4.1 still has a combinatorial complexity with respect to the control horizon and the number of uncontrollable events.

Remark 1. The SHOC and RHOC approaches are different from the more common control approach for stochastic systems, where the *average* state is controlled. In our setting, the uncertainty affecting DHSA has a discrete nature, so that taking averages may lead to unsatisfactory solutions. Consider the following problem: control to the origin the state of the system having three modes with dynamics $x(k+1) = x(k)$, $x(k+1) = x(k) + u(k) - 1$, $x(k+1) = x(k) + u(k) + 1$, respectively mode $1, 2, 3$. Consider the system starting in $x(0) = 0$ in mode 1 and assume at time $\bar{k}$ the mode switches to state 2 or 3, both with probability 0.5. An average state control policy would choose $u(k) = 0$, $\forall k$, with the consequence that the trajectories of the system will always diverge from the desired state. On the other hand, SHOC and RHOC would choose one of the two possible behaviors and optimize the system for that situation, e.g. by setting $u(k) = 1$ if the system is predicted to switch to mode 2. In 50% of the cases the state would be brought to the origin (clearly, in the remaining 50% the error would be larger than in the case of the average control policy).

5   Application Example

As a benchmark test we consider a problem in production systems where the goal is to control a small factory production facility subject to random failures depending on wear.

5.1   Modeling

The considered production facility is constituted by two lines having different fixed production rates. The factory production rate must track a given reference forecasted demand.

The production system accumulates wear. When the wear is above a certain level, there is a probability p_{break} that the system breaks. Maintenance can be decided and executed to reduce wear, at the price of stopping the production. Production is interrupted when the system is damaged and the system must be repaired before production starts again.

The production rate dynamics $\psi(k)$ is modeled as a first order asymptotically stable linear system, the wear dynamics $\nu(k)$ as an integrator. The production facility can be in three discrete states: *Normal, Danger* (=risk of damage) and *Damaged*. The sFSM describing the possible discrete state transitions is presented in Figure 1, where the events e_1, e_2 represents the *risky* threshold crossing ($\nu(k) \geq 5.1$) and the completion of the repairing ($\nu(k) \leq 0.1$), respectively. There are three binary control commands, two for activating independently the production lines and the third, mutually exclusive with the others, activating maintenance. A more detailed description of the system can be found in [11].

5.2   Control Design and Results

All the tests presented here have been performed on an Intel Pentium Xeon 2.8 MHz running Matlab 6.5 and Cplex 9.0. We set $N = 8$, $\tilde{p} = 0.4$ and the

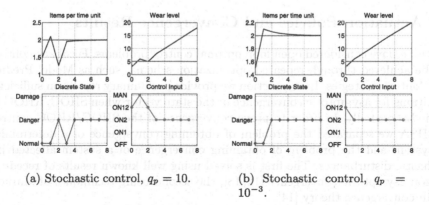

(a) Stochastic control, $q_p = 10$.   (b) Stochastic control, $q_p = 10^{-3}$.

Fig. 2. Stochastic control of a production system

objective function $\sum_{i=0}^{N} |(\psi(k) - r(k))|$, in which r is the forecasted demand, $r(k) = 2, \forall k \in [0,8]$. The constraints involve the discrete and continuous dynamics of the system and the additional mutual exclusivity constraint among production line activation signals and maintenance execution signal. The trade off coefficient q_p is used as a tuning parameter and set either to 10 or to 10^{-3}, while $p_{break} = 0.1$. The initial state is $\psi(0) = 1.5$, $\nu(0) = 3$ and the discrete state is *Normal*. The optimal control sequence found is applied in open loop.

The expected trajectory for $q_p = 10$ has probability 0.66 and it is shown in Figure 2(a). Note that the probability is higher than the limit $\tilde{p}$ because of the probability cost C_p. In Figure 2(b) the expected trajectory for $q_p = 10^{-3}$ is reported: it has higher performance but the probability of the optimal trajectory decreases to 0.53. In both cases the computation time to solve the associated MIP is less than 0.1 seconds.

The stochastic control does not ensure that constraints will be met when u^* is implemented. If we require that the production rate remains above a certain threshold $\tilde{\psi}_m = 0.92$ items per time unit in all possible situations during the whole horizon, a RHOC approach must be used. For $q_p = 10^{-3}$, the robust algorithm requires two additional iterations to solve the problem and a computation time of 0.68 seconds. The predicted trajectory is reported in Figure 3(a).

In Figure 3(b) the robust control solution is reported for $q_p = 10$. In this case only one additional iteration is required with respect to the stochastic control under the same conditions and the computation time is 0.49 seconds.

Figures 3(c), 3(d) depict the worst case situation in which the system suddenly breaks down when it is in danger, in order to compare SHOC and RHOC. Probability coefficients $q_p = 10^{-3}$ (Figure 3(c)) and $q_p = 10$ (Figure 3(d)) are tested in both approaches. The trajectory obtained by stochastic control (dashed line) is initially closer to the desired production rate, but it crosses the line of minimum desired rate. Instead, when the input profile obtained by robust control algorithm (solid line) is applied, the production rate remains in the desired region during the whole control horizon.

6   Actuation Policies and Convergence Results

So far we have considered open loop optimal control problems. Feedback control can be achieved through repeated optimization schema, such as Model Predictive Control strategies. In this section we provide preliminary results on sufficient conditions for asymptotic convergence of the state vector when SHOC/RHOC is applied repeatedly. In order to prove convergence of the SHOC/RHOC control of DHSA we separated the problem of obtaining convergence of a deterministic system and the problem of obtaining convergence of a system affected by stochastic disturbances. The first is solved using well known results of receding horizon asymptotic convergence [12, 18], the second using techniques of Markov Chain convergence theory [14].

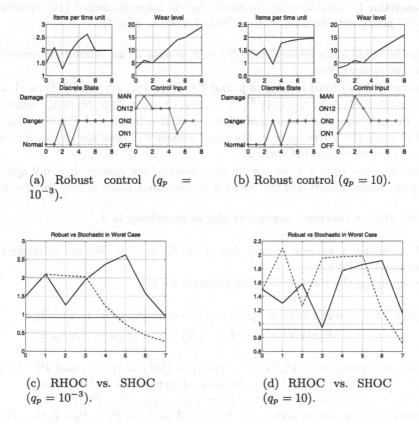

(a) Robust control ($q_p = 10^{-3}$).

(b) Robust control ($q_p = 10$).

(c) RHOC vs. SHOC ($q_p = 10^{-3}$).

(d) RHOC vs. SHOC ($q_p = 10$).

Fig. 3. Robust control (solid) and comparison with stochastic control (dashed)

6.1   Repeated Open-Loop Optimal Control

The simpler policy is Repeated Open-Loop Optimal Control (ROLOC): from a given state $x(0)$ an SHOC/RHOC problem is solved and the whole input sequence $u^* = \{u^*(i)\}_{i=0}^{N-1}$ is applied. Then, a new problem is solved from $x(N)$, and so on.

Since the system is stochastic, asymptotic convergence in probability is considered here. A sequence of random variables $\{\phi(i)\}_{i=0}^{\infty}$ converges in probability to a random variable $\bar{\phi}$ if $\forall \varepsilon > 0, \lim_{i \to \infty} \mathbf{P}[|\phi(i) - \bar{\phi}| > \varepsilon] = 0$ (see [19]).

Consider a DHSA in initial state x_0, stochastic hybrid optimal control with ROLOC policy and a target state $\bar{x}$. Let $\mathcal{X} = \mathcal{X}_r \times \{0,1\}^{n_b}$ be the full (continuous and discrete) state set and let $\mathcal{R}(\bar{x}, N) \subseteq \mathcal{X}$ be the set of states from which the state $\bar{x}$ is reachable within N steps. Define $\tilde{p}$ such that $0 < \tilde{p} \leq \min_{x \in \mathcal{R}(\bar{x}, N)} \{P[\mathcal{T}(x, \bar{x})]\} < 1$, where $\mathcal{T}(x, \bar{x})$ is the trajectory with maximum probability from state x to $\bar{x}$. Let $\mathcal{X}_s \subseteq \mathcal{X}$ be the set of states x_0 for which problem (14) is feasible from $x(0) = x_0$ and let the initial state be $x_0 \in \mathcal{R}(\bar{x}, N) \cap \mathcal{X}_s$.

Proposition 1. *Consider the stochastic hybrid optimal control* (14) *applied in ROLOC policy with horizon N from initial state $x_0 \neq \bar{x}$. If:*

1. *the terminal state constraint $x(N) = \bar{x}$ is used as an additional constraint in the optimization,*
2. *the probability limit is fixed to $\tilde{p}$ and $0 < \tilde{p} \leq \min_{x \in \mathcal{R}(\bar{x},N)}\{P[\mathcal{T}(x,\bar{x})]\} < 1$,*
3. *$\forall x \in \mathcal{R}(\bar{x}, N) \cap \mathcal{X}_s, \forall w \in W^N$, $\tilde{x} = F(x, u^*, w) \in \mathcal{R}(\bar{x}, N) \cap \mathcal{X}_s$, where u^* is the deterministic component of the optimal solution and F is the function that maps the initial state x, the input sequence u^* and the stochastic event sequence w in the final state $\tilde{x}$,*
4. *the objective state $\bar{x}$ is an equilibrium point of the system, it is not affected by stochastic events and the optimal performance index is zero for $x = \bar{x}$,*

then the state x converges asymptotically in probability to $\bar{x}$.

Proof. Consider a generic instant kN, $k \in \mathbb{K}$, $k > 0$. We are interested in computing $\mathbf{P}[x(kN) = \bar{x}]$.

By applying the total probability theorem we get

$$\mathbf{P}[x(kN) = \bar{x}] = \mathbf{P}[x(kN) = \bar{x}|x((k-1)N) = \bar{x}]\,\mathbf{P}[x((k-1)N) = \bar{x}] + \\ \mathbf{P}[x(kN) = \bar{x}|x((k-1)N) \neq \bar{x}]\,\mathbf{P}[x((k-1)N) \neq \bar{x}]\,. \quad (19)$$

Because of hypothesis 4, $\mathbf{P}[x(kN) = \bar{x}|x((k-1)N) = \bar{x}] = 1$, and $\mathbf{P}[x(kN) = \bar{x}|x((k-1)N) \neq \bar{x}] = \hat{p}_{k-1} \geq \tilde{p}$ because of hypothesis 2. Denoting by $P_k = \mathbf{P}[x(kN) = \bar{x}]$, we can write (19) as $P_k = P_{k-1} + \hat{p}_{k-1}(1 - P_{k-1})$.

We prove convergence by induction. For $k = 1$ we have $P_1 = P_0 + \hat{p}_0(1 - P_0) = \hat{p}_0 \geq \tilde{p} = \sum_{i=0}^{0}\tilde{p}(1-\tilde{p})^i$ where $P_0 = 0$ because $x_0 \neq \bar{x}$. Assume that

$$P_{k-1} \geq \sum_{i=0}^{k-2}\tilde{p}(1-\tilde{p})^i. \quad (20)$$

Then $P_k = P_{k-1} + \hat{p}_{k-1}(1 - P_{k-1}) \geq P_{k-1} + \tilde{p}(1 - P_{k-1}) = P_{k-1}(1 - \tilde{p}) + \tilde{p}$. By the induction hypothesis (20), $P_k \geq \sum_{i=0}^{k-2}\tilde{p}(1-\tilde{p})^{i+1} + \tilde{p} = \sum_{i=1}^{k-1}\tilde{p}(1-\tilde{p})^i + \tilde{p}(1-\tilde{p})^0 = \sum_{i=0}^{k-1}\tilde{p}(1-\tilde{p})^i$, and thus we have $\sum_{i=0}^{k-1}\tilde{p}(1-\tilde{p})^i \leq P_k \leq 1$. Since $\lim_{k\to\infty}\sum_{i=0}^{k-1}\tilde{p}(1-\tilde{p})^i = 1$, we conclude that $\lim_{k\to\infty}\mathbf{P}[x(kN) = \bar{x}] = 1$.   □

Note that hypothesis 1 forces convergence to $\bar{x}$, hypothesis 2 ensures feasibility of (13) in optimization and hypothesis 3 ensures not to lose feasibility because of an unexpected stochastic event; this hypothesis might be difficult to verify, thus it can be convenient to verify a condition including it (e.g. that the condition is feasible for each valid input sequence and not only for the optimal one), and it can be removed if RHOC is used. Hypothesis 4 ensures that the objective state will never be left, once it is reached. We can note that the larger is $\tilde{p}$, the faster the probability of reaching the target state converges to one.

6.2   Model Predictive Control

We now consider a Model Predictive Control (MPC) policy, where an optimal control problem is repeated at each step k and only $u^*(0)$ is applied as the input $u(k)$, while $\{u^*(1), \dots u^*(N-1)\}$ are discarded. In order to obtain convergence of such an MPC policy, we make the probability limit $\tilde{p}$ time varying.

Consider solving problem (14) from the initial state $x(0) = x_0$, with probability limit $\tilde{p}(0) = \tilde{p}$ as defined in hypothesis 2. Let (u^*, w^*) be the optimizer, and let the predicted next state be $\hat{x}(1) = f(x(0), u^*(0), w^*(0))$. After applying the first input $u^*(0)$ we get a new state $x(1)$, from which a new optimization problem is solved with probability limit $\tilde{p}(1)$ defined by

$$\tilde{p}(k+1) = \begin{cases} \frac{\tilde{p}(k)}{\mathbf{P}[w^*(k)]} & \text{if} \quad x_b(k+1) = \hat{x}_b(k+1) \\ \tilde{p}(0) & \text{if} \quad x_b(k+1) \neq \hat{x}_b(k+1). \end{cases} \tag{21}$$

The value $\mathbf{P}[w^*(k)]$ represents the probability of the transition predicted at step k and it is known from the result of the MIP, while x_b is the discrete component of the state. The purpose of updating the probability limit is to force the probability of a path between two unexpected transitions to be greater or equal than $\tilde{p}$, therefore avoiding the generation of trajectories having "almost-0" probability.

Assumption 1. The "deterministic behavior" of the MPC closed-loop system, where both u and w are manipulated variables, is asymptotically stable.

Assumption 1 can be satisfied by using final state constraints and defining cost weight matrices in the objective function as reported in [12, 18], since the problem is that of stabilizing a deterministic ueDHA by manipulating the inputs u and w in a receding horizon fashion. When the above strategy is applied, we can prove convergence using the same arguments of Proposition 1. A path that reaches the objective without unexpected transitions in the worst case has probability $\tilde{p}$, thus the probability of having one or more of them is $1 - \tilde{p}$.

Proposition 2. *The stochastic hybrid optimal control* (14) *applied to the DHSA with MPC policy and probability limit update* (21), *under the same hypotheses of Proposition 1 and Assumption 1, converges asymptotically in probability to the objective state $\bar{x}$.*

Proof. The final state constraint and preliminary assumption on ueDHA ensure that, if there are no unexpected transitions in an interval "long enough", the system state converges to the objective, as shown in [18]. The probability of having no unexpected transitions in the worst case is $\tilde{p}$, and the probability of having h of them is $\tilde{p}(1 - \tilde{p})^h$. The probability of converging with not more than m unexpected transition is $\sum_{h=0}^{m} \tilde{p}(1 - \tilde{p})^h$. As $k \to \infty$, there might be $m \to \infty$ unexpected transitions, but the probability of converging is $\sum_{h=0}^{\infty} \tilde{p}(1-\tilde{p})^h$. This series has been shown to converge at value 1, thus $\lim_{k\to\infty} \mathbf{P}[x(k) = \bar{x}] = 1$. □

Even in this case we can relax hypothesis 3 if the RHOC approach is used.

7   Conclusions

In this paper we have shown that by modeling hybrid systems affected by stochastic uncertainty as DHSA several classes of optimal control problems can be solved. We have shown how to trade off between performance and probability, how to impose the chance constraints and how to satisfy constraints robustly. The approach was exemplified on an application study and a set of sufficient conditions, under which asymptotic convergence of repeated optimization schemes can be proved, has been given.

References

1. Antsaklis, P.: A brief introduction to the theory and applications of hybrid systems. Proc. IEEE, Special Issue on Hybrid Systems: Theory and Applications **88** (2000) 879–886
2. Pola, G., Bujorianu, M., Lygeros, J., Di Benedetto, M.: Stochastic hybrid models: an overview with application to air traffic management. In: IFAC–ADHS03,IFAC conference on analysis and design of hybrid systems. (2003)
3. Hu, J., Lygeros, J., Sastry, S.: Towards a theory of stochastic hybrid systems. In Krogh, B., Lynch, N., eds.: Hybrid Systems: Computation and Control. Volume 1790 of Lecture Notes in Computer Science. Springer-Verlag (2000) 160–173
4. Bujorianu, M., Lygeros, J.: Reachability questions in piecewise deterministic markov processes. In Maler, O., Pnueli, A., eds.: Hybrid Systems: Computation and Control. Number 2623 in Lecture Notes in Computer Science, Springer-Verlag (2003) 126–140
5. Liberzon, D., Chatterjee, D.: On stability of stochastic switched systems. In: Proc. 43th IEEE Conf. on Decision and Control, Paradise Island, Bahamas (2004)
6. Strubbe, S., Julius, A., van der Schaft, A.: Communicating piecewise deterministic markov processes. In: in Proc. IFAC Conf. Analysis and Design of Hybrid Systems. (2003) 349–354
7. Prandini, M., Hu, J., Lygeros, J., Sastry, S.: A probabilistic approach to aircraft conflict detection. IEEE Transactions on Intelligent Transportation Systems **1** (2000) 199–220
8. Cassandras, C., Mookherje, R.: Receding horizon optimal control for some stochastic hybrid systems. In: Proc. 41th IEEE Conf. on Decision and Control. (2003) 2162–2167
9. Hespanha, J.: Stochastic hybrid systems: application to communication networks. In Alur, R., Pappas, G., eds.: Hybrid Systems: Computation and Control. Volume 2993 of Lecture Notes in Computer Science. Springer-Verlag (2004) 387–401
10. Torrisi, F., Bemporad, A.: HYSDEL — A tool for generating computational hybrid models. IEEE Trans. Contr. Systems Technology **12** (2004) 235–249
11. Bemporad, A., Di Cairano, S.: Modelling and optimal control of hybrid systems with event uncertainty. Technical report, University of Siena (02/04, 2004) Available at www.dii.unisi.it/~dicairano/papers/tr0204.pdf.
12. Bemporad, A., Morari, M.: Control of systems integrating logic, dynamics, and constraints. Automatica **35** (1999) 407–427
13. Davis, M.: Markov models and optimization. Chapman-Hall, London (1993)
14. Cassandras, C.: Discrete event systems. Aksen associates (1993)

15. Birge, J., Louveaux, F.: Introduction to Stochastic Programming. Springer, New York (1997)
16. Bemporad, A.: Hybrid Toolbox – User's Guide. (2003) http://www.dii.unisi.it/hybrid/toolbox.
17. ILOG, Inc.: CPLEX 8.1 User Manual, Gentilly Cedex, France. (2003)
18. Lazar, M., Heemels, W., Weiland, S., Bemporad, A.: Stability of hybrid model predictive control. In: Proc. 43th IEEE Conf. on Decision and Control, Paradise Island, Bahamas (2004)
19. Papoulis, A.: Probability, random variables and stochastic processes. McGraw-Hill (1991)

Hybrid Decentralized Control of
Large Scale Systems

Francesco Borrelli[1], Tamás Keviczky[2], Gary J. Balas[2], Greg Stewart[3],
Kingsley Fregene[3], and Datta Godbole[3]

[1] Dipartimento di Ingegneria, Università del Sannio,
82100 Benevento, Italy
francesco.borrelli@unisannio.it
[2] Department of Aerospace Engineering and Mechanics,
University of Minnesota,
Minneapolis, MN 55455, United States
[3] Honeywell Laboratories, Minneapolis, MN 55418, United States

Abstract. Motivated by three applications which are under investigation at the Honeywell Research Laboratory in Minneapolis, we introduce a class of large scale control problems. In particular we show that a formation flight problem, a paper machine control problem and the coordination of cameras in a monitoring network can be cast into this class. In the second part of the paper we propose a decentralized control scheme to tackle the complexity of the problem. The scheme makes use of logic rules which improve stability and feasibility of the decentralized method by enforcing coordination. The decentralized control laws which respect the rules are computed using hybrid control design.

1 Introduction

Past years have seen a significant interest in techniques for analyzing and controlling hybrid systems. For certain classes of hybrid systems, it is possible to solve control problems, to compute reachability and invariant sets and to verify properties such as stability, controllability and observability [1, 2, 3, 4, 5, 6]. Large part of current research is focused on exploring new methods, theory and algorithms which are applicable to larger classes of systems and under less restrictive assumptions. Recently, we have started to explore the use of current results in hybrid control methodologies in order to simplify the design of controllers for large scale dynamical systems.

Motivated by three applications which are under investigation at the Honeywell Research Laboratory, we present a class of large scale control problems and show how hybrid control can help in designing decentralized control strategies. The three applications share the following characteristics: (i) they involve large number of subsystems (order of hundreds) which can be independently actuated, (ii) the subsystems are dynamically decoupled, (iii) the control objective can only be achieved through a collective behavior, and (iv) the feasible

M. Morari and L. Thiele (Eds.): HSCC 2005, LNCS 3414, pp. 168–183, 2005.
© Springer-Verlag Berlin Heidelberg 2005

set of states of each subsystem is a function of other subsystems' states. These applications fall under the general class of optimal control problems for a set of decoupled dynamical systems where cost function and constraints couple the dynamical behavior of the systems.

The interest in decentralized control goes back to the seventies. Wang and Davison were probably the first in [7] to envision the "increasing interest in decentralized control systems..." when "...control theory is applied to solve problems for large scale systems". Decentralized control techniques today can be found in a broad spectrum of applications ranging from robotics and formation flight to civil engineering. Such a wide interest makes a survey of all the approaches that have appeared in the literature very difficult and goes also beyond the scope of this paper. Approaches to decentralized control design differ from each other in the assumptions they make on: (i) the kind of interaction between different systems or different components of the same system (dynamics, constraints, objective), (ii) the model of the system (linear, nonlinear, constrained, continuous-time, discrete-time), (iii) the model of information exchange between the systems, and (iv) the control design technique used.

The ubiquity of sensor and actuator networks has been envisioned several years ago [8]. The main focus of this paper is to propose a decentralized control design technique which can be very efficient when hybrid control methodologies are used. In this paper we focus on *decoupled systems*. The problem of decentralized control for decoupled systems can be formulated as follows. A dynamical system is composed of (or can be decomposed into) distinct dynamical subsystems that can be independently actuated. The subsystems are dynamically decoupled but have common objectives and constraints which make them interact between each other. Typically the *interaction* is local, i.e. the objective and the constraints of a subsystem are function of only a subset of other subsystems' states. The interaction will be represented by an "interaction graph", where the nodes represent the subsystems and an arc between two nodes denotes a coupling term in the objectives and/or in the constraints associated to the nodes. Also, typically it is assumed that the *exchange of information* has a special structure, i.e., it is assumed that each subsystem can sense and/or exchange information with only a subset of other subsystems. Often the *interaction graph* and the *information exchange graph* coincide. A decentralized control scheme consists of distinct controllers, one for each subsystem, where the inputs to each subsystem are computed only based on local information, i.e. on the states of the subsystem and its neighbors.

Due to the complexity of the problem, control of large scale systems is usually approached using decentralization. Along with the benefits of a decentralized design, one has to face inherent issues such as difficulties in ensuring stability and feasibility of the system. *One of the main objectives of this paper is to show how coordination rules can be included in the decentralized control design by using hybrid system techniques.* Such rules improve the overall behavior of the systems and make the control subproblems feasible where traditional design is either infeasible or too conservative. Theoretical proofs of stability and feasibility in such design schemes are under investigation but in general difficult to give. Nevertheless, the benefits and practicality of these techniques have been proven by extensive simulations.

We will formulate hybrid constrained optimal control problems in discrete time [3]. In particular, computational results are obtained by using on-line mixed-integer optimization [3] or the evaluation of an equivalent lookup table obtained by means of parametric programming [9]. However, the main concepts presented in this paper are applicable to any control scheme and design methodology as long as it can cope with continuous dynamics and logic rules.

2   Problem Formulation

Consider a set of N_v linear decoupled dynamical systems, where the i-th system is described by the discrete-time time-invariant state equations:

$$x_{k+1}^i = f^i(x_k^i, u_k^i) \tag{1}$$
$$y_k^i = h^i(x_k^i)$$

where $x_k^i \in \mathbb{R}^{n^i}$, $u_k^i \in \mathbb{R}^{m^i}$, $f^i : \mathbb{R}^{n^i} \times \mathbb{R}^{m^i} \to \mathbb{R}^{n^i}$, $h^i : \mathbb{R}^{n^i} \to \mathbb{R}^{p^i}$ are states, inputs, state update function and output function of the i-th system, respectively. Let $\mathcal{U}^i \subseteq \mathbb{R}^{m^i}$ and $\mathcal{Y}^i \subseteq \mathbb{R}^{p^i}$ denote the set of feasible inputs and outputs of the i-th system

$$y_k^i \in \mathcal{Y}^i, \ u_k^i \in \mathcal{U}^i, \ k \geq 0 \tag{2}$$

where $\mathcal{Y}^i$ and $\mathcal{U}^i$ are given polytopes.

We will refer to the set of N_v constrained systems as *team system*. Let $\tilde{x}_k \in \mathbb{R}^{N_v \times n^i}$ and $\tilde{u}_k \in \mathbb{R}^{N_v \times m^i}$ be the vectors which collect the states and inputs of the team system at time k, i.e. $\tilde{x}_k = [x_k^1, \ldots, x_k^{N_v}]$, $\tilde{u}_k = [u_k^1, \ldots, u_k^{N_v}]$, with

$$\tilde{x}_{k+1} = f(\tilde{x}_k, \tilde{u}_k) \tag{3}$$

We denote by (x_e^i, u_e^i) the equilibrium pair of the i-th system and $(\tilde{x}_e, \tilde{u}_e)$ the corresponding equilibrium for the team system.

So far the individual systems belonging to the team system are completely decoupled. We consider an optimal control problem for the team system where cost function and constraints couple the dynamic behavior of individual systems. We use a graph topology to represent the coupling in the following way. We associate the i-th system to the i-th node of the graph, and if an edge (i,j) connecting the i-th and j-th node is present, then the cost and the constraints of the optimal control problem will have a component which is a function of both x^i and x^j. The graph will be *undirected*, i.e. $(i,j) \in \mathcal{A} \Rightarrow (j,i) \in \mathcal{A}$ and furthermore, the edges representing coupling change with time. Therefore, before defining the optimal control problem, we need to define a graph (which can be time-varying)

$$\mathcal{G}(t) = \{\mathcal{V}, \mathcal{A}(t)\} \tag{4}$$

where $\mathcal{V}$ is the set of nodes $\mathcal{V} = \{1, \ldots, N_v\}$ and $\mathcal{A}(t) \subseteq \mathcal{V} \times \mathcal{V}$ the set of time-varying arcs (i, j) with $i \in \mathcal{V}$, $j \in \mathcal{V}$.

Once the graph has been defined, the optimization problem is formulated as follows. Denote with $\tilde{x}_k^i$ the states of all neighbors of the i-th system at time k, i.e. $\tilde{x}_k^i = \{x_k^j \in \mathbb{R}^{n^j} | (j, i) \in \mathcal{A}(k)\}$, $\tilde{x}_k^i \in \mathbb{R}^{\tilde{n}_k^i}$ with $\tilde{n}_k^i = \sum_{j|(j,i)\in\mathcal{A}(k)} n_k^j$. Analogously, $\tilde{u}_k^i \in \mathbb{R}^{\tilde{m}_k^i}$ denotes the inputs to all the neighbors of the i-th system at time k. Let

$$g^{i,j}(x^i, x^j) \le 0 \tag{5}$$

define interconnection constraints between the i-th and the j-th systems, with $g^{i,j} : \mathbb{R}^{n^i} \times \mathbb{R}^{n^j} \to \mathbb{R}^{nc_{i,j}}$. We will often use the following shorter form of the interconnection constraints defined between the i-th system and all its neighbors:

$$g_k^i(x_k^i, \tilde{x}_k^i) \le 0 \tag{6}$$

with $g_k^i : \mathbb{R}^{n^i} \times \mathbb{R}^{\tilde{n}_k^i} \to \mathbb{R}^{nc_{i,k}}$.

Consider the following cost

$$l(\tilde{x}, \tilde{u}) = \sum_{i=1}^{N_v} l_k^i(x^i, u^i, \tilde{x}_k^i, \tilde{u}_k^i) \tag{7}$$

where $l^i : \mathbb{R}^{n^i} \times \mathbb{R}^{m^i} \times \mathbb{R}^{\tilde{n}_k^i} \times \mathbb{R}^{\tilde{m}_k^i} \to \mathbb{R}$ is the cost associated to the i-th system and is a function of its states and the states of its neighbor nodes. Assume that l is a positive convex function with $l(\tilde{x}_e, \tilde{u}_e) = 0$.

Consider the infinite time optimal control problem

$$\tilde{J}_\infty^*(\tilde{x}) \triangleq \min_{\{\tilde{u}_0, \tilde{u}_1, \ldots\}} \sum_{k=0}^{\infty} l(\tilde{x}_k, \tilde{u}_k) \tag{8a}$$

$$\text{subj. to} \begin{cases} x_{k+1}^i = f^i(x_k^i, u_k^i), \\ y_k^i = h^i(x_k^i), \\ \quad i = 1, \ldots, N_v, \quad k \ge 0 \\ g^{i,j}(x_k^i, x_k^j) \le 0, \\ \quad i = 1, \ldots, N_v, \quad k \ge 0, \\ \quad (i, j) \in \mathcal{A}(k) \\ y_k^i \in \mathcal{Y}^i, \quad u_k^i \in \mathcal{U}^i, \\ \quad i = 1, \ldots, N_v, \quad k \ge 0 \\ \tilde{x}_0 = \tilde{x} \end{cases} \tag{8b}$$

For all $\tilde{x} \in \mathbb{R}^{N_v \times n^i}$, if problem (8) is feasible, then the optimal input $\tilde{u}_0^*, \tilde{u}_1^*, \ldots$ will drive the N_v systems to their equilibrium points x_e^i while satisfying state, input and interconnection constraints.

Remark 1. Since we assumed that the graph is undirected, there will be redundant constraints in problem (8). Note the form of constraints (6) is rather general and it will include the case when only partial information about states of neighboring nodes is involved.

With the exception of a few cases, solving an infinite horizon optimal control problem is computationally prohibitive. An infinite horizon controller can be designed by repeatedly solving finite time optimal control problems in a receding horizon fashion as described next. At each sampling time, starting at the current state, an open-loop optimal control problem is solved over a finite horizon. The optimal command signal is applied to the process only during the following sampling interval. At the next time step a new optimal control problem based on new measurements of the state is solved over a shifted horizon. The resultant controller is often referred to as Receding Horizon Controller (RHC). Assume at time t the current state $\tilde{x}_t$ to be available. Consider the following constrained finite time optimal control problem

$$\tilde{J}_N^*(\tilde{x}_t) \triangleq \min_{\{U_t\}} \sum_{k=0}^{N-1} l(\tilde{x}_{k,t}, \tilde{u}_{k,t}) + l_N(\tilde{x}_{N,t}) \tag{9a}$$

$$\text{subj. to} \begin{cases} x_{k+1,t}^i = f^i(x_{k,t}^i, u_{k,t}^i), \\ \quad y_{k,t}^i = h^i(x_{k,t}^i), \\ \quad\quad i = 1, \ldots, N_v, \quad k \geq 0 \\ g^{i,j}(x_{k,t}^i, x_{k,t}^j) \leq 0, \\ \quad\quad i = 1, \ldots, N_v, \quad (i,j) \in \mathcal{A}(t), \\ \quad\quad k = 1, \ldots, N-1 \\ y_{k,t}^i \in \mathcal{Y}^i, \quad u_{k,t}^i \in \mathcal{U}^i \\ \quad\quad i = 1, \ldots, N_v, \\ \quad\quad k = 1, \ldots, N-1 \\ \tilde{x}_{N,t} \in \mathcal{X}_f, \\ \tilde{x}_{0,t} = \tilde{x}_t \end{cases} \tag{9b}$$

where N is the prediction horizon, $\mathcal{X}_f \subseteq \mathbb{R}^{N_v \times n^i}$ is a terminal region, l_N is the cost on the terminal state. In (9) we denote with $U_t \triangleq [\tilde{u}_{0,t}, \ldots, \tilde{u}_{N-1,t}]' \in \mathbb{R}^s$, $s \triangleq N_v \times mN$ the optimization vector, $x_{k,t}^i$ denotes the state vector of the i-th node predicted at time $t+k$ obtained by starting from the state x_t^i and applying to system (1) the input sequence $u_{0,t}^i, \ldots, u_{k-1,t}^i$. The tilded vectors will denote the prediction vectors associated to the team system.

Let $U_t^* = \{\tilde{u}_{0,t}^*, \ldots, \tilde{u}_{N-1,t}^*\}$ be the optimal solution of (9) at time t and $\tilde{J}_N^*(\tilde{x}_t)$ the corresponding value function. Then, the first sample of U_t^* is applied to the team system (3)

$$\tilde{u}_t = \tilde{u}_{0,t}^*. \tag{10}$$

The optimization (9) is repeated at time $t+1$, based on the new state x_{t+1}.

It is well known that stability is not ensured by the RHC law (9)–(10). Usually the terminal cost l_N and the terminal constraint set $\mathcal{X}_f$ are chosen to ensure closed-loop stability. A treatment of sufficient stability conditions goes beyond the scope of this work and can be found in the survey [10]. We assume that the reader is familiar with the basic concept of RHC and its main issues, we refer to [10] for a comprehensive treatment of the topic. In this paper we will assume that terminal cost l_N and the terminal constraint set $\mathcal{X}_f$ can be appropriately chosen in order to ensure the stability of the closed-loop system.

In general, the optimal input u_t^i to the i-th system computed by solving (9) at time t, will be a function of the overall state information $\tilde{x}_t$.

3   Motivating Examples

In this section we present three distinct applications that represent the class of systems and control problems studied in this manuscript. All the examples involve a significant number of subsystems for which the coupling cost and constraints are formulated in different ways. Next we discuss the main features of each problem and refer the reader to appropriate publications for complete details. More details can be found in [11].

3.1   OAV Formation Flight

Formation flight can be viewed as a large control problem which computes the control inputs to Unmanned Aerial Vehicles (UAVs) in order to fly challenging maneuvers while maintaining relative positions as well as safe distances between each UAV pair.

Centralized and decentralized optimal control has been the most successful technique to formulate and tackle such a problem [12, 13, 14, 15]. Centralized optimal or suboptimal approaches have been used in different studies. However, as the number of UAVs increases, the solution of big, centralized, non-convex optimization problems becomes prohibitive, even having the most advanced optimization solver, or using oversimplified linear vehicle dynamics. Decentralized control for UAV formation flight with collision avoidance guarantees is attracting significant research interest and is currently a very active area within the aerospace control field.

Honeywell Research Laboratory in Minneapolis is studying formation flight for a scalable autonomous ducted-fan UAV called Organic Air Vehicle (OAV). The OAV is a highly nonlinear, constrained multi-input, multi-output (MIMO) system. OAV formation flight is a complex task which is rendered tractable via a hierarchical decomposition of the problem. In such a decomposition, the lower level is made up of the OAV dynamics equipped with efficient guidance and control loops. At the higher level, the controlled OAV can be represented sufficiently well as a constrained MIMO linear system where the inputs to the system dynamics are accelerations along the N, E, h-axes, and the states are velocities and positions along the N, E, h-axes.

Future scenarios will implement hundreds of OAVs flying in formation. Detailed information about the OAV and an exhaustive list of references to formation flight can be found in [16]. The main message of this section is that OAV formation flight falls in the class of problems (8) where f^i and h^i model the high-level dynamics of the i-th OAV. The cost function will depend on the formation's mission and will include terms that minimize relative distances and/or velocities between neighboring vehicles. The coupling constraints arise from collision avoidance. The interaction graph is full (each vehicle has to avoid all other vehicles) but it is often approximated with a time-varying graph based on a "closest spatial neighbors" model. In summary, the formation flight application example is identified by the following characteristics

- *Subsystems*: Independently actuated, decoupled vehicle dynamics with acceleration inputs along the N, E, h-axes. The states of each vehicle represent velocities and positions along the N, E, h-axes.
- *Subsystem Constraints*: Bounds on speed and acceleration of the vehicles.
- *Interaction Constraints*: Collision avoidance constraints between vehicles.
- *Objective Function*: Minimization of relative distance and absolute position errors in order to achieve a desired formation and arrive at a specified target, respectively.
- *Graph*: Time-varying graph based on a "closest spatial neighbors" model.

3.2   Paper Machine

The papermaking process employs large arrays of actuators spread across a continuously moving web to control the cross-directional (CD) profiles of the paper properties as measured by a scanning gauge downstream from the actuators. A CD control system calculates actuator moves to maintain the measured CD profiles of paper properties on target. An overview of industrial CD control systems can be found in [17]. The wet pulp slurry enters the machine where it is distributed over a wide area and forced through a gap governed by the slice lip where it is extruded onto a moving wire screen. The rest of the paper machine first drains then dries the majority of the water from the pulp and a formed sheet of paper is rolled up. The three main properties of interest are weight, moisture, and caliper. We will consider the CD weight control problem using a slice lip actuator array. CD control of the weight of a paper sheet is accomplished by actuators at the headbox. The function of weight control actuators is to achieve an even distribution of the pulp fibers across the width of the wire belt, despite changing pulp properties. In a typical industrial CD control system controller computations are performed at the spatial resolution of the actuator profile. Such profiles have from 30 up to 300 elements, corresponding to the number of actuators. The measurement signals are obtained from the scanning sensor at a much higher spatial resolution with up to 2000 elements.

The dynamics of each actuator in the headbox is modeled as a first order system with deadtime. The deadtime models the transport delay equivalent to the time taken for the paper to travel from the actuators to the scanning sensor. The model of each actuator system is described by the linear state update function

$$x_{k+1}^i = Ax_k^i + Bu_k^i \tag{11}$$

where x_k^i represents the position of the i-th actuator at time k and at previous time instants $k-1, \ldots, k-p$ (where p is the order of the deadtime), and u_k^i is the desired position of the actuators. The output y_k^j is the weight measured by the j-th sensor

$$y_k^j = C\tilde{x}_k + Dd_k^j \tag{12}$$

and it is ideally a function of all the actuator positions. The overall system model includes additive disturbances $d_k^1, \ldots, d_k^m$, which act on the measurements and represent an inhomogeneous pulp weight distribution. Typically, the impulse response of individual actuators, also known as the cross-directional (CD) bump response is much narrower than the width of the paper sheet. This implies that y_k^j is a function of spatially "close" actuators only. Denoting the set of such actuators with $\mathcal{S}^j$, the output equation can be written as

$$y_k^j = \sum_{l \in \mathcal{S}^j} C_l \tilde{x}_{l,k} + Dd_k^j \tag{13}$$

where C_l is the l-th element of the row vector C. An important factor in CD control is the presence of actuator constraints, which represent maximum-minimum actuator positions and the presence of limits on relative positions between neighboring actuators. This latter restricts the bending of the slice lip (i.e. neighboring actuator positions cannot be too far from each other).

The control problem can be arranged in the form (8) by considering independent actuator dynamics and an objective function which minimizes the error between the desired and actual paper weight profile. In summary, the paper machine application example can be described by the following features

- *Subsystems*: Independently actuated elements along the slice lip profile in the paper headbox, where the inputs are the desired actuator movements and the outputs are the actual actuator positions.
- *Subsystem Constraints*: Bounds on actuator positions.
- *Interaction Constraints*: Bounded deviation between neighboring valve movements to prevent excessive bending and eventual breaking of the slice lip profile.
- *Objective Function*: Tracking of paper weight profiles in the presence of changing pulp properties. The paper weight measured by downstream sensors is a function of neighboring actuator positions.
- *Graph*: Depending on the bending restrictions for the slice lip, a time-invariant line graph or n closest neighbor interconnection gives the underlying topology such as the one shown in Figure 1.

Fig. 1. Typical interconnection topology in the paper machine example

3.3   Monitoring Network of Cameras

Monitoring and surveillance in public areas is nowadays accomplished by using a plethora of cameras. As an example, main international airports can be equipped with more than hundreds of cameras. Future monitored areas will be outfitted with fixed wide-angle cameras and "Pan-Tilt-Zoom" (PTZ) cameras which can communicate within a distributed network. These two types of cameras can be used to achieve different goals such as identifying multiple targets or identifying details on a moving target (e.g. the faces of several walking persons or the numberplates on moving cars). Pan, tilt and zoom factors can be controlled by PTZ cameras in order to achieve the desired goals. The accuracy and precision of the captured detail will depend on properties such as size, position and speed of the moving objects. These properties are better tracked by the wide-angle cameras. The goal is to design control strategies for achieving "good" tracking of the details.

The controller receives information about size, position and speed of the objects from wide-angle cameras and information about the current tracking accuracy and quality of the zoomed images from PTZ cameras. Based on such information, pan, tilt and zoom factors will be commanded to achieve optimal multi-objective tracking. In such a scenario, PTZ cameras are independently actuated systems, which need to cooperate to achieve a certain goal. (A typical example is tracking a walking person through the rooms and floors of a building). The interaction constraints between cameras will ensure that the orientation and zooming factors of neighboring cameras do not create a blind spot allowing unmonitored intrusion into the environment. The characteristics of problem (8) are easily identified for this example as well

- *Subsystems*: Independently actuated cameras where Pan, Tilt and Zooming factors are controlled.
- *Subsystem Constraints*: Physical PTZ ranges of cameras.
- *Interaction Constraints*: Relative orientation and zooming factors have to be constrained to avoid (or minimize the size of) blind spots in a given area.
- *Objective Function*: Tracking of multiple targets and details on a target.
- *Graph*: The graph connection will depend on the physical position of cameras. Cameras in two adjacent rooms need to exchange information if the rooms can be accessed from each other. There will be no need for communication if the rooms are far away and on different floors.

4   Decentralized Control Scheme

The previous examples are all characterized by the presence of a large number of states (on the order of hundreds). We tackle the complexity associated to the design of controllers for such class of large scale systems by using decentralized optimal control schemes. In this section we present a possible way to decentralize the RHC problem in (9). In Section 5 we show how feasibility and stability can be practically improved by using coordination rules. Decentralization of RHC problems raises issues of stability and feasibility to be addressed, which are topics of current research in decentralized control design [18, 19, 20, 21, 22, 23].

As presented in the preliminary study [21], we decompose problem (9) into N_v finite time optimal control problems, each one associated to a different node as detailed next. Each node has information about its current states and its neighbors' current states. Based on such information, each node computes its optimal inputs and its neighbors' optimal inputs. The input to the neighbors will only be used to predict their trajectories and then discarded, while the first component of the optimal input to the node will be implemented where it was computed.

Considering the overall problem description given by systems (1), graph $\mathcal{G}(t)$, and RHC policy (9)-(10), let the following finite time optimal control problem $\mathcal{P}_i(t)$ be associated to the i-th system at time t

$$\min_{\tilde{U}_t^i} \sum_{k=0}^{N-1} l_t^i(x_{k,t}^i, u_{k,t}^i, \tilde{x}_{k,t}^i, \tilde{u}_{k,t}^i) + l_N^i(x_{N,t}^i, \tilde{x}_{N,t}^i) \tag{14a}$$

$$\text{subj. to } x_{k+1,t}^i = f^i(x_{k,t}^i, u_{k,t}^i), \tag{14b}$$

$$y_{k,t}^i = h^i(x_{k,t}^i), \quad k \geq 0$$

$$y_{k,t}^i \in \mathcal{Y}^i, \quad u_{k,t}^i \in \mathcal{U}^i, \tag{14c}$$

$$k = 1, \ldots, N - 1$$

$$x_{k+1,t}^j = f^j(x_{k,t}^j, u_{k,t}^j), \quad (j, i) \in \mathcal{A}(t), \tag{14d}$$

$$y_{k,t}^j = h^j(x_{k,t}^j), \quad k \geq 0$$

$$y_{k,t}^j \in \mathcal{Y}^i, \quad u_{k,t}^j \in \mathcal{U}^j, \quad (j, i) \in \mathcal{A}(t), \tag{14e}$$

$$k = 1, \ldots, N - 1$$

$$g^{i,j}(x_{k,t}^i, u_{k,t}^i, x_{k,t}^j, u_{k,t}^j) \leq 0, \quad (i, j) \in \mathcal{A}(t), \tag{14f}$$

$$k = 1, \ldots, N - 1$$

$$g^{q,r}(x_{k,t}^q, u_{k,t}^q, x_{k,t}^r, u_{k,t}^r) \leq 0, \tag{14g}$$

$$(q, i) \in \mathcal{A}(t), \quad (r, i) \in \mathcal{A}(t),$$

$$k = 1, \ldots, N - 1$$

$$x_{N,t}^i \in \mathcal{X}_f^i, \quad x_{N,t}^j \in \mathcal{X}_f^j, \quad (i, j) \in \mathcal{A}(t) \tag{14h}$$

$$x_{0,t}^i = x_t^i, \quad \tilde{x}_{0,t}^i = \tilde{x}_t^i \tag{14i}$$

where $\tilde{U}_t^i \triangleq [u_{0,t}^i, \tilde{u}_{0,t}^i, \ldots, u_{N-1,t}^i, \tilde{u}_{N-1,t}^i]' \in \mathbb{R}^s$, $s \triangleq (\tilde{m}^i + m^i)N$ denotes the optimization vector, $x_{k,t}^i$ denotes the state vector of the i-th node predicted at time $t + k$ obtained by starting from the state x_t^i and applying to system (1) the input sequence $u_{0,t}^i, \ldots, u_{k-1,t}^i$. The tilded vectors denote the prediction vectors associated to the neighboring systems *assuming a constant interconnection graph*. Denote by $\tilde{U}_t^{i*} = [u_{0,t}^{*i}, \tilde{u}_{0,t}^{*i}, \ldots, u_{N-1,t}^{*i}, \tilde{u}_{N-1,t}^{*i}]$ the optimizer of problem $\mathcal{P}_i(t)$. Note that problem $\mathcal{P}_i(t)$ involves only the state and input variables of the i-th node and its neighbors at time t.

We will define the following decentralized RHC control scheme. At time t

1. Compute graph connection $\mathcal{A}(t)$ according to a chosen policy.
2. Each node i solves problem $\mathcal{P}_i(t)$ based on measurements of its state x_t^i and the states of all its neighbors $\tilde{x}_t^i$.
3. Each node i implements the first sample of $\tilde{U}_t^{i*}$

$$u_t^i = u_{0,t}^{*i}. \tag{15}$$

4. Each node repeats steps 1 to 4 at time $t + 1$, based on the new state information x_{t+1}^i, $\tilde{x}_{t+1}^i$.

In order to solve problem $\mathcal{P}_i(t)$ each node needs to know its current states, its neighbors' current states, its terminal region, its neighbors' terminal regions and models and constraints of its neighbors. Based on such information each node computes its optimal inputs and its neighbors' optimal inputs assuming a constant set of neighbors over the horizon. The input to the neighbors will only be used to predict their trajectories and then discarded, while the first component of the i-th optimal input of problem $\mathcal{P}_i(t)$ will be implemented on the i-th node. The solution of the i-th subproblem will yield a control policy for the i-th node of the form $u_t^i = k_t^i(x_t^i, \tilde{x}_t^i)$.

Even if we assume N to be infinite, the decentralized RHC approach described so far does not guarantee that solutions computed locally are globally feasible and stable (i.e. feasible for problem (9)). The reason is simple: At the i-th node the prediction of the neighboring state x^j is done independently from the prediction of problem $\mathcal{P}_j(t)$. Therefore, the trajectory of x^j predicted by problem $\mathcal{P}_i(t)$ and the one predicted by problem $\mathcal{P}_j(t)$, based on the same initial conditions, are different (since in general, $\mathcal{P}_i(t)$ and $\mathcal{P}_j(t)$ will be different). This will imply that constraint fulfillment will be ensured by the optimizer u_t^{*i} for problem $\mathcal{P}_i(t)$ but not for the overall problem (9).

A detailed discussion on feasibility and stability issues of decentralized RHC schemes goes beyond the scope of this paper. Some important observations can be found in [21, 19, 18, 20]. The main research topics include: (i) the choice of the graph topology when it is not fixed or unique, (ii) the choice of local prediction horizons, terminal weights and terminal regions and its effect on the global performance and feasibility.

5   Application of Hybrid Theory in Decentralized Control

In general, it is very difficult to provide feasibility guarantees in a constrained decentralized control problem. Nevertheless everyday life is full of decentralized control problems. Although feasible solutions are not always found or even possible at all, these problems are solved day-by-day relying on certain rules that help coordinate the single subsystem efforts. Examples range from traffic laws to behavior of individuals in a community.

This suggests that it can be beneficial to make use of coordination rules in some decentralized engineering control problems as well. Hybrid control design techniques are able to cope with the hybrid nature of a problem governed by differential equations and logic rules. For this reason we investigate the benefits of hybrid system techniques in implementing coordination rules within the decentralized control framework presented in Section 4. A more formal discussion follows.

We define a *rule element* to be a Boolean-valued function operating on the states of a node and its neighbors' states

$$\varrho \ : \ (x^i, \tilde{x}^i) \to X, \quad X = \{true, false\}. \tag{16}$$

We define a *rule* to be a propositional logic statement involving rule elements

$$\mathcal{R} \ : \ (\varrho_1, \varrho_1, \dots, \varrho_{n-1}) \to X, \quad X = \{true, false\}. \tag{17}$$

The logic statement $\mathcal{R}$ is a combination of "not" ($\neg$), "and" ($\wedge$), "or" ($\vee$), "exclusive or" ($\oplus$), "implies" ($\to$), and "iff" ($\leftrightarrow$) operators. For instance, the following logic expression of

$$\mathcal{R}(X_1, \dots, X_{n-1}) \leftrightarrow X_n \tag{18}$$

involving Boolean variables $X_1, \dots, X_n$ can be expressed equivalently with its conjunctive normal form (CNF)

$$\bigwedge_{j=1}^{k} \left(\left(\bigvee_{i \in P_j} X_i \right) \vee \left(\bigvee_{i \in N_j} \neg X_i \right) \right), \quad N_j, P_j \subseteq \{1, \dots, n\}. \tag{19}$$

The rule holds and its value is "true" if the statement is evaluated as true based on the rule elements. The rule is not respected and its value is "false" when the underlying statement is false.

We introduce two abstract function classes called *coordinating functions*, which operate on a set of rules and the states of a node and its neighbors

$$\mathscr{F}_c^{\mathcal{C}} \ : \ (\mathfrak{R}, x^i, \tilde{x}^i) \to \mathbb{R} \tag{20}$$

$$\mathscr{F}_c^{bin} \ : \ (\mathfrak{R}, x^i, \tilde{x}^i) \to \{0, 1\} \tag{21}$$

where $\mathfrak{R}$ is a set of rules defined in (17). The coordinating functions can be defined to have either continuous or binary values. These function classes rely on rules and states of the system and can be included in the cost function ($\mathscr{F}_c^{\mathcal{C}}$) or constraints ($\mathscr{F}_c^{bin}$) of subproblems. This means that the decentralized problem (14) is modified in the following way

$$\min_{\tilde{U}_t^i} \ J_N^{dec}(x_t^i, \tilde{x}_t^i) + \mathscr{F}_c^{\mathcal{C}}(\mathfrak{R}, x_t^i, \tilde{x}_t^i)$$

$$\text{subj. to} \quad \text{constraints (14b)} - (14i)$$

$$g_c\left(x_{t,k}^i, \tilde{x}_{t,k}^i, \mathscr{F}_c^{bin}(\mathfrak{R}, x_{t,k}^i, \tilde{x}_{t,k}^i)\right) \leq 0, \quad k = 1, \dots, N-1$$

where $J_N^{dec}(x_t^i, \tilde{x}_t^i)$ denotes the cost function in (14a).

If chosen appropriately, coordinating functions have the benefit of guiding towards feasible sequences of decentralized solutions. When $\mathscr{F}_c^C$ is used in the cost function, trajectories which respect rules can be penalized less and have a cost which is less than the cost of trajectories, which do not enforce the rules. When $\mathscr{F}_c^{bin}$ is used in the constraints, the local domain of feasibility is reduced to the domain where only trajectories respecting rules are feasible. A crucial assumption underlying this idea is that each component has to abide by the same or at least similar set of rules.

Remark 2. We point out that the approach of this paper to large-scale control problems is independent of the problem formulation. Continuous-time formulations and other hybrid control design techniques could be used.

Simulation results of the decentralized control scheme applied to the paper machine example are reported in [11] and show that similar performance is achieved compared to a centralized solution.

6   Formation Flight Example

This section presents details of the decentralized control scheme (14)-(15) described in Section 4 applied to the formation flight of vehicles flying at a certain altitude. Each vehicle is modeled as a point mass in two dimensions with constraints on states and inputs. The coupling between vehicles stems from the common objective of the team (moving in formation) and its constraints (vehicles are not allowed to violate each others protection zones). Our intention is to illustrate the use of hybrid system techniques that aid in retaining feasibility of the decentralized scheme.

The autonomous aerial vehicle dynamical model used in this paper reflects the simplified dynamics of the Organic Air Vehicle (OAV) mentioned in Section 3.1. We describe the OAV dynamics by using the following linear discrete-time model

$$x_{k+1} = f(x_k, u_k) \qquad (23)$$

where the state update function $f : \mathbb{R}^6 \times \mathbb{R}^3 \to \mathbb{R}^6$ is a linear function of its inputs and $x_k \in \mathbb{R}^6$, $u_k \in \mathbb{R}^3$ are states and inputs of the vehicle at time k, respectively. In particular,

$$x_k = \begin{bmatrix} x_{k,pos} \\ x_{k,vel} \end{bmatrix}, \quad u = \begin{bmatrix} x\text{-axis acceleration} \\ y\text{-axis acceleration} \\ z\text{-axis acceleration} \end{bmatrix}$$

and $x_{k,pos} \in \mathbb{R}^3$ is the vector of x, y and z coordinates and $x_{k,vel} \in \mathbb{R}^3$ is the vector of x-axis, y-axis and z-axis velocity components at time k. It is important to emphasize that the approach proposed in this paper can easily accommodate higher order, more complex linear or piecewise-linear models that describe the OAV dynamics with higher fidelity.

In order to improve coordination and the likelihood of feasibility of the decentralized scheme, different "right-of-way" priorities can be introduced which allow to have better prediction about neighbors' trajectories. This can be easily achieved if protection zones are modeled as parallelepipeds and the disjunctions are modeled as binary variables. "Right-of-way" priorities can be translated into weights and constraints on the binary variables which describe the location of a vehicle with respect to a parallelepipedal protection zone of another vehicle (six binary variables in three dimensions for each vehicle couple).

The main idea behind inter-vehicle coordination is to make use of "preferred" decisions in the hybrid control problem that arises due to the non-convex collision avoidance constraints. For illustration, consider the following scenario. Assume that protection zones around vehicles are specified as square exclusion regions centered around each vehicle's position as depicted in Figure 2. If the edges of the protection zones are of size p, then collision avoidance can be represented by introducing binary decision variables associated to the feasibility of linear inequalities defined over the system states. Disjunctions of the protection zones can then be easily described by propositional logic statements involving the binary decision variables. This mixture of logic states and dynamics is then modeled in the MLD framework [3] by translating logic relations into mixed-integer linear inequalities. Part of this translation is illustrated in Table 1 for the purpose of describing the idea behind implementing inter-vehicle coordination rules in two dimensions. The superscripts "E, W, N, S" stand for "east", "west", "north" and "south" corresponding to positive x, negative x, positive y and negative y directions, respectively. For instance, the value of the $\delta_{i,j}^N$ variable is true if the i-th vehicle is "north" of the j-th vehicle, or in other words if $y_i - \frac{p}{2} > y_j + \frac{p}{2}$.

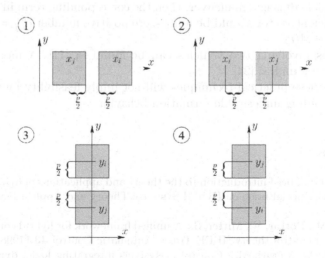

Fig. 2. Square protection exclusion zones

Table 1. Use of binary variables to express disjunctions

Disjunction inequality	Binary variable	Big-M technique
$1: \quad x_i - \frac{p}{2} \geq x_j + \frac{p}{2}$	$\delta_{ij}^E = \begin{cases} 1 \text{ if ineq. TRUE} \\ 0 \text{ if ineq. FALSE} \end{cases}$	$x_j - x_i + p \leq M(1 - \delta_{ij}^E)$ $x_j - x_i + p > m\delta_{ij}^E$
$2: \quad x_i + \frac{p}{2} \leq x_j - \frac{p}{2}$	$\delta_{ij}^W = \begin{cases} 1 \text{ if ineq. TRUE} \\ 0 \text{ if ineq. FALSE} \end{cases}$	$x_i - x_j + p \leq M(1 - \delta_{ij}^W)$ $x_i - x_j + p > m\delta_{ij}^W$
$3: \quad y_i - \frac{p}{2} \geq y_j + \frac{p}{2}$	$\delta_{ij}^N = \begin{cases} 1 \text{ if ineq. TRUE} \\ 0 \text{ if ineq. FALSE} \end{cases}$	$y_j - y_i + p \leq M(1 - \delta_{ij}^N)$ $y_j - y_i + p > m\delta_{ij}^N$
$4: \quad y_i + \frac{p}{2} \leq y_j - \frac{p}{2}$	$\delta_{ij}^S = \begin{cases} 1 \text{ if ineq. TRUE} \\ 0 \text{ if ineq. FALSE} \end{cases}$	$y_i - y_j + p \leq M(1 - \delta_{ij}^S)$ $y_i - y_j + p > m\delta_{ij}^S$

Using the binary variables introduced in Table 1, the condition to be satisfied for avoiding collision is

$$\delta_{ij}^E \text{ OR } \delta_{ij}^W \text{ OR } \delta_{ij}^N \text{ OR } \delta_{ij}^S \tag{24}$$

In order to establish desired coordination rules, we add a linear term of the binary variables in the cost function that penalizes certain undesired relative positions between the i-th vehicle and its neighbors determined by the disjunction associated to a particular binary variable.

For instance, if we would like to penalize having neighbors to the "east" side of the i-th vehicle during a maneuver, then the corresponding term in the binary variable coefficient vector should be a non-zero positive number $c_{i,j}^\delta = [* \ 0 \ 0 \ 0]$ for all $j|(i,j) \in \mathcal{A}(t)$.

Simulations involving two vehicles can be found in [11]. A more complex example can be found at [24].

Note that these practical techniques will not imply feasibility by themselves but help in avoiding undesirable formation behavior.

References

1. Antsaklis, P.: A brief introduction to the theory and applications of hybrid systems. Proc. IEEE, Special Issue on Hybrid Systems: Theory and Applications **88** (2000) 879–886
2. Branicky, M., Borkar, V., Mitter, S.: A unified framework for hybrid control: model and optimal control theory. IEEE Trans. Automatic Control **43** (1998) 31–45
3. Bemporad, A., Morari, M.: Control of systems integrating logic, dynamics, and constraints. Automatica **35** (1999) 407–427
4. Lygeros, J., Tomlin, C., Sastry, S.: Controllers for reachability specifications for hybrid systems. Automatica **35** (1999) 349–370

5. Tomlin, C., Mitchell, I., Bayen, A., Oishi, M.: Computational techniques for the verification of hybrid systems. Proceedings of the IEEE **91** (2003) 986–1001
6. Bemporad, A., Ferrari-Trecate, G., Morari, M.: Observability and controllability of piecewise affine and hybrid systems. IEEE Trans. Automatic Control **45** (2000) 1864–1876
7. Wang, S., Davison, E.J.: On the stabilization of decentralized control systems. IEEE Trans. Automatic Control **18** (1973) 473–478
8. Murray, E.R.M.: Control in an Information Rich World: Future Directions in Control, Dynamics, and Systems. SIAM, (to appear) (2003)
9. Borrelli, F.: Constrained Optimal Control of Linear and Hybrid Systems. Volume 290 of Lecture Notes in Control and Information Sciences. Springer (2003)
10. Mayne, D., Rawlings, J., Rao, C., Scokaert, P.: Constrained model predictive control: Stability and optimality. Automatica **36** (2000) 789–814
11. Borrelli, F., Keviczky, T.: Hybrid decentralized control of large scale systems. Technical report, Università del Sannio. Benevento (IT). (2004, Downloadable at http://www.ing.unisannio.it/grace/HomepageFB/HSCC05Full.pdf)
12. Stipanovic, D., Inalhan, G., Teo, R., Tomlin, C.J.: Decentralized overlapping control of a formation of unmanned aerial vehicles. Automatica **40** (2004) 1285–1296
13. Richards, A., Bellingham, J., Tillerson, M., How, J.P.: Coordination and control of multiple uavs. In: AIAA Guidance, Navigation, and Control Conference, Monterey, CA. (2002)
14. Shim, D., Kim, H., Sastry, S.: Decentralized reflective model predictive control of multiple flying robots in dynamic enviroment. Technical report, Department of Electical Engineering and Computer Sciences. University of California at Berkeley (2003)
15. Dunbar, W.B., Murray, R.M.: Model predictive control of coordinated multi-vehicle formation. In: Proc. 41th IEEE Conf. on Decision and Control. (2002)
16. Fregene, K., Borrelli, F.: OAV formation flight: a decentralized optimization based approach. Technical report, Honeywell Laboratories, Minneapolis (2004, Downloadable at http://www.aem.umn.edu/people/others/borrelli)
17. Stewart, G.E., Gorinevsky, D.M., Dumont, G.A.: Feedback controller design for a spatially distributed system: The paper machine problem. IEEE Trans. Control Systems Technology **11** (2003) 612–628
18. Camponogara, E., Jia, D., Krogh, B., Talukdar, S.: Distributed model predictive control. IEEE Control Systems Magazine (2002)
19. Dunbar, W.B., Murray, R.M.: Receding horizon control of multi-vehicle formations: A distributed implementation. In: Proc. 43th IEEE Conf. on Decision and Control. (2004)
20. Richards, A., How, J.: A decentralized algorithm for robust constrained model predictive control. In: Proc. American Contr. Conf. (2004)
21. Keviczky, T., Borrelli, F., Balas, G.J.: A study on decentralized receding horizon control for decoupled systems. In: Proc. American Contr. Conf. (2004)
22. Keviczky, T., Borrelli, F., Balas, G.J.: Hierarchical design of decentralized receding horizon controllers for decoupled systems. In: Proc. 43th IEEE Conf. on Decision and Control. (2004)
23. Borrelli, F., Keviczky, T., Balas, G.J.: Collision-free UAV formation flight using decentralized optimization and invariant sets. In: Proc. 43th IEEE Conf. on Decision and Control. (2004)
24. Online: http://www.aem.umn.edu/people/others/borrelli/ff.htm (2004)

On the Stabilisation of Switching Electrical Power Converters

Jean Buisson, Pierre-Yves Richard, and Hervé Cormerais

Hybrid System Group, Supélec-IETR, Avenue de la Boulaie,
35511 Cesson Sévigné, France
Jean.Buisson@rennes.supelec.fr
http://www.supelec.fr

Abstract. This paper considers the control of switching power converters which are a particular class of hybrid systems. Such systems, which are controlled by switches, can be modeled using physical principles. Taking advantage of the energetical properties of their models, a Lyapunov function is proposed. This function, which has not to be computed but is systematically deduced from the physical model, allows to derive different stabilizing switching sequences. From a theoretical point of view, asymptotic stability can be obtained, but it requires null intervals between switching times. In order to ensure a minimum time between switchings, this Lyapunov function has to be increasing for a small duration by using a delay or a dead zone. A control law principle that guarantees the invariance of a specified domain with respect to state trajectories is proposed. Two examples are provided at the end of this paper that demonstrate the efficiency of the proposed approach.

1 Introduction

Devices like power converters (Boost, Buck, Ćuk, multilevel converters) are widespread industrial devices. They are used in many applications such as variable speed DC motor drives, computer power supply, cell phone and cameras. Those devices are electrical circuits controlled by switches (transistors, diodes). Aiming at reducing switching losses and EMI (Electromagnetic Interference) of power converters, a lot of soft switching techniques are developed so that high efficiency, small size and low weight can be achieved. When they are operating in normal conditions, those circuits have been designed and switches are used in such a way that there is no discontinuity. Those devices are good candidate for hybrid modelling, analysis and control. In this context, they can be modelled by switched systems (without jump).

Those systems have received the attention of many researchers in the area of control and hybrid systems. Some approaches use continuous models. From a practical point of view, those devices are often controlled through a Pulse-Width-Modulation (PWM). The models of power converters associated to PWM can be approximated by an average model [1] [2], which is often non-linear. Continuous control approaches are then used [2], some of them based on physical

M. Morari and L. Thiele (Eds.): HSCC 2005, LNCS 3414, pp. 184–197, 2005.

principles such as passivity based control [3], which takes into account energy dissipation properties to design the controller. Sliding mode has also been used to control such systems. This technique uses a high speed switched control law to drive state trajectories onto a specified manifold and then maintains them on this manifold for all susbequent time. Associated control actions can be either piecewise continuous, requiring a PWM regulation scheme, or directly boolean [2], [4], [3].

In [5], a Lyapunov approach is proposed in order to generate a stabilizing continuous control. The associated Lyapunov function is obtained through a constructive procedure requiring a partial differential equation to be solved. This approach is restricted to non-singular systems.

A hybrid approach is proposed in [6] where the continuous model is discretized. The PWM period is divided in N subperiods allowing to take into account the model switching during the period. A N-step model allows describing more precisely the state evolution during a period. The MLD framework is used and a model predictive control is applied.

In [7] the circuit is modelled with a general piecewise affine model (PWA). A hybrid automaton is used to take into account the control: guards are designed in order to guarantee that the state trajectories will remain in a safe ball centered on the set point. An iterative numerical algorithm is proposed to compute the maximum radius of a ball such that at the boundary of the ball, control action can force the trajectory to go inside the ball. To solve this problem, a grid is defined on the ball boundary.

Studies on stability and stabilization of hybrid systems are mainly based on the establishment of common or multiple Lyapunov functions, either in a continuous time [8], [9] or in a discrete time [9] context. Those functions are generally computed using a linear matrix inequality (LMI) problem formulation [8]. However most of those works are concerned with free linear systems or with systems sharing a common equilibrium. The systems studied here present a common characteristic: in their different operating modes they have no common equilibrium or no equilibrium. However, with a suitable control, they can exhibit a behaviour similar to those of conventional stable systems near equilibrium. The case of switched systems with no common equilibrium point may be dealt with, using the concept of practical stability where the objective is to bring the system trajectories to stay within given boundaries. In [10] a necessary and sufficient condition for practical stabilizability of integrator switched systems is proposed. Those results are extended to more general systems in [11] where a sufficient condition is established and a switching law is built.

The approach proposed in this paper is a hybrid one based on physical considerations. The objective is to design a Lyapunov function, which allows defining switching sequences to stabilize such systems around prescribed references, which are not equilibrium points for all the configurations. The paper is organized in the following way: in Section 2 the characteristics of the models for the class of systems under consideration are presented. Section 3 presents the main contribution of this paper, which is the definition of the references and of a common

Lyapunov function that has not to be computed but is directly deduced from the physical model. Different state feedback control laws based on this function are proposed in section 4, and the problem of parameter uncertainties is also addressed. Section 5 presents two examples, the Buck-Boost and the 3-level converters, illustrating the approach. Finally, in section 6 conclusion and further research directions are discussed.

2   Models of the Systems with Switching Power Converters

The systems under consideration are electrical or electromechanical systems, including electrical power converters, which are used to adapt the energy supplied by a power source to a load. Those systems include power sources, energy storage elements (inductances or capacitors), dissipative elements (resistances), transformers, gyrators and switching components. In the following, the storage and dissipative elements are supposed to be linear and the transformers and gyrators are supposed to be constant. The physical switches are considered to be ideal: in the state *on*, their voltage is null and in the state *off*, their current is null. In most of those systems, physical switches are associated by pairs. In each pair, one physical switch is controlled (e.g. transistor) while the other one may be not (e.g. diode). In a normal operating mode both physical switches commutate at the same time. Their association constitutes a commutation cell, which will be called switch in the following.

In order to derive models for physical systems, different energy based approaches, such as circuit theory, bond graphs [12], Euler Lagrange, Hamiltonian approach [13] can be used. For switching systems, extensions have been proposed in [14] for the Hamiltonian approach or in [15] [16] among many other references for the bond graph approach.

If storage elements are independent, all those approaches can lead, for one mode, to model (1), which is called "port controlled Hamiltonian systems with dissipation" [14].

$$\dot{x} = (J - R)z + gu \qquad (1)$$

Vector $u \in \mathbb{R}^m$ corresponds to the energy sources which are generally either constant in DC-DC or DC-AC converters or sinusoidal in AC-DC or AC-AC converters. This vector is supposed constant in the following. Vector $x \in \mathbb{R}^n$ is the state vector and n is the number of energy storage elements. State variables are the energy variables (fluxes linkage in the inductors, charges in the capacitors), $z \in \mathbb{R}^n$ is the co-state vector. Co-state variables are the corresponding coenergy variables (currents, voltages). In the case where the components are linear, the relation between those two vectors is given by:

$$z = Fx \qquad (2)$$

where $F = F^T \succ 0$. In simple cases, F is a diagonal matrix the elements of which are the inverse of the values of capacitances or inductances. The quantity

$\dot{x}^T z$ represents the power entering the storage elements. The energy, which is stored in the system, can be expressed as:

$$E(x) = \tfrac{1}{2}\, x^T F x \qquad (3)$$

Both $n \times n$ matrices J and R are called structure matrices. Matrix J is skew symetric, $J = -J^T$; it corresponds to a power continuous interconnection in the network model. Matrix R is nonnegative; it corresponds to the energy dissipating part of the circuit.

For any other mode, as physical switches commutate by pairs, storage elements are still independent and the state and costate keep the same components. It also results that, for those systems, there is no jump on state variable when switching [15]. Those hybrid systems can be considered from the hybrid point of view as switching systems. As J, R and g may depend upon the mode, the model can be expressed as:

$$\dot{x} = (J(\rho) - R(\rho))z + g(\rho)u \qquad (4)$$

$\rho \in \{0,1\}^p$ is a boolean vector describing the configuration or mode of the system, p is the number of switches (or pairs of physical switches). Matrixes $J(\rho)$ and $R(\rho)$ have the same properties than J and R .

For this class of physical systems with pairs of physical switches, it is assumed in the following that the three matrixes in (4) can be expressed using an affine relationship:

$$J(\rho) = J_0 + \sum_1^p \rho_i J_i, \quad R(\rho) = R_0 + \sum_1^p \rho_i R_i, \quad g(\rho) = g_0 + \sum_1^p \rho_i g_i \qquad (5)$$

where ρ_i are the components of ρ. This property which has been verified on many usual devices (Buck, Boost, Ćuck) [17] [14] has also been formally proved for multicellular serial converters [18].

3   Lyapunov Function

The control approach which is proposed in this paper is based on a common Lyapunov function for the different modes. In the case of systems with a common equilibrium, they are stabilized around this equilibrium. Here, as there is no common equilibrium, the point around which the system will be stabilized has to be defined first.

3.1   Admissible Reference

The objective is to design a switching control law such that the output of the system take some specified value. Using the same approach as with an average model where the control ρ is considered continuous but constrained, the following definition of an admissible reference is proposed.

Definition 1. $z_0 = F x_0$ *is called an admissible reference for system (4)-(2) where u is constant, if there exits $\rho_0 \in \mathbb{R}^p$, $0 \leq \rho_{0i} \leq 1$ such that constraint (6):*

$$0 = (J(\rho_0) - R(\rho_0))z_0 + g(\rho_0)u \tag{6}$$

is satisfied.

Remark 1. That admissible reference is an equilibrium for the average model. For that control value, since $\dot{x} = 0$, the energy stored in each storage element of the system corresponding to the average model remains constant.

If $p < n$, the admissible reference belongs to a subspace of $\mathbb{R}^n$. p state variables that are considered as the output of the model will be specified. The other state variables as well as ρ_0 are fixed by constraint (6).

In other cases, (6) is still verified, but $(J(\rho_0) - R(\rho_0))$ may be singular, x_0 is not necessarily unique and some state variables can be chosen arbitrarily.

3.2   Lyapunov Function

A function V is a Lyapunov function for system (1) in x_0 if

- $V(x, x_0) > 0$ anywhere excepted in x_0 where $V(x_0, x_0) = 0$,
- V is radially unbounded,
- for any x, a control ρ can be chosen such that $\dot{V}(x, x_0) < 0$.

If such a control law is applied, then x will converge asymptotically towards x_0. A contribution of this paper is to propose such a function.

Theorem 1 (Lyapunov function). *Considering system (4)-(2), it is always possible to find a boolean state feedback $\rho(x)$ such that the function defined by $V(x, x_0) = \frac{1}{2}(x - x_0)^T F(x - x_0)$, where x_0 is an admissible reference according to definition 1, is a Lyapunov function for the resulting closed-loop system.*

Proof. Since there is no jump, V is positive, continuous and null only for $x = x_0$. The time derivative of V depends on the value of the control ρ and will be denoted by $\dot{V}_\rho$.

$$\dot{V}_\rho = (x - x_0)^T F \dot{x} = (z - z_0)^T ((J(\rho) - R(\rho))z + g(\rho)u) \tag{7}$$

Using the skew symetry property of $J(\rho)$, this expression becomes

$$\dot{V}_\rho = -(z - z_0)^T R(\rho)(z - z_0) + (z - z_0)^T ((J(\rho) - R(\rho))z_0 + g(\rho)u) \tag{8}$$

Using the property of the admissible reference (6), this expression can be rewritten:

$$\dot{V}_\rho = -(z - z_0)^T R(\rho)(z - z_0) +$$
$$(z - z_0)^T (((J(\rho) - R(\rho)) - (J(\rho_0) - R(\rho_0)))z_0 + (g(\rho) - g(\rho_0))u) \tag{9}$$

And finally, replacing R, J, g using (5)

$$\dot{V}_\rho = -(z - z_0)^T R(\rho)(z - z_0) + \sum_1^p (z - z_0)^T ((J_i - R_i)z_0 + g_i u)(\rho_i - \rho_{0i}) \tag{10}$$

Since $R(\rho)$ is a nonnegative matrix, the first term of this expression is never positive, and since $0 \leq \rho_{0i} \leq 1$, the second term can be made negative by choosing each ρ_i according to the sign of $(z - z_0)^T((J_i - R_i)z_0 + g_i u)$.   □

For that class of systems, it is then possible to define without any computation, but only on physical consideration, a common Lyapunov function. Since there is no jump, this function is continuous. Its time derivative is continuous except on switching. The following section examines how this function can be used in order to define control laws.

4   Control Strategies

State feedback control laws can be deduced from this Lyapunov function. By state feedback, we mean that the control laws which define the switching sequences are dependent on system state. They may be classified in two classes: the first one consists in choosing at each time a value of the control ρ such that $\dot{V}_\rho \leq 0$. In the second one, $\dot{V}_\rho$ can take small positive values during a limited time.

4.1   Asymptotically Stable Control

Analysing equation (10), it can be observed that, for a given value of the state, at least one value of ρ can be choosen such that $\dot{V}_\rho \leq 0$. In general, more than one value will fulfill this condition. If any of those values is applied, asymptotic stability is guaranteed. So different strategies can be used in order to satisfy other specifications under the constraint $\dot{V}_\rho \leq 0$.

Maximum descent strategy. One strategy consists in choosing, at each time, the value of ρ such that all the terms in the sum are negative or null, which gives, if R is constant, the lowest value of $\dot{V}$. Commutation surfaces are then p hyperplanes defined by

$$(z - z_0)^T((J_i - R_i)z_0 + g_i u) = 0 \tag{11}$$

This strategy will lead to sliding mode or zeno phenomena. Sliding mode will take place if on a switching surface (11) both following reachability conditions are satisfied:

$$((J_i - R_i)z_0 + g_i u)^T F\dot{x} < 0 \quad \text{if} \quad \rho_i = 0 \tag{12}$$

$$((J_i - R_i)z_0 + g_i u)^T F\dot{x} > 0 \quad \text{if} \quad \rho_i = 1 \tag{13}$$

For this approach, and more generally, for all the strategies such that the sum ($\sum$) in (10) is negative, we get:

$$\dot{V}_\rho \leq -(z - z_0)^T R(\rho)(z - z_0) \tag{14}$$

and for systems for which $R(\rho) \succ 0$ for any value of the control ρ , it leads to

$$\dot{V} \leq -\inf_{\rho} \underline{\sigma}(FR(\rho)F)(x - x_0)^T(x - x_0) \qquad (15)$$

where $\underline{\sigma}(.)$ denotes the smallest singular value. In this case, the system is exponentially stable cf. theorem 3.3 in [8].

Minimum switching strategy. A second approach, which may be used in order to decrease the number of switchings consists in keeping the same value of ρ until the trajectory hits the switching surface defined by $\dot{V}_\rho = 0$ and to choose on that surface a new value of ρ such that $\dot{V}_\rho < 0$. Even if it does not lead to zeno phenomena, this approach will lead to faster and faster switching when getting closer to the admissible reference.

4.2   Non Asymptotically Stable Control

Preceding strategies require an infinite bandwidth. But in practice, switching frequency is limited. In order to reduce the switching frequency, different approaches can be used: include a delay (dwell time) between switching instants, add a dead zone to the switching surfaces, use a synchronised approach and switch only on sample instants. Those strategies lead to possibly switch when $\dot{V}_\rho > 0$ and to oscillations around the reference. Typical behaviour will be presented in the examples. Relations between the amplitude of the oscillations and the delay, the sampling time or the dead zone have still to be studied. The following strategy allows mastering the amplitude of the oscillations.

ϵ-**practically asymptotically stable control.** The objective of this control is to guarantee that the system state trajectories remain in a specified domain around the reference. A ball is defined using the Lyapunov function:

$$B[x_0, \epsilon] = \left\{ x \in \mathbb{R}^n \mid (x - x_0)^T F(x - x_0) \leq \epsilon \right\} \qquad (16)$$

The ball is attractive if, when the state is outside the ball, one of the switching laws defined in 4.1 is applied. In order to avoid sliding motion the second strategy can be applied. The ball will thus be reached in a finite time. Next, since the boundary is a level surface for the Lyapunov function, the ball can be made invariant if whenever a trajectory hits its boundary, the control switches to a new value such that $\dot{V}_\rho < 0$ and keeps this value till the next meeting of the ball boundary. With such a switching law, the system is ϵ-practically asymptotically stable such as defined in [10], [11]. This solution allows to control the amplitude of the oscillations, but not the interval between switchings.

4.3   Robust Control

In practice, there is always uncertainty about the values of the model parameters. Let suppose that this uncertainty is modelled by disturbances d on the parameters of the model equations (4)-(2), bounded in some set D. Let define

$$\Omega_\rho = \left\{ x \in \mathbb{R}^n \mid \forall d \in D, \ \dot{V}_\rho < 0 \right\} \qquad (17)$$

This domain defines a subset of the state space where, for a given configuration ρ, the derivative of function V, such as defined in (10) under the constraint (6), is negative whatever the disturbance is. It follows immediately:

Proposition 1. *Let $\Omega = \bigcup_\rho \Omega_\rho$. Ω defines the domain where a control ρ can be chosen such that $\dot{V}_\rho < 0$ whatever the perturbation $d \in D$ is. Any domain O such that $O \supseteq \bar{\Omega}$ can be made attractive and stable with an appropriate control $\rho(x)$.*

If $x \notin O$ then $x \in \Omega$, any ρ such that $x \in \Omega_\rho$ may be applied and the Lyapunov function will be robustly decreasing.

5 Examples

Two examples are presented in order to illustrate the proposed approach. The first one is simple enough to make some computations by hand. The second one allows to show the applicability on more complex systems.

Example 1 (Buck-Boost converter). Figure 1 represents a simplified circuit of a well known power converter called Buck-Boost converter. Under normal operating conditions, the diode is conducting when the controlled physical switch is open ($\rho = 1$) and blocked when the controlled physical switch is closed ($\rho = 0$). The state vector $x = (p, q)^T$ is composed of the flux linkage in the inductance

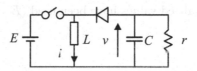

Fig. 1. Buck-Boost converter

and the charge in the capacitor. The co-state vector $z = (i, v)^T$ is composed of the current in the inductance and voltage on the capacitor with the sign conventions represented on the figure. The matrixes corresponding to model (4), (5) are:

$$J(\rho) = \begin{pmatrix} 0 & \rho \\ -\rho & 0 \end{pmatrix}, \quad R(\rho) = \begin{pmatrix} 0 & 0 \\ 0 & 1/r \end{pmatrix}, \quad g(\rho) = \begin{pmatrix} 1 - \rho \\ 0 \end{pmatrix}, \quad F = \begin{pmatrix} \frac{1}{L} & 0 \\ 0 & \frac{1}{C} \end{pmatrix}$$

State equation is:

$$\begin{pmatrix} \dot{p} \\ \dot{q} \end{pmatrix} = \begin{pmatrix} 0 & \frac{\rho}{C} \\ -\frac{\rho}{L} & -\frac{1}{rC} \end{pmatrix} \begin{pmatrix} p \\ q \end{pmatrix} + \begin{pmatrix} 1 - \rho \\ 0 \end{pmatrix} E$$

Co-state equation is:

$$\begin{pmatrix} \dot{i} \\ \dot{v} \end{pmatrix} = \begin{pmatrix} 0 & \frac{\rho}{L} \\ -\frac{\rho}{C} & -\frac{1}{rC} \end{pmatrix} \begin{pmatrix} i \\ v \end{pmatrix} + \begin{pmatrix} \frac{1-\rho}{L} \\ 0 \end{pmatrix} E$$

The set point is defined by :

$$v_0 = \left(1 - \frac{1}{\rho_0}\right) E$$

$$i_0 = -\frac{1}{\rho_0 r}\left(1 - \frac{1}{\rho_0}\right) E$$

In this example it can be seen that the admissible reference necessarily belongs to a subspace of $\mathbb{R}^2$. Usually, it is the output voltage v_0 that is specified, allowing to define:

$$\rho_0 = \frac{E}{E - v_0}$$

$$i_0 = \frac{v_0(v_0 - E)}{rE}$$

The proposed Lyapunov function is:

$$V = \frac{1}{2}\frac{(p - p_0)^2}{L} + \frac{1}{2}\frac{(q - q_0)^2}{C}$$

And its derivative:

$$\dot{V}_\rho = -\frac{(v - v_0)^2}{r} + (v_0 i - i_0 v - E(i - i_0))(\rho - \rho_0)$$

In the simulation, normalized values have been used ($E = 1\text{V}$, $r = 1\Omega$, $L = 1\text{H}$,

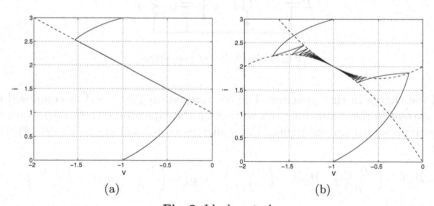

(a)   (b)

Fig. 2. Ideal control

$C = 1\text{F}$). First the output voltage is specified $v_0 = -1\text{V}$. Then $\rho_0 = 0.5$ and $i_0 = 2\text{A}$.

In the following, the state space trajectories corresponding to two different initial conditions (-1,0) and (-1,3) are presented. Figure 2.a presents the case where at each time, the value of ρ leading to the lowest value of $\dot{V}$ is used. The switching surface is depicted on the same figure in dashed line. It is then given by (11):

$$0 = (v_0 i - i_0 v - E(i - i_0))$$

We can observe a sliding mode. Sliding conditions are :

$$\left. \begin{array}{c} (v_0 - E)\frac{E}{L} + \frac{i_0}{C}\left(i + \frac{v}{r}\right) \leq 0 \\ (v_0 - E)\frac{E}{L} + i_0 \frac{v}{rC} \geq 0 \end{array} \right\} \Rightarrow v < 1$$

Figure 2.b presents state trajectories when switching only if $\dot{V}$ becomes null. Switching surfaces, represented with dashed lines, are given for both values of ρ by:

$$-\frac{(v - v_0)^2}{r} + (v_0 i - i_0 v - E(i - i_0))(\rho - \rho_0) = 0$$

In this case, there is no sliding mode, but the time between two switchings decreases towards zero when the state comes closer to the set point.

Figure 3 represents the two same cases but using an hysteresis $\epsilon = 0.2$ on switching surfaces in both cases. It results in both cases in a minimum time between two switchings as well as oscillations on the output.

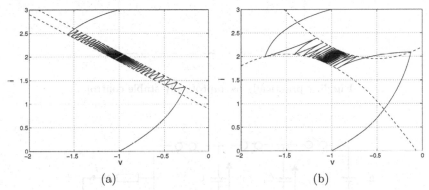

(a)   (b)

Fig. 3. Control with hysteresis on switching surface

Figure 4 represents the two same cases but with discrete time control where the sampling time is 0.1s. Figure 5 represents state space trajectories corresponding to the ϵ-practically asymptotically stable control.

Example 2 (3-level converter). The 3-level converter of figure 6, is constituted of three pairs of physical switches (1-2), (3-4) and (5-6). In each pair, when one switch is on, the other one is closed. The control vector is $\rho = (\rho_1 \ \rho_2 \ \rho_3)^T$. $\rho_i = 1$ if physical switch $2i$ is off and 0 if it is on. The state vector $x = (p \ q_1 \ q_2)^T$ is composed of the flux linkage in the inductance and the charges in the capacitors. The co-state vector $z = (i \ v_1 \ v_2)^T$ is composed of the current in the inductance

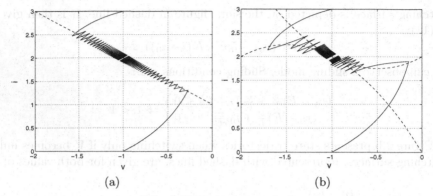

(a)   (b)

Fig. 4. Discrete time control

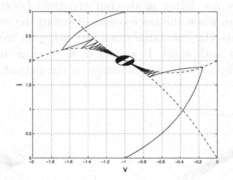

Fig. 5. ϵ-practically asymptotically stable control

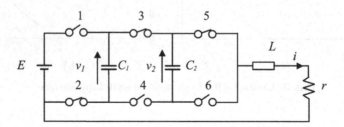

Fig. 6. 3-level converter in the configuration $\rho = (0\ 1\ 1)$

and voltages on the capacitors with the sign conventions represented on the figure. The matrixes corresponding to the model (4), (5) are

$$J(\rho) = \begin{pmatrix} 0 & 1 - \rho_1 - \rho_2 & -1 + \rho_2 + \rho_3 \\ -1 + \rho_1 + \rho_2 & 0 & 0 \\ 1 - \rho_2 - \rho_3 & 0 & 0 \end{pmatrix}$$

then

$$J_0 = \begin{pmatrix} 0 & 1 & -1 \\ -1 & 0 & 0 \\ 1 & 0 & 0 \end{pmatrix}, \; J_1 = \begin{pmatrix} 0 & -1 & 0 \\ 1 & 0 & 0 \\ 0 & 0 & 0 \end{pmatrix}, \; J_2 = \begin{pmatrix} 0 & -1 & 1 \\ 1 & 0 & 0 \\ -1 & 0 & 0 \end{pmatrix}, \; J_3 = \begin{pmatrix} 0 & 0 & 1 \\ 0 & 0 & 0 \\ -1 & 0 & 0 \end{pmatrix}$$

and

$$R(\rho) = R_0 = \begin{pmatrix} r & 0 & 0 \\ 0 & 0 & 0 \\ 0 & 0 & 0 \end{pmatrix}, \; g(\rho) = \begin{pmatrix} \rho_1 \\ 0 \\ 0 \end{pmatrix}, \; g_1 = \begin{pmatrix} 1 \\ 0 \\ 0 \end{pmatrix}, \; F = \begin{pmatrix} \frac{1}{L} & 0 & 0 \\ 0 & \frac{1}{C_1} & 0 \\ 0 & 0 & \frac{1}{C_2} \end{pmatrix}$$

Then the state equation is

$$\begin{pmatrix} \dot{p} \\ \dot{q}_1 \\ \dot{q}_2 \end{pmatrix} = \begin{pmatrix} -\frac{r}{L} & \frac{1-\rho_1-\rho_2}{C_1} & -\frac{1-\rho_2-\rho_3}{C_2} \\ -\frac{1-\rho_1-\rho_2}{L} & 0 & 0 \\ \frac{1-\rho_2-\rho_3}{L} & 0 & 0 \end{pmatrix} \begin{pmatrix} p \\ q_1 \\ q_2 \end{pmatrix} + \begin{pmatrix} \rho_1 \\ 0 \\ 0 \end{pmatrix} E$$

The constraint imposed for the reference are:

$$\rho_{10} + \rho_{20} = 1, \; \rho_{20} + \rho_{30} = 1 \text{ and } \begin{cases} p_0 = \rho_{10} \frac{EL}{E} \\ i_0 = \rho_{10} \frac{E}{r} \end{cases}$$

At the equilibrium, the average model is not asymptotically stable; there are two eigenvalues equal to zero. This implies, as explained in the remark of definition 1, that q_{10} and q_{20} (or v_{10} and v_{20}) can be chosen arbitrarily. It is usual in order to have a regular distribution of voltages to take $v_{10} = \frac{2}{3}E$ and $v_{10} = \frac{1}{3}E$.

In the simulation, the following values are used: $E = 90$V, $r = 20\Omega$, $L =$ 75mH , $C_1 = C_2 = 0.001$F . The reference is $v_{10} = 60$V , $v_{20} = 30$V, and $i_0 = 2$A.

Two strategies have been used. The first one consists in choosing the value of ρ minimizing $\dot{V}_\rho$. In the second one, the value of ρ minimizing $(z - z_0)^T \dot{z}$ under the constraint $\dot{V}_\rho < 0$ is used in order to cause maximal descent of the function $(z - z_0)^T (z - z_0)$.

Figure 7 and 8 present the results. Curve A corresponds to the first strategy and B the second one. It can be noticed that the speed has been improved in the second case.

6   Conclusion

In this paper a hybrid approach for the control of switching power converters with linear components has been presented. Since those systems have no common equilibrium, the admissible references around which the system can be stabilized have been defined. We have proposed a Lyapunov function, which is directly deduced from the physical model. Using this Lyapunov function, some examples of switching laws providing asymptotic stability have been proposed. Theses strategies imply a switching interval which can become null when reaching the

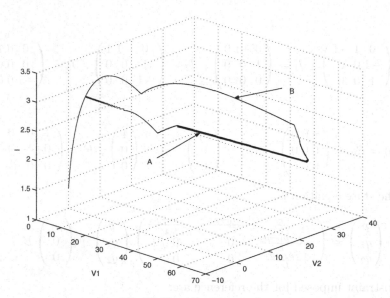

Fig. 7. Co-state trajectories

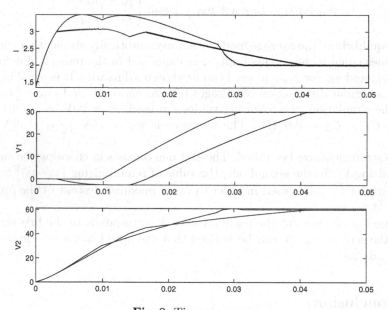

Fig. 8. Time responses

reference. In order to avoid this difficulty, relaxed strategies have been proposed. Two examples have proven the efficiency of this approach. Further works concern the study of control laws combining different criteria as well as the study of the relation between the hysteresis, the amplitude of the oscillation, the time between switchings or the sample time. Another point which has to be studied is the application of this approach to reference tracking.

References

1. Middlebrook, R., Ćuk, S.: A general unified approach to modeling switching converter power stages. In: IEEE Power Electronics Specialists Conference. (1976) 18–34
2. Sira-Ramirez, H.: Non linear p-i controller design for switch-mode dc-to-dc power converters. IEEE Transaction on circuits and systems **38** (1991) 410–417
3. Sira-Ramirez, H., Moreno, R.P., Ortega, R., Esteban, M.G.: Passivity-based controllers for the stabilization of dc-t-dc power converters. Automatica **33** (1997) 499–513
4. Sira-Ramirez, H., Rios-Bolivar, M.: Sliding mode control of dc-to-dc power converters via extended linearization. IEEE Transaction on circuits and systems-1 **41** (1994) 652–661
5. Maschke, B., Ortega, R., van der Schaft, A., Escobar, G.: Lyapunov functions for forced systems with application to stabilizing control. In: Proceedings 14th IFAC World Congress. Volume E. (1999) 409–414
6. Geyer, T., Papafotiou, G., Morari, M.: On the optimal control of switch-mode dc-dc converters. hybrid systems. In Alur, R., Pappas, G., eds.: Proc. 7th International Workshop on Hybrid Systems: Computation and Control. Volume 2993 of Lecture Notes in Computer Science., Springer (2004) 342–356
7. Senesky, M., Eirea, G., Koo, T.: Hybrid modelling and control of power electronics. In Maler, O., Pnueli, A., eds.: Proc. 6th International Workshop on Hybrid Systems: Computation and Control. Volume 2623 of Lecture Notes in Computer Science., Springer (2003) 450–465
8. DeCarlo, R., Branicky, M., Pettersson, S., Lennartson, B.: Perspectives and results on the stability and stabilizability of hybrid systems. Proceedings of the IEEE **88** (2000) 1069–1082
9. Liberzon, D., Morse, A.S.: Basic problems in stability and design of switched systems. IEEE Control Systems Magazine **19** (1999) 59–70
10. Xu, X., Antsaklis, P.J.: Practical stabilization of integrator switched systems. In: Proceedings of the 2003 American Control Conference. (2003) 2767–2772
11. Xu, X., Zhai, G.: On practical stability and stabilization of hybrid and switched systems. In: Proc. 7th International Workshop on Hybrid Systems: Computation and Control. Lecture Notes in Computer Science, Springer (2004) 615–630
12. Karnopp, D., Margolis, D., Rosenberg, R.: System Dynamics : a Unified Approach. 2 edn. Wiley Interscience (1990)
13. van der Schaft, A.: L2 gain and passivity techniques in nonlinear control. Volume 218 of Lecture Notes in Control and Information Sciences. Springer-Verlag (1996)
14. Escobar, G., van der Schaft, A., Ortega, R.: A hamiltonian viewpoint in the modeling of switching power converters. Automatica **35** (1999) 445–452
15. Buisson, J., Cormerais, H., Richard, P.: Analysis of the bond graph model of hybrid physical systems with ideal switches. Journal of Systems and Control Engineering **216** (2002) 47–72
16. Strömberg, J.E.: A mode Switching Modelling Philosophy. PhD thesis, Linkping (1994)
17. Buisson, J., Cormerais, H., Richard, P.: Bond graph modelling of power converters with switches commutating by pairs. In Granda, J., Granda, J., eds.: Proc. ICBGM. Volume 216. (2001) 47–72
18. Cormerais, H., Richard, P., Buisson, J.: A generic passivity based control for multicellular serial converters. IFAC, Prague (submitted) (2005)

Bisimulation for General Stochastic Hybrid Systems*

Manuela L. Bujorianu[1], John Lygeros[2], and Marius C. Bujorianu[3]

[1]Department of Engineering, University of Cambridge,
Cambridge, CB2 1PZ, UK
lmb56@eng.cam.ac.uk
[2]Department of Electrical and Computer Engineering,
University of Patras, Patras, GR26500, Greece
lygeros@ee.upatras.gr
[3]Computing Laboratory, University of Kent,
Canterbury CT2 7NF, UK
mcb8@kent.ac.uk

Abstract. In this paper we define a bisimulation concept for some very general models for stochastic hybrid systems (general stochastic hybrid systems). The definition of bisimulation builds on the ideas of Edalat and of Larsen and Skou and of Joyal, Nielsen and Winskel. The main result is that this bisimulation for GSHS is indeed an equivalence relation. The secondary result is that this bisimulation relation for the stochastic hybrid system models used in this paper implies the same kind of bisimulation for their continuous parts and respectively for their jumping structures.

Keywords: stochastic hybrid systems, Markov processes, simulation morphism, zigzag morphism, bisimulation, category theory.

1 Introduction

Significant progress in verification of probabilistic systems has been done mostly for discrete distributions or Markov chains. Continuous stochastic processes are incomparable more difficult to verify. It is notorious that theorem proving of stochastic properties (with the probability one) can be carried out on the unit circle only. Model checking and reachability analysis are strongly conditioned by abstraction techniques. When the state space is not only infinite but also continuous, abstraction techniques must be very strong. Hybrid systems add an extra level of complexity because of the hybrid nature of the state space (discrete and continuous states coexist) and stochastic hybrid systems push further this

---

* This work has been supported by the European Commission under HYBRIDGE project, IST-2001-32460.

M. Morari and L. Thiele (Eds.): HSCC 2005, LNCS 3414, pp. 198–214, 2005.

complexity by adding non-determinism and uncertainty. Therefore, it is imperious necessary to have an abstraction theory for stochastic processes that can be used for verification and analysis of stochastic hybrid systems.

Reachability analysis and model checking are much easier when a concept of bisimulation is available. The state space can be drastically abstracted in some cases. In this paper, we focus on defining bisimulation relations for stochastic hybrid systems, as a first step towards creating a framework for verification.

Besides of different bisimulation concepts in the concurrency theory, the notion of bisimulation is present

• in the 'deterministic world': continuous and dynamical systems [21] or hybrid systems [15];
• or in the 'probabilistic world': probabilistic discrete systems [18], labelled Markov processes [5], piecewise deterministic Markov processes [22].

In this paper we define a bisimulation concept for some very general models for stochastic hybrid systems (general stochastic hybrid systems, abbreviated GSHS, introduced in [12, 9]). The definition of bisimulation builds on the ideas of Edalat [5, 14] and of Larsen and Skou [18] and of Joyal, Nielsen and Winskel [17]. The main result is that this bisimulation for GSHS, which extends the Edalat definition for labelled Markov processes, is indeed an equivalence relation. This turns out to be a rather hard mathematical result, which employs the whole stochastic analysis apparatus associated to a GSHS (viewed as a strong Markov process defined on Borel space).

Being defined in a category theory context, this stochastic bisimulation, as a notion of system equivalence, enjoys some fundamental mathematical properties. Moreover, we prove that this is a natural notion of bisimulation for GSHS because the bisimilarity of two GSHS implies the bisimilarity of their diffusion components and respectively of their jumping parts.

The rest of the paper is organized as follows. Next section gives a quick tour on stochastic bisimulation. Moreover, it presents the main difficulties, which we have to overcome when we have to define a concept of bisimulation for very general Markov processes. As well, it is stressed that the key point in the construction of bisimulation is the definition of morphism. Section 3 gives a short presentation of GSHS. In section 4 we present different kind of morphism, which might be associated to GSHS. In section 5 we define the concepts of simulation morphism, zigzag morphism and stochastic bisimulation for GSHS. Also, we prove that this bisimulation is an equivalence relation. Section 6 points out the specific features of the bisimulation for GSHS. The paper ends with some conclusions and further work.

2   A Quick Tour in Stochastic Bisimulation

The classical paper of Joyal, Nielsen and Winskel [17] presents a general categorical view of what bisimulation is for deterministic systems. This paper works with a general category of models **M**, whose objects are the systems in question, and the arrows are the simulation morphisms. More, it is distinguished a sub-category of the $\mathbf{M}$ called the *path category* $\mathbf{P}$ of path objects (with morphims expressing how they can be extended). The meaning of a simulation morphism $\psi : X^2 \to X^1$ between two objects X^2, X^1 of $\mathbf{M}$ is that any path p of X^2 is matched by the path $\psi \circ p$ in X^1. The abstract notion of bisimulation is for-mulated in terms of certain special morphisms called $\mathbf{P}$-*open maps* (which are a stronger version of the simulation morphisms). Two objects X^2 and X^1 are called $\mathbf{P}$-bisimilar if and only if there exists an object X together with a span of $\mathbf{P}$-*open maps* between them: $\psi^1 : X \to X^1$ and $\psi^2 : X \to X^2$.

For the probabilistic case it is not easy to generalize this bisimulation. The probabilistic bisimulation (for probabilistic systems) in the case of a discrete state space has been developed by Larsen and Skou in [18].

For the continuous case (for Markov processes) this definition can not be adapted straightforward. The main problem is how to define the simulation morphisms and the open maps. In this case, we say that a Markov process M^1 *simulates* another Markov M^2 if there exist a surjective continuous morphism $\psi : X^2 \to X^1$ between their state spaces such that each transition probability on X^2 'is matched' by a transition probability on X^1. The meaning of this 'matching' is that for each measurable set $A \subset X^1$ and for each $u \in X^2$ we have

$$p_t^2(u, \psi^{-1}(A)) \leq p_t^1(\psi(u), A), \forall t \geq 0. \tag{1}$$

where (p_t^2) and (p_t^1) are the transition functions corresponding to M^2, respec-tively to M^1. A such morphism ψ is called a *simulation morphism*.
The open maps are replaced by the so-called *zigzag morphisms*, which are sim-ulation morphism for which the condition (1) holds with equality.

Practically, a simulation condition as (1) is hard to be checked because the time t runs in a 'continuous' set. Then, it is necessary to require supplementary assumptions about the transition probabilities of the processes we are talking about. This kind of simulation morphisms and zigzag morphisms have been de-fined for some particular Markov processes: for labelled Markov processes [5] and for stationary Markov processes with discrete time (defined on Polish or an-alytic spaces) [14]. In these papers, the authors consider the categories of above Markov processes as objects and the zigzag morphisms as morphisms. Then the bisimulation notion for these processes is given in a 'classical' way. Two labelled Markov processes, for example, are probabilistically bisimilar if there exists a *span of zigzag morphisms* between them. In this context, we can point out an-other reason why only some special kind of Markov processes are considered, as follows. This bisimulation relation is always reflexive and symmetric. But, the transitivity of a such relation (the bisimulation must be an equivalence relation) is usually implied by the existence of *semi-pullbacks* in the Markov process cat-egory considered [17, 14]. That means, in the respective category, for any pair of morphisms $\varphi^1 : M^1 \to M$ and $\varphi^2 : M^2 \to M$ (M^1, M^2, M are objects in that category) there exist an object M^0 and morphisms $\pi^i : M^0 \to M^i$ ($i = 1, 2$) such that $\varphi^1 \circ \pi^1 = \varphi^2 \circ \pi^2$ as in the following diagram.

$$M^0$$

$$\pi^1 \swarrow \qquad \searrow \pi^2$$

$$M^1 \qquad\qquad M^2$$

$$\searrow \varphi^1 \qquad \swarrow \varphi^2$$

$$M$$

The construction of the semi-pullback in the above categories of Markov processes is strongly based on the stationarity property of the Markov processes considered [5, 14]. In this case the transition probabilities do not depend on time! Then the construction mechanism of the semi-pullback in a such categories of Markov processes is reduced to the construction of the semi-pullback in the category of transition probability functions and surjective transition probability preserving Borel maps (as morphisms in the respective category) (see [14] for the detailed construction).

In this paper, we develop a novel concept of *stochastic bisimulation* for general stochastic hybrid systems. This concept of bisimulation might be formulated, as well, for strong Markov processes defined on Borel spaces. Instead of restricting ourself to some specific categories of Markov processes, we chose to change the definitions of simulation morphisms and the zigzag morphisms. The novelty consists of the way to define these morphisms. Specifically, we replace the condition (1) by a 'global condition' which illustrate that the executions of the simulated process can be matched by the execution of the simulator process. Since, these process are not stationary, we require for these morphisms to 'preserve' the kernel operators (or, dual the infinitesimal generators) of the processes considered. Since the expressions of the generators are known [12], these kind of conditions can be easily checked. Then the bisimulation relation is naturally given via zigzag morphism spans between GSHS. Dually, this bisimulation can be defined using morphisms between the excessive function cones associated to the Markov processes. Moreover, the category of strong Markov processes defined on Borel spaces with these zigzag morphisms as morphisms has semi-pullback, then the bisimulation relation is an equivalence relation (the category of GSHS as objects and with same zigzag morphisms as morphisms is a full subcategory in the above category).

The probabilistic bisimulation (for labelled Markov processes) defined in [5] can be derived from our concept of bisimulation, based on the whole theory that relates the infinitesimal generators and the transition probabilities.

3   Stochastic Hybrid Systems

In this section we give a short presentation of the general model for stochastic hybrid systems, introduced in [12], which is used in the following sections. It is notably that in [4], a quite general model of stochastic hybrid systems that can be related to GSHS as a particular case, has been implemented in Charon [1]).

Definition 1. *A General Stochastic Hybrid System (GSHS) is a collection* $H = ((Q, d, \mathcal{X}), b, \sigma, Init, \lambda, R)$ *where*

- Q *is a countable set of discrete variables;*
- $d : Q \to \mathbb{N}$ *is a map giving the dimensions of the continuous state spaces;*
- $\mathcal{X} : Q \to \mathbb{R}^{d(\cdot)}$ *maps each* $q \in Q$ *into an open subset* X^q *of* $\mathbb{R}^{d(q)}$;
- $b : X(Q, d, \mathcal{X}) \to \mathbb{R}^{d(\cdot)}$ *is a vector field;*
- $\sigma : X(Q, d, \mathcal{X}) \to \mathbb{R}^{d(\cdot) \times m}$ *is a* $X^{(\cdot)}$-valued matrix, $m \in \mathbb{N}$;
- $Init : \mathcal{B}(X) \to [0, 1]$ *is an initial probability measure on* $(X, \mathcal{B}(S))$;
- $\lambda : \overline{X}(Q, d, \mathcal{X}) \to \mathbb{R}^{+}$ *is a transition rate function;*
- $R : \overline{X} \times \mathcal{B}(\overline{X}) \to [0, 1]$ *is a transition measure.*

We call the set $X(Q, d, \mathcal{X}) = \bigcup_{i \in Q} \{i\} \times X^i$ the hybrid state space of the GSHS and $x = (i, x^i) \in X(Q, d, \mathcal{X})$ the hybrid state. The closure of the hybrid state space will be $\overline{X} = X \cup \partial X$, where $\partial X = \bigcup_{i \in Q} \{i\} \times \partial X^i$. It is known that X can be endowed with a metric ρ whose restriction to any component X^i is equivalent to the usual component metric [13]. Then $(X, \mathcal{B}(X))$ is a Borel space (homeomorphic to a Borel subset of a complete separable metric space), where $\mathcal{B}(X)$ is the Borel σ-algebra of X.

We built a GSHS as a *Markov string* H [10] obtained by the concatenation of some diffusion processes (x_t^i), $i \in Q$ together with a jumping mechanism given by a family of stopping times (S^i). Let ω_i be a diffusion trajectory, which starts in $(i, x^i) \in X$. Let $t_*(\omega_i)$ be the first hitting time of ∂X^i of the process (x_t^i). Define the function

$$F(t, \omega_i) = I_{(t < t_*(\omega_i))} \exp(- \int_0^t \lambda(i, x_s^i(\omega_i))) ds. \tag{2}$$

This function will be the survivor function for the stopping time S^i associated to the diffusions (x_t^i).

Definition 2 (GSHS Execution). *A stochastic process* $x_t = (q(t), x(t))$ *is called a GSHS execution if there exists a sequence of stopping times* $T_0 = 0 < T_1 < T_2 \leq \ldots$ *such that for each* $k \in \mathbb{N}$,

- $x_0 = (q_0, x_0^{q_0})$ *is a* $Q \times X$-valued random variable extracted according to the probability measure Init;
- *For* $t \in [T_k, T_{k+1})$, $q_t = q_{T_k}$ *is constant and* $x(t)$ *is a solution of the SDE:*

$$dx(t) = b(q_{T_k}, x(t))dt + \sigma(q_{T_k}, x(t))dW_t \tag{3}$$

where W_t *is a the* m-dimensional standard Wiener;

- $T_{k+1} = T_k + S^{i_k}$ *where* S^{i_k} *is chosen according with the survivor function (2).*
- *The probability distribution of* $x(T_{k+1})$ *is governed by the law* $R((q_{T_k}, x(T_{k+1}^{-})), \cdot)$.

It is known, from [9], that any GSHS, H, under standard assumptions (about the diffusion coefficients, non-Zeno executions, transition measure, etc see [9] for a detailed presentation) is a strong Markov process [19] and it has the càdlàg property (i.e. for all $\omega \in \Omega$ the trajectories $t \mapsto x_t(\omega)$ are right continuous on $[0, \infty)$ with left limits on $(0, \infty)$). Here, $(\Omega, \mathcal{F}, P)$ is the underlying probability space associated to H as a Markov process. The model H can be thought of as a family of random variables $(x_t)_{t \geq 0}$. For any $x \in X$, the measure P_x (Wiener probability) is the law of $(x_t)_{t \geq 0}$ under the initial condition $x_0 = x$.

Let (P_t) denote the operator semigroup associated to H which maps $\mathcal{B}^b(X)$ (the set of all bounded measurable functions $f : X \to \mathbb{R}$) into itself given by

$$P_t f(x) = E_x f(x_t), \tag{4}$$

where E_x is the expectation w.r.t. P_x. As well, we define the *resolvent operators* associated to the semigroup (4) by $V^\alpha f := \int_0^\infty e^{-\alpha t} P_t f dt$, $\alpha \geq 0$ for all positive $\mathcal{B}$-measurable functions f. We write V for V^0 and we call it the *kernel operator*. Then a function f is *excessive* (w.r.t. the semigroup (P_t) or the resolvent (V^α)) if it is measurable, non-negative and $P_t f \leq f$ for all $t \geq 0$ and $P_t f \nearrow f$ as $t \searrow 0$. Let denote by $\mathcal{E}_H$ the set of all excessive functions associated to H. The strong Markov property can be characterized in terms of excessive functions [19].

For a GSHS, H, as a Markov process, the expression of the infinitesimal generator L is given in [12]. For $f \in \mathcal{D}(L)$ (the domain of generator) Lf is given by

$$Lf(x) = L_{cont} f(x) + \lambda(x) \int_X (f(y) - f(x)) R(x, dy) \tag{5}$$

where:

$$L_{cont} f(x) = \mathcal{L}_b f(x) + \frac{1}{2} Tr(\sigma(x)\sigma(x)^T \mathbb{H}^f(x)). \tag{6}$$

For a strong Markov process defined on a Borel space (which is the case for CSHS), the opus of the kernel operator is the inverse operator of the infinitesimal generator of the process [19].

A stochastic differential equation generates a much richer structure than just a family of stochastic processes, each solving the stochastic differential equation for a given value. In fact, it gives a flow of random diffeomorphism, i.e. it generates a random dynamical system (RDS) [2]. Therefore, the construction of a GSHS as a Markov string (see [10]) of diffusions does not only generate a Markov process, but it also generates an RDS (which is a 'string' of the RDS components). The theory of random dynamical systems is relatively new and we refer to [2], as the first systematic presentation of this theory. We present only the necessary definitions that we need in this paper.

Let $\theta_t : \Omega \to \Omega$ for all $t \in [0, \infty)$. $(\Omega, \mathcal{F}, P, \theta_t)$ (abbreviated θ) is called a *metric dynamical system*, if: 1.The map $\theta : \Omega \times [0, \infty) \to \Omega$, $(\omega, t) \mapsto \theta_t(\omega)$ is measurable from $(\Omega \times [0, \infty), \mathcal{F} \otimes \mathcal{B}([0, \infty))$ to $(\Omega, \mathcal{F})$; 2. θ satisfies the flow properties: (i) $\theta_0 = id_\Omega$ and (ii) $\theta(t + s) = \theta_t \circ \theta_s$ $\forall s, t \in [0, \infty)$; 3. θ is measure preserving, i.e. $\theta_t P = P$ $\forall t \in [0, \infty)$ (where $fP := P \circ f^{-1}$). The metric dynamical system is necessary to model the random perturbations of an RDS.

A measurable *random dynamical system* on the measurable space $(X, \mathcal{B})$ over the metric dynamical system θ with time $[0, \infty)$ is a map $\varphi : [0, \infty) \times \Omega \times X \to X$, $(t, \omega, x) \mapsto \varphi(t, \omega, x)$ with the following properties: 1. φ is $\mathcal{B}([0, \infty)) \otimes \mathcal{F} \otimes \mathcal{B}/\mathcal{B}$

- measurable; 2. If $\varphi(t,\omega) = \varphi(t,\omega,\cdot)$ then φ forms a perfect cocycle over θ, i.e. φ has the properties: (i) $\varphi(0,\omega) = id_X$ and (ii) $\varphi(t+s,\omega) = \varphi(t,\theta_s\omega) \circ \varphi(s,\omega)$ $\forall \omega \in \Omega$ $\forall s, t \in [0,\infty)$.

The RDS associated to a GSHS arises from its construction as a Markov string: the shift operator (θ_t) of the corresponding Markov string is exactly the metric dynamical system for the RDS and for each $x \in X$, $\omega \in \Omega$, $t \geq 0$ the value of the RDS cocycle $\varphi(t,\omega,x)$ is exactly $x_t(\omega)$ with x as the starting point (or $\varphi(t,\omega,x)$ is the execution of GSHS with x as the starting point). In other words, the cocycle φ is a replacement of the flow from the determinist case.

In the next section we will define some concepts of morphism for stochastic hybrid systems. The definitions will employ notions specific to the Markov process theory as: kernel operator, excessive functions, etc. The three faces of a stochastic hybrid system - Markov process, random dynamical system or dynamical system - will give more intuitions about the notion of morphism which will be proposed next. Some connections with theory of dynamical systems might be available.

4   Morphisms Associated to GSHS

In this section we define a concept of morphism between GSHS intimately connected with the morphisms between the associated cones of excessive functions.

Let H a GSHS defined as in section 3. We assume that H as Markov process is transient (i.e. there exists a strict positive Borel measurable function q such that Vq is a bounded function). We define a preorder relation $\prec_H$ on X as

$$x \prec_H y \iff Vf(y) \leq Vf(x), \forall f \in \mathcal{B}^b(X), f \geq 0.$$

$\prec_H$ is an order on the trajectories of H. That means: $x \prec_H y$ if and only if there exist some time $t \in [0,+\infty)$ and $\omega \in \Omega$ such that $y = \varphi(t,\omega,x)$. For each fixed ω, the trajectory $[\varphi(t,\omega,\cdot)]_{t\geq 0}$ is totally ordered w.r.t. $\prec_H$. If H degenerates in a dynamical system then the relation $\prec_H$ is an order relation because H is supposed to be transient. We will call $\prec_H$ the *trajectory (pre)order* of H.

One can define on X the *fine topology*, denoted by τ_H^f, which consists of the sets $G \subseteq X$ with the following property: $\forall x \in G$, $\forall \omega \in \Omega$ $\exists t_0 \in (0,\zeta(\omega))$ such that $\varphi(t,\omega,x) \in G, \forall t \in (0,t_0)$ (each trajectory starting from x remains for a while in G)[1]. The fine topology is the coarsest topology on X, which makes continuous all excessive functions. The fine topology τ_H^f is separated and is finer than the initial topology.

In the first step, we define the morphisms between the cones of excessive functions. Let H^1, H^2 be two GSHS with state spaces $X^{(1)}$, respectively $X^{(2)}$. Let

---

[1] Note that the fine topology can be defined in terms of hitting times for a Markov process.

$\mathcal{E}_{H^1}, \mathcal{E}_{H^2}$ the associated cones of excessive functions. An *$\mathcal{E}$-morphism* (between these two cones) can be defined as an application

$$\Psi : \mathcal{E}_{H^1} \to \mathcal{E}_{H^2} \tag{7}$$

such that the following properties hold: (i) $\Psi(f+g) = \Psi(f) + \Psi(g)$, $\forall f, g \in \mathcal{E}_{H^1}$; (ii) $f \le g \Rightarrow \Psi(f) \le \Psi(g)$; $f_k \nearrow f \Rightarrow \Psi(f_k) \nearrow \Psi(f)$; (iv) $\Psi(f \cdot g) = \Psi(f) \cdot \Psi(g)$, $\forall f, g \in \mathcal{E}_{H^1}$; (v) $\Psi(1) = 1$. An $\mathcal{E}$-morphism Ψ is called *finite* if $f < +\infty \Rightarrow \Psi(f) < +\infty$.

Proposition 1. *If $\psi : X^{(2)} \to X^{(1)}$ is measurable, monotone (i.e. $u \prec_{H^2} v \Rightarrow \psi(u) \prec_{H^1} \psi(v)$) and finely continuous then $\Psi : \mathcal{E}_{H^1} \to \mathcal{E}_{H^2}$ given by*

$$\Psi(f) = f \circ \psi \tag{8}$$

for all $f \in \mathcal{E}_{H^1}$, is a finite $\mathcal{E}$-morphism.

In some papers [20], an application ψ as in the Prop. 1 is called *H-map*. Intuitively, in the formula (8) the H-map ψ can be thought of as a *variable change*, i.e. for all $f \in \mathcal{E}_{H^1}$

$$\Psi(f)(u) = f(\psi(u)), \forall u \in X^{(2)}. \tag{9}$$

Remark 1. (i) The map Ψ defined by (8) can be extended as a map between the two cones of measurable positive functions defined on $X^{(1)}$, respectively $X^{(2)}$, loosing the property of finely continuity. Prop.1 shows how a function between the state spaces of H^1, H^2 can provide an $\mathcal{E}$-morphism.

(ii) Conversely, if Ψ is an $\mathcal{E}$-morphism as in (7) then there exists a unique measurable monotone and finely continuous application $\overline{\psi}$ from $X^{(2)}$ to an extension of $X^{(1)}$ such that: $\Psi(f) = f \circ \overline{\psi}, \forall f \in \mathcal{E}_{H^1}$. To obtain this result one can use results from [20].

In the next section the notion of stochastic bisimulation will be defined based on the concept of H-map. For this purpose the following results will guide us in building the notions of simulation morphism and zigzag morphism. A surjective H-map $\psi : X^{(2)} \to X^{(1)}$ induces an equivalence relation $\sim_\psi$ on $X^{(2)}$

$$u \sim_\psi v \Leftrightarrow \psi(u) = \psi(v). \tag{10}$$

In this way, to each $x \in X^{(1)}$ we can associate an equivalence class $\hat{u}$ w.r.t. $\sim_\psi$ such that $\hat{u} = \psi^{-1}(x)$. Then, using (9), each function g belonging to the range of Ψ can be extended to $X^{(2)}/_{\sim_\psi}$, i.e. $g(\hat{u}) = f(x)$ provided that $\hat{u} = \psi^{-1}(x)$ and $g = \Psi(f)$.

Proposition 2. *If $\psi : X^{(2)} \to X^{(1)}$ is a surjective and finely open H-map such that each excessive function $g \in \mathcal{E}_{H^2}$ has the property*

$$u \sim_\psi v \Rightarrow g(u) = g(v) \tag{11}$$

then the $\mathcal{E}$-morphism $\Psi : \mathcal{E}_{H^1} \to \mathcal{E}_{H^2}$ given by formula (8) is surjective.

Proof. For each $g \in \mathcal{E}_{H^2}$ we have to define $f \in \mathcal{E}_{H^1}$ such that $\Psi(f) = g$. Let $f : X^{(1)} \to [0, \infty)$ defined by $f(x) = g(u)$ for each $x \in X^{(1)}$, where $u \in X^{(2)}$ is such that $\psi(u) = x$ (there exists a such u since ψ is surjective). The function f is well defined because of (11). Then f can be written as $f = g \circ \psi^{-1}$ and for any open set $D \subset [0, \infty)$ we have $f^{-1}(D) = \psi(g^{-1}(D))$. Since ψ is a finely open map we obtain that $f^{-1}(D)$ is finely open in $X^{(1)}$. Then $f \in \mathcal{E}_{H^1}$.   □

Remark 2. It is easy to check that if in the Prop. 1 both ψ and Ψ are surjective then Ψ must be bijective. Therefore the two excessive function cones can be identified and the two processes are equivalent.

5   Stochastic Bisimulation

In this section we develop a novel concept of bisimulation for GSHS. This concept is inspired by the bisimulation concept for labelled Markov processes [5] or stationary Markov processes with discrete time [14]. Because, our models *are not stationary* Markov processes, we can not use the Edalat's bisimulation.

To define the notion of bisimulation for GSHS, we need to give the definition of *simulation morphism and zigzag morphisms* between GSHS. The main difference from the similar notions from [5] is that we replace the conditions about the transition probabilities (which, in the non-stationary case, should depend on time) with *global conditions* written in terms of kernel operators or excessive functions associated to the GSHS. Similarly, these morphisms can be defined for strong Markov processes with càdlàg property defined on Borel spaces.

Definition 3. *A simulation morphism between two GSHS, H^1 and H^2 (the process H^1 simulates the process H^2), is a H-map (i.e. measurable, monotone, finely continuous application) $\psi : X^{(2)} \to X^{(1)}$ such that*

$$V^2(f \circ \psi) \leq V^1 f \circ \psi, \forall f \in \mathcal{B}^b(X^{(1)}), \ f \geq 0, \tag{12}$$

where V^1 (resp. V^2) is the kernel operator associated to H^1 (resp. H^2).

The definition 3 illustrates, in terms of kernel operators, that the simulating process can make all the transitions of the simulated process with greater probability than in the process being simulated. More intuitively, a simulation morphism ψ is not only monotone, but it also refines the "distances" on the trajectories since the trajectory order relations are defined by means of the kernel operators. On the other hand, the finely continuity of ψ illustrates the fact that to a trajectory of H^1 corresponds a class of trajectories of H^2.

Remark 3. Replacing the simulation condition (12) with an weaker one, using the $\mathcal{E}$-morphism Ψ generated by ψ with formula (8), one can define a simulation morphism as follows

$$V^2 \circ \Psi \leq \Psi \circ V^1. \tag{13}$$

Definition 4. *A surjective simulation morphism ψ between two GSHS, H^1 and H^2 is called zigzag morphism if the formula (12) holds with equality, i.e.*

$$V^2(f \circ \psi) = V^1 f \circ \psi, \forall f \in \mathcal{B}^b(X^{(1)}), \ f \geq 0. \tag{14}$$

Remark 4. For a zigzag morphims the monotony is already implied by the zigzag condition (14) (easy consequence of the way to define the order relations on the spaces $X^{(2)}$ and $X^{(1)}$).

Using the $\mathcal{E}$-morphism Ψ generated by ψ, the condition (14) becomes

$$V^2 \circ \Psi = \Psi \circ V^1 \tag{15}$$

i.e. the following diagram commutes

$$
\begin{array}{ccc}
\mathcal{E}_{H^1} & \xrightarrow{\Psi} & \mathcal{E}_{H^2} \\
V^1 \uparrow & & \uparrow V^2 \\
\mathcal{E}_{H^1} & \xrightarrow{\Psi} & \mathcal{E}_{H^2}
\end{array}
$$

Then we can define a *zigzag $\mathcal{E}$-morphim Ψ* (between two GSHS, H^1 and H^2) as a surjective $\mathcal{E}$-morphism such that the condition (15) yields.

Next, we define the *stochastic bisimulation* for GSHS as the existence of a span of zigzag morphisms.

Definition 5. *Let H^1 and H^2 be two GSHS. H^1 is stochastic bisimilar to H^2 (written $H^1 \sim H^2$) if there exists a span of zigzag morphisms between them, i.e. there exists a GSHS H^{12} and zigzag morphisms ψ^1 (where $\psi^1 : X^{12} \to X^{(1)}$) and ψ^2 (where $\psi^2 : X^{12} \to X^{(2)}$) such that*

$$
\begin{array}{ccc}
 & H^{12} & \\
\psi^1 \swarrow & & \searrow \psi^2 \\
H^1 & & H^2
\end{array}
$$

Notice that if there is a zigzag morphism between two systems, they are bisimilar since the identity is a zigzag morphism.

Remark 5. The notions of simulation morphism, zigzag morphism and stochastic bisimulation can be formulated in a similar way for strong Markov processes defined on Polish spaces (a Polish space is a homeomorphic image of complete separable metric space) or analytic spaces (an analytic space is the continuous image of a Polish space into another Polish space and is equipped with the subspace topology of the latter space). In this paper, since the GSHS state space is a Borel space, we consider only Markov processes defined on Borel spaces.

Remark 6. We can define a weak version of the stochastic bisimulation via $\mathcal{E}$-morphisms, i.e. $H^1 \sim H^2$ if there exist a cospan of zigzag $\mathcal{E}$-morphisms Ψ^1 and Ψ^2 between their excessive function cones

$$\mathcal{E}_{H^{12}}$$
$$\psi^1 \nearrow \qquad \nwarrow \psi^2$$
$$\mathcal{E}_{H^1} \qquad\qquad \mathcal{E}_{H^2}$$

Let us consider the category of the strong Markov processes defined on Borel spaces as the objects and zigzag morphisms as the morphisms. This category contains as a full subcategory the category of GSHS as the objects and zigzag morphisms as the morphisms.

Proposition 3. *The category of the strong Markov processes on Borel spaces as the objects and zigzag morphisms as the morphisms has semi-pullbacks.*

Proof. Let M^1, M^2, M be strong Markov processes defined on the Borel spaces $X^{(1)}, X^{(2)}, X$, respectively. Suppose that there exist two zigzag morphisms

$$\psi^1 : X^{(1)} \to X, \ \psi^2 : X^{(2)} \to X. \tag{16}$$

We have to prove that there exist another object M^0 (a strong Markov process defined on a Borel space $X^{(0)}$) and two zigzag morphisms $\pi^1 : X^{(0)} \to X^{(1)}$ and $\pi^2 : X^{(0)} \to X^{(2)}$ such that the following diagram commutes

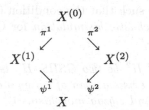

Let $X^{(0)} = \{(x^1, x^2) | \psi^1(x^1) = \psi^2(x^2)\}$ equipped with the subspace topology of the product topology on $X^{(1)} \times X^{(2)}$. Note that $X^{(0)}$ is nonempty since ψ^1 and ψ^2 are supposed surjective. As well, $X^{(0)}$ is a measurable set of $X^{(1)} \times X^{(2)}$ (equipped with its Borel σ-algebra). We take M^0 as the part of the product of the Markov processes M^1, M^2 restricted to $X^{(0)}$, the process product is "killed" outside of $X^{(0)}$ [13] For the relationships which exist between the kernel operators of the processes M^1, M^2 and the kernel operator of their product, see [11] and the references therein. Then π^1 and π^2 can be taken as the projection maps and the equality $\psi^1 \circ \pi^1 = \psi^2 \circ \pi^2$ trivially holds.

On the other hand, if we define the stochastic bisimulation defined via zigzag $\mathcal{E}$-morphisms, then the pullback existence for the category of Markov processes (with morphisms given by zigzag $\mathcal{E}$-morphisms) is equivalent with the *pushout existence* in the category of their excessive function cones (with the morphisms given by zigzag $\mathcal{E}$-morphisms). Let us take the following span of morphims between the excessive function cones

$$\mathcal{E}_M$$
$$\psi^1 \swarrow \qquad \searrow \psi^2$$
$$\mathcal{E}_{M^1} \qquad\qquad \mathcal{E}_{M^2}$$

Naturally, we consider $\mathcal{E}$ as the tensor product $\mathcal{E}_{M^1} \otimes \mathcal{E}_{M^1}$ of the cones $\mathcal{E}_{M^1}, \mathcal{E}_{M^1}$ (which correspond to the product of operator semigroups or to Markov process product defined on $X^{(1)} \times X^{(2)}$). Then the 'inclusions' $\mathcal{E}_{M^1} \overset{\Gamma^1}{\hookrightarrow} \mathcal{E}$, $\Gamma^1(f^1) = \Psi^1(f) \otimes \Psi^2(f)$ if $f^1 = \Psi^1(f)$ and $\mathcal{E}_{M^2} \overset{\Gamma^2}{\hookrightarrow} \mathcal{E}$, $\Gamma^2(f^2) = \Psi^1(f) \otimes \Psi^2(f)$ if $f^2 = \Psi^2(f)$ (essentially, Ψ^1 and Ψ^2 are surjective) gives the desired pushout construction, i.e. the following diagram commutes

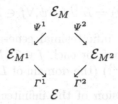

Proposition 4. *The stochastic bisimulation defined by Def. 5 on GSHS (or strong Markov processes on Borel spaces) is an equivalence relation.*

6   Specific Features of Bisimulation for GSHS

A zigzag morphism $\psi : X^{(2)} \to X^{(1)}$ between two GSHS, H^1 and H^2, induces a relation $\mathcal{R} \subset X^{(2)} \times X^{(1)}$ as follows: $u\mathcal{R}x \Leftrightarrow \psi(u) = x$. Then the equivalence relation $\sim_\psi$ on $X^{(2)}$ can be thought of as the equivalence relation induced by $\mathcal{R}$ in sense of [22], i.e. $u \sim_\psi v$ iff there exists $x \in X^{(1)}$ such that $u\mathcal{R}x$ and $v\mathcal{R}x$ (which is exact the meaning of (10)). The equivalence relation induced by $\mathcal{R}$ on $X^{(2)}$ is the trivial one (x can be equivalent only with itself).

The space $X^{(2)}/_{\sim_\psi}$ can be endowed with the σ algebra $\mathcal{B}^*(X^{(2)})$, which is the "saturation" of the Borel σ-algebra of $X^{(2)}$ w.r.t. $\sim_\psi$ (i.e. the collection of all Borel sets of $X^{(2)}$ in which any equivalence class of $X^{(2)}$ is either totally contained or totally not contained). A function on $g : X^{(2)} \to \mathbb{R}$, which is measurable w.r.t. $\mathcal{B}^*(X^{(2)})$ will be called *saturated measurable function*. It is clear that a function measurable g is saturated measurable iff (11) holds. Each function $f : X^{(1)} \to \mathbb{R}$ measurable w.r.t. $\mathcal{B}(X^{(1)})$ can be identified with a saturated measurable function g such that $g = f \circ \psi$.

The morphism ψ can be viewed as a bijective mapping $\psi : X^{(2)}/_{\sim_\psi} \to X^{(1)}$. It is clear that ψ is a measurable application. To identify the two above measurable spaces ψ^{-1} must be measurable. The main idea, which results from this reasoning, is that the measurable space $(X^{(1)}, \mathcal{B}(X^{(1)}))$ can be embedded in the measurable space $(X^{(2)}, \mathcal{B}(X^{(2)}))$ and the measurable function on $X^{(1)}$ can be identified with the saturated measurable functions on $X^{(2)}$.

Based on the theory of semigroups of Markov processes, one can obtain from the zigzag condition (14): for almost all $t \geq 0$ (i.e. except with a zero Lebesgue measure set of times) the following equalities (versions of (1)) hold

$$p_t^2(u, \psi^{-1}(A)) = p_t^1(x, A), \forall x \in X^{(1)}, \forall u \in \hat{u} = \psi^{-1}(x), \forall A \in \mathcal{B}(X^{(1)}) \quad (17)$$
$$P_t^2(f \circ \psi)(u) = P_t^1 f(x), \forall x \in X^{(1)}, \forall u \in \hat{u} = \psi^{-1}(x), \forall f \in \mathcal{B}^b(X^{(1)})$$

Note that $\psi^{-1}(A) \in \mathcal{B}^*(X^{(2)})$. Therefore the transition probabilities of H^1 simulates 'equivalence classes' of transition probabilities of H^2.

Remark 7. The connection between the kernel operator and the infinitesimal generator of the strong process Markov process allows us transform the conditions (15) and (14) as follows

$$L^{(2)} \circ \Psi = \Psi \circ L^{(1)}$$

$$L^{(2)}(f \circ \psi) = L^{(1)} f \circ \psi, \forall f \in \mathcal{D}(L^{(1)}) \tag{18}$$

where $L^{(1)}$ (resp. $L^{(2)}$) is the infinitesimal generator of H^1 (resp. H^2). The equality (18) holds provided that for each $f \in \mathcal{D}(L^{(1)})$ (the domain of L^1) the function $f \circ \psi$ belongs to $\mathcal{D}(L^{(2)})$ (the domain of $L^{(2)}$).

Since for GSHS the expression of the infinitesimal generator is known, to check if the formula (18) is true for two given GSHS is only a computation exercice.
Recall that a GSHS has been constructed as a Markov string, i.e. a sequence of diffusion processes with a jumping structure. Then the cone of excessive functions associated to a GSHS can be characterized as a 'sum' of the excessive function cones associated to the diffusion components. This characterization 'explains' the following result.

Proposition 5. *A zigzag morphism ψ between two GSHS H^1 and H^2 defined as in Def. 4 preserves the continuous parts of the two models.*

Proof. Suppose that the two GSHS state spaces are $X^{(1)} = \bigcup_{i \in Q^1} \{i\} \times X^{i(1)}$ and $X^{(2)} = \bigcup_{q \in Q^2} \{q\} \times X^{q(2)}$. We can suppose without loosing the generality that each two modes have empty intersection and therefore $X^{(1)} = \bigcup_{i \in Q^1} X^{i(1)}$ and $X^{(2)} = \bigcup_{q \in Q^2} X^{q(2)}$. The function ψ maps $X^{(2)}$ into $X^{(1)}$. From the construction of H^1, as Markov string, we have $V^1 f = \sum_{i \in Q^1} V^{i1} f^i, \forall f \in \mathcal{B}^b(X^{(1)})$, where, for each $i \in Q^1$, V^{i1} is the kernel operators of the component diffusion of H^1 which operates on $X^{i(1)}$ and $f^i = f|_{X^{i(1)}} \in \mathcal{B}^b(X^{i(1)})$. A similar expression can be written for V^2 (i.e. $V^2 g = \sum_{q \in Q^2} V^{q2} g^q$, $g \in \mathcal{B}^b(X^{(2)})$).

Let f be an arbitrary positive bounded measurable function on $X^{(1)}$. Then for each $i \in Q^1$ consider f^i as before. Let $Y^{i(2)} = \psi^{-1}(X^{i(1)})$ (note that $Y^{i(2)}$ is an open set) and ψ^i be the restriction of ψ, which maps $Y^{i(2)}$ into $X^{i(1)}$. Denote $g^i = f^i \circ \psi^i \in \mathcal{B}^b(Y^{i(2)})$ and $g^{iq} = g^i|_{Y^{i(2)} \cap X^{q(2)}}$. The zigzag condition (14) becomes $W^{i2}(f^i \circ \psi^i) = V^{i1} f^i \circ \psi^i$, where W^{i2} is the 'restriction' of V^2 to $Y^{i(2)}$, i.e. $W^{i2} g^i = \sum_{q \in Q^2} V^{q2} g^{iq}$ (more intuitively, W^{i2} is the sum of kernels associated to the component diffusions of H^2, which operate on $Y^{i(2)}$). Then, for all $x \in X^{i(1)}$ we have

$$W^{i2} g^i(u) = V^{i1} f^i(x), \tag{19}$$

provided that $\psi^i(u) = x$. Because V^{i1} corresponds to a diffusion process, it must be the case that in the left hand side of (19) the 'jumping part' to not longer exist (at least for the saturated measurable functions). Then the kernel W^{i2} corresponds to a continuous process (which might be a diffusion or a switching diffusion process). □

Any zigzag morphism ψ can be extended by (finely) continuity to the boundary of the state spaces. Or, we can suppose from the beginning that the zigzag morphims operate on the closures of the state spaces. We have to assume that the zigzag morphims 'keep' the boundary points, or, in other words, $\psi : \partial X^{(2)} \to \partial X^{(1)}$ is surjective.

Remark 8. The finely continuity of a zigzag morphism between two GSHS is important only when we use the connection with the associated excessive function cones. Otherwise, we can replace this continuity with the continuity w.r.t. to the initial topologies of the state spaces.

Proposition 6. *A zigzag morphism ψ between two GSHS H^1 and H^2 defined as in Def. 4 preserves the jumping structure of the two models.*

Proof. For each $x \in X^{(1)}$ there exist, by surjectivity of ψ, some elements $u \in X^{(2)}$ such that $\psi(u) = x$. Then, for each $f \in \mathcal{D}(L^{(1)})$, a simple computation of the right hand side of (18) gives

$$L^{(1)}f(x) = L^{(1)}_{cont}f(x) + \lambda^1(x) \int_{\overline{X}^{(1)}} (f(y) - f(x))R^1(x, dy) \tag{20}$$

and after, the left hand side of (18) is

$$L^{(2)}(f \circ \psi)(u) = L^{(2)}_{cont}(f \circ \psi)(u) + \lambda^2(u) \int_{\overline{X}^{(2)}} [(f \circ \psi)(v) - (f \circ \psi)(u)]R^2(u, dv). \tag{21}$$

From the Prop. 5 we have the equality of the continuous parts of (20) and (21). Then the jumping parts (20) and (21) must coincide. Then

$$\lambda^1(x) \int_{\overline{X}^{(1)}} (f(y) - f(x))R^1(x, dy) = \lambda^2(u) \int_{\overline{X}^{(2)}} [(f \circ \psi)(v) - (f \circ \psi)(u)]R^2(u, dv).$$

The construction of GSHS H^1 and H^2, as Markov strings, shows that the transition measures R^1 and R^2 play the role of the transition probabilities when the processes jump from one diffusion to another (see Def.2). Then they satisfy (17), i.e. $R^2(u, \psi^{-1}(A)) = R^1(x, A), \forall A \in \mathcal{B}(X^{(1)})$. It easily follows that $\lambda^1(x) = \lambda^2(u), \forall u \in \hat{u} = \psi^{-1}(x)$. □

Therefore, the stochastic bisimulation between two GSHS reduces to the bisimulations between their continuous components and between their jump structures. In this way our concept of bisimulation can be related with the bisimulation for piecewise deterministic Markov processes (which are particular class of GSHS) defined in terms of an equivalence relation between the deterministic flows and the probabilistic jumps [22].

7 Conclusions

In this paper we develop a notion of stochastic bisimulation for a category of general models for stochastic hybrid systems (which are Markov processes) or, more generally, for the category of strong Markov processes defined on Borel spaces. The morphisms in this category are the zigzag morphims. A zigzag morphism between two Markov processes is a surjective (finely) continuous measurable functions between their state spaces which 'commutes' with the kernel operators of the processes considered. The fundamental technical contribution is the proof that this stochastic bisimulation is indeed an equivalence relation.

The secondary result of the paper is that this bisimulation relation for GSHS (the stochastic hybrid system models we are dealing in this paper) implies the same kind of bisimulation for their continuous parts and respectively for their jumping structures.

This work is intended to be a foundation for applying formal methods to stochastic hybrid systems. The category of GSHS we have introduced can be used to employ various methodologies from formal methods that admit a categorical support, like viewpoints and formal testing [6].

8 Further Work

From stochastic analysis viewpoint, most of the models of stochastic hybrid systems are strong Markov processes. Then, many tools available for the Markov process studying can be used to characterize their main features. On the other hand, some of them can be included in the class of random dynamical systems (stochastic extensions of the dynamical systems). Therefore the whole ergodic theory or stability results available for random dynamical systems might be applied to them. As well, stability results of random dynamical systems [3] can be lifted to these models of stochastic hybrid systems. Moreover, because in the deterministic case there are characterizations of the Lyapunov functions in terms of excessive function [16], it might be possible to investigate similar connections in the stochastic case.

From the verification and analysis of stochastic hybrid systems perspective, a concept of stochastic bisimulation can facilitate the way towards a model checking of stochastic hybrid systems.

The work presented in this paper and the above discussion allow us to point out some possible research directions in the stochastic hybrid system framework:

- Use the stochastic bisimulation to get manageable sized system abstractions;
- Use the stochastic bisimulation to investigate the reachability problem;
- Make a comparative study of the different approaches on reachability analysis for stochastic hybrid systems: 1. the approach based on the hitting times and hitting probabilities for a target set [7]; 2. the approach based on the so-called Dirichlet forms and excessive functions [8]; 3. the approach based on Lyapunov function (for the switching diffusion processes) [23].

References

1. Alur, R., Grosu, R., Hur, Y., Kumar, V., Lee, I.: *Modular Specifications of Hybrid Systems in CHARON*, Proc. 3rd International Workshop on *Hybrid Systems: Computation and Control*, LNCS 1790 (2000), 6-19.
2. Arnold, L.: Random Dynamical systems. Springer-Verlag, Berlin, (1998).
3. Arnold, L.: *Lyapunov's Second Method for Random Dynamical Systems*. J. of Diff. Eq. **177** (2001), 235-265.
4. Bernadskiy, M., Sharykin, R., Alur, R.: *Structured Modelling of Concurrent Stochastic Hybrid Systems*. In Y. Lakhnech, Y. Sergio Eds., Proc. FORMATS'04 (2004), Springer LNCS 3253, 309-324.
5. Blute, R., Desharnais, J., Edalat, A., Panangaden, P.: *Bisimulation for Labelled Markov Processes*. In Logic in Comp. Sc., IEEE Press (1997), 149-158.
6. Bujorianu, M.C., Bujorianu, M.L., Maharaj, S.: *Towards a Formalization of Viewpoints Testing*. In R. Hierons, T. Jeron Eds., Proceedings of Formal Approaches to Testing of Software (2002), 137-151.
7. Bujorianu, M.L., Lygeros, J.: *Reachability Questions in Piecewise Deterministic Markov Processes*. In O. Maler, A. Pnueli Eds., *Hybrid Systems: Computation and Control*, 6th International Workshop, HSCC03, LNCS 2623 (2003), 126-140.
8. Bujorianu M.L : *Extended Stochastic Hybrid Systems and their Reachability Problem*. In R. Alur, G. Pappas Eds., *Hybrid Systems: Computation and Control* 7th International Workshop, HSCC04, Springer LNCS 2993 (2004), 234-249.
9. Bujorianu, M.L., Lygeros, J.: *General Stochastic Hybrid Systems*. IEEE Mediterranean Conference on Control and Automation MED'04, Turkey, (2004).
10. Bujorianu, M.L., Lygeros, J.: *Theoretical Foundations of General Stochastic Hybrid Processes*. Proc. 6th International Symposium on Mathematical Theory of Networks and Systems (MTNS 2004).
11. Bujorianu, M.L.: *Capacities and Markov Processes*. Libertas Math., **24** (2004), 201-210.
12. Bujorianu, M.L., Lygeros, J.: *General Stochastic Hybrid Systems: Modelling and Optimal Control*. Proc. 43th Conference in Decision and Control (2004).
13. Davis, M.H.A.: *Markov Models and Optimization*, Chapman & Hall, London (1993).
14. Edalat, A.: *Semi-pullbacks and Bisimulation in Categories of Markov Processes*. Math. Struct. in Comp. Science. **9** (1999), no.5, 523-543.
15. Haghverdi, E., Tabuada, P., Pappas, G.J.: *Bisimulation Relations for Dynamical, Control and Hybrid Systems*. Submitted to Theor. Comput. Science.
16. Hmissi, M.: *Semi-groupes Deterministes*. Sem. Th. Potentiel **9** (1989), Paris, LNM 1393, 135-144.
17. Joyal, A., Nielsen, M., Winskel, G.: *Bisimulation from Open Maps*. Inf. and Comp., **127(2)** (1996), 164-185.
18. Larsen, K.G., Skou, A.: *Bisimulation through Probabilistic Testing*. Inf. and Comp., **94** (1991), 1-28.
19. Meyer, P.A.: Processus de Markov. LNM., **26**, Springer Verlag, Berlin, (1976).
20. Popa, E., Popa, L.: *Morphisms for Semi-dynamical Systems*. An. St. Univ. Iasi, t.**XLIV**, f.2 (1998), 335-349.

214   M.L. Bujorianu, J. Lygeros, and M.C. Bujorianu

21. Schaft, A.J. van der: *Bisimulation of Dynamical Systems*. In R. Alur, G. Pappas Eds., Hybrid Systems: Computation and Control, 7th International Workshop, HSCC 2004, Springer LNCS 2993, 559-569.
22. Strubbe, S.N., Schaft, A.J. van der: *Bisimulation for Communicating PDPs*. (2005), Proc. of *Hybrid Systems: Computation and Control*, HSCC05, to appear.
23. Yuan, C., Lygeros, J.: *Stochastic Markovian Switching Hybrid Processes*. (2004) WP SHS, Public Deliverable DSHS3, EU project COLUMBUS (IST-2001-38314).

Position and Force Control of Nonsmooth Lagrangian Dynamical Systems Without Friction

Sophie Chareyron and Pierre-Brice Wieber

INRIA Rhône-Alpes 38334 St-Ismier Cedex, France
{Sophie.Chareyron, Pierre-Brice.Wieber}@inria.fr
http://www.inrialpes.fr/bipop/

Abstract. Analyses of position and force control laws in the case of perfectly rigid bodies have been made so far with strong assumptions on the state of the contacts such as supposing that they are permanent. We're interested here in having a look at what happens when no such assumptions is made: we are led therefore to propose a Lyapunov stability analysis of a position and force control law in the mathematical framework of nonsmooth Lagrangian dynamical systems, a typical example of hybrid dynamical systems.

1 Introduction

Many applications of robot manipulators require contact phases between the robots and their environments, and a regulation of both the position of the robots and the reaction forces at the contact points is usually demanded in this case. So far, analyses of the corresponding position and force control laws have been either focusing on robot manipulators and environments with finite stiffnesses [1] or they have been made in the case of perfectly rigid bodies with strong assumptions on the state of the contacts [2] such as supposing that they are permanent [3]. Note that with such assumptions, the dynamical system solutions are ensured to be continuous, so that they fit into the classical framework of control theory [4]. In the case of perfectly rigid bodies, when the assumption of permanent contact is relaxed, the analysis of dynamical systems turns out to be greatly complicated, we're interested in this paper in having a look at what happens in this case, and more precisely what happens with the propositions of [3].

As we will see in section 2, the dynamical behaviour of mechanical systems with non permanent contact may present impacts, discrete events that intertwine with the continuous dynamics, the landmark of hybrid dynamical system [5]. More precisely, the frictionless contact law that we will consider fits into the smaller subclass of complementarity systems [5], [6]. Now, instead of considering piecewise smooth solutions as is usually done for hybrid systems [7, 8], we will consider here the wider class of nonsmooth solutions that has been proposed in [9], [10], [11], [12], [13]. These solutions are introduced through an extensive use of convex and nonsmooth analysis, and since these mathematical tools are still unusual in control theory, we are going to spend some time in section 2 to present

M. Morari and L. Thiele (Eds.): HSCC 2005, LNCS 3414, pp. 215–225, 2005.
© Springer-Verlag Berlin Heidelberg 2005

them, and to see how this relates to the usual framework of hybrid systems. Section 3 is then entirely devoted to analysing in this nonsmooth dynamics framework the Lyapunov stability of the position and force control law proposed in [3] without the strong assumption of permanent contacts.

2   Nonsmooth Lagrangian Dynamical Systems

2.1   Systems with Non-permanent Contacts

With n the number of degrees of freedom of the dynamical system, let us consider a time-variation of generalized coordinates $q : \mathbb{R} \to \mathbb{R}^n$ and the related velocity $\dot{q} : \mathbb{R} \to \mathbb{R}^n$:

$$\forall t, t_0 \in \mathbb{R}, \ q(t) = q(t_0) + \int_{t_0}^{t} \dot{q}(\tau) \, d\tau.$$

We're interested here with Lagrangian dynamical systems which may experience non-permanent contacts of perfectly rigid bodies. Geometrically speaking, the non-overlapping of rigid bodies can be expressed as a constraint on the position of the corresponding dynamical system, a constraint that will take the form here of a closed set $\Phi \subset \mathbb{R}^n$ in which the generalized coordinates are bound to stay [11]:

$$\forall t \in \mathbb{R}, \ q(t) \in \Phi.$$

This way, contact phases correspond to phases when $q(t)$ lies on the boundary of Φ, and non-contact phases to phases when $q(t)$ lies in the interior of Φ. We will suppose that this closed set is time-invariant, and we will have to suppose that it is convex for the stability analysis of section 3.

We can define then for all $q \in \Phi$ the tangent cone [14]

$$\mathcal{T}(q) = \{ v \in \mathbb{R}^n : \ \exists \tau_k \to 0, \ \tau_k > 0,$$
$$\exists q_k \to q, \ q_k \in \Phi$$
$$\text{with } \tfrac{q_k - q}{\tau_k} \to v \},$$

and we can readily observe that if the velocity $\dot{q}(t)$ has a left and right limit at an instant t, then obviously $-\dot{q}^-(t) \in \mathcal{T}(q(t))$ and $\dot{q}^+(t) \in \mathcal{T}(q(t))$.

Now, note that $\mathcal{T}(q) = \mathbb{R}^n$ in the interior of the domain Φ, but it reduces to a half-space or even less on its boundary (Fig. 1): if the system reaches this boundary with a velocity $\dot{q}^- \notin \mathcal{T}(q)$, it won't be able to continue its movement with a velocity $\dot{q}^+ = \dot{q}^-$ and still stay in Φ (Fig. 1). A discontinuity of the velocity will have to occur then, corresponding to an impact between contacting rigid bodies, the landmark of *nonsmooth* dynamical systems.

We can also define for all $q \in \Phi$ the normal cone [14]

$$\mathcal{N}(q) = \{ v \in \mathbb{R}^n : \ \forall q' \in \Phi, \ v^T(q' - q) \leq 0 \},$$

and we will see in the inclusion (4) of section 2.3 that it is directly related to the reaction forces arising from the contacts between rigid bodies.

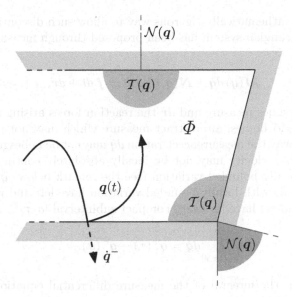

Fig. 1. Examples of tangent cones $\mathcal{T}(q)$ and normal cones $\mathcal{N}(q)$ on the boundary of the domain Φ, and example of a trajectory $q(t) \in \Phi$ that reaches this boundary with a velocity $\dot{q}^- \notin \mathcal{T}(q)$

Now, note that $\mathcal{N}(q) = \{0\}$ in the interior of the domain Φ, and it contains at least a half-line of $\mathbb{R}^n$ on its boundary (Fig. 1): this will imply the obvious observation that non-zero contact forces may be experienced only on the boundary of the domain Φ, precisely when there is a contact. Discontinuities of the contact forces might be induced because of that, what will be discussed later.

In the end, note that with these definitions, the state $(q(t), \dot{q}(t))$ appears now to stay inside the set

$$\Omega = \{(q, \dot{q}) : \; q \in \Phi, \; \dot{q} \in \mathcal{T}(q)\}.$$

2.2   Nonsmooth Lagrangian Dynamics

The dynamics of Lagrangian systems subject to Lebesgues-integrable forces are usually expressed as differential equations,

$$M(q) \frac{d\dot{q}}{dt} + N(q, \dot{q}) \, \dot{q} = f,$$

with $M(q)$ the symmetric positive definite inertia matrix that we will suppose to be a C^1 function of q, $N(q, \dot{q}) \, \dot{q}$ the corresponding nonlinear effects and f the Lebesgues-integrable forces. Classical solutions to these differential equations lead to smooth motions, with a locally absolutely continuous velocity $\dot{q}(t)$.

But we have seen that discontinuities of the velocity may have to occur in the case of Lagrangian systems experiencing non-permanent contacts between rigid bodies. A mathematically rigorous way to allow such discontinuities in the dynamics of Lagrangian system has been proposed through measure differential equations [11], [15],

$$M(q)\,d\dot{q} + N(q,\dot{q})\,\dot{q}\,dt = f\,dt + dr, \tag{1}$$

with dt the Lebesgues measure and dr the reaction forces arising from the contacts between rigid bodies, an abstract measure which may not be Lebesgues-integrable. This way, the measure acceleration $d\dot{q}$ may not be Lebesgues-integrable either so that the velocity may not be locally absolutely continuous anymore but only with locally bounded variation (see the remark below) $\dot{q} \in \mathrm{lbv}(\mathbb{R},\mathbb{R}^n)$ [11] [15]. Functions with locally bounded variation have left and right limits at every instant, and we have for every compact subinterval $[\sigma,\tau] \subset \mathbb{R}$

$$\int_{[\sigma,\tau]} d\dot{q} = \dot{q}^+(\tau) - \dot{q}^-(\sigma).$$

Considering then the integral of the measure differential equations (1) over a singleton $\{\tau\}$, we have

$$\int_{\{\tau\}} M(q)\,d\dot{q} = M(q)\int_{\{\tau\}} d\dot{q} = M(q)(\dot{q}^+(\tau) - \dot{q}^-(\tau)),$$

$$\int_{\{\tau\}} \big(N(q,\dot{q})\,\dot{q} - f\big)dt = \big(N(q,\dot{q})\,\dot{q} - f\big)\int_{\{\tau\}} dt = 0,$$

leading to the following relationship between possible discontinuities of the velocities and possible atoms of the contact forces,

$$M(q)\,\big(\dot{q}^+(\tau) - \dot{q}^-(\tau)\big) = \int_{\{\tau\}} dr,$$

or, $M(q)$ being invertible,

$$\dot{q}^+(\tau) = \dot{q}^-(\tau) + M(q)^{-1}\int_{\{\tau\}} dr. \tag{2}$$

Remark 1. *A function f is of locally bounded variation on $\mathbb{R}$ if its variation on any compact subinterval I of $\mathbb{R}$ is finite:*

$$\mathrm{Var}(f;I) = \sup_{\substack{t_0 \le t_1 \le \ldots \le t_n \\ \forall\, t_i \in I}} \sum_{i=1}^n \|f(t_i) - f(t_{i-1})\| < +\infty.$$

Note that in the framework of nonsmooth analysis, properties of functions with bounded variation are far more important than their definition, we are particularly interested in the following two properties. First as we have already seen, *functions with locally bounded variation have left and right limits at every instant, and if $d\dot{q}$ denotes their differential measure (an abstract measure that may not be Lebesgues-integrable), we have for every compact subinterval $[\sigma, \tau] \subset \mathbb{R}$*

$$\int_{[\sigma,\tau]} d\dot{q} = \dot{q}^+(\tau) - \dot{q}^-(\sigma).$$

Then, functions with locally bounded variation can be decomposed into the sum of a continuous function and a countable set of discontinuous step functions [16]. In specific cases, as when data are piecewise analytic [12], the solution to the dynamics (1) can be shown to be piecewise continuous with possibly infinitely (countably) many discontinuities. In this case, it is possible to focus distinctly on each continuous piece and each discontinuity as in the framework of hybrid systems [8],[17]. But this is usually done through an ordering of the discontinuities strictly increasing with time, which can pose problem in particular when having to go through accumulations of impacts. The framework of nonsmooth analysis appears therefore more appropriate for obtaining results in the case of impacting systems, even though the calculus rules for functions with bounded variation require some care, as shown with the following Proposition that will be used in section 3.2,

Proposition 1. *If $x \in lbv(I, \mathbb{R})$ and $y \in lbv(I, \mathbb{R})$, then the continuous function $\Phi(x, y)$, $t \longrightarrow \Phi(x(t), y(t))$ is an element of $lbv(I, \mathbb{R})$ whose differential measure equals*

$$d\Phi(x, y) = \Phi(dx, \frac{y^+ + y^-}{2}) + \Phi(dy, \frac{x^+ + x^-}{2}).$$

2.3   Inelastic Frictionless Unilateral Contacts

Following [11], we will consider that the non-permanent contacts that may be experienced by our Lagrangian systems are perfectly unilateral, frictionless and inelastic. Expressing the $\mathbb{R}^n$ valued measure dr as the product of a non-negative real measure $d\mu$ and a $\mathbb{R}^n$ valued function $r'_\mu \in L^1_{loc}(\mathbb{R}, d\mu; \mathbb{R}^n)$,

$$dr = r'_\mu \, d\mu, \tag{3}$$

the unilaterality of the contacts (no adhesive forces) together with the absence of friction corresponds to the inclusion

$$\forall t \in \mathbb{R}, \ -r'_\mu(t) \in \mathcal{N}(q(t)), \tag{4}$$

and the inelasticity of the contacts corresponds to the complementarity condition

$$\forall t \in \mathbb{R}, \ \dot{q}^+(t)^T r'_\mu(t) = 0. \tag{5}$$

One can note that on top of this complementarity condition, the inclusion (4) also induces a complementarity between $r'_\mu(t)$ and $q(t)$, but for a more in-depth presentation of these concepts and equations which are quite subtle, the interested reader should definitely refer to [11].

2.4   Some Lyapunov Stability Theory

The Lyapunov stability theory is usually presented for dynamical systems with states that vary continuously with time [4], [17], [18], Fillipov systems for example [19], [20], but we have seen that in the case of nonsmooth mechanics, the velocity and thus the state $x(t) = (q(t), \dot{q}(t))$ may present discontinuities. Lyapunov stability theory is hopefully not strictly bound to continuity properties, some results for discontinuous dynamical systems can still be derived both in the usual framework of hybrid systems [21] and in the framework of nonsmooth analysis [22]. In the following we will prefer this latter for the reasons mentioned in Remark 1, which provides for example the following theorem.

Theorem 1. *A closed invariant set $S \subset \Omega$ is globally stable if and only if there exists a function $V : \Omega \to \mathbb{R}$ such that*

(i) *there exist two continuous strictly increasing functions $\alpha(.)$ and $\beta(.)$ satisfying $\alpha(0) = 0, \beta(0) = 0$ such that*

$$\forall x \in \Omega, \ \alpha(d(x, S)) \le V(x) \le \beta(d(x, S)),$$

with $d(x, S)$ the distance between the state x and the set S, and
(ii) *for all solutions $x(t)$ to the nonsmooth dynamics (1), the function $V(x(t))$ is non-increasing with time.*

Such a function is called a Lyapunov function with respect to the stable set S.

Note now that the position and force control law that we are going to study in the next section is proved to be asymptotically stable in [3] through the use of LaSalle's invariance theorem. This latter is tightly bound to the continuity of trajectories of the systems with respect to initial conditions, a property of nonsmooth dynamical systems that holds only in some specific cases [13],[23]. For dynamical systems satisfying this continuity property, it is still possible to propose a theorem equivalent to LaSalle's [22],[24]. However in this paper, we will only consider the global stability proposed in the previous theorem.

3   Lyapunov Stability Analysis of a Position and Force Control Law

This section aims at analysing the Lyapunov stability of the position and force control law proposed in [3] without the assumption of permanent contacts between the end-effector and its environment. Based on the nonsmooth analysis framework and in particular in Theorem 1, we will be able to conclude on the stability of this control law with no need for any assumptions concerning the state of the contact experienced by the systems. Note that [3] proved that both the desired position and the desired contact forces were stable, but non-permanent contacts unfortunately won't allow to conclude on the stability of the contact forces.

3.1   A Position and Force Control Law

Let us consider now that the Lebesgues-integrable forces f acting on the dynamics (1) consist of some external forces e_f and a control u,

$$f = e_f + u.$$

With the help of this control u, we would like to stabilize both the position q of the dynamical systems and the reaction forces dr to some desired constant values q_d and $r_d\, dt$ (following (3), the desired contact forces are defined through the product of the Lebesgues measure dt and a constant vector $r_d \in \mathbb{R}^n$). First of all, these desired position and reaction forces have to be consistent with the contact model (4),

$$-r_d \in \mathcal{N}(q_d). \tag{6}$$

Following then the proposition of [3], we define the control u through the derivative of a strictly convex C^1 potential function $P(q)$, a dissipative term $C\,\dot{q}$ with C a positive definite matrix, and a compensation of the external forces,

$$u = -\frac{dP}{dq}(q) - C\,\dot{q} - e_f. \tag{7}$$

With this control law, the dynamics (1) becomes

$$M(q)\,d\dot{q} + N(q,\dot{q})\,\dot{q}\,dt = -\frac{dP}{dq}(q)\,dt - C\,\dot{q}\,dt + dr, \tag{8}$$

the equilibria of which, with $\dot{q} = 0$, are positions for which

$$0 = -\frac{dP}{dq}(q)\,dt + r'_\mu\,d\mu.$$

This equation of measures is satisfied if and only if $d\mu = dt$ and

$$0 = -\frac{dP}{dq}(q) + r'_\mu, \tag{9}$$

and through theorem VII.1.1.1 of [14], this corresponds together with (4) to the specification of the minima of $P(q)$ over the domain Φ: the equilibria of the closed loop dynamics correspond to the minima of the potential function. More precisely, since Φ is assumed to be convex and $P(q)$ strictly convex, if there is such a minimum then it is reached at a unique position: if there is an equilibrium position of the closed loop dynamics, then it is unique.

If we assume now that the potential function satisfies explicitly

$$\frac{dP}{dq}(q_d) = r_d,$$

then there is such a minimum through (6) and the same theorem of [14]: this minimum is $P(q_d)$, reached at the position q_d, and equation (9) becomes

$$0 = -r_d + r'_\mu,$$

so that the contact forces will be as desired at this equilibrium,

$$dr = r_d\,dt.$$

3.2   Lyapunov Stability Analysis

Since $P(q)$ has a global minimum reached at the unique position q_d, with

$$K(q, \dot{q}) = \frac{1}{2} \dot{q}^T M(q) \dot{q}$$

the kinetic energy of the dynamical system, the function

$$V(q, \dot{q}) = K(q, \dot{q}) + P(q) - P(q_d)$$

has 0 as a global minimum, reached at the unique state $(q_d, 0)$.

Since it is convex with a minimum reached at a unique position, we know from proposition IV.3.2.5 and definition IV.3.2.6 of [14] that the function $P(q)$ is radially unbounded. Excluding pathological behaviours of the inertia matrix, we can suppose quite directly then that the function $V(q, \dot{q})$ is also radially unbounded. Lemma 3.5 of [4] allows then to conclude that it satisfies condition (i) of the theorem of section 2.4 with respect to the set $\mathcal{S} = \{(q_d, 0)\}$, appearing therefore as a possible Lyapunov function.

Indeed, through Proposition 1 given in Remark 1, classical differentiation rules of lbv allow to compute the time-derivative of the kinetic energy,

$$dK = \frac{1}{2} \dot{q}^T \dot{M}(q, \dot{q}) \dot{q}\, dt + \frac{(\dot{q}^+ + \dot{q}^-)}{2}^T M(q)\, d\dot{q}.$$

For the closed loop dynamics (8), this time-derivative is

$$dK = \frac{1}{2} \dot{q}^T \left(\dot{M}(q, \dot{q}) - 2\, N(q, \dot{q}) \right) \dot{q}\, dt - \dot{q}^T \frac{dP}{dq}(q)\, dt$$

$$- \dot{q}^T C \dot{q}\, dt + \frac{(\dot{q}^+ + \dot{q}^-)}{2}^T dr,$$

(note that $\dot{q}^+ dt = \dot{q}^- dt = \dot{q}\, dt$) where the first term is identically 0 since $\dot{M}(q, \dot{q}) - 2\, N(q, \dot{q})$ is an antisymmetric matrix and $-\dot{q}^T C \dot{q}$ is non-positive since C is a positive matrix. Recalling then relations (2) and (3), we have

$$\frac{(\dot{q}^+ + \dot{q}^-)}{2}^T dr = \dot{q}^{+T} dr - \frac{1}{2} \left[\int_{\{\tau\}} dr \right]^T M(q)^{-1} dr$$

$$= \dot{q}^{+T} r'_\mu\, d\mu$$

$$- \frac{1}{2} \left[\int_{\{\tau\}} d\mu \right] r'_\mu{}^T M(q)^{-1} r'_\mu\, d\mu$$

where the first term is identically 0 because of the complementarity condition (5) and the second term is non-positive since the inertia matrix is positive and $d\mu \geq 0$. All this ends up with

$$dK \leq -\dot{q}^T \frac{dP}{dq}(q)\, dt,$$

and since the time-derivative of the potential function is precisely

$$dP = \dot{q}^T \frac{dP}{dq}(q)\, dt,$$

we are led to

$$dV = dK + dP \leq 0.$$

The function $V(x(t))$ is therefore non-increasing with time, condition (ii) of the theorem of section 2.4 is also satisfied, and the proof that the state $(q_d, 0)$ is globally stable with the closed loop dynamics (8) is completed.

Note that what we have proved here is the stability of the state $(q_d, 0)$ only, and not of the contact forces $r_d\, dt$: on the contrary to what appears in [3], non-zero contact forces can't be stable in our case since, as we have seen in section 2.1, non-zero contact forces may be experienced only on the boundary of the domain Φ, when there is a contact. These forces may therefore jump to zero in every neighbourhood of any equilibrium position, what is not compatible with Lyapunov stability.

3.3   An Example

Following [3], we can see for example that with a strictly convex quadratic potential function

$$P(q) = \frac{1}{2}(q - q_d)^T\, W\,(q - q_d) + r_d^T(q - q_d)$$

with a symmetric positive definite matrix W, the control law (7) becomes a strictly linear feedback

$$u = -W\,(q - q_d) - r_d - C\,\dot{q} - e_f$$

for which we know now that the equilibrium state $(q_d, 0)$, where the contact forces are $r_d\, dt$, is globally stable.

4   Conclusion

The stability of nonsmooth mechanical systems, a typical example of hybrid dynamical systems, has been studied here in the framework of convex and nonsmooth analysis.

The position and force control law proposed in [3] can be proved to be stable in this framework with no need for any assumptions concerning the state of the contacts experienced by the systems. This result is obtained with the help of differentiation rules for functions with locally bounded variations which are somehow different from the more usual ones for locally absolutely continuous functions, but which can be practiced in a very similar way, allowing to derive a Lyapunov stability analysis for nonsmooth dynamical systems very similar to what appears in the smooth case.

Extreme care must be taken though about the particularities of nonsmooth dynamical systems: if we can propose a stability theorem such as the one of section 2.4, which is very similar to usual theorems for smooth dynamical systems, it doesn't mean that the whole stability theory for smooth dynamics can be translated to the nonsmooth case without specific and sometimes subtle adaptations. The example of Lasalle's theorem discussed in section 2.4 or the fact that the contact forces can't be stable for physical reasons speak for themselves.

References

1. Yabuta, T.: Nonlinear basic stability concept of the hybrid position/force control scheme for robot manipulators. IEEE Trans. Robot. Automat. **8** (1992) 663–670
2. Bourgeot, J.M., Brogliato, B.: Tracking control of Lagrangian complementarity systems. Int. J. of Bifurcation and Chaos, special issue on Nonsmooth Dynamical Systems **15** (2005)
3. Wang, D., McClamroch, H.: Position and force control for constrained manipulator motion: Lyapunov's direct method. IEEE Trans. Robot. Automat. **9** (1993) 308–313
4. Khalil, H.: Nonlinear systems. Prentice-Hall (1996)
5. Brogliato, B.: Some perspectives on the analysis and control of complementarity systems. IEEE Transactions on Automatic Control **48** (2003) 918–935
6. Brogliato, B., Heemels, W.: Hybrid systems modeling and control. European Journal of Control. Special issue on "fundamental issues in control" **9** (2003) 177–189
7. De Carlo, R. Branicky, S.P.S., Lennartson, B.: Perspectives and results on the stability and stabilizability of hybrid systems. Proc. IEEE **88** (2000) 1069–1082
8. Lygeros, J. Johansson, K.S.S.J.Z., Sastry, S.: Dynamical properties of hybrid automata. IEEE Transactions on Automatic Control **48** (2003) 2–17
9. Schatzman, M.: A class of nonlinear differential equations of second order in time. Nonlinear Analysis, Theory, Methods & Applications **2** (1978) 355–373
10. Moreau, J.J.: Liaisons unilatérales sans frottements et chocs inélastiques. C.R. Acad.Sc.Paris **296** (1983) 1473–1476
11. Moreau, J.J.: Unilateral contact and dry friction in finite freedom dynamics. In Moreau, J.J., Panagiotopulos, P., eds.: Nonsmooth mechanics and Applications. Volume 302. Springer Verlag (1988) 1–82
12. Ballard, P.: The dynamics of discrete mechanical systems with perfect unilateral constraints. Archive for Rational Mechanics and Analysis (2000) 199–274
13. Ballard, P.: Formulation and well-posedness of the dynamics of rigid-body systems with perfect unilateral constraints. Philosophical Transactions: Mathematical, Physical & Engineering Sciences **359** (2001) 2327–2346
14. Hiriart-Urruty, J.B., Lemaréchal, C.: Convex Analysis and Minimization Algorithms. Springer Verlag, Heidelberg (1996) Two volumes - 2nd printing.
15. Moreau, J.J.: An introduction to unilateral dynamics. In Fremond, M., Maceri, F., eds.: Novel approaches in civil engineering. Springer Verlag (2001)
16. Moreau, J.J.: Bounded variation in time. In Moreau, J.J., Panagiotopulos, P., Strang, G., eds.: Topics in Nonsmooth Mechanics. Birkhäuser, Basel Boston Berlin (1988) 1–74

17. Branicky, S.: Multiple lyapunov functions and other analysis tools for switched and hybrid systems. IEEE Transactions on Automatic Control **43** (1998) 475–482
18. Zubov, V.: Methods of A.M. Lyapunov and their application. Noordhoff (1964)
19. Orlov, Y.: Extended invariance principle for nonautonomous switched systems. IEEE Transactions on Automatic Control **48** (2003) 1448–1452
20. Bacciotti, A., Ceragioli, F.: Stability and stabilization of discontinuous systems and nonsmooth lyapunov functions. ESAIM: COCV **4** (1999) 361–376
21. Ye, H. Michel, A., Hou, L.: Stability theory for hybrid dynamical systems. IEEE Transactions on Automatic Control **43** (1998) 461–474
22. Chareyron, S., Wieber, P.: Stabilization and regulation of nonsmooth lagrangain systems. Technical report, INRIA Rhône-Alpes (2004) submitted.
23. Paoli, L.: Problemes de vibro-impact: etude de la dépendance par rapport aux donnees. C.R. Acad. Sci. Paris **339** (2004) 27–32
24. Tornambè, A.: Modeling and control of impact in mechanicl systems: theory and experimental results. IEEE Transactions on Automatic Control **44** (1999) 294–309

Existence of Cascade Discrete-Continuous State Estimators for Systems on a Partial Order

Domitilla Del Vecchio and Richard M. Murray

Control and Dynamical Systems,
California Institute of Technology,
1200 E California Boulevard, Mail Stop 107-81,
Pasadena, CA 91125
{ddomitilla, murray}@cds.caltech.edu

Abstract. In this paper, a cascade discrete-continuous state estimator on a partial order is proposed and its existence investigated. The continuous state estimation error is bounded by a monotonically nonincreasing function of the discrete state estimation error, with both the estimation errors converging to zero. This work shows that the lattice approach to estimation is general as the proposed estimator can be constructed for any observable and discrete state observable system. The main advantage of using the lattice approach for estimation becomes clear when the system has monotone properties that can be exploited in the estimator design. In such a case, the computational complexity of the estimator can be drastically reduced and tractability can be achieved. Some examples are proposed to illustrate these ideas.

1   Introduction

The analysis of systems that show "hybrid" behavior is precious to several engineering areas. Embedded systems and complex systems such as the Internet, biological systems, multi-agent systems, and many others provide examples of such a hybrid behavior. The problem of estimating the state becomes relevant when asking to control these systems or to verify the correctness of their behavior as is in the case of air-traffic control systems (see for example [12] and [2]).

The coupling of continuous and discrete dynamics renders the analysis of these systems hard. As pointed out by Bemporad [3], one of the biggest issues is complexity. There are several causes of such complexity, and some are specific to the application domain. Among these, there is the absence of mathematical tools able to handle a uniform analysis of both the logic evolution and of the continuous evolution. In Del Vecchio et al. [6], it was shown that a partial order on the discrete variables can be used in order to reduce complexity of the discrete state estimator and achieve scalability in the number of variables to be estimated. In this paper, similar ideas are applied in order to estimate the continuous and the discrete variables in a unified framework.

There is a wealth of research on hybrid observer design. The pioneering work of Caines [4] proposes the observer tree method for the estimation of the discrete state of a finite state machine. The observer tree method is used also in Balluchi et al. [1] for the

M. Morari and L. Thiele (Eds.): HSCC 2005, LNCS 3414, pp. 226–241, 2005.
© Springer-Verlag Berlin Heidelberg 2005

estimation of the discrete state. The estimator proposed in this paper is similar to the decoupled estimator design proposed by [1], except that in the present work the continuous and the discrete states are estimated simultaneously and asymptotic convergence and thus tracking of the state is achieved. If the dimension of the discrete variables set is very large, the estimation problem relying on observer-tree methods becomes intractable. If the system has some order preserving properties with respect to a suitable partial order, the method that is proposed in this paper generates a computationally efficient estimator. As opposed to [13], which proposes to detect the discrete state change *a posteriori*, here estimation and tracking of the state is sought.

The basic assumption this paper relies on is that the discrete state can be estimated without the aid of the continuous state estimate. This assumption has already practical interest for example in the case of multi-robot systems. In these systems, the discrete variables (used in the control or communication protocol) are often updated on the basis of their values and of the values of measurable continuous variables, such as position. This way, the continuous state estimate can be driven by the discrete state estimate. Thus, a cascade discrete-continuous state estimator is constructed that achieves convergence of the estimation error to zero and thus tracks the value of the state. The estimator is constructed on a larger variable space equipped with a partial order, where the extended system has some properties that are referred to as order compatibility for the discrete state dynamics and induced order compatibility for the continuous state dynamics. The proposed estimator can be constructed for any system that is observable and discrete state observable, and thus the lattice approach to estimation is general. The main advantage of this method is clear when the system enjoys some monotonic properties that the estimator can exploit directly. In such a case the complexity of the estimator is drastically reduced and a scalability property can be achieved in the number of variables to be estimated. This is shown in simulation examples.

This paper is organized as follows. In Section 2, basic notions on partial orders and on observability are reviewed. In Section 3, the model is introduced. In Section 4, the estimation problem is stated formally, and a solution is proposed in Section 5. The existence result of the proposed estimator is in Section 6. To show the generality of the proposed estimation scheme, the estimator is constructed for three different examples in Section 7. Section 8 gives some computational complexity estimates that clearly show the cases where the developed approach reduces the computational burden.

2   Basic Concepts

This section reviews basic notions on partial order theory (see [5] for more details) and on observability of deterministic transition systems.

2.1   Partial Orders

A partial order is a set χ with a partial order relation "$\leq$", and it is denoted $(\chi, \leq)$. The *join* "$\vee$" and the *meet* "$\wedge$" of two elements x and w in χ are defined as $x \vee w = \sup\{x, w\}$ and $x \wedge w = \inf\{x, w\}$, if $S \subseteq \chi$, $\bigvee S = \sup S$ and $\bigwedge S = \inf S$, where $\sup\{x, w\}$ denotes the smallest element in χ that is bigger than both x and w, and $\inf\{x, w\}$ denotes the largest element in χ that is smaller than both x and w. If $x < w$ and there is no other element in between x and w, we write $x \ll w$.

Let $(\chi, \leq)$ be a partial order. If $x \wedge w \in \chi$ and $x \vee w \in \chi$ for any $x, w \in \chi$, then $(\chi, \leq)$ is a *lattice*. Let $(\chi, \leq)$ be a lattice and let $S \subseteq \chi$ be a non-empty subset of χ. Then $(S, \leq)$ is a *sublattice* of χ if $a, b \in S$ implies that $a \vee b \in S$ and $a \wedge b \in S$. If any sublattice of χ contains its least and greatest elements, then $(\chi, \leq)$ is called *complete*. Given a complete lattice $(\chi, \leq)$, we will be concerned with a special kind of a sublattice called an *interval sublattice* defined as follows. Any interval sublattice of $(\chi, \leq)$ is given by $[L, U] = \{w \in \chi : L \leq w \leq U\}$ for $L, U \in \chi$. That is, this special sublattice can be represented by only two elements. For example, the intervals of $(\mathbb{R}, \leq)$ are just the familiar closed intervals on the real line. The cardinality of an interval sublattice $[L, U]$ is denoted $\|[L, U]\|$.

The *power lattice* of a set $\mathcal{U}$, denoted $(\mathcal{P}(\mathcal{U}), \subseteq)$, is given by the power set of $\mathcal{U}$, $\mathcal{P}(\mathcal{U})$ (the set of all subsets of $\mathcal{U}$), ordered according to the set inclusion $\subseteq$. The meet and join of the power lattice is given by intersection and union. The bottom element is the empty set, that is $\perp = \emptyset$, and the top element is $\mathcal{U}$ itself, that is $\top = \mathcal{U}$.

Let $(P, \leq)$ and $(Q, \leq)$ be partially ordered sets. A map $f : P \to Q$ is (i) an *order preserving map* if $x \leq w \implies f(x) \leq f(w)$; (ii) an *order embedding* if $x \leq w \iff f(x) \leq f(w)$; (iii) an *order isomorphism* if it is order embedding and it maps P *onto* Q.

A partial order induces a notion of distance between elements in the space. In this paper, the distance function on a partial order is defined as follows.

Definition 1. (Distance on a partial order) Let $(P, \leq)$ be a partial order. A distance d on $(P, \leq)$ is a function $d : P \times P \to \mathbb{R}$ such that the following properties are verified:

  (i) $d(x, y) \geq 0$ for any $x, y \in P$ and $d(x, y) = 0$ if and only if $x = y$;
 (ii) $d(x, y) = d(y, x)$;
(iii) if $x \leq y \leq z$ then $d(x, y) \leq d(x, z)$.

Because this paper is concerned with a partial order on the space of the discrete variables as well as with a partial order on the space of the continuous variables, it is useful to introduce the Cartesian product of two partial orders (see [10] for example).

Definition 2. (Cartesian product of partial orders) Let $(P_1, \leq)$ and $(P_2, \leq)$ be two partial orders. Their Cartesian product is given by $(P_1 \times P_2, \leq)$, where $P_1 \times P_2 = \{(x, y) \mid x \in P_1 \text{ and } y \in P_2\}$ and $(x, y) \leq (x', y')$ if and only if $x \leq x'$ and $y \leq y'$. For any $(p_1, p_2) \in P_1 \times P_2$ the standard projections $\pi_1 : P_1 \times P_2 \to P_1$ and $\pi_2 : P_1 \times P_2 \to P_2$ are such that $\pi_1(p_1, p_2) = p_1$ and $\pi_2(p_1, p_2) = p_2$.

2.2   Deterministic Transition Systems and Observability

The class of systems this work is concerned with are deterministic, infinite state systems with output defined as follows. A *deterministic transition system* (DTS) is the tuple $\Sigma = (S, \mathcal{Y}, F, g)$, where S is a set of states with $s \in S$; $\mathcal{Y}$ is a set of outputs with $y \in \mathcal{Y}$; $F : S \to S$ is the state transition function; $g : S \to \mathcal{Y}$ is the output function. An execution of Σ is any sequence $\sigma = \{s(k)\}_{k \in \mathbb{N}}$ such that $s(0) \in S$ and $s(k + 1) = F(s(k))$ for all $k \in \mathbb{N}$. The set of all executions of Σ is denoted $\mathcal{E}(\Sigma)$.

Definition 3. (Observability) The deterministic transition system $\Sigma = (S, \mathcal{Y}, F, g)$ is said to be *observable* if any two different executions $\sigma_1, \sigma_2 \in \mathcal{E}(\Sigma)$ are such that there exists a k such that $g(\sigma_1(k)) \neq g(\sigma_2(k))$.

In the next section, the class of observable systems is restricted to the class of systems that are independent discrete state observable.

3   The Model

In this section, the distinction between the portion of the state that takes values in a finite set and the portion that takes values in an infinite possibly dense set is explicitly made. For a system $\Sigma = (S, \mathcal{Y}, F, g)$, suppose that $S = \mathcal{U} \times \mathcal{Z}$ with $\mathcal{U}$ a finite set, and $\mathcal{Z}$ an infinite possibly dense set; $\mathcal{Y}$ is a finite or infinite set; $F = (f, h)$, where $f : \mathcal{U} \times \mathcal{Y} \to \mathcal{U}$ and $h : \mathcal{U} \times \mathcal{Z} \to \mathcal{Z}$; $g : \mathcal{U} \times \mathcal{Z} \to \mathcal{Y}$ is the output map. These systems have the form

$$\alpha(k+1) = f(\alpha(k), y(k)) \tag{1}$$

$$z(k+1) = h(\alpha(k), z(k)) \tag{2}$$

$$y(k) = g(\alpha(k), z(k)),$$

and they are referred to as the tuple $\Sigma = (\mathcal{U} \times \mathcal{Z}, \mathcal{Y}, (f, h), g)$. The function f that updates the discrete variable α can be represented by a set of logic statements, or, in the case $\mathcal{Y}$ is finite, by a look-up table or recursive formula as is the case of finite state machines ([9]). For each value of α, the equation (2) is a difference equation. Before stating the problem in more detail, an additional definition is given.

Definition 4. (Independent discrete state observability) The system $\Sigma = (\mathcal{U} \times \mathcal{Z}, \mathcal{Y}, (f, h), g)$ is said to be *independent discrete state observable* if for any execution with output sequence $\{y(k)\}_{k \in \mathbb{N}}$, the following are verified

(i) The set of α compatible with the pair $(y(k), y(k+1))$, that is $\{\alpha \in \mathcal{U} \mid y(k) = g(\alpha, z(k))$ and $y(k+1) = g(f(\alpha, y(k)), h(\alpha, z(k)))\} := \mathcal{S}(k)$ does not depend on $z(k)$;
(ii) if two executions $\sigma_1 = \{\alpha_1(k), z_1(k)\}_{k \in \mathbb{N}}$ and $\sigma_2 = \{\alpha_2(k), z_2(k)\}_{k \in \mathbb{N}}$ are such that the sequences $\{\alpha_1(k)\}_{k \in \mathbb{N}} \neq \{\alpha_2(k)\}_{k \in \mathbb{N}}$, then there is $k > 0$ such that $\alpha_1(k) \in \mathcal{S}(k)$ and $\alpha_2(k) \notin \mathcal{S}(k)$.

Item (i) is trivially verified if $g(\alpha, z) = (g_\alpha(\alpha), g_z(\alpha, z))$, where $g_\alpha : \mathcal{U} \to \{Y_1, Y_2, ..., Y_m\}$ partitions the set $\mathcal{U}$ in equivalence classes. We allow two steps in order to have an equivalence class that is independent of $z(k)$, as this is often the case when α acts in the z dynamics. This assumption is made for the sake of simplicity. It can be relaxed to allow a finite number of steps for obtaining a set $\mathcal{S}(k)$ that does not depend on z with minor modifications to the estimator structure. From this definition, it follows that an independent discrete state observable system admits a discrete state estimator that does not involve the continuous state estimate. This property will allow to construct a cascade discrete-continuous state estimator as defined in the following section.

4   Problem Statement

Consider the deterministic transition system $\Sigma = (\mathcal{U} \times \mathcal{Z}, \mathcal{Y}, (f, h), g)$, with the output sequence $\{y(k)\}_{k \in \mathbb{N}}$. It is desirable to determine and track the value of the current state $(\alpha(k), z(k))$ of the system. This is more formally stated in the following problem.

Problem 1. (Cascade discrete-continuous state estimator) Given the deterministic transition system $\Sigma = (\mathcal{U} \times \mathcal{Z}, \mathcal{Y}, (f, h), g)$, find functions f_1, f_2, f_3, f_4, f_5 with $f_1 : \chi \times \mathcal{Y} \times \mathcal{Y} \to \chi$, $f_2 : \chi \times \mathcal{Y} \times \mathcal{Y} \to \chi$, $f_3 : \mathcal{L} \times \chi \times \mathcal{Y} \times \mathcal{Y} \to \mathcal{L}$, $f_4 : \mathcal{L} \times \chi \times \mathcal{Y} \times \mathcal{Y} \to \mathcal{L}$, $f_5 : \mathcal{L} \to \mathcal{Z}_E$, with $\mathcal{U} \subseteq \chi$, $(\chi, \leq)$ a lattice, $\mathcal{Z} \subseteq \mathcal{Z}_E$ with $(\mathcal{Z}_E, \leq)$ a lattice, $\chi \times \mathcal{Z}_E \subseteq \mathcal{L}$, $(\mathcal{L}, \leq)$ a lattice, such that the update laws

$$L(k + 1) = f_1(L(k), y(k), y(k + 1))$$
$$U(k + 1) = f_2(U(k), y(k), y(k + 1))$$
$$q_L(k + 1) = f_3(q_L(k), L(k), y(k), y(k + 1))$$
$$q_U(k + 1) = f_4(q_U(k), U(k), y(k), y(k + 1)) \tag{3}$$

with $z_L(k) = f_5(q_L(k))$ and $z_U(k) = f_5(q_U(k))$, where $L(k), U(k) \in \chi$, $L(0) := \bigwedge \chi$, $U(0) := \bigvee \chi$, $q_L(k), q_U(k) \in \mathcal{L}$, $q_L(0) = \bigwedge \mathcal{L}$, $q_U(0) = \bigvee \mathcal{L}$, and $z_L(k), z_U(k) \in \mathcal{Z}_E$, have the following properties

(i) $L(k) \leq \alpha(k) \leq U(k)$ (correctness);
(ii) $\|[L(k + 1), U(k + 1)]\| \leq \|[L(k), U(k)]\|$ (non-increasing error);
(iii) There exists $k_0 > 0$ such that $[L(k), U(k)] \cap \mathcal{U} = \alpha(k)$ for any $k \geq k_0$ (convergence);
(i') $z_L(k) \leq z(k) \leq z_U(k)$;
(ii') there is a nonnegative function $V : \mathbb{N} \to \mathbb{R}$ such that $d(z_L(k), z_U(k)) \leq V(k)$, with $V(k + 1) \leq V(k)$;
(iii') There exists $k_0' > k_0$ such that $d(z_{L'}(k), z_{U'}(k)) = 0$ for any $k \geq k_0'$, where $L' = \bigwedge([L, U] \cap \mathcal{U})$, $U' = \bigvee([L, U] \cap \mathcal{U})$, $z_{L'}(k) = f_5(q_{L'}(k))$, $z_{U'}(k) = f_5(q_{U'}(k))$, $q_{L'}(k+1) = f_3(q_{L'}(k), L'(k), y(k), y(k + 1))$, and $q_{U'}(k + 1) = f_4(q_{U'}(k), U'(k), y(k), y(k + 1))$, with $q_{L'}(0) = q_L(0)$ and $q_{U'}(0) = q_U(0)$, for some distance function "d".

The update laws (3) are in cascade form as the variables L and U are updated on the basis of their previous values and on the basis of the output, while the variables q_L and q_U are updated on the basis of their previous values and on the basis of the values of L and U respectively. Note that the lower and the upper bound estimates of $z(k)$ are outputs of the laws that update $q_L(k)$ and $q_U(k)$, which lie in the space $\mathcal{L}$. Properties (iii) and (iii') roughly ask that the lower and upper bounds shrink to $\alpha(k)$ and $z(k)$. Property (ii') gives a monotonic bound on the continuous variable estimation error.

Note that the distance function "d" has been left unspecified for the moment, as its form depends on the particular partial order chosen $(\mathcal{Z}_E, \leq)$. In the case in which $\mathcal{Z} = \mathcal{Z}_E$ and the order is established component-wise, the distance can be the classical euclidean distance. In the following section, a solution to the Problem 1 is proposed.

5   Estimator Construction

Given the deterministic transition system $\Sigma = (\mathcal{U} \times \mathcal{Z}, \mathcal{Y}, (f,h), g)$, a set of sufficient conditions that allow a solution to Problem 1 is provided. With this respect, some definitions involving the extension of the system Σ to a lattice are useful.

Definition 5. (System extension) Consider the system $\Sigma = (\mathcal{U} \times \mathcal{Z}, \mathcal{Y}, (f,h), g)$. Let $(\chi, \leq)$, $(\mathcal{Z}_E, \leq)$, and $(\mathcal{L}, \leq)$ be lattices with $\mathcal{U} \subseteq \chi$, $\mathcal{Z} \subseteq \mathcal{Z}_E$, and $\chi \times \mathcal{Z}_E \subseteq \mathcal{L}$. An extension of Σ on the lattice $(\mathcal{L}, \leq)$ is given by $\tilde{\Sigma} = (\mathcal{L}, \mathcal{Y}, \tilde{F}, \tilde{g})$ such that

(i) $\tilde{F} : \mathcal{L} \times \mathcal{Y} \to \mathcal{L}$ and $\tilde{F}|_{\mathcal{U} \times \mathcal{Z} \times \mathcal{Y}} = (f,h)$, and $\mathcal{L} - (\mathcal{U} \times \mathcal{Z})$ is invariant under $\tilde{F}$;
(ii) $\tilde{F}|_{\chi \times \mathcal{Z}_E \times \mathcal{Y}} = (\tilde{f}, \tilde{h})$ where $\tilde{f} : \chi \times \mathcal{Y} \to \chi$, $\tilde{f}|_{\mathcal{U} \times \mathcal{Y}} = f$, $\tilde{h} : \chi \times \mathcal{Z}_E \to \mathcal{Z}_E$, and $\tilde{h}|_{\mathcal{U} \times \mathcal{Z}} = h$;
(iii) $\tilde{g} : \mathcal{L} \to \mathcal{Y}$ and $\tilde{g}|_{\mathcal{U} \times \mathcal{Z}} = g$;
(iv) for any $q \in \mathcal{L}$ there exist $(w_1, \bar{z}_1), (w_2, \bar{z}_2) \in \chi \times \mathcal{Z}_E$ such that $(w_1, \bar{z}_1) \leq q \leq (w_2, \bar{z}_2)$, where $a_L(q) := \max_{(\mathcal{L}, \leq)}\{(w,\bar{z}) \in \chi \times \mathcal{Z}_E \mid q \geq (w,\bar{z})\}$ and $a_U(q) := \min_{(\mathcal{L}, \leq)}\{(w,\bar{z}) \in \chi \times \mathcal{Z}_E \mid q \leq (w,\bar{z})\}$.

Item (iv) of the above definition establishes that the chosen lattices are such that any element in $\mathcal{L}$ that is not in $\chi \times \mathcal{Z}_E$ can be approximated by two elements in $\chi \times \mathcal{Z}_E$, $a_L(q)$ and $a_U(q)$. These are the lower and upper approximation of q respectively. Note that if $q \in \chi \times \mathcal{Z}_E$, then $a_L(q) = a_U(q) = q$. The next definition links the discrete state dynamics of $\tilde{\Sigma}$ with the partial order $(\chi, \leq)$.

Definition 6. (Order compatibility) The pair $(\tilde{\Sigma}, (\chi, \leq))$ is said to be *order compatible* if the following are verified

(i) $\{w \in \chi \mid y(k+1) = \tilde{g}(\tilde{f}(w, y(k)), \tilde{h}(w, z(k)))$ and $y(k) = \tilde{g}(w, z(k))\} = [l_w(k), u_w(k)]$ for $l_w(k), u_w(k) \in \chi$;
(ii) $\tilde{f} : ([l_w(k), u_w(k)], y(k)) \to [\tilde{f}(l_w(k), y(k)), \tilde{f}(u_w(k), y(k))]$ is order isomorphic.

Item (i) in the above definition establishes that the set of $w \in \chi$ compatible with the pair $(y(k), y(k+1))$ for any execution σ with output sequence $\{y(k)\}_{k \in \mathbb{N}}$ is a sublattice interval in χ. Note that $S(k) = [l_w(k), u_w(k)] \cap \mathcal{U}$ by definition. Two steps $k, k+1$ are allowed to obtain a set of $w \in \chi$ compatible with the output that does not depend on the values of z. For the construction of a cascade discrete-continuous state estimator, the case in which the partial order $(\mathcal{L}, \leq)$ is induced by the partial order $(\chi, \leq)$ by means of the system dynamics is of interest. Thus, a new notion of order compatibility is introduced in the next definition.

Definition 7. (Induced order compatibility) The pair $(\tilde{\Sigma}, (\mathcal{L}, \leq))$ is said to be *induced order compatible* if

(i) for any $w_1 \leq w_2$ in $[l_w(k), u_w(k)]$, there are $l_q(k, w_1), u_q(k, w_2) \in \mathcal{L}$ such that

$$\{q \in \mathcal{L} \mid \pi_1 \circ a_L(q) = w_1, \ \pi_1 \circ a_U(q) = w_2, \ y(k+1) = \tilde{g}(\tilde{F}(q, y(k))), \text{ and } y(k) = \tilde{g}$$
$$(q)\} \subseteq [l_q(k, w_1), u_q(k, w_2)];$$

(ii) $a_L(l_q(k, w_1)) = (w_1, l_z(k, w_1))$ and $a_U(u_q(k, w_2)) = (w_2, u_z(k, w_2))$, for $l_z(k, w_1), u_z(k, w_2) \in \mathcal{Z}_E$;

(iii) $\tilde{F}$: $([l_q(k, w_1), u_q(k, w_2)], y(k)) \rightarrow [\bar{F}(l_q(k, w_1), y(k)), \bar{F}(u_q(k, w_2), y(k))]$ is order preserving, and $\tilde{F}$: $(\alpha \times [l_z(k, \alpha), u_z(k, \alpha)], y(k)) \rightarrow [\bar{F}(\alpha, l_z(k, \alpha), y(k)),$
$\bar{F}(\alpha, u_z(k, \alpha), y(k))]$ is order isomorphic;
(iv) for any $[L, U] \subseteq [l_w(k), u_w(k)]$

$$d\left(\pi_2 \circ a_L \circ \tilde{F}(l_q(k, L), y(k)), \pi_2 \circ a_U \circ \tilde{F}(u_q(k, U), y(k))\right) \leq \gamma(\|[L, U]\|),$$

for some distance function "d",$\gamma : \mathbb{N} \rightarrow \mathbb{R}$ a monotonic function of its argument.

Item (i) of this definition means that a sublattice interval in $(\chi, \leq)$ compatible with the output pair $(y(k), y(k + 1))$ induces a sublattice interval in $(\mathcal{L}, \leq)$ corresponding to the same output pair. Item (ii) specifies that such output interval is approximated by the Cartesian product of two sublattice intervals in $(\chi, \leq)$ and in $(\mathcal{Z}_E, \leq)$. Item (iii) establishes the usual order preserving properties of the extension, and item (iv) establishes that the size of the interval lattice in $(\mathcal{Z}_E, \leq)$ induced by an interval $[L, U] \in \chi$ increases with the size of $[L, U]$. A solution to the Problem 1 is proposed by the following theorem.

Theorem 1. *Given the system* $\Sigma = (\mathcal{U} \times \mathcal{Z}, \mathcal{Y}, (f, h), g)$, *assume that there are lattices* $(\chi, \leq)$, $(\mathcal{Z}_E, \leq)$, *and* $(\mathcal{L}, \leq)$, *with* $\mathcal{U} \subseteq \chi$, $\mathcal{Z} \subseteq \mathcal{Z}_E$, *and* $\chi \times \mathcal{Z}_E \subseteq \mathcal{L}$ *such that the pairs* $(\tilde{\Sigma}, (\chi, \leq))$ *and* $(\tilde{\Sigma}, (\mathcal{L}, \leq))$ *are order compatible and induced order compatible respectively. Then a solution to Problem 1 is provided by*

$$L(k + 1) = \tilde{f}(l_w(k) \vee L(k), y(k))$$
$$U(k + 1) = \tilde{f}(u_w(k) \wedge U(k), y(k))$$
$$q_L(k + 1) = \tilde{F}(q_L(k) \vee l_q(k, l_w(k) \vee L(k)), y(k))$$
$$q_U(k + 1) = \tilde{F}(q_U(k) \wedge u_q(k, u_w(k) \wedge U(k)), y(k)). \tag{4}$$

with $z_L(k) = \pi_2 \circ a_L(q_L(k))$ *and* $z_U(k) = \pi_2 \circ a_U(q_U(k))$.

Proof. The idea of the proof is analogous to the one proposed in [8]. Here, a sketch is provided, which highlights the differences due to the more general framework considered in this paper. For the proof of (i)-(ii)-(iii), the reader is deferred to [6]. Define $U^* = u_w(k) \wedge U(k)$, $L^* = l_w(k) \vee L(k)$, $q_U^* = q_U(k) \wedge l_q(k, U^*)$, and $q_L^* = q_L(k) \vee l_q(k, L^*)$. The dependence of u_q and l_q on their arguments is omitted, as well as the dependence of $\tilde{F}$ on y.

Proof of (i'). By using induction argument on k and exploiting the order preserving property of $\tilde{F}$, one can show that $q_L(k) \leq (\alpha(k), z(k)) \leq q_U(k)$ (see Figure 1) for any k. By the the fact that $\pi_2 \circ a_L$ and $\pi_2 \circ a_U$ are order preserving functions, (i') follows (see Figure 1).

Proof of (ii'). Using the order preserving property of $\tilde{F}$, of $\pi_2 \circ a_L$, and of $\pi_2 \circ a_U$, one deduces that $z_L(k + 1) \geq \pi_2 \circ a_L \circ \tilde{F}(l_q(k, L^*))$ and $z_U(k + 1) \leq \pi_2 \circ a_U \circ \tilde{F}(u_q(k, U^*))$ (see Figure 1). By exploiting the property (iii) of the distance function in Definition 1, and the property (iv) given in Definition 7, one can infer that $d(z_L(k + 1), z_U(k + 1)) \leq \gamma(\|[L^*, U^*]\|)$. Since $\tilde{f}$ is order isomorphic, it follows that $\|[L^*, U^*]\| = \|[\tilde{f}(L^*, y), \tilde{f}(U^*, y)]\|$. Thus, (ii') of Problem 1 is satisfied with $V(k) = \gamma(\|[L(k), U(k)]\|)$.

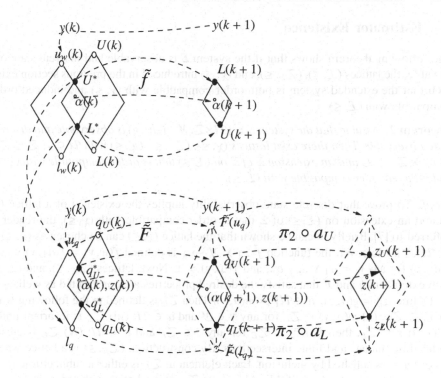

Fig. 1. Hasse diagrams representing the updates of the estimator in Theorem 1

Proof of (iii'). For $k > k_0$, $L'(k) = \alpha(k) = U'(k)$ as $[L(k), U(k)] \cap \mathcal{U} = \alpha(k)$. As a consequence, $q_{L'}(k+1) = F(q_{L'}(k) \vee l_q(k, \alpha(k)))$ and $q_{U'}(k+1) = \ddot{F}(q_{U'}(k) \vee u_q(k, \alpha(k)))$, where $l_q(k, \alpha) = (\alpha, l_z(k, \alpha))$ and $u_q(k, \alpha) = (\alpha, u_z(k, \alpha))$. One then uses the facts that $(\alpha, l_z(k, \alpha)) \le q_{L'}(k) \vee l_q(k, \alpha(k))$, $q_{U'}(k) \vee u_q(k, \alpha(k)) \le (\alpha, u_z(k, \alpha))$, the fact that $\tilde{F}$: $(\alpha \times [l_z(k, \alpha), u_z(k, \alpha)]) \to [\tilde{F}(\alpha, l_z(k, \alpha)), \tilde{F}(\alpha, u_z(k, \alpha))]$ is order isomorphic, and the fact that $\mathcal{L} - (\mathcal{U} \times \mathcal{Z})$ is invariant under $\tilde{F}$. Proceeding by contradiction, if for any k there are $(\alpha', z_1'), (\alpha', z_2')$ in $[q_{L'}(k), q_{U'}(k)] \cap (\mathcal{U} \times \mathcal{Z})$ that are compatible with the output, there must be $(\alpha, z_1), (\alpha, z_2) \in [q_{L'}(k-1), q_{U'}(k-1)] \cap (\mathcal{U} \times \mathcal{Z})$ such that $(\alpha', z_1') = F(\alpha, z_1)$ and $(\alpha', z_2') = F(\alpha, z_2)$. Also, $(\alpha, z_1), (\alpha, z_2)$ are compatible with the output as well (see Figure 1). Since this is true for any k, one can construct two executions of Σ that are different and share the same output sequence. This contradicts observability of Σ. Then there must be $k > k_0$ such that $[q_{L'}(k), q_{U'}(k)] \cap (\mathcal{U} \times \mathcal{Z}) = (\alpha(k), z(k))$, and therefore $z_{L'}(k) = z_{U'}(k) = z(k)$.

In the following section, conditions in order to verify the assumptions needed for the construction of the estimator given in Theorem 1 are given. I particular, observability and discrete state observability are sufficient conditions for the estimator construction, and therefore the proposed estimation approach on a lattice is general.

6   Estimator Existence

The following theorem shows that if the system Σ is observable and discrete state observable, the lattices $(\mathcal{L}, \leq)$, $(\mathcal{Z}_E, \leq)$, and $(\chi, \leq)$ introduced in the previous section exist, such that the extended system is both order compatible with $(\chi, \leq)$ and induced order compatible with $(\mathcal{L}, \leq)$.

Theorem 2. *Assume that the system* $\Sigma = (\mathcal{U} \times \mathcal{Z}, \mathcal{Y}, (f, h), g)$ *is observable and discrete state observable. Then there exist lattices* $(\chi, \leq)$, $(\mathcal{Z}_E, \leq)$, $(\mathcal{L}, \leq)$ *with* $\mathcal{U} \subseteq \chi$, $\mathcal{Z} \subseteq \mathcal{Z}_E$, *and* $\chi \times \mathcal{Z}_E \subseteq \mathcal{L}$, *and an extension* $\tilde{\Sigma}$ *of* Σ *on* $(\mathcal{L}, \leq)$ *that is order compatible with* $(\chi, \leq)$ *and induced order compatible with* $(\mathcal{L}, \leq)$.

Proof. To prove that discrete state observability implies the existence of a lattice $(\chi, \leq)$ and an extension on $(\mathcal{L}, \leq)$ of Σ that is order compatible with $(\chi, \leq)$, the reader is deferred to [7]. Briefly, it can be shown that the lattice $(\chi, \leq)$ can be chosen as $(\chi, \leq) = (\mathcal{P}(\mathcal{U}), \subseteq)$. Moreover, the function $\tilde{f} : \chi \times \mathcal{Y} \to \chi$ is defined $\tilde{f}(w, y) = f(\alpha_1, y) \vee \ldots \vee f(\alpha_n, y)$ for any $w = \alpha_1 \vee \ldots \vee \alpha_n$, and $\tilde{f}(\perp, y) = \perp$. Next, lattices $(\mathcal{Z}_E, \leq)$, and $(\mathcal{L}, \leq)$ with extensions $\tilde{h}$ and $\tilde{F}$ that satisfy the desired properties are constructed as well.

Define $\{z | y = g(\alpha, z), \ \alpha \in \mathcal{U}\} := m(\alpha, y)$. Then $\mathcal{Z}_E$ is defined in the following way: (i) $\mathcal{Z} \subseteq \mathcal{Z}_E$; (ii) $m(\alpha, y) \in \mathcal{Z}_E$ for any $y \in \mathcal{Y}$ and $\alpha \in \mathcal{U}$; (iii) $\mathcal{Z}_E$ is invariant under h, i.e. if $\bar{z} \in \mathcal{Z}_E$, then $h(\alpha, \bar{z}) \in \mathcal{Z}_E$ for any $\bar{z} \in \mathcal{Z}_E$ and $\alpha \in \mathcal{U}$; (iv) $\mathcal{Z}_E$ is closed under finite unions and finite intersections. By construction, $(\mathcal{Z}_E, \leq)$ is a lattice where the order is established by inclusion. Each element in $\mathcal{Z}_E$ is either a submanifold of $\mathcal{Z}$ or a union of disjoint submanifolds. Also, $(\chi \times \mathcal{Z}_E, \leq)$ is a lattice with order established component-wise. Define $(\mathcal{L}, \leq) := (\mathcal{P}(\chi \times \mathcal{Z}_E), \subseteq)$. Obviously, $\chi \times \mathcal{Z}_E \subseteq \mathcal{L}$. Any element $q \in \mathcal{L}$ has the form $q = (w_1, \bar{z}_1) \vee \ldots \vee (w_k, \bar{z}_k)$, where $\bar{z}_j \in \mathcal{Z}_E$ and $w_i \in \chi$.

Define the function $\tilde{F} : \mathcal{L} \times \mathcal{Y} \to \mathcal{L}$ in the following way. For any $q = (w_1, \bar{z}_1) \vee \ldots \vee (w_k, \bar{z}_k) \in \mathcal{L}$, define (omit the dependence on y for simplifying notation)

$$\tilde{F}(q) := \tilde{F}(w_1, \bar{z}_1) \vee \ldots \vee (\tilde{F}(w_k, \bar{z}_n),$$

where $\tilde{F}(w_i, \bar{z}_i) := (\tilde{f}(w_i), \tilde{h}(w_i, \bar{z}_i))$. Let $w_i = \alpha_{i,1} \vee \ldots \vee \alpha_{i,p_i}$ and $\bar{z}_i = m_{i,1} \vee \ldots \vee m_{i,n_i}$ with $m_{i,1}$ submanifolds of $\mathcal{Z}$, then $\tilde{h} : \chi \times \mathcal{Z}_E \to \mathcal{Z}_E$ is defined such that $\tilde{h}(w_i, \bar{z}_i) := \vee_{l,j} h(\alpha_{i,l}, m_{i,j})$. From this definition, it follows that $\tilde{F}$ is order preserving. Also, $\tilde{F}(\perp) := \perp$.

The function $\tilde{g} : \mathcal{L} \to \mathcal{Y}$ is defined in the following way. For any $q \in \mathcal{L}$ for $q = (w_1, \bar{z}_1) \vee \ldots \vee (w_k, \bar{z}_k)$, $w_i = \alpha_{i,1} \vee \ldots \vee \alpha_{i,p_i}$, and $\bar{z}_i = m_{i,1} \vee \ldots \vee m_{i,n_i}$

$$\tilde{g}(q) := y \text{ iff } \tilde{g}(w_i, \bar{z}_i) = y,$$

with $\tilde{g}(w_i, \bar{z}_i) = y$ iff $g(\alpha_{i,l}, m_{i,j}) = y$ for any l, j, where $g(\alpha_{i,l}, m_{i,j}) = y$ if and only if $m_{i,j} \subseteq m(\alpha_{i,j}, y)$ by definition of $m(\alpha_{i,j}, y)$.

For any $q = (w_1, \bar{z}_1) \vee \ldots \vee (w_k, \bar{z}_k) \in \mathcal{L}$, its lower and upper approximations are defined as $a_L(q) := (w_1 \wedge \ldots \wedge w_k, \bar{z}_1 \wedge \ldots \wedge \bar{z}_k)$ and $a_U(q) := (w_1 \vee \ldots \vee w_k, \bar{z}_1 \vee \ldots \vee \bar{z}_k)$. An example of elements in the lattice $(\mathcal{L}, \leq)$ with lower and upper approximations is shown in Figure 2.

The lattices and the system extension have been constructed. Now, the items of Definition 6 and Definition 7 can be checked. Item (i) of Definition 6 is satisfied with

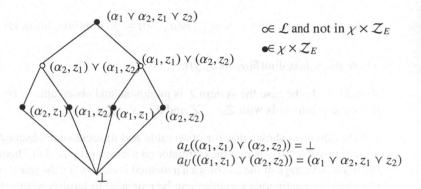

$\in \mathcal{L}$ and not in $\chi \times \mathcal{Z}_E$

$\in \chi \times \mathcal{Z}_E$

$a_L((\alpha_1, z_1) \vee (\alpha_2, z_2)) = \bot$

$a_U((\alpha_1, z_1) \vee (\alpha_2, z_2)) = (\alpha_1 \vee \alpha_2, z_1 \vee z_2)$

Fig. 2. Hasse diagram representing elements in the lattice $(\mathcal{L}, \leq)$

$[l_w, u_w] = [\bot, w]$ for $w = \alpha_1 \vee \ldots \vee \alpha_n$, with α_i such that $g(\alpha_i, z(k)) = y(k)$ and $\tilde{g}(f(\alpha_i, y(k)), \tilde{h}(\alpha_i, z(k))) = y(k + 1)$. Items (i)-(ii) of Definition 7 are satisfied with $\{q \in \mathcal{L} \mid y(k) = \tilde{g}(q), \pi_1 \circ a_L(q) = \bot, \pi_1 \circ a_U(q) = w\} = [\bot, u_q(k, w)]$ with $u_q(k, w) = (\alpha_1, m(\alpha_1, y(k))) \vee \ldots \vee (\alpha_n, m(\alpha_n, y(k)))$ if $w = \alpha_1 \vee \ldots \vee \alpha_n$. Also, $a_L(\bot) = \bot$ and $\pi_2 \circ a_U(u_q(k, w)) = m(\alpha_1, y(k)) \vee \ldots \vee m(\alpha_n, y(k))$.

Item (iii) of Definition 7 is satisfied because $\tilde{F}$ is order preserving by construction and because $\tilde{F} : \alpha \times [\bot, m(\alpha, y)] \rightarrow [\bot, \tilde{F}(\alpha, m(\alpha, y))]$ is one-one because the system is observable.

To verify (iv) of Definition 7, a distance function on $\mathcal{Z}_E$ is defined. For any $\bar{z}_1, \bar{z}_2 \in \mathcal{Z}_E$, define

$$d(\bar{z}_1, \bar{z}_2) := \begin{cases} |\dim(\bar{z}_1) - \dim(\bar{z}_2)| & \text{if } \bar{z}_1 \text{ and } \bar{z}_2 \text{ are related} \\ 1 & \text{if } \bar{z}_1 \text{ and } \bar{z}_2 \text{ are not related,} \end{cases} \tag{5}$$

where if $\bar{z} = m_1 \vee \ldots \vee m_n$, $\dim(\bar{z}) := \sum_i \dim(m_i)$, and $\dim(m_i)$ denotes the dimension of the submanifold $m_i \subset \mathcal{Z}$. Define $\dim(\bot) = 0$, $\dim(z) = 1$ for any $z \in \mathcal{Z}$, thus a submanifold isomorphic to $\mathbb{R}^m$ has dimension $m + 1$. Properties (i)-(ii) of Definition 1 are verified. (Note that any two points in $\mathcal{Z}$ are not related.) To verify (iii) of the Definition 1, consider $\bar{z}_1 \leq \bar{z}_2$ for $\bar{z}_1, \bar{z}_2 \in \mathcal{Z}_E$, and compute $d(\bot, \bar{z}_1)$ and $d(\bot, \bar{z}_2)$. If $\bar{z}_1 \leq \bar{z}_2$, by the way $\mathcal{Z}_E$ has been constructed, it means that there are m_i and m'_i submanifolds in $\mathcal{Z}_E$ such that $\bar{z}_1 = m_1 \vee \ldots \vee m_n$, and $\bar{z}_2 = m'_1 \vee \ldots \vee m'_p$ with $n \leq p$, and for any i there is a j such that $m_i \subseteq m'_j$. Thus, $\dim(\bar{z}_1) = \dim(m_1) + \ldots + \dim(m_n)$ and $\dim(\bar{z}_2) = \dim(m'_1) + \ldots + \dim(m'_p)$ with $n \leq p$ and $\dim(m_i) \leq \dim(m'_i)$. Thus expression (5) defines a distance function according to Definition 1. Thus, for any $[\bot, U] \subseteq [\bot, u_w]$ with $U = \alpha_1 \vee \ldots \vee \alpha_n$

$$d(\bot, \pi_2 \circ a_U \circ \tilde{F}(u_q(k, U))) = d(\bot, h(\alpha_1, m(\alpha_1, y)) \vee \ldots \vee h(\alpha_n, m(\alpha_n, y))),$$

as $\tilde{F}(u_q(k, U)) = (f(\alpha_1), h(\alpha_1, m(\alpha_1, y)) \vee \ldots \vee (f(\alpha_n), h(\alpha_n, m(\alpha_n, y)))$, $a_U \circ \tilde{F}(u_q(k, U)) = (f(\alpha_1) \vee \ldots \vee f(\alpha_n), h(\alpha_1, m(\alpha_1, y)) \vee \ldots \vee h(\alpha_n, m(\alpha_n, y)))$, and thus $\pi_2 \circ a_U \circ \tilde{F}(u_q(k, U)) = h(\alpha_1, m(\alpha_1, y)) \vee \ldots \vee h(\alpha_n, m(\alpha_n, y))$. Concluding, the definition of distance yields to

$$d(\bot, h(\alpha_1, m(\alpha_1, y)) \vee \dots \vee h(\alpha_n, m(\alpha_n, y))) = \sum_{i=1}^{n} \dim(h(\alpha_i, m(\alpha_i, y)) \le d_M |[\bot, U]|,$$

where $d_M = \max_i \dim(h(\alpha_i, m(\alpha_i, y))$.

Remark 1. In the case the system Σ is monotone and observable in two steps (see [8]), the same result holds with $\mathcal{Z}_E = \mathcal{Z}$ and $\mathcal{L} = \chi \times \mathcal{Z}$.

This theorem shows that for observable and discrete state observable systems it is always possible to construct the estimator on a lattice proposed in Theorem 1. However, the main advantage of the use of such a method is clear when the space of discrete and/or the space of continuous variables can be extended to lattices where the order relation can be efficiently computed using algebraic properties. This is the case of the monotone deterministic transition systems considered in [8]. To illustrate this point, in the next section three examples are proposed.

7   Simulation Examples

The first example is a linear hybrid automaton where a lattice of the type constructed in the proof of Theorem 2 is used. The second example is characterized by a continuous dynamics which is monotone (see [11]), and this allows to have $\mathcal{Z}_E = \mathcal{Z}$ with a cone partial order. The third example is a multi-robot example proposed in [8], which is a monotone DTS, and thus it allows the largest complexity reduction.

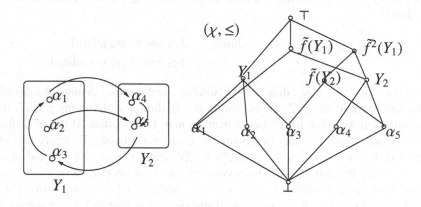

Fig. 3. Map f and output function for the automaton of Example 1 (left). Lattice $(\chi, \le)$ and the extended function $\tilde{f}$ (right)

Example 1. Linear discrete time hybrid automaton. Define $\mathcal{U} = \{\alpha_1, \alpha_2, \alpha_3, \alpha_4, \alpha_5\}$, and $\alpha(k + 1) = f(\alpha(k))$ where f is defined in the Figure 3 left. Assume $\mathcal{Z} = \mathbb{R}^n$, $z(k + 1) = A(\alpha(k))z(k) + B(\alpha(k))$, where $A(\alpha_i) = A_i \in \mathbb{R}^n \times \mathbb{R}^n$ and $B(\alpha_i) = B_i \in \mathcal{Z}$. The output function g is such that $g(\alpha, z) = (g_\alpha(\alpha), g_z(\alpha, z))$, where $g_\alpha : \mathcal{U} \to \{Y_1, Y_2\}$ and $g_z(\alpha, z) = C(\alpha)z$, with $C(\alpha_i) = C_i \in \mathbb{R}^m \times \mathcal{Z}$.

An instance of such an example is considered with $n = 3$, where $A_1 = ((1, 1, 1)', (0, 1, 1)', (0, 0, 1)')'$, $A_2 = ((1/2, 1/2, 1/2)', (1, 2, 2)', (0, 0, 1)')'$, $A_3 = ((2, 1, 1)', (0, 1, 1)', (2, 0, 0)')'$, $A_4 = ((1, 1, 1)', (1, 1, 0)', (0, 0, 1)')'$, $A_5 = ((1, 0, 0)', (1, 1, 1)', (1, 1, 0)')'$, $C_1 = (1, 0, 0)$, $C_2 = (1, 1, 2)$, $C_3 = (0, 0, 0)$, $C_4 = (1, 0, 0)$, and $C_5 = (0, 1, 1)$. The values of B_i are not relevant for computing the estimator performance, and thus they are omitted.

For the discrete state estimate, the minimal lattice $(\chi, \leq)$ where the system is extended is shown in Figure 3 right. Its size is always smaller than $|\mathcal{U}|^2$ as pointed out in [7], and its construction is analogous to the construction of the observer tree as done in [4] and [1].

For the continuous state estimate, the lattice $(\mathcal{Z}_E, \leq)$ is constructed according to the proof of Theorem 2, where the submanifolds are affine linear subspaces. Thus, $z_U(k)$ at each step k is a collection of affine linear subspaces, each given by the set of $z \in \mathbb{R}^3$ such that $M_i(k)z = (Y(k) - V_i(k))$, where $M_i(k) = (C(\alpha_i)', (C(f(\alpha_i))A(\alpha_i))', ..., (C(f^{k-1}(\alpha_i))A(f^{k-2}(\alpha_i)))')'$, $V_i(k) = (0, C(f(\alpha_i))B(\alpha_i), ...C(f^{k-1}(\alpha_i))B(f^{k-2}(\alpha_i)))'$, $Y(k) = (y(0), ..., y(k-1))'$, and α_i is such that $f^{k-1}(\alpha_i) \in [\bot, U(k)]$, for $U(k) \in \chi$ and $i \in \{1, .., 5\}$. When only one α_i is left in $[\bot, U(k)]$ and the corresponding matrix $M_i(k)$ has rank equal to n, the estimator has converged. Thus, define $d(\bot, z_U(k)) = \sum_{i=1}^{5} \beta(M_i(k))$ where

$$\beta(M_i(k)) := \begin{cases} 0 & \text{if } f^{k-1}(\alpha_i) \notin [\bot, U(k)] \\ (n+1) - \text{rank}(M_i(k)) & \text{otherwise} \end{cases}$$

As a consequence, when $d(\bot, z_U(k)) = 1$, the estimator has converged and $z(k) = M_j(k)^\dagger (Y(k) - V_j(k))$ for some $j \in \{1, ..., 5\}$, where $M_j(k)^\dagger$ is the pseudoinverse of $M_j(k)$. Note that, after the first k at which $d(\bot, z_U(k)) = 1$, the state of the system is tracked. The behavior of $d(\bot, U(k)) := |[\bot, U(k)]|$ and of $d(\bot, z_U(k))$ are illustrated in the left plot of Figure 4. Note that a simultaneous discrete-continuous state estimation allows faster convergence rates of the continuous estimate with respect to the case in which the continuous estimate takes place after the discrete estimate has converged.

In this example, the continuous variable space does not have monotone properties. As a consequence, the representation of the elements of $(\chi, \leq)$ and of $(\mathcal{Z}_E, \leq)$ involves a listing of objects: for χ, there is a listing of α_is and for $\mathcal{Z}$ we have a listing of linear subspaces. Moreover, to represent each linear subspace, a number of constants larger than n (the number of constants needed for representing an element in $\mathbb{R}^n$) is needed. A measure of the complexity of the estimator is given in the sequel. If $|\mathcal{U}|$ is very large, this choice of the partial orders renders the estimation process prohibitive. A case in which a different partial order must be used for computational tractability, is presented in Example 3.

Example 2. This example considers the case in which it is possible to choose $\mathcal{Z}_E = \mathcal{Z}$ because the system is monotone (see [8] for a formal definition). Let again $\mathcal{U} = \{\alpha_1, \alpha_2, \alpha_3, \alpha_4, \alpha_5\}$, and $\alpha(k+1) = f(\alpha(k))$ where f is defined in Figure 3 (left). The continuous dynamics is given by

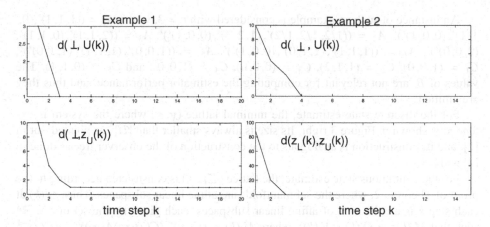

Fig. 4. Estimator performance: example 1 (left) and example 2 (right)

$$z_1(k + 1) = (1 - \beta)z_1(k) - \beta z_{i,2}(k) + 2\beta X(\alpha(k))$$
$$z_2(k + 1) = (1 - \lambda)z_2(k) + \lambda X(\alpha(k)), \qquad (6)$$

where $\beta = 0.1$, $\lambda = 0.1$, $X(\alpha_i) := 10i$ for $i \in \{1, ..., 5\}$. The minimal lattice $(\chi, \leq)$ is shown in Figure 3 (right). In this case $\mathcal{L} = \chi \times \mathcal{Z}$, where $\mathcal{Z} = \mathbb{R}^2$, and the order $(\mathcal{Z}, \leq)$ is chosen such that $(z_1^a, z_2^a) \leq (z_1^b, z_2^b)$ if and only if $z_2^a \leq z_2^b$. The function $\tilde{h}$: $\chi \times \mathcal{Z} \to \mathcal{Z}$ is defined by defining the function $\tilde{X} : \chi \to \mathbb{R}$ in the following way. $\tilde{X}(Y_1) := \max(X(\alpha_1), X(\alpha_2), X(\alpha_3)) = 30$, $\tilde{X}(Y_2) := \max(X(\alpha_3), X(\alpha_5)) = 50$, and in analogous way for the others, that is $\tilde{X}(\tilde{f}(Y_2)) = 50$, $\tilde{X}(\tilde{f}^2(Y_1)) = 50$, $\tilde{X}(\tilde{f}(Y_1)) = 50$, and $\tilde{X}(\perp) := 0$. With this choice, $\tilde{h}(w_1, z^a) \leq \tilde{h}(w_2, z^b)$ for any $(w_1, z^a) \leq (w_2, z^b)$, that is the system is monotone. Convergence plots are shown in Figure 4 (right).

As opposite to Example 1, in this case the representation of the elements in $\mathcal{Z}_E$ requires only n scalar numbers, and the computation of the order relation is straightforward. This alleviates the computational burden with respect to the previous example.

Example 3. This example shows the case in which there is a $(\chi, \leq)$, whose order relation can be computed algebraically, and $\mathcal{Z}_E = \mathcal{Z} = \mathbb{R}^{20}$, with order established according to the cone order. There are $N = 10$ discrete variables updated in a highly coupled fashion (the assignments), each living in the set $\{1, ..., N\}$. As a consequence $\mathcal{U} = [1, N]^N$. This example is the multi-robot example described in detail in [8], and it is a monotone DTS. Here, only convergence plots are shown, and they are in Figure 5. The size of $\mathcal{U}$ is of the order of N^N, but thanks to the monotonic properties of the system, the computational complexity of the estimator is linear with N.

8   Complexity Considerations

The scope of the proposed examples is two-fold. First, they give an idea of the range of systems to which the lattice estimation approach applies (just observable and discrete state observable systems). Second, they point out that the lattice approach alleviates the

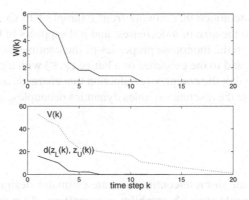

Fig. 5. Estimator performance: example 3. $W(k)$ represents the discrete state estimation error and $V(k)$ is the monotonic function bounding the continuous state estimation error

computational burden of the estimator and even renders intractable problems tractable when the system has monotone properties and a good choice of the lattices is made. To make this point more formal, the computational complexity in each of the examples is estimated as function of the continuous variables, the discrete variables, and the sizes of the sets where the discrete variables lie. This section is not meant to be a formal treatment of computational complexity, but has the scope of giving a qualitative measure of the computational complexity diversity of the proposed examples. Let n be the number of continuous variables (3 for the first example, 2 for the second, and 20 in the third), N be the number of discrete variables (1 in the first example, 1 in the second example, and 10 in the third example), and u be the set where each discrete variable lie (in the first and second example $u = \mathcal{U}$, and in the third $u = \{1, ..., N\}$ and $\mathcal{U} = u^N$). The computational cost of the estimator is computed as

$$\text{computational cost} \propto S + a_{UC}$$

where S is the sum of the sizes of the look-up tables used at each update of the estimator, and a_{UC} is the algebraic update cost of each estimator update. The cost of any set of algebraic computation is set to 1. One can verify that $S \propto |u|^{2N}$ in the first two examples, and that $S \propto 2N$ in the third one. In the first example, $a_{UC} \propto |u|^N n$, and $a_{UC} \propto 2n$ in the second and third examples. This is shown in the following table.

Table 1. Estimator computational cost

Example 1	$|u|^{2N} + |u|^N n$
Example 2	$|u|^{2N} + 2n$
Example 3	$2N + 2n$

From the table, one notice that moving from Example 1 to Example 3 the computational burden due to the size of u decreases, and it disappears in the case of the third example. This is due to the monotone properties of the continuous dynamics in Example 2 and Example 3, and to the existence of a lattice $(\chi, \leq)$ with algebraic properties in Example 3. Note also that the complexity reduction that characterizes the third example does not occur because the discrete variables dynamics decouples, as in fact it is heavily coupled.

9   Conclusions

In this paper, a cascade discrete-continuous state estimator design is proposed under observability and discrete state observability assumptions. As pointed out also in the simulation examples section, the proposed approach is general. The main advantage of using a lattice approach to the estimation problem is clear when the system has monotone properties that can be exploited in the estimator construction. In this case, the computational complexity is drastically reduced and a scalability property holds in the number of variables to be estimated. Thanks to this feature, the estimator can be efficiently designed even for systems with large discrete state spaces, for which the state estimation problem is intractable if the monotone properties are not directly exploited (see Example 3).

The results obtained in this paper suggest that a partial order structure is a possible way for overcoming complexity issues in the estimation of hybrid systems. A future research trust will try to generalize these ideas to the coupled discrete-continuous state estimation problem. Given the promising results obtained using partial order theory for state estimation problems, the authors will explore the possibility of applying similar tools for other control and analysis problems in hybrid systems.

Acknowledgements

This work has been partially supported by AFOSR under grants F49620-01-1-0460 and FA9550-04-1-0169.

References

1. A. Balluchi, L. Benvenuti, M. D. Di Benedetto, and A. Sangiovanni-Vincentelli. Design of observers for hybrid systems. In *Lecture Notes in Computer Science* 2289,C. J. Tomlin and M. R. Greensreet Eds. Springer Verlag, pages 76–89, 2002.
2. Alexandre Bayen, Jiawei Zhang, Claire Tomlin, and Yinyu Ye. Milp formulation and polynomial time algorithm for an aircraft scheduling problem. In *Proc. of American Control Conference*, 2003.
3. A. Bemporad, G. Ferrari-Trecate, and M. Morari. Observability and controllability of piecewise affine and hybrid systems. *IEEE Transactions on Automatic Control*, 45:1864–1876, 1999.
4. P. E. Caines. Classical and logic-based dynamic observers for finite automata. *IMA J. of Mathematical Control and Information*, pages 45–80, 1991.

5. B. A. Davey and H. A. Priesteley. *Introduction to Lattices and Order*. Cambridge University Press, 2002.
6. D. DelVecchio and R. M. Murray. Discrete state estimators for a class of hybrid systems on a lattice. In *Lecture Notes in Computer Science* 2993, R. Alur and G. Pappas Eds. Springer Verlag, pages 311–325, 2004.
7. D. DelVecchio and R. M. Murray. Existence of discrete state estimators for hybrid systems on a lattice. In *Conf. on Decision and Control*, 2004.
8. D. DelVecchio and R. M. Murray. Cascade discrete-continuous state estimators for a class of monotone systems. In *IFAC (Submitted)*, pages 76–89, 2005.
9. J. E. Hopcroft, R. Motwani, and J. D. Ullman. *Introduction to Automata Theory, languages, and Computation*. Addison Wesley, 2001.
10. A. Jung S. Abramsky. *Domain Theory*. Handbook of Logic in Computer Science Volume 3. 1994.
11. H. L. Smith. *Monotone Dynamical Systems*. Mathematical Surveys and Monographs. American Mathematical Society, 1995.
12. Claire Tomlin, Ian Mitchell, , and Ronojoy Ghosh. Safety verification of conflict resolution maneuvers. *IEEE Transactions on Intelligent Transportation Systems*, 2001.
13. R. Vidal, A. Chiuso, and S. Soatto. Observability and identifiability of jump linear systems. In *Conf. on Decision and Control*, pages 3614 – 3619, Las Vegas, 2002.

Refining Abstractions of Hybrid Systems Using Counterexample Fragments

Ansgar Fehnker[1], Edmund Clarke[2], Sumit Kumar Jha[2], and Bruce Krogh[2]

[1] National ICT Australia and University of New South Wales, Sydney, Australia
ansgar.fehnker@nicta.com.au
[2] Carnegie Mellon University, Pittsburgh, USA
{emc, jha}@cs.cmu.edu
krogh@ece.cmu.edu

Abstract. Counterexample guided abstraction refinement, a powerful technique for verifying properties of discrete-state systems, has been extended recently to hybrid systems verification. Unlike in discrete systems, however, establishing the successor relation for hybrid systems can be a fairly expensive step since it requires evaluation and over-approximation of the continuous dynamics. It has been observed that it is often sufficient to consider fragments of counterexamples rather than complete counterexamples. In this paper we further develop the idea of fragments. We extend the notion of cut sets in directed graphs to cutting sets of fragments in abstractions. Cutting sets of fragments are then used to guide the abstraction refinement in order to prove safety properties for hybrid systems.

1 Introduction

Model checking for hybrid systems requires finite abstractions [1, 2, 3, 4]. Abstractions of hybrid systems are usually quotient transition systems for the infinite-state transition system that provides the semantics for the hybrid system. The two principal issues in constructing these quotient transition systems are: (i) identifying and representing the sets of hybrid system states that comprise the states for the abstraction; and (ii) computing the transition relation for the abstraction. Step (ii) is usually the most difficult and time-consuming step because it involves the computation of reachable sets for the continuous dynamics in the hybrid system. The time involved in computing reachable sets for the continuous dynamics makes the time required to perform model checking on the abstraction negligible in the overall time required to perform the verify-refine iteration described above.

Counterexample guided abstraction refinement (CEGAR) has been proposed to guide the refinement process. This refinement strategy, originally developed for discrete-state systems, uses counterexamples in the abstraction (runs that violate the specification) to determine how to refine the abstraction so that known counterexamples are eliminated [5, 6]. This approach was extended to hybrid

M. Morari and L. Thiele (Eds.): HSCC 2005, LNCS 3414, pp. 242–257, 2005.
© Springer-Verlag Berlin Heidelberg 2005

systems [1, 3] as follows. The abstraction is created based only on the discrete transitions in the hybrid system. For a given counterexample in this abstraction, reachability computations are performed to see if the counterexample could occur in the hybrid system. This process is called *validation*. If the reachability computations show that the counterexample cannot occur in the hybrid system, the counterexample in the abstraction is *refuted* and is said to be *spurious*. Information from the overapproximated reachability computations is then used to refine the abstraction. For most hybrid systems, reachability computations are necessarily over-approximations, so the validity of a counterexample is always relative to the currently used over-approximation method.

We made two observations in our work on CEGAR for hybrid systems. First, rather than refuting a complete counterexample, it is sufficient and often a lot cheaper to refute a *fragment* of the counterexample. Second, coarse over-approximation methods to compute reachable sets are not only computationally faster, but can also lead to smaller refinements and produce conclusive results more quickly than those obtained with exact (but computationally expensive) methods. These observations are the basis for the new approach to abstraction refinement proposed in this paper. The overall goal is to obtain as much information as possible from an analysis of the graph representing *all* abstract counterexamples, and to use this information to minimize the amount of time for expensive reachability computations for the underlying hybrid system dynamics.

2   Preliminaries

Definition 1. *A hybrid automaton is a tuple* $HA = (Z, z_0, z_f, X, inv, X_0, T, g, j, f)$ *where*

- Z *is a finite set of* locations *with initial location* $z_0 \in Z$, *and final location* z_f.
- $X \subseteq \mathbb{R}^n$ *is the continuous state space.*
- $inv : Z \to 2^X$ *assigns to each location* $z \in Z$ *an invariant* $inv(z) \subseteq X$.
- $X_0 \subseteq X$ *is the set of initial continuous states.*
- $T \subseteq Z \times Z$ *is the set of* discrete transitions *between locations.*
- $g : T \to 2^X$ *assigns a guard set* $g((z_1, z_2)) \subseteq X$ *to* $(z_1, z_2) \in T$.
- $j : T \to (X \to 2^X)$ *assigns to each* $(z_1, z_2) \in T$ *and a reset or* jump *mapping from* X *to* 2^X. *The notation* $j_{(z_1, z_2)}$ *is used for* $j((z_1, z_2))$
- $f : Z \to (X \to \mathbb{R}^n)$ *assigns to each location* $z \in Z$ *a continuous vector field* $f(z)$. *The notation* f_z *is used for* $f(z)$. *The evolution of the continuous behavior in location* z *is governed by the differential equation* $\dot{\chi}(t) = f_z(\chi(t))$. *The differential equation is assumed to have a unique solution for each initial value* $\chi(0) \in inv(z)$.

Definition 2. *A transition system* TS *is a tuple* (S, S^0, S^f, R) *with a set of states* S, *a set of initial states* $S^0 \subseteq S$, *a set of accepting states* $S^f \subseteq S$, *and a transition relation* $R \subseteq S \times S$.

Definition 3. *The semantics of a hybrid automaton HA is a transition system* $TS(HA) = (\bar{S}, \bar{S}^0, \bar{S}^f, \bar{R})$ *with:*

- *the set of all hybrid states* $\bar{S} = \{(z,x)|z \in Z, x \in X, x \in inv(z)\}$,
- *the set of initial hybrid states* $\bar{S}^0 = \{z_0\} \times (X_0 \cap inv(z_0))$,
- *the set of accepting hybrid states* $\bar{S}^f = \{z_f\} \times inv(z_f)$
- *transitions* $\bar{R}$ *with* $((z_1,x_1),(z_2,x_2)) \in \bar{R}$, *iff* $(z_1,z_2) \in T$ *and there exist a trajectory* $\chi : [0,\tau] \to X$ *for some* $\tau \in \mathbb{R}^{>0}$ *such that:* $\chi(0) = x_1$, $\chi(\tau) \in g((z_1,z_2))$, $x_2 \in j_{(z_1,z_2)}(\chi(\tau))$, *and* $\dot{\chi}(t) = f_{z_1}(\chi(t))$ *for* $t \in [0,\tau]$, $\chi(t) \in inv(z_1)$ *for* $t \in [0,\tau]$.

The first step in model checking hybrid systems is to find a suitable finite abstraction, where the notion of abstraction for transition systems is defined as follows.

Definition 4. *Given a transition system* $C = (\bar{S}, \bar{S}^0, \bar{S}^f, \bar{R})$, *a transition system* $A = (S, S^0, S^f, R)$ *is an abstraction of transition system* C, *denoted by* $A \succeq C$, *if there exist an abstraction function* $\alpha : \bar{S} \to S$ *such that* $S^0 = \alpha(\bar{S}^0)$, $S^f = \alpha(\bar{S}^f)$ *(where* α *is extended to subsets of* $\bar{S}$ *in the usual way),and*

$$R \supseteq \{(s_1, s_2)|\exists(\bar{s}_1, \bar{s}_2) \in \bar{R}, \alpha(\bar{s}_1) = s_1, \alpha(\bar{s}_2) = s_2\}$$

In this paper, we are interested in constructing finite abstractions for $C = TS(HA)$, where HA is a given hybrid automaton. This given infinite-state transition system is referred to as the *concrete system*. An abstraction A may include transitions that have no counterpart in C. Such *spurious transitions* may arise in abstractions of hybrid systems because sets of reachable states for hybrid systems cannot, except for simple dynamics [7], be computed exactly, but have to be overapproximated. The computations of sets of reachable states required for our procedure are represented formally as follows.

For an abstraction function α, let $\bar{S}_\alpha$ denote the partition of the set of hybrid states $\bar{S}$ defined by the inverse mapping α^{-1}. Our procedure requires a method for computing the set of states that can be reached from one element of $\bar{S}_\alpha$ in another element of $\bar{S}_\alpha$. That is, given two sets of hybrid states, $\bar{S}_1, \bar{S}_2$ in $\bar{S}_\alpha$, we require a method for computing a subset of states in $\bar{S}_2$ that contains the set of hybrid states that can be reached from states in $\bar{S}_1$. We denote such a method by $\overline{succ}$. Given a set of hybrid states $\bar{S}_1 \subset \bar{S}$ the set of *successor states* is denoted by $succ(\bar{S}_1) = \{\bar{s}'|\exists \bar{s} \in \bar{S}_1. (\bar{s}, \bar{s}') \in \bar{R}\}$. With this notation, an over-approximation method $\overline{succ}$ is defined as:

Definition 5. *Let HA be a hybrid automaton with* $TS(HA) = (\bar{S}, \bar{S}^0, \bar{S}^f, \bar{R})$, *and let* $A = (S, S^0, S^f, R)$ *and* α *as in Defn. 4. Let* $\bar{S}_1 = \alpha^{-1}(s_1)$, *and* $\bar{S}_2 = \alpha^{-1}(s_2)$. *Then* $\overline{succ} : \bar{S}_\alpha \times \bar{S}_\alpha \to 2^{\bar{S}}$ *is the over-approximation of the set of hybrid successors of* $\bar{S}_1$ *in* $\bar{S}_2$ *iff* $\overline{succ}(\bar{S}_1, \bar{S}_2) \subseteq \bar{S}_2$ *and* $\overline{succ}(\bar{S}_1, \bar{S}_2) \supseteq succ(\bar{S}_1) \cap \bar{S}_2$.

Our abstraction refinement procedure provides a framework to use the fact that different over-approximation techniques have different computational loads and accuracy. It was observed in [3] that combinations of coarse and precise methods can improve the efficiency of the verify-refine iterations significantly. In the following we assume a series of over-approximation methods $\overline{succ}_1, \ldots, \overline{succ}_n$ is given that provides a hierarchy of coarse to tight approximations. This hierarchy will be used to assign weights to fragments that reflect the computational effort required to apply the various over-approximation methods.

Our procedure is based on the analysis of sequences of states in abstractions called *fragments*.

Definition 6. *A* fragment *of a transition system* $TS = (S, S^0, S^f, R)$ *is a finite sequence* $(s_0, \ldots, s_n)$ *such that* $(s_{i-1}, s_i) \in R$ *for* $i = 1, \ldots, n$. *A* run *is a fragment with* $s_0 \in S^0$. *A state* s *is* reachable *if the there exists a run that ends in* s. *An* accepting run *is a run* $(s_0, \ldots, s_n)$ *with* $s_n \in S^f$. *The set of all accepting runs of* TS *will be denoted by* $\mathcal{R}(TS)$. *A run* $(s_0, \ldots, s_n)$ *is* loop-free *if for all* $i, j \in \{0, \ldots, n\}$, $i \neq j$ *implies* $s_i \neq s_j$.

We consider the verification of *safety properties*. The set of states S^f should not be reachable, that is, the transition system should not have any accepting run. We refer to S^f as the *set of bad states* and to accepting runs as *counterexamples*. Our analysis of counterexamples for abstractions will focus on sets of fragments, using the following notions of cutting fragments and cutting sets of fragments.

Definition 7. *For* $n_2 \geq n_1 \geq 0$, *fragment* $\varrho_1 = (s_0, \ldots, s_{n_1})$ cuts *a fragment* $\varrho_2 = (t_0, \ldots, t_{n_2})$, *denoted by* $\varrho_1 \sqsubseteq \varrho_2$, *if there exists a* $i \in \{0, \ldots, n_2 - n_1\}$ *such that* $t_{i+j} = s_j$ *for* $j = 0, \ldots, n_1$.

Definition 8. *A set* $\mathcal{F}_1$ *of fragments* cuts *a set of fragments* $\mathcal{F}_2$, *denoted by* $\mathcal{F}_1 \sqsubseteq \mathcal{F}_2$, *if for each fragment* $\varrho_2 \in \mathcal{F}_2$ *there exist* $\varrho_1 \in \mathcal{F}_1$ *such that* $\varrho_1 \sqsubseteq \varrho_2$. *Set* $\mathcal{F}_1$ *is* minimal *if* $\mathcal{F}_1 \sqsubseteq \mathcal{F}_2$ *and* $\mathcal{F}_1 \setminus \varrho \not\sqsubseteq \mathcal{F}_2$ *for all* $\varrho \in \mathcal{F}_1$. *Given a transition system* TS, *a set of fragments* $\mathcal{F}$ *cuts* TS *if* $\mathcal{F} \sqsubseteq \mathcal{R}(A)$.

In words, a fragment ϱ_1 cuts another fragment ϱ_2 if ϱ_1 is a subsequence ϱ_2. When a transition system is an abstraction of a hybrid system, a set of fragments $\mathcal{F}$ that cuts the abstraction covers all counterexamples for the abstraction, that is, any path from the initial state to the bad state (a counterexample) is cut by one of the fragments in $\mathcal{F}$. Any set of fragments that cuts $\mathcal{F}$ also cuts the abstraction. The remainder of the paper shows how the minimal cutting sets of fragments can be used to guide the refinement of abstractions for hybrid systems.

3   Validating Fragments

Abstractions can be represented as directed graphs, with states as nodes and transitions as edges. The initial states can be considered as sources and the final states as sinks. A cut set is a set of edges such that all paths from source to sink contain at least one edge in the set. For example, for the graph in Fig. 1.(a) transitions (G, J) and (B, E) are a cut set. All paths from source to sink pass

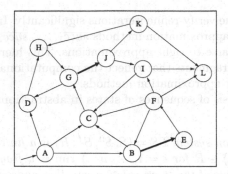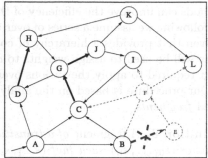

Fig. 1. The initial state of this transition system is A, the accepting state is L. Figure 1.(a) depicts a pair of transitions that cut the transition system. Cutting set can also contain fragments of length greater than two (Fig. 1.(b))

through one of those edges. All accepting runs are cut, if those edges are deleted from the graph.

This paper generalizes the idea of cut sets to sets of fragments that cut the abstraction. For example, fragments (D, H) and (C, G, J) in Fig. 1.(b) form a cut set since all runs from source to sink contain either (D, H) or (C, G, J). If both fragments were spurious, then there would exist no run in the concrete system that connects source to sink. Hence, the concrete system would satisfy the safety property.

The process of determining whether or not a fragment is spurious is called *validating a fragment*. For a given fragment $(s_0, \ldots, s_n)$ of an abstraction A with abstraction function α, the objective is to determine if there exists a fragment $(\bar{s}_0, \ldots, \bar{s}_n)$ of hybrid system C, such that $s_i = \alpha(\bar{s}_i)$, for all $i = 0, \ldots, n$. Computation of hybrid successors is the key step in the validation procedure. The validation procedure uses methods $\overline{succ}_1, \ldots, \overline{succ}_m$ for the validation step. The procedure maintains a mapping $\mathcal{X} : (\mathcal{F} \times \mathbb{N}) \to \{1, \ldots, m\}$ that assigns method $\mathcal{X}((s_0, \ldots, s_n), i)$ to validate transition i of fragment $(s_0, \ldots, s_n)$. Also, $\bar{\mathcal{X}}$ denotes the assignment of the least conservative method to every transition in the given fragment.

The validation is performed as follows. Given abstraction A, concrete system C, abstraction function α, and fragment $(s_0, \ldots, s_n)$:

$$\bar{S}_0 := \alpha^{-1}(s_0)$$
for $i = 1, \ldots, n - 1$
$$\bar{S}_i := \alpha^{-1}(s_i)$$
$$\bar{S}_i := \overline{succ}_{\mathcal{X}((s_0, \ldots, s_n), i)}(\bar{S}_{i-1}, \bar{S}_i)$$
if $\bar{S}_i = \emptyset$
    return("Fragment not valid")
end % if
end % for
return"Fragment valid with respect to method ")

This procedure computes the hybrid successors along the fragment. There exist no corresponding run to $(s_0, \ldots, s_n)$ if a set of successors $\bar{S}_i$ becomes empty.

The need to consider fragments of length two or longer arises when all single-transition fragments have been validated and some are found to be non-spurious. Suppose for example, that (B, E) in Fig. 1.(a) has been shown to be spurious, while (G, J) has been shown to be non-spurious. The next iteration has to choose a cutting set from the abstraction in Fig. 1.(b). Fragment (G, J) however can not be part of the next cutting set, since it is known to be non-spurious. Suppose that (D, H) and (C, G, J) have not been validated yet. The set of fragments (D, H) and (C, G, J) can then be chosen as the next cutting set, and one must then check if they are spurious.

4   Using Sets of Fragments for Abstraction Refinement

Figure 2 presents our procedure for model checking hybrid systems using sets of fragments to guide the abstraction refinement. The inputs to the procedure are: C, a given concrete (hybrid) system; A, an initial abstraction for C; $\mathcal{F}$, a set of loop-free fragments that cuts A; and $\mathcal{P} : \mathcal{F} \to \mathbb{N}$, an assignment of weights reflecting the computational effort required to validate each fragment. The concrete system is represented implicitly through the equations of the underlying hybrid automaton. The initial abstraction includes the abstraction function and a representation of the associated partition of hybrid states. In this paper we assume the initial abstraction $A = (S, S^0, S^f, R)$ is defined as in [3]. This initial abstraction has one abstract state for each control location, with the exception of the initial location. For the initial location the abstraction includes two states, one to represent the set of hybrid states $S^0 = z_0 \times (inv(z_0) \cap X_0)$, and one state to represent $z_0 \times (inv(z_0) \setminus X_0)$. Given the initial abstraction $A = (S, S^0, S^f, R)$, the initial set of fragments $\mathcal{F}$ is defined to be the set of transitions R. Initially, $\mathcal{X}$ assigns the computationally cheapest method to all transitions in the initial set $\mathcal{F}$, and $\mathcal{P}$ initially assigns the weight associated with this method.

In each iteration through the main loop, a new abstraction is constructed based on the results of validating sets of fragments. If there are no accepting runs for the abstraction coming into the main loop $(\mathcal{R}(A) = \emptyset)$ the verification terminates with a positive result: the bad state is not reachable in the hybrid system.

The first step in each iteration is to compute a minimal cutting set of fragments $\mathcal{F}_{opt}$ for which the set sum of the weights is minimized (Fig. 2(i)). Section 5 describes the algorithm for finding $\mathcal{F}_{opt}$, which is a generalization of algorithms for finding minimal cut sets of links in a graph.

Given the set of fragments $\mathcal{F}_{opt}$, the inner loop iterates through the elements of $\mathcal{F}_{opt}$ one at a time. Each fragment in $\mathcal{F}_{opt}$ will be validated (Fig. 2(ii)). This iteration continues until all fragments have been validated $(\mathcal{F}_{opt} = \emptyset)$ or an abstraction has been constructed for which the remaining fragments no longer constitute fragments for the abstraction $(\mathcal{F}_{opt} \not\subseteq \mathcal{F})$. If the current fragment is a valid accepting run, the procedure stops. Otherwise, if it is a valid fragment, the

```
while R(A) ≠ ∅
    F_opt := cutset(A, F, P)                                          (i)
    while F_opt ≠ ∅ ∧ F_opt ⊆ F
        (s_0, ..., s_n) :∈ F_opt, F_opt := F_opt \ (s_0, ..., s_n)
        valid := validate((s_0, ..., s_n), A, C, X)                   (ii)
        if valid ∧ s_0 ∈ S^0 ∧ s_n ∈ S^f ∧ X = X̄
            exit("Found valid accepting run of A")
        elseif valid
            (F, P, X) := augment(F, P, X, (s_0, ..., s_n), A)         (iii)
            break
        else
            (A, F, P, X) := refine(A, F, P, X, (s_0, ..., s_n))       (iv)
        end % if
    end % for
end % while

exit("z_f is not reachable for the HA")
```

Fig. 2. Validation-refinement loop that uses cutting sets of fragments F_{opt} to guide the refinement. Inputs to this procedure are: Concrete hybrid system C, initial abstraction A, initial set of loop-free fragments F that cuts A, an assignment to estimated computational cost of validation P and, finally, an assignment to validation methods X

procedure augments the set of fragments as well as the assignment of weights and methods (iii), leaves the inner while loop, and recomputes F_{opt}. If the fragment is not valid, the abstraction, fragments, weights and method assignment are refined (Fig. 2(iv)). This refinement may change F such that $F_{opt} \nsubseteq F$. In this case the procedure exits the inner while loop and recomputes F_{opt}.

Augmentation (iii) and refinement (iv) depend on the outcome of the validation procedure (ii): either the procedure finds an empty set of successors, i.e. there exists no corresponding fragment in C to $(s_0, ..., s_n)$, or the procedure could not find an empty set of hybrid successors. The latter may be caused by the over-approximation error of the selected methods. In this case there are two options on how to proceed: Either, the over-approximation can be improved by using a different approximation method, or the current fragment must be replaced by extensions of the current fragment.

Choosing a different over-approximation method. The result of the validation might be improved by a different approximation method in future iterations. Changing the validation methods for fragment $(s_0, ..., s_n)$ is done by changing the mapping X (which maps transitions in a fragment to the method that should be used to validate them) for at least one transition in $(s_0, ..., s_n)$. If the procedure changes the mix of methods used to validate $(s_0, ..., s_n)$ it has to update function P accordingly.

Extending the fragment. If the over-approximation cannot improve, the current fragment $(s_0, ..., s_n)$ will be replaced by new, extended fragments. This be-

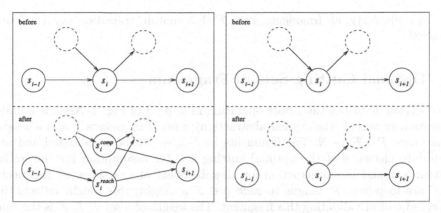

Fig. 3. Left: Refinement by splitting states. Right: Refinement by purging transitions. For a formal definition of the refinement operations see [3]

comes necessary if the validation step uses for each fragment the best available over-approximation method. The new fragments will extend $(s_0, \ldots, s_n)$ in both directions of the transition relation, i.e. sets $\{(s', s_0, \ldots, s_n) | (s', s_0) \in R\}$ and $\{(s_0, \ldots, s_n, s') | (s_n, s') \in R\}$ are added to $\mathcal{F}$. Recall the requirement that for all $\varrho_1, \varrho_2 \in \mathcal{F}$, $\varrho_1 \not\sqsubseteq \varrho_2$. The procedure enforces this requirement by removing all fragments from $\mathcal{F}$ that are cut by some other fragment. It also removes all fragments that contain self-loops. The set of new fragment ensures that there are a sufficient number of fragments in $\mathcal{F}$ to cut $\mathcal{R}A$, although one fragment was removed. Finally, $\mathcal{X}$ and $\mathcal{P}$ are updated for all new fragments of $\mathcal{F}$.

To avoid fragments of unlimited length the augmentation might extend fragments only up to a certain length. First experiments show that an upper bound of 2 to 4 is reasonable. Adding only a limited number of fragments may lead to a situation in which a certain counterexample is not cut by any fragment. In this case the procedure might add the complete counterexample to the cutting set, and validate it in the next iteration.

Refinement. If the current fragment is not valid, the refinement step (iv) in Fig. 2 uses the sets $\bar{S}_i$ that were computed in the validation step (ii), for $i = 1, \ldots, k$. For $i = 1, \ldots, k - 1$ the following steps are performed. If $\bar{S}_i$ is a proper subset of $\alpha^{-1}(s_i)$, split s_i into two abstract states, one, s_i^{reach}, to represent the states in $\bar{S}_i$, and one, s_i^{comp} to represent the states in $\alpha^{-1}(s_i) \setminus \bar{S}_i$ (Fig. 3). The new states s_i^{reach} and s_i^{comp} will have the same ingoing and outgoing transitions as S_i, with one exception. The transition from s_{i-1} to s_i^{comp} can be omitted, since there exists no hybrid transition from any state in $\bar{S}_{i-1}$ to some state in $\alpha^{-1}(s_i) \setminus \bar{S}_i$. All fragments from $\mathcal{F}$ that involve state s_i are removed, and the new transitions of the abstraction are added to $\mathcal{F}$. $\mathcal{X}$ assigns to the new fragments the default method for single transitions, and $\mathcal{P}$ the weight that is associated with this method. If $\bar{S}_i$ is equal to $\alpha^{-1}(s_i)$, then there is no need to refine the abstraction.

For $i = k$ the transition (s_{k-1}, s_k) is omitted from the abstraction (Fig. 3), since there exists no hybrid transition from any state in $\bar{S}_{k-1}$ to some state in

$\alpha^{-1}(s_k)$. Similarly, all fragments from $\mathcal{F}$ that contain transition (s_{k-1}, s_k) are removed.

5   Optimal Cutting Sets of Fragments

This section describes the cutset operation in step (i) of Fig. 2. Assume a finite transition system A (the current abstraction), a set of fragments $\mathcal{F}$ and a weight assignment $\mathcal{P} : \mathcal{F} \to \mathbb{N}$. The fragments in $\mathcal{F}$ have not been validated and are candidate elements of the optimal cutting set. By assumption for the initial abstraction, and by construction for all subsequent abstractions, all fragments in $\mathcal{F}$ are loop-free. $\mathcal{P}$ assigns to each $\varrho \in \mathcal{F}$ a weight; this weight reflects the expected cost of validating this fragment. The weight of a set $\mathcal{F}' \subseteq \mathcal{F}$ is the sum of the weights of the elements. Furthermore, it is assumed that $\varrho_1 \sqsubseteq \varrho_2$ implies $\mathcal{P}(\varrho_1) \leq \mathcal{P}(\varrho_2)$. As a consequence it is required for all $\varrho_1, \varrho_2 \in \mathcal{F}$ that $\varrho_1 \not\sqsubseteq \varrho_2$, i.e. no fragments in $\mathcal{F}$ cuts another.

Step (i) of the procedure in Fig. 2 computes a cutting set $\mathcal{F}_{opt} \subseteq \mathcal{F}$ of A that is minimal w.r.t. to $\mathcal{P}$, i.e. it satisfies

$$\sum_{f \in \mathcal{F}_{opt}} \mathcal{P}(f) = \min_{\substack{\mathcal{F}' \subseteq \mathcal{F} \\ \mathcal{F}' \sqsubseteq \mathcal{R}(A)}} \sum_{f \in \mathcal{F}'} \mathcal{P}(f) \qquad (1)$$

Example. Suppose that we are given transition system A in Fig. 4 as abstraction. Suppose furthermore that fragments $(0, 4, 5)$, $(1, 2, 4)$, $(0, 1)$ and $(4, 3)$ have not been validated yet. Assume an associated weight of 2 with validating fragment $(0, 4, 5)$, a weight of 3 with $(1, 2, 4)$, and a weight of 1 with fragments $(0, 1)$ and $(4, 3)$. What subset of these fragments is the cutting set with the lowest sum of weights? Obviously, we have to include fragment $(0, 4, 5)$ in any cutting set. But is the set with fragments $(0, 4, 5)$ and $(0, 1)$ sufficient? After all, this set cuts all loop-free accepting runs.

Somewhat surprisingly, there exist an accepting run that is not covered by fragment $(0, 4, 5)$ or fragment $(0, 1)$. Neither cuts accepting run $(0, 4, 3, 1, 2, 4, 5)$, although fragment $(0, 4, 5)$ cuts it trivially once we remove loop $(4, 3, 1, 2, 4)$. This demonstrates that the problem of finding cutting sets of fragments is not a simple cut set problem in a directed graph, for which it would be sufficient to cut all loop-free runs. ■

A standard cut set algorithm cannot be applied directly, since fragments in $\mathcal{F}$ are not represented by single transitions in A. To solve this problem, we define a collection of transition systems that *observe* A. The purpose of these observers is to record the occurrence of a fragment in A. For example, the observer for fragment $(0, 4, 5)$ will help to distinguish between occurrence of a sequence $(0, 4, 5)$ and $(2, 4, 5)$. The observers, one observer for each fragment in $\mathcal{F}$, are composed with a labelled version of abstraction A. Labelled transition systems, which are called *automata*, and the composition of automata is defined as follows.

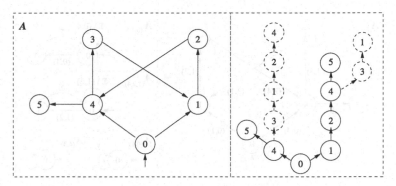

Fig. 4. Left: A finite transition system A. Right: The depth-first unrolling of A. The unrolling stops if either the final state 5 is reached (solid), or if a loop has been detected (dashed)

Definition 9. *Given a set of labels Σ, an* automaton *A is a tuple $(\Sigma, S, S^0, S^f, R, L)$ where (S, S^0, S^f, R) is a transition system and $L : R \to 2^{\Sigma}$ a labelling function.*

Definition 10. *Let $A_i = (\Sigma_i, S_i, S_i^0, S_i^f, R_i)$ be a finite number of automata, $i = 1, \ldots, n$. The* synchronous composition *$A = A_1 \| \ldots \| A_n$ is an automaton (Σ, S, S^0, S^f, R) with*

- $\Sigma = \bigcup_{i \in \{1, \ldots, n\}} \Sigma_i$, *the union of all alphabets.*
- $S = S_1 \times \ldots \times S_n$, $S^0 = S_1^0 \times \ldots \times S_n^0$, *and* $S^f = S_1^f \times \ldots \times S_n^f$. *The projection $s|_{S_i}$ will be denoted as s_i.*
- $(s, s') \in R$ *if* $\bigcap_{i \in \{1, \ldots, n\}} L_i(s_i, s_i')$ *is nonempty.*
- $L(s, s') = \bigcap_{i \in \{1, \ldots, n\}} L_i(s_i, s_i')$.

This is a very restricted notion of composition. The composition automaton can only take a transition if all automata can take a transition with the same label. However, the observing automata will be constructed such that they can always synchronize with any transition in the observed automaton. Given a transition system A and a set of fragments $\mathcal{F}$ of A, the procedure first extends A with labels, and then introduces for each fragment in $\mathcal{F}$ a small automaton that observes the occurrence of a fragment. The steps to obtain the observing automata are the following:

1. Extend $A = (S, S^0, S^f, R)$ to an automaton $A_l = (\Sigma, S, S^0, S^f, R)$ with $\Sigma = R$ and L mapping $(s, s') \mapsto \{(s, s')\}$.
2. For each $\varrho \in \mathcal{F}$, $\varrho = (s_0, \ldots, s_{n-1})$, introduce an observer automaton $A_\varrho = (\Sigma_\varrho, S_\varrho, S_\varrho^0, S_\varrho^f, R_\varrho, L_\varrho)$ with
   - $\Sigma_\varrho = \Sigma$
   - $S_\varrho = \{t_0, \ldots, t_{n-1}\}$, where n is the length of fragment ϱ.
   - $S_\varrho^0 = \{t_0\}$ and $S_\varrho^f = S_\varrho$
   - R_ϱ is the set $\{(t_i, t_{i+1}) | i = 0, \ldots, n - 2\} \cup \{(t_i, t_0) | i = 0, \ldots, n - 1\}\}$
   - and L_ϱ is the following mapping

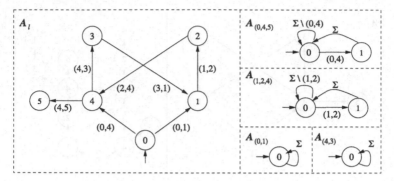

Fig. 5. The automata $A_{(0,4,5)}$, $A_{(1,2,4)}$, $A_{(0,1)}$, and $A_{(4,3)}$ observe the transitions in A_l. The only accepting state of A_l is the state 5

$$(t,t') \mapsto \begin{cases} (s_{i-1}, s_i) & \text{if } (t,t') = (t_i, t_{i+1}), \ i = 0, \dots, n-2 \\ \Sigma \setminus (s_{i-1}, s_i) & \text{if } (t,t') \neq (t_i, t_{i+1}), \ i = 0, \dots, n-2 \\ \Sigma & \text{if } (t,t') = (t_{n-1}, t_n) \end{cases}$$

The next step composes the labelled transition system A_l with the observer automata A_ϱ for all $\varrho \in \mathcal{F}$. This composition will be denoted as $A_{\mathcal{F}}$.

Example (Cont). Given the transition system A in Fig. 4, the first step is to obtain A_l by adding labels (Fig. 5). Recall that $\mathcal{F} = \{(0,4,5), (1,2,4), (0,1), (4,3)\}$, and $\mathcal{P}(0,4,5) = 2$, $\mathcal{P}(1,2,4) = 3$, $\mathcal{P}(0,1) = 1$ and $\mathcal{P}(4,3) = 1$. The next step includes a small observing automaton for each fragment (Fig. 5). The automaton for fragment $(0,4,5)$ has as many states as the fragment has transitions. In each state the observer automaton can synchronize with any transition in A_l.

If transition $(0,4)$ occurs in A_l the observing automaton $A_{(0,4,5)}$ takes a transition from state 0 to state 1. If transition $(4,5)$ occurs right after the first transition, the observing automaton will take a transition back to the initial state. This corresponds to the transition from $(4,1,0,0,0)^T$ to $(5,0,0,0,0)^T$ in composition $A_{\mathcal{F}}$ in Fig. 6. This transition marks an occurrence of the fragment $(0,4,5)$ in A_l.

Figure 6 depicts the composition automaton $A_{\mathcal{F}}$, and the tree of all loop-free counterexamples. There are two transitions labelled $(4,3)$ in $A_{\mathcal{F}}$. Transition $(4,3)$ is an element of the set of fragments $\mathcal{F}$ that have not been validated yet. If one could show that $(4,3)$ is spurious, it would eliminate both arcs in the graph in one go. Obviously, the cut set algorithms for directed graphs cannot be used, since several arcs in $A_{\mathcal{F}}$ can represent the same fragment of A_l.

The set with $((4,1,0,0,0)^T, (5,0,0,0,0)^T)$ and $((2,0,1,0,0)^T, (4,0,0,0,0)^T)$ cuts composition $A_{\mathcal{F}}$.[1] These transitions in $A_{\mathcal{F}}$ mark the occurrence of fragments $(0,4,5)$ and $(1,2,4)$ in A. The overall weight of this set is 5. The tree also shows that the set containing fragments $(0,4,5)$ and $(0,1)$ does not cut A_l,

---

[1] Column vectors are used for elements of product state spaces to distinguish them from tuples of states that are fragments.

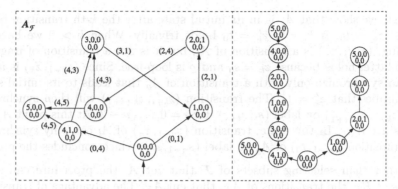

Fig. 6. Composition automaton $A_\mathcal{F}$, and the tree of all loop-free accepting runs

since transitions $((4, 1, 0, 0, 0)^T, (5, 0, 0, 0, 0)^T)$ and $((0, 0, 0, 0, 0)^T, (1, 0, 0, 0, 0)^T)$ do not cut $A_\mathcal{F}$. It also shows that $(0, 4, 5)$, $(1, 0)$ and $(4, 3)$ are a cutting set of A, with an associated weight of 4. This is the optimal cutting set for this example.

The observers for the fragments $(0, 1)$ and $(4, 3)$ do not add anything and could be omitted. Likewise, one observer for fragments that are equal except for the last transition would be sufficient. However, maintaining those observers docs not increase the size of the composition, and we choose to maintain them in this paper to treat the different fragments consistently. ∎

The construction of A_l ensures that each transition has a unique label. Consequently A_l is deterministic. All observers are deterministic, too, and can synchronize in each state with any transition of A_l. The behavior of A_l is not restricted by the observers. This yields a close relationship between $A_\mathcal{F}$ and A_l, and thus between $A_\mathcal{F}$ and A. As a matter of fact for each $\pi \in \mathcal{R}(A)$ there exist a $\pi_\mathcal{F} \in \mathcal{R}(A_\mathcal{F})$ such that $\pi_\mathcal{F}|_S = \pi$, and for each $\pi_\mathcal{F} \in \mathcal{R}(A_\mathcal{F})$ there exist a $\pi \in \mathcal{R}(A)$ such that such that $\pi_\mathcal{F}|_S = \pi$, where $\pi_\mathcal{F}|_S$ is the projection of $\pi_\mathcal{F}$ to the states S of A_l.

Lemma 1. *Given a transition system A, a set of fragments $\mathcal{F}$ of A and the composition automaton $A_\mathcal{F}$, the following holds.*

(i) A subset $\mathcal{F}' \subseteq \mathcal{F}$ cuts transition system A, i.e. $\mathcal{F}' \sqsubseteq \mathcal{R}(A)$ iff for all $\pi_\mathcal{F} \in \mathcal{R}(A_\mathcal{F})$ there exists $\varrho \in \mathcal{F}'$ such that $\varrho \sqsubseteq \pi_\mathcal{F}|_S$.

(ii) Given $\varrho = (s_0, \ldots, s_n)$, $\pi_\mathcal{F} \in \mathcal{R}(A_\mathcal{F})$ the following holds: $\varrho \sqsubseteq \pi_\mathcal{F}|_S$ iff the projection of the path $\pi_\mathcal{F}$ to $S \times S_\varrho$ contains a transition from $(s_{n-1}, t_{n-1})^T$ to $(s_n, t_0)^T$.

Proof: (i) This follows directly from the observation that $\pi_\mathcal{F}|_S$ is in $\mathcal{R}(A)$ for all $\pi_\mathcal{F} \in \mathcal{R}(A_\mathcal{F})$, and that for all path $\pi \in \mathcal{R}(A)$ there exists a $\pi_\mathcal{F}$, with $\pi_\mathcal{F}|_S = \pi$.
(ii)"$\Rightarrow$" Transition $(s_{n-1}, t_{n-1})^T$ to $(s_n, t_0)^T$ can only be taken if it was immediately preceded by transitions synchronizing on labels $(s_{n-i-1}, s_{n-i})^T$, for $i = 1, \ldots, n - 1$.
"$\Leftarrow$". Let $\pi_\mathcal{F}|_S = (z_0, \ldots, z_m)$ and $\pi_\mathcal{F}|_{S_\varrho} = (z'_0, \ldots, z'_m)$. By definition, $\varrho \sqsubseteq \pi_\mathcal{F}|_S$ iff there exists a k such that $z_{k+i} = s_i$ for $i = 0, \ldots, n$.

First, we show that A_ϱ is in its initial state after the k-th transition of $\pi_\mathcal{F}$, that is, $z'_k = t_0$. If $k = 0$, $z'_k = t_0$ holds trivially. When $k > 0$ we have the following: (z_{k-1}, z_k) is a transition of A_l, but it is not a transition of fragment ϱ. The latter holds because $z_k = s_0$ and ϱ is loop-free. Since (z_{k-1}, z_k) is not in ϱ it can synchronize only with a transition of A_ϱ that leads to its initial state. This implies that $z'_k = t_0$. The transition (z_{k+i}, z_{k+i+1}) will then synchronize with (z'_{k+i}, z'_{k+i+1}) on label (s_i, s_{i+1}), for $i = 0, \ldots, n-2$. At this point A_ϱ will be in state t_{n-1}. In this state, transition (z_{n-1}, z_n) of A_l can only synchronize with transition (t_{n-1}, t_0) of A_ϱ on label (s_{n-1}, s_n), which concludes the proof. ∎

Rather than selecting subsets of $\mathcal{F}$ that cut A, the procedure can select subsets of $R_\mathcal{F}$, the transitions of $A_\mathcal{F}$, that cut $A_\mathcal{F}$. The advantage of transitions above fragments is that it becomes sufficient to look at loop-free accepting runs. A set $R'_\mathcal{F} \subseteq R_\mathcal{F}$ that cuts all loop-free accepting runs, also cuts all accepting runs. Let $\mathcal{R}_{lf}(A_\mathcal{F})$ be the set of all loop-free accepting runs.

Lemma 2. *Given a transition system A, a set of fragments $\mathcal{F}$ of A and the composition automaton $A_\mathcal{F}$. Let $R'_\mathcal{F} \subseteq R_\mathcal{F}$, then $R'_\mathcal{F} \sqsubseteq \mathcal{R}_{lf}(A_\mathcal{F})$ iff $R'_\mathcal{F} \sqsubseteq \mathcal{R}(A_\mathcal{F})$.*

Proof: "⇒" Suppose that we have an accepting run $\pi_\mathcal{F} \in \mathcal{R}(A_\mathcal{F})$. From this we can obtain a loop-free accepting run $\pi'_\mathcal{F}$ by eliminating all loops. According to the precondition there exists a $\varrho \in R'_\mathcal{F}$ such that $\varrho \sqsubseteq \pi'_\mathcal{F}$, which means that ϱ appears somewhere in $\pi'_\mathcal{F}$. Since the transitions that occur in $\pi_\mathcal{F}$ are a super-set of those that appear in $\pi'_\mathcal{F}$ we have $\varrho \sqsubseteq \pi_\mathcal{F}$, too. "⇐" If a set of transitions cuts all accepting runs, it will cut all loop-free accepting runs. ∎

Lemma 2 allows the consideration of only loop-free accepting runs of $A_\mathcal{F}$. However, the example demonstrates that a cut set algorithm for directed graphs cannot be used to find a cut set of $A_\mathcal{F}$, since fragments of A may be represented by multiple transitions in $A_\mathcal{F}$. The cutting set problem can be solved by a translation to a set cover problem. A similar approach has been used in [8] to find cut sets for *attack graphs*.

Given a finite (universal) set $\mathcal{U}$ and a set of sets $\mathcal{C} = \{\mathcal{C}_1, \ldots, \mathcal{C}_n\}$ with $\mathcal{C}_i \subseteq \mathcal{U}$ as input, a set cover algorithm computes the smallest subset $\mathcal{C}_{opt} \subseteq \mathcal{C}$ such that $\bigcup_{\mathcal{C}_i \in \mathcal{C}_{opt}} \mathcal{C}_i = \mathcal{U}$. The set cover problem is NP-complete, but a greedy approach is guaranteed to find an solution that is at most $\lg n$ as bad as the optimal solution in polynomial time (where n is the number of elements of $\mathcal{U}$) [9]. The greedy algorithm picks in each iteration the set from $\mathcal{S}$ that covers the greatest number of uncovered elements of $\mathcal{U}$, until the complete set $\mathcal{U}$ is covered.

The problem of finding a cutting set of fragments is a set cover problem, where the universal set is $\mathcal{R}_{lf}(A_\mathcal{F})$, and $\mathcal{C}$ contains for each fragment ϱ in $\mathcal{F}$ set $\mathcal{C}_\varrho = \{\pi_\mathcal{F} \in \mathcal{R}_{lf}(A_\mathcal{F}) | \varrho \sqsubseteq \pi_\mathcal{F}|_S\}$. The problem is to find an optimal subset of $\mathcal{C}$ that covers $\mathcal{R}_{lf}(A_\mathcal{F})$. We compute the sets $\mathcal{C}_\varrho$ by a depth-first exploration of $A_\mathcal{F}$, that starts backtracking if it either finds a loop, or reaches an accepting state. In the latter case it adds the accepting run to $\mathcal{C}_\varrho$ if $\varrho \sqsubseteq \pi$.

We modify the greedy algorithm to accommodate the fact that we are not looking for the smallest cover of $\mathcal{R}_{lf}(A_\mathcal{F})$, but for an optimal one. In each iteration the algorithm adds the set $\mathcal{C}_\varrho$ to $\mathcal{C}_{opt}$ that has the smallest associated cost $\mathcal{P}(\varrho)$ per covered run. In the latter it considers only runs that have not been covered in earlier iterations. When all runs in $\mathcal{R}_{lf}(A_{\mathcal{F}})$ are covered the procedure tests if the set obtained by removing some $\mathcal{C}_\varrho$ from $\mathcal{C}_{opt}$ covers all runs. If this is the case, $\mathcal{C}_\varrho$ will be omitted from $\mathcal{C}_{opt}$.

The overall procedure to compute cutting sets of fragments can be summarized as follows. Given a finite transition system A and a set of loop-free fragments $\mathcal{F}$, construct the composition automaton $A_{\mathcal{F}}$. Then, compute all loop-free accepting runs $\mathcal{R}_{lf}(A_{\mathcal{F}})$. For each fragment ϱ compute the corresponding set $\mathcal{C}_\varrho$, which contains $\pi_{\mathcal{F}} \in \mathcal{R}_{lf}(A_{\mathcal{F}})$, if $\varrho \sqsubseteq \pi_{\mathcal{F}}|_S$. Finally, compute the optimal set cover $\mathcal{C}_{opt}$. The optimal cutting set of fragments $\mathcal{F}_{opt}$ contains all fragments ϱ with $\mathcal{C}_\varrho \in \mathcal{C}_{opt}$.

Example (cont). The composition automaton $A_{\mathcal{F}}$ has only three loop-free counterexamples (Fig. 6). The following table shows which of these, projected to S, is cut by what fragment:

	$(0,4,5)$	$(1,2,4)$	$(0,1)$	$(4,3)$
$(0,4,5)$	✓			
$(0,4,3,1,2,4,5)$		✓		✓
$(0,1,2,4,5)$		✓	✓	

Given the set $\mathcal{F} = \{(0,4,5), (1,2,4), (0,1), (4,3)\}$ there are two sets of fragments that cover all accepting runs: $\{(0,4,5),(1,2,4)\}$ and $\{(0,4,5),(0,1),(4,3)\}$. The latter is optimal with an overall weight of 4.   ∎

6   Example

This section uses an adaptive cruise control system to illustrate the proposed cut set approach. The results in [3] for this example show that analyzing fragments of counterexamples rather than complete counterexamples can reduce the computation time in CEGAR by an order of magnitude. Here we apply the concept of cutting sets of counterexample graphs to guide the abstraction.

The adaptive cruise control system is part of a vehicle-to-vehicle coordination system [10]. This system has two modes: cruise control mode (cc-mode) and adaptive cruise control mode (acc-mode). The acc-mode tries to keep a safe distance to the vehicle ahead, while the cc-mode tries to keep a constant speed. The hybrid automaton is the composition of a four-gear automatic transmission with the two mode acc-controller. An additional error state represents collisions.

Two different methods are used for validation. The first method, $\overline{succ}_{coarse}$, formulates the question if a trajectory between S_1 and S_2 exists as an optimization problem. The second method $\overline{succ}_{tight}$ computes polyhedra which enclose all trajectories that originate in S_1. This over-approximation with polyhedra is based on work presented in [2]. Both methods were discussed in [11]. The default method for single transitions, $\overline{succ}_{coarse}$, has an associated weight of 1. If this method fails to refute a fragment, the fragment is extended to a path of length

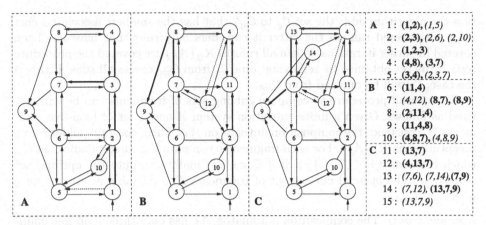

Fig. 7. Adaptive cruise control example. The initial state is 1, the final state, that models collision, is state 9. Figure **A** depicts the initial abstraction. **B** and **C** depict refinements. To the right, the sequence of cutting sets computed during verification. Valid fragments in bold face, spurious ones in italics

two. For pairs of transitions $\overline{succ}_{coarse}$ is applied first, with an associated weight of 2. If this method fails to refute the fragment, method $\overline{succ}_{tight}$ will be applied to the fragment next, with an associated weight of 6.

Our prototype implementation of the cut set method computes 15 cutting sets to reach a conclusive result. The sequences of cut sets and abstraction refinements are shown in Fig. 7. Three fragments were found to be spurious: $(2, 3, 7)$ of the fifth cut set for the first abstraction in Fig. 7.A, leading to the refinement show in Fig. 7.B; $(4, 8, 9)$ of the 10th cut set, leading to the refinement in Fig. 7.C, and $(13, 7, 9)$ of the 15th cut set. This final fragment was validated before in the 14th iteration with $\overline{succ}_{coarse}$ and found to be non-spurious. The validation method for this fragment was consequently updated to $\overline{succ}_{tight}$ with an associated weight of 6. The more accurate method then found in the 15th iteration that $(13, 7, 9)$ is spurious. This was the only time that $\overline{succ}_{tight}$ was invoked. Because the only fragment of the cutting set is not valid, state 9 is proven to be not reachable, which concludes the verification.

Note that the cut set in iteration 7 is not the optimal cut set; the 8th set would have been optimal at this stage. Although the greedy approach fails to compute the optimal cut set in this case, it does not compromise the final result, since the computed sets are always cutting sets.

A complete analysis of the ACC example with the prototype implementation of the cut set method in MATLAB takes 27.8 secs. on 1.2GHz Celeron processor, compared to 28.1 secs. for our implementation of the CEGAR approach from [3]. Although the runtimes are very similar, the cut set approach invokes the coarse-over-approximation 24 times vs. 29 invocations by CEGAR with fragments. Both invoke $\overline{succ}_{tight}$ once. An analysis of the experimental results using the MATLAB profiler indicates that only 2.3% of the computation time is spent computing cut sets.

7   Conclusions and Future Work

This paper presents a method for guiding abstraction refinement for hybrid systems using sets of fragments of counterexamples, building on the notion of fragment that was introduced in [3]. We use the concept of cutting sets of fragments. These cutting sets of fragments focus on the analysis similar to the way in which cut sets in directed graphs focus on bottlenecks. The aim is to refute as many counterexamples as possible while minimizing the expected computational effort.

The procedure presented in this paper leaves room for many heuristic choices, for example what mix of over-approximation methods is useful for what fragments, and how to assign weights to validations. Effective heuristics will be developed as we gain experience and insight with our prototype tool.

References

1. Alur, R., Dang, T., Ivančić, F.: Counter-example guided predicate abstraction of hybrid system. In: TACAS. Volume 2619 of LNCS., Springer (2003)
2. Chutinan, A., Krogh, B.: Verification of polyhedral-invariant hybrid automata using polygonal flow pipe approximations. In Vaandrager, F., van Schuppen, J., eds.: Hybrid Systems: Computation and Control. LNCS 1569, Springer Verlag (1999) 76–90
3. Clarke, E., Fehnker, A., Han, Z., Krogh, B., Ouaknine, J., Stursberg, O., Theobald, M.: Abstraction and counterexample-guided refinement in model checking of hybrid systems. International Journal of Foundations of Computer Science 14 (2003) 583–604
4. Tiwari, A., Khanna, G.: Series of abstractions for hybrid automata. In Tomlin, C.J., Greenstreet, M.R., eds.: Hybrid Systems: Computation and Control HSCC. Volume 2289 of LNCS., Springer (2002) 465–478
5. Clarke, E., Grumberg, O., Jha, S., Lu, Y., Veith, H.: Counterexample-guided abstraction refinement. In: Computer-Aided Verification. Volume 1855 of LNCS., Springer (2000) 154–169
6. Kurshan, R.: Computer-Aided Verification of Coordinating Processes: The Automata-Theoretic Approach. Princeton University Press (1994)
7. Henzinger, T., Kopke, P., Puri, A., Varaiya, P.: What's decidable about hybrid automata? In: Proceedings of the 27th Annual Symposium on Theory of Computing, ACM Press (1995) 373–382
8. Sheyner, O.: Scenario Graphs and Attack Graphs. PhD thesis, SCS, Carnegie Mellon University (2004)
9. Skiena, S.: The Algorithm Design Manual. Telos/Springer-Verlag (1998)
10. Girard, A., Souza, J., Misener, J., Hedrick, J.: A control architecture for integrated cooperative cruise control and collision warning systems. In: Proc. 40th IEEE Conf. on Decision and Control. (2001)
11. Stursberg, O., Fehnker, A., Han, Z., Krogh, B.: Specification-guided analysis of hybrid systems using a hierachy of validation methods. In: Proc. IFAC Conference ADHS, Elsevier (2003)

PHAVer: Algorithmic Verification of Hybrid Systems Past HyTech

Goran Frehse

Dept. of Electrical and Computer Engineering,
Carnegie Mellon University, Pittsburgh, PA 15213, USA
gfrehse@ece.cmu.edu
http://www.andrew.cmu.edu/~gfrehse

Abstract. In 1995, HyTech broke new ground as a potentially powerful tool for verifying hybrid systems – yet it has remained severely limited in its applicability to more complex systems. We address the main problems of HyTech with PHAVer, a new tool for the exact verification of safety properties of hybrid systems with piecewise constant bounds on the derivatives. Affine dynamics are handled by on-the-fly overapproximation and by partitioning the state space based on user-definable constraints and the dynamics of the system. PHAVer's exact arithmetic is robust due to the use of the Parma Polyhedra Library, which supports arbitrarily large numbers. To manage the complexity of the polyhedral computations, we propose methods to conservatively limit the number of bits and constraints of polyhedra. Experimental results for a navigation benchmark and a tunnel diode circuit show the effectiveness of the approach.

1 Introduction

Systems with discrete as well as continuous dynamics, i.e., hybrid systems, are notoriously complex to analyze, and the algorithmic verification of hybrid systems remains a challenging problem, both from a theoretic point of view as well as from the implementation side. Ideally, one would like to obtain either an exact result or a conservative overapproximation of the behavior of the system, e.g., as the set of reachable states. An exact computation is possible with linear hybrid automata (LHA) [1], which are defined by linear predicates and piecewise constant bounds on the derivatives. They were proposed and studied in detail by Henzinger et al., see [2] for an extensive discussion, who presented in 1995 a tool called HyTech that could perform various computations with such systems [3]. It featured a powerful input language and functionality, but suffered from a major flaw: its exact arithmetic was using limited digits, which can quickly lead to overflow errors. While it was successfully used to analyze a number examples, see [4, 5] and references therein, the overflow problem prohibits any application to more complex systems.

The valuable experiences with HyTech have prompted a number of suggestions for improvement, a summary of which can be found in [4]. We address the

M. Morari and L. Thiele (Eds.): HSCC 2005, LNCS 3414, pp. 258–273, 2005.

most pressing ones with PHAVer (Polyhedral Hybrid Automaton Verifyer), a new tool for analyzing linear hybrid automata with the following characteristics:

- exact and robust arithmetic based on the Parma Polyhedra Library [6],
- on-the-fly overapproximation of piecewise affine dynamics,
- conservative limiting of bits and constraints in polyhedral computations,
- support for compositional and assume-guarantee reasoning. [1]

PHAVer's extended functionality and computational robustness open up new application domains as well as research issues that were abandoned because of the limits of previous implementations. Exact arithmetic entails, in addition to the security and beauty of formal correctness, the significant advantage of a separation of concerns. Problems of convergence, combinatorial explosion and nondeterminism can be identified as such, which is very difficult if they are intertwined with numerical difficulties. We present PHAVer's algorithm for overapproximating piecewise affine dynamics with LHA, which refines locations with user-specified constraints. The constraints allow the user to include expert knowledge in refining certain variables to a specified detail, and can be adapted to the dynamics by prioritizing the size or the spread angle of the derivatives of a location. Due to the exact arithmetic, the size of coefficients as well as the number of constraints that define polyhedra can grow excessively. We propose methods to simplify polyhedra by limiting both the number of bits and contraints. The applicability of PHAVer and the effectiveness of the proposed methods are demonstrated with a navigation benchmark [7], and a tunnel diode circuit [8]. In addition to the reachability algorithm, PHAVer includes a separate engine for computing simulation relations between hybrid automata. It can be used to verify equivalence or abstraction between different models, and for assume-guarantee reasoning. For lack of space, the reader is referred to [9] for further details on the approach.

Earlier attempts to improve over HyTech include the use of interval arithmetic [10], which can quickly lead to prohibitively large overapproximations. An algorithm specialized on rectangular automata was proposed in [11] and implemented based on the HyTech engine. Unfortunately, it therefore also suffered from the same flaws. While most tools for timed automata use exact computations, we are not aware of tools for hybrid systems, other than HyTech, to do so. The first HyTech prototype was implemented in Mathematica and did not have any numerical restrictions, but it was also 50–1000 times slower than the later version written in C++ [12]. Our on-the-fly overapproximation essentially performs a partitioning of the state space similar to the approach in [13]. For the simplification of polyhedra it has been suggested to use bounding boxes or oriented rectangular hulls [14]. Instead, we propose to simply drop the least significant of the constraints, as this seems a good compromise in terms of accuracy and speed. For a survey of verification tools for hybrid automata, see [15].

---

[1] Not addressed are more advanced input capabilities like hierarchy, templates and directional communication labels, since we consider these easily and more appropriately handled by a GUI-frontend or editor.

In the next section, we will briefly introduce the hybrid automaton model used by PHAVer, which has a simple Input/Output structure to support compositional reasoning. In Sect. 3 we present the reachability analysis algorithm of PHAVer, and its on-the-fly overapproximation of affine dynamics. Experimental results are provided for a navigation benchmark. Methods to manage the complexity of polyhedra by limiting the bits and constraints are proposed in Sect., 4, and illustrated with a tunnel diode circuit. We sum up the results with some conclusions in Sect. 5.

2 Hybrid I/O-Automata with Affine Dynamics

The theory of hybrid I/O-automata has been developed extensively by Lynch, Segala, Vaandrager and Weinberg [16]. It is a very general framework that is based on (almost) arbitrary trajectories of a set of variables, which can have different dynamic types. Since our focus is on obtaining a computable framework for compositional reasoning, we have proposed a simple concept of I/O-automata in [9], which is largely based on the hybrid automata in [1]. Given a set Var of variables, a valuation is a function $v : Var \rightarrow \mathbb{R}$. Let $V(Var)$ denote the set of valuations over Var. An *activity* is a function $f : \mathbb{R}^{\geq 0} \rightarrow V(Var)$. Let $act(Var)$ denote the set of activities over the variables in Var. A set S of activities is *time-invariant* if for all $f \in S, d \in \mathbb{R}^{\geq 0} : f_d(t) := f(t+d) \in S$. Let $\downarrow_{Var})$ be the projection onto the variables in Var.

Definition 1 (Hybrid I/O-Automaton). *[9]A hybrid Input/Output-auto-maton (HIOA) $H = (Loc, Var_S, Var_I, Var_O, Lab, \rightarrow, Act, Inv, Init)$ consists of the following:*

- *A finite set Loc of locations.*
- *Finite and disjoint sets of state and input variables, Var_S and Var_I, and of output variables $Var_O \subseteq Var_S$. Let $Var = Var_S \cup Var_I$.*
- *A finite set Lab of synchronization labels.*
- *A finite set of discrete transitions $\rightarrow \subseteq Loc \times Lab \times 2^{V(Var) \times V(Var)} \times Loc$. A transition $(l, a, \mu, l') \in \rightarrow$ is also written as $l \xrightarrow{a,\mu}_H l'$.*
- *A mapping $Act : Loc \rightarrow 2^{act(Var)}$ to time-invariant sets of activities.*
- *A mapping $Inv : Loc \rightarrow 2^{V(Var)}$ from locations to sets of valuations.*
- *Initial states $Init \subseteq Loc \times V(Var)$ s.t. $(l, v) \in Init \Rightarrow v \in Inv(l)$.*

In PHAVer, we deal with hybrid automata that can be analyzed using polyhedra, i.e., finite linear formulas. A *linear expression* is of the form $\sum_i a_i x_i + b$, and a *convex linear formula* is a finite conjunction of constraints $\sum_i a_i x_i + b \bowtie 0$, with $a_i, b \in \mathbb{Z}$, $x_i \in Var$ and a sign $\bowtie \in \{<, \leq, =\}$. A *non-convex linear formula*, or *linear formula*, is a finite disjunction of convex linear formulas. A *linear hybrid automaton* (LHA) [1] is a hybrid automaton in which the invariants and the continuous transition relation are given by linear formulas over Var, and the activities are given by linear formulas over the time derivatives of the variables. If the dynamics are given by linear formulas over the derivatives and the variables, we call it an *affine hybrid automaton*. [2]

3   Reachability Analysis in PHAVer

A reachability analysis computes all states that are connected to the initial states by a run. We enhances the fixpoint computation algorithm for reachability with operators for the refinement of locations and the simplification of sets of states described by polyhedra. The refinement of locations is used when affine dynamics are overapproximated with LHA-dynamics, where locations are split into smaller parts to improve the accuracy. The simplification operator fulfills two purposes: Firstly, the overapproximation of sets of states with a simpler representation keeps the complexity from growing beyond computationally manageable limits. Secondly, since termination is not guaranteed for linear hybrid automata, over-approximation of the sets of states as well as the set of derivatives can be used to accelerate convergence and possibly force termination by reducing the model to a class where reachability is decidable. The challenge lies in trading speed, termination and resource consumption against the loss of accuracy. The algorithm used in PHAVer for computing the set of reachable states is shown in Fig. 1. We

procedure *GetReach*
> **Input:** a set of initial states S_I
> **Output:** the set of states S_R reachable from S_I
> $(S_I, \{S_I\}) := refine\_loc(S_I, \{S_I\});$
> $W, S_R := time\_elapse(S_I);$
> **while** $W \neq \emptyset$ **do**
>> $N := trans\_post(W);$
>> $(N, (S_I, S_R, W)) := refine\_loc(N, (S_I, S_R, W));$
>> $N := cheap\_difference(N, S_R);$
>> $N := union\_approx(N, S_R);$
>> $N := simplify(N);$
>> $N := time\_post(N, simplify(time\_deriv(N, Inv)));$
>> $S_R := S_R \cup N;$
>> $W := N$
> **od.**

Fig. 1. Reachability Algorithm in PHAVer

give a brief summary of the operators used. Let X, Y and $Y_1, \dots, Y_z$ be arbitrary sets of states, each described by a set of convex polyhedra for each location.

Post-operators: The operator $time\_elapse(X, Y)$ computes the successors of a set of states X by letting time elapse according to a set Y that attributes a set

---

[2] In literature, a LHA is also referred to as a *piecewise constant* HA, and an affine HA as a *linear* HA.

of derivatives to each location. The successors of discrete transitions are given by *trans_post*(X). A detailed description can be found in [2].

Overapproximating Operators: The operator *cheap_difference*(X, Y) computes a overapproximation of $X \setminus Y$ by returning the polyhedra in Y that are not individually contained in some polyhedra of X. The gain in speed usually far outweighs the fact that more states are iterated than necessary [2]. With *union_approx*(X, Y), the union of new states X and old states Y can optionally be overapproximated, e.g., by using the convex hull. If there are no new states for a location, the operator returns the empty set for that location. The *simplify* operator is used to reduce the complexity the representation of states by overapproximation. It can also be applied to the set of derivatives in the location. Current options in PHAVer for *simplify* include a bounding box overapproximation, limiting the number of bits used by the coefficients of constraints, and limiting the number of constraints.

Refinement Operators: The operator *refine_loc*(X, (Y_1, ..., Y_z)) partitions the locations with states in X as described in Sect. 3.1 and maps the states in $Y_1, ..., Y_z$ to the new set of locations. The operator *time_deriv*(X, Y) computes the set of derivatives that any state in X might exhibit, provided that the states are confined to Y:

$$time\_deriv(X, Y) = \{(l, \dot{f}(t)) | \exists (l, v) \in X, f \in Act(l), t \in \mathbb{R}^{\geq 0} :$$
$$(f(0) = v \wedge \forall t', 0 \leq t' \leq t : f(t') \in Y)\}$$

In the following section we give a more detailed description of the refinement operator and its parameters.

3.1   On-the-Fly Over-Approximation of Affine Dynamics

While PHAVer's computations are based on linear hybrid automata models, it also accepts affine dynamics, which are then overapproximated conservatively. The approximation error depends on the size of the location and the dynamics, so PHAVer offers to partition reachable locations during the analysis. The partitioning takes place by splitting locations recursively along user-defined hyperplanes until a minimum size is reached or the dynamics are sufficiently refined.

The *relaxed affine dynamics* are given by a convex linear formula for its derivatives, i.e., a conjunction of constraints

$$a_i^T \dot{x} + \hat{a}_i^T x \bowtie_i b_i, \qquad a_i, \hat{a}_i \in \mathbb{Z}^n, b_i \in \mathbb{Z}, \bowtie_i \in \{<, \leq, =\}, \ i = 1, ..., m. \quad (1)$$

for each location. In the following, we assume the equalities to be modeled using conjuncts of pairs of inequalities. In a location *loc*, the constraints (1) are overapproximated conservatively with constraints of the form $\alpha_i \dot{x} \bowtie_i \beta_i$, $\alpha_i \in \mathbb{Z}^n, \beta_i \in \mathbb{Z}$, by finding the infimum of (1) inside the invariant $Inv(loc)$. Let

$$p/q = \inf_{x \in Inv(loc)} \hat{a}_i^T x, \qquad p, q \in \mathbb{Z}.$$

If p/q exists, the set of $\dot{x}$ that fulfill (1) is bounded by $a_i^T \dot{x} \bowtie_i b_i - p/q$, otherwise the constraint must be dropped. The linear constraint on $\dot{x}$ is then given by $\alpha_i = qa_i$, $\beta_i = qb_i - p$.

The resulting overapproximation error depends on the size of the locations and the dynamics but can be made arbitrarily small by defining suitably small locations. PHAVer does so by recursively splitting a location along a suitable hyperplane chosen from a user-provided set. The splitting is repeated in reachable locations until a certain threshold, e.g., a minimum size, is reached. We account for the dynamics of the system using the spatial angle that is spanned by the derivatives in a location. Let the *spread* $\sphericalangle(X)$ of a set of valuations be defined as

$$\sphericalangle(X) = \arccos \min_{x,y \in X} x^T y / |x||y|\}$$

and the spread $\sphericalangle_{deriv}(loc, X, Y)$ of the derivatives of states X confined to states Y in location loc as

$$\sphericalangle_{deriv}(loc, X, Y) = \sphericalangle \left(\{v | (loc, v) \in time\_deriv(X, Y)\}\right).$$

The spread of the derivatives is used in two ways: The refinement of a location is stopped once the spread is smaller than a given minimum, or the constraints are prioritized according to the spread of the derivatives in the location after the splitting.

Recall that a hyperplane h is defined by an equation $a_h^T x = b_h$, where the normal vector a_h determines its direction and the inhomogeneous term b_h its position, for which we choose the center of the location. Let the *slack* of h in a location loc be defined by

$$\Delta(a_h) = \max_{x \in Inv(loc)} a_h^T x - \min_{x \in Inv(loc)} a_h^T x.$$

In PHAVer, the user provides a list of candidate normal vectors $a_{h,i}$ and the minimum and maximum slack that the hyperplanes will have in the refined locations, i.e.,

$$Cand = \{(a_{h,1}, \Delta_{min,1}, \Delta_{max,1}), \ldots, (a_{h,m}, \Delta_{min,m}, \Delta_{max,m})\}.$$

This allows the user to include expert knowledge by choosing planes and location sizes suitable for the system. The candidate hyperplanes are prioritized according to a user-controlled list of criteria. We consider the criteria to be a map

$$split\_crit : \{a^T x \bowtie b | a \in \mathbb{Z}^n, b \in \mathbb{Z}\} \times Loc \times 2^{S_H} \mapsto (\mathbb{R} \cup \infty \cup -\infty)^z$$

that attributes a z-tuple of prioritizing measures, evaluated lexicographically, to each constraint, and takes into account a set of valuations considered of interest. Two special symbols are included: ∞ voids the constraint, but it can be overruled by $-\infty$, which takes precedence over all other factors. The currently implemented measure $split\_crit(a^T x \bowtie b, loc, N)$ takes into account the set N of reachable states in the location, and offers the following choices:

1. Prioritize constraints according to their slack:

$$split\_crit_1 = \begin{cases} \Delta(a_h)/\Delta_{min,h} & \text{if} \Delta(a_h) > \Delta_{min,h}, \\ \infty & \text{otherwise.} \end{cases}$$

2. Prioritize constraints that have reachable states only on one side:

$$split\_crit_2 = \begin{cases} 1 \text{ if } \exists x, x' \in N : a^T x < b \wedge a^T x' > b \\ 0 \text{ otherwise.} \end{cases}$$

3. Prioritize constraints according to the spread of the derivatives. Discard constraint if a minimum spread $\lessdot_{min}$ is reached and the slack is smaller than $\Delta_{max,h}$:

$$split\_crit_3 = \begin{cases} -\lessdot_{deriv}(loc, N, Inv) & \text{if } \lessdot_{deriv}(loc, N, Inv) \geq \lessdot_{min} \\ & \vee\ \Delta(a_h) > \Delta_{max,h}, \\ \infty & \text{otherwise.} \end{cases}$$

4. Prioritize constraints according to the derivative spread after the constraint is applied:

$$split\_crit_4 = -\max\{\lessdot_{deriv}(loc, N, \{(l, x) \in Inv \mid a^T x \leq b\}),$$
$$\lessdot_{deriv}(loc, N, \{(l, x) \in Inv \mid a^T x \geq b\})\}.$$

For efficiency, the refinement is applied on the fly as shown in the reachability algorithm of Fig. 1. The algorithms for splitting a location, and refining the location with the prioritized candidate constraints are shown in Fig. 2 and Fig. 3.

procedure *SplitLocation*
  Input: HIOA $H = (Loc, Var_S, Var_I, Var_O, Lab, \rightarrow, Act, Inv, Init)$,
      location loc, constraint $a_i^T x \bowtie_i b_i$, splitting label τ_H,
      list $\{Y_1, \ldots, Y_n\}$ of set of states of H for remapping
  Output: Hybrid I/O-automaton H with split location loc
  $Loc := \{l \in Loc \mid l \neq loc\} \cup \{(loc, \leq), (loc, \geq)\}$;
  $\rightarrow := \{(l, a, \mu, l') \in \rightarrow \mid l \neq loc \wedge l' \neq loc\}$
      $\cup \{(l, a, \mu, (loc, \leq)), (l, a, \mu, (loc, \geq)) \mid (l, a, \mu, loc) \in \rightarrow\}$
      $\cup \{((loc, \leq), a, \mu, l'), ((loc, \geq), a, \mu, l') \mid (loc, a, \mu, l) \in \rightarrow\}$
      $\cup \{(l, \tau_H, \{x' = x | x \in Var\}, l') \mid l, l' \in \{(loc, \leq), (loc, \geq)\}\}$;
  $Act := \{l \mapsto x(t) \in Act \mid l \neq loc\}$
      $\cup \{(loc, \bowtie) \mapsto x(t) \mid loc \mapsto x(t) \in Act, \bowtie \in \{\leq, \geq\}\}$;
  for $S \in \{Y_1, \ldots, Y_n\} \cup \{Inv, Init\}$ **do**
    $S := \{(l, x) \in S \mid l \neq loc\}$
      $\cup \{((loc, \bowtie), x) \mid (loc, x) \in S \wedge a_i^T x \bowtie b_i, \bowtie \in \{\leq, \geq\}\}$
  od.

Fig. 2. Splitting a location along a hyperplane

procedure *refine_loc*
    Input: HIOA $H = (Loc, Var_S, Var_I, Var_O, Lab, \rightarrow, Act, Inv, Init)$,
        set of investigated states N, set of candidate constraints
        $Cand = \{(a_{h,1}, \Delta_{min,1}, \Delta_{max,1}), \ldots, (a_{h,m}, \Delta_{min,m}, \Delta_{max,m})\}$,
        list $\{Y_1, \ldots, Y_n\}$ of set of states of H for remapping
    Output: Hybrid I/O-automaton H with locations in N refined

    for $loc \in \{l \in Loc | \exists x : (l, x) \in N\}$ **do**
        do
            for $i = 1, \ldots, m$ **do**

$$b_i := 1/2 \left(\max_{x \in Inv(loc)} a_{h,i}^T x + \min_{x \in Inv(loc)} a_{h,i}^T x \right);$$

$$c_i := split\_crit(a_{h,i}^T x = b_i, loc, N)$$

            od;
            $k := \underset{i=1,\ldots,m}{\operatorname{argmin}} c_i$;
            if $\infty \notin c_k \vee -\infty \in c_k$ **then**
                $SplitLocation(H, loc, a_{h,k}^T x = b_k, \tau_H, \{Y_1, \ldots, Y_n\})$
        od
        while k **exists and** $\infty \notin c_k \vee -\infty \in c_k$ **od**
    od.

Fig. 3. Refining states with a set of candidate constraints

3.2 Example: Navigation Benchmark

We illustrate the reachability analysis of PHAVer with a benchmark proposed in [7]. It models an object moving in a plane, and following dynamically a set of desired velocities $v_d(i) = (sin(i\pi/4), cos(i\pi/4))^T$, $i = 0, \ldots, 7$, where i is attributed to each unit square in the plane by a given map M. A special symbol A denotes the set of target states, and B denotes the set of forbidden states for the object. We verified that the forbidden states are not reachable for the instances shown in Fig. 4, whose maps are given by:

$$M_{NAV01} = M_{NAV02} = M_{NAV03} = \begin{pmatrix} B & 2 & 4 \\ 2 & 3 & 4 \\ 2 & 2 & A \end{pmatrix}, M_{NAV04} = \begin{pmatrix} B & 2 & 4 \\ 2 & 2 & 4 \\ 1 & 1 & A \end{pmatrix}.$$

The dynamics of the 4-dimensional state vector $(x_1, x_2, v_1, v_2)^T$ are given by

$$\begin{pmatrix} \dot{x} \\ \dot{v} \end{pmatrix} = \begin{pmatrix} 0 & I \\ 0 & A \end{pmatrix} \begin{pmatrix} x \\ v \end{pmatrix} - \begin{pmatrix} 0 \\ A \end{pmatrix} \begin{pmatrix} 0 \\ v_d(i) \end{pmatrix}, \text{ with } A = \begin{pmatrix} -1.2 & 0.1 \\ 0.1 & -1.2 \end{pmatrix}.$$

The initial states for the instances are defined by $x_0 \in [2, 3] \times [1, 2]$ and

$$v_{0,NAV01} \in [-0.3, 0.3] \times [-0.3, 0], \quad v_{0,NAV02} \in [-0.3, 0.3] \times [-0.3, 0.3],$$
$$v_{0,NAV03} \in [-0.4, 0.4] \times [-0.4, 0.4], \quad v_{0,NAV04} \in [0.1, 0.5] \times [0.05, 0.25].$$

As splitting constraints we use $Cand = \{(v_1, \delta_1, \infty), (v_2, \delta_2, \infty)\}$, where appropriate δ_i were established by some trial-and-error runs, and $(split\_crit_1)$ as splitting criterion. Note that x_1, x_2 need not be refined, since they depend only on v.

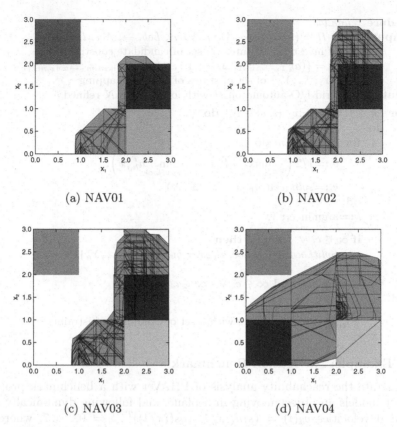

(a) NAV01   (b) NAV02

(c) NAV03   (d) NAV04

Fig. 4. Reachable states in the x_1, x_2-plane (initial states darkest)

The other analysis parameters were left at their default setting. While we need to specify bounds for the analysis region, we can handle the unbounded case by checking that the reachable state space is strictly contained in the analysis region. All instances shown were obtained with a-priori bounds of $[-2, 2]$ on the velocities, and the reachable velocities remained within an interval $[-1.1, 1.1]$, which confirms our a-priori bounds as valid. Figure 4 shows the set of reachable states computed by PHAVer as a result. Computation times and memory consumption are shown in Table 1, and were obtained on a Pentium IV, 1.9GHz with 768 MB RAM running Linux. For the instances NAV01–NAV03, the analysis was fairly straightforward, with $\delta_i = 0.5$. For the instance NAV04 we had to set $\delta_i = 0.25$, and the analysis did not terminate at first. We applied a heuristic: The convex hull was computed for the first 20 iterations for speed, then switched to normal reachability, and at iteration 40 a bounding box simplification was triggered manually. In comparison, for a predicate abstraction tool the following times were reported in [17]: For NAV01–NAV03 $34s$, $153s$ (68MB) and $152s$ (180MB), respectively, on a Sun Enterprise 3000 (4 x 250 MHz UltraSPARC) with 1 GB RAM.

Table 1. Computation times and memory requirements

Instance	Time	Memory	Automaton Iter.	Loc.	Trans.	Reachable Set Loc.	Polyh.
NAV01	34.73 s	62.6 MB	13	141	3452	79	646
NAV02	62.16 s	89.7 MB	13	153	3716	84	1406
NAV02^i	41.05 s	53.7 MB	13	148	3661	84	84
NAV03	61.88 s	90.0 MB	13	153	3716	84	1406
NAV04^{ii}	225.08 s	116.3 MB	45	267	7773	167	362

^{i} convex hull, ^{ii} convex hull up to iter. 20, bounding box at iter. 40

4   Managing the Complexity of Polyhedra

A set of symbolic states is described by a linear formula, the convex sub-formulas of which define convex polyhedra, which in turn are described by a set of constraints. In exact fixpoint computations with polyhedra, the size of numbers in the formula as well as the number of constraints typically increases unless the structure of the hybrid system imposes boundaries, e.g., by resets or invariants. To keep the complexity manageable, we propose the simplification of complex polyhedra in a strictly conservative fashion by limiting the number of bits, i.e., the size of coefficients, and the number of constraints. We reduce only inequalities to preserve the affine dimension of the polyhedron. In practice, both simplifications are applied when the number of bits or constraints exceeds a given threshold that is significantly higher than the reduction level. The resulting hysteresis between exact computations and overapproximations gives cyclic dependencies time to stabilize.

4.1   Limiting the Number of Bits

We consider the ith constraint $a_i^T x \bowtie_i b_i$ of a polyhedron of the form $Ax + b \bowtie 0$, where a_i is a vector of the coefficients $a_{ij} \in \mathbb{Z}$ of A, $i = 1, \ldots, m$, $j = 1, \ldots, n$, $\bowtie$ is a vector of signs $\bowtie_i \in \{\leq, <, =\}$, and b is a vector of inhomogeneous coefficients $b_i \in \mathbb{Z}$. We assume that the a_{ij} and b_i have no common factor and that there are no redundant constraints. The goal is to find a new constraint $\alpha_i^T x \bowtie_i \beta_i$ with coefficients α_{ij} having less than z bits, i.e., $|\alpha_{ij}|, |\beta_i| \leq 2^{z+1} - 1$, with the least overapproximation possible. Expressing the new coefficients in terms of a scaling factor $f > 0$, rounding errors r_{ij}, $|r_{ij}| \leq 0.5$ and an error r_i for the inhomogeneous term we get $\alpha_{ij} = f a_{ij} + r_{ij}$ and $\beta_i = f b_i + r_i$. There is no a-priori bound on r_i, since it depends on the new direction α_i and the other constraints that define the polyhedron. With the bounds on the r_{ij}, we get $|f a_{ij} + r_{ij}| \leq 2^{z+1} - 1$, and get upper bounds on f using $|r_{ij}| \leq 0.5$ and, in the best case, we expect β_i to be close to $f b_i$. Since β_i must be rounded strictly upwards to guarantee conservativeness, we get $|r_i| \leq 1$ as an optimistic estimate:

$$f \leq (2^{z+1} - 3/2)/|a_{ij}|, \text{ and} \tag{2}$$

$$f \leq (2^{z+1} - 2)/|b_i|. \tag{3}$$

To predict the effects of rounding precisely is difficult and would lead to a mixed integer linear program, so we employ a heuristic algorithm, shown in Fig. 5. Let $round(x)$ be a function that returns the next integer between x and zero, and $ceil(x)$ be a function that rounds to the next larger integer. First, we estimate f based on (2),(3), then we compute a new β_i using linear programming. If β_i has more than z bit, we decrease f and start over. The procedure is repeated until all coefficients $\alpha_{ij} = 0$, in which case the problem is infeasible. Note that it is not

procedure *LimitConstraintBits*

    Input: Polyhedron as a set of constraints $P = \{a_k^T x \bowtie_k b_k | k = 1, \ldots, m\}$,
                 index i to constraint to be limited, desired number of bits z
    Output: new constraint $\alpha_i^T x \bowtie_i b_i$

    $success := false$;
    $f := min\{(2^{z+1} - 3/2)/|a_{kj}|, (2^{z+1} - 2)/|b_i| \mid j = 1, \ldots, n\}$;
    while $\neg success$ **do**
        for $j = 1, \ldots, n$ **do** $\alpha_{ij} := round(f a_{ij})$ **od**;
        $q := \min\limits_{x \in P} \alpha_i^T x$;
        if $\alpha_i = 0$ **or** $q = -\infty$ **then abort fi**;
        $\beta_i := ceil(q)$;
        if $|\beta_i| \leq 2^{z+1} - 1$ **then** $success := true$
        else $f := min\{f/2 - 3/(4|a_{kj}|), (2^{z+1} - 2)/|\beta_i| \mid j = 1, \ldots, n\}$ **fi**;
    od.

Fig. 5. Limiting the number of bits of a constraint

guaranteed that the new polyhedron is bounded. Figure 6 illustrates the basic scheme. The normal vector a_i of the constraint, shown in (a), is approximated by α_i, as shown in (b). Linear programming yields the inhomogeneous term q that makes the constraint tangent to the polyhedron, as in (c). Rounding of q yields β_i, and the polyhedron outlined in (d).

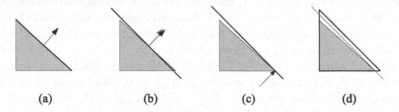

      (a)   (b)   (c)   (d)

Fig. 6. Limiting the number of bits of a constraint

4.2 Limiting the Number of Constraints

To reduce the complexity of a polyhedron, we propose to drop constraints based on a criterion *crit* that measures the the difference between the polyhedron with and without the constraint. As with limiting the number of bits, we usually chose

procedure *LimitConstraintsByAngle*

    Input: Polyhedron P as a set of constraints $a_i^T x \bowtie_i b_i$, $i = 1, \ldots, m$,

         desired number of constraints z

    Output: Polyhedron H

    for $i = 1, \ldots, m$, $j = 1, \ldots, m$, $j > i$ **do** $\alpha(i,j) := a_i^T a_j$ **od;**

    $H := \{a_k^T x \bowtie_k b_k \mid k = \operatorname{argmin}_k (\max_j |a_{kj}|)\} \cup \{a_i^T x \bowtie_i b_i \mid \bowtie_i \in \{=\}\};$

    $C := P \setminus H;$

    while $(|C| > 0 \wedge (|H| < z \vee (bounded(P) \wedge \neg bounded(H))))$ **do**

        $j = \operatorname{argmin}_j (\max_i \alpha(i,j))$ **s.t.** $a_i^T x \bowtie_i b_i \in H, a_j^T x \bowtie_j b_j \in C;$

        $H := H \cup \{a_j^T x \bowtie_j b_j\};$

        $C := C \setminus \{a_j^T x \bowtie_j b_j\}$

    od.

Fig. 7. Reconstructing a polyhedron with a limited number of constraints by angle prioritization

to not limit equalities in order to preserve the affine dimension of the polyhedron. If an equality is to be limited, it must be replaced by two inequalities.

Let P be a set of linear constraints describing a convex polyhedron, and $P^{\setminus i} = P \setminus \{a_i^T x \bowtie_i b_i\}$ be the polyhedron without it's ith constraint. Then the difference between the points contained P and $P^{\setminus i}$ is the polyhedron $P^{\neg i} = P^{\setminus i} \cup \{-a_i^T x \overline{\bowtie}_i - b_i\}$, where $(\bowtie_i, \overline{\bowtie}_i) \in \{(<, \leq), (\leq, <)\}$, obtained by simply replacing the ith constraint with its complement. It has less non-redundant constraints than P and is therefore preferable in the formulations below. We consider three methods:

1. volumetric: Let $V(P)$ be the volume of the points contained in P. Then $crit = V(P^{\setminus i}) - V(P) = V(P^{\neg i})$. Requires $P^{\neg i}$ to be bounded.
2. slack: Let $b_{max} = \max_x a_i^T x$ s.t. $x \in P^{\neg i}$. Then $crit = (b_{max} - b_i)/||a_i||$, i.e., the distance, measured in the direction of a_i, between the points farthest apart in $P^{\neg i}$. Requires $P^{\neg i}$ to be bounded in the direction of a_i.
3. angle: $crit = -\max_{j \neq i} a_j^T a_i$. Measures the negative cosine of the closest angle between the normal vector of the ith constraint and all others.

We consider two general procedures of selecting the z most important out of m original constraints:

1. deconstruction: Starting from the entire set of constraints, drop the $m - z$ constraints with the least effect according to $crit$.
2. construction: Starting from an empty set of constraints, add the z constraints with the greatest effect according to $crit$.

While deconstruction is more likely to preserve as much as possible of the original polyhedron, construction requires less iterations if $m > 2z$. The criteria based on volume and slack require the initial polyhedron to be bounded, for which one could use, e.g., the invariant of the location.

The construction method with an angle criterion was the fastest in our experiments. The algorithm is shown in Fig. 7, where C is the set of candidate constraints and H is the set of chosen constraints. H is initialized with the set of equalities and an arbitrary initial constraint. Here we choose the one with the smallest coefficients. In a while-loop, the constraint is chosen based on the best of the worst-cases, i.e., the smallest angle with the constraints in H. Since $a_j^T a_i$ is the cosine of the angle, choosing the smallest angle translates into maximizing $a_j^T a_i$. The constraint is added to H and removed from the candidates C, and the procedures is repeated until $|H| \geq z$ and the boundedness of P implies boundedness of H.

4.3   Example: Tunnel-Diode Oscillator Circuit

Consider a tunnel-diode oscillator circuit [8]. It models the current I and the voltage drop V of a tunnel diode in parallel to the capacitor of a serial RLC circuit, which are in stable oscillation for the given parameters. The state equations are given by

$$\dot{V} = 1/C(-I_d(V) + I),$$
$$\dot{I} = 1/L(-V - 1/G \cdot I + V_{in}),$$

where $C = 1\ pF$, $L = 1\ \mu H$, $G = 5\ m\Omega^{-1}$, $V_{in} = 0.3\ V$, and the diode current

$$I_d(V) = \begin{cases} 6.0105V^3 - 0.9917V^2 + 0.0545V & \text{if } V \leq 0.055, \\ 0.0692V^3 - 0.0421V^2 + 0.004V + 8.9579e{-}4 & \text{if } 0.055 \leq V \leq 0.35, \\ 0.2634V^3 - 0.2765V^2 + 0.0968V - 0.0112 & \text{if } 0.35 \leq V. \end{cases}$$

The dynamics were approximated with LHA, similar to the approach in Sect. 3.1. Figure 8(a) shows the convex hull of the reachable states starting from $V \in [0.42V, 0.52V]$, $I = 0.6mA$. It also shows the invariants (dashed) generated by the refinement algorithm using constraints $Cand = \{(V, 0.7/128, 0.7/16),$ $(I, 1.5/128, 1.5/16)\}$, i.e., max. 128 partitions in both directions, and splitting criterion $(split\_crit_3, split\_crit_1)$ with $\sphericalangle_{min} = \arccos(0.99)$. The analysis with PHAVer took $52.63s$ and 55MB RAM, with the largest coefficient taking up 7352 bits and at most 7 constraints per polyhedron.

A stopwatch was added to the system to measure the cycle time, i.e., the maximum time it takes any state to cross the threshold $I = 0.6\mu A$, $V > 0.25V$ twice. For the clocked circuit, the number of bits and constraints grows rapidly and a more precise analysis, such as shown in Fig. 8(b) is only possible with limits on both. We compare the exact analysis for constraints $Cand = \{(V, 0.7/32, 0.7/16),$ $(I, 1.5/32, 1.5/16)\}$ with an analysis limiting the bits to 16 when a threshold of 300 bits is reached, and a limit of 32 constraints at a threshold of 56. Figures 9(a) and 9(b) show a linear increase in the number of constraints, and an exponential increase of the number of bits in the new polyhedra found at each iteration. The analysis takes $979s$ (210MB) when exact, and $79s$ (39.6MB) when limited. At a more than tenfold increase in speed, the overapproximation is negligible and results in a cycle time estimate that is only 0.25 percent larger.

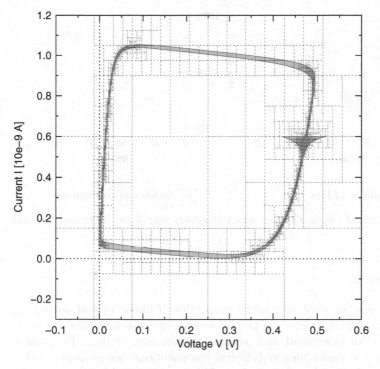

(a) *V-I*-Plane, invariants dashed

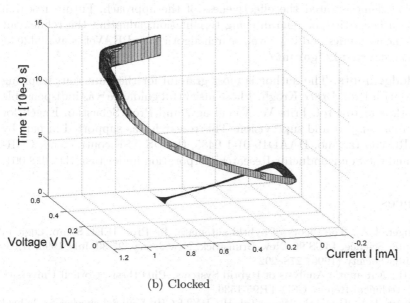

(b) Clocked

Fig. 8. Reachable states of Tunnel Diode Circuit

272   G. Frehse

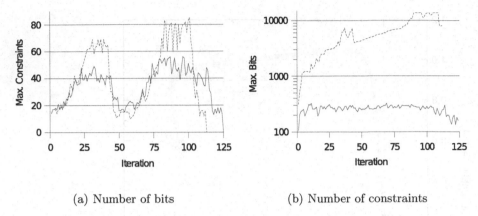

(a) Number of bits   (b) Number of constraints

Fig. 9. Clocked Tunnel Diode Circuit, exact (dashed) and with limits on bits and constraints (solid)

5   Conclusions

PHAVer, a new tool for verifying safety properties of linear hybrid automata, provides exact, robust arithmetic, on-the-fly overapproximation of affine dynamics, and supports compositional and assume/guarantee-reasoning. To manage the complexity of the underlying polyhedral computations, we proposed methods for conservatively limiting the number of bits and constraints that describe a polyhedron. Experimental results for a navigation benchmark and a tunnel diode circuit demonstrated the effectiveness of the approach. Future research will focus on heuristics for guaranteeing termination, adapting the refinement further to the dynamics and improved search algorithms. PHAVer is available at http://www.cs.ru.nl/~goranf/.

Acknowledgements. The author is most grateful for the numerous inspiring discussions with Prof. Bruce Krogh, whose insightful guidance was indispensable in this work, and to Prof. Frits W. Vaandrager and Prof. Sebastian Engell for their generous support and supervision. This research was supported in part by the US ARO contract no. DAAD19-01-1-0485, the US NSF contract no. CCR-0121547, and the Semiconductor Research Corporation under task ID 1028.001.

References

1. Henzinger, T.A.: The theory of hybrid automata. In: Proc. IEEE Symp. Logic in Computer Science, LICS'96, New Brunswick, New Jersey, 27-30 July 1996, IEEE Computer Society (1996) 278–292
2. Ho, P.H.: Automatic Analysis of Hybrid Systems. PhD thesis, Cornell University (1995) Technical Report CSD-TR95-1536.
3. Henzinger, T.A., Ho, P.H., Wong-Toi, H.: HYTECH: A model checker for hybrid systems. Int. Journal on Software Tools for Technology Transfer **1** (1997) 110–122

4. Henzinger, T.A., Preussig, J., Wong-Toi, H.: Some lessons from the hytech experience. In: Proceedings of the 40th Annual Conference on Decision and Control (CDC'01), IEEE Press (2001) pp. 2887–2892
5. Cofer, D.D., Engstrom, E., Goldman, R.P., Musliner, D.J., Vestal, S.: Applications of model checking at Honeywell Laboratories. In Dwyer, M.B., ed.: SPIN. Volume 2057 of LNCS., Springer (2001) 296–303
6. Bagnara, R., Ricci, E., Zaffanella, E., Hill, P.M.: Possibly not closed convex polyhedra and the Parma Polyhedra Library. In Hermenegildo, M.V., Puebla, G., eds.: Static Analysis: Proc. Int. Symp. Volume 2477 of LNCS., Springer (2002) 213–229
7. Fehnker, A., Ivancic, F.: Benchmarks for hybrid systems verification. In Alur, R., Pappas, G.J., eds.: HSCC'04. Volume 2993 of LNCS., Springer (2004) 326–341
8. Gupta, S., Krogh, B.H., Rutenbar, R.A.: Towards formal verification of analog designs. In: Proc. IEEE Intl. Conf. on Computer-Aided Design (ICCAD-2004), Nov. 7–11, 2004, San Jose CA (USA). (2004)
9. Frehse, G., Han, Z., Krogh, B.H.: Assume-guarantee reasoning for hybrid i/o-automata by over-approximation of continuous interaction. In: Proc. IEEE Conf. Decision and Control (CDC'04), Dec. 14–17, 2004, Atlantis, Bahamas. (2004)
10. Henzinger, T.A., Horowitz, B., Majumdar, R., Wong-Toi, H.: Beyond HYTECH: Hybrid systems analysis using interval numerical methods. In Lynch, N.A., Krogh, B.H., eds.: HSCC. Volume 1790 of LNCS., Springer (2000) 130–144
11. Preussig, J., Kowalewski, S., Wong-Toi, H., Henzinger, T.A.: An algorithm for the approximative analysis of rectangular automata. In: Proceedings of the Fifth International Symposium on Formal Techniques in Real-Time and Fault-Tolerant Systems (FTRTFT). Number 1486 in LNCS, Springer-Verlag (1998) 228–240
12. Henzinger, T.A., Ho, P.H., Wong-Toi, H.: Hytech: the next generation. In: Proc. IEEE Real-Time Systems Symp. (RTSS'95), IEEE Computer Society (1995) 56–65
13. Henzinger, T.A., Ho, P.H., Wong-Toi, H.: Algorithmic analysis of nonlinear hybrid systems. IEEE Transactions on Automatic Control **43** (1998) 540–554
14. Stursberg, O., Krogh, B.H.: Efficient representation and computation of reachable sets for hybrid systems. In Maler, O., Pnueli, A., eds.: HSCC'03. Volume 2623 of LNCS., Springer (2003) 482–497
15. Silva, B.I., Stursberg, O., Krogh, B.H., Engell, S.: An assessment of the current status of algorithmic approaches to the verification of hybrid systems. In: Proc. 40th Conference on Decision and Control (CDC'01). (2001)
16. Lynch, N.A., Segala, R., Vaandrager, F.W.: Hybrid I/O automata. Information and Computation **185** (2003) 105–157
17. Ivancic, F.: Modeling and Analysis of Hybrid Systems. PhD thesis, University of Pennsylvania, Philadelphia, PA (2003)

Direct Torque Control for Induction Motor Drives: A Model Predictive Control Approach Based on Feasibility

Tobias Geyer and Georgios Papafotiou

Automatic Control Laboratory,
Swiss Federal Institute of Technology (ETH),
CH-8092 Zurich, Switzerland
{geyer, papafotiou}@control.ee.ethz.ch

Abstract. In this paper, we present a new approach to the Direct Torque Control (DTC) problem of three-phase induction motor drives. This approach is based on Model Predictive Control (MPC) exploiting the specific structure of the DTC problem and using a systematic design procedure. Specifically, by observing that the DTC objectives, which require the controlled variables to remain within certain bounds, are related to feasibility rather than optimality, and by using a blocking control inputs regime for the whole prediction horizon we derive a low complexity controller. The derived controller is an explicit state-feedback control law that can be implemented as a look-up table. Even though the controller is derived here for a DTC drive featuring a two-level inverter, the control scheme can be extended to also tackle three-level inverters. Simulation results demonstrate that the proposed controller leads to performance improvements despite its simple structure.

1 Introduction

Enabled by significant technological developments in the area of power electronics, variable speed induction motor drives have evolved to a state of the art technology within the last decades. These systems, in which DC-AC inverters are used to drive induction motors as variable frequency three-phase voltage or current sources, are used in a wide spectrum of industrial applications. One of the methods for controlling the induction motor's torque and speed is Direct Torque Control (DTC), which was first introduced in 1985 by Takahashi and Noguchi [13] and is nowadays a industrial standard for induction motor drives [14, 11].

The basic characteristic of DTC is that the positions of the inverter switches are directly determined rather than indirectly, thus refraining from using a modulation technique like Pulse Width (PWM) or Space Vector (SVM) modulation. In the generic scheme, the control objective is to keep the motor's torque and the amplitude of the stator flux within pre-specified bounds. The inverter is triggered by hysteresis controllers to switch whenever these bounds are violated.

M. Morari and L. Thiele (Eds.): HSCC 2005, LNCS 3414, pp. 274–290, 2005.

The choice of the new switch positions is made using a pre-designed look-up table that has been derived using geometric insight in the problem and additional heuristics.

The main reason that makes the design of the switching table difficult is the fact that the DTC drive constitutes a hybrid system, i.e. a system incorporating both continuous and discrete dynamics - in particular discrete-valued manipulated variables. Additionally, constraints on states, inputs and outputs are present imposing further complications on the controller design, since the underlying mathematical problems are intrinsically complex and hard to solve.

Recently, we have proposed in [9, 10] a systematic procedure for the design of the DTC switching table by reformulating the control problem as a *Model Predictive Control* (MPC) [8] problem for a two- and a three-level inverter. Modelling the DTC drive as a hybrid system, introducing integer variables for the inverter switch positions that represent the manipulated variables of the control problem and expressing the control objectives in a cost function led to a constrained finite time optimal control problem. By solving the underlying optimization problem on-line and comparing the results with the behavior of ABB's ACS6000 drive [1] featuring a three-level inverter, we have demonstrated a potential performance improvement in the range of 20 %. Subsequently, moving towards the practical implementation of the method, we have pre-computed off-line the optimal control problem for all feasible states and thus derived the explicit state-feedback control law. The latter was done for a DTC drive featuring a two-level inverter and for a specific operating point.

Nevertheless, the complexity of the derived state-feedback controller prohibits the practical implementation on the currently employed controller hardware. On the other hand, two observations suggest the existence of a low complexity controller resulting from a systematic design procedure. Firstly, albeit their very simple controller structure, the existing DTC schemes have proven to yield a satisfactory control performance. Secondly, the post analysis of the derived state-feedback control law reveals a simple and robust pattern in the solution to the optimal control problem.

These observations have motivated the control scheme presented in this paper which is based on the following fundamental property of DTC. The control objectives only weakly relate to optimality but rather to feasibility, in the sense that the main objective is to find a control input that keeps the controlled variables within their bounds, i.e. a control input that is feasible. The second, weaker objective is to select among the set of feasible control inputs the one that minimizes the average switching frequency. The latter can be approximated by the number of switch transitions over the (short) horizon.

We therefore propose an MPC scheme based on feasibility with a prediction horizon N and an internal model of the DTC drive for the predictions. We propose to switch only at the current time-step and to disregard switching within the prediction horizon, which is equivalent to a move blocking strategy. This greatly reduces the number of control input sequences from 8^N to 8 and allows us to evaluate a small number of input sequences by moving forward in time. For each input sequence, we determine the number of steps the controlled variables are kept within their bounds, i.e. remain feasible. Next we define the number of switch transitions divided by the number of predicted time-steps an input remains feasible as a cost function emulating the switching frequency. In a last step, the control input is chosen that minimizes the cost function. We refer to this concept as the *Feasibility Approach*. The simplicity of the control methodology (with the only design parameter N) translates into a state-feedback control law with a complexity that is of an order of magnitude lower than the one of its counterpart obtained through solving the optimal control problem [9].

The paper is organized as follows. Starting with the derivation of a low complexity piecewise affine model for the DTC drive in Section 2, we pose in Section 3 the control objectives. In Section 4, we first present the Feasibility Approach as a control scheme that is evaluated on-line, and subsequently, we show how the control problem can be pre-solved off-line and translated into a state-feedback control law. Simulation results for the case of a two-level inverter are shown in Section 5, while Section 6 summarizes the results and discusses the extendability of the control approach to DTC drives featuring three-level inverters.

Due to the page limitation the paper had to be shortened by a few pages (mostly Section 2). The full paper is available as technical report [4].

2   Modelling

2.1   Physical Setup

For the modelling of the DTC drive, all variables are transformed from the three-phase system (abc) to an orthogonal dq0 reference frame with a direct (d), a quadrature (q) and a zero (0) axis, that can be either stationary or rotating [6]. For the needs of this paper, the transformation of a vector $\xi_{abc} = [\xi_a \; \xi_b \; \xi_c]^T$ from the three-phase system to the vector $\xi_{dq0} = [\xi_d \; \xi_q \; \xi_0]^T$ in the dq0 frame is

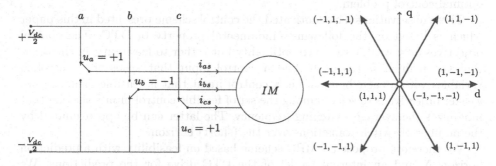

(a) The equivalent representation of a three-phase two-level inverter driving an induction motor

(b) The voltage vectors on the dq plane with switch positions

Fig. 1. Physical setup and voltage vectors

carried out through $\xi_{dq0} = P(\varphi)\xi_{abc}$, where φ is the angle between the a-axis of the three-phase system and the d-axis of the reference frame, and $P(\varphi)$ is the Park transformation [6].

An equivalent representation of a three-phase two-level inverter driving an induction motor is shown in Fig. 1(a). At each phase, the inverter can produce two different voltages $-\frac{V_{dc}}{2}, \frac{V_{dc}}{2}$, where V_{dc} denotes the voltage of the dc-link. The switch positions of the inverter can therefore be fully described using the three integer variables u_a, u_b, $u_c \in \{-1, 1\}$, where each variable corresponds to one phase of the inverter, and the values $-1, 1$ correspond to the phase potentials $-\frac{V_{dc}}{2}, \frac{V_{dc}}{2}$, respectively.

There are $2^3 = 8$ different vectors of the form $u_{abc} = [u_a \; u_b \; u_c]^T$. Using the Park transformation these vectors can be transformed into the dq0 frame resulting in vectors of the form $u_{dq0} = [u_d \; u_q \; u_0]^T$. The latter are shown in Fig. 1(b), where they are mapped into the (two-dimensional) dq plane. Even though they are commonly referred to as voltage vectors, this term describes the switch positions rather than the actual voltages applied to the machine terminals.

The dynamics of the squirrel-cage rotor induction motor are commonly modelled in a dq0 reference frame that can be either stationary or rotating. The standard modelling approach, which can be found in detail in [6], yields a 5-dimensional nonlinear state-space model, that uses as state variables the d- and q-components of the stator and rotor flux linkages per second ψ_{ds}, ψ_{qs}, ψ_{dr} and ψ_{qr}, respectively, and the rotor's rotational speed ω_r. The 0-axis components are neglected, since they do not contribute to the electromagnetic torque and are decoupled from the dynamics in the d- and q-axis. The model parameters are the stator and rotor resistances r_s and r_r, the stator, rotor and mutual inductive reactances x_{ls}, x_{lr} and x_m, respectively, the inertia constant H expressed in seconds, and the mechanical load torque T_ℓ.

In this standard dynamical model of the induction motor, the saturation of the machine's magnetic material, the changes of the rotor resistance due to the skin effect and the temperature changes of the stator resistance are ignored. A more elaborate presentation of the induction motor's modelling procedure is out of the scope of this paper. For details, the reader is referred to [6].

2.2   Low Complexity Modelling

In [9, 10], we have derived a low-complexity model of the DTC drive taking into account that the stator flux dynamics are significantly faster than the dynamics of the rotor flux and the rotational speed, and that the length of the stator flux vector and the electromagnetic torque are invariant under a rotation of the flux vectors. This model has the state vector

$$x(k) = \left[\psi_{ds}^{\vartheta}(k) \; \psi_{qs}^{\vartheta}(k) \; \cos(\varphi(k))\right]^T, \qquad (1)$$

where $\psi_{ds}^{\vartheta}(k)$ and $\psi_{qs}^{\vartheta}(k)$ denote the d- and q-component of the rotated and mapped stator flux vector, and $\varphi(k)$ captures the position of the rotating reference frame with $\varphi(k+1) = \varphi(k) + \omega_r T_s$. The output vector

$$y(k) = \left[T_e(k) \; \Psi_s^2(k)\right]^T \tag{2}$$

comprises the electromagnetic torque and the squared length of the stator flux vector, and the input vector is composed of the integer variables u_a, u_b and u_c

$$u(k) = u_{abc}(k) = \left[u_a(k) \; u_b(k) \; u_c(k)\right]^T \in \{-1, 1\}^3. \tag{3}$$

For a summary of the low-complexity modelling, the reader is referred to [4], whereas the complete modelling can be found in [9].

2.3   Piecewise Affine Model

In a subsequent step, we have computed in [9] a piecewise affine (PWA) model for a DTC drive featuring a two-level inverter. PWA models [12] are defined by partitioning the state-space into polyhedra and associating with each polyhedron an affine state-update and output function

$$x(k+1) = f_{j(k)}(x(k), u(k)) \tag{4a}$$
$$y(k) = g_{j(k)}(x(k)) \tag{4b}$$
$$\text{with } j(k) \text{ such that } \begin{bmatrix} x(k) \\ u(k) \end{bmatrix} \in \mathcal{P}_{j(k)}, \tag{4c}$$

where $x(k)$, $u(k)$, $y(k)$ denote at time k the real and binary states, inputs and outputs, respectively, the polyhedra $\mathcal{P}_{j(k)}$ define a set of polyhedra $\{\mathcal{P}_j\}_{j \in \mathcal{J}}$ on the state-input space, and the real time-invariant functions $f_{j(k)}$ and $g_{j(k)}$ are affine in the states and inputs, with $j(k) \in \mathcal{J}$, $\mathcal{J}$ finite. For simplicity, we will later drop the index $j(k)$ and (4c), and use $x(k+1) = f(x(k), u(k))$ and $y(k) = g(x(k))$ to denote the PWA system (4). Note that the PWA system (4) has no throughput, i.e. $y(k)$ is independent of $u(k)$.

To derive such a PWA model, all nonlinearities need to be replaced by PWA approximation over a bounded set of (feasible) states $\mathcal{X}^0$. The set $\mathcal{X}^0$ can be easily determined by translating the output hysteresis bounds imposed by the control objectives into constraints on the state-space. Introducing the lower and upper bounds on the electromagnetic torque $T_{e,min}$ and $T_{e,max}$, respectively, and noting that in the low-complexity model the torque is a linear expression of the second state, the torque bounds can be directly translated into linear bounds on $x_2(k)$

$$\frac{D}{x_m \psi_{dr}^{\vartheta}} T_{e,min} \leq x_2(k) \leq \frac{D}{x_m \psi_{dr}^{\vartheta}} T_{e,max}, \tag{5}$$

where ψ_{dr}^{ϑ} is equal to the length of the rotor flux, which is treated as a parameter in the low-complexity model. Similarly for the stator flux, its lower and upper bounds $\Psi_{s,min}^2$ and $\Psi_{s,max}^2$ turn into the quadratic state constraint

$$\Psi_{s,min}^2 \leq x_1^2(k) + x_2^2(k) \leq \Psi_{s,max}^2. \tag{6}$$

To account for measurement noise and small disturbances causing the torque or the stator flux to slightly violate the imposed bounds, we relax (5) and (6) by 20 % of the corresponding bound width.

The bounds on the third state are derived from the angle $\varphi(k)$. To ensure that the model remains feasible for at least N time-steps when starting with a $\varphi(k)$ close to $\frac{\pi}{3}$, the bounds on $\varphi(k)$ are set to $0 \leq \varphi(k) \leq \frac{\pi}{3} + N\omega_r T_s$, which translate into the following bounds on $x_3(k)$

$$\cos(\frac{\pi}{3} + N\omega_r T_s) \leq x_3(k) \leq 1. \tag{7}$$

Summing up, the constraints (5), (6) and (7) define the set of states $\mathcal{X}^0$ for which the PWA model is to be defined. Thus, the nonlinearities of the DTC drive need to be approximated for $x \in \mathcal{X}^0$ as shown in [9, 10].

Starting from a model description in the HYbrid Systems DEscription Language HYSDEL [15], and fixing the operating point, namely the parameters ω_r and ψ_{dr}^ϑ, the model can be transformed into PWA form with the mode enumeration algorithm [5]. This procedure yields a PWA model defined on a polyhedral partition with 48 polyhedra in the six-dimensional state-input space.

3   Control Problem

The most prominent control objective concerning the induction motor is to keep the electromechanical torque within bounds around its reference. In order to avoid the saturation or demagnetization of the motor, the amplitude of the stator flux has to be kept between certain pre-specified bounds around the reference which are in general time-invariant. The control objective concerning the inverter is to minimize the average switching frequency.

4   Feasibility Approach

Traditionally, based on the imposed bounds, the next voltage vector to be applied to the induction motor is selected by evaluating a look-up table every $T_s = 25\,\mu s$. The goal of this paper is to replace the look-up table by a new DTC scheme that is based on a systematic design procedure. This controller needs to address the above formulated objectives, i.e. to minimize the average switching frequency while keeping the controlled variables (torque and length of the stator flux) within the given bounds.

Similar to [9, 10], this controller is based on predictive control with a receding horizon policy. Minimizing the average switching frequency leads to a prediction horizon with an infinite number of steps. As such a problem in the context of hybrid systems is computationally not tractable, we need to approximate this objective. In [9, 10], we have done this by restricting the prediction horizon N to a small number of steps (three or four) and by formulating an objective function that postpones switching and penalizes the violation of the bounds using soft constraints. In particular, we have allowed for switch transitions within the prediction interval. Dynamic programming [3] allowed us to compute off-line the explicit state-feedback control law for the whole state-space.

4.1   On-line Computation of the Control Input

On the other hand, the underlying optimization problem of the above stated control problem is not so much based on optimality but rather on feasibility, meaning that the controlled variables have to be kept within their bounds, i.e. feasible. This insight greatly simplifies the control problem. Furthermore, we propose to switch only at the current time-step k and to disregard switching within the prediction horizon, which is equivalent to a move blocking strategy. This greatly reduces the number of control input sequences from 8^N to 8 and allows us to evaluate a small number of control sequences by moving forward in time. As a result, dynamic programming moving backwards in time becomes obsolete.

More formally, let $u(k-1)$ denote the last voltage vector. If $u(k-1)$ is also feasible at time-instant k, i.e. all controlled variables are predicted to lie within their bounds at time-instant $k+1$, a reasonable choice is to apply it again, i.e. $u(k) = u(k-1)$. If not, however, the controller must choose another voltage vector. For each of the remaining seven voltage vectors, one can easily compute through open-loop predictions the number of time-steps this voltage vector would keep the controlled variables within their bounds. This step reduces the optimal control problem to a feasibility problem. The voltage vector is chosen that minimizes the average switching frequency over the prediction interval, i.e. the number of switch transitions over the number of time-steps, thus re-introducing the notion of optimality. This control concept, to which we refer as the Feasibility Approach, is summarized in Algorithm 1, where f and g refer to the PWA model (4). An output vector $y(k)$ is said to be feasible, if the corresponding bounds are met, and $U = \{-1, 1\}^3$ denotes the set of available voltage vectors.

Algorithm 1

function $u(k) = \text{Algo1} \ (\ x(k), \ u(k-1) \ )$

  $x(k+1) = f(x(k), u(k-1))$

  if $y(k+1) = g(x(k+1))$ feasible

    $u(k) = u(k-1)$

  else

    for all $u(k) \in U \setminus u(k-1)$

      $n_u = -1$

      repeat

        $n_u = n_u + 1$

        $x(k+n_u+1) = f(x(k+n_u), u(k))$

        until $\big(y(k+n_u+1) = g(x(k+n_u+1))$ infeasible $\big)$ **or** $\big(n_u = N \big)$

    endfor

    $u(k) = \arg\min_{u(k)} \frac{\|u(k)-u(k-1)\|}{n_u}$

  endif

Compared to MPC, this control policy is by definition significantly simpler, as only eight control sequences (or control strategies) need to be compared with each other. Unlike in MPC, switch transitions within the prediction interval are not considered, and can only be performed at the current time-instant k. Furthermore, the length of the prediction horizon is time-varying, ranging from one step to 10 or even 20 steps. As the next section will show, an explicit form of the proposed controller can be computed easily. Even more important, the explicit form has a low complexity but maintains or improves the control performance with respect to MPC.

4.2   Off-line Computation of the State-Feedback Control Law

We restrict the computation of the explicit state-feedback control law to the set of states $\mathcal{X}^0$, which we have obtained by relaxing the bounds on the torque and the flux by 20 %. Furthermore, we fix the operating point, namely the rotor speed ω_r and the length of the rotor flux ψ_{dr}^ϑ, and set the lower and upper bounds on the outputs (torque and stator flux). Next, we derive the PWA model defined on $\mathcal{X}^0$. Rewriting (5) and (6), let $\mathcal{C}$ denote the set of states whose corresponding outputs are feasible

$$ \mathcal{C} = \{x \in \mathcal{X}^0 \mid \begin{bmatrix} T_{e,min} \\ \Psi_{s,min}^2 \end{bmatrix} \leq g(x) \leq \begin{bmatrix} T_{e,max} \\ \Psi_{s,max}^2 \end{bmatrix}, \tag{8} $$

where we have replaced the quadratic expression in (6) by the PWA approximation for the stator flux.

Before presenting the computation of the state-feedback control law in three stages, we introduce the following notation. Let n denote the time-step within the prediction horizon N, $\mathcal{X}_{feas}^n$ the set of states at time-step $k+n$ corresponding to feasible outputs $y(k+\ell)$ for all $\ell \in \{1, \dots, n\}$, $\mathcal{X}_{infs}^n$ the set of states at time-step $k+n$ with feasible outputs $y(k+\ell)$ for all $\ell \in \{1, \dots, n-1\}$, but infeasible outputs $y(k+n)$, and $\mathcal{Q}_u^n$ the set of states at time-step k that keep the outputs for n time-steps feasible when applying the voltage vector u.

Stage I. First, we determine the set of states $x(k) \in \mathcal{X}^0$ for which the controlled variables are feasible at time-step $k+1$ when applying $u(k) = u(k-1)$. We denote this set of states as the *core*

$$ \mathcal{Q}_u^c = \{x \in \mathcal{X}^0 \mid f(x, u) \in \mathcal{C}\}, \tag{9} $$

and its complement in $\mathcal{X}^0$ as the *ring*

$$ \mathcal{Q}_u^r = \mathcal{X}^0 \setminus \mathcal{Q}_u^c. \tag{10} $$

Example 1. To visualize the algorithm, consider as an example a two-level inverter driving an induction machine with the rated voltage 3.3 kV and the rated real power 1.587 MW. All parameters can be found in [9] in Tables 3 and 4. The operating point is given by the rotor speed $\omega_r = 0.8$ p.u., the load torque

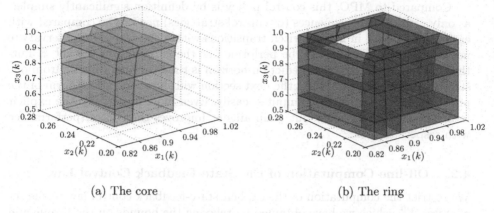

(a) The core   (b) The ring

Fig. 2. Core and ring for $u(k-1) = [1 \; -1 \; -1]$

$T_\ell = 0.8$ p.u., the torque bounds $T_{e,min} = 0.72$ p.u. and $T_{e,max} = 0.88$ p.u., and the flux bounds $\Psi^2_{s,min} = 0.82$ p.u. and $\Psi^2_{s,max} = 1.04$ p.u.. After deriving the PWA model on $\mathcal{X}^0$ (enlarged by 20 % as in Section 2.3), and determining the set $\mathcal{C}$, the core and the ring can be easily computed as shown in Fig. 2 for the voltage vector $u(k-1) = [1 \; -1 \; -1]$. This operation takes on a Pentium IV roughly 1 s.   ∎

Stage II. For each new voltage vector $u(k) \in U \backslash u(k-1)$, the following procedure is performed for the initial set[1] $\mathcal{X}^0$. Initially, we set $n = 0$. Next, we map the polyhedra $\mathcal{X}^n$ from time-step $k + n$ to $k + n + 1$ yielding $\mathcal{X}^{n+1}$. The states corresponding to infeasible outputs form the set $\mathcal{X}^{n+1}_{\text{infs}}$. Consequently, we map $\mathcal{X}^{n+1}_{\text{infs}}$ back to the time-step k and associate with them the number of time-steps n. We denote these polyhedra by $\mathcal{Q}^n_u$, where u corresponds to the chosen voltage vector $u(k)$, and n denotes the number of time-steps this voltage vector $u(k)$ can be applied to the set of states before any of the outputs violates a bound. If there remain any feasible states, we move one time-step forward in the future by increasing n by one and repeat the above procedure.

This yields for each new voltage vector a polyhedral partition of the ring $\{\mathcal{Q}^n_u\}^N_{n=0}$, where each polyhedron is associated with a unique number indicating for how many time-steps the respective voltage vector can be applied before any of the controlled variables violates a bound.

---

[1] Conceptually, this stage of the algorithm should be initialized with the ring $\mathcal{Q}^r_u$ rather than $\mathcal{X}^0$. Let us note though that since the facets of the initial set are mapped forward and backward in time, in the worst case, the complexity of the algorithm both in terms of the computation time and the number of resulting polyhedra $\{\mathcal{Q}^n_u\}^N_{n=0}$ is exponential in the number of facets of the initial set. Therefore, as $\mathcal{X}^0$ is by definition a very simple polytopic set with only a few facets, whereas the ring is a non-convex set with possibly many facets, we initialize Algorithm 2 with $\mathcal{X}^0$ rather than the ring.

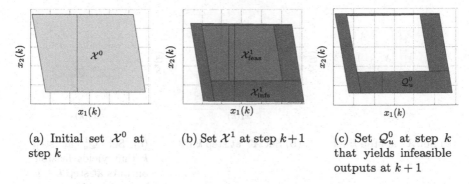

(a) Initial set $\mathcal{X}^0$ at step k

(b) Set $\mathcal{X}^1$ at step $k+1$

(c) Set $\mathcal{Q}_u^0$ at step k that yields infeasible outputs at $k + 1$

Fig. 3. First step of Algorithm 2 in the $x_1 x_2$ plane for $u(k) = [1 \ -1 \ -1]$

Next, the algorithm is summarized, where the two subfunctions mapForw and mapBack are affine transformations of polyhedra using the PWA model (4) for a fixed voltage vector $u(k)$. Specifically, mapForw yields $\mathcal{X}^{n+1} = \{f(x, u) \mid x \in \mathcal{X}^n, u = u(k)\}$, and mapBack yields $\mathcal{Q}_u^n = \{x \mid (f_u \circ \ldots \circ f_u)(x) \in \mathcal{X}_{\text{infs}}^{n+1}\}$, where we have set $f_u(x) = f(x, u)$ and concatenated f_u n times. Note that mapForw maps a set of states by one time-step forward in time, whereas mapBack maps a set of states by n time-steps backwards. The subscript feas (infs) refers to sets of states corresponding to feasible (infeasible) outputs.

Algorithm 2

function $\{\mathcal{Q}_u^n\}_{n=0}^N$ = Algo2 ($\mathcal{C}$, $\mathcal{X}^0$, u, N)

    $n = 0$

    while $\mathcal{X}^n \neq \emptyset$ **and** $n < N$

        $\mathcal{X}^{n+1}$ = mapForw ($\mathcal{X}^n$, u)

        $\mathcal{X}_{\text{feas}}^{n+1} = \mathcal{X}^{n+1} \cap \mathcal{C}$

        $\mathcal{X}_{\text{infs}}^{n+1} = \mathcal{X}^{n+1} \setminus \mathcal{X}_{\text{feas}}^{n+1}$

        $\mathcal{Q}_u^n$ = mapBack ($\mathcal{X}_{\text{infs}}^{n+1}$, u)

        $\mathcal{X}^{n+1} = \mathcal{X}_{\text{feas}}^{n+1}$

        $n = n + 1$

    endwhile

    $\mathcal{Q}_u^n$ = mapBack ($\mathcal{X}^n$, u)

Example 1 (continued). Setting $N = 4$, we proceed with Example 1. Fig. 3 visualizes the first step ($n = 0$) of Algorithm 2 in the $x_1 x_2$ plane, where the same scaling is used for all three figures. Starting with the initial set of states $\mathcal{X}^0$ in Fig. 3(a), the voltage vector $u(k) = [1 \ -1 \ -1]$ maps $\mathcal{X}^0$ from time-step k to $k + 1$ as shown in Fig. 3(b). The set $\mathcal{X}^1$ comprises two parts. $\mathcal{X}_{\text{feas}}^1$ ($\mathcal{X}_{\text{infs}}^1$) contains the states corresponding to feasible (infeasible) outputs. This set $\mathcal{X}_{\text{infs}}^1$

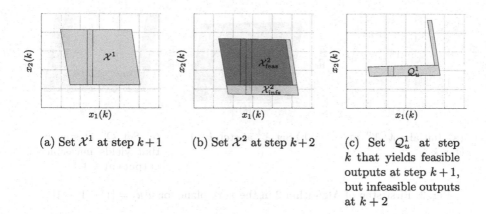

(a) Set $\mathcal{X}^1$ at step $k+1$ (b) Set $\mathcal{X}^2$ at step $k+2$ (c) Set $\mathcal{Q}_u^1$ at step k that yields feasible outputs at step $k+1$, but infeasible outputs at $k+2$

Fig. 4. Second step of Algorithm 2 in the $x_1 x_2$ plane for $u(k) = [1 \ -1 \ -1]$

is consequently mapped back from time-step $k+1$ to k resulting in $\mathcal{Q}_u^0$ and indicating that this set is zero-step feasible for the chosen $u(k)$. Furthermore, we set $\mathcal{X}^1 = \mathcal{X}_{\text{feas}}^1$.

The second step ($n = 1$) is shown in Fig. 4 starting from the set $\mathcal{X}^1$ at time-step $k+1$ in Fig. 4(a). Applying $u(k) = [1 \ -1 \ -1]$ to this set maps it from time-step $k+1$ to $k+2$ as shown in Fig. 4(b). Again, $\mathcal{X}_{\text{feas}}^2$ ($\mathcal{X}_{\text{infs}}^2$) contains the states corresponding to feasible (infeasible) outputs. The states in $\mathcal{X}_{\text{infs}}^2$ are mapped back for two steps from $k+2$ to k yielding $\mathcal{Q}_u^1$ which is shown in Fig. 4(c) and refers to states which are one-step feasible for $u(k)$.

Repeating the above procedure for $n = 2, 3, 4$ and collecting the sets $\mathcal{Q}_u^n$ yields the polyhedral partition $\{\mathcal{Q}_u^n\}_{n=0}^4$ shown in Fig. 5. The outer polyhedra correspond to outputs that are feasible for zero time-steps when applying $u(k) = [1 \ -1 \ -1]$, while the inner polyhedra are feasible for one, two, three and four time-steps as $x_2(k)$ is increasing. Note that $\{\mathcal{Q}_u^n\}_{n=0}^4$ is by construction a polyhedral partition of the set $\mathcal{X}^0$.

The computation time for the second stage for the given example is approximately 2 min on a Pentium IV.   ∎

Summing up, Stages I and II yield a semi-explicit control law that is evaluated by following Algorithm 1, with the main difference that the number of steps n_u is not calculated by mapping operations but rather by set membership tests evaluating if the given state lies in the respective polyhedron. Specifically, if for the given $u(k-1)$, the state $x(k)$ lies in the core, reapply the last voltage vector again. Else determine for each new voltage vector the polyhedron in $\{\mathcal{Q}_u^n\}_{n=0}^N$ containing $x(k)$, evaluate the associated number of time-steps n_u, and find the voltage vector $u(k)$ with the lowest cost as defined in Algorithm 1. This is formalized in Algorithm 3.

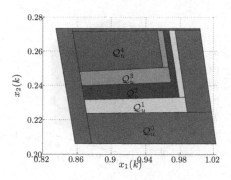

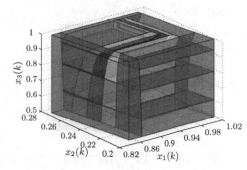

(a) Polyhedral partition in the $x_1 x_2$ plane for $x_3 = 0.95$

(b) Polyhedral partition in the three-dimensional state space

Fig. 5. The resulting polyhedral partition $\{Q_u^n\}_{n=0}^N$ of Algorithm 2 for $u(k) = [1 \ -1 \ -1]$ and $N = 4$, where the colors correspond to the number of steps n

Algorithm 3

function $u(k) = \mathsf{Algo3} \ (\ x(k), \ u(k-1) \ )$

  if $x(k) \in Q_u^c$

    $u(k) = u(k-1)$

  else

    for all $u(k) \in U \setminus u(k-1)$

      determine n_u such that $x(k) \in Q_u^{n_u}$

    endfor

    $u(k) = \arg\min_{u(k)} \frac{||u(k)-u(k-1)||}{n_u}$

  endif

Regarding the computational burden for the on-line computation of the control input, in the worst case, one core needs to be evaluated and the seven polyhedral partitions of $U \setminus u(k-1)$ which feature in general a low number of polyhedra.

Stage III. In the third stage we pre-compute Algorithm 3 and derive the fully explicit control law as a function of the last voltage vector $u(k-1)$ and the current state $x(k)$. For $u(k-1) \in U$, we evaluate for each polyhedron in $\{Q_u^n\}_{n=0}^N$ the cost and associate with it the voltage vector $u(k)$. Next, the core Q_u^c is added with zero cost and the voltage vector $u(k) = u(k-1)$. Finally, we compare the cost expressions and iteratively remove (parts of) polyhedra with inferior

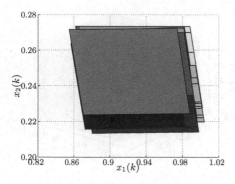
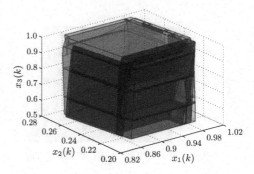

(a) Polyhedral partition in the x_1x_2 plane for $x_3 = 0.95$

(b) Polyhedral partition in the three-dimensional state-space

Fig. 6. Polyhedral partitions of the state-feedback control law resulting from Stage III for $u(k-1) = [1 \ -1 \ -1]$, where each color corresponds to a voltage vector $u(k) \in U$

costs[2]. A detailed exposition and analysis of this algorithm can be found in [2]. This yields one polyhedral partition, where each polyhedron refers to a voltage vector $u(k)$ (and not to a number of time-steps). This procedure is repeated for all the eight former voltage vectors $u(k-1)$ yielding eight different fully explicit state-feedback control laws. As a result, the computational burden of evaluating the control law is reduced, as $u(k-1)$ directly defines the one polyhedral partition that needs to be searched through in order to obtain $u(k)$. However, the memory requirements are higher since the polyhedral partitions of the fully explicit control law are in general more complex than the one of the semi-explicit control law.

Example 1 (continued). Applying Stage III to Example 1 yields for $u(k-1) = [1 \ -1 \ -1]$ the explicit control law shown in Fig. 6. Each color corresponds to a voltage vector $u(k) \in U$. In particular, the large polyhedron in the center of the three-dimensional state space refers to $u(k) = u(k-1)$. The explicit control law comprises a total of eight control laws similar to Fig. 6, where each one corresponds to a formerly applied voltage vector $u(k-1) \in U$.

---

[2] As the cost expressions used in Algorithms 1 and 3 are rational, where the nominator (in the case of a two-level inverter) is restricted to the integers two, four and six, and the denominator to $0, \ldots, N$, the costs take only a few different values. This increases the possibility that at a given time two or more voltage vectors have the same associated cost leading to ambiguities in the choice of the next voltage vector. In such cases, we suggest to remove the ambiguity by imposing an additional heuristic selection criterion. Examples for such rules are to select the vector that keeps the controlled variables feasible for the maximal number of steps, or to favor zero vectors. Obviously, these ambiguities occur less frequently when the maximal horizon N is increased.

The computation was performed using the function mpt_removeOverlaps of the Multi-Parametric Toolbox [7]. The computation time was 15 min.   ∎

5   Simulation Results

The simulation results presented in this section were derived for a DTC drive featuring a two-level inverter. The parameters of the drive are the same as in [9], and the operating point we consider is as in Example 1. As mentioned before, the only design parameter which influences the calculation of the state-feedback controller and consequently the performance of the drive, is the maximal horizon N over which the feasibility of each voltage vector is considered.

In the following, we evaluate the performance of the proposed Feasibility Approach in terms of the average inverter switching frequency. As a benchmark, we employ the Optimal DTC scheme presented in [9]. The corresponding state-feedback controller [9], which was derived for a prediction horizon of two and features a total of 47'000 polyhedra, yields for the above setup an average switching frequency of 525 Hz. Note that in the Optimal DTC scheme switching is allowed at every time-step within the prediction horizon, and that the comparison is based on the same case study as in [9]. In particular, the same drive parameters, operating point and bounds imposed on the torque and the stator flux are used.

The results obtained with the Feasibility Approach are summarized in Table 1 for eight different values of the maximal horizon N. For the horizon used in [9], i.e. $N = 2$, the switching frequency is significantly increased with respect to the benchmark. This is to be expected, since the move blocking strategy (no switching of the control input within the horizon) reduces the degrees of freedom of the control algorithm. However, setting the maximal horizon to $N = 5$ yields a switching frequency that is comparable to the one obtained with the Optimal DTC approach, and the choices of $N = 6$ and $N = 7$ reduce the

Table 1. Performance and complexity of the state-feedback control law

N	switching frequency [Hz]	total number of polyhedra in semi-explicit control law	total number of polyhedra in fully explicit control law
2	632	292	1192
3	606	440	1891
4	572	625	2226
5	540	860	2907
6	510	1051	3362
7	495	1256	3737
8	547	1467	4443
9	574	1694	4758

switching frequency. Most important, this performance improvement is achieved despite the complexity reduction of the state-feedback controller by an order of magnitude with respect to its Optimal DTC counterpart.

Focusing on the case of $N = 7$, the relative switching frequency improvement with respect to the benchmark amounts to 5.7 %. Furthermore, we should point out that using the Feasibility Approach the bounds on the torque and the stator flux are very strictly respected. The Optimal DTC scheme, however, allows for small violations of the bounds; the degree of the violations can be adjusted using a design parameter (penalty on the soft constraints for the bounds) that affects the switching frequency. As tightening the bounds increases the switching frequency, the expected performance improvement is even more pronounced.

For completeness, one should note that the switching frequency does not monotonically decrease with N. This phenomenon has also been observed with the Optimal DTC scheme and is currently under investigation. In particular, a further increase of the horizon to $N = 8$ or $N = 9$ leads to a performance deterioration with respect to $N = 7$.

6   Conclusions and Outlook

In this paper, we have presented the derivation and performance analysis of a state-feedback controller based on MPC for the DTC problem of induction motors driven by a two-level inverter. The proposed controller features a significantly lower complexity (by an order of magnitude) than its counterpart in [9] for the same fixed operating point. It is derived through a simple and systematic design procedure and maintains and even improves the favorable control performance properties obtained by the use of predictive control.

The controller presented in this paper could be extended in the following two ways. Firstly, by considering changes in the operating point. This necessitates the parametrization of the drive's PWA model over the rotational speed ω_r and the torque and flux bounds. Concerning the bounds, only one parameter is needed for the median of the torque bounds. The flux bounds and the width of the torque bounds can be assumed to be in general time-invariant. Obviously, the complexity of the resulting controller would be increased. Yet it is to be expected that the low complexity with respect to an accordingly extended optimal controller in [9] is maintained.

Secondly, this paper can be extended by applying the presented method to a DTC drive with a three-level inverter. As a result, two additional control objectives, namely the regulation of the inverter's neutral point potential and the even distribution of the switching effort between the upper and the lower half of the inverter, arise. A straightforward approach would be to accurately model the nonlinear dynamics of the neutral point potential. To avoid such a substantially more complex PWA model, a favorable approach is to refrain from deriving the fully explicit controller and to rather use the semi-explicit realization in combination with time-varying weights on the voltage vectors. An outer loop should monitor the neutral point potential and set the weights accordingly to favor the selection of voltage vectors that keep the potential within given bounds around zero. The same approach can be also used for the even distribution of the switching effort. Since these control objectives are roughly and heuristically defined, they do not require to be strictly met thus rendering the above approach a sufficient approximation.

The full version of this paper is available as technical report [4] extending the modelling in Section 2.

Acknowledgements

This work was supported by ABB Switzerland Ltd., and by the IST research project IST-2001-33520 *Control and Computation* of the EU. The authors would like to thank Christian Stulz, Pieder Joerg and Petri Schroderus of ABB ATDD, Turgi, Switzerland, and Andreas Poncet of ABB Corporate Research, Baden-Dättwil, Switzerland, for their continuous advice. Most importantly, we would like to acknowledge the contribution of Manfred Morari from ETH Zürich, Switzerland.

References

1. ABB Asea Brown Boveri Ltd. Product webpage of ACS 6000. online document. www.abb.com/motors&drives.
2. M. Baotić and F.D. Torrisi. Polycover. Technical Report AUT03-11, Automatic Control Laboratory ETH Zurich, http://control.ee.ethz.ch/, 2003.
3. D.P. Bertsekas. *Dynamic Programming and Optimal Control*. Athena Scientific, 1995.
4. T. Geyer, G. Papafotiou, and M. Morari. Direct torque control for induction motor drives: A model predictive control approach based on feasibility. Technical Report AUT04-09, Automatic Control Laboratory ETH Zurich, http://control.ee.ethz.ch/, 2004.
5. T. Geyer, F.D. Torrisi, and M. Morari. Efficient mode enumeration of compositional hybrid systems. In A. Pnueli and O. Maler, editors, *Hybrid Systems: Computation and Control*, volume 2623 of *Lecture Notes in Computer Science*, pages 216–232. Springer-Verlag, 2003.
6. P.C. Krause. *Analysis of Electric Machinery*. McGraw-Hill, NY, 1986.
7. M. Kvasnica, P. Grieder, M. Baotić, and M. Morari. Multi parametric toolbox (MPT). In R. Alur and G. Pappas, editors, *Hybrid Systems: Computation and Control*, volume 2993 of *Lecture Notes in Computer Science*, pages 448–462. Springer-Verlag, 2004. http://control.ee.ethz.ch/~mpt.
8. J.M. Maciejowski. *Predictive Control*. Prentice Hall, 2002.
9. G. Papafotiou, T. Geyer, and M. Morari. Optimal direct torque control of three-phase symmetric induction motors. Technical Report AUT03-07, Automatic Control Laboratory ETH Zurich, http://control.ee.ethz.ch/, 2003.
10. G. Papafotiou, T. Geyer, and M. Morari. Optimal direct torque control of three-phase symmetric induction motors. In *Proceedings of the 43th IEEE Conference on Decision and Control*, Atlantis, Bahamas, December 2004.

11. P. Pohjalainen, P. Tiitinen, and J. Lulu. The next generation motor control method - direct torque control, DTC. In *Proceedings of the European Power Electronics Chapter Symposium*, volume 1, pages 115–120, Lausanne, Switzerland, 1994.
12. E.D. Sontag. Nonlinear regulation: The piecewise linear approach. *IEEE Transactions on Automatic Control*, 26(2):346–358, April 1981.
13. I. Takahashi and T. Noguchi. A new quick response and high efficiency control strategy for the induction motor. *IEEE Transactions on Industry Applications*, 22(2):820–827, September/October 1986.
14. I. Takahashi and Y. Ohmori. High-performance direct torque control of an induction motor. *IEEE Transactions on Industry Applications*, 25(2):257–264, March/April 1989.
15. F.D. Torrisi and A. Bemporad. Hysdel — a tool for generating computational hybrid models for analysis and synthesis problems. *IEEE Transactions on Control Systems Technology*, 12(2):235–249, March 2004.

Reachability of Uncertain Linear Systems Using Zonotopes[*]

Antoine Girard

Department of Electrical and Systems Engineering,
University of Pennsylvania, Philadelphia, PA 19104
agirard@seas.upenn.edu

Abstract. We present a method for the computation of reachable sets of uncertain linear systems. The main innovation of the method consists in the use of zonotopes for reachable set representation. Zonotopes are special polytopes with several interesting properties : they can be encoded efficiently, they are closed under linear transformations and Minkowski sum. The resulting method has been used to treat several examples and has shown great performances for high dimensional systems. An extension of the method for the verification of piecewise linear hybrid systems is proposed.

1 Introduction

Reachability computation is required in several tasks such as verification or synthesis of hybrid systems [10, 19]. Except for very specific classes of hybrid systems [4, 15], exact computation of the reachable sets is impossible. The main difficulty lies in the computation of the reachable sets of the continuous dynamics. The importance of the problem has motivated much research on approximate reachability analysis. Two main approaches have been developped. The first one includes all abstraction methods (see for instance [1, 20]). The main idea is to process the reachability analysis on a simple abstract system which approximates a more complex one. The second approach consists in computing directly approximations of the reachable sets of the system [2, 5, 7, 14, 16, 18].

The success of such methods lies in the choice of an efficient representation of the approximations of the reachable sets. Methods have been proposed using several set representations such as general polytopes [7] oriented hyperrectangles [18], orthogonal polyhedra [2], ellipsoids [14] or level sets [16]. These methods have been used and have succeeded in solving some case studies. However, they remain expensive and their use is only limited to small systems.

Thus, today, the challenge for new work on reachability is to find how we can handle large-scale (or even middle-scale) systems. Recently [21], a new method has been proposed allowing to process safety verification for linear systems of high dimension (up to dimension 100 in a reasonnable time).

---

[*] Research partially supported by the Région Rhône-Alpes (Projet CalCel).

M. Morari and L. Thiele (Eds.): HSCC 2005, LNCS 3414, pp. 291–305, 2005.
© Springer-Verlag Berlin Heidelberg 2005

In this paper, we propose a method for the computation of an over-approximation of the reachable sets of uncertain linear systems. The reachable sets are represented as the union of zonotopes (special polytopes). The resulting approximations are of good quality. Moreover, the method can be used for large-scale systems.

The paper is organized as follows. First, we introduce the mathematical notion of zonotope. Then, we explain our algorithm for the computation of approximate reachable sets of uncertain linear systems. Afterwards, we present some experimental results. Finally, we use it for hybrid system verification. For a better readability, the proofs are state in the appendix.

2   Zonotopes: Definition and Properties

Zonotopes are a special class of convex polytopes. Traditionally, a zonotope is defined as the image of a cube under an affine projection [22]. Equivalently, a zonotope is a Minkowski sum of a finite set of line segments. In this paper, we will use the following definition:

Definition 1 (Zonotope). *A zonotope Z is a set such that:*

$$Z = \left\{ x \in \mathbb{R}^n : x = c + \sum_{i=1}^{i=p} x_i g_i, \ -1 \le x_i \le 1 \right\}$$

where $c, g_1, \ldots, g_p$ are vectors of $\mathbb{R}^n$. We note $Z = (c, < g_1, \ldots, g_p >)$.

Thus, it is clear that a zonotope is a polytope. Parallelepipeds and hyper-rectangles are particular zonotopes.

Note that a zonotope $Z = (c, < g_1, \ldots, g_p >)$ is always centrally symmetric and that the point $c \in \mathbb{R}^n$ is the center of Z. The collection of vectors $g_1, \ldots, g_p$ is called the set of generators of Z. On figure 1, we represented a planar zonotope with three generators. For a zonotope with p generators in $\mathbb{R}^n$, the value of p/n is called the order of the zonotope. For instance, a parallelepiped is a zonotope of order 1. From a practical point of view, the definition 1 gives an efficient representation of the set since the number of faces of a zonotope in $\mathbb{R}^n$ with p

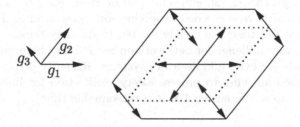

Fig. 1. Example of a zonotope with three generators

generators is in $O(p^{n-1})$ [11]. Zonotopes have long been studied in combinatorial geometry [22]. Practical application of zonotopes have been shown in various domains such as systems of polynomial equations [12], computational geometry [11] or rigorous approximation of dynamical systems [13, 9].

In this paper, we propose using zonotopes to over-approximate the reachable sets of uncertain linear systems. The use of zonotopes has been motivated by two main properties:

1. Zonotopes are closed under linear transformation. Let $\mathcal{L}$ be a linear map and $Z = (c, < g_1, \ldots, g_p >)$ a zonotope,

$$\mathcal{L}Z = \left\{ \mathcal{L}x : x = c + \sum_{i=1}^{i=p} x_i g_i, \ -1 \leq x_i \leq 1 \right\}$$
$$= (\mathcal{L}c, < \mathcal{L}g_1, \ldots, \mathcal{L}g_p >).$$

The image of a zonotope by a linear map can be computed in linear time with regard to the order of the zonotope.

2. Zonotopes are closed under Minkowski sum. Let $Z_1 = (c_1, < g_1, \ldots, g_p >)$ and $Z_2 = (c_2, < h_1, \ldots, h_q >)$ be two zonotopes,

$$Z_1 + Z_2 = (c_1 + c_2, < g_1, \ldots, g_p, h_1, \ldots, h_q >).$$

Thus, the Minkowski sum of two zonotopes can be computed by the concatenation of two lists.

3   Approximation of Reachable Sets

Let us consider the following uncertain linear system :

$$x'(t) = Ax(t) + u(t), \ \|u(t)\| \leq \mu \tag{1}$$

where A is an $n \times n$ matrix and $\|.\|$ denotes the infinity norm on $\mathbb{R}^n$ ($\|x\| = \max_{i=1}^{i=n} |x_i|$). Given a set of possible initial values I, the reachable set of the system at the time t is

$$\Phi_t(I) = \{y \in \mathbb{R}^n : \exists x \text{ solution of } (1) \ , \ x(0) \in I \wedge x(t) = y\}.$$

The reachable set on the interval $[\underline{t}, \overline{t}]$ from the set of initial values I can therefore be defined by

$$\mathcal{R}_{[\underline{t},\overline{t}]}(I) = \bigcup_{t \in [\underline{t},\overline{t}]} \Phi_t(I).$$

In [10], a method using the maximum principle has been proposed for the computation of the reachable sets of uncertain linear systems such as (1). In [5], a general method for uncertain systems is proposed. This method works for any uncertain system provided you can compute the reachable sets of an associated deterministic system. This technique makes intensive use of the Minkowski sum.

Hence, it is generally expensive (particularly for high dimensional systems). For the reasons mentioned in the previous section, the use of zonotopes may be a good solution to avoid expensive computations of the Minkowski sum.

Let T be a positive real number, we want to compute an over-approximation of the reachable set $\mathcal{R}_{[0,T]}(I)$. Our method has similarities with the flow pipe technique [7] which has been used successfully for deterministic systems. Let $r > 0$ be the time step, we assume that $N = T/r$ is an integer. The reachable set $\mathcal{R}_{[0,T]}(I)$ can be decomposed in the following way:

$$\mathcal{R}_{[0,T]}(I) = \bigcup_{i=0}^{i=N-1} \mathcal{R}_{[ir,(i+1)r]}(I). \tag{2}$$

Thus, if we are able to compute over-approximations of the sets $\mathcal{R}_{[ir,(i+1)r]}(I)$, we can compute an over-approximation of the set $\mathcal{R}_{[0,T]}(I)$. Moreover, we have

$$\mathcal{R}_{[ir,(i+1)r]}(I) = \Phi_r(\mathcal{R}_{[(i-1)r,ir]}(I)).$$

Therefore, we need to define conservative approximations of the maps $\mathcal{R}_{[0,r]}$ and Φ_r, for r arbitrary small. Moreover, since we aim to use zonotopes, these conservative approximations must map zonotopes into zonotopes.

3.1   Conservative Approximation of Φ_r

Let Z be a zonotope in $\mathbb{R}^n$. Let $x \in Z$, $y \in \Phi_r(x)$, there exists an admissible input u such that

$$y = e^{rA}x + \int_0^r e^{(r-s)A}u(s)ds.$$

Therefore,

$$\|y - e^{rA}x\| \leq \int_0^r e^{(r-s)\|A\|}\mu ds = \frac{e^{r\|A\|} - 1}{\|A\|}\mu. \tag{3}$$

Let us note $\beta_r = \frac{e^{r\|A\|}-1}{\|A\|}\mu$, from the previous equation, $\Phi_r(Z)$ is included in the set $e^{rA}Z + \square(\beta_r)$ where $\square(\beta_r)$ denotes the ball of center 0 and of radius β_r for the infinite norm. Note that $\square(\beta_r)$ is actually a hypercube and consequently it is a zonotope. Hence, the set $e^{rA}Z + \square(\beta_r)$ over-approximating $\Phi_r(Z)$ is a zonotope. Moreover, we can show that the quality of the approximation is good for the Hausdorff distance.

Definition 2 (Hausdorff distance). *The Hausdorff distance between two subsets of $\mathbb{R}^n$, S_1 and S_2 is*

$$d_H(S_1, S_2) = \max\left(\sup_{x_1 \in S_1}\inf_{x_2 \in S_2}\|x_1 - x_2\|, \sup_{x_2 \in S_2}\inf_{x_1 \in S_1}\|x_1 - x_2\|\right).$$

Lemma 1 (Conservative approximation of Φ_r)

1. *Conservative approximation:* $\Phi_r(Z) \subseteq e^{rA}Z + \square(\beta_r)$
2. *Convergence:* $d_H(\Phi_r(Z), e^{rA}Z + \square(\beta_r)) \leq \mu\|A\|e^{r\|A\|}r^2$.

3.2   Conservative Approximation of $\mathcal{R}_{[0,r]}$

The over-approximation process of $\mathcal{R}_{[0,r]}$ is a bit more complex. Let $Z = (c, < g_1, \ldots, g_p >)$ be a zonotope; using (3) it is clear that

$$\mathcal{R}_{[0,r]}(Z) \subseteq (\bigcup_{t \in [0,r]} e^{tA} Z) + \Box(\beta_r). \tag{4}$$

Thus, we shall over-approximate the reachable set of the deterministic linear system $x' = Ax$ using a zonotope, and then add the set $\Box(\beta_r)$. Our method for the approximation of the reachable set of the deterministic system is quite similar to the one of [7] or [10] but with zonotopes.

In [10], for instance, the method proposed is the following. First, the reachable set is approximated by the convex hull of Z and $e^{rA}Z$. Secondly, this set is bloated in order to over-approximate the reachable set. The convex hull of two zonotopes is generally not a zonotope, hence, we can not apply directly this method to our problem. For instance, we can replace the convex hull by the smallest zonotope enclosing Z and $e^{rA}Z$. This problem is complex and might be very expensive to solve for high dimensional systems (see [11]). Therefore, we take a rougher approximation which is very simple to compute:

$$P = (\tfrac{c+e^{rA}c}{2}, < \tfrac{g_1+e^{rA}g_1}{2}, \ldots, \tfrac{g_p+e^{rA}g_p}{2}, \tfrac{c-e^{rA}c}{2}, \tfrac{g_1-e^{rA}g_1}{2}, \ldots, \tfrac{g_p-e^{rA}g_p}{2} >). \tag{5}$$

The center and the p first generators of the zonotope gives the mean value of the zonotopes Z and $e^{rA}Z$. The $p+1$ other generators are small (their norm is $O(r)$) and allow to enclose both sets Z and $e^{rA}Z$. Afterwards, this set is bloated. This is done by adding a ball of radius α_r to the zonotope P. α_r must be big enough so that $P + \Box\alpha_r$ contains the reachable set of the deterministic system (the computation of the value of α_r can be found in appendix). The principle of the over-approximation of the reachable set is shown on figure 2.

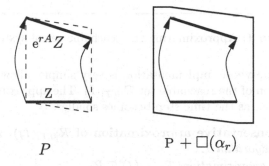

Fig. 2. Principle of the over-approximation of the reachable set

Lemma 2 (Conservative approximation of $\mathcal{R}_{[0,r]}$). *Let P be defined as in equation 5.*

1. *Conservative approximation:* $\mathcal{R}_{[0,r]}(Z) \subseteq P + \square(\alpha_r + \beta_r)$
2. *Convergence:*

$$d_H(\mathcal{R}_{[0,r]}(Z), P + \square(\alpha_r + \beta_r)) \leq r\|A\|e^{r\|A\|}\left(\frac{\mu}{\|A\|} + (\frac{1}{2} + r)\sup_{x\in Z}\|x\|\right)$$

with $\alpha_r = (e^{r\|A\|} - 1 - r\|A\|)\sup_{x\in Z}\|x\|$.

3.3   Reachability Algorithm

We can now present the reachability algorithm. The principle is similar to the one of the method presented in [5]. First, the reachable set is initialized using the method presented in the section 3.2. Afterwards, the image of the reachable set by the flow of the deterministic system $x' = Ax$ is computed and bloated as explained in the section 3.1.

Input: A zonotope of initial values $I = (c, < g_1, \ldots, g_p >)$
Result: An approximation of the reachable set $\mathcal{R}_{[0,T]}(I)$

$N = \frac{T}{r}$
$\alpha_r = (e^{r\|A\|} - 1 - r\|A\|)\sup_{x\in I}\|x\|$
$\beta_r = \frac{e^{r\|A\|}-1}{\|A\|}\mu$

$P_0 = (\frac{c+e^{rA}c}{2}, < \frac{g_1+e^{rA}g_1}{2}, \ldots, \frac{g_p+e^{rA}g_p}{2}, \frac{c-e^{rA}c}{2}, \frac{g_1-e^{rA}g_1}{2}, \ldots, \frac{g_p-e^{rA}g_p}{2} >)$
$Q_0 = P_0 + \square(\alpha_r + \beta_r)$
$R_0 = Q_0$
for $i \leftarrow 1$ **to** $N-1$ **do**
$\quad\left|\begin{array}{l} P_i = e^{rA}Q_{i-1} \\ Q_i = P_i + \square(\beta_r) \\ R_i = R_{i-1} \cup Q_i \end{array}\right.$
end
return R_N

Algorithm 1: Approximating the reachable set of system (1)

This algorithm, whose implementation is very simple, allows to compute an over-approximation of the reachable set $\mathcal{R}_{[0,T]}(I)$. The approximation converges to the reachable set as the time step becomes smaller.

Theorem 1 (Conservative approximation of $\mathcal{R}_{[0,T]}(I)$). *Let R_{N-1} be the set computed by algorithm 1.*

1. *Conservative approximation:* $\mathcal{R}_{[0,T]}(I) \subseteq R_{N-1}$
2. *Convergence:*

$$d_H(\mathcal{R}_{[0,T]}(I), R_{N-1}) \leq r\|A\|e^{\|A\|T}\left(\frac{2\mu}{\|A\|} + (\frac{1}{2} + r)\sup_{x\in Z}\|x\|\right).$$

3.4   Controlling the Expansion of the Order of Zonotopes

At each iteration of the loop of algorithm 1, the set Q_{i+1} is obtained by computing the image of Q_i by a linear map and by adding the set $\square(\beta_r)$. Consequently, the order of the zonotope Q_{i+1} equals the order of Q_i plus 1. Therefore, the order of the zonotope Q_i is $O(i)$. The memory allocation needed to encode the over-approximation of the set $\mathcal{R}_{[0,T]}(I)$ is in $O(N^2)$. We can also show that the time needed for its computation is also $O(N^2)$. For large value of N the over-approximation of $\mathcal{R}_{[0,T]}(I)$ can thus be quite expensive in memory and in time.

A solution to avoid this quadratic expansion is to limit the order of the zonotopes Q_i. Let m be the maximum order allowed for the zonotopes Q_i. If the order of the zonotope Q_i is m, then following algorithm 1, the order of Q_{i+1} should be $m+1$ which is greater to the maximum order allowed. We must have recourse to a reduction step. It consists in taking $2n$ generators of Q_{i+1}, $h_1, \ldots, h_{2n}$, and to replace them by n generators, such that the new zonotope of order m contains Q_{i+1} (see figure 3). Equivalently, we have to over-approximate the zonotope $(0, < h_1, \ldots, h_{2n} >)$ by a zonotope with n generators and whose center is 0. Let x be a point of the zonotope $(0, < h_1, \ldots, h_{2n} >)$, then $x = \sum_{i=1}^{i=2n} x_i h_i$, where $x_i \in [-1, 1]$. x^j, the j-th component of x, is bounded in absolute value by $\sum_{i=1}^{i=2n} |h_i^j|$ where h_i^j is the j-th component of h_i. Therefore, $(0, < h_1, \ldots, h_{2n} >)$ is included in the interval hull

$$\left[-\sum_{i=1}^{i=2n} |h_i^1| , \sum_{i=1}^{i=2n} |h_i^1| \right] \times \cdots \times \left[[-\sum_{i=1}^{i=2n} |h_i^n| , \sum_{i=1}^{i=2n} |h_i^n| \right]$$

which is a zonotope with n generators $h'_1, \ldots, h'_n$ such that all the components of the vector h'_j are equal to 0 except the j-th one which is given by $\sum_{i=1}^{i=2n} |h_i^j|$.

The choice of the $2n$ generators of Q_{i+1} to be replaced is important for the quality of the approximation. The best selection consists in taking the vectors $h_1, \ldots, h_{2n}$ such that the over-approximation of the zonotope $(0, < h_1, \ldots, h_{2n} >)$ by an intervall hull is as good as possible (intervall hulls are zonotopes whose generators have only one non zero component). Let $Q_{i+1} = (c, < g_1, \ldots, g_{(m+1)n} >)$ and let us assume that the generators have been sorted so that:

$$\|g_1\|_1 - \|g_1\|_\infty \leq \|g_2\|_1 - \|g_2\|_\infty \leq \cdots \leq \|g_{(m+1)n}\|_1 - \|g_{(m+1)n}\|_\infty.$$

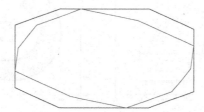

Fig. 3. Example of over-approximation of a zonotope by a zonotope of lower order

We choose for $i \in \{1, \ldots, 2n\}$, $h_i = g_i$. These vectors are closed to vectors with only one non zero component and therefore $(0, < h_1, \ldots, h_{2n} >)$ is well approximated by an intervall hull.

Other heuristics for the reduction step can be found in [13, 9].

4   Experimental Results

The method has been implemented in the free scientific software package Scilab. We used our method to compute the reachable set of numerous uncertain linear systems of various size. In this section, we present some of our results.

First, we considered the two dimensional system defined by :

$$A = \begin{pmatrix} -1 & -4 \\ 4 & -1 \end{pmatrix}, \ \mu = 0.05.$$

We computed an over-approximation of the reachable set $\mathcal{R}_{[0,2]}(I)$ for the set of initial values $I = [0.9, 1.1] \times [-0.1, 0.1]$. The over-approximation has been computed using a time step of 0.02 (100 iterations). The maximum order allowed for zonotopes is 10 (20 generators). The result is shown on figure 4. We can see that the quality of the approximation is good.

We also computed an over-approximation of the reachable set $\mathcal{R}_{[0,1]}(I)$ of a five dimensional system where the Jordan form of the matrix A is

$$\begin{pmatrix} -1 & -4 & 0 & 0 & 0 \\ 4 & -1 & 0 & 0 & 0 \\ 0 & 0 & -3 & 1 & 0 \\ 0 & 0 & -1 & -3 & 0 \\ 0 & 0 & 0 & 0 & -2 \end{pmatrix}$$

The perturbations are bounded by $\mu = 0.01$. The over-approximation has been computed using a time step of 0.005 (200 iterations) and the maximum order

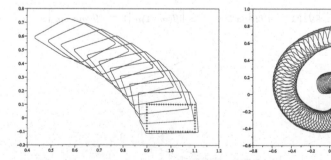

Fig. 4. Reachable set of the two dimensional example. Left: first iterations of the algorithm. Right: over-approximation of the reachable set $\mathcal{R}_{[0,2]}(I)$

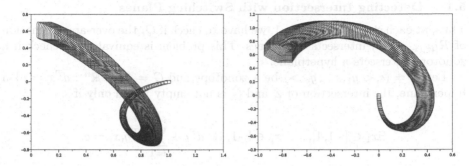

Fig. 5. Reachable set of the five dimensional example: projection on coordinates x_1 and x_2 (left), x_4 and x_5 (right)

Table 1. Computation times of the reachable set of uncertain linear systems of several dimensions. (Implementation: Scilab; Machine: Pentium III, 1 GHz)

Dimension	5	10	20	50	100
Cputime (s)	0.05	0.33	1.5	9.91	43.7

allowed for zonotopes is 40 (200 generators). Projections of the reachable set are shown on figure 4.

We also used our method for high dimensional systems. Experimental results are shown in table 1. We computed an over-approximation of the reachable set $\mathcal{R}_{[0,1]}(I)$ of uncertain linear systems of several dimensions (with $\mu = 0.01$). We used a time step equal to 0.01 (100 iterations) and the maximum order allowed for zonotopes is 5. The matrices were chosen at random and then normalized (for the infinity norm). We can see that our algorithm has great performances. Moreover, it particularly fits high-dimensional systems since it computes the reachable set of a hundred dimensional system in less than 1 minute.

5   Verification of Hybrid Systems

Our method can of course be incorporated in a hybrid system verification process. It is compatible with high level algorithms used by the toolboxes d/dt [3] and CheckMate [8]. Let us consider hybrid systems where the continuous dynamics are given by uncertain linear differential equations such as (1). In each mode, the reachable set of the hybrid system can be computed efficiently by our method. It remains for us to incorporate an event detection process which checks at each step wether the reachable set intersects the guards of the system or not. We will assume that the guards are specified by switching planes:

$$G_{q,q'} = \{x \in \mathbb{R}^n : d_{q,q'}^T x = e_{q,q'}\}, \text{ where } d_{q,q'} \in \mathbb{R}^n, e_{q,q'} \in \mathbb{R}.$$

5.1   Detecting Intersection with Switching Planes

Thus, at each step of algorithm 1, we have to check if Q_i the over-approximation of $\mathcal{R}_{[ir,(i+1)r]}(I)$ intersects the planes. This problem is equivalent to check if a zonotope intersects a hyperplane.

Let $Z = (c, < g_1, \ldots, g_p >)$ be a zonotope and $G = \{x \in \mathbb{R}^n : d^T x = e\}$ a hyperplane, the intersection of Z and G is not empty if and only if

$$\exists x_1 \in [-1,1], \ldots, x_p \in [-1,1], \; d^T c + \sum_{i=1}^{i=p} d^T g_i x_i = e.$$

Thus, the zonotope Z intersects the hyperplane G, if and only if

$$(e - d^T c) \in \left[-\sum_{i=1}^{i=p} |d^T g_i|, \sum_{i=1}^{i=p} |d^T g_i| \right].$$

Hence, we can see that it is very easy to check if a zonotope intersects a hyperplane. Moreover, this is done in linear time with regard to the number of generators of the zonotope as well as the dimension of the system.

5.2   Checking Robustness of the Two Tank System

The two-tank system (see figure 6) has been presented in [17] as an illustration of limit cycles arising in hybrid systems. The system consists of two tanks and two valves. The first valve allows to add water in the first tank, while the second one allows to drain off the second tank. There are also a constant inflow in tank 1 and a constant outflow in tank 2. The system is obtained by linearization about an operating point. The objective is to keep the water levels within some limits using a feedback on/off switching strategy for the valves.

The two valve settings result in four discrete states for our piecewise linear hybrid system. The discrete dynamics are given by the automaton presented on figure 6. The continuous dynamics are given by affine differential equations $x' = A_q x + b_q$, $q \in \{1, 2, 3, 4\}$ with

$$A_1 = \begin{pmatrix} -1 & 0 \\ 1 & 0 \end{pmatrix} \; A_2 = \begin{pmatrix} -1 & 0 \\ 1 & 0 \end{pmatrix} \; A_3 = \begin{pmatrix} -1 & 0 \\ 1 & -1 \end{pmatrix} \; A_4 = \begin{pmatrix} -1 & 0 \\ 1 & -1 \end{pmatrix}$$

$$b_1 = \begin{pmatrix} -2 & 0 \end{pmatrix}^t \; b_2 = \begin{pmatrix} 3 & 0 \end{pmatrix}^t \; b_3 = \begin{pmatrix} -2 & -5 \end{pmatrix}^t \; b_4 = \begin{pmatrix} 3 & -5 \end{pmatrix}^t$$

It is well known that this system has a stable limit cycle. In this part, we propose to use our method to check the robustness of this limit cycle. Indeed, the real continuous dynamics can not be exactly known, there are uncertainties on the characteristics of the valves, variations of the inflow and of the outflow. These uncertainties can be modeled by adding a small perturbation term:

$$x'(t) = A_{q(t)} x(t) + b_{q(t)} + u(t), \; \|u(t)\| \le \mu.$$

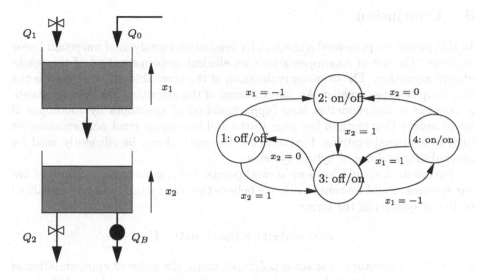

Fig. 6. The two tank system

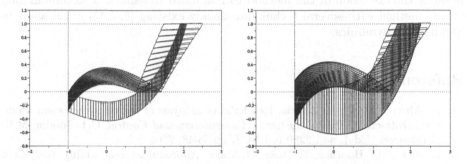

Fig. 7. Reachable set of the two tank system. Left: $\mu = 0.01$. Right: $\mu = 0.1$

The goal for us is to check if the periodic behaviour remains when we replace the deterministic dynamics by the uncertain ones. It is easy to generalize the method presented in the previous sections in order to handle uncertain affine dynamics.

We computed the reachable set of the two tank system, for the initial discrete state 3, and for the set of initial values of the continuous variable $I = [1.5, 2.5] \times \{1\}$. The reachable set has been computed for uncertainties bounded by 0.01 and then by 0.1. The result is shown on figure 7. In both cases, we can check that the periodic behaviour is conserved. Thus, the switching strategy is acceptable since the water levels in each tank remain bounded.

6   Conclusion

In this paper, we presented a method for reachability analysis of uncertain linear systems. The use of zonotopes allows an efficient implementation of the reachability algorithm. The over-approximation of the reachable set converges as the time step becomes smaller. An improvement of the algorithm has been proposed, it consists in the reduction step (approximation of zonotopes by zonotopes of lower order). Our method has been tested and has shown great performances for high-dimensional systems. Furthermore, the method can be efficiently used for reachability analysis of hybrid systems.

Future work should focus on several points. First, more general classes of linear systems should be considered. We believe that our method can be generalized to linear systems of the form:

$$x'(t) = Ax(t) + Bu(t), \; u(t) \in U$$

where U is a zonotope. For some polytopic norm, the order of approximation of the reachable set should be conserved. Secondly, a rigorous analysis of the error introduced by the reduction step should be done. It is important to quantify the influence of the maximum order allowed for zonotopes. The third important point is the extension of the method to non-linear dynamics. The combination of our method with several techniques already existing [5, 7, 13] could allow to handle such dynamics.

References

1. R. Alur, T. Dang, F. Ivancic, Reachability analysis of hybrid systems via predicate abstraction, *Hybrid Systems : Computation and Control*, C.J. Tomlin, M.R. Greenstreet (Eds), no . 2289 in LNCS, pp 35-48, 2002.
2. E. Asarin, O. Bournez, T. Dang, O. Maler, Approximate reachability analysis of piecewise linear dynamical systems, *Hybrid Systems : Computation and Control*, N. Lynch, B. H. Krogh (Eds), no. 1790 in LNCS, pp 21-31, Springer, 2000.
3. E. Asarin, T. Dang, O. Maler, d/dt: A verification tool for hybrid systems, *in the Proc. of CDC'01*, 2001.
4. E. Asarin, G. Schneider, S.Yovine. Towards computing phase portraits of polygonal differential inclusions, *Hybrid Systems : Computation and Control*, C.J. Tomlin, M.R. Greenstreet (Eds), no . 2289 in LNCS, pp 49-61, 2002.
5. E. Asarin, T. Dang, A. Girard, Reachability of non-linear systems using conservative approximations, *Hybrid Systems : Computation and Control*, O. Maler, A. Pnueli (Eds), no. 2623 in LNCS, pp 22-35, Spinger, 2003.
6. E. Asarin, T. Dang, Abstraction by projection and application to multi-affine systems, *Hybrid Systems : Computation and Control*, R. Alur, G.J. Pappas (Eds), no. 2993 in LNCS, pp 32-47, Springer, 2004.
7. A. Chutinan, B.H. Krogh, Verification of polyhedral invariant hybrid automata using polygonal flow pipe approximations. *Hybrid Systems : Computation and Control*, F. Vaandrager, J. van Schuppen (Eds), no. 1569 in LNCS, pp 76-90, Springer, 1999.

8. A. Chutinan, B.H. Krogh, Computational techniques for hybrid system verification, *IEEE Trans. on Automatic Control*, vol. 48, no. 1, 2003, pp. 64-75.
9. Combastel C., A state bounding observer based on zonotopes, in *Proc. of European Control Conference*, 2003.
10. T. Dang, Vérification et synthèse des systèmes hybrides, *Thèse de Doctorat*, Institut National Polytechnique de Grenoble, 2000.
11. L.J. Guibas, A. Nguyen , L. Zhang, Zonotopes as bounding volumes, in *Proc. of Symposium on Discrete Algorithms*, pp 803-812.
12. B. Huber and B. Sturmfels, A polyhedral method for solving sparse polynomial systems, *Math. of Computation*, 64:1541-1555, 1995.
13. W. Kühn, Zonotope dynamics in numerical quality control, in *Mathematical Visualization*, H.-C. Hege, K. Polthier (Eds), pp 125-134, Springer, 1998.
14. A. Kurzhanski, P. Varaiya, Ellipsoidal tehcniques for reachability analysis, *Hybrid Systems : Computation and Control*, N. Lynch, B. H. Krogh (Eds), no. 1790 in LNCS, Springer, 2000.
15. G. Lafferriere, G. Pappas, S. Yovine, Reachability computation for linear systems, *Proc. IFAC World Congress*, E:7-12, 1999.
16. I. Mitchell, C. Tomlin, Level set methods for computation in hybrid systems, *Hybrid Systems : Computation and Control*, N. Lynch, B. H. Krogh (Eds), no. 1790 in LNCS, Springer, 2000.
17. M. Rubensson, B. Lennartson, S. Pettersson, Convergence to limit cycles in hybrid systems: an example, *Large Scale Systems: Theory and Applications*, pp 704-709, 1998.
18. O. Stursberg, B.H. Krogh, Efficient representation and computation of reachable sets for hybrid systems, *Hybrid Systems : Computation and Control*, O. Maler, A. Pnueli (Eds), no. 2623 in LNCS, pp 482-497, Spinger, 2003.
19. C. Tomlin, I. Mitchell, A. Bayen, and M. Oishi, Computational techniques for the verification and control of hybrid systems, *Proc. of the IEEE*, 91(7):986-1001, July 2003.
20. A. Tiwari, G. Khanna, Series of abstractions for hybrid automata, *Hybrid Systems : Computation and Control*, C.J. Tomlin, M.R. Greenstreet (Eds), no . 2289 in LNCS, pp 465-478, 2002.
21. H. Yazarel, G.J. Pappas, Geometric programming relaxations for linear system reachability, in *Proc. American Control Conference*, 2004.
22. G.M. Ziegler, Lectures on polytopes, *Graduate texts in Mathematics*, Springer-Verlag, 1995.

Appendix

Proof of Lemma 1 (Adapted from [5])

The proof of the first part of the lemma is a consequence of equation (3). Let us prove the second part.

Let $x \in e^{rA}Z + \Box\beta_r$, there exists $z \in Z$ such that $\|e^{rA}z - x\| \le \beta_r$. Let us consider the constant input function u such that $u(s) = \frac{\|A\|}{e^{r\|A\|}-1}(x - e^{rA}z)$ for all $s \in [0,r]$. We can check that $\|u(s)\| \le \mu$, therefore,

$$x_u = e^{rA}z + \int_0^r e^{(r-s)A}u(s)\, ds \in \Phi_r(Z).$$

Then,

$$x_u - x = e^{rA}z - x + \int_0^r e^{(r-s)A}u(s)\,ds = \int_0^r e^{(r-s)A}u(s) - \frac{1}{r}(x - e^{rA}z)\,ds$$

$$= \int_0^r e^{(r-s)A}u(s) - \frac{e^{r\|A\|} - 1}{r\|A\|}u(s)\,ds$$

$$= \int_0^r e^{(r-s)A}u(s) - u(s) - \frac{e^{r\|A\|} - r\|A\| - 1}{r\|A\|}u(s)\,ds.$$

Therefore,

$$\|x_u - x\| \le \mu \int_0^r (r-s)\|A\|e^{\|A\|(r-s)} + \frac{r\|A\|e^{r\|A\|}}{2}\,ds \le \mu r^2 \|A\| e^{r\|A\|}.$$

Proof of Lemma 2

Let x be an element of Z, $t \in [0,r]$, it is reasonable to approximate the value of $e^{tA}x$ by $x + \frac{t}{r}(e^{rA}x - x)$. Indeed,

$$e^{tA}x - x - \frac{t}{r}(e^{rA}x - x) = \sum_{k=2}^{k=\infty} \frac{t(t^{k-1} - r^{k-1})}{k!}A^k x.$$

It follows that

$$\|e^{tA}x - x - \frac{t}{r}(e^{rA}x - x)\| \le (e^{r\|A\|} - 1 - r\|A\|)\|x\|. \tag{6}$$

Let $\alpha_r = (e^{r\|A\|} - 1 - r\|A\|)\sup_{x \in Z}\|x\|$, from (4) and (6), we have $\mathcal{R}_{[0,r]}(Z) \subseteq Q + \Box(\alpha_r + \beta_r)$ where $Q = \{x + \frac{t}{r}(e^{rA}x - x) : x \in Z, t \in [0,r]\}$. We can check that the zonotope P defined by equation (5) contains the set Q. Therefore, the first part of the lemma is proved.

Before proving the second part of the lemma, let us compute the distance between P and Q. Let $x \in P$, there exist $-1 \le x_i \le 1$, $-1 \le \lambda \le 1$, $-1 \le y_i \le 1$,

$$x = \frac{c + e^{rA}c}{2} + \sum_{i=1}^{i=p} \frac{g_i + e^{rA}g_i}{2}x_i + \frac{c - e^{rA}c}{2}\lambda + \sum_{i=1}^{i=p} \frac{g_i - e^{rA}g_i}{2}y_i.$$

Let y be the point defined by $y = \frac{c + e^{rA}c}{2} + \sum_{i=1}^{i=p} \frac{g_i + e^{rA}g_i}{2}x_i$. We can check that y is an element of Q. Moreover,

$$\|x - y\| \le \|\frac{c - e^{rA}c}{2}\lambda + \sum_{i=1}^{i=p} \frac{g_i - e^{rA}g_i}{2}y_i\| \le \frac{e^{r\|A\|} - 1}{2}\|c\lambda + \sum_{i=1}^{i=p} g_i y_i\|.$$

Therefore, $d_H(P, Q) \le \frac{e^{r\|A\|} - 1}{2}\sup_{x \in Z}\|x\|$. Now let us remark that,

$$d_H(\mathcal{R}_{[0,r]}(Z), P + \Box(\alpha_r + \beta_r)) \le d_H(\mathcal{R}_{[0,r]}(Z), Q + \Box(\alpha_r + \beta_r)) + d_H(P, Q).$$

Thus, let $x \in Q + \square(\alpha_r + \beta_r)$, there exists $y \in Q$ such that $\|x - y\| \leq \alpha_r + \beta_r$. There exist $z \in Z$, $t \in [0, r]$ such that $y = z + \frac{t}{r}(e^{rA}z - z)$. Let $x' = e^{tA}z$, from equation (6), $\|x' - y\| \leq \alpha_r$. Moreover since $x' \in \mathcal{R}_{[0,r]}(Z)$ we have

$$d_H(\mathcal{R}_{[0,r]}(Z), Q + \square(\alpha_r + \beta_r)) \leq 2\alpha_r + \beta_r \leq e^{r\|A\|}r^2 \sup_{x \in Z} \|x\| + e^{r\|A\|}r\mu.$$

Proof of Theorem 1 (Adapted from [5])

From lemma 2, $\mathcal{R}_{[0,r]}(I) \subseteq Q_0$. Assume that $\mathcal{R}_{[(i-1)r,ir]}(I) \subseteq Q_{i-1}$, using lemma 1

$$\mathcal{R}_{[ir,(i+1)r]}(I) = \Phi_r(\mathcal{R}_{[(i-1)r,ir]}(I)) \subseteq \Phi_r(Q_{i-1}) \subseteq e^{rA}Q_{i-1} + \square(\beta_r) = Q_i.$$

Thus, by induction, the first part of the theorem is proved. Let us note $\delta_{i-1} = d_H(\mathcal{R}_{[(i-1)r,ir]}(I), Q_{i-1})$.

$$\delta_i = d_H(\Phi_r(\mathcal{R}_{[(i-1)r,ir]}(I)), e^{rA}Q_{i-1} + \square(\beta_r))$$
$$\leq d_H(\Phi_r(\mathcal{R}_{[(i-1)r,ir]}(I)), \Phi_r(Q_{i-1})) + d_H(\Phi_r(Q_{i-1}), e^{rA}Q_{i-1} + \square(\beta_r)).$$

From lemma 1, $d_H(\Phi_r(Q_{i-1}), e^{rA}Q_{i-1} + \square(\beta_r))$ is bounded by $\mu\|A\|e^{r\|A\|}r^2$. Furthermore, it is easy to show that

$$d_H(\Phi_r(\mathcal{R}_{[(i-1)r,ir]}(I)), \Phi_r(Q_{i-1})) \leq e^{r\|A\|}d_H(\mathcal{R}_{[(i-1)r,ir]}(I), Q_{i-1}).$$

Consequently, we have $\delta_i \leq e^{r\|A\|}\delta_{i-1} + \mu\|A\|e^{r\|A\|}r^2$. Therefore, for all $i \in \{0, \ldots, N-1\}$

$$\delta_i \leq e^{ir\|A\|}\delta_0 + \mu\|A\|e^{r\|A\|}r^2 \sum_{k=0}^{k=i-1} e^{k\|A\|r}$$
$$\leq e^{ir\|A\|}\delta_0 + \mu\|A\|e^{r\|A\|}r^2 \frac{e^{ir\|A\|} - 1}{e^{r\|A\|} - 1} \leq e^{\|A\|(T-r)}\delta_0 + \mu r e^{\|A\|T}.$$

The use of lemma 2 ends the proof of the second part of the theorem.

Safety Verification of Controlled Advanced Life Support System Using Barrier Certificates

Sonja Glavaski[1], Antonis Papachristodoulou[2], and Kartik Ariyur[1]

[1] Honeywell Laboratories, MN65-2810,
3660 Technology Dr., Minneapolis, MN 55418 - USA
{sonja.glavaski, kartik.ariyur}@honeywell.com
[2] Control and Dynamical Systems,
California Institute of Technology, Pasadena, CA 91125 - USA
antonis@cds.caltech.edu

Abstract. In this paper we demonstrate how to construct barrier certificates for safety verification of nonlinear hybrid systems using sum of squares methodologies, with particular emphasis on the computational challenges of the technique when applied to an Advanced Life Support System. The controlled system aims to ensure that the carbon dioxide and oxygen concentrations in a Variable Configuration CO_2 Removal (VCCR) subsystem never reach unacceptable values. The model we use is in the form of a hybrid automaton consisting of six modes each with nonlinear continuous dynamics of state dimension 10. The sheer size of the system makes the task of safety verification difficult to tackle with any other methodology. This is the first application of the sum of squares techniques to the safety verification of an intrinsically hybrid system with such high dimensional continuous dynamics.

1 Introduction

Hybrid automata provide a unique modeling framework for the study of several real world applications including the control of "systems of systems" along with the concomitant hierarchical decision processes. The analysis of these systems was initiated primarily in the theoretical computer science community, and several methods have been developed to handle systems with large scale discrete dynamics and simple continuous dynamics [1]. These approaches break down in the face of more complicated continuous dynamics combined with complex decision rules. Recently, control synthesis tools have been developed for hybrid systems whose continuous dynamics are linear and time invariant [2]. However most real controlled applications that can be modeled as hybrid automata consist of several modes each with high dimensional nonlinear continuous dynamics; the stability analysis, performance and safety verification of the overall design becomes a cumbersome task indeed.

In this paper we are interested in the safety verification of a controlled advanced life support system. A description of the system specifics can be found

M. Morari and L. Thiele (Eds.): HSCC 2005, LNCS 3414, pp. 306–321, 2005.

in [3] and [4]. We focus our attention on the Variable Configuration CO_2 Removal (VCCR) subsystem that consists of the main crew cabin and two adsorb/desorb beds. The main purpose of VCCR subsystem is to keep the levels of O_2 and CO_2 inside the two beds at acceptable levels, something that a simple feedback controller aims to achieve. The controlled system was simulated using SIMULINK®, but a formal safety verification proof is desired, as the system is safety-critical. We stress that no simulation procedure can ever guarantee the safety of the system, however fine the gridding of the initial condition space is. Because of the nature of the system these concentrations oscillate about the desired values; our wish is to ensure the safe functionality of the system, so that the oscillatory concentrations do not reach unacceptable values. After some modeling assumptions, the simplest adequate model for the system is in the form of a 6-mode automaton, each subsystem described by 10-dimensional continuous state dynamics.

In order to verify the safety of the system, we resorted to the construction of a so-called barrier certificate, through a methodology that was developed recently in [5]. The idea behind safety verification using barrier certificates is that their existence guarantees that trajectories starting from a set of initial conditions never enter unsafe operating conditions; in our case, given a fairly large set of initial cabin concentrations we can verify the safety of the controlled system. Moreover, a scenario in which the performance of one of the system parts is degraded is considered, and safety is verified in this case too by constructing another barrier certificate.

The computation of barrier functions is performed with the sum of squares decomposition, which is in turn computed using semidefinite programming. This is the first successful attempt to compute barrier functions for an intrinsically hybrid system with high dimensional continuous dynamics. Finally, this method of verification holds promise for safety verification of "systems of systems" where switching control laws are already operational.

This paper is organized as follows. Section 2 states the relevant results used in this paper. Due to space limitations, it is not possible to include all the details. An interested reader is referred to [5] for more details. Section 3 describes Advanced Life Support testbed and presents in detail the switching controller used. In section 4 we discuss how the barrier certificates are constructed and what computational challenges are encountered. Conclusions and future work are presented in section 5.

2   Hybrid System Safety Verification Using the Sum of Squares Decomposition

In this section we review briefly certain notions that will be used in the sequel, such as how a so-called barrier certificate satisfying certain conditions can guarantee the safety of a system modeled as a hybrid automaton. We then present briefly how these conditions can be tested efficiently using the sum of squares technique, leading to the algorithmic construction of the actual certificate.

The framework we use to model the system is presented in more detail in [6]. The verification problem and solution is presented in detail in [5].

2.1   Problem Formulation

The continuous state of a hybrid dynamical system evolves according to a set of continuous time differential equations determined by its discrete states, which in turn are governed by a discrete event process (such as a finite automaton). In this framework, a hybrid system is a tuple $H = (\mathcal{X}, L, X_0, I, F, T)$ with the following components.

- $\mathcal{X} \subset \mathbb{R}^n$ is the continuous state-space.
- L is a finite set of *locations* or *modes*. The overall state-space of the system is $X = L \times \mathcal{X}$, and a state of the system is denoted by $(l, x) \in L \times \mathcal{X}$.
- $X_0 \subset X$ is a set of initial states.
- $I : L \rightarrow 2^{\mathcal{X}}$ is the invariant, i.e. the set of all possible continuous states while at location l.
- $F : X \rightarrow 2^{\mathbb{R}^n}$ is a set of vector fields, one for each location.
- $T \subset X \times X$ is a relation describing discrete transitions between two locations, when a *guard* relation is satisfied.

The system evolves from the initial conditions in the set X_0, through a sequence of continuous flows and discrete transitions that are described by the map T. A set of unsafe states is denoted $X_u \subset X$. In addition for each location $l \in L$ we define the set of initial and unsafe continuous states as $\text{Init}(l) = \{x \in \mathcal{X} : (l, x) \in X_0\}$ and $\text{Unsafe}(l) = \{x \in \mathcal{X} : (l, x) \in X_u\}$. To each tuple $(l', l) \in L \times L$ with $l \neq l'$, we associate a guard set $\text{Guard}(l', l) = \{x' \in \mathcal{X} : ((l', x'), (l, x)) \in T \text{ for some } x \in \mathcal{X}\}$. The guard set describes when a discrete transition between two locations should occur.

The safety verification problem aims in deciding whether the system can reach a set of unsafe states X_u, given an initial set X_0. To answer this question, we use a recently developed tool, *Barrier Certificates* [5].

Theorem 1. *[5] Let the hybrid system $H = (\mathcal{X}, L, X_0, I, F, T)$ and the unsafe set X_u be given. Suppose there exists a* barrier certificate, *i.e. a collection $\{B_l(x)\}$ of functions $B_l(x)$ for all $l \in L$, each of which is differentiable with respect to its argument and satisfies*

$$B_l(x) > 0 \ \forall \ x \in Unsafe(l) \tag{1}$$

$$B_l(x) \leq 0 \ \forall \ x \in Init(l) \tag{2}$$

$$\frac{\partial B_l(x)}{\partial x} f_l(x) \leq 0 \ \forall \ x \in I(l) \tag{3}$$

$$B_l(x) \leq 0 \ \text{for some } l' \in L \text{ and } x \in Guard(l', l) \text{ with } B_{l'}(x) \leq 0. \tag{4}$$

Then the safety of the hybrid system H is guaranteed.

Proof. Let such a barrier certificate be given and consider a trajectory of the hybrid system from some initial condition $(l_0, x_0) \in X_0$ and the evolution of $B_{l(t)}(x(t))$ along this trajectory. The second condition asserts that $B_l(x(t)) \leq 0$, and the third and fourth conditions assert that $\{B_l(x)\}$ is non-increasing along jumps, and therefore can never attain a positive value. Consequently no such trajectory can ever reach an unsafe state $(l_u, x_u) \in X_u$, as there $B_{l_u}(x_u)$ is positive according to the first condition. Therefore the safety of the system is guaranteed.

The last condition in the above theorem is not convex, but can be relaxed to a convex condition as follows:

Proposition 1. *Let the hybrid system* $H = (\mathcal{X}, L, X_0, I, F, T)$, *the unsafe set* X_u *and some nonnegative constants* $\sigma_{l,l'}$ *be given. Suppose there exists a barrier certificate, i.e. a collection* $\{B_l(x)\}$ *of functions* $B_l(x)$ *for all* $l \in L$, *each of which is differentiable with respect to its argument and satisfies (1–3) and*

$$B_l(x) - \sigma_{l,l'} B_{l'}(x) \leq 0 \ \text{for some } l' \in L \text{ and } x \in Guard(l', l). \tag{5}$$

Then the safety of the hybrid system H *is guaranteed.*

Construction of barrier certificates is in general not easy, especially when the continuous state dynamics are nonlinear. This is because testing non-negativity even in the case of *polynomial* functions of degree greater than or equal to 4 is NP-hard [7]. However, for systems whose continuous dynamics are polynomial and for which initial and unsafe set descriptions are semialgebraic (i.e. described by polynomial equalities and inequalities) the Sum of Squares decomposition [8] can be used to construct polynomial barriers by solving a relevant semidefinite programme (SDP) [9]. This technique inherits the worst-case polynomial time complexity property of solving an SDP, and is therefore computationally attractive. This procedure is described in detail in [5].

We therefore restrict our attention to the case in which the continuous state dynamics have a polynomial description and the unsafe, initial invariant and guard sets as captured as semi-algebraic sets, i.e. they are captured by a vector of polynomial inequalities $g_{Unsafe(l)} \leq 0$, $g_{Init(l)}(x) \leq 0$, $g_{I(l)}(x) \leq 0$, and $g_{Guard(l,l')}(x) \leq 0$. The search for a barrier certificate can then be formulated as a Sum of Squares feasibility problem, given by the following proposition:

Proposition 2. *Let the hybrid system* H *and the descriptions of all the sets* $I(l), Init(l)$ $Unsafe(l)$ *and* $Guard(l)$ *be given. Suppose there exist polynomials* $B_l(x)$, *a positive number* ε *and vectors of sums of squares* $\sigma_{Unsafe(l)}(x)$, $\sigma_{Init(l)}(x)$, $\sigma_{I(l)}(x)$ *and* $\sigma_{Guard(l,l')}(x)$ *and* $\sigma_{B'_l}(x)$ *such that the following expressions*

$$B_l(x) - \varepsilon + \sigma_{Unsafe(l)}^T(x) g_{Unsafe(l)}(x) \tag{6}$$

$$-B_l(x) + \sigma_{Init(l)}^T(x) g_{Init(l)}(x) \tag{7}$$

$$-\frac{\partial B_l(x)}{\partial x} f_l(x) + \sigma_{I(l)}^T(x) g_{I(l)}(x) \tag{8}$$

$$-B_l(x) + \sigma_{B_l'}(x) B_{l'}(x) + \sigma_{Guard(l,l')}^T(x) g_{Guard(l,l')}(x) \tag{9}$$

are sums of squares for each $(l, l') \in L^2$, $l \neq l'$. Then $B_l(x)$ satisfies the conditions of Theorem 1 and the safety of the system is guaranteed.

Each of the above four conditions is a computational relaxation to testing the relevant condition in Proposition 1. For example condition (1) guarantees that for all $x \in \text{Unsafe}(l)$ we have:

$$B_l(x) \geq \varepsilon - \sigma_{\text{Unsafe}(l)}^T(x) g_{\text{Unsafe}(l)} > 0$$

since $\epsilon > 0$, $\sigma_{\text{Unsafe}(l)}$ are sum of squares and $g_{\text{Unsafe}(l)} \leq 0$ in the unsafe region. A similar rationale holds for the other conditions.

The construction of the barrier certificates in this paper is done with the aid of SOSTOOLS, a sum of squares programming solver [10] and SeDuMi, a semidefinite programming solver [11].

3   The Advanced Life Support System

The Advanced Life Support test-bed is used to support large-scale, long-duration testing of integrated regenerative life support systems under a closed and controlled environment. This shall be used as the basis for future long duration manned space exploration missions on the moon and other planetary surfaces. An important goal is to maximize recovery of reusable resources from waste products, generated by humans and plants, in order to create a self-sustainable life support system during space exploration. One of the main components of the life support system is the Air Revitalization system (ARS).

The Air Revitalization System provides fresh air to the crew chamber atmosphere, by the following operations:

- Recovery and generation of oxygen;
- Removal of carbon dioxide from the crew cabin;
- Intermediate gaseous products processing and storage;
- Provisions for control during degraded operations.

The ARS comprises of three major subsystems that accomplish the above functions - namely:

- Variable Configuration Carbon Dioxide Removal (VCCR);
- Carbon Dioxide Reduction System (CRS);
- Oxygen Generation System (OGS).

The basic function of the VCCR is to recover CO_2 from the crew cabin by adsorption into an adsorber, desorb the accumulated CO_2 and send it to an accumulator for recovery of O_2. It consists of the main crew cabin and two adsorb/desorb beds, whose purpose is to keep the levels of CO_2 and O_2 inside the two beds at acceptable levels, while tracking a desired reference concentration of O_2 and CO_2. To achieve this, each bed goes into a 3 phase cycle in the following sequence:

- An *adsorb* phase, in which CO_2 is removed from the cabin and gets adsorbed on the bed surface. The adsorbing bed returns CO_2 lean air back in the cabin.
- An *airsave* phase in which the desorbing bed recycles CO_2-lean air back to the cabin from its gas phase. It is assumed that the solid phase CO_2 is frozen in this process, so that no gas escapes from the bed.
- The *desorb* phase, in which the adsorbed CO_2 is removed from the adsorbent, which is accumulated in the CO_2 buffer.

The adsorber beds have a saturation capacity of solid-phase CO_2 they can adsorb. The system is configured in such a way so that when one of the beds is connected to the crew cabin adsorbing CO_2, the other one is undergoing airsave/desorption. After every half-cycle, the beds change their roles and the adsorbing bed goes through airsave/desorption and the desorbing bed goes through adsorption. It is assumed that all desorb/adsorb processes occur at a constant rate.

As seen from the above descriptions, this overall system provides a fairly complex and rich set of interesting scenarios to model, simulate and control. A more detailed description of the system specifics can be found in [4].

3.1   VCCR System Dynamics

The equations that describe the state evolution (i.e. the concentrations of CO_2, O_2 and inerts in the beds and cabin) are different for the airsave, adsorb and desorb processes. They are however simple mass balance equations, described below in detail.

We denote $x_1 - \rho_c(CO_2)$, the concentration of CO_2 in the cabin, $x_2 = \rho(CO_2, 1)$, $x_3 = \rho(CO_2, 2)$, the concentrations of CO_2 in bed 1 and bed 2 respectively and $x_4 = \dot{m}_{CO_2}$ the make-up mass flow of CO_2 in the cabin. Similarly, we denote $z_1 = \rho_c(O_2)$ the concentration of O_2 in the cabin, $z_2 = \rho(O_2, 1)$ and $z_3 = \rho(O_2, 2)$ the concentrations of O_2 in the two beds and $z_4 = \dot{m}_{O_2}$ the make-up mass flow of O_2 in the cabin.

The control variables are the volumetric flow rates of the two streams and the make-up mass flow rate of the CO_2 and O_2 streams. We have the following control laws:

- Volumetric flow rate from the cabin to the bed undergoing adsorption:

$$v_{ad} = v_{ad,n} + k_p^{ads}(x_1 - x_{1,r}) \tag{10}$$

where $v_{ad,n}$ and k_p^{ads} are constants and $x_{1,r}$ is a reference value for the desired concentration of CO_2 in the cabin.

- Volumetric flow rate from the cabin to the bed undergoing airsave is a constant, v_{as}.
- Volumetric flow rate from the cabin to the bed undergoing desorption:

$$v_{des,i} = k_p^{des} x_i, \quad i \in \{2,3\} \tag{11}$$

where k_p^{des} is a constant.

- The make-up mass flow rate of CO_2 in the cabin is given by a PID controller. In the frequency domain we have:

$$x_4(s) = (k_p + \frac{k_i}{s} + k_d s)(x_1(s) - x_{1,r}) \tag{12}$$

To proceed we approximate the derivative term by a term with limited D action, as follows:

$$x_4(s) = (k_p + \frac{k_i}{s} + \frac{k_d s}{\tau s + 1})(x_1(s) - x_{1,r})$$
$$= \frac{s^2(\tau k_p + k_d) + s(k_p + k_i \tau) + k_i}{s(\tau s + 1)}(x_1(s) - x_{1,r}) \tag{13}$$

Going back to the time domain, we get:

$$\tau \ddddot{x}_4 = -\dot{x}_4 + (\tau k_p + k_d)\ddot{x}_1 + (k_p + k_i \tau)\dot{x}_1 + k_i(x_1 - x_{1,r}) \tag{14}$$

Defining $x_5 = \dot{x}_4$, we have the following 2-state system:

$$\dot{x}_4 = x_5 \tag{15}$$
$$\tau \dot{x}_5 = -x_5 + (\tau k_p + k_d)\ddot{x}_1 + (k_p + k_i \tau)\dot{x}_1 + k_i(x_1 - x_{1,r}) \tag{16}$$

The value of $\ddot{x}_1$ is found by differentiating in time the respective equation in the relevant mode.

- The make-up mass flow rate of O_2 in the cabin is given by a PID controller of the similar structure as for CO_2:

$$\dot{z}_4 = z_5 \tag{17}$$
$$\tau \dot{z}_5 = -z_5 + (\tau k_p + k_d)\ddot{z}_1 + (k_p + k_i \tau)\dot{z}_1 + k_i(z_1 - z_{1,r}) \tag{18}$$

where $z_{1,r}$ is a reference point for the desired O_2 concentration in the cabin.

We will formulate the problem in the time-domain using a PID controller for the make-up streams, although the analysis will be done using a PI controller, for reasons that will be explained later. The system switches between 4 different modes.

Mode 1: Adsorber 1 adsorbing, Adsorber 2 in airsave In this first cycle, bed 1 is adsorbing CO_2 from the cabin. Bed 2 has just finished this cycle, and the CO_2-lean air in the bed is pumped back in the cabin, before the CO_2 that was accumulated in the bed is desorbed and removed. The equations describing the system in this phase are given by:

$$V_c\dot{x}_1 = (v_{\text{ad,n}} + k_p^{\text{ads}}(x_1 - x_{1,r}))(x_2 - x_1) + v_{\text{as,n}}x_3 + r_c(CO_2) + x_4$$

$$V_1\dot{x}_2 = -(v_{\text{ad,n}} + k_p^{\text{ads}}(x_1 - x_{1,r}))(x_2 - x_1) - r_{\text{ads}}(CO_2, 1)$$

$$V_2\dot{x}_3 = -v_{\text{as,n}}x_3$$

$$\dot{x}_4 = x_5$$

$$\tau\dot{x}_5 = -x_5 + (\tau k_p + k_d)\ddot{x}_1 + (k_p + k_i\tau)\dot{x}_1 + k_i(x_1 - x_{1,r})$$

$$V_c\dot{z}_1 = (v_{\text{ad,n}} + k_p^{\text{ads}}(x_1 - x_{1,r}))(z_2 - z_1) + v_{\text{as,n}}z_3 + r_c(O_2) + z_4$$

$$V_1\dot{z}_2 = -(v_{\text{ad,n}} + k_p^{\text{ads}}(x_1 - x_{1,r}))(z_2 - z_1)$$

$$V_2\dot{z}_3 = -v_{\text{as,n}}z_3$$

$$\dot{z}_4 = z_5$$

$$\tau\dot{z}_5 = -z_5 + (\tau k_p + k_d)\ddot{z}_1 + (k_p + k_i\tau)\dot{z}_1 + k_i(z_1 - z_{1,r})$$

Mode 2: Adsorber 1 adsorbing, Adsorber 2 desorbing In this mode bed 1 is still adsorbing, but bed 2 has pumped all CO_2-free gas in the cabin and is now desorbing. The switching from Mode 1 to Mode 2 is done when the concentration of CO_2 in bed 2 falls below a certain level, $x_3 \leq x^c$.

$$V_c\dot{x}_1 = (v_{\text{ad,n}} + k_p^{\text{ads}}(x_1 - x_{1,r}))(x_2 - x_1) + r_c(CO_2) + x_4$$

$$V_1\dot{x}_2 = -(v_{\text{ad,n}} + k_p^{\text{ads}}(x_1 - x_{1,r}))(x_2 - x_1) - r_{\text{ads}}(CO_2, 1)$$

$$V_2\dot{x}_3 = -k_p^{\text{des}}x_3^2 + r_{\text{des}}(CO_2, 2)$$

$$\dot{x}_4 = x_5$$

$$\tau\dot{x}_5 = -x_5 + (\tau k_p + k_d)\ddot{x}_1 + (k_p + k_i\tau)\dot{x}_1 + k_i(x_1 - x_{1,r})$$

$$V_c\dot{z}_1 = (v_{\text{ad,n}} + k_p^{\text{ads}}(x_1 - x_{1,r}))(z_2 - z_1) + r_c(O_2) + z_4$$

$$V_1\dot{z}_2 = -(v_{\text{ad,n}} + k_p^{\text{ads}}(x_1 - x_{1,r}))(z_2 - z_1)$$

$$V_2\dot{z}_3 = -k_p^{\text{des}}x_3 z_3$$

$$\dot{z}_4 = z_5$$

$$\tau\dot{z}_5 = -z_5 + (\tau k_p + k_d)\ddot{z}_1 + (k_p + k_i\tau)\dot{z}_1 + k_i(z_1 - z_{1,r})$$

Mode 3: Adsorber 2 adsorbing, Adsorber 1 in airsave This mode is the same as Mode 1, under the intuitive symmetry. Switching from Mode 2 to Mode 3 is done when both adsorption and desorption processes are complete. Because of the saturation in these processes, the transition is done through an intermediate stage, as will be discussed later on.

$$V_c\dot{x}_1 = v_{\text{ad,n}}x_2 + (v_{\text{ad,n}} + k_p^{\text{ads}}(x_1 - x_{1,r}))(x_3 - x_1) + r_c(CO_2) + x_4$$

$$V_1\dot{x}_2 = -v_{\text{ad,n}}x_2$$

$$V_2\dot{x}_3 = -(v_{\text{ad,n}} + k_p^{\text{ads}}(x_1 - x_{1,r}))(x_3 - x_1) - r_{\text{ads}}(CO_2, 2)$$

$$\dot{x}_4 = x_5$$

$$\tau\dot{x}_5 = -x_5 + (\tau k_p + k_d)\ddot{x}_1 + (k_p + k_i\tau)\dot{x}_1 + k_i(x_1 - x_{1,r})$$

$$V_c\dot{z}_1 = (v_{\text{ad,n}} + k_p^{\text{ads}}(x_1 - x_{1,r}))(z_3 - z_1) + v_{\text{as,n}}z_2 + r_c(O_2) + z_4$$

$$V_1\dot{z}_2 = -v_{\text{as,n}}z_2$$

$$V_2\dot{z}_3 = -(v_{\text{ad,n}} + k_p^{\text{ads}}(x_1 - x_{1,r}))(z_3 - z_1)$$

$$\dot{z}_4 = z_5$$

$$\tau\dot{z}_5 = -z_5 + (\tau k_p + k_d)\ddot{z}_1 + (k_p + k_i\tau)\dot{z}_1 + k_i(z_1 - z_{1,r})$$

Mode 4: Adsorber 2 adsorbing, Adsorber 1 desorbing This mode is the same as Mode 3 modulo the implied symmetry.

$$V_c\dot{x}_1 = (v_{\text{ad,n}} + k_p^{\text{ads}}(x_1 - x_{1,r}))(x_3 - x_1) + r_c(CO_2) + x_4$$

$$V_1\dot{x}_2 = -k_p^{\text{des}}x_2^2 + r_{\text{des}}(CO_2, 1)$$

$$V_2\dot{x}_3 = -(v_{\text{ad,n}} + k_p^{\text{ads}}(x_1 - x_{1,r}))(x_3 - x_1) - r_{\text{ads}}(CO_2, 2)$$

$$\dot{x}_4 = x_5$$

$$\tau\dot{x}_5 = -x_5 + (\tau k_p + k_d)\ddot{x}_1 + (k_p + k_i\tau)\dot{x}_1 + k_i(x_1 - x_{1,r})$$

$$V_c\dot{z}_1 = (v_{\text{ad,n}} + k_p^{\text{ads}}(x_1 - x_{1,r}))(z_3 - z_1) + r_c(O_2) + z_4$$

$$V_1\dot{z}_2 = -k_p^{\text{des}}x_2 z_2$$

$$V_2\dot{z}_3 = -(v_{\text{ad,n}} + k_p^{\text{ads}}(x_1 - x_{1,r}))(z_3 - z_1)$$

$$\dot{z}_4 = z_5$$

$$\tau\dot{z}_5 = -z_5 + (\tau k_p + k_d)\ddot{z}_1 + (k_p + k_i\tau)\dot{z}_1 + k_i(z_1 - z_{1,r})$$

3.2   Controller Switching Rules

The switching rules are as per Figure 1. We initialize the system in Mode 1, at a configuration in which the initial concentration of CO_2 in the cabin and bed 1 is about atmospheric ($9.13g/m^3$) and in bed 2 is below atmospheric, $2.56g/m^3$. Bed 1 is in adsorber mode and bed 2 is in airsave mode. In the next mode, airsave ends and bed 2 starts desorbing. Switching from Mode 1 to Mode 2 should then happen when the level of CO_2 in bed 2 has reduced significantly. We set this level to $5.5g/m^3$. For the switching from Mode 2 to Mode 3 the deciding factor is the level of CO_2 that has been adsorbed in bed 1, i.e. whether it has saturated, and whether the level of CO_2 is almost zero in bed 2, which is desorbing. Switching to Mode 3 from Mode 2 happens when *both* of the following happen:

1. Bed 1 has saturated, i.e. it cannot adsorb more CO_2.
2. Bed 2 cannot desorb further.

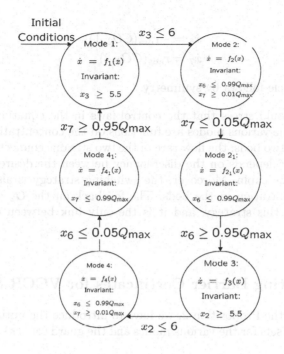

Fig. 1. Switching rule with saturation

As the adsorption happens at a much slower rate than desorption, the bed that is desorbing will reach saturation before the bed that is adsorbing. This necessitates the introduction of an intermediate mode, mode 2_1, depicted in Figure 1. The solid phase concentration for beds 1 and 2, x_6 and x_7 respectively, which decide when switching occurs can be calculated as follows:

– Mode 1:

$$\dot{x}_6 = r_{\text{ads}}(CO_2, 1)$$
$$\dot{x}_7 = 0$$

– Mode 2:

$$\dot{x}_6 = r_{\text{ads}}(CO_2, 1)$$
$$\dot{x}_7 = -r_{\text{des}}(CO_2, 2)$$

– Mode 3:

$$\dot{x}_6 = 0$$
$$\dot{x}_7 = r_{\text{ads}}(CO_2, 2)$$

– Mode 4:

$$\dot{x}_6 = -r_{\text{des}}(CO_2, 1)$$
$$\dot{x}_7 = r_{\text{ads}}(CO_2, 2)$$

The rest of the cycle follows by symmetry.

Remark 1. We should stress that the control laws in the equations describing the dynamics in the various modes are functions on the concentration of CO_2 in the cabin and the two beds: the flow rate of the two streams connecting the cabin with the two beds depends on the discrepancy between the desired and actual level of CO_2 in the cabin. Moreover, the switching strategy is also a function of the CO_2 concentration in the beds. The feedback on the O_2 concentration is a "follower" of this strategy, and it is the only link between O_2 and CO_2 dynamics.

4   Constructing Barrier Certificates for VCCR System

In order to apply the Proposition 2, we have to introduce the initial and unsafe sets, the invariant sets for the various modes and the guard sets as semi-algebraic sets.

The initial conditions will be assumed to be in the following set:

$$\begin{aligned}
X_0 = \{x \in \mathcal{X} \mid & (x_1 - 9)^2 + (x_2 - 9)^2 + (x_3 - 2.5)^2 + (x_4 - 16)^2 - 0.5^2 \le 0, \\
& (z_1 - 280)^2 + (z_2 - 280)^2 + (z_3 - 280)^2 + (z_4 - 80)^2 - 5^2 \le 0, \\
& (x_6 - 20)(x_6 - 30) \le 0, \\
& (x_7 - 220)(x_7 - 240) \le 0\}
\end{aligned} \tag{19}$$

The unsafe set is given by:

$$X_u = \{x \in \mathcal{X} \mid (x_1 - 7.1)(x_1 - 12.6) \ge 0, (z_1 - 271)(z_1 - 305) \ge 0\} \tag{20}$$

If we assume that the inerts have a concentration of around $913 g/m^3$ then the above unsafe set corresponds to:

– CO_2 in the range $0.59 - 1.05$ %.
– O_2 in the range $22.5 - 25.4$ %.

We already mentioned that we assume that the system switches between 6 states, the intermediate states 2_1 and 4_1 shown in Figure 1 take into account the saturations in the beds. In all modes, part of the invariant set is described by:

$$\begin{aligned}
I_{\text{com}} = \{x \in \mathcal{X} \mid & (x_1 - 9)^2 + (x_2 - 7)^2 + (x_3 - 7)^2 + (x_4 - 16)^2 - 7^2 \le 0, \\
& (z_1 - 280)^2 + (z_2 - 280)^2 + (z_3 - 280)^2 - 40^2 \le 0, \\
& z_4(z_4 - 200) \le 0\}
\end{aligned}$$

For the various modes we further have:

$$I_{1,p} = \{x \in \mathcal{X} | 5.5 - x_3 \leq 0, x_6(x_6 - Q_{max}) \leq 0, x_7(x_7 - Q_{max}) \leq 0\}$$
$$I_{2,p} = \{x \in \mathcal{X} | x_6(x_6 - 0.99Q_{max}) \leq 0, (x_7 - 0.01Q_{max})(x_7 - Q_{max}) \leq 0\}$$
$$I_{2_1,p} = \{x \in \mathcal{X} | x_6(x_6 - 0.99Q_{max}) \leq 0, x_7(x_7 - 0.01Q_{max}) \leq 0\}$$
$$I_{3,p} = \{x \in \mathcal{X} | 5.5 - x_2 \leq 0, x_6(x_6 - Q_{max}) \leq 0, x_7(x_7 - Q_{max}) \leq 0\}$$
$$I_{4,p} = \{x \in \mathcal{X} | (x_6 - 0.01Q_{max})(x_6 - Q_{max}) \leq 0, x_7(x_7 - 0.99Q_{max}) \leq 0\}$$
$$I_{4_1,p} = \{x \in \mathcal{X} | x_7(x_7 - 0.99Q_{max}) \leq 0, x_6(x_6 - 0.01Q_{max}) \leq 0\}$$

The invariant set for each mode is then $I_l = I_{com} \cap I_{l,p}$.

Switching between the various modes happens when the state in the particular mode finds itself in the guard set. The guard sets are shown in Figure 1, reproduced here for convenience:

$$\text{Guard}(1,2) = \{x \in \mathcal{X} | x_3 - 6 \leq 0\}$$
$$\text{Guard}(2,2_1) = \{x \in \mathcal{X} | x_7(x_7 - 0.05Q_{max}) \leq 0\}$$
$$\text{Guard}(2_1,3) = \{x \in \mathcal{X} | (x_6 - 0.95Q_{max})(x_6 - Q_{max}) \leq 0\}$$
$$\text{Guard}(3,4) = \{x \in \mathcal{X} | x_2 - 6 \leq 0\}$$
$$\text{Guard}(4,4_1) = \{x \in \mathcal{X} | x_6(x_6 - 0.05Q_{max}) \leq 0\}$$
$$\text{Guard}(4_1,1) = \{x \in \mathcal{X} | (x_7 - 0.95Q_{max})(x_7 - Q_{max}) \leq 0\}$$

4.1   Computational Considerations

The system consists of 6 modes with continuous dynamics in each mode of state dimension 12. The vector fields are already polynomial in their variables, which facilitates the use of the Sum of Squares decomposition for the analysis, and are of highest order 2. What is required therefore is to construct 6 functions B_l as required by Proposition 1 each of which satisfies 4 SOS conditions.

Here we describe the computational challenges that were faced when these barrier functions were constructed. The first issue that has to be dealt with is numerical conditioning of the problem itself. Indeed the state variables have equilibria that are orders of magnitude apart, which introduces an artificial numerical conditioning. This can be removed by rescaling all states so that they are of the same order of magnitude.

Secondly, the system with 12 states produces a semidefinite programme that is on the boundary of what can be solved using any current SDP solver [11]. The situation is even worse, because the two states that represent the derivative action z_5 and x_5 evolve on a different time scale than the rest of the system, owing to the parameter τ which has to be small so that the derivative action extends to high frequencies; this produces numerical stiffness in the resulting semidefinite programme on top of increasing the state dimension by 2. We had to proceed by removing these states from consideration and instead we considered the control law that determines the make-up flow streams of O_2 and CO_2 as a pure PI controller (setting the derivative term to zero).

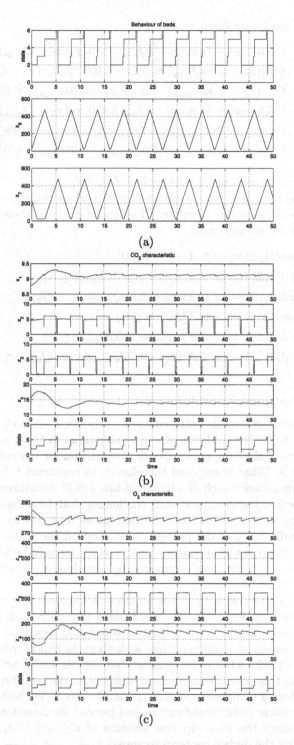

Fig. 2. Controlled VCCR System Simulation outputs

With these two modifications in place, we still had to choose the values $\sigma_{B'_l}(x)$ in Proposition 2, due to the fact that their value cannot be computed using SOS since that would result to a non-convex problem. We chose these values to be 0.5, values that were found to result in a feasible solution.

4.2 Simulation and Verification Results

Sample simulations of the system (with PI controllers) are presented in Figure 2. Figure 2(a) shows how the concentration of solid CO_2 changes as the beds switch from adsorb to desorb. Figure 2(b) shows how the concentrations of CO_2 in the main cabin and the two beds, as well as the mass flow rate of the make-up stream vary with time. Figure 2(c) shows the same behavior for O_2. The locations here represents the cycle from 1 to 6, as the modes are shown in Figure 1.

Given the initial, unsafe, invariant and guard sets and the considerations explained above a set of quadratic Barrier functions was constructed using SOS-TOOLS that proves the safe functionality of the system. Note that when B_l is quadratic all conditions but condition (3) are of order 2 if B is of order 2. Condition (3) is 4th order in this case. The certificates contain many terms, and are therefore not reproduced here. For example, B_1 is given by:

$$
\begin{aligned}
B_1 = &-9.1x_5 - 29.0x_6 - 2809.2z_1 - 6.3x_2 - 25.3x_3 - 133.0x_1 - 41.1z_2 - 41.0z_3 \\
&-12.8z_4 + 4248.3 + .41x_3z_2 + 0.1x_4z_2 - 0.1x_5z_2 + 0.1x_6z_2 + 10z_1z_2 \\
&-76x_4 + 0.2x_2z_4 - 0.2x_3z_4 - 2x_4z_4 - 0.1x_5z_4 - 0.1x_6z_4 + 5.6z_1z_4 - 0.4z_2z_4 \\
&+0.1z_3z_4 - 0.3x_1z_3 + 0.4x_2z_3 - 0.1x_3z_3 - 0.1x_4z_3 + 0.7x_5z_3 + 0.3x_6z_3 \\
&-27.9x_1z_1 + 2.8x_2z_1 + 7.5x_3z_1 - 10.8x_4z_1 - 1.1x_5z_1 + 4.9x_6z_1 - 1.1x_1z_2 \\
&-0.1x_2z_2 - 0.2x_1x_6 + 0.6x_3x_6 + 2.3x_4x_6 + 3.7x_5x_6 - 0.3x_2x_6 - 1.2x_3x_4 \\
&-1.6x_1x_5 + 0.4x_2x_5 - 0.4x_3x_5 + 1.5x_4x_5 - 3.8x_1x_2 - 2.3x_1x_3 + 5.6x_3^2 \\
&+19.2x_4^2 + 2.0x_5^2 + 2.6x_6^2 + 488.1z_1^2 + 2.6z_2^2 + 1.2z_3^2 + 3.6z_4^2 + 80.5x_1^2 + 3.3x_2^2 \\
&+3.6x_2x_3 + 47.7x_1x_4 - 2.4x_2x_4 + 13z_1z_3 + 0.1z_2z_3 - 3.9x_1z_4.
\end{aligned}
$$

The same verification was performed in the case of a degraded adsorption rate for the two beds; this was set to a 6.5% lower value than the nominal value. The control law provides safe functionality in this case too, which is verified by constructing a Barrier certificate.

5 Conclusion and Future Work

We demonstrated how the construction of a barrier certificate can verify the safe functionality of a controller applied to a safety-critical hybrid system. It should be appreciated that even though the controller and its switching rules are simple, there is no other efficient methodology for verifying the safety of such a system. On the other hand, construction of a barrier certificate for the controlled system proves that the system will never enter an unsafe operating condition. Such a conclusion would be impossible with any simulation procedure.

Though we have been able to provide a barrier certificate for our controlled system, the description complexity of the system was on the limits of what can be tackled with current semidefinite programming solvers. In such cases, the special structure of the resulting sum of squares program should be taken into account before solving it using semidefinite programming, as this will not only reduce the computational burden but also remove numerical ill-conditioning.

This work has given us the opportunity to demonstrate the applicability of rigorous analytical methods for verifying controllers for complex hybrid, non linear dynamical systems. The above methodology can be applied to verification problems in other applications.

Acknowledgements

This material is based on work supported by NASA Ames Research Center under Contract No. NAS2-01067. We wish to acknowledge our program monitor, Dr. Robert Morris at the NASA Ames Research Center, for his support, suggestions and encouragement throughout the course of this project. We also acknowledge the rest of our team, Ranjana Deshpande, Nitin Lamba, and Shankar Subramanian for their contribution to overall project on designing verifiable hybrid controllers.

References

1. Wong-Toi, H.: The synthesis of controllers for linear hybrid automata. In: Proceedings of Conference on Decision and Control. (1997)
2. Bemporad, A., Morari, M.: Control of systems integrating logic, dynamics, and constraints. Automatica **35** (1999) 407–427
3. Malin, J., Nieten, J., Schreckenghost, D., MacMahon, M., Graham, J., Thronesbery, C., Bonasso, R., Kowing, J.: Multi-agent diagnosis and control of an air revitalization system for life support in space. Proceedings of the IEEE Aerospace Conference (2000)
4. Subramanian, D., Ariyur, K., Lamba, N., Deshpande, R., Glavaski, S.: Control design for a hybrid dynamical system: A nasa life support system. In: Hybrid Systems: Computation and Control, LNCS 2293, Springer–Verlag (2004) 570–584
5. Prajna, S., Jadbabaie, A.: Safety verification of hybrid systems using barrier certificates. In: Hybrid Systems: Computation and Control, LNCS 2293, Springer–Verlag (2004) 477–492
6. Alur, R., Courcoubetis, C., Halbwachs, N., Henzinger, T.A., Ho, P.H., Nicolin, X., Oliviero, A., Sifakis, J., Yovine, S.: The algorithmic analysis of hybrid systems. Theoretical Computer Science **138** (1995) 3–34
7. Murty, K.G., Kabadi, S.N.: Some NP-complete problems in quadratic and nonlinear programming. Mathematical Programming **39** (1987) 117–129

8. Parrilo, P.A.:   Structured Semidefinite Programs and Semialgebraic Geometry Methods in Robustness and Optimization.   PhD thesis, California Institute of Technology, Pasadena, CA (2000) Available at http://www.control.ethz.ch/~parrilo/pubs/index.html.
9. Vandenberghe, L., Boyd, S.: Semidefinite programming. SIAM Review **38** (1996) 49–95
10. Prajna, S., Papachristodoulou, A., Parrilo, P.A.: SOSTOOLS – Sum of Squares Optimization Toolbox, User's Guide. Available at http://www.cds.caltech.edu/sostools and http://www.aut.ee.ethz.ch/parrilo/sostools (2002)
11. Sturm, J.F.: Using SeDuMi 1.02, a MATLAB toolbox for optimization over symmetric cones. Optimization Methods and Software **11–12** (1999) 625–653 Available at http://fewcal.kub.nl/sturm/software/sedumi.html.

Polynomial Stochastic Hybrid Systems

João Pedro Hespanha*

Center for Control Engineering and Computation,
University of California, Santa Barbara, CA 93101

Abstract. This paper deals with polynomial stochastic hybrid systems (pSHSs), which generally correspond to stochastic hybrid systems with polynomial continuous vector fields, reset maps, and transition intensities. For pSHSs, the dynamics of the statistical moments of the continuous states evolve according to infinite-dimensional linear ordinary differential equations (ODEs). We show that these ODEs can be approximated by finite-dimensional nonlinear ODEs with arbitrary precision. Based on this result, we provide a procedure to build this type of approximations for certain classes of pSHSs. We apply this procedure for several examples of pSHSs and evaluate the accuracy of the results obtained through comparisons with Monte Carlo simulations. These examples include: the modeling of TCP congestion control both for long-lived and on-off flows; state-estimation for networked control systems; and the stochastic modeling of chemical reactions.

1 Introduction

Hybrid systems are characterized by a state-space that can be partitioned into a continuous domain (typically $\mathbb{R}^n$) and a discrete set (typically finite). For the stochastic hybrid systems considered here, both the continuous and the discrete components of the state are stochastic processes. The evolution of the continuous-state is determined by a stochastic differential equation and the evolution of the discrete-state by a transition or reset map. The discrete transitions are triggered by stochastic events much like transitions between states of a continuous-time Markov chains. However, the rate at which these transitions occur may depend on the continuous-state. The model used here for SHSs, whose formal definition can be found in Sec. 2, was introduced in [1] and is heavily inspired by the Piecewise-Deterministic Markov Processes (PDPs) in [2]. Alternative models can be found in [3, 4, 5].

The extended generator of a stochastic hybrid system allows one to compute the time-derivative of a "test function" of the state of the SHS along solutions to the system, and can be viewed as a generalization of the Lie derivative for deterministic systems [1, 2]. Polynomial stochastic hybrid systems (pSHSs) are characterized by extended generators that map polynomial test functions into

* Supported by the National Science Foundation under grants CCR-0311084, ANI-0322476.

M. Morari and L. Thiele (Eds.): HSCC 2005, LNCS 3414, pp. 322–338, 2005.
© Springer-Verlag Berlin Heidelberg 2005

polynomials. This happens, e.g., when the continuous vector fields, the reset maps, and the transition intensities are all polynomial functions of the continuous state. An important property of pSHSs is that if one creates an infinite vector containing the probabilities of all discrete modes, as well as all the multi-variable statistical moments of the continuous state, the dynamics of this vector are governed by an infinite-dimensional linear ordinary differential equation (ODE), which we call the *infinite-dimensional moment dynamics* (cf. Sec. 3).

SHSs can model large classes of systems but their formal analysis presents significant challenges. Although it is straightforward to write partial differential equations (PDEs) that express the evolution of the probability distribution function for their states, generally these PDEs do not admit analytical solutions. The infinite-dimensional moment dynamics provides an alternative characterization for the distribution of the state of a pSHS. Although generally statistical moments do not provide a description of a stochastic process as accurate as the probability distribution, results such as Tchebycheff, Markoff, or Bienaymé inequalities can be used to infer properties of the distribution from its moments.

In general, the infinite-dimensional *linear* ODEs that describe the moment dynamics for pSHSs are still not easy to solve analytically. However, sometimes they can be accurately approximated by a finite-dimensional *nonlinear* ODE, which we call the *truncated moment dynamics*. We show in Sec. 3 that, under suitable stability assumptions, it is in principle possible for a finite-dimensional nonlinear ODE to approximate the infinite-dimensional moment dynamics, up to an error that can be made arbitrarily small. Aside from its theoretical interest, this result motivates a procedure to actually construct these finite-dimensional approximations for certain classes of pSHSs. This procedure, which is described in Sec. 4, is applicable to pSHS for which the (infinite) matrix that characterizes the moment dynamics exhibits a certain diagonal-band structure and appropriate decoupling between certain moments of distinct discrete modes. The details of this structure can be found in Lemma 1.

To illustrate the applicability of the results, we consider several systems that appeared in the literature and that can be modeled by pSHSs. For each example, we construct in Sec. 5 truncated moment dynamics and evaluate how they compare with estimates for the moments obtained from a large number of Monte Carlo simulations. The examples considered include:

1. The modeling of network traffic under TCP congestion control. We consider two distinct cases: long-lived traffic corresponding to the transfer of files with infinite length; and on-off traffic consisting of file transfers with exponentially distributed lengths, alternated by times of inactivity (also exponentially distributed). These examples are motivated by [1, 6].

2. The modeling of the state-estimation error in a networked control system that occasionally receives state measurements over a communication network. The rate at which the measurements are transmitted depends on the current estimation error. This type of scheme was shown to out-perform

periodic transmission and can actually be used to approximate an optimal transmission scheme [7, 8].

3. Gillespie's stochastic modeling for chemical reactions [9], which describes the evolution of the number of particles involved in a set of reactions. The reactions analyzed were taken from [10, 11] and are particularly difficult to simulate due to the existence of two very distinct time scales.

2   Polynomial Stochastic Hybrid Systems

A SHS is defined by a stochastic differential equation (SDE)

$$\dot{x} = f(\mathbf{q}, \mathbf{x}, t) + g(\mathbf{q}, \mathbf{x}, t)\dot{\mathbf{n}}, \qquad f : \mathcal{Q} \times \mathbb{R}^n \times [0, \infty) \to \mathbb{R}^n, \qquad (1)$$
$$g : \mathcal{Q} \times \mathbb{R}^n \times [0, \infty) \to \mathbb{R}^{n \times k},$$

a family of m *discrete transition/reset maps*

$$(\mathbf{q}, \mathbf{x}) = \phi_\ell(\mathbf{q}^-, \mathbf{x}^-, t), \qquad \phi_\ell : \mathcal{Q} \times \mathbb{R}^n \times [0, \infty) \to \mathcal{Q} \times \mathbb{R}^n, \qquad (2)$$

$\forall \ell \in \{1, \dots, m\}$, and a family of m *transition intensities*

$$\lambda_\ell(\mathbf{q}, \mathbf{x}, t), \qquad \lambda_\ell : \mathcal{Q} \times \mathbb{R}^n \times [0, \infty) \to [0, \infty), \qquad (3)$$

$\forall \ell \in \{1, \dots, m\}$, where $\mathbf{n}$ denotes a k-vector of independent Brownian motion processes and $\mathcal{Q}$ a (typically finite) discrete set. A SHS characterizes a jump process $\mathbf{q} : [0, \infty) \to \mathcal{Q}$ called the *discrete state*; a stochastic process $\mathbf{x} : [0, \infty) \to \mathbb{R}^n$ with piecewise continuous sample paths called the *continuous state*; and m stochastic counters $\mathbf{N}_\ell : [0, \infty) \to \mathbb{N}_{\geq 0}$ called the *transition counters*.

In essence, between transition counter increments the discrete state remains constant whereas the continuous state flows according to (1). At transition times, the continuous and discrete states are reset according to (2). Each transition counter $\mathbf{N}_\ell$ counts the number of times that the corresponding discrete transition/reset map ϕ_ℓ is "activated." The frequency at which this occurs is determined by the transition intensities (3). In particular, the probability that the counter $\mathbf{N}_\ell$ will increment in an "elementary interval" $(t, t + dt]$, and therefore that the corresponding transition takes place, is given by $\lambda_\ell(\mathbf{q}(t), \mathbf{x}(t), t)dt$. In practice, one can think of the intensity of a transition as the instantaneous rate at which that transition occurs. The reader is referred to [1] for a mathematically precise characterization of this SHS. The following result can be used to compute expectations on the state of a SHS. For briefness, we omit a few technical assumptions that are straightforward to verify for the SHSs considered here:

Theorem 1 ([1]). *Given a function* $\psi : \mathcal{Q} \times \mathbb{R}^n \times [0, \infty) \to \mathbb{R}$ *that is twice continuously differentiable with respect to its second argument and once continuously differentiable with respect to the third one, we have that*

$$\frac{\partial \, \mathrm{E}[\psi(\mathbf{q}(t), \mathbf{x}(t), t)]}{\partial t} = \mathrm{E}[(L\psi)(\mathbf{q}(t), \mathbf{x}(t), t)], \qquad (4)$$

where $\forall (q, x, t) \in \mathcal{Q} \times \mathbb{R}^n \times [0, \infty)$

$$(L\psi)(q,x,t) := \frac{\partial\psi(q,x,t)}{\partial x}f(q,x,t) + \frac{\partial\psi(q,x,t)}{\partial t} +$$

$$+ \frac{1}{2}\operatorname{trace}\left(\frac{\partial^2\psi(q,x)}{\partial x^2}g(q,x,t)g(q,x,t)'\right) +$$

$$+ \sum_{\ell=1}^{m}\left(\psi(\phi_\ell(q,x,t),t) - \psi(q,x,t)\right)\lambda_\ell(q,x,t), \quad (5)$$

and $\frac{\partial\psi(q,x,t)}{\partial t}$, $\frac{\partial\psi(q,x,t)}{\partial x}$, and $\frac{\partial^2\psi(q,x)}{\partial x^2}$ denote the partial derivative of $\psi(q,x,t)$ with respect to t, the gradient of $\psi(q,x,t)$ with respect to x, and the Hessian matrix of ψ with respect to x, respectively. The operator $\psi \mapsto L\psi$ defined by (5) is called the extended generator of the SHS.   □

We say that a SHS is *polynomial (pSHS)* if its extended generator L is closed on the set of finite-polynomials in x, i.e., $(L\psi)(q,x,t)$ is a finite-polynomial in x for every finite-polynomial $\psi(q,x,t)$ in x. By a *finite-polynomials in x* we mean a function $\psi(q,x,t)$ such that $x \mapsto \psi(q,x,t)$ is a (multi-variable) polynomial of finite degree for each fixed $q \in \mathcal{Q}$, $t \in [0,\infty)$. A pSHS is obtained, e.g., when the vector fields f and g, the reset maps ϕ_ℓ, and the transition intensities λ_ℓ are all finite-polynomials in x.

Examples of Polynomial Stochastic Hybrid Systems

Example 1 (TCP long-lived [12]). The congestion window size $\mathbf{w} \in [0,\infty)$ of a long-lived TCP flow can be generated by a SHS with continuous dynamics $\dot{\mathbf{w}} = \frac{1}{RTT}$ and a reset map $\mathbf{w} \mapsto \frac{\mathbf{w}}{2}$, with intensity $\lambda(\mathbf{w}) := \frac{p\,\mathbf{w}}{RTT}$. The round-trip-time RTT and the drop-rate p are parameters that we assume constant. This SHS has a single discrete mode that we omit for simplicity and its generator is given by

$$(L\psi)(w) = \frac{1}{RTT}\frac{\partial\psi(w)}{\partial w} + \frac{pw\bigl(\psi(w/2) - \psi(w)\bigr)}{RTT},$$

which is closed on the set of finite-polynomials in w.   □

Example 2 (TCP on-off [12]). The congestion window size $\mathbf{w} \in [0,\infty)$ for a stream of TCP flows separated by inactivity periods can be generated by a SHS with three discrete modes $\mathcal{Q} := \{\text{ss}, \text{ca}, \text{off}\}$, one corresponding to slow-start, another to congestion avoidance, and the final one to flow inactivity. Its continuous dynamics are defined by

$$\dot{\mathbf{w}} = \begin{cases} \frac{(\log 2)\mathbf{w}}{RTT} & \mathbf{q} = \text{ss} \\ \frac{1}{RTT} & \mathbf{q} = \text{ca} \\ 0 & \mathbf{q} = \text{off}; \end{cases}$$

the reset maps associated with packet drops, end of flows, and start of flows are given by $\phi_1(\mathbf{q},\mathbf{w}) := \bigl(\text{ca}, \frac{\mathbf{w}}{2}\bigr)$, $\phi_2(\mathbf{q},\mathbf{w}) := (\text{off}, 0)$, and $\phi_3(\mathbf{q},\mathbf{w}) := (\text{ss}, w_0)$, respectively; and the corresponding intensities are

$$\lambda_1(\mathbf{q},\mathbf{w}) := \begin{cases} \frac{p\,w}{RTT} & \mathbf{q} \in \{\mathrm{ss},\mathrm{ca}\} \\ 0 & \mathbf{q} = \mathrm{off} \end{cases} \qquad \lambda_2(\mathbf{q},\mathbf{w}) := \begin{cases} \frac{w}{kRTT} & \mathbf{q} \in \{\mathrm{ss},\mathrm{ca}\} \\ 0 & \mathbf{q} = \mathrm{off} \end{cases}$$

$$\lambda_3(\mathbf{q},\mathbf{w}) := \begin{cases} \frac{1}{\tau_{\mathrm{off}}} & \mathbf{q} = \mathrm{off} \\ 0 & \mathbf{q} \in \{\mathrm{ss},\mathrm{ca}\}. \end{cases}$$

The round-trip-time RTT, the drop-rate p, the average file size k (exponentially distributed), the average off-time τ_{off} (also exponentially distributed), and the initial window size w_0 are parameters that we assume constant. The generator for this SHS is given by

$$(L\psi)(q,w) = \begin{cases} \frac{(\log 2)w}{RTT}\frac{\partial\psi(\mathrm{ss},w)}{\partial w} + \frac{pw\big(\psi(\mathrm{ca},w/2)-\psi(\mathrm{ss},w)\big)}{RTT} + \frac{w\big(\psi(\mathrm{off},0)-\psi(\mathrm{ss},w)\big)}{k\,RTT} & q = \mathrm{ss} \\ \frac{1}{RTT}\frac{\partial\psi(\mathrm{ca},w)}{\partial w} + \frac{pw\big(\psi(\mathrm{ca},w/2)-\psi(\mathrm{ca},w)\big)}{RTT} + \frac{w\big(\psi(\mathrm{off},0)-\psi(\mathrm{ca},w)\big)}{k\,RTT} & q = \mathrm{ca} \\ \frac{\psi(\mathrm{ss},w_0)-\psi(\mathrm{off},w)}{\tau_{\mathrm{off}}} & q = \mathrm{off}, \end{cases}$$

which is closed on the set of finite-polynomials in w.   □

Example 3 (Networked control system [7]). Suppose that the state of a stochastic scalar linear system $\dot{\mathbf{x}} = a\mathbf{x} + b\dot{\mathbf{n}}$ is estimated based on state-measurements received through a network. For simplicity we assume that state measurements are noiseless and delay free. The corresponding state estimation error $\mathbf{e} \in \mathbb{R}$ can be generated by a SHS with continuous dynamics $\dot{\mathbf{e}} = a\mathbf{e} + b\dot{\mathbf{n}}$ and one reset map $\mathbf{e} \mapsto 0$ that is activated whenever a state measurement is received. It was conjectured in [7] and later shown in [8] that transmitting measurements at a rate that depends on the state-estimation error is optimal when one wants to minimize the variance of the estimation error, while penalizing the average rate at which messages are transmitted. This motivates considering the following reset intensity $\lambda(\mathbf{e}) := \mathbf{e}^{2\rho}$, $\rho \in \mathbb{N}_{\geq 0}$. This SHS has a single discrete mode that we omitted for simplicity and its generator is given by

$$(L\psi)(e) := a\,e\frac{\partial\psi(e)}{\partial e} + \frac{b^2}{2}\frac{\partial^2\psi(e)}{\partial e^2} + (\psi(0)-\psi(e))e^{2\rho},$$

which is closed on the set of finite-polynomials in e.   □

Example 4 (Decaying-dimerizing reaction set [10, 11]). The number of particles $\mathbf{x} := (\mathbf{x}_1,\mathbf{x}_2,\mathbf{x}_3)$ of three species involved in the following set of decaying-dimerizing reactions

$$S_1 \xrightarrow{c_1} 0, \qquad 2S_1 \xrightarrow{c_2} S_2, \qquad S_2 \xrightarrow{c_3} 2S_1, \qquad S_2 \xrightarrow{c_4} S_3 \qquad (6)$$

can be generated by a SHS with continuous dynamics $\dot{\mathbf{x}} = 0$ and four reset maps

$$\phi_1(\mathbf{x}) := \begin{bmatrix} \mathbf{x}_1-1 \\ \mathbf{x}_2 \\ \mathbf{x}_3 \end{bmatrix} \quad \phi_2(\mathbf{x}) := \begin{bmatrix} \mathbf{x}_1-2 \\ \mathbf{x}_2+1 \\ \mathbf{x}_3 \end{bmatrix} \quad \phi_3(\mathbf{x}) := \begin{bmatrix} \mathbf{x}_1+2 \\ \mathbf{x}_2-1 \\ \mathbf{x}_3 \end{bmatrix} \quad \phi_4(\mathbf{x}) := \begin{bmatrix} \mathbf{x}_1 \\ \mathbf{x}_2-1 \\ \mathbf{x}_3+1 \end{bmatrix}$$

with intensities $\lambda_1(\mathbf{x}) := c_1\mathbf{x}_1$, $\lambda_2(\mathbf{x}) := \frac{c_2}{2}\mathbf{x}_1(\mathbf{x}_1-1)$, $\lambda_3(\mathbf{x}) := c_3\mathbf{x}_2$, and $\lambda_4(\mathbf{x}) := c_4\mathbf{x}_2$, respectively. Since the numbers of particles take values in the discrete set of integers, we can regard the $\mathbf{x}_i$ as either part of the discrete or continuous state. We choose to regard them as continuous variables because we are interested in studying their statistical moments. In this case, the SHS has a single discrete mode that we omit for simplicity and its generator is given by

$$(L\psi)(x) = c_1 x_1 \big(\psi(x_1 - 1, x_2, x_3) - \psi(x)\big) + \frac{c_2}{2} x_1 (x_1 - 1)\big(\psi(x_1 - 2, x_2 + 1, x_3) - \psi(x)\big)$$
$$+ c_3 x_2 \big(\psi(x_1 + 2, x_2 - 1, x_3) - \psi(x)\big) + c_4 x_2 \big(\psi(x_1, x_2 - 1, x_3 + 1) - \psi(x)\big),$$

which is closed on the set of finite-polynomials in x. $\square$

3   Moment Dynamics

To fully characterize the dynamics of a SHS one would like to determine the evolution of the probability distribution for its state $(\mathbf{q}, \mathbf{x})$. In general, this is difficult so a more reasonable goal is to determine the evolution of (i) the probability of $\mathbf{q}(t)$ being on each mode and (ii) the moments of $\mathbf{x}(t)$ conditioned to $\mathbf{q}(t)$. In fact, often one can even get away with only determining a few low-order moments and then using results such as Tchebycheff, Markoff, or Bienaymé inequalities to infer properties of the overall distribution.

Given a discrete state $\bar{q} \in \mathcal{Q}$ and a vector of n integers $m = (m_1, m_2, \ldots, m_n)$ $\in \mathbb{N}_{\geq 0}^n$, we define the *test-function associated with $\bar{q}$ and m* to be

$$\psi_{\bar{q}}^{(m)}(q, x) := \begin{cases} x^{(m)} & q = \bar{q} \\ 0 & q \neq \bar{q}, \end{cases} \qquad \forall q \in \mathcal{Q}, x \in \mathbb{R}^n$$

and the *(uncentered) moment associated with $\bar{q}$ and m* to be

$$\mu_{\bar{q}}^{(m)}(t) := \mathrm{E}\left[\psi_{\bar{q}}^{(m)}\big(\mathbf{q}(t), \mathbf{x}(t)\big)\right] \qquad \forall t \geq 0. \tag{7}$$

Here and in the sequel, given a vector $x = (x_1, x_2, \ldots, x_n)$, we use $x^{(m)}$ to denote the monomial $x_1^{m_1} x_2^{m_2} \cdots x_n^{m_n}$.

PSHSs have the property that if one stacks all moments in an infinite vector μ_∞, its dynamics can be written as

$$\dot{\mu}_\infty = A_\infty(t)\mu_\infty \qquad \forall t \geq 0, \tag{8}$$

for some appropriately defined infinite matrix $A_\infty(t)$. This is because $\forall \bar{q} \in \mathcal{Q}, m = (m_1, \ldots, m_n) \in \mathbb{N}_{\geq 0}^n$, the expression $(L\psi_{\bar{q}}^{(m)})(q, x, t)$ is a finite-polynomial in x and therefore can be written as a finite linear combination of test-functions (possibly with time-varying coefficients). Taking expectations on this linear combination and using (4), (7), we conclude that $\dot{\mu}_{\bar{q}}^{(m)}$ can be written as linear combination of uncentered moments in μ_∞, leading to (8). In the sequel, we refer to (8) as the *infinite-dimensional moment dynamics*. Analyzing (and even simulating) (8) is generally difficult. However, as mentioned above one can often get away with just computing a few low-order moments. One would therefore like to determine a finite-dimensional system of ODEs that describes the evolution of a few low-order models, perhaps only approximately.

When the matrix A_∞ is lower triangular (e.g., as in Example 3 with $\rho = 0$), one can simply truncate the vector μ_∞ by dropping all but its first k elements and obtain a finite-dimensional system that exactly describes the evolution of the moments. However, in general A_∞ has nonzero elements above the main diagonal and therefore if one defines $\mu \in \mathbb{R}^k$ to contain the top k elements of μ_∞, one obtains from (8) that

$$\dot{\mu} = I_{k\times\infty} A_\infty(t)\mu_\infty = A(t)\mu + B(t)\bar{\mu}, \qquad \bar{\mu} = C\mu_\infty, \tag{9}$$

where $I_{k\times\infty}$ denotes a matrix composed of the first k rows of the infinite identity matrix, $\bar{\mu} \in \mathbb{R}^r$ contains all the moments that appear in the first k elements of $A_\infty(t)\mu_\infty$ but that do not appear in μ, and C is the projection matrix that extracts $\bar{\mu}$ from μ_∞. Our goal is to approximate the infinite dimensional system (8) by a finite-dimensional nonlinear ODE of the form

$$\dot{\nu} = A(t)\nu + B(t)\bar{\nu}(t), \qquad \bar{\nu} = \varphi(\nu, t), \tag{10}$$

where the map $\varphi : \mathbb{R}^k \times [0, \infty) \to \mathbb{R}^r$ should be chosen so as to keep $\nu(t)$ close to $\mu(t)$. We call (10) the *truncated moment dynamics* and φ the *truncation function*. We need the following two stability assumptions to establish sufficient conditions for the approximation to be valid.

Assumption 1 (Boundedness). *There exist sets Ω_μ and Ω_ν such that all solutions to (8) and (10) starting at some time $t_0 \geq 0$ in Ω_μ and Ω_ν, respectively, exist and are smooth on $[t_0, \infty)$ with all derivatives of their first k elements uniformly bounded. The set Ω_ν is assumed to be forward invariant.* ☐

Assumption 2 (Incremental Stability). *There exists a function[1] $\beta \in \mathcal{KL}$ such that, for every solution μ_∞ to (8) starting in Ω_μ at some time $t_0 \geq 0$, and every $t_1 \geq t_0$, $\nu_1 \in \Omega_\nu$ there exists some $\hat{\mu}_\infty(t_1) \in \Omega_\mu$ whose first k elements match ν_1 and*

$$\|\mu(t) - \hat{\mu}(t)\| \leq \beta(\|\mu(t_1) - \hat{\mu}(t_1)\|, t - t_1), \qquad \forall t \geq t_1, \tag{11}$$

where $\mu(t)$ and $\hat{\mu}(t)$ denote the first k elements of the solutions to (8) starting at $\mu_\infty(t_1)$ and $\hat{\mu}_\infty(t_1)$, respectively. ☐

Remark 1. Assumption 2 was purposely formulated without requiring Ω_μ to be a subset of a normed space to avoid having to choose a norm under which the (infinite) vectors of moments are bounded. ☐

The result that follows establishes that the difference between solutions to (8) and (10) converges to an arbitrarily small ball, provided that a sufficiently large but *finite* number of derivatives of these signals match point-wise. To state this

---

[1] A function $\beta : [0, \infty) \times [0, \infty) \to [0, \infty)$ is of *class $\mathcal{KL}$* if $\beta(0, t) = 0$, $\forall t \geq 0$; $\beta(s, t)$ is continuous and strictly increasing on s, $\forall t \geq 0$; and $\lim_{t\to\infty} \beta(s, t) = 0$, $\forall s \geq 0$.

result, the following notation is needed: We define the matrices $C^i(t)$, $i \in \mathbb{N}_{\geq 0}$ recursively by

$$C^0(t) = C, \qquad C^{i+1}(t) = C^i(t)A_\infty(t) + \dot{C}^i(t), \qquad \forall t \geq 0, \ i \in \mathbb{N}_{\geq 0},$$

and the family of functions $L^i\varphi : \mathbb{R}^k \times [0, \infty) \to \mathbb{R}^r$, $i \in \mathbb{N}_{\geq 0}$ recursively by

$$(L^0\varphi)(\nu, t) = \varphi(\nu, t), \ (L^{i+1}\varphi)(\nu, t) = \frac{\partial(L^i\varphi)(\nu, t)}{\partial \nu}(A(t)\nu + B(t)\varphi(\nu, t)) + \frac{\partial(L^i\varphi)(\nu, t)}{\partial t},$$

$\forall t \geq 0$, $\nu \in \mathbb{R}^k$, $i \in \mathbb{N}_{\geq 0}$. These definitions allow us to compute time derivatives of $\bar{\mu}(\tau)$ and $\bar{\nu}(\tau)$ along solutions to (8) and (10), respectively, because

$$\frac{\mathrm{d}^i \bar{\mu}(t)}{\mathrm{d}t^i} = C^i(t)\mu_\infty(t), \qquad \frac{\mathrm{d}^i \bar{\nu}(t)}{\mathrm{d}t^i} = (L^i\varphi)(\nu(t), t), \qquad \forall t \geq 0, \ i \in \mathbb{N}_{\geq 0}. \qquad (12)$$

Theorem 2 ([13]). *For every $\delta > 0$, there exists an integer N sufficiently large for which the following result holds: Assuming that for every $\tau \geq 0$, $\mu_\infty \in \Omega_\mu$*

$$C^i(\tau)\mu_\infty = (L^i\varphi)(\mu, \tau), \qquad \forall i \in \{0, 1, \dots, N\}, \qquad (13)$$

where μ denotes the first k elements of μ_∞, then

$$\|\mu(t) - \nu(t)\| \leq \beta(\|\mu(t_0) - \nu(t_0)\|, t - t_0) + \delta, \qquad \forall t \geq t_0 \geq 0, \qquad (14)$$

along all solutions to (8) and (10) with initial conditions $\mu_\infty(t_0) \in \Omega_\mu$ and $\nu(t_0) \in \Omega_\nu$, respectively, where $\mu(t)$ denotes the first k elements of $\mu_\infty(t)$. $\qquad \square$

4 Construction of Approximate Truncations

Given a constant $\delta > 0$ and sets Ω_μ, Ω_ν, it may be very difficult to determine the integer N for which the approximation bound (14) holds. This is because, although the proof of Theorem 2 is constructive, the computation of N requires explicit knowledge of the function $\beta \in \mathcal{KL}$ in Assumption 2 and, at least for most of the examples considered here, this assumption is difficult to verify. Nevertheless, Theorem 2 is still useful because it provides the explicit conditions (13) that the truncation function φ should satisfy for the solution to the truncated system to approximate the one of the original system. For the problems considered here we require (13) to hold for $N = 1$, for which (13) simply becomes

$$C\mu_\infty = \varphi(\mu, \tau), \quad CA_\infty(\tau)\mu_\infty = \frac{\partial\varphi(\mu, \tau)}{\partial \mu}I_{k \times \infty}A_\infty(\tau)\mu_\infty + \frac{\partial\varphi(\mu, \tau)}{\partial t}, \qquad (15)$$

$\forall \mu_\infty \in \Omega_\mu$, $\tau \geq 0$. Lacking knowledge of β, we will not be able to explicitly compute for which values of δ (14) will hold, but we will show by simulation that the truncation obtained provides a very accurate approximation to the infinite-dimensional system (8), even for such a small choice of N. We restrict our attention to functions φ and sets Ω_μ for which it is simple to use (15) to explicitly compute truncated systems.

Separable truncation functions: For all the examples considered, we consider functions φ of the form

$$\varphi(\nu, t) = \Lambda \nu^{(\Gamma)} := \Lambda \begin{bmatrix} \nu_1^{\gamma_{11}} \nu_2^{\gamma_{12}} \dots \nu_k^{\gamma_{1k}} \\ \vdots \\ \nu_1^{\gamma_{r1}} \nu_2^{\gamma_{r2}} \dots \nu_k^{\gamma_{rk}} \end{bmatrix}, \tag{16}$$

for appropriately chosen constant matrices $\Gamma := [\gamma_{ij}] \in \mathbb{R}^{r \times k}$ and $\Lambda \in \mathbb{R}^{r \times r}$, with Λ diagonal. In this case, (15) becomes

$$C\mu_\infty = \Lambda \mu^{(\Gamma)}, \tag{17a}$$

$$C A_\infty(\tau)\mu_\infty = \Lambda \operatorname{diag}[C\mu_\infty] \Gamma \operatorname{diag}[\mu_1^{-1}, \mu_2^{-1}, \dots, \mu_k^{-1}] I_{k \times \infty} A_\infty(\tau)\mu_\infty. \tag{17b}$$

Deterministic distributions: A set Ω_μ that is particularly tractable corresponds to deterministic distributions $\mathcal{F}_{\text{det}} := \{P(\cdot\,; q, x) : x \in \Omega_x, q \in \mathcal{Q}\}$, where $P(\cdot\,; q, x)$ denotes the distribution of $(\mathbf{q}, \mathbf{x})$ for which $\mathbf{q} = q$ and $\mathbf{x} = x$ with probability one; and Ω_x a subset of the continuous state space $\mathbb{R}^n$. For a particular distribution $P(\cdot\,; q, x)$, the (uncentered) moment associated with $\bar{q}$ and $m \in \mathbb{N}_{\geq 0}^n$ is given by

$$\mu_{\bar{q}}^{(m)} := \int \psi_{\bar{q}}^{(m)}(\tilde{q}, \tilde{x}) P(d\tilde{q}\,d\tilde{x}; q, x) := \psi_{\bar{q}}^{(m)}(q, x) := \begin{cases} x^{(m)} & q = \bar{q} \\ 0 & q \neq \bar{q}, \end{cases}$$

and therefore the vectors μ_∞ in Ω_μ have this form. Although this family of distributions may seem very restrictive, it will provide us with truncations that are accurate even when the pSHSs evolve towards very "nondeterministic" distributions, i.e., with significant variance. For this set Ω_μ, (17) takes a particularly simple form and the following result provides a simple set of conditions to test if a truncation is possible.

Lemma 1 ([13]). *Let Ω_μ be the set of deterministic distributions $\mathcal{F}_{\text{det}}$ with Ω_x containing some open ball in $\mathbb{R}^n$ and consider truncation functions φ of the form (16). The following conditions are necessary for the existence of a function φ of the form (16) that satisfies (15):*

1. *For every moment $\mu_{q_\ell}^{(m_\ell)}$ in $\bar{\mu}$ the polynomial[2] $\sum_{\substack{i=1 \\ q_i = q_\ell}}^{\infty} a_{\ell,i} x^{(m_i)}$ must belong to the linear subspace generated by the polynomials*

$$\left\{ \sum_{\substack{i=1 \\ q_i = q_\ell}}^{\infty} a_{j,i} x^{(m_\ell - m_j + m_i)} : 1 \leq j \leq k, \ q_j = q_\ell \right\}.$$

2. *For every moment $\mu_{q_\ell}^{(m_\ell)}$ in $\bar{\mu}$ and every moment $\mu_{q_i}^{(m_i)}$ in μ_∞ with $q_i \neq q_\ell$, we must have $a_{\ell,i} = 0$. Here we are denoting by $a_{j,i}$ the jth row, ith column entry of A_∞.* □

---

[2] We are considering polynomials with integer (both positive and negative) powers.

Condition 1 imposes a diagonal-band-like structure on the submatrices of A_∞ consisting of the rows/columns that correspond to each moment that appears in $\bar{\mu}$. This condition holds for Examples 1, 2, and 3, but not for Example 4. However, we will see that the moment dynamics of this example can be simplified so as to satisfy this condition without introducing a significant error. Condition 2 imposes a form of decoupling between different modes in the equations for $\dot{\bar{\mu}}$. This condition holds trivially for all examples that have a single discrete mode. It does not hold for Example 2, but also here it is possible to simplify the moment dynamics to satisfy this condition without introducing a significant error.

5   Examples of Truncations

We now present truncated systems for the several examples considered before and discuss how the truncated models compare to estimates of the moments obtained from Monte Carlo simulations. All Monte Carlo simulations were carried out using the algorithm described in [1]. Estimates of the moments were obtained by averaging a large number of Monte Carlo simulations. In most plots, we used a sufficiently large number of simulations so that the 99% confidence intervals for the mean cannot be distinguished from the point estimates at the resolution used for the plots. Ir is worth to emphasize that the results obtained through Monte Carlo simulations required computational efforts orders of magnitude higher than those obtained using the truncated systems.

Example 1 (TCP long-lived). Since for this system it is particularly meaningful to consider moments of the packet sending rate $\mathbf{r} := \frac{\mathbf{w}}{RTT}$, we choose $\psi^{(m)}(w) = \frac{w^m}{RTT^m}$, $\forall m \in \mathbb{N}_{\geq 0}$. We consider a truncation whose state contains the first and second moments of the sending rate. In this case, (9) can be written as follows:

$$\begin{bmatrix} \dot{\mu}^{(1)} \\ \dot{\mu}^{(2)} \end{bmatrix} = \begin{bmatrix} 0 & -\frac{p}{2} \\ \frac{2}{RTT^2} & 0 \end{bmatrix} \begin{bmatrix} \mu^{(1)} \\ \mu^{(2)} \end{bmatrix} + \begin{bmatrix} \frac{1}{RTT^2} \\ 0 \end{bmatrix} + \begin{bmatrix} 0 \\ -\frac{3p}{4} \end{bmatrix} \bar{\mu}, \qquad (18)$$

where $\mu := \mu^{(3)}$ evolves according to $\dot{\mu}^{(3)} = \frac{3\mu^{(2)}}{RTT^2} - \frac{7p\mu^{(4)}}{8}$. In this case, (17) has a unique solution φ, resulting in a truncated system given by (18) and

$$\bar{\mu} = \varphi(\mu^{(1)}, \mu^{(2)}) := \frac{(\mu^{(2)})^{\frac{5}{2}}}{(\mu^{(1)})^2}. \qquad (19)$$

Figure 1 shows a comparison between Monte Carlo simulations and this truncated model. A step in the drop probability was introduced at time $t = 5$sec to show that the truncated model also captures well transient behavior.   □

Example 2 (TCP on-off). For this system we also consider moments of the sending rate $\mathbf{r} := \frac{\mathbf{w}}{RTT}$ on the ss and ca modes, and therefore we use

$$\psi_{\text{off}}^{(0)}(q, w) = \begin{cases} 1 & q = \text{off} \\ 0 & q \in \{\text{ca}, \text{ss}\} \end{cases} \qquad \psi_{\text{ss}}^{(m)}(q, w) = \begin{cases} \frac{w^m}{RTT^m} & q = \text{ss} \\ 0 & q \in \{\text{ca}, \text{off}\} \end{cases}$$

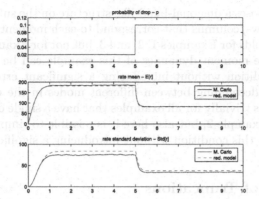

Fig. 1. Comparison between Monte Carlo simulations and the truncated model (18), (19) for Example 1, with $RTT = 50$ms and a step in the drop-rate p from 2% to 10%

$$\psi_{ca}^{(m)}(q,w) = \begin{cases} \frac{w^m}{RTT^m} & q = ca \\ 0 & q \in \{ss, off\} \end{cases}$$

We consider a truncation whose state contains the zeroth, first, and second moments of the sending rate. In this case, (9) can be written as follows:

$$
\begin{bmatrix} \dot{\mu}_{off}^{(0)} \\ \dot{\mu}_{ss}^{(0)} \\ \dot{\mu}_{ca}^{(0)} \\ \dot{\mu}_{ss}^{(1)} \\ \dot{\mu}_{ca}^{(1)} \\ \dot{\mu}_{ss}^{(2)} \\ \dot{\mu}_{ca}^{(2)} \end{bmatrix} =
\begin{bmatrix}
-\tau_{off}^{-1} & 0 & 0 & \frac{1}{k} & \frac{1}{k} & 0 & 0 \\
\tau_{off}^{-1} & 0 & 0 & -\frac{1}{k}-p & 0 & 0 & 0 \\
0 & 0 & 0 & p & -\frac{1}{k} & 0 & 0 \\
\frac{\tau_{off}^{-1}w_0}{RTT} & 0 & 0 & \frac{\log 2}{RTT} & 0 & -\frac{1}{k}-p & 0 \\
0 & 0 & \frac{1}{RTT^2} & 0 & 0 & \frac{p}{2} & -\frac{1}{k}-\frac{p}{2} \\
\frac{\tau_{off}^{-1}w_0^2}{RTT^2} & 0 & 0 & 0 & \frac{\log 4}{RTT} & 0 & 0 \\
0 & 0 & 0 & 0 & \frac{2}{RTT^2} & 0 & 0
\end{bmatrix}
\begin{bmatrix} \mu_{off}^{(0)} \\ \mu_{ss}^{(0)} \\ \mu_{ca}^{(0)} \\ \mu_{ss}^{(1)} \\ \mu_{ca}^{(1)} \\ \mu_{ss}^{(2)} \\ \mu_{ca}^{(2)} \end{bmatrix} +
\begin{bmatrix} 0 & 0 \\ 0 & 0 \\ 0 & 0 \\ 0 & 0 \\ -\frac{1}{k}-p & 0 \\ \frac{p}{4} & -\frac{1}{k}-\frac{3p}{4} \end{bmatrix} \bar{\mu},
$$

(20)

where $\bar{\mu} := [\,\mu_{ss}^{(3)}\ \mu_{ca}^{(3)}\,]'$ evolves according to

$$\dot{\mu}_{ss}^{(3)} = \frac{\tau_{off}^{-1}w_0^3}{RTT^3}\mu_{off}^{(0)} + \frac{\log 8}{RTT}\mu_{ss}^{(3)} - (\frac{1}{k}+p)\mu_{ss}^{(4)},$$ (21a)

$$\dot{\mu}_{ca}^{(3)} = \frac{3}{RTT^2}\mu_{ca}^{(2)} + \frac{p}{8}\mu_{ss}^{(4)} - (\frac{1}{k}+\frac{7p}{8})\mu_{ca}^{(4)}.$$ (21b)

However, (21) does not satisfy condition 2 in Lemma 1 because the different discrete modes do not appear decoupled: $\dot{\mu}_{ss}^{(3)}$ depends on $\mu_{off}^{(0)}$, and $\dot{\mu}_{ca}^{(3)}$ depends on $\mu_{ss}^{(4)}$. For the purpose of determining φ, we ignore the cross coupling terms and approximate (21) by

$$\dot{\mu}_{ss}^{(3)} \approx \frac{\log 8}{RTT}\mu_{ss}^{(3)} - (\frac{1}{k}+p)\mu_{ss}^{(4)}, \qquad \dot{\mu}_{ca}^{(3)} \approx \frac{3}{RTT^2}\mu_{ca}^{(2)} - (\frac{1}{k}+\frac{7p}{8})\mu_{ca}^{(4)}.$$ (22)

The validity of these approximations generally depends on the network parameters. When (22) is used, it is straightforward to verify that (17) has a unique solution φ, resulting in a truncated system given by (20) and

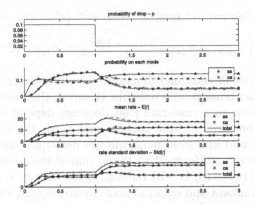

Fig. 2. Comparison between Monte Carlo simulations (solid lines) and the truncated model (20), (23) (dashed lines) for Example 2, with $RTT = 50$ms, $\tau_{\text{off}} = 1$sec, $k = 20.39$ packets (corresponding to 30.58KB files broken into 1500bytes packets, which is consistent with the file-size distribution of the UNIX file system reported in [14]), and a step in the drop-rate p from 10% to 2% at $t = 1$sec

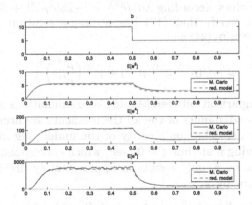

Fig. 3. Comparison between Monte Carlo simulations (solid lines) and the truncated model (24), (25) (dashed lines) for Example 3, with $a = 1$, $q = 1$, and a step in the parameter b from 10 to 2 at time $t = 0.5$sec

$$\bar{\mu} = \varphi(\mu) = \left[\frac{\mu_{\text{ss}}^{(0)} (\mu_{\text{ss}}^{(2)})^3}{(\mu_{\text{ss}}^{(1)})^3} \quad \frac{(\mu_{\text{ca}}^{(0)})^{\frac{1}{2}} (\mu_{\text{ca}}^{(2)})^{\frac{5}{2}}}{(\mu_{\text{ca}}^{(1)})^2} \right]'. \tag{23}$$

Figure 2 shows a comparison between Monte Carlo simulations and the truncated model (20), (23). The dynamics of the first and second order moments are accurately predicted by the truncated model. In preparing this paper, several simulation were executed for different network parameters and initial conditions. Figure 2 shows typical best-case (before $t = 1$) and worst-case (after $t = 1$) results. □

Example 3 (Networked control system). Now $\psi^{(m)}(e) = e^m$, $m \in \mathbb{N}_{\geq 0}$ and

$$(L\psi^{(m)})(e) = a\,m\,\psi^{(m)}(e) + \frac{m(m-1)b^2}{2}\psi^{(m-2)}(e) - \psi^{(m+2\rho)}(e).$$

For $\rho = 0$, the infinite-dimensional dynamics have a lower-triangular structure and therefore an exact truncation is possible. However, this case is less interesting because it corresponds to a reset-rate that does not depend on the continuous state and is therefore farther from the optimal [7, 8]. We consider here $\rho = 1$. In this case, the odd and even moments are decoupled and can be studied independently. It is straightforward to check that if the initial distribution of **e** is symmetric around zero, it will remain so for all times and therefore all odd moments are constant and equal to zero. Regarding the even moments, the smallest truncation for which condition 1 in Lemma 1 holds is a third order one, for which (9) can be written as follows:

$$\begin{bmatrix} \dot{\mu}^{(2)} \\ \dot{\mu}^{(4)} \\ \dot{\mu}^{(6)} \end{bmatrix} = \begin{bmatrix} 2a & -1 & 0 \\ 6b^2 & 4a & -1 \\ 0 & 15b^2 & 6a \end{bmatrix} \begin{bmatrix} \mu^{(2)} \\ \mu^{(4)} \\ \mu^{(6)} \end{bmatrix} + \begin{bmatrix} b^2 \\ 0 \\ 0 \end{bmatrix} + \begin{bmatrix} 0 \\ 0 \\ -1 \end{bmatrix} \bar{\mu}, \tag{24}$$

where $\bar{\mu} := \mu^{(8)}$ evolves according to $\dot{\mu}^{(8)} = -28b^2\mu^{(6)} + 8a\mu^{(8)} - \mu^{(10)}$. It is straightforward to verify that (17) has a unique solution φ, resulting in a truncated system given by (24) and

$$\bar{\mu} = \varphi(\mu^{(2)}, \mu^{(4)}, \mu^{(6)}) = \mu^{(2)}\left(\frac{\mu^{(6)}}{\mu^{(4)}}\right)^3. \tag{25}$$

Figure 3 shows a comparison between Monte Carlo simulations and the truncated model (24), (25). The dynamics of the all the moments are accurately predicted by the truncated model. The nonlinearity of the underlying model is apparent by the fact that halving b at time $t = 0.5$sec, which corresponds to dividing the variance of the noise by 4, only results in approximately dividing the variance of the estimation error by 2.   □

Example 4 (Decaying-dimerizing reaction set). For this system the test functions are of the form $\psi^{(m_1,m_2,m_2)}(x) = x_1^{m_1} x_2^{m_2} x_3^{m_3}$, $\forall m_1, m_2, m_3 \in \mathbb{N}_{\geq 0}$ and

$$(L\psi^{(m_1,m_2,m_2)})(x) = c_1 \sum_{i=0}^{m_1-1} \binom{m_1}{i}(-1)^{m_1-i}\psi^{(i+1,m_2,m_3)}(x)$$

$$+ \frac{c_2}{2} \sum_{\substack{i,j=0 \\ (i,j)\neq(m_1,m_2)}}^{m_1,m_2} \binom{m_1}{i}\binom{m_2}{j}(-2)^{m_1-i}\left(\psi^{(i+2,j,m_3)}(x) - \psi^{(i+1,j,m_3)}(x)\right)$$

$$+ c_3 \sum_{\substack{i,j=0 \\ (i,j)\neq(m_1,m_2)}}^{m_1,m_2} \binom{m_1}{i}\binom{m_2}{j}2^{m_1-i}(-1)^{m_2-j}\psi^{(i,j+1,m_3)}(x)$$

$$+ c_4 \sum_{\substack{i,j=0 \\ (i,j)\neq(m_2,m_3)}}^{m_2,m_3} \binom{m_2}{i}\binom{m_3}{j}(-1)^{m_2-i}\psi^{(m_1,i+1,j)}(x), \tag{26}$$

Table 1. Comparison between estimates obtained from Monte Carlo simulations and the truncated model for Example 4. The Monte Carlo data was taken from [11]

Source for the estimates	$E[\mathbf{x}_1(0.2)]$	$E[\mathbf{x}_2(0.2)]$	StdDev$[\mathbf{x}_1(0.2)]$	StdDev$[\mathbf{x}_2(0.2)]$
10,000 MC. simul.	387.3	749.5	18.42	10.49
model (27), (29)	387.2	749.6	18.54	10.60

where the summations result from the power expansions of the terms $(x_i - c)^{m_i}$. For this example we consider a truncation whose state contains all the first and second order moments for the number of particles of the first and second species. To keep the formulas small, we omit from the truncation the second moments of the third species, which does not appear as a reactant in any reaction and therefore its higher order statistics do not affect the first two. In this case, (9) can be written as follows:

$$
\begin{bmatrix} \dot{\mu}^{(1,0,0)} \\ \dot{\mu}^{(0,1,0)} \\ \dot{\mu}^{(0,0,1)} \\ \dot{\mu}^{(2,0,0)} \\ \dot{\mu}^{(0,2,0)} \\ \dot{\mu}^{(1,1,0)} \end{bmatrix} =
\begin{bmatrix}
-c_1+c_2 & 2c_3 & 0 & -c_2 & 0 & 0 \\
-\frac{c_2}{2} & -c_3\ c_4 & 0 & \frac{c_2}{2} & 0 & 0 \\
0 & c_4 & 0 & 0 & 0 & 0 \\
c_1-2c_2 & 4c_3 & 0 & 4c_2-2c_1 & 0 & 4c_3 \\
-\frac{c_2}{2} & c_3+c_4 & 0 & \frac{c_2}{2} & -2c_3-2c_4 & -c_2 \\
c_2 & -2c_3 & 0 & -\frac{3c_2}{2} & 2c_3 & c_2-c_1-c_3-c_4
\end{bmatrix}
\begin{bmatrix} \mu^{(1,0,0)} \\ \mu^{(0,1,0)} \\ \mu^{(0,0,1)} \\ \mu^{(2,0,0)} \\ \mu^{(0,2,0)} \\ \mu^{(1,1,0)} \end{bmatrix} +
\begin{bmatrix} 0 & 0 \\ 0 & 0 \\ 0 & 0 \\ -2c_2 & 0 \\ 0 & c_2 \\ \frac{c_2}{2} & -c_2 \end{bmatrix} \bar{\mu},
$$
(27)

where $\bar{\mu} := \begin{bmatrix} \mu^{(3,0,0)} & \mu^{(2,1,0)} \end{bmatrix}'$ evolves according to

$$
\dot{\mu}^{(3,0,0)} = (-c_1 + 4c_2)\mu^{(1,0,0)} + 8c_3\mu^{(0,1,0)} + (3c_1 - 10c_2)\mu^{(2,0,0)} + 12c_3\mu^{(1,1,0)}
$$
$$
+ (-3c_1 + 9c_2)\mu^{(3,0,0)} + 6c_3\mu^{(2,1,0)} - 3c_2\mu^{(4,0,0)}
$$
(28a)

$$
\dot{\mu}^{(2,1,0)} = -2c_2\mu^{(1,0,0)} - 4c_3\mu^{(0,1,0)} + 4c_3\mu^{(2,0,0)} + 4c_3\mu^{(0,2,0)} + (c_1 - 2c_2 - 4c_3)\mu^{(1,1,0)}
$$
$$
- \frac{5c_2\mu^{(3,0,0)}}{2} + (4c_2 - 2c_1 - c_3 - c_4)\mu^{(2,1,0)} + 4c_3\mu^{(1,2,0)} + \frac{c_2\mu^{(4,0,0)}}{2} - 2c_2\mu^{(3,1,0)}.
$$
(28b)

This system does not satisfy condition 1 in Lemma 1 because the $\mu^{(1,0,0)}$, $\mu^{(0,1,0)}$ terms in the right-hand sides of (28) lead to monomials in x_1 and x_2 that do not exist in any of the polynomials $\left\{ \sum_{i=1}^{\infty} a_{j,i}\, x^{(m_\ell - m_j + m_i)} : 1 \le j \le 6 \right\}$. These terms can be traced back to the lowest-order terms in power expansions in (26) and disappear if we discard them. This leads to a simplified version of (27) for which condition 1 in Lemma 1 does hold, allowing us to find a unique solution φ to (17), resulting in a truncated system given (27) and

$$
\bar{\mu} = \varphi(\mu) = \left[\left(\frac{\mu^{(2,0,0)}}{\mu^{(1,0,0)}} \right)^3 \quad \frac{\mu^{(2,0,0)}}{\mu^{(0,1,0)}} \left(\frac{\mu^{(1,1,0)}}{\mu^{(1,0,0)}} \right)^2 \right]'.
$$
(29)

Ignoring the lowest-order powers of x_1 and x_2 in the power expansions is valid when the populations of these species are high. In practice, the approximation still seems to yield good results even when the populations are fairly small. Figure 4 shows a comparison between Monte Carlo simulations and the truncated model (27), (29). The coefficients used were taken from [11–Example 1]: $c_1 = 1$,

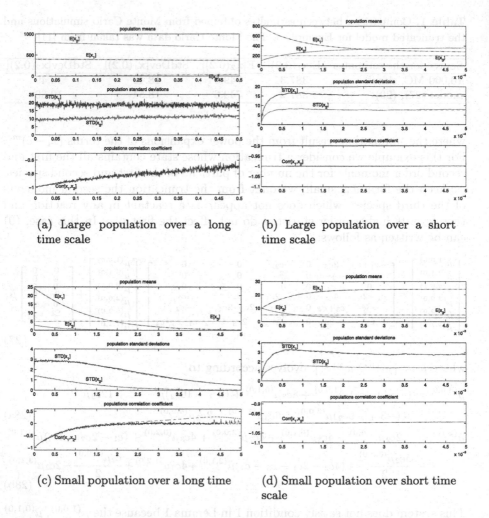

(a) Large population over a long time scale

(b) Large population over a short time scale

(c) Small population over a long time

(d) Small population over short time scale

Fig. 4. Comparison between Monte Carlo simulations (solid lines) and the truncated model (27), (29) (dashed lines) for Example 4

$c_2 = 10$, $c_3 = 1000$, $c_4 = 10^{-1}$. In Fig. 4(a), we used the same initial conditions as in [11–Example 1]: $x_1(0) = 400$, $x_2(0) = 798$, $x_3(0) = 0$. The match is very accurate, as can be confirmed from Table 1. The values of the parameters chosen result in a pSHS with two distinct time scales, which makes this pSHS computationally difficult to simulate ("stiff" in the terminology of [11]). Fig. 4(a) shows the evolution of the system on the "slow manifold," whereas Fig. 4(b) zooms in on the interval $[0, 5 \times 10^{-4}]$ and shows the evolution of the system towards this manifold when it starts away from it at $x_1(0) = 800$, $x_2(0) = 100$, $x_3(0) = 200$. Figures 4(c)–4(d) shows another simulation of the same reactions but for much smaller initial populations: $x_1(0) = 10$, $x_2(0) = 10$, $x_3(0) = 5$. The truncated model still provides an extremely good approximation, with significant error only in the covariance between x_1 and x_2 when the averages and standard deviation of these variables get below one.   □

6   Conclusions and Future Work

In this paper, we showed that the infinite-dimensional linear moment dynamics of a pSHS can be approximated by a finite-dimensional nonlinear ODE with arbitrary precision. Moreover, we provided a procedure to build this type of approximation. The methodology was illustrated using a varied pool of examples, demonstrating its wide applicability. Several observations arise from these examples, which point to directions for future research:

1. In all the examples presented, we restricted our attention to truncation functions φ of the form (16) and we only used deterministic distributions to compute φ. Mostly likely, better results could be obtained by considering more general distributions, which may require more general forms for φ.
2. The truncation of pSHSs that model chemical reactions proved especially accurate. This motivates the search for systematic procedures to automatically construct a truncated system from chemical equations such as (6). Another direction for future research consists of comparing the truncated models obtains here with those in [15].

An additional direction for future research consists of establishing computable bounds on the error between solutions to the infinite-dimensional moments dynamics and to its finite-dimensional truncations.

References

1. Hespanha, J.: Stochastic hybrid systems: Applications to communication networks. In Alur, R., Pappas, G., eds.: Hybrid Systems: Computation and Control. Number 2993 in Lect. Notes in Comput. Science. Springer-Verlag, Berlin (2004) 387–401
2. Davis, M.H.A.: Markov models and optimization. Monographs on statistics and applied probability. Chapman & Hall, London, UK (1993)
3. Hu, J., Lygeros, J., Sastry, S.: Towards a theory of stochastic hybrid systems. In Lynch, N.A., Krogh, B.H., eds.: Hybrid Systems: Computation and Control. Volume 1790 of Lect. Notes in Comput. Science., Springer (2000) 160–173
4. Pola, G., Bujorianu, M., Lygeros, J., Benedetto, M.D.: Stochastic hybrid models: An overview. In: Proc. of IFAC Conf. on Anal. and Design of Hybrid Syst. (2003)
5. Bujorianu, M.: Extended stochastic hybrid systems and their reachability problem. In: Hybrid Systems: Computation and Control. Lect. Notes in Comput. Science. Springer-Verlag, Berlin (2004) 234–249
6. Bohacek, S., Hespanha, J., Lee, J., Obraczka, K.: A hybrid systems modeling framework for fast and accurate simulation of data communication networks. In: Proc. of ACM SIGMETRICS. (2003)

7. Xu, Y., Hespanha, J.: Communication logics for networked control systems. In: Proc. of 2004 Amer. Contr. Conf. (2004)
8. Xu, Y., Hespanha, J.: Optimal communication logics for networked control systems. In: Proc. of 43rd Conf. on Decision and Contr. (2004)
9. Gillespie, D.T.: A general method for numerically simulating the stochastic time evolution of coupled chemical reactions. J. Comp. Physics **22** (1976) 403–434
10. Gillespie, D., Petzold, L.: Improved leap-size selection for accelerated stochastic simulation. J. of Chemical Physics **119** (2003) 8229–8234
11. Rathinam, M., Petzold, L., Cao, Y., Gillespie, D.: Stiffness in stochastic chemically reacting systems: The implicit tau-leaping method. J. of Chemical Physics **119** (2003) 12784–12794
12. Hespanha, J.: A model for stochastic hybrid systems with application to communication networks. Submitted to the *Int. Journal of Hybrid Systems* (2004)
13. Hespanha, J.P.: Polynomial stochastic hybrid systems (extended version). Technical report, University of California, Santa Barbara, Santa Barbara (2004) Available at http://www.ece.ucsb.edu/~hespanha/techreps.html.
14. Irlam, G.: Unix file size survey – 1993. Available at http://www.base.com/gordoni/ufs93.html (1994)
15. Van Kampen, N.: Stochastic Processes in Physics and Chemistry. Elsevier (2001)

Non-uniqueness in Reverse Time of Hybrid System Trajectories

Ian A. Hiskens*

Department of Electrical and Computer Engineering,
University of Wisconsin-Madison, Madison, WI 53706
hiskens@engr.wisc.edu

Abstract. Under standard Lipschitz conditions, trajectories of systems described by ordinary differential equations are well defined in both forward and reverse time. (The flow map is invertible.) However for hybrid systems, uniqueness of trajectories in forward time does not guarantee flow-map invertibility, allowing non-uniqueness in reverse time. The paper establishes a necessary and sufficient condition that governs invertibility through events. It is shown that this condition is equivalent to requiring reverse-time trajectories to transversally encounter event triggering hypersurfaces. This analysis motivates a homotopy algorithm that traces a one-manifold of initial conditions that give rise to trajectories which all reach a common point at the same time.

1 Introduction

Uniqueness is a fundamental property of solutions of dynamical systems. Intuitively, uniqueness in forward time should imply reverse time uniqueness[1]. That is certainly the case for systems described by ordinary differential equations, as discussed in the background presentation in Section 2. However it is not necessarily true for hybrid systems.

Hybrid system solutions are composed of periods of smooth behaviour separated by discrete events [2]. Standard transversality conditions can be established to ensure transitions through events are well behaved. An overview is provided in Section 4. However those conditions are not sufficient to ensure reverse-time mappings through events are well defined. It is shown in the paper that another transversality-type condition must be satisfied to ensure uniqueness in reverse-time (or equivalently flow-map invertibility.)

Recent investigations have established conditions governing the well-posedness of solutions for various hybrid system formalisms. A complementarity modelling framework [3] underlies the characterization of solutions of linear relay systems [4, 5] and further extensions to piecewise-linear systems [6, 7]. A more general hybrid automata framework is considered in [8]. In all cases, well-posedness is

---

* Research supported by the National Science Foundation through grant ECS-0332777.
[1] In other words, invertibility of the flow map [1]. This is discussed further in Section 3.

M. Morari and L. Thiele (Eds.): HSCC 2005, LNCS 3414, pp. 339–353, 2005.

addressed in the context of forward solutions, i.e., whether there exists a unique (forward) solution for every initial state x_0. It is noted in [5], though without discussion, that forward-time well-posedness does not imply well-defined behaviour in reverse time. That reverse-time issue is addressed in this paper, in the context of flow-map invertibility. It is shown in Section 7 that non-invertibility gives rise to a manifold of initial conditions for trajectories which all reach a common point at the same time. Such concepts have not previously been explored.

Analysis of system dynamic behaviour is normally only concerned with trajectory evolution in forward time. In such cases, the issues raised here are inconsequential. However reverse-time trajectories form the basis for the adjoint system equations, which underlie algorithms for solving boundary value and dynamic embedded optimization problems [9, 10, 11]. Application of such algorithms to hybrid systems must therefore consider these uniqueness issues.

2   Background

Existence and uniqueness properties for systems of the form

$$\dot{x} = f(x), \qquad x(0) = x_0 \tag{1}$$

where $f : \mathbb{R}^n \to \mathbb{R}^n$ are well known [12, 13]. In particular, if $f \in C^1$, i.e., is continuous in x and has continuous first partial derivatives with respect to x over $\mathbb{R}^n$, then (1) has a unique solution

$$x(t) = \phi(t, x_0) \equiv \phi_t(x_0), \tag{2}$$

with $\phi(0, x_0) = x_0$. Furthermore, the *flow map* $\phi(t, x_0)$ is differentiable with respect to x_0. The *sensitivity transition matrix* is defined as

$$\Phi(t, x_0) \triangleq \frac{\partial \phi(t, x_0)}{\partial x_0}. \tag{3}$$

It is obtained by differentiating (1) with respect to x_0 to give

$$\dot{\Phi}(t, x_0) = Df(t)\Phi(t, x_0), \qquad \Phi(0, x_0) = I \tag{4}$$

where

$$Df(t) \triangleq \left. \frac{\partial f(x)}{\partial x} \right|_{x = \phi(t, x_0)}.$$

The transition matrix $\Phi(t, x_0)$ is the solution of a set of linear time-varying differential equations (4), so has the property

$$\det \Phi(t, x_0) = \exp \left\{ \int_0^t \text{Trace}\{Df(\tau)\} d\tau \right\}, \tag{5}$$

which implies $\Phi(t, x_0)$ is nonsingular for all t.

Expanding $\phi(t, x_0)$ in a Taylor series, and neglecting higher order terms, results in

$$\phi(t, \bar{x}_0) - \phi(t, x_0) \approx \Phi(t, x_0)(\bar{x}_0 - x_0) \qquad (6)$$

$$\Rightarrow \delta x(t) \approx \Phi(t, x_0)\delta x_0. \qquad (7)$$

In other words a change δx_0 in initial conditions[2] induces a change $\delta x(t)$ in the trajectory at time t, with that change described (approximately) by $\Phi(t, x_0)$. Because $\Phi(t, x_0)$ is nonsingular for all t, it may be concluded that given any $\delta x(t)$, it is always possible to find the corresponding δx_0, i.e.,

$$\delta x_0 = \Phi(t, x_0)^{-1}\delta x(t). \qquad (8)$$

3 Reverse Time Trajectories

For systems of the form (1), the map $\phi_t \in C^1$. Furthermore, according to (5), its derivative $D\phi_t(x) = \Phi(t, x)$ is always invertible. Therefore, by the inverse function theorem [1], ϕ_t is a one-parameter family of diffeomorphisms. It follows that ϕ_t has a C^1 inverse ϕ_{-t}, such that $\phi_{-t}(\phi_t(x)) = \phi_0(x) = x$. This inverse ϕ_{-t} is referred to as the *reverse time* trajectory.

4 Hybrid Systems

Hybrid systems have the form

$$\dot{x} = f_p(x), \qquad p \in \mathcal{P} \qquad (9)$$

where $f_p : \mathbb{R}^n \to \mathbb{R}^n$, and $\mathcal{P}$ is some finite index set. Transitions between the various subsystems $f_i \to f_j$ occur when the state x evolves to a point that satisfies an event triggering condition,

$$s_{ij}(x) = 0 \qquad (10)$$

where $s_{ij} : \mathbb{R}^n \to \mathbb{R}$. We shall assume $s_{ij} \in C^1$. A more elaborate differential-algebraic model, that incorporates switching and impulse effects, is described in [14].

Assume all f_p satisfy the differentiability condition of f in (1), and x is continuous at events, i.e., impulses do not occur. Furthermore, assume that event triggers are encountered transversally[3],

$$\nabla s_{ij}^T \dot{x} = \nabla s_{ij}^T f_i \neq 0 \qquad (11)$$

---

[2] Parameter sensitivity can be incorporated through initial conditions by introducing trivial equations
$$\dot{\lambda} = 0, \quad \lambda(0) = \lambda_0.$$

[3] Tangential encounters are associated with grazing phenomena [15].

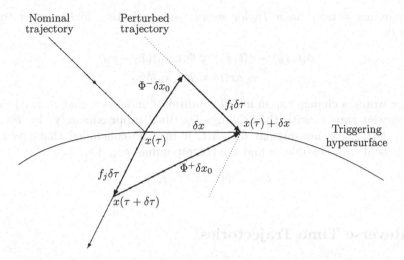

Fig. 1. Jump conditions

and that event switching is well defined, in the sense that accumulation effects do not occur. Under those conditions, (9) has a unique solution that can be expressed in the same form as (2).

Away from events, the sensitivity transition matrix $\Phi(t, x_0)$ is defined according to (4). It is shown in [14] that at an event $i \rightarrow j$, occurring at time τ, sensitivities Φ generically jump[4] according to

$$\Phi(\tau^+, x_0) = \Phi(\tau^-, x_0) + (f_j - f_i) \frac{\nabla s_{ij}^T \Phi(\tau^-, x_0)}{\nabla s_{ij}^T f_i} \tag{12}$$

$$= \left(I + (f_j - f_i) \frac{\nabla s_{ij}^T}{\nabla s_{ij}^T f_i} \right) \Phi(\tau^-, x_0) \tag{13}$$

$$= \Phi(\delta, x(\tau^-)) \Phi(\tau^-, x_0) \tag{14}$$

where δ in (14) signifies the time increment $\tau^+ - \tau^-$. Notice that the transversality condition (11) ensures that the denominator of (12) is non-zero.

Equation (12) can be rewritten

$$\Phi^+ = \Phi^- - (f_j - f_i) \frac{\partial \tau}{\partial x_0} \tag{15}$$

where

$$\frac{\partial \tau}{\partial x_0} = -\frac{\nabla s_{ij}^T \Phi^-}{\nabla s_{ij}^T f_i}$$

---

[4] No jump occurs if $f_i = f_j$ or $\nabla s_{ij}^T \Phi(\tau^-, x_0) = 0$.

gives the sensitivity of event triggering time to initial conditions. For a perturbation δx_0, (15) gives

$$\delta x = \Phi^- \delta x_0 + f_i \delta \tau = \Phi^+ \delta x_0 + f_j \delta \tau,$$

which is illustrated in Figure 1.

5   Uniqueness in Forward and Reverse Time

Generalizing (14) to a sequence of events occurring at times $0 < \tau_1 < \tau_2 < \cdots < \tau_\ell$ results in the sensitivity transition matrix at $t > \tau_\ell$ having composition

$$\Phi(t, x_0) = \Phi(t - \tau_\ell^+, x(\tau_\ell^+)) \times \Phi(\delta, x(\tau_\ell^-)) \times \Phi(\tau_\ell^- - \tau_{\ell-1}^+, x(\tau_{\ell-1}^+)) \times \cdots$$
$$\times \Phi(\tau_1^-, x_0)$$

where $\Phi(\tau_\ell^- - \tau_{\ell-1}^+, x(\tau_{\ell-1}^+))$ corresponds to transitions along smooth sections of the flow, and $\Phi(\delta, x(\tau_\ell^-))$ describes the transition through an event at time τ_ℓ. Property (5) ensures that matrices $\Phi(\tau_\ell^- - \tau_{\ell-1}^+, x(\tau_{\ell-1}^+))$ are always nonsingular. However the following theorem establishes conditions governing the singularity of transition matrices $\Phi(\delta, x(\tau_\ell^-))$.

Theorem 1. *The sensitivity transition matrix* $\Phi(\delta, x(\tau^-))$ *is singular if and only if* $\nabla s_{ij}^T f_j = 0$.

Proof: The proof makes use of the fact that $\det(I + ab^T) = 1 + b^T a$, which is a special case of $\det(I + AB) = \det(I + BA)$ [16]. Then

$$\det \Phi(\delta, x(\tau^-)) = \det \left(I + (f_j - f_i) \frac{\nabla s_{ij}^T}{\nabla s_{ij}^T f_i} \right)$$

$$= 1 + \frac{\nabla s_{ij}^T}{\nabla s_{ij}^T f_i} (f_j - f_i)$$

$$= \frac{\nabla s_{ij}^T f_j}{\nabla s_{ij}^T f_i},$$

which is zero if and only if $\nabla s_{ij}^T f_j = 0$.

$\square$

Therefore, for a hybrid system, $\Phi(t, x_0)$ will be singular if the conditions of Theorem 1 occur at *any* event. But if $\Phi(t, x_0)$ is singular, the hybrid system flow ϕ_t is not a diffeomorphism, and the reverse time trajectory ϕ_{-t} is not well defined.

Recalling (7), a perturbation δx_0 in initial conditions will always result in a well defined perturbation $\delta x(t)$ in the trajectory at time t. However if $\Phi(t, x_0)$ is not invertible, the reverse mapping (8) is not valid. A general perturbation $\delta x(t)$ cannot be mapped backwards to a corresponding unique δx_0. More specif-

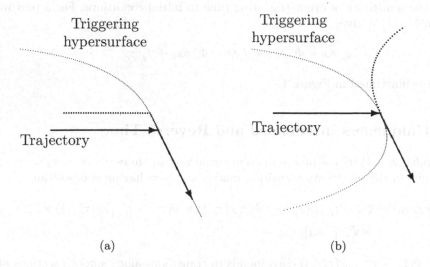

Triggering
hypersurface

Triggering
hypersurface

Trajectory

Trajectory

(a)   (b)

Fig. 2. Conditions inducing singularity

ically though, if $\delta x(t)$ lies in the range space of $\Phi(t, x_0)$, then it can be mapped backwards to a continuum of δx_0[5].

It may be concluded that for hybrid systems, uniqueness of trajectories in forward time does not guarantee uniqueness in reverse time.

Note that there is a subtle but important difference between the transversality condition (11) and the singularity condition of Theorem 1, even though they have a similar form. Transversality (11) ensures the trajectory has a well defined (forward) encounter with the triggering hypersurface. Theorem 1 establishes conditions that relate to the trajectory's departure from the event. Furthermore, it should be emphasised that the triggering condition $s_{ij}(x) = 0$ is only active for subsystem i, before the event. After the event, in subsystem j, it is no longer relevant.

Figure 2 illustrates ways in which the singularity condition of Theorem 1, $\nabla s_{ij}^T f_j = 0$, may arise. In Figure 2(a), the post-event trajectory remains on the triggering hypersurface for a non-zero time interval. This situation is relatively common in practice, for example the action of anti-wind-up limits [17]. In Figure 2(b), the post-event trajectory leaves the triggering hypersurface tangentially. The examples of Section 8 consider both situations further.

These two cases motivate an interesting corollary of Theorem 1.

Corollary 2. *The sensitivity transition matrix $\Phi(\delta, x(\tau^-))$ is nonsingular if and only if the reverse-time trajectory $\phi_{-t}(x(\tau^+))$ is transversal to the triggering hypersurface s_{ij} that induces the event at time τ.*

---

[5] Let u and v be the left and right eigenvectors of $\Phi(t, x_0)$ corresponding to a zero eigenvalue. Then if $u^T \delta x(t) = 0$, δx_0 will lie in the one-dimensional subspace defined by $\delta x_0 = w + \alpha v$ where $\delta x(t) = \Phi(t, x_0)w$ and α is a scalar.

In other words, to ensure uniqueness in reverse time, the reverse-time trajectory must "encounter" triggering hypersurfaces transversally. (Though keep in mind these hypersurfaces are really only defined for the forward trajectory.) The situations presented in Figure 2 illustrate reverse-time non-uniqueness when this transversality condition is not satisfied. In both illustrations, the post-event segment of the trajectory could have originated from the dotted trajectory, rather than the actual pre-event (solid) trajectory.

Note that the two cases depicted in Figure 2 are structurally quite different. In Figure 2(a), reverse-time non-uniqueness persists under perturbations in the initial conditions, whereas for Figure 2(b), perturbations destroy that property. However this latter case has an interesting sliding interpretation when the triggering hypersurface is common to both the pre- and post-trigger subsystems. Referring to Figure 2(b), consider trajectories that emanate from either subsystem and encounter the triggering hypersurface just above the switching point of the nominal trajectory (the switching that induces reverse-time non-uniqueness). Those trajectories will slide along the hypersurface until they reach that pivotal switching point. From there they will depart the hypersurface and follow the post-switching trajectory shown in the figure. The pivotal switching point separates the sliding region from that associated with well-behaved switching.

Keep in mind that this sliding interpretation is only appropriate when the triggering hypersurface is common to both subsystems. Corollary 2 is more generally applicable.

6   Impulses at Events

The hybrid system model established in Section 4 and used through Section 5 assumed continuity of x at events. However results can be generalized to allow impulses at events. Assume the impulse mapping at event $i \to j$ has the form

$$x^+ = h_{ij}(x^-)$$

where $h_{ij} : \mathbb{R}^n \to \mathbb{R}^n$ is a diffeomorphism, and x^+, x^- refer to the values of the state just after, and just prior to, the event respectively[6].

It is shown in [14] that with the inclusion of impulse effects, the sensitivity transition matrix jump conditions (12)-(14) become

$$\Phi(\delta, x(\tau^-)) = Dh + (f_j - Dh f_i)\frac{\nabla s_{ij}^T}{\nabla s_{ij}^T f_i} \tag{16}$$

where $Dh \triangleq \frac{\partial h_{ij}}{\partial x}$. In this case, Theorem 1 takes a slightly modified form.

Theorem 3. *For nonsingular Dh, the sensitivity transition matrix $\Phi(\delta, x(\tau^-))$ is singular if and only if $\nabla s_{ij}^T Dh^{-1} f_j = 0$.*

---

[6] An implicit impulse mapping $\check{h}_{ij}(x^+, x^-) = 0$ is also acceptable, though not used here.

Proof: The proof is similar to that of Theorem 1. With Dh nonsingular,

$$\det \Phi(\delta, x(\tau^-)) = \det(Dh) \det \left(I + (Dh^{-1}f_j - f_i) \frac{\nabla s_{ij}^T}{\nabla s_{ij}^T f_i} \right)$$

$$= \det(Dh) \left(1 + \frac{\nabla s_{ij}^T}{\nabla s_{ij}^T f_i} (Dh^{-1}f_j - f_i) \right)$$

$$= \det(Dh) \left(\frac{\nabla s_{ij}^T Dh^{-1} f_j}{\nabla s_{ij}^T f_i} \right).$$

Given that Dh is nonsingular, singularity of $\Phi(\delta, x(\tau^-))$ corresponds to $\nabla s_{ij}^T Dh^{-1} f_j = 0$.   □

The condition established in Theorem 3 has a very similar interpretation to that of Theorem 1. Now though, the post-event vector field f_j is translated via Dh^{-1} back to a pre-event coordinate system, where transversality is again required for nonsingularity.

7   Homotopy Algorithm

To first order, deviations in a trajectory at time t are given by (7). If $\Phi(t, x_0)$ is singular then a deviation δx_0 that coincides with the null-space[7] of $\Phi(t, x_0)$ results in $\delta x(t) = 0$. As mentioned in Section 5, under such conditions $\phi(t, x_0)$ maps a continuum of x_0 to a single point $x(t)$. In fact, if $\Phi(t_*, x_0)$ has rank deficiency k, then $x(t_*) = \phi(t_*, x_0)$ defines a k-manifold.

If $\Phi(t_*, x_0)$ has a single zero eigenvalue, then

$$\Sigma = \{x_0 : \phi(t_*, x_0) - x(t_*) = 0\} \qquad (17)$$

describes a 1-manifold, or curve. Homotopy methods can be used to generate successive points along such curves. An Euler homotopy provides a robust predictor-corrector algorithm [18].

Assume a point $\bar{x}_0$ on Σ is known. (This is a straightforward initial value problem.) The first step of the homotopy algorithm is the (first order) prediction of the next point on the curve. This is achieved by finding the vector that is tangent to Σ at $\bar{x}_0$. This tangent vector is nothing more than the (normalized) right eigenvector v of $\Phi(t_*, \bar{x}_0)$ corresponding to the zero eigenvalue. The prediction of the next point is obtained by moving along v a predefined distance τ,

$$x_{0,pred} = \bar{x}_0 + \tau v,$$

where

$$\Phi(t_*, \bar{x}_0)v = 0 \qquad (18)$$

$$\|v\| = 1. \qquad (19)$$

---

[7] The null-space is spanned by the right eigenvectors corresponding to zero eigenvalues.

Having found the prediction point, we now need to correct to a point x_0 on the curve. The Euler method does this by solving for the point of intersection of the curve and a hyperplane that passes through $x_{0,pred}$ and that is orthogonal to v. Points x_0 on this hyperplane are given by,

$$(x_0 - \bar{x}_0)^T v = \tau. \tag{20}$$

The point of intersection of the curve and the hyperplane is therefore given by

$$\phi(t_*, x_0) - x(t_*) = 0 \tag{21}$$

$$(x_0 - \bar{x}_0)^T v = \tau. \tag{22}$$

Note though that (21)-(22) describe $n + 1$ equations in n unknowns. However the rank deficiency of (21) suggests that one of those equations is redundant, and so can be discarded. It remains to determine which equation to discard.

Newton-Raphson solution of (21)-(22) proceeds via the iteration formula

$$\begin{bmatrix} \Phi(t_*, x_0) \\ v^T \end{bmatrix} \Delta x_0 = \begin{bmatrix} \phi(t_*, x_0) - x(t_*) \\ (x_0 - \bar{x}_0)^T v - \tau \end{bmatrix} \tag{23}$$

where $\Phi(t_*, x_0)$ is singular, with a single zero eigenvalue. Solution of (23) requires that $u^T(\phi(t_*, x_0) - x(t_*)) = 0$, where u is the left eigenvector of $\Phi(t_*, x_0)$ corresponding to the zero eigenvalue. In other words, u describes the linear dependence between the first n equations of (23). This implies that the best equation to discard from (21) is that corresponding to the element of u with the largest absolute value.

The next point on the curve is therefore given by Newton-Raphson solution of

$$F(x_0) \equiv \begin{bmatrix} \underline{\phi(t_*, x_0) - x(t_*)} \\ (x_0 - \bar{x}_0)^T v - \tau \end{bmatrix} = 0 \tag{24}$$

which utilizes the (nonsingular) Jacobian

$$DF(x_0) = \begin{bmatrix} \underline{\Phi(t_*, x_0)} \\ v^T \end{bmatrix}, \tag{25}$$

where underlining in (24) and (25) indicates that the appropriate equation has been discarded.

8   Examples

8.1   Example 1

As indicated in Section 5, anti-wind-up limits provide a common situation where reverse-time transversality is not possible. This can be illustrated using a simple example that consists of a linear continuous-time system

$$\dot{x} = \begin{bmatrix} -1 & 2 \\ -2 & -1 \end{bmatrix} x$$

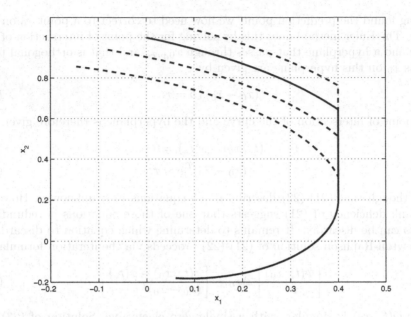

Fig. 3. Example 1 response

together with an anti-wind-up limit restricting $x_1 \leq 0.4$. In terms of the hybrid system representation of Section 4, this system may be modelled as

$$\dot{x} = f_1(x) = \begin{bmatrix} -1 & 2 \\ -2 & -1 \end{bmatrix} x \qquad \text{(subsystem 1)}$$

$$\dot{x} = f_2(x) = \begin{bmatrix} 0 & 0 \\ -2 & -1 \end{bmatrix} x \qquad \text{(subsystem 2)}$$

with transitions from subsystem 1 to 2 triggered when

$$s_{12}(x) = x_1 - 0.4 = 0$$

and from subsystem 2 to 1 when

$$s_{21}(x) = [-1 \ 2]x = 0.$$

This latter condition ensures $\dot{x}_1 < 0$ after switching, so behaviour is directed away from the limit surface. The response of this system for initial conditions $x_0 = [0 \ 1]^T$ is shown as a solid line in Figure 3.

At the instant prior to the limit being encountered (event triggering), the sensitivity transition matrix $\Phi(\tau^-, x_0)$ had eigenvalues $0.64 \pm j0.40$. However for this event,

$$\Phi(\delta, x(\tau^-)) = \begin{bmatrix} 0 & 0 \\ 0 & 1 \end{bmatrix}$$

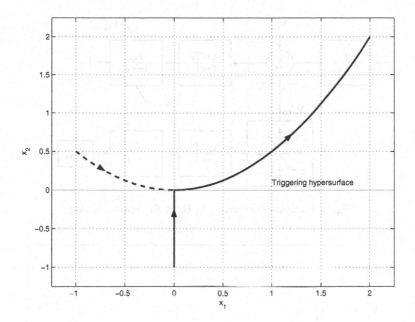

Fig. 4. Example 2 response

which clearly has a zero eigenvalue, with corresponding left eigenvector $\nabla s_{ij} = [1\ 0]^T$.

The homotopy algorithm was used to locate other initial points that reached the same final point at the same time. These are shown in Figure 3 as dashed lines. Once the limit is encountered, the trajectories are indistinguishable. All are well defined in forward time, but there is no unique reverse-time trajectory.

8.2   Example 2

Behaviour of the form shown in Figure 2(b) can be illustrated using the simple hybrid system,

$$\dot{x} = f_1(x) = \begin{bmatrix} 0 \\ 1 \end{bmatrix} \qquad \text{(subsystem 1)}$$

$$\dot{x} = f_2(x) = \begin{bmatrix} 1 \\ x_1 \end{bmatrix} \qquad \text{(subsystem 2)}$$

with transitions from subsystem 1 to 2 triggered when

$$s_{12}(x) = x_2 = 0.$$

The solid line in Figure 4 shows the trajectory given by initial conditions $x_0 = [0\ -1]^T$. The singularity condition of Theorem 1 occurs at the switching point

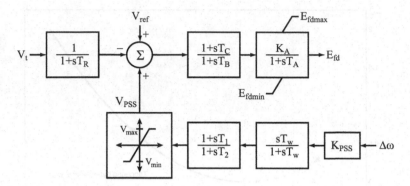

Fig. 5. Excitation system (AVR/PSS) representation

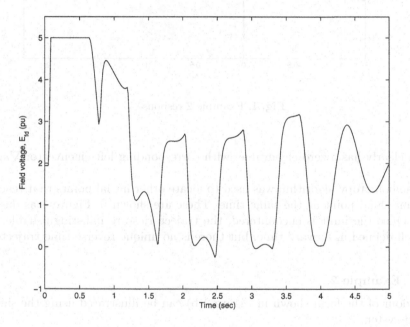

Fig. 6. Generator field voltage response

$x = [0 \ 0]^T$, implying the trajectory is not unique in reverse time. This non-uniqueness is confirmed by the dashed trajectory which starts at $x_0 = [-1 \ 0.5]^T$, but coincides with the nominal trajectory from the point $x = [0 \ 0]^T$ onwards.

If transitions from subsystem 2 to 1 were triggered when

$$s_{21}(x) = s_{12}(x)$$

then all trajectories emanating from below the dashed line would slide along the x_1-axis until reaching the point $x = [0 \ 0]^T$. From there they would all follow the nominal trajectory shown.

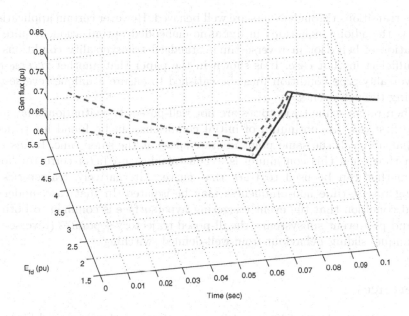

Fig. 7. Trajectories given by homotopy algorithm

8.3   Example 3

A more elaborate power system case has also been considered. In this case, generators were represented by a sixth order nonlinear model [19], and equipped with the excitation system shown in Figure 5. This system includes clipping limits on the stabilizer output V_{PSS}, and anti-windup limits on the field voltage E_{fd}. The response of the generator field voltage E_{fd} to a fault is shown in Figure 6. Note that this trajectory is quite non-smooth, as is typical for power systems.

At 0.086 sec, the anti-windup limit was encountered. As anticipated, the sensitivity transition matrix $\Phi(\delta, x(0.086^-))$ was singular, with a single zero eigenvalue at that event. The homotopy algorithm was again used to locate initial points that converged to the same final point at the same final time. Results are shown in Figure 7. The solid line corresponds to the original case. The dashed trajectories originate from points given by the homotopy. Note that all curves converge at 0.086 sec.

9   Conclusions

Hybrid system solutions are composed of periods of smooth behaviour separated by discrete events. Standard transversality conditions can be established to ensure transitions through events are well behaved. However certain applications, such as the adjoint equations in dynamic embedded optimization, require the evaluation of behavior in reverse time. Standard transversality conditions are not sufficient in that case. It is shown in the paper that another *reverse-time* transversality-type condition must be satisfied to ensure a unique reverse-time mapping through events.

When reverse-time trajectories are not well-posed, two situations may arise. In the first case, a continuum of initial conditions can be found for trajectories that all reach the same point in state-space at the same time. It has been shown that when this continuum is a 1-manifold, a predictor-corrector homotopy method can be used to trace that curve. Alternatively, trajectories exhibiting reverse-time non-uniqueness may be isolated. In that case, under the special condition that the event triggering hypersurface is common to both the pre- and post-event subsystems, the ill-posed trajectory separates (reverse-time non-unique) sliding behaviour from well-defined switching.

References

1. Hirsch, M., Smale, S.: Differential Equations, Dynamical Systems and Linear Algebra. Academic Press, Orlando, FL (1974)
2. Liberzon, D.: Switching in Systems and Control. Birkhauser, Boston (2003)
3. van der Schaft, A., Schumacher, J.: Complementarity modeling of hybrid systems. IEEE Transactions on Automatic Control **43** (1998) 483–490
4. Lootsma, Y., van der Schaft, A., Çamlibel, M.: Uniqueness of solutions of linear relay systems. Automatica **35** (1999) 467–478
5. Pogromsky, A., Heemels, W., Nijmeijer, H.: On solution concepts and well-posedness of linear relay systems. Automatica **39** (2003) 2139–2147
6. Heemels, W., Çamlibel, M., Schumacher, J.: On the dynamic analysis of piecewise-linear networks. IEEE Transactions on Circuits and Systems-I **49** (2002) 315–327
7. Imura, J.I., van der Schaft, A.: Characterization of well-posedness of piecewise-linear systems. IEEE Transactions on Automatic Control **45** (2000) 1600–1619
8. Lygeros, J., Johansson, K., Simić, S., Zhang, J., Sastry, S.: Dynamical properties of hybrid automata. IEEE Transactions on Automatic Control **48** (2003) 2–17
9. Errico, R.: What is an adjoint model? Bulletin of the American Meteorological Society **78** (1997) 2577–2591
10. Cao, Y., Li, S., Petzold, L., Serban, R.: Adjoint sensitivity analysis for differential-algebraic equations: The adjoint DAE system and its numerical solution. SIAM Journal on Scientific Computing **24** (2003) 1076–1089
11. Wardi, Y., Egerstedt, M., Boccadoro, M., Verriest, E.: Optimal control of switching surfaces. In: Proceedings of the 43rd Conference on Decision and Control, Paradise Island, Bahamas (2004) 1854–1859
12. Khalil, H.: Nonlinear Systems. 2nd edn. Prentice Hall, Upper Saddle River, NJ (1996)
13. Perko, L.: Differential Equations and Dynamical Systems. Springer-Verlag, New York, NY (1996)

14. Hiskens, I., Pai, M.: Trajectory sensitivity analysis of hybrid systems. IEEE Transactions on Circuits and Systems I: Fundamental Theory and Applications **47** (2000) 204–220
15. Donde, V., Hiskens, I.: Shooting methods for locating grazing phenomena in hybrid systems. International Journal of Bifurcation and Chaos (2004) Submitted.
16. Kailath, T.: Linear Systems. Prentice Hall, Upper Saddle River, NJ (1980)
17. Goodwin, G., Graebe, S., Salgado, M.: Control System Design. Upper Saddle River, New Jersey: Prentice Hall (2001)
18. Garcia, C., Zangwill, W.: Pathways to Solutions, Fixed Points and Equilibria. Prentice Hall, Englewood Cliffs, NJ (1981)
19. Sauer, P., Pai, M.: Power System Dynamics and Stability. Prentice Hall, Upper Saddle River, NJ (1998)

Comparison of Four Procedures for the Identification of Hybrid Systems

Aleksandar Lj. Juloski[1], W.P.M.H. Heemels[2], Giancarlo Ferrari-Trecate[3],
René Vidal[4], Simone Paoletti[5], and J.H.G. Niessen[6]

[1] Department of Electrical Engineering, Eindhoven University of Technology,
PO Box 513, 5600MB Eindhoven, The Netherlands
a.juloski@tue.nl
[2] Embedded Systems Institute, PO Box 513,
5600 MB Eindhoven, The Netherlands
maurice.heemels@embeddedsystems.nl
[3] INRIA, Domaine de Voluceau, Rocquencourt - B.P.105,
78153, Le Chesnay Cedex, France
Giancarlo.Ferrari-Trecate@inria.fr
[4] Center for Imaging Science, Johns Hopkins University,
308B Clark Hall, 3400 N Charles St, Baltimore, MD 21218, USA
rvidal@cis.jhu.edu
[5] Dipartimento di Ingegneria dell'Informazione, Universita' di Siena,
Via Roma 56, 53100 Siena, Italy
paoletti@dii.unisi.it
[6] Nyquist, Industrial Control, P.O. Box 7170,
5605 JD Eindhoven, The Netherlands
h.niessen@nyquist.com

Abstract. In this paper we compare four recently proposed procedures for the identification of PieceWise AutoRegressive eXogenous (PWARX) and switched ARX models. We consider the clustering-based procedure, the bounded-error procedure, and the Bayesian procedure which all identify PWARX models. We also study the algebraic procedure, which identifies switched linear models. We introduce quantitative measures for assessing the quality of the obtained models. Specific behaviors of the procedures are pointed out, using suitably constructed one dimensional examples. The methods are also applied to the experimental identification of the electronic component placement process in pick-and-place machines.

1 Introduction

In this paper we study four recently proposed procedures for the identification of discrete time piecewise affine (PWA) models. The identification procedures that we compare are the clustering-based procedure [1], the bounded-error procedure [2,3], the Bayesian procedure [4] and the algebraic procedure [5,6] (see section 2 for brief descriptions). Of course, there are other methods available in

M. Morari and L. Thiele (Eds.): HSCC 2005, LNCS 3414, pp. 354–369, 2005.

literature, for instance the work given in [7] and [8]. However, due to the specific knowledge of the authors and space limitations, the attention is restricted to the four procedures mentioned before.

There is not much known how the procedures compare in particular situations. Some features of the clustering-based procedure have been analyzed theoretically in [9], but a formal analysis of the properties of the bounded-error, algebraic and Bayesian procedures for noisy data is currently not available. Therefore, we will study specific examples of PWA models that can help us better understand properties of the methods in practical situations.

To be precise, the PWA models that the clustering-based, bounded-error and the Bayesian procedures identify are PieceWise ARX (PWARX) models of the form:

$$y(k) = f(x(k)) + e(k), \tag{1}$$

where $e(k)$ is the error term and the PWA map $f(\cdot)$ is defined as:

$$f(x) = \begin{cases} [\, x' \quad 1\,]\, \theta_1 \text{ if } x \in \mathcal{X}_1, \\ \quad \vdots \\ [\, x' \quad 1\,]\, \theta_s \text{ if } x \in \mathcal{X}_s. \end{cases} \tag{2}$$

In (2) $x(k)$ is a vector of regressors defined as

$$x(k) \triangleq [\, y(k-1)\, y(k-2) \, \dots \, y(k-n_a) \\ u'(k-1)\, u'(k-2) \, \dots \, u'(k-n_b)\,]', \tag{3}$$

where k is the time index and $y \in \mathbb{R}$, $u \in \mathbb{R}^m$ are the outputs and the inputs of the system, respectively. For $i = 1, \dots s$, $\theta_i \in \mathbb{R}^{n+1}$ is a parameter vector (PV) with $n = n_a + n_b$.

The bounded regressor space $\mathbb{X}$ is partitioned into s convex polyhedral regions $\{\mathcal{X}_i\}_{i=1}^s$, i.e.

$$\bigcup_{i=1}^{s} \mathcal{X}_i = \mathbb{X} \subset \mathbb{R}^n \quad \text{and} \quad \mathcal{X}_i \cap \mathcal{X}_j = \varnothing \quad i \neq j. \tag{4}$$

When the partition $\{\mathcal{X}_i\}_{i=1}^s$ is known we can define the mode $\mu(k)$ of the data pair $(x(k), y(k))$, $k = 1, \dots, N$ uniquely as:

$$\mu(k) := i \text{ if } x(k) \in \mathcal{X}_i. \tag{5}$$

The algebraic procedure identifies switched linear models of the form (1), where

$$f(x) = [\, x' \quad 1\,]\, \theta_i,$$

and $i \in \{1, \dots s\}$ is arbitrary for each time index k. The problems of estimation of parameters $\theta_1, \dots, \theta_s$ for switched linear and PWARX models are closely related, and in the sequel we will treat them in parallel. In addition, the identification of PWARX models requires also the estimation of the regions $\mathcal{X}_i$, which would form an extension of the algebraic procedure.

The general identification problem reads as follows: given the data set $\mathcal{N} = \{(x(k), y(k))\}_{k=1}^{N}$ reconstruct the PWA map $f(\cdot)$, i.e. determine the PVs $\{\theta_i\}_{i=1}^{s}$ and the polyhedral partition $\{\mathcal{X}_i\}_{i=1}^{s}$.

Identification of PWARX models is a challenging problem since it involves the estimation of both the PVs $\{\theta_i\}_{i=1}^{s}$ and the regions of the regressor space $\{\mathcal{X}_i\}_{i=1}^{s}$ on the basis of the available data set $\mathcal{N}$. In case that regions of the regressor space are known a priori the problem complexity reduces to that of s linear system identification problems [1].

In order to compare the procedures and asses the quality of the obtained models we propose several quantitative measures in section 2. These measures are "common sense" criteria (not the ones optimized by the methods themselves) and reflect practical needs for identification. In section 3 we will address different approaches to data classification of each of the procedures, and consequences on the accuracy of the identified model. In section 4 we will investigate the effects of the overestimation of model orders. In section 5 we will study the effects of noise. In section 6 we will apply the procedures for the experimental identification of the component placement process in pick-and-place machines. Finally, summary and conclusions are presented in section 7.

2   The Compared Procedures

In this section we briefly discuss the four procedures we compare. The basic steps that each method performs are: the estimation of the PVs $\{\theta_i\}_{i=1}^{s}$, the classification of the data points (grouping data points attributed to the i-th mode to the set $\mathcal{F}_i$, $i = 1, \ldots, s$) and the estimation of the corresponding regions $\{\mathcal{X}_i\}_{i=1}^{s}$, for PWARX models.

The first two steps are performed in a different way by each procedure, as discussed in the sequel, while the estimation of the regions can be done in the same way for all methods. The basic idea is as follows. Having the data points that are attributed to sets $\mathcal{F}_i$ and $\mathcal{F}_j$, we are looking for a separating hyperplane in the regressor space $\mathbb{X}$ described by:

$$M_{ij}'x = m_{ij}, \qquad (6)$$

where M_{ij} is a vector, and m_{ij} is a scalar, so that for each $x(k) \in \mathcal{X}_i$, $M_{ij}'x(k) \leq m_{ij}$, and for each $x(k) \in \mathcal{X}_j$ $M_{ij}'x(k) > m_{ij}$. If such a hyperplane can not be found (i.e. the data set is not linearly separable) we are interested in a generalized separating hyperplane which minimizes the number of misclassified data points. The method we use for estimating the separating hyperplanes in this paper is Multicategory Robust Linear Programming (MRLP). This method can solve the classification problem with more than two data classes. For a detailed discussion on MRLP see [10].

2.1   Clustering-Based Procedure

The clustering-based procedure [1] is based on the rationale that regressors that lie close together are likely to belong to the same partition and the same ARX model. The main steps of the procedure are:

- For each data pair $(x(k), y(k))$ a local data set (LD) $\mathcal{C}_k$ is built containing its $c-1$ nearest datapoints[1] in the regressor space $\mathbb{X}$. LDs that only contain data pairs belonging to a single subsystem are referred to as *pure* LDs, while LDs containing data generated by different subsystems are called *mixed* LDs.
- Calculate θ_k^{LS} for each LD using least squares on $\mathcal{C}_k$ and compute the mean m_k of $\mathcal{C}_k$. Each datapoint $(x(k), y(k))$ is thereby mapped onto the feature vectors $\xi_k = [(\theta_k^{LS})', m_k']'$.
- Cluster the points $\{\xi_k\}_{k=1}^{N}$ in s clusters $\mathcal{D}_i$ by minimizing a suitable cost function.
- Since the mapping of the datapoints onto the feature space is bijective, the data subsets $\{\mathcal{F}_i\}_{i=1}^{s}$ can be built using the clusters $\{\mathcal{D}_i\}_{i=1}^{s}$. The PVs $\{\theta_i\}_{i=1}^{s}$ are estimated from data subsets $\mathcal{F}_i$ by least squares.

The clustering procedure requires the model orders n_a, n_b, and the number of models s. The parameter c is the tuning knob of this procedure.

2.2   Bounded-Error Procedure

The main feature of the bounded-error procedure [2, 3] is to impose that the error $e(k)$ in (1) is bounded by a given quantity $\delta > 0$ for all the samples in the estimation data set $\mathcal{N}$. At *initialization*, the estimation of the number of submodels s, data classification and parameter estimation are performed simultaneously by partitioning the (typically infeasible) set of N linear complementary inequalities

$$|y(k) - \varphi(k)'\theta| \le \delta, \quad k = 1, \dots, N, \tag{7}$$

where $\varphi(k)' = [x(k)'\ 1]$, into a minimum number of feasible subsystems (MIN PFS problem). MIN PFS problem is $\mathcal{NP}$-hard, and the suboptimal algorithm based on thermal relaxations is used. Then, an iterative *refinement* procedure is applied in order to deal with data points $(y(k), x(k))$ satisfying $|y(k) - \varphi(k)'\theta_i| \le \delta$ for more than one θ_i. These data are termed *undecidable*. The refinement procedure alternates between data reassignment and parameter update, and, if desirable, enables the reduction of the number of submodels. For given positive thresholds α and β, submodels i and j are merged if $\alpha_{i,j} < \alpha$, with

$$\alpha_{i,j} = \|\theta_i - \theta_j\|_2 / \min\{\|\theta_i\|_2, \|\theta_j\|_2\}, \tag{8}$$

whereas submodel i is discarded if the cardinality of the corresponding data cluster $\mathcal{F}_i$ is less than βN. In [2, 3] parameter estimates are computed through

---

[1] According to the Euclidean distance.

the ℓ_∞ projection estimator, but any other projection estimate, such as least squares, can be used [11].

The bounded-error procedure requires that the model orders n_a and n_b are fixed. The main tuning parameter is the bound δ: The larger δ, the smaller the required number of submodels at the price of a worse fit of the data. The optional parameters α and β, if used, also implicitly determine the final number of submodels returned by the procedure. Another tuning parameter is the number of nearest neighbors c used to attribute undecidable data points to submodels in the refinement step.

2.3   Bayesian Procedure

The Bayesian procedure [4] is based on the idea of refining the available a priori knowledge about the modes and parameters of the hybrid system. Parameters θ_i of the piece-wise affine map (2) are treated as random variables, and described with their probability density functions (pdfs) $p_{\theta_i}(\cdot)$. A priori knowledge on the parameters can be supplied to the procedure by choosing appropriate a priori parameter pdfs. The data classification problem is posed as the problem of finding the data classification with the highest probability. Since this problem is combinatorial, an iterative suboptimal algorithm is derived in [4], based on sequential processing of data points in the collected data set. It is assumed that the probability density function of the additive noise term e, $p_e(\cdot)$ is given.

The parameter estimation algorithm has N iterations, and in each iteration the pdf of one of the parameters is refined. In the k-th iteration of the algorithm the most probable mode $\mu(k)$ of the data pair $(x(k), y(k))$ is computed, using the available pdfs of the parameter vectors from step $k - 1$. Subsequently, the data pair $(x(k), y(k))$ is assigned to the mode i that most likely generated it, and the a posteriori pdf of parameter vector θ_i is computed, using as a fact that the pair $(x(k), y(k))$ was generated by mode i. To numerically implement the Bayesian procedure particle filtering algorithms are used (see e.g. [12]). In order to have a good representation of the pdf a large number of particles may be needed. This accounts for the majority of the computational burden.

After the parameter estimation phase, data points are attributed to the mode that most likely generated them. For the estimation of regions a modification of the standard MRLP procedure is proposed in [4]. Assume that the data point attributed to the mode i ends up in the region $\mathcal{X}_j$. If the probabilities that the data point is generated by both modes are approximately equal, this misclassification should not be penalized highly. Following this idea we introduce the non-negative valued *pricing functions*, which assign price to misclassification of data points. Pricing functions are plugged into the MRLP procedure.

The Bayesian procedure requires model orders n_a and n_b, and the number of modes s. The most important tuning parameters of the procedure are the a priori parameter pdfs $p_{\theta_i}(\cdot, 0)$, and the pdf of the additive noise p_e. Also, the particle filtering algorithm has several tuning parameters.

2.4   Algebraic Procedure

The method proposed in [5, 6] approaches the problem of identifying the class of Switched ARX (SARX) models in an algebraic fashion. For deterministic models, it provides a global solution that is provably correct in the noiseless case, even when the number of models and the model orders are unknown and different. For stochastic models, it provides a sub-optimal solution that can be used to initialize any of the iterative approaches. The algebraic method exploits the fact that in the noiseless case ($e = 0$), the data pair $(x(k), y(k))$ satisfies $z'(k)[1 \ \theta_i']' \doteq [y(k) \ -\varphi'(k)][1 \ \theta_i']' = y(k) - \varphi'(k)\theta_i = 0$ for a suitable PV θ_i. Hence the following homogeneous polynomial of degree s holds for all k[2]

$$p_s(z(k)) = \prod_{i=1}^{s}(z'(k)[1 \ \theta_i']') = \nu_s(z(k))'h_s = 0, \qquad (9)$$

where $\nu_n(z(k))$ contains all $M_s(n_a, n_b) \doteq \binom{n_a+n_b+s+1}{s}$ monomials of degree s in $z(k)$ and $h_s \in \mathbb{R}^{M_s(n_a,n_b)}$ contains the coefficients of p_s. Therefore, the identification of multiple ARX models can be viewed as the identification of a single, though more complex, hybrid ARX model $\nu_s(z(k))'h_s = 0$ whose hybrid PV h_s depends on the parameters of the ARX models $\{\theta_i\}_{i=1}^{s}$, but not on the switching sequence or the switching mechanism. Since the polynomial $h_s'\nu_s(z(k)) = 0$ holds for all k, the hybrid PV can be identified by solving the following linear system (using least squares with noisy data)

$$[\nu_s(z(1)) \cdots \nu_s(z(k)) \cdots]'h_s = 0 \quad \text{and} \quad h_s(1) = 1. \qquad (10)$$

This linear system has a unique solution when the data are sufficiently exciting and s, n_a and n_b are known perfectly. When only upper bounds $\bar{s}$, $\bar{n}_a$ and $\bar{n}_b$ for s, n_a and n_b, respectively, are available, one can still obtain a unique solution by noticing that the last entries of each θ_i are zero, hence the last entries of $h_{\bar{s}}$ must also be zero. Determining the number of zero entries requires a tuning parameter in the case of noisy data. Given $h_{\bar{s}}$, the number of models s is the number of non-repeated factors in $p_{\bar{s}}$ and the PVs of the original ARX models correspond to the last $\bar{n}_a + \bar{n}_b + 1$ entries of the vector of partial derivatives of $p_{\bar{s}}$, $\frac{\partial p_{\bar{s}}(z)}{\partial z} \in \mathbb{R}^{\bar{n}_a+\bar{n}_b+2}$, evaluated at a point $z_i \in \mathbb{R}^{\bar{n}_a+\bar{n}_b+2}$ that is generated by the ith ARX model and can be chosen automatically once p_s is known. Given the PVs, data pairs $(x(k), y(k)$ are attributed to the model λ satisfying the rule

$$\lambda(k) = \arg \min_{1 \le i \le s} (y(k) - \varphi(k)'\theta_i)^2. \qquad (11)$$

This rule is applicable to SARX models, and by extension to all switching mechanisms. However, if additional knowledge about the switching mechanism (e.g. PWARX models) is available, more appropriate classification rules can be used.

---

[2] This product equation was introduced independently in [13] in the particular case of $s = 2$ models.

2.5   Quality Measures

Since our aim is to compare the procedures, some quantitative measures for the quality of the identification results are introduced. These measures will capture the accuracy of the estimated PVs $\{\hat{\theta}_i\}_{i=1}^s$ and the accuracy of the estimated partitions $\{\hat{\mathcal{X}}_i\}_{i=1}^s$.

When the model that generated the data is known, one can measure the accuracy of the identified PV through the quantity:

$$\Delta_\theta = \max_{1 \leq i \leq s} \left(\min_{1 \leq j \leq s} \frac{\|\hat{\theta}_i - \theta_j\|_2}{\|\theta_j\|_2} \right), \tag{12}$$

where $\hat{\theta}_i$ are the reconstructed PVs and θ_j are the PVs of the generating model. This measure is only applicable for the cases where the number of submodels is the same for the generating and identified model. Δ_θ is zero for the perfect estimates, and increases as the estimates worsen.

A sensible quality measure for the estimated regions is much harder to define. For the case where $n = 1$ and $s = 2$ we propose the following index:

$$\Delta_\mathcal{X} = \left| \frac{m_{12}}{M_{12}} - \frac{\hat{m}_{12}}{\hat{M}_{12}} \right|, \tag{13}$$

where M_{12}, m_{12}, $\hat{M}_{12}$, $\hat{m}_{12}$ are the coefficients of the separating hyperplanes, defined in (6), of the original and reconstructed model, respectively.

An overall quality measure which is also applicable when the generating model is not known is provided by the sum of squared residuals (one step ahead prediction errors):

$$\hat{\sigma}_\varepsilon^2 = \frac{1}{s} \sum_{i=1}^s \frac{\text{SSR}_{\mathcal{F}_i}}{|\mathcal{F}_i|}, \tag{14}$$

where the set $\mathcal{F}_i$ contains the datapoints classified to submodel i and the sum of squared residuals (SSR) of submodel i is defined as:

$$\text{SSR}_{\mathcal{F}_i} = \sum_{x(k) \in \mathcal{F}_i} (y(k) - [x(k)' \, 1]\theta_i)^2.$$

The value of the estimated model is considered acceptable if $\hat{\sigma}_\varepsilon^2$ is small and/or near the expected noise of the identified system.

Models with good one-step ahead prediction properties may perform poorly in simulation. To measure the model performance in simulation we propose to use the averaged Sum of the Squared simulation Errors (SSE_{sim}),

$$\text{SSE}_{\text{sim}} = \frac{1}{N-n} \sum_{k=n+1}^N (y(k) - \hat{y}(k))^2, \tag{15}$$

where $\hat{y}(k)$ is the output of the simulation obtained by building $x(k)$ from the real inputs and previously estimated outputs. The idea behind (15) is that poorly estimated regions may increase the simulation error, since these poor estimates may lead to wrong choices of the next submodel.

When doing experimental identification $\hat{\sigma}_\varepsilon^2$ and SSE_{sim} are useful for selecting acceptable models from a set of identified models obtained by using the procedures with different tuning parameters and estimates of the system orders.

3   Intersecting Hyperplanes

If the hyperplanes over the regressor space defined by PVs θ_i and θ_j intersect over $\mathcal{X}_j$, datapoints may be wrongly attributed to the data subset $\mathcal{F}_i$. To shed some light on this issue, consider the PWARX model $y(k) = f(x(k)) + e(k)$ where f is defined as:

$$f(x) = \begin{cases} [\, x \quad 1\,] \begin{bmatrix} 0.5 \\ 0.5 \end{bmatrix} & \text{if } x \in [-2.5,\, 0] \\[4mm] [\, x \quad 1\,] \begin{bmatrix} -1 \\ 2 \end{bmatrix} & \text{if } x \subset (0,\, 2.5] \end{cases} \tag{16}$$

The data set used for identification is depicted in figure 1, together with the data classification obtained from the clustering-based and bounded error procedures. It is seen that the clustering-based and the bounded-error procedures do not experience problems with the intersecting PVs in this particular example. The data classification using the algebraic procedure and the minimum prediction error rule (11) is given in figure 1, right. It is seen that the minimum error prediction rule can lead to misclassifications, and hence it is not the most appropriate rule for the case of PWARX models.

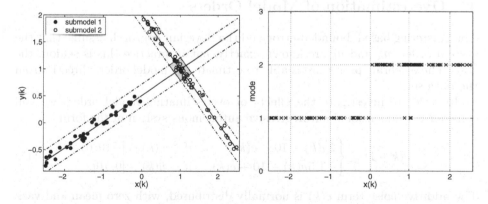

Fig. 1. left: Classification with clustering-based and the bounded-error procedures. Both procedures yield $\Delta_\theta = 0.0186$ and $\Delta_\mathcal{X} = 0.0055$ **right:** Data classification obtained by using the algebraic procedure (yielding $\Delta_\theta = 0.0276$) and attributing each data point to the submodel which generates the smallest prediction error

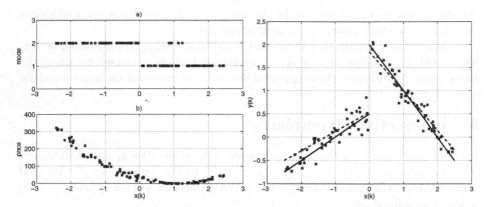

Fig. 2. Identification results for Bayesian procedure, initialized with a priori parameter pdfs $p_{\theta_1}(\cdot; 0) = p_{\theta_2}(\cdot; 0) \sim \mathcal{U}[-2.5, 2.5] \times [-2.5, 2.5]$, yielding $\Delta_\theta = 0.1366$ and $\Delta_\chi = 0.0228$ **left:** a) Data points attributed to modes b) Price function for the wrong classification **right:** Data set used for identification, the true model (solid) and the identified model (dashed)

The data classification and the price function for misclassification using the Bayesian procedure is depicted in figure 2, left. The price for misclassification of wrongly attributed points is small in comparison to the weight for misclassification of the correctly attributed points. The identified model with the Bayesian procedure, together with the true model is depicted in the figure 2, right.

We stress that the classification methods employed by the clustering-based, bounded-error and the Bayesian methods are based on heuristics. Theoretical analysis of this issue is needed.

4   Overestimation of Model Orders

The clustering based, bounded-error and the Bayesian approach assume that the system orders n_a and n_b are known exactly, but in practice this is seldom the case. The algebraic procedure is able to estimate the model orders directly from the data set.

In order to investigate the effects of overestimating model orders we will consider a 1-dimensional autoregressive autonomous system of the form

$$y(k+1) = \begin{cases} 2y(k) + 10 + e(k), & \text{if} \quad y(k) \in [-10, 0) \\ -1.5y(k) + 10 + e(k), & \text{if} \quad y(k) \in [0, 10]. \end{cases} \tag{17}$$

The additive noise term $e(k)$ is normally distributed, with zero mean and variance $\sigma_e^2 = 0.01$. The sequence $y(k)$ was generated with $y(0) = -10$, and the input was generated as $u(k) \sim \mathcal{U}[-10, 10]$.

The true model orders are $n_a = 1, n_b = 0$. Identification procedures were applied for all combinations of $n_a = 1, \ldots, 4$ and $n_b = 1, \ldots, 5$. Note that for overes-

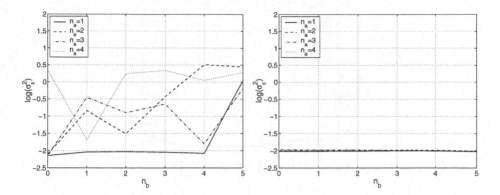

Fig. 3. left: $\hat{\sigma}_\varepsilon^2$ for the clustering procedure with $s = 2$ and $c = 20$ **right:** $\hat{\sigma}_\varepsilon^2$ for the bounded error procedure

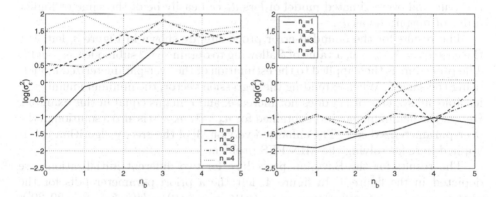

Fig. 4. $\hat{\sigma}_\varepsilon^2$ for the Bayesian procedure **left:** with unprecise initial parameter pdfs **right:** with precise initial parameter pdfs

timated model orders, the correct model is obtained by setting to zeroes the entries in θ_i, M_{ij}, m_{ij} on positions corresponding to superfluous elements in the regressor.

Figure 3 shows the values of the criterion $\hat{\sigma}_\varepsilon^2$ on the logarithmic scale, for models with different model orders identified by the clustering-based procedure. From figure 3 it is seen that the clustering procedure identifies the model with $\hat{\sigma}_\varepsilon^2$ value close to the noise in the system for true system orders, but that the performance rapidly deteriorates when the model order is overestimated. The problem with the overestimated order lies in the assumption that datapoints close to each other in the regressor space belong to the same subsystem. When overestimating the order of the model regressor is extended with elements which do not contain relevant information for the estimation of the subsystems, but change the distance between the regressors. If the true distance is denoted by d_0, the distance between the extended regressors is $d_e^2 = d_0^2 + d_*^2$, where d_*^2 is due to the added elements, and contains no useful information. Depending on

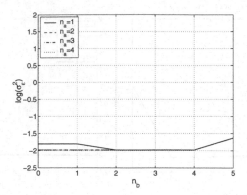

Fig. 5. $\hat{\sigma}_\varepsilon^2$ for the algebraic procedure

the true and overestimated model orders d_* can easily be of the same or higher order of magnitude as d_0.

The results for the bounded-error procedure are shown in Figure 3, left. For the case $n_a = 1$, $n_b = 0$, a value of δ allowing to obtain $s = 2$ submodels is sought. The procedure is then applied to the estimation of the over-parameterized models using the same δ. When extending the regression vector, the minimum number of feasible subsystems of (7) does not increase, and remains equal in this example. Hence, the minimum partition obtained for $n_a = 1$, $n_b = 0$ is also a solution in the over-parameterized case. The enhanced version [3] of the greedy algorithm [14] is applied here for solving the MIN PFS problem.

The results for the Bayesian procedure for two different initializations are depicted in the figure 4. In figure 4, left the a priori parameter pdfs for the case $n_a = 1, n_b = 0$ are chosen as $p_{\theta_1}(\cdot; 0) = p_{\theta_2}(\cdot; 0) = \mathcal{U}([-5,5] \times [-20,20])$. For increased orders, added elements in the parameter vector are taken to be uniformly distributed in the interval $[-5,5]$ (while the true value is 0). In figure (4), right for the case $n_a = 1, n_b = 0$ the a priori parameter pdfs are chosen as $p_{\theta_1}(\cdot; 0) = \mathcal{U}([0,4] \times [8,12])$, $p_{\theta_2}(\cdot; 0) = \mathcal{U}([-4,0] \times [8,12])$, and all added elements are taken to be uniformly distributed in the interval $[-0.5, 0.5]$. This example shows the importance of proper choice of initial parameter pdfs for the Bayesian procedure. With precise initial pdfs the algorithm manages to estimate relatively accurate over-parameterized models. In the case when the a priori information is not adequate the performance of the algorithm deteriorates rapidly.

The algebraic procedure is applied to the data set with $s = 2$, but unknown model orders. The results are depicted in the figure 5. From 5 we see that the procedure has no difficulties in estimating the over-parameterized model.

5   Effects of Noise

In this section we study effects of noise e on the identification procedures. The first issue of interest is the effect that different realizations of noise with the

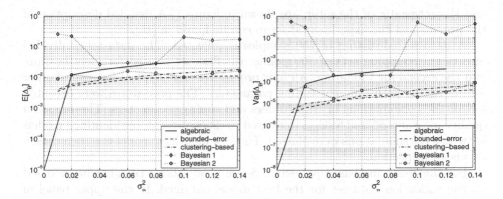

Fig. 6. Means (left) and variances (right) of the Δ_θ distributions for several variances of noise σ_η^2

same statistical properties have on the identification results. The second issue is how statistical properties of noise influence identification results.

To shed some light on these issues we designed an experiment with the PWARX model of section 4 (see (17)). For this model we generated a noise-less data set of 100 datapoints. The procedures are applied 100 times on this data set, after adding a different realization of normally distributed noise with zero mean and variance σ_e^2 to the outputs $y(k)$. For each identified model the index Δ_θ is computed. In this way an approximate distribution of Δ_θ for each σ_e^2 can be constructed. For each such distribution we computed its mean and variance. For more details see [15]

Figure 6 depicts means and variances of Δ_θ distributions as functions of σ_e^2 for all four procedures. Again, we have two different initializations for the Bayesian procedure, denoted in figure as "Bayesian 1" and "Bayesian 2". For "Bayesian 1" we used $p_{\theta_1}(\cdot; 0) = p_{\theta_2}(\cdot; 0) = \mathcal{U}([-5, 5] \times [-20, 20])$, and for "Bayesian 2" we used $p_{\theta_1}(\cdot; 0) = \mathcal{U}([0, 4] \times [8, 12])$, $p_{\theta_1}(\cdot; 0) = \mathcal{U}([-4, 0] \times [8, 12])$.

From figure 6 we can conclude that the clustering-based procedure and the bounded-error procedure achieve similar performance with respect to noise. The algebraic procedure is more sensitive to noise, as compared to the clustering-based and bounded-error procedures. With precise initialization ("Bayesian 1") the Bayesian procedure achieves performance comparable to clustering-based and bounded-error, while with imprecise initialization ("Bayesian 2") the quality measures are the worst of all procedures.

6   Experimental Example

In this section we show the results of the identification of the component placement process in pick-and-place machines. The pick-and-place machine is used for automatically placing electronic components on a Printed Circuit Board (PCB). To study the placement process, an experimental setup was made. The photo and the schematic of the setup are shown in figure 7. A detailed description of the process and the experimental setup can be found in [16].

A data set consisting of 750 samples is collected. The data set is divided into two overlapping sets of 500 points, the first set is used for identification, and the second for validation. All four procedures were applied for several order estimates and with different tuning parameters. The procedures were executed for all the combinations of these orders and tuning parameters. The proposed quality measures $\hat{\sigma}_\varepsilon^2$ and $\mathrm{SSE_{sim}}$ were used to choose acceptable identified models for which the simulations were plotted. The best identified model was then chosen by visual inspection.

For the clustering-based procedure figure 8, left shows the *simulation* based on the validation data set for the best model obtained. In the upper panel of the figure measured output y_{id} and the simulated output y_{sim} are depicted. The lower panel shows which of the identified submodels is active at each time instant. It turns out that the best models are obtained for high values of c. The same was observed in [16]. A possible explanation is the following: because of the presence of dry friction neither the free nor the impact mode are linear, but with large LD's the effects of dry friction can be 'averaged out' as a process noise. Note that the difference between the measured and simulated responses, which is due to unmodeled dry friction, is clearly visible, e.g. on the time interval $[225, 300]$.

As the number of modes s for the bounded-error procedure is not fixed, in order to identify two modes, the right combination of the parameters α, γ and δ has to be found. For the initial error bound δ we used $3\hat{\sigma}_\varepsilon \approx 1$, obtained from the clustering-based procedure, assuming that this value would be a good estimate for the variance of the measurement noise. Executing the bounded-error procedure with δ's in the vicinity of this $3\hat{\sigma}_\varepsilon^2$ resulted in identified models with only one parameter vector, and a large number of infeasible points. Therefore, we had to lower the error bound to $\delta = 0.30$. For this value of δ the procedure identified a model that distinguishes two submodels. Model identified with this δ had a smaller values of both $\hat{\sigma}_\varepsilon^2$ for the identification data set and SSE_{sim}

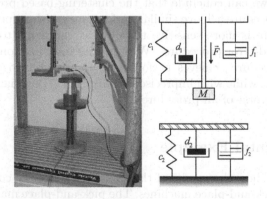

Fig. 7. Photo and the schematic representation of the experimental setup

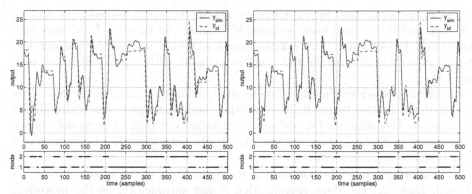

Fig. 8. left: Simulation of the PWARX model generated by the clustering procedure with $n_a = 2$, $n_b = 2$, $s = 2$ and $c = 90$ for the validation data set with $SSE_{sim} = 1.98$ **right:** Simulation of the PWARX model generated by the bounded-error procedure with $n_a = 2$, $n_b = 2$, $\delta = 0.3$, $\alpha = 0.10$, $\beta = 0.01$ and $c = 40$ for the validation data set with $SSE_{sim} = 1.72$ **upper fig.:** solid line: predicted response, dashed line: measured response **lower fig.:** active mode

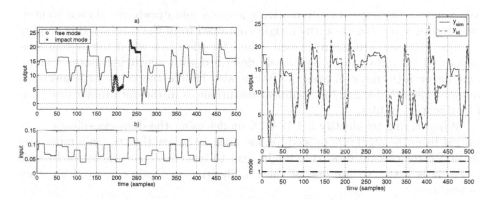

Fig. 9. Bayesian procedure. **left:** Data set used for identification a) position (portion marked with o: data points used for the initialization of the free mode; portion marked with ×: data points used for initialization of impact mode b) input signal **right: upper fig.:** Simulation of the identified model (solid line: simulated response, dashed line: measured response), $SSE_{sim} = 1.56$ **lower fig.:** modes active during the simulation

for the validation data set than the model identified with the clustering-based procedure. The simulation of the validation data set for the best identified model is shown in the figure 8, right.

Physical insight into the operation of the setup facilitates the initialization of the Bayesian procedure. For instance, although the mode switch does not occur at a fixed height of the head, with a degree of certainty data points below certain height may be attributed to the free mode, and, analogously data points above certain height may be attributed to the impact mode. This a priori information may be exploited to obtain the rough estimate of each of the parameters through least squares, θ_i^{LS}. Also, the variance $\tilde{V}_i$ of such estimate may be obtained. This information is sufficient to describe the parameter θ_i as a normally distributed random variable, with a mean θ_i^{LS} and variance $\tilde{V}_i$.

Portions of the identification data set that are used to initialize the procedure are depicted in the figure 9, left, together with the input signal. Results of simulation of the identified model are given in figure 9, right. The model yields a lower value of SSE_{sim} than the two models obtained with the clustering-based and bounded-error procedures.

The algebraic procedure identified the parameters of the model, with $\hat{\sigma}_\varepsilon^2 = 0.0803$. However, the data classification is not satisfactory, as the procedure predicts rapidly oscillating mode values, while in the physical system such oscillations are impossible. It remains for the future work to check if estimated parameters can be used to obtain the satisfactory PWARX model.

7   Conclusions

We conclude the paper by summarizing features and drawbacks of each identification procedure, based on the insights obtained from the considered examples.

The algebraic procedure is well suited for the cases when the system that generated the data can be accurately described with a switched linear system, and no or little noise is present. It can also handle the cases with unknown model orders. Noise and/or nonlinear disturbances in the data may cause poor identification results.

When trying to identify a PWARX model using the data classification obtained from the algebraic procedure one must be aware that the minimum prediction error classification rule might lead to inaccurate classification. In such cases, it is better to use one of the classification methods employed by other procedures.

The Bayesian procedure is well suited for the cases where the sufficient physical insight into the underlying data generating process is available. By appropriate choice of the initial parameter pdfs the user might steer the procedure towards identifying the model where the modes of the identified model represent different modes of the physical system. On the other hand, poor initialization may lead to poor identification results.

The bounded error procedure is well suited for the cases when there is no a priori knowledge on the physical system and one needs to identify a model with a prescribed bounded prediction error (e.g. approximation of nonlinear systems). Tuning parameters allow for the tradeoff between the model complexity and accuracy. However, finding the right combination of tuning parameters to get the model with the prescribed structure (number of modes) may be difficult.

The clustering-based procedure is well suited for the cases when there is no a priori knowledge on the physical system, and one needs to identify a model with a prescribed structure. When using the clustering-based procedure one must be aware of the possible erratic behavior (as described in section 4) in the cases when the model orders are not known exactly.

References

1. Ferrari-Trecate, G., Muselli, M., Liberati, D., Morari, M.: A clustering technique for the identification of piecewise affine and hybrid systems. Automatica **39** (2003) 205–217
2. Bemporad, A., Garulli, A., Paoletti, S., Vicino, A.: A greedy approach to identification of piecewise affine models. In Maler, O., Pnueli, A., eds.: Hybrid Systems: Computation and Control. Lecture Notes on Computer Science. Springer Verlag (2003) 97–112
3. Bemporad, A., Garulli, A., Paoletti, S., Vicino, A.: Data classification and parameter estimation for the identification of piecewise affine models. In: Proceedings of the 43rd IEEE Conference on Decision and Control, Paradise Island, Bahamas (2004) 20–25
4. Juloski, A., Weiland, S., Heemels, W.: A Bayesian approach to identification of hybrid systems. In: Proceedings of the 43rd Conference on Decision and Control, Paradise Island, Bahamas (2004) 13–19
5. Vidal, R., Soatto, S., Ma, Y., Sastry, S.: An algebraic geometric approach to the identification of a class of linear hybrid systems. In: Proc. of IEEE Conference on Decision and Control. (2003)
6. Vidal, R.: Identification of PWARX hybrid models with unknown and possibly different orders. In: Proc. of IEEE American Control Conference. (2004)
7. Roll, J., Bemporad, A., Ljung, L.: Identification of piecewise affine systems via mixed-integer programming. Automatica **40** (2004) 37–50
8. Munz, E., Krebs, V.: Identification of hybrid systems using a priori knowledge. In: Preprints of the 15th IFAC world congress, Barcelona, Spain (2002)
9. Ferrari-Trecate, G., Schinkel, M.: Conditions of optimal classification for piecewise affine regression. In Maler, O., Pnueli, A., eds.: Proc. 6th International Workshop on Hybrid Systems: Computation and Control. Volume 2623 of Lecture Notes in Computer Science. Springer-Verlag (2003) 188–202
10. Bennett, K., Mangasarian, O.: Multicategory discrimination via linear programming. Optimization Methods and Software **3** (1993) 27–39
11. Milanese, M., Vicino, A.: Optimal estimation theory for dynamic systems with set membership uncertainty: an overview. Automatica **27** (1991) 997–1009
12. Arulampalam, M., Maskell, S., Gordon, N., Clapp, T.: A tutorial on particle filters for online nonlinear/non-Gaussian Bayesian tracking. IEEE Transactions on Signal Processing **50** (2002) 174–188
13. Verriest, E., Moor, B.D.: Multi-mode system identification. In: Proc. of European Conference on Control. (1999)
14. Amaldi, E., Mattavelli, M.: The MIN PFS problem and piecewise linear model estimation. Discrete Applied Mathematics **118** (2002) 115–143
15. Niessen, H., Juloski, A., Ferrari-Trecate, G., Heemels, W.: Comparison of three procedures for the identification of hybrid systems. In: Proceedings of the Conference on Control Applications, Taipei, Taiwan (2004)
16. Juloski, A., Heemels, W., Ferrari-Trecate, G.: Data-based hybrid modelling of the component placement process in pick-and-place machines. Control Engineering Practice **12** (2004) 1241–1252

An Ontology-Based Approach to Heterogeneous Verification of Embedded Control Systems

Rajesh Kumar, Bruce H. Krogh, and Peter Feiler

Carnegie Mellon University, Pittsburgh, PA 15213-3890, USA
{rajeshk, krogh@ece.cmu.edu}, phf@sei.cmu.edu

Abstract. This paper presents an ontology-based approach to *heterogeneous verification* of embedded systems, that is, the integration of verification results from different tools and different models of embedded system applications. We present an overview of our proposed framework and explain the key components. We then describe an initial ontology for embedded control applications and its mapping to a knowledge base. We illustrate this initial framework using an example of an automotive power window controller. The concluding discussion describes our current work and future research directions.

Keywords: ontology, knowledge base, knowledge integration, theorem proving.

1 Introduction

Since the 1980s tools based on formal methods, particularly model checking, have emerged as powerful aids for the verification of digital hardware designs [1]. Model checking of software has also advanced greatly with programs running into thousands of lines having been verified [2]. Formal techniques provide more rigorous guarantees about the correctness of a system than informal testing.

Much of the research in hybrid systems has been directed toward extending the rigor of formal methods to applications where continuous dynamics need to be accommodated, as in many embedded control system designs [3,4]. While this is a laudable goal, it is clear that the application of hybrid systems tools will always require significant abstraction and simplification of models. This means that complete verification of designs must incorporate information from other sources, ranging from engineering insight to simulation studies. This is not surprising since even for discrete systems abstraction, extensive simulation, and engineering judgement are required for complete debugging and verification.

Our tool SVM (*System Verification Manager*) makes it possible to record the relationships between requirements, models and verification processes, and perform requirements-driven verification (formal and informal) using multiple models and tools [5,6]. This paper proposes a formal framework for collecting verification information from many sources, including new tools for hybrid system verification, and for using the information to verify system properties that

M. Morari and L. Thiele (Eds.): HSCC 2005, LNCS 3414, pp. 370–385, 2005.

are beyond the reach of any one tool or modelling formalism. We call this process *heterogeneous verification*.

Heterogeneous verification currently occurs in an ad hoc fashion. This is mainly due to the difficulty of keeping track of information as the system is built,due to the volume of data as well as the distributed nature of development. We propose an *ontology-based approach* as a foundation of a framework to capture development data formally and derive new information from heterogeneous sources.

Section 2 defines the terminology in this paper and presents an overview of some related research. Section 3 gives an overview of the proposed approach and describes the overall process flow for performing heterogeneous verification. Section 4 describes a base ontology for embedded control systems. Section 5 illustrates the concepts of heterogeneous verification for an example of a power window controller. The concluding section summarizes the contributions of this paper and describes our current work on realizing the complete framework described in this paper.

2   Definitions and Related Work

This section defines the key concepts on which our framework draws and discusses related research on knowledge representation and reasoning.

An *ontology* is an "explicit specification of a conceptualization" [7]. A conceptualization is a set of definitions that allows one to construct expressions about some particular domain. A *knowledge base* is a collection of knowledge expressed using some formal knowledge representation language [8]. In any application that manipulates a large body of knowledge, knowledge management tools are needed that integrate the disparate sources of data into a coherent body of interrelated information. This is the problem of *knowledge integration*. New knowledge can be obtained through automated deduction or automated reasoning [9].

Deductive databases deduce new facts from the facts in the database using reasoning rules [10]. Our verification support framework extends the idea of deductive databases with an ontology-based, user-extensible interface for programming the reasoning logic. *Mediators* [11] and *ontology extended databases* [12] address the problem of "semantic interoperation" among different data sources, that is, combining information from different data sources even though they may be represented in different formats. The formalism of *hybrid knowledge bases* forms a theoretical framework in which mediators can be expressed in a declarative way [13]. Using an ontology, we essentially bypass the problem of mediation between data sources since an ontology provides a formal structure for the information obtained from different sources.

MILAN is an integrated simulation framework that allows a developer to build different components of a system using different tools [14]. The Metropolis toolset supports multiple analysis tools for design and simulation [15]; the only formal verification tool it supports is SPIN. MILAN and Metropolis address the problem of system design when components may be modelled using different formalisms, and hence they address a different aspect of the larger problem that we can call "heterogeneous system engineering." Our framework aims to support compositional verification across analysis tools. In addition to verification, our framework would also facilitate activities such as consistency checking, assumption tracking, and "what-if" kinds of analysis.

Our approach aims to fuse ontology technologies (which enable the capture and representation of arbitrary domains) with theorem proving (which enable analysis of the stored information to come up with newer pieces of information). There are logic programming languages with special constructs to specify ontologies, such as F-logic [16]. Rules can also be represented in logic-based ontology specification languages such as and ONION [17]. We use the ontology editing tool Protegé [18], which supports the use of Prolog for logical analysis and deduction.

3 Approach

Figure 1 presents the major components and flow of activities in the proposed framework. An initial implementation of the proposed framework is presented in Sect. 5.

Knowledge about the system verification that is relevant to managing the system verification process is extracted from the verification activities and put into a knowledge base. The structure of the knowledge base is defined by an ontology in two stages. A *base ontology* reflects the fact that we are dealing with a model-based system verification process and with the domain of embedded systems. The ontology consists of a *static ontology*, a definition of knowledge structure, and an *epistemic ontology*, a set of dependencies, conditions, and constraints on the facts in the knowledge base. The base ontology is defined once as part of our framework. It is then augmented and refined by domain experts (such as requirements engineers, verification engineers and designers) to reflect knowledge of the application domain that is relevant to the verification process. This process of ontology specialization is a continuous, ongoing process.

Once the knowledge base is defined, it is populated with verification facts from disparate information sources (heterogeneous knowledge assimilation). The heterogeneous information sources shown on the right in Fig. 1 include requirements documents stating properties of the system to be verified, models of the system in different representations and different degrees of fidelity, and the results of performing various kinds of verification ranging from model checking to simulation. These information sources evolve over time as developers create and update models and perform various verification activities.

A *verification manager* operates on the knowledge base to determine the state of system verification and to provide guidance on what verification activities developers should focus on depending on the *requirements*. This activity involves reasoning about the facts in the knowledge base (knowledge composition and deduction). This activity is supported by a query language that operates on the knowledge base. We are currently using the Horn clause language as our

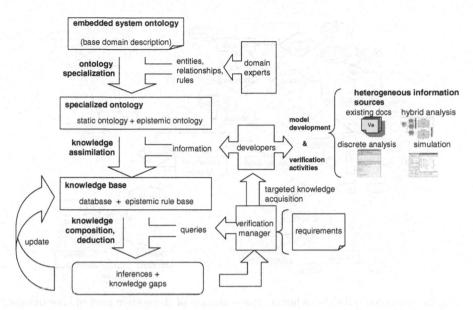

Fig. 1. Elements of the ontology-based framework for heterogeneous verification

query language. A query processor takes (i) a query and (ii) the knowledge base and generates a logic program by slicing the knowledge base; that is, it extracts the information (facts as well as rules) that is relevant to the query. This logic program is then fed to the inference engine.

The *inference engine* derives new facts and answers questions of interest about the verification scenario using the stored information and the specified epistemic rules. We are currently using Prolog as our inference engine. The new pieces of information augment the knowledge base. Reasoning with incomplete knowledge, the inference engine also identifies knowledge gaps, i.e., missing pieces of information in the knowledge base in order to draw desired conclusions. These knowledge gaps are then prioritized by the verification manager to guide developers to perform targeted verifications and re-verifications that focus on critical system requirements. Thus, our ontology-based system verification framework supports an evolutionary process of managing system verification throughout the development life cycle.

4   An Ontology for Embedded Control Systems

This section describes a base ontology for verification of embedded control systems. The ontology consists of two parts: the *static ontology* and the *epistemic ontology*. The static ontology defines the concepts of interest in embedded control systems through the entities and relations shown in Figs. 2 and 3. Our static ontology describes the high level domain objects such as *systems*, *models*, *constraints*, and their interrelationships. A heterogeneous verification scenario

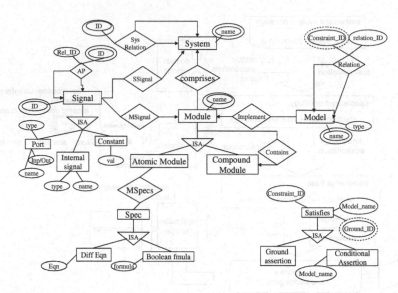

Fig. 2. Relational database schema representation of the system part of base ontology (see Fig. 3 for legend)

consists of one or more *systems*. A *system* can *comprise* one or more *modules*. A module may either be *atomic* or *compound*. A compound module contains other modules. Modules are *implemented* by *models*. Models may be related to one another via relations such as *abstraction, equivalence, sub-model* and so forth. All the relations are identified by unique relation identifiers. In Sect. 5 we illustrate how inferences may be drawn from this information.

Requirements are represented in the form of constraints. A constraint may either be a *logical constraint, timing constraint*, or *structural constraint*. A constraint may be *compound* in that it may consist of other *sub-constraints*.

Constraints are true or false on models, i.e. a model may *satisfy* a constraint. A constraint being satisfied by a model is based on four classes of *grounds* or causes: *model checking, simulation, relation* and *analysis*.

We use the term *epistemic* in the same sense as in [19]. The epistemic ontology captures the expert's understanding of the domain and can be regarded as the logical rules that govern the reasoning on the concepts captured by the static ontology.

The following rules comprise the base epistemic ontology for our example:

- signal relations and causality are transitive.
- any cut of the constraint coverage tree covers nodes above the cut.
- If constraint set A covers B and B is equivalent to C then set A covers C.

The above base domain ontology is specialized for the verification application depending on the types of analyses that need to be considered. For the example scenario we consider we need to refine the epistemic ontology to include the

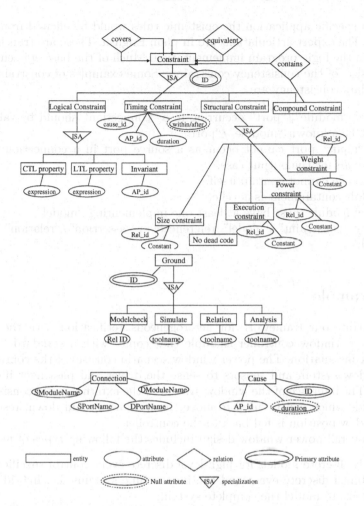

Fig. 3. Relational database schema representation of the constraint part of the base ontology

following constraint satisfaction rules with respect to different relations between models.

- the *equivalence* relation among models is reflexive and transitive.
- The *abstraction* relation on models (with or without respect to a given constraint) is transitive.
- A model satisfies a constraint if an abstraction of it (with or without respect to a given constraint) satisfies that constraint.
- A system (model) satisfies a constraint if any of its subsystems (sub-models) satisfies that constraint.

The ontology is further refined to incorporate sampling time information (see the next section).

For a specific application the epistemic rules would be elicited from domain experts. The expert articulations are in plain English. These are translated into clauses in the logic program implementation. Much of the base epistemic ontology consists of the consistency constraints. Some examples of constraints which govern data consistency are

- Every "module"/"port" occurring in a "connection" should be valid, i.e. it must be a known "module"/"port".
- An "input" port cannot occur as a source port in a connection; *mutatus mutandis* for the output case.
- A module cannot contain itself.
- Module containment is acyclic.
- Every module must have at least one implementing "model".
- Every "constraint"/"model" referenced in "assertion"/"relation" must be valid.

5   Example

We illustrate our framework for heterogeneous verification with the automotive power window controller example that comes with a standard MATLAB Simulink installation. The power window scenario consists of the controller and the window system and sensors to sense the driver and passenger inputs (see Fig. 4). The interface of the window system to the external world consists of two commands which can be used to move the window up and down, respectively. The window position is fed back to the controller.

The overall power window design includes the following types of models:

- purely discrete models for high-level discrete event control specification;
- combined discrete event and continuous time systems, i.e. hybrid dynamic systems, to model the complete system;

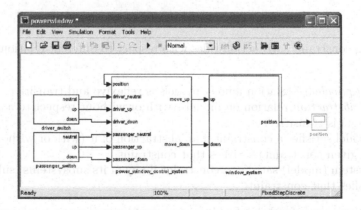

Fig. 4. power window controller

Table 1. Models of interest in the window controller application

Model	Type
discrete-controller	Stateflow
second-order-plant	Simulink
multi-body-plant	Simulink
discrete-controller-2nd-order-plant	Simulink
discrete-controller-multi-body-plant	Simulink

- energy domain models for the plant;
- automatically generated controller source code for the control subsystem.

The requirement for the up button function is stated as:

Req1: The driver/passenger move-up button when pressed shall cause the window to move up within 4s and the window shall never exert a force of more than 100N. The driver button has priority.

The above requirement is composed of two constraints. One is a safety constraint regarding the force and the other is a timing constraint. This is captured in the knowledge base as a compound constraint having two 'sub-constraint's.

The models of interest in the power window scenario are shown in Table 1. The second-order plant and the discrete-controller-second-order-plant models are built for initial testing of the control algorithm. These models do not include any of the actual physics of the plant. After an initial analysis of the discrete event control and continuous dynamics using these models, a detailed plant model can be used to evaluate performance in more realistic situations. Models at such a level of detail are best designed in the power domain, i.e., as energy flows. The detailed plant model uses energy-based components. Power Electronics are used to model the actuator dynamics and the Multibody Toolset in Simulink is used to model the power window plant. This is the multi-body plant model which is included in the discrete-controller-multi-body-plant model. More specifically

- The discrete controller is model-checked against the discrete properties (e.g., the passenger move-up button when pushed causes the window to start moving up).
- The second-order plant is analyzed to check the time taken to close and open the window.
- The full detailed model of the multi-body plant is simulated to check force constraints on the system.

The detailed multi-body-plant model cannot be model-checked because it contains a variety of continuous dynamic elements (e.g., friction in the system, models of the DC motor, and the physical components such as gears with non-linearities). To model check such a system, the usual process is to perform a manual simplification in order to build a model in a formalism that can be input to a model checking tool, e.g., Charon [20]. These simplified models are often based on sweeping, simplifying assumptions that are not documented. For example, to model check the force constraint one would have to construct a hybrid automaton model of the discrete controller coupled to the continuous plant model and introduce new continuous variables and their dynamics to model the window force. Further simplifications are typically needed to construct a model that can actually be analysed (e.g., approximating dynamics by simpler ones, reducing the order, etc.).

Our heterogeneous verification approach makes it possible to pull in the individual analysis results for sub-models (the bullets above) to reason about the complete system and infer results on models and systems for others. The tool also documents the relations between different models constructed during the course of the verification exercise. We illustrate this process now in the context of the power windows example.

Heterogeneous Knowledge Assimilation

Figure 5 shows a screenshot of the Protégé tool. The static ontology defines the database, which stores *facts* about the verification scenario. The static ontology is implemented as class definitions in Protégé. The verification scenario facts are entered in the knowledge base as instances of the class definitions and these instances are accessed by the Prolog reasoning engine. Protégé supports the construction of the static ontology and provides an extensible architecture for extended functionality. The Protégé Prolog plugin has been used to encode epistemic ontology as Horn clauses. These clauses are imported into the knowledge base as the reasoning rules. See Appendix A for the details of the logic program implementation for the epistemic ontology.

Once the knowledge base is defined, it is populated with information about the verification scenario as such information becomes available. For example, the models store of the knowledge base is built by entering the model information (Table 1) as the models are built.

Knowledge Inferencing

We now illustrate the reasoning abilities of the knowledge base with respect to compositional deduction and multi-fidelity reasoning using the requirement relating to the window force.

The models of interest (given in Table 1) are known to the knowledge base. We also know the following facts:

- The window force constraint is true on the `multi-body-plant`. This is obtained from simulation as discussed earlier.
- The `multi-body-plant` is a submodel of the `discrete-controller-multi-body-plant`.
- The `second-order-plant` is a submodel of the `discrete-controller-second-order-plant`.
- The `multi-body-plant` model is an abstraction of the `second-order-plant` model with regard to the window force constraint.

Class definition   Instances   Rules in Prolog

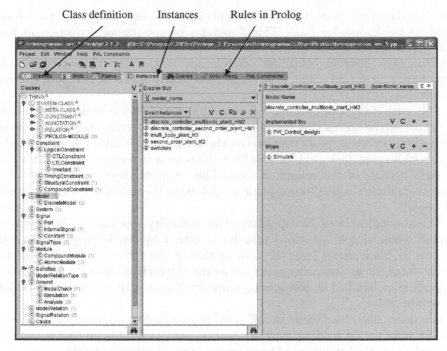

Fig. 5. Knowledge base implementation in Protegé

We have rules that state how properties propagate across abstractions and also from submodels to higher-level models (see Appendix A, item 2).

Given the above information we can query the knowledge base for the models that satisfy the window force sub-requirement. This constraint is identified by the identifier `frame(heterogeneous_ver_2_Instance_41)` in the knowledge base. [1] The following is the Prolog session for this query.

```
?-satisfies(frame(heterogeneous_ver_2_Instance_41), Y),model_name(Y, Name).
Y = frame(heterogeneous_ver_2_Instance_28); Name = multi_body_plant_M3;        (i)
SUCCESS. redo (y/n/a)?y
Y = frame(heterogeneous_ver_2_Instance_27); Name =
                              discrete_controller_second_order_plant_HM1; (ii)
SUCCESS. redo (y/n/a)?y
Y = frame(heterogeneous_ver_2_Instance_29); Name =
                              discrete_controller_multibody_plant_HM2;    (iii)
SUCCESS. redo (y/n/a)?y
Y = frame(heterogeneous_ver_2_Instance_25); Name= second_order_plant_M2;  (iv)
SUCCESS. redo (y/n/a)?y
FAIL
?-
```

The multi-body plant satisfies the requirement (item (i) above) because it is one of known facts provided to the knowledge base.

Since the `multi-body-plant` is a submodel of the `discrete-controller-multi-body-plant` model,the requirement is true on the `discrete-controller-`

---

[1] The identifiers are assigned by Protegé automatically as the knowledge base is built.

`multi-body-plant` (item (iii) above). This inference uses one of the rules provided to the knowledge base. This illustrates compositional deduction in the framework. Similarly the truth/falsity of the discrete properties from model checking the discrete controller propagates to the `discrete-controller` `-second-order-plant` and the `discrete-controller-multi-body-plant` models.

The truth of the window force constraint propagates to the second-order-plant model across the abstraction relation between it and the multi-body-plant model (item (iv)). Inferring properties across the abstraction relation is an example of a bookkeeping task that is usually tedious in a heterogeneous verification scenario because of the volume of data. This property then propagates to the discrete-controller-second-order-plant model using the submodel relation (item (ii) above).

The above illustrates the capability of multi-fidelity reasoning in the proposed scheme. Some simple questions may be answered by considering models and systems as black boxes (e.g. the propagation of the force sub-requirement to the model of the second-order plant across the abstraction relation), while other properties are handled by considering more detail (the example of compositional deduction above).

If a query fails, the failed "proof" may be analyzed to arrive at the pieces of missing information to drive new verification activities. This process is manual currently since Prolog does not have a notion of proof objects. Identifying missing information is one of the directions of future research.

Note that the relationships between the entities are simply *stated* and nothing is specified about how they should be used - this is handled by the Prolog engine. In other words, the encoding of the entities and relationships in the logic program is declarative rather than functional. This enables a flexible use of the knowledge base. For example, we can have queries going the opposite way to those described above, such as the following query that requests the constraints that are true on the discrete controller-second-order plant model.

```
satisfies(X, frame(heterogeneous_ver_2_Instance_27)).
X = frame(heterogeneous_ver_2_Instance_41);    --- the force constraint.
SUCCESS. redo (y/n/a)?y
......
```

The knowledge base returns `frame(heterogeneous_ver_2_Instance_41)`, which corresponds to window force sub-requirement.

Ontology Specialization

Finally we illustrate how our proposed scheme provides the flexibility of knowledge base augmentation, incorporating newer kinds of information/reasoning capabilities by extending the ontology and the knowledge base. The initial knowledge base does not have any sampling time related information about the models. We extend the ontology to include:

- sampling time information for models - this is done by extending the static ontology to add an additional attribute called `sampling time` for `discrete models`.;

- the semantics of the sampling time is added to the epistemic ontology leading to new rules in the knowledge base (see discrete system sampling time related information in Appendix A).

The sampling time information for models is then inserted into the knowledge base and the corresponding rules enable propagation of discrete properties across discrete models. Extensions of the ontology and the knowledge base enables the handling of newer classes of analysis.

To summarize, we have shown how the knowledge base derived from the ontology that we built for the power windows example can be used for the purposes of compositional deduction and heterogeneous reasoning in a verification scenario. We also showed how the framework offers the flexibility to incorporate new types of information. We could also run consistency checks, e.g. to check whether the interconnections in a system are type consistent. Such a query would be handled using the available information about the ports of subsystems and their types. We can do 'what-if' analysis by asserting and de-asserting facts in the knowledge base and re-entering queries.

6   Discussion

This paper presents an illustration of how an ontology-based knowledge management scheme can address some of the problems of verification and validation of hybrid systems. The natural question to ask is whether this approach is feasible for real-scale systems. We believe that the answer to this question is 'yes', because of the success of some recent tools and applications reported in the literature. For example, the European Computer Research Centre (ECRC) started the MegaLog and ECRC Knowledge Base System (EKS) projects to demonstrate the viability of deductive database technology for real-world applications. The work in [21] shows how generic architectures for building large scale knowledge bases are feasible . In [22], the application of deductive databases to standard benchmarks like the Muenchner Verkehrs Verbund (MVV) knowledge base [23] and the Wisconsin database benchmarks [24] is demonstrated.

Our work currently stands as follows. We have adopted the entity-relationship diagram definition as our static ontology specification. There is a simple mapping of the static ontology specification into the class diagram implementation in the tool we used (Protegé). Only parts of the knowledge base are accessed through the Prolog interface for handling queries. We have shown examples of applications of the knowledge base and also the extensibility of our framework to handle newer analyses in Sect. 5.

As mentioned in Sect. 2, many ontology definition languages use Horn clause language (or similar languages) to encode rules. We need a formal language for the epistemic ontology. There exist notations for the static ontology (such as RDF [25] , F-Logic [16]), but there is no equivalent one for the epistemic part. We have used the Horn clause language. A language to specify the epistemic ontology touches on aspects of semantic meta-modelling. A theory of operations on ontology-driven knowledge bases will extend the work of Wiederhold et al. [11]. A higher-level language is required since the framework we propose is meant to be used in a large-scale, distributed verification scenario where it is unreasonable to assume that the users will be familiar with logic programming.

We have used Prolog for the inference engine in our framework because Prolog is a decidable system of logic based on Horn clauses derived from predicate logic. The other attraction of using Prolog is that it is a declarative language. It is quite clear that the full power of first-order predicate calculus is not required for our domain since first-order logic works on the open world assumption where variables can range over infinite domains. Logic programming with its closed-world assumption is more useful because we want to reason using the *existing* information at any point of time. Logic programs without negation can only handle monotonic queries, however, which is insufficient for our purpose since the ability to retract old conclusions is required. In addition, some of the functionality required in such a knowledge management framework calls for constraint solving (over the reals for example). Logic programming languages have been extended to handle constraints, including non-monotonic modes of reasoning as well as inconsistencies and uncertainties [26, 27, 28, 29]. Computational issues become more important as the expressiveness increases, even when the logic remains decidable. We plan to use the enhanced logic programming languages in the future to support these additional concerns that arise in embedded control applications.

References

1. J.R. Burch, E.M. Clarke, D.E. Long, K.L. MacMillan, D.L. Dill: Symbolic model checking for sequential circuit verification. IEEE Transactions on Computer-Aided Design of Integrated Circuits and Systems **13** (1994) 401–424
2. Clarke, E., Kroening, D., Lerda, F.: A tool for checking ANSI-C programs. In Jensen, K., Podelski, A., eds.: Tools and Algorithms for the Construction and Analysis of Systems (TACAS 2004). Volume 2988 of Lecture Notes in Computer Science., Springer (2004) 168–176
3. Alur, R., Courcoubetis, C., Halbwachs, N., Henzinger, T.A., Ho, P.H., Nicollin, X., Olivero, A., Sifakis, J., Yovine, S.: The algorithmic analysis of hybrid systems. Theoretical Computer Science **138** (1995) 3–34
4. Alur, R., Henzinger, T., Wong-Toi, H.: Symbolic analysis of hybrid systems. In: Proc. 37-th IEEE Conference on Decision and Control, 1997. (1997)
5. Aldrich, B., Fehnker, A., Krogh, B.H., Feiler, P.H., Han, Z., Lim, E., Sivashankar;, S.: Managing verification activities with svm. Sixth International Conference on Formal Engineering Methods (2004)
6. (http://www.ece.cmu.edu/~webk/svm)
7. Gruber, T.: A translation approach to portable ontology specification. Knowledge Acquisition **5** (1993) 199–220
8. Levesque, H.J., Lakemeyer, G.: The Logic of Knowledge Bases. The MIT Press (2001)
9. Fitting, M.: First-Order Logic and Automated Theorem Proving. Springer-Verlag (1995)
10. Ramamohanarao, K., Harland, J.: An introduction to deductive database languages and systems. The VLDB Journal **3** (1994) 107–122

11. Wiederhold, G.: Interoperation, mediation and ontologies. International Symposium on Fifth Generation Computer Systems (FGCS94), Tokyo, Japan (1994)
12. Bonatti, P., Deng, Y., Subrahmanian, V.: An ontology-extended relational algebra. Proc. 2003 IEEE Intl. Conference on Information Reuse and Integration, Las Vegas, Nevada (2003) 192–199
13. Lu, J.J., Nerode, A., Subrahmanian, V.S.: Hybrid knowledge bases. IEEE Transactions on Knowledge and Data Engineering, **8** (1996) 773–785
14. Ledeczi, A., Davis, J., Neema, S., Agrawal, A.: Modeling methodology for integrated simulation of embedded systems. ACM Transactions on Modeling and Computer Simulation (2003)
15. Balarin, F., Watanabe, Y., Hsieh, H., Lavagno, L., Passerone, C., Sangiovanni-Vincentelli, A.: Metropolis: An integrated electronic system design environment. (Transactions of IEEE Computer Society, April 2003 (Vol. 36, No. 4))
16. Maedche, A., Staab, S.: Ontologies in f-logic. (In: S. Staab, R. Studer (Eds.): Handbook of Ontologies. Springer)
17. Gyssens, M., Paredaens, J., den Bussche, J.V., van Gucht, D.: A graph-oriented object database model. IEEE Transactions on Knowledge and Data Engineering **6** (1994) 572–586
18. ⟨http://protege.stanford.edu/⟩
19. Freiling, M.: Designing an inference engine: From ontology to control. Proceedings of the International Workshop on Artificial Intelligence for Industrial Applications (1988) 20–26
20. Alur, R., Grosu, R., Hur, Y., Kumar, V., Lee, I.: Modular specification of hybrid systems in CHARON. In: HSCC. (2000) 6–19
21. Mylopoulos, J., Chaudhri, V.K., Plexousakis, D., Shrufi, A., Topologlou, T.: Building knowledge base management systems. VLDB Journal: Very Large Data Bases **5** (1996) 238–263
22. Bocca, J.B.: Compilation of logic programs to implement very large knowledge base systems - a case study: Educe*. In: Proceedings of the Sixth International Conference on Data Engineering, February 5-9, 1990, Los Angeles, California, USA, IEEE Computer Society (1990) 361–369
23. Bocca, J., Pearson, P.J.: On prolog - dbms connections: a step forward from educe. In: Peter M. D. Gray, Robert J. Lucas (Eds.): Prolog and Databases - Implementations and New Directions. Ellis Horwood / John Wiley (1988) 55–66
24. Bitton, D., DeWitt, D.J., Turbyfill, C.: Benchmarking database systems a systematic approach. In: Proceedings of the 9th International Conference on Very Large Data Bases, Morgan Kaufmann Publishers Inc. (1983) 8–19
25. ⟨http://www.w3.org/RDF/⟩
26. Jaffar, J., Maher, M.J.: Constraint logic programming: A survey. Journal of Logic Programming **19/20** (1994) 503–581
27. Subrahmanian, V.S.: Nonmonotonic logic programming. IEEE Transactions on Knowledge and Data Engineering **11** (1999) 143–152
28. Blair, H.A., Subrahmanian, V.S.: Paraconsistent logic programming. Theor. Comput. Sci. **68** (1989) 135–154
29. Kifer, M., Subrahmanian, V.S.: Theory of generalized annotated logic programming and its applications. Journal of Logic Programming **12** (1992) 335–367

Appendix A

Logic program implementation of epistemic ontology illustrated in the examples section.

1. Some utility libraries defining set and list summation operations.

```
member(X,[X|_]).
member(X,[_|Y]) :- member(X,Y).
subset([A|X], Y):- member(A,Y), subset(X,Y).
subset([],Y).
intersection([],X,[]).
intersection([X|R], Y, [X|Z]) :- member(X,Y), !,
                                        intersection(R,Y,Z).
intersection([X|R], Y, Z) :- intersection(R, Y, Z).
union([], X, X).
union([X|R], Y, Z) :- member(X, Y), !, union(R, Y, Z).
union([X|R], Y, [X|Z]) :- union(R, Y, Z).

sumlist([],0).
sumlist([H|T],N) :- sumlist(T,N1), N is N1+H.
```

2. Rules relating to constraint satisfaction

```
% Constraint satisfaction properties
        not(Goal) :- \+ Goal.

        satisfies_fact(X, Y) :-
                instanceof(X, frame('Constraint')),
                instanceof(Y, frame('Model')),
                instanceof(Z, frame('Satisfies')),
                constraint_satisfied(Z, X),
                model_satisfied(Z, Y).

        satisfies(X, Y) :-
                (
                satisfies_fact(X,Y) % X is known to be true on Y
                )
                ;
                ( % A submodel of Y satisfies X
                instanceof(X, frame('Constraint')),
                instanceof(Y, frame('Model')),
                instanceof(Z, frame('ModelRelation')),
                model_relation(Z, frame(heterogeneous_ver_2_Instance_18)),
                instanceof(P, frame('Model')),
                model1(Z, P),
                model2(Z, Y),
                satisfies(X, P)
                )
                ;
                ( % An abstraction of Y satisfies X
                instanceof(X, frame('Constraint')),
                instanceof(Y, frame('Model')),
                instanceof(Z, frame('ModelRelation')),
                model_relation(Z, frame(heterogeneous_ver_2_Instance_21)),
                instanceof(P, frame('Model')),
                model1(Z, P),
                model2(Z, Y),
                satisfies(X, P)
                )
                ;
                ( % X is a compound constraint and Y satisfies all its subconstraints
                instanceof(X, frame('CompoundConstraint')),
                instanceof(Y, frame('Model')),
                subconstraints(X, SubconstraintList),
                not((member(C, SubconstraintList), not(satisfies(C, Y))))
                ).
```

3. discrete system sampling time related information

```
satisfies(X, Y) :-
        ( % Y is a discrete model, and a discrete model Z with a
          % lower sampling time than Y satisfies X
          instanceof(X, frame('Constraint')),
          instanceof(Y, frame('DiscreteModel')),
          instanceof(Z, frame('DiscreteModel')),
          constraint_ID(X, 3003),
          satisfies_fact(X, Z),
          sampling_time(Y, Yvalue), sampling_time(Z, Zvalue),
          (Yvalue > Zvalue),
          (implemented_sys(Y, Sys), implemented_sys(Z, Sys))
        )
```

Mode-Automata Based Methodology for Scade

Ouassila Labbani, Jean-Luc Dekeyser, and Pierre Boulet

Laboratoire d'Informatique Fondamentale de Lille,
Université des Sciences et Technologies de Lille, Bâtiment M3,
Cité Scientifique, 59655 Villeneuve d'Ascq Cedex, France
{labbani, dekeyser, boulet}@lifl.fr

Abstract. In this paper, we present a new design methodology for synchronous reactive systems, based on a clear separation between control and data flow parts. This methodology allows to facilitate the specification of different kinds of systems and to have a better readability. It also permits to separate the study of the different parts by using the most appropriate existing tools for each of them.

Following this idea, we are particularly interested in the notion of running modes and in the Scade tool. Scade is a graphical development environment coupling data processing and state machines (modeled by the synchronous languages Lustre and Esterel). It can be used to specify, simulate, verify and generate C code. However, this tool does not follow any design methodology, which often makes difficult the understanding and the re-use of existing applications. We will show that it is also difficult to separate control and data flow parts using Scade. Regulation systems are better specified using mode-automata which allow adding an automaton structure to data flow specifications written in Lustre. When we observe the mode-structure of the mode-automaton, we clearly see where the modes differ and the conditions for changing modes. This makes it possible to better understand the behavior of the system.

In this work, we try to combine the advantages of Scade and running modes, in order to develop a new design methodology which facilitates the study of several systems by respecting the separation between control and data flows. This schema is illustrated through the Climate case study suggested by Esterel Technologies[1], in order to exhibit the benefits of our approch compared to the one advocated in Scade.

1   Introduction

Development of complex and critical reactive systems requires reliable and efficient tools and methods. Some failures and crashes of these systems can lead to data or time losses, incidents that can potentially be catastrophic. For this reason, these systems are often submitted to severe requirements of good functioning, aiming the *zero error* quality. Their reliability becomes at the same time

---

[1] www.esterel-technologies.com

M. Morari and L. Thiele (Eds.): HSCC 2005, LNCS 3414, pp. 386–401, 2005.

a more and more important stake and a problem which gets harder and harder to solve.

To address those needs, several studies have been launched in the reactive system domain. We often speak about approaches and tools for modeling, simulating, and checking of these systems. These tools are based on different models, depending on their basic hypotheses (synchronous or asynchronous, control or data flow, ...) and use formal techniques having a well defined syntax accompanied by a rigorous semantics based on mathematical models.

In this paper, we study synchronous reactive systems and we propose a new approach for modeling these systems. Our study is inspired by the principles used in Scade (Lustre + Esterel) and mode-automata. It is based on the precise and clear separation between control and data flow parts, that allow us, on the one hand, to avoid the use of conditional structure of Lustre and to have a best readability, and on the other hand, to facilitate the separated study of the different parts by using the most appropriate tools for each part.

2   Context

2.1   Reactive Systems and Synchronous Approach

Reactive Systems are computer systems that react continuously to their environment, by producing results at each invocation [1]. These results depend on data provided by the environment during the invocation, and on the internal state of the system. This class of systems contrasts with *transformational systems* and *interactive systems*. Transformational systems are classical programs whose inputs are available at the beginning of their execution, and which deliver their outputs when terminating, as compilers for instance. Interactive systems are programs which react continuously to their environment, but at their own speed, as operating systems for instance.

D. Harel and A. Pnueli [1] have given to reactive systems the image of a black box that react to its environment at a speed determined by the latter (figure 1).

Specification of software or hardware reactive systems behavior is complex. It can lead to difficult and important errors. Indeed, such systems are not only described by transformational relationships, specifying outputs from inputs, but also by the links between outputs and inputs via their possible combinations in one step [3]. Modeling reactive systems is therefore a difficult activity.

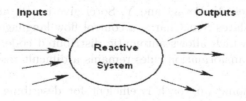

Fig. 1. Reactive System

In the beginning of the 80's, the family of synchronous languages and formalisms has been a very important contribution to the reactive system area [2]. Synchronous languages have been introduced to make programming reactive systems easier [4]. They are based on the *synchrony hypothesis* that does not take reaction time in consideration. Each activity can then be dated on the discrete time scale. This hypothesis considers that the computer is infinitely fast and each reaction is instantanous and atomic.

Synchronous languages are devoted to the design, programming and validation of reactive systems. They have a formal semantics and can be efficiently compiled into C code, for instance. These languages can be classified into two main families: *declarative languages* and *imperative languages*.

Declarative or data flow languages like Lustre ([5] and [6]) or Signal ([7] and [10]) are used when the behavior of the system to be described has some regularity like in signal-processing. Their main task consists in consuming data, performing calculations and producing results.

Imperative or control flow languages like Esterel ([9], [8] and [16]) or Argos [11] are more appropriate for programming systems with discrete changes and whose control is dominant: for instance coffee machines. Their purpose is to manage the processing of data by imposing an execution order to operations and by choosing one operation among several exclusive.

However, rarely these systems have an exclusively regular or discrete behavior. The most realistic and used embedded systems combine control and data processing. Such global systems may be totally specified with imperative languages, but data dependences between operations can not be clearly specified and furthermore problems may occur due to shared variables. Similarly, they may be totally specified with declarative languages, but the control is hidden in data dependences making it difficult to specify tests and branchings necessary for verification or optimization purposes. For these reasons, we need efficient tools and methods taking in consideration this kind of systems.

Several approaches have been proposed in this domain. We can find the *multi-languages* approach which combines imperative and declarative languages, like using Lustre and Argos [18]. It is based on a linking mechanism and allows the re-use of existing code. However, when using several languages it is very difficult to ensure that the set of corresponding generated codes will satisfy the global specification. Another design method consists in using a *transformational* approach which allows the use of both types of languages for specification but, before code generation, the imperative specifications must be translated into declarative specifications, or vice-versa, allowing to generate a unique code instead of multiple ones. N. Pernet and Y. Sorel give in [19] an example of this approch which translates SyncCharts, a control flow language, into SynDEx, a data flow language which allows automatic distributed code generation. However, definition of transformation rules remains a difficult task and can induce several errors.

The transformational approach is efficient for describing reactive systems combining control and data processing. However, there are systems whose behavior is mainly regular but can switch instantaneously from a behavior to another. They are the systems with running modes. The most adapted method to describe this kind of system consists in using a *multi-styles* approach which makes it possible to describe with only one language the various behaviors of the system. The mode-automata represent a significant contribution in this field. Their goal consists in adding an automaton structure to the Lustre programs.

In our work we choose to study the transformational approach using Scade, where Esterel code is transformed into Lustre, and the concept of mode-automata allowing the description of different running modes of the system. The goal of our work consists in proposing a mixed approach which can facilitate the specification of a variety of synchronous reactive systems.

2.2   Scade

Scade (Safety Critical Application Development Environment) [13] is a graphical development environment commercialized by Esterel Technologies. The Scade environment was defined to help and assist the development of critical embedded systems. This environment is composed of several tools such as a graphical editor, a simulator, a model checker and a code generator that automatically translates graphical specifications into C code.

The Scade language is a graphical data flow specification language that can be translated into Lustre. Scade is built on formal foundations. It is deterministic and provides efficient solutions for the development of reactive systems. Thus, Scade enables the saving of a significant amount of verification efforts, essentially because it supports a *correct by construction* process [14] and automated production of the life cycle elements. It has been used in important European avionic projects (Airbus A340-600, A380, Eurocopter) and is also becoming a de-facto standard in this field.

Scade uses two specification formalisms: *block diagrams* for continuous control and *state machines* for discrete control [12]. It adds a rigorous view of these formalisms which includes a precise definition of concurrency and a proof that all Scade programs behave deterministically.

By *continuous control* we mean sampling sensors at regular time intervals, performing signal-processing computations on their values, and outputting values often using complex mathematical formulas. Data is continuously subject to the same transformation. In Scade, continuous control is graphically specified using block diagrams. Scade blocks are fully hierarchical: blocks at a description level can themselves be composed of smaller blocks interconnected by local flows.

By *discrete control* we mean changing the behavior according to external events originating either from discrete sensors and user inputs or from internal program events. Discrete control is generally represented by state machines. A richer concept of hierarchical state machines has been introduced in Scade to avoid the state explosion problems. The Esterel Technologies hierarchical state machines are called *Safe State Machines* (SSMs). These evolved from the Esterel programming language and the SyncCharts state machine [15].

Large applications contain cooperating continuous and discrete control parts. To make the specification of such systems easier, Scade makes it possible to seamlessly couple both data flow and state machine styles. Most often, one includes SSMs into block-diagram design to compute and propagate functioning modes. Then, the discrete signals to which a SSM reacts and which it sends back are simply transformed into boolean data flows in the block diagram.

Scade does not give any design methodology. It does not impose a well defined technique or rules to follow for the construction of the system, which gives more freedom to users. However, users can specify their system in a not very organized way which makes it difficult to understand and to re-use existing specifications. Thus, the application of formal verification techniques on such models is very difficult and even impossible. Errors are more and more serious and the resulting system will be unstable. It is also difficult to specify mainly regular systems which change instantaneously their behavior with Scade. These systems are more easily specified using mode-automata. In [20], F. Maraninchi and Y. Rémond show through a production-cell case study that real industrial applications can be better specified by using a mode-structure if their behavior is mainly regular. For these reasons, it becomes necessary to introduce a design methodology and the concept of running modes in Scade to facilitate the specification, the verification and the re-use of various applications.

2.3   Mode-Automata

Informal Presentation. One way of facing the complexity of a system is to decompose it into several "independent" tasks. Of course the tasks are never completely independent, but it should be possible to find a decomposition in which the tasks are not too strongly connected with each other. Different formalisms are used in the reliability engineering framework in order to design these models of systems under study: *Boolean formalisms* like block diagrams, and *states/transitions formalisms* like Petri nets.

Mode automata have been proposed in [17]. They introduce, in the domain-specific data-flow language Lustre for reactive systems, a new construct devoted to the expression of *running modes*. It corresponds to the fact that several definitions (equations) may exist for the same output, that should be used at distinct periods of time.

A mode automaton is an input/output automaton. It has a finite number of states, that are called *modes*. At each moment, it is in one (and only one) mode. It may change its mode when an event occurs. In each mode, a transfer function determines the values of output flows from the values of input flows. Mode automaton can be combined in order to design hierarchical models. They generalize both bounded Petri nets and block diagrams.

Figure 2 represents a simple example of mode-automaton. It has two states, and equations attached to them. The transitions are labeled by conditions on X. The important point is that X and its memory are *global* to all states. The only thing that changes when the automaton changes states is the transition function; the memory is preserved.

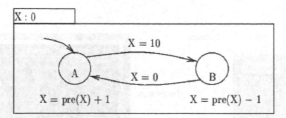

Fig. 2. Mode-automaton: simple example

Formal Definition. A mode-automaton is a tuple $(Q, q_0, V_i, V_o, I, f, T)$ where:

- Q is the set of states of the automaton part;
- $q_0 \in Q$ is the initial state;
- V_i and V_o are the sets of input and output variables, respectively. Input and output variables form disjoint sets (i.e. $V_i \cap V_o = \emptyset$);
- $I : V_o \longrightarrow D$ is a function defining the default value of output variables;
- $T \in Q \times C(V) \times Q$ is the set of transitions, labeled by conditions on the variables of $V = V_i \cup V_o$
- $f : V_o \longrightarrow (Q \longrightarrow EqR(V))$ is a function used to define the labeling of states by total functions from V_o to the set $EqR(v_i \cup V_o)$ of expressions that constitute the right parts of the equations.

$EqR(V)$ has the following syntax: $e ::= c|x|op(e,\dots,e)|pre(y)$ where c stands for constants, x stands for a name in $V_i \cup V_o$, y stands for a name in V_o and op stands for all combinational operators. The condition in $C(V)$ are Boolean expressions of the same form, but without pre operators.

3   Case Study: Climate

3.1   Climate Description

In this section, we present our approach through a case study. We chose to study the *Climate* example that contains both pure control logic and data handling. In this example, we consider the simple case where the system responds to only four inputs of Boolean type. These inputs correspond to the buttons Climate, Left, Right and Ok (figure 3.a). As output, we can have: the climate mode, the temperature, the level of ventilation and the ventilation mode (figure 3.b). The types of the output values are as follows:

- **ClimateMode**: enum {Auto, Manual} initially Auto;
- **Temperature**: integer in [17, 27] initially 19;
- **VentilationLevel**: integer in [0, 100] initially 0;
- **VentilationMode**: enum{CAR, FACE, FEET,DEFROST,CIRCULATION} initially CAR.

Initially, the climate is in automatic (Auto) mode. The switch to Manual mode will be after the Adjust state that allows to confirm a choice using the OK button (figure 4).

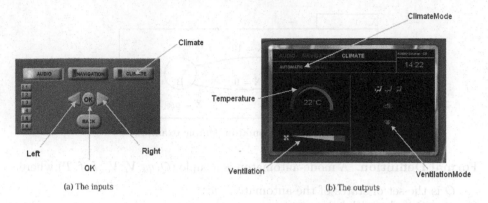

(a) The inputs   (b) The outputs

Fig. 3. Climate: inputs and outputs

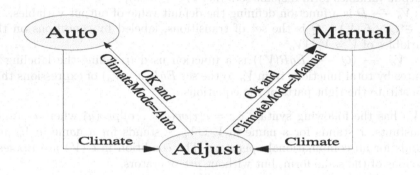

Fig. 4. The different states of Climate

The Auto State

- Set the temperature:
  - Left button decrease the temperature by 1 down to 17;
  - Right button increase the temperature by 1 up to 27.
- Climate button goes to state Adjust.

The Adjust State

- Navigate with Left/Right buttons through the ventilation mode and climate mode in the following order: CAR, FACE, FEET, DEFROST, CIRCULA-TION, Auto, Manual.
- OK button select the activated state and leave the Adjust mode. It goes to the Auto state if ClimateMode is Auto, and to the Manual state otherwise.

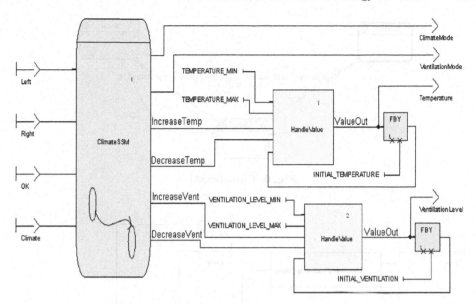

Fig. 5. Climate in Scade

The Manual State

- Set the ventilation level:
    - Left button decrease the ventilation level by 1 down to 0;
    - Right button increase the ventilation level by 1 up to 100.
- Climate button goes to state Adjust.

The specification of the Climate system contains control and calculation. The goal of our work consists in having a clear design of this specification, in which we separate control and data parts.

3.2   Conception of Climate System with Scade

The solution proposed by Esterel Technologies using Scade for the conception of Climate system is represented by figure 5.

This system possesses four inputs relative to buttons: Left, Right, Ok and Climate. As output, it provides four results: `ClimateMode`, `VentilationMode`, `Temperature` and `VentilationLevel`. Input values pass through a control part represented by the SSM `ClimateSSM` of figure 6. This SSM gives ventilation and climate modes as result. It also allows to activate the calculation part `HandleValue` by two different signals: `Incr` and `Decr` which correspond to the increase and decrease of the temperature or ventilation level. The activation of `HandleValue` depends on input values (buttons pushed) and the present state of the system. Each state in `ClimateSSM` represents a macro-state which specify the behavior of the global state.

The operator `FBY` (followed by) which appears on figure 5 is a predefined temporal operator in Scade. It makes it possible to preserve the value of a

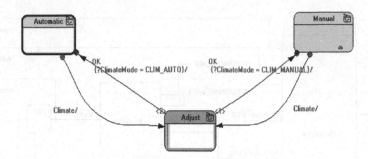

Fig. 6. ClimateSSM

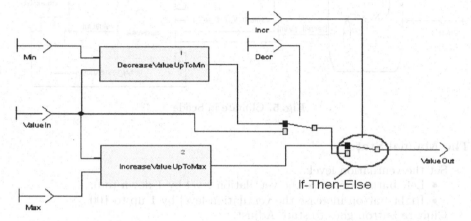

Fig. 7. HandleValue in Scade

given expression on several cycles. In Scade, $FBY(E, n, Init)$ is equivalent to $Init \rightarrow pre(Init \rightarrow pre(\cdots \rightarrow pre(E)))$ in Lustre, where E is an expression which defines the sequence $(e_1, e_2, \ldots e_n)$ and n is a static expression which value is strictly positive.

In the Climate example, FBY allows to keep the preceding value of Temperature or VentilationLevel which will be transmitted to HandleValue operator. Initially, FBY transmits the initial value of the temperature (INITIAL_TEMPERATURE) or that of the ventilation level (INITIAL_VENTILATION).

By descending to a lower level of the hierarchy, the conception model that corresponds to the operator HandleValue is indicated by figure 7. HandleValue allows to increase or decrease a given value depending on the values of signals Incr and Decr[2].

In Scade, the correspondence between various levels of the hierarchy does not use a naming mechanism but rather the link between inputs and outputs. For example, inputs values: TEMPERATURE_MIN, IncreaseTemp _MAX, TEMPERATURE

---

[2] Incr and Decr can not be activated at the same time.

and `DecreaseTemp` of the `HandleValue` operator which appear on figure 5 correspond respectively to the values of `Min, Max, Inc` and `Dec` of the `HandleValue` operator appearing on figure 7.

In this model, we notice that the calculation part `HandleValue` contains a mixture of calculation (`DecreaseValueUpToMin` and `IncreaseValueUpToMax`) and control (*If_Then_Else*). This mixture can make difficult the comprehension of the system, as well as the use of already existing tools, dedicated exclusively to processing the calculation part or the control part. Thus, as shown in the figures 7, `HandleValue` is composed of two calculation parts: `DecreaseValueUpToMin` and `IncreaseValueUpToMax`. Independently of the values of `Inc` and `Dec`, the two parts are activated and the output value will be chosen depending on signal's values of `Inc` and `Dec`. This corresponds to the strict and compound nature of the conditional structure *If_Then_Else* in Lustre. In this case, the two branches of the conditional structure are always evaluated which can introduce side-effect problems.

The goal of our work consists in proposing a conceptual model that allows to have a clear separation between control and data parts. This will allow us, on the one hand, to avoid the use of the Lustre conditional structure and to have a best readability, and on the other hand, to facilitate the separated study of the different parts by using the most appropriate tools for each category, notably concerning the application of the different formal verification techniques.

4   Control/Data Flow Separation Using Scade

First, we have tried to apply the concept of separated Control/Data Flow by using Scade. To make this, we have studied the Climate example by separating control and data parts. The diagram corresponding to our approach is shown on figure 8.

In this example, we have divided the problem into three sub-problems that correspond to the different states of the system: Auto, Adjust and Manual. The activation of each state is made by the SSM `ControlClimate` depending on the input values of Ok and Climate.

In this approach, we can clearly distinguish inputs and outputs of the system, control parts, and data parts. Contrary to what its name indicates, the data part does not only designate an exclusive data processing. It can also contain a SSM followed by a data part, or only the control part. The lowest level in the hierarchy represents an homogeneous part that can exclusively contain the control or the elementary calculation.

The application of this approach in Scade raises some issues. For example, the value of `ClimateMode` can be modified by two different states: Auto and Adjust. However, in Scade it is impossible to link the same output to two different operators. In Scade, each data must have a unique definition at a given time, which makes the connection of the same output to several different operators impossible. This requires the introduction of the *If_Then_Else* operators, which complicate the model and break the control/data flow separation concept. To fill

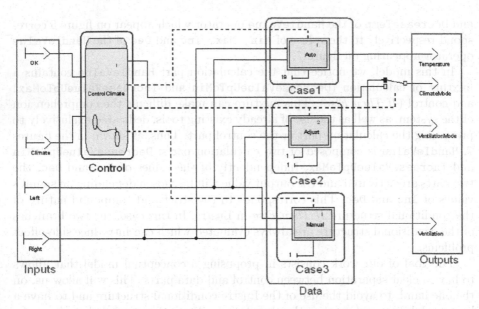

Fig. 8. Climate: trying the separation control/data flow with Scade

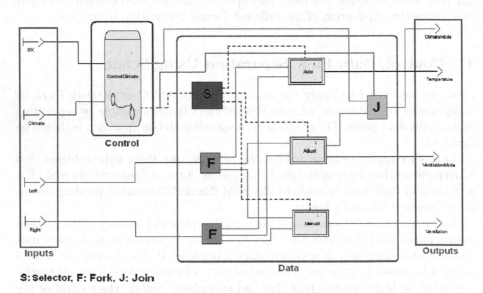

S: Selector, F: Fork, J: Join

Fig. 9. Control/data flow separation model using Scade and Fork/Join operators

this gap, we have proposed to add special operators that play the role of **Fork** and **Join** which allow the division of data between several operators. We have also added a *selector* operator that receives as input a value provided by a SSM, according to which it can choose the state to activate (figure 9).

The function of the *Fork* operator consists in diffusing the input value on all its output points, while the role of the *Join* operator consists in giving an

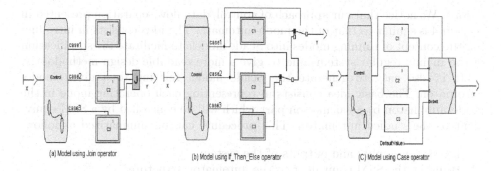

(a) Model using Join operator   (b) Model using If_Then_Else operator   (C) Model using Case operator

Fig. 10. Example of the Join operator and its equivalent in Scade

output value among those received as inputs and according to the value provided by the SSM.

Selector and Fork operators represent only an optimization of notations used in Scade because, in this tool, it is possible to connect the same value to several operator's inputs. However, the Join operator replace the conditional structures *If_Then_Else* and *Switch_Case* used in Scade. In this context, one Join operator with n inputs can be used to replace a structure of $n-1$ *If_Then_Else* operators or one *Switch_Case* operator with n inputs.

In the case of the *If_Then_Else* operators, it is obvious that the complexity of the model increases according to the number of inputs which makes difficult the comprehension of the model. Thus, if we use the *Switch_Case* operator, calculation blocks are not conditioned and then all inputs must be computed before the operator chooses the selected one. This behavior leads to difficult problems and can be very expensive regarding time and memory. Moreover, the default value used in *Switch_Case* operator does not have any interest because we suppose that one and only one component must be activated at a given time[3]. For these reasons, we prefer introducing a Join operator which allows an implicit use of conditional structures and facilitates the comprehension of the model. Figure 10 gives an example of Join operator and its equivalent in Scade.

The model suggested in figure 9 makes it possible to have a better design methodology based on the separation between control and calculation parts. This representation gives a possible solution to complete the Scade model of figure 8 and facilitates the use of separation control/data flow model with Scade.

5 Using Mode-Automata with Scade

As indicated in section 2.3, the mode-automata makes it possible to divide the specification of the system into several running modes. The switch between the modes is made accordingly to the activation conditions which appear on the tran-

---

[3] This concept enable us to avoid the introduction of the default value relating to the **condact** operators in Scade.

sitions. We notice that our approach of control/data flow separation presented in section 4 is similar to that of the mode-automata. The idea consists in introducing the concept of running modes into Scade models to facilitate the specification of the mainly regular systems and to give a more readable design methodology.

It is also easy to generate the Scade model relating to a given mode-automaton. The basic idea consists in representing each operating mode in the mode-automaton by a calculation part which will be controlled by a SSM equivalent to the studied automaton. This procedure can be summarized as follow:

1. Extracting inputs and outputs of the system.
2. Building the SSM equivalent to the automaton structure.
3. Modeling each operating part of mode-automaton (Lustre equations) by a calculation block in Scade.
4. Connecting the SSM and calculation parts using Selector, Fork and Join operators.
5. adding the Delay operators if necessary.

Figure 11 gives an example of a mode-automaton and its equivalent in control/data flow separation model with Scade. In this example, the modes A and B are respectively replaced by the components AC and BC. The switch between the various modes is done via the SSM Control which, according to the value of X and the state of the system, makes it possible to choose the component to be activated. In this context, the Lustre equations of the mode-automatons are replaced by calculation components in our design model, while the structure of

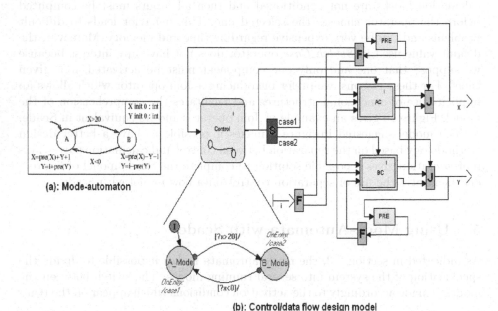

(a): Mode-automaton

(b): Control/data flow design model

Fig. 11. Mode-automaton and its equivalent in control/data flow model

the automaton is replaced by a SSM responsible for the activation of the various parts of calculation.

6   New Formalism for Scade

In this section, we propose a new formalism for Scade based on the running modes concept. This formalism allows to have a clearer and easy to re-use model. For that, we introduce the concept of components with *same interface* to facilitate the introduction and deletion of components. In this context, the operators or states of execution in a given level of hierarchy must have the same inputs and outputs. Thus, if an operator does not modify an output value, its role only consists in giving its preceding value. A global view of the model that we wish to have for the Climate example is represented by figure 12.

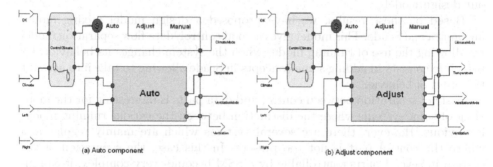

Fig. 12. Control/Data Flow Separation: use of the components with single assignment

In this model, the various situations of the system are represented in tabs. The activation of each case is done by the selector according to the value provided by the control part (SSM). In other words, the part controled by a SSM can be seen as a black box with a set of inputs and outputs. In this box and according to the value provided by the selector we can connect various components having a single assignment and the same type and number of inputs and outputs.

In the Climate example, the controllable part is made of three tabs corresponding to the different states of the system: Auto, Adjust and Manual. These three components have the same number and type of inputs and outputs. Their role consists in providing output values according to input ones. This representation makes it possible to give a more readable model and facilitates the update and re-use of various existing components. It is also important to note that our model supports a hierarchical construction in all its design levels. This concept is similar to that used in Scade.

7   Conclusion and Future Work

In this paper, we have introduced a new formalism to specify complex synchronous reactive systems. The goal of our works consists in having a clear model separating control and data parts, which enables us to have a more readable and reusable specification and a better use of the various existing tools.

First, we have studied the possibility of separation between control and data parts using Scade. This study has shown that it is very difficult and even impossible to have a strict control/data flow separation with Scade, because each variable can only have one definition at the same time and it is then impossible to share the same variable between several operators. Thus, the ternary and strict nature of the conditional structure *If_Then_Else* in Lustre can induce several side-effect problems. We have also shown that the principle of the model that we wish to have is very similar to that of running modes. For this reason we have studied the mode-automata and the possibility of their integration in our design model.

Based on these results, we have proposed a design model mixing mode-automata and Scade. This model gives a good control/data flow separation model by allowing the use of running modes when the system changes its behavior. Its principle consists in adding some concepts in Scade allowing to take into account this kind of behavior.

A strict separation between control and data parts is interesting for the modeling of some systems where the distinction between the various running modes is obvious. However, there are several systems which are mainly regular and where the control part is not too present. In this case, the separation of the system in several parts controllable by a SSM becomes very complex, it can introduce problems of redundancy and unverifiable errors. In future work, to face this problem, we will propose to use the concept of running mode locally for a sub-part of the system which contains the control. We also wish to give an internal format and to provide transformation rules making possible the switch between our model and the internal format used in Scade. This would enable the use of different services existing in Scade, in particular for formal verification and code generation.

References

1. D. Harel and A. Pnueli: On the development of reactive systems. Logics and Models of Concurrent Systems (NATO ASI Series). **13** (1985) 477–498
2. N. Halbwachs: Synchronous programming of reactive systems. Kluwer Academic Pub. (1993)
3. L. Zaffalon and P. Breguet: Conception de Systèmes Réactifs. Revue Scientifique de l'EIVD. (2001)
4. G. Berry and A. Benveniste: The synchronous approach to reactive and real-time systems. Proceedings of the IEEE. September. **79** (1991) 1270–1282

5. P. Caspi, D. Pilaud, N. Halbwachs and J. A. Plaice: Lustre, a declarative language for real time programming. Proceedings ACM Conference on Principles of Programming Languages (1987)
6. N. Halbwachs and P. Caspi and P. Raymond and D. Pilaud: The synchronous data-flow programming language LUSTRE. Proceedings of the IEEE. September. **79** (1991) 1305–1320
7. Albert Benveniste, Patricia Bournai, Thierry Gautier and Paul Le Guernic: SIGNAL: a Data Flow Oriented Language for Signal Processing. INRIA, centre de Rennes IRISA. March. (1985)
8. Gerard Berry and Georges Gonthier: The Esterel Synchronous Programming Language: Design, Semantics, Implementation. Science of Computer Programming. **19** (1992) 87–152
9. Frédéric Boussinot and Robert De Simone: The Esterel Language. Another Look at Real-Time Programming. Proceedings of the IEEE. September. **79** (1991) 1293–1304
10. P. Le Guernic and T. Gautier and M.Le Borgne and C. Le Maire: Programming Real-Time applications with SIGNAL. Another Look at Real-Time Programming. Proceedings of the IEEE. September. **79** (1991) 1321–1336
11. F. Maraninchi and Y. Rémond: Argos: an Automaton-Based Synchronous Language. Computer Languages. Elsevier. **27** (2001) 61–92
12. Esterel Technologies: Efficient Development of Airborn Software with SCADE $Suite^{TM}$. (2003). http://www.esterel-technologies.com/v3/?id=41490
13. Esterel Technologies: SCADE Language Reference Manual. (2004)
14. Peter Amey: Correctness by Construction: better can also be cheaper. Journal of Defense Software Engineering. March. (2002)
15. Charle Andrés: Representation and Analysis of Reactive Behaviors: A Synchronous Approach. Computational Engineering in Systems Applications (CESA). IEEE-SMC. July. (1996) 19–29
16. Gérard Berry: The Foundations of Esterel. Proofs, Languages, and Interaction, Essays in Honour of Robin Milner. MIT Press. (2000)
17. F. Maraninchi and Y. Rémond: Mode-automata: About modes and states for reactive systems. European Symposium On Programming. LNCS 1381. March. (1998)
18. M. Jourdan and F. Lagnier and F. Maraninchi and P. Raymond: A multiparadigm language for reactive systems. IEEE International Conference on Computer Languages (ICCL). Toulouse, France. (1994)
19. Nicolas Pernet and Yves Sorel: Optimized Implementation of Distributed Real-Time Embedded Systems Mixing Control and Data Processing. International Conference: Computer Applications in Industry and Engineering. Las Vegas, USA. November. (2003)
20. Florence Maraninchi and Yann Rémond: Applying Formal Methods to Industrial Cases: The Language Approach (The Production-Cell and Mode-Automata). Proc. 5th International Workshop on Formal Methods for Industrial Critical Systems. Berlin. April. (2000)

Taylor Approximation for Hybrid Systems

Ruggero Lanotte and Simone Tini

Dipartimento di Scienze della Cultura, Politiche e dell'Informazione,
Università dell'Insubria, Via Valleggio 11, I-22100, Como, Italy
{ruggero.lanotte, simone.tini}@uninsubria.it

Abstract. We propose a new approximation technique for Hybrid Automata. Given any Hybrid Automaton H, we call $Approx(H, k)$ the Polynomial Hybrid Automaton obtained by approximating each formula ϕ in H with the formulae ϕ_k obtained by replacing the functions in ϕ with their Taylor polynomial of degree k. We prove that $Approx(H, k)$ is an over–approximation of H. We study the conditions ensuring that, given any $\epsilon > 0$, some k_0 exists such that, for all $k > k_0$, the "distance" between any vector satisfying ϕ_k and at least one vector satisfying ϕ is less than ϵ. We study also conditions ensuring that, given any $\epsilon > 0$, some k_0 exists such that, for all $k > k_0$, the "distance" between any configuration reached by $Approx(H, k)$ in n steps and at least one configuration reached by H in n steps is less than ϵ.

1 Introduction

Hybrid automata [1, 3] are a widely studied model for *hybrid systems* [18], i.e. dynamical systems combining discrete and continuous state changes. Hybrid automata combine finite state machines with continuously evolving *variables*, and exhibit two kinds of state changes: discrete jump transitions, occurring instantaneously, and continuous flow transitions, occurring while time elapses. These two kinds of transitions are guarded by *transition labels* and *activity functions*, respectively, which are constraints on the source and target value of the variables.

1.1 Reachability

Most of hybrid system applications are safety critical and require guarantees of safe operation. To analyze *safety properties* (i.e. properties requiring that a given set of *bad configurations* cannot be reached), the decidability of *reachability* problem (i.e. whether or not a given configuration can be reached) is determinant. Unfortunately, for most classes of hybrid systems, reachability is undecidable [11]. However, for some of these classes, computing the successors (or predecessors) of configurations sets in the underlying transition system is reasonably efficient, and, therefore, reachability *in a limited number of steps* is decidable.

Now, there are also classes of hybrid systems for which the successors of configuration sets are not computable. A new methodology has been proposed

M. Morari and L. Thiele (Eds.): HSCC 2005, LNCS 3414, pp. 402–416, 2005.

in [10] to fill this gap. First of all, according to [10], an automaton A is an
approximation of another automaton B iff A is obtained from B by weakening
activity functions and transition labels. In such a way, all computations of B are
also computation of A, and, hence, if we prove that a *bad* configuration cannot
be reached by A in n steps, then we can infer that it cannot be reached by B
in n steps. Now, such a proof is possible since the approximation A is always
a *linear hybrid automaton*, for which the successors of configuration sets are
computable. The notion of approximation is then strengthened by the notion
of ε-*approximation*: Given any $\epsilon > 0$, A is an ε-*approximation* of B iff, given
any vector v_A satisfying an activity function (resp. transition label) in A, there
is a vector v_B satisfying the corresponding activity function (resp. transition
label) in B such that the *distance* between v_A and v_B is below ϵ. This notion of
ε-approximation is motivated by the need to limit the *error* introduced by the
approximation. Finally, any *approximation operator* γ mapping automata into
their approximations is *asymptotically complete* iff, for any $\epsilon > 0$ and for any
hybrid automaton B, an ε-approximation of B can be given by γ. In [10] an
asymptotically complete approximation operator, called *rationally rectangular
phase-portrait approximation operator*, is given which approximate all transition
labels and activity functions by products of intervals with rational endpoints.

1.2   Our Contribution

In the present paper, we propose a new approximation technique. Our idea is
to weaken transition labels and activity functions by replacing functions over
variables with their polynomial of Taylor. More precisely, given any hybrid automaton A and natural k, $Approx(A, k)$ is the automaton obtained by replacing
in transition labels and activity functions each function $f(\overrightarrow{x})$ over the variables
$\overrightarrow{x}$ with the *polynomial of Mac Laurin for f of degree k*, denoted $P^k(f, \overrightarrow{x})$,
i.e. the polynomial of Taylor for f of degree k w.r.t. vector $\overrightarrow{0}$. Of course, to
define $Approx(A, k)$ we require that all functions $f(\overrightarrow{x})$ are derivable k times.
Notice that $Approx(A, k)$ is in the class of *polynomial hybrid automata*, for which
computing the successors of configuration sets is decidable [8, 9].

We shall prove that $Approx(A, k)$ is an approximation for A according to
[10], i.e. that all transition labels and activity functions of $Approx(A, k)$ are less
demanding than those of A. We shall study the conditions ensuring that our approximation is asymptotically complete, in the sense that, for each $\epsilon > 0$ there
exists some k_0 such that, for all $k > k_0$, $Approx(A, k)$ is an ε-approximation
for A. We note that looking for more accurate approximations for A is in some
sense mechanizable, since it simply requires taking increasing values for k. Moreover, we will argue that for most classical functions, computing the Mac Laurin
polynomial of degree k is quite efficient (i.e., polynomial w.r.t. k).

Now, looking for ε-approximations for small values of ϵ is a strategy suggested
in [10] to limit the error of the approximation. We observe that this analysis of
the error is *syntactic*, in the sense that it does not consider the behavior of A
and its approximation. In this paper we take a step toward a *semantic* analysis
of the error. We study conditions ensuring that, when k tends to the infinity,

the behavior of $Approx(A,k)$ gets close to the behavior of A. More precisely, these conditions ensure that, for each $\epsilon > 0$, there is some k_0 such that, for all $k > k_0$, if $Approx(A,k)$ reaches a configuration c in n steps, then A reaches a configuration c' in n steps such that the *distance* between c and c' is below ϵ.

1.3   Related Works

Approximation is a strategy widely used for the analysis of hybrid systems. However, the literature presents different notions of approximations, that we briefly comment in this section. Several papers (see, e.g., [2, 1, 4, 11, 12, 14, 15, 16]) show that for some classes of hybrid automata it is possible to map a given automaton A into an approximation B and a property P_A (like, for instance, reachability) over A into a property P_B over B such that: 1) A satisfies P_A iff B satisfies P_B; 2) the problem "B satisfies P_B" is decidable.

Other papers (see, e.g., [5, 6, 7, 13, 17, 19, 20, 21]) consider classes of hybrid systems for which the strategy previously described does not work, and study how one can compute under-approximations and/or over-approximations of the set of the reachable configurations.

Also [10] considers a class of hybrid automata for which the strategy of [2, 1, 4, 11, 12, 14, 15, 16]) does not work, but, instead of computing an approximation of the reachable set of configurations of the original automaton, the idea is to approximate syntactically the automaton, by weakening activity functions and transition labels, so that the obtained automaton falls in the class of linear hybrid automata, for which reachability in n steps is decidable.

As in [10], in this paper we approximate syntactically an automaton A with another automaton, that we call $Approx(A,k)$. Moreover, we study also how close the behaviors of A and $Approx(A,k)$ are.

1.4   Organization of the Paper

The paper is organized as follows. In Sect. 2 and Sect. 3 we recall the notions on the theory of Hybrid Automata and Taylor approximation that will be employed in the paper. In Sect. 4 we introduce our definition of approximation of an Hybrid Automaton, in Sect. 5 we do the syntactical analysis of the error, and in Sect. 6 we do the semantical analysis of the error. In Sect. 7 we discuss efficiency issues. Finally, in Sect. 8 we outline some future developments of our paper. Let us note that for lack of space proofs of propositions and theorems are omitted. Proofs can be found in the draft at the following URL: http://www.di.unipi.it/~lanotte/pub.html.

2   Hybrid Automata

In this section we recall the formalism of Hybrid Automata (see, e.g., [18]).

2.1   Formulae

A *vector* of dimension n on a given set U is a tuple $\vec{u} = (u_1, \ldots, u_n)$ in U^n.

For a vector of real variables $\overrightarrow{x} = (x_1, \ldots, x_n)$, let $\Phi(\overrightarrow{x})$ denote the set of *formulae* over $\overrightarrow{x}$ defined as follows:

$$\phi ::= f(x_1, \ldots, x_n) \sim c \mid \neg\phi_1 \mid \phi_1 \vee \phi_2 \mid \phi_1 \wedge \phi_2$$

where $\phi, \phi_1, \phi_2 \in \Phi(\overrightarrow{x})$, $f : \mathbb{R}^n \to \mathbb{R}$, $c \in \mathbb{R}$, and $\sim \in \{<, \leq, =, \geq, >\}$.

We say that *a formula* $\phi \in \Phi(\overrightarrow{x})$ *is polynomial* iff, for each subformula $f(x_1, \ldots, x_n) \sim c$ appearing in ϕ, f is a polynomial on the variables $\overrightarrow{x}$.

Let $\phi \in \Phi(\overrightarrow{x})$ and $\overrightarrow{u} \in \mathbb{R}^n$; we say that *the vector* $\overrightarrow{u}$ *satisfies the formula* ϕ, written $\overrightarrow{u} \models \phi$, iff the following conditions hold:

$$
\begin{aligned}
\overrightarrow{u} &\models f(x_1, \ldots, x_n) \sim c && \text{iff } f(\overrightarrow{u}) \sim c \\
\overrightarrow{u} &\models \neg\phi_1 && \text{iff } \overrightarrow{u} \models \phi_1 \text{ does not hold} \\
\overrightarrow{u} &\models \phi_1 \vee \phi_2 && \text{iff either } \overrightarrow{u} \models \phi_1 \text{ or } \overrightarrow{u} \models \phi_2 \\
\overrightarrow{u} &\models \phi_1 \wedge \phi_2 && \text{iff both } \overrightarrow{u} \models \phi_1 \text{ and } \overrightarrow{u} \models \phi_2
\end{aligned}
$$

For a formula ϕ in $\Phi(\overrightarrow{x})$, let $[\![\phi]\!]$ denote the set $\{\overrightarrow{u} \in \mathbb{R}^n \mid \overrightarrow{u} \models \phi\}$ of the vectors in $\mathbb{R}^n$ satisfying ϕ.

Without loss of generality, we shall assume that negation does not appear in any formula, and that each relation symbol $\sim$ is in $\{\leq, <\}$. Actually, given any formula, negation can be removed by rewriting $\neg(\neg\phi)$ as ϕ, $\neg(\phi_1 \wedge \phi_2)$ as $\neg\phi_1 \vee \neg\phi_2$, $\neg(\phi_1 \vee \phi_2)$ as $\neg\phi_1 \wedge \neg\phi_2$, $\neg(f(\overrightarrow{x}) < c)$ as $f(\overrightarrow{x}) \geq c$, $\neg(f(\overrightarrow{x}) \leq c)$ as $f(\overrightarrow{x}) > c$, $\neg(f(\overrightarrow{x}) > c)$ as $f(\overrightarrow{x}) \leq c$, $\neg(f(\overrightarrow{x}) \geq c)$ as $f(\overrightarrow{x}) < c$, and $\neg(f(\overrightarrow{x}) = c)$ as $f(\overrightarrow{x}) > c \vee f(\overrightarrow{x}) < c$. Then, relation symbols $=, \geq$ and $>$ can be removed by rewriting $f(\overrightarrow{x}) = c$ as $f(\overrightarrow{x}) \leq c \wedge f(\overrightarrow{x}) \geq c$, $f(\overrightarrow{x}) \geq c$ as $-f(\overrightarrow{x}) \leq -c$, and $f(\overrightarrow{x}) > c$ as $-f(\overrightarrow{x}) < -c$.

2.2   The Formalism

Definition 1. *An Hybrid Automaton H is a tuple $(\overrightarrow{x}, \phi_{init}, Q, q_0, T, Act)$ s.t.:*

- $\overrightarrow{x} = (x_1, \ldots, x_n)$ *is a vector of* real *variables.*
- $\phi_{init} \in \Phi((x_1, \ldots, x_n))$ *is the initial condition.*
- Q *is a finite set of states.*
- $q_0 \in Q$ *is the initial state.*
- $T \subseteq Q \times \Phi((x_1, \ldots, x_n, x'_1, \ldots, x'_n)) \times Q$ *is a finite set of transitions. Variables $x'_1, \ldots, x'_n$ represent the new values taken by the variables $x_1, \ldots, x_n$ after the firing of the transition.*
- $Act : Q \to \Phi((x_1, \ldots, x_n, t, x'_1, \ldots, x'_n))$ *is the activity function assigning to each state q a formula $Act(q)$. The variable t represents time elapsing.*

Example 1 (Alur et al., [1]). The temperature of a room is controlled by a thermostat, which continuously senses the temperature and turns the heater on and off. When the heater is off, the temperature, denoted by variable x, decreases according to the exponential function xe^{-Kt}, where K is a constant determined by the room; when the heater is on, the temperature follows the function $xe^{-Kt} + h(1 - e^{-Kt})$, where h is a constant that depends on the power

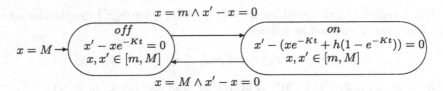

Fig. 1. The thermostat of [1] ($x \in [m, M]$ stays for $x \geq m \wedge x \leq M$)

of the heater. We wish to keep the temperature between m and M degrees and turn the heater on and off accordingly. The resulting Hybrid Automaton is in Fig. 1.

Definition 2 (Fränzle, [8,9]). *An Hybrid Automaton is a Polynomial Hybrid Automaton iff ϕ_{init} is a polynomial formula, for each state q, $Act(q)$ is a polynomial formula, and, for each transition (q, ϕ, q'), ϕ is a polynomial formula.*

Let us explain now the behavior of an Hybrid Automaton H. A *configuration* is a pair $(q, \overrightarrow{u})$, where q is a state in Q and $\overrightarrow{u}$ is a vector in $\mathbb{R}^n$ representing the value of the variables $\overrightarrow{x}$. H can evolve from $(q, \overrightarrow{u})$ to another configuration $(q', \overrightarrow{u}')$, written $(q, \overrightarrow{u}) \rightarrow (q', \overrightarrow{u}')$, by performing either an activity step or a transition step, where:

- an *activity step* describes the evolution from configuration $(q, \overrightarrow{u})$ due to remaining in state q and passing of time. In u units of time, the activity $Act(q)$ takes H to a new valuation of the variables, more precisely:

$$\frac{u \geq 0 \text{ and } (\overrightarrow{u}, u, \overrightarrow{u}') \models Act(q)}{(q, \overrightarrow{u}) \rightarrow (q, \overrightarrow{u}')}$$

- a *transition step* describes the evolution from configuration $(q, \overrightarrow{u})$ due to the firing of a transition from state q. More precisely:

$$\frac{(q, \phi, q') \in T \text{ and } (\overrightarrow{u}, \overrightarrow{u}') \models \phi}{(q, \overrightarrow{u}) \rightarrow (q', \overrightarrow{u}')}$$

A *run* r of H is a sequence of (activity and transition) steps $(q_0, \overrightarrow{u_0}) \rightarrow (q_1, \overrightarrow{u_1}) \rightarrow \cdots \rightarrow (q_n, \overrightarrow{u_n})$, where q_0 is the initial state and $\overrightarrow{u_0} \in [\![\phi_{init}]\!]$.
A configuration $(q_n, \overrightarrow{u_n})$ is *reachable* iff there is a run $(q_0, \overrightarrow{u_0}) \rightarrow (q_1, \overrightarrow{u_1}) \rightarrow \cdots \rightarrow (q_n, \overrightarrow{u_n})$ leading to $(q_n, \overrightarrow{u_n})$.

2.3   Regions

A *region* R of an Hybrid Automaton H is a set of configurations of H. The set of the regions of H is denoted $\mathcal{R}(H)$. The set of the configurations reachable by H from the configurations in region R is denoted $Post(R, H)$. More precisely:

$$Post(R, H) = \{(q', \overrightarrow{u}') \mid \exists (q, \overrightarrow{u}) \in R \text{ such that } (q, \overrightarrow{u}) \rightarrow (q', \overrightarrow{u}')\}$$

Let $Post^n(H)$ denote either the region $\{(q_0, \overrightarrow{u_0}) \mid \overrightarrow{u_0} \in [\![\phi_{init}]\!]\}$, if $n = 0$, or the region $Post(Post^{n-1}(H), H)$, if $n > 0$. Moreover, let $Post(H)$ denote the region $\bigcup_{n \in \mathbb{N}} Post^n(H)$. The following result is folklore.

Theorem 1. *A configuration* $(q, \overrightarrow{u})$ *is reachable in n steps from some configuration* $(q_0, \overrightarrow{u_0})$ *with* $\overrightarrow{u_0} \in [\![\phi_{init}]\!]$ *iff* $(q, \overrightarrow{u}) \in Post^n(H)$. *Hence* $(q, \overrightarrow{u})$ *is reachable iff* $(q, \overrightarrow{u}) \in Post(H)$.

The following result is proved in [8, 9].

Theorem 2 (Fränzle, [8, 9]). *The problem of reachability in n steps for Polynomial Hybrid Automata is decidable.*

3   Taylor Approximation

Let C_n denote the set of the possibly partial functions $f : \mathbb{R}^n \to \mathbb{R}$. Given a function $f \in C_n$, let $Dom(f)$ denote the domain of f.

Let $D_j^i f$ denote the ith derivate of f with respect to the coordinate j^{th}.

Let C_n^k denote the subset of the functions in C_n that are derivable k times, i.e., $f \in C_n^k$ iff, for any $i_1, \ldots, i_n$ with $i_1 + \cdots + i_n = k$, $(D_1^{i_1} \ldots D_n^{i_n} f)$ exists.

Definition 3. *Given a function $f \in C_n^k$ and a vector $\overrightarrow{v} \in Dom(f)$, the polynomial of Taylor of degree k for f with respect to vector $\overrightarrow{v}$ is defined as follows:*

$$P^k(f, \overrightarrow{x}, \overrightarrow{v}) = \sum_{i_1 + \ldots + i_n \leq k} \frac{((D_1^{i_1} \ldots D_n^{i_n} f)(\overrightarrow{v})) \cdot ((x_1 - v_1)^{i_1} \cdot \cdots \cdot (x_n - v_n)^{i_n})}{i_1! \cdot \cdots \cdot i_n!}$$

Given a vector $\overrightarrow{u} \in Dom(f)$, *let* $r^k(f, \overrightarrow{u}, \overrightarrow{v})$ *denote the* remainder *(or error)* $f(\overrightarrow{u}) - P^k(f, \overrightarrow{u}, \overrightarrow{v})$.

Hence, for all $\overrightarrow{u} \in Dom(f)$, $P^k(f, \overrightarrow{u}, \overrightarrow{v})$ is a polynomial that approximates $f(\overrightarrow{u})$, and $r^k(f, \overrightarrow{u}, \overrightarrow{v})$ quantifies the error of the approximation. The following result, known as Lagrange Remainder Theorem, estimates $r^k(f, \overrightarrow{u}, \overrightarrow{v})$.

Theorem 3 (Lagrange). *Given a function $f \in C_n^{k+1}$ and two vectors $\overrightarrow{u}, \overrightarrow{v} \subset Dom(f)$, there exists a vector $\overrightarrow{v}'$ on the segment linking $\overrightarrow{u}$ and $\overrightarrow{v}$ such that:*

$$r^k(f, \overrightarrow{u}, \overrightarrow{v}) = \sum_{i_1 + \ldots + i_n = k+1} \frac{((D_1^{i_1} \ldots D_n^{i_n} f)(\overrightarrow{v}')) \cdot ((u_1 - v_1)^{i_1} \cdot \cdots \cdot (u_n - v_n)^{i_n})}{i_1! \cdot \cdots \cdot i_n!}$$

From now on, for simplicity, we shall consider the *polynomial of Mac Laurin of degree k for f*, i.e. the polynomial of Taylor of degree k for f with respect to the vector $\overrightarrow{0}$. This polynomial will be denoted $P^k(f, \overrightarrow{x})$ instead of $P^k(f, \overrightarrow{x}, \overrightarrow{0})$.

Definition 4. *Given a formula $\phi \in \Phi(\overrightarrow{x})$ and a function $f \in C_n^{k+1}$, f is analytic in $[\![\phi]\!]$ if there exist two naturals C and L such that, for any $i_1, \ldots, i_n$ and $\overrightarrow{u} \in [\![\phi]\!]$, it holds that:*

$$\left| (D_1^{i_1} \ldots D_n^{i_n} f)(\overrightarrow{u}) \right| \leq L \cdot C^{i_1 + \cdots + i_n}$$

If f is analytic in $[\![\phi]\!]$, given $\hat{C}$ and $\hat{L}$ the minimal values satisfying the condition of Def. 4 , for any k we shall denote with $C(f, \phi, k)$ the value $\hat{L} \cdot \hat{C}^{k+1}$.

Intuitively, if f is analytic in $[\![\phi]\!]$, $\hat{C}$ and $\hat{L}$ permit us to have an upper bound to $\left| (D_1^{i_1} \ldots D_n^{i_n} f)(\overrightarrow{u}) \right|$, for all $\overrightarrow{u} \in [\![\phi]\!]$ and for all $i_1, \ldots, i_n$.

Example 2. Trigonometric functions are analytic in any $[\![\phi]\!]$. As an example, for the function $\sin(x)$ it is sufficient to take the constants $L = C = 1$. Exponential and logarithmic functions are analytic in $[\![\phi]\!]$ if ϕ constraints variables within finite intervals. As an example, for function e^{2x} and $[\![\phi]\!] \subseteq [0, 10]$, it is sufficient to take the constants $C = 2$ and $L = e^{20}$.

If f is analytic in $[\![\phi]\!]$, let $R^k(f, \overrightarrow{x}, \phi)$ denote the polynomial

$$R^k(f, \overrightarrow{x}, \phi) = \frac{C(f, \phi, k) \cdot n^{k+1} \cdot \prod_{i=1}^n \left((x_i)^{2 \cdot \lceil \frac{k+1}{2} \rceil} + 1 \right)}{\lfloor \frac{k+1}{n} \rfloor !}$$

Otherwise, if f is not analytic in $[\![\phi]\!]$, let $R^k(f, \overrightarrow{x}, \phi)$ be ∞.

Hence, $R^k(f, \overrightarrow{u}, \phi)$ is an upper bound to the remainder $r^k(f, \overrightarrow{u}, \overrightarrow{0})$, for all $\overrightarrow{u} \in [\![\phi]\!]$. Moreover, if f is analytic in $[\![\phi]\!]$, $R^k(f, \overrightarrow{u}, \phi)$ gets close to 0 when k tends to the infinity. Let us formalize these two intuitions.

Proposition 1. *Let f be analytic in $[\![\phi]\!]$. It holds that:*

- $|r^k(f, \overrightarrow{u}, \overrightarrow{0})| \leq R^k(f, \overrightarrow{u}, \phi)$, *for all $\overrightarrow{u} \in [\![\phi]\!]$*
- *for all $\overrightarrow{u} \in [\![\phi]\!]$, $\lim_{k \to \infty} R^k(f, \overrightarrow{u}, \phi) = 0$.*

4   Approximation of Hybrid Automata

Let us introduce now our notion of approximation for an Hybrid Automaton H.

Definition 5. *Let H be an Hybrid Automaton where all functions appearing in formulae are derivable $k + 1$ times. The approximation of degree k for H is the Polynomial Hybrid Automaton $Approx(H, k)$ that is obtained from H by replacing each formula ϕ with a formula ϕ_k, which, in turn, is derived from ϕ by replacing each non-polynomial subformula $f(\overrightarrow{y}) \sim c$ in ϕ with:*

$$\begin{cases} P^k(f, \overrightarrow{y}) - R^k(f, \overrightarrow{y}, \phi) \sim c \text{ if } R^k(f, \overrightarrow{y}, \phi) \neq \infty \\ true \hspace{3.3cm} \text{if } R^k(f, \overrightarrow{y}, \phi) = \infty \end{cases}$$

where $\overrightarrow{y}$ stays for either $\overrightarrow{x}$, if ϕ is ϕ_{init}, or $(\overrightarrow{x}, \overrightarrow{x}')$, if ϕ is a transition label, or $(\overrightarrow{x}, t, \overrightarrow{x}')$, if ϕ is an activity function.

Since $f(\overrightarrow{y}) = P^k(f, \overrightarrow{y}) + r^k(f, \overrightarrow{y}, \overrightarrow{0})$, for some remainder $r^k(f, \overrightarrow{y}, \overrightarrow{0}) \in [-R^k(f, \overrightarrow{y}, \phi), R^k(f, \overrightarrow{y}, \phi)]$, and since we have assumed w.l.o.g. that $\sim \in \{<, \leq\}$, it holds that, for all $\overrightarrow{u} \in \mathbb{R}^n$, $f(\overrightarrow{u}) \sim c$ implies $P^k(f, \overrightarrow{u}) - R^k(f, \overrightarrow{u}, \phi) \sim c$.

Hence, $Approx(H, k)$ is obtained from H by replacing formulae with less demanding formulae (this fact will be formalized in Thm. 4).

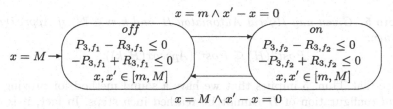

Fig. 2. $Approx(H, 3)$, where H is the thermostat of [1]

Example 3. Let H be the thermostat of Fig. 1. Let us suppose that $M, m > 0$. Let us call $f_1(x, t, x')$ and $f_2(x, t, x')$ the two functions $x' - xe^{-Kt}$ and $x' - (xe^{-Kt} + h(1 - e^{-Kt}))$ of Fig. 1, respectively, and let us call ϕ_1 and ϕ_2 the two activity functions $f_1(x, t, x') = 0$ and $f_2(x, t, x') = 0$, respectively. In Fig. 2 we show the Polynomial Hybrid Automaton $Approx(H, 3)$. Here, we have that:

- $P_{3, f_1} = P^3(f_1, (x, t, x')) = x' - x + Ktx - \frac{K^2}{2}xt^2$
- $P_{3, f_2} = P^3(f_2, (x, t, x')) = x' - x + Ktx - \frac{K^2}{2}xt^2 - hKt + \frac{hK^2}{2}t^2 - \frac{hK^3}{6}t^3$.

Moreover, let us compute the polynomials $R_{3, f_1} = R^3(f_1, (x, t, x'), \phi_1)$ and $R_{3, f_2} = R^3(f_2, (x, t, x'), \phi_2)$ of Fig. 2. We note that in states *off* and *on* we have that $t \in \left[0, \frac{ln(m) - ln(M)}{K}\right]$. Therefore the absolute value of derivate n^{th} of $-e^{-Kt}$ is less or equal than $max(\frac{M}{m}, 1)K^n$, and hence, the derivate n^{th} of f_1 is less or equal than $C_1(2K)^n$, where $C_1 = max\left(\frac{m+1}{m}M, 1 + M\right)$.

The absolute value of the derivate n^{th} of $h(1 - e^{-Kt})$ is less or equal than $max\left(\frac{hM+m}{m}, 2\right)K^n$, and hence, the derivate n^{th} of f_2 is less or equal than $C_2(2K)^n$, where $C_2 = \left(max\left(\frac{hM+m}{m}, 2\right) + max\left(\frac{m+1}{m}M, 1 + M\right)\right)$.

As a consequence $R_{3, f_i} = C_i \cdot (6K)^4 \cdot (x^4 + 1) \cdot (t^4 + 1) \cdot ((x')^4 + 1)$, for $i = 1, 2$.

We can recall now the notion of approximation of [10], which simply requires that all formulae in the approximation H' are weaker than those in the original automaton H, and prove that it is respected by our notion of approximation.

Definition 6 (Henzinger et al., [10]). *An Hybrid Automaton H' is an approximation of an Hybrid Automaton H if H' is obtained from H by replacing each formula ϕ with a formula ϕ' such that $[\![\phi']\!] \supseteq [\![\phi]\!]$.*

Theorem 4. *Given any Hybrid Automaton H and $k \in \mathbb{N}$, the Polynomial Hybrid Automaton $Approx(H, k)$ is an approximation of H according to Def. 6.*

With the notion of syntactic approximation given in Def. 5, a notion of behavioral approximation can be associated. Intuitively, the behavior of $Approx(H, k)$ approximates the behavior of H in the sense that all configurations that are reachable by H are reachable also by $Approx(H, k)$, in the same number of steps. In Sect. 6 we will study conditions over H ensuring that, if k tends to the infinity, then the behavior of $Approx(H, k)$ gets close to the behavior of H.

Theorem 5. *Given any Hybrid Automaton H and $k, n \in \mathbb{N}$, if $Approx(H, k)$ exists, then:*

$$Post^n(H) \subseteq Post^n(Approx(H, k))$$

Notice that Thm. 5 implies that we have a sound method for proving that some *bad* configuration of H cannot be reached in n steps. In fact, it is computable whether some configuration can be reached in n steps by a Polynomial Hybrid Automaton (see Thm. 2). Hence, if we prove that some bad configuration cannot be reached by $Approx(H, k)$ in n steps, then we infer that this configuration cannot be reached by H in n steps.

5   Syntactical Analysis of the Error

In [10], Def. 6 is strengthened by the notion of ϵ-approximation, which requires that any vector in $\mathbb{R}^n$ satisfying a formula ϕ' of the approximation H' must be "close" to at least one vector in $\mathbb{R}^n$ satisfying the corresponding formula ϕ in the original automaton H, where "close" means that the "distance" between the two vectors is bounded by ϵ. Intuitively, ϵ-approximations are motivated by the need to limit the error introduced by the approximation.

Here, we reformulate the notion of ϵ-approximation of [10] in terms of a notion of neighborhood of ray ϵ of a space in $\mathbb{R}^n$.

Given two vectors $\vec{u} = (u_1, \ldots, u_n)$ and $\vec{v} = (v_1, \ldots, v_n)$ in $\mathbb{R}^n$, let $d(\vec{u}, \vec{v})$ denote their *distance* $\sqrt{(u_1 - v_1)^2 + \cdots + (u_n - v_n)^2}$.

A *space* S in $\mathbb{R}^n$ is a set of vectors in $\mathbb{R}^n$.

Definition 7. *Given a space S in $\mathbb{R}^n$ and a real $\epsilon \geq 0$, the neighborhood of ray ϵ of space S is the set of spaces*

$$N(S, \epsilon) = \{S' \supseteq S \mid \forall \vec{v}' \in S' \; \exists \vec{v} \in S \text{ such that } d(\vec{v}, \vec{v}') \leq \epsilon\}$$

The following properties demonstrate the solidity of Def. 7.

Proposition 2. *Given spaces S_1 and S_2, and some $\epsilon, \xi \geq 0$, it holds that:*

1. *$S_1 \subseteq S_2$ implies $\forall S_1' \in N(S_1, \epsilon) \; \exists S_2' \in N(S_2, \epsilon)$ such that $S_1' \subseteq S_2'$*
2. *$\epsilon < \xi$ implies $N(S_1, \epsilon) \subset N(S_1, \xi)$*
3. *$\forall S' \in N(S_1 \cup S_2, \epsilon) \; \exists S_1' \in N(S_1, \epsilon), S_2' \in N(S_2, \epsilon)$ such that $S' = S_1' \cup S_2'$*
4. *$\forall S' \in N(S_1 \cap S_2, \epsilon) \; \exists S_1' \in N(S_1, \epsilon), S_2' \in N(S_2, \epsilon)$ such that $S' = S_1' \cap S_2'$*
5. *$N(S_1, 0) = \{S_1\}$.*

We can now reformulate the notion of ϵ-approximation of [10] by exploiting Def. 7.

Definition 8 (Henzinger et al., [10], reformulated). *An Hybrid Automaton H' is an ϵ-approximation of an Hybrid Automaton H if H' is obtained from H by replacing each formula ϕ with a formula ϕ' such that $[\![\phi']\!] \in N([\![\phi]\!], \epsilon)$.*

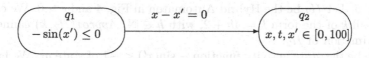

Fig. 3. The Hybrid Automaton H_1

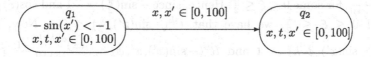

Fig. 4. The Hybrid Automaton H_2

Our aim is now to study the conditions over H ensuring that Def. 5 permits us to define ϵ-approximations for H, for all $\epsilon > 0$. We begin with two examples showing that in some cases ϵ-approximations cannot be given.

The first examples suggests to consider only formulae ϕ constraining variables within bounded intervals, thus avoiding variables that can tend to the infinity. (This does not represent a critical issue, since the definition of convergence for Taylor series requires that variables belong to bounded intervals.)

Example 4. Let H_1 be the Hybrid Automaton in Fig. 3 and $0 < \epsilon < \frac{\pi}{2}$. We can show that there is no k such that $Approx(H_1, k)$ is an ϵ-approximation for H_1. Let ϕ be the activity function $-\sin(x') \le 0$ of state q_1. We have that

$$\llbracket \phi \rrbracket = \{[2i \cdot \pi, (2i+1) \cdot \pi] \mid i \in \mathbb{N}\} \cup \{[-2i \cdot \pi, -(2i-1) \cdot \pi] \mid i \in \mathbb{N}^{\ge 0}\}$$

For any k, since $P^k(\sin(x'), x') - R^k(\sin(x'), x', \phi)$ is a polynomial, it holds that

$$\lim_{x' \to \infty} |P^k(-\sin(x'), x') - R^k(-\sin(x'), x', \phi)| = \infty.$$

Therefore, there exists some x_0 such that either $(-\infty, -x_0] \subseteq \llbracket \phi_k \rrbracket$ or $[x_0, \infty) \subseteq \llbracket \phi_k \rrbracket$. Given any $v - (2 \cdot i + \frac{3}{2}) \cdot \pi$, for some $i \in \mathbb{Z}$ such that $v \subset (\ \infty, \ x_0]$ or $v \in [x_0, \infty)$, there is no $v' \in \llbracket \phi \rrbracket$ with $d(v, v') \le \epsilon$, thus implying $\llbracket \phi_k \rrbracket \notin N(\llbracket \phi \rrbracket, \epsilon)$.

As suggested by Ex. 4, let us introduce the notion of bounded formula.

Definition 9. *A formula $\phi \in \Phi(\overrightarrow{x})$ is bounded iff any function f appearing in ϕ is analytic in $\llbracket \phi \rrbracket$, and*

$$\phi \equiv \phi' \wedge \bigwedge_{i \in [1,n]} x_i \in [l_{x_i}, u_{x_i}],$$

for some $\phi' \in \Phi(\overrightarrow{x})$ and $l_{x_1}, u_{x_1}, \ldots, l_{x_n}, u_{x_n} \in \mathbb{R}$. In such a case we denote with l_i^ϕ and u_i^ϕ the lower and the upper bound of x_i in ϕ.

The second example suggests to take care with formulae $f(\overrightarrow{x}) \sim c$ with $\sim \in \{<, >\}$.

Example 5. Let H_2 be the Hybrid Automaton in Fig. 4 and $\epsilon > 0$. We can show that for all k of the form $k = 4h + 2$, with $h \in \mathbb{N}$, $Approx(H_2, k)$ cannot be an ϵ-approximation of H_2.

Let ϕ be the state activity function $-\sin(x') < -1$ of state q_1. We have that $[\![\phi]\!] = \emptyset$. For each k of the form $k = 4h + 2$, $D^{k+1}(-\sin(x')) = \cos(x')$. Therefore, Lagrange Remainder Theorem ensures that $-\sin(\frac{\pi}{2}) - P^k(-\sin(x'), \frac{\pi}{2}) = \cos(\xi)\frac{\frac{\pi}{2}^{k+1}}{(k+1)!}$, for some $0 \le \xi \le \frac{\pi}{2}$. Hence, since $-\sin(\frac{\pi}{2}) = -1$ and $\cos(\xi)\frac{\frac{\pi}{2}^{k+1}}{(k+1)!} \ge 0$ for all $0 \le \xi \le \frac{\pi}{2}$, we have that $P^k(-\sin(x'), \frac{\pi}{2}) \le -1$. Now, it holds that $C(-\sin(x'), \phi, k) = 1$ and $R^k(-\sin(x'), x', \phi) = \frac{(x')^{2\lceil\frac{k+1}{2}\rceil+1}}{(k+1)!} \ge 0$. So, $P^k(-\sin(x'), x') - R^k(-\sin(x'), x', \phi) < -1$ is satisfied in a neighborhood of $\frac{\pi}{2}$, thus implying that $[\![\phi_k]\!] \neq \emptyset$ and $[\![\phi_k]\!] \notin N([\![\phi]\!], \epsilon)$ for any $\epsilon \ge 0$.

Notice that if we replace the activity function $\sin(x') < -1$ of state q_1 with $\sin(x') \le -1$, the argument of Ex. 5 falls. In fact, in such a case $\frac{\pi}{2} \in [\![\phi]\!]$, and, if k tends to the infinity, $R^k(-\sin(x'), x', \phi)$ tends to 0 and $P^k(-\sin(x'), x') - R^k(-\sin(x'), x', \phi) \le -1$ is satisfied only for values v that tend to $\frac{\pi}{2}$. Now, if we fix ϵ, we can choose some k_0 such that, if $k > k_0$, $d(v, \frac{\pi}{2}) \le \epsilon$.

We prove now that for all H satisfying the restrictions suggested by Ex. 4 and Ex. 5 we are able to find ϵ-approximations for all $\epsilon > 0$.

Theorem 6. *Consider an Hybrid Automaton H for which $Approx(H, k)$ exists for all $k > 0$. If the following conditions hold:*

- *each formula appearing in H is bounded*
- *each formula $f(x_1, \ldots, x_n) \sim c$ appearing in H is such that $\sim$ is $\le$*

then, for each $\epsilon > 0$ there exists some k_0 such that, for each $k > k_0$, $Approx(H, k)$ is an ϵ-approximation of H.

Note that Thm. 6 can capture also formulae $f(\overrightarrow{x}) = c$ and $f(\overrightarrow{x}) \ge c$, which can be rewritten as $f(\overrightarrow{x}) \le c \wedge -f(\overrightarrow{x}) \le -c$ and $-f(\overrightarrow{x}) \le -c$, respectively.

Actually, formulae $f(\overrightarrow{x}) \sim c$ with $\sim \in \{<, >\}$ considered in Ex. 5 can be admitted, provided that the hypothesis of Thm. 6 are strengthened.

Theorem 7. *Consider an Hybrid Automaton H for which $Approx(H, k)$ exists for all $k > 0$. If the following conditions hold:*

1. *each formula appearing in H is bounded*
2. *each formula $f(x_1, \ldots, x_n) \sim c$ appearing in H is such that $\sim \in \{<, \le\}$*
3. *for any formula $f(x_1, \ldots, x_n) < c$ appearing in a formula ϕ of H, and vector $\overrightarrow{u} \in [l_1^\phi, u_1^\phi] \times \cdots \times [l_n^\phi, u_n^\phi]$, if $f(\overrightarrow{u}) = c$, then $\overrightarrow{u} \in (l_1^\phi, u_1^\phi) \times \cdots \times (l_n^\phi, u_n^\phi)$.*
4. *for any formula ϕ appearing in H, and vector $\overrightarrow{u} \in [l_1^\phi, u_1^\phi] \times \cdots \times [l_n^\phi, u_n^\phi]$, there exists an index $j \in [1, n]$ such that one of the following facts hold:*
   (a) *for each $f(x_1, \ldots, x_n) \sim c$ appearing in ϕ such that $f(\overrightarrow{u}) = c$, there exists a neighborhood $N(\overrightarrow{u}, \epsilon)$ with $\epsilon > 0$ such that the function f is strictly increasing on j in $N(\overrightarrow{u}, \epsilon)$*

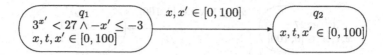

Fig. 5. The Hybrid Automaton H_3

(b) *for each $f(x_1, \ldots, x_n) \sim c$ appearing in ϕ such that $f(\overrightarrow{u}) = c$, there exists a neighborhood $N(\overrightarrow{u}, \epsilon)$ with $\epsilon > 0$ such that the function f is strictly decreasing on j in $N(\overrightarrow{u}, \epsilon)$*

then, for each $\epsilon > 0$ there exists some k_0 such that, for each $k > k_0$, $Approx(H, k)$ is an ϵ-approximation of H.

Note that Thm. 7 captures also formulae $f(\overrightarrow{x}) = c$, $f(\overrightarrow{x}) \geq c$ and $f(\overrightarrow{x}) > c$.

The following example shows that conditions 4a and 4b of Thm. 7 cannot be relaxed by simply requiring that "for each $f(x_1, \ldots, x_n) \sim c$ appearing in ϕ such that $f(\overrightarrow{u}) = c$, there exists a neighborhood $N(\overrightarrow{u}, \epsilon)$ with $\epsilon > 0$ such that the function f is strictly monotonic on j in $N(\overrightarrow{u}, \epsilon)$".

Example 6. Let H_3 be the Hybrid Automaton in Fig. 5 and $\epsilon > 0$. We can show that there is no k such that $Approx(H_3, k)$ is an ϵ-approximation of H_3.

Let ϕ be the activity function $3^{x'} < 27 \wedge -x' \leq -3$ of state q_1. Since $-x'$ is decreasing and $3^{x'}$ is increasing, the fourth condition of Thm. 7 is violated for $u = 3$. We have that $[\![\phi]\!] = \emptyset$.

For each k, $D^k(3^{x'}) = ln(3)^k \cdot 3^{x'}$. Therefore, Lagrange Remainder Theorem ensures that, for all u, $3^u - P^k(3^{x'}, u) = ln(3)^{k+1} \cdot 3^{\xi} \cdot \frac{(u)^{k+1}}{(k+1)!}$, for some $0 \leq \xi \leq u$. Hence, the remainder is greater than zero for all $u > 0$, thus implying $3^u > P^k(3^{x'}, u)$. Now, it holds that $C(3^{x'}, \phi, k) = 3^{100} \cdot ln(3)^{k+1}$ and $R^k(3^{x'}, x', \phi) = 3^{100} \cdot ln(3)^{k+1} \cdot \frac{(u)^{2\lceil \frac{k+1}{2} \rceil}}{(k+1)!}$. Since $R^k(3^{x'}, u, \phi)$ is greater than 0 for all $u > 0$, $P^k(3^{x'}, u) - R^k(3^{x'}, u, \phi) < 3^u$, thus implying that, for each k, $P^k(3^{x'}, u) - R^k(3^{x'}, u, \phi) < 27$ iff $u < 3 + e_k$, for some $e_k > 0$. Now, $[\![\phi_k]\!] = (3, 3 + e_k)$ is not empty, thus implying $[\![\phi_k]\!] \not\subseteq N([\![\phi]\!], \epsilon)$, for any $\epsilon \geq 0$.

6   Semantical Analysis of the Error

The notion of ϵ-approximation permits us to do a syntactical analysis of the error. Our aim is now to do a semantical analysis of the error, i.e. we wish to measure how the behavior of $Approx(H, k)$ is close to the behavior of H.

We need before the preliminary notions of neighborhood of a region and of asymptotic behavior for the class of functions $f : \mathbb{N} \to \mathcal{R}(H)$.

Definition 10. *Given a region R and a real $\epsilon \geq 0$, the neighborhood of ray ϵ of region R is the set of regions*

$$N(R, \epsilon) = \{R' \supseteq R \mid \forall(q, \overrightarrow{v'}) \in R' \setminus R \; \exists(q, \overrightarrow{v}) \in R \text{ such that } d(\overrightarrow{v}, \overrightarrow{v'}) \leq \epsilon\}$$

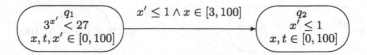

Fig. 6. The Hybrid Automaton H_4

The following properties, analogous to those of Prop. 2, demonstrate the solidity of Def. 10.

Proposition 3. *Given regions R_1 and R_2, and some $\epsilon, \xi \geq 0$, it holds that:*

1. $R_1 \subseteq R_2$ *implies* $\forall R_1' \in N(R_1, \epsilon)$ $\exists R_2' \in N(R_2, \epsilon)$ *such that* $R_1' \subseteq R_2'$
2. $\epsilon < \xi$ *implies* $N(R_1, \epsilon) \subset N(R_1, \xi)$
3. $\forall R' \in N(R_1 \cup R_2, \epsilon)$ $\exists R_1' \in N(R_1, \epsilon), R_2' \in N(R_2, \epsilon)$ *such that* $R' = R_1' \cup R_2'$
4. $\forall R' \in N(R_1 \cap R_2, \epsilon)$ $\exists R_1' \in N(R_1, \epsilon), R_2' \in N(R_2, \epsilon)$ *such that* $R' = R_1' \cap R_2'$
5. $N(R_1, 0) = \{R_1\}$.

Definition 11. *Let f be any function $f : \mathbb{N} \to \mathcal{R}(H)$. Function $f(k)$ asymptotically tends to region R, denoted $f(k) \approx_{k \to \infty} R$, iff:*

$$\forall \epsilon > 0 \ \exists k_0 \geq 0 \text{ such that } \forall k > k_0 \ f(k) \in N(R, \epsilon)$$

Intuitively, Def. 11 says that $f(k)$ gets close to R when k tends to the infinity.

Let us prove that, under a suitable hypothesis, if k tends to the infinity, then the behavior of $Approx(H, k)$ gets close to the behavior of H, in the sense that $Post^n(Approx(H, k))$ asymptotically tends to $Post^n(H)$.

Theorem 8. *Consider an Hybrid Automaton H satisfying the hypothesis of Thm. 6. For each $n \in \mathbb{N}$, it holds that*

$$Post^n(Approx(H, k)) \approx_{k \to \infty} Post^n(H).$$

As in the case of Thm. 6, Thm. 8 admits also formulae $f(\overrightarrow{x}) = c$ and $f(\overrightarrow{x}) \geq c$.

We show now that the result of Thm. 8 does not hold if we take the hypothesis of Thm. 7.

Example 7. Let H_4 be the Hybrid Automaton in Fig. 6. H_4 satisfies the hypothesis of Thm. 7, whereas the activity function $3^{x'} < 27$ of state q_1 violates the second condition of Thm. 6. We note that no configuration (q_2, v) can be reached by H_4, for any v. On the contrary, we have already seen in Ex. 6 that $P^k(3^{x'}) - R^k(3^{x'}, x', \phi) < 27$ iff $x' < 3 + e_k$, for some $e_k > 0$, and, hence, $Post^2(Approx(H, k))$ contains all (q_2, v) such that $v \leq 1$. We conclude that $Post^2(Approx(H, k)) \approx_{k \to \infty} Post^2(H)$ does not hold.

7   Efficient Implementation of *Approx(H, k)*

An effective algorithm for building $Approx(H, k)$ from H requires an effective algorithm for computing $P(f, \overrightarrow{x})$ and $C(f, \phi, k)$ from f. Hence, we are interested in the set $\mathcal{P}$ of the functions f for which $P(f, \overrightarrow{x})$ and $C(f, \phi, k)$ are computable in polynomial time w.r.t. k, for all formulae ϕ. Fortunately, $\mathcal{P}$ contains most of the functions used in the applications considered in the literature.

We note firstly that $\mathcal{P}$ contains all functions $p(\overrightarrow{x})$, with p any polynomial.

Then, $\mathcal{P}$ contains most of functions over one variable that are used in the examples in the literature, such as c^x, $log_c(x)$, $sin(x)$, $cos(x)$, $tg(x)$, with $c \in \mathbb{R}$.

Finally, $\mathcal{P}$ contains functions $y + f(\overrightarrow{x})$, where f is, in turn, a function in $\mathcal{P}$. Functions in this form permit us to simulate sum, composition and product of functions by introducing new variables, as showed in the following example.

Example 8. The bounded formula $x' - xe^{-Kt} = 0 \wedge x \in [m, M] \wedge x' \in [m, M]$ of state *off* in Fig. 1 can be replaced with the following (also bounded) formula ϕ:

$$x' - xy = 0 \wedge y - e^z = 0 \wedge z + Kt = 0 \wedge x, x' \in [m, M] \wedge y \in \left[\frac{m}{M}, 1\right] \wedge z \in \left[ln\left(\frac{m}{M}\right), 0\right]$$

Now, the polynomial $P^k(y - e^z, (y, z)) - R^k(y - e^z, (y, z), \phi)$ is equal to:

$$y - 1 - z - \frac{z^2}{2} - \cdots - \frac{z^k}{k!} - \frac{(M - m) \cdot 2^k \cdot \left(y^{2\lceil \frac{k+1}{2} \rceil} + 1\right)\left(z^{2\lceil \frac{k+1}{2} \rceil} + 1\right)}{M \cdot \lfloor \frac{k+1}{2} \rfloor!}$$

and it is polynomially computable w.r.t. k.

8   Future Works

In this paper we have defined syntactical over–approximations for hybrid automata by means of Taylor polynomials, and we have studied their syntactical and semantical convergence w.r.t. the original specifications.

As future work we will study also under–approximations based on this technique. Moreover, we will study also the function binding the approximation degree k to the error measure ϵ. Finally, we will study strategies to approximate only *partially* a function, to obtain a more accurate approximation. For instance, the function $y - e^z$ of Ex. 8 can be approximated by the function

$$y - 1 - z - \frac{z^2}{2} - \cdots - \frac{z^k}{k!} - \frac{(M - m) \cdot \left(z^{2 \cdot \lceil \frac{k+1}{2} \rceil} + 1\right)}{M \cdot (k + 1)!}$$

that approximates only e^z.

References

1. R. Alur, C. Courcoubetis, N. Halbwachs, T.A. Henzinger, P.H. Ho, X. Nicollin, A. Olivero, J. Sifakis, and S. Yovine: The algorithmic analysis of hybrid systems. Theor. Comput. Sci. 138(1), 1995, 3–34.

2. R. Alur and D.L. Dill: A theory of timed automata. Theor. Comput. Sci. 126(2), 1994, 183–235.
3. R. Alur, T.A. Henzinger, and P.H. Ho: Automatic symbolic verification of embedded systems. IEEE Trans. Software Eng. 22(6), 1996, 181–201.
4. R. Alur, T.A. Henzinger, G. Lafferriere, and G.J. Pappas: Discrete abstractions of hybrid systems. Proc. IEEE 88(7), 2000, 971–984.
5. E. Asarin, O. Bournez, T. Dang, O. Maler, and A. Pnueli: Effective synthesis of switching controllers for linear systems. Proc. IEEE 88(7), 2000, 1011-1025.
6. A.M. Bayen, E. Crück, and C.J. Tomlin: Guaranteed overapproximations of unsafe sets for continuous and hybrid systems: Solving the Hamilton-Jacobi equation using viability techniques. Proc. Hybrid Systems: Computation and Control, Lecture Notes in Computer Science 2289, Springer, Berlin, 2002, 90–104.
7. A. Chutinan and B.H. Krogh: Verification of polyhedral-invariant hybrid automata using polygonal flow pipe approximation. Proc. Hybrid Systems: Computation and Control, Lecture Notes in Computer Science 1569, Springer, Berlin, 1999, 76–90.
8. M. Fränzle: Analysis of hybrid systems: An ounce of realism can save an infinity of states. Proc. Computer Science Logic, Lecture Notes in Computer Science 1683, Springer, Berlin, 1999, 126–140.
9. M. Fränzle: What will be eventually true of polynomial hybrid automata. Proc. Theoretical Aspects of Computer Software, Lecture Notes in Computer Science 2215, Springer, Berlin, 2001, 340–359.
10. T.A. Henzinger, P.H. Ho, and H. Wong-Toi: Algorithmic analysis of nonlinear hybrid systems. IEEE Trans. Automat. Contr. 43(4), 1998, 540-554.
11. T.A. Henzinger, P.W. Kopke, A. Puri, and P. Varaiya: What's decidable about hybrid automata? J. Comput. Syst. Sci. 57(1), 1998, 94–124.
12. T.A. Henzinger and R. Majumdar: Symbolic model checking for rectangular hybrid systems. Proc. Tools and Algorithms for the Construction and Analysis of Systems, Lecture Notes in Computer Science 1785, Springer, Berlin, 2000, 142–156.
13. A.B. Kurzhanski and P. Varaiya: Reachability under uncertainty. Proc IEEE Conference on Decision and Control, 2002.
14. G. Lafferriere, G.J. Pappas, and S. Sastry: O-minimal hybrid systems. Math. Contr. Sign. Syst. 13(1), 2000, 1–21.
15. G. Lafferriere, G.J. Pappas, and S. Yovine: A new class of decidable hybrid systems. Proc. Hybrid Systems: Computation and Control, Lecture Notes in Computer Science 1569, Springer, Berlin, 1999, 137–151.
16. G. Lafferriere, G.J. Pappas, and S. Yovine: Reachability computation for linear hybrid systems. Proc. IFAC World Congress, 1999, 7–12.
17. I. Mitchell, A.M. Bayen, and C.J. Tomlin: Validating a Hamilton-Jacobi approximation to hybrid system reachable sets. Proc. Hybrid Systems: Computation and Control, Lecture Notes in Computer Science 2034, Springer, Berlin, 2001, 418–432.
18. A. Pnueli and J. Sifakis (Eds.): Special issue on hybrid systems. Theor. Comput. Sci. 138(1), 1995.
19. A. Puri, V. Borkar, and P. Varaiya: ε-approximation of differential inclusions. Proc. Hybrid Systems: Verification and Control, Lecture Notes in Computer Science 1066, Springer, Berlin, 1996, 362–376.
20. C. Tomlin, I. Mitchell, A. Bayen, and M. Oishi: Computational techniques for the verification and control of hybrid systems. Proc. IEEE 91(7), 2003, 986–1001.
21. H. Yazarel and G.J. Pappas: Geometric programming relaxations for non linear system reachability. Proc. American Control Conference, 2004.

Infinity Norms as Lyapunov Functions for Model Predictive Control of Constrained PWA Systems

Mircea Lazar[1], W.P.M.H. Heemels[2], Siep Weiland[1], Alberto Bemporad[3], and Octavian Pastravanu[4]

[1] Dept. of Electrical Eng., Eindhoven Univ. of Technology,
P.O. Box 513, 5600 MB Eindhoven, The Netherlands
m.lazar@tue.nl
[2] Embedded Systems Institute, P.O. Box 513,
5600 MB Eindhoven, The Netherlands
[3] Dip. Ingegneria dell'Informazione, Università di Siena,
Via Roma 56, 53100 Siena, Italy
[4] Dept. of Automatic Control and Industrial Informatics,
Technical Univ. "Gh. Asachi" of Iasi, Iasi 700050, Romania

Abstract. In this paper we develop *a priori* stabilization conditions for infinity norm based hybrid MPC in the terminal cost and constraint set fashion. Closed-loop stability is achieved using infinity norm inequalities that guarantee that the value function corresponding to the MPC cost is a Lyapunov function of the controlled system. We show that Lyapunov asymptotic stability can be achieved even though the MPC value function may be discontinuous. One of the advantages of this hybrid MPC scheme is that the terminal constraint set can be directly obtained as a sublevel set of the calculated terminal cost, which is also a local piecewise linear Lyapunov function. This yields a new method to obtain positively invariant sets for PWA systems.

1 Introduction

Hybrid systems provide a unified framework for modeling complex processes that include both continuous and discrete dynamics. The large variety of practical situations where hybrid systems are encountered (e.g., physical processes interacting with discrete actuators) led to an increasing interest in modeling and control of hybrid systems. Several modeling formalisms have been developed for describing hybrid systems, such as Mixed Logical Dynamical (MLD) systems [1] or Piecewise Affine (PWA) systems [2], and several control strategies have been proposed for relevant classes of hybrid systems. Many of the control schemes for hybrid systems are based on optimal control, e.g., like the ones in [3], [4], or on Model Predictive Control (MPC), e.g., as the ones in [1], [5], [6], [7]. In this paper we focus on the implementation of MPC for constrained PWA systems. This is motivated by the fact that PWA systems can model a broad class of hybrid systems, as shown in [8].

M. Morari and L. Thiele (Eds.): HSCC 2005, LNCS 3414, pp. 417–432, 2005.

The implementation of MPC for hybrid systems faces two difficult problems: how to reduce the computational complexity of the constrained optimization problem that has to be solved on-line and how to guarantee closed-loop stability. Most of the MPC algorithms are based on the optimization of a cost function which is defined using either quadratic forms or infinity norms. If a quadratic form is used to define the cost function, the MPC constrained optimization problem becomes a Mixed Integer Quadratic Programming (MIQP) problem, e.g., see [1] for details. This choice has led to fruitful results with respect to the stability problem of hybrid MPC, mainly due to the fact that in this case, the stabilization conditions can be reduced to a set of Linear Matrix Inequalities (LMI). Such results have been initially derived in the context of state feedback stabilization of PWA systems, as done in [3], [9]. The extension of the terminal cost and constraint set method for guaranteeing stability in MPC (e.g., see [10] for details) to the class of constrained PWA systems has been worked out in [7]. The terminal weight is calculated in [7] using semi-definite programming and the terminal state is constrained to a polyhedral positively invariant set in order to guarantee stability.

In the case when the infinity norm is used to define the cost function, the MPC constrained optimization problem leads to a Mixed Integer Linear Programming (MILP) problem, as pointed out in [5]. A piecewise affine explicit solution to this problem can be obtained using multi-parametric programming, as shown in [5], [6], [11], which may result in a reduction of the on-line computational complexity (one still has to check in which state space region the measured state resides). Regarding the stability problem, an a priori heuristic test for guaranteeing stability of infinity norm based MPC of PWA systems has been developed in [5]. Recently, an *a posteriori* procedure for guaranteeing stability of hybrid systems with a linear performance index has been derived in [12] by analyzing the explicit PWA closed-loop system. Another option to guarantee stability is to impose a terminal *equality* constraint, as done in [1] for hybrid MPC based on a quadratic form. However, this method has the disadvantage that the system must be brought to the origin in finite time, over the prediction horizon (this requires that the PWA system is controllable, while stabilizability should be sufficient in general). As a result, a longer prediction horizon may be needed for ensuring feasibility of the MPC optimization problem (fact which increases the computational burden). Also, the terminal equality constraint is only proven to guarantee attractivity. Lyapunov stability [13], next to attractivity, is a desirable property from a practical point of view.

In this paper we guarantee asymptotic stability (including Lyapunov stability) for infinity norm based hybrid MPC in the terminal cost and constraint set fashion. *A priori* stabilization conditions are developed using infinity norm inequalities, in contrast with the *a posteriori* verification proposed in [12]. If the considered infinity norm inequalities are satisfied, then the value function of the MPC cost is a Lyapunov function of the controlled PWA system. We show that Lyapunov asymptotic stability can be achieved even though the MPC value function may be discontinuous. This fact has been pointed out in [14] for nonlinear discrete-time systems and it has been used in [9] to derive a state-feedback based stabilizing controller for discrete-time PWA systems. We calculate the terminal weight by solving off-line an optimization problem. Several two-step methods to transform this problem into a Linear Programming (LP) problem are also presented. The terminal constraint set can be automatically obtained as a polyhedron (or as a finite union of polyhedra) by simply taking one of the sublevel sets of the calculated terminal cost, which is a local piecewise linear Lyapunov function. Then the MPC constrained optimization problem that has to be solved on-line still leads to a MILP problem.

The paper is organized as follows. Section 2 deals with preliminary notions and Section 3 provides a precise problem formulation. The main result concerning infinity norms as Lyapunov functions for MPC of constrained PWA systems is presented in Section 4. Several possibilities to obtain the terminal weight matrix are indicated in Section 5 and relaxations are developed in Section 6. The conclusions are summarized in Section 7.

2   Preliminaries

Consider the time-invariant discrete-time autonomous nonlinear system described by

$$x_{k+1} = g(x_k), \tag{1}$$

where $g(\cdot)$ is an arbitrary nonlinear function.

Definition 1. *Given* λ, $0 \le \lambda \le 1$, *a set* $\mathcal{P} \subset \mathbb{R}^n$ *is a* λ*-contractive set for system* (1) *if for all* $x \in \mathcal{P}$ *it holds that* $g(x) \in \lambda\mathcal{P}$. *For* $\lambda = 1$ *a* λ*-contractive set is called a* positively invariant set.

A polyhedron is a convex set obtained as the intersection of a finite number of open and/or closed half-spaces. Moreover, a convex and compact set in $\mathbb{R}^n$ that contains the origin in its interior is called a C-set [15].

For a vector $x \in \mathbb{R}^n$ we define $\|x\|_\infty := \max_{i=1,\ldots,n} |x_i|$, where x_i is the i-th component of x, and for a matrix $Z \in \mathbb{R}^{m \times n}$ we define

$$\|Z\|_\infty \triangleq \sup_{x \neq 0} \frac{\|Zx\|_\infty}{\|x\|_\infty}.$$

It is well known [16] that $\|Z\|_\infty = \max_{1 \le i \le m} \sum_{j=1}^n |Z^{\{ij\}}|$, where $Z^{\{ij\}}$ is the ij-th entry of Z. Also, for a matrix $Z \in \mathbb{R}^{m \times n}$ with full-column rank we define $Z^{-L} := (Z^\top Z)^{-1} Z^\top$, which is a left inverse of Z (i.e. $Z^{-L} Z = I_n$).

3   Problem Statement

Consider the time-invariant discrete-time PWA system [2] described by equations of the form

$$x_{k+1} = A_j x_k + B_j u_k + f_j \quad \text{when} \quad x_k \in \Omega_j. \tag{2}$$

Here, $x_k \in \mathbb{X} \subseteq \mathbb{R}^n$ is the state and $u_k \in \mathbb{U} \subseteq \mathbb{R}^m$ is the control input at the discrete-time instant $k \geq 0$. $A_j \in \mathbb{R}^{n \times n}$, $B_j \in \mathbb{R}^{n \times m}$, $f_j \in \mathbb{R}^n$, $j \in \mathcal{S}$ with $\mathcal{S} := \{1, 2, \ldots, s\}$ and s denoting the number of discrete modes. The sets $\mathbb{X}$ and $\mathbb{U}$ specify state and input constraints and it is assumed that they are polyhedral C-sets. The collection $\{\Omega_j \mid j \in \mathcal{S}\}$ defines a partition of $\mathbb{X}$, meaning that $\cup_{j \in \mathcal{S}} \Omega_j = \mathbb{X}$ and $\Omega_i \cap \Omega_j = \emptyset$ for $i \neq j$. Each Ω_j is assumed to be a polyhedron (not necessarily closed). Let $\mathcal{S}_0 := \{j \in \mathcal{S} \mid 0 \in \mathrm{cl}(\Omega_j)\}$ and let $\mathcal{S}_1 := \{j \in \mathcal{S} \mid 0 \notin \mathrm{cl}(\Omega_j)\}$, where $\mathrm{cl}(\Omega_j)$ denotes the closure of Ω_j. Note that $\mathcal{S} = \mathcal{S}_0 \cup \mathcal{S}_1$. In the sequel we assume that the origin is an equilibrium state for (2) with $u = 0$, and therefore, we require that

$$f_j = 0 \text{ for all } j \in \mathcal{S}_0. \tag{3}$$

Note that the class of hybrid systems described by (2)-(3) contains PWA systems which *may be discontinuous over the boundaries* and which are PWL in the regions whose closure contains the origin. The goal of this paper is to develop for system (2) an *asymptotically stabilizing* infinity norm based MPC scheme that leads to a MILP problem. For a fixed $N \in \mathbb{N}$, $N \geq 1$, let $\mathbf{x}_k(x_k, \mathbf{u}_k) = (x_{k+1}, \ldots, x_{k+N})$ denote a state sequence generated by system (2) from initial state x_k and by applying the input sequence $\mathbf{u}_k := (u_k, \ldots, u_{k+N-1}) \in \mathbb{U}^N$. Furthermore, let $\mathbb{X}_N \subseteq \mathbb{X}$ denote a desired target set that contains the origin.

Definition 2. *The class of* admissible input sequences *defined with respect to* $\mathbb{X}_N$ *and state* $x_k \in \mathbb{X}$ *is* $\mathcal{U}_N(x_k) := \{\mathbf{u}_k \in \mathbb{U}^N \mid \mathbf{x}_k(x_k, \mathbf{u}_k) \in \mathbb{X}^N, x_{k+N} \in \mathbb{X}_N\}$.

Stated differently, the input sequence $\mathbf{u}_k \in \mathbb{U}^N$ is admissible with respect to $\mathbb{X}_N$ and $x_k \in \mathbb{X}$ if the following conditions are satisfied:

$$x_{k+1+i} = A_j x_{k+i} + B_j u_{k+i} + f_j \text{ when } x_{k+i} \in \Omega_j, \tag{4a}$$

$$u_{k+i} \in \mathbb{U}, \quad x_{k+i} \in \mathbb{X} \quad \text{for } i = 0, \ldots, N-1, \tag{4b}$$

$$x_{k+N} \in \mathbb{X}_N. \tag{4c}$$

Now consider the following problem.

Problem 1. At time $k \geq 0$ let $x_k \in \mathbb{X}$ be given. Minimize the cost function

$$J(x_k, \mathbf{u}_k) \triangleq \|P x_{k+N}\|_\infty + \sum_{i=0}^{N-1} \|Q x_{k+i}\|_\infty + \|R u_{k+i}\|_\infty \tag{5}$$

over all input sequences $\mathbf{u}_k \in \mathcal{U}_N(x_k)$.

Here, N denotes the prediction horizon, and $P \in \mathbb{R}^{p \times n}$, $Q \in \mathbb{R}^{q \times n}$ and $R \in \mathbb{R}^{r \times m}$ are matrices which have full-column rank. The rank condition is necessary in order to ensure that $\|Px\|_\infty \neq 0$ for $x \neq 0$. We call an initial state $x_k \in \mathbb{X}$ *feasible* if $\mathcal{U}_N(x_k) \neq \emptyset$. Similarly, Problem 1 is said to be feasible (or *solvable*) for $x_k \in \mathbb{X}$ if $\mathcal{U}_N(x_k) \neq \emptyset$. Let

$$V_{\mathrm{MPC}}(x_k) \triangleq \min_{\mathbf{u}_k \in \mathcal{U}_N(x_k)} J(x_k, \mathbf{u}_k) \tag{6}$$

denote the value function corresponding to (5) and consider an optimal sequence of controls calculated for state $x_k \in \mathbb{X}$ by solving Problem 1, i.e.,

$$\mathbf{u}_k^* \triangleq (u_k^*, u_{k+1}^*, \ldots, u_{k+N-1}^*), \tag{7}$$

which minimizes (5). Let $\mathbf{u}_k^*(1)$ denote the first element of the sequence (7). According to the receding horizon strategy, the MPC control law is defined as

$$u_k^{\text{MPC}} = \mathbf{u}_k^*(1); \quad k \in \mathbb{Z}_+. \tag{8}$$

A more precise problem formulation can now be stated as follows.

Problem 2. Given Q, R and system (2) the objective is to determine P, N and $\mathbb{X}_N$ such that system (2) in closed-loop with the MPC control (8) is asymptotically stable in the Lyapunov sense and Problem 1 leads to a MILP problem.

Note that many of the hybrid MPC schemes only guarantee attractivity, e.g., see [1], [5], and not Lyapunov stability, which is important in practice (we thank the reviewer for this remark).

Remark 1. A partial solution to Problem 2 has been presented in [5], where a test criterion has been developed to *a priori* guarantee attractivity of the origin for the closed-loop system. Unfortunately, the results of [5] did not yield a systematic way for calculating the matrix P, but only a heuristic procedure. Another option to guarantee stability in infinity norm based hybrid MPC is to perform an *a posteriori* check of stability, after computing (8) as an explicit PWA control law, as it has been done in [12].

4   Infinity Norms as Lyapunov Functions for Hybrid MPC

In order to solve Problem 2 we aim at using the value function (6) as a candidate Lyapunov function for the closed-loop system (2)-(8) and we employ a terminal cost and constraint set method [10]. We also consider an auxiliary PWL control action of the form

$$\tilde{u}_k \triangleq K_j x_k, \quad x_k \in \Omega_j, \quad k \in \mathbb{Z}_+, \quad K_j \in \mathbb{R}^{m \times n}, \quad j \in \mathcal{S}. \tag{9}$$

Let $\mathbb{X}_U := \cup_{j \in \mathcal{S}} \{x \in \Omega_j \mid K_j x \in \mathbb{U}\}$ denote the safe set with respect to *state and input* constraints for this controller and let $\mathbb{X}_N \subseteq \mathbb{X}_U$ be a positively invariant set for the PWA system (2) in closed-loop with (9). In the sequel we require that $\mathbb{X}_N$ contains the origin in its interior. Now consider the following inequalities:

$$\|P(A_j + B_j K_j)P^{-L}\|_\infty + \|QP^{-L}\|_\infty + \|RK_j P^{-L}\|_\infty \leq 1 - \gamma_j, \quad j \in \mathcal{S} \tag{10}$$

and

$$\|Pf_j\|_\infty \leq \gamma_j \|Px\|_\infty, \quad \forall x \in \mathbb{X}_N \cap \Omega_j, \quad j \in \mathcal{S}, \tag{11}$$

where $\{\gamma_j \mid j \in \mathcal{S}\}$ are scaling factors that satisfy $0 \leq \gamma_j < 1$ for all $j \in \mathcal{S}$. Note that, because of (3), (11) trivially holds if $\mathcal{S} = \mathcal{S}_0$.

Theorem 1. *Suppose* (10)-(11) *is solvable in* (P, K_j, γ_j) *for* P *with full-column rank and* $j \in \mathcal{S}$, $\mathbb{X}_N \subseteq \mathbb{X}_{\mathbb{U}}$ *is a positively invariant set for the closed-loop system* (2)-(9) *that contains the origin in its interior and fix* $N \geq 1$. *Then it holds that*

1. *If Problem 1 is feasible at time* $k \in \mathbb{Z}_+$ *for state* $x_k \in \Omega_j$, *then Problem 1 is feasible at time* $k + 1$ *for state* $x_{k+1} = A_j x_k + B_j \mathbf{u}_k^*(1) + f_j$.
2. *The MPC control* (8) *asymptotically stabilizes the PWA system* (2) *for all feasible initial states (including the set* $\mathbb{X}_N$), *while satisfying the state and input constraints* (4).
3. *The origin of the PWA system* (2) *in closed-loop with feedback* (9) *is locally asymptotically stable, while satisfying the state and input constraints* (4).
4. *If* $\mathbb{X} = \mathbb{R}^n$, $\mathbb{U} = \mathbb{R}^m$ *and* (11) *holds for* $\mathbb{X}_N = \mathbb{R}^n$, *then the origin of the PWA system* (2) *in closed-loop with feedback* (9) *is globally asymptotically stable.*

In order to prove Theorem 1 we will need the following result, the proof of which can be found in the appendix.

Lemma 1. *Consider the closed-loop PWA system* (2)-(9):

$$x_{k+1} = (A_j + B_j K_j)x_k + f_j \quad when \quad x_k \in \Omega_j, \quad j \in \mathcal{S}. \tag{12}$$

Assume that (11) *is solvable for some* P *with full-column rank. Then for any* $l = 0, 1, 2, \ldots$ *there exists an* $\alpha_l > 0$ *such that for all* $x_k \in \mathbb{X}_N$

$$\|x_{k+l}\|_\infty \leq \alpha_l \|x_k\|_\infty, \tag{13}$$

if $(x_k, x_{k+1}, \ldots, x_{k+l})$ *is a solution of* (12).

Now we prove Theorem 1.

Proof. Consider (7) and the shifted sequence of controls

$$\mathbf{u}_{k+1} \triangleq (u_{k+1}^*, u_{k+2}^*, \ldots, u_{k+N-1}^*, \tilde{u}_{k+N}), \tag{14}$$

where the auxiliary control $\tilde{u}_{k+N}$ denotes the control law (9) at time $k + N$.

1) If Problem 1 is feasible at time $k \in \mathbb{Z}_+$ for state $x_k \in \Omega_j$ then there exists $\mathbf{u}_k^* \in \mathcal{U}_N(x_k)$ that solves Problem 1. Then x_{k+N} satisfies constraint (4c). Since $\mathbb{X}_N \subseteq \mathbb{X}_{\mathbb{U}}$ is positively invariant for system (2) in closed-loop with (9), it follows that $\mathbf{u}_{k+1} \in \mathcal{U}_N(x_{k+1})$. Hence, Problem 1 is feasible for state $x_{k+1} = A_j x_k + B_j \mathbf{u}_k^*(1) + f_j$. Moreover, all states in the set $\mathbb{X}_N \subseteq \mathbb{X}_{\mathbb{U}}$ are feasible with respect to Problem 1, as the PWL feedback (9) can be applied for any N.

2) In order to achieve stability we require for all *feasible* initial conditions $x_0 \in \mathbb{X} \backslash \{0\}$ that the forward difference $\Delta V_{\text{MPC}}(x_k) := V_{\text{MPC}}(x_{k+1}) - V_{\text{MPC}}(x_k)$ is strictly negative for all $k \in \mathbb{Z}_+$, which can be written as:

$$\begin{aligned} \Delta V_{\text{MPC}}(x_k) &= J(x_{k+1}, \mathbf{u}_{k+1}^*) - J(x_k, \mathbf{u}_k^*) \leq J(x_{k+1}, \mathbf{u}_{k+1}) - J(x_k, \mathbf{u}_k^*) = \\ &= -\|Qx_k\|_\infty - \|Ru_k^*\|_\infty + \|Px_{k+N+1}\|_\infty + \|R\tilde{u}_{k+N}\|_\infty \\ &\quad + \|Qx_{k+N}^*\|_\infty - \|Px_{k+N}^*\|_\infty < 0, \quad \forall x_{k+N}^* \in \mathbb{X}_N \backslash \{0\}. \end{aligned} \tag{15}$$

Here, $x_k \in \Omega_j$ is the measured state at the sampling instant k and $x^*_{k+1} = A_j x_k + B_j u^*_k + f_j$. Hence, it suffices to determine the matrix P such that there exists $\tilde{u}_{k+N}$ with

$$\|Px_{k+N+1}\|_\infty + \|R\tilde{u}_{k+N}\|_\infty + \|Qx^*_{k+N}\|_\infty - \|Px^*_{k+N}\|_\infty \leq 0, \ \forall x^*_{k+N} \in \mathbb{X}_N, \tag{16}$$

in order to guarantee that $\Delta V_{\mathrm{MPC}}(x_k) \leq -\|Qx_k\|_\infty$ for all *feasible* initial conditions $x_0 \in \mathbb{X}\backslash\{0\}$. Since Q has full-column rank, there exists a positive number τ such that $\|Qx\|_\infty \geq \tau\|x\|_\infty$ for all $x \in \mathbb{X}$. Hence, it follows that (16) implies that V_{MPC} possesses a *negative definite forward difference* (see [13] for details). Substituting (9) at time $k + N$ and (2) in (16) yields the equivalent

$$\|P(A_j + B_j K_j)x^*_{k+N} + Pf_j\|_\infty + \|RK_j x^*_{k+N}\|_\infty$$
$$+ \|Qx^*_{k+N}\|_\infty - \|Px^*_{k+N}\|_\infty \leq 0, \quad \forall x^*_{k+N} \in \mathbb{X}_N \cap \Omega_j, \quad j \in \mathcal{S}. \tag{17}$$

Now we prove that if (10)-(11) holds, then (17) holds. Since P and $\{K_j \mid j \in \mathcal{S}\}$ satisfy (10) we have that

$$\|P(A_j + B_j K_j)P^{-L}\|_\infty + \|QP^{-L}\|_\infty + \|RK_j P^{-L}\|_\infty + \gamma_j - 1 \leq 0, \quad j \in \mathcal{S}. \tag{18}$$

Right multiplying the inequality (18) with $\|Px^*_{k+N}\|_\infty$ and using the inequality (11) yields:

$$0 \geq \|P(A_j + B_j K_j)P^{-L}\|_\infty \|Px^*_{k+N}\|_\infty + \|QP^{-L}\|_\infty \|Px^*_{k+N}\|_\infty$$
$$+ \gamma_j\|Px^*_{k+N}\|_\infty + \|RK_j P^{-L}\|_\infty \|Px^*_{k+N}\|_\infty - \|Px^*_{k+N}\|_\infty \geq$$
$$\geq \|P(A_j + B_j K_j)P^{-L}Px^*_{k+N}\|_\infty + \|QP^{-L}Px^*_{k+N}\|_\infty$$
$$+ \|Pf_j\|_\infty + \|RK_j P^{-L}Px^*_{k+N}\|_\infty - \|Px^*_{k+N}\|_\infty \geq$$
$$\geq \|P(A_j + B_j K_j)x^*_{k+N} + Pf_j\|_\infty + \|RK_j x^*_{k+N}\|_\infty$$
$$+ \|Qx^*_{k+N}\|_\infty - \|Px^*_{k+N}\|_\infty. \tag{19}$$

Hence, inequality (17) holds and consequently $\Delta V_{\mathrm{MPC}}(x_k) \leq -\tau\|x_k\|_\infty$. Next, we show that $V_{\mathrm{MPC}}(x_k)$ is a positive definite, radially unbounded and decrescent function [13]. From (6) and (5) we have that

$$V_{\mathrm{MPC}}(x_k) \geq \|Qx_k\|_\infty \geq \tau\|x_k\|_\infty, \quad \forall N \geq 1, \quad \forall x \in \mathbb{X}. \tag{20}$$

Hence, $V_{\mathrm{MPC}}(x_k)$ is a *positive definite* and *radially unbounded* function.

For $x_k \in \mathbb{X}_N$ we have that the control law $\tilde{u}_k = K_j x_k$ when $x_k \in \mathbb{X}_N \cap \Omega_j$ is admissible. Then it follows that the control sequence $\tilde{\mathbf{u}}_k := (\tilde{u}_k, \ldots, \tilde{u}_{k+N-1}) \in \mathbb{U}^N$ is contained in $\mathcal{U}_N(x_k)$. Since there always exist some positive constants γ_P and γ_Q such that $\|Px_k\|_\infty \leq \gamma_P\|x_k\|_\infty$ and $\|Qx_k\|_\infty \leq \gamma_Q\|x_k\|_\infty$ (e.g., $\gamma_P = \|P\|_\infty$ and $\gamma_Q = \|Q\|_\infty$), we have that

$$V_{\mathrm{MPC}}(x_k) \leq J(x_k, \tilde{\mathbf{u}}_k) = \|Px_{k+N}\|_\infty + \sum_{i=0}^{N-1} \|Qx_{k+i}\|_\infty + \|RK_{j_i}x_{k+i}\|_\infty \leq$$

$$\leq \gamma_P \|x_{k+N}\|_\infty + (\gamma_Q + \kappa) \sum_{i=0}^{N-1} \|x_{k+i}\|_\infty, \quad \forall x_k \in \mathbb{X}_N, \tag{21}$$

where $\kappa = \max_{j \in \mathcal{S}} \|RK_j\|_\infty$ and $j_i \in \mathcal{S}$ is such that $x_{k+i} \in \Omega_{j_i}$. From Lemma 1 it follows that there exist constants $\alpha_i > 0$ such that $\|x_{k+i}\|_\infty \leq \alpha_i \|x_k\|_\infty$, $i = 1, \ldots, N$, and by letting $\beta := \gamma_P \alpha_N + (\gamma_Q + \kappa)(1 + \sum_{i=1}^{N-1} \alpha_i)$ it follows that

$$V_{\mathrm{MPC}}(x_k) \leq \beta \|x_k\|_\infty, \quad \forall x_k \in \mathbb{X}_N.$$

Hence, $V_{\mathrm{MPC}}(x_k)$ is a *decrescent* function [13] on $\mathbb{X}_N$ (note that $\mathbb{X}_N$ contains the origin in its interior). Since $V_{\mathrm{MPC}}(x_k)$ is also positive definite it follows that

$$\tau \|x_k\|_\infty \leq V_{\mathrm{MPC}}(x_k) \leq \beta \|x_k\|_\infty, \quad \forall x_k \in \mathbb{X}_N. \tag{22}$$

Then, by applying the reasoning used in the proof of Theorem 3 and Theorem 4 from [9] (note that for any $\epsilon > 0$ we can choose $\delta = (\tau/\beta)\epsilon < \epsilon$ and hence, continuity of $V_{\mathrm{MPC}}(x_k)$ is not necessary, see [9] and [13] for details) it follows that the infinity norm inequalities (10)-(11) are sufficient for guaranteeing Lyapunov asymptotic stability [13] for the PWA system (2) in closed-loop with the MPC control (8).

3) Since $\{(P, K_j) \mid j \in \mathcal{S}\}$ satisfy (17) we have that

$$\|P(A_j + B_j K_j)x_k + P f_j\|_\infty - \|Px_k\|_\infty \leq -\|Qx_k\|_\infty < 0, \quad \forall x_k \in \mathbb{X}_N \setminus \{0\}, j \in \mathcal{S}. \tag{23}$$

Then it follows that $V(x) := \|Px\|_\infty$, which is a radially unbounded, positive definite and decrescent function, possesses a negative definite forward difference. Hence, $V(x_k)$ is a common polyhedral Lyapunov function for the dynamics $x_{k+1} = (A_j + B_j K_j)x_k + f_j$, $j \in \mathcal{S}$. Then, the origin of the PWA system (2) with feedback (9) is asymptotically stable on some region of attraction, e.g., the *polyhedral* sublevel set given by the largest $\varphi > 0$ for which $\{x \in \mathbb{X} \mid V(x) \leq \varphi\}$ is contained in $\mathbb{X}_U$.

4) For the PWA system (2) with $\mathbb{X} = \mathbb{R}^n$ and $\mathbb{U} = \mathbb{R}^m$ we have that $\mathbb{X}_U = \mathbb{R}^n$. Since (23) holds for $\mathbb{X}_N = \mathbb{R}^n$, it follows that the origin of the PWA system (2) with feedback (9) is globally asymptotically stable. $\square$

It follows from Theorem 1 that a terminal set $\mathbb{X}_N$ can be easily obtained as a sublevel set

$$\mathbb{X}_N \triangleq \{x \in \mathbb{X} \mid \|Px\|_\infty \leq \varphi^*\}, \tag{24}$$

where $\varphi^* = \sup_\varphi \{\{x \in \mathbb{X} \mid \|Px\|_\infty \leq \varphi\} \subset \mathbb{X}_U\}$. Since this set is a polyhedron, Problem 1 leads to a MILP problem, which can be solved by standard tools developed in the context of infinity norm based hybrid MPC [4].

Remark 2. We have shown that Lyapunov asymptotic stability can be guaranteed for the closed-loop system (2)-(8) and all *feasible* initial states, even though the MPC value function and the PWA dynamics (2) may be discontinuous. This results from the fact that V_{MPC} is radially unbounded, it possesses a negative definite forward difference and the inequality (22) holds on $\mathbb{X}_N$ (note that $V_{\text{MPC}}(0) = 0$ and (22) implies that $V_{\text{MPC}}(x)$ is continuous at $x = 0$). Moreover, it follows from Theorem 2 of [14] that the origin of the closed-loop system (2)-(8) is locally *exponentially stable* (i.e. this property holds for all states in $\mathbb{X}_N$).

Remark 3. The set of feasible initial states with respect to Problem 1 depends on the value of the prediction horizon N, due to the terminal constraint (4c). The larger N, the larger the set of feasible states is. For a given terminal constraint set $\mathbb{X}_N$ and an assigned set of initial conditions, one can perform a reachability (controllability) analysis in order to obtain the minimum prediction horizon needed to achieve feasibility of Problem 1 for the desired set of initial states. A procedure that can be employed to solve this problem for constrained PWA systems is given in [6].

Finding the matrix P and the feedback matrices $\{K_j \mid j \in \mathcal{S}\}$ that satisfy the infinity norm inequality (10) amounts to solving an optimization problem subject to the constraint $\text{rank}(P) = n$. Note that this constraint can be replaced by the convex constraint $P^\top P > 0$. Once a matrix P satisfying (10) has been found, one still has to check that P also satisfies inequality (11), provided that $\mathcal{S} \neq \mathcal{S}_0$. For example, this can be verified by checking the inequality

$$\|Pf_j\|_\infty \leq \gamma_j \min_{x \in \mathbb{X}_N \cap \Omega_j} \|Px\|_\infty, \quad j \in \mathcal{S}(\mathbb{X}_N),$$

where $\mathcal{S}(\mathbb{X}_N) := \{j \mid \mathbb{X}_N \cap \Omega_j \neq \emptyset\} \cap \mathcal{S}_1$. In order not to perform this additional check, the inequality (11) can be removed by requiring that $\mathbb{X}_N \subseteq \cup_{j \in \mathcal{S}_0} \Omega_j$ is a positively invariant set only for the PWL sub-system of the closed-loop PWA system (2)-(9), i.e., for the system $x_{k+1} = (A_j + B_j K_j)x_k$ when $x_k \in \Omega_j$, $j \in \mathcal{S}_0$, as done in [7] for hybrid MPC based on quadratic forms. Note that the auxiliary control action (9) defines now a local state feedback, instead of a global state feedback, as in Theorem 1. In this case Theorem 1 can be reformulated as follows.

Corollary 1. *Suppose that the inequality*

$$\|P(A_j + B_j K_j)P^{-L}\|_\infty + \|QP^{-L}\|_\infty + \|RK_j P^{-L}\|_\infty \leq 1 \qquad (25)$$

is solvable in (P, K_j) for P with full-column rank and $j \in \mathcal{S}_0$. Let $\mathbb{X}_N \subseteq \mathbb{X}_U \cap \{\cup_{j \in \mathcal{S}_0} \Omega_j\}$ be a positively invariant set for the closed-loop system $x_{k+1} = (A_j + B_j K_j)x_k$ when $x_k \in \Omega_j$, $j \in \mathcal{S}_0$ and assume that $\mathbb{X}_N$ contains the origin in its interior. Fix $N \geq 1$. Then the first three statements of Theorem 1 hold.

Proof. From the fact that the terminal state is constrained to lie in $\mathbb{X}_N \subseteq \mathbb{X}_U \cap \{\cup_{j \in \mathcal{S}_0} \Omega_j\}$ and from (3) we have that $f_j = 0$ for all $j \in \mathcal{S}_0$. Then it follows that (11) holds with equality for $\gamma_j = 0$, $\forall j \in \mathcal{S}_0$. Since (P, K_j) satisfy (25) for all $j \in \mathcal{S}_0$ it follows that (P, K_j) satisfy (10)-(11) for all $j \in \mathcal{S}_0$. Then the results follow from Theorem 1. $\qquad\square$

Example 1. Consider the following third order chain of integrators with a varying sampling rate:

$$x_{k+1} = \begin{cases} A_1 x_k + B_1 u_k & \text{if } [0\ 1\ 1]x_k \leq 0 \,,\ [1\ 0\ 0]x_k < 4 \,,\ [-1\ 0\ 0]x_k < 4 \\ A_2 x_k + B_2 u_k & \text{if } [0\ 1\ 1]x_k > 0 \,,\ [1\ 0\ 0]x_k < 4 \,,\ [-1\ 0\ 0]x_k < 4 \\ A_3 x_k + B_3 u_k + f & \text{otherwise} \end{cases}$$

(26)

subject to the constraints $x_k \in \mathbb{X} = [-15, 15]^3$ and $u_k \in \mathbb{U} = [-1, 1]$, where

$$A_1 = \begin{bmatrix} 1 & 0.4 & 0.08 \\ 0 & 1 & 0.4 \\ 0 & 0 & 1 \end{bmatrix},\ A_2 = \begin{bmatrix} 1 & 0.7 & 0.245 \\ 0 & 1 & 0.7 \\ 0 & 0 & 1 \end{bmatrix},\ A_3 = \begin{bmatrix} 1 & 0.8 & 0.32 \\ 0 & 1 & 0.8 \\ 0 & 0 & 1 \end{bmatrix},$$

$$B_1 = \begin{bmatrix} 0.0107 \\ 0.08 \\ 0.4 \end{bmatrix},\ B_2 = \begin{bmatrix} 0.0572 \\ 0.245 \\ 0.7 \end{bmatrix},\ B_3 = \begin{bmatrix} 0.0853 \\ 0.32 \\ 0.8 \end{bmatrix},\ f = \begin{bmatrix} 0.3 \\ 0.1 \\ 0.1 \end{bmatrix}.$$

The MPC tuning parameters are $Q = I_3$ and $R = 0.1$. The following solution to the inequality (10) has been found using a min-max formulation and the Matlab `fmincon` solver (CPU time was 5.65 seconds on a Pentium III at 700MHz):

$$P = \begin{bmatrix} 24.1304 & 20.3234 & 4.9959 \\ 20.3764 & 35.9684 & 10.5832 \\ 6.3709 & 9.21 & 9.9118 \end{bmatrix},\ K_3 = \begin{bmatrix} -0.8434 & -2.063 & -1.9809 \end{bmatrix},\ \gamma = 0.174,$$

$$K_1 = \begin{bmatrix} -2.3843 & -4.5862 & -3.1858 \end{bmatrix},\ K_2 = \begin{bmatrix} -0.8386 & -2.1077 & -2.1084 \end{bmatrix}. \tag{27}$$

$\mathbb{X}_N$ has been obtained as in (24) for $\varphi^* = 2.64$. Due to the input constraints we have that $\mathbb{X}_N \subset \cup_{j \in S_0} \Omega_j$ for system (26). However, inequality (11) holds for system (26) and all $x \in \mathbb{X}$. The initial state is $x_0 = [3\ -1\ 2]^\top$ and the prediction horizon of $N = 8$ is obtained as in Remark 3 for the matrices P, Q and R given above. The simulation results are plotted in Figure 1 for system (26) in closed-loop with the MPC control (8). As guaranteed by Theorem 1, the MPC control law (8) stabilizes the unstable system (26) while satisfying the state and input constraints.   □

5   Solving the Stabilization Conditions

This section gives some techniques to approach the computationally challenging problem associated with inequality (10). All these methods start from the fact that if the matrix P is known in (10), then the optimization problem can be recast as an LP problem. In the sequel we will indicate three ways to find an educated guess of P. The first two methods are based on the observation that a matrix P that satisfies (10)-(11) (for some K_j, $j \in S$) has the property that $V(x) = \|Px\|_\infty$ is a common polyhedral Laypunov function of the PWA system (2) in closed-loop with some PWL feedback (9). Using this observation, an educated guess of P is now based on functions $V(x) = \|Px\|_\infty$ that satisfy this necessary condition and thus, induce positively invariant sets for the closed-loop system (2)-(9).

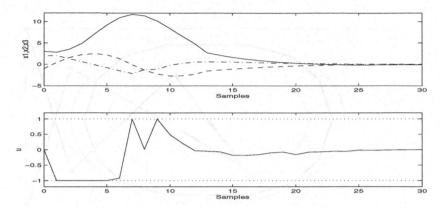

Fig. 1. Example 1: State trajectory and Input history

5.1   A Quadratic Approach

One possibility to fix the terminal weight matrix is to use the approach of [7] to calculate a polyhedral positively invariant set for the PWL sub-system of the PWA system (2)-(9), i.e., for the system $x_{k+1} = (A_j + B_j K_j)x_k$ when $x_k \in \Omega_j$, $j \in \mathcal{S}_0$. If the algorithm of [7] terminates in finite time and the resulting polyhedral set is symmetric, then a good choice for P is the matrix that induces this polyhedral set, i.e. $\{x \in \mathbb{X} \mid \|Px\|_\infty \leq c\}$ for some $c > 0$. Note that this type of approach to obtain P is based on the fact that the feedback matrices $\{K_j \mid j \in \mathcal{S}_0\}$ are already known, e.g., in [7] they are calculated via semi-definite programming in order to obtain a common quadratic Lyapunov function. The approach of [9] can also be used to compute the feedbacks that guarantee quadratic stability and then, the algorithm of [7] can be employed to obtain a polyhedral positively invariant set. Fixing P in (10) and solving in $\{K_j \mid j \in \mathcal{S}_0\}$ (and γ_j) amounts to looking for a different state feedback control law, which not only renders the employed polyhedral set positively invariant, but also ensures that $V_{\mathrm{MPC}}(x_k)$ possesses a negative definite forward difference.

5.2   "Squaring the Circle"

Another way to obtain polyhedral (or piecewise polyhedral) positively invariant sets for closed-loop PWA systems that admit a common (or a piecewise) quadratic Lyapunov function has been recently developed in [17]. In this approach, the polyhedral set can be constructed by solving the problem of fitting a polyhedron in between two ellipsoidal sublevel sets of a quadratic Lyapunov function, where one is contained in the interior of the other and the states on the boundary of the outer ellipsoid are mapped by the closed-loop dynamics into the interior of the inner ellipsoid. This problem can be solved using the recent algorithm developed in [18] in the context of DC programming. The polyhedral set is constructed by treating the ellipsoids as sublevel sets of convex functions, and by exploiting upper and lower piecewise affine bounds on such functions.

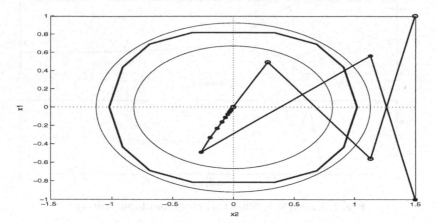

Fig. 2. Example 2: State trajectory

Giving additional structure to the algorithm of [18] such that it generates a polyhedron with a finite number of facets, a polyhedral positively invariant set is obtained for system (2) and then P can be chosen as the matrix that induces this polyhedron.

Example 2. Consider the example proposed in [5], i.e.,

$$x_{k+1} = \begin{cases} A_1 x_k + Bu_k & \text{if } [1\ 0]x_k \geq 0 \\ A_2 x_k + Bu_k & \text{if } [1\ 0]x_k < 0 \end{cases} \tag{28}$$

subject to the constraints $x_k \in \mathbb{X} = [-5,5] \times [-5,5]$, $u_k \in \mathbb{U} = [-1,1]$ and with

$$A_1 = \begin{bmatrix} 0.35 & -0.6062 \\ 0.6062 & 0.35 \end{bmatrix}, \quad A_2 = \begin{bmatrix} 0.35 & 0.6062 \\ -0.6062 & 0.35 \end{bmatrix}, \quad B = \begin{bmatrix} 0 \\ 1 \end{bmatrix}.$$

The common *quadratic* Lypunov function calculated in [7] for system (28)-(9) with feedback matrices $K_1 = [-0.611\ -0.3572]$, $K_2 = [0.611\ -0.3572]$ and the algorithm of [18] have been used to compute a polyhedral positively invariant set for system (28). The two ellipsoidal sublevel sets of the quadratic Lyapunov function plotted in Figure 2 are such that all the states on the boundary of the outer ellipsoid go inside the inner ellipsoid in one discrete-time step. The matrix P has been chosen as the matrix that induces the polyhedron plotted in Figure 2. Then (10) has been solved for the MPC tuning parameters $Q = \text{diag}([0.6\ 1])$ and $R = 0.1$, yielding the new state feedback matrices $K_1 = [-0.6897\ -0.1416]$ and $K_2 = [0.1454\ -0.7461]$. The simulation results obtained for $N = 2$ and the initial states $x_0 = [1\ 1.5]^\top$ (circle line) and $x_0 = [-1\ 1.5]^\top$ (star line) are shown in Figure 2 together with a plot of the polyhedral positively invariant set.   □

5.3   Square Matrices Q and P

If Q is square and invertible, a different way to simplify (10) is to parameterize the terminal weight as $P = \frac{1}{\epsilon}Q$, where $0 < \epsilon < 1$.

Lemma 2. *Assume that $\{K_j, \gamma_j \mid j \in \mathcal{S}\}$ with $0 \le \gamma_j < 1$ and ϵ satisfy the inequality*

$$\|Q(A_j + B_j K_j)Q^{-1}\|_\infty + \epsilon\|RK_j Q^{-1}\|_\infty \le 1 - \epsilon - \gamma_j, \quad j \in \mathcal{S}. \qquad (29)$$

Then $P = \frac{1}{\epsilon}Q$ and $\{K_j, \gamma_j \mid j \in \mathcal{S}\}$ satisfy the inequality (10).

Proof. From the fact that Q is square and invertible it follows that $P = \frac{1}{\epsilon}Q$ is square and invertible. Then the inequality (10) can be written as

$$\|P(A_j + B_j K_j)P^{-1}\|_\infty + \|QP^{-1}\|_\infty + \|RK_j P^{-1}\|_\infty \le 1 - \gamma_j, \quad j \in \mathcal{S}.$$

By replacing $P = \frac{1}{\epsilon}Q$ and $P^{-1} = \epsilon Q^{-1}$ in the above inequality yields the equivalent inequality (29). □

For a fixed ϵ, finding $\{K_j, \gamma_j \mid j \in \mathcal{S}\}$ that satisfy the inequality (29) amounts to solving an LP problem. Then the matrix P can be simply chosen as $P = \frac{1}{\epsilon}Q$.

6   Relaxations

The *a priori* stabilization conditions for infinity norm based MPC of constrained PWA systems developed in Section 4 amount to searching for a common Lyapunov function and a common polyhedral positively invariant set for all subsystems of (2). Since in general there is no guarantee that such a function and such a set exist, in the sequel we relax the conditions of Section 4 by employing different terminal weight matrices in cost (5), depending on the state space region where the terminal state resides. Now consider the following problem.

Problem 3. At time $k \ge 0$ let $x_k \in \mathbb{X}$ be given. Minimize the cost function

$$J(x_k, \mathbf{u}_k) \triangleq \|P_j x_{k+N}\|_\infty + \sum_{i=0}^{N-1} \|Qx_{k+i}\|_\infty + \|Ru_{k+i}\|_\infty \text{ when } x_{k+N} \in \Omega_j, j \in \mathcal{S}$$

$$(30)$$

over all input sequences $\mathbf{u}_k \in \mathcal{U}_N(x_k)$.

Let $\mathcal{Q}_{ji} := \{x \in \Omega_j \mid \exists u \in \mathbb{U} : A_j x + B_j u + f_j \in \Omega_i\}$, $(j, i) \in \mathcal{S} \times \mathcal{S}$ and let $\mathcal{X} := \{(j, i) \in \mathcal{S} \times \mathcal{S} \mid \mathcal{Q}_{ji} \ne \emptyset\}$. The set of pairs of indices $\mathcal{X}$ can be determined off-line by performing a one-step rechability analysis for the PWA system (2) (note that the *one-step* rechability analysis does not yield a combinatorial drawback). The set $\mathcal{X}$ contains all discrete mode transitions that can occur in the PWA system (2), i.e. a transition from Ω_j to Ω_i can occur if and only if $(j, i) \in \mathcal{X}$. The infinity norm inequalities (10) and (11) become:

$$\|P_i(A_j + B_j K_j)P_j^{-L}\|_\infty + \|QP_j^{-L}\|_\infty + \|RK_j P_j^{-L}\|_\infty \le 1 - \gamma_{ji}, \quad (j, i) \in \mathcal{X}$$

$$(31)$$

and

$$\|P_i f_j\|_\infty \le \gamma_{ji} \|P_j x\|_\infty, \quad \forall x \in \mathbb{X}_N \cap \Omega_j, \quad (j,i) \in \mathcal{X}, \qquad (32)$$

where γ_{ji} are scaling factors that satisfy $0 \le \gamma_{ji} < 1$, $(j,i) \in \mathcal{X}$. Now Theorem 1 can be extended as follows.

Theorem 2. *Suppose* (31)-(32) *is solvable in* (P_j, K_j, γ_{ji}) *for* P_j *with full-column rank and* $(j,i) \in \mathcal{X}$. *Let* $\mathbb{X}_N \subseteq \mathbb{X}_U$ *be a positively invariant set for the closed-loop system* (2)-(9) *that contains the origin in its interior. Fix* $N \ge 1$ *and calculate the MPC control* (8) *by solving at each sampling instant Problem 3 instead of Problem 1. Then the four statements of Theorem 1 hold for Problem 3.*

The proof is similar to the proof of Theorem 1 and is omitted here for brevity.

Since $\{(P_j, K_j) \mid j \in \mathcal{S}\}$ satisfy (31) and (32) we have that

$$\|P_i(A_j + B_j K_j)x_k + P_i f_j\|_\infty - \|P_j x_k\|_\infty \le -\|Q x_k\|_\infty < 0,$$
$$\forall x_k \in \mathbb{X}_N \setminus \{0\}, \quad (j,i) \in \mathcal{X}. \qquad (33)$$

Then, it can be proven along the lines of the proof of Theorem 1 that the *discontinuous* function $V(x) := \|P_j x\|_\infty$ when $x \in \Omega_j$ is a (piecewise linear) Lyapunov function for the dynamics $x_{k+1} = (A_j + B_j K_j)x_k + f_j$, $j \in \mathcal{S}$. Hence, the origin of the PWA system (2) with feedback (9) is asymptotically stable on some region of attraction, e.g., the *piecewise polyhedral* sublevel set given by the largest $\varphi > 0$ for which $\{x \in \mathbb{X} \mid V(x) \le \varphi\}$ is contained in $\mathbb{X}_U$. The terminal set $\mathbb{X}_N$ can be obtained in this case as

$$\mathbb{X}_N \triangleq \cup_{j \in \mathcal{S}}\{x \in \Omega_j \mid \|P_j x\|_\infty \le \varphi^*\}, \qquad (34)$$

where $\varphi^* = \sup_\varphi \{\{x \in \Omega_j \mid \|P_j x\|_\infty \le \varphi\} \subset \mathbb{X}_U\}$. Since this set is a finite union of polyhedra, Problem 3 still leads to a MILP problem, which is a standard tool in the context of infinity norm based hybrid MPC [4].

Note that the methods of Section 5.2 and Section 5.3 can also be applied to reduce the optimization problem associated with the infinity norm inequality (31) to an LP problem.

Remark 4. The sublevel sets of the Lyapunov function $V(x) = \|P_j x\|_\infty$ when $x \in \Omega_j$ with P_j satisfying (33) are λ-contractive sets [15] and they are finite unions of polyhedra (i.e. they are represented by a polyhedron in each region of the PWA system). Hence, this yields a new method to obtain (in finite time) a *piecewise polyhedral* λ-*contractive set* for the class of PWA systems, which takes into account also the affine terms f_j for $j \in \mathcal{S}_1$. If we set $P_j = P$ for all $j \in \mathcal{S}$ (as done in Section 4), this yields a new way to obtain *polyhedral* λ-*contractive sets* for PWA systems.

7 Conclusions

In this paper we have developed *a priori* stabilization conditions for infinity norm based MPC of constrained PWA systems. Stability has been achieved using infinity norm inequalities. If the considered inequalities are satisfied, then the possibly discontinuous value function of the MPC cost is a Lyapunov function of the controlled PWA system. The terminal weight(s) are obtained by solving off-line an optimization problem. Several possibilities to reduce this problem to an LP problem via a two-step procedure have been indicated. The terminal constraint set is simply obtained by taking one of the sublevel sets of the terminal cost, which is a local piecewise linear Lyapunov function. As a by-product we have also obtained a new approach for the calculation of positively invariant sets for PWA systems.

Acknowledgements. The authors would like to thank the reviewers for their helpful comments. They are also grateful for the financial support received from the Dutch Science Foundation (STW), Grant "Model Predictive Control for Hybrid Systems" (DMR. 5675) and from the Control Training Site program (Contract HPMT-CT-2001-00278).

A   Proof of Lemma 1

We will use induction to prove Lemma 1. For $l = 0$, the inequality (13) holds for any $\alpha_0 \geq 1$. Suppose (13) holds for some $l \geq 0$. Now we will prove that (13) holds for $l + 1$. We have that

$$\|x_{k+l+1}\|_\infty = \|(A_j + B_j K_j)x_{k+l} + f_j\|_\infty \quad \text{when} \quad x_{k+l} \in \mathbb{X}_N \cap \Omega_j.$$

Due to the full-column rank of P, there exist positive numbers μ_P and γ_P such that $\mu_P\|z\|_\infty \leq \|Pz\|_\infty \leq \gamma_P\|z\|_\infty$ for all $z \in \mathbb{R}^n$. Then it follows that

$$\|x_{k+l+1}\|_\infty \leq \|(A_j + B_j K_j)x_{k+l}\|_\infty + \|f_j\|_\infty \leq$$
$$\leq \eta\|x_{k+l}\|_\infty + \mu_P^{-1}\|Pf_j\|_\infty \leq \eta\|x_{k+l}\|_\infty + \mu_P^{-1}\|Px_{k+l}\|_\infty,$$

where $\eta = \max_{j\in\mathcal{S}} \|A_j + B_j K_j\|_\infty$ and in the last inequality we used (11) and $0 \leq \gamma_j < 1$ for all $j \in \mathcal{S}$. The above inequality yields

$$\|x_{k+l+1}\|_\infty \leq (\eta + \mu_P^{-1}\gamma_P)\|x_{k+l}\|_\infty.$$

By the induction hypothesis there exists $\alpha_l > 0$ such that (13) holds for x_{k+l} and by letting $\alpha_{l+1} := (\eta + \mu_P^{-1}\gamma_P)\alpha_l > 0$ it follows that

$$\|x_{k+l+1}\|_\infty \leq \alpha_{l+1}\|x_k\|_\infty.$$

$\square$

References

1. Bemporad, A., Morari, M.: Control of systems integrating logic, dynamics, and constraints. Automatica **35** (1999) 407–427
2. Sontag, E.: Nonlinear regulation: the piecewise linear approach. IEEE Transactions on Automatic Control **26** (1981) 346–357

3. Rantzer, A., Johansson, M.: Piecewise linear quadratic optimal control. IEEE Transactions on Automatic Control **45** (2000) 629–637
4. Borrelli, F.: Constrained optimal control of linear and hybrid systems. Volume 290 of Lecture Notes in Control and Information Sciences. Springer (2003)
5. Bemporad, A., Borrelli, F., Morari, M.: Optimal controllers for hybrid systems: Stability and piecewise linear explicit form. In: 39th IEEE Conference on Decision and Control, Sydney, Australia (2000) 1810–1815
6. Kerrigan, E., Mayne, D.: Optimal control of constrained, piecewise affine systems with bounded disturbances. In: 41st IEEE Conference on Decision and Control, Las Vegas, Nevada (2002) 1552–1557
7. Lazar, M., Heemels, W., Weiland, S., Bemporad, A.: Stabilization conditions for model predictive control of constrained PWA systems. In: 43rd IEEE Conference on Decision and Control, Paradise Island, Bahamas (2004) 4595–4600
8. Heemels, W., De Schutter, B., Bemporad, A.: Equivalence of hybrid dynamical models. Automatica **37** (2001) 1085–1091
9. Mignone, D., Ferrari-Trecate, G., Morari, M.: Stability and stabilization of piecewise affine systems: An LMI approach. Technical Report AUT00-12, Automatic Control Laboratory, ETH Zürich, Switzerland (2000)
10. Mayne, D., Rawlings, J., Rao, C., Scokaert, P.: Constrained model predictive control: Stability and optimality. Automatica **36** (2000) 789–814
11. Baotic, M., Christophersen, F., Morari, M.: A new algorithm for constrained finite time optimal control of hybrid systems with a linear performance index. In: European Control Conference, Cambridge, UK (2003)
12. Christophersen, F., Baotic, M., Morari, M.: Stability analysis of hybrid systems with a linear performance index. In: 43rd IEEE Conference on Decision and Control, Paradise Island, Bahamas (2004) 4589–4594
13. Freeman, H.: Discrete-time systems. John Wiley & Sons, Inc. (1965)
14. Scokaert, P., Rawlings, J., Meadows, E.: Discrete-time Stability with Perturbations: Application to Model Predictive Control. Automatica **33** (1997) 463–470
15. Blanchini, F.: Ultimate boundedness control for uncertain discrete-time systems via set-induced Lyapunov functions. IEEE Transactions on Automatic Control **39** (1994) 428–433
16. Kiendl, H., Adamy, J., Stelzner, P.: Vector norms as Lyapunov functions for linear systems. IEEE Transactions on Automatic Control **37** (1992) 839–842
17. Lazar, M., Heemels, W.P.M.H, Weiland, S., Bemporad, A.: On the Stability of Quadratic Forms based Model Predictive Control of Constrained PWA Systems. In: 24th American Control Conference, Portland, Oregon (2005)
18. Alessio, A., Bemporad, A.: A Recursive Algorithm for DC Programming and Applications in Computational Geometry. Technical report, Dipartimento di Ingegneria dell'Informazione, Universitá di Siena, Via Roma 56, 53100 Siena, Italy (2004)

Air-Traffic Control in Approach Sectors: Simulation Examples and Optimisation

Andrea Lecchini[1], William Glover[1], John Lygeros[2], and Jan Maciejowski[1]

[1] Control Lab, Department of Engineering,
University of Cambridge, CB2 1PZ Cambridge, UK
{al394, wg214, jmm}@eng.cam.ac.uk
http://www-control.eng.cam.ac.uk/
[2] Department of Electrical Engineering, University of Patras, Rio,
26500 Patras, Greece
lygeros@ee.upatras.gr
http://www.sml.ee.upatras.gr/lygeros

Abstract. In this contribution we consider the approach to the runway as a case study of our research on conflict resolution for Air-Traffic Control with stochastic models. We simulate the approach for landing and optimise the maneuver through a simulation based optimisation strategy.

1 Introduction

In the current organisation of Air-Traffic Management the centralised Air-Traffic Control is in complete control of the air-traffic and ultimately responsible for safety. The main objective of Air-Traffic Control is to maintain safe separation between aircraft by issuing proper instructions to the pilots. A *conflict* is defined as the situation of loss of minimum safe separation between two aircraft. If it is possible, Air-Traffic Control tries also to fulfil the (possibly conflicting) requests of aircraft and airlines; for example, desired paths to avoid turbulence or desired time of arrivals to meet schedule. In order to improve performance of Air-Traffic Control, mainly in anticipation of increasing levels of traffic, research effort has been spent in the last decade on creating tools for conflict detection and resolution. A review of research work in this area of Air-Traffic Control is presented in [1].

Uncertainty is introduced in air-traffic by the action of the wind field, incomplete knowledge of the physical coefficients of the aircraft and unavoidable imprecision in the execution of Air-Traffic Control instructions. In conflict detection the objective is to evaluate conflict probability over a certain future horizon starting from the current positions and flight plans of the aircraft. In conflict resolution the objective is to calculate suitable maneuvers to avoid a predicted conflict. A number of conflict resolution algorithms have been proposed for a deterministic setting, for example [2, 3, 4]. In a stochastic setting, research has concentrated mainly on conflict detection [5, 6, 7, 8]. The main reason for this is the complexity of stochastic prediction models which, even if it does not make

M. Morari and L. Thiele (Eds.): HSCC 2005, LNCS 3414, pp. 433–448, 2005.

it impossible to estimate conflict probability through Monte Carlo methods, it makes the quantification of the effects of possible control actions intractable.

Air-traffic conflict resolution involves several hybrid aspects related either to the nature of the system and to the control problem. The system itself contains continuous dynamics, arising from the physical motion of the aircraft, discrete dynamics, arising from the logic embedded in the Flight Management System, and stochastic dynamics, arising from the effect of wind on the aircraft tracks and uncertainty in the physical parameters of the aircraft (for example the mass). Other hybrid aspects, from the point of view of Air-Traffic Control, are the fact that aircraft follow a nominal path that is a sequence of straight lines and that the motion of aircraft can not be freely adjusted. For example descending aircraft follow a prespecified speed profile and therefore "descent" can be seen as a discrete state with only a "1/0" value. Moreover, in conflict resolution, there are two rather separate problems one has to solve: (i) coordination between aircraft (e.g. selecting a landing sequence), which is typically a discrete combinatorial problem, and (ii) selecting the parameters of the resolution maneuver within the constraints imposed by the coordination, which is typically an optimisation problem over a continuous set.

We are currently investigating — see also [9] — on the use a Monte Carlo approach for conflict resolution in order to extend to this task the advantages of the Monte Carlo framework, in terms of flexibility and complexity of the prediction models that can be used. To this end, we adopt a Monte Carlo Markov Chain randomised optimisation method introduced originally in [10, 11].

Here we illustrate our approach in the solution of a typical Air-Traffic Control situation involving aircraft approaching the runway in Approach Sectors. In Section 1 we give a general formulation of the problem. The Monte Carlo Markov Chain optimisation procedure is described in Section 2. In Section 3 and 4 respectively we illustrate Air-Traffic Control in Approach Sectors and the air-traffic simulator. A simulation example with optimisation is presented in Section 5. Section 6 contains conclusion and future objectives.

2   Penalty Formulation of an Expected Value Optimisation Problem with Constraints

In this paper we formulate conflict resolution as a constrained optimisation problem. Given a set of aircraft involved in a conflict, the conflict resolution maneuver is determined by a parameter ω which defines the nominal paths of the aircraft The actual execution of the maneuver is affected by uncertainty. Therefore, the sequence of actual positions of the aircraft during the resolution maneuver (for example: the sequence of positions every 6 seconds which is a typical time interval between two successive radar sweeps) *a-priori* of its execution is a random variable denoted by X. A conflict is defined as the event that the positions of two aircraft during the execution of the maneuver are too close. The objective is to select ω in order to maximise the expected value of some measure of performance associated to the execution of the resolution maneuver while ensuring a small probability of conflict. In this section we introduce the formulation of the problem in a general fashion.

Let X be a random variable whose distribution depends on some parameter ω. The distribution of X is denoted by $p_\omega(x)$ with $x \in \mathbf{X}$. The set of all possible values of ω is denoted by $\boldsymbol{\Omega}$. We assume that a constraint on the random variable X is given in terms of a feasible set $\mathbf{X_f} \subseteq \mathbf{X}$. We say that a realisation x, of random variable X, violates the constraint if $x \notin \mathbf{X_f}$. Moreover, we assume that for a realisation $x \in \mathbf{X_f}$ some definition of performance of x is given. In general performance can depend also on the value of ω, therefore performance is measured by a function $\mathrm{perf}(\omega, x)$, $x \in \mathbf{X_f}$, $\omega \in \boldsymbol{\Omega}$. We assume that $\mathrm{perf}(\omega, x)$ takes values in $(0, 1]$. The probability of satisfying the constraint is denoted by $P(\omega)$

$$P(\omega) = \int_{x \in \mathbf{X_f}} p_\omega(x)dx. \tag{1}$$

The probability of violating the constraint is denoted by $\bar{P}(\omega) = 1 - P(\omega)$. The expected performance for a given $\omega \in \boldsymbol{\Omega}$ is denoted by $\mathrm{PERF}(\omega)$, where

$$\mathrm{PERF}(\omega) = \int_{x \in \mathbf{X_f}} \mathrm{perf}(\omega, x)p_\omega(x)dx. \tag{2}$$

Ideally one would like to maximise the performance over all ω, subject to a bound on the probability of constraint satisfaction. Given a bound $\bar{\mathbf{P}} \in [0, 1]$, this corresponds to solving the constrained optimization problem

$$\mathrm{PERF}_{\max | \bar{\mathbf{P}}} = \sup_{\omega \in \boldsymbol{\Omega}} \mathrm{PERF}(\omega) \tag{3}$$

$$\text{subject to } \bar{P}(\omega) < \bar{\mathbf{P}}. \tag{4}$$

Clearly, a necessary condition for the problem to have a solution is that there exists $\omega \in \boldsymbol{\Omega}$ such that $\bar{P}(\omega) \le \bar{\mathbf{P}}$, or, equivalently,

$$\bar{P}_{\min} = \inf_{\omega \in \boldsymbol{\Omega}} \bar{P}(\omega) < \bar{\mathbf{P}}. \tag{5}$$

This optimization problem is generally difficult to solve, or even to approximate by randomised methods. Here we approximate this problem by an optimisation problem with penalty terms. We show that with a proper choice of the penalty term we can enforce the desired maximum bound on the probability of violating the constraint, provided that such a bound is feasible, at the price of sub-optimality in the resulting expected performance.

Let us introduce the function $u(\omega, x)$ defined as

$$u(\omega, x) = \begin{cases} \mathrm{perf}(\omega, x) + \Lambda & x \in \mathbf{X_f} \\ 1 & x \notin \mathbf{X_f}, \end{cases} \tag{6}$$

where $\Lambda > 1$. The parameter Λ represents a reward for constraint satisfaction. The expected value of $u(\omega, x)$ is given by

$$U(\omega) = \int_{x \in X} u(\omega, x) p_\omega(x) dx \qquad \omega \in \Omega. \tag{7}$$

Instead of the constrained optimization problem (3)–(4) we solve the unconstrained optimization problem:

$$U_{\max} = \sup_{\omega \in \Omega} U(\omega). \tag{8}$$

Assume the supremum is attained and let $\bar{\omega}$ denote the optimum solution, i.e. $U_{\max} = U(\bar{\omega})$. For $\bar{\omega}$ we would like to obtain bounds on the probability of violating the constraints and the level of suboptimality of $\text{PERF}(\bar{\omega})$ over $\text{PERF}_{\max | \bar{\text{P}}}$. A basic bound on the probability of violating the constraint at $\bar{\omega}$ is the following.

Proposition 1. $\bar{\text{P}}(\bar{\omega})$ *satisfies*

$$\bar{\text{P}}(\bar{\omega}) \le \frac{1}{\Lambda} + \frac{\Lambda - 1}{\Lambda} \bar{\text{P}}_{\min}. \tag{9}$$

Proof. The optimisation criterion $U(\omega)$ can be written in the form

$$U(\omega) = \int_{x \in X_f} (\text{perf}(\omega, x) + \Lambda) p_\omega(x) dx + \int_{x \notin X_f} p_\omega(x) dx$$
$$= \text{PERF}(\omega) + \Lambda - (\Lambda - 1)\bar{\text{P}}(\omega).$$

By the definition of $\bar{\omega}$ we have that $U(\bar{\omega}) \ge U(\omega)$ for all $\omega \in \Omega$. We therefore can write

$$\text{PERF}(\bar{\omega}) + \Lambda - (\Lambda - 1)\bar{\text{P}}(\bar{\omega}) \ge \text{PERF}(\omega) + \Lambda - (\Lambda - 1)\bar{\text{P}}(\omega) \qquad \forall \omega$$

which can be rewritten as

$$\bar{\text{P}}(\bar{\omega}) \le \frac{\text{PERF}(\bar{\omega}) - \text{PERF}(\omega)}{\Lambda - 1} + \bar{\text{P}}(\omega) \qquad \forall \omega. \tag{10}$$

Since $0 < \text{perf}(\omega, x) \le 1$, $\text{PERF}(\omega)$ satisfies

$$0 < \text{PERF}(\omega) \le P(\omega). \tag{11}$$

Therefore we can use (11) to obtain an upper bound on the right-hand side of (10) from which we obtain

$$\bar{\text{P}}(\bar{\omega}) \le \frac{1}{\Lambda} + \frac{\Lambda - 1}{\Lambda} \bar{\text{P}}(\omega) \qquad \forall \omega \in \Omega.$$

We eventually obtain (9) by taking a minimum to eliminate the quantifier on the right-hand side of the above inequality.

Proposition 1 suggests a method for choosing Λ to ensure that the solution $\bar{\omega}$ of the optimization problem will satisfy $\bar{P}(\bar{\omega}) \leq \bar{P}$. The following immediate corollaries make this observation more explicit.

Corollary 1. *Any*

$$\Lambda \geq \frac{1 - \bar{P}_{\min}}{\bar{P} - \bar{P}_{\min}} \tag{12}$$

ensures that $\bar{P}(\bar{\omega}) \leq \bar{P}$.

Typically such a bound will not be useful in practice, since the value of $\bar{P}_{\min}$ will be unknown. If we know that there exists a parameter $\omega \in \Omega$ for which the constraints are satisfied almost surely a tighter (and potentially more useful) bound can be obtained.

Corollary 2. *If there exists* $\omega \in \Omega$ *such that* $\bar{P}(\omega) = 0$, *then any*

$$\Lambda \geq \frac{1}{\bar{P}} \tag{13}$$

ensures that $\bar{P}(\bar{\omega}) \leq \bar{P}$.

For cases where the existence of such an ω cannot be guaranteed, it suffices to know $\bar{P}(\omega)$ for some $\omega \in \Omega$ with $\bar{P}(\omega) < \bar{P}$ to obtain a bound.

Corollary 3. *If there exists* $\omega \in \Omega$ *for which* $\hat{P} = \bar{P}(\omega)$ *is known, then any*

$$\Lambda \geq \frac{1 - \hat{P}}{\bar{P} - \hat{P}} \tag{14}$$

ensures that $\bar{P}(\bar{\omega}) \leq \bar{P}$.

The last bound will of course be more conservative than those of the previous two corollaries. In addition to bounds on the probability that $\bar{\omega}$ satisfies the constraints, we would also like to obtain a bound on how far the performance $\mathrm{PERF}(\bar{\omega})$ is from the ideal performance $\mathrm{PERF}_{\max \,|\bar{P}}$. The following proposition provides a basic bound in this direction.

Proposition 2. *The performance of the maximiser,* $\bar{\omega}$, *of* $U(\omega)$ *satisfies*

$$\mathrm{PERF}(\bar{\omega}) \geq \mathrm{PERF}_{\max \,|\bar{P}} - (\Lambda - 1)(\bar{P} - \bar{P}_{\min}). \tag{15}$$

Proof. By definition of $\bar{\omega}$ we have that $U(\bar{\omega}) \geq U(\omega)$ for all $\omega \in \Omega$. In particular, we know that

$$\mathrm{PERF}(\bar{\omega}) \geq \mathrm{PERF}(\omega) - (\Lambda - 1)\left[\bar{P}(\omega) - \bar{P}(\bar{\omega})\right] \qquad \forall \omega : \bar{P}(\omega) \leq \bar{P}.$$

Taking a lower bound of the right-hand side, we obtain

$$\mathrm{PERF}(\bar{\omega}) \geq \mathrm{PERF}(\omega) - (\Lambda - 1)\left[\bar{P} - \bar{P}_{\min}\right] \qquad \forall \omega : \bar{P}(\omega) \leq \bar{P}.$$

Taking the maximum and eliminating the quantifier on the right-hand side we obtain the desired inequality.

Clearly to minimise the gap between the optimal performance and the performance of $\bar{\omega}$ we need to select Λ as small as possible.

3   Simulation-Based Optimisation

In this section we recall a simulation-based procedure, to find approximate optimisers of $U(\omega)$. The only requirement for applicability of the procedure is to be able to obtain realisations of the random variable X with distribution $p_\omega(x)$ and to evaluate $u(\omega, x)$ pointwise. This optimisation procedure is in fact a general procedure for the optimisation of expected value criteria. It has been originally proposed in the Bayesian statistics literature [10].

The optimisation strategy relies on extractions of a random variable Ω whose distribution has modes which coincide with the optimal points of $U(\omega)$. These extractions are obtained through Monte Carlo Markov Chain (MCMC) simulation [12]. The problem of optimising the expected criterion is then reformulated as the problem of estimating the optimal points from extractions concentrated around them. In the optimisation procedure, there exists a tunable trade-off between estimation accuracy of the optimiser and computational effort. In particular, the distribution of Ω is proportional to $U(\omega)^J$ where J is a positive integer which allows the user to increase the "peakedness" of the distribution and concentrate the extractions around the modes at the price of an increased computational load. If the tunable parameter J is increased during the optimisation procedure, this approach can be seen as the counterpart of Simulated Annealing for a stochastic setting. Simulated Annealing is a randomised optimisation strategy developed to find tractable approximate solutions to complex deterministic combinatorial optimisation problems [13]. A formal parallel between these two strategies has been derived in [11].

The MCMC optimisation procedure can be described as follows. Consider a stochastic model formed by a random variable Ω, whose distribution has not been defined yet, and J conditionally independent replicas of random variable X with distribution $p_\Omega(x)$. Let us denote $h(\omega, x_1, x_2, \ldots, x_J)$ the joint distribution of $(\Omega, X_1, X_2, X_3, \ldots, X_J)$. It is straightforward to see that if

$$h(\omega, x_1, x_2, \ldots, x_J) \propto \prod_j u(\omega, x_j) p_\omega(x_j) \qquad (16)$$

then the marginal distribution of Ω, say $h(\omega)$, satisfies

$$h(\omega) \propto \left[\int u(\omega, x) p_\omega(x) dx \right]^J = U(\omega)^J. \qquad (17)$$

This means that if we can extract realisations of $(\Omega, X_1, X_2, X_3, \ldots, X_J)$ then the extracted Ω's will be concentrated around the optimal points of $U(\Omega)$ for a sufficiently high J. These extractions can be used to find an approximate solution to the optimisation of $U(\omega)$.

Realisations of the random variables $(\Omega, X_1, X_2, X_3, \ldots, X_J)$, with the desired joint probability density given by (16), can be obtained through Monte Carlo Markov Chain simulation. The algorithm is presented below. In the algorithm, $g(\omega)$ is known as the instrumental (or *proposal*) distribution and is freely chosen by the user; the only requirement is that $g(\omega)$ covers the support of $h(\omega)$.

MCMC Algorithm

Given $\omega(k)$, $x_j(k)$, $j = 1, \ldots, J$ realisations of random variable $X(k)$ with distribution $p_{\omega(k)}(x)$, and $u_J(k) = \prod_{j=1}^{J} u(\omega(k), x_j(k))$:

1 Extract

$$\tilde{\Omega} \sim g(\omega)$$

2 Extract

$$\tilde{X}_j \sim p_{\tilde{\Omega}}(x) \quad j = 1, \ldots, J$$

and calculate

$$\tilde{U}_J = \prod_j u(\tilde{\Omega}, \tilde{X}_j)$$

3 Extract the new state of the chain as

$$[\omega(k+1), \, u_J(k+1)] = \begin{cases} [\tilde{\Omega}, \tilde{U}_J] & \text{with probability } \rho(\omega(k), u_J(k), \tilde{\Omega}, \tilde{U}_J) \\ [\omega(k), \, u_J(k)] & \text{with probability } 1 - \rho(\omega(k), u_J(k), \tilde{\Omega}, \tilde{U}_J) \end{cases}$$

where

$$\rho(\omega, u_J, \tilde{\omega}, \tilde{u}_J) = \min\left\{1, \frac{\tilde{u}_J}{u_J} \frac{g(\omega)}{g(\tilde{\omega})}\right\}$$

This algorithm is a formulation of the Metropolis-Hasting algorithm for a desired distribution given by $h(\omega, x_1, x_2, \ldots, x_J)$ and proposal distribution given by

$$g(\omega) \prod_j p_\omega(x_j).$$

In this case, the acceptance probability for the standard Metropolis-Hastings algorithm is

$$\frac{h(\tilde{\omega}, \tilde{x}_1, \tilde{x}_2, \ldots, \tilde{x}_J)}{h(\omega, x_1, x_2, \ldots, x_J)} \frac{g(\omega) \prod_j p_\omega(x_j)}{g(\tilde{\omega}) \prod_j p_\omega(\tilde{x}_j)}.$$

By inserting (16) in the above expression one obtains the probability $\rho(\omega, u_J, \tilde{\omega}, \tilde{u}_J)$. Under minimal assumptions, the Markov Chain $\Omega(k)$ is uniformly ergodic with stationary distribution $h(\omega)$ given by (17). Results that characterise the convergence rate to the stationary distribution can be found for example in [12].

A general guideline to obtain faster convergence is to concentrate the search distribution $g(\omega)$ where $U(\omega)$ assumes nearly optimal values. The algorithm represents a trade-off between computational effort and the "peakedness" of the target distribution. This trade-off is tuned by the parameter J which is the power of the target distribution and also the number of extractions of X at each step of the chain. Increasing J concentrates the distribution more around the optimisers of $U(\omega)$, but also increases the number of simulations one needs to perform at each step. Obviously if the peaks of $U(\omega)$ are already quite sharp, this implies some advantages in terms of computation, since there is no need to increase further the peakedness of the criterion by running more simulations. For the specific $U(\omega)$ proposed in the previous section, a trade-off exists between its peakedness and the parameter Λ, which is related to probability of constraint violation. In particular, the greater Λ is the less peaked the criterion $U(\omega)$ becomes, because the relative variation of $u(\omega, x)$ is reduced, and therefore more computational effort is required for the optimisation of $U(\omega)$.

4   Air-Traffic Control in Terminal Airspace and Approach Sectors

Terminal Airspace and Approach Sectors are perhaps the most difficult scenarios in Air-Traffic Control. The management of traffic, in this case, includes tasks such as determining landing sequences and issuing of "vector" maneuvers to avoid collisions, holding the aircraft in "stacks" in case of congested traffic, etc. Here, we give a schematic representation of the problem as described in [14].

During most of the flight, aircraft stay at cruising altitudes, above 30000 ft. In the current organisation, the traffic at these altitudes has an *en-route* structure, which facilitates the action of Air-Traffic Control. Aircraft follow prespecified corridors at different *flight levels*. Two adjacent flight levels are separated by 100 ft; for example, the altitude of 30000 ft is denoted by FL300.

Towards the end of the flight, aircraft enter the Terminal Airspace where air-traffic controllers guide them from cruising altitudes to the entry points of the Approach Sector, between FL50 and FL150. Ideally, aircraft should enter the Approach Sector in a sequence properly spaced in time. Air-traffic controllers of the Approach Sector are then responsible for guiding the aircraft towards the proper runway. The tasks of Air-Traffic Control in the Approach Sectors include:

1) Maintain safe separation between aircraft. This is the most important requirement for safety, in any sector, during all parts of the flight. Aircraft must always maintain a minimum level of separation. A *conflict* between two aircraft is defined as the situation of loss of minimum safe separation between them. Safe separation is defined by a protected zone centred around each aircraft. The

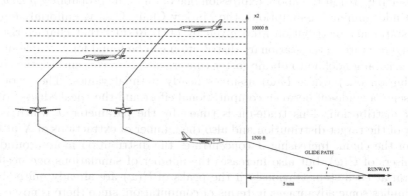

Fig. 1. Schematic representation of approach maneuver: elevation view

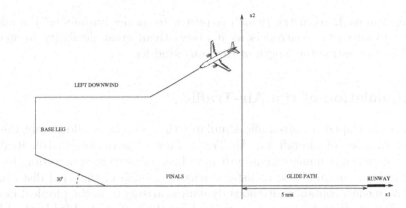

Fig. 2. Schematic representation of approach maneuver: plan view

level of accepted minimum separation can vary with the density of the traffic and the region of the airspace. A largely accepted shape of the protected zone is defined by a vertical cylinder, centred on the aircraft with having radius 5 nmi and height 2000 ft, so that aircraft which do not have 5 nmi of horizontal separation must have 1000 ft of vertical separation.

2) Descend aircraft from entry altitude to intercept localiser. Once aircraft have entered the Approach Sector, Air-Traffic Control must guide them from the entry altitude (FL50 to FL150) to FL15. This is the altitude at which they can intercept the *localiser*, i.e. the radio beacons which will guide them onto the runway. The point at which the aircraft will actually start the descent towards the runway is an important variable which has to be carefully chosen since it can affect the rest of the manouver and the coordination with other aircraft. The reason is that aircraft fly following prespecified speed profiles which depend on the altitude; they fly faster at high altitudes and slower at low altitudes. This implies that aircraft, flying at lower altitudes, are slower in joining the landing queue.

3) Sequence aircraft towards the runway. The air-traffic controllers must direct the aircraft towards the runway in a properly spaced queue. This is done by adjusting the waypoints (corners) of a standard approach route (STAR) — see Figures 1 and 2. Typically the route is composed of four legs. During their descent, aircraft are first aligned, on one of the two sides of the runway, in the direction of the runway but with opposite heading. This leg is called the *left/right downwind leg*, since aircraft are expected to land against the wind. Aircraft then they perform a turn of approximately 90°, to approach the localiser. This second segment is called the *base leg*. Aircraft perform an additional turn in order to intercept the plane of the localiser with an angle of incidence of approximately 30°. The reason is that 30° is a suitable angle for pilots to perform the final turn in the direction of the runway as soon as possible when the localiser has been intercepted. It is required that aircraft intercept the localiser plane at least 5 nmi from the beginning of the runway and at an altitude of $1000 - -1500$ ft, so that they can follow a $3° - -5°$ glide path to the runway.

This approach geometry (which is referee to as the "trombone") is advantageous to air-traffic controllers as it allows them great flexibility in spacing aircraft by adjusting the length of the downwind leg.

5   Simulation of the Air-Traffic

We have developed an air-traffic simulator that simulates adequately the behaviour of a set of aircraft for Air-Traffic Control purposes [15, 16]. Realistic models of current commercial aircraft have been implemented according to [17]. The simulator contains also realistic stochastic models of the wind disturbance [18]. The models contain continuous dynamics, arising from the physical motion of the aircraft, discrete dynamics, arising from the logic embedded in the Flight Management System, and stochastic dynamics, arising from the effect of the wind and incomplete knowledge of physical parameters (for example the aircraft mass, which depends on fuel, cargo and number of passengers). The simulator has been coded in Java and can be used in different operation modes either to generate accurate data, for validation of the performance of conflict detection and resolution algorithm, or to run faster simulations of simplified models.

The nominal path for each aircraft is entered in the simulator as a sequence of waypoints. The actual trajectories of the aircraft are then a perturbed version of the nominal path, depending on the particular realisations of wind disturbances and uncertain parameters. In Figures 3 and 4 several trajectory realisations corresponding to the same nominal path are displayed. In this example, the aircraft, initially at 15000 ft, performs the approach maneuver described in the previous section. In addition to stochastic wind terms, uncertainty about the mass of the aircraft is introduced as an uniform distribution between two extreme values. The figures suggest that the resulting uncertainty in the position of aircraft is of the order of magnitude of a few kilometres.

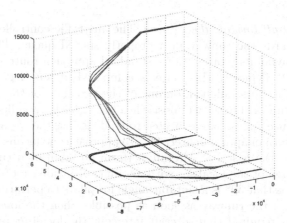

Fig. 3. Several trajectory realisations of an approach maneuver (altitude is expressed in feet and plan coordinates are expressed in meters)

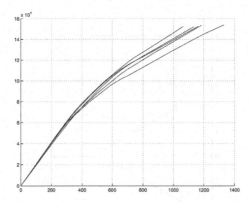

Fig. 4. Travelled distance (meters) versus time (seconds) for several trajectory realisations of an approach maneuver

6   Simulation of Arrivals and Optimisation

In this section, we optimise an approach maneuver with coordination between two aircraft. We consider Aircraft One (A1) and Aircraft Two (A2) approaching the runway as illustrated in Figure 5. In the figure, the glide path towards the runway starts at the origin of the reference frame and coordinates are expressed in meters. The aircraft are initially in level flight. The parameters of the approach maneuver are the distance, from initial position, of the start of the final descent (ω_1) and the length of the downwind leg (ω_2).

The initial position of A1 is [0 50000] and altitude 10000 *ft*. The approach maneuver of this aircraft is fixed to $\bar{\omega}_1 = 30000$ and $\bar{\omega}_2 = 50000$. The initial position of A2 is [0 50000] and altitude 10000 *ft*. The parameters of its approach maneuver will be selected using the optimization algorithm. The range of the optimisation parameters is $\omega_2 \in [35000, 60000]$ and $\omega_1 \in [0, \omega_2]$. The motion of the two aircraft is affected by the same uncertainty as in the simulation example of Section 5.

We assume that the performance of the approach maneuver is measured by the arrival time of A2 at the start of the glide path (T_2). The measure of performance is given by perf $= e^{-a \cdot T_2}$ with $a = 5 \cdot 10^{-4}$. The constraint is that the trajectory of A2 is not in conflict with the trajectory of A1. Aircraft 2 must also reach the altitude of 1500 *ft* before the start of the glide path. We optimise initially with an upper bound on probability of constraint violation given by $\bar{P} = 0.3$. It is easy to see that there exists a maneuver in the set of optimisation parameters that gives negligible conflict probability. Therefore, based on inequality (13), we select $\Lambda = 3.5$ in the optimisation criterion.

The results of the optimisation procedure are illustrated in Figures 6-9 for different values of J and proposal distribution g. Each figure shows the scatter plot of the accepted parameters during MCMC simulation. In all cases the first 10% of accepted parameters was discarded as a *burn in* period to allow convergence of the chain to its stationary distribution. Figure 6 illustrates the case

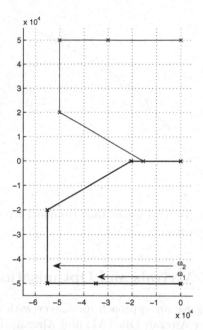

Fig. 5. Approach maneuvers for A1 (thin) and A2 (bold)

$J = 5$ and proposal distribution g uniform over the parameter space. In this case, the ratio between accepted and proposed parameters during MCMC simulation was 0.36. A region characterised by a low density of accepted parameters can be clearly seen in the figure. These are parameters which correspond to a conflicting maneuver where the aircraft are performing an almost symmetrical approach. The figure also shows two distinct "clouds" of accepted maneuvers. They correspond to a discrete choice that the air traffic controller has to make: either land A2 before A1 (bottom right cloud) or land A1 before A2 (top left cloud).

Figure 7 illustrates the case $J = 50$ and g uniform. In this case the ratio between accepted and proposed states was 0.08. The case $J = 50$ is illustrated also in Figure 8. In this case, however, the proposal distribution g was a sum of 100 Gaussian distributions $N(\mu, \sigma^2 I)$ with variance $\sigma^2 = 10^5 \, m^2$. The means of Gaussian distributions were 100 parameters chosen from those accepted in the MCMC simulation for $J = 5$ and belonging to the cloud corresponding to "A2 arrives before A1". This appears to be the more promising cloud because of the higher density of points; recall that the distribution of accepted points is concentrated around the maximisers of $U(\omega)$. The choice of this proposal distribution gives clear computational advantages since less computational time is spent searching over regions of non optimal parameters. For this choice of g the ratio between accepted and proposed parameters increased to 0.2. Figure 9 illustrates the case $J = 100$ and proposal distribution constructed as before from states accepted for $J = 50$. In this case the ratio between accepted and

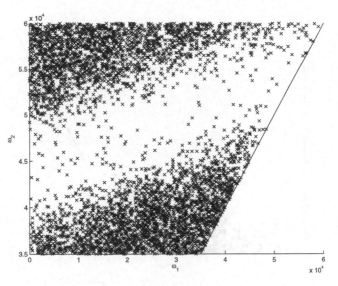

Fig. 6. Accepted states (50000) during MCMC simulation ($J = 5$, g uniform)

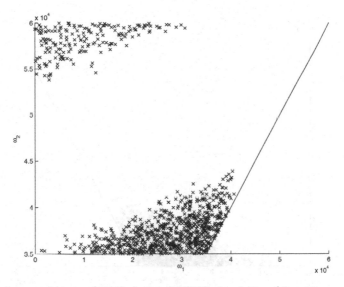

Fig. 7. Accepted states (1000) during MCMC simulation ($J = 50$, g uniform)

proposed parameters was 0.5. Figure 9 indicates that a nearly optimal maneuver is $\omega_1 = 35000$ and $\omega_2 = 35000$. The probability of conflict for this maneuver, estimated by 1000 Monte-Carlo runs, was zero.

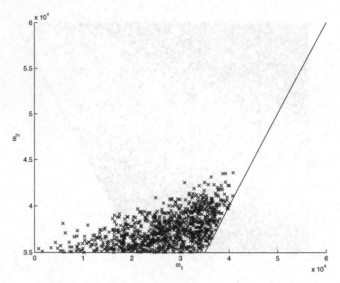

Fig. 8. Accepted states (1000) during MCMC simulation ($J = 50$, g sum of Gaussian distributions)

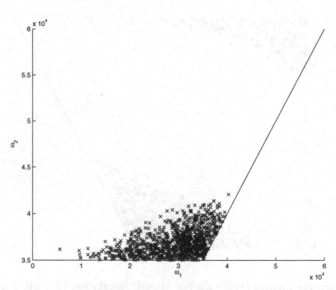

Fig. 9. Accepted states (1000) during MCMC simulation ($J = 100$, g = sum of Gaussian distributions)

7   Conclusions

In this paper we illustrated a Monte Carlo approach to air traffic conflict resolution in a stochastic setting. The main motivation for our approach is to enable the use of realistic stochastic hybrid models of aircraft flight; Monte Carlo methods appear to be the only ones that allow such models. We have formulated conflict resolution as the optimisation of an expected value criterion with probabilistic constraints. Here, a penalty formulation of the problem has been considered which guarantees constraint satisfaction but delivers a suboptimal solution. A side effect of the optimization procedure is that structural differences between maneuvers (e.g. the sequencing choices in the landing example considered here) are highlighted as "clouds" of maneuvers accepted by the algorithm.

Our current research is concerned with overcoming the suboptimality imposed by the need to provide constraint satisfaction guarantees. A possible way is to use the Monte Carlo Markov Chain procedure presented in Section 3 to obtain optimisation parameters that satisfy the constraint and then to optimise over this set in a successive step.

Acknowledgement: This work was supported by the European Commission under project HYBRIDGE IST-2001-32460 and EUROCONTROL under contract C20051E/BM/03. The authors would like to thank EUROCONTROL Experimental Centre for having provided places to 'Air-Traffic Control Familiarisation Course' from which the case study considered in this paper has been inspired.

References

1. Kuchar, J., Yang, L.: A review of conflict detection and resolution methods. IEEE Transactions on Intelligent Transportation Systems **1** (2000) 179–189
2. Frazzoli, E., Mao, Z., Oh, J., Feron, E.: Aircraft conflict resolution via semi-definite programming. AIAA Journal of Guidance, Control, and Dynamics **24** (2001) 79–86
3. Hu, J., Prandini, M., Sastry, S.: Optimal Coordinated Maneuvers for Three-Dimensional Aircraft Conflict Resolution. AIAA Journal of Guidance, Control and Dynamics **25** (2002)
4. Tomlin, C., Pappas, G., Sastry, S.: Conflict resolution for Air Traffic Management: a case study in multi-agent hybrid systems. IEEE Transactions on Automatic Control **43** (1998) 509–521
5. Paielli, R., Erzberger, H.: Conflict probability estimation for free flight. Journal of Guidance, Control and Dynamics **20** (1997) 588–596 Available from World wide Web: http://www.ctas.arc.nasa.gov/publications/papers/.
6. Irvine, R.: A geometrical approach to conflict probability estimation. In: 4th USA/Europe Air Traffic Management R&D seminar, Santa Fe (2001) Available from World Wide Web: http://atm2001.eurocontrol.fr/finalpapers/pap137.pdf.
7. Krystul, J., Bagchi, A., Blom, H.: Risk decomposition and assessment methods. Technical Report WP8, Deliverable D8.1, HYBRIDGE (2003) Available from World Wide Web: http://www.nlr.nl/public/hosted-sites/hybridge/.
8. Hu, J., Prandini, M., Sastry, S.: Aircraft conflict detection in presence of spatially correlated wind perturbations. In: AIAA Guidance, Navigation and Control Conf., Austin, Texas, USA (2003)

9. Lecchini, A., Glover, W., Lygeros, J., Maciejowski, J.: Air Traffic Control with an expected value criterion. Technical Report WP5, Deliverable D5.2, HYBRIDGE (2004) Accepted for presentation at IFAC World Congress 2005. Available from World Wide Web: http://www.nlr.nl/public/hosted-sites/hybridge.
10. Mueller, P.: Simulation based optimal design. In: Bayesian Statistics 6, J.O. Berger, J.M. Bernardo, A.P. Dawid and A.F.M. Smith (eds.), Oxford University Press (1999) 459–474
11. Mueller, P., Sanso, B., De Iorio, M.: Optimal Bayesian design by inhomogeneous Markov chain simulation. Technical report (2003) Available from World Wide Web: http://www.ams.ucsc.edu.
12. Robert, C., Casella, G.: Monte Carlo Statistical Methods. Springer-Verlag (1999)
13. van Laarhoven, P., Aarts, E.: Simulated Annealing: Theory and Applications. D.Reidel Publishing Company (1987)
14. EUROCONTROL Experimental Centre: Air-Traffic Control Familiarisation Course. (2004)
15. Glover, W., Lygeros, J.: A multi-aircraft model for conflict detection and resolution algorithm validation. Technical Report WP1, Deliverable D1.3, HYBRIDGE (2003) Available from World Wide Web: http://www.nlr.nl/public/hosted-sites/hybridge/.
16. Glover, W., Lygeros, J.: A stochastic hybrid model for air traffic control simulation. In: Hybrid Systems: Computation and Control, 7th International Workshop. Volume 2993 of Lecture Notes in Computer Science., Philadelphia, PA, USA, Springer (2004) 372–386
17. EUROCONTROL Experimental Centre: User Manual for the Base of Aircraft Data (BADA) — Revision 3.3. (2002) Available from World Wide Web: http://www.eurocontrol.fr/projects/bada/.
18. Cole, R., Richard, C., Kim, S., Bailey, D.: An assessment of the 60 km rapid update cycle (ruc) with near real-time aircraft reports. Technical Report NASA/A-1, MIT Lincoln Laboratory (July 15, 1998)

Identification of Deterministic Switched ARX Systems via Identification of Algebraic Varieties[*]

Yi Ma[1] and René Vidal[2]

[1] Dept. of Elect. & Comp. Eng., UIUC, Urbana, IL 61801, USA
yima@uiuc.edu
[2] Dept. of BME, J. Hopkins U., Baltimore MD 21218, USA
rvidal@cis.jhu.edu

Abstract. We present a closed-form (linear-algebraic) solution to the identification of deterministic switched ARX systems and characterize conditions that guarantee the uniqueness of the solution. We show that the simultaneous identification of the number of ARX systems, the (possibly different) model orders, the ARX model parameters, and the switching sequence is equivalent to the identification and decomposition of a projective algebraic variety whose degree and dimension depend on the number of ARX systems and the model orders, respectively. Given an upper bound for the number of systems, our algorithm identifies the variety and the maximum orders by fitting a polynomial to the data, and the number of systems, the model parameters, and the switching sequence by differentiating this polynomial. Our method is provably correct in the deterministic case, provides a good sub-optimal solution in the stochastic case, and can handle large low-dimensional data sets (up to tens of thousands points) in a batch fashion.

1 Introduction

Hybrid systems are mathematical models that are used to describe continuous processes that occasionally exhibit discontinuous behaviors due to sudden changes of dynamics. In recent years, there has been significant interest and progress in the study of the analysis, stability, and control of hybrid systems. Knowing the system parameters, many successful theories have been developed to characterize the behaviors of hybrid systems under different switching mechanisms. However, in practice, the parameters and the switching mechanism of a hybrid system are often not known and we are faced with the task of identifying the system from its input and output measurements.

In this paper, we propose an algebraic approach to the identification of a class of discrete-time hybrid systems known as Switched Auto Regressive eXogenous (HARX) systems, i.e., systems whose evolution is described as

---

[*] This work is supported by the NSF grant IIS-0347456 and the research startup funds from UIUC ECE Dept. and Hopkins WSE. The authors thank Prof. R. Fossum for valuable comments and Prof. A. Juloski for providing datasets for the experiments.

M. Morari and L. Thiele (Eds.): HSCC 2005, LNCS 3414, pp. 449–465, 2005.
© Springer-Verlag Berlin Heidelberg 2005

$$y_t = \sum_{j=1}^{n_a(\lambda_t)} a_j(\lambda_t) y_{t-j} + \sum_{j=1}^{n_c(\lambda_t)} c_j(\lambda_t) u_{t-j} \quad (+ w_t), \tag{1}$$

where $u_t \in \mathbb{R}$ is the *input* and $y_t \in \mathbb{R}$ is the *output* of the system. The *discrete state* λ_t, also called the *mode* of the system, can evolve due to a variety of switching mechanisms. In this paper, we consider the least restrictive case:[1] $\{\lambda_t\}$ is a deterministic but unknown sequence that can take a finite number of possible values: $\lambda : \mathbb{Z} \to \{1, 2, \ldots, n\}$. The last term w_t is zero for a deterministic switched ARX system and is a white-noise random process for a stochastic system. The purpose of this paper is to characterize sufficient conditions and develop efficient algorithms for solving the following problem:

Problem 1 (*Identification of Switched Auto Regressive eXogenous Systems*).
Given input/output data $\{u_t, y_t\}_{t=0}^T$ generated by an HARX system (1), identify the number of ARX models n, the orders of each ARX system $\{n_a(i), n_c(i)\}_{i=1}^n$, the system parameters $\{a_j(i)\}_{j=1}^{n_a(i)}$ and $\{c_j(i)\}_{j=1}^{n_c(i)}$, and the discrete states $\{\lambda_t\}$.

We know from classic identification theory of linear systems that the configuration space of the input/output data generated by a linear system is a subspace whose dimension equals the order of the system. The problem of identifying the system is equivalent to identifying this subspace from a finite number of samples on the subspace. As we will show in this paper, for multiple linear systems the configuration space is a union of subspaces (possibly of different dimensions), which can be naturally described as a (projective) algebraic variety Z in an ambient space $\mathbb{P}^K$. To some extent, there is a one-to-one correspondence between a hybrid linear system and the variety of its configuration space. Hence the system identification problem can be cast as a special case of the problem of identifying a low-degree (projective) algebraic variety from a finite number of samples. Once the variety Z is known or retrieved from the input/output data, the constituent systems correspond to the *irreducible sub-varieties* Z_i of the variety $Z = Z_1 \cup Z_2 \cup \cdots \cup Z_n \subseteq \mathbb{P}^K$, and can be obtained from the *decomposition* of the ideal $\mathfrak{a}(Z)$ of (homogeneous) polynomials associated with the variety Z into prime ideals: $\mathfrak{a} = \mathfrak{p}_1 \cap \mathfrak{p}_2 \cap \cdots \cap \mathfrak{p}_n \subseteq \mathbb{C}[z_1, z_2, \ldots, z_K]$.

When the orders of the constituents ARX systems are equal and known, our previous work [23] has shown that $\mathfrak{a}$ is a principal ideal whose decomposition is equivalent to the factorization of its generator. However, when the orders of the constituent ARX systems are *different*, depending on the switching sequence, the configuration space of the HARX system may not simply be a union of the configuration spaces of the constituent ARX systems, and the ideal $\mathfrak{a}$ is in general *not* a principal ideal, as demonstrated in [19] under the additional assumption that the number of systems is known.

---

[1] Least restrictive in the sense that there is no constraint on the temporal evolution of the discrete state, hence our results also apply to other switching mechanisms, such as Jump-Markov Linear Systems (JMLS) and PieceWise ARX (PWARX) systems.

Paper Contributions. In this paper, we consider the most general case of HARX systems with unknown number of models and unknown and possibly different orders. We show that if the input/output data are sufficiently exciting, the HARX system can be identified from a special polynomial p whose last nonzero term has the lowest degree-lexicographic order in the ideal $\mathfrak{a}$. This polynomial is unique, factorable, and independent of the switching sequence. Furthermore, the non-repeated factors of this polynomial correspond to the constituent ARX systems. Therefore, given an upper bound for the number of systems and the system orders, our algorithm automatically identifies the number of systems and the ARX model parameters using linear-algebraic techniques, and subsequently the system orders and the switching sequence. Although the algorithm is developed primarily for the noise-free deterministic case, the algorithm is numerically stable and provides a good sub-optimal solution for the stochastic case with moderate noises (see Remarks 1 and 4 in the sequel). We deal with larger noises by iteratively refining the algebraic solution using Expectation Maximization (EM).

Relations to Previous Work. Work on identification (and filtering) of hybrid systems first appeared in the seventies; a review of the state of the art as of 1982 can be found in [16]. After a decade-long hiatus, the problem has recently been enjoying considerable interest in the hybrid systems community (see e.g., [4, 21, 22]) and also in the machine learning community (see e.g., [7, 15]). When the model parameters and the switching mechanism (not the discrete states) are *known*, the identification problem reduces to the design of observers for the hybrid state [1, 3, 8, 17], together with the study of observability conditions under which hybrid observers operate correctly (see [21, 22] and references therein). When the model parameters and the discrete states are both *unknown*, the identification problem becomes much more challenging. Existing batch methods concentrate on the class of piecewise affine and piecewise ARX systems, i.e., models in which the regressor space is partitioned into polyhedra with affine or ARX submodels for each polyhedron. For instance, [9] assumes that the number of systems is known, and proposes an identification algorithm that combines clustering, regression and classification techniques; [6] solves for the model parameters and the partition of the state space using mixed-integer linear and quadratic programming; [5] uses a greedy approach for partitioning a set of infeasible inequalities into a minimum number of feasible subsystems; [12] iterates between assigning data points to models and computing the model parameters using a Bayesian approach. The only existing recursive method is for the class of switched ARX models [20].

2   Identification of a Single ARX System

For the sake of completeness and comparison, let us first review some classic results for the identification of a single discrete-time ARX system

$$y_t = a_1 y_{t-1} + \cdots + a_{n_a} y_{t-n_a} + c_1 u_{t-1} + \cdots + c_{n_c} u_{t-n_c}. \qquad (2)$$

The transfer function $\hat{H}(z) \doteq \hat{y}(z)/\hat{u}(z)$ of the system (2) is given by:

$$\hat{H}(z) = z^{\max(n_a-n_c,0)}\tilde{H}(z) = \frac{z^{\max(n_a-n_c,0)}(z^{n_c-1}c_1 + z^{n_c-2}c_2 + \cdots + c_{n_c})}{z^{\max(n_c-n_a,0)}(z^{n_a} - z^{n_a-1}a_1 - z^{n_a-2}a_2 - \cdots - a_{n_a})}. \quad (3)$$

In principle, given an infinite input/output sequence, we can identify the parameters of the ARX model by directly computing $\hat{H}(z)$ as $\hat{y}(z)/\hat{u}(z)$.[2] This requires the ARX model to be *identifiable*, i.e., $\tilde{H}(z)$ must have no pole-zero cancellation, and $\hat{u}(z)$ to have no zero in common with a pole of $\hat{H}(z)$ and vice versa.

Alternatively, we may identify the system by identifying a *subspace* associated with the input/output data. Let us define the vector of *regressors* as:

$$x_t \doteq [y_t, y_{t-1}, \ldots, y_{t-n_a}, u_{t-1}, u_{t-2}, \ldots, u_{t-n_c}]^T \in \mathbb{R}^K. \quad (4)$$

where $K \doteq n_a + n_c + 1$. Thus, for all time t, the so-defined x_t is orthogonal to the vector that consists of the parameters of the ARX system:

$$b \doteq [1, -a_1, -a_2, \ldots, -a_{n_a}, -c_1, -c_2, \ldots, -c_{n_c}]^T \in \mathbb{R}^K. \quad (5)$$

i.e. $\forall t$ x_t and b satisfy the equation $b^T x_t = 0$. In other words, b is the normal vector to the hyperplane spanned by (the rows of) the following *data matrix*:

$$L(n_a, n_c) \doteq [x_{\max(n_a,n_c)}, \ldots, x_{t-1}, x_t, x_{t+1}, \ldots]^T \in \mathbb{R}^{\infty \times K}. \quad (6)$$

When the model orders n_a, n_c are known, we can readily solve for b from the null space of $L(n_a, n_c)$. In practice, the model orders may be unknown, and only upper bounds $\bar{n}_a$ and $\bar{n}_c$ may be available, hence the vector of regressors x_t is

$$x_t \doteq [y_t, y_{t-1}, y_{t-2}, \ldots, y_{t-\bar{n}_a}, u_{t-1}, u_{t-2}, \ldots, u_{t-\bar{n}_c}]^T \in \mathbb{R}^K, \quad (7)$$

where $K = \bar{n}_a + \bar{n}_c + 1$. Obviously, for all t the following vector

$$b \doteq [1, -a_1, -a_2, \ldots, -a_{n_a}, 0_{1\times(\bar{n}_a-n_a)}, -c_1, -c_2, \ldots, -c_{n_c}, 0_{1\times(\bar{n}_c-n_c)}]^T \quad (8)$$

satisfies $x_t^T b = 0$. Notice that here the vector b is the one in (5) with additional $\bar{n}_a - n_a$ and $\bar{n}_c - n_c$ zeros filled in after the terms $-a_{n_a}$ and $-c_{n_c}$, respectively.

Let us define the data matrix $L(\bar{n}_a.\bar{n}_c)$ in the same way as in equation (6). Because of the redundant embedding (7), the vector b is no longer the only one in null(L). It is easy to verify that all the following vectors are also in null(L):

$$b^1 = [0_{1\times1}, 1, -a_1, \ldots, -a_{n_a}, 0_{1\times(\bar{n}_a-n_a-1)}, 0_{1\times1}, -c_1, \ldots, -c_{n_c}, 0_{1\times(\bar{n}_c-n_c-1)}]^T,$$

$$b^2 = [0_{1\times2}, 1, -a_1, \ldots, -a_{n_a}, 0_{1\times(\bar{n}_a-n_a-2)}, 0_{1\times2}, -c_1, \ldots, -c_{n_c}, 0_{1\times(\bar{n}_c-n_c-2)}]^T,$$

$$\vdots \qquad\qquad\qquad \vdots \qquad\qquad\qquad (9)$$

Therefore, the data $\{x_t\}$ span a low-dimensional linear subspace S of $\mathbb{R}^K$. Each of the vectors in (8)-(9) uniquely determines the original system (2), including its order and coefficients. However, a vector in the null space of L is in general a linear combination of all such vectors and it is not necessarily one of the above.

In order to identify the original system from the data matrix L, we need to seek a vector in null(L) that has certain desired structure. To this end, notice that the last $\bar{n}_c - n_c$ entries of b in (8) are zero, hence the last non-zero entry of

---

[2] Notice that this scheme is not practical, because computing $\hat{y}(z)$ usually requires an infinitely-long output sequence $\{y_t\}$.

b has the lowest order – in terms of the ordering of the entries of x_t – among all vectors that are in null(L). Therefore, we can obtain the first $\bar{n}_a + n_c + 1$ entries of b from the null space of the submatrix of L defined by its first $\bar{n}_a + n_c + 1$ columns. Since n_c is unknown, we can incrementally take the first $j = 1, 2, \ldots$ columns of the matrix L from the left to the right:

$$L^1 \doteq L(:, 1:1), \quad L^2 \doteq L(:, 1:2), \quad \ldots, \quad L^j \doteq L(:, 1:j), \qquad (10)$$

until the rank of the submatrix L^j stops increasing for some $j = m$. Under the additional assumption that $\hat{u}(z)$ has no zeros at $z = 0$, null(L^m) gives the first m entries of the desired vector b, because $z^{n_c-1}c_1 + z^{n_c-2}c_2 + \cdots + c_{n_c}$ and $z^{d+\max(n_c-n_a,0)}(z^{n_a} - z^{n_a-1}a_1 - z^{n_a-2}a_2 - \cdots - a_{n_a})$ are co-prime polynomials.[3]

Remark 1 (Identifying b and m in the Stochastic Case). In the stochastic case (i.e., $w_t \neq 0$), the ultimate goal is to minimize the (squared) modeling error $\sum_t w_t^2 = \sum_t (b^T x_t)^2$, which corresponds to the maximum-likelihood estimate when w_t is white-noise. The optimal solution b^* can be found in a least-square sense as the singular vector that corresponds to the smallest singular value of L^m. However, in the noisy case, we cannot directly estimate m from the rank of L^j since it might be full rank for all j. Based on model selection techniques [13], m can be estimated from a noisy L^j by minimizing the sum of a data fitting term and a model complexity term as

$$m = \operatorname*{argmin}_{j=1,\ldots,K} \left\{ \frac{\sigma_j^2(L^j)}{\sum_{k=1}^{j-1} \sigma_k^2(L^j)} + \kappa \cdot j \right\}, \qquad (11)$$

where $\sigma_k(L^j)$ is the kth singular value of L^j and $\kappa \in \mathbb{R}$ is a parameter weighting the two terms. The data fitting term measures how well the data is approximated by the model – in this case how close the matrix L^j is to dropping rank. The model complexity term penalizes choosing models of high complexity – in this case choosing a large rank.

There is, however, a much more direct way of dealing with the case of unknown orders. The following lemma shows that the system orders n_a and n_c together with the system parameters b can all be simultaneously and uniquely computed from the data.

Lemma 1 (Identifying the Orders of an ARX System). *Suppose we are given data generated by an identifiable ARX model whose input $\hat{u}(z)$ shares no poles or zeros with the zeros or poles, respectively, of the model transfer function $\hat{H}(z)$. If $\bar{n}_a + \bar{n}_c + 1 \leq n_a + n_c + 1$, then*

$$\operatorname{rank}\left(L(\bar{n}_a, \bar{n}_c)\right) = \begin{cases} \bar{n}_a + \bar{n}_c & \text{if and only if} \quad \bar{n}_a = n_a \text{ and } \bar{n}_c = n_c, \\ \bar{n}_a + \bar{n}_c + 1 & \text{otherwise.} \end{cases} \qquad (12)$$

---

[3] Similar arguments and conclusions hold if in the definition of x_t, we put the inputs $u_{t-1}, \ldots, u_{t-\bar{n}_c}$ in front of the outputs $y_{t-1}, \ldots, y_{t-\bar{n}_a}$ instead.

Therefore the systems orders can be computed as:

$$(n_a, n_c) = \arg \min_{(\bar{n}_a, \bar{n}_c) \in \mathbb{Z}^2} \{\bar{n}_a + \bar{n}_c : \text{rank}(L(\bar{n}_a, \bar{n}_c)) = \bar{n}_a + \bar{n}_c\}. \tag{13}$$

The parameter vector $\boldsymbol{b}$ is the unique vector in the null space of $L(n_a, n_c)$.

We omit the proof here due to the limit of space. In principle, the lemma allows us to identify the precise orders n_a, n_c and the vector $\boldsymbol{b}$ of the ARX system from the (infinite) sequences of input $\{u_t\}$ and output $\{y_t\}$. In practice, we are usually given a finite input/output sequence. In such cases, we need to assume that the sequence of regressors is *sufficiently exciting*, i.e., the $T \times (n_a + n_c + 1)$ submatrix

$$L \doteq [\boldsymbol{x}_{\max(n_a, n_c)}, \dots, \boldsymbol{x}_{\max(n_a, n_c) + T - 1}]^T \tag{14}$$

has the same rank $n_a + n_c$ as the "full" L matrix defined in (6).[4] This condition for identifiability from finite data can also be expressed in terms of the input sequence. As shown in [2], the regressors are sufficiently exciting if the input sequence $\{u_t\}$ is, i.e., if the following vectors

$$\boldsymbol{u}_t \doteq [u_t, u_{t-1}, \dots, u_{t-n_a-n_c+1}]^T \in \mathbb{R}^{n_a+n_c}, \qquad n_a + n_c - 1 \le t \le T, \tag{15}$$

span an $(n_a + n_c)$-dimensional subspace.

3   Identification of Switched ARX Systems

From our discussion in section 2, we know that the regressors generated by a sufficiently excited and identifiable ARX system live in a linear subspace in $\mathbb{R}^K$ where $K = \bar{n}_a + \bar{n}_c + 1$ and $\bar{n}_a, \bar{n}_c$ are upper bounds on the orders of the system. The problem of identifying the ARX system becomes one of seeking a vector in the orthogonal complement to this subspace that has certain desired structure.

In this section we show how to generalize these concepts to the more challenging problem of identifying a switched ARX system (Problem 1). More specifically, we consider an input/output sequence $\{u_t, y_t\}$ generated by a switched ARX system switching among a set of n ARX systems with parameters $\{\boldsymbol{b}_i\}_{i=1}^n$ and possibly different orders $\{n_a(i), n_c(i)\}_{i=1}^n$. We assume that the HARX system is *identifiable*, i.e., for all $i = 1, \dots, n$, the rational function $\tilde{H}_i(z)$ associated with the ith ARX model has no zero-pole cancellation and the configuration subspaces of all the ARX models do not contain one another.[5] In general, we also assume that we do not know the exact number of systems and system orders, but we know certain upper bounds $\bar{n}, \bar{n}_a$ and $\bar{n}_c$, i.e.,

---

[4] In the case of a redundant embedding, the sequence of regressors is said to be sufficiently exciting if $\text{rank}(L) = \bar{n}_a + \bar{n}_c + 1$.

[5] One way to ensure this is to assume that for all $i \ne j = 1, \dots, n$, $\tilde{H}_i(z)$ and $\tilde{H}_j(z)$ do not have all their zeros and poles in common. That is, there is no ARX system that can simulate another ARX system with a smaller order. However, this is not necessary because two ARX systems can have different configuration spaces even if one system's zeros and poles are a subset of the other's. Determining both necessary and sufficient conditions for the identifiability remains an open issue.

$$\bar{n} \geq n, \quad \bar{n}_a \geq n_a \doteq \max\{n_a(1), \ldots, n_a(n)\}, \quad \bar{n}_c \geq n_c \doteq \max\{n_c(1), \ldots, n_c(n)\}. \quad (16)$$

We now show how to identify a switched ARX system despite these uncertainties.

3.1   The Hybrid Decoupling Polynomial

One of the difficulties in identifying switched ARX systems is that we do not know the switching sequence λ_t, hence we cannot directly apply the subspace identification technique described in the previous section to each of the n ARX systems. As we will soon see, in fact both the number of subspaces and their dimensions depend not only on the number of systems and their orders but also on the switching sequence. This motivates us to look for relationships between the data $\{\boldsymbol{x}_t \in \mathbb{R}^K\}$ and the system parameters $\{\boldsymbol{b}_i \in \mathbb{R}^K\}$ that do not depend on the switching sequence. To this end, recall that for every t there exists a mode $\lambda_t = i \in \{1, 2, \ldots, n\}$ such that $\boldsymbol{b}_i^T \boldsymbol{x}_t = 0$. Therefore, the following polynomial equation [23] must be satisfied by the system parameters and the input/output data for any switching sequence and mechanism (JMLS or PWARX):

$$p_n(\boldsymbol{x}_t) \doteq \prod_{i=1}^{n} (\boldsymbol{b}_i^T \boldsymbol{x}_t) = 0. \quad (17)$$

We call p_n the *hybrid decoupling polynomial* (HDP). This polynomial equation was introduced independently in [18] in the case of two models ($n = 2$).

The HDP eliminates the discrete state by taking the product of the equations defining each one of the ARX systems. While taking the product is not the only way of algebraically eliminating the discrete state, this leads to an algebraic equation with a very nice algebraic structure. The HDP is simply a homogeneous multivariate polynomial of degree n in K variables, which can be written linearly in terms of its coefficients as

$$p_n(\boldsymbol{z}) \doteq \prod_{i=1}^{n} (\boldsymbol{b}_i^T \boldsymbol{z}) = \sum h_{n_1,\ldots,n_K} z_1^{n_1} \cdots z_K^{n_K} = \boldsymbol{h}_n^T \nu_n(\boldsymbol{z}) = 0. \quad (18)$$

In eqn. (18), $h_I = h_{n_1,\ldots,n_K} \in \mathbb{R}$ is the coefficient of the monomial $\boldsymbol{z}^I = z_1^{n_1} z_2^{n_2} \cdots z_K^{n_K}$, where $0 \leq n_j \leq n$ for $j = 1, \ldots, K$, and $n_1 + n_2 + \cdots + n_K = n$; $\nu_n : \mathbb{R}^K \to \mathbb{R}^{M_n(K)}$ is the *Veronese map* of degree n which is defined as [10]:

$$\nu_n : [z_1, \ldots, z_K]^T \mapsto [\ldots, \boldsymbol{z}^I, \ldots]^T, \quad (19)$$

with I chosen in the degree-lexicographic order (assuming the order $z_1 < z_2 < \cdots < z_K$); and $M_n(K) \doteq \binom{n+K-1}{K-1} = \binom{n+K-1}{n}$ is the total number of independent monomials. As shown in [10], the vector of coefficients $\boldsymbol{h}_n \in \mathbb{R}^{M_n(K)}$ is simply a vector representation of the symmetric tensor product of the individual system parameters $\{\boldsymbol{b}_i\}_{i=1}^{n}$, i.e.,

$$\text{Sym}(\boldsymbol{b}_1 \otimes \boldsymbol{b}_2 \otimes \cdots \otimes \boldsymbol{b}_n) \doteq \sum_{\sigma \in \mathfrak{S}_n} \boldsymbol{b}_{\sigma(1)} \otimes \boldsymbol{b}_{\sigma(2)} \otimes \cdots \otimes \boldsymbol{b}_{\sigma(n)} \in \mathbb{R}^{M_n(K)}, \quad (20)$$

where $\mathfrak{S}_n$ is the permutation group of n elements. We will show in the sequel how $\boldsymbol{h}_n$ can be recovered from the data and how the parameters of each individual ARX system $\{\boldsymbol{b}_i\}_{i=1}^{n}$ can be further retrieved from it.

3.2   Identifying the Number and Orders of ARX Systems

Assume for now that we know the number of systems n. We will show later how to relax this assumption. Since the HDP (17)–(18) is satisfied by all the data points $\{x_t\}_{t=1}^T$, we can use it to derive the following linear system on h_n:

$$L_n(\bar{n}_a, \bar{n}_c)\, h_n \doteq \left[\nu_n(x_{\max\{\bar{n}_a, \bar{n}_c\}}) \cdots \nu_n(x_{\max\{\bar{n}_a, \bar{n}_c\}+T-1})\right]^T h_n = 0_{T \times 1}, \qquad (21)$$

where $L_n(\bar{n}_a, \bar{n}_c) \in \mathbb{R}^{T \times M_n(K)}$ is the matrix of the input/output data embedded via the Veronese map.

Notice that to construct the matrix L_n, one needs to choose $\bar{n}_a$ and $\bar{n}_c$. If the constituent ARX systems have different orders, the choice can never be the most compact for every ARX system. Nevertheless, there will always be less redundancy in the embedding if $\bar{n}_a$, $\bar{n}_c$ are the maximum orders n_a, n_c for all the ARX systems. To identify the maximum orders, we need some extra conditions on the switching and input sequences.

Definition 1 (Sufficiently Exciting Switching and Input Sequences). *A switching and input sequence $\{\lambda_t, u_t\}$ is called* sufficiently exciting *for a switched ARX system, if the data points $\{x_t\}$ generated by $\{\lambda_t, u_t\}$ are sufficient to determine the union of the subspaces associated with the constituent ARX systems as an algebraic variety.*

Remark 2. When $\bar{n}_a < n_a$ or $\bar{n}_c < n_c$, the above condition requires $L_n(\bar{n}_a, \bar{n}_c)$ to be full rank, because at least one of the subspaces must have full dimension $\bar{n}_a + \bar{n}_c + 1$. When $\bar{n}_a \geq n_a$ and $\bar{n}_c \geq n_c$, the above condition implies that the null space of $L_n(\bar{n}_a, \bar{n}_c)$ is contained in the span of the vectors $\{h\}$, where h is the symmetric tensor product of any choice of n vectors of the form (8) or (9), each one associated with one of the n ARX models.

Remark 3. The above condition is not as strong as it seems to be, as the set of input and switching sequences that are not sufficiently exciting are a zero-measure set. Notice, however, that the definition does not explicitly characterize the set of sufficiently exciting input and switching sequences. Intuitively the switching sequence should visit each one of the n modes frequently enough [20] and the input sequence should be sufficiently exciting, as defined in the previous section. A more precise characterization of sufficiently exciting input and switching sequences remains elusive at this point.

Under the assumption of sufficiently exiting input and switching sequences, the following theorem gives a formula for the maximum orders. The theorem is a natural generalization of Lemma 1 from one to multiple ARX systems.

Theorem 1 (Identifying the Maximum Orders). *Let $\{u_t, y_t\}$ be input/ output data generated by an identifiable HARX system. Let $L_n(i, j) \in \mathbb{R}^{T \times M_n(i+j+1)}$ be the embedded data matrix defined in (21), but computed with system orders i and j. If T is large enough and the input and switching sequences are sufficiently exciting, then the maximum orders of the constituent ARX systems are given by:*

$$(n_a, n_c) = \underset{(i,j):M_n(i+j+1) < T}{\arg\min} \left\{(i+j) : \mathrm{rank}(L_n(i,j)) < M_n(i+j+1)\right\}. \qquad (22)$$

Proof. First notice that the maximum orders n_a and n_c maybe achieved separately by different ARX systems. Nevertheless, for any ARX system, if either $i < n_a$ or $j < n_c$ is true, at least one of the subspaces must be of dimension $i + j + 1$. Therefore if the input and switching sequences are sufficiently exciting so that this subspace is visited enough, then there is a large enough T such that the entries of $L_n(i,j)$ are independent monomials of degree n on these regressors. The matrix $L_n(i,j)$ drops rank only for a zero measure set of such regressors. Therefore in general, for a sufficiently large T, there is no polynomial of degree n that vanishes on the set of all regressors and we must have $\text{rank}(L_n(i,j)) = M_n(i+j+1)$. If $i = n_a$ and $j = n_c$, then there is exactly one vector, i.e., h_n, in the null space of $L_n(i,j)$. Therefore, the maximum orders n_a, n_c are the ones for which $n_a + n_c$ is minimum and $L_n(n_a, n_c)$ drops rank, as claimed.   ∎

Given the data matrix $L_n(n_a, n_c)$ embedded with the correct maximum orders, we would like to retrieve the coefficient vector h_n from its null space. There are two potential difficulties. First, since the maximum orders n_a, n_c may not be tight for every constituent ARX system, the null space of $L_n(n_a, n_c)$ may be more than one-dimensional, as we have known from a single ARX system. Second, even if we know the discrete state for each time, the structure of the data associated with each state is not exactly the same as that of the ARX system itself: Suppose we switch to the ith system at time t_0, then we have $b_i^T x_{t_0} = 0$. However, the vectors b given in equation (9) are no longer orthogonal to x_{t_0} even if the embedding is redundant for the ith system. In a sense, the regressor at a switching time usually lives in a subspace whose dimension is higher than that of the subspace associated with the ARX model generating the regressor. Therefore, the configuration space of the data $\{x_t\}$ of an HARX system will *not* exactly be the union of all the subspaces associated with the constituent ARX systems. Let us denote the former as an algebraic variety Z' and the latter as Z. Then in general, we have $Z' \supseteq Z$. In order to retrieve h_n uniquely from the data matrix L_n, we need to utilize its additional structure.

Lemma 2 (Structure of the Hybrid Decoupling Polynomial). *The monomial associated with the last non-zero entry of the coefficient vector h_n of the HDP $p_n(z) = h_n^T \nu_n(z)$ has the lowest degree-lexicographic order in all the polynomials in $\mathfrak{a}(Z) \cap S_n$, where S_n is the set of polynomials of degree up to n.*

Proof. Any polynomial of degree n in $\mathfrak{a}(Z)$ is a superposition of $\prod_{i=1}^{n}(b_{\sigma(i)}^T z)$ where $b_{\sigma(i)}$ is a normal vector to the subspace associated with the ith ARX system. Notice that h_n is the symmetric tensor of $b_1, b_2, \ldots, b_n$ defined in (8). For the ith ARX system, the last non-zero entry of the vector b_i always has the lowest degree-lexicographic order among all normal vectors that are orthogonal to the regressors $z = x_t$ associated to the ith system, see equations (8) and (9). Therefore, the last non-zero entry of h_n must have the lowest degree-lexicographic order.   ∎

Theorem 2 (Identifying the Hybrid Decoupling Polynomial). *Let $\{u_t, y_t\}_{t=0}^{T}$ be the input/output data generated by an identifiable HARX system. Let*

$L_n^j \in \mathbb{R}^{T \times j}$ be the first j columns of the embedded data matrix $L_n(n_a, n_c)$, and let $m \doteq \min \{ j : \mathrm{rank}(L_n^j) = j - 1 \}$. If T is sufficiently large and the input and switching sequences are sufficiently exciting, then the coefficient vector h_n of the hybrid decoupling polynomial is

$$h_n = \left[(h_n^m)^T, \ 0_{1 \times (M_n(K) - m)} \right]^T \in \mathbb{R}^{M_n(K)}, \tag{23}$$

where $h_n^m \in \mathbb{R}^m$ is the unique vector that satisfies

$$L_n^m h_n^m = 0 \quad \text{and} \quad h_n^m(1) = 1. \tag{24}$$

Proof. Let Z to be the union of the subspaces associated with the n constituent ARX systems. Since the input and switching sequence is sufficiently exciting in the sense of Definition 1, any polynomial of degree less than and equal to n that vanishes on all the data points must be in the set $\mathfrak{a}(Z) \cap S_n$.

From our discussion before the theorem, the configuration space Z' of the data $\{x_t\}$ associated with the switched ARX system is in general a superset of Z. The ideal $\mathfrak{a}'(Z')$ of polynomials that vanish on the configuration space Z' is then a sub-ideal of the ideal $\mathfrak{a}(Z)$ associated with the union of the subspaces. Furthermore, regardless of the switching sequence, the hybrid decoupling polynomial $p_n(z)$ is always in $\mathfrak{a}' \cap S_n \subseteq \mathfrak{a} \cap S_n$. According to Lemma 2, the last non-zero term of $p_n(z)$ has the lowest degree-lexicographic order among all polynomials of degree n in $\mathfrak{a}$, so does it in $\mathfrak{a}'$. Since every solution $L_n \tilde{h} = 0$ gives a polynomial $\tilde{p}_n(z) = \tilde{h}_n^T \nu_n(z) \in \mathfrak{a} \cap S_n$ of degree n that vanishes on all data points, the last non-zero entry of h_n given by (23) obviously has the lowest degree-lexicographic order. Therefore, we have $p_n(z) = h_n^T \nu_n(z)$. ∎

In fact, in order to compute the coefficients h_n of the hybrid decoupling polynomial, we can do better than checking the rank of the submatrix L_n^j for every $j = 1, 2, \ldots$. The following corollary provides one alternative scheme.

Corollary 1 (Zero Coefficients of the Decoupling Polynomial). *Let $\{b_i\}_{i=1}^n$ be a set of K-vectors. Suppose that one of the b_i has a maximal number of zeros on its right, and without loss of generality, assume $b_1 = [b_{11}, \ldots, b_{1n_1}, 0, \ldots, 0]^T$, with $b_{1n_1} \neq 0$. The multivariate polynomial $p_n(z) \doteq (b_1^T z)(b_2^T z) \cdots (b_n^T z)$ has zero coefficients for all the monomials of $\nu_n([z_{n_1+1}, z_{n_1+2}, \ldots, z_K])$; but the coefficients cannot all be zeros for the monomials of $\nu_n([z_{n_1}, z_{n_1+1}, \ldots, z_K])$.*

This corollary allows us to narrow down the range for m (where L_n^j first drops rank) because m must fall between two consecutive values of the following: $1, M_n(K) - M_n(K-1), M_n(K) - M_n(K-2), \ldots, M_n(K) - 1$.

Remark 4 (Sub-Optimality in the Stochastic Case). In the stochastic case (i.e., $w_t \neq 0$), we can still solve for h_n^m in (24) in a least-squares sense as the singular vector of L_n^m associated with its smallest singular value, using a similar model selection criterion for m as in Remark 1. However, unlike the single system case, the so-found h_n no longer minimizes the sum of least-square errors $\sum_t w_t^2 = \sum_t (b_{\lambda_t}^T x_t)^2$. Instead, it minimizes (in a least-square sense) a "weighted version" of this objective:

$$\sum_t \alpha_t (b_{\lambda_t}^T x_t)^2 \doteq \sum_t \prod_{i \neq \lambda_t} (b_i^T x_t)^2 (b_{\lambda_t}^T x_t)^2, \tag{25}$$

where the weight α_t is conveniently chosen to be $\prod_{i \neq \lambda_t}(b_i^T x_t)^2$. Such a "softening" of the objective function allows a global algebraic solution. It offers a sub-optimal approximation for the original stochastic objective when the variance of w_t is small. One can use the solution as the initialization for any other iterative optimization scheme (such as EM) to further minimize the original stochastic objective.

Notice that in the above theorem, we have assumed that the switching sequence is such that all the ARX systems are sufficiently visited. What if only a subset of the n systems are sufficiently visited? Furthermore, in practice, we sometimes do not even know the correct number of systems involved and only know an upper bound for it. The question is whether the above theorem still applies when the degree n we choose for the Veronese embedding is strictly larger than the actually number of systems. This is answered by the following corollary whose proof is straightforward.

Corollary 2 (Identifying the Number of ARX Systems). *Let $\{u_t, y_t\}_{t=0}^T$ be input/output data generated by an HARX system with $n < \bar{n}$ discrete states. If T is sufficiently large and the input and switching sequences are sufficiently exciting, then the vector $h_{\bar{n}}$ found by Theorem 2 is the symmetric tensor product $h_{\bar{n}} = \mathrm{Sym}\big(b_1 \otimes b_2 \cdots \otimes b_n \otimes \underbrace{e_1 \otimes \cdots \otimes e_1}_{\bar{n}-n}\big)$, where $e_1 \doteq [1, 0, \ldots, 0]^T \in \mathbb{R}^K$, i.e., $h_{\bar{n}}$ is the coefficients of the polynomial $p_{\bar{n}}(z) = h_{\bar{n}}^T \nu_{\bar{n}}(z) = (b_1^T z)(b_2^T z) \cdots (b_n^T z) z_1^{\bar{n}-n}$.*

Therefore, if we over-estimate the number of constituent systems or the switching sequence does not visit all the systems, the solution given by Theorem 2 will simply treat the nonexistent (or not visited) systems as if they had zero order[6] and the information about the rest of the systems will be conveniently recovered.

3.3 Identifying the System Parameters and Discrete States

Theorem 2 allows us to determine the HDP $p_n(z) = h_n^T \nu_n(z)$, from input/output data $\{u_t, y_t\}_{t=0}^T$. The rest of the problem is to recover the system parameters $\{b_i\}_{i=1}^n$ from h_n. As shown in [23], one can obtain the system parameters directly from the derivatives of the HDP $p_n(z)$ at a collection of n points as

$$b_i = \left.\frac{Dp_n(z)}{e_1^T Dp_n(z)}\right|_{z \in \mathcal{H}_i}, \qquad i = 1, \ldots, n, \tag{26}$$

where $\mathcal{H}_i = \{z : b_i^T z = 0\}$ and $e_1 = [1, 0, \ldots, 0]^T \in \mathbb{R}^K$. However, since the value of the discrete state λ_t is unknown, we do not know which data points $\{x_t\}$ belong to which hyperplane. In order to choose one point per hyperplane, notice that we can always choose a point z_n lying on one of the hyperplanes as any of the points in the data set. However, in the presence of noise and outliers,

---

[6] That is, the coefficient vector $b = e_1$ corresponds to the "system" $y_t = 0$ with $n_a = n_c = 0$, which is a trivial ARX system.

an arbitrary point in may be far from the hyperplanes. The question is then how to compute the *distance* from each data point to its closest hyperplane, *without* knowing the normals to the hyperplanes. The following lemma allows us to compute a first order approximation to such a distance:

Lemma 3. *Let $\tilde{z} \in \mathcal{H}_i$ be the projection of a point $z \in \mathbb{R}^K$ onto its closest hyperplane $\mathcal{H}_i$. The Euclidean distance from z to $\mathcal{H}_i$ is given by*

$$\|z - \tilde{z}\| = \frac{|p_n(z)|}{\|(I - e_1 e_1^T) D p_n(z)\|} + O(\|z - \tilde{z}\|^2). \qquad (27)$$

Therefore, we can choose a point in the data set close to one of the subspaces as:

$$z_n = \underset{z \in \{x_t\}}{\arg\min} \frac{|p_n(z)|}{\|(I - e_1 e_1^T) D p_n(z)\|}, \qquad (28)$$

and then compute the normal vector at z_n as $b_n = D p_n(z_n)/(e_1^T D p_n(z_n))$. In order to find a point z_{n-1} in one of the remaining hyperplanes, we penalize choosing a point from $\mathcal{H}_n$ in (28) by dividing the objective function by the distance from z to $\mathcal{H}_n$, namely $|b_n^T z|/\|\Pi b_n\|$. That is, we can choose a point on or close to $\cup_{i=1}^{n-1} \mathcal{H}_i$ as

$$z_{n-1} = \arg\min_{z \in \{x_t\}} \frac{\frac{|p_n(z)|}{\|\Pi D p_n(z)\|}}{\frac{|b_n^T z|}{\|\Pi b_n\|}}, \qquad (29)$$

By repeating this process for the remaining hyperplanes, we obtain one point per hyperplane, hence the system parameters $\{b_i\}_{i=1}^n$. We can then reconstruct the discrete state trajectory $\{\lambda_t\}$ from input/output data $\{x_t\}_{t=0}^T$ as

$$\lambda_t = \underset{i=1,\dots,n}{\arg\min} \left(b_i^T x_t\right)^2, \qquad (30)$$

because for each time t there exists a generally unique i such that $b_i^T x_t = 0$. There will be ambiguity in the value of λ_t only if x_t happens to be at (or close to) the intersection of more than one subspace associated to the constituent ARX systems. However, the set of all such points is a zero measure set of the variety $Z \subseteq \{z : p_n(z) = 0\}$.

3.4   The Basic Algorithm and Its Extensions

Based on the results that we have derived so far, we summarize the main steps for solving the identification of an HARX system (Problem 1) as the following Algorithm 1.

Different Embedding Orders. The ordering of $\{y_t\}$ and $\{u_t\}$ in (7) is more efficient for the algorithm when $n_a(i)$ are approximately the same for all the constituent systems and $n_c(i)$ are much smaller than $n_a(i)$. However, if $n_a(i)$ are rather different for different systems and $n_c(i)$ and $n_a(i)$ are roughly the same, the following ordering in time t

$$x_t \doteq [y_t, y_{t-1}, u_{t-1}, y_{t-2}, u_{t-2}, \dots, y_{t-n_a}, u_{t-n_a}]^T \in \mathbb{R}^K \qquad (31)$$

results in less non-zero leading coefficients in h_n, thus making Algorithm 1 more efficient. However, if all the systems have the same $n_a = n_c$, both embeddings have the same efficiency.

Algorithm 1 (Identification of HARX Systems).

Given input/output data $\{y_t, u_t\}$ from a sufficiently excited switched ARX system, and the upper bounds on the number $\bar{n}$ and orders $(\bar{n}_a, \bar{n}_c)$ of its constituent ARX systems:

1. **Maximum System Orders.** Identify the maximum orders (n_a, n_c) according to Theorem 1.
2. **Veronese Embedding.** Construct the data matrix $L_{\bar{n}}(n_a, n_c)$ via the Veronese map (19) based on the given number $\bar{n}$ of systems and the maximum orders (n_a, n_c) identified from the previous step.
3. **Hybrid Decoupling Polynomial.** Compute the coefficients of the polynomial $p_{\bar{n}}(z) \doteq h_{\bar{n}}^T \nu_{\bar{n}}(z) = \prod_{i=1}^n \left(b_i^T z\right) z_1^{\bar{n}-n} = 0$ from the data matrix $L_{\bar{n}}$ according to Theorem 2 and Corollary 2. In the stochastic case, comply with Remarks 1 and 4.
4. **Constituent System Parameters.** Retrieve the parameters $\{b_i\}_{i=1}^n$ of each constituent ARX system from the derivatives of $p_{\bar{n}}(z)$ as described in the previous subsection.
5. **Key System Parameters.** The correct number of system n is the number of $b_i \neq e_1$; The correct orders $n_a(i), n_c(i)$ are determined from such b_i according to their definition (8); The discrete state λ_t for each time t is given by equation (30).

Inferring the Switching Mechanisms. Once the system parameters and the discrete state have been identified, the problem of estimating the switching mechanisms, e.g., the partition of the state space for PWARX or the parameters of the jump Markov process for JMLS, becomes a simpler problem. We refer interested readers to [5, 9] for specific algorithms.

4   Simulations and Experiments

In this section we evaluate the performance of the proposed algorithm with respect to the amount of noise in the data and the choice of the model orders. We also present experiments on real data from a component placement process in a pick-and-place machine.

Error as a Function of Noise. Consider the PWAR model taken from [14]

$$y_t = \begin{cases} 2u_{t-1} + 10 + w_t & \text{if } u_{t-1} \in [-10, 0], \\ -1.5u_{t-1} + 10 + w_t & \text{if } u_{t-1} \in (0, 10], \end{cases} \tag{32}$$

with input $u_t \overset{\text{i.i.d.}}{\sim} \mathcal{U}(-10, 10)$ and noise $w_t \overset{\text{i.i.d.}}{\sim} \mathcal{N}(0, \sigma_\eta^2)$. We run our algorithm with $n = 2$, $n_a = 0$ and $n_c = 1$ for 10 different values of σ_η and compute the mean and the variance of the error in the estimated model parameters, as shown in Figure 1. The algebraic algorithm without any iterative refinement estimates the parameters with an error[7] of less than 3.7% for the levels of noise considered. These errors are comparable to those of the Ferrari-Trecate and Bemporad's

---

[7] The error between the estimated parameters $\hat{b}$ and the true parameters b is computed as $\max_{i=1,\dots,m} . \min_{j=1,\dots,n} . \frac{\left\| \hat{b}_i - b_j \right\|}{\left\| [0_{(K-1) \times 1} \ I_{K-1}] b_j \right\|}$.

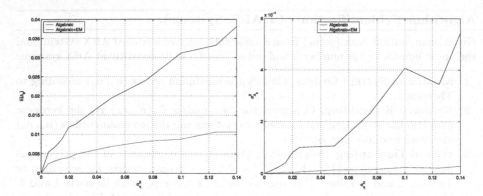

Fig. 1. Means (left) and variances (right) of the error in the estimation of the model parameters for different levels of noise. Blue curves are for the purely algebraic Algorithm 1; Green curves are for the EM algorithm initialized with the solutions from Algorithm 1

algorithms reported in [14] which are about $1.5 \sim 2.5\%$. The error is reduced significantly to about 1% (see Figure 1 left) by using the algebraic algorithm with iterative refinement via Expectation and Maximization (EM).

Error as a Function of the Model Orders. Consider the PWAR system taken from [14]

$$y_t = \begin{cases} 2y_{t-1} + 0u_{t-1} + 10 + w_t & \text{if } y_{t-1} \in [-10, 0], \\ -1.5y_{t-1} + 0u_{t-1} + 10 + w_t & \text{if } y_{t-1} \in (0, 10], \end{cases} \tag{33}$$

with initial condition $y_0 = -10$, input $u_t \overset{\text{i.i.d.}}{\sim} \mathcal{U}(-10, 10)$ and noise $w_t \overset{\text{i.i.d.}}{\sim} \mathcal{N}(0, 0.01)$.

We applied our algorithm[8] with known number of models $n = 2$, but unknown model orders (n_a, n_c). For all $\kappa > 1.3 \cdot 10^{-8}$, our algorithm correctly estimates the orders as $n_a = 1$ and $n_c = 0$. For such orders, the estimates of the ARX model parameters are $[1.9878, 0, 10.0161]^T$ and $[-1.4810, 0, 10.0052]^T$, which have an error of 0.0020.

We also evaluated the performance of our algorithm as a function of the orders (n_a, n_c) for a known number of models $n = 2$. Rather than estimating the orders using formula (22), we use a fixed value for (n_a, n_c) and search for the polynomial in the null space of $L_n(n_a, n_c)$ with the smallest degree-lexicographic order. We repeat the experiment for multiple values of $n_a = 1, \ldots, 4$ and $n_c = 1, \ldots, 10$, to evaluate the effectiveness of equation (11) at finding the "correct" null space of $L_n(n_a, n_c)$. Figure 2 shows the results for $\kappa = 10^{-5}$. Notice that for all the range of values of n_a and n_c, the algorithm gives an error that is

---

[8] Since the ARX model is an affine model with a constant input, we slightly modify our algorithm by using homogeneous coordinates for the regressor x_t, i.e., appending an entry of "1."

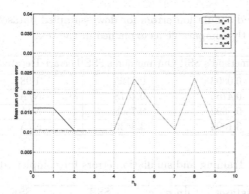

Fig. 2. Mean sum of squares error for various orders of the ARX models

very close to the theoretical bound of 0.01 (the noise variance). These results are significantly better than those reported in [14] for the Ferrari-Trecate and Bemporad's algorithms when applied with wrong model orders. The results are comparable to those of Ferrari-Trecate and Bemporad's algorithms when applied with the true model orders.

Experimental Results on Test Datasets. We applied our algorithm with $n = n_a = n_c = 2$ to four datasets of $T = 60,000$ measurements from a component placement process in a pick-and-place machine [11]. For comparison with the results in [14], we first report results on a down-sampled dataset of 750 consisting of one out of every 80 samples. The 750 points are separated in two overlapping groups of points. The first 500 points are used for identification, and the last 500 points are used for validation. Table 1 shows the average sum of squared residuals (SSR) – one step ahead prediction errors, and the average sum of squared simulation errors (SSE) obtained by our method for all four datasets, as well as the SSE of Ferrari-Trecate's and Bemporad's algorithm for the first dataset as reported in [14]. It is worth mentioning that the SSE and SSR errors provided by our method are not strictly comparable to those [14]. This is because Ferrari-Trecate's and Bemporad's algorithms apply to PWARX models in which the mode λ_t is a piecewise linear function of the past inputs and outputs, while our method applies to switched ARX models in which λ_t can evolve arbitrarily. Therefore, for PWARX models λ_t is known automatically once the piece-wise linear map has been learned, while for switched ARX models one must use the measured output y_t to determine λ_t as in (30).

We also tested our algorithm on the 60,000 measurements. We split the data in two groups of 30,000 points each. The first group is used for identification and the last group for simulation. Table 2 shows the average sum of squared residual error (SSR) and the average sum of squared simulation error (SSE) for all four datasets. Figure 3 shows the true and simulated outputs for dataset 1.

Overall, the algorithm demonstrates a very good performance in all four datasets. The running time of a MATLAB implementation of our algorithm is 0.15 second for the 500 data points and 0.841 second for 30,000 data points.

Table 1. Training and simulation errors for down-sampled datasets. Note that these numbers are not strictly comparable as explained in the text

Dataset	n n_a n_c	Our method's SSR	Our method's SSE	Ferrari-Trecate SSE	Bemporad SSE
1	2 2 2	0.0803	0.1195	1.98	2.15
2	2 2 2	0.4765	0.4678	N/A	N/A
3	2 2 2	0.6692	0.7368	N/A	N/A
4	2 2 2	3.1004	3.8430	N/A	N/A

Table 2. Training and simulation errors for complete datasets

Dataset	n n_a n_c	SSR	SSE
1 with all points	2 2 2	$4.9696 \cdot 10^{-6}$	$5.3426 \cdot 10^{-6}$
2 with all points	2 2 2	$9.2464 \cdot 10^{-6}$	$7.9081 \cdot 10^{-6}$
3 with all points	2 2 2	$2.3010 \cdot 10^{-5}$	$2.5290 \cdot 10^{-5}$
4 with all points	2 2 2	$7.5906 \cdot 10^{-6}$	$9.6362 \cdot 10^{-6}$

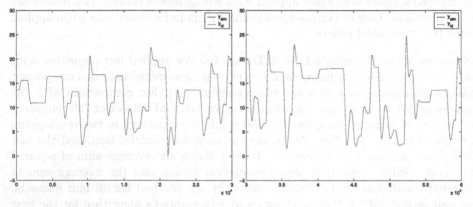

Fig. 3. Training and simulation sequences for complete datasets – the simulated and the identified sequences overlap almost exactly

5   Conclusions

We have proposed a linear-algebraic solution to the problem of identifying (deterministic) switched ARX systems. The algorithm can deal with the general case in which the switches are arbitrary and the number and orders of the constituent ARX systems are unknown. It can also tolerate moderate noises in the data. In the future, we would like to investigate efficient ways for on-line implementation of the algorithm as well as generalize our methods to state-space models.

References

1. A. Alessandri and P. Coletta. Design of Luenberger observers for a class of hybrid linear systems. In *Hybrid Systems: Computation and Control*, pages 7–18. 2001.

2. B.D.O. Anderson and C.R. Johnson. Exponential convergence of adaptive identification and control algorithms. *Automatica*, 18(1):1–13, 1982.
3. A. Balluchi, L. Benvenuti, M. Di Benedetto, and A. Sangiovanni-Vincentelli. Design of observers for hybrid systems. In *Hybrid Systems: Computation and Control*, volume 2289 of *LNCS*, pages 76–89. Springer Verlag, 2002.
4. A. Bemporad, G. Ferrari, and M. Morari. Observability and controllability of piecewise affine and hybrid systems. *IEEE Trans. on Aut. Cont.*, 45(10):1864–76, 2000.
5. A. Bemporad, A. Garulli, S. Paoletti, and A. Vicino. A greedy approach to identification of piecewise affine models. In *Hybrid Systems: Computation and Control*, LNCS, pages 97–112. Springer Verlag, 2003.
6. A. Bemporad, J. Roll, and L. Ljung. Identification of hybrid systems via mixed-integer programming. In *IEEE Conf. on Decision & Control*, pages 786–792, 2001.
7. A. Doucet, A. Logothetis, and V. Krishnamurthy. Stochastic sampling algorithms for state estimation of jump Markov linear systems. *IEEE Transactions on Automatic Control*, 45(1):188–202, 2000.
8. G. Ferrari-Trecate, D. Mignone, and M. Morari. Moving horizon estimation for hybrid systems. *IEEE Transactions on Automatic Control*, 47(10):1663–1676, 2002.
9. G. Ferrari-Trecate, M. Muselli, D. Liberati, and M. Morari. A clustering technique for the identification of piecewise affine systems. *Automatica*, 39(2):205–217, 2003.
10. J. Harris. *Algebraic Geometry: A First Course*. Springer-Verlag, 1992.
11. A. Juloski, W. Heemels, and G. Ferrari-Trecate. Data-based hybrid modelling of the component placement process in pick-and-place machines. In *Control Engineering Practice*. To appear.
12. A. Juloski, S. Weiland, and M. Heemels. A Bayesian approach to identification of hybrid systems. In *IEEE Conf. on Decision & Control*, 2004.
13. K. Kanatani and C. Matsunaga. Estimating the number of independent motions for multibody motion segmentation. In *Asian Conf. on Computer Vision*, 2002.
14. H. Niessen and A.Juloski. Comparison of three procedures for identification of hybrid systems. In *Conference on Control Applications*, 2004.
15. V. Pavlovic, J. M. Rehg, T. J. Cham, and K. P. Murphy. A dynamic Bayesian network approach to figure tracking using learned dynamic models. In *Proc. of the Intl. Conf. on Comp. Vision*, pages 94–101, 1999.
16. J. K. Tugnait. Detection and estimation for abruptly changing systems. *Automatica*, 18(5):607–615, 1982.
17. D. Del Vecchio and R. Murray. Observers for a class of hybrid systems on a lattice. In *Hybrid Systems: Computation and Control.* 2004.
18. E.I. Verriest and B. De Moor. Multi-mode system identification. In *European Control Conference*, 1999.
19. R. Vidal. Identification of PWARX hybrid models with unknown and possibly different orders. In *IEEE Conf. on Decision & Control*, 2004.
20. R. Vidal and B.D.O. Anderson. Recursive identification of switched ARX hybrid models: Exponential convergence and persistence of excitation. In *CDC*, 2004.
21. R. Vidal, A. Chiuso, and S. Soatto. Observability and identifiability of jump linear systems. In *IEEE Conf. on Decision & Control*, pages 3614–3619, 2002.
22. R. Vidal, A. Chiuso, S. Soatto, and S. Sastry. Observability of linear hybrid systems. In *Hybrid Systems: Computation and Control*, pages 526–539. 2003.
23. R. Vidal, S. Soatto, Y. Ma, and S. Sastry. An algebraic geometric approach to the identification of a class of linear hybrid systems. In *Proceedings of CDC*, 2003.

Learning Multi-modal Control Programs

Tejas R. Mehta and Magnus Egerstedt

Georgia Institute of Technology,
School of Electrical and Computer Engineering,
Atlanta, GA 30332, USA
{tmehta, magnus}@ece.gatech.edu

Abstract. Multi-modal control is a commonly used design tool for breaking up complex control tasks into sequences of simpler tasks. In this paper, we show that by viewing the control space as a set of such tokenized instructions rather than as real-valued signals, reinforcement learning becomes applicable to continuous-time control systems. In fact, we show how a combination of state-space exploration and multi-modal control converts the original system into a finite state machine, on which Q-learning can be utilized.

1 Introduction

In this paper we study the problem of controlling complex systems through the decomposition of the control task into a sequence of control modes. Such a divide and conquer approach has proved useful in that it allows the control designer to construct a number of relatively simple control laws, rather than one complex law. Successful examples of this approach include flight mode control in avionics and behavior based control of autonomous robots.

The aim of this paper is to show that such multi-modal control design strategies allow us to use standard reinforcement learning techniques on previously computationally intractable problems, namely for continuous-time control systems, where the states and control signals take on values in uncountably large sets. To see how this can be done, it should be noted that reinforcement learning is readily applicable when the state space and the input set are finite sets and the system is event driven (e.g. finite state machines or Markov decision processes). See for example [9, 11, 16, 17].

However, by considering a finite number of feedback laws κ_i, $i = 1, \ldots, M$ (i.e. mappings from the state space to the input set), together with interrupts ξ_j, $j = 1, \ldots, N$, which are the conditions for the termination of the current mode, a finite quantization of the control space is obtained. Note that the control set itself is not quantized but rather that the quantization acts at a functional level. This observation takes care of the problem of quantizing the control inputs. Moreover, by adopting a Lebesque sampling strategy where a new state is sampled only when the interrupts trigger, the continuous time problem is transformed into an event-driven problem. The final piece of the puzzle is the

M. Morari and L. Thiele (Eds.): HSCC 2005, LNCS 3414, pp. 466–479, 2005.

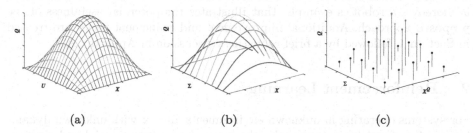

(a)   (b)   (c)

Fig. 1. Depicted is the progression from X and U being smooth manifolds (a) to the case when both the state space and the input set are finite (c) through the introduction of multi-modal control procedures and Lebesque sampling

observation that, given an initial state x_0 and a finite length multi-modal program, only a finite number of states are reachable. These ideas are illustrated in Figure 1, where the first figure corresponds to a case where the state space $X \sim \mathbb{R}^n$ and the input set $U \sim \mathbb{R}^m$. Depicted as a function of x and u is the so-called Q-function that characterizes the utility of using control input u at state x. In the next figure, U is replaced by Σ, which corresponds to a finite set of control-interrupt pairs. Without discretizing U, a finite control space is obtained by defining a finite set of available control modes. The final figure shows a situation where both the state space and the input space are finite. The input space is again given by Σ, while X^Q is the quantized state space obtained through an exploration of the states that are reachable from x_0 (in N steps) at the distinct times at which the interrupts may trigger.

To go from a continuous time control system to a finite state machine is certainly not a new idea. In particular, discretizations of the space-time domain are routinely used for establishing reachability properties. However, such discretizations do not reflect the underlying dynamics in any meaningful way. Alternatives are given in [2], where tokenized control symbols result in reachable lattices, and in [15], where LTL specifications are defined for a quantized system while guaranteeing that the specifications still hold for the original system. The idea of structured state space explorations was pursued in [1], where the reachable part of the state space was implicitly discretized using rapidly-exploring random trees. Additional results on motion description languages and tokenized control strategies can be found in [3, 6, 7, 8]. Moreover, it is not necessary to let the state space and input set be finite in order to apply learning techniques [14]. For example, a set of basis functions can be defines for supporting the Q-function such as sigmoids, wavelets, or Gaussian kernel functions. However, the computational burden associated with these methods of often prohibitive.

In this paper we will make these preliminary, informal observations rigorous, and the outline of the paper is as follows: In Section 2 we will discuss reinforcement learning for discrete event-driven systems and see how these techniques can be modified in order to incorporate multi-modal feedback strategies. In Sec-

tion 3 we switch our attention to continuous-time control systems, where the
state and control spaces are $\mathbb{R}^n$ and $\mathbb{R}^m$ respectively. Contained in this section
is moreover a robotics example, that illustrates the potential usefulness of the
proposed approach. Additional improvement and refinement issues are treated
in Section 4, followed by a brief robustness discussion in Appendix A.

2   Reinforcement Learning

For systems operating in unknown environments and/or with unknown dynamics, reinforcement learning provides the means for systematic trial-and-error interactions with the environment. Although the contribution of this paper is to
apply learning techniques to multi-modal hybrid systems, we will here briefly
cover the standard reinforcement-learning model.

2.1   Standard Reinforcement Learning

In the standard reinforcement-learning model, at each step (discrete time), the
agent chooses an action, $u \in U_F$, based on the current state, $x \in X_F$, of the
environment, where U_F and X_F are finite sets (Hence the subscript F). The
corresponding result is given by $x_{k+1} = \delta(x_k, u_k)$, where $\delta : X_F \times U_F \to X_F$
is the state transition function that encodes the system dynamics. Moreover,
a cost $c : X_F \times U_F \to \mathbb{R}$ is associated with taking action u at state x. The
agent should choose actions in order to minimize the overall cost. Given a policy
$\pi : X_F \to U_F$, the discounted cost that we wish to minimize is given by

$$V^\pi(x_0) = \sum_{k=0}^{\infty} \gamma^k c(x_k, \pi(x_k)),$$

where $\gamma \in (0, 1)$ is the discount factor and $x_{k+1} = \delta(x_k, \pi(x_k))$, $k = 0, 1, \ldots$
We will use $V^*(x)$ to denote the minimum discounted cost incurred if the
agent starts in state x and executes the optimal policy, denoted by π^*. In other
words, the optimal value function is defined through the Bellman equation

$$V^*(x) = \min_{u \in U_F} \left[c(x, u) + \gamma V^*(\delta(x, u)) \right], \forall x \in X_F.$$

This equation simply states that the optimal value is obtained by taking the
action that minimizes the instantaneous cost plus the remaining discounted cost.
Once V^* is known, the optimal policy, π^*, follows directly through

$$\pi^*(x) = \min_{u \in U_F} \left[c(x, u) + \gamma V^*(\delta(x, u)) \right],$$

which shows why knowing V^* is equivalent to knowing the optimal policy.
If we now let $Q^*(x, u)$ be the discounted cost for taking action u in state x
and then continuing to act optimally, we observe that $V^*(x) = min_u Q^*(x, u)$,
and therefore

$$Q^*(x, u) = c(x, u) + \gamma \min_{u' \in U_F} Q^*(\delta(x, u), u').$$

To find Q^*, we start by assigning a uniform value to every state-action pair, and then randomly select state-action pairs (x, u) and update the Q-table using the following Q-learning law

$$Q_k(x, u) := Q_{k-1}(x, u) + \alpha_k \left(c(x, u) + \gamma \min_{u' \in U_F} \left\{ Q_{k-1}(\delta(x, u), u') - Q_{k-1}(x, u) \right\} \right).$$

If each action is selected at each state an infinite number of times on an infinite run and α_k, the learning rate, is decayed appropriately, the Q values will converge to Q^* with probability 1. By appropriate decay of α_k we mean that $\sum_k \alpha_k = \infty$ while $\sum_k \alpha_k^2 < \infty$, hence decreasing the learning rate over time (e.g. $\alpha_k = 1/k$) will guarantee convergence. (For more details regarding reinforcement learning, see for example [9, 11, 14, 16, 17].)

2.2   Learning Control Programs

We now define a new input space that corresponds to tokenized descriptions of feedback laws and interrupts, as prescribed within the motion description language (MDL) framework. Instead of interacting with the environment at each step, the agent takes actions based on a feedback law κ, which is a function of the state x. The agent furthermore continues to act on the feedback control law κ until the interrupt ξ triggers, at which point a scalar cost is incurred.

Formally, let X_F and U_F be finite sets, as defined earlier, and let $\Sigma = K \times \Xi$, where $K \subseteq U_F{}^{X_F}$ (the set of all maps from X_F to U_F) and $\Xi \subseteq \{0, 1\}^{X_F}$. Moreover, let $\tilde{\delta} : X_F \times \Sigma \to X_F$ be the state transition mapping, $\tilde{x}_{k+1} = \tilde{\delta}(\tilde{x}_k, (\kappa_k, \xi_k))$, obtained through the following free-running, feedback mechanism [8]: Let $\tilde{x}_0 = x_0$ and evolve x according to $x_{k+1} = \delta(x_k, \kappa_0(x_k))$ until the interrupt triggers, i.e. $\xi_0(x_{k_0}) = 1$ for some index k_0. Now let $\tilde{x}_1 = x(k_0)$ and repeat the process, i.e. $x_{k+1} = \delta(x_k, \kappa_1(x_k))$ until $\xi_1(x_{k_1}) = 1$. Now let $\tilde{x}_2 = x(k_1)$, and so on. Also let $\zeta : X_F \times \Sigma \to \mathbb{R}$ be the cost associated with the transition.

We want to apply reinforcement learning to this model. To accomplish this we must make a few modifications. First, note that $card(\Sigma)$ is potentially much larger than $card(U_F)$, where $card(\cdot)$ denotes the cardinality. This directly affects the number of entries in our Q table. If all possible feedback laws and interrupts were available, the cardinality of the new input space would be $[2card(U_F)]^{card(X_F)}$ with obvious implications for the numerical tractability of the problem.

Second, in order to find Q^*, we start again by assigning a uniform value to every state-action pair, and then iteratively update the Q values by randomly selecting a state-action pair with the action comprising of one of the possible feedback laws in K and interrupts in Ξ. The consequent Q-learning law is

$$Q_k(x, (\kappa, \xi)) := Q_{k-1}(x, (\kappa, \xi))$$
$$+ \alpha_k \left(\zeta(x, (\kappa, \xi)) + \gamma \min_{(\kappa', \xi')} \left\{ Q_{k-1}(\tilde{\delta}(x, (\kappa, \xi)), (\kappa', \xi')) - Q_{k-1}(x, (\kappa, \xi)) \right\} \right).$$

Since Ξ and K are finite, the set of all possible modes Σ is finite as well. Hence the convergence results still hold, as long as each mode is selected for each state an infinite number of times, and α_k decays appropriately.

2.3   Example: Maze

Consider the problem of an agent navigating a $M \times M$ planar grid (we will let $M = 10$) with obstacles. For any of the M^2 possible positions, the agent can move either north (N), south (S), east (E), west (W), or not at all (ϵ). Each such action, except of course ϵ, advances the agent one step, and it is understood that there is a boundary along the perimeter of the grid that the agent can not cross. Moreover the agent can advance through obstacles even though a hefty cost is incurred whenever this happens. Starting from an arbitrary location, the agent needs to find the shortest path to a specified goal, while avoiding obstacles.

We can restate this problem as a reinforcement learning problem, where the agent must learn the optimal policy given the model of the environment. Formally, we have

- $x = (x_1, x_2)$, where $x_1, x_2 \in \{0, 1, 2, \ldots, M - 1\}$;
- $u \in \{N, S, E, W, \epsilon\}$;
- $\delta(x, u) = \begin{cases} (x_1, \min\{x_2 + 1, M - 1\}) & \text{if } u = N \\ (x_1, \max\{x_2 - 1, 0\}) & \text{if } u = S \\ (\min\{x_1 + 1, M - 1\}, x_2) & \text{if } u = E \\ (\max\{x_1 - 1, 0\}, x_2) & \text{if } u = W \\ (x_1, x_2) & \text{if } u = \epsilon \end{cases}$
- $c(x, u) = \begin{cases} 0 & \text{if } \delta(x, u) = x_{goal} \\ 100 & \text{if } \delta(x, u) \in \mathcal{O} \\ 1 & \text{otherwise} \end{cases}$

Here, x_{goal} is the goal state, while $\mathcal{O} \subset X$ is the set of obstacles. Using standard Q-learning, as previously described, the agent quickly learns the shortest path to the goal and the resulting simulation result is shown in Figure 2(a).

In this example, each input corresponds to one step in the maze. However, one could ask the question about the shortest mode string that makes the agent reach the goal, following the development in [8]. Unfortunately, the total number of feedback laws is $card(K) = card(U_F)^{card(X_F)}$, i.e. in this example we have 5^{100} possible control modes, which is a numerically intractably large number. Hence, we have to reduce the size of K, and our particular choice is the set of constant feedback laws, i.e. $K = \{\kappa_N, \kappa_S, \kappa_E, \kappa_W, \kappa_\epsilon\}$, where $\kappa_N(x) = N$, $\forall x \in X_F$, and so on. Similarly, we need to limit the size of the interrupt set, and we simply let Ξ be set of interrupts that trigger after m steps, $m = 1, 2, \ldots, N$. (We denote these interrupts by $\Xi = \{\xi_1, \ldots, \xi_N\}$.) In this case $card(\Xi) = N$, and for the particular problem we are interested in, we let $N = 9$ (since $M = 10$), so we need $9 \times 5 \times 100 = 4500$ entries in the Q-table. Note that, in order to keep track of the number of steps, the state space has to be augmented in a straightforward manner.

Now in order to find Q^*, and consequently the optimal policy, we start by assigning a uniform value to every state-action pair (recall we have 4500 possible such pairs). We then randomly select a state-action pair and update its Q-value according to the previously discussed, modified Q-learning law. The result of the simulation is shown in Figure 2(b). Note that this may not always be the

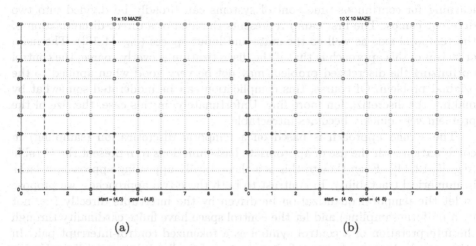

Fig. 2. Robot navigating through a maze using a standard reinforcement-learning model (left) and using modes with interrupts as the control set (right)

shortest path in terms of length (even though it happens to be the shortest in this particular case), but it is the optimal path in terms of the length of the mode string.

3   Learning Control Programs for Continuous Systems

Now that the discrete-time case with finite state and input spaces is covered, we shift focus to the main contribution of this paper, namely the solution to the problem of learning multi-modal control programs for continuous-time systems. Suppose we have the following system:

$$\dot{x} = f(x, u), \qquad x \in X = \mathbb{R}^n, \qquad u \in U = \mathbb{R}^m, \qquad \text{where } x(t_0) = x_0 \text{ is given.}$$

If at time t_0, the system receives the input string $\sigma = (\kappa_1, \xi_1), \ldots, (\kappa_q, \xi_q)$, where $\kappa_i : X \to U$ is the feedback control law, and $\xi_i : X \to \{0, 1\}$ is the interrupt, then x evolves according to

$$\dot{x} = f(x, \kappa_1(x)); \quad t_0 \leq t < \tau_1$$
$$\vdots \qquad\qquad \vdots$$
$$\dot{x} = f(x, \kappa_q(x)); \quad \tau_{q-1} \leq t < \tau_q,$$

where τ_i denotes the time when the interrupt ξ_i triggers (i.e. changes from 0 to 1).

We are interested in finding a sequence of control-interrupt pairs that minimizes a given cost for such a system. For example, we might be interested in driving the system to a certain part of the state space (e.g. to the origin), and penalize the final deviation from this target set. Previous work on reinforcement learning for continuous-time control systems can broadly be divided into two different camps. The first camp represents the idea of a direct discretization of the temporal axis as well as the state and input spaces (e.g. [4, 13]). The main criticism of this approach is that if the discretization is overly coarse, the control optimizing the discretized problem may not be very good when applied to the original problem. Of course, this complication can be moderated somewhat by making the discretization more fine. Unfortunately, in this case, the size of the problem very quickly becomes intractable.

The second approach is based on a temporal discretization (sampling) in combination with the use of appropriate basis functions to represent the Q-table (e.g. [5, 12, 14]). Even though this is a theoretically appealing approach, it lacks in numerical tractability. In contrast to both these two approaches, we propose to let the temporal quantization be driven by the interrupts directly (i.e. not by a uniform sampling) and let the control space have finite cardinality through the interpretation of a control symbol as a tokenized control-interrupt pair. In other words, by considering a finite number of feedback laws $\kappa_i : X \to U$, $i = 1, \ldots, M$, together with interrupts ξ_j, $j = 1, \ldots, N$, the control space (viewed at a functional level) is finite even though the actual control signals take on values in $\mathbb{R}^m$. Another effect of the finite mode-set assumption is that it provides a natural quantization of the state space. Moreover, if we bound the length of the mode sequences, this quantization is in fact resulting in a finite set of reachable states.

Given an input $\sigma = (\kappa, \xi) \in \Sigma$, where $\Sigma \subseteq U^X \times \{0,1\}^X$, the flow is given by

$$\phi(x_0, \sigma, t) = x_0 + \int_0^t f(x(s), \kappa(x(s)))ds.$$

If there exists a finite time $T \geq 0$ such that $\xi(\phi(x_0, \sigma, T)) = 1$, then we let the interrupt time be given by

$$\tau(\sigma, x_0) = min\{t \geq 0 \mid \xi(\phi(x_0, \sigma, t)) = 1\}.$$

If no such finite time T exists then we say that $\tau(\sigma, x_0) = \tau_\infty$ for some distinguishable symbol τ_∞. Furthermore, we let the final point on the trajectory generated by σ be

$$\chi(\sigma, x_0) = \phi(x_0, \sigma, \tau(\sigma, x_0))$$

if $\tau(\sigma, x_0) \neq \tau_\infty$ and use the notation $\chi(\sigma, x_0) = \chi_\infty$ otherwise. Moreover let $\chi(\sigma, \chi_\infty) = \chi_\infty, \forall \sigma \in \Sigma$.

This construction allows us to define the Lebesque sampled finite state machine $(X_N^Q, \Sigma, \tilde{\delta}, \tilde{x}_0)$, where N is the longest allowable mode string, and where the state transition is given by

$$\tilde{x}_0 = x_0$$
$$\tilde{x}_{k+1} = \tilde{\delta}(\tilde{x}_k, \sigma_k) = \chi(\sigma_k, \tilde{x}_k), k = 0, 1, \ldots$$

The state space X_N^Q is given by the set of all states that are reachable from $\tilde{x}_0$ using mode strings of length less than or equal to N.

Now that we have a finite state machine describing of the dynamics, we can run our learning algorithm, with an appropriate cost function, in order to obtain the optimal control program as discussed earlier. However, in order to preserve computing resources, we run this in parallel with the state exploration, and the general algorithm for accomplishing this is given by

$$\mathcal{X} := \{\tilde{x}_0, \tilde{\delta}(\tilde{x}_0, \sigma)\}, \ \forall \sigma \in \Sigma$$
$$step(\tilde{x}_0) := 0$$
$$step(\tilde{\delta}(\tilde{x}_0, \sigma)) := 1, \ \forall \sigma \in \Sigma$$
$$p := 1$$
$$Q_p(\tilde{x}, \sigma) := const \ \forall \tilde{x} \in \mathcal{X}, \sigma \in \Sigma$$
repeat
$$\quad p := p + 1$$
$$\quad \tilde{x} := rand(\chi \in \mathcal{X} \mid step(\chi) < N)$$
$$\quad \sigma := rand(\Sigma)$$
$$\quad \tilde{x}' := \tilde{\delta}(\tilde{x}, \sigma)$$
$$\quad \textbf{if } \tilde{x}' \notin \mathcal{X} \textbf{ then}$$
$$\quad\quad step(\tilde{x}') := step(\tilde{x}) + 1$$
$$\quad\quad \mathcal{X} := \mathcal{X} \cup \{\tilde{x}'\}$$
$$\quad\quad Q(\tilde{x}', \sigma) := const \ \forall \sigma \in \Sigma$$
$$\quad \textbf{end if}$$
$$\quad Q_p(\tilde{x}, \sigma) := Q_{p-1}(\tilde{x}, \sigma)$$
$$\quad\quad\quad + \alpha_p \Big(\zeta(\tilde{x}, \sigma) + \gamma \min_{\sigma' \in \Sigma} \big\{ Q_{p-1}(\tilde{x}', \sigma') - Q_{p-1}(\tilde{x}, \sigma) \big\} \Big)$$
until $mod(p, L) = 0 \ \ and \ \ |Q_p(\tilde{x}, \sigma) - Q_{p-L}(\tilde{x}, \sigma)| < \epsilon, \ \forall \tilde{x} \in \mathcal{X}, \sigma \in \Sigma$
$$X_N^Q = \mathcal{X}$$

Unlike the earlier Q-learning algorithm, the state space is initially unknown for this case, and we thus begin learning/exploring from the states we know (namely $\tilde{x}_0$ and all the states reachable in one step). At each iteration of the learning process, we select a state randomly from the set of known states and we select a mode randomly from the set of modes. In the algorithm, the function $step(\tilde{x})$ represents the length of the shortest control program used so far to reach state $\tilde{x}$ from the initial state $\tilde{x}_0$. This is to ensure we only explore states that are reachable from $\tilde{x}_0$ using mode strings of length less than or equal to N, i.e. $\mathcal{X} \subseteq X_N^Q$. We then calculate the next state and determine if it is a member of our known state space (In practice, it is necessary to check if the next state belongs to a neighborhood of a previously visited state). If not, add this state to the known state space and make the corresponding change in the Q-table. We continue to explore and update the state space and our Q-table (or value function) in this manner until the Q-table is stationary. Note that in the algorithm, $\epsilon > 0$ is a small positive scalar and L is a large number needed to ensure that sufficiently many state-action pairs are visited.

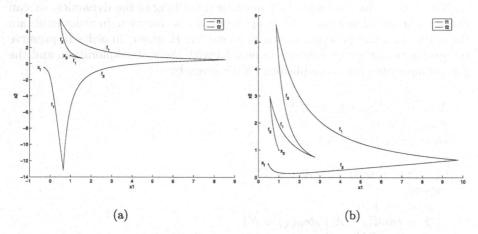

(a)   (b)

Fig. 3. In this example, $M = 1$ and $\delta = 0.75$ and the resulting optimal mode strings are (cost = final distance to the origin) $\hat{\sigma} = (\kappa_1, \xi_{13}) \cdot (\kappa_2, \xi_{25}) \cdot (\kappa_1, \xi_{15}) \cdot (\kappa_2, \xi_{23}) \cdot (\kappa_1, \xi_{15})$ (left) and (cost = final distance to the origin combined with total distance travelled) $\hat{\sigma} = (\kappa_2, \xi_{24}) \cdot (\kappa_1, \xi_{12}) \cdot (\kappa_1, \xi_{21}) \cdot (\kappa_2, \xi_{13}) \cdot (\kappa_1, \xi_{25})$ (right)

Fig. 4. Experimental setup

3.1   Example

Consider the following simple planar integrator system:

$$\dot{x} = u, \qquad x, u \in \mathbb{R}^2, \qquad x_0 = \begin{pmatrix} 1 \\ 1 \end{pmatrix}.$$

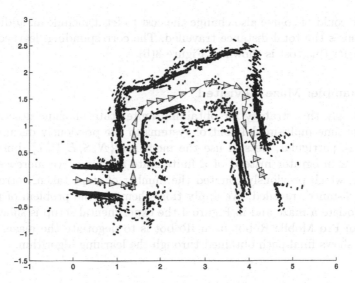

Fig. 5. The final trajectory. Depicted is the path of the robot together with the range sensor readings (IR-based) obtained throughout the final run. Note how the odometric drift makes the maze look somewhat distorted

Moreover, let the modes be given by $\Sigma = \{\sigma_{ij} = (\kappa_i, \xi_{ij}),\ i = 1, 2,\ j = 1, \ldots, 5\}$, where

$$\kappa_1(x) = \begin{pmatrix} 1 & 0.1 \\ 0 & -1 \end{pmatrix} x$$

$$\kappa_2(x) = \begin{pmatrix} -1 & 0 \\ -0.2 & 2 \end{pmatrix} x$$

$$\xi_{1j} = \begin{cases} 1 \text{ if } x_2^2 < M\delta^j \\ 0 \text{ otherwise} \end{cases}$$

$$\xi_{2j} = \begin{cases} 1 \text{ if } x_1^2 < M\delta^j \\ 0 \text{ otherwise} \end{cases}$$

$$for\ j = 1, 2, \ldots, 5,$$

where $M, \delta > 0$. Note that the system is unstable in either mode. We want to learn a mode string that will stabilize the system, i.e. drive it to the origin. Although it may not be possible to drive the system to $x = 0$ with these particular control-interrupt pairs, we want to select a string of modes which bring the system to a neighborhood of $x = 0$.

For the particular choice of modes, the reachable set has cardinality $2\sum_{i=0}^{N} 5^i$, where N is the maximum number of steps (or string length) and as can be expected, the cardinality of the state space increases exponentially with respect to the length of the control program. The resulting plot from solving the learning problem using the combined state space exploration and Q-learning is shown in Figure 3(a) in which $N = 5$ and the cost is given solely by the final distance to the origin. We could of course also change the cost to let it include an additive term that measures the total distance travelled. The corresponding, learned optimal trajectory for this cost is shown in Figure 3(b).

3.2   Example: Maze Revisited

We now apply this strategy for obtaining finite state machine descriptions of continuous time multi-modal control systems to the previously discussed maze problem. In particular, we still use the mode set $\{N, S, E, W, \epsilon\}$, but define it for a planar integrator instead of a finite state machine. We moreover let the interrupts, which previously counted the number of steps taken, correspond to a certain distance travelled. We apply this scheme to the problem of making a robot negotiate a maze and in Figure 4 the experimental setup is shown, where a Magellan Pro Mobile Robot from iRobot is to negotiate the maze. Figure 5 moreover shows final path obtained through the learning algorithm.

4   Refining the Learning Process

In this section we discuss some methods for enhancing the learning process. In particular, for problems with large state and input spaces (basically all interesting problems), the convergence is typically slow when using a purely random exploration strategy. However, it is well-known that one can use knowledge about the problem in order to speed up the learning process. The idea is to start out the learning process completely at random, but as the system gains "experience" the state space exploration becomes less and less random. In other words, we bias the selection of the state-action pairs to explore and update based on current values of the Q-table.

In order to formalize this, some notation is needed. We let $P(x, u)$ denote the probability of selecting state-action pair (x, u) from $X_F \times U_F$, with $\sum_{x \in X} \sum_{u \in U} P(x, u) = 1$. Initially we begin with

$$P_0(x, u) = \frac{1}{card(X) card(U)}.$$

In other words, every state-action pair has an equal likelihood of being selected. As we gain experience, we can change these probabilities to bias the selection in favor of state-action pairs with lower Q-values (potentially "good" state-action pairs). There may be many appropriate methods for biasing these probabilities, and one simple approach is to let the probability of selection state-action pair (x, u) be given by

$$P_k(x, u) = \frac{Q_{k-1}(x, u)}{\sum_{x' \in X_F} \sum_{u' \in U_F} Q_{k-1}(x', u')}.$$

Given such a biased probability distribution, we do not want to use it prematurely, for this may lead us to not learn the optimal policy. Instead we want to introduce a confidence value, $c \in [0, 1]$, which is based on the time step k and the past Q-values. With a lower value of c, the exploration strategy should be more random (i.e. use $P_0(x, u)$ when selecting a state-action pair), while higher value of c suggest using a more biased exploration strategy (i.e. use $P_k(x, u)$). Note that we still want to leave some amount of randomness in the selection process in order to ensure that the entire state and input space is explored. Hence, c should never equal 1. The degree of bias in the selection process and the necessary experience will vary from problem to problem.

Based on our knowledge of the problem we can also start pruning the state-space as we gain experience. This means that we could exclude states that we are certain are not part of the optimal trajectory. This reduction in the size of the state-space enables the learning process to converge faster since all the plausible state-action pairs can be selected more often. However, great caution and high degree of accuracy must be used when pruning the state-space to ensure that the optimal policy is still learned since incorrectly pruning a potentially useful state may mean that only a sub-optimal policy is learned.

5   Conclusions

In this paper we present a method for going from continuous time control systems to finite state machines in a structured manner. In particular, by only considering a finite number of modes, i.e. control-interrupt pairs, the input space is finite and the continuous time dynamics has been replaced by a Lebesque sampled, discrete time system. Moreover, by only allowing mode strings of a certain length, the reachable state space (at the interrupt times) is finite as well. This construction means that previously unavailable computational methods, such as reinforcement learning, are now applicable in a straight forward manner.

Acknowledgements

This work was sponsored by the National Science Foundation through the program ECS NSF-CAREER award (grant # 0237971).

References

1. A. Bhatia, and E. Frazzoli. Incremental Search Methods for Reachability Analysis of Continuous and Hybrid Systems. *Hybrid Systems: Computation and Control. Springer-Verlag*, 2004.
2. A. Bicchi, A. Marigo, and B. Piccoli. On the reachability of quantized control systems. *IEEE Transactions on Automatic Control*, 4(47):546-563, April 2002.
3. A. Bicchi, A. Marigo, and B. Piccoli. Encoding steering control with symbols. *IEEE International Conference on Decision and Control*, pages 3343-3348, 2003.
4. S.J. Bradtke, B.E. Ydstie, and A.G. Barto. Adaptive linear quadratic control using policy iteration. *American Control Conference*, pages 3475-3479, 1994.

5. L. Crawford, and S.S. Sastry. Learning Controllers for Complex Behavioral Systems. *Neural Information Processing Systems Tenth Annual Conference(NIPS 96)*, 1996.
6. M. Egerstedt. On the Specification Complexity of Linguistic Control Procedures. *International Journal of Hybrid Systems*, Vol. 2, No. 1-2, pp. 129-140, March & June, 2002.
7. M. Egerstedt, and D. Hristu-Varsakelis. Observability and Policy Optimization for Mobile Robots. *IEEE Conference on Decision and Control, Las Vegas, NV*, Dec. 2002.
8. M. Egerstedt, and R.W. Brockett. Feedback Can Reduce the Specification Complexity of Motor Programs. *IEEE Transactions on Automatic Control*, Vol. 48, No. 2, pp. 213–223, Feb. 2003
9. T. Jaakkola, M.I. Jordan, and S.P. Singh. On the Convergence of stochastic iterative dynamic programming algorithms. *Neural Computation* 6(6), 1994.
10. L.P. Kaebling, M.L. Littman, and A.R. Cassandra. Learning Policies for Partially Observable Environments: Scaling Up. *Proceedings of the Twelfth International Conference on Machine Learning*, 1995.
11. L.P. Kaebling, M.L. Littman, and A.W. Moore. Reinforcement learning: A survey. *Journal Of Artificial Intelligence Research*, 1996.
12. K. Morgansen, and R.W. Brockett. Optimal Regulation and Reinforcement Learning for the Nonholonomic Integrator. *Proceedings of the American Control Conference*, pp. 462-6, June 2000
13. R.S. Sutton. Generalization in Reinforcement Learning: Successful Examples Using Sparse Coarse Coding. *Neural Information Processing Systems 8*, 1996.
14. R.S. Sutton, and A.G. Barto. *Reinforcement Learning, An Introduction*. MIT Press, Cambridge, MA, 1998.
15. P. Tabuada and G. Pappas. Model Checking LTL over Controllable Linear Systems is Decidable. *Hybrid Systems: Computation and Control*, Springer-Verlag, Prague, Czech Republic, 2003.
16. J.N. Tsitsiklis. Asynchronous stochastic approximation and Q-learning. *Machine Learning*, 16(3), 1994.
17. C.J.C.H. Watkins, and P. Dayan. Q-learning. *Machine Learning* 8(3/4):257-277, May 1992.

Appendix A.   Robustness Analysis

Note that the entire argument presented in this paper concerning the finite state space model hinges on the fact that we start from a fixed initial state. In this section we will conduct a sensitivity analysis to show that if the mode string $\hat{\sigma}$ is optimal when starting at x_0, it is in fact still optimal for $\tilde{x}_0 = x_0 + \Delta x_0$, for some small perturbation Δx_0. It is sufficient to show that if x_0 is perturbed a little, then $\tilde{x}_f$, the point obtained after executing $\hat{\sigma}$ from $\tilde{x}_0$, lies within a small neighborhood of x_f, i.e. we need to show that $\Delta x_f = x_f - \tilde{x}_f$ is small.

In order to simplify the notation, we let the interrupt surfaces be encoded by smooth functions $g_i(x) = 0$, i.e. $\xi_i(x) = 1$ when $g_i(x) = 0$ and $\xi_i(x) = 0$ otherwise. Also, the trajectory of x is given by $x(t) = \Phi_1(t, t_0)$ until $g_1(x) = 0$. Then it is given by $x(t) = \Phi_2(t, \tau_1)$ until $g_2(x) = 0$, and so on. Here Φ_i is the state-transition function associated with $\dot{x} = f(x, \kappa_i(x))$, and τ_i is the time that interrupt ξ_i triggers, i.e. $g_i(x(\tau_i)) = 0$. Moreover we will denote this point $x_{h_i} = x(\tau_i)$. So for $t \in [0, \tau_1)$, we get

$$\dot{\tilde{x}} = f_1(\tilde{x}, u) = f_1(x + \Delta x_0, u)$$
$$= f_1(x, u) + \frac{\partial f_1}{\partial x} \Delta x_0 + o(\Delta x).$$

Hence,

$$\dot{\Delta x} = \frac{\partial f_1}{\partial x} \Delta x_0 + o(\Delta x),$$

meaning that for $t \in [0, \tau_1)$, $\Delta x(t) = \Phi_1(t, t_0)\Delta x_0 + o(\Delta x)$. To examine the trajectory after the interrupt, we have to calculate the change in the interrupt time τ_1 and the position at this time, namely x_{h_1}. Again, using the first order approximation, we get

$$\tilde{x}(\tau_1 + \Delta\tau_1) = x(\tau_1 + \Delta\tau_1) + \Delta x(\tau_1 + \Delta\tau_1)$$
$$= x(\tau_1) + f_1(x(\tau_1))\Delta\tau_1 + \Delta x(\tau_1) + o(\Delta\tau_1).$$

Here $t = \tau_1 + \Delta\tau_1$ is the time that the trajectory of $\tilde{x}$ hits the interrupt surface, so we must have

$$g_1(\tilde{x}(\tau_1 + \Delta\tau_1)) = 0,$$

which implies that

$$g_1(x(\tau_1)) + \frac{\partial g_1}{\partial x}(x(\tau_1))\left[f_1(x(\tau_1))\Delta\tau_1\right] + \frac{\partial g_1}{\partial x}(x(\tau_1))\Delta x(\tau_1) + o(\Delta\tau_1) = 0.$$

Letting $L_{f_1}g_1(x(\tau)) := \frac{\partial g_1}{\partial x}(x(\tau_1))\left[f_1(x(\tau_1))\Delta\tau_1\right]$, which is the Lie derivative of g_1 along f_1, and assuming that this quantity is non-zero, we get

$$\Delta\tau_1 = \frac{\frac{\partial g_1}{\partial x}(x(\tau_1))\Phi_1(\tau_1, t_0)\Delta x_0}{L_{f_1}g_1(x(\tau_1))},$$

where we have ignored higher order terms. Hence,

$$\Delta x_{h_1} = \tilde{x}(\tau_1 + \Delta\tau_1)$$
$$= \left[I - \frac{f_1\frac{\partial g_1}{\partial x}(x(\tau_1))}{L_{f_1}g_1(x(\tau_1))}\right]\Phi_1(\tau_1, t_0)\Delta x_0.$$

Now, based on the assumption that $L_{f_1}g_1(x(\tau_1)) \neq 0$ (i.e. the interrupt triggers non-tangentially), Δx_{h_1} is small. Similarly we get that Δx_{h_2} is small under the assumption that $L_{f_2}g_2(x(\tau_2)) \neq 0$. Continuing in this manner, we deduce that Δx_f will be small as long as $L_{f_i}g_i(x(\tau_i)) \neq 0$, for $i = 1, \ldots, M$, and the result follows.

A Toolbox of Hamilton-Jacobi Solvers for Analysis of Nondeterministic Continuous and Hybrid Systems

Ian M. Mitchell[1] and Jeremy A. Templeton[2]

[1] Department of Computer Science, University of British Columbia,
2366 Main Mall, Vancouver, BC, Canada V6T 1Z4
mitchell@cs.ubc.ca
http://www.cs.ubc.ca/~mitchell
[2] Department of Mechanical Engineering, Stanford University,
Bldg. 500, Stanford, CA, 94305
temple@stanford.edu
http://www.stanford.edu/~temple

Abstract. Hamilton-Jacobi partial differential equations have many applications in the analysis of nondeterministic continuous and hybrid systems. Unfortunately, analytic solutions are seldom available and numerical approximation requires a great deal of programming infrastructure. In this paper we describe the first publicly available toolbox for approximating the solution of such equations, and discuss three examples of how these equations can be used in system analysis: cost to go, stochastic differential games, and stochastic hybrid systems. For each example we briefly summarize the relevant theory, describe the toolbox implementation, and provide results.

1 Introduction

Hamilton-Jacobi (HJ) *partial differential equations* (PDEs) have a long history in optimal control and zero sum differential games; for example, see [1, 2, 3]. Unfortunately, analytic solutions of these equations can rarely be found for systems with nonlinear dynamics, and numerical approximation of such solutions requires development of a significant code base to support tasks such as gridding, initial conditions, approximation of spatial and temporal derivatives, temporal integration and visualization.

Until now, no such collection of code was publicly available. In the next section, we briefly describe the Toolbox of Level Set Methods, which the first author has released [4] and which contains the algorithms necessary to approximate solutions of a broad class of time-dependent HJ PDEs. We have previously described methods whereby these PDEs can be used to find reach sets for hybrid and continuous systems [5, 6], and the toolbox documentation [7] examines several of these computations in detail.

The remainder of this paper discusses three different examples of how the HJ PDE can be used to analyze nondeterministic continuous and hybrid systems:

M. Morari and L. Thiele (Eds.): HSCC 2005, LNCS 3414, pp. 480–494, 2005.

cost to go, stochastic differential games for continuous systems, and hybrid systems with stochastic switching between discrete modes. The underlying system dynamics may be nonlinear in all cases. By nondeterminism, we mean more than just stochastic perturbations to the system dynamics. While the latter two examples do include stochastic continuous evolution governed by Brownian motion and stochastic discrete evolution governed by Poisson point processes respectively, the first two examples also include bounded input parameters whose probabilistic distribution is unspecified. Such nondeterministic input parameters are typically used to model best-case control and/or worst-case disturbance in a robust fashion.

Approximations are computed by the toolbox on a Cartesian grid of the state space, and hence these algorithms are subject to the curse of dimensionality: costs rise exponentially with the dimension of the system. In practice, systems of dimensions 1–3 can be examined interactively, while dimensions 4–5 are slow but feasible.

Despite this limitation on dimension, we feel that the toolbox and the techniques described below may prove useful in at least three ways. First, as a pedagogical tool for exploring optimal control and differential games in nonlinear settings—until now examples of such methods have been extremely simplistic because of the difficulty in finding analytic solutions. Second, as a method for checking the results of faster but more specialized algorithms and solutions; for example, the reduced order solution of a TCP transmission rate model proposed in [8] and validated in section 5. Finally, there are some systems of interest which are of sufficiently low dimension to be directly analyzed, such as the aforementioned TCP transmission rate model, or simple mobile robots.

2   The Toolbox of Level Set Methods

Level set methods are a collection of numerical algorithms for approximating the solution of time-dependent HJ PDEs. The Toolbox of Level Set Methods implements many of the basic level set algorithms in MATLAB[1] for any number of dimensions. Visualization, scripting and debugging tools are provided by MATLAB, and no additional toolboxes are required. Source code (in the form of m-files) and documentation are provided [4, 7]. The algorithms on which the toolbox is based are taken primarily from [9].

2.1   The Equations

The toolbox is designed to compute approximations of certain types of *time-dependent* HJ PDEs, a class of equations whose most general form is

$$D_t\varphi(x,t) + G(x,t,\varphi,D_x\varphi,D_x^2\varphi) = 0, \tag{1}$$

---

[1] MATLAB is a product and trademark of The Mathworks Incorporated of Natick, Massachusetts. For more details see http://www.mathworks.com/products/matlab/. The level set toolbox described in this document was developed by the first author, and is neither endorsed by nor a product of The Mathworks.

subject to bounded and continuous initial conditions $\varphi(x,0) = g(x)$ and the monotonicity requirement [10]

$$G(x,t,r,p,\mathbf{X}) \leq G(x,t,s,p,\mathbf{Y}), \text{ whenever } r \leq s \text{ and } \mathbf{Y} \leq \mathbf{X}, \tag{2}$$

where $\mathbf{X}$ and $\mathbf{Y}$ are symmetric matrices of appropriate dimension. Since the initial conditions may not satisfy (1), they are the limit as $t \to 0$ of the solution $\varphi(x,t)$. This PDE is also sometimes called *first order hyperbolic* (if there is no $D_x^2\varphi$ term) or *degenerate parabolic* (if the term involving $D_x^2\varphi$ is not of full rank). Unless G is linear and of full rank in the highest order derivative which is present, even with smooth initial conditions φ may not remain differentiable and hence (1) will have no classical solution. The appropriate weak solution for the problems studied below is the viscosity solution [11], and the algorithms of the toolbox are designed to approximate this solution.

A key feature of the viscosity solution of (1) is that under suitable conditions φ remains bounded and continuous for all time. This property may not hold for other types of HJ PDE, such as some instances of the minimum time to reach function examined in section 3. The algorithms in the toolbox make use of the continuity assumption to achieve improved accuracy. The terms presently implemented in the toolbox, and the constraints placed on the dynamics—essentially boundedness and continuity—are designed to maintain this assumption.

Although we focus below on methods of analysing continuous and hybrid systems with HJ PDEs, these equations have many other applications including dynamic implicit surfaces, fluid simulation, image processing, financial mathematics, and resource management [9, 12, 13].

2.2   Using the Toolbox

The specific forms of (1) currently implemented by the toolbox and discussed further below are

$$0 = D_t\varphi(x,t) \tag{3}$$
$$+ v(x,t) \cdot \nabla\varphi(x,t) \tag{4}$$
$$+ H(x,t,\varphi,\nabla\varphi) \tag{5}$$
$$- \text{trace}[\mathbf{L}(x,t)D_x^2\varphi(x,t)\mathbf{R}(x,t)] \tag{6}$$
$$+ \lambda(x,t)\varphi(x,t) \tag{7}$$
$$+ F(x,t,\varphi), \tag{8}$$

potentially subject to constraints

$$D_t\varphi(x,t) \geq 0, \qquad\qquad D_t\varphi(x,t) \leq 0, \tag{9}$$
$$\varphi(x,t) \leq \psi(x,t), \qquad\qquad \varphi(x,t) \geq \psi(x,t), \tag{10}$$

where $x \in \mathbb{R}^d$ is the d dimensional state, $\varphi : \mathbb{R}^d \times \mathbb{R} \to \mathbb{R}$ is the level set function, $\nabla\varphi(x,t) = D_x\varphi(x,t)$ is the gradient or vector of first partial derivatives of φ, and $D_x^2\varphi(x,t)$ is the Hessian matrix of second partial derivatives of φ. Note that the time derivative (3) and at least one term involving a spatial derivative (4)–(6) must appear, otherwise the equation is not a time-dependent HJ PDE. While the toolbox includes other types of terms, these are the ones most relevant to analysis of nondeterministic continuous and hybrid systems, so we restrict our exposition to them. Other types of terms are described in the toolbox documentation [7]. We now discuss the application(s) of each of these terms in system analysis.

Motion by a constant velocity field (4) is used for solving Hamilton-Jacobi equations for systems without input parameters. The velocity field v : $\mathbb{R}^d \times \mathbb{R} \to \mathbb{R}^d$ must be continuous, and describes the deterministic trajectories $\dot{x} = v(x,t)$ of the system to be analyzed. This term is essentially a special case of the next one. Although not discussed in detail, the example in section 5 uses this term for its continuous evolution.

General Hamilton-Jacobi terms (5) can be used for any first order spatially dependent term that is continuous in x and t, satisfies the monotonicity requirement (2) with respect to φ, and is homogenous of degree one in $\nabla\varphi(x,t)$. Such terms arise in optimal control and zero sum differential games [14]. The examples in sections 3 and 4 make use of this term.

The trace of the Hessian (6), which arises in Kolmogorov or Fokker-Plank equations when working with stochastic differential equations [12]. The matrices $\mathbf{L}$ and $\mathbf{R}$ must be continuous. This term appears in the PDEs in section 4.

Discounting terms (7), which arise in some types of optimal control problems [2] and in hybrid systems with nondeterminism arising from continuous Markov chain-like switching between discrete modes [8]. The discount factor $\lambda : \mathbb{R}^d \times \mathbb{R} \to [0, +\infty)$ must be continuous in x and t. Section 5 examines the communication network model from [8], where λ can be thought of as the rate of switching between modes.

Forcing terms (8), a catch-all for any part of the PDE that is independent of the derivatives of φ. The forcing function must be continuous in x and t and satisfy (2) with respect to φ. In a hybrid system analysis—such as the communication model in section 5—we solve a collection of HJ PDEs, one PDE for each mode of the hybrid system. In this case, (8) can be used for components of one mode's PDE that depend on the value of another mode's solution. However, its use must be carefully considered. Although it may look like the correct way to handle a running cost in a cost to go type example, section 3 demonstrates an alternative formulation that does not require a forcing term and maintains continuity of φ, even if the resulting cost to go is not continuous.

Constraints on the sign of the temporal derivative of φ (9). Such constraints impose the condition that the implicit surface represented by the level sets of φ should not grow or should not shrink. These constraints are used in continuous reach set computations [5, 6].

Constraints on the value of φ (10), via the externally supplied continuous function $\psi : \mathbb{R}^d \times \mathbb{R} \to \mathbb{R}$. In hybrid system analysis, such constraints arise in finding reach-avoid sets [5].

The toolbox is written as a collection of components, so the process of computing an approximate solution to an HJ PDE consists of choosing the appropriate components, providing appropriate parameters, calling a single function, and visualizing the results. Part of the goal of the toolbox's design is to emulate the experience of using MATLAB's ordinary differential equation (ODE) solvers as closely as possible, although the complexity of PDEs means that more parameters must be provided and few defaults are available. Consequently, we recommend that modification of and/or cutting and pasting from one or more of the many documented examples is the best way to proceed when analyzing a new system.

Among the parameters that the user must provide are a grid for the computational domain, initial conditions for φ, order of accuracy of derivative approximations, types of terms (4)–(10), and any parameters needed by those terms. The toolbox download [4] includes the source m-files for each of the components. Source codes for all of the examples presented in this paper are also available at the same web site, some as part of the base toolbox download and some as separate downloads. Users are encouraged to modify or add components if the available ones do not cover the case of interest; for example, the input dependent stochastic term mentioned at the end of section 4.

Hybrid systems are not directly supported by the toolbox, because there is no consistent modeling language or notation for general nondeterministic, nonlinear hybrid systems. Until such time as one is available, we hope that the example in section 5 and those in [7] make clear that analysis of such systems using the toolbox is still quite feasible even if the discrete dynamics must coded by hand.

3   Cost to Go

For our first example, we look at a *time-independent* HJ PDE, also called a *stationary* [6] or *degenerate elliptic* [10] equation. Consider a closed target set $\mathcal{T}$ for a system evolving according to dynamics $\dot{x} = f(x, b)$. The single input parameter $b \in \mathcal{B}$, where $\mathcal{B} \subset \mathbb{R}^{d_b}$ is compact and $b(\cdot) : [0, T] \to \mathcal{B}$ is measurable, is attempting to minimize the cost to go to arrive at the target

$$\vartheta(x) = \min_{b(\cdot)} \int_0^T \ell(x(t), b(t)) dt, \tag{11}$$

where the running cost $\ell(x, b) > 0$ is continuous and $T = \min\{t \geq 0 \mid x(t) \in \mathcal{T}\}$ is the time of arrival at the target set. If $\ell \equiv 1$, then $\vartheta(x)$ is the minimum time to reach function.

Following standard procedures [2] it can be shown that the cost to go function is the viscosity solution of the time-independent HJ PDE

$$\begin{aligned}
\hat{H}(x, D_x \vartheta(x)) &= \ell(x, b) &&\text{in } \mathbb{R}^d \setminus \mathcal{T}, \\
\vartheta(x) &= 0 &&\text{on } \partial \mathcal{T}, \\
\hat{H}(x, p) &= \min_{b \in \mathcal{B}} p \cdot f(x, b).
\end{aligned} \tag{12}$$

Clearly this PDE is not of a form directly supported by the toolbox—it does not even contain a temporal derivative. However, following [15] we can solve an auxiliary time-dependent HJ PDE using the toolbox and extract an approximation of the solution to (12). To summarize those results, let

$$G(x, \vartheta(x), \nabla\vartheta(x)) = 0 \quad \text{in } \mathbb{R}^d \setminus \mathcal{T},$$
$$\vartheta(x) = 0 \quad \text{on } \partial\mathcal{T}, \tag{13}$$

be a general first order stationary HJ PDE, and assume that the boundary conditions are noncharacteristic

$$\sum_{i=1}^{d} p_i \frac{\partial G(x, \vartheta, p)}{\partial p_i} \neq 0 \text{ on } \partial\mathcal{T}. \tag{14}$$

A time-dependent HJ PDE is found by making the changes of variables

$$\vartheta(x) \leftarrow t \quad \text{and} \quad \nabla\vartheta(x) \leftarrow \frac{\nabla\varphi(x,t)}{D_t\varphi(x,t)}$$

in (13) and algebraic manipulation of the resulting equation into the form

$$D_t\varphi(x,t) + H(x, t, \nabla\varphi(x,t)) = 0, \tag{15}$$

where (14) ensures that this manipulation is locally feasible. The corresponding initial conditions are $\varphi(x,0) = 0$ on $\partial\mathcal{T}$, $\varphi(x,0) < 0$ inside $\mathcal{T}$ and $\varphi(x,0) > 0$ on $\mathbb{R}^d \setminus \mathcal{T}$, with $\varphi(x,0)$ a continuous and strictly monotone function of distance to $\mathcal{T}$ near its boundary. Typically $\varphi(x,0)$ is chosen as a signed distance function for $\mathcal{T}$.

Returning to the cost to go example, we find that the transformation process described above leads to the time-dependent HJ PDE (15) with Hamiltonian

$$H(x, t, p) = \min_{b \in \mathcal{B}} \frac{p \cdot f(x, b)}{\ell(x, b)}, \tag{16}$$

which is solved using a combination of terms (3) and (5) from the toolbox. The condition (14) in this case requires that $\nabla\varphi(x,0) \cdot f(x,b) \neq 0$ on $\partial\mathcal{T}$, which is equivalent to requiring that the vector field f not be tangent to the target set.

As a concrete example, we consider the minimum time to reach the origin for a double integrator [16, 17]. The two dimensions are position x_1 and velocity x_2. The system parameters are

$$f(x, b) = \begin{bmatrix} x_2 \\ b \end{bmatrix}, \quad \mathcal{T} = \left\{ \begin{bmatrix} 0 \\ 0 \end{bmatrix} \right\},$$
$$\ell(x, b) = 1, \quad \mathcal{B} = [-1, +1],$$
$$\varphi(x, 0) = \|x\|_2.$$

After solving (15), we set

$$\vartheta(x) = \{t \mid \varphi(x, t) = 0\}. \tag{17}$$

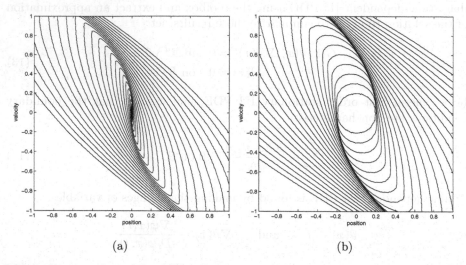

$$\text{(a)} \qquad\qquad\qquad\qquad \text{(b)}$$

Fig. 1. Contour plots of the minimum time to reach a target at the origin for a double integrator with unit magnitude input. The largest contour represents a time to reach of 2.4. In figure 1(a), the target is the origin. In figure 1(b), the target is the circle of radius 0.2 centered at the origin

In practice, $\vartheta(x)$ is constructed during the integration of (15) so that the entire time history of φ need not be stored at once. Figure 1(a) shows a contour plot of $\vartheta(x)$.

Interestingly, in this particular case (cost to go with no discount), it is possible to derive the same HJ PDE (15) with Hamiltonian (16) starting from the reach set theory [6], but without the noncharacteristic assumption (14). The resulting φ function is still continuous in time and space, but it may be constant with respect to t at fixed x; consequently, we cannot uniquely define ϑ using (17). Choosing $\vartheta(x) = \min\{t \mid \varphi(x,t) = 0\}$ is a reasonable alternative, although this ϑ will no longer be continuous (and hence the standard viscosity solution theory does not apply). Figure 1(b) shows a contour plot of such a ϑ for $\mathcal{T} = \{x \mid \|x\|_2 \le 0.2\}$. The contour lines of the approximation become very tightly packed along the curves where the analytic ϑ is discontinuous.

A variety of different algorithms have been more recently proposed for approximating minimum time to reach, cost to go or general stationary HJ PDE solutions for systems with inputs and nonlinear dynamics [18, 19, 20, 21]. Because the explicit time-dependent solvers of the toolbox are timestep restricted by a CFL condition, it is likely that the method described above is the slowest of the algorithms. However, it is quite general—although not derived above, this method works for zero sum differential games, where (11) and (16) are modified to include a maximization over an input $a \in \mathcal{A}$ which may appear in both the dynamics f and the running cost ℓ. The resulting Hamiltonian is nonconvex in $\nabla\varphi$. Furthermore, because the function φ on which derivative approximations are taken is continuous, this algorithm has the potential for better accuracy than those methods which depend on differentiating the sometimes discontinuous ϑ function directly. Quantitative comparisons are challenging, because implementations of the other algorithms are not publicly available at the present time.

4   Stochastic Continuous Systems

The nondeterminism in the previous example was entirely due to input parameter b (and possibly a) whose value is bounded (and measurable with respect to time), but otherwise unconstrained. Another class of nondeterminism which appears often in models involves parameters whose values are drawn probabilistically from some distribution. A popular model of system evolution in such cases is the *stochastic differential equation* (SDE)

$$dx(t) = f(x(t), t, a, b)dt + \sigma(x(t), t)dB(t), \qquad x(t_0) = x_0, \qquad (18)$$

where $B(t)$ is a Brownian motion process of appropriate dimension, the *drift* term f represents the deterministic component of the system evolution, and the *diffusion* term $\sigma dB(t)$ represents the probabilistic component of the system evolution. The functions f and σ must be continuous in x and t. If present, the input parameters a and/or b are treated the same manner as in the previous section. We interpret (18) in the Itô sense [12].

The mechanism by which we analyze the behavior of the system is the *stochastic differential game* (SDG), whose expected cost is defined as

$$\varphi(x_0, t_0) = E\left[\inf_{b(\cdot)} \sup_{a(\cdot)} \left(\int_{t_0}^{T} \ell(x(s), s, a(s), b(s))ds + g(x(T))\right)\right], \qquad (19)$$

where the finite horizon T is a constant. The order of the optimization can be swapped, and if the optimal choice of the outer input (b in this case) depends on the choice of the inner input (a in this case), then a suitable definition of nonanticipative strategies must be introduced [14]. The running cost ℓ and terminal cost g should be continuous in their parameters. The theory of first order viscosity solutions was extended [22,23] to determine that this expected cost is the viscosity solution of the second order PDE

$$D_t\varphi(x, t) + H(x, t, \nabla\varphi(x, t)) + \tfrac{1}{2}\operatorname{trace}\left[\sigma(x, t)\sigma^T(x, t)D_x^2\varphi(x, t)\right] = 0. \qquad (20)$$

with Hamiltonian

$$H(x, t, p) = \max_{a \in \mathcal{A}} \min_{b \in \mathcal{B}} \left[p \cdot f(x, t, a, b) + \ell(x, t, a, b)\right], \qquad (21)$$

and terminal conditions $\varphi(x, T) = g(x)$. If the order of the optimization in (19) was swapped, so is the order of the optimization in (21). Transformation of (20) into an initial value problem is accomplished by the change of variables $t \leftarrow T - t$. Provided that the user can perform the static optimization in (21) for fixed x, t and p, the initial value version of (20) can be solved in the toolbox by combining terms (3), (5) and (6).

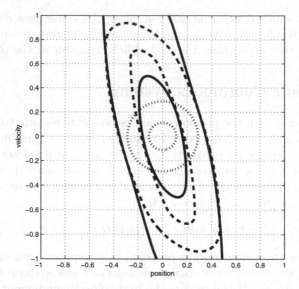

Fig. 2. Expected cost contours for the double integrator with stochastic viscosity. Dotted lines show the 0.1 (inner circle) and 0.9 (outer circle) terminal cost contours. Dashed lines show the same contours of the expected cost at $T-t=0.5$ for the system without stochastic viscosity. Solid lines show the expected cost at the same time for the system with stochastic viscosity

As a quantitative example we return to the double integrator, but this time impose a stochastically varying force whose standard deviation is proportional to the velocity (akin to a stochastically varying viscosity)

$$dx(t) = \begin{bmatrix} x_2 \\ b - k_1 x_2 \end{bmatrix} dt - \begin{bmatrix} 0 \\ k_2 x_2 \end{bmatrix} dB(t).$$

The goal of the input will be to drive the system to the origin. To reward terminal states close to the origin and penalize those further away, we use a terminal cost criterion that is near zero close to the origin, and grows quickly and smoothly towards one as distance increases. Mathematically,

$$\varphi(x,T) = g(x) = 1 - \left[1 + \exp\left(\frac{\|x\|_2 - \rho}{\epsilon \rho} \right) \right]^{-1},$$

where smaller ρ encourages the system closer to the origin, and smaller ϵ narrows the region where the cost changes from zero to one. The parameters chosen for simulation are

$$\ell(x,t,b) = 0, \qquad \mathcal{B} = [-1,+1],$$
$$k_1 = 0.5, \quad k_2 = 1.0,$$
$$\rho = 0.2, \qquad \epsilon = 0.2.$$

Results shown in figure 2 compare the expected cost at $T - t = 0.5$ with (k_2 as above) and without ($k_2 = 0$) stochastic viscosity. Note that the region expected to achieve very low cost ($\varphi(x,t) \leq 0.1$) shrinks when $k_2 > 0$, but the region able to achieve at least some cost reduction ($\varphi(x,t) \leq 0.9$) grows.

The theory [22, 23] is more general than (18) would imply—it allows σ to depend on differential game inputs a and b as well; for example, perhaps the noise is multiplicative in the inputs. The resulting HJ PDE includes optimization over a and b on a single term containing both $\nabla\varphi$ and $D_x^2\varphi$. The toolbox does not presently support such a term, but one could be added.

5   Stochastic Hybrid Systems

For our final application of the toolbox, we choose an example from the growing theory of stochastic hybrid systems. In particular, we take a model of the transmission window size for the Transmission Control Protocol (TCP) that handles reliable end-to-end delivery of packets between computers on the Internet [8]. In this model a continuous approximation of the window size evolves deterministically in one of several modes of the hybrid system, but jumps stochastically between the modes at a state-dependent rate.

Following [24] a *stochastic hybrid system* (SHS) for a set of discrete modes $q \in Q$ and continuous states $x \in \mathbb{R}^d$ is defined by a continuous differential equation $\dot{x} = f(q,x,t)$, a collection of m discrete transition maps $(q,x) = \phi_j(q^-, x^-, t)$ for $j = 1,\ldots,m$, and for each transition map a continuous $\lambda_j(q,x,t) \geq 0$ that can be thought of as a transition rate for that map.

If the resets ϕ_j are identity maps with respect to the continuous state $(q,x) = \phi_j(q^-, x, t)$, it is relatively straightforward to derive a Kolmogorov or Fokker-Planck like PDE for this system

$$D_t\varphi(q,x,t) + \nabla\varphi(q,x,t) \cdot f(q,x,t)$$
$$+ \sum_{j=1}^{m} \lambda_j(q,x,t)\left(\varphi(\phi_j(q,x,t),t) - \varphi(q,x,t)\right) = 0 \tag{22}$$

This PDE can be solved with the toolbox using terms (3), (4), (7) and (8) on a vector of level set functions, with one function and PDE for each mode q. Although it looks like a discounting term, $\lambda_j(q,x,t)\varphi(\phi_j(q,x,t),t)$ is treated as a forcing function with (8) because it depends on the value of another mode's φ. Given fixed finite horizon $T > 0$ and continuous terminal condition $\varphi_T(q,x)$, the solution of (22) at $t_0 < T$ is

$$\varphi(q_0,x_0,t_0) = E[\varphi_T(q(T),x(T))] \quad \text{where } q(t_0) = q_0 \text{ and } x(t_0) = x_0.$$

Extensions of this simplistic model to nonidentity reset maps and to stochastic continuous dynamics are explored in [8]. The PDEs thereby identified have so far been implementable using components of the toolbox.

To demonstrate the process of implementing such PDEs in the toolbox, we use the first TCP example from [8]. In this model, the files to be transmitted are drawn from a mixture of M exponential distributions characterized by their

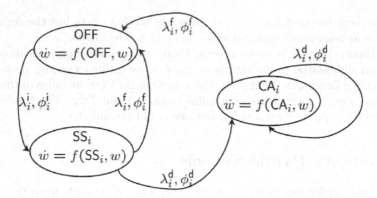

Fig. 3. Stochastic hybrid system model of TCP flow. The only continuous variable is window size w, whose continuous dynamics are deterministic. Nondeterminism enters through the switches, which occur stochastically at rate λ and modify the window size according to reset map ϕ. Modes SS_i and CA_i and the corresponding mode switches will be replicated for each file size $i = 1, \dots, M$. This model is taken from [8]

mean file sizes k_i, $i = 1, \dots, M$ (in packets). The TCP connection has three basic modes: no current transmission (OFF), slow-start (SS), and congestion avoidance (CA). Because the rate at which transmissions are completed depends on the size of the file being transmitted, however, the SHS has a copy of each of the latter two modes (SS_i and CA_i) for every element of the file size distribution; consequently, there are $2M + 1$ modes in the SHS.

A sketch of the SHS is shown in figure 3 (for $M = 1$). In every mode, the only continuous state variable is the transmission window size w (in packets), whose deterministic dynamics depend on the mode

$$f(\text{OFF}, w) = 0, \qquad f(SS_i, w) = \frac{(\log 2)w}{n_{\text{ack}}\text{RTT}}, \qquad f(CA_i, w) = \frac{1}{n_{\text{ack}}\text{RTT}},$$

where n_{ack} is the number of packets acknowledged for each ack packet received and RTT is the round trip time (in seconds). There are three types of discrete mode switches. From OFF to each of the CA_i modes there is a switch corresponding to transmission initiation with

$$\lambda_i^{\text{i}}(\text{OFF}, w) = \frac{p_i}{\tau_{\text{off}}}, \qquad \phi_i^{\text{i}}(\text{OFF}, w) = (CA_i, w_0),$$

where p_i is the probability that the size of the next file will be drawn from the distribution of mean size k_i ($\sum_i p_i = 1$), τ_{off} is the average quiescent period (actual quiescent times are drawn from an exponential distribution with this mean) and w_0 is the initial window size. From CA_i and SS_i to the same SS_i there are switches corresponding to dropped packets

$$\lambda_i^{\text{d}}(q, w) = \frac{p_{\text{drop}}w}{\text{RTT}}, \qquad \phi_i^{\text{d}}(q, w) = (SS_i, w/2), \qquad q \in \{SS_i, CA_i\},$$

where p_{drop} is the probability of dropping a packet. Finally, from CA_i and SS_i to OFF there are switches corresponding to finishing a transmission

$$\lambda_i^f(q,w) = \frac{w}{k_i\mathsf{RTT}}, \qquad \phi_i^f(q,w) = (\mathsf{OFF},0), \qquad q \in \{\mathsf{SS}_i, \mathsf{CA}_i\}.$$

The total is $5M$ distinct switches. For more details on the SHS, see [8, 24].

The variable of interest in this model is the transmission rate $r = w/\mathsf{RTT}$. Because the reset maps affect the continuous state, we must solve a modified version of (22), although the same basic terms are involved. To determine the mean rate over a collection of modes $\mathcal{Q}' \subset \mathcal{Q}$, we use terminal conditions

$$\varphi_T(q,w) = \begin{cases} r = \frac{w}{\mathsf{RTT}}, & \text{if } q \in \mathcal{Q}'; \\ 0, & \text{otherwise.} \end{cases} \tag{23}$$

We examine $3 + M$ different cases: $\mathcal{Q}_{\text{total}} = \mathcal{Q} \setminus \mathsf{OFF}$, $\mathcal{Q}_{\mathsf{SS}} = \{\mathsf{SS}_i\}_{i=1}^M$, $\mathcal{Q}_{\mathsf{CA}} = \{\mathsf{CA}_i\}_{i=1}^M$, and for each $i = 1, \ldots, M$ a $\mathcal{Q}_i = \{\mathsf{SS}_i, \mathsf{CA}_i\}$.

Because the window size is reset upon completion of the transmission of each file, we can expect that along any trajectory of the system the effect of that trajectory's initial window size will eventually disappear. Therefore, to find the mean rate we solve the appropriate HJ PDEs until they converge to a constant value, which will be the expected long term rate over the modes in $\mathcal{Q}'$. The standard deviation of the rate $\sigma(r)$ is found by substituing r^2 for r in (23) and the formula $\sigma^2(r) = E[r^2] - E[r]^2$. We calculate the rate mean and standard deviation for each of the 5 cases (total, SS, CA, small files, and medium files) over a variety of packet drop rates using the parameters for the $M = 2$ case from [8]

$$\tau_{\text{off}} = 5 \text{ sec}, \qquad \mathsf{RTT} = 0.05 \text{ sec},$$
$$w_0 = 0.693, \qquad n_{\text{ack}} = 1,$$
$$k_1 = \frac{3.5}{\mathsf{ps}}, \qquad k_2 = \frac{246}{\mathsf{ps}},$$
$$p_1 = 0.8887, \qquad p_2 = 0.1113,$$
$$\mathsf{ps} = \frac{1500}{1024}, \qquad p_{\text{drop}} \in [3(10^{-4}), 3(10^{-1})],$$

where ps is the packet size in kilobytes. Results are shown in figure 4, and correspond well with those in [8–figure 4].

While the procedure outlined above is much more computationally intense than the analytic formulas deduced in [8], it is more general in several respects. First, as the SHS theory develops the numerical solution can be extended through other terms in the toolbox to treat stochastic continuous evolution and potentially evolution dependent on control and/or disturbance input parameters. Second, it provides a method of checking the analytic solution, which made assumptions regarding the third moment of the rate distribution in order to find closed form equations.

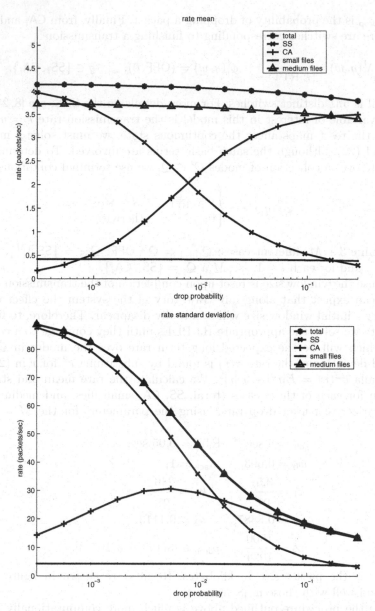

Fig. 4. Expected rates and standard deviations as estimated by the toolbox for the stochastic hybrid system model of TCP flow, using the two component model of transfer file sizes. Compare with [8–figure 4]

6   Conclusions

We have demonstrated several applications of HJ PDEs to the analysis of non-deterministic continuous and hybrid systems, and how the Toolbox of Level Set

Methods can be used to approximate the solution of these nonlinear PDEs. Furthermore, we have only touched on a small fraction of the problems in which such PDEs could prove useful. Examples of extensions include SDGs with boundary conditions [12, 10] and SHSs where both the continuous and discrete evolution is stochastically driven [24, 25, 26, 27]. We encourage others to modify and contribute to the toolbox, and we look forward to adding appropriate new features as the theory advances and compelling examples become available.

Acknowledgements. The first author would like to thank Andrew L. Zimdars for collaborative work examining HJ PDEs for stochastic continuous and hybrid systems, and Professor João P. Hespanha for providing parameter values used in his SHS model of TCP.

References

1. Isaacs, R.: Differential Games. John Wiley (1967)
2. Bardi, M., Capuzzo-Dolcetta, I.: Optimal Control and Viscosity Solutions of Hamilton-Jacobi-Bellman equations. Birkhäuser, Boston (1997)
3. Souganidis, P.E.: Two-player, zero-sum differential games and viscosity solutions. In Bardi, M., Raghavan, T.E.S., Parthasarathy, T., eds.: Stochastic and Differential Games: Theory and Numerical Methods. Volume 4 of Annals of International Society of Dynamic Games. Birkhäuser (1999) 69–104
4. http://www.cs.ubc.ca/~mitchell/ToolboxLS.
5. Tomlin, C., Mitchell, I., Bayen, A., Oishi, M.: Computational techniques for the verification of hybrid systems. Proceedings of the IEEE **91** (2003) 986–1001
6. Mitchell, I., Bayen, A., Tomlin, C.J.: A time-dependent Hamilton-Jacobi formulation of reachable sets for continuous dynamic games. Submitted to *IEEE Transactions on Automatic Control* (2004)
7. Mitchell, I.M.: A toolbox of level set methods. Technical Report TR-2004-09, Department of Computer Science, University of British Columbia, Vancouver, BC, Canada (2004)
8. Hespanha, J.P.: Stochastic hybrid systems: Application to communication networks. In Alur, R., Pappas, G.J., eds.: Hybrid Systems: Computation and Control. Number 2993 in Lecture Notes in Computer Science. Springer Verlag (2004) 397–401
9. Osher, S., Fedkiw, R.: Level Set Methods and Dynamic Implicit Surfaces. Springer-Verlag (2002)
10. Crandall, M.G., Ishii, H., Lions, P.L.: User's guide to viscosity solutions of second order partial differential equations. Bulletin of the American Mathematical Society **27** (1992) 1–67
11. Crandall, M.G., Evans, L.C., Lions, P.L.: Some properties of viscosity solutions of Hamilton-Jacobi equations. Transactions of the American Mathematical Society **282** (1984) 487–502
12. Øksendal, B.: Stochastic Differential Equations: an Introduction with Applications. Sixth edn. Springer (2003)
13. Mangel, M.: Decision and Control in Uncertain Resource Systems. Academic Press, Orlando, Fl (1985)

14. Evans, L.C., Souganidis, P.E.: Differential games and representation formulas for solutions of Hamilton-Jacobi-Isaacs equations. Indiana University Mathematics Journal **33** (1984) 773–797
15. Osher, S.: A level set formulation for the solution of the Dirichlet problem for Hamilton-Jacobi equations. SIAM Journal of Mathematical Analysis **24** (1993) 1145–1152
16. Athans, M., Falb, P.L.: Optimal Control. McGraw-Hill, New York (1966)
17. Broucke, M., Benedetto, M.D.D., Gennaro, S.D., Sangiovanni-Vincentelli, A.: Optimal control using bisimulations: Implementation. In Benedetto, M.D.D., Sangiovanni-Vincentelli, A., eds.: Hybrid Systems: Computation and Control. Number 2034 in Lecture Notes in Computer Science. Springer Verlag (2001) 175–188
18. Tsai, Y.H.R., Cheng, L.T., Osher, S., Zhao, H.K.: Fast sweeping methods for a class of Hamilton-Jacobi equations. SIAM Journal on Numerical Analysis **41** (2003) 673–694
19. Sethian, J.A., Vladimirsky, A.: Ordered upwind methods for static Hamilton-Jacobi equations: Theory and algorithms. SIAM Journal on Numerical Analysis **41** (2003) 325–363
20. Cardaliaguet, P., Quincampoix, M., Saint-Pierre, P.: Optimal times for constrained nonlinear control problems without local controllability. Applied Mathematics and Optimization **35** (1997) 1–22
21. Falcone, M.: Numerical solution of dynamic programming equations. In: Optimal Control and Viscosity Solutions of Hamilton-Jacobi-Bellman equations. Birkhäuser (1997) Appendix A of [2].
22. Ishii, H.: On uniqueness and existence of viscosity solutions of fully nonlinear second-order elliptic PDEs. Communications on Pure and Applied Mathematics **42** (1989) 15–45
23. Fleming, W.H., Souganidis, P.E.: On the existence of value functions of two-player, zero-sum stochastic differential games. Indiana University Mathematics Journal **38** (1989) 293–313
24. Hespanha, J.P.: A model for stochastic hybrid systems with application to communication networks. Submitted to the *International Journal of Hybrid Systems* (2004)
25. Ghosh, M.K., Arapostathis, A., Marcus, S.I.: Ergodic control of switching diffusions. SIAM Journal of Control and Optimization **35** (1997) 1952–1988
26. Filar, J.A., Gaitsgory, V., Haurie, A.B.: Control of singularly perturbed hybrid stochastic systems. IEEE Transactions on Automatic Control **46** (2001) 179–190
27. Kushner, H.J., Dupuis, P.: Numerical Methods for Stochastic Control Problems in Continuous Time. Springer-Verlag, Berlin, New York (1992)

On Transfinite Hybrid Automata

Katsunori Nakamura and Akira Fusaoka

Department of Computer Science,
Ritsumeikan University,
Nojihigashi, Kusatsu-city, SIGA, Japan 525-8577
fusaoka@cs.ritsumei.ac.jp

Abstract. In this paper, we propose a new method to deal with hybrid systems based on the concept of the nonstandard analysis and the Büchi's transfinite automata. An essential point of the method is a generalization of hybrid automata with hyperfinite iteration of an infinitesimal transition in $^*\mathbb{R}$. This nonstandard model of hybrid automata allows discrete but hyperfinite state transition, so that we can describe and reason about the interaction of the continuous and discrete dynamics in the algebraic framework. In this enlarged perspective of the hybrid automata, we discuss about the asymptotic orbit of the dynamics that is peculiar to the hybrid systems such as Zeno.

1 Introduction

A hybrid automaton is a well known as a standard framework in the formalization of the hybrid system in which continuous and discrete dynamics are interacting each other [1, 13]. Especially, it has been providing a useful basis for the analysis or verification for the dynamical property of the hybrid systems such as the automotive engine [2] or the robotics [9]. However, the hybrid automaton has several limitations due to its simplicity and it is sometimes insufficient for the fully treatment of hybrid dynamics. Among them, we focus on two problems: the description of continuous dynamics and Zeno problem. The continuous dynamics is described in the form of differential equations in the hybrid automata. This is one of advantages of the hybrid automata because many mathematical methods and techniques are available in the fully established fields of control theory. However, it is also one of reasons for the difficulty in the logical or mechanical treatment of hybrid dynamics. In the automatic synthesis or automatic verification for the engine controllers, for example, the axiomatic framework is necessary for the differential equation of the combustion dynamics in cylinder. But we have no efficient reasoning system till now for the analysis and the real number theory which is actually available for the complex differential equations. On the other hands, so-called Zeno problem is related to the state transition of automata. Namely, it is incomplete in the meaning that the limiting state cannot be defined for the infinite sequence of discrete state transitions. The Zeno is a phenomenon in which the infinite iteration of a discrete value change occurs in the finite time that is familiar not only in the industrial hybrid system but

M. Morari and L. Thiele (Eds.): HSCC 2005, LNCS 3414, pp. 495–510, 2005.
© Springer-Verlag Berlin Heidelberg 2005

also in our daily life [8, 12]. For example, a bouncing ball shows the Zeno orbit in which a ball becomes to be rest in the finite time after the infinite iteration of bouncing (discontinuous change of velocity). It is often pointed out that the Zeno is a significant but hard problem from the standard treatment of the hybrid system, so that the non-Zeno condition is prerequisite assumption at many studies of hybrid system. There have been many studies to deal with Zeno in the hybrid automata [14, 17, 6], and the timed automata [3].

In this paper, we propose a new type of hybrid automata called a transfinite hybrid automaton, which is a generalization of the standard one at two points. First, we use the infinite recurrence equation instead of the differential equation based on the nonstandard analysis so that the whole behaviors of systems including the continuous dynamics are represented by the discrete transition of states. Secondly, the construction of Büchi's transfinite automaton is introduced in the frame of hybrid automata, which allows the infinite transitions among the set of states [5]. In comparison with other methods, the transfinite hybrid automaton has the following advantages:

(1) Since the continuous change is defined by the sequence of the actions with the infinitesimal effect in the very small duration, we can deal with both the continuous and discrete dynamics uniformly in the discrete but hyperfinite state transition paradigm. Therefore, we need not deal with the derivative and integration. Instead, we use only arithmetic and simple algebra for $\mathbb{R}$ and $^*\mathbb{R}$ so that it is appropriate for the logical treatment of the hybrid system.
(2) The completeness in the space of discrete and continuous dynamics is naturally introduced so that it allows to deal with the fixed point, for example, an asymptotic behavior toward limits such as Zeno.

1.1   A Bouncing Ball

Let consider the motion of a bouncing ball. It is described by two variables x, v which denote the height and velocity of a ball.

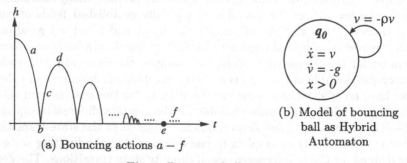

(a) Bouncing actions $a - f$

(b) Model of bouncing ball as Hybrid Automaton

Fig. 1. Bouncing ball system

Figure 1 gives the motion of the bouncing ball and its corresponding hybrid automaton. In this paper, we keep the word "state" for the automaton, and use

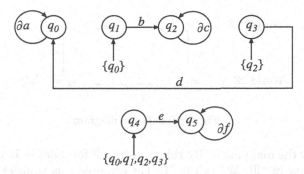

Fig. 2. Model of bouncing ball as Transfinite Automaton

the word "situation" to denote the physical status of the system. In Figure 1(b), the system continuously evolves within the state q_0 according to the differential equation while it satisfies the invariant condition in q_0. The state transition occurs whenever the condition is violated. Although this model gives a simple and elegant formulation, it is sometimes weak. For example, the state transition eventually halts after the infinite repetition of bouncing but we cannot find out this property from the visual representation. Figure 2 gives the automaton proposed here for the bouncing ball. We use two types of transition. The first is the usual transition represented by the arc from one state to another. The second type is represented by the arc from a set of states to another state, which means that after infinite visits to all states of the set, the machine transfers to the designated state. Every transition is instantaneous. We denote by ∂a the infinitesimal segment of the action a. Therefore, the ball moves to the situation q_1 after iterating the small falling ∂a infinitely at q_0. The action b represents the instantaneous motion of the ball bouncing. In the situation q_2, it ascends toward the highest point by repeating ∂c and reaches to the point at q_3. Then it moves to falling again. After the infinite iteration of these behaviors, the ball is at rest in q_4 and repeats the halting action forever in q_5. The rational expression $((\partial a)^\omega b (\partial c)^\omega d)^\omega e (\partial f)^\omega$ gives the action schema for the behavior of the ball.

1.2   Outline of the Methodology

The proposed method is essentially to build the transfinite automata which simulate the standard hybrid automata. It is schematically illustrated in Figure 3. We have two worlds, $\mathbb{Z}$ (a world of a hybrid automata $\mathcal{A}$ moving in $\mathbb{R}$) and $^*\mathbb{Z}$ (a world of a transfinite hybrid automata $^*\mathcal{A}$ moving in $^*\mathbb{R}$). The two mappings α and β gives the simulation condition. Namely, we can use $\beta(^*\mathcal{A}(\alpha(s_1)))$ in $^*\mathbb{Z}$ instead of $s_2 = \mathcal{A}(s_1)$ in $\mathbb{Z}$.

From a logical point of view, this method corresponds to the nonstandard model of hybrid automata. Let's assume that an action is decomposable into a sequence of n action-steps via the equi-distant discretization. We describe the dynamics of each action-step in the standard world $\mathbb{Z}$. We denote by **L** the logical closure of the axioms and theorems in $\mathbb{Z}$. We re-interpret the all formulas

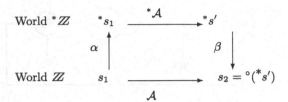

Fig. 3. Simulation diagram

of **L** in *$\mathbb{R}$ by the mapping α. By this transfer, all formulas in **L** are transformed to the formulas in *$\mathbb{R}$. We call it ***L**. For example n is transfer to the infinite integer *n. Since *$\mathbb{R}$ allows a discrete but hyperfinite state transition, *$\mathcal{A}$ gives a new situation as the result of performing the infinitesimal action or the infinite iteration of action. Since the situations in *$\mathbb{Z}$ contains infinitesimal or infinite values of system variables and these values have no actual meaning from the physical point of view, the nonstandard situation must be pulled back to the standard one by the mapping β. The mapping β must designate a standard situation which is close to the given nonstandard situation.

Note that ***L** is syntactically equivalent to **L** because we alter only its interpretation. So that all theorems in **L** hold even in ***L**(Transfer principle [16]). This is an essential point of this method.

2 Nonstandard Discretization

In this paper, we treat the continuous dynamics in terms of hyperfinite recurrence equations. Therefore, we introduce the infinite division of an action with continuous motion based on the nonstandard analysis. The infinitesimal segment of action is called an infinitesimal action. We prove that any standard action is equivalent to an infinite iteration of the infinitesimal action.

2.1 Nonstandard Real *$\mathbb{R}$

The nonstandard real number *$\mathbb{R}$ is constructed from the real number $\mathbb{R}$ via the ultra product formation [16].

Definition 1 (Ultra filter). *Let $\mathcal{F}$ be a family of the subsets of $\mathbb{N}$ which satisfy the following conditions, where $\mathbb{N}$ is the set of all natural numbers.*

(1) $\mathbb{N} \in \mathcal{F}$, $\phi \notin \mathcal{F}$
(2) if $A \in \mathcal{F}$ and $A \subset B$ then $B \in \mathcal{F}$
(3) if $A \in \mathcal{F}$ and $B \in \mathcal{F}$ then $A \cap B \in \mathcal{F}$
(4) for any $A \subset \mathbb{N}$, $A \in \mathcal{F}$ or $\mathbb{N} - A \in \mathcal{F}$
(5) if $A \subset \mathbb{N}$ is finite then $\mathbb{N} - A \in \mathcal{F}$

$\mathcal{F}$ *is called an ultra filter. For example, the set of all co-finite sets $\{\mathbb{N} - A \mid A \text{ is finite }\}$ is an ultra filter.*

Definition 2 (Hyperreal number). *We fix an ultra filter $\mathcal{F}$.*

(1) Let W denote a set of sequences of real numbers $(a_1, a_2, \cdots)$. The nonstandard real number $^*\mathbb{R}$ is defined by introducing the following equivalence relation into W

$$(a_1, a_2, \cdots) \sim (b_1, b_2, \cdots) \Leftrightarrow \{k \mid a_k = b_k\} \in \mathcal{F}$$

Namely, $^*\mathbb{R} = W/\sim$. We denote the equivalence class of $(a_1, a_2, \cdots)$ by $[(a_1, a_2, \cdots)]$.
This means that the hyperreal number is regarded as the infinite sequence of real numbers ignoring the difference of finite part.
(2) the nonstandard integer $^*\mathbb{N} \subseteq {}^*\mathbb{R}$ is also introduced via the ultra product formation. A set $A \subseteq {}^*\mathbb{N}$ is hyperfinite if there exists $N \in {}^*\mathbb{N}$ such that for every $x \in A, x < N$.

We distinguish the nonstandard variables and function symbols from the standard one by attaching $*$ to them, although it is omitted in the clear cases. The usual real number a is treated by $[(a, a, a, ...)]$, so that $^*\mathbb{R}$ contains $\mathbb{R}$ itself. An element of $\mathbb{R}$ in $^*\mathbb{R}$ is called a standard number. For the elements of $^*\mathbb{R}$, we can define arithmetic operations and relations in the following way [10].
The usual arithmetic operations such as $+, -, \times, /$ are given by

$$[(a_1, a_2, ...)] + [(b_1, b_2, ...)] = [(a_1 + b_1, a_2 + b_2, ...)]$$

The usual relations such as $<$ are given by

$$[(a_1, a_2, ...)] < [(b_1, b_2, ...)] \equiv \{n \mid a_n < b_n\} \in \mathcal{F}$$

Note that an element $[(1, \frac{1}{2}, \frac{1}{3}, ...)]$ is smaller than any real number $[(a, a, ...)]$, namely it is an infinitesimal. Also, a number $\omega = [(1, 2, 3, ...)]$ is infinite.

Definition 3 (Closeness). *We define a relation $a \approx b$ if the distance from a to b is infinitesimal, that is*

$$(\forall a, b \in {}^*\mathbb{R})[a \approx b \text{ iff } a - b \text{ is infinitesimal}]$$

A relation $a \approx b$ is an equivalence relation.
From the construction of $^*\mathbb{R}$, every standard function $f(x)$ is extended to the nonstandard function $^*f(x)$, which holds any properties of the original function. This is called the transfer principle. Dual to the transfer principle, the finite hyperreal number satisfying a certain property has the corresponding real number with this property [10].

Theorem 1 (Transfer Principle). *If a property holds for all real numbers, then it holds for all hyperreal numbers.*

Theorem 2 (monad, shadow). *For every finite number $a \in {}^*\mathbb{R}$, there is only one standard number $b \in \mathbb{R}$ such that $a \approx b$. b is called a monad of a and denoted by $b = {}^\circ a$.*

The continuity, differentiation and Riemann integral of the $\mathbb{R}$-valued function is defined in the $^*\mathbb{R}$ in the following way.

Definition 4 (Continuity, Differentiation and Riemann integral).

(1) A standard function $f(x)$ is continuous at a standard number x if and only if for all $y \in {}^*\mathbb{R}$, $^*f(y) \approx {}^*f(x)$ if $y \approx x$.

(2) A standard function $f(x)$ is differentiable at a standard number x if and only if there exists some $d \in \mathbb{R}$ such that for every nonzero infinitesimal ε,

$$\frac{1}{\varepsilon}[{}^*f(x+\varepsilon) - f(x)] \approx d$$

(3) Let A standard function $f(x)$ be continuous over $[a, b]$. For the nonstandard sequence, $x_0 = a, x_1, x_2 \cdots, x_\omega = b$ such that $x_{i+1} - xi = \frac{b-a}{\omega}$ for every i,

$$\int_a^b f(x)dx = {}^\circ \left(\sum_{k=0}^{\omega-1} {}^*f(x_k)\frac{b-a}{\omega} \right)$$

2.2   Description of the Dynamics

Situation: The behavior of the hybrid system is represented in the terms of the situation and the action. The situation is the physical status of the system at each time instance and the action causes the time evolution via changing the situation. The situation is described by the vector of $\mathbb{R}$-valued variables $(x_1, x_2, \cdots, x_n)$. We denote the set of situations by **Sit**. We assume that the situation contains a special variable *time*. The set of action is **Act** $\subseteq$ **Sit** $\times$ **Sit**. We define the duration of action a at the situation s as $\tau(a, s) = time(a(s)) - time(s)$.

The nonstandard extension of situation is introduced via the similar way to $^*\mathbb{R}$.

Definition 5 (Nonstandard situation). *We fix an ultra filter $\mathcal{F}$. Let $s_1 = (x_1^1, x_2^1, ..., x_m^1), s_2 = (x_1^2, x_2^2, ..., x_m^2), \cdots$ be a sequence of situations. Then the nonstandard situation is defined by*

$$^*\mathbf{Sit} = \{([(x_1^1, x_1^2, \cdots)], [(x_2^1, x_2^2, \cdots)], \cdots, [(x_m^1, x_m^2, \cdots)] >$$
$$| \{n \mid (x_1^n, x_2^n, \cdots, x_m^n) \in \mathbf{Sit}\} \in \mathcal{F}\}$$

From this definition, we can always find the limiting situation $[(s_1, s_2, ...)] \in {}^*\mathbf{Sit}$ of any sequence of standard situations $s_1, s_2, ... \in \mathbf{Sit}$. Namely,

$$[(s_1, s_2, ...)] = ([(x_1^1, x_1^2, ...)], [(x_2^1, x_2^2, ...)], ..., [(x_m^1, x_m^2, ...)])$$
$$\text{where } s_n = (x_1^n, x_2^n, ..., x_m^n) \text{ for each } n$$

Action: A dynamical system can be characterized generally as an infinite iteration of an action a, namely $(s, a(s), a(a(s)), ...)$. In the following theorem, we prove that there always exists the nonstandard situation which is the result of infinite iteration of action.

Theorem 3 (Infinite iteration of action). *For any standard action a and any situation* $s \in$ **Sit**, $a^\omega(s) \in$ ****Sit** *for* $\omega = [(1, 2, ...)]$.

Proof. Clearly, $a^\omega(s) = [(a^1(s), a^2(s), ...)]$ by the definition. From Definition 5, $a^\omega(s) \in$ ****Sit**.

Definition 6 (Fixed point). *An action a has a fixed point if and only if*

$$\forall n \in \mathbb{N}[a^\omega(s) \approx a^{\omega+n}(s)]$$

A fixed point s is **attractive** *if and only if there exists* $Z \subseteq$ ****Sit** *such that*

$$s \in Z \text{ and } \forall s' \in Z[s' \neq s \rightarrow (\forall n \in \mathbb{N}[a^n(s') \in Z]) \wedge a^\omega(s') \approx s]$$

The fixed point s is **repelling** *if and only if there exists* $Z \subseteq$ ****Sit** *such that*

$$s \in Z \text{ and } \exists n \in \mathbb{N} \forall s' \in Z[s' \neq s \wedge a^n(s') \notin Z]$$

A fixed point $s = a^\omega(s_0)$ *is* **Zeno** *related to* a, x *if and only if*

$$\exists r \in \mathbb{N}[x(s) \not\approx x(a^r(s)) \wedge time(s) \text{ is finite}$$

Definition 7 (Equi-time division of action). *A standard action a is* $n-$*divisible for any* $n \in N$ *if there exists an action* a_n *such that* $a_n{}^n(s) = a(s)$ *and* $\tau(a_n, s_k)$ *is constant for every* $s_k = a_n{}^k(s)$ *for* $k < n$.

Theorem 4 (Infinite division of action). *Assume that the action a is n-divisible for every n. There exists* $\partial a \in$ **Act such that* $\partial a^k(s) \in$ ****Sit** *for each* $k = 1, 2, ..., \omega$.

Proof. Let $\xi(n, k) = a_n{}^k(s)$ for finite n, k. We define nonstandard situations $\xi(\omega, k) = [(\xi(1, k_1), \xi(2, k_2), ..., \xi(n, k_n), ...)]$, where $k_\omega = k$ and if $k_m < \frac{m}{2}$ then $k_{m-1} = k_m$ else $k_{m-1} = k_m - 1$.

By the definition 5, $\xi(\omega, k) \in$ ****Sit**. And also,
$time(\xi(\omega, k)) = [(time(\xi(1, k_1), time(\xi(2, k_2), ...,)] = time(s) + \frac{[(k_1, k_2, ...)]}{\omega} \tau$.
Therefore, we can conclude $\xi(\omega, k) = \partial a^k(s)$.

In the following, we denote the duration of ∂a by ν, that is $\nu = \frac{\tau}{\omega}$ for the duration τ of action a.

Clearly, $a(s) = \partial a^\omega(s)$. Namely, we can regard any standard action as an infinite iteration of the infinitesimal action.

2.3   Nonstandard Recurrence Equation

The continuous parts of the hybrid dynamics can be easily transformed to the hyperfinite recurrence equations via the infinite iteration of the infinitesimal action if their differential equations satisfy the Lipschitz condition.

Theorem 5 (Discretization). *Let* $f : \mathbb{R}^n \to \mathbb{R}^n$ *be a standard function which satisfies the Lipschitz condition:* $|f(x) - f(y)| < c|x - y|$

Let ∂a *be an infinitesimal action with the duration* $\nu = \frac{T}{\omega}$ *such that*
$\partial a : x' = x + f(x)\nu$
Then the function $g(t) = {}^{\circ}z(t)$ *where* $z(t) = (\partial a)^i(x_0)$ *for* $(i+1)\nu > t \geq i\nu$
gives a solution at $t \in [0, T]$ *for*

$$\frac{dx}{dt} = f(x); \quad x(t_0) = x_0$$

Proof. Let $\xi_i = (\partial a)^i(x_0)$, namely $\xi_{i+1} = \xi_i + f(\xi_i)\nu$.
$|\xi_{i+1} - \xi_i| = |\xi_i + f(\xi_i)\nu - (\xi_{i-1} + f(\xi_{i-1})\nu)| < |\xi_i - \xi_{i-1}| + |f(\xi_i)\nu - f(\xi_{i-1})\nu| < (1 + c\nu)|\xi_i - \xi_{i-1}|$. Therefore,
$|\xi_{i+1} - \xi_i| < (1 + c\nu)^i|\xi_1 - \xi_0| = (1 + c\frac{T}{\omega})^{\frac{t}{T}\omega}|\xi_1 - \xi_0| < e^{cT}|f(\xi_0)|\nu \approx 0$. Namely, $\xi_{i+1} \approx \xi_i$, so that $z(t) \approx z(t')$ if $t \approx t'$. This means that $z(t)$ is an S-continuous function. It is known that every S-continuous function $h(t)$ has a continuous function ${}^{\circ}h(t)$ as a shadow [10]. Therefore, there exists a standard continuous function $g(t) = {}^{\circ}z(t)$. Clearly, $g(t_0) = x_0$ and

$$\int_{t_0}^{t} f(x)dt \approx \sum_{k=0}^{i} f(\xi_k)\nu = \xi_i - \xi_0 \approx {}^{\circ}z(t) - {}^{\circ}z(t_0) = g(t) - g(t_0)$$

Example 1. Consider the differential equation of the action a for the situation $(x, time)$

$$\frac{dx}{dt} + kx = p, \quad x(s_0) = x_0, time(s_0) = 0$$

Let assume that we want to predict the situation s' after t seconds. We deal with this differential equation by using the piecewise constant model. The dynamics for the variable x is described by an action ∂a with duration ν.

For every situation s_i,
$x(s_{i+1})) = (1 - k\nu)x(s_i) + p\nu, \ time(s_i) = time(s_i) + \nu$ for $i = 1, 2, ..., \omega$
where $\nu = \frac{t}{\omega}$.

The desired situation s' is given by s_ω. By mathematical Induction rule (the mathematical induction is also available in *$\mathbb{N}$ [16]), we have

$$x(s_\omega) = x_0(1 - k\frac{t}{\omega})^\omega$$

We must find out the standard value near $x(s_\omega)$. We use a knowledge related to infinitesimal arithmetic: $(1 - \frac{1}{n})^n \approx e^{-1}$ if n is infinite. From this equation, we have $(1 - k\frac{t}{\omega})^\omega \approx e^{-kt}$

Finally, we have the desired situation $s' = (x_0 e^{-kt}, t)$

Note that we use only the simple arithmetic rules for real and hyperreal numbers in the above argument.

3   Transfinite Hybrid Automata

Büchi introduces the automaton on the infinite words indexed by ordinals [5], which is a generalization of the usual automaton. Namely, Büchi's transfinite automaton contains the transition rules for the limit ordinals in addition to the usual successor transitions. We use this construction to define the automata which recognize the hyperfinite words whose letters are indexed by the nonstandard integer. Since the hyperfinite integer has a similar linear and discrete order structure to the ordinals, the idea of limit transitions can be used also to the automata on hyperfinite words. Although the hybrid automaton defined here is based on the nonstandard integers rather than ordinals, we call it "transfinite" hybrid automata because it inherits the limit transition rules from Büchi's transfinite automaton.

In the following, we use n instead of $*n$ to represent the hyper integer, that is $n \in {}^*\mathbb{N}$).

Definition 8 (word). *Let Σ is a finite set of letters (called alphabet).*

(1) For a (nonstandard) integer n, the n-sequence of letters $a_1 a_2, \cdots a_n$ is called a word on Σ with the length n. ϵ is the word with the length 0.

(2) For the sets U, V of words of Σ, we define the rational operation

$U + V = \{x \mid x \in U \cup V\}$

$U \cdot V = \{x_1 x_2 \mid x_1 \in U \wedge x_2 \in V\}$

$U^\omega = \{x^\omega \mid x \in U\}$

$U^\dagger = \{\epsilon\} \cup U \cup U \cdot U \cdots \cup U^\omega \cdots$, $U^\dagger$ *is the nonstandard extension of closure* U^*

(3) $S \subseteq \Sigma^\dagger$ is called rational if and only if it can be obtained from finite subsets using a hyperfine number of rational operations.

Definition 9 (Transfinite Hybrid Automaton).
A transfinite hybrid automaton $\mathcal{A}$ is an 8-tuple $(Q, A, E, I, F, X, X_0, D)$ where

1. *Q is the finite set of states.*
2. *A is the finite set of infinitesimal actions.*
3. *E is the finite set of transition rules ; $E \subseteq (Q \times A \times Q) \cup (\mathcal{P}(Q) \times Q)$ where $(P, q) \notin E$ if $q \in P$*
4. *$I \in Q$ is the initial state. $X_0 \in X$ is the initial situation.*
5. *$F \subset Q$ is the set of the final states.*
6. *For the sequence of states $q_1, q_2, \cdots, q_n$,*
   $Inf(\{q_1, q_2, \cdots, q_n\}) = \{q \mid \{k \mid q_k = q\}$ is infinite $\}$
7. *$X \subseteq \mathbb{R}^m$ where $m \in {}^*\mathbb{N}$ is the set of situations. Namely, $x = (x_1, x_2, \cdots, x_m) \in X$ is a vector of the continuous or discrete values of physical entities. We use $x' = (x'_1, x'_2, \cdots, x'_m) \in X'$ for the result situation of the action. The situation contains the special variable time or t.*
8. *D is the set of dynamics for each action of A. The dynamics of each action is given by specifying its precondition and effect in the form of $p(x) \rightarrow x' = f(x)$ where $f(x)$ is given by the algebraic formula formed from the arithmetic operations of ${}^*\mathbb{R}$.*

Example 2 (A bouncing ball automaton). (Figure 2)
$\mathcal{A} = (\{q_0, q_1, q_2, q_3, q_4, q_5\}, E, q_0, \{q_5\}, \{(x, v, t)\}, D)$ where
$E = \{(q_0, \partial a, q_0), (q_1, b, q_2), (q_2, \partial c, q_2), (q_3, d, q_0), (q_4, e, q_5), (q_5, \partial f, q_5),$
$(\{q_0\}, q_1), (\{q_2\}, q_3), (\{q_0, q_1, q_2, q_3\}, q_4)\}$
The dynamics D for each action is
$a : x \not\approx 0 \rightarrow (x' = x - v\tau(\partial a); v' = v - g\tau(\partial a); t' = t + \tau(\partial a);)$
$b : x \approx 0 \rightarrow (x' = x; v' = -v\rho; t' = t + \tau(b);)$, where $0 < \rho < 1$
$c : v \not\approx 0 \rightarrow (x' = x - v\tau(\partial c); v' = v - g\tau(\partial c); t' = t + \tau(\partial c);)$
$d : v \not\approx 0 \rightarrow (x' = x; v' = -v; t' = t + \tau(d);)$
$e : x \approx 0 \rightarrow (x' = 0; v' = 0; t' = t + \tau(e);)$
$f : x = 0 \rightarrow (x' = 0; v' = 0; t' = t + \tau(\partial f);)$

Definition 10 (Transition).

(1) A word $\alpha = a_1 a_2 \cdots a_n \in A^\dagger$ has a transition $(q_0, q_1, \cdots q_n)$ of the automaton $\mathcal{A} = (Q, A, E, q_0, F, X, X_0, D)$ if and only if there exists either $(q_i, a_i, q_{i+1}) \in E$ or $\{q_{i1}, q_{i2}, \cdots, q_{ir}\} \subseteq Inf(\{q_0, q_1, \cdots q_i\})$ such that $(\{q_{i1}, q_{i2}, \cdots, q_{ir}\}, q_{i+1}) \in E$

(2) $\alpha = a_1 a_2 \cdots a_n \in A^\dagger$ is recognizable if its transition $(q_0, q_1, \cdots q_n)$ ends at the final state $q_n \in F$. The set of all recognizable words of $\mathcal{A}$ is called the language of $\mathcal{A}$ which we denote by $L(\mathcal{A})$.

Kleene's theorem gives the fundamental result that the language $L(\mathcal{A})$ of a finite automaton $\mathcal{A}$ is equivalent to some rational expression. This corresponding theorem is extended to the case of the transfinite automata [7, 18]. For the transfinite automata defined here, the theorem also holds because of the straightforward application of the transfer principle in the nonstandard analysis.

Theorem 6 (Action schema). *For given transfinite hybrid automata $\mathcal{A} = (Q, E, q_0, F, X, X_0, D)$, there exists the rational expression $\mathcal{E}$, $\mathcal{E} = L(\mathcal{A})$. A set $AS \subseteq A^\dagger$ is called a set of an action schema if it is rational.*

Theorem 7 (Boolean operation of automata). *Let $\mathcal{A}, \mathcal{B}$ be two transfinite hybrid automata over A. There exist transfinite hybrid automata which recognize $L(\mathcal{A} \cup \mathcal{B}), L(\mathcal{A} \cap \mathcal{B}), A^\dagger - \mathcal{A} \cup L(\mathcal{B})$.*

Definition 11 (Execution).

*(1) **nonstandard execution.** Let $\alpha = a_1 a_2, \cdots a_n \in AS$ be an action schema of $\mathcal{A} = (Q, E, q_0, F, X, X_0, D)$ with the transition $q_0, q_1, \cdots q_n$. α is $*-executable$ if and only if there exists a sequence of situations $w_0, w_1, \cdots, w_n \subseteq X$ such that*
(a) $w_0 = X_0$
(b) for all $i = 1, 2, \cdots, n$
*   case 1: If $(q_i, a_i, q_{i+1}) \in E$ and $p(x(w_i))$ holds where $p(x)$ is the precondition of action a_i, then $x(w_{i+1}) = x'(w_i)$.*
*   case 2: if $(\{q_{i1}, q_{i2}, \cdots, q_{ir}\}, q_{i+1}) \in E$ and $x(w_{ij}) \approx x(w_{ik})$ for any $r \geq i, j > 0$, then $x(w_{i+1}) = x(w_{ij})$ for some $j = 1, 2, \cdots, r$.*

(2) **execution in the standard sense.** *Note that each situation w_i of α is always defined over $^*\mathbb{R}$ if it is $*-$executable. However, it is feasible only when all values in w_i have their shadows in the standard world. Namely, α is executable in the standard sense if and only if it is $*-$executable and the all situations $w_0, w_1, \cdots, w_n \subseteq X$ have finite values. Especially, $time(w_{ij})$ must be finite for each ij in every limit transition $(\{q_{i1}, q_{i2}, \cdots, q_{ir}\}, q_{i+1}) \in E$. This means that a state is actually reachable after the limit transition only when the machine spent finite time for the previous ω-iteration).*

4 The Description of Hybrid System

4.1 Alternative Water Tank

Consider a coupling of two water tanks [14]. Let x, y denotes the level of water in Tank A and Tank B. We assume that the tap in the bottom of each tank discharges the water at a rate proportional to the level of each tank. Also the constant flow denoted by p of the water is poured exclusively to either Tank A (we call the state A) or Tank B (the state B) at each time (Figure 4).We use the control strategy.

$$\text{if } st = A \wedge x \geq h \wedge y < h \text{ then switch to } B$$
$$\text{if } st = B \wedge y \geq h \wedge x < h \text{ then switch to } A$$

The levels of water x, y are described below: (where st is the state of Tank)

$$\text{if } st = A \text{ then } \frac{dx}{dt} + kx - p = 0 \wedge \frac{dy}{dt} + ky = 0$$
$$\text{if } st = B \text{ then } \frac{dx}{dt} + kx = 0 \wedge \frac{dy}{dt} + ky - p = 0$$

The corresponding hybrid automaton is given in Figure 5).

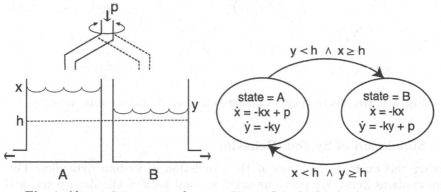

Fig. 4. Alternative water tank   **Fig. 5.** Standard hybrid automaton

4.2   The System Description in a Transfinite Hybrid Automaton

We can describe this system in a transfinite hybrid automaton as below.

$\mathbf{Q} = \{q_0, q_1, q_2, q_3, q_4, q_5, q_6\}$

$\mathbf{A} = \{\partial a, a, \partial b, b, c, d, e, f, g\}$

$\mathbf{E} = \{\{q_0, \partial a, q_0\}, \{q_2, \partial b, q_2\}, \{q_1, c, q_2\}, \{q_3, d, q_0\}, \{q_4, e, q_5\}, \{q_5, f, q_0\}, \{q_5, g, q_2\},$
$\{\{q_0\}, q_1\}, \{\{q_2\}, q_3\}, \{\{q_0, q_1, q_2, q_3\}, q_4\}, \{\{q_0, q_1, q_2, q_3\}, q_6\}\}$

$\mathbf{I} = \{Q = q_0, x = h_A, y = h_B, t = 0\}$

$\mathbf{F} = \{q_6\}$

$\mathbf{X} = \{x, y, t\}$

$\mathbf{D} = \{$

$\partial a : y \not\approx h \rightarrow (x' = (1 - k\tau(\partial a))x + p\tau(\partial a)), y' = (1 - k\tau(\partial a))y, t' = t + \tau(\partial a))$

$\partial b : x \not\approx h \rightarrow (x' = (1 - k\tau(\partial b))x, y' = (1 - k\tau(\partial b))y + p\tau(\partial b), t' = t + \tau(\partial b))$

$c : y \approx h \rightarrow (x' = x, y' = h, t' = t + \Delta)$

$d : x \approx h \rightarrow (x' = h, y' = y, t' = t + \Delta)$

$e : x \approx h \wedge y \approx h \rightarrow (x' = h, y' = h, t' = t + \Delta)$

$f : x' = (1 - k\Delta)x + p\Delta, y' = (1 - k\Delta)y, t' = t + \Delta$

$g : \ x' = (1 - k\Delta)x, y' = (1 - k\Delta)y + p\Delta, t' = t + \Delta$

$\}$

where Δ is the infinitesimal which denotes the minimal unit time of the system
(the minimal clock or sampling time).

We present this automaton in Figure 6. The action schema of this
automaton is

$$((\partial a)^{\omega} c(\partial b)^{\omega} d)^{\omega} e(f((\partial a)^{\omega} c(\partial b)^{\omega} d)^{\omega} + g((\partial b)^{\omega} d(\partial a)^{\omega} c)^{\omega})$$

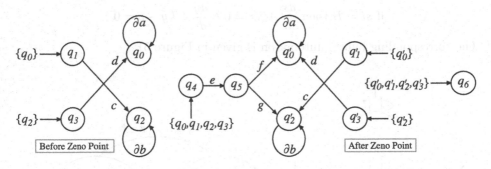

Fig. 6. A transfinite hybrid automaton for the alternative water tanks

4.3   Simulation of System Behavior

By using this example, we present the simulation of system dynamics. This
system contains Zeno. We prove its existence and localize the Zeno point, and
discuss about how we can escape from it.

[The existence of Zeno point]

The level of water x, y at the end of the action $(\partial a)^\omega, (\partial b)^\omega$ was shown below.

$$x_1 = \frac{p}{k} + \frac{h(h_A - \frac{p}{k})}{h_A}, y_1 = h \text{ when } (\partial a)^\omega \text{ was executed}$$

$$x_1 = h, y_1 = \frac{p}{k} + \frac{h(h_B - \frac{p}{k})}{h_B}, \text{ when } (\partial b)^\omega \text{ was executed}$$

If we assume that the index $2n$ of values means n times iteration of $(\partial a)^\omega \cdot (\partial b)^\omega$ and $2n + 1$ means the execution of $(\partial a)^\omega$ after n times iteration of $(\partial a)^\omega \cdot (\partial b)^\omega$, then

$$x_{2n+1} = \frac{p}{k} + \frac{h(h-\frac{p}{k})}{y_{2n}}, \qquad y_{2n+1} = h, \qquad \tau_{2n+1} = \frac{1}{k}log(\frac{y_{2n}}{h})$$

$$x_{2n} = h, \qquad y_{2n} = \frac{p}{k} + \frac{h(h-\frac{p}{k})}{x_{2n-1}}, \quad \tau_{2n} = \frac{1}{k}log(\frac{x_{2n-1}}{h}, t_n) = \sum_{i=1}^{n} \tau_i$$

The symbolic simulator gives the values x_{2n+1}, y_{2n} in the form of infinite continued fraction.

$$x_{2n+1} = y_{2n} = \frac{p}{k} + \cfrac{h\left(h - \frac{p}{k}\right)}{\frac{p}{k} + \cfrac{h\left(h-\frac{p}{k}\right)}{\frac{p}{k} + \cfrac{h\left(h-\frac{p}{k}\right)}{\frac{p}{k} + \cfrac{h\left(h-\frac{p}{k}\right)}{\vdots}}}}$$

We can prove the relations $h < x_{2n+1} < x_{2n-1}, h < y_{2n} < y_{2n-2}$ from the mathematical induction. Namely, the sequences of x, y are monotonously decreasing but bounded so that x, y have a limit point by the Weierstrass's theorem. Namely, we have a standard $\hat{x}, \hat{y}, \hat{t}$ such that $x_{2n+1} \approx \hat{x}, y_{2n} \approx \hat{y}, t_n \approx \hat{t}$. From $x_{2n+1} \approx x_{2n-1} \approx \hat{x}$ and a recurrence equation $x_{2n+1} = \frac{p}{k} + \frac{h(h-\frac{p}{k})}{\frac{p}{k}+\frac{h(h-\frac{p}{k})}{x_{2n-1}}}$, we have $\hat{x} = h$. Similarly, we can get $\hat{y} = h$. On the other hand, we have $(x_{n+1} + y_{n+1}) = (1 - k\Delta)(x_n + y_n) + p\tau$ from the system description. By solving this recurrence equation, we have $\hat{t} = \frac{1}{k}log(\frac{(h_A+h_B)k-p}{2hk-p})$. $\hat{t}$ is finite so that we can prove that the situation $\hat{s} = < h, h, \frac{1}{k}log(\frac{(h_A+h_B)k-p}{2hk-p}) >$ is Zeno point.

[Escape from Zeno]

This Zeno point is repelling for $t > \hat{t}$ so that the behavior of the system at $t > \hat{t}$ depends on the situation immediately after the Zeno point. Assume that ∂a is currently performed. Since the duration of any action should not be smaller than the minimal sampling time Δ, the action ∂a continues during Δ even $\partial a(\tau)$ becomes smaller than Δ. After passing Δ, the next value of y becomes lower than h and the next system time is over $\hat{t}$ (See Figure 7). So we can jump out from the fixed point.

[Uncertainty]

It is uncertain which action f or g will be selected at the state q_5 after Zeno. If ∂a is executed immediately before q_5, f is selected, and otherwise g is taken.

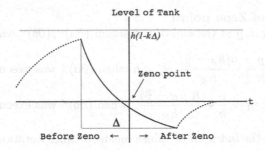

Fig. 7. Monad around Zeno point

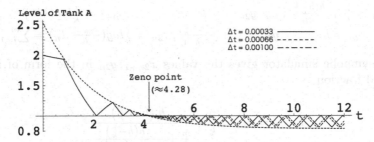

Fig. 8. The orbit of the water level of Tank A

However, ∂a and ∂b are exchanged intensively at the state q_4, so that the next state is undecidable. This is the inherent uncertainty in after-Zeno due to the infinite discrete value change within a finite time.

The Figure 8 shows a result of the numerical simulation. We use some very small numbers for Δ, and the other parameters are $x_0 = 2.0 \wedge y_0 = 1.5 \wedge k = 0.5 \wedge h = 1.0 \wedge p = 0.9$. The excursion of the level of tank is contained in the envelope $u = (h_A + h_B - \frac{p}{k})e^{-kt} + \frac{p}{k}$.

5   Concluding Remarks

We propose a new type of hybrid automata which aims at the formal analysis and synthesis of the control plan for hybrid systems. In this system, executions can be represented by transfinite sequences of infinitesimal actions over $^*\mathbb{R}$ for the both continuous and discrete dynamics. We can deal with the convergent (even also divergent) sequences such as Zeno in this framework. Although Büchi's transfinite automaton is formed over the countable ordinal, we use his idea for the hypernumber $^*\mathbb{N}$ and $^*\mathbb{R}$. The formulation based on the nonstandard analysis is required because the state and its physical situation is defined after the limit transition depending on the times of iteration $(\omega, 2\omega, \omega^2, \cdots)$. Namely, we need to incorporate the limit of functions over $\mathbb{R}$ with the limit transition. The transfinite transition on ordinal is possibly introduced to the standard hybrid automata directly, but it may be weak in this sense. The nonstandard formulation always allows the transfinite state transition to be complete.

In order to deal with the hybrid dynamics in the transfinite hybrid automata, the following inferential devices are required:

(1) a reasoning system for the extended arithmetic of the hyperfinite integer and $^*\mathbb{R}$

(2) a set of transfer rules between $^*\mathbb{R}$ and $\mathbb{R}$ such as

$$^\circ(x+y) = {^\circ}x + {^\circ}y, {^\circ}(xy) = {^\circ}x{^\circ}y,$$
$$^\circ x \neq 0 \to {^\circ}(1/x) = 1/{^\circ}x, {^\circ}(1 + \frac{x}{\omega})^\omega = e^x$$

A symbolic and numerical simulator is partially developed on $Mathematica^{TM}$ of Wolfram Research Inc. The symbolic simulation of the recurrence equation is troublesome because its solution is usually given in the form of very long arithmetic formula.

Many problems remains for the future study. Especially, the synthesis or verification of the transfinite hybrid automata may not necessarily be easy. Büchi proved the equivalence of the transfinite automata to the formulas of some second order language for the countable ordinals [5]. This suggests that it may be possibly used as the specification language for the transfinite behaviors of dynamics.

References

1. Alur,R., Courcoubetis,C. Henzinger,T.A. and Ho, P.,1993. Hybrid Automata: An algorithmic Approach to the Specification and Verification of Hybrid Systems, *Hybrid Systems (Grossman, R.L., et al. eds) LNCS 736*, 209-229.
2. Balluci,A., Natale,F.Di., Sangiovanni-Vincentelli,A. and Schuppen, J.H.,2004. Synthesis for Idle Speed Control of an Automotive Engine, *Proc HSCC2004 LNCS 2993*, 80-94.
3. Bérard,B., Picaronny,C.,1997. Accepting Zeno words without making time stand still, *Mathematical Foundations of Computer Science 1997, LNCS 1295*, 149-158.
4. Bruyére,V. and Carton,O.,2001. Automata on Linear Orderings : in *DLT2002 (Ito, M., et al. eds) LNCS 2450*, 103-115.
5. Büchi J.R.,1965. Transfinite Automata recursions and weak second order theory of ordinals, *In Proc. Int. Congress Logic, Methodology, and Philosophy of Science*, 2-23.
6. Cassez F., Henzinger,T.A. and Raskn, JF.,2002. A Comparison of Control Problems for Timed and Hybrid Systems, *Proc. HSCC2002 LNCS 2289*, 134-148.
7. Choueka Y.,1978. Finite automata, definable sets, and regular expressions over ω^n-tape, *J. Compute. System Sci.*, 17(1) 81-97.
8. Davis, Y. 1992. Infinite Loops in Finite Time: Some Observations, *Proc.Int. Conf. Principle of Knowledge Representation and Reasoning*, 47-58.
9. Egerstedt M.,2000. Behavior Based Robotics Using Hybrid Automata, *In Proc. HSCC2000. LNCS 1790*, 103-116.

10. Goldblatt, R. 1998. *Lecture on the Hyperreals: An Introduction to Nonstandard Analysis*, New York, Springer.
11. Grossman, R.L.,Larson R.G.,1995.An algebraic approach to hybrid systems, *Theoretical Computer Science*, 138:101-112.
12. Hansen, M.R.,Pandya P.K. and Chaochen,Z,1995. Finite divergence, *Theoretical Computer Science*, 138:113-139.
13. Henzinger, T.A.,1996. The Theory of Hybrid Automata, *Proc. 11th Annual Sympo. on Logic and Computer Science LNCS 96*, 278-292.
14. Johansson, K.H.,Egerstedt,M.,Lygeros,J. and Sasty,S.,1994. On the Regularization of Zeno Hybrid Automata, *System & Control Letters*, 38:141-150.
15. Iwasaki,Y.,Farquhar,A.,Saraswat,V.,Bobrow,D. and Gupta,V.,1995. Modeling Time in Hybrid System: How Fast Is " Instantaneous", *Proc. 14th Int. Conf. Artificial Intelligence*, 1773-1781.
16. Robinson, A. 1974. *Non-standard analysis*, Amsterdam, North Holland.
17. Zhang, J., Johansson, K.H., Lygeros, J. and Sasty,S., 2000. Dynamical System Revisited: Hybrid Systems with Zeno Execution, *Proc.HSCC2000. LNCS 1790*, 451-464.
18. Wojciechowski J.,1985. Finite automata on transfinite sequences and regular expressions, *Fundamenta informaticæ*, 8(3-4) 379-396.

Design of Optimal Autonomous Switching Circuits to Suppress Mechanical Vibration

Dominik Niederberger

Automatic Control Laboratory, Swiss Federal Institute of Technology (ETH),
CH–8092 Zürich, Switzerland
niederberger@control.ee.ethz.ch
http://control.ethz.ch

Abstract. This paper demonstrates the use of a hybrid system approach to design optimal controllers for smart damping materials. Recently, controllers have been used to switch piezoelectric materials for mechanical vibration suppression. These controllers allow a small implementation and require little or no power. However, the control laws to switch these circuits are derived heuristically and it remains unclear, if better control laws exist. We present a new control approach based on a hybrid system framework. This allows to derive optimal switching laws by solving a receding horizon optimal control problem with multi-parametric programming. Additionally, we show how to implement the optimal switching laws with analog electronic circuitry such that the resulting damping circuits do not require power for operation. Simulations show the improvement of the damping compared with heuristically derived circuits and experiments demonstrate that the autonomous damping circuits can suppress vibration without requiring additional power.

1 Introduction

Generally, the performance of passive damping materials to suppress mechanical vibration is very poor for low frequencies. The resulting strong vibration can cause malfunction or even damage the material. In other cases, the vibration can reduce the precision of machinery tools or unwanted noise radiation from the material can occur. Therefore active vibration control was introduced [1, 2]. However, conventional active vibration control requires many bulky electronic devices and power supply for its operation making this technology expensive and not suitable for applications in highly integrated smart damping materials. Thus, piezoelectric shunt damping was suggested where an electrical network is attached to the terminals of a piezoelectric transducer as shown in Figure 1. These shunt circuits Z can dissipate the transformed mechanical vibration energy or store the energy and give it back to the mechanical system in the optimal moment. Several electrical shunt topologies were proposed, for example the R shunt[3] that is very easy to implement and does not require a power supply, but its damping performance is very poor. More efficient are resonant shunts[3, 4, 5, 6], like $R - L$ shunts. However, these shunts lack from the drawback that

M. Morari and L. Thiele (Eds.): HSCC 2005, LNCS 3414, pp. 511–525, 2005.
© Springer-Verlag Berlin Heidelberg 2005

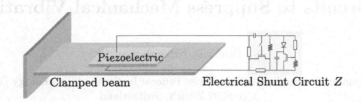

Fig. 1. Shunt Damping

they are very hard to tune and the inductance L needs to be very high (from 1 H to more than 100 H). Such a high inductance can only be implemented with virtual[7] or synthetic[8] impedances and thus the $R - L$ shunt requires power for operation. Other shunts, like negative capacitor shunts [9], also require power and are even more difficult to implement and tune.

In this paper, we will show how to implement a damping circuit that can efficiently suppress structure vibration without requiring power for operation. The idea is based on so called switching shunts as shown in Figure 2a), where the first two cases will be investigated in this paper. We will demonstrate how to design optimal switching controllers S for these shunts using a hybrid system approach and how to implement these controllers completely autonomous, i.e. without power supply. Experiments will show that these new shunts can damp vibration without electrical power requirement.

2   Model and Control Problem Formulation

The aim of this paper is to develop an autonomous control device that can efficiently damp structural vibration and does not require any extra power for operation. The model for the design of the optimal switching control is kept as simple as possible. Only one or later two structural modes and the piezoelectric transducer are modelled. It was shown in [10] that composite structures with an electrically shunted piezoelectric transducer can be modelled as an electrical equivalent system. In Figure 2b), the electrical equivalent circuit for one

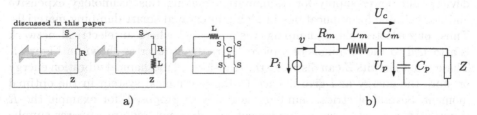

Fig. 2. a) Different switching shunt topologies b) Electrical equivalent model of the shunted piezoelectric composite structure

structural mode with a shunted piezoelectric patch is shown. The state-space representation of this system is

$$\dot{\mathbf{x}} = \underbrace{\begin{bmatrix} 0 & 1/C_m & 0 \\ -1/L_m & -R_m/L_m & -1/L_m \\ 0 & 1/C_p & -1/(C_pZ) \end{bmatrix}}_{\mathbf{A}} \mathbf{x} + \underbrace{\begin{bmatrix} 0 \\ 1/L_m \\ 0 \end{bmatrix}}_{\mathbf{B}} P \text{ and } y = \underbrace{\begin{bmatrix} 0 & 1 & 0 \end{bmatrix}}_{\mathbf{C}} \mathbf{x}, \quad (1)$$

with the state vector $\mathbf{x} = [U_c, v, U_p]^T$, where v denotes the velocity and P, R_m, L_m, C_m, C_p, and Z the corresponding disturbance force, the equivalent damping, mass, stiffness, piezoelectric capacitance and the shunt impedance that has to be designed. For more details, the reader is referred to Niederberger et al. [10]. The transfer function of the electrical equivalent system is equal to other models considered for shunt damping[3, 11]. However, the electrical equivalent model allows easy simulations of the shunted composite structure using electronic circuit simulators like Saber[1] or PSpice[2]. For models with several structure modes, the method by Moheimani et al. [5] may be preferred. Using subspace identification, the parameters of this model can easily be identified from experimental data. We will consider both modelling techniques for the optimal control design in Section 4. In the following, we want to find a switching sequence or switching law S that minimizes the vibration using the switching R or $R-L$ shunt shown in Figure 2a). The objective is to solve the optimization problem

$$\min_{S(t)} \int_0^\infty \left(\mathbf{C}x(t)\right)^2 dt = \min_{S(t)} \int_0^\infty v^2(t) dt, \quad (2)$$

where the disturbance force P is either a Dirac-impulse or a colored noise disturbance.

3   Heuristic Control Laws

3.1   Switching R Shunt Circuit

Figure 3a) shows the switching R shunt, where a resistor R is shunted to the piezoelectric transducer depending on the switch state S. Based on the work of Larson[12] to change the stiffness of acoustic drivers, Clark et al.[11] introduced the State-Switching technique for shunt damping. First, the switch controller was derived for a mechanical single degree of freedom ($SDOF$) system like in Figure 3c). The aim is to suppress the vibration of mass M, that is attached by a variable spring with either $k = k_0$ or $k = k_0 + \Delta k$ where $\Delta k > 0$. Additionally, the mass is damped by a damper d. The mass M is subjected to a tonal excitation force with a frequency equal to the resonance frequency of the system. The idea of State Switching is that the mass starts off in the high-stiffness ($k = k_0 + \Delta k$).

---

[1] SaberSketch, V2.4, Avant! Corp., 9205 S.W. Gemini Drive, Beaverton, Or 97008.
[2] PSpice Schematics, Evaluation V9.1, Cadence Design Systems, www.cadence.com.

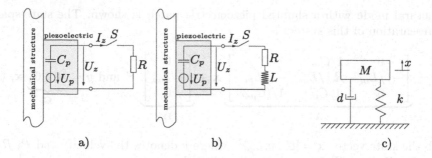

Fig. 3. a) Switching R Shunt, b) Switching $R - L$ Shunt c) Single degree of freedom (SDOF) system whose stiffness can either be $k = k_0 + \Delta k$ or $k = k_0$

When the mass reaches the maximum displacement, the potential energy is also at a maximum, defined by

$$E_{pot}^{max} = \frac{1}{2} \underbrace{(k_0 + \Delta k)}_{k} x_{max}^2. \tag{3}$$

At this point, the stiffness is switched to a low stiffness state ($k = k_0$) such that the potential energy is $E_{pot}^{max'} = k_0 x_{max}^2/2$, which is less than before. The difference in energy is

$$\Delta E = \frac{1}{2}(\Delta k) x_{max}^2. \tag{4}$$

This energy is released from the system, when switching occurs. The spring is kept in the low stiffness state until the modal displacement returns to equilibrium (i.e. $x(t) = 0$). Then the spring is switched back to the high stiffness state and the entire cycle repeats. The control law for the stiffness k can be expressed as

$$k(t) = \begin{cases} k_0 + \Delta k & : \quad x(t) \cdot \dot{x}(t) \geq 0 \\ k_0 & : \quad x(t) \cdot \dot{x}(t) < 0. \end{cases} \tag{5}$$

This heuristic control law was then applied for shunted piezoelectric structures, because one structural mode of the piezoelectric composite structure can be modelled as a $SDOF$ system and the corresponding stiffness is changed by the piezoelectric actuator between its open and closed-circuit states by approximately $1/(1 - k_{ij})$, where k_{ij} is the appropriate piezoelectric coupling factor. The control law of the shunt impedance is then

$$Z(t) = \begin{cases} \infty \ \Omega & \text{if} \quad x(t) \cdot \dot{x}(t) \geq 0 \\ 0 \ \Omega & \text{if} \quad x(t) \cdot \dot{x}(t) < 0 \end{cases} \text{ or } S(t) = \begin{cases} 0 & \text{if} \quad x(t) \cdot \dot{x}(t) \geq 0 \\ 1 & \text{if} \quad x(t) \cdot \dot{x}(t) < 0, \end{cases} \tag{6}$$

for the ideal switch in Figure 3a) with $R = 0 \ \Omega$. In real applications, R that represents the switch is not $0 \ \Omega$ and therefore it remains unclear if the heuristically derived control law still holds, since $R \neq 0$ was not taken into account in the derivation of the State-Switching law.

3.2   Switching R-L Shunt - The SSDI Technique

A switching $R - L$ shunt is shown in Figure 3b). Depending on the switch state S, an $R - L$ network is connected to the terminals of a piezoelectric transducer with the view of minimizing the vibration of the structure. The synchronized switch damping inductor (SSDI)[13, 14] technique says that if the product of the velocity $v(t)$ and U_z becomes greater than zero, the switch is shut. The switch is opened again, when the applied charge reaches a peak with the opposite sign from where it began (about $1/2$ of the time period of the $C_p - L$ resonance). In the SSDI technique, the optimal value of L is more than 20 times smaller than for the standard $R - L$ shunt. Therefore, virtual or synthetic inductors may not be required.

4   Hybrid System Optimal Control Approach

4.1   Hybrid System Model

The systems with the switching electrical shunt circuits can be represented by a piecewise affine (PWA) system like it was shown in Morari et al. [15]. For the switching R or $R - L$ shunted system, one obtains

$$x(t + 1) = \mathbf{A}_d^i x(t) + \mathbf{B}_d^i u(t) \text{ IF } S \in \mathbf{P}^i, \tag{7}$$

where $S \in [0, 1]$ is the state of the switch, $i \in [1, 2]$, $P^1 = 0$, $P^1 = 1$, $\mathbf{A}_d^1$ is the time discretized Matrix $\mathbf{A}$ in Equation 1 where $Z \to \infty$, $\mathbf{A}_d^2$ and Z is either a resistor or a serial inductor-resistor network. Notice that the controller can only affect S, whereas u is regarded as disturbance input. Although PWA systems represent a modelling environment for a wide variety of hybrid systems, they are not suitable for recasting the problem into a compact optimization problem. Therefore, the model is transformed into a Mixed Logical Dynamical (MLD) form (Bemporat and Morari) [16]. It can be used to recast the problem into a mixed integer linear (MILP) or quadratic program (MIQP). The procedure to reformulate the PWA system in Equation 7 is automated with the compiler HYS-DEL (HYbrid System DEscription Language) [17], that generates the matrices of the MLD.

4.2   Implicit Solution

In a first step, the optimal switch sequence is calculated for an impulse disturbance. This is done by using the model predictive control methodology with online optimization. The idea is to use the model of the plant to predict the future evolution of the system. At each time step t the controller chooses a sequence of optimal future switch inputs through an online optimization procedure. Afterwards, only the first sample of the optimal sequence is implemented. Then at

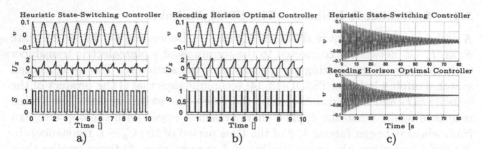

Fig. 4. a) Implicit optimal control and b) heuristic control of the switching R shunt. c) comparison of the performance for an impulse disturbance

time $t + 1$, a new set of measurements is taken and a new sequence is computed based on the current state. This procedure is expressed in the following formula

$$\min_{S \subset S_t(0),...,S_t(m-1)} \sum_{k=0}^{m-1} \| \mathbf{C}x(k) \|_2^2$$

$$\text{subj. to} \begin{cases} S_t(k) \quad \in [0,1] \\ x(t+1) = \mathbf{A}_{\mathbf{d}}^{\mathbf{i}} x(t) + \mathbf{B}_{\mathbf{d}}^{\mathbf{i}} u(t) \text{ IF } S \in \mathbf{P^i}, \end{cases} \tag{8}$$

where m is the prediction horizon. The cost function is the 2-norm of $\mathbf{C}x(k)$. The difference to the ∞-norm is that in the 2-norm case, the larger amplitudes of the vibration get more weighted. However, in simulation it could be shown that the optimal switching sequence is the same for both norms. Therefore, the ∞-norm is used for the explicit solution in section 4.3, since in this case the optimization problem can be cast as a (MILP) that can be solved faster. The optimization problem was solved with either Cplex[3] or the free available GLPK (GNU Linear Programming Kit)[4]. For this class of problem, one has to choose a prediction horizon m and a sampling time T_s. Very small sampling times result in a larger number of prediction steps m and that makes the computation extremely long. On the other hand, long sampling times prohibit the switching controller to switch when it is optimal since it is not possible to switch within two samples. Therefore, a tradeoff has to be made. This is done by plotting the optimized cost function in Equation 8 as a function of T_s and m and choosing the optimal parameters from that plot.

Model with one structural mode: In a first study, the optimization program is run with a model that captures one structural mode, the piezoelectric transducer and the electrical shunt circuit. For the switching R shunt, the simulation results for an impulse response are shown in Figure 4 in comparison with

---

[3] CPLEX 7.0, ILOG Inc., Gentilly Cedex, France.

[4] GLPK, A. Makhorin, Department for Applied Informatics, Moscow Aviation Institute, Russia, http://www.gnu.org/software/glpk/glpk.html.

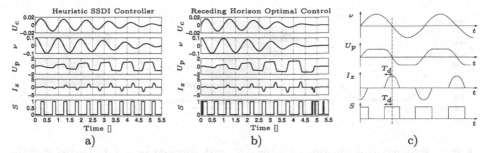

Fig. 5. Heuristic versus RHOC with $T_s = 0.02$s. a) Heuristic Controller, b) RHOC with $m = 22$. c) According to the RHOC, the switch is turned on $T_d = \pi\sqrt{LC_p}/2$ before the product of the velocity $v(t)$ and U_z becomes greater than zero

the heuristic switching controller. One can see that the performance is slightly improved. The difference to the heuristic controller is that the optimal controller only briefly shuts the switch. In Figure 5, the results with the switching $R - L$ shunt are shown. It can be seen that the optimal controller behaves very similar like the heuristic controller. However, it shuts the switch earlier than the heuristic controller does. This is better shown in Figure 5c), where the optimal controller shuts T_d before $v(t) \cdot U_z(t)$ changes its sign. On the other hand, the standard heuristic controller would shut exactly when $v(t) \cdot U_z(t)$ becomes zero.

Model with two structural modes: In these simulations, the model captures two structural modes. Since the switching R shunt did not show promising damping performance with either the heuristic or the receding horizon optimal controller, we will only show the results with the switching $R - L$ shunt. In Figure 6, it can be seen that it is possible to damp two structural modes with only one switching $R - L$ shunt. Figure 6a) shows the result for an impulse disturbance and Figure 6b) and c) show the time response to a colored noise disturbance and the frequency spectrum of the corresponding response.

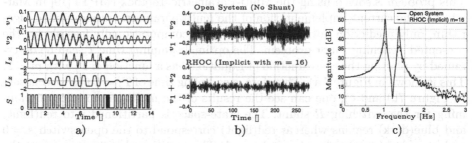

Fig. 6. System with 2 structural modes: a) Impulse response: Open system (dashed line), switching $R - L$ shunt (solid line) b) broadband disturbance c) spectrum of the broadband response

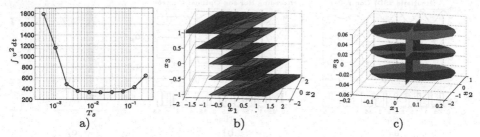

Fig. 7. R-Shunt: a) Evaluation of optimal T_s with constant $m = 2$. b) Partition of the state-space ($m = 2$, $T_s = 0.08$s). Red (light) corresponds to $S = 0$ and blue (dark) to $S = 1$. c) Zoom into the origin of the partitioned state-space

4.3   Explicit Solution

Since the computation of the optimization problem at one time step takes several seconds and the sampling time of real damping applications is generally in the range of milliseconds, the implicit optimal control approach cannot be applied. Therefore, a multi-parametric programming algorithm is used [18] to avoid the online computation of the MILP. This is referred as to the explicit solution. The idea of multi-parametric programming is to calculate the optimal $s^*(0)$ as a function of the state $x(0)$. In this case, the state space gets partitioned into regions where $s^*(0)$ is either 0 or 1. This means that once the partition of the state space is calculated, one can easily look-up the optimal switch state s^* for the actual state $x(t)$ of the system. Moreover, the partition of the state-space allows to derive the optimal control law. The multi-parametric programming to compute the explicit optimal switching law can be formulated as

$$\mathbf{J}_N^*(x_0) = \min_{S_t(0),\dots,S_t(m-1)} \sum_{k=0}^{m-1} \| \mathbf{C}x(k) \|_\infty \qquad (9)$$

$$\text{subj. to} \quad \mathbf{GS}_m \leq \mathbf{W} + \mathbf{E}x_0. \qquad (10)$$

This problem is solved using the Multi-Parametric Toolbox (MPT) [19] in Matlab. For the current implementation of the multi-parametric programming algorithm, only prediction horizons m below 2 are computationally feasible for the presented switching shunt problem. The optimal sampling time T_s can be determined by plotting the cost-function of Equation 8 as a function of T_s with $m = 2$. This is shown in Figure 7 a). Therefore, a sampling time of $T_s = 0.08$s was chosen. In Figure 7b) and c), one can see the results of the multi-parametric programming for the switching R shunt. The state-space is partitioned into red(light) and blue(dark) regions whereas red(light) correspond to the open switch $s = 0$ and blue(dark) to the closed switch $s = 1$. The partitioned state-space gives the information whether the switch should be shut or not. This is similar like a look-up table. The same procedure is performed for the switching $R - L$ shunt. In Figure 8, one can see the simulation results with the explicit optimal controller (off-line) and the implicit optimal controller (on-line) for the switching $R - L$

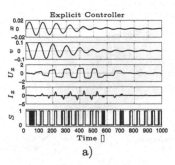
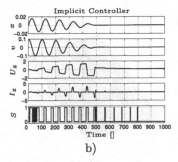

Fig. 8. Switching $R-L$ Shunt: a) Explicit solution with $m=2$, $T_s=0.08$s, b) Implicit solution with $m=20$, $T_s=0.02$s

shunt. The results are very similar. The small difference appears due to the fact that the explicit controller was designed for a sampling-time $T_s=0.08$s, which prohibits to switch at exactly the optimal time. On the other hand, the implicit controller was simulated for $T_s=0.02$s and a prediction horizon $m=10$ that explains the slightly better performance.

4.4   Approximation of the Optimal Switching Law

A quasi-optimal and continuous control law for the switching R or $R-L$ shunt can be deduced by inspecting the explicit and implicit solution of sections 4.2 and 4.3. The quasi-optimal control law should approximate the optimal controller as good as possible, but its implementation as an electronic analog circuit should be kept very easy.

Approximated Switching Law for Switching R Shunt: In simulations, a strong correlation between x_2 and x_3, i.e. $x_2 = \alpha x_3$, can be observed. If this correlation is taken into account, the 3 dimensional regions in Figure 7 b) can be cut along $x_2 = \alpha x_3$ into regions of dimension 2. The obtained approximated regions are plotted in Figure 9a). The switching law defined by these regions can be described by

$$S(t) = \begin{cases} 1 & \text{if} \quad x_1(t) \cdot x_2(t) \geq 0 \\ 0 & \text{if} \quad x_1(t) \cdot x_2(t) < 0, \end{cases} \tag{11}$$

where $x_2 \sim \dot{x}_1$. One can see that this is the same switching law like that of the State-Switching in Equation (6) proposed by [11].

Approximated Switching Law for Switching $R-L$ Shunt: It is more difficult to obtain an approximated switching law for the $R-L$ shunt, because the regions of the explicit solution are of dimension 4. One possibility would be to plot the regions in 2 dimensions by keeping two states constant. But even in this case, it is tricky to formulate an approximated switching law. Therefore, we will have a closer look at the simulated solution in the time domain. In Figure 5 where the optimal switching sequence is computed implicitly, it can be seen that

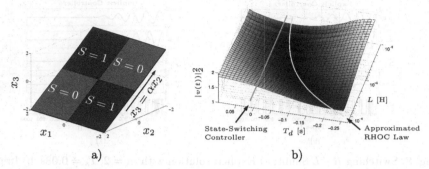

a)   b)

Fig. 9. a) Resulting regions, if the 3 dimensional regions are cut along $x_2 = \alpha x_3$. b) Vibration energy as a function of the switch on time T_d and the inductor L. One can see that the heuristic State-Switching Controller is not optimal, whereas the approximated Receding Horizon Optimal Controller (RHOC) achieves optimal vibration reduction

the switch is turned on $T_d = \pi\sqrt{LC_p}/2$ before $v(t) = 0$ or the strain $x(t)$ is at a maximum, i.e. a quarter of the period of the $L - C_p$ resonance. The switch is turned off whenever the current I_z becomes zero after the switch was turned on. Therefore one can formulate the following law:

$$S(t) = \begin{cases} 1 & \text{if } t \geq T_i - \underbrace{\frac{\pi\sqrt{LC_p}}{2}}_{T_d} \wedge I_z \neq 0 \\ 0 & \text{else,} \end{cases} \tag{12}$$

with T_i defined by $v(T_i) = 0$. This new switching law is very similar like that of Richard et al. [13], but the time-shift T_d is new and improves the damping performance. The improvement can also be seen in Figure 9b), where the vibration energy is plotted for different T_d and L. The heuristic control law would keep $T_d = 0$, whereas the approximated optimal control law keeps T_d on the curved line where the vibration energy is minimal.

5 Implementation as an Autonomous Electrical Circuit

5.1 Circuit Design

Simulations in Section 4 showed that switching $R - L$ shunts can efficiently suppress vibration. On the other hand, switching R shunts are not very promising, although they are more efficient than simple R shunts. In the following, we will demonstrate how to implement the switching $R - L$ shunt such that the resulting circuit does not require electrical power for its operation. The scope is to design a circuit comprising an inductor, resistor and switch with corresponding logic such that the switch is shut according to the rules derived from the approximated optimal control design in Section 4.4. The problem can be solved by using a second collocated piezoelectric patch as shown in Figure 10a). The voltage across

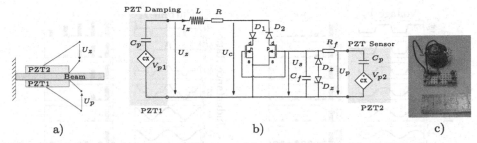

Fig. 10. a) Set-up of the clamped beam with 2 PZTs b) Sketch of the autonomous shunt circuit that does not require power for operation. c) Photo of the circuit

this patch is related to the strain with $U_p = \alpha x$, where α is a constant. We assume that the signal U_p consists only of the structure mode that has to be damped. This can be achieved by placing the piezoelectric patch at a location where almost only the corresponding mode is observable. From Section 4.4, we know that the switch is shut T_d before the strain reaches its maximum. This is implemented with a low-pass filter that changes the phase of U_p such that the filtered $\tilde{U}_p$ reaches its maximum T_d before U_p reaches its next maximum (Figure 10b). Two Z-diodes convert the sinusoidal signal into a rectangular signal U_c that is supplied to the switch. The switch is designed to automatically turn off when the current changes its sign according to Section 4.4. For this purpose, two complementary field-effect transistors (MOSFETs) are used. When the signal U_c is positive, M_1 is on, if it is negative, M_2 is on. The diodes D_1 and D_2 make that the transistors turn off whenever the current changes its sign. In this case, the whole switch remains off until U_c changes its sign. In this case the other transistor turns on. This corresponds to the switching law derived from the optimal control design. The functionality of the circuit was successfully validated by simulations in PSpice and Saber. A photo of the implemented circuit is shown in Figure 10c).

5.2   Excitation of Higher Harmonics

Because of the switching, higher structural modes can be excited. The level of excitation depends on the inductor value. The higher the inductance, the smoother is the waveform of U_z and I_z and therefore the smaller is the excitation of higher harmonics. The waveforms of U_z and I_z can be expressed as Fourier-series

$$U_z(t) = \sum_{k=1}^{\infty} a_k \sin\left(\frac{2\pi k t}{T_m}\right),$$ (13)

with the period T_m. The calculated Fourier coefficients a_k are shown in Figure 11. One can see that with an increase of the inductance ratio, the excitation of higher harmonics decreases. For the design of the switching $R - L$ shunt, one has to check if there exist higher harmonics corresponding to structural resonances that could be excited.

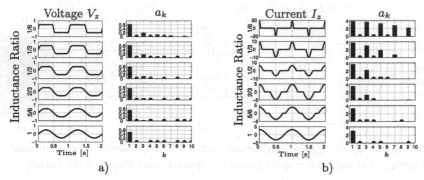

Fig. 11. Fourier coefficients for a) U_z and b) I_z. An inductor ratio of 1 corresponds to the standard $R - L$ shunt configuration

5.3   Experiments

This section shows some experimental results with the analog switching $R - L$ shunt that does not require power for operation. For simplicity, the first experiment was carried out on a one-side clamped beam (Figure 10a). Two identical collocated piezoelectric patches (Midé QP25N[5]) are used for shunt damping. The positions of the patches are determined by maximizing the strain of the corresponding structural mode to be damped (here 2nd mode). The beam is excited by either an additional piezoelectric patch or an electromechanical shaker. The results are shown in Figure 12a) and b) for tonal excitation where a vibration suppression of about 8 dB is achieved. In Figure 12c), one can see that the vibration suppression depends on the magnitude of the vibration, i.e. on the magnitude of the excitation force. If the magnitude of the excitation is too low, the transistors do not work, because the generated voltages are to small for the transistor's threshold. On the other hand, if the excitation is too high and thus the vibration is very high, the hysteresis of the piezoelectric material starts to play a role. In this case, the vibration suppression is not very effective anymore and the vibration suppression decreases for increasing excitation force. In Figure 13, the response for broadband excitation is plotted. It can be seen that the vibration suppression of the autonomous switching shunt is around 8dB, whereas the $R - L$ shunt with power supply achieves 18dB. On the other hand, the standard R that is autonomous like the switching shunt, achieves only 1.5dB of vibration suppression.

The second experiment was conducted on a plate mounted in a duct system as shown in Figure 14a). The scope is to minimize the sound transmission of the plate. This is done by using two bonded piezoelectric patches on the plate that are connected to the autonomous switching $R - L$ shunt. A QP25N from Midé is used for damping and a QP10Ni for driving the switch. The QP10Ni is based on the direct 3-3 piezoelectric effect and thus it provides higher output

[5] Midé Technology Corporation, 200 Boston Ave, Suite 1000 Medford, MA 02155 U.S.A, www.mide.com

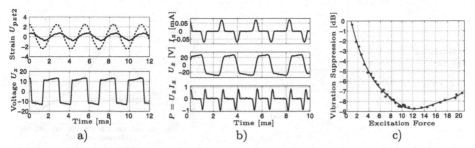

Fig. 12. Tonal excitation of the beam. a) open loop (dashed) and shunted system (solid) and corresponding voltage U_z. b) Current I_z, voltage U_z and power $I_z U_z$. c) Vibration suppression of the shunted system as a function of the excitation's magnitude. The vibration suppression is measured at 314.2 Hz and the measurement points are approximated by a 4th order polynomial

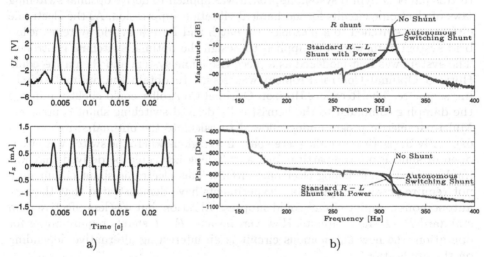

Fig. 13. Broadband excitation of the beam: a) Signals U_z and I_z of the shunt b) Transfer-function from excitation to strain on the beam with different shunts

voltages and one can expect better performance since the transistors only work after a certain threshold voltage. The results for broadband excitation are shown in Figure 14b), where the magnitude of the sound-pressure transfer-function P_{out}/P_{in} is plotted. One can see that a decrease of around 2dB is achieved. The performance of a standard $R-L$ shunt is around 8dB, but it requires additional power for operation since the inductor L is very big and can only be implemented with virtual inductors. Therefore, the autonomous switching $R-L$ shunt could be preferred depending on the application.

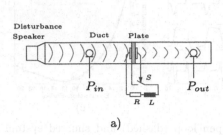

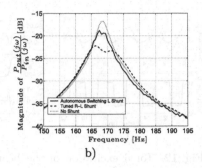

a)   b)

Fig. 14. a) Set-up of the duct system with shunted plate b) Magnitude of the transfer-function from P_{in} to P_{out} with different shunts

6   Conclusion

In this paper, a hybrid system approach was applied to derive optimal switching laws of electronic circuits for mechanical vibration suppression. As the electronic circuits are switched to a piezoelectric patch and form a hybrid systems, a hybrid system framework was applied to design the optimal switching controller. The system was first modelled as a piecewise affine system and then a Receding Horizon Optimal Control Problem was solved to obtain the optimal switching sequence. The Receding Horizon Optimal Controller could slightly improve the damping compared to the heuristically derived switching shunt controllers. Multi-parametric programming allowed to calculate the optimal switching law explicitly by partitioning the state-space into regions where the switch was either open or shut. From the partitioning, a switching law could be derived that was implemented in an analog electronic circuit. This electronic shunt circuit does not require power for operation. Experiments have demonstrated that the new autonomous damping circuit could suppress vibration, but was less effective than standard $R - L$ shunt circuits. However, because $R - L$ shunts require power for operation, the new autonomous circuit is an interesting alternative depending on the application.

Acknowledgments

The author wishes to thank his supervisor Prof. Manfred Morari for his continuous help and encouraging discussions. Support for this research has been provided by grants from ETH (Zürich) and EMPA (Dübendorf). The experimental facilities were provided by the EMPA (Dübendorf). Special thanks go to Michal Kvasnika, Mato Baotic and Stanislaw Pietrzko for technical assistance.

References

1. Fuller, C.R., Elliott, S.J., Nelson, P.A.: Active Control of Vibration. Academic Press Limited, 24-28 Oval Road, London (1996)

2. Elliott, S., Nelson, P.: Active noise control. IEEE-Signal-Processing-Magazine **10** (1993) 12–35
3. Hagood, N.W., von Flotow, A.: Piezoelectric materials and passive electrical networks. Journal of Sound and Vibration **146(2)** (1991) 243–268
4. Tsai, M.S., Wang, K.W.: On the structural damping characteristics of active piezoelectric actuators with passive shunt. Journal of Sound and Vibration **221** (1999) 1–22
5. Moheimani, S.: A survey of recent innovations in vibration damping and control using shunted piezoelectric transducers. IEEE Transactions on Control Systems Technology **11** (2003) 482–494
6. Niederberger, D., Fleming, A., Moheimani, S., Morari, M.: Adaptive multi-mode resonant piezoelectric shunt damping. Smart Materials and Structures, Institute of Physics Publishing **13** (2004) 1025–1035
7. Antoniou, A.: Realization of gyrators using operational amplifiers and their use in rc-active networks synthesis. Proc. IEE **116** (1969) 1838–1850
8. Fleming, A.J., Behrens, S., Moheimani, S.O.R.: Synthetic impedance for implementation of piezoelectric shunt-damping circuits. IEE Electronics Letters **36** (2000) 1525–1526
9. Wu, S.Y.: Broadband piezoelectric shunts for structural vibration control. Patent No. 6,075,309 (2000)
10. Niederberger, D., Morari, M., Pietrzko, S.: Adaptive resonant shunted piezoelectric devices for vibration suppression. In: Proc. SPIE Smart Structures and Materials - Smart Structures and Integrated Systems, Vol.5056, San Diego, CA USA (2003) 213–224
11. Clark, W.W.: Vibration control with state-switched piezoelectric materials. Journal of intelligent material systems and structures. **11** (2000) 263–271
12. Larson, G., Rogers, P., Munk, W.: State switched transducers: a new approach to high-power, low-frequency, underwater projectors. Journal-of-the-Acoustical-Society-of-America **103** (1998)
13. Richard, C., Guyomar, D., Audigier, D., Bassaler, H.: Enhanced semi-passive damping using continuous switching of a piezoelectric devices on an inductor. In: Proc. SPIE Smart Structures and Materials, Damping and Isolation, SPIE Vol.3989, Newport Beach, CA (2000) 288–299
14. Corr, L., Clark, W.W.: A novel semi-active multi-modal vibration control law for a piezoelectric actuator. Journal of Vibration and Acoustics, Transactions on the ASME **125** (2003) 214–222
15. Morari, M., Baotic, M., Borelli, F.: Hybrid systems modelling and control. European Journal of Control (2003) 177–189
16. Bemporad, A., Morari, M.: Control of systems integrating logic. Automatica **35** (1999) 407–427
17. Torrisi, F., Bemporad, A., Mignone, D.: Hysdel - a tool for generating hybrid models. Technical Report AUT00-03, Automatic Control Laboratory, ETH Zurich (2000)
18. Sakizlis, V., Dua, V., Perkins, J., Pistikopoulos, E.: The explicit control law for hybrid systems via parametric programming. In: Proc. of the 2002 American Control Conference, Anchorage. (2002)
19. Kvasnica, M., Grieder, P., Baotic, M., Morari, M.: Multi-Parametric Toolbox (MPT). (2003)

Interchange Formats for Hybrid Systems: Review and Proposal

Alessandro Pinto[1], Alberto L. Sangiovanni-Vincentelli[1], Luca P. Carloni[3], and Roberto Passerone[2]

[1] Department of Electrical Engineering and Computer Sciences,
University of California at Berkeley, Berkeley, CA 94720
{apinto, alberto}@eecs.berkeley.edu
[2] Cadence Berkeley Labs, Berkeley, CA 94704
robp@cadence.com
[3] Department of Computer Science,
Columbia University in the City of New York, NY 10027-7003
luca@cs.columbia.edu

Abstract. Interchange formats have been the backbone of the EDA industry for several years. They are used as a way of helping the development of design flows that integrate foreign tools using formats with different syntax and, more importantly, different semantics. The need for integrating tools coming from different communities is even more severe for hybrid systems because of the relative immaturity of the field and the intrinsic difficulty of the mathematical underpinnings. In this paper, we provide a discussion about interchange formats for hybrid systems, we survey the approaches used by different tools for analysis (simulation and formal verification) and synthesis of hybrid systems, and we give a recommendation for an interchange format for hybrid systems based on the METROPOLIS metamodel. The proposed interchange format has rigorous semantics and can accommodate the translation to and from the formats of the tools we have surveyed while providing a formal reasoning framework.

1 Introduction

Hybrid systems have proven to be powerful design representations for system-level design in particular for embedded controllers. The term *hybrid* refers to the use of multiple models of computation in a unified framework. Often, hybrid refers to a mix of continuous dynamical systems and finite-state machines even though compositions of heterogeneous systems may be defined in larger semantic domains. The needs for a way of mixing and matching different tools is very much felt because of the relative novelty of this design representation and of the immaturity of the tools available today. There are two camps in the community who deals with hybrid systems: one would prefer to define a common model of computation for hybrid systems that should be used uniformly across different tools, the other pushes for an *interchange format*, i.e., a file, or a set of files, which

M. Morari and L. Thiele (Eds.): HSCC 2005, LNCS 3414, pp. 526–541, 2005.
© Springer-Verlag Berlin Heidelberg 2005

contains data in a given syntax that is understood by different interacting tools. It is not a database nor a data structure, but a simpler object whose goal is to foster the exchange of data among different tools and research groups. Of course, the approach fostered by the first group has innumerable advantages but it faces an uphill battle with respect to the existing tool vendors or providers such as research groups since embracing this approach would require a substantial rewrite of their tools. The second approach could be strengthened by providing rigorous semantics to the interchange format, thereby allowing a formal analysis of the properties of the translation between different hybrid models.

Our goal in this paper is to provide a survey of models of computation used in a number of tools for the design of hybrid systems and to propose a prototype interchange format based on the Metropolis MetaModel (MMM) that should favor the interaction among the groups involved in hybrid system research and development.

In the U.S., the DARPA MoBIES project had the importance of an interchange format very clear and supported the development of HSIF as a way of fostering interactions among its participants. However, limitations to its semantics make the interchange of data between foreign tools difficult (for example, HSIF does not support some of the features of SIMULINK/STATEFLOW model). To motivate our views, we offer here some considerations about interchange formats that are the result of our experience in the field of Electronic Design Automation (EDA) and of a long history in participating to the formation of standard languages and models for hardware design as well as of Columbus [1], a research project supported by the European Community that spearheaded collaboration across the ocean between European and US research groups.

We believe that an interchange format for tools and designs should:

- support all existing tools, modeling approaches and languages in a coherent global view of the applications and of the theory;
- be open, i.e., be available to the entire community at no cost and with full documentation;
- support a variety of export and import mechanisms;
- support hierarchy and object orientation (compact representation, entry error prevention).

By having these fundamental properties, an interchange format can become the formal backbone for the development of sound design methodologies through the assembly of various tools. The process of moving from the design representation used by tool A to the one used by tool B is structured in two steps: first, a representation in the standard interchange format is derived from the design entry that is used by A, then a preprocessing step is applied to produce the design entry on which B can operate. Notice that tool B may not need all the information on the design that were used by A and, as it operates on the design, it may very well produce new data that will be written into the interchange format but that will not ever be used by A. Naturally, the semantics of the interchange format must be rich enough to capture and "protect" the different properties of the design at the various stages of the design process. This guarantees that there will be no loss going from one design environment to another due to the interchange format itself. The format is indeed a neutral go-between.

In our opinion, HSIF is an excellent model for supporting clean design of hybrid systems but not yet a true interchange format. SIMULINK/STATEFLOW internal format could be a de facto standard but it is not open nor it has features that favor easy import and export. MODELICA has full support of hierarchy and of general semantics that subsumes most if not all existing languages and tools. As such, it is indeed an excellent candidate but it is not open. In addition, all of them have not been developed with the goal of supporting heterogeneous implementations.

On the other hand, the METROPOLIS metamodel (MMM) has generality and can be used to represent a very wide class of models of computation. It has a clear separation between communication and computation as well as architecture and function. While the metamodel itself is perfectly capable to express continuous time systems, there is no tool today that can manage this information in METROPOLIS.

In conclusion, we believe that no approach is mature enough today to recommend its general adoption. However, we believe also that combining and leveraging HSIF, MODELICA, and the METROPOLIS metamodel, we can push for the foundations of a standard interchange format as well as a standard design capture language where semantics is favored over syntax. The discussion of this approach is the main goal of the paper.

2   Preliminaries

This section contains the definitions of hybrid systems and the METROPOLIS metamodel language.

Hybrid Systems. The notion of a hybrid system that has been used in the control community is centered around a particular composition of discrete and continuous dynamics. In particular, the system has a continuous evolution and occasional jumps. The jumps correspond to the change of state in an automaton whose transitions are caused either by controllable or uncontrollable external events or by the continuous evolution. A continuous evolution is associated to each state by means of ordinary differential equations. The structure of the equations and the initial condition may be different for each automaton state. In the sequel, we follow the classic work of Lygeros et al. [2] to define a hybrid system as used in the control literature. In this definition, a hybrid system is a tuple $\mathcal{H} = (\mathbf{Q}, \mathbf{U}_D, X, U, V, \mathbf{S}_C, \mathcal{S}, E, Inv, R, G)$. Without going into the detailed definition of each element of the tuple, we just recall that the triple $(\mathbf{Q}, \mathbf{U}_D, E)$ can be viewed as a Finite State Machine (FSM) having state set $\mathbf{Q}$, inputs $\mathbf{U}_D$ and transitions defined by E. This FSM characterizes the structure of the discrete transitions. A dynamical system is associated to each state and characterized by a set of differential equations. Of particular interest are the mappings Inv, R, G. $Inv : \mathbf{Q} \to 2^{X \times \mathbf{U}_D \times U \times V}$ is a mapping called *invariant* that is defined over each state of the automaton and states the conditions under which a transition from a state to another in the automaton *must occur*. $R : E \times X \times U \times V \rightarrow 2^X$ is the reset mapping that defines the initial state of the continuous dynamics after a particular transition has occurred. $G : E \rightarrow 2^{X \times U \times V}$ is a mapping called *guard*. G determines the conditions under which a transition *may occur*. The guard and the invariant mappings are complex to analyze with respect to the behavior of the hybrid system. Guards are partly responsible for the non-deterministic behavior of a hybrid system since when a guard allows a transition to occur, the hybrid system may or may not take that transition. The full semantics of a hybrid system are beyond the scope of this paper and can be found in [2].

Metropolis and Its Meta-model. The METROPOLIS metamodel [3] is a formalism with precise semantics, yet general enough to support the models of computation [4] proposed so far and, at the same time, to allow the invention of new ones. A behavior can be defined as concurrent occurrences of sequences of *actions*. Some action may follow another action, which may take place concurrently with other actions. The occurrences of these actions constitute the behavior of a system that the actions belong to.

In the metamodel, special types of objects called *process* and *medium* are used to describe computation and communication, respectively. Processes are active objects characterized by a thread that specifies the possible sequence of actions (or better of events, where an event is the beginning or ending of an action) of the process. Medium, instead, are passive objects that offer services and are used for implementing specialized communication protocols. For coordination, one can write formulas in linear temporal logic [5], or use quantity managers to describe a particular algorithmic implementation of constraints. Operationally, a building block called *quantity* is defined in the metamodel language. Its task is to attach tags to events. An execution is then divided in two steps. First, processes issue requests to the quantity managers to annotate their events with particular values of the quantities. Second, the control passes to the quantity managers that order the event depending on the values that have been requested, and decide which requests to grant. In a complex system, multiple quantities could be needed. A quantity manager has to be defined for each quantity. Since their scheduling decisions could depend on each other, the metamodel language provides an interaction mechanism that the user can fully customize to give a specific semantics to the model.

The semantics of the interchange format must be carefully defined to cover all the languages of interest, while still providing efficient and tractable access to subsets corresponding to particular domains of application. The Metropolis metamodel serves this purpose. In fact, states and continuous processes are defined in abstract terms, and can be tailored for the individual needs of a particular model of hybrid behavior. In particular, the mechanisms that determine the operational semantics of the model can be customized by simply encoding the appropriate scheduling policies as the resolution function of the quantity managers dedicated to handling the transition relation and the discretized solution of the continuous dynamics. This flexibility is essential to cleanly, and natively, support different semantic models in a unified environment. In addition, the metamodel is in itself executable, and provides the high level abstract semantics that regulates the scheduling and interaction of processes and quantity managers. Thus, if different models of hybrid behavior are translated into our interchange format, they can also be executed together. Their execution is regulated by the specific choice of managers and resolution functions that are used to glue the system together.

In addition, the full power of the metamodel constraint capabilities and declarative specification can be used to ensure and/or verify that certain properties of interest are satisfied at the border of the domains. This capability is especially important, as it provides a single unified environment for co-simulation and co-analysis.

Note, in particular, that the semantics of interaction between different models of computation is not fixed, but can be defined according to the implementation strategy. The metamodel is first used to define a common semantic domain. Then, the appropriate refinement maps are used to embed each specific model into the common refinement. The semantics of interaction is then the result of applying the metamodel abstract semantics (defined in terms of action automata [3]) to the instances of the models. Thus, different model interactions can be obtained by not only changing the common refinement, but also by playing with the refinement maps. Experimenting with this technique is part of our future work. In particular we aim at integrating different formalisms by showing their individual strengths and weaknesses.

3   A Survey of Languages and Tools for Hybrid Systems

Table 1 shows the approach adopted by each language for modeling the basic hybrid system structure. The first column indicates how discrete and continuous signals are declared in each language. Some languages like CHARON [6] and MODELICA [7] use special type modifiers to specify whether a variable is discrete or continuous. However, the **semantics is different** in the two cases. While CHARON defines a discrete variable constant between two events, hence having derivative equal to zero, the derivative of discrete variables in MODELICA is not defined. Graphical languages like HYVISUAL [8], SIMULINK [9], and SCICOS [10] rely on attributes associated with ports. Type of signals can be automatically inferred during compilation. HYSDEL [11] and CHECKMATE [12] describe the hybrid system as a finite state machine connected to a set of dynamical systems making the interface between discrete and continuous signals fixed and explicit.

Another basic feature is the association of a dynamical system to a specific state of the hybrid automata. HYVISUAL and CHARON seem to have the most intuitive syntax and semantics for this purpose. In HYVISUAL a state of the hybrid automata can be refined into a continuous time system. CHARON allows a mode to be described by a set of algebraic and differential equations. In CHECKMATE, SIMULINK, and HYSDEL a hybrid system is modeled with two blocks: a state machine and a set of dynamical systems. A discrete state tran-

Table 1. Various approaches to modeling hybrid systems

Name	Continuous/Discrete Specification	State/Dynamics Mapping	Continuous/Discrete Interface
CHARON	defined by language modifier	modes refinenement into continuous dynamics	indirect
CHECKMATE	separation between FSMs and dynamical systems	discrete output from FSMs to dynamical systems	event generator first order hold
HYSDEL	real and boolean signals	discrete output from FSMs to dynamical systems	event generator first order hold
HYVISUAL	signal attribute, automatic type detection	state refinement into continuous models	toContinuous, toDiscrete actors
MODELICA	defined by language modifier	different equation sets depending on events	indirect (when statements)
SCICOS	defined by port attribute	implemented by connections of event selectors	interaction between continuous/discrete states
SIMULINK	automatic type detection	discrete output from FSMs to dynamical systems	library blocks like zero-order hold.

Table 2. Main features offered by the languages/tools of Table 1

Name	Derivative	Automata Definition	Hierarachy	Object Oriented	Non-Causal Modeling	Algebraic Loops	Dirac Pulses
CHARON	yes	modes of operation	yes	yes	no	no	no
CHECKMATE	yes	STATEFLOW specification	no	no	no	no	no
HYSDEL	discrete differences	logic functions	no	no	no	no	no
HYVISUAL	integration	graphical editor	yes	yes	no	no	no
MODELICA	yes	algorithm sections	yes	yes	yes	no	not yet
SCICOS	integration	network of condit. blocks	yes	no	no	no	no
SIMULINK	derivative and integration	STATEFLOW specification	yes	no	no	no	no

sition can be triggered by an event coming from a particular event-generation block that monitors the values of the variables of the dynamical system. On the other hand, the finite state machine can generate events that are sent to a mode-change that selects a particular dynamics depending on the event. SCI-COS implements the automata as an interconnection of blocks whose discrete state can affect the continuous state of blocks implementing the continuous dynamics. Finally, MODELICA provides a set of conditional statements that can change the set of equations describing the continuous state. The last column in Table 1 describes how discrete and continuous signals and blocks interact with each other. CHECKMATE and HYSDEL use an event-generator and a mode-change block. HYVISUAL and SIMULINK provide special library blocks to convert a discrete signal into a continuous and vice versa. In SCICOS, a block can have both continuous and discrete inputs as well as continuous and discrete states.

Discrete states can influence continuous states. CHARON and MODELICA have special modifiers for distinguishing between discrete and continuous signals. As in all other languages, assignments of one to the other is not possible and can be statically checked (by a simple type checker).

Table 2 shows the features provided by the different tools. All of them support the derivative operator. The specification of the discrete automata has different interpretations. Again, the most intuitive way of describing the discrete automata is implemented by HYVISUAL and CHARON. HYVISUAL, for instance, has a finite state machine editor where a state machine can be described with bubbles and arcs. Each bubble can then be refined into a continuous time system or into another hybrid system.

Two features are very useful: Object orientation (OO), i.e. the possibility of defining objects and extending them through inheritance and field/method extension, and non-causal modeling, i.e. the possibility of using implicit equations to describe a dynamical system. None of the languages discussed above has a clear definition of the semantics of programs that contain algebraic loops. All of them rely on the simulation engine that, in presence of algebraic loops, either stops with an error message or solves them using specialized algorithms. We believe that a language has to give a meaning to programs containing algebraic loops and the meaning should be independent from the simulation engine.

4   The Interchange Format

In this section, we present a set of requirements for an Interchange Format (IF) and then we proceed to suggest a prototype IF, based on the MMM, by defining its syntax and semantics.

Requirements. An interchange format should be able to capture all the main features of the languages that have been already developed. It has to be a sort of "maximum common denominator" among all hybrid system modeling environments. Specification in the interchange format are not supposed to be written directly by designers. Instead, they should be produced by automatic tools that translate specifications written with other languages into the interchange format. The set of supported features has to be rich enough to guarantee lossless translations. For instance, if the interchange format did not support hierarchy, only flat designs could be described. A translation from one language that supports hierarchy to the interchange format would still be possible but it would inevitably flatten out the design structure, making it impossible to retrieve the original description (the translation process then would be lossy in the sense that the design structure would be lost forever).

We describe the set of features that we believe are essential for an interchange format.

- **Object orientation** is used to group common properties of a set of objects in a base class. It includes the features for defining complex data structures as well as incompletely specified processes. It is possible to extend processes and add/determine part of their behaviors.

- **Hierarchy** is an essential feature for organizing, structuring and encapsulating designs. Flat designs are too complicated to handle because they expose all their complexity in a single view. Even if the interchange format is not supposed to be manipulated directly by designers, it has to retain the original structure.
- **Heterogeneous modeling** is the ability of representing and mixing different models of computation.
- **Refinement** is a language feature for specifying a formal relation between components described at different levels of abstraction. Similarly to Ptolemy, refinement can be used to associate a continuous time dynamics to a discrete state. Since a design can be expressed at different levels of abstraction, formal refinement is definitely an important feature.
- **Implicit equations** are naturally used by designers to describe dynamical systems. An equation represents a constraint on a set of variables.
- **Explicit declaration of discrete states and transitions manager.** A transition manager determines the possible sequence of discrete states of a hybrid automata. Transitions from one state to another, even if defined by the designer, are handled by the simulator, which is hidden. In order for the sequence of states to be preserved across tools, a transition manager should be explicitly described in the interchange format.
- **Explicit declaration of invariant constraints.** Invariants are constraints on the state variables. A set of invariant constraints can be associated with each state of a hybrid system. A specific logic should be supported by the interchange format to specify invariants. METROPOLIS, for instance, defines the logic of constraints (LOC) as a general way of declaring relations among quantities.
- **Explicit non-determinism** must be supported by the interchange format. Languages like the METROPOLIS metamodel have a keyword to specify non-deterministic variables. It is up to the simulation engine to implement non-deterministic choices and return, for instance, one of the possible simulation traces. At the specification level the semantics of a non-deterministic system should include all admissible traces. Non-determinism is important for modeling the environment and for the emergent field of stochastic hybrid systems.
- **Explicit declaration of causality relations and scheduling for variables resolution.** When a system is described with implicit equations, sophisticated techniques are required to understand dependency among variables. After the dependency analysis has been performed, an imperative program can be written that evaluates variables with a specific order. This step is usually hidden but should be explicit in the interchange format since it contributes to the operational semantics of the language.
- **General continuous/discrete interface.** Each modeling environment defines its own communication semantics between continuous and discrete domains. Instead of defining a communication semantics, the interchange for-

mat should provide a set of language primitives that allow the designer to implement any possible communication scheme.

Language syntax. Rather than focusing on object orientation and scoping, we focus on the definition of a few base classes and synchronization statements that should be provided by the interchange format. In order to support heterogeneous modeling, the interchange format should provide a set of basic building blocks that can be used to build several models of computation. The METROPOLIS metamodel provides three basic components: `processes` for doing computation, `media` for communication and `quantity managers` for synchronization and scheduling and starting form this basic classes, we define the following:

- `State` is a process that extends the basic process class. It contains ports representing input and output transitions. These ports are connected to other states and are used to communicate output actions and reset maps.
- `AnalogProcess` is a continuous time process which extends the basic process class. It contains: ports to access external variables that are stored in communication media, and a set of `equation` statements that define the process behavior.
- `TManager` (TM) is the transitions manager which implements the transitions logic of the finite state machine. It defines a `resolve` method which determines the current state.
- `EManager` (EM) is the equation manager. Each equation has a scheduler associated with it. The scheduler defines a `resolve` method that computes unknown values starting from known ones. It uses causality constraints to determine inputs and outputs.
- `ERManager` (ERM) is a manager associated with each dynamical system. It defines a `resolve` method that implements the algorithm to schedule the equation resolution.
- `Transition` is a communication medium used to connect states.
- `AnalogVar` is a communication medium used to connect analog processes.

Besides the basic elements, few other keywords are needed:

- `refine(Object, Netlist)` creates a formal relation between an object and a netlist of components. It is used to build models at different levels of abstraction.
- `invariant{ <formula on state variables> }` is used to specify invariants. `<formula>` is a relation on the state variables.
- `causality(P,var_1 -> var_2)` states that var_1 depends on var_2. The two variables must be in the scope of the process P.
- `scheduling(P_1,P_2,...,P_N)` specifies the scheduling order among processes $P_1,...,P_N$ belonging to a dynamical system.

Language semantics. Figure 1 shows a simple example of hybrid system described in the interchange format. Following the METROPOLIS metamodel formalism, we graphically represent processes (analog and states) with squares, communication media with circles and managers with diamonds. The system

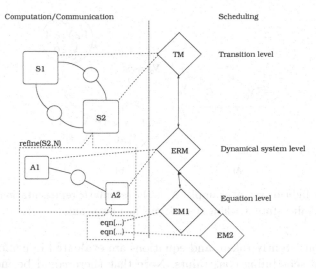

Computation/Communication

Scheduling

Transition level

Dynamical system level

Equation level

Fig. 1. Graphical representation of an hybrid system using the interchange format

has two discrete states which communicate through media. Each state is refined into a dynamical system (or into another hybrid system). State $S2$, for instance, is refined into a dynamical system composed of two analog processes, $A1$ and $A2$. The behavior of an analog process is specified by equations. The netlist is partitioned in the *computation/communication netlist* $\mathcal{CN}$, which represents the structure of the system, and the the *managers netlist* $\mathcal{MN}$ which limits the possible executions of $\mathcal{CN}$ by imposing scheduling constraints. $\mathcal{CN}$ contains processes and communication media. The set of processes $P = \{S, A\}$ is partitioned in the set of states S and the set of analog processes A. Each process behavior is a sequence of events $\{e_i\}$ where an event can have an annotation associated with it (e.g. time).

The execution of a program is defined as a sequence of event vectors $v = [E_S, E_A]$ where $E_S(i)$ is the event executed by the i-th state process and $E_A(i)$ by the i-th analog process. A special event called NOP corresponds to the stalling of a process (refer to [3] for a detailed explanation of the METROPOLIS metamodel semantics). In this setting, an execution is valid if the transition event $E_S(i)$ from state s_i to s_j implies that the set of values associated with events in E_A satisfies the guard conditions defined on the transition. In addition, if the current state is s_i and all events in E_S are equal to NOP, then the set of values associated with events in E_A must satisfy the invariant constraints defined in s_i.

Operationally, the execution consists of a sequence of iterations during which, processes in $\mathcal{CN}$ issue requests to $\mathcal{MN}$ which in turn grants only the requests that are consistent with constraints like guards and invariants. The type of a request depend on the process that issues it. **State** processes issue requests to execute their output transitions while **AnalogProcess** processes issue requests to evaluate their equations sets.

When requests are issued the control is passed to $\mathcal{MN}$ and a coordination between TM, EM and ERM starts to ensure that invariants are satisfied, tran-

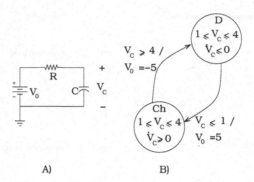

A)   B)

Fig. 2. Simple hybrid system example. A) is the schematic representation of the circuit, B) shows the finite state machine, transitions and invariants

sitions are consistently taken, and equations are evaluated in conformance with causality and scheduling constraints. Note that there could be more than one event vector satisfying all constraints and choosing one is a simulation choice and not a restriction imposed by the language.

Example. Consider the continuous time system of Figure 2. Resistor R and capacitor C are two continuous time processes.

Capacitor is a process derived from a general analog process (figure 3). The AnalogProcess base class defines special functions for establishing connections to quantity managers. The process has two ports to connect to communication media and read/write variables value. The port type is an interface that declares services that are defined (implemented) by communication media. Note that the ports are not associated with a direction, which implies that the component does not have a causality constraint associated with its description. A resistor is described in the same way but the current/voltage relation is governed by Ohm's law v = R*i.

For the description of the system, we refer the reader to Figure 3. The entire continuous time subsystem results from the interconnection of analog processes into a netlist, called RCCircuit. Causality constraints and scheduling constraints are specified in this netlist and are used to build the scheduling netlist.

Following is an example corresponding to the charge state of the circuit. Reset maps as well as shared state variables are all accessed through ports. A media has to provide a place to store these variables and also has to implement services to access them. Depending on the implementation of these services, it is possible to customize the communication semantics.

A finite state machine is represented as interconnection of states and transitions. The first part of the netlist instantiates all components including states and communication media. The second part connects states to channels. The last part describes the transitions. Each state declares a set of output transitions that can be connected to the target state in the FSM netlist.

A top level netlist is needed for instantiation of the finite state machine and association of dynamical systems to states. A snippet of the code is also shown

```
process Capacitor extends AnalogProcess {        process Charge extends State {
  parameter double C;                              port AnalogChannel vOout, vOin, vc;
  port AnalogInterface i, v;                       OutTransition vcth(vc >= 4, vOout = -5);
  equations {                                      constraints {
    i = c * der(v);                                  invariant(vc>=1 && vc <= 4 && der(vc) >= 0);
  }                                                }
}                                                }


netlist RCCircuit extends AnalogNetlist {
  port AnalogInterface VO;
  AnalogChannel current, voltagec, voltager = new AnalogChannel(0.0);
  Sub S = new Sub();
  Capacitor C = new Capacitor(1uF);
  Resistor  R = new Resistor(1K);
  connect(S.in1,VO); connect(S.in2,voltagec); connect(S.out,voltager);
  connect(R.v,voltager); connect(R.i,current); connect(C.i,current); connect(C.v,voltagec);
  constraints {
    causality(R,v->i); causality(C,i->v); causality(S,out-> in1 && in2); scheduling(S->R->C);
  }
}


netlist RCFSM extends FSMNetlist {
  Charge ch = new Charge();
  Discharge dch = new Discharge();
  AnalogChannel vOc2d, vOd2c = new AnalogChannel(0.0);
  connect(ch.vOout,vOc2d); connect(ch.vOin,vOd2c);
  connect(dch.vOout,vOd2c); connect(dch.vOin,vOc2d);
  transition(ch.vcth,dch); transition(dch.vcth,ch);
}


netlist Top {
  RCFSM myfsm = new RCFSM();
  refine(myfsm.ch,RCCircuit);
  refine(myfsm.dch,RCCircuit);
  refineconnect(myfsm.ch.vOin, refinementof(myfsm.ch).VO);
  refineconnect(myfsm.dch.vOin, refinementof(myfsm.dch).VO);
  connect(myfsm.ch.vc,refinementof(myfsm.ch).voltagec);
  connect(myfsm.dch.vc,refinementof(myfsm.dch).voltagec);
}
```

Fig. 3. Example of code describing an analog netlist, a state, an FSM and the top netlist

in Figure 3. The top netlist uses the **refine** keyword to associate a dynamical system to a state. A few more connections are specified in the top netlist. First of all we have to connect the reset maps to the dynamical system input. In this case the variable V_0 is an input of the RCCircuit netlist. Also we have to connect the variable corresponding to voltage across the capacitor to the state input port. This variable will be checked during simulation for evaluating guards conditions and invariant constraints.

5   Application Scenarios

Consider three hypothetical flows: one where a system is specified and simulated using HYVISUAL, and then is formally validated using CHECKMATE. The second is a similar flow where MODELICA is used as design entry and simulation tool instead of HYVISUAL. The third is when a design consists of two parts, one modeled in MODELICA and one in HYVISUAL and we wish to simulate the entire system in MODELICA.

To implement these flows, the basic operations are importing into the interchange format from HYVISUAL and MODELICA models and exporting the interchange format into a CHECKMATE and a MODELICA model. Using the interchange format allows a linear number of translations and relative constraints versus a quadratic number of translators if the interchange format is not used.

HYVISUAL **to Interchange Format.** Translating an HYVISUAL model into the interchange format is straightforward.

Computation. There is a one-to-one correspondence between HYVISUAL states and state processes in the interchange format. Each state can be refined into another hybrid model or into a dynamical systems. This is possible because the interchange format supports refinement of a generic object into a netlist. Also a dynamical system in HYVISUAL is constructed as the interconnection of library elements, each of them having a well defined input-output behavior. Each component is mapped into an analog process whose set of equations is defined by the behavior of the respective HYVISUAL component.

Communication. Each state process has input and output ports representing respectively input and output transitions. Each HYVISUAL transition from state s_i to s_j is mapped into a transition medium between state process s_i and s_j in the interchange format. If a refinement is associated with the HYVISUAL transition, then the correspondent transition medium is refined into a netlist.

For each variable v appearing in guard condition c on transition t, there has to be an analog channel from the dynamical system that computes v to the state having t as output transition.

Communication between analog processes in the same dynamical system are implemented by analog communication channels.

Coordination. Each component in HYVISUAL is causal, i.e. it has inputs and outputs and output values are computed as a function of the inputs. For each analog process a set of causality constraints is added in such a way that outputs depend on the inputs.

Causality and scheduling constraints are used respectively by the equation resolution manager and the equation manager for computing the values of variables at a given time. These two managers in cooperation with the transition manger implement all the algorithms that determine the system operational behavior. For instance, the Runge-Kutta solver can be implemented by the cooperation of ERM and EM. The transition manager, instead, can be implemented so that a request for backtracking is issued to the ERM when a threshold is missed.

MODELICA **to Interchange Format.** A MODELICA `model` has one or more equation sections that describe its behavior. An equation section can contain `if` and `when` statements whose condition expression generates events. Depending on which event happens, different branches of the conditional statements (and, therefore, a different set of equations) become active. There are several additional restrictions. In particular, the number of variables has always to be equal to the number of equations (non-determinism is avoided by construction).

The translation of a MODELICA program into the interchange format can be done as follows.

Computation. Each MODELICA model is a hybrid system. The number of state processes and the transitions between them are determined by the number of branches resulting from the combination of `if` and `when` statements in the equation sections of the model. Each state process is refined into a dynamical system whose set of equations corresponds to the branch that is active in that state. Since the interchange format supports hierarchy and non-causal modeling (as well as object orientation) translation of the computation aspect does not require special analysis of the original program.

Communication. The only communication mechanism that we should pay attention to is the `connection` primitive that MODELICA defines. Variables involved in a connection are subject to an implicit equation. If the variables are defined as `flow` variables that their sum as to be zero, otherwise they have to be equal. This semantics can be implemented in the interchange format by an analog process that explicitly declares the equations of a connection.

Coordination. Since MODELICA allows non-causal modeling, causality analysis must be performed on the original program to determine the causality and scheduling constraints for each model. In the case of MODELICA functions, this is not needed since inputs and outputs are defined by special keywords.

Interchange Format to MODELICA. Each process in the interchange format is mapped to a MODELICA model. If the process is a unrefined analog process then the MODELICA model only contains an equation section where all the equations of the analog process are directly rewritten using the MODELICA syntax.

An interconnection of state processes modeling an hybrid automata (where each process is refined into a dynamical system) is mapped into a MODELICA model presenting a `when` statement with as many branches as states. Each branch is guarded by the guard conditions on the automata transitions. Also each dynamical system that refines a state s is described as a set of equations in the correspondent branch of the when statement representing s.

Note that a model in the interchange format always comes with causality constraints on the variables. Instead of using model then, it is better to use functions in MODELICA that distinguish between input and output.

A composition of hybrid systems in the interchange format is a MODELICA model that instantiates all the systems and interconnects them.

Note that a translation from MODELICA to the interchange format and back will only lose the connection statements since they are translated into analog processes. However, a smart translator could recognize connection processes (e.g., by name) and generate a connection relation among the inputs of the analog connection process.

Interchange Format to CHECKMATE. CHECKMATE models hybrid systems using three basic blocks:

- Switched continuous system block (SCSB) of the form $\dot{x} = f(x, \sigma)$ where σ is a discrete variable.
- Polyhedral threshold block (PTHB) whose output is a Boolean variable which is true if $Cx \leq d$ is satisfied. This block represents the conjunction of all guard conditions.
- Finite state machine block (FSMB) that takes the output of PTHB and generates σ.

The function f can be of three types: $x = c$, $\dot{x} = Ax + b$ and $\dot{x} = f(x)$ where f is a non linear function.

Before translating a model from the interchange format to CHECKMATE, we must verify that the limitations on the guard conditions and on the fields are not violated by the model to be translated. If this is not the case, an error should be notified saying that the target language lacks properties that are required for the description of the original model. After this step, we flatten the design hierarchy. The program in the interchange format has to be analyzed and rewritten in the form of a finite state machine where each state is refined into a dynamical system. The CHECKMATE FSMB has the same states and transitions of the interchange format one. To build the FSMB we replace each guard condition with a Boolean input coming from the PTHB. The FSMB has an output σ denoting the current state. For each dynamical system d_i which refines state s_i we derive its state space representation. The CHECKMATE SCSB is the juxtaposition of all this systems and the input σ decides which of this systems is used for computing the state variables. Finally the CHECKMATE PTHB is obtained as the conjunction of all guard conditions, state variables as inputs and as many Boolean outputs as guard conditions.

6   Conclusions

Hybrid systems are important to a number of applications of great scientific and industrial interest. Being hybrid systems at the same time complex and relatively new, several tools are today available based on different assumptions and modeling strategies. We reviewed the most visible tools for hybrid systems and we presented the case for a novel interchange format based on the METROPOLIS metamodel (MMM). To do so, we first gave a formal definition of the MMM. We proceeded in listing the requirements and the formal definition of the format. We concluded with examples of use of the interchange format in defining a design flow that includes HYVISUAL, MODELICA and CHECKMATE to enter the design, simulate it and formally verifying its properties. The interchange format is at this point a proposal, since work still needs to be done to support it with the appropriate debugging and analysis tools and to provide translators to and from the new IF from and to existing tools.

We are confident that a variation of our proposal will be eventually adopted by the community interested in designing embedded systems with particular emphasis on control. We are open to any suggestion and recommendation to improve our proposal.

Acknowledgements. We gratefully acknowledge the discussions on this topic with Janos Stzipanovits of Vanderbilt University and its team, Ed Lee of UC Berkeley, Marika Di Benedetto of University of L'Aquila, Albert Benveniste of INRIA, and the PARADES team (Andrea Balluchi, Alberto Ferrari, Massimo Baleani, Leonardo Mangeruca and Paolo Murrieri). This work has been supported in part by the Columbus Project of the European Community, CHESS ITR, and the GSRC.

References

1. (http://www.columbus.gr/)
2. Lygeros, J., Tomlin, C., Sastry, S.: Controllers for reachability specifications for hybrid systems. In: Automatica, Special Issue on Hybrid Systems. (1999)
3. Balarin, F., Lavagno, L., Passerone, C., Sangiovanni-Vincentelli, A., Sgroi, M., Watanabe, Y.: Modeling and designing heterogeneous systems. Technical Report 2002/01, Cadence Berkeley Laboratories (2002)
4. Lee, E., Sangiovanni-Vincentelli, A.: A framework for comparing models of computation. IEEE Trans. Comput.-Aided Design Integrated Circuits **17** (1998) 1217–1229
5. Pnueli, A.: The temporal logic of programs. In: Proc. 18th Annual IEEE Symposium on Foundations of Computer Sciences. (1977) 46–57
6. Alur, R., Dang, T., Esposito, J., Hur, Y., Ivancic, F., Kumar, V., Lee, I., Mishra, P., Pappas, G.J., Sokolsky, O.: Hierarchical modeling and analysis of embedded systems. Proceedings of the IEEE (2002)
7. Fritzson, P.: Principles of Object-Oriented Modeling and Simulation with Modelica 2.1. J. Wiley & Sons (2004)
8. Hylands, C., Lee, E.A., Liu, J., Liu, X., Neuendorffer, S., Zheng, H.: Hyvisual: A hybrid system visual modeler. Technical Report UCB/ERL M03/1, UC Berkeley (2003) available at http://ptolemy.eecs.berkeley.edu/hyvisual/.
9. Dabney, J.B., Harman, T.L.: Mastering Simulink. Prentice Hall (2003)
10. Nikoukhah, R., Steer, S.: SCICOS A dynamic system builder and simulator user's guide - version 1.0. Technical Report Technical Report 0207. INRIA, (Rocquencourt, France, June) (1997)
11. Torrisi, F.D., Bemporad, A., Bertini, G., Hertach, P., Jost, D., Mignone, D.: Hysdel 2.0.5 - user manual. Technical report, ETH Zurich (2002)
12. Silva, B.I., Richeson, K., Krogh, B., Chutinan, A.: Modeling and verifying hybrid dynamic systems using checkmate. In: ADPM. (2000)

Primal–Dual Tests for Safety and Reachability

Stephen Prajna[1] and Anders Rantzer[2]

[1] Control and Dynamical Systems,
California Institute of Technology,
Pasadena, CA 91125 – USA
prajna@cds.caltech.edu

[2] Department of Automatic Control,
Lund Institute of Technology,
SE 221 00 Lund – Sweden
rantzer@control.lth.se

Abstract. A methodology for safety verification using barrier certificates has been proposed recently. Conditions that must be satisfied by a barrier certificate can be formulated as a convex program, and the feasibility of the program implies system safety, in the sense that there is no trajectory starting from a given set of initial states that reaches a given unsafe region. The dual of this problem, i.e., the reachability problem, concerns proving the existence of a trajectory starting from the initial set that reaches another given set. Using insights from convex duality and the concept of density functions, in this paper we show that reachability can also be verified through convex programming. Several convex programs for verifying safety, reachability, and other properties such as eventuality are formulated. Some examples are provided to illustrate their applications.

1 Introduction

Safety verification or reachability analysis addresses the question whether an unsafe region in the state space is reachable by some system trajectories starting from a set of initial states. The need for safety verification arises as the complexity of the system increases, and is also underscored by the safety critical nature of the system. This is particularly important for modern engineering systems, many of which have hybrid (i.e., a mixture of discrete and continuous) dynamics.

Various methods have been proposed for safety verification. For verification of discrete (finite state) systems, model checking techniques [1] have been very successful and have garnered a popularity that prompts the development of analogous approaches for verification of continuous systems, which mostly require computing the propagation of initial states (see e.g. [2, 3, 4, 5, 6, 7, 8, 9, 10, 11]). Unfortunately, while these techniques allow us to compute an exact or near exact approximation of reachable sets, it is difficult to perform such a computation due to the infinite number of states. Not only that, the complexity is worse when the system is nonlinear and uncertain.

M. Morari and L. Thiele (Eds.): HSCC 2005, LNCS 3414, pp. 542–556, 2005.

Recently, we proposed a method for safety verification that does not require propagating the initial set, based on what we term barrier certificates [12]. Our conditions for safety can be stated as follows. Given a system $\dot{x} = f(x)$ with the state x taking its value in $\mathcal{X}$, a set of initial states $\mathcal{X}_0 \subset \mathcal{X}$, and an unsafe set $\mathcal{X}_u \subset \mathcal{X}$, suppose there exists a continuously differentiable function $B : \mathcal{X} \to \mathbb{R}$ such that the inequalities

$$B(x) \leq 0 \qquad\qquad \forall x \in \mathcal{X}_0, \tag{1}$$

$$B(x) > 0 \qquad\qquad \forall x \in \mathcal{X}_u, \tag{2}$$

$$\frac{\partial B}{\partial x} f(x) \leq 0 \qquad\qquad \forall x \in \mathcal{X}. \tag{3}$$

are satisfied. Then the *safety* of the system is verified, namely, there is no trajectory $x(t)$ of the system such that $x(0) \in \mathcal{X}_0$, $x(T) \in \mathcal{X}_u$ for some $T \geq 0$, and $x(t) \in \mathcal{X}$ for all $t \in [0, T]$. In this case, the function $B(x)$ is called a barrier certificate.

The above method is analogous to the Lyapunov method for stability analysis [13], and is closely related to the viability theory [14] and invariant sets [15] approaches to safety verification. We would like to note that ideas parallel to ours also appear in [16, 17]. When the vector field $f(x)$ is polynomial and the sets $\mathcal{X}$, $\mathcal{X}_0$, $\mathcal{X}_u$ are semialgebraic, a polynomial barrier certificate $B(x)$ can be searched using sum of squares techniques [18, 19] in conjunction with semidefinite programming [20]. The method can also be extended to handle hybrid, uncertain, and stochastic systems [12, 21] and successful application to a hybrid system with 6 locations and 10 continuous state variables has been reported [22].

For hybrid systems, safety verification can also be performed by first constructing a discrete abstraction of the system [23, 2, 6, 7, 8, 9] and then performing verification on the resulting abstraction. This approach provides a nice hierarchical way for managing the complexity of verification: start with a coarse abstraction and successively refine it until safety is verified or a non-spurious counter-example is found. However, a crucial and computationally demanding component of the abstracting process is still the continuous reachability analysis, which is required to determine whether or not a transition between two discrete states in the abstraction is possible.

In constructing discrete abstractions of hybrid systems, barrier-certificate-based analysis can be used for ruling out transitions between discrete states. What is still missing is a method for proving that other transitions are indeed possible. This is the problem of *reachability*, which for a system $\dot{x} = f(x)$, the state set $\mathcal{X}$, the initial set $\mathcal{X}_0 \subset \mathcal{X}$, and the target set $\mathcal{X}_r \subset \mathcal{X}$, amounts to proving that there exists a trajectory $x(t)$ of the system such that $x(0) \in \mathcal{X}_0$, $x(T) \in \mathcal{X}_r$ for some $T \geq 0$, and $x(t) \in \mathcal{X}$ for all $t \in [0, T]$. It is important to note that failure in computing a barrier certificate that proves the unreachability of the target set from the initial set does not by itself mean that the target set is reachable from the initial set. For example, when using polynomial parameterization for $B(x)$, it may be the case that we fail to find $B(x)$ because the degree of the polynomial is not high enough.

In the present paper, we use the ideas of duality and density functions [24, 25] to formulate a "dual" test for reachability, thus forming a primal and dual pair of safety and reachability tests. We show that reachability can be verified through convex optimization, e.g., sum of squares technique and semidefinite programming when the vector field is polynomial and the sets are semialgebraic. In addition, another pair of convex programs for safety and reachability tests will also be formulated, where the primal test now proves reachability and the dual test proves safety. Either of these pairs can be used to rule out or establish transitions between discrete states when creating abstractions of hybrid systems. We will also show that this convex programming approach can be used to prove properties such as eventuality or weak eventuality — whose definitions will be presented later, or even other simple combinations of reachability/eventuality and safety.

The outline of the paper is as follows. In Section 2, we give an intuitive illustration of the duality idea by addressing the verification of a simple discrete system. The main results of the paper are presented and proven in Section 3. In Section 4, some examples will be presented to illustrate the applications of the tests. Finally, some conclusions will be given in Section 5.

2   A Discrete Verification Example

To give an intuitive flavor of the duality ideas used in this paper, let us consider the verification of a simple discrete system, shown in Figure 1. The system has four states, labelled 1 through 4, and three transitions between states, represented by the directed edges in the graph. We assume that node 1 is the initial state and node 4 is the unsafe state.

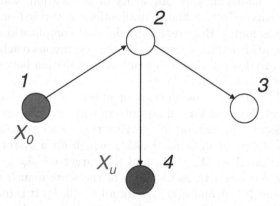

Fig. 1. A simple discrete system. The nodes represent the states of the system, while the directed edges represent transitions between states

For this system, conditions analogous to (1)–(3) that must be satisfied by a barrier certificate can be formulated. One way to find a barrier certificate is by solving the linear program

$$\max B_4 - B_1$$
$$\text{subject to } B_2 - B_1 \leq 0,$$
$$B_3 - B_2 \leq 0,$$
$$B_4 - B_2 \leq 0,$$

where the decision variables B_1, B_2, B_3, B_4 take values in the reals. This formulation is similar to the continuous case: analogous to (3), we ask that $B_i \leq B_j$ if there is a directed edge from node i to node j, whereas the objective function in this case is the difference between the values of B at the unsafe state and at the initial state. If there is a feasible solution of the above problem such that the objective function is strictly positive, then the value of B at the unsafe state is strictly greater than that at the initial state, i.e., there exists a barrier certificate for the system, and consequently we prove that there is no path going from node 1 to node 4.

The dual of the above linear program is as follows:

$$\min 0$$
$$\text{subject to } \rho_{12} \geq 0, \rho_{23} \geq 0, \rho_{24} \geq 0,$$
$$\rho_{12} = 1,$$
$$\rho_{24} + \rho_{23} - \rho_{12} = 0,$$
$$\rho_{24} = 1,$$
$$\rho_{23} = 0.$$

The dual decision variable ρ_{ij} can be interpreted as the transportation density from node i to node j. The equality constraints basically state that conservation of flows holds at each node – the total flow into a node is equal to the total flow out. In addition, the first and third equality constraints indicate that there exist a unit source at node 1, i.e., the initial state, and a unit sink at node 4, i.e., the unsafe state. This duality interpretation has been studied extensively in the past, see e.g. [26] and references therein.

The existence of a feasible solution to the dual linear program implies the existence of a path from the initial state to the unsafe state. This can be shown using the facts that the flows are conserved and that there are a unit source and a unit sink at the initial state and unsafe state, respectively. Hence, showing that the dual linear program is feasible can be used for verifying reachability. As a matter of fact, if we also add the objective function $\sum \rho_{ij}$ to the dual linear program, we obtain a linear programming formulation of the shortest path problem. In this case, the nonzero entries corresponding to any optimal vertex solution of the linear program will indicate a shortest path from the initial node to the unsafe node.

The duality argument above can also be used to prove that the existence of a barrier certificate is both sufficient and necessary for safety. For this, suppose that there exists no barrier certificate for the system, which is equivalent to the maximum objective value of the primal linear program being equal to zero. This objective value is attained by e.g., $B_i = 0$ for all i. The linear programming duality [20] implies that there exists a feasible solution to the dual linear program, from which we can further conclude the existence of a path from the initial state to the unsafe state, as explained in the previous paragraph. In the continuous case, a converse theorem for barrier certificates is proven in [27].

For the above example, the optimal objective value of the primal linear program is equal to zero. The unique feasible solution to the dual linear program is given by $\rho_{12} = 1$, $\rho_{23} = 0$, $\rho_{24} = 1$, which shows the path from node 1 to node 4. Had the direction of the edge from node 2 to node 4 been reversed, for example, the optimal objective value of the corresponding primal linear program will be ∞, and there will be no feasible solution to the dual linear program.

3   Main Results

We denote the space of m-times continuously differentiable functions mapping $X \subseteq \mathbb{R}^n$ to $\mathbb{R}^p$ by $C^m(X, \mathbb{R}^p)$. The solution $x(t)$ of $\dot{x} = f(x)$ starting from $x(0) = x_0$ is denoted by $\phi_t(x_0)$. For a set Z, we define $\phi_t(Z) = \{\phi_t(x) : x \in Z\}$. The divergence of a vector field $f \in C^1(X, \mathbb{R}^n)$ is denoted by $\nabla \cdot f(x)$. Finally, let $\mathrm{cl}(X)$ denote the closure of a set X, and ∂X denote the boundary of X.

The following version of Liouville's theorem (from [24]) will be used in the proofs of the main theorems.

Lemma 1. *Let $f \in C^1(D, \mathbb{R}^n)$ where $D \subseteq \mathbb{R}^n$ is open and let $\rho \in C^1(D, \mathbb{R})$ be integrable. Consider the system $\dot{x} = f(x)$. For a measurable set Z, assume that $\phi_\tau(Z)$ is a subset of D for all τ between 0 and t. Then*

$$\int_{\phi_t(Z)} \rho(x)dx - \int_Z \rho(z)dz = \int_0^t \int_{\phi_\tau(Z)} [\nabla \cdot (f\rho)](x)dxd\tau. \tag{4}$$

At this point, we are ready to state and prove the first pair of tests for safety and reachability.

Theorem 1. *Consider the differential equation $\dot{x} = f(x)$ with $f \in C^1(\mathbb{R}^n, \mathbb{R}^n)$. Let $\mathcal{X} \subset \mathbb{R}^n$ and $\mathcal{X}_0, \mathcal{X}_u, \mathcal{X}_r \subset \mathcal{X}$ be bounded open sets, and suppose that there exists a function $B \in C^1(\mathbb{R}^n, \mathbb{R})$ satisfying*

$$B(x) \leq 0 \qquad\qquad \forall x \in \mathcal{X}_0, \tag{5}$$

$$B(x) > 0 \qquad\qquad \forall x \in \mathcal{X}_u, \tag{6}$$

$$\frac{\partial B}{\partial x} f(x) \leq 0 \qquad\qquad \forall x \in \mathcal{X}. \tag{7}$$

Then the safety property holds, i.e., there exists no trajectory $x(t)$ of the system such that $x(0) \in \mathcal{X}_0$, $x(T) \in \mathcal{X}_u$ for some $T \geq 0$, and $x(t) \in \mathcal{X}$ for all $t \in [0, T]$.

On the other hand, if there exists a function $\rho \in C^1(\mathbb{R}^n, \mathbb{R})$ satisfying

$$\int_{\mathcal{X}_0} \rho(x)dx > 0, \tag{8}$$

$$\rho(x) < 0 \qquad \forall x \in \mathrm{cl}(\partial\mathcal{X} \setminus \partial\mathcal{X}_r), \tag{9}$$

$$\nabla \cdot (\rho f)(x) > 0 \qquad \forall x \in \mathrm{cl}(\mathcal{X} \setminus \mathcal{X}_r), \tag{10}$$

then the reachability property holds, i.e., there exists a trajectory $x(t)$ of the system such that $x(0) \in \mathcal{X}_0$, $x(T) \in \mathcal{X}_r$ for some $T \geq 0$, and $x(t) \in \mathcal{X}$ for all $t \in [0, T]$.

Proof. For a proof of the first statement, assume that there exists a $B(x)$ satisfying (5)–(7), while at the same time there is an initial condition $x_0 \in \mathcal{X}_0$ such that the trajectory $x(t)$ of $\dot{x} = f(x)$ starting at $x(0) = x_0$ satisfies $x(t) \in \mathcal{X}$ for all $t \in [0, T]$ and $x(T) \in \mathcal{X}_u$. Condition (7) states that the Lie derivative of $B(x)$ along this flow is non-positive. A direct consequence of this is that $B(x(T))$ must be less than or equal to $B(x(0))$, which is contradictory to (5)–(6). Thus we conclude that the system is safe.

To prove the second statement, let $X \subset \mathcal{X}_0$ be an open set on which $\rho(x) > 0$. We will first prove that there must be an initial condition $x_0 \in X$ whose flow $\phi_t(x_0)$ leaves $\mathcal{X} \setminus \mathcal{X}_r$ in finite time. In fact, the set of all initial conditions in X whose flows do not leave $\mathcal{X} \setminus \mathcal{X}_r$ in finite time is a set of measure zero. To show this, let Y be an open neighborhood of $\mathcal{X} \setminus \mathcal{X}_r$ such that $\nabla \cdot (\rho f)(x) > 0$ on $\mathrm{cl}(Y)$. Now define

$$Z = \bigcap_{i=1,2,\dots} \{x_0 \in X : \phi_t(x_0) \in Y \quad \forall t \in [0, i]\}.$$

The set Z is an intersection of countable open sets and hence is measurable. It contains all initial conditions in X for which the trajectories stay in Y for all $t \geq 0$. That Z is a set of measure zero can be shown using Lemma 1 as follows. Since $\phi_t(Z) \subset Y$, Y is bounded, and $\rho(x)$ is continuous, the left hand side of (4) is bounded. For (4) to hold, we must have $\int_{\phi_\tau(Z)} [\nabla \cdot (f\rho)](x)dx \to 0$ as $\tau \to \infty$, or equivalently, the measure of $\phi_\tau(Z)$ converges to zero as $\tau \to \infty$. Suppose now that Z has non-zero measure. We have a contradiction since $\lim_{t\to\infty} \int_{\phi_t(Z)} \rho(x)dx = 0$ whereas $\lim_{t\to\infty} \int_Z \rho(x)dx + \int_0^t \int_{\phi_\tau(Z)} [\nabla \cdot (f\rho)](x)dxd\tau$ is strictly positive. Thus Z must have zero measure. Since $\mathcal{X} \setminus \mathcal{X}_r \subset Y$, it follows immediately that the set of all initial conditions in X whose flows stay in $\mathcal{X} \setminus \mathcal{X}_r$ for all time is a set of measure zero.

Now take any x_0 whose flow leaves $\mathcal{X} \setminus \mathcal{X}_r$ in finite time, and assume that the flow $\phi_t(x_0)$ leaves $\mathcal{X}$ without entering $\mathcal{X}_r$ first. Let $T > 0$ be the first time instant $\phi_t(x_0)$ leaves $\mathcal{X}$. That is, let $\phi_t(x_0) \in \mathcal{X} \setminus \mathcal{X}_r$ for all $t \in [0, T)$ and $\phi_T(x_0) \notin \mathcal{X}$. Choose a neighborhood Z of x_0 such that

$$\rho(x) > 0 \quad \forall x \in Z,$$

$$\rho(x) < 0 \quad \forall x \in \phi_T(Z),$$

$$\nabla \cdot (\rho f)(x) > 0 \quad \forall x \in \phi_\tau(Z), \tau \in [0, T].$$

Now apply Lemma 1 again with $t = T$ to obtain a contradiction. According to the above, the left hand side of (4) is negative while the right hand side is positive. Thus there is a contradiction, and we conclude that for $x(0) = x_0$ there must exist $T \geq 0$ such that $x(T) \in \mathcal{X}_r$ and $x(t) \in \mathcal{X}$ for all $t \in [0, T]$.

It is interesting to see that the roles of $B(x)$ and $\rho(x)$ in proving safety and reachability can be interchanged, as in the second pair of tests stated in the next theorem. The possibility of using the density function $\rho(x)$ to prove safety was first suggested in [28].

Theorem 2. *Consider the differential equation $\dot{x} = f(x)$ with $f \in C^1(\mathbb{R}^n, \mathbb{R}^n)$. Let $\mathcal{X} \subset \mathbb{R}^n$ and $\mathcal{X}_0, \mathcal{X}_u, \mathcal{X}_r \subset \mathcal{X}$ be bounded open sets, and suppose that there exists a function $B \in C^1(\mathbb{R}^n, \mathbb{R})$ satisfying*

$$\int_{\mathcal{X}_0} B(x)dx < 0, \tag{11}$$

$$B(x) > 0 \qquad\qquad \forall x \in \partial\mathcal{X} \setminus \partial\mathcal{X}_r, \tag{12}$$

$$\frac{\partial B}{\partial x} f(x) < 0 \qquad\qquad \forall x \in \mathrm{cl}(\mathcal{X} \setminus \mathcal{X}_r). \tag{13}$$

Then the reachability property holds, i.e., there exists a trajectory $x(t)$ of the system such that $x(0) \in \mathcal{X}_0$, $x(T) \in \mathcal{X}_r$ for some $T \geq 0$, and $x(t) \in \mathcal{X}$ for all $t \in [0, T]$.

On the other hand, if there exists a function $\rho \in C^1(\mathbb{R}^n, \mathbb{R})$ satisfying

$$\rho(x) \geq 0 \qquad\qquad \forall x \in \mathcal{X}_0, \tag{14}$$

$$\rho(x) < 0 \qquad\qquad \forall x \in \mathcal{X}_u, \tag{15}$$

$$\nabla \cdot (\rho f)(x) \geq 0 \qquad\qquad \forall x \in \mathcal{X}, \tag{16}$$

then the safety property holds, i.e., there exists no trajectory $x(t)$ of the system such that $x(0) \in \mathcal{X}_0$, $x(T) \in \mathcal{X}_u$ for some $T \geq 0$, and $x(t) \in \mathcal{X}$ for all $t \in [0, T]$.

Proof. To prove the first statement, consider a point $x_0 \in \mathcal{X}_0$ such that $B(x_0) < 0$. The flow $\phi_t(x_0)$ must leave $\mathcal{X} \setminus \mathcal{X}_r$ in finite time, since the Lie derivative inequality (13) holds and $B(x)$ is bounded below on $\mathcal{X}$. Now assume that $\phi_t(x_0)$ leaves $\mathcal{X}$ without entering $\mathcal{X}_r$ first, and consider the first time instant $t = T$ at which it happens. From (13), it follows that $B(\phi_T(x_0))$ is strictly less than zero, which is contradictory to (12). Thus we conclude that for $x(0) = x_0$ there must exist $T \geq 0$ such that $x(T) \in \mathcal{X}_r$ and $x(t) \in \mathcal{X}$ for all $t \in [0, T]$.

We proceed to proving the second statement. Assume that there is a $\rho(x)$ satisfying the conditions of the theorem, while at the same time there exists an $x_0 \in \mathcal{X}_0$ such that $\phi_T(x_0) \in \mathcal{X}_u$ for some $T \geq 0$ and $\phi_t(x_0) \in \mathcal{X}$ for $t \in [0, T]$. Let $Z \subset \mathcal{X}_0$ be a ball surrounding x_0 such that also $\phi_T(Z) \subset \mathcal{X}_u$ and $\phi_t(Z) \subset \mathcal{X}$ for $t \in [0, T]$. Now apply Lemma 1 with $t = T$ to obtain a contradiction. According to the assumptions of the theorem, the left hand side of (4) is negative and the right hand side is non-negative. Hence there is a contradiction and the proof is complete.

Remark 1. Modulo the following modifications on the assertions of the theorems, the conclusions will still hold even when the sets are not bounded. In particular, for the second part of Theorem 1, we need to add the condition that $\rho(x)$ is integrable on $\mathcal{X}$ and replace (10) by

$$\nabla \cdot (\rho f)(x) \geq \epsilon \qquad\qquad \forall x \in \mathrm{cl}(\mathcal{X} \setminus \mathcal{X}_r)$$

for a positive number ϵ. In the first part of Theorem 2, we need to add the condition that $B(x)$ is bounded below on $\mathcal{X}$ and replace (13) by

$$\frac{\partial B}{\partial x} f(x) \leq -\epsilon \qquad\qquad \forall x \in \mathrm{cl}(\mathcal{X} \setminus \mathcal{X}_r)$$

for a positive number ϵ.

In applications where the system has stable equilibrium points, it is often convenient to exclude a neighborhood of the equilibria from the region where the divergence inequality (16) must be satisfied, since the inequality is otherwise impossible to satisfy without a singularity in $\rho(x)$. This does not make the conclusion of the theorem weaker, as long as the excluded set does not intersect $\mathcal{X}_u$ and is entirely surrounded by a region of positive $\rho(x)$.

Similarly, the Lie derivative inequality (13) is impossible to satisfy when the system has equilibrium points in $\mathcal{X} \setminus \mathcal{X}_r$. In this case, a neighborhood of the equilibria should also be excluded from the region where the inequality is to be satisfied. The conclusion of the theorem is still valid as long as the excluded set is entirely surrounded by a region of positive $B(x)$.

Notice in particular that all the tests presented above are convex programming problems. This opens the possibility of computing $B(x)$ and $\rho(x)$ using convex optimization. For systems whose vector fields are polynomial and whose set descriptions are semialgebraic (i.e., described by polynomial equalities and inequalities), a computational method called sum of squares optimization is available if we use polynomial parameterizations for $B(x)$ or $\rho(x)$. The method is based on the sum of squares decomposition of multivariate polynomials [18] and semidefinite programming [20]. Software tools [19] are helpful for this purpose. See [12] for details.

Remark 2. Strictly speaking, it should be noted that the tests in the above theorems are not pairs of *Lagrange dual* problems [20] in the sense of convex optimization. We deliberately do not use Lagrange dual problems to avoid computational problems when we postulate $B(x)$ or $\rho(x)$ as polynomials. For example, the Lagrange dual problem of the safety test in Theorem 1 will require $\nabla \cdot (\rho f)(x)$ to be zero on $\mathcal{X} \setminus (\mathcal{X}_0 \cup \mathcal{X}_u)$ (see [27]). Although useful for theoretical purposes, this will hinder the computation of $\rho(x)$ through polynomial parameterization and sum of squares optimization. In this regard, some interesting future directions would be to see if a pair of Lagrange dual problems can be formulated so that both problems can be solved using sum of squares optimization, or more importantly, to see if the dual infeasibility certificate of one convex program can be interpreted directly as a feasible solution to the dual convex program.

In the reachability test of Theorem 2, the set of states $\{x \in \mathcal{X}_0 : B(x) < 0\}$ is said to satisfy the *eventuality*[1] property: all trajectories starting from this set will eventually reach $\mathcal{X}_r$ in a finite time. Analogously, in Theorem 1, the set of states $\{x \in \mathcal{X}_0 : \rho(x) > 0\}$ is said to satisfy the *weak eventuality* property: almost all trajectories starting from this set will eventually reach $\mathcal{X}_r$ in a finite time. These facts are evident from the proofs of the theorems. In many applications, it is of paramount importance to prove eventuality (or even weak eventuality), e.g., to prove that something "good" will happen. The eventuality or weak eventuality tests for the whole initial set $\mathcal{X}_0$ can be performed simply by replacing (11) and (8) by $B(x) < 0 \ \forall x \in \mathcal{X}_0$ and $\rho(x) > 0 \ \forall x \in \mathcal{X}_0$, respectively.

Example 1. To show that the weak eventuality property mentioned above cannot in general be strengthened to eventuality, consider the system $\dot{x} = x$, with $\mathcal{X} = (-5, 5) \subset \mathbb{R}$, $\mathcal{X}_0 = (-1, 1)$, $\mathcal{X}_r = (-5, -4) \cup (4, 5)$. The function $\rho(x) = 1$ satisfies all the conditions that guarantee weak eventuality, hence almost all trajectories starting from $\mathcal{X}_0$ will reach $\mathcal{X}_r$ in finite time. The only exception in this case is the trajectory $x(t) = 0$.

While one may argue that the reachability property can be shown by running a numerical simulation of $\dot{x} = f(x)$ starting from a properly chosen $x_0 \in \mathcal{X}_0$, the merit of the tests in Theorems 1 and 2 is twofold. First, a solution to the convex programs for reachability will automatically indicate which state x_0 can be chosen as the initial state (or a set of states from which almost all points can be chosen as the initial state). Second, the use of these convex programs allows us to also consider the worst-case analysis of systems with disturbance or the controller design problem. For example, consider a system $\dot{x} = f(x, d)$, where the disturbance signal $d(t)$ is assumed to be piecewise continuous, bounded, and take its value in a set D. Then solving (11)–(13) with the Lie derivative inequality replaced by

$$\frac{\partial B}{\partial x} f(x, d) < 0 \qquad\qquad \forall (x, d) \in \mathrm{cl}(\mathcal{X} \setminus \mathcal{X}_r) \times D$$

will prove reachability under all possible disturbance $d(t)$, which obviously *cannot be proven using simulation*. The same remark applies to eventuality, which cannot be proven using simulation even when there exists no disturbance. On the other hand, the density function $\rho(x)$ is more appropriate for controller design, as pointed out in [24]. For a system $\dot{x} = f(x) + g(x)u$ where u is the control input, the inequalities (8)–(9) and

$$\nabla \cdot [\rho(f + ug)](x) > 0 \qquad\qquad \forall x \in \mathrm{cl}(\mathcal{X} \setminus \mathcal{X}_r),$$

(and similarly for (14)–(16)) are certainly convex conditions on the pair $(\rho, \rho u)$. It is therefore natural to introduce $\psi = \rho u$ as a search variable and use convex

---

[1] This property is also termed the *liveness* property in temporal logics [29]. We use "eventuality" to avoid possible confusion with "liveness" in the sense of viability theory.

optimization to find a feasible pair (ρ, ψ), then recover the control law as $u(x) = \psi(x)/\rho(x)$; see [28].

It is clear that the above tests can be combined to prove the reachability – safety property:

> there exists a trajectory $x(t)$ such that $x(0) \in \mathcal{X}_0$, $x(T) \in \mathcal{X}_r$ for some $T \geq 0$, and $x(t) \notin \mathcal{X}_u$, $x(t) \in \mathcal{X}$ for all $t \in [0, T]$,

or the eventuality – safety (or weak eventuality – safety) property:

> for all (or almost all) initial states $x_0 \in \mathcal{X}_0$, the trajectory $x(t)$ starting at $x(0) = x_0$ will satisfy $x(T) \in \mathcal{X}_r$ for some $T \geq 0$ and $x(t) \notin \mathcal{X}_u$, $x(t) \in \mathcal{X}$ for all $t \in [0, T]$.

For instance, the tests for eventuality – safety and weak eventuality – safety properties are stated in the following corollary.

Corollary 1. *Consider the differential equation $\dot{x} = f(x)$ with $f \in C^1(\mathbb{R}^n, \mathbb{R}^n)$. Let $\mathcal{X} \subset \mathbb{R}^n$ and $\mathcal{X}_0, \mathcal{X}_u, \mathcal{X}_r \subset \mathcal{X}$ be bounded open sets, and suppose that there exists a function $B \in C^1(\mathbb{R}^n, \mathbb{R})$ satisfying*

$$B(x) < 0 \qquad \forall x \in \mathcal{X}_0, \tag{17}$$

$$B(x) > 0 \qquad \forall x \in (\partial\mathcal{X} \setminus \partial\mathcal{X}_r) \cup \mathcal{X}_u, \tag{18}$$

$$\frac{\partial B}{\partial x} f(x) < 0 \qquad \forall x \in \mathrm{cl}(\mathcal{X} \setminus \mathcal{X}_r). \tag{19}$$

Then the eventuality – safety property holds. Similarly, if there exists a function $\rho \in C^1(\mathbb{R}^n, \mathbb{R})$ satisfying

$$\rho(x) > 0 \qquad \forall x \in \mathcal{X}_0, \tag{20}$$

$$\rho(x) < 0 \qquad \forall x \in \mathrm{cl}(\partial\mathcal{X} \setminus \partial\mathcal{X}_r) \cup \mathcal{X}_u, \tag{21}$$

$$\nabla \cdot (\rho f)(x) > 0 \qquad \forall x \in \mathrm{cl}(\mathcal{X} \setminus \mathcal{X}_r), \tag{22}$$

then the weak eventuality – safety property holds. In this case, the safety property holds also for trajectories that does not reach $\mathcal{X}_r$ in finite time.

4   Examples

4.1   Successive Primal–Dual Refinement

Consider the system

$$\dot{x}_1 = x_2,$$

$$\dot{x}_2 = -x_1 + \frac{1}{3}x_1^3 - x_2,$$

and let the set of states be $\mathcal{X} = (-3.5, 3.5) \times (-3.5, 3.5) \subset \mathbb{R}^2$. Furthermore, define

$$\mathcal{X}_0 = (-3.4, 3.4) \times (3.35, 3.45), \qquad \mathcal{X}_2 = (-3.5, 3.5) \times (-3.5, -3.45),$$

$$\mathcal{X}_1 = (3.45, 3.5) \times (-3.5, 3.5), \qquad \mathcal{X}_3 = (-3.5, -3.45) \times (-3.5, 3.5).$$

In this example, we will investigate the reachability of $\mathcal{X}_1$, $\mathcal{X}_2$, $\mathcal{X}_3$ from $\mathcal{X}_0$ (cf. Figure 3). This kind of analysis is encountered when constructing a discrete abstraction of continuous or hybrid systems, or when analyzing a counterexample found during the verification of such an abstraction.

The tests in Theorem 1 will be used for our analysis. Since the vector field is polynomial and the sets are semialgebraic, we use polynomial parameterization for $B(x)$ and $\rho(x)$, and then apply the sum of squares method to compute them. Degree bound is imposed on $B(x)$ and $\rho(x)$. Because of this, we might not be able to find a single $B(x)$ or $\rho(x)$ that prove safety/reachability for the whole $\mathcal{X}_0$. If neither $B(x)$ nor $\rho(x)$ can be found, we divide the interval of x_1 into two parts and apply the tests again to the smaller sets. A set is pruned if $B(x)$ is found, and this process is repeated until a $\rho(x)$ is found or the whole $\mathcal{X}_0$ is proven safe.

The result is as follows.

1. We prove that the set $\mathcal{X}_1$ is reachable from $\mathcal{X}_0$. The verification progress is shown in Figure 2 (a).
2. It can be proven directly that $\mathcal{X}_2$ is not reachable from $\mathcal{X}_0$.
3. It is proven that the set $\mathcal{X}_3$ is reachable from $\mathcal{X}_0$. See Figure 2 (b).

For proofs of the corresponding reachability and safety, see Figure 3.

Obviously, the above bisection algorithm is just a simple, straightforward approach to refine and prune the initial set, and other algorithms that are more efficient can be proposed in the future.

4.2   Proving Eventuality

For the second example, consider the four dimensional system

$$\dot{x}_1 = x_2, \qquad\qquad \dot{x}_3 = x_4,$$
$$\dot{x}_2 = -x_3, \qquad\qquad \dot{x}_4 = x_1^2 - x_4 + 2 + d,$$

where the time-varying disturbance input $d(t)$ is assumed to take value in the interval $[-1, 1]$. Let the set of states and the initial set be

$$\mathcal{X} = \{x \in \mathbb{R}^4 : x_1^2 + x_2^2 + x_3^2 + x_4^2 < 7^2\},$$
$$\mathcal{X}_0 = \{x \in \mathbb{R}^4 : x_1^2 + x_2^2 + x_3^2 + x_4^2 < 0.1^2\}.$$

When there is no disturbance input, simulation indicates that the trajectory of the system starting from the origin reaches the set

$$\mathcal{X}_{r,1} = \{x \in \mathbb{R}^4 : (x_1 + 1)^2 + (x_2 + 1.75)^2 + (x_3 - 2.25)^2 + (x_4 - 2)^2 < 0.2^2\}$$

in finite time. As we introduce the disturbance input and also the uncertainty in the initial condition, some trajectories of the system will no longer reach the above set. However, it is expected that these trajectories will still reach a larger ball with the same center as $\mathcal{X}_{r,1}$. Using $B(x)$ of degree 4, it can be verified that the set

$$\mathcal{X}_{r,2} = \{x \in \mathbb{R}^4 : (x_1 + 1)^2 + (x_2 + 1.75)^2 + (x_3 - 2.25)^2 + (x_4 - 2)^2 < 3^2\}$$

is reached in finite time by all trajectories of the system starting from $\mathcal{X}_0$.

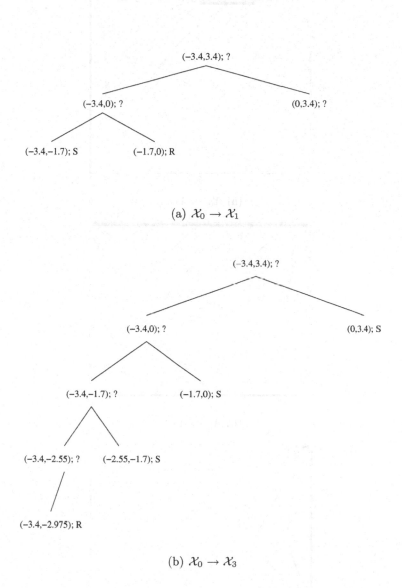

(a) $\mathcal{X}_0 \rightarrow \mathcal{X}_1$

(b) $\mathcal{X}_0 \rightarrow \mathcal{X}_3$

Fig. 2. Proving the reachability of $\mathcal{X}_1$ and $\mathcal{X}_3$ from $\mathcal{X}_0$ in the example of Section 4.1. At each node we indicate the range of x_1 on $\mathcal{X}_0$ for which safety and reachability are tested. If neither is verified (denoted by ?), then the x_1-interval is divided into two and the tests are applied to the smaller sets. The annotation S (respectively R) indicates that $B(x)$ (respectively $\rho(x)$) is found. Breadth-first search starting from the leftmost branch is used. When the degree of $B(x)$ or $\rho(x)$ is chosen equal to 8, the semidefinite program for each safety or reachability test at any node can be solved in less than 4 seconds on a Pentium III 600 MHz laptop. The verification of $\mathcal{X}_0 \nrightarrow \mathcal{X}_2$ terminates at the top node, since a barrier certificate $B(x)$ can be found directly

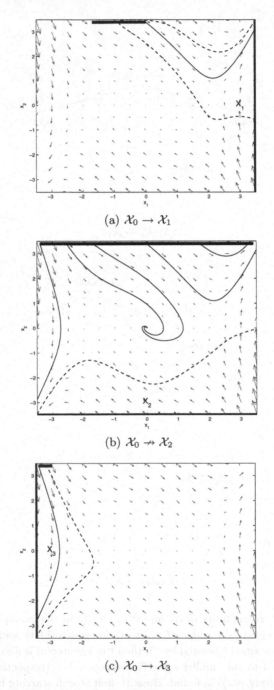

(a) $\mathcal{X}_0 \to \mathcal{X}_1$

(b) $\mathcal{X}_0 \nrightarrow \mathcal{X}_2$

(c) $\mathcal{X}_0 \to \mathcal{X}_3$

Fig. 3. Possible transitions from $\mathcal{X}_0$ to $\mathcal{X}_1$, $\mathcal{X}_2$, $\mathcal{X}_3$ for the example in Section 4.1. In (a) and (c), dashed curves are the zero level sets of $\rho(x)$'s that certify reachability. In (b), dashed curve is the zero level set of $B(x)$ that certifies safety. Thick solid lines at the top of the figures are the initial sets for which the certificates are computed. Some trajectories of the system are depicted by solid curves

5   Conclusions

In the previous sections, we use the insight from convex duality and the concept of density functions to formulate a test for reachability, which together with safety analysis using barrier certificates form a pair of convex programs for safety and reachability tests. We have additionally presented another pair of safety and reachability tests, also in the form of convex programs. This opens the possibility to perform these tests using convex optimization. In particular, sum of squares optimization can be used for this purpose when the vector field of the system is polynomial and the sets are semialgebraic.

We have further commented on the use of this methodology for worst-case reachability analysis or controller synthesis. It is pointed out that similar tests can be derived for proving eventuality or weak eventuality, and the tests can be combined to verify properties such as reachability–safety and eventuality–safety. Some examples have been presented for illustration. While the present tests are aimed for continuous reachability or safety analysis and hence are useful for constructing abstractions of hybrid systems, we expect that all of them can also be extended to handle hybrid systems directly, using an approach similar to the one presented in [12].

References

1. Clarke, Jr., E.M., Grumberg, O., Peled, D.A.: Model Checking. MIT Press, Cambridge, MA (2000)
2. Bemporad, A., Torrisi, F.D., Morari, M.: Optimization-based verification and stability characterization of piecewise affine and hybrid systems. In: Hybrid Systems: Computation and Control, LNCS 1790. Springer-Verlag (2000) 45–58
3. Kurzhanski, A., Varaiya, P.: Ellipsoidal techniques for reachability analysis. In: Hybrid Systems: Computation and Control, LNCS 1790. Springer-Verlag, Heidelberg (2000) 203–213
4. Lafferriere, G., Pappas, G.J., Yovine, S.: Symbolic reachability computations for families of linear vector fields. Journal of Symbolic Computation 32 (2001) 231–253
5. Anai, H., Weispfenning, V.: Reach set computations using real quantifier elimination. In: Hybrid Systems: Computation and Control, LNCS 2034. Springer-Verlag (2001) 63–76
6. Asarin, E., Dang, T., Maler, O.: The d/dt tool for verification of hybrid systems. In: Computer Aided Verification, LNCS 2404. Springer-Verlag (2002) 365–370
7. Alur, R., Dang, T., Ivancic, F.: Progress on reachability analysis of hybrid systems using predicate abstraction. In: Hybrid Systems: Computation and Control, LNCS 2623. Springer-Verlag, Heidelberg (2003) 4–19
8. Tomlin, C.J., Mitchell, I., Bayen, A.M., Oishi, M.: Computational techniques for the verification of hybrid systems. Proceedings of the IEEE 91 (2003) 986–1001
9. Chutinan, A., Krogh, B.H.: Computational techniques for hybrid system verification. IEEE Transactions on Automatic Control 48 (2003) 64–75
10. Tiwari, A.: Approximate reachability for linear systems. In: Hybrid Systems: Computation and Control, LNCS 2623. Springer-Verlag (2003) 514–525

11. Yazarel, H., Pappas, G.: Geometric programming relaxations for linear systems reachability. In: Proceedings of the American Control Conference. (2004)
12. Prajna, S., Jadbabaie, A.: Safety verification of hybrid systems using barrier certificates. In: Hybrid Systems: Computation and Control, LNCS 2993. Springer-Verlag, Heidelberg (2004) 477–492
13. Khalil, H.K.: Nonlinear Systems. Second edn. Prentice-Hall, Inc., Upper Saddle River, NJ (1996)
14. Aubin, J.P.: Viability Theory. Birkhäuser, Boston, MA (1991)
15. Jirstrand, M.: Invariant sets for a class of hybrid systems. In: Proceedings of the IEEE Conference on Decision and Control. (1998)
16. Sankaranarayanan, S., Sipma, H., Manna, Z.: Constructing invariants for hybrid systems. In: Hybrid Systems: Computation and Control, LNCS 2993. Springer-Verlag (2004) 539–554
17. Tiwari, A., Khanna, G.: Nonlinear systems: Approximating reach sets. In: Hybrid Systems: Computation and Control, LNCS 2993. Springer-Verlag (2004) 600–614
18. Parrilo, P.A.: Structured Semidefinite Programs and Semialgebraic Geometry Methods in Robustness and Optimization. PhD thesis, California Institute of Technology, Pasadena, CA (2000)
19. Prajna, S., Papachristodoulou, A., Parrilo, P.A.: Introducing SOS-TOOLS: A general purpose sum of squares programming solver. In: Proceedings of the IEEE Conference on Decision and Control. (2002) Available at http://www.cds.caltech.edu/sostools and http://www.aut.ee.ethz.ch/~parrilo/sostools.
20. Boyd, S., Vandenberghe, L.: Convex Optimization. Cambridge University Press, Cambridge (2004)
21. Prajna, S., Jadbabaie, A., Pappas, G.J.: Stochastic safety verification using barrier certificates. In: Proceedings of the IEEE Conference on Decision and Control. (2004)
22. Glavaski, S., Papachristodoulou, A., Ariyur, K.: Controlled hybrid system safety verification: Advanced life support system testbed. Submitted (2005)
23. Alur, R., Henzinger, T., Lafferriere, G., Pappas, G.J.: Discrete abstractions of hybrid systems. Proceedings of the IEEE 88 (2000) 971–984
24. Rantzer, A.: A dual to Lyapunov's stability theorem. Systems and Control Letters 42 (2001) 161–168
25. Rantzer, A., Hedlund, S.: Duality between cost and density in optimal control. In: Proceedings of the IEEE Conference on Decision and Control. (2003)
26. Papadimitriou, C.H., Steiglitz, K.: Combinatorial Optimization: Algorithms and Complexity. Dover Publications Inc., Mineola, NY (1998)
27. Prajna, S., Rantzer, A.: On the necessity of barrier certificates. In: Proceedings of the IFAC World Congress. (2005) To appear.
28. Rantzer, A., Prajna, S.: On analysis and synthesis of safe control laws. In: Proceedings of the Allerton Conference on Communication, Control, and Computing. (2004)
29. Manna, Z., Pnueli, A.: The Temporal Logic of Reactive and Concurrent Systems: Specification. Springer-Verlag, New York, NY (1992)

Adjoint-Based Optimal Control of the Expected Exit Time for Stochastic Hybrid Systems

Robin L. Raffard[1], Jianghai Hu[2], and Claire J. Tomlin[1]

[1] Dept. of Aeronautics and Astronautics, Stanford University
{rraffard, tomlin}@stanford.edu
[2] School of Electrical and Computer Engineering, Purdue University
jianghai@ecn.purdue.edu

Abstract. In this paper, we study the problem of controlling the expected exit time from a region for a class of stochastic hybrid systems. That is, we find the least costly feedback control for a stochastic hybrid system that can keep its state inside a prescribed region for at least an expected amount of time. The stochastic hybrid systems considered are quite general: the continuous dynamics are governed by stochastic differential equations, and the discrete mode evolves according to a continuous time Markov chain. Instead of adopting the usual Hamilton-Jacobi viewpoint, we study the problem directly by formulating it as a PDE constrained optimization problem, and propose a solution using adjoint-based gradient descent methods. Numerical results of the proposed approach are presented for several representative examples, and, for the simple case, compared with analytical results.

1 Introduction

There has been considerable current research interest in stochastic hybrid systems (SHSs) [1, 2, 3, 4, 5] due to their ability to represent such systems as maneuvering aircraft [6], switching communication networks [7], etc. Most efforts have been devoted to the analysis of such systems: for control, the main approach to date relies on solving a dynamic programming problem using a Hamilton-Jacobi formulation [1]. In this paper, we propose an alternative method for optimal control of SHSs. The approach poses the optimal control problem as a partial differential equation (PDE) constrained optimization program, and uses an adjoint method to solve this optimization program. The adjoint method, introduced by Lions [8] and developed by Jameson [9] in the context of aerodynamic design, computes the gradient of an objective function whose variables are subject to PDE constraints. It is a powerful method, due mainly to the flexibility with which the optimal control problem can be formulated. Indeed, once the governing PDE, encoding the dynamics of the system, has been derived, many types of optimization problems can be posed. For instance, any constraints on the control input or on the state variable can be handled, contrary to Hamilton-Jacobi formulations.

M. Morari and L. Thiele (Eds.): HSCC 2005, LNCS 3414, pp. 557–572, 2005.

In this paper, we focus on a particular practical optimal control problem. Given a domain of the state space of a SHS, we aim to maintain the expected sojourn time of the state within this domain above a certain threshold, while minimizing the cost of the control input. Different stochastic differential equations govern the continuous state in each mode, and a continuous time Markov chain dictates possible mode switches based on state and/or time. We first review the SHS model [1], and transform the optimal control problem into a PDE optimization problem. Then, we present and apply the adjoint method to this optimization problem. We present a set of interesting examples illustrating, through numerical solution, the resulting control policies, and we conclude with a note on further applications of the adjoint-based method in the context of SHSs.

2   Problem Formulation

2.1   Stochastic Hybrid Systems

General frameworks of stochastic hybrid systems have been proposed in [2,3]. In this paper we focus on a special class called switched diffusions [1]. The state (X_t, m_t) of a switched diffusion system $\mathcal{H}$ consists of two parts: $X_t \in \mathbb{R}^n$ is the continuous state, and $m_t \in S = \{1, \ldots, M\}$ is the discrete state (or mode). The dynamics of the state (X_t, m_t) is characterized by the following:

- **Continuous Dynamics.** The continuous state X_t evolves according to a stochastic differential equation (SDE) whose drift and variance terms depend on the discrete mode m_t.

$$dX_t = u(X_t, m_t)\, dt + \sigma(X_t, m_t)\, dB_t. \tag{1}$$

  B_t is a d-dimensional Brownian motion in some probability space $(\Omega, \mathcal{F}, P)$, with Ω the sample space, $\mathcal{F}$ the σ-field, and P the probability measure, and $u : \mathbb{R}^n \times S \to \mathbb{R}^n$ and $\sigma : \mathbb{R}^n \times S \to \mathbb{R}^{n \times d}$ are functions that are bounded and Lipschitz continuous in the first argument. Moreover, we assume that the possible values of σ are bounded away from zero.

- **Discrete Dynamics.** The discrete mode m_t evolves according to a continuous time Markov chain with a generator matrix $\Lambda(x) = [\lambda_{kl}(x)]_{1 \le k,l \le M}$ whose components depend on the continuous state $X_t = x$. Note that, $\forall k \ne l$, $\lambda_{kl}(x) \ge 0$ and $\lambda_{kk}(x) = -\sum_{l \ne k} \lambda_{kl}(x) \le 0$. Equivalently, for $\Delta t > 0$, we have

$$P(m_{t+\Delta t} = l \mid m_t = k, X_t = x) = \begin{cases} \lambda_{kl}(x)\Delta t + o(\Delta t), & \text{if } l \ne k, \\ 1 + \lambda_{kk}(x)\Delta t + o(\Delta t), & \text{if } l = k. \end{cases} \tag{2}$$

  Thus, given that $\mathcal{H}$ is in discrete mode k and continuous state x at time t, within a short time period Δt, $m_{t+\Delta t}$ jumps to a new mode $l \ne k$ with an approximate probability $\lambda_{kl}(x)\Delta t$.

 – **Reset Condition.** For simplicity, we assume trivial reset condition. In other words, whenever a jump in m_t occurs, X_t remains unchanged. Note that the methodology developed in this paper is still applicable with general deterministic reset conditions.

We now outline the procedures to obtain stochastic solutions (executions) to the above stochastic hybrid system. Starting from an initial condition $X_0 = x$ and $m_0 = k$, the discrete state m_t remains in mode k for a random amount of time T_k while the continuous state evolves according to equation (1) with $m_t \equiv k$ until it reaches X_{T_k}. Then at time T_k the discrete state jumps to a new mode $l \neq k$ with probability $-\lambda_{kl}(X_{T_k})/\lambda_{kk}(X_{T_k})$ while the continuous state remains unchanged at X_{T_k}. This step is then repeated an infinite number of times. Note that if Λ is independent of x, the distribution of T_k is exponential with rate $-\lambda_{kk}$; however, in general, the random time T_k has a distribution dependent on the outcome of X_t.

In many practical applications, the variance term σ in the continuous dynamics (1) characterizing the environment noises and the λ_{kl} terms in (2) governing the transitions among operational modes are given and not adjustable, while the drift term u in (1) can be controlled by users to a certain degree. In this perspective, u can be treated as the control input of system $\mathcal{H}$.

In the following, we shall use $P^{(x,k)}$ and $E^{(x,k)}$ to denote the probability and expectation under the initial condition $X_0 = x$ and $m_0 = k$.

2.2   Optimal Exit Time Control

Given a switched diffusion system $\mathcal{H}$, we now formulate the problem studied in this paper. Let U be an open set of $\mathbb{R}^n$ with compact support. Let (X_t, m_t) be a stochastic solution to $\mathcal{H}$ starting from $X_0 = x$ and $m_0 = k$ at time 0. We consider the following stopping time:

$$\tau = \inf\{t > 0 : X_t \notin U\}, \tag{3}$$

which is called the exit time from U (or the sojourn time in U).

Remark 1. Note that the definition of τ in (3) does not involve m_t. Therefore, at exit time τ, the switched diffusion can be in any discrete mode $m_t \in S$.

Define $V(x, k)$ as the expected exit time from U, starting from (x, k):

$$V(x, k) = E^{(x,k)}[\tau]. \tag{4}$$

Treating u as the feedback control of the system $\mathcal{H}$, $V(x, k)$ is determined by the design of u. In practical situations, U is often referred to as the *safe set* in which one wants the system state to stay. Then a natural problem is to find the least expensive control $u : U \times S \to \mathbb{R}^n$ that can keep the system in U for at least an expected amount of time. Specifically, let $\rho, \xi : U \times S \to \mathbb{R}_+$ be two positive functions representing weights. The cost of the control, $J(u)$, is written as

$$J(u) \triangleq \sum_{k=1}^{M} \int_U \xi(x, k) \|u(x, k)\|^2 \, dx, \tag{5}$$

and the (weighted) cumulative expected exit time from U, $V_{cee}(u)$, is defined as

$$V_{cee}(u) = \sum_{k=1}^{M} \int_{U} \rho(x,k)V(x,k)\,dx. \tag{6}$$

In particular, if ρ is the probability density function of (X_0, m_0) over $U \times S$, then $V_{cee}(u)$ coincides with the expected exit time from U with uncertain (X_0, m_0).

Problem 1. The problem studied in this paper is

$$\text{Minimize } J(u) \text{ subject to } V_{cee}(u) \geq V_0, \tag{7}$$

for some constant $V_0 > 0$.

For simplicity, but without loss of generality, we shall assume that $\rho = \xi \equiv 1$, unless otherwise stated.

2.3   Reformulation as a PDE Constrained Optimization Problem

Problem (1) in its current form is not easy to analyze as the dependence of $V_{cee}(u)$ on the control u is implicit. In this section, we shall derive the PDE satisfied by $V(x,k)$ defined in (4), where u will appear as a coefficient to be controlled.

Definition 1 (Generator of the Switched Diffusion). *To the switched diffusion $(X_t, m_t)_{t \geq 0}$, we associate an operator L (referred to as the generator) that maps a function $f \in C_0^2(\mathbb{R}^n \times S)$ to a new function $Lf \in C_0^0(\mathbb{R}^n \times S)$ defined by*

$$Lf(x,m) \triangleq \sum_{i=1}^{n} u_i(x,m) \frac{\partial f(x,m)}{\partial x_i} + \frac{1}{2} \sum_{i,j=1}^{n} (\sigma(x,m)\sigma(x,m)^T)_{ij} \frac{\partial^2 f(x,m)}{\partial x_i \partial x_j}$$
$$+ \sum_{k=1}^{M} \lambda_{mk}(x) f(x,k), \quad \forall x \in \mathbb{R}^n, \ \forall m = 1, \ldots, M. \tag{8}$$

Here $C_0^2(\mathbb{R}^n \times S)$ (resp. $C_0^0(\mathbb{R}^n \times S)$) denotes the set of functions on $\mathbb{R}^n \times S$ with compact support that are twice differentiable (resp. continuous) with respect to the first argument. $u_i(x,m)$ denotes the i-th component of the vector $u(x,m) \in \mathbb{R}^n$.

Lemma 1. *For all $(x,m) \in \mathbb{R}^n \times S$, and for any $f \in C_0^2(\mathbb{R}^n \times S)$, $M_t \triangleq f(X_t, m_t) - f(X_0, m_0) - \int_0^t Lf(X_s, m_s)\,ds$ is a Martingale on $(\Omega, \mathcal{F}, P^{(x,m)})$.*

A proof of the above lemma can be found in [3].

Theorem 1. *For all $(x,m) \in U \times S$, $V(x,m) = E^{x,m}[\tau]$ is finite, and is a solution of the following system of PDEs:*

$$LV(x,m) = -1, \quad \forall x \in U, \ \forall m \in S,$$
$$V(x,m) = 0, \quad \forall x \in \partial U, \ \forall m \in S. \tag{9}$$

Proof. 1. By assumption, for each $m \in S$, $\sigma(\cdot, m) : x \in U \mapsto \sigma(x, m) \in \mathbb{R}^{n \times d}$ is a continuous function whose values are bounded away from zero. Therefore the PDE system (9) admits a unique solution V twice differentiable in its first argument [10]. Since $V_{\partial U \times S} \equiv 0$, we can construct $\tilde{V} \in C_0^2(\mathbb{R}^n \times S)$, such that $\tilde{V} = V$ on $\bar{U} \times S$. Applying Lemma 1 to $\tilde{V}$, we have that

$$M_t \triangleq \tilde{V}(X_t, m_t) - \tilde{V}(X_0, m_0) - \int_0^t L\tilde{V}(X_s, m_s) \, ds \qquad (10)$$

is a Martingale on $(\Omega, \mathcal{F}, P^{(x,m)})$.

Now, for each integer $N \in \mathbb{N}^+$, define $\tau_N \triangleq \tau \wedge N = \min(\tau, N)$. Then τ_N is a stopping time with finite expectation $E^{x,m}[\tau_N] \leq N < \infty$. Therefore, applying the optional sampling theorem to the Martingale M_t stopped at time τ_N, we deduce that $E^{x,m}[M_{\tau_N}] = 0$. In addition, $\forall s \in [0, \tau_N]$, $X_s \in \bar{U}$; therefore, $\int_0^{\tau_N} L\tilde{V}(X_s, m_s) \, ds = \int_0^{\tau_N} LV(X_s, m_s) \, ds = -\tau_N$, and thus, $E^{x,m}[\tau_N] = E^{x,m}[\tilde{V}(X_0, m_0) - \tilde{V}(X_{\tau_N}, m_{\tau_N})] \leq 2 \sup_{(x,m) \in U \times S} \{|\tilde{V}(x, m)|\} < \infty.$

Applying the monotone convergence theorem, with $\tau_N \to \tau$ almost surely, we deduce that $E^{x,m}[\tau] = \sup_N \{E^{x,m}[\tau_N]\} \leq 2 \sup_{(x,m) \in U \times S} \{|\tilde{V}(x, m)|\} < \infty.$

2. Since $E^{x,m}[\tau] < \infty$, we can now apply the optional sampling theorem to M_t stopped at time τ. We obtain $E^{x,m}[\tilde{V}(X_\tau, m_\tau)] - E^{x,m}[\tilde{V}(x, m)] + E^{x,m}[\tau] = 0.$ Given the boundary conditions satisfied by V, we have $\tilde{V}_{\partial U \times S} = 0$ and therefore, $\tilde{V}(X_\tau, m_\tau) \equiv 0$. It follows that $\forall (x, m) \in U \times S$, $V(x, m) = \tilde{V}(x, m) = E^{x,m}[\tau]$, which proves the theorem. $\qquad \square$

As a result of Theorem 1, Problem (1) can now be reformulated as follows:

$$\begin{aligned} \text{Minimize} \quad & J(u) = \sum_{m=1}^M \int_U \|u(x, m)\|^2 \, dx \\ \text{Subject to} \quad & \sum_{m=1}^M \int_U V(x, m) \, dx \geq V_0; \\ & \begin{cases} LV(x, m) = -1, & \forall x \in U, \ m \in S; \\ V(x, m) = 0, & \forall x \in \partial U, \ m \in S. \end{cases} \end{aligned} \qquad (11)$$

Note that the constraint on V in the above problem is written explicitly as a system of coupled PDEs with boundary condition. In the next section, we shall introduce tools to solve this kind of optimization problem.

3   PDE Constrained Optimization via Adjoint Method

The adjoint method is a gradient-based method which can numerically solve optimization problems subject to PDE constraints [9, 8]. In Section 3.1, we will first briefly review the adjoint method in its most general setting, and then apply it to the optimal exit time control problem for switched diffusions in Section 3.2.

3.1   Adjoint Method for Solving PDE Constrained Optimization

Consider the following general PDE constrained optimization program.

$$
\begin{aligned}
\text{Minimize} \quad & J(u,v) \\
\text{Subject to} \quad & \mathcal{N}(u,v) = 0 \\
& r(u,v) \leq 0.
\end{aligned}
\tag{12}
$$

Here, $\mathcal{N}(u,v) = 0$ denotes a PDE; v denotes the solution of the PDE; u is the control variable, which is in general an adjustable coefficient of the PDE or an adjustable term in the boundary conditions; J is the objective function of the optimization program and has to be real valued; r is a function of u and v which characterizes all the inequality constraints of the problem, such as bounds on the control variable u or on the solution v. J and r are assumed to be differentiable in u and v.

In order to apply the adjoint-method, we first need to reduce (12) into an unconstrained optimization problem. For this purpose, we use a (logarithm) barrier method:

$$
\begin{aligned}
\text{Minimize} \quad & I(u,v) = J(u,v) - \epsilon \mathbf{1}^T \log(-r(u,v)) \\
\text{Subject to} \quad & \mathcal{N}(u,v) = 0,
\end{aligned}
\tag{13}
$$

where $\mathbf{1}^T \log(-r(u,v))$ represents the inner product between the identity $\mathbf{1}$ and $\log(-r(u,v))$. Problem (12) and Problem (13) are equivalent when $\epsilon \to 0$. Therefore solving (13) with $\epsilon \simeq 0$ will approximately solve (12). The adjoint method can then be used to derive the gradient of the cost function I with respect to the control input u, subject to the constraint $\mathcal{N}(u,v) = 0$, thus deriving a descent direction for u in Problem (13). First, take a first variation of I:

$$
\delta I = \left(\frac{\partial I}{\partial u}\right)^T \delta u + \left(\frac{\partial I}{\partial v}\right)^T \delta v.
\tag{14}
$$

Similarly, a first order variation of the PDE gives the dependence of δv on δu:

$$
\delta \mathcal{N} = \left(\frac{\partial \mathcal{N}}{\partial u}\right) \delta u + \left(\frac{\partial \mathcal{N}}{\partial v}\right) \delta v = 0,
\tag{15}
$$

in which $\frac{\partial \mathcal{N}}{\partial u}$ and $\frac{\partial \mathcal{N}}{\partial v}$ are linear operators. Taking the inner product of (15) with any differentiable function q (named *costate*) and subtracting it from (14), we have

$$
\forall q, \quad \delta I = \left(\left(\frac{\partial I}{\partial u}\right)^T - q^T \frac{\partial \mathcal{N}}{\partial u}\right) \delta u + \left(\left(\frac{\partial I}{\partial v}\right)^T - q^T \frac{\partial \mathcal{N}}{\partial v}\right) \delta v.
\tag{16}
$$

Choosing q such that it satisfies the following adjoint PDE:

$$
\left(\frac{\partial \mathcal{N}}{\partial v}\right)^T q = \frac{\partial I}{\partial v},
\tag{17}
$$

we derive δI as a function of δu only:

$$
\delta I = \left(\left(\frac{\partial I}{\partial u}\right)^T - q^T \frac{\partial \mathcal{N}}{\partial u}\right) \delta u,
\tag{18}
$$

which precisely defines the gradient of I with respect to the control variable u:

$$\nabla I(u) = \frac{\partial I}{\partial u} - \left(\frac{\partial \mathcal{N}}{\partial u}\right)^T q. \tag{19}$$

With the gradient $\nabla I(u)$ in hand, one can then design an iterative algorithm using gradient descent to solve Problem (13) numerically. Note that in each step one has to solve the PDE and the adjoint PDE (17) in order to obtain the gradient.

3.2   Adjoint Method Applied to Optimal Sojourn Time Control

We now demonstrate how the adjoint method can be applied to solve the optimal sojourn time control Problem (11). We assume that $\xi = \rho \equiv 1$ on U.

First, we transform Problem (11) into the form of (13) as:

Minimize $I(u) = \sum_{m=1}^{M} \int_{U} \|u(x,m)\|^2 \, dx - \epsilon \log(\sum_{m=1}^{M} \int_{U} V(x,m) \, dx - V_0)$

Subject to $\begin{cases} LV(x,m) = -1, \ \forall x \in U, \ m \in S; \\ V(x,m) = 0, \ \forall x \in \partial U, \ m \in S. \end{cases}$

$$\tag{20}$$

Note that instead of writing $I(u,V)$, we omit V since it depends on u implicitly. A first variation of the cost function I gives:

$$\delta I(u) = 2 \sum_{m=1}^{M} \int_{U} u(x,m)^T \delta u(x,m) \, dx - \epsilon \frac{\sum_{m=1}^{M} \int_{U} \delta V(x,m) \, dx}{\sum_{m=1}^{M} \int_{U} V(x,m) \, dx - V_0}. \tag{21}$$

To compute δI as a function of δu only (and not as a function of δV, which is not directly controllable), one needs to eliminate δV. For this purpose, we take the first variation of the PDE constraint $LV(x,m) = -1$, which gives the dependence of δV on δu:

$$\sum_{i=1}^{n} \left[\delta u_i(x,m) \frac{\partial V(x,m)}{\partial x_i} + u_i(x,m) \frac{\partial \delta V(x,m)}{\partial x_i} \right] +$$

$$\sum_{i,j=1}^{n} \frac{1}{2} (\sigma(x,m)\sigma(x,m)^T)_{ij} \frac{\partial^2 \delta V(x,m)}{\partial x_i \partial x_j} + \sum_{k=1}^{M} \lambda_{mk}(x) \delta V(x,k) = 0. \tag{22}$$

For each m, multiplying (22) by a costate function $q(x,m)$ which is twice differentiable in x and which is identically zero on ∂U (required for the integration by parts in (24)), integrating over the domain U, and then summing over all m, we obtain:

$$\sum_{m=1}^{M} \int_{U} \left(q^m \sum_{i=1}^{n} u_i^m \frac{\partial \delta V^m}{\partial x_i} + \frac{q^m}{2} \sum_{i,j=1}^{n} (\sigma^m \sigma^{mT})_{ij} \frac{\partial^2 \delta V^m}{\partial x_i \partial x_j} \right.$$

$$\left. + q^m \sum_{k=1}^{M} \lambda_{mk} \delta V^k \right) dx = - \sum_{m=1}^{M} \int_{U} \sum_{i=1}^{n} q^m \frac{\partial V^m}{\partial x_i} \delta u_i^m \, dx, \tag{23}$$

where for simplicity we drop the explicit dependence on x, and use V^m for $V(\cdot, m)$, u_i^m for $u_i(\cdot, m)$, etc... Integrating by parts in (23) and using the boundary condition that, on ∂U, $V^m \equiv 0$ and $q^m \equiv 0$, we have

$$
\sum_{m=1}^{M} \int_U \left(-\sum_{i=1}^{n} \frac{\partial(q^m u_i^m)}{\partial x_i} + \frac{1}{2} \sum_{i,j=1}^{n} \frac{\partial^2[q^m(\sigma^m \sigma^{mT})_{ij}]}{\partial x_i \partial x_j} \right.
$$
$$
\left. + \sum_{k=1}^{M} \lambda_{km} q^k \right) \delta V^m \, dx = -\sum_{m=1}^{M} \int_U q^m \sum_{i=1}^{n} \frac{\partial V^m}{\partial x_i} \delta u_i^m \, dx.
\tag{24}
$$

Suppose for each m we choose q^m so that the following adjoint PDE holds:

$$
\frac{1}{2} \sum_{i,j=1}^{n} \frac{\partial^2[q^m(\sigma^m \sigma^{mT})_{ij}]}{\partial x_i \partial x_j} - \sum_{i=1}^{n} \frac{\partial(q^m u_i^m)}{\partial x_i} + \sum_{k=1}^{M} \lambda_{km} q^k
$$
$$
= \frac{\epsilon}{\sum_{m=1}^{M} \int_U V^m \, dx - V_0}.
\tag{25}
$$

First substituting (25) into (24), and then the result into (21), we have

$$
\delta I(u) = \sum_{m=1}^{M} \int_U \left(2u^m + q^m \nabla V^m \right)^T \delta u^m \, dx.
$$

So the gradient of I with respect to the control u for the discrete mode m is

$$
\nabla I^m = 2u^m + q^m \nabla V^m, \quad m = 1, \ldots, M.
\tag{26}
$$

We emphasize here that q^m in equation (26) is the solution to the adjoint equation (25) with boundary condition $q^m \equiv 0$ on ∂U. Furthermore, the quantities q^m, u^m, etc. represent q, u, etc. in mode m; and not q or u to the power m.

Having obtained the gradient of I with respect to the control u, the gradient descent algorithm for finding the optimal u can be formulated as follows.

Algorithm 1 (Adjoint based algorithm). *Set $\epsilon = 1$ and guess an initial value for u.*
Repeat (loop a)
   Repeat (loop b)
      1. Solve equation (9) for V, using the current control u.
      2. Solve the adjoint equation (25) for q, using the current u and V.
      3. Determine the gradient ∇I according to equation (26).
      4. Line search: compute $\beta > 0$ so that $I(u - \beta \nabla I)$ is minimized.
      5. Update $u := u - \beta \nabla I$.
   Terminate loop b *when $\|\nabla I\|$ is smaller than the stopping criteria α_b.*
   Decrease ϵ by letting $\epsilon := \mu \epsilon$, where $\mu \in [0.1, 0.5]$.
Terminate loop a *when ϵ is smaller than the stopping criteria α_a.*
Return *$u_{opt} = u$.*

Remark 2. According to the analysis of Section 2, the admissible control u has to be bounded and Lipschitz continuous on U. Thus, to be rigorous, a constraint of the type $u_{\min} \leq u(x,m) \leq u_{\max}$ should be added to the optimization problem to ensure the boundedness of u. Regarding the Lipschitz continuity, the gradient ∇I should be projected on a functional subspace of Lipschitz continuous functions after step 3 of Algorithm 1.

3.3   Validation Against Analytical Solution in a Simple Case

It is possible to solve Problem (1) analytically in some simple cases. In this section, we shall present such a case studied in [11], and compare the analytical result with the numerical ones obtained using Algorithm 1.

Suppose that $M = 1$, $U = [-a, a] \subset \mathbb{R}$, and $\sigma = 1$ on U. Then the stochastic hybrid system degenerates into a simple diffusion on the interval $[-a, a]$:

$$dX_t = u(X_t)\, dt + dB_t.$$

The expected exit time $V(x)$ from U starting from $x \in U$ satisfies

$$\frac{1}{2}V''(x) + u(x)V'(x) + 1 = 0, \quad V(-a) = V(a) = 0. \tag{27}$$

Assume $\xi \equiv 1$, and $\rho(x)$ is a unit pulse centered at the origin. Then Problem (11), which is equivalent to Problem (1), can then be formulated as

$$\text{Minimize } \int_{-a}^{a} u^2(x)\, dx, \text{ subject to equation (27) and } V(0) \geq V_0.$$

Suppose in addition that the control u is odd in x, i.e., $u(-x) = -u(x)$, $\forall x \in U$. Then V as a solution to (27) is even in x. Because of the symmetry, it suffices to study the problem on the left half interval $[-a, 0]$ only:

$$\text{Minimize } \int_{-a}^{0} u^2(x)\, dx, \text{ subject to equation (27) and } V(0) \geq V_0. \tag{28}$$

Denote $y_1 = V$ and $y_2 = V'$. Then the above problem is equivalent to the following optimal control problem:

$$\text{Minimize } \int_{-a}^{0} u^2(x)\, dx, \text{ subject to } \begin{cases} y_1' = y_2, & y_1(-a) = 0, y_1(0) = V_0, \\ y_2' = -2uy_2 - 2, & y_2(0) = 0. \end{cases}$$

Using the Maximum Principle, and identifying two first integrals in the Hamiltonian equations, we can determine the optimal trajectory (y_1, y_2) as

$$y_2(x) = \Phi^{-1}(x), \quad y_1(x) = \int_{-a}^{x} y_2(x)\, dx, \tag{29}$$

where Φ is a function defined by $\Phi(y) = \int_0^y \dfrac{dx}{-2\sqrt{1+x^2(c_1 x + c_2)}}$ for some suitably chosen constants c_1 and c_2. The optimal control u in this case can be determined from y_1 and y_2 accordingly. For more details, see [11].

In Figure 1, we plot the analytic and the numerical results for the above problem. One can see that Algorithm 1 generates results that fit the analytical one exceedingly well.

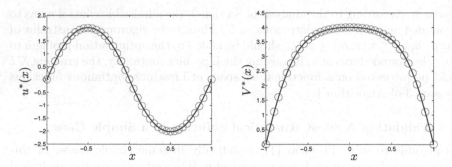

Fig. 1. *Validation against analytical results. Left*: Optimal control u^* returned by Algorithm 1 (solid) and by the analytical solution (circles). *Right*: Optimal expected sojourn time returned by Algorithm 1 (solid) and by analytical solution (circles)

4   Simulation Examples for Stochastic Hybrid Systems

We now apply our algorithm to investigate the optimal exit time control problem for switched diffusions. Two main categories of switched diffusions are considered: time switching and state switching.

4.1   Time Switching

The time switching case refers to the case in which the variance $\sigma(x, m)$ and the mode transition rate $\Lambda(x)$ are both independent of the continuous state x. Therefore, for each mode m, the variance $\sigma\sigma^T$ is a constant matrix, and the time the system spends in mode m before jumping to a new mode has an exponential distribution.

For simplicity, in this section we assume that there are only two modes: $S = \{1, 2\}$, and that, for each mode $m = 1, 2$, the variance $\sigma(\cdot, m) \equiv \sigma_m I_n$ for constants $\sigma_1^2 = 1$ and $\sigma_2^2 = 2$, where I_n is the n-by-n identity matrix. The problem is then to determine the control $u(\cdot, 1)$ and $u(\cdot, 2)$ for the two modes.

Example 1 (Switching Between Two Modes in a 2-D Disk). Suppose $U = B(0, a)$ is the disk of radius $a > 0$ around the origin in $\mathbb{R}^2$. In cylindrical coordinates $x = (r, \theta)$, the control $u = (u_r, u_\theta)$ is decomposed into the radial component u_r and ortho-radial component r_θ, and the PDE (9) governing the expected sojourn time $V(x, m) = V((r, \theta), m)$ in U becomes

$$\frac{\sigma_m^2}{2}\left(\frac{\partial^2 V((r, \theta), m)}{\partial r^2} + \frac{1}{r}\frac{\partial V((r, \theta), m)}{\partial r} + \frac{1}{r^2}\frac{\partial^2 V((r, \theta), m)}{\partial \theta^2}\right) +$$
$$u_r\frac{\partial V((r, \theta), m)}{\partial r} + \frac{u_\theta}{r}\frac{\partial V((r, \theta), m)}{\partial \theta} + \sum_{k=1}^{2}\lambda_{mk}V((r, \theta), k) + 1 = 0, \qquad (30)$$
$$V((a, \theta), m) = 0, \, \forall \theta \in [0, 2\pi]; \quad V((r, 2\pi), m) = V((r, 0), m), \, \forall r \in [0, a].$$

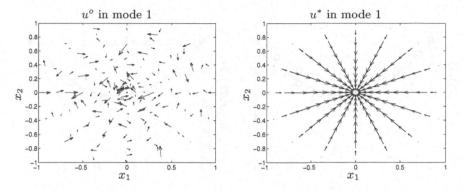

Fig. 2. *Left*: Initial guess for the control u in mode 1. Arrows represent the directions and the amplitudes of the randomly generated control u. *Right*: Optimal control u^* in mode 1 returned by Algorithm 1. Note that it is radially-invariant

So the equivalent PDE-constrained optimization Problem (11) becomes

$$\text{Minimize } \sum_{m=1}^{2} \int_0^{2\pi} \int_0^a \left(u_r^2((r,\theta), m) + u_\theta^2((r,\theta), m) \right) \, r \, dr \, d\theta$$
$$\text{Subject to } \sum_{m=1}^{2} \int_0^{2\pi} \int_0^a V((r,\theta), m) \, r \, dr \, d\theta \geq 2V_0; \qquad (31)$$
$$\text{Equation (30)}.$$

Due to the rotational symmetry of the problem: the domain U, the cost function and the constraints are all invariant under the rotations around the origin, we conjecture that the optimal solutions are also radially symmetric:

Conjecture 1. *The optimal control u^* is of the form $u^* = u_r(r)e_r$, where e_r is the radius unit vector.*

We verify this conjecture numerically by applying the adjoint algorithm 1 using randomly generated initial guesses for the control u. We assume that the switching rates are given by $\Lambda = \begin{bmatrix} -10 & 10 \\ 10 & -10 \end{bmatrix}$. On the left of Fig. 2 we show a typical initial guess for the control u in mode 1 (guesses for control in mode 2 are similar). The optimal control u^* returned by the algorithm is shown on the right of the figure, which is radially symmetric. That the algorithm converges to the same solution from a wide selection of initial u demonstrates its robustness with respect to initial guesses.

Two more scenarios are also simulated, one with a higher switching rate $\Lambda = \begin{bmatrix} -20 & 20 \\ 20 & -20 \end{bmatrix}$, and the other with no switching at all: $\Lambda = \begin{bmatrix} 0 & 0 \\ 0 & 0 \end{bmatrix}$. In both cases, the algorithm produces radially symmetric solutions. Thus we only plot the radial component u_r^* of the solution u^* in Fig. 3, with controls in mode 1 and 2 on the left and right, respectively. The higher switching rate case is plotted in circles, and the no switching case in squares. For comparisons, we also plot the simulation results for the non-hybrid case (only one mode) for three different σ: $\sigma = \sigma_1$ (dash dot lines), $\sigma = \frac{\sigma_1 + \sigma_2}{2}$ (solid lines), and $\sigma = \sigma_2$ (dot lines).

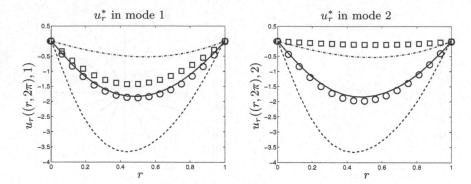

Fig. 3. Radial component u_r^* of the optimal control u^* in mode 1 (*left*) and mode 2 (*right*) for the high switching rate case (circles) and no switching case (squares). Also included are the u_r^* for the non-hybrid case (only one mode) with variance $\sigma = \sigma_1$ (dash dot), $\sigma = \frac{\sigma_1 + \sigma_2}{2}$ (solid), and $\sigma = \sigma_2$ (dot)

In the higher switching rate case, the optimal controls in the two modes are almost the same, and also close to the optimal control in the non-hybrid case with variance $\sigma = \frac{\sigma_1 + \sigma_2}{2}$. This is because, due to the very frequent switchings between the two modes, and the fact that quickly the distribution of m_t will converge to the stationary distribution of equal probability $\frac{1}{2}$ in each mode, the stochastic hybrid system switching between diffusions of variances σ_1 and σ_2, can be approximated by a single diffusion with variance $\sigma = \frac{\sigma_1 + \sigma_2}{2}$.

For the zero switching rate case, the optimal controls in the two modes are quite different from each other, and from the other cases as well. Barely any control is exerted in mode 2 compared with in mode 1. The reason is that it costs less control input to maintain the expected sojourn time above $2V_0$ in mode 1, than maintaining the expected sojourn time above V_0 in mode 2.

4.2   State Switching

Consider the following situation. The domain U is partitioned into a finite number of subdomains U_α. Consider a diffusion process X_t evolving on U accordingly to $dX_t = u(X_t)dt + \sigma(X_t)dB_t$, where the variance $\sigma(x)$ takes the constant value σ_α for $x \in U_\alpha$. Thus σ is piecewise constant on U. Assume that there is only one mode $m = 1$.

Rigorously speaking, for the above X_t to be well defined one needs $\sigma(x)$ to be Lipschitz continuous in x, which is not the case here. However, one can "smooth out" the transition of σ near the boundary of U_α to satisfy this requirement. Specifically, one can make σ to be constant σ_α in a compact subset of U_α approximately equal to U_α, and determine the value of σ for points near the boundary with other subdomains via interpolation. The σ thus obtained is Lipschitz continuous in x, and using it one gets an approximate of the original process. As an example, we partition the domain $U = [-a, a] \times [-b, b]$ into two subdomains: $U_a = [-a, 0] \times [-b, b]$, and $U_b = (0, a] \times [-b, b]$. We can choose the variance $\sigma(x)$

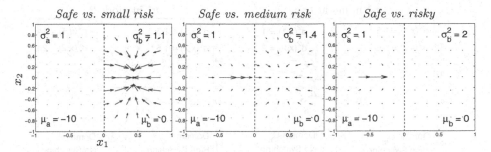

Fig. 4. Optimal control u^* for Example 2. A constant nominal drift exists in domain U_a. $\sigma_a^2 = 1$, while $\sigma_b^2 = 1.1$ (*left*); $\sigma_b^2 = 1.4$ (*center*); $\sigma_b^2 = 2$ (*right*). Note that in different figures the sizes of the arrows representing the magnitude of the control u^* are not in the same scale: *Left:* $\|u^*\|_{\max} = 4.3$. *Center:* $\|u^*\|_{\max} = 14.2$. *Right:* $\|u^*\|_{\max} = 16.1$

to be constant σ_a on $U_a^\epsilon = [-a, -\epsilon] \times [-b, b]$ and σ_b on $U_b^\epsilon = [\epsilon, a] \times [-b, b]$, with $\epsilon > 0$, and determine $\sigma(x)$ on $(-\epsilon, \epsilon) \times [-b, b]$ by interpolation.

Example 2 (Safe vs. Risky in a 2-D Box). Suppose that $U = [-a, a] \times [-b, b] = U_a \cup U_b$ as defined above. In this example, we would like to study whether it is more advantageous to try to stay in U_a with a low uncertainty (low variance) but a constant drift pushing toward the left boundary, or to try to stay in U_b with no uncontrollable drift but with high uncertainty (high variance). For this purpose, we set the following conditions. $\sigma(x)$ is constant equal to $\sigma_a I_2$ on U_a for $\sigma_a^2 = 1$, and constant equal to $\sigma_b I_2$ on U_b for $\sigma_b^2 = 2$. To smooth out the transition of $\sigma(x)$, we use the parameter $\epsilon = 0.02$. Furthermore, assume that on subdomain U_a there is an uncontrollable constant drift $(-10, 0)^T$ to the left, while on U_a there is no such drift. Thus X_t is governed by $dX_t = [\mu(X_t) + u(X_t)] dt + \sigma(X_t) dB_t$, with $\mu(x) = (-10, 0)^T$ if $x \in U_a$ and $\mu(x) = 0$ if $x \in U_b$.

First write the PDE governing the expected sojourn time $V(x)$ as

$$\frac{\sigma^2}{2}\left(\frac{\partial^2 V}{\partial x_1^2} + \frac{\partial^2 V}{\partial x_2^2}\right) + (\mu_1 + u_1)\frac{\partial V}{\partial x_1} + (\mu_2 + u_2)\frac{\partial V}{\partial x_2} = -1, \quad \forall x \in U, \quad (32)$$

with boundary condition $V(x) \equiv 0$ for $x \in \partial U$. Thus the problem becomes

$$
\begin{aligned}
&\text{Minimize} \quad \int_{-a}^{a} \int_{-b}^{b} (u_1^2 + u_2^2)\, dx_1\, dx_2 \\
&\text{Subject to} \quad \int_{-a}^{a} \int_{-b}^{b} V(x)\, dx_1\, dx_2 \geq V_0, \text{ and equation (32)},
\end{aligned} \quad (33)
$$

Algorithm 1 can be extended easily to deal with the uncontrollable drift term. The results are shown in Fig. 4 and are quite interesting. For very small values of σ_b, $(\sigma_b^2 = 1.1)$, the optimal control concentrates all the energy in the domain U_b, trying to contain X_t near the center of U_b. However, as $\sigma_b^2 = 1.4$, the optimal control is distributed on both U_a and U_b. If σ_b^2 increases further to 2, the optimal control applies very little force on U_b and concentrates most of its energy near the center horizontal line in U_a.

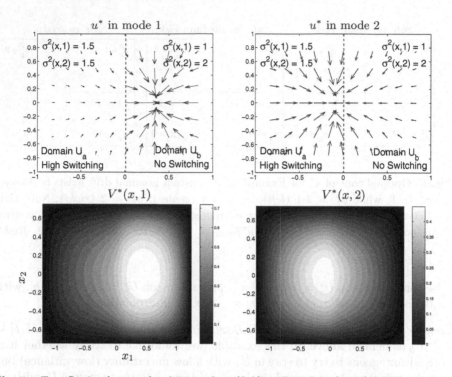

Fig. 5. *Top*: Optimal controls u^* in mode 1 (*left*) and mode 2 (*right*) for Example 3. *Bottom*: Optimal expected exit time $V^*(x, 1)$ (*left*) and $V^*(x, 2)$ (*right*)

4.3   General Switching

We now consider a general scenario that encompasses the previous two cases as special instances. In this case, sudden changes in variance can occur either due to the random discrete mode transitions or due to the state evolving into different subdomains of U.

Example 3 (General Switching in a 2-D box). Let $U = U_a \cup U_b$ be as before. Suppose that there are two discrete modes ($M = 2$). In subdomain U_a, the switching rate between the two modes due to the continuous time Markov chain m_t is high, so the diffusion switches rapidly between mode 1 and mode 2. On the other hand, the switching rate is zero on U_b so that once X_t enters U_b, m_t will remain in the same mode. In addition, assume that the variance on domain U_a is $\sigma_a I_2$ with $\sigma_a^2 = 1.5$, regardless of the discrete mode, while on U_b, the variance is $\sigma_b I_2$, with $\sigma_b^2 = 1$ if $m = 1$ and $\sigma_b^2 = 2$ if $m = 2$. To sum up, we have $\sigma(x, 1) = \sigma(x, 2) = \sqrt{1.5} I_2$, $\Lambda(x) = \begin{bmatrix} -20 & 20 \\ 20 & -20 \end{bmatrix}$, $\forall x \in U_a$; $\sigma(x, 1) = I_2$, $\sigma(x, 2) = \sqrt{2} I_2$, $\Lambda(x) = \begin{bmatrix} 0 & 0 \\ 0 & 0 \end{bmatrix}$, $\forall x \in U_b$. The optimal control u^* for this problem as obtained by Algorithm 1 is shown in Fig. 5. Under mode 1, u^* tends to drive X_t towards subdomain U_b where the variance is lower than in U_a. In mode 2, u^* tends to drive X_t towards U_a, in which the average variance is lower than the variance in U_b. However, the optimal control does not drive the diffusion near the center of U_a (as it drives the diffusion near the center of U_b, under mode 1). The interpretation is that the diffusion originally in mode 2, in U_b, will tend to be driven to U_a, switch mode and then go back to U_b in mode 1. This is a smart optimal control.

5   Conclusions and Extensions

In this paper we proposed to use the adjoint method to solve the optimal sojourn time control problem for a class of stochastic hybrid systems. We formulated the problem as a PDE-constrained optimization problem, and devised an algorithm to solve it using the gradients computed via the adjoint method.

The adjoint method is a powerful tool that can be applied to many other optimal control problems. Examples include optimal control of expected reward over an infinite time horizon: $V(x,m) = E^{x,m}[\int_0^\infty e^{-\alpha s} r(X_s, m)\, ds]$, which satisfies

$$LV(x,m) - \alpha V(x,m) = -r(x,m)\,, \quad m = 1, \ldots, M.$$

As another example, we can choose $V(x,t,m) = E^{x,m}[f(X_t, m)]$, which solves the backward Kolmogorov equation:

$$\frac{\partial V(x,t,m)}{\partial t} = LV(x,t,m). \quad V(x,0,m) = f(x,m).$$

Nevertheless, the adjoint method is not without its shortcomings. First, the dimension of the state of the stochastic hybrid system sets the dimension of the PDE to optimize. In implementation, PDEs can be numerically solved in dimension 3 or 4 – for higher dimensions, the memory requirement becomes problematic. Therefore, the adjoint method, which runs on a modern single processor computer in a few seconds for the application presented above, can be applied only for stochastic hybrid systems of continuous dimension say less than 4. Second, gradient descent methods for large scale optimization programs (n dimensions usually results in 100^n grid points) might be very slow. Therefore, second order optimization should be adopted. We are currently investigating these issues. The first might be overcome by applying directly the adjoint method in the Monte-Carlo space. Regarding the second, we are currently developing a Newton method implementation.

References

1. GHOSH, M., ARAPOSTATHIS, A., MARCUS, S.I.: Optimal control of switching diffusions with applications to flexible manufacturing systems. (SIAM J. Control Optim. 31 (1993), 1183–1204)

2. HU, J., LYGEROS, J., SASTRY, S.: Towards a theory of stochastic hybrid systems. In Lynch, N.A., Krogh, B.H., eds.: Hybrid Systems: Computation and Control (HSCC). Lecture Notes in Computer Science 1790, (Springer-Verlag) 160–173.
3. BUJORIANU, M.L., LYGEROS, J.: General stochastic hybrid systems: Modelling and optimal control. (Proceedings of the IEEE Int. Conference on Decision and Control, Atlantis, Bahamas, 2004)
4. BUJORIANU, M.L.: Extended stochastic hybrid systems and their reachability problem. In Alur, R., Pappas, G.J., eds.: Hybrid Systems: Computation and Control (HSCC). Lecture Notes in Computer Science (LNCS 2993), (Springer-Verlag) 234–249.
5. YUAN, C., LYGEROS, J.: Asymptotic stability and boundeness of delay switching diffusions. In Alur, R., Pappas, G.J., eds.: Hybrid Systems: Computation and Control (HSCC). Lecture Notes in Computer Science (LNCS 2993), (Springer-Verlag) 646–659.
6. HWANG, I., HWANG, J., TOMLIN, C.J.: Flight-mode-based aircraft conflict detection using a residual-mean interacting multiple model algorithm. In: Proceedings of the AIAA Guidance, Navigation, and Control Conference. AIAA-2003-5340 (2003)
7. HESPANHA, J.P.: Stochastic hybrid systems: Application to communication networks. In Alur, R., Pappas, G.J., eds.: Hybrid Systems: Computation and Control (HSCC). Lecture Notes in Computer Science (LNCS 2993), (Springer-Verlag) 387–401.
8. LIONS, J.L.: Optimal Control of Systems Governed by Partial Differential Equations. (translated by S.K. Mitter, Springer Verlag, New York)
9. JAMESON, A.: Aerodynamic design via control theory. (Princeton University Report MAE 1824, ICASE Report No. 88-64, November 1988, also, J. of Scientific Computing, Vol. 3, 1988, pp. 233-260)
10. EVANS, L.: Partial Differential Equations. AMS Press (2002)
11. HU, J., SASTRY, S.: Optimal sojourn time control within an interval. (Proceedings of the American Control Conference, Denver, CO. 3478-3483. 2003)
12. ETHIER, S.N., KURTZ, T.G.: Markov Processes: Characterization and Convergence. Wiley (1986)
13. GILL, P.E., MURRAY, W., WRIGHT, M.H.: Practical Optimization. Academic Press. Harcourt Brace and Company (1999)
14. ROGERS, L., WILLIAMS, D.: Diffusions, Markov processes and Martingales. Vol.1, 2nd Ed., Cambridge (2000)
15. DURRETT, R.: Stochastic Calculus: A Practical Introduction. CRC Press (1996)
16. OKSENDAL, B.: Stochastic Differential Equations. An Introduction with Applications. Springer-Verlag, Sixth Edition (2003)

Safety Verification of Hybrid Systems by Constraint Propagation Based Abstraction Refinement[*]

Stefan Ratschan[1] and Zhikun She[2]

[1] Max-Planck-Institut für Informatik, Saarbrücken, Germany
stefan.ratschan@mpi-sb.mpg.de
http://www.mpi-sb.mpg.de/~ratschan
[2] Max-Planck-Institut für Informatik, Saarbrücken, Germany
zhikun.she@mpi-sb.mpg.de
http://www.mpi-sb.mpg.de/~zhikun

Abstract. This paper deals with the problem of safety verification of non-linear hybrid systems. We start from a classical method that uses interval arithmetic to check whether trajectories can move over the boundaries in a rectangular grid. We put this method into an abstraction refinement framework and improve it by developing an additional refinement step that employs constraint propagation to add information to the abstraction without introducing new grid elements. Moreover, the resulting method allows switching conditions, initial states and unsafe states to be described by complex constraints instead of sets that correspond to grid elements. Nevertheless, the method can be easily implemented since it is based on a well-defined set of constraints, on which one can run any constraint propagation based solver. First tests of such an implementation are promising.

1 Introduction

In this paper we provide a method for verifying that a given non-linear hybrid system has no trajectory that starts from an initial state and reaches an unsafe state. Our approach builds upon a known method that decomposes the state space according to a rectangular grid, and uses interval arithmetic to check the flow on the boundary between neighboring grid elements.

The reasons for choosing this method as a starting point are: it can do verification instead of verification modulo rounding errors, it can deal with constants that are only known up to intervals, and it uses a check that is less costly than

---

[*] This work was partly supported by the German Research Council (DFG) as part of the Transregional Collaborative Research Center "Automatic Verification and Analysis of Complex Systems" (SFB/TR 14 AVACS). See www.avacs.org for more information.

M. Morari and L. Thiele (Eds.): HSCC 2005, LNCS 3414, pp. 573–589, 2005.
© Springer-Verlag Berlin Heidelberg 2005

explicit computation of continuous reach sets, or checks based on quantifier elimination. However, this method has the drawback that it may require a very fine grid to provide an affirmative answer, and that it ignores the continuous behavior within the grid elements. In this paper we provide a remedy to this problem.

In our solution we put the classical interval method into an abstraction refinement framework where the abstract states represent hyper-rectangles (*boxes*) in the continuous part of the state space. Here refinement corresponds to splitting boxes into pieces and recomputing the possible transitions. In order to avoid splitting into too many boxes, we employ an idea that is at the core of the field of constraint programming: instead of a splitting process that is potentially exponential in the dimension of the problem, try to deduce information without splitting, in an efficient, but possibly incomplete, constraint propagation step. Here we use conditions on the motion of the trajectories within these boxes to construct a constraint without a differentiation operator, whose solution contains the reach set. Then we employ a constraint propagation algorithm to remove elements from the boxes that do not fulfill this constraint.

Many algorithms for checking the safety of hybrid systems are based on floating point computation that involve rounding errors. This is a perfectly valid approach. However, in some safety critical applications one would like to *verify* safety. Experience shows that just replacing floating point computation by faithfully rounded interval operations either results in too wide intervals, or—in combination with splitting—in inefficient algorithms. So we tried to develop a genuine interval based approach here.

Our implementation of the algorithms is publically available [31].

The structure of the paper is as follows: in Section 2 we formalize our safety verification problem; in Section 3 we put the classical interval based method into an abstraction refinement framework; in Section 4 we improve the method, using constraint propagation techniques; in Section 5 we discuss our implementation; in Section 6 we illustrate the behavior of the implementation using a few example problems; and in Section 8 we conclude the paper.

2 Problem Definition

We fix a variable s ranging over a finite set of discrete modes $\{s_1, \ldots, s_n\}$ and variables $x_1, \ldots, x_k$ ranging over closed real intervals $I_1, \ldots, I_k$. We denote by Φ the resulting state space $\{s_1, \ldots, s_n\} \times I_1 \times \cdots \times I_k$. In addition, for denoting the derivatives of $x_1, \ldots, x_k$ we assume variables $\dot{x}_1, \ldots, \dot{x}_k$, ranging over $\mathbb{R}$ each, and for denoting the targets of jumps, variables $s', x'_1, \ldots, x'_k$ ranging over $\{s_1, \ldots, s_n\}$ and $I_1, \ldots, I_k$, correspondingly.

In order to describe hybrid systems we use constraints that are arbitrary Boolean combinations of equalities and inequalities over terms that may contain function symbols like $+$, $\times$, exp, sin and cos (which further function symbols might be allowed will become clear in Section 5). These constraints are used, on the one hand, to describe the possible flow and jumps, and on the other hand, to mark certain parts of the state space (e.g., the set of initial states).

Definition 1. *A state space constraint is a constraint over the variables* $x_1, \ldots x_k$. *A flow constraint is a constraint over the variables* s, $x_1, \ldots, x_k$, $\dot{x}_1, \ldots, \dot{x}_k$. *A jump constraint is a constraint over the variables* s, $x_1, \ldots, x_k$ *and* s', $x'_1, \ldots, x'_k$. *A hybrid system description (or short: description) is a tuple consisting of a flow constraint, a jump constraint, a state space constraint describing the set of initial states, and a state space constraint describing the set of unsafe states.*

Example of a flow constraint for the case $n = 2$ and $k = 1$:

$$\left((s = \mathsf{s}_1 \to \dot{x} = x) \bigwedge (s = \mathsf{s}_2 \to \dot{x} = -x) \right)$$

We use these constraints to describe the following:

Definition 2. *A hybrid system is a tuple* $(Flow, Jump, Init, UnSafe)$ *where* $Flow \subseteq \Phi \times \mathbb{R}^k$, $Jump \subseteq \Phi \times \Phi$, $Init \subseteq \Phi$, *and* $UnSafe \subseteq \Phi$.

A hybrid system description gives rise to the hybrid system, for which each constituting set is the solution set of the corresponding constraint of the hybrid system description. For unrolling such a hybrid system to trajectories we employ the following notation: for a function $r : \mathbb{R}_{\geq 0} \mapsto \Phi$, $\lim_{t' \to t_-} r(t')$ is the left limit of r at t.

Definition 3. *A continuous time trajectory is a function in* $\mathbb{R}_{\geq 0} \mapsto \Phi$. *A trajectory of a hybrid system* $(Flow, Jump, Init, UnSafe)$ *is a continuous time trajectory r such that*

- *if the real-valued component f of r is differentiable at t, and $\lim_{t' \to t_-} r(t')$ and $r(t)$ have an equal mode s, then $((s, f(t)), \dot{f}(t)) \in Flow$, and*
- *otherwise,* $(\lim_{t' \to t_-} r(t'), r(t)) \in Jump$.

A trajectory from a state x to a state y is a trajectory r such that $r(0) = x$ and there is a $t \in \mathbb{R}_{\geq 0}$ such that $r(t) = y$.

Note that in this definition we can enforce jumps by formulating a flow constraint that does not allow continuous evolution in a certain region. A *flow* is a trajectory without a jump (i.e., without an evolution according to the relation *Jump*).

Definition 4. *A system is* safe *if and only if there is no trajectory from an initial to an unsafe state.*

We would like to have an algorithm that, given a hybrid system description, decides whether the corresponding system is safe. However, this is an undecidable problem [16]. So we aim at an algorithm for which we know that, if it terminates, the hybrid system described by the input is safe, and otherwise, we do not know anything.

3   An Interval Based Method

In this section we give an algorithm for verifying safety. Basically, it is the result of taking a classical method for safety verification, and putting it in an abstraction refinement framework. It seems that this classical method is in the folklore of the hybrid systems community, and appears the first time in the literature as a basis for a method that abstracts to timed automata [34]. It checks the flow at the boundary of boxes using interval arithmetic and requires that switching conditions, initial states and unsafe states be aligned to the box grid. In contrast, our resulting algorithm allows these sets to be described by complex constraints as introduced by Definition 1. We assume that we have an algorithm that can test such constraints for falsehood, that is an algorithm that either returns "false" or "unknown". On details how to arrive at such an algorithm see Section 5.

We abstract to systems of the following form:

Definition 5. *A* discrete system *over a finite set S is a tuple $(Trans, Init, UnSafe)$ where $Trans \subseteq S \times S$ and $Init \subseteq S$, $UnSafe \subseteq S$. We call the set S the* state space *of the system.*

In contrast to Definition 2, here the state space is a parameter. This will allow us to add new states to the state space during abstraction refinement.

Trajectories of such systems employ discrete time:

Definition 6. *A* trajectory of a discrete system $(Trans, Init, UnSafe)$ over a *set S is a function $r : \mathbb{N}_0 \mapsto S$ such that for all $t \in \mathbb{N}_0$, $(r(t), r(t+1)) \in Trans$.*

When analyzing discrete systems, we would like to ignore details not relevant to the property we want to verify, that is we would like to use abstractions. This has to be done in a conservative way, that is, if the abstraction is safe, then the original system should also be safe:

Definition 7. *An* abstraction function *between a discrete system $(Trans_1, Init_1, UnSafe_1)$ over S_1 and a discrete system $(Trans_2, Init_2, UnSafe_2)$ over S_2 is a function $\alpha : S_1 \mapsto S_2$ such that for every transition $(x, y) \in Trans_1$, $(\alpha(x), \alpha(y)) \in Trans_2$, for every $q \in Init_1$, $\alpha(q) \in Init_2$, and for every $q \in UnSafe_1$, $\alpha(q) \in UnSafe_2$. A system is an* abstraction *of another one iff there exists an abstraction function between the two.*

Given a system that abstracts another one, we call the former the abstract system and the latter the concrete system.

In our case we want to use abstraction to analyze hybrid instead of discrete systems. Here we have the problem that in a hybrid system we have no notion of transition. Usually, this problem is solved by defining an abstract transition to correspond to either a jump or a (arbitrarily long) flow [2], or to a jump followed by a flow [9]. For both methods one has to follow a flow over potentially unbounded time, which can be extremely costly. Therefore, in our definition, we only require that every concrete trajectory have a corresponding abstract one.

Definition 8. *An abstraction function between a hybrid system $(Flow_1, Jump_1,$ $Init_1, UnSafe_1)$ and a discrete system $(Trans_2, Init_2, UnSafe_2)$ over S is a function $\alpha : \Phi \mapsto S$ such that:*

- *for all p, q in Φ, if there is a trajectory from p to q according to $Flow_1$ and $Jump_1$, then there is a trajectory from $\alpha(p)$ to $\alpha(q)$ according to $Trans_2$.*
- *for all $q \in Init_1$, $\alpha(q) \in Init_2$, and for every $q \in UnSafe_1$, $\alpha(q) \in UnSafe_2$.*

A discrete system is an abstraction of a hybrid system, iff there exists an abstraction function between the two.

Since for every trajectory from Init to Unsafe of the first system there is a corresponding trajectory from Init to Unsafe in the second system, we have:

Property 1. For a system C, for every abstraction C_α of C, if C_α is safe, then C is safe.

Therefore we can prove safety on the abstraction instead of the concrete system. If this does not succeed, we refine the abstraction, that is, we include more information about the concrete system into it. This results in Algorithm 1.

Algorithm 1 Abstraction Refinement

---
let A be a discrete abstraction of the hybrid system represented by a description D
while A is not safe **do**
    refine the abstraction A
end while

In order to implement the above algorithm, we need to fix the state space of the abstract system. Here we use pairs (s, B), where s is one of the modes $\{s_1, \ldots, s_n\}$ and B is a hyper-rectangle (*box*), representing subsets of the concrete state space Φ. More specifically, for the initial abstraction we use the state space $\{(s_1, \{x \mid (s_1, x) \in \Phi\}) \mid 1 \leq i \leq n\}$. When refining the abstraction we split a box into two parts, creating two abstract states (s, B_1) and (s, B_2) with $B_1 \cup B_2 = B$, from an abstract state (s, B).

In order to compute a discrete abstraction over this state space, we have to show how to compute the transitions of the resulting abstraction, and its set of initial and unsafe states. Here we assume that the input consists of a hybrid system description with flow constraint $Flow(s, x, \dot{x})$, jump constraint $Jump(s, x, s', x')$, initial constraint $Init(s, x)$ and unsafety constraint $UnSafe(s, x)$. Now

- we mark an abstract state (s, B) as initial iff we cannot disprove the constraint $\exists x \in B \ Init(s, x)$, and
- we mark an abstract state (s, B) as unsafe iff we cannot disprove the constraint $\exists x \in B \ UnSafe(s, x)$.

In order to compute the possible transitions between two neighboring boxes in the same mode, we first consider the flow on common boundary points. For a box $B = [\underline{x}_1, \overline{x}_1] \times \cdots \times [\underline{x}_k, \overline{x}_k]$, we let its j-th lower face be $[\underline{x}_1, \overline{x}_1] \times \cdots \times [\underline{x}_j, \underline{x}_j] \times \cdots \times [\underline{x}_k, \overline{x}_k]$ and its j-th upper face be $[\underline{x}_1, \overline{x}_1] \times \cdots \times [\overline{x}_j, \overline{x}_j] \times \cdots \times [\underline{x}_k, \overline{x}_k]$. Two boxes are *non-overlapping* if their interiors are disjoint.

Lemma 1. *For a mode s, and two non-overlapping boxes $B \subseteq \mathbb{R}^k$ and $B' \subseteq \mathbb{R}^k$ with $B \cap B' \neq \emptyset$, let F be a face of B s.t. $B \cap B' \subseteq F$. If a flow in s leaves B and enters B' through a point $x \in (B \cap B')$, then*

- $\exists \dot{x}_j [Flow(s, x, (\dot{x}_1, \ldots, \dot{x}_k)) \wedge \dot{x}_j \leq 0]$, *if F is the j-th lower face of B, and*
- $\exists \dot{x}_j [Flow(s, x, (\dot{x}_1, \ldots, \dot{x}_k)) \wedge \dot{x}_j \geq 0]$, *if F is the j-th upper face of B*

We denote the above constraint by $outgoing^F_{s,B}(x)$. Using this constraint we can now construct a constraint for checking the possible transition between two boxes in the same mode.

Lemma 2. *For a mode s, two non-overlapping boxes $B, B' \subseteq \mathbb{R}^k$, if there is a flow in mode s that comes from B and enters B' through a common point of B and B', then*

$$\exists a \left[a \in B \wedge a \in B' \wedge \left[\forall F \subseteq B \left[a \in F \Rightarrow outgoing^F_{s,B}(a) \right] \right] \right]$$

This is an immediate result of Lemma 1. We denote the corresponding constraint by $transition_{s,B,B'}$.

Now we compute a transition from (s, B) to (s', B') iff

- $s = s'$ and $B = B'$, or
- $s = s'$, $B \neq B'$, and we cannot disprove $transition_{s,B,B'}$ of Lemma 2, or
- there are $x \in B$ and $x' \in B'$ such that $Jump(s, x, s', x')$ holds.

So, given a hybrid system description D and a set $\mathcal{B}$ of abstract states (i.e., mode/box pairs) such that all boxes corresponding to the same mode are non-overlapping, we have a method for computing the set of initial states, set of unsafe states, and transitions of a corresponding abstraction. We denote the resulting discrete system by $Abstract_D(\mathcal{B})$.

Theorem 1. *For all hybrid system descriptions D and sets of abstract states $\mathcal{B}$ covering the whole state space such that all boxes corresponding to the same mode are non-overlapping, $Abstract_D(\mathcal{B})$ is an abstraction of the hybrid system denoted by D.*

Proof. Let D be an arbitrary, but fixed hybrid system description, and let $\mathcal{B}$ be arbitrary, but fixed set of abstract states covering the whole state space such that all boxes corresponding to the same mode are non-overlapping. Denote the hybrid system described by D by $C_1 = (Flow_1, Jump_1, Init_1, UnSafe_1)$ and $Abstract_D(\mathcal{B})$ by $C_2 = (Trans_2, Init_2, UnSafe_2)$. We first assume that the jump relation $Jump_1$ of the hybrid system C_1 is empty. According to Definition 8 we need to construct an abstraction function $\alpha : \Phi \mapsto \mathcal{B}$ between C_1 and C_2. Let

$\alpha : \Phi \mapsto \mathcal{B}$ be such that $\alpha(s, b) = (s, B)$ where $(s, B) \in \mathcal{B}$ with $b \in B$ (the set $\mathcal{B}$ might contain several such abstract states since the boxes might have common boundaries, in that case one can choose any of these). Clearly, such an α exists since the whole state space is covered by $\mathcal{B}$.

Now we prove that α fulfills the two conditions stated in Definition 8:

- Assume that there is a trajectory from p to q. Since there are no jumps, both p and q have the same mode s. We have to prove that there is an abstract trajectory from $\alpha(p)$ to $\alpha(q)$. Suppose that the trajectory from p to q is covered by abstract states $(s, B_1), \ldots, (s, B_t)$ in the following order according to $Flow_1$: $\alpha(p) = (s, B_1), \ldots, (s, B_t) = \alpha(q)$. By Lemma 2, $transition_{s, B_1, B_2}$, $transition_{s, B_2, B_3}, \ldots$, and $transition_{s, B_{t-1}, B_t}$ hold. Therefore, $Abstract_D(\mathcal{B})$ will contain all the transitions over these abstract states. This implies that there is a trajectory from $\alpha(p)$ to $\alpha(q)$ according to $Trans_2$.
- Let $x \in Init_1$ be arbitrary but fixed. Let $(s, B) = \alpha(x)$. Then, since $x \in B$, by the definition of $Abstract_D(\mathcal{B})$, $\alpha(x) \in Init_2$. A similar argument holds for $UnSafe_1$ and $UnSafe_2$.

For a hybrid system with jump relation, we partition the trajectory into parts according to where a jump occurs. Thus, a jump does not occur during each part. Moreover, for each part, its end point and the starting point of the next part satisfy the jump constraint. Therefore, the algorithm will compute these transitions from an abstract state containing the end point to an abstract state containing the starting point of the next part. Combining the above proof, we can deduce that if there is a trajectory from x to y, then there is an abstract trajectory from $\alpha(x)$ to $\alpha(y)$. □

If the differential equations in the flow constraint are in explicit form $\dot{x} = Flow(x)$ then one can disprove the above constraints using interval arithmetic. According to Lemma 2 one can take all faces F of the common boundary of two boxes B and B', evaluate $Flow$ on F using interval arithmetic, and check whether the resulting intervals have a sign that does not allow flows over the boundary—as described by Lemma 1. In Section 5 a method will be described that allows the flow constraints also to be in implicit form.

Now a concrete instantiation of Algorithm 1 can maintain the abstract state space $\mathcal{B}$ as described earlier, compute a corresponding abstract system $Abstract_D$ $(\mathcal{B})$, and (since this abstract system is finite) check its safety—either by a brute force algorithm or using more sophisticated model checking technology. We can either recompute the abstract system $Abstract_D(\mathcal{B})$ each time we want to check its safety, or we can do this incrementally, just recomputing the elements corresponding to a changed element of the abstract state space (i.e., a box resulting from splitting).

4   A Constraint Propagation Based Improvement

The method introduced in the previous section has two main problems: First, splitting can result in a huge number of boxes, especially for high-dimensional problems; second, the method considers the flow only on the box boundaries and ignores the behavior inside of the boxes. In this section we will try to remove these problems.

In order to remove the first problem, we will refine the abstraction without creating more boxes by splitting. Here we can use the observation that, for safety verification, the unreachable state space is uninteresting, and there is no need to include it into the abstraction. Therefore, instead of requiring an abstraction function (Definition 8), we allow it to be a relation:

Definition 9. *An* abstraction relation *between a hybrid system* $(Flow_1, Jump_1, Init_1, UnSafe_1)$ *and a discrete system* $(Trans_2, Init_2, UnSafe_2)$ *over S is a relation* $\alpha \subseteq \Phi \times S$ *such that:*

- *for all $q \in \Phi$, if there is a trajectory from an element of $Init_1$ to q according to $Flow_1$ and $Jump_1$, then for all q_α with $\alpha(q, q_\alpha)$ there is a trajectory from an element of $Init_2$ to q_α according to $Trans_2$,*
- *for all $q \in Init_1$, there is a $q_\alpha \in Init_2$, with $\alpha(q, q_\alpha)$ and*
- *for all $q \in UnSafe_1$, if q is reachable from $Init_1$, then there is a $q_\alpha \in UnSafe_2$ with $\alpha(q, q_\alpha)$.*

A discrete system is an abstraction *of a hybrid system iff there exists an abstraction relation between the two.*

Clearly Property 1 also holds for this adapted definition.

Note that in the literature there is a similar notion of simulation relation [26, 10]. However, a simulation relation relates transitions between arbitrary states instead of only trajectories that start from the initial set. Now we can modify Theorem 1 as follows:

Theorem 2. *For all hybrid system descriptions D and sets of abstract states $\mathcal{B}$ containing all elements of the state space reachable from the initial set such that all boxes corresponding to the same mode are non-overlapping, $Abstract_D(\mathcal{B})$ is an abstraction of the hybrid system denoted by D.*

Proof. We proceed in a similar way as in the proof of Theorem 1. We let D and $\mathcal{B}$ be arbitrary, but fixed, fulfilling the conditions of the theorem, and denote the continuous time hybrid system by $C_1 = (Flow_1, Jump_1, Init_1, UnSafe_1)$ and $Abstract_D(\mathcal{B})$ by $C_2 = (Trans_2, Init_2, UnSafe_2)$. We first assume that the hybrid system has no jump relation. According to Definition 9 we have to construct an abstraction relation $\alpha \subseteq \Phi \times \mathcal{B}$ between C_1 and C_2.

Let α be such that $\alpha((s, x), (s_\alpha, B))$ iff $s = s_\alpha$ and $x \in B$.

- We prove that for every concrete trajectory from a p that is reachable from $Init_1$ to a q, there is a corresponding abstract trajectory (we cannot assume $p \in Init_1$ since, when introducing jumps later, this property has to hold for all jump-less fragments). Since there are no jumps, both p and q have the same mode s. Let p_α and q_α be arbitrary, but fixed, such that $\alpha(p, p_\alpha)$ and $\alpha(q, q_\alpha)$. We prove that there is an abstract trajectory from

p_α to q_α. Now let $(s, B_1), \ldots, (s, B_t)$ be abstract states in $\mathcal{B}$ such that the trajectory from p to q passes them in the following order according to $Flow_1 : p_\alpha = (s, B_1), \ldots, (s, B_t) = q_\alpha$. Such boxes exist, since $\mathcal{B}$ covers the reach set of C_1. By Lemma 2, $transition_{s,B_1,B_2}$, $transition_{s,B_2,B_3}$, $\ldots$, and $transition_{s,B_{t-1},B_t}$ hold. Therefore, $Abstract_D(\mathcal{B})$ will contain all the transitions over these abstract states. This implies that there is a trajectory from p_α to q_α according to $Trans_2$.

- For all $q \in Init_1$, there is a $q_\alpha \in Init_2$, with $\alpha(q, q_\alpha)$ holds by definition of $Abstract_D(\mathcal{B})$ since q is reachable and therefore covered by an element of $\mathcal{B}$. In the same way, for every reachable $q \in UnSafe_1$ there is a $q_\alpha \in UnSafe_2$ with $\alpha(q, q_\alpha)$.

For a hybrid system with jump relation we proceed analogously to Theorem 1. $\square$

So we can exclude parts of the state space from the abstraction process, for which we can show that they are not reachable. In order to do this, we observe that a point in a box B is reachable only if it is reachable either from the initial set via a flow in B, from a jump via a flow in B, or from a neighboring box via a flow in B.

We will now formulate constraints corresponding to each of these conditions. Then we can remove points from boxes that do not fulfill at least one of these constraints. For this, we first give a constraint describing flows within boxes:

Lemma 3. *For a box $B \subseteq \mathbb{R}^k$ and a mode s, if a point $y = (y_1, \ldots, y_k) \in B$ is reachable from a point $x = (x_1, \ldots, x_k) \in B$ via a flow in B and s, then*

$$\bigwedge_{1 \leq m < n \leq k} \exists a, \dot{a} \, [a \in B \wedge Flow(s, a, \dot{a}) \wedge \dot{a}_n \cdot (y_m - x_m) = \dot{a}_m \cdot (y_n - x_n)]$$

Proof. Assume that $r(t) = (r_1(t), \ldots, r_k(t))$ is a flow in B from x to y. So $r(0) = x$ and for a certain $t \in \mathbb{R}_{\geq 0}$, $r(t) = y$. Then, for $i, j \in \{1, \ldots, k\}$ arbitrary, but fixed, by the Extended Mean Value Theorem we have:

$$\exists t' \in [0, t] \, [\dot{r}_j(t')(y_i - x_i) = \dot{r}_i(t')(y_j - x_j)] \, .$$

Now choose such a t' and let $a = r(t')$ and $\dot{a} = \dot{r}(t')$. Then, since r is a flow, $Flow(s, a, \dot{a})$ and hence the whole constraint holds. $\square$

The intuition behind the above Lemma is that whenever we have a flow from a 2-dimensional point (x_n, x_m) to a 2-dimensional point (y_n, y_m), then there must be a point on the trajectory, where the vector field points exactly in the direction $(y_n - x_n, y_m - x_m)$. Therefore the box must contain such a point.

We denote the above constraint by $flow_B(s, x, y)$. Now we can write down a constraint describing the first condition—reachability from the initial set:

Lemma 4. *For a mode s and a box $B \subseteq \mathbb{R}^k$, if $z \in B$ is reachable from the initial set via a flow in s and B, then*

$$\exists y \in B \, [Init(s, y) \wedge flow_B(s, y, z)]$$

The proof is trivial since it is an immediate consequence of Lemma 3. We denote the above constraint by $initflow_B(s, z)$.

We also have a constraint describing the second condition—reachability from a jump:

Lemma 5. *For modes s and s', boxes $B, B' \subseteq \mathbb{R}^k$, and $z \in B'$, if (s', z) is reachable from a jump from (s, B) via a flow in B', then*

$$\exists x \in B \exists x' \in B' \left[Jump(s, x, s', x') \wedge flow_{B'}(s', x', z) \right]$$

The proof is trivial since it is also consequence of Lemma 3. We denote the above constraint by $jumpflow_{B,B'}(s, s', z)$.

And finally, we strengthen the condition mentioned in Lemma 2, to a constraint describing the third condition—reachability from a neighboring box.

Lemma 6. *For a mode s and boxes $B, B' \subseteq \mathbb{R}^k$, if $z \in B'$ is reachable from a common point of B and B' via a flow in s and B, then*

$$\exists a \left[a \in B \wedge a \in B' \wedge \left[\forall F \subseteq B [a \in F \Rightarrow outgoing_{s,B}^F(a)] \right] \wedge flow_{B'}(s, a, z) \right]$$

This is a consequence of Lemma 3 and Lemma 1. We denote the above constraint by $boundaryflow_{B,B'}(s, z)$.

Now a point in a box is only reachable if it is reachable according to Lemma 4, Lemma 5, or Lemma 6:

Theorem 3. *For a set of abstract states $\mathcal{B}$, a pair $(s', B') \in \mathcal{B}$ and a point $z \in B'$, if (s', z) is reachable, then*

$$initflow_{B'}(s', z) \vee \bigvee_{(s,B) \in \mathcal{B}} jumpflow_{B,B'}(s, s', z) \vee \bigvee_{(s,B) \in \mathcal{B}, s=s', B \neq B'}$$

$$boundaryflow_{B,B'}(s', z)$$

We denote this constraint by $reachable_{B'}(s', z)$. Now, if we can prove that a certain point does not fulfill this constraint, we know that it is not reachable from the set of initial states. For now we assume that we have an algorithm (a *pruning algorithm*) that takes such a constraint, and an abstract state (s', B') and returns a sub-box of B' that still contains all the solutions of the constraint in B'. See the next section for details on such algorithms.

Since the constraint $reachable_{B'}(s', z)$ depends on all current abstract states, a change of B' might allow further pruning of other abstract states. So we can repeat pruning until a fixpoint is reached. This terminates since we use floating point computation here and there are only finitely many floating point numbers. Given a set of abstract states $\mathcal{B}$, we denote the resulting fixpoint by $Prune_D(\mathcal{B})$.

Now, since according to Theorem 2, we do not need to consider unreachable parts of the state space in abstraction, we can do the operation $\mathcal{B} \leftarrow Prune_D(\mathcal{B})$ anywhere in Algorithm 1. So we do this at the beginning, and each time $\mathcal{B}$ is refined by splitting a box.

So our method can in some cases refine the abstraction without splitting, which is a remedy for the first problem identified at the beginning of the section. For doing so, it considers the flow not only on the boundary but also inside of the boxes. Therefore, in addition, the result also provides a remedy for the second problem!

Now observe that in the computation of $Abstract_D(\mathcal{B})$ we check whether one abstract state is reachable from another one. But this information has already been computed by $Prune_D(\mathcal{B})$. More precisely, we get this information from the individual disjuncts of Theorem 3, and we do not need to recompute it. Clearly this does not change the correctness of our abstraction process.

Moreover, we do not need to completely recompute $Abstract_D(\mathcal{B})$ after each refinement step: for this we observe that our solver might prove that one of the disjuncts of the constraint of Theorem 3 has an empty solution. For example, this is trivially the case for *boundary flow* and non-neighboring boxes. In such a case we can remove the corresponding disjunct from the disjunction. Afterwards, the constraint only depends on some, but not necessarily all other abstract states in $\mathcal{B}$, and we only have to re-compute it, if one of these changed (cf. the constraint propagation algorithm AC-3 [25]).

5   Implementation

In this section we discuss our implementation of the algorithms introduced in the previous sections.

First, we show how to arrive at a pruning algorithm as required by the previous section. Such algorithms are one of the main topics of the area of constraint programming (for more information see http://slash.math.unipd.it/cp/). Usually these work on conjunctions of atomic constraints over a certain domain. For the domain of the real numbers, given a constraint ϕ and a floating-point box B, they compute another floating-point box $N(\phi, B)$ such that $N(\phi, B) \subseteq B$ (contractance), and such that $N(\phi, B)$ contains all solutions of ϕ in B (cf. the notion of *narrowing operator* [5,4], sometimes also called *contractor*). There are several methods for implementing such a pruning algorithm. The most basic method [13,11,6] decomposes all atomic constraints (i.e., constraints of the form $t \geq 0$ or $t = 0$, where t is a term) into conjunctions of so-called primitive constraints (i.e., constraints such as $x + y = z$, $xy = z$, $z \in [\underline{a}, \overline{a}]$, or $z \geq 0$) by introducing additional auxiliary variables (e.g., decomposing $x + 2y \geq 0$ to $2y = v_1 \wedge x + v_1 = v_2 \wedge v_2 \geq 0$). Then it applies a pruning algorithm for these primitive constraints [21] until a fixpoint is reached. Here the floating point results are always rounded outwards, such that the result remains correct also under rounding errors. There are several variants, improvements and alternatives in the literature [22,5,23,24,20].

The constraints introduced in the previous sections also contain existential quantifiers. These can be treated by simply pruning the Cartesian product of the box corresponding to the free variables and the box bounding the quantified variables [29]. For disjunctions one can prune the disjuncts and take the union of the result [29]. Moreover, the constraints contain variables s and s' ranging over a finite set. These can be easily eliminated by a trivial substitution and simplification.

We have implemented the algorithm on top of our RSOLVER [30] package that provides pruning and solving of quantified constraints of the real numbers, a graphical user interface, and several other features, and that uses the smathlib library [18] for pruning primitive constraints. The implementation is publically available [31], and we will make the source code open, which will make it easy to extend it or to experiment with changes.

6   Computation Results

In this section we illustrate the behavior of our implementation on a few examples. Here we use the following splitting strategy: we split several boxes at a time, one box per mode, choosing a box with widest side-length for each mode and then bisecting it along its widest variable. In this way, we can avoid that we keep splitting boxes in the same mode. Of course, one can choose other splitting techniques.

Now we compare the computation results obtained by the basic method of Section 3 and our improved method of Section 4 on some examples. The computations were performed on a Pentium M 1.7 GHz notebook with 512 MB memory. Note that we used the straightforward implementation described in the last section, without any special optimizations whatsoever.

Example 1:

Flow: $\dot{x}_1 = x_1 - x_2, \dot{x}_2 = x_1 + x_2$
Empty jump relation
Init: $2.5 \leq x_1 \leq 3.0 \wedge x_2 = 0$
Unsafe: $x_1 \geq 0 \wedge x_2 \geq 0 \wedge x_2 < -x_1 + 2$
The state space: $[0, 4] \times [0, 4]$

For the basic method, after the 7-th splitting, one can get eight boxes and prove that the region $[0, 1] \times [0, 1]$ can not be reached. After the 15-th splitting, one gets sixteen boxes and prove that the set $\{x_1 \geq 0 \wedge 0 \leq x_2 < -x_1 + 2\}$ cannot be reached. However, for the improved method, after splitting for the 7-th time and calling the pruning method, we get seven boxes and can prove that the set $\{x_1 \geq 0 \wedge 0 \leq x_2 < -x_1 + 2\}$ can not be reached.

The reason is that the improved method not only removes the box $[0, 2] \times [0, 1]$, but also removes part of the box $[0, 2] \times [1, 2]$, both of which do not fulfill the constraint in Theorem 3. The algorithm calls the pruning algorithm for 378 times and costs 0.826 seconds.

Example 2: from a paper by J. Preussig and co-workers [27].

Flow: $\dot{x} = \dot{y} = \dot{t} = 1$
Empty jump relation
Init: $0 \leq x \leq 1 \wedge y = t = 0$
Unsafe: $0 \leq x \leq 2 \wedge 1 < y \leq 2 \wedge 0 \leq t < 1$
The state space: $[0, 2] \times [0, 2] \times [0, 4]$

For the basic method, splitting does not improve the abstraction. However, the improved method can prove that the trajectories starting from initial set do not enter the unsafe states. The algorithm only executes the splitting once, calls the pruning algorithm 10 times, gets 2 boxes, and costs 0.339 seconds.

Example 3: The flow constraints are constructed by setting all the parameters in the two tanks problem [34] to 1.

Flow: $\left(s = 1 \rightarrow \binom{\dot{x}_1}{\dot{x}_2} = \binom{1 - \sqrt{x_1}}{\sqrt{x_1} - \sqrt{x_2}}\right) \wedge \left(s = 2 \rightarrow \binom{\dot{x}_1}{\dot{x}_2} = \binom{1 - \sqrt{x_1 - x_2 + 1}}{\sqrt{x_1 - x_2 + 1} - \sqrt{x_2}}\right)$
Jump: $(s = 1 \wedge 0.99 \leq x_2 \leq 1) \rightarrow (s' = 2 \wedge x_1' = x_1 \wedge x_2' = 1)$
Init: $s = 1 \wedge (x_1 - 5.5)^2 + (x_2 - 0.25)^2 \leq 0.0625$
Unsafe: $\left(s = 1 \wedge (x_1 - 4.5)^2 + (x_2 - 0.25)^2 < 0.0625\right)$
The state space: $(1, [4, 6] \times [0, 1]) \cup (2, [4, 6] \times [1, 2])$

The basic method cannot prove that the trajectories starting from the initial states do not enter the unsafe states. The reason is that splitting does not improve the abstraction. But the improved method can prove that the trajectories starting from initial do not enter the unsafe states. The algorithm does 11 splitting steps, calls the pruning algorithm 5658 times, gets 11 boxes in the first mode and 12 boxes in the second mode, and costs 4.620 seconds.

Example 4: A predator-prey example

Flow: $\left(s = 1 \rightarrow \binom{\dot{x}_1}{\dot{x}_2} = \binom{-x_1 + x_1 x_2}{x_2 - x_1 x_2}\right) \wedge \left(s = 2 \rightarrow \binom{\dot{x}_1}{\dot{x}_2} = \binom{-x_1 + x_1 x_2}{x_2 - x_1 x_2}\right)$
Jump: $\left((s = 1 \wedge 0.875 \leq x_2 \leq 0.9) \rightarrow (s' = 2 \wedge (x_1' - 1.2)^2 + (x_2' - 1.8)^2 \leq 0.01)\right.$
$\left. \vee \left((s = 2 \wedge 1.1 \leq x_2 \leq 1.125) \rightarrow (s' = 1 \wedge (x_1' - 0.7)^2 + (x_2' - 0.7)^2 \leq 0.01)\right)\right)$
Init: $s = 1 \wedge (x_1 - 0.8)^2 + (x_2 - 0.2)^2 \leq 0.01$
Unsafe: $\left(s = 1 \wedge x_1 > 0.8 \wedge x_2 > 0.8 \wedge x_1 \leq 0.9 \wedge x_2 \leq 0.9\right)$
The state space: $(1, [0.1, 0.9] \times [0.1, 0.9]) \cup (2, [1.1, 1.9] \times [1.1, 1.9])$

Again, splitting does not improve the abstraction for the basic method. However, it does in our improved method. The algorithm proves safety, using 61 splitting steps, and 478533 calls to the pruning algorithm, resulting in 56 boxes in the first mode and 61 boxes in the second mode, costing 117 seconds.

The main remaining problem of our improved method is that even in some simple cases it still cannot prove that certain elements of the state space are unreachable. For example, applying our method to the following example: Flow: $\dot{x} = \dot{y} = 1$, Init: $x = y = 0$, State space: $[0, 4] \times [0, 4]$, when we start with splitting along the variable x, we cannot remove parts below the $x = y$ line. If we start with splitting along y, we cannot remove parts above the $x = y$ line. The reason is, that we do not follow trajectories over more than one box.

7   Related Work

The idea of using abstraction to compute the reach set of hybrid systems is not new. Here the basic choice is, which data-structure to use for representing subsets of the continuous part of the state space.

Kowalewski, Stursberg and co-workers pioneered the use of box representations [34, 32, 27, 28, 33]. Also in their method, interval arithmetic is used to check the flow on the boundaries of a rectangular grid. Then timing information is added by checking the flow within these boxes. As a result one arrives at rectangular or timed automata. All appearing switching conditions, initial states and unsafe states have to be aligned to the predefined grid, whereas in this paper, we allow complex constraints. Moreover, their method has been designed for a fixed grid, and a refinement of the abstraction requires a complete re-computation, whereas in the present work, this can be done incrementally. Also, their method does not include a step for refining the abstraction without splitting, and it is harder to implement, since it does not build upon an existing constraint solver. However, they generate additional timing information, and use additional information on reachable subsets of faces.

Another frequently used technique for representing parts of the state space are polyhedra [8, 1, 9, 2, 3]. This has the advantage of being flexible, but requires involved algorithms for handling these polyhedra and for approximating reachable sets. In contrast to that, boxes are less flexible, but the corresponding operations are simple to implement efficiently, even with validated handling of floating-point rounding errors. It is not clear how one could adapt the pruning mechanism of this paper to polyhedra.

Another method uses semi-algebraic sets for representation [35]. This is even more flexible, and can produce symbolic output, but requires highly complex quantifier elimination tools [12]. Again, it is not clear how one could employ a pruning mechanism for such a representation.

There are also methods that use interval arithmetic to compute the reach set explicitly, without abstraction. In one approach [15] an interval ODE solver is used, and in another one [17] a constraint logic programming language [19] that allows constraints with differentiation operators.

8   Conclusion

In this paper we have put a classical method for verifying safety of hybrid systems into an abstraction refinement framework, and we have provided a constraint propagation based remedy for some of the problems of the method. As a result, we need to split into less boxes, we retain information on the flow within boxes, and we can use complex constraints for specifying the hybrid system. Since the method is based on a clear set of constraints, it can be easily implemented using a pruning algorithm based on constraint propagation.

Our long term goal is to arrive at a method for which one can prove termination for all, but numerically ill-posed cases, in a similar way as can be done for quantified inequality constraints [29], and hybrid systems in which all trajectories follow polynomials [14]. Moreover, we will use counterexamples to guide the refinement process [9, 2].

Interesting further questions are, whether work on constraint propagation in the discrete domain can be useful in a similar way for pruning the discrete state space, and whether similar pruning of the state space can be done for more complex verification tasks, (i.e., for general ACTL queries).

Acknowledgement. The authors thank Martin Fränzle for carefully removing some of our initial ignorance about the intricacies of hybrid systems.

References

1. R. Alur, T. Dang, and F. Ivančić. Reachability analysis of hybrid systems via predicate abstraction. In Tomlin and Greenstreet [36].
2. R. Alur, T. Dang, and F. Ivančić. Counter-example guided predicate abstraction of hybrid systems. In H. Garavel and J. Hatcliff, editors, *TACAS*, volume 2619 of *LNCS*, pages 208–223. Springer, 2003.
3. E. Asarin, T. Dang, and O. Maler. The d/dt tool for verification of hybrid systems. In *CAV'02 - Computer Aided Verification*, number 2404 in LNCS, pages 365–370. Springer, 2002.
4. F. Benhamou. Heterogeneous constraint solving. In *Proc. of the Fifth International Conference on Algebraic and Logic Programming*, 1996.
5. F. Benhamou, D. McAllester, and P. Van Hentenryck. CLP(Intervals) revisited. In *International Symposium on Logic Programming*, pages 124–138, Ithaca, NY, USA, 1994. MIT Press.
6. F. Benhamou and W. J. Older. Applying interval arithmetic to real, integer and Boolean constraints. *Journal of Logic Programming*, 32(1):1–24, 1997.
7. B. F. Caviness and J. R. Johnson, editors. *Quantifier Elimination and Cylindrical Algebraic Decomposition.* Springer, Wien, 1998.
8. A. Chutinan and B. H. Krogh. Verification of polyhedral-invariant hybrid automata using polygonal flow pipe approximations. In Vaandrager and van Schuppen [37], pages 76–90.
9. E. Clarke, A. Fehnker, Z. Han, B. Krogh, J. Ouaknine, O. Stursberg, and M. Theobald. Abstraction and counterexample-guided refinement in model checking of hybrid systems. *International Journal of Foundations of Computer Science*, 14(4), 2003.
10. E. M. Clarke, O. Grumberg, and D. A. Peled. *Model Checking.* MIT Press, 1999.
11. J. G. Cleary. Logical arithmetic. *Future Computing Systems*, 2(2):125–149, 1987.
12. G. E. Collins and H. Hong. Partial cylindrical algebraic decomposition for quantifier elimination. *Journal of Symbolic Computation*, 12:299–328, 1991. Also in [7].
13. E. Davis. Constraint propagation with interval labels. *Artificial Intelligence*, 32(3):281–331, 1987.
14. M. Fränzle. Analysis of hybrid systems: An ounce of realism can save an infinity of states. In J. Flum and M. Rodriguez-Artalejo, editors, *Computer Science Logic (CSL'99)*, number 1683 in LNCS. Springer, 1999.

15. T. A. Henzinger, B. Horowitz, R. Majumdar, and H. Wong-Toi. Beyond HyTech: hybrid systems analysis using interval numerical methods. In N. Lynch and B. Krogh, editors, *Proceedings of the Third International Workshop on Hybrid Systems: Computation and Control (HSCC '00)*, volume 1790 of *LNCS*. Springer, 2000.

16. T. A. Henzinger, P. W. Kopke, A. Puri, and P. Varaiya. What's decidable about hybrid automata. *Journal of Computer and System Sciences*, 57:94–124, 1998.

17. T. Hickey and D. Wittenberg. Rigorous modeling of hybrid systems using interval arithmetic constraints. In R. Alur and G. J. Pappas, editors, *Hybrid Systems: Computation and Control*, number 2993 in LNCS. Springer, 2004.

18. T. J. Hickey.   smathlib.   http://interval.sourceforge.net/interval/C /smathlib/README.html.

19. T. J. Hickey. Analytic constraint solving and interval arithmetic. In *Proceedings of the 27th Annual ACM SIGACT-SIGPLAN Symposium on Principles of Programming Languages*, 2000.

20. T. J. Hickey. Metalevel interval arithmetic and verifiable constraint solving. *Journal of Functional and Logic Programming*, 2001(7), October 2001.

21. T. J. Hickey, M. H. van Emden, and H. Wu. A unified framework for interval constraint and interval arithmetic. In M. Maher and J. Puget, editors, *CP'98*, number 1520 in LNCS, pages 250–264, 1998.

22. L. Jaulin, M. Kieffer, O. Didrit, and É. Walter. *Applied Interval Analysis, with Examples in Parameter and State Estimation, Robust Control and Robotics*. Springer, Berlin, 2001.

23. O. Lhomme. Consistency techniques for numeric CSPs. In *Proc. 13th Intl. Joint Conf. on Artificial Intelligence*, 1993.

24. O. Lhomme, A. Gotlieb, and M. Rueher. Dynamic optimization of interval narrowing algorithms. *Journal of Logic Programming*, 37(1–3):165–183, 1998.

25. A. K. Mackworth. Consistency in networks of relations. *Artificial Intelligence*, 8:99–118, 1977.

26. R. Milner. An algebraic definition of simulation between programs. In *Proc. of the 2nd International Joint Conference on Artificial Intelligence*, pages 481–489, 1971.

27. J. Preußig, S. Kowalewski, H. Wong-Toi, and T. Henzinger. An algorithm for the approximative analysis of rectangular automata. In *5th Int. School and Symp. on Formal Techniques in Fault Tolerant and Real Time Systems*, number 1486 in LNCS, 1998.

28. J. Preußig, O. Stursberg, and S. Kowalewski. Reachability analysis of a class of switched continuous systems by integrating rectangular approximation and rectangular analysis. In Vaandrager and van Schuppen [37].

29. S. Ratschan. Continuous first-order constraint satisfaction. In J. Calmet, B. Benhamou, O. Caprotti, L. Henocque, and V. Sorge, editors, *Artificial Intelligence, Automated Reasoning, and Symbolic Computation*, number 2385 in LNCS, pages 181–195. Springer, 2002.

30. S. Ratschan. Rsolver. http://www.mpi-sb.mpg.de/~{}ratschan/rsolver, 2004. Software package.

31. S. Ratschan and Z. She. Hsolver. http://www.mpi-sb.mpg.de/~{}ratschan /hsolver, 2004. Software package.

32. O. Stursberg and S. Kowalewski. Analysis of controlled hybrid processing systems based on approximation by timed automata using interval arithmetic. In *Proceedings of the 8th IEEE Mediterranean Conference on Control and Automation (MED 2000)*, 2000.

33. O. Stursberg, S. Kowalewski, and S. Engell. On the generation of timed discrete approximations for continuous systems. *Mathematical and Computer Models of Dynamical Systems*, 6:51–70, 2000.

34. O. Stursberg, S. Kowalewski, I. Hoffmann, and J. Preußig. Comparing timed and hybrid automata as approximations of continuous systems. In P. J. Antsaklis, W. Kohn, A. Nerode, and S. Sastry, editors, *Hybrid Systems*, number 1273 in LNCS, pages 361–377. Springer, 1997.

35. A. Tiwari and G. Khanna. Series of abstractions for hybrid automata. In Tomlin and Greenstreet [36].

36. C. J. Tomlin and M. R. Greenstreet, editors. *Hybrid Systems: Computation and Control HSCC*, number 2289 in LNCS, 2002.

37. F. Vaandrager and J. van Schuppen, editors. *Hybrid Systems: Computation and Control – HSCC'99*, number 1569 in LNCS. Springer, 1999.

Generating Polynomial Invariants for Hybrid Systems*

Enric Rodríguez-Carbonell[1] and Ashish Tiwari[2]

[1] LSI Department, Technical University of Catalonia,
Jordi Girona, 1-3 08034 Barcelona, Spain
erodri@lsi.upc.es
[2] SRI International, 333 Ravenswood Ave, Menlo Park, CA, U.S.A.
Tel:+1.650.859.4774, Fax:+1.650.859.2844
tiwari@csl.sri.com

Abstract. We present a powerful computational method for automatically generating polynomial invariants of hybrid systems with linear continuous dynamics. When restricted to linear continuous dynamical systems, our method generates a set of polynomial equations (algebraic set) that is the best such over-approximation of the reach set. This shows that the set of algebraic invariants of a linear system is computable. The extension to hybrid systems is achieved using the abstract interpretation framework over the lattice defined by algebraic sets. Algebraic sets are represented using canonical Gröbner bases and the lattice operations are effectively computed via appropriate Gröbner basis manipulations.

1   Introduction

Verification of hybrid systems is a challenging problem. While testing can guarantee the correctness of a specific behavior of the system, verification attempts to provide correctness guarantee for *all* possible behaviors of the system. This extensive coverage is achieved, in most cases, by representing and manipulating *sets of states* of the system, rather than a single state. This jump from working with a single state, as in testing, to working with sets of states, as in verification, is also the main source of computational challenges in verification.

Arguably the most significant strides in the development of formal methods and verification technology were made in the form of developing effective representations for sets of states. The binary decision diagram representation provided a crucial breakthrough for hardware circuit verification, and region construction

* The research of the first author was partially supported by Spanish FPU grant ref. AP2002-3693 and the projects Maverish (MCYT TIC2001-2476-C03-01) and Logic-Tools (TIN2004-03382) funded by the Spanish Ministry of Education and Science. The second author was supported in part by the National Science Foundation under grants CCR-0311348 and CCR-ITR-0326540 and NASA Langley Research Center contract NAS1-00108 to Rannoch Corporation.

M. Morari and L. Thiele (Eds.): HSCC 2005, LNCS 3414, pp. 590–605, 2005.

played a similar role for timed systems. In this paper, we argue that a canonical basis representation for algebraic sets provides an effective choice for a class of hybrid systems with linear continuous dynamics.

A good representation for a set of states is one that allows efficient computation of some basic operations. In the case of discrete state transition systems, these operations are well understood. Depending on the exact verification procedure, some or all of the set union, set intersection, set complement, subset, and projection operators may be required [11]. In the case of hybrid systems, we additionally require that the representation behaves "nicely" along the continuous evolutions at different locations of the hybrid system.

This paper explores the representation of sets of states $Set \subseteq \mathbb{R}^n$ by the set of polynomials $P \in \mathbb{Q}[X_1, \ldots, X_n]$ that form the kernel of Set, that is, $P(s) = 0$ for all $s \in Set$. Such a set of polynomials has several nice algebraic properties. It is an *ideal* and has a finite basis representation. Furthermore, there is a canonical fully-reduced basis, called a Gröbner basis, which can be effectively computed (cf. ordered binary decision diagrams [4]). The set union, set intersection, and set inclusion operators are efficiently computable on these canonical bases. The same is also true of the quantifier-elimination (projection) operator.

Using the above properties of the canonical ideal basis, we show that both continuous and discrete behaviors of hybrid systems can be processed. The main contributions of this paper are:

(i) We show that, for *any* linear continuous dynamical system CS, the *best* algebraic over-approximation of the reach set of CS can be computed (Section 3). The proof of this result borrows some key insights from Lafferriere, Pappas and Yovine [16], who use *semi-algebraic* sets and show that *exact* reach sets can be computed for more restricted classes of linear vector fields.

(ii) We show that the method for over-approximating reach sets for linear dynamical systems can be extended to hybrid systems using an abstract interpretation framework, thanks to the various nice computational properties of Gröbner bases (Section 4). We also present some experimental results obtained by using our method to generate polynomial invariants for hybrid systems (Section 5).

1.1   Related Work

Sankaranarayanan et al. [18] presented an approach for generating polynomial equational invariants for hybrid systems with more general (nonlinear) polynomial dynamics. However, their approach is based on *guessing* a template for the invariant and generating constraints that would guarantee that the guessed parametric polynomial equation is an *inductive* invariant. We restrict ourselves to linear dynamics, but our method is not based on guessing a template. In fact, it is complete for linear systems. On the other hand, any extension of our method to hybrid systems with more general continuous dynamics would require the use of heuristics, such as [21, 18].

Region graphs suffice to compute exact reach sets for timed automata [2]. Polygonal sets have been used as representations for computing reachable states for linear hybrid automata [1]. For more complex continuous dynamics, various representations have been used for computing over-approximations of the reach sets, such as, union of convex polytopes [5], union of hyper-rectangles [8], and ellipsoids [14]. Similar in the spirit of the result presented here, Kurzhanski and Varaiya [14] show that the best ellipsoidal over-approximation of the reach set for certain linear systems can be computed. We also note here that some of the above works use abstract interpretation ideas, most notably in the form of widening to accelerate reachability (or fixpoint) computation [12, 8].

Exact reach sets for a class of linear vector fields were computed as semi-algebraic sets over state variables and special variables representing exponential or trigonometric functions [16]. We contrast algebraic sets with semi-algebraic sets as a choice for representing sets of states. Algebraic sets are defined as the zeros of a finite set of polynomial equations. They admit unique canonical representations on which various set operations and quantifier-elimination operation can be efficiently performed. Semi-algebraic sets, on the other hand, are boolean combinations of sets defined by polynomial equations and inequalities. By definition, they are closed under boolean operations. However, there is no standard notion of canonical representation. There is a quantifier-elimination procedure, but it is quite complex, both in theory and practice.

2   Preliminaries: Ideals of Polynomials

Let $\mathbb{K}[X]$ denote the set of polynomials over the variables $X = \{x_1, \ldots, x_n\}$ with coefficients in the field $\mathbb{K}$ ($\mathbb{K} = \mathbb{R}, \mathbb{Q}$). Given a set $S \subseteq \mathbb{K}^n$ of points, we are interested in those polynomials P that evaluate to 0 at S, that is, $P(s) = 0, \forall s \in S$. These polynomials form an *ideal*: an ideal is a set $I \subseteq \mathbb{K}[X]$ such that it includes 0, is closed under addition and if $P \in \mathbb{K}[X]$ and $Q \in I$, then $PQ \in I$.

Given a set of polynomials $B \subseteq \mathbb{K}[X]$, the *ideal generated by B* is

$$\langle B \rangle = \{f \in \mathbb{K}[X] \mid f = \sum_{j=1}^{k} P_j Q_j \text{ with } P_j \in \mathbb{K}[X], Q_j \in B, k \geq 1\}.$$

For an ideal I, a set of polynomials B such that $I = \langle B \rangle$ is called a *basis* of I. By Hilbert's basis theorem, all ideals of polynomials admit a *finite* basis. Thus, any ideal is associated to a finite system of polynomial equalities: the ideal $I = \langle P_1(X), \ldots, P_k(X) \rangle$ corresponds naturally to the system $\{P_1(X) = 0, \ldots, P_k(X) = 0\}$. The solutions to this system are the common zeroes of all the polynomials in I; this set of points, denoted by $\mathbf{V}(I) = \{s \in \mathbb{K}^n \mid P(s) = 0 \, \forall P \in I\}$, is called the *variety* of I (over $\mathbb{K}^n$). A variety is also called an *algebraic set*.

For instance, the ideal $\langle x(x^2 + y^2 - 1), y(x^2 + y^2 - 1) \rangle$ is associated to the system $\{x(x^2 + y^2 - 1) = 0, \ y(x^2 + y^2 - 1) = 0\}$. Its solution, which defines the variety $\mathbf{V}(\langle x(x^2 + y^2 - 1), y(x^2 + y^2 - 1) \rangle)$, is the union of the circle $x^2 + y^2 = 1$ and the origin. Notice that this set, unlike convex polyhedra [10, 5], is not convex or even connected.

Reciprocally, given a set of points $S \subseteq \mathbb{K}^n$, the polynomials vanishing on this set form the ideal $\mathbf{I}(S) = \{P \in \mathbb{K}[X] \mid P(s) = 0 \, \forall s \in S\}$, called the *ideal of*

S. Notice that, for arbitrary ideals, the inclusion $I \subseteq \mathbf{IV}(I)^1$ may be strict: the variety of the ideal of all multiples of x^2 is just the origin, $\mathbf{V}(\langle x^2 \rangle) = \{0\}$; but $\mathbf{I}(\{0\}) = \langle x \rangle$, and $x \notin \langle x^2 \rangle$. We are interested in the ideals for which the equality $\mathbf{IV}(I) = I$ holds; these ideals are *complete* in the sense that they include *all* polynomials that evaluate to 0 at the points of the variety $\mathbf{V}(I)$ they represent. Since any ideal I satisfying $\mathbf{IV}(I) = I$ is the ideal of the variety $\mathbf{V}(I)$, such an ideal is called an *ideal of variety*.

3 Linear Systems

A *linear (continuous dynamical) system CS* is a tuple (X, Init, A, b) where $X = \{x_1, ..., x_n\}$ is a finite set of variables interpreted over the reals $\mathbb{R}$, $\mathbf{X} = \mathbb{R}^n$ is the set of all valuations of the variables X, $\mathit{Init} \subseteq \mathbf{X}$ is the set of initial states, and $A \in \mathbb{Q}^{n \times n}$ and $b \in \mathbb{Q}^{n \times 1}$ are the matrices that constrain the dynamics of CS by the differential equation $\dot{x} = Ax + b$. Since interest is in computational feasibility, the matrices A and b are assumed to contain rational entries.

The semantics, $[[CS]]$, of a linear system $CS = (X, \mathit{Init}, A, b)$ over an interval $I = [t_0, t_1] \subseteq \mathbb{R}$ is a collection of mappings $x : I \mapsto \mathbf{X}$ satisfying (i) the initial condition: $x(t_0) \in \mathit{Init}$, and (ii) the continuous dynamics: for all $t \in [t_0, t_1]$, $\dot{x}(t) = Ax(t) + b$. In case the interval I is left unspecified, it is assumed to be the interval $[0, \infty)$.

We say that a state $s \in \mathbf{X}$ is *reachable* in a continuous dynamical system CS if there exists a function $x \in [[CS]]$ such that $s = x(t)$ for some $t \in I$. The set, $\mathit{Reach}(CS)$, is defined as the set of all reachable states of the system CS.

The problem of computing the exact reachability set $\mathit{Reach}(CS)$ for a given dynamical system CS is intractable in general. However, for purposes of verification of safety properties, it often suffices to compute an *over-approximation* (or superset) of the reachable set of states—if the over-approximation does not intersect the set of bad states, then the original system will never reach a bad state. An over-approximation of the reachable states is also called an *invariant* of the system. The most precise invariant of a system is its exact reach set.

Lafferriere, Pappas and Yovine showed that the exact reach set can be computed for a subclass of linear continuous dynamical systems [16]. Subsequently, it was shown that invariants could be effectively constructed for more general classes of linear systems [20]. We show here that the most precise *equational invariant* for arbitrary linear systems can be computed. We focus on a special case in Section 3.1, and generalize to arbitrary linear systems in Section 3.2.

3.1 Eigenvalues with Rational Components

Assume that the eigenvalues of A are of the form $a + bi$, where $a, b \in \mathbb{Q}$ and $i^2 = -1$. We do *not* assume that A is diagonalizable. The solution to the system of differential equations $\dot{x} = Ax + b$ is

---

[1] We write $\mathbf{IV}$ instead of $\mathbf{I} \circ \mathbf{V}$ to denote the composition of $\mathbf{I}$ and $\mathbf{V}$.

$$\Phi(s^*, t) = e^{At}s^* + e^{At}\left(\int_0^t e^{-A\tau}d\tau\right)b \, , s^* \in Init \tag{1}$$

where Φ is the flow of the vector field. It can be easily proved that both e^{At} and $\int_0^t e^{-A\tau}d\tau$ can be written as sums of terms of the form $ct^k e^{\pm at}\cos(bt)$, $ct^k e^{\pm at}\sin(bt)$, where $c \in \mathbb{Q}$, $k \in \mathbb{N}$ and the complex numbers $\lambda = a + bi$ are the eigenvalues of the matrix A.

The set of reachable states of CS is

$$Reach(CS) = \{s \in \mathbb{R}^n : \exists s^*, t. \, (t \geq 0 \, \wedge \, s^* \in Init \, \wedge \, s = \Phi(s^*, t))\} \tag{2}$$

We can express the solution $\Phi(s^*, t)$ given in Equation 1 in terms of polynomials using up to four auxiliary variables u, v, w, z. Specifically, since we assume that all eigenvalues of A are of the form $a + bi$ with $a, b \in \mathbb{Q}$, we can find positive rational numbers p, q such that, for any eigenvalue $\lambda = a + bi$ of A, there exist integers c_λ, d_λ such that $c_\lambda = a/p$ and $d_\lambda = b/q$. Now we just need to replace e^{pt} by u, e^{-pt} by v, $\cos(qt)$ by w and $\sin(qt)$ by z: for any eigenvalue $\lambda = a + bi$, we replace e^{at} by $u^{|c_\lambda|}$ or $v^{|c_\lambda|}$ depending on whether $a > 0$ or $a < 0$ respectively; $\cos(bt)$ and $\sin(bt)$ can be similarly expressed in terms of w and z. Therefore, we can express the flow Φ as a polynomial over the initial conditions and the dummy variables t, u, v, w, z [16]. The reach set from Equation 2 can now be written as

$$\exists s^*, t, u, v, w, z \,.\, (t \geq 0 \, \wedge \, s^* \in Init \, \wedge \, s = \Phi(s^*, t, u, v, w, z) \, \wedge$$
$$u = e^{pt} \, \wedge \, v = e^{-pt} \, \wedge \, w = \cos(qt) \, \wedge \, z = \sin(qt)) \tag{3}$$

The exponentials and the trigonometric functions are eliminated by introducing new equations $uv = 1$ and $w^2 + z^2 = 1$ that capture the dependencies between e^{pt}, e^{-pt}, $\cos(qt)$ and $\sin(qt)$. Clearly, the resulting formula, given below, represents an invariant of CS.

$$\exists s^*, t, u, v, w, z \,.\, (t \geq 0 \, \wedge \, u \geq 1 \, \wedge \, s^* \in Init \, \wedge \, s = \Phi(s^*, t, u, v, w, z) \, \wedge$$
$$uv = 1 \, \wedge \, w^2 + z^2 = 1) \tag{4}$$

Using quantifier elimination for reals, this method gives a semi-algebraic invariant for the linear system CS. Unfortunately, the formula above does not capture all semi-algebraic relationships that exist between t, u, v, w and z.

One of the main observations of this paper is that the two equations $uv = 1$ and $w^2 + z^2 = 1$ are sufficient to capture all algebraic invariants of CS. Furthermore, to compute the algebraic invariants, the expensive step that involves doing quantifier elimination over the reals can be replaced by a Gröbner basis [7] computation step, which is simpler and often more efficient in practice. Since we use Gröbner bases to eliminate variables, we need to employ an elimination term ordering in which the auxiliary variables are the biggest. In summary, the method to compute the strongest algebraic invariants of CS is to use Gröbner bases to eliminate the quantified variables in Equation 4.

The main result of the paper is that, if the initial conditions are described by means of an ideal of variety, we obtain *all* polynomials that evaluate to 0 at the exact reachability set of CS.

Theorem 1. *Let* $CS = (X, \mathbf{V}(I^*), A, \mathbf{b})$ *be a linear system, where* $I^* \subseteq \mathbb{Q}[X^*]$ *is the ideal of variety of initial states. Let* $P_1, ..., P_n \in \mathbb{Q}[X^*, t, u, v, w, z]$ *be the polynomials approximating the flow* Φ *defined above. Then,*

$$\mathbf{I}(Reach(CS)) = \langle I^*, -x_1 + P_1, \ldots, -x_n + P_n, uv - 1, w^2 + z^2 - 1\rangle \cap \mathbb{R}[X]$$

Proof. The $\supseteq$ inclusion is obvious. For the $\subseteq$ inclusion, take an arbitrary polynomial $q \in \mathbf{I}(Reach(CS))$. Normalize the polynomial q using the following rewrite rules[2] to get a new polynomial r:

$$x_1 \to P_1, \ldots, x_n \to P_n, \ uv \to 1, \ w^2 \to -z^2 + 1$$

Our goal is to prove that $r \in \langle I^* \rangle$ (as an ideal in $\mathbb{R}[X, X^*, t, u, v, w, z]$). Since we have eliminated all occurrences of uv, w^2 and x_i, the polynomial r must be of the form

$$\sum_{l,m,n \geq 0} a_{lmn}(X^*)t^l u^m z^n + b_{lmn}(X^*)t^l u^m wz^n + c_{lmn}(X^*)t^l v^m z^n + d_{lmn}(X^*)t^l v^m wz^n$$

with a finite number of non-vanishing terms. We need to prove that the polynomials $a_{lmn}(X^*)$, $b_{lmn}(X^*)$, $c_{lmn}(X^*)$, and $d_{lmn}(X^*)$ are in $\mathbf{IV}(I^*) = I^*$. So, we will prove that $\forall s^* \in \mathbf{V}(I^*)$, $a_{lmn}(s^*) = b_{lmn}(s^*) = c_{lmn}(s^*) = d_{lmn}(s^*) = 0$.

Fix $s^* \in \mathbf{V}(I^*)$. Under the substitution $x_i \mapsto P_i, u \mapsto e^{pt}, v \mapsto e^{-pt}, w \mapsto \cos(qt), z \mapsto \sin(qt), X^* \mapsto s^*$, the polynomial q evaluates to 0 (for all $t \geq 0$), and so do the polynomials $uv - 1, w^2 + z^2 - 1, -x_i + P_i$. Therefore, we have that for all $t \geq 0$, $R(t) := r(s^*, t, e^{pt}, e^{-pt}, \cos(qt), \sin(qt)) = 0$, or equivalently

$$\sum_{l,m \geq 0} t^l e^{mpt}\left(\sum_{n \geq 0} a_{lmn}(s^*)\sin^n(qt) + b_{lmn}(s^*)\sin^n(qt)\cos(qt)\right) +$$

$$t^l e^{-mpt}\left(\sum_{n \geq 0} c_{lmn}(s^*)\sin^n(qt) + d_{lmn}(s^*)\sin^n(qt)\cos(qt)\right) = 0$$

Since this function evaluates to 0 for *all* $t \geq 0$, we claim without proof that $a_{lmn}(s^*) = b_{lmn}(s^*) = c_{lmn}(s^*) = d_{lmn}(s^*) = 0$. This completes the proof. $\square$

Example 1. Consider the following system of differential equations, which describes the dynamics of a charged particle under the influence of a magnetic field:

$$\begin{pmatrix} \dot{x} \\ \dot{y} \\ \dot{v}_x \\ \dot{v}_y \end{pmatrix} = \begin{pmatrix} 0 & 0 & 1 & 0 \\ 0 & 0 & 0 & 1 \\ 0 & 0 & 0 & -1/2 \\ 0 & 0 & 1/2 & 0 \end{pmatrix} \begin{pmatrix} x \\ y \\ v_x \\ v_y \end{pmatrix}$$

---

[2] Simplification of q by a rewrite rule $l \to r$ simply means that you replace l by r in q. Experts in Gröbner bases will notice that we are using the term ordering lex($X > u > v > w > z > t > X^*$).

The solution is given by

$$\begin{cases} x = x^* + 2\sin(t/2)\,v_x^* + (2\cos(t/2)-2)\,v_y^* & v_x = \cos(t/2)\,v_x^* - \sin(t/2)\,v_y^* \\ y = y^* + (-2\cos(t/2)+2)\,v_x^* + 2\sin(t/2)\,v_y^* & v_y = \sin(t/2)\,v_x^* + \cos(t/2)\,v_y^* \end{cases}$$

where x^*, y^*, v_x^*, v_y^* stand for the initial values. In this case the eigenvalues of the system matrix are 0, $i/2$ and $-i/2$, which is consistent with the fact that the non-algebraic terms in the solution are $\cos(t/2)$, $\sin(t/2)$. By introducing the variables w and z to replace $\cos(t/2)$ and $\sin(t/2)$ respectively, we can rewrite the solution as follows (there are no exponential terms in this case):

$$\begin{cases} x = x^* + 2zv_x^* + (2w-2)v_y^* & v_x = wv_x^* - zv_y^* \\ y = y^* + (-2w+2)\,v_x^* + 2zv_y^* & v_y = zv_x^* + wv_y^* \end{cases}$$

Now assume that the initial conditions satisfy $v_x^* = 2$, $v_y^* = -2$. Therefore we have to eliminate x^*, y^*, v_x^*, v_y^*, w, z from the ideal

$$\langle v_x^* - 2, v_y^* + 2, -x + x^* + 2zv_x^* + (2w-2)v_y^*, -y + y^* + (-2w+2)\,v_x^* + 2zv_y^*,$$

$$-v_x + wv_x^* - zv_y^*, -v_y + zv_x^* + wv_y^*, w^2 + z^2 - 1\rangle$$

The elimination of the auxiliary variables yields the ideal $\langle v_x^2 + v_y^2 - 8\rangle$, which corresponds to the law of conservation of energy.   □

The method for generating the most precise equational (algebraic) invariants of linear systems can be extended to handle state invariants that are specified as polynomial equations. Before eliminating the quantified variables from Equation 4, we add all the equations representing any state invariant that may be true.

It is difficult to generalize the method to compute the best semi-algebraic invariant. Whereas the two equations $uv = 1$ and $w^2 + z^2 = 1$ capture all algebraic relationships between the functions $e^{pt}, e^{-pt}, \sin(qt)$ and $\cos(qt)$, there is no *finite* set (basis) of inequalities that captures all the semi-algebraic relationships between these functions. This also partly explains why the decidability results [15, 16] are not easy to generalize.

3.2   Generalization to Arbitrary Eigenvalues

Let $\mathcal{L}$ be the set of all eigenvalues of the matrix A. We now drop the assumption that $a, b \in \mathbb{Q}$ for all $a + bi \in \mathcal{L}$ by generalizing the above ideas. First, let us deal with the exponential terms $e^{\pm at}$. To that end, we define $\mathcal{R} = \{\pm \mathrm{Re}(\lambda) \,|\, \lambda \in \mathcal{L}\} \setminus \{0\}$. Since $\mathcal{R}$ is finite, we can obtain a finite basis $\mathcal{B} = \{p_1, ..., p_k\}$ of the $\mathbb{Q}$-vector space generated by $\mathcal{R}$. By definition, this set has the properties that:

1. $\forall a \in \mathcal{R}$, $\exists c_1^a, ..., c_k^a \in \mathbb{Q}$ such that $a = \sum_{i=1}^{k} c_i^a p_i$.
   ($\mathcal{B}$ is a system of generators)
2. $\forall c_1, ..., c_k \in \mathbb{Q}$, if $\sum_{i=1}^{k} c_i p_i = 0$, then necessarily $c_1 = \cdots = c_k = 0$.
   ($\mathcal{B}$ is $\mathbb{Q}$-linearly independent)

Further, by multiplying the elements in $\mathcal{B}$ by appropriate correction factors, we can ensure that the coefficients c_i^a are *integers*, i.e. $\forall a \in \mathcal{R}, \exists c_1^a, ..., c_k^a \in \mathbb{Z}$ such that $a = \sum_{i=1}^k c_i^a p_i$. By introducing the auxiliary variables $u_i = e^{p_i t}, v_i = e^{-p_i t}$:

$$e^{at} = e^{\sum_{i=1}^k c_i^a p_i t} = \prod_{i=1}^k e^{c_i^a p_i t} = \prod_{i=1}^k \begin{cases} u_i^{|c_i^a|} & \text{if } \text{sign}(c_i^a) = 1 \\ v_i^{|c_i^a|} & \text{if } \text{sign}(c_i^a) = -1 \end{cases}$$

So we can substitute the exponentials by means of the auxiliary variables.

Example 2. Let us consider that $\mathcal{L} = \{\lambda_1, \lambda_2, \lambda_3, \lambda_4\} = \{1+\sqrt{2}, 1-\sqrt{2}, 1/2, 1/3\}$. Taking $\mathcal{B} = \{p_1, p_2\} = \{1 + \sqrt{2}, 1/6\}$ as a basis, all coefficients are integers: $\lambda_1 = p_1, \lambda_2 = -p_1 + 12p_2, \lambda_3 = 3p_2, \lambda_4 = 2p_2$. So, if $u_1 = e^{(1+\sqrt{2})t}, v_1 = e^{-(1+\sqrt{2})t}, u_2 = e^{(1/6)t}, v_2 = e^{-(1/6)t}$, then for instance $e^{(1-\sqrt{2})t} = v_1 u_2^{12}$. □

Trigonometric terms are handled likewise. Define $\mathcal{I} = \{\text{Im}(\lambda) \mid \lambda \in \mathcal{L}\} \setminus \{0\}$ and introduce $2l$ auxiliary variables w_j, z_j, representing $\cos(q_j t), \sin(q_j t)$ for $1 \leq j \leq l$, where $q_1, ..., q_l \in \mathbb{R}$ form a finite basis of $\mathcal{I}$.

Theorem 1 can now be extended by replacing the four auxiliary variables by $2k + 2l$ auxiliary variables. The main observation is that the $k + l$ equations, $u_i v_i = 1$ and $w_i^2 + z_i^2 = 1$, capture *all* the algebraic relationships between the auxiliary variables. We state the following theorem without proof.

Theorem 2. *Let $CS = (X, \mathbf{V}(I^*), A, \mathbf{b})$ be a linear system, where $I^* \subseteq \mathbb{Q}[X^*]$ is the ideal of variety of initial states. Let $P_1, ..., P_n \in \mathbb{Q}[X^*, t, u_1, v_1, ..., u_k, v_k, w_1, z_1, ..., w_l, z_l]$ be the polynomials approximating the flow Φ. Then,*

$$\mathbf{I}(Reach(CS)) = \langle I^*, -x_1 + P_1, \ldots, -x_n + P_n,$$
$$u_1 v_1 - 1, ..., u_k v_k - 1, w_1^2 + z_1^2 - 1, ..., w_l^2 + z_l^2 - 1 \rangle \cap \mathbb{R}[X]$$

4 Hybrid Systems

In this section we extend the technique for generating algebraic invariants to hybrid systems using abstract interpretation [6]. At each location, we restrict ourselves to linear continuous dynamics.

A *hybrid system* $HS = (\mathcal{L}, X, \mathcal{T}, (Init)_{\ell \in \mathcal{L}}, (A)_{\ell \in \mathcal{L}}, (\mathbf{b})_{\ell \in \mathcal{L}})$ consists of a finite set $\mathcal{L}$ of *locations*; a finite set of continuous dynamical systems $(X, Init_\ell, A_\ell, \mathbf{b}_\ell)$, one associated with each location $\ell \in \mathcal{L}$; and a finite set $\mathcal{T} \subset \mathcal{L} \times \mathcal{L} \times 2^{\mathbf{X}} \times (\mathbf{X} \rightarrow \mathbf{X})$ of discrete *transitions*. A discrete transition $\tau = (\ell, \ell', \gamma, \alpha) \in \mathcal{T}$ consists of a *source location* $\ell \in \mathcal{L}$, a *target location* $\ell' \in \mathcal{L}$, a *guard* γ which is a boolean function of the variables X, and an *action* α which is a multiple assignment of the variables. A *state* of the system HS is given by a location $\ell \in \mathcal{L}$ and a valuation $\mathbf{s} \in \mathbf{X} = \mathbb{R}^n$ of the variables over the real numbers.

The semantics, $[[HS]]$, of a hybrid system HS is a collection of infinite sequences of states $(\ell, \mathbf{s}) \in \mathcal{L} \times \mathbf{X}$ of the form $(\ell_0, \mathbf{s_0}), (\ell_1, \mathbf{s_1}), (\ell_2, \mathbf{s_2}), \ldots$ such that $\mathbf{s_0} \in Init_{\ell_0}$ specifies an *initial state*, and for each pair of consecutive states $(\ell_i, \mathbf{s_i}), (\ell_{i+1}, \mathbf{s_{i+1}})$ one of the two *transition conditions* holds:

- *discrete transition*: there exists a transition $\tau = (\ell_i, \ell_{i+1}, \gamma, \alpha) \in \mathcal{T}$ which is enabled, i.e. $\gamma(s_i) = true$, and such that $s_{i+1} = \alpha(s_i)$.

- *continuous transition*: the control location does not change, in other words $\ell_i = \ell_{i+1} = \ell$; and there is a trajectory going from s_i to s_{i+1} along the flow determined by A_ℓ, b_ℓ, i.e. there exist a time interval $\delta \geq 0$ and a differentiable function $x : [0, \delta] \to \mathbf{X}$ such that $x(0) = s_i$, $x(\delta) = s_{i+1}$ and $\dot{x}(t) = A_\ell x + b_\ell$ (and the state invariant, if any, holds).

A state (ℓ, s) is *reachable* if there exists a sequence in $[[HS]]$ where it appears. The set of all reachable states of a hybrid system HS is denoted by $Reach(HS)$.

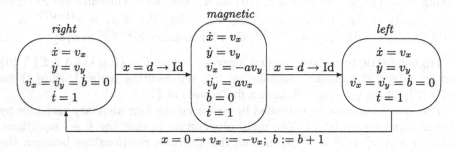

Fig. 1. Dynamics of a charged particle

Example 3. The hybrid system in Figure 1, taken from [19], models the position (x, y) and the velocity (v_x, v_y) of a charged particle on a plane with a reflecting barrier at $x = 0$ and a magnetic field perpendicular to the plane in the region $x \geq d$ (where $d \geq 0$ is a parameter of the system). The variable b counts the number of times the particle has collided against the reflecting barrier, and t is a clock that measures the total time elapsed.

The hybrid system has three locations: in locations *left* and *right*, the particle is moving freely under no external force, either toward or away from the barrier, while in location *magnetic* it is moving under the effect of the magnetic field. The three discrete transitions model the movement of the particle in and out of the magnetic field and its collision with the barrier. In our analysis, we assume that initially the particle is moving *right* with $v_x = 2$, $v_y = -2$ and $x = y = t = b = 0$; also, the parameters d and a are set to 2 and $1/2$ respectively.   □

4.1   Reachable States as Fixpoints

Let us denote by $Reach = Reach(HS)$ the set of all reachable states of a hybrid system HS. Given a location ℓ, we also write $Reach_\ell$ to represent the set of all reachable states at location ℓ, i.e. $Reach_\ell = \{s \mid (\ell, s) \in Reach\}$.

We first characterize the (tuple of) reachable states $(Reach_\ell)_{\ell \in \mathcal{L}}$ using a system of fixpoint equations. Consider a discrete transition $\tau = (\ell, \ell', \gamma, \alpha)$. The states at location ℓ where transition τ is enabled are given by $Reach_\ell \cap \gamma$. After firing the transition, the new states reached are given by $\alpha(Reach_\ell \cap \gamma)$, where α represents the mapping that updates the values of the variables. The set of states in which location ℓ' is entered is obtained by summing up over all discrete transitions that lead to ℓ':

$$Init_{\ell'} \cup \left(\bigcup_{(\ell,\ell',\gamma,\alpha)\in\mathcal{T}} \alpha(Reach_\ell \cap \gamma) \right).$$

The above states provide the initial conditions for the continuous evolution at ℓ'. Now, $Reach_{\ell'}$ is obtained thus:

$$Reach_{\ell'} = \bigcup_{t\geq 0} \Phi_{\ell'}\left(Init_{\ell'} \cup \left(\bigcup_{(\ell,\ell',\gamma,\alpha)\in\mathcal{T}} \alpha(Reach_\ell \cap \gamma) \right), t\right). \qquad (5)$$

The above system of equations defines $(Reach)_{\ell\in\mathcal{L}}$ in terms of itself. The least fixpoint of this system of equations (with respect to the inclusion $\subseteq$ ordering) is the *exact* set of reachable states of HS. However, any fixpoint (not necessarily the least) will give an over-approximation of the exact reach set.

The ability to compute a fixpoint of the above equations depends on the choice of the representation for sets of states. Some choices are convex polyhedra [5], algebraic sets, semi-algebraic sets [16], and ellipsoidal sets [14]. Using the results from Section 3, in the next subsections we will show how algebraic solutions of the Fixpoint Equation 5 can be computed. The general framework (originally defined for discrete transition systems) is called *abstract interpretation* [6].

4.2   Abstract Interpretation

Abstract interpretation [6] is a general framework for discovering invariant properties for a given discrete transition system. It works by solving a fixpoint equation $X = F(X)$ (which determines the reachable sets for that system) over an *abstract domain*. The abstract domain is defined by the representation used for specifying sets of states. The application of abstract interpretation involves:

1. *Choosing an abstract domain A*: Each element in the abstract domain represents a set of states. The original fixpoint equation $X = F(X)$ (defined over arbitrary sets of states X) is transformed into a fixpoint equation $Y = G(Y)$ over the sets of states Y *defined* by the abstract domain.
2. *Computing a solution of the fixpoint equation $Y = G(Y)$ over the abstract domain iteratively*: A solution of the equation $Y = G(Y)$ is obtained by computing a fixpoint of the recurrence $Y_0 = \bot$ (the least element of the abstract domain), $Y_{k+1} = G(Y_k)$. This recurrence may not necessarily converge in a finite number of steps; in this case the termination is forced by means of the application of a *widening* operator $\nabla : A \times A \to A$, at the cost of further over-approximation. Such an operator must satisfy:
   - $\forall Y_1, Y_2 \in A,\ Y_1 \subseteq Y_1 \nabla Y_2$ and $Y_2 \subseteq Y_1 \nabla Y_2$.
   - For any increasing chain $Y_0 \subseteq Y_1 \subseteq \cdots$, the new increasing chain defined by $Y_0' = Y_0$, $Y_{k+1}' = Y_k' \nabla Y_{k+1}$ is not strictly increasing (that is, it finitely converges).
   Under these hypotheses, the last element of the finite sequence $Y_0', Y_1', Y_2', \ldots$ yields a solution of the fixpoint equation.

4.3   Operations with Ideals of Variety

We now show that the abstract domain of algebraic sets, represented as ideals of variety, can be used to compute polynomial invariants for hybrid systems. In Section 2 we presented this domain, and Section 3 showed how to handle continuous evolution (that is, the Φ function in the Fixpoint Equation 5). We now show how the rest of the operators used in Equation 5, viz. the assignment transformation α, the set union $\cup$ and the set intersection $\cap$, can be effectively computed over our choice of abstract domain. We will also present a widening operator to guarantee termination.

Specifically, we use the following operations on algebraic sets (represented as ideals) to abstract the corresponding operations on (arbitrary) sets, see [17]:

Assignment Transformation → *Elimination of Variables.* Given an ideal of variety $I = \langle P_1(X), ..., P_k(X) \rangle$ and a multiple (polynomial) assignment $(x_1, ..., x_n) := (\alpha_1(X), ..., \alpha_n(X))$, we introduce auxiliary variables $\bar{X} = \{\bar{x}_1, ..., \bar{x}_n\}$, to denote the values of the variables *before* the assignment. Then the relationship between the values before and after the assignment is described by the ideal

$$\langle P_1(\bar{X}), ..., P_k(\bar{X}), x_1 - \alpha_1(\bar{X}), ..., x_n - \alpha_n(\bar{X}) \rangle.$$

The output ideal of variety can be obtained by eliminating the auxiliary variables $\bar{X}$ in the ideal above by means of well-known elimination techniques based on Gröbner bases [7].

Union of States → *Intersection of Ideals.* Given two ideals of variety I and J, the union of the states represented by I and J is represented by the ideal $\mathbf{I}(\mathbf{V}(I) \cup \mathbf{V}(J))$, which is equal to $I \cap J$ by duality. Therefore, the output ideal of variety is the intersection ideal $I \cap J$.

Intersection of States → *Sum and Quotient of Ideals.* Given two ideals of variety $I = \langle P_1, ..., P_k \rangle$ and $J = \langle Q_1, ..., Q_l \rangle$, we distinguish two cases:

– We want to represent $\mathbf{V}(I) \cap \mathbf{V}(J)$ (this is the case when guards have *polynomial equalities* like $x = 0$). The *sum* of ideals $I + J = \langle P_1, ..., P_k, Q_1, ..., Q_l \rangle$, which is generated by the union of the bases, has the property that $\mathbf{V}(I + J) = \mathbf{V}(I) \cap \mathbf{V}(J)$. However, $I + J$ may not be an ideal of variety; therefore we have to compute its closure $\mathbf{IV}(I + J)^3$.
– We want to represent $\mathbf{V}(I) \cap (\mathbb{K}^n \setminus \mathbf{V}(J)) = \mathbf{V}(I) \setminus \mathbf{V}(J)$ (this is the case when guards have *polynomial disequalities* like $x \neq 0$). The *quotient* $I : J$ of ideals satisfies that $I : J = \mathbf{I}(\mathbf{V}(I) \setminus \mathbf{V}(J))$, i.e. it is the maximal set of polynomials that evaluate to 0 at $\mathbf{V}(I) \setminus \mathbf{V}(J)$. Thus we take $I : J$ as the output ideal of variety.

---

[3] If we take the complex numbers $\mathbb{C}$ as the field for the coefficients instead of $\mathbb{R}$, by Hilbert's Nullstellensatz $\mathbf{IV} = Rad$, the radical operator, which can be effectively computed.

Widening Operator. Given two ideals of variety I and J, we are interested in *under*-approximating the ideal $I \cap J$ so that we can guarantee termination of the fixpoint computation. One way to achieve this is to restrict $I \cap J$ to polynomials that have degree less or equal than a prefixed degree bound d. As the ideal generated by these polynomials may not be an ideal of variety, the closure operator **IV** must be applied. Formally, given two ideals of variety I, J and a degree bound d, the widening is defined as:

$$I \nabla_d J = \mathbf{IV}(\{P \in GB(I \cap J, \succ) \mid \mathrm{degree}(P) \leq d\}),$$

where $GB(K, \succ)$ stands for a Gröbner basis of an ideal K with respect to the graded term ordering[4] $\succ$. We are experimenting with other widening operators that would allow the generalization of Theorem 1 to hybrid systems.

It is well-known in computational algebraic geometry that canonical representation for $I \cap J, I \cup J, I : J$, and elimination ideals can be effectively computed from the corresponding representations for I and J.

Example 4. In the hybrid system model of the charged particle, let us denote by $I_{right}, I_{magnetic}$ and I_{left} the ideals of variety corresponding to the states *right*, *magnetic* and *left* respectively. As the initial state is *right* with $v_x = 2$, $v_y = -2$, $x = y = b = t = 0$, we get the following system of fixpoint equations:

$$\begin{cases} I_{right} = \phi_{right}(\langle v_x - 2, v_y + 2, x, y, t, b \rangle \cap \alpha(\mathbf{IV}(I_{left} + \langle x \rangle))) \\ I_{magnetic} = \phi_{magnetic}(\mathbf{IV}(I_{right} + \langle x - d \rangle)) \\ I_{left} = \phi_{left}(\mathbf{IV}(I_{magnetic} + \langle x - d \rangle)) \end{cases}$$

where α transforms (v_x, b) into $(-v_x, b + 1)$ and leaves the rest of the variables unchanged, and the ϕ's are the mappings abstracting the flows in continuous transitions, taking as input an ideal of initial conditions and returning an ideal of invariant polynomials (computed using the technique described in Section 3).

We approximate the fixpoint of this equation by using the widening operator ∇_2. We get the following invariants:

$$I_{right} = \langle v_y + 2, v_x^2 - 4 \rangle \qquad I_{left} = \langle v_y + 2, v_x^2 - 4 \rangle$$
$$I_{magnetic} = \langle x - 2v_y - 4 - d, v_x^2 + v_y^2 - 8 \rangle$$

The reason why we get $v_x^2 = 4$ both at *right* and *left* is that our hybrid system allows undesired behaviors, such as the particle in mode *right* making a transition to *magnetic* and then instantly moving again to *left* with no time elapse. However, using the implicit invariants $v_x \geq 0$ at *right* and $v_x \leq 0$ at *left*, we deduce that $v_x = 2$ at *right* and $v_x = -2$ at *left*. We add these invariants to the guards and finally get the following more precise invariant:

$$\begin{cases} I_{right} = \langle v_y + 2, v_x - 2, 2db - 8b + y + x \rangle \\ I_{magnetic} = \langle x - 2v_y - 4 - d, v_x^2 + v_y^2 - 8, 2v_x + y + 2db - 8b - 4 + d \rangle \\ I_{left} = \langle v_y + 2, v_x + 2, 2db - 8b + y - 8 - x \rangle \end{cases}$$

---

[4] Gröbner bases and graded term orderings are used in this definition because they allow us to prove that, when employing this widening operator, the fixpoint computation yields all the polynomial invariants of degree $\leq d$, see [7, 17].

5 Examples

We illustrate our method for generating polynomial invariants on some hybrid systems taken from the literature. As an optimization, we did not compute the closure **IV** always; nonetheless, the obtained invariants sufficed for proving the properties of interest. We implemented our techniques in the algebraic geometry tool Macaulay 2 [9] using a PC running Linux with a 2.5 GHz. processor and 512 MB of memory.

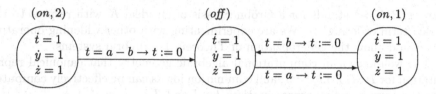

Fig. 2. Hybrid system for a thermostat

Thermostat. Figure 2 shows a hybrid system, taken from [13], modeling a thermostat. The system has three locations: in $(on, 1)$ and $(on, 2)$ the thermostat is on, while in (off) the thermostat is off. There are three clocks: t tracks the time elapsed at the current location, y tracks the total time, and z tracks the time the thermostat has been on. There are also two parameters a and b that limit the maximum time the thermostat is in the locations. The initial state is $(on, 2)$ with $t = y = z = 0$. Using ∇_2, in 0.44 seconds we get the invariants

$$\begin{cases} I_{(on,2)} = \langle y - t, z - t \rangle \\ I_{(off)} = \langle -a^2 + ab + az + bz - by + bt \rangle \\ I_{(on,1)} = \langle a^2 - 2ab - az - bz + by + at \rangle \end{cases}$$

In [13] it was proved that, for $a = \ln(3)$, $b = \ln(2)$, the thermostat is on between $23.17/60 \approx 38.6\%$ and $23.51/60 \approx 39.2\%$ of the time within the first 60 time units of operation. We can use the polynomial invariants above to refine these bounds. At location (off), from the implicit invariant $0 \le t \le a$ and $-a^2 + ab + az + bz - by + bt = 0$ we get that

$$\frac{a^2 - 2ab + by}{a + b} \le z \le \frac{a^2 - ab + by}{a + b}.$$

We also get the same inequalities at location $(on, 1)$ by using the implicit invariant $0 \le t \le b$ and $a^2 - 2ab - az - bz + by + at = 0$. Substituting $a = \ln(3)$, $b = \ln(2)$, $y = 60$, we get the interval $[23.03/60, 23.46/60] \approx [38.4\%, 39.1\%]$, which provides us with a better upper bound.

Train System. The hybrid system shown in Figure 3 and taken from [19] models a train accelerating (location acc), moving at constant speed (location $cons$) and decelerating until stopping (location dec). Once the train has halted, it remains quiet for 2 seconds. There are four variables: the position of the train x, its velocity v, a clock t and a counter s of the number of stops made so far. The initial state is acc with $x = v = s = t = 0$.

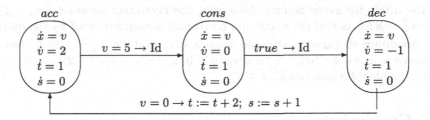

Fig. 3. Train system

We obtain the following invariants in 0.32 seconds using ∇_2:

$$I_{acc} = \langle -4x + v^2 - 115s + 20t - 10v \rangle$$
$$I_{dec} = \langle 4x + 115s - 20t - 20v + 75 + 2v^2 \rangle$$
$$I_{cons} = \langle v - 5, 4x + 115s - 20t + 25 \rangle$$

Note that these invariants, e.g. $4x + 115s - 20t - 20v + 75 + 2v^2 = 0$ at dec, can be found analytically by computing the distance covered x in terms of the other variables.

Charged Particle Revisited. Consider the hybrid system of the charged particle. Assume now that both the distance parameter d and the magnetic field magnitude a are left unknown (which is a more general setting than in [19]). Under these conditions the vector field in *magnetic* is no longer linear. However, notice that, since a is constant, the solution to the system of differential equations still has the same structure as in Section 3, with the difference that a may appear in a denominator. We overcome this problem by introducing a new auxiliary variable a' to represent the value a^{-1} (we assume that $a \neq 0$; the case $a = 0$ is straightforward to analyze). We also employ the polynomial $aa' - 1$ to represent the equation $aa^{-1} = 1$.

As before, due to imprecisions in our modeling, we first obtain the following invariants (in 1.80 seconds using ∇_2):

$$I_{right} = \langle v_y + 2, v_x^2 - 4 \rangle \qquad I_{left} = \langle v_y + 2, v_x^2 - 4 \rangle$$
$$I_{magnetic} = \langle ax - ad - v_y - 2, v_x^2 + v_y^2 - 8 \rangle$$

Strengthening this invariant as in Example 4 and re-computing the fixpoint, in 0.70 seconds we get:

$$\begin{cases} I_{right} = \langle v_y + 2, v_x - 2, -ax + 4b - 2adb - ay \rangle \\ I_{magnetic} = \langle ax - ad - v_y - 2, v_x^2 + v_y^2 - 8, ay - 4b + 2adb - 2 + ad + v_x \rangle \\ I_{left} = \langle v_y + 2, v_x + 2, 4b - 2adb - ay + 4 - 2ad + ax \rangle \end{cases}$$

Let us see some properties of the system that these invariants allow us to prove. First, by using the invariant $ax + ay = 4b - 2adb$ at $right$ we can compute the height where the particle collides as a function of the bounce counter b: by setting $x = 0$ we get $y = 2b(2 - ad)/a$. In particular, if $ad = 2$ the particle returns to the origin for every bounce. Moreover, the invariants $ax = ad + v_y + 2$ and $v_x^2 + v_y^2 = 8$ let us find the maximum horizontal distance covered by the particle: the maximum distance is achieved when $\dot{x} = v_x = 0$, i.e. $v_y = \pm 2\sqrt{2}$; then this distance is $x = d + (2\sqrt{2} + 2)/a$ when $a > 0$, $x = d + (-2\sqrt{2} + 2)/a$ when $a < 0$ (the feasible solutions satisfy $x \geq d$).

6   Conclusions

We presented a computational method for generating the most precise algebraic invariant for linear dynamical systems. We then extended this method to compute equational invariants for hybrid systems using an abstract interpretation approach. The main computational technique is based on Gröbner basis computation and we do not use the prohibitively expensive (quantifier elimination) decision procedure for the reals. Canonical Gröbner bases provide a useful representation for sets of states as they have several important properties such as canonicity, closure under boolean operations and quantifier elimination.

As future work, we plan to integrate our techniques with other approaches for dealing with inequalities. The resulting method would perform a much more precise analysis of hybrid systems with a wider range of applicability.

Acknowledgments

The authors would like to thank the reviewers for insightful comments.

References

1. R. Alur, C. Courcoubetis, T. A. Henzinger, and P.-H. Ho. Hybrid automata: An algorithmic approach to the specification and verification of hybrid systems. In R. L. Grossman, A. Nerode, A. P. Ravn, and H. Rischel, editors, *Hybrid Systems*, volume 736 of *LNCS*, pages 209–229. Springer, 1993.
2. R. Alur and D. Dill. A theory of timed automata. *Theoretical Computer Science*, 126:183–235, 1994.
3. R. Alur and G. J. Pappas, editors. *Hybrid Systems: Computation and Control, 7th International Workshop, HSCC 2004, Philadelphia, PA, USA, March 25-27, 2004, Proceedings*, volume 2993 of *Lecture Notes in Computer Science*. Springer, 2004.
4. R. Bryant. Symbolic boolean manipulation with ordered binary-decision diagrams. *ACM Computing Surveys*, 24(3):293–318, 1992.
5. A. Chutinan and B. H. Krogh. Computing polyhedral approximations to flow pipes for dynamic systems. In *37th IEEE Conference on Decision and Control*, 1998.
6. P. Cousot and R. Cousot. Abstract interpretation: A unified lattice model for static analysis of programs by construction or approximation of fixpoints. In *4th ACM Symp. on Principles of Programming Languages, POPL 1977*, pages 238–252, 1977.

7. D. Cox, J. Little, and D. O'Shea. *Ideals, varieties, and algorithms*. Springer-Verlag, New York, 1996.
8. T. Dang and O. Maler. Reachability analysis via face lifting. In T. A. Henzinger and S. Sastry, editors, *HSCC*, volume 1386 of *LNCS*, pages 96–109. Springer, 1998.
9. D. R. Grayson and M. E. Stillman. Macaulay 2: A software system for research in algebraic geometry. Available at http://www.math.uiuc.edu/Macaulay2/.
10. N. Halbwachs, Y.-E. Proy, and P. Raymond. Verification of linear hybrid systems by means of convex approximations. In B. Le Charlier, editor, *SAS*, volume 864 of *LNCS*, pages 223–237. Springer, 1994.
11. T. A. Henzinger. The symbolic approach to hybrid systems. Invited tutorial at Intl. Conf. on Computer-Aided Verification, CAV 2002. http://www-cad.eecs.berkeley.edu/~tah/.
12. T. A. Henzinger and P.-H. Ho. A note on abstract interpretation strategies for hybrid automata. In P. Antsaklis, W. Kohn, A. Nerode, and S. Sastry (eds.), editors, *Hybrid Systems II*, volume 999 of *LNCS*, pages 252–264, Berlin, 1995. Springer-Verlag.
13. T. A. Henzinger, P.-H. Ho, and H. Wong-Toi. Algorithmic analysis of nonlinear hybrid systems. *IEEE Transactions on Automatic Control*, 43:540–554, 1998.
14. A. B. Kurzhanski and P. Varaiya. On ellipsoidal techniques for reachability analysis. *Dynamics of Continuous, Discrete and Impulsive Systems Series B: Applications and Algorithms*, 9:347–367, 2002.
15. G. Lafferriere, G. J. Pappas, and S. Yovine. A new class of decidable hybrid systems. In F. W. Vaandrager and J. H. van Schuppen, editors, *HSCC*, volume 1569 of *Lecture Notes in Computer Science*, pages 137–151. Springer, 1999.
16. G. Lafferriere, G. J. Pappas, and S. Yovine. Symbolic reachability computations for families of linear vector fields. *J. Symbolic Computation*, 32(3):231–253, 2001.
17. E. Rodriguez-Carbonell and D. Kapur. An abstract interpretation approach for automatic generation of polynomial invariants. In *11th Static Analysis Symposium (SAS'04)*, volume 3148 of *LNCS*, 2004.
18. S. Sankaranarayanan, H. Sipma, and Z. Manna. Constructing invariants for hybrid systems. In Alur and Pappas [3], pages 539–554.
19. S. Sankaranarayanan, H. Sipma, and Z. Manna. Constructing invariants for hybrid systems. *Formal Methods in System Design*, 2004. Preprint submitted for publication.
20. A. Tiwari. Approximate reachability for linear systems. In O. Maler and A. Pnueli, editors, *Hybrid Systems: Computation and Control, HSCC 2003*, volume 2623 of *Lecture Notes in Computer Science*, pages 514–525. Springer, 2003.
21. A. Tiwari and G. Khanna. Nonlinear systems: Approximating reach sets. In Alur and Pappas [3], pages 600–614.

Modeling, Optimization and Computation for Software Verification*

Mardavij Roozbehani, Eric Feron, and Alexandre Megrestki

Laboratory for Information and Decision Systems (LIDS),
Massachusetts Institute of Technology, Cambridge, MA, U.S.A.
{mardavij, feron, ameg}@mit.edu

Abstract. Modeling and analysis techniques are presented for real-time, safety-critical software. Software analysis is the task of verifying whether the computer code will execute safely, free of run-time errors. The critical properties that prove safe execution include bounded-ness of variables and termination of the program in finite time. In this paper, dynamical system representations of computer programs along with specific models that are pertinent to analysis via an optimization-based search for system invariants are developed. It is shown that the automatic search for system invariants that establish the desired properties of computer code, can be formulated as a convex optimization problem, such as linear programming, semidefinite programming, and/or sum of squares programming.

1 Introduction

Failure of real-time control systems, such as those used in spacecrafts, satellites, multiple coordinating UAVs, automobiles and therapy machines may lead to loss of human life or a huge loss in capital and products. However, safe operation of these safety-critical control systems relies heavily on the embedded software. According to Boeing Co. and Honeywell Inc., software development accounts for $60-80\%$ of the effort spent on the development of complex control systems, while much of this effort is expended on validation and verification of the software after or during its development [10].

While real-time software must satisfy various resource allocation, timing, computation and performance constraints, the very least to require is that the software must execute safely, free of run-time errors. The critical software properties that must be verified/validated for safe execution include: (1) absence of variable overflow, (2) absence of 'array index out-of-bounds' calls, and (3) termination of the functions and sub-functions and if required, the program itself in finite time. Some additional properties that might be desired in a reliable, safety-critical software include: (4) robustness to uncertain inputs, including feedback

---

* This work was supported by the National Science Foundation under Grant CNS-0451865 and by the Boeing Co. under Grant MIT-BA-GTA-1.

M. Morari and L. Thiele (Eds.): HSCC 2005, LNCS 3414, pp. 606–622, 2005.

from analog systems, (5) validity of certain inequalities relating inputs and outputs, for instance, passivity and (6) absence of 'dead-code'. Software analysis, is the task of verification of some or all of the above properties.

Cousot [6],[8], published one of the most noteworthy approaches in the literature that deal with software analysis. The main method of verification is based on the notion of *abstract interpretation* of computer programs. See also [9],[21]. According to [6, 7], abstract interpretation is defined as an approximate program semantics derived from the domain of concrete semantic operations by replacing it with a domain of abstract semantic operations. A limitation associated with these methods is the introduction of a narrowing or widening operator, which often causes the method to generate weak invariants, resulting in considerable conservatism in analysis [5]. Nevertheless, these methods have shown to be practical for the verification of several properties of real-time, safety-critical systems such as large-sized avionics systems. Alternative methods aiming at generating stronger statements about the evolution of variables in software systems might be found, for example, in the model-checking literature; however, the trade-off often achieved by these methods is that of increased accuracy and the generation of stronger properties of software (or software model) variables, often at the cost of increased computational requirements and limited scalability to large systems. Moreover, construction of the program models often cannot be fully automated. Recently, there have been renewed efforts at establishing properties of software systems by the combined use of abstractions or, better, bisimulation mechanisms, and applying control theoretic principles to them. Much of the relevant literature in that regard may be found in the recent field of *hybrid systems* [16]. See for instance [11]. In general, it was found that many methods developed in system and control theory for systems driven by differential equations were in principle applicable to hybrid systems, possibly at the price of having to re-develop some elements of theory, e.g. optimal control theory on hybrid systems [20, 15, 4] or control of hybrid systems using bisimulations [18, 17].

In this paper we introduce a systems theoretic approach for software analysis. We present modeling techniques through the introduction of linear-like models that may represent a broad range of computer programs of interest to this paper. These include single flow programs and gain scheduled piecewise linear systems, used to control physical devices such as aerospace systems or automotive control systems. The main method of verification is an optimization-based search for system invariants. We; therefore, suggest specific Lyapunov-like functions, whose properties guarantee variable bounded-ness as well as other desired properties, such as guaranteed program termination. We also show how the search for these system invariants may be formulated as a convex optimization problem, such as linear programming, semi-definite programming and/or a sums of squares problem. At the end, we sketch the *block-wise analysis* procedure for improving the scalability of the proposed methods as analysis of large-size computer programs is undertaken.

2   Automated Software Analysis: Preliminaries

In this section we introduce the fundamentals of software analysis through dynamical system models. We consider computer programs as dynamical systems and introduce certain Lyapunov-like functions as certificates for the behavior of these systems.

2.1   Computer Programs as Dynamical Systems

We view a computer program as a dynamical system which defines the rules for iterative modification of operating memory, possibly in response to real-time inputs. In particular, we consider models defined in general by a *state space* set X with selected subsets $X_0 \subset X$ of *initial states* and $X_\infty \subset X$ of *terminal states*, and by a set-valued function $f : X \mapsto 2^X$, such that $f(x) \subset X_\infty, \forall x \in X_\infty$. The dynamical system $\mathcal{S} = \mathcal{S}(X, f, X_0, X_\infty)$ defined by X, f, X_0, X_∞ is understood as the set of all sequences $\mathcal{X} = (x(0), x(1), \ldots, x(t), \ldots)$ of elements from X satisfying

$$
\begin{aligned}
& x\,(0) \in X_0, \qquad x\,(t+1) \in f\,(x\,(t)) \quad \forall t \in \mathbb{Z}_+ \\
& \text{s.t. } f(x) \subset X_\infty, \forall x \in X_\infty
\end{aligned}
\tag{1}
$$

The uncertainty in the definition of $x(0)$ represents the programs's dependence on parameters, and the uncertainty in the definition of $x(t+1)$ represents program's ability to respond to real-time inputs. From this viewpoint, analysis of software means verification of certain properties of system (1). In Section 4, we elaborate on the dynamical systems view of computer programs and suggest specific models that are essentially equivalent to (1), yet are more suitable for analysis purposes.

Definition 1. *A computer program represented by a dynamical system $\mathcal{S} = \mathcal{S}(X, f, X_0, X_\infty)$ is said to terminate in finite time if every solution $\mathcal{X} = x(t)$ of (1) satisfies $x(t) \in X_\infty$ for some $t \in \mathbb{Z}_+$. In addition, we say that the state variables remain bounded (do not overflow) if $\forall t \in \mathbb{Z}_+$, $x(t)$ does not belong to a certain (unsafe) subset X_- of X for every solution $\mathcal{X} = x(t)$ of (1).*

2.2   Lyapunov Functions as Behavior Certificates

Definition 2. *A Lyapunov function for system (1) is defined to be a function $V : X \mapsto \mathbb{R}$ such that*

$$
V\,(\bar{x}) < \theta V\,(x) \quad \forall x \in X, \ \bar{x} \in f\,(x) : x \notin X_\infty.
\tag{2}
$$

where θ is a positive constant.

Remark 1. The parameter θ in the above definition, is very important in providing the flexibility required for designing appropriate Lyapunov functions that establish finite-time termination and/or bounded-ness. For instance if $V\,(x_0) < 0$ and $\theta \geq 1$, (2) implies that V must strictly monotonically decrease along the trajectories of (1) until they reach a terminal state. As we will see in the sequel, this is suitable for establishing finite-time termination. However, with $V(x_0) < 0$ and $\theta < 1$, V is not required to decrease along the trajectories of (1), while it remains negative. This is very important in proving absence of overflow in computer programs without the finite-time termination property.

Termination in finite time. The following Theorem provides a useful criterion for verifying finite-time termination in software analysis.

Theorem 1. *If there exists a bounded function $V : X \mapsto \mathbb{R}^-$, and a constant $\theta > 1$ satisfying*

$$V(\bar{x}) < \theta V(x) \quad \forall x \in X, \ \bar{x} \in f(x) : x \notin X_\infty. \tag{3}$$

then a terminal state X_∞ will be reached in a finite number of steps.

Proof. Since V is bounded, there exists $M \in \mathbb{R}^+$, such that $-M \leq V(x) < 0$, $\forall x \in X$. Now, assume that there exists a sequence $\mathcal{X} = (x(0), x(1), \ldots, x(t), \ldots)$ of elements from X satisfying (1) that does not reach a terminal state in finite time. I.e. $x(t) \notin X_\infty, \forall t \in \mathbb{Z}^+$. Then, $V(x(t)) < -M$ for

$$t > \frac{\log M - \log |V(x(0))|}{\log \theta}, \tag{4}$$

which contradicts bounded-ness of V.

Absence of overflow. We already saw that absence of overflow can be characterized by avoidance of an unsafe subset X_- of the state space X. Consider a Lyapunov function V, defined according to (2). Define the level sets $\mathcal{L}_r(V)$ of V, by

$$\mathcal{L}_r(V) = \{x \in X : V(x) < r\}$$

These level sets are invariant with respect to (1), in the sense that $x(t+1) \in \mathcal{L}_r(V)$ whenever $x(t) \in \mathcal{L}_r(V)$. We use this fact, along with the monotonicity property of V, to establish a separation between the reachable set and the unsafe region of the state space.

Theorem 2. *Consider the system (1) and let $\mathcal{V}$ denote the space of all Lyapunov functions for this system satisfying (2) with some $\theta \geq 1$. An unsafe subset X_- of the state space X can never be reached along all the trajectories of (1) if there exists $V \in \mathcal{V}$ satisfying*

$$\inf_{x \in X_-} V(x) \geq \sup_{x \in X_0} V(x) \tag{5}$$

In addition, if

$$\inf_{x \in X_-} V(x) \geq 0 \tag{6}$$

then, $\theta > 0$ is sufficient.

Proof. The proof proceeds by contradiction. First consider the $\theta \geq 1$ case and assume that (1) has a solution $\mathcal{X} = (x\,(0)\,, x\,(1)\,, ..., x\,(t_-)\,, ...)$, where $x\,(0) \in X_0$ and $x\,(t_-) \in X_-$. Since $V\,(x)$ is strictly monotonically decreasing along any solution of (1), we must have:

$$\inf_{x \in X_-} V(x) \leq V\,(x\,(t_-)) < V\,(x\,(0)) \leq \sup_{x \in X_0} V(x) \qquad (7)$$

which contradicts (5). Now, consider the case $\theta < 1$ for which monotonicity of V is not always implied. Partition X_0 into subsets $\overline{X}_0$ and $\underline{X}_0$ such that $X_0 = \overline{X}_0 \cup \underline{X}_0$ and

$$V\,(x) \leq 0 \qquad \forall x \in \underline{X}_0$$
$$V\,(x) > 0 \qquad \forall x \in \overline{X}_0$$

Note that either of $\overline{X}_0$ and $\underline{X}_0$ may happen to be empty. Now, assume that (1) has a solution $\overline{\mathcal{X}} = (\overline{x}\,(0)\,, x\,(1)\,, ..., x\,(t_-)\,, ...)$, where $\overline{x}\,(0) \in \overline{X}_0$ and $x\,(t_-) \in X_-$. Note that by assumption, $V\,(x\,(t_-)) \geq 0$ and thus

$$V\,(x\,(t)) > 0 \qquad \forall t < t_-$$

$V\,(x\,(t))$ is therefore strictly monotonically decreasing over the sequence $\overline{x}\,(0)$ to $x\,(t_-)$. Hence, (7) must hold, which contradicts (5). Finally, assume that (1) has a solution $\underline{\mathcal{X}} = (\underline{x}\,(0)\,, x\,(1)\,, ..., x\,(t_-)\,, ...)$, where $\underline{x}\,(0) \in \underline{X}_0$ and $x\,(t_-) \in X_-$. In this case, we must have $V\,(x\,(t)) \leq 0, \forall t$. This implies that $V\,(x\,(t_-)) < 0$, which contradicts (6). Proof is complete.

Now, we turn our attention to development of general forms for system invariants that establish the desired properties and are appropriate for use in a convex optimization framework. Among several properties of a reliable software mentioned earlier, absence of overflow and finite-time termination are expected in most applications.

Theorem 3. *Consider the dynamical system* $\mathcal{S} = \mathcal{S}(X, f, X_0, X_\infty)$ *defined by* *(1) and assume that there exists a real-valued function* $V : X \mapsto \mathbb{R}$ *such that*

$$V\,(x) < 0 \quad \forall x \in X_0. \qquad (8)$$
$$V\,(\overline{x}) < \theta V\,(x) \quad \forall x \in X,\ \overline{x} \in f\,(x) : x \notin X_\infty. \qquad (9)$$
$$V\,(x) > \left\| \frac{x}{M} \right\|^2 - 1 \quad \forall x \in X. \qquad (10)$$

where $\theta \in \mathbb{R}^+$ *is a constant, and no constraint on finiteness of the state space* X *is imposed. Then, every solution* $\mathcal{X} = x\,(t)$ *of (1) remains bounded in the safe region defined by* $|x_i| < M$, *where each* x_i *is a component of the state vector* x. *Moreover, if* $\theta > 1$, *every solution* $\mathcal{X} = x\,(t)$ *reaches a terminal state* X_∞ *in finite time.*

Proof. Note that (8) and (9) imply non-positivity of $V(x)$ on $X \setminus X_\infty$. Moreover, by (10), $V(x)$ is bounded from below by -1. Therefore, $V(x) \in (-1, 0)$. By Theorem 1, (9) implies finite-time termination. Also, the unsafe region X_- is defined by $|x_i| \geq M$. Therefore,

$$\left\| \frac{x}{M} \right\|^2 \geq 1, \ \forall x \in X_-,$$

$$\inf_{x \in X_-} V(x) = 0 \geq 0 = \sup_{x \in X_0} V(x)$$

Theorem 2 then completes the proof.

Remark 2. By imposing a quadratic form on V, the search for a Lyapunov-like function satisfying (8) $-$ (10) reduces to a semidefinite program [1]. As an alternative, imposing a linear or piecewise linear form on V, along with replacing condition (10) with $2n$ constraints

$$V(x) > \frac{x_i}{M} - 1 \ \forall x \in X, \ i = 1..n$$

$$V(x) > -\frac{x_i}{M} - 1 \ \forall x \in X, \ i = 1..n$$

converts the problem of finding an appropriate system invariant to linear or mixed integer/linear programming [3]. Another possibility is to let V be a polynomial function of the state variables x_i. In this case, the search for system invariants restricted to the class of polynomials with real coefficients can be formulated as a sums of squares problem [22],[23].

3   Models of Computer Programs

In this section we develop specific models of software that are convenient for analysis purposes. Practical considerations such as convenience for automated parsing/compiling, availability of an efficient relaxation technique and compatibility with a particular numerical engine for convex optimization influence the choice of modeling language.

3.1   Mixed Integer/Linear Systems

With the following Proposition, we first provide the motivation/intuition behind using this model for software systems. (The statement of the proposition was formulated in [14]. The authors were not able to find a published proof of the proposition as stated below. Also, compare with [2].)

Proposition 1. *Universality of mixed-integer linear models. Let f be any arbitrary piece-wise affine function defined on a compact state space X, which consists of finite unions of finite polytopes. Then, f can be defined precisely, by* *imposing linear equality constraints on a finite number of binary variables and a finite number of analog variables ranging over bounded intervals. I.e.*

There exists matrices F and H, such that

$$f(x) = \{F[x; w; v; 1] : \text{ s.t. } \exists w \in [-1, 1]^q, \exists v \in \{-1, 1\}^r \text{ s.t. } H[x; w; v; 1] = 0\}$$

Proof. The proof is by construction. First, notice that without loss of generality we may assume that $x \in [-1, 1]^n$. Now, let $X = \bigcup_{i=1}^{i=N} X_k$, where each X_i is defined by a finite set of linear inequality constraints. I.e.

$$X_i := \{x \mid \mathbf{a}_{ki}^T x \le b_{ki}, \ k = 1, ..., N_i\} \tag{11}$$

Note that by definition $f(x) = 2A_i x + 2B_i \quad x \in X_i$, where the constant 2 appears for convenience in notation only. Now, assign a binary variable $v_i \in \{-1, 1\}$, to each X_i, $i = 1...N - 1$, according to the following rule,

$$v_i = 1 \iff x \in X_i, \ v_i = -1 \iff x \notin X_i, i = 1, ...N - 1 \tag{12}$$

$$\sum_{i=1}^{i=N-1} v_i = -N + 1 \iff x \in X_N, \quad \sum_{i=1}^{i=N-1} v_i = -N + 3 \iff x \notin X_N$$

Then we have

$$f(x) = \sum_{i=1}^{N-1} (1 + v_i)(A_i x + B_i) - (N - 3)(A_N x + B_N) - \sum_{i=1}^{N-1} v_i (A_N x + B_N),$$

subject to

$$\sum_{i=1}^{i=N-1} v_i \le -N + 3, \text{ and } (12), \text{ and } v_i \in \{-1, 1\}, \ i = 1...N \tag{13}$$

Now, we need to relate (11) and (12), which is done in the following way;

$$x \in X_i \iff (\mathbf{a}_{ki}^T x - b_{ki})(v_i + 1) \le 0, \ k = 1, ..., N_i \tag{14}$$

Since by assumption, each X_i is bounded,

$$\underline{R}_{ki} := \min_{x \in X_i} \mathbf{a}_{ki}^T x - b_{ki}$$

exists and is finite. Therefore, the condition $x \in X_i$, is equivalent to,

$$\mathbf{a}_{ki}^T x v_i + \mathbf{a}_{ki}^T x - b_{ki} v_i - b_{ki} - \underline{R}_{ki}(w_{ki} + 1) = 0, \ w_{ki} \in [-1, 1], \ k = 1, ..., N_i \tag{15}$$

Next, define auxiliary state vectors $y_i := x v_i \in \mathbb{R}^n$. Notice that y_i is the multiplication of an analog variable x, and a binary variable v_i. We represent this (nonlinear) transformation by an affine transformation involving auxiliary analog variables $z_i \in [-1, 1]^n$, and $\overline{z}_i \in [-1, 1]^n$, subject to a set of linear constraints, in the following way,

$$y_i = 4z_i - x - v_i \mathbf{1}_n - \mathbf{1}_n, \quad z_i \le \frac{(v_i + 1)}{2} \mathbf{1}_n$$

$$z_i \ge 0, \quad \overline{z}_i \le -v_i \mathbf{1}_n, \quad z_i = \frac{1}{2}(x - \overline{z}_i)$$

equivalently,

$$y_i = 4z_i - x - v_i \mathbf{1}_n - \mathbf{1}_n, \quad i = 1, .., N \tag{16a}$$

$$z_i + \frac{1}{2}\left(W_i^1 + I_n\right)\mathbf{1}_n = \frac{(v_i + 1)}{2}\mathbf{1}_n \tag{16b}$$

$$z_i = \frac{1}{2}\left(W_i^2 + I_n\right)\mathbf{1}_n \tag{16c}$$

$$\overline{z}_i + \frac{1}{2}\left(W_i^3 + I_n\right)\mathbf{1}_n = -v_i \mathbf{1}_n \tag{16d}$$

$$z_i = \frac{1}{2}(x - \overline{z}_i) \tag{16e}$$

where W_i^k is defined by

$$W_i^k = \mathrm{diag}\left\{w_{ji}^k, \ j = 1, .., n\right\}, \ i = 1, .., N, \ k = 1, .., 3, \ w_{ij}^k \in [-1, 1]$$

Now, let $X_e = \begin{bmatrix} x & y_1 & \cdots & y_n & z_1 & \cdots & z_n & \overline{z}_1 & \cdots & \overline{z}_n & w & v & 1 \end{bmatrix}^T$, where $w = \begin{bmatrix} w_{11} & \cdots & w_{NN} & w_{11}^1 & \cdots & w_{Nn}^1 & \cdots & w_{Nn}^3 \end{bmatrix}$, and $v = \begin{bmatrix} v_1 & \cdots & v_n \end{bmatrix}$. Then,

$$f(x) := \left[\sum_{i=1}^{N-1} A_i - (N-3)A_N\right] x + \begin{bmatrix} A_1 - A_N & \cdots & A_{N-1} - A_N \end{bmatrix} y \tag{17}$$

$$+ \begin{bmatrix} B_1 - B_N & \cdots & B_{N-1} - B_N \end{bmatrix} v + \sum_{i=1}^{N-1} B_i + (-N+3)B_N$$

which is linear in x, y, v. Moreover, (17) is subject to constraints (13), (15), (16), which are all linear equality constraints in X_e. This completes the proof.

So far, we have shown that imposing linear equality constraints on Boolean variables and on analog variables ranging over bounded intervals allows one to define arbitrary piecewise linear functions on finite unions of polytopes. This observation serves as the basis for introducing the widely used class of models which will be referred to as *mixed integer/linear systems* here. These models are capable of providing relatively brief descriptions of complicated dependencies.

A mixed integer/linear system model has state space $X \subset \mathbb{R}^n$. Its state transition function $f : X \mapsto 2^X$ is defined by two matrices F, H of dimensions n-by-$(n + q + r + 1)$ and p-by-$(n + q + r + 1)$, according to

$$f(x) = \{F[x; w; v; 1] :$$

$$\exists w \in [-1, 1]^q, \exists v \in \{-1, 1\}^r \text{ s.t. } H[x; w; v; 1] = 0\}$$

Natural Lyapunov function candidates for mixed integer/linear systems are quadratic functionals. Within this class, checking monotonicity of Lyapunov functions along system trajectories can be done by application of the traditional quadratic relaxation techniques, starting with those used in deriving the bounds for the MAX-CUT problem [19], which leads to semidefinite programming as the Lyapunov function design tool.

Search for Lyapunov invariants using linear or semidefinite programming. This section details our approach to compute Lyapunov invariants for mixed integer/linear software models. Looking for a function V satisfying (8) – (10), may be seen an infinite-dimensional convex programming problem in the unknown V. This may be solved by first defining an appropriate, finite-dimensional parameterization of V and then solving the resulting finite-dimensional, convex optimization problem.

Linear parameterization of quadratic Lyapunov functions appear as

$$V(x) := \begin{bmatrix} x \\ 1 \end{bmatrix}^T P \begin{bmatrix} x \\ 1 \end{bmatrix}$$

where P is a constant, symmetric matrix.

For the Lyapunov invariant parameterization considered above, the problem of finding an invariant that satisfies the conditions (8)−(10) is about solving a set of nonlinear constraints arising from these conditions. These conditions are often non-convex conditions, which makes their exact solution often impractical, but, fortunately also unnecessary. Instead, we will focus on using relaxed versions of these conditions, which are much easier to solve using either linear or semidefinite optimization routines. The main tool used towards obtaining these relaxations is a Lagrangian relaxation procedure also known as S-procedure.

For example, the first of the three conditions does not require such a procedure, since it is a linear constraint on the coefficients of P: Indeed, the requirement $V(x(0)) < 0$ may also be written as,

$$\begin{bmatrix} \frac{x(0)}{M} \\ 1 \end{bmatrix}^T P \begin{bmatrix} \frac{x(0)}{M} \\ 1 \end{bmatrix} < 0. \tag{18}$$

where M is the overflow limit. The second condition, (9), may be written as

$$\begin{bmatrix} \frac{F.[x(k)\ v(k)\ w(k)\ 1]}{M} \\ 1 \end{bmatrix}^T P \begin{bmatrix} \frac{F.[x(k)\ v(k)\ w(k)\ 1]}{M} \\ 1 \end{bmatrix} < \theta \begin{bmatrix} \frac{x(k)}{M} \\ 1 \end{bmatrix} P \begin{bmatrix} \frac{x(k)}{M} \\ 1 \end{bmatrix} \tag{19}$$

for any $x(k)$, $v(k)$, $w(k)$ satisfying

$$H.\left[x(k)\ w(k)\ v(k)\ 1 \right]^T = 0 \text{ and } w(k) \in [-1,1]^q,\ v(k) \in \{-1,1\}^r \tag{20}$$

The constraint $v \in \{-1,1\}^r$ is equivalent to the quadratic constraint

$$v^T M_1 v - \sum_{i=1}^{r} \mu_{i,1} = 0, \text{ with } M_1 = \text{diag}\left\{\mu_{1,1},\ \mu_{2,1},\ \cdots \mu_{r,1}\right\}$$

for arbitrary $\mu_{i,1} \in \mathbb{R}$, $i = 1, \ldots r$. Likewise, the constraint $w \in [1,1]^q$ is equivalent to

$$w^T E_1 w - \sum_{i=1}^{q} \eta_{i,1} \leq 0, \text{ with } E_1 = \text{diag}\left\{\eta_{1,1}, \eta_{2,1}, \ldots \eta_{q,1}\right\}$$

for arbitrary $\eta_{i,1} > 0$, $i = 1, \ldots q$. Formulating the proper Lagrangian relaxation, condition (19) holds whenever condition (20) holds if there exists $P, M_1, E_1 \geq 0$ and $y_1 \in \mathbb{R}^{s_x \times n_H}$ such that

$$L_1^T P L_1 - \theta L_2^T P L_2 < y_1 H_M + H_M^T y_1^T + L_3^T M_1 L_3 + L_4^T E_1 L_4 - L_5^T \left(\text{Tr } M_1 + \text{Tr } E_1\right) L_5 \tag{21}$$

where

$$H_M := [M h_x \ h_w \ h_v \ h_1], \quad F_M := \left[f_x \ \frac{f_w}{M} \ \frac{f_v}{M} \ \frac{f_1}{M}\right]$$

$$L_1 := \begin{bmatrix} F_M \\ 0_{1 \times (s_x - 1)} \ 1 \end{bmatrix}, \quad L_2 := \begin{bmatrix} I_n & 0_{n \times (s_x - n)} \\ 0_{1 \times (s_x - 1)} & 1 \end{bmatrix}$$

$$L_3 := [I_{n+q} \ 0_{(n+q) \times (r+1)}], \quad L_4 := [0_{(r+1) \times (n+q)} \ I_{r+1}], \quad L_5 := [0_{1 \times (s_x - 1)} \ 1]$$

Likewise, (10) may be written as

$$\begin{bmatrix} \frac{x(k)}{M} \\ 1 \end{bmatrix}^T \begin{bmatrix} I_n & 0 \\ 0 & -1 \end{bmatrix} \begin{bmatrix} \frac{x(k)}{M} \\ 1 \end{bmatrix} < \begin{bmatrix} \frac{x(k)}{M} \\ 1 \end{bmatrix}^T P \begin{bmatrix} \frac{x(k)}{M} \\ 1 \end{bmatrix} \tag{22}$$

for any $x(k)$, $v(k)$, $w(k)$ satisfying

$$H. \left[x(k) \ w(k) \ v(k) \ 1\right]^T = 0 \text{ and } w(k) \in [-1, 1]^q, \ v(k) \in \{-1, 1\}^r \tag{23}$$

Thus condition (22) holds whenever condition (23) holds if there exists $P, M_2, E_2 \geq 0$ and $y_2 \in \mathbb{R}^{s_x \times n_H}$ such that

$$L_2^T P_0 L_2 - L_2^T P L_2 < y_2 H_M + H_M^T y_2^T + L_3^T M_2 L_3 + L_4^T E_2 L_4 - L_5^T \left(\text{Tr } M_2 + \text{Tr } E_2\right) L_5 \tag{24}$$

Thus, absence of overflow and finite execution time are guaranteed if there exist $P, M_1, M_2, E_1 \geq 0, E_2 \geq 0, y_1$, and y_2 satisfying constraints (18, 21 and 24).

3.2   Linear Systems with Conditional Switching

In this model the state space of the system is the direct product

$$X = \{0, 1, 2, \ldots, m\} \times \mathbb{R}^n$$
$$= \{(k, v) : k \in \mathbb{Z}, \ 0 \leq k \leq m, \ v \in \mathbb{R}^n\}$$

of a discrete set and an n-dimensional Euclidean space, $X_0 = \{(0, v_0)\}$, $X_\infty = \{m\} \times \mathbb{R}^n$. The set-valued state transition map $f : \ X \mapsto 2^X$ is defined by matrices $A_k, B_k, L_k, G_k, H_k, I_k, C_k, D_k$, where $k \in \{0, 1, \ldots, m - 1\}$, as well as by a function $p : \{0, 1, \ldots, m-1\} \mapsto \{0, 1, \ldots, m\}$, according to the following rule:

$$f(k, v) = \{(k+1, A_k v + B_k w + L_k) : \ w \in [-1, 1]\}$$

when $C_k v + D_k \leq 0$ and $k < m$,

$$f(k, v) = \{(p(k), G_k x + H_k w + I_k) : \ w \in [-1, 1]\}$$

when $C_k v + D_k > 0$ and $k < m$, and $f(k, v) = \{m, v\}$ when $k = m$.

In this model, the discrete component k of the state vector $x = (k, v)$ represents the "current line of the code", while v is the real state vector being processed and w represents bounded real-valued input data. All operations allowed are affine, except for the conditional "go to $p(k)$" statements allowed on every line. This model appears to be suitable for programs with simple flow, as well as real-time interactions between simple logic and gain scheduled linear systems.

Natural Lyapunov function candidates for linear systems with conditional switching have the piecewise quadratic or piecewise linear form $V(k, v) = \sigma_k(v)$, where for every $k \in \{0, 1, \ldots, m\}$ the function $\sigma_k : \mathbb{R}^n \mapsto \mathbb{R}$ is a quadratic or an affine functional.

3.3   Trigonometric Polynomial Models

The models described in the previous sections are only capable of describing piecewise linear transformations of analog variables. This is not always convenient: for example, multiplication of two analog state variables can be represented this way only approximately and this representation is particularly cumbersome. In order to cover a larger class of analog operations, the *trigonometric polynomial models* could be useful.

A trigonometric polynomial model has state space X which is a closed subgroup of a poly-thorus $\mathbb{T}^n$, where $\mathbb{T}$ denotes the unit circle in the complex plane. Equivalently, one can think of X as a direct product of sets of the form $\mathbb{T}^k$ or $\mathbb{Z}_q^k$, where $\mathbb{Z}_q$ denotes the set of all complex numbers z such that $z^q = 1$. The word "trigonometric" refers to the natural parameterizations

$$\mathbb{T} = \{\cos(t) + j\sin(t) : \ t \in \mathbb{R}\}$$

of the unit circle. The state transition map $f : X \mapsto 2^X$ is defined by a vector polynomial p with respect to $2 * n + k$ complex variables, according to

$$f(x) = \{y \in X : \ p(y, x, z) = 0 \text{ for some } z \in \mathbb{T}^k\}.$$

Natural Lyapunov function candidates for trigonometric polynomial models are real-valued trigonometric polynomials. Checking validity of a Lyapunov function candidate reduces to verification of positivity of a trigonometric polynomial subject to a set of polynomial constraints, which can be done using the Shor's "sums of squares" argument: A polynomial is positive if it can be represented as a sum of squares of polynomials. While it is not true that a positive polynomial can always be represented as a sum of squares of polynomials, it can be shown that the equivalence holds in the case of *trigonometric polynomials*.

4   A Numerical Example

Consider the following program:

$$x_1 = 0; x_2 = 0;$$
$$\text{while } x_2 \leq 100,$$
$$\quad \text{if } x_1 \geq 0,$$
$$\qquad x_1 = x_1 - a;$$
$$\quad \text{else}$$
$$\qquad x_1 = x_1 + b;$$
$$\quad \text{end}$$
$$\quad x_2 = x_2 + 1;$$
$$\text{end}$$

where $a \in [100, 900]$ and $b \in [200, 800]$, are uncertain input parameters. Using 2 slack variables and 1 binary variable, a mixed integer/linear model of this piece of code is defined by matrices F, and H, given as:

$$x(0) = \begin{bmatrix} 0 \\ 0 \end{bmatrix}, \; n = 2, \; q = 2, \; r = 1.$$

$$F = \begin{bmatrix} 1 & 0 & 0 & 0 & -\frac{a+b}{2} & \frac{b-a}{2} \\ 0 & 1 & 0 & 0 & 0 & 1 \end{bmatrix}, \; H = \begin{bmatrix} 1 & 0 & -\frac{M}{2} & 0 & -\frac{M}{2} & 0 \\ 0 & 1 & 0 & R & 0 & R - 100 \end{bmatrix}, \; R = \frac{M+100}{2},$$

Given $M = 1000$ as the overflow limit, using $(18), (21), (24)$, the quadratic Lyapunov function

$$V(x) = \frac{1}{2000} x_1^2 - \frac{1}{5000} x_1 - \frac{1777}{1000} x_2 - \frac{201}{10000} x_2^2 - \frac{3}{10000}$$

was found to prove bounded-ness and finite-time termination for all a and b.

5   Block-Wise Analysis of Computer Programs

Block-wise analysis is a method for improving the scalability/computational cost of the above techniques as analysis of large size computer programs is undertaken. The basic idea here is to consider large-size software as the interconnection of smaller size dynamical systems (functions, subfunctions and procedures that we call them "blocks"). These so called blocks interact via a subset of the program states called "global variables". Correctness of each block is established separately, known *a priori*, or assumed temporarily. The dynamics of each block is then abstracted/approximated by equalities and/or inequalities relating the inputs and the outputs. In obvious cases, abstractions of this level may be provided by the programmer to facilitate the analysis task. This way, the states/variables that are local to each block are eliminated from the global model. Correctness of the software will be established by verifying bounded-ness of global variables, as well as verifying that when required, a final global state will be reached in finite-time. In case correctness of some of the blocks were assumed temporarily, their correctness need to be established rigorously, subject to the bounds available now, for global variables. To further clarify the concept, we implement the method on the following example.

```
typedef enum {FALSE = 0, TRUE = 1} BOOLEAN;
BOOLEAN INIT1, INIT2; float P, X;

void filter1 () {
    static float E[2], S[2];
    if (INIT1) {
        S[0] = X;      P = X;
        E[0] = X;      E[1]=0;      S[1]=0;
    } else {
        P =0.5*X–0.7*E[0]+0.4*E[1]+1.5*S[0]–S[1]*0.7;
        E[1] = E[0];
        E[0] = X;
        S[1] = S[0];
        S[0] = P;
        X=P/6+S[1]/5;
    }
}

void filter2 () {
    static float E2[2], S2[2];
    if (INIT2) {
        S2[0] =0.5*X;    P = X;
        E2[0] = 0.8*X;    E2[1]=0;    S2[1]=0;
    } else {
        P =0.3*X–E2[0]*0.2+E2[1]*1.4+S2[0]*0.5–S2[1]*1.7;
        E2[1] = 0.5*E2[0];
        E2[0] = 2*X;
        S2[1] = S2[0]+10;
        S2[0] = P/2+S2[1]/3;
        X=P/8+S2[1]/10;
    }
}

void main () {
    X = 0;    INIT1 = TRUE;    INIT2=TRUE;
    while (1) {
        X = 0.98 * X + 85;
        if (abs(X)<= 400) {
            filter1 ();
            X=X+100;
            INIT1=FALSE;
        } else if (abs(X)<=800) {
```

```
        filter 2();
        X=X-50;
        INIT2=FALSE;
    }
}}
```

For automated (block-wise) analysis of this program, the analyzer must be provided (either by a compiler or by the programmer) with the system invariant that prior to each execution of filter1(), $|X| \leq 400$. Next, filter() is modeled in the following abstracted way:

$w_x \in [-1, 1]$, $s_0(0) \in [-400, 400]$, $e_0(0) \in [-400, 400]$,
$P(0) \in [-400, 400]$, $s_1(0) = 0$, $e_1(0) = 0$.

$$\begin{bmatrix} P(k+1) \\ e_1(k+1) \\ e_0(k+1) \\ s_1(k+1) \\ s_0(k+1) \end{bmatrix} = \begin{bmatrix} 0 & 0.4 & -0.7 & -0.7 & 1.5 & 0.5 \times 400 & 0 \\ 0 & 0 & 1 & 0 & 0 & 0 & 0 \\ 0 & 0 & 0 & 0 & 0 & 1 \times 400 & 0 \\ 0 & 0 & 0 & 0 & 1 & 0 & 0 \\ 0 & 0.4 & -0.7 & -0.7 & 1.5 & 0.5 \times 400 & 0 \end{bmatrix} \begin{bmatrix} P(k) \\ e_1(k) \\ e_0(k) \\ s_1(k) \\ s_0(k) \\ w_x(k) \\ 1 \end{bmatrix}$$

Due to the presence of static variables e and s, bounded-ness of the above recursion for an infinite number of iteration must be verified. Using LMIs $(18) - (24)$ with $\theta = 0.9$, $\left\| \begin{bmatrix} P & e_1 & e_0 & s_1 & s_0 \end{bmatrix} \right\| \leq 2038$ was proved.

$$\left\| \begin{bmatrix} P & e_1 & e_0 & s_1 & s_0 \end{bmatrix} \right\| \leq 2038 \rightarrow \left\| \begin{bmatrix} P & s_1 \end{bmatrix} \right\| \leq 2038$$

$$|X| = \left| \frac{P}{6} + \frac{s_1}{5} \right| \leq 2038 \sqrt{\left(\frac{1}{6} \right)^2 + \left(\frac{1}{5} \right)^2} \simeq 531$$

This proves that in the worst case, the value of X, after execution of filter1() cannot be greater than 531. Similarly, prior to each execution of filter2(), $|X| \leq 800$ is invariant. Next, filter2() is modeled in the following abstracted way:

$w_x \in [-1, 1]$, $s2_0(0) \in [-400, 400]$, $e2_0(0) \in [-640, 640]$,
$P(0) \in [-800, 800]$, $s2_1(0) = 0$, $e2_1(0) = 0$.

$$\begin{bmatrix} P(k+1) \\ e2_1(k+1) \\ e2_0(k+1) \\ s2_1(k+1) \\ s2_0(k+1) \end{bmatrix} = \begin{bmatrix} 0 & 1.4 & -0.2 & -1.7 & 0.5 & 0.3 \times 800 & 0 \\ 0 & 0 & 0.5 & 0 & 0 & 0 & 0 \\ 0 & 0 & 0 & 0 & 0 & 2 \times 800 & 0 \\ 0 & 0 & 0 & 0 & 1 & 0 & 10 \\ 0 & \frac{1.4}{2} & \frac{-0.2}{2} & \frac{-1.7}{2} & \frac{1}{3} + \frac{0.5}{2} & \frac{0.3 \times 800}{2} & \frac{10}{3} \end{bmatrix} \begin{bmatrix} P(k) \\ e2_1(k) \\ e2_0(k) \\ s2_1(k) \\ s2_0(k) \\ w_x(k) \\ 1 \end{bmatrix}$$

Again, using LMIs $(18) - (24)$ with $\theta = 0.9$, $\left\| \begin{bmatrix} P & e_1 & e_0 & s_1 & s_0 \end{bmatrix} \right\| \leq 9935$ was proved.

$$\left\|\left[P\ e_1\ e_0\ s_1\ s_0\right]\right\| \le 9935 \to \left\|\left[P\ s_1\right]\right\| \le 9935$$

$$|X| = \left|\frac{P}{8} + \frac{s_1}{10}\right| \le 9935\sqrt{\left(\frac{1}{8}\right)^2 + \left(\frac{1}{10}\right)^2} \simeq 1591$$

This in turn, proves that in the worst case, the value of X, after execution of filter2() cannot be greater than 1591. The main program is now abstracted in the following way.

```
void main () {
    X = 0;
    while (1) {
        X = 0.98 * X + 85;
        if (abs(X)<= 400) {
            X=531*w1; % w1∈ [−1, 1], for block-wise analysis filter1() is
                       % abstracted by a simple input-output map.
            X=X+100;
        } else if (abs(X)<=800) {
            X=1591*w2; % w2∈ [−1, 1], for block-wise analysis filter2() is
                       % abstracted by a simple input-output map.
            X=X−50;
        }
}}
```

Using the explained methods, analysis of this program in turn proves that $|X| \le 4560$. Therefore, regarding that X, P, S, E are *floating point* variables, we proved that a run-time error due to an overflow in program variables cannot occur.

6   Conclusions

A new framework for analysis of real-time software was introduced. It was shown that software can be viewed/modeled as a dynamical system. Specific models carrying this task were also introduced. System invariants, found by convex optimization of certain Lyapunov-like functions prove the desired properties of the software. These properties include bounded-ness of all variables within safe regions and finite time termination of the program. To improve scalability of these techniques for application to large-size computer programs, the method of block-wise analysis of computer code was suggested. It was shown through a numerical example, how this method can be applied.

References

1. S. Boyd, L.E. Ghaoui, E. Feron, and V. Balakrishnan. Linear Matrix Inequalities in Systems and Control Theory. Society for Industrial and Applied Mathematics, 1994.

2. A. Bemporad, D. Mignone, and M. Morari. Moving horizon estimation for hybrid systems and fault detection. In Proc. American Control Conference, June 1999, Pages:2471–2475.
3. D. Bertsimas, and J. Tsitsikilis. Introduction to Linear Optimization. Athena Scientific, 1997.
4. M. S. Branicky, V. S. Borkar, and S. K. Mitter. A unified framework for hybrid control: model and optimal control theory. IEEE Transactions on Automatic Control, 43(1):31-45, 1998.
5. M. A. Colon, S. Sankaranarayanan, H. B. Sipma. Linear invariant generation using non-linear constraint solving. In Computer Aided Verification (CAV 2003), vol. 2725 of Lecture Notes in Computer Science, Springer Verlag, pp. 420-433.
6. P. Cousot and R. Cousot. Abstract interpretation: a unified lattice model for static analysis of programs by construction or approximation of fixpoints. In Proc. 4th ACM SIGPLAN-SIGACT Symposium on Principles of Programming Languages, POPL '77, pages 238–252, 1977.
7. P. Cousot, and R. Cousot. Systematic design of program analysis frameworks. In Conference Record of the Sixth Annual ACM SIGPLAN-SIGACT Symposium on Principles of Programming Languages, pages 269–282, San Antonio, Texas, 1979. ACM Press, New York.
8. P. Cousot. Semantic foundations of program analysis. In S. Muchnick and N. Jones, editors, Program Flow Analysis: Theory and Applications, chapter 10, pages 303–342. Prentice-Hall, 1981.
9. D. Dams. Abstract interpretation and partition refinement for Model Checking. Ph.D. Thesis, Eindhoven University of Technology, 1996.
10. B. S. Heck, L. M. Wills, and G. J. Vachtsevanos. Software technology for implementing reusable, distributed control systems. IEEE Control Systems Magazine, 23(1): 21–35, 2003.
11. S. Prajna, and A. Jadbabaie. Safety verification of hybrid systems using barrier certificates. Hybrid Systems: Computation and Control. Springer-Verlag lecture notes in computer science, March 2004.
12. M. Johansson, and A. Rantzer. On the computation of piecewise quadratic Lyapunov functions. In Proc. 36th IEEE Conference on Decision and Control, San Diego, California, December 1997.
13. M. Johansson, and A. Rantzer. Computation of piecewise quadratic Lyapunov functions for hybrid systems. IEEE Transactions on Automatic Control, 43(4), pp. 555-559, April 1998.
14. J. Harper, A. Megretski. Personal communication, 2000.
15. S. Hedlund and A. Rantzer. Optimal control of hybrid systems. In Proc. 38th IEEE Conference on Decision and Control, Phoenix, Arizona, December 1999.
16. R. Alur, and G. J. Pappas (Eds.): Hybrid Systems: Computation and Control, 7th International Workshop, Lecture Notes in Computer Science, volume 2993, Springer Verlag, March 2004.
17. G. Lafferriere, G. J. Pappas, and S. Sastry. Hybrid systems with finite bisimulations. Hybrid Systems V, Lecture Notes in Computer Science, volume 1567, Springer 1999.
18. G. Lafferriere, G. J. Pappas, and S. Sastry. Reachability analysis of hybrid systems using bisimulations. In Proc. of the 37th IEEE Conference on Decision and Control, pages 1623-1628, Tampa, 1998.
19. M. Laurent. Tighter linear and semidefinite relaxations for max-cut based on the Lovász–Schrijver Lift-and-Project procedure. SIAM Journal on Optimization, 12(2):345–375.

20. J. Lygeros, C. Tomlin, and S. Sastry. Controllers for reachability specifications for hybrid systems. Automatica, 35(3):349-370, 1999.
21. D. Monniaux. Abstract interpretation of programs as Markov decision processes. In Static Analysis Symposium, volume 2694 in Lecture Notes in Computer Science, pages 237-254, Springer Verlag, 2003.
22. P. A. Parrilo. Minimizing Polynomial Functions. In Algorithmic and Quantitative Real Algebraic Geometry, DIMACS Series in Discrete Mathematics and Theoretical Computer Science, Vol. 60, pp. 83–99, AMS.
23. K. Gatermann, and P.A. Parrilo. Symmetry groups, semidefinite programs, and sums of squares. Journal of Pure and Appl. Algebra, Vol. 192, No. 1-3, pp. 95-128, 2004.

Bisimulation for Communicating Piecewise Deterministic Markov Processes (CPDPs)

Stefan Strubbe and Arjan van der Schaft*

Twente University, PO BOX 217, 7500AE Enschede, The Netherlands
{s.n.strubbe, a.j.vanderschaft}@math.utwente.nl

Abstract. CPDPs (Communicating Piecewise Deterministic Markov Processes) can be used for compositional specification of systems from the class of stochastic hybrid processes formed by PDPs (Piecewise Deterministic Markov Processes). We define CPDPs and the composition of CPDPs, and prove that the class of CPDPs is closed under composition. Then we introduce a notion of bisimulation for PDPs and CPDPs and we prove that bisimilar PDPs as well as bisimilar CPDPs have equal stochastic behavior. Finally, as main result, we prove the congruence property that, for a composite CPDP, substituting components by different but bisimilar components results in a CPDP that is bisimilar to the original composite CPDP (and therefore has equal stochastic behavior).

1 Introduction

Many real-life systems nowadays are complex hybrid systems. They consist of multiple components 'running' simultaneously, having both continuous and discrete dynamics and interacting with each other. Also, many of these systems have a stochastic nature. An interesting class of stochastic hybrid systems is formed by the Piecewise Deterministic Markov Processes (PDPs), which were introduced in 1984 by Davis (see [1, 2]). Motivation for considering PDP systems is two-fold. First, almost all stochastic hybrid processes that do not include diffusions can be modelled as a PDP, and second, PDP processes have very nice properties (such as the strong Markov property) when it comes to stochastic analysis. (In [2] powerful analysis techniques for PDPs have been developed). However, PDPs cannot communicate or interact with other PDPs and therefore, from a compositional modelling point of view, we should find a way of opening the structure of PDPs to let them communicate/interact.

In [3], the automata formalism CPDP, which stands for Communicating Piecewise Deterministic Markov Processes, is introduced. Basically, a CPDP is a PDP-type system that can communicate (or interact) with other CPDPs. In [3], this communication is formalized by means of a composition operator. In this way, we may model complex stochastic hybrid systems (without diffusions) as PDPs, based on the description of their components. Furthermore, in [4], it

---

* Both authors were supported by the EU-project HYBRIDGE (IST-2001-32460).

M. Morari and L. Thiele (Eds.): HSCC 2005, LNCS 3414, pp. 623–639, 2005.

is proven that for any CPDP that is closed, i.e. does not communicate anymore with the environment, we can construct a corresponding PDP that expresses the same stochastic process. Therefore, analysis techniques for PDPs can be used for analyzing CPDPs.

In this paper we give a slightly different definition of CPDPs than the definition in [3]. This new definition is more convenient in the context of composition. As in [3], we formalize the communication between CPDPs by means of a composition operator, and we prove that the composition of two CPDPs is again a CPDP. (A partial proof of this was already given in [3]).

The main part of this paper is about bisimulation for CPDPs. It is well-known that the composition of multiple subsystems leads to state space explosion. One tool that has proved to be effective in dealing with the state space explosion problem is bisimulation. Bisimulation can be seen as a state space reduction technique: By bisimulation we can find systems with smaller state spaces, that still have the same external behavior. Two systems have the same external behavior if they cannot be distinguished in any composition context. The notion of bisimulation was introduced by Milner [5] in the context of discrete state processes. Since then, bisimulation has also been established in the context of probabilistic and stochastic automata [6, 7], continuous time interactive Markov chains (IMC) [8], continuous dynamical systems [9, 10] and general (non-stochastic) hybrid systems [11, 12].

In this paper, we define bisimulation in the context of CPDPs. In some sense, this notion of bisimulation for CPDPs integrates the notions of bisimulation for IMC, stochastic automata and continuous/hybrid systems.

An important point is that CPDPs have a stochastic processes semantics (see [4]). This implies that we want to define bisimulation in such a way that two bisimilar CPDPs express equivalent stochastic processes. Therefore, we define bisimulation such that certain analytical properties of stochastic processes still remain in the quotient systems obtained by bisimulation (by factoring out equivalence classes). In particular, we prove that two bisimilar CPDPs have the same stochastic (PDP) behavior. We also prove the congruence property that, in the composition of multiple CPDPs, substitution of a component by a different bisimilar component does not change the stochastic behavior of the composite system.

From an analysis point of view, we can then reduce the state space of a composite CPDP in a compositional way by substituting components by state-reduced bisimilar components. To analyze the original composite CPDP, we can then (because of the equivalence result of CPDPs and PDPs) use the PDP analysis techniques on the state reduced composite CPDP.

The organization of the paper is as follows. In Section 2 we give the definition of the PDP stochastic process. In Section 3 we give the definition of the CPDP model. In Section 4 we define composition for CPDP and we prove that, under certain conditions, the composition of two CPDPs is again a CPDP. In Section 5 we prepare the bisimulation notion for CPDPs by first defining bisimulation for PDPs with output functions (called weighted PDPs). We prove that bisimilar

weighted PDPs have equivalent stochastic behavior. Then in Section 6 we extend
the PDP bisimulation notion to CPDPs. Using the results of Section 5, we prove
that weighted bisimilar CPDPs have equivalent stochastic behavior. After that,
we prove that, in the composition of multiple weighted CPDPs, substitution of
a component by a different bisimilar component does not change the stochastic
behavior of the composite system. In the final section conclusions are drawn and
future research directions are discussed.

2 Definition of the PDP

The state space and the dynamics of a PDP are defined as follows: K is a
countable set of locations. For each $\nu \in K$, $d(\nu) \in \mathbb{N}$ denotes the dimension of
the continuous state space of location ν. For each $\nu \in K$, let E_ν be an open
subset of $\mathbb{R}^{d(\nu)}$ and let $g_\nu : \mathbb{R}^{d(\nu)} \rightarrow \mathbb{R}^{d(\nu)}$ be a locally Lipschitz continuous
function on E_ν. The flow $\phi_\nu(t, \zeta)$ is uniquely determined by the differential
equation $\dot{\hat{\zeta}} = g_\nu(\hat{\zeta})$ and equals $\hat{\zeta}(t)$, assumed that $\hat{\zeta}(0) = \zeta$. The hybrid state
space of the PDP is now defined as

$$E = \{(\nu, \zeta) | \nu \in K, \zeta \in E_\nu\}.$$

Remark 1. In fact, the state space E of the PDP is in [2] extended such that E
also contains the boundary points that are backward reachable (via flow ϕ) but
not forward reachable from the interior of E.

For $x = (\nu, \zeta) \in E$ define

$$t_*(x) = \begin{cases} \inf\{t > 0 | \phi_\nu(t, \zeta) \in \partial E_\nu\}, \\ \infty \text{ if no such time exists.} \end{cases}$$

where $\partial E_\nu = \bar{E}_\nu \backslash E_\nu$ is the boundary of E_ν, $\bar{E}_\nu$ is the closure of E_ν.

The jump mechanism of the PDP is determined by a jump rate function λ
and a transition measure Q. The jump rate $\lambda : E \rightarrow \mathbb{R}_+$ is a measurable function
such that for each $x = (\nu, \zeta) \in E$, there exists $\epsilon(x) > 0$ such that the function
$s \rightarrow \lambda(\nu, \phi_\nu(s, \zeta))$ is integrable on $[0, \epsilon(x)[$. With Γ^* we denote the boundary of
E that is reachable from the interior of E. The transition measure Q maps $E \cup \Gamma^*$
into the set $\mathcal{P}(E)$ of probability measures on the Borel space $(E, \mathcal{E})$, where $\mathcal{E}$ is
the set containing all Borel sets of E (according to a 'natural' topology, defined
in [2]), with the properties that for each fixed $A \in \mathcal{E}$ the map $x \rightarrow Q(A, x)$, where
$Q(A, x)$ denotes the probability of A according to the probability measure $Q(x)$,
is measurable, and $Q(\{x\}, x) = 0$ for all $x \in E \cup \Gamma^*$.

A PDP process, starting from initial state $x_0 = (\nu_0, \zeta_0)$, can be 'executed'
as follows: The dynamics of x_t from $t = 0$ is determined by the vectorfield g_{ν_0}
until either the boundary (i.e. the set ∂E_{ν_0}) is hit at time $t_*(x_0)$ or until a point
is generated by the Poisson process that has density $\lambda(x_t)$. In either case, a
jump takes place and the target hybrid state is determined by the probability

measure $Q(\cdot, (\nu_0, \phi_{\nu_0}(\hat{t}, \zeta_0)))$, where $\hat{t}$ is the jump time. From the target state this execution procedure can be repeated.

For a PDP it is assumed that there are no explosions (i.e. $|\phi_\nu(t, \zeta)| \not\to \infty$ if $t \not\to \infty$) and that there is no Zeno behavior (i.e. for every starting point $x \in E$, $EN_t < \infty$ for all $t \in \mathbb{R}_+$, where N_t is a random variable 'counting' the number of jumps up to time t and EN_t is the expectation of N_t).

3   Definition of the CPDP

A CPDP automaton is a tuple $(L, V, v, Inv, G, \Sigma, A, P, S, C)$, where

- L is a countable set of locations
- V is a set of variables. With $d(y)$ for $y \in V$ we denote the dimension of variable y. $y \in V$ takes its values in $\mathbb{R}^{d(y)}$. We also say that $\mathbb{R}^{d(y)}$ is the valuation space of y.
- $v : L \to 2^V$ maps each location to a subset of V, which is the set of active variables of the corresponding location
- Inv assigns to each location l and each variable $y \in v(l)$ an open subset of $\mathbb{R}^{d(y)}$, i.e. $Inv(l, y) \subset \mathbb{R}^{d(y)}$. With Inv_l we denote the subset of the valuation space of $v(l)$ that is built from (or loosely speaking: is the product of) the invariants of the individual variables. With ∂Inv_l we denote the set of boundary points of l, which is equal to the set of valuations of $v(l)$ where each $y \in v(l)$ takes value in $\overline{Inv(l, y)}$ and at least one $y \in v(l)$ takes value in $\partial Inv(l, y) := \overline{Inv(l, y)} \backslash Inv(l, y)$.
- G assigns to each location l and each $y \in v(l)$ a locally Lipschitz continuous function from $\mathbb{R}^{d(y)}$ to $\mathbb{R}^{d(y)}$, i.e. $G(l, y) : \mathbb{R}^{d(y)} \to \mathbb{R}^{d(y)}$. This vectorfield uniquely determines a flow $\phi_{l,y}(t, y_0)$ along this vectorfield.
- Σ is the set of communication labels. $\bar{\Sigma}$ denotes the 'passive' mirror of Σ and is defined as $\bar{\Sigma} = \{\bar{a} | a \in \Sigma\}$.
- B is a finite set of boundary hit transitions and consists of 4-tuples (l, a, l', R), denoting a transition from location $l \in L$ to location $l' \in L$ with communication label $a \in \Sigma$ and reset map R. This reset map R assigns to each boundary point of l for each active variable $y \in v(l')$ a probability measure on the invariant (and its Borel sets) of y for location l'. We will denote the measure of R for variable y at boundary point ζ by $R^y(\zeta)$.
- P is a finite set of passive transitions and consists of 4-tuples $(l, \bar{a}, l', R)$, denoting a transition from location $l \in L$ to location $l' \in L$ with passive communication label $\bar{a} \in \bar{\Sigma}$ and reset map R. R assigns to each interior point of location l for each active variable $y \in v(l')$ a probability measure on the invariant (and its Borel sets) of y for location l'.
- S is a finite set of spontaneous (also called Poisson) transitions and consists of 5-tuples (l, λ, a, l', R), denoting a transition from location $l \in L$ to location $l' \in L$ with communication label $a \in \Sigma$, jump-rate function λ and reset map R. The jump rate $\lambda : Inv_l \to \mathbb{R}_+$ is a measurable function such that for each $\zeta \in Inv_l$, there exists $\epsilon(\zeta) > 0$ such that the function $s \to \lambda(\phi_l(s, \zeta))$ is

integrable on $[0, \epsilon(\zeta)[$, where ϕ_l denotes the flow of the valuations of variables $v(l)$ for location l. R is defined on all interior points of l as it is done for passive transitions.

- C is the choice function. C assigns to each boundary point (l, ζ) of the CPDP a probability measure on the set of outgoing boundary hit transitions, i.e. $C(l, \zeta)$ (with $\zeta \in \partial Inv_l$) is a probability measure on B_l, where B_l is the set of boundary hit transitions that have l as origin location. Furthermore, for all $l \in L$ and all $\bar{a} \in \bar{\Sigma}$, such that for location l there is an outgoing passive transition labelled $\bar{a}$, C assigns to each triplet $(l, \zeta, \bar{a})$ (with $\zeta \in Inv_l$) a probability measure on the set of passive transitions leaving l and labelled $\bar{a}$.

We also impose the standard PDP conditions on a CPDP. For the details of how this is done, we refer to [4].

Passive transitions are used to interact with the environment (see [3] for an explanation of the communication mechanism established by the interplay of boundary hit, spontaneous and passive transitions). The environment can activate/trigger these passive transitions. When a CPDP does not have passive transitions, then it can not be influenced by the environment, which means that it is autonomous and can be executed 'on its own'.

Execution of a CPDP $(L, V, v, Inv, G, \Sigma, A, P, S, C)$ without passive transitions (i.e. $P = \emptyset$), starting from initial state $x_0 = (l_0, \zeta_0)$, is done as follows: The dynamics at $t = 0$ is determined by the vectorfield $G(l_0)$ until either the boundary $(\partial Inv(l_0))$ is hit at time $t_*(x_0)$ (which is defined similarly as t_* for the PDP) or until a point is generated by a Poisson process of one of the spontaneous transitions. For each spontaneous transition $\alpha = (l_0, \lambda_\alpha, l', R_\alpha)$ a Poisson process is 'running' with density $\lambda_\alpha(x_t)$. As soon as one of these Poisson processes generates a point, the corresponding spontaneous transition will be taken. If the first jump is caused by a boundary-hit at boundary point ζ, a boundary hit transition will be selected according to the probability measure $C(l_0, \zeta)$. The new continuous state in the target location of the active transition, will be selected according to the probability measures of the reset map R of the boundary hit transition. If the first jump is caused by one of the Poisson processes, the reset map of the corresponding spontaneous transition will select the new continuous state in the target location. From the new hybrid state on, this execution procedure can be repeated.

4   Composition of CPDPs

In this section we define a composition operator for CPDPs. We prove that, under certain conditions, the class of CPDPs is closed under this composition operation. We also prove that the composition operator is commutative and associative. For an explanation of the active/passive communication mechanism, established by this composition operator, we refer to [3].

Suppose CPDPs $\mathcal{A}_i = (L_i, V_i, v_i, Inv_i, G_i, \Sigma, B_i, P_i, S_i, C_i)$ are given. We assume that the sets of communication labels are the same for $\mathcal{A}_1$ and $\mathcal{A}_2$ and we assume that V_1 and V_2 are disjoint. The composition $\mathcal{A}_1 \| \mathcal{A}_2$ of $\mathcal{A}_1$ with $\mathcal{A}_2$ is defined as follows:

$\mathcal{A}_1 \| \mathcal{A}_2 := (L, V, v, Inv, G, \Sigma, B, P, S, C)$, where $L = L_1 \times L_2$, $V = V_1 \cup V_2$, $v(l_1, l_2) := v(l_1) \cup v(l_2)$, $Inv((l_1, l_2), y) = Inv_1(l_1, y)$ if $y \in V_1$ and $Inv((l_1, l_2), y) = Inv_2(l_2, y)$ if $y \in V_2$, $G((l_1, l_2), y) = G_1(l_1, y)$ if $y \in V_1$ and $G((l_1, l_2), y) = G_2(l_2, y)$ if $y \in V_2$. The sets B, P and S are determined by the following structural operational rules, where $l_1, l_1' \in L_1$ and $l_2, l_2' \in L_2$. For the boundary hit transitions we have the rules

$$\mathbf{r1.} \quad \frac{l_1 \xrightarrow{a, R_1} l_1', l_2 \xrightarrow{\bar{a}}}{(l_1, l_2) \xrightarrow{a, R} (l_1', l_2)}, \mathbf{r2.} \quad \frac{l_1 \xrightarrow{a, R_1} l_1', l_2 \xrightarrow{\bar{a}, R_2} l_2'}{(l_1, l_2) \xrightarrow{a, R} (l_1', l_2')}$$

These rules should be interpreted as, **r1**: If $(l_1, a, l_1', R) \in B_1$ and there exist no l_2' and R_2 such that $(l_2, \bar{a}, l_2', R_2) \in P_2$, then $((l_1, l_2), a, (l_1', l_2), R) \in B$ (R will be defined next). **r2**: If $(l_1, a, l_1', R) \in B_1$ and $(l_2, \bar{a}, l_2', R_2) \in P_2$, then $((l_1, l_2), a, (l_1', l_2'), R) \in B$. The rules **r3** till **r6** should be interpreted likewise. R in rule **r1** equals R_1 for the variables of l_1' (and thus ignores the valuation of the variables of l_2 before the jump) and equals the 'identity' map for the variables in l_2 (i.e. the values of the variables of l_2 do not change with probability one). R in rule **r2** equals R_1 for the variables of l_1' and equals R_2 for the variables of l_2'. For the spontaneous transitions we have the rules

$$\mathbf{r3.} \quad \frac{l_1 \xrightarrow{a, R_1, \lambda} l_1', l_2 \xrightarrow{\bar{a}}}{(l_1, l_2) \xrightarrow{a, R, \lambda} (l_1', l_2)}, \mathbf{r4.} \quad \frac{l_1 \xrightarrow{a, R_1, \lambda} l_1', l_2 \xrightarrow{\bar{a}, R_2} l_2'}{(l_1, l_2) \xrightarrow{a, R, \lambda} (l_1', l_2')},$$

where R in rule **r3** is derived from R_1 as in rule **r1** and R in rule **r4** is derived from R_1 and R_2 as in rule **r2**. For the passive transitions we have the rules

$$\mathbf{r5.} \quad \frac{l_1 \xrightarrow{\bar{a}, R_1} l_1', l_2 \xrightarrow{\bar{a}}}{(l_1, l_2) \xrightarrow{\bar{a}, R} (l_1', l_2)}, \mathbf{r6.} \quad \frac{l_1 \xrightarrow{\bar{a}, R_1} l_1', l_2 \xrightarrow{\bar{a}, R_2} l_2'}{(l_1, l_2) \xrightarrow{\bar{a}, R} (l_1', l_2')},$$

where R in rule **r5** is derived from R_1 as in rule **r1** and R in rule **r6** is derived from R_1 and R_2 as in rule **r2**.

The reset maps of the boundary hit transitions (as a result of rules **r1** and **r2**) are defined well for boundary points where the variables of the second location l_2 are in the interior of the invariant of l_2. However, for 'double boundary points', i.e. for boundary points where both the variables of the first location and the variables of the second location are on the boundaries of the invariants (of l_1 and l_2 respectively), the reset map is ill-defined because the target continuous state is again a boundary state, which is not allowed for CPDPs. For now, we say that the reset maps for these double boundary points are undefined.

Beside the rules **r1** till **r6**, there are also the rules **r1'** till **r5'** which are the mirrored versions of **r1** till **r5**. This means that

$$\mathbf{r1'.} \quad \frac{l_1 \xrightarrow{\bar{a}}, l_2 \xrightarrow{a, R_2} l_2'}{(l_1, l_2) \xrightarrow{a, R} (l_1, l_2')}, \mathbf{r2'.} \quad \frac{l_1 \xrightarrow{\bar{a}, R_1} l_1', l_2 \xrightarrow{a, R_2} l_2'}{(l_1, l_2) \xrightarrow{a, R} (l_1', l_2')},$$

etc. For active transitions, the choice function C is defined as follows: If $\alpha \in B$ is derived from an active transition $\alpha_1 \in B_1$ (via rule **r1** or **r2**), then $C((l_1, l_2), (\zeta_1, \zeta_2))(\alpha)$ equals $C(l_1, \zeta_1)(\alpha_1)$ (in case **r1**) and $C(l_1, \zeta_1)(\alpha_1) C(l_2, \zeta_2, \bar{a})(\alpha_2)$ (in case **r2** with passive transition α_2) for ζ_1 a boundary point and ζ_2 an interior point, equals zero for ζ_1 an interior point and ζ_2 a boundary point, and is 'undefined' for ζ_1 and ζ_2 both boundary points. For the case that $\alpha \in B$ is derived from an active transition $\alpha_2 \in B_2$ (via rule **r1'** or **r2'**), $C((l_1, l_2), (\zeta_1, \zeta_2))(\alpha)$ is defined vice versa. For passive transitions, the choice function C is defined as follows: If $\alpha \in P$ with label $\bar{a}$ is derived from a passive transition $\alpha_1 \in P_1$ (via rule **r5** or **r6**), then $C((l_1, l_2), (\zeta_1, \zeta_2))(\alpha)$ equals $C(l_1, \zeta_1, \bar{a})(\alpha_1)$ (in case **r5**) and $C(l_1, \zeta_1, \bar{a})(\alpha_1) C(l_2, \zeta_2, \bar{a})(\alpha_2)$ (in case **r6** with passive transition α_2) for ζ_1 and ζ_2 interior points. This ends the definition of composition of CPDPs.

In the definition of composition above, reset maps and choice function are not defined for double boundary points. If our model would allow non-determinism and the possibility to jump onto the boundary (like the more general CPDP model of [13]), we expect that this 'problem' can be solved in a more satisfactory way.

Theorem 1. *The composition of two CPDPs is a CPDP that is undefined on double boundary points assumed that there is no zeno-behavior. With other words, if for the composition of two CPDPs we assign proper reset maps to the double boundary points for the boundary hit transitions and properly define the choice function for the double boundary points, then the composition is a CPDP assumed that this completed composition is non-zeno.*

Proof. It can directly be seen that the elements L, V, v, Inv and G are proper CPDP elements. It can also easily be seen that the transitions that are generated by the rules **r1** till **r6** (and their mirror rules) have proper reset maps (except on the double boundary points) and are therefore proper CPDP transitions (except on the double boundary points). The only element that needs a closer look is the choice function C. For C to be a proper CPDP element, for each boundary point the values that C assigns to the boundary hit transitions should add up to one and also for each interior point (l, ζ) and each passive label $\bar{a}$ that is used by at least one transition of location l, the values that C assigns to the passive transitions in l with label $\bar{a}$ should add up to one. Concerning the active transitions: At a boundary point $(l_1, \partial\zeta_1, l_2, \zeta_2)$, with $\partial\zeta_1 \in \partial Inv_1(l_1)$ and $\zeta_2 \in Inv_2(l_2)$, the value of any active transition α of $\mathcal{A}_1$ with label a is carried over to the corresponding active transition in $\mathcal{A}$ in case that $l_2 \overset{\bar{a}}{\nrightarrow}$ and in case that $l_2 \overset{\bar{a}}{\rightarrow}$, this value is spread over the different active transitions that are the result of α synchronizing with the passive $\bar{a}$-transitions in l_2 (i.e. we get $C(l_1, \partial\zeta_1)(\alpha_1) C(l_2, \zeta_2, \bar{a})(\tilde{\alpha}_1) + \cdots + C(l_1, \partial\zeta_1)(\alpha_1) C(l_2, \zeta_2, \bar{a})(\tilde{\alpha}_n) = C(l_1, \partial\zeta_1)(\alpha_1)$, with $\tilde{\alpha}_i$ the passive $\bar{a}$-transitions from l_2). Therefore, because the active transitions corresponding to active transitions in l_2 get value zero, the values add up to one. For boundary points $(l_1, \zeta_1, l_2, \partial\zeta_2)$ we have the symmetric case. For boundary points $(l_1, \partial\zeta_1, l_2, \partial\zeta_2)$, C is undefined. Concerning the passive transitions: With a similar argument it can be shown that values of passive transitions of $\mathcal{A}_i$ either carry over to passive transitions of $\mathcal{A}$ or are spread over a set of passive transitions of $\mathcal{A}$ such that the sum of the values does not change. This ends the proof.

Remark 2. In the composition of CPDPs $\mathcal{A}_1$ and $\mathcal{A}_2$ we get for each joint location (l_1, l_2) a combination of vectorfields from $\mathcal{A}_1$ and $\mathcal{A}_1$. In order to maintain the PDP properties, this composition of vectorfields should be locally Lipschitz continuous. We also get a composition of reset-maps which should result in proper reset maps etc. Because the CPDP is now, as opposed to [3], defined as having multiple variables in one location, these 'properties maintained in composition' are already proved in the PDP/CPDP-equivalence proof from [4].

Corollary 1. *If the probability that two CPDPs (which are composed with each other) reach their boundaries at the same time is zero, then the stochastic behavior of the composite system is fully specified and is equal to the behavior of a PDP. Thus, if we then complete the composition of these two CPDPs to form a new CPDP (which can always be done) in two different ways, then the stochastic behaviors of these two completed CPDPs will be the same.*

Theorem 2. *The composition operator* $||$*, which operates on the class of CPDPs, is commutative and associative.*

Proof. We identify joint locations (l_1, l_2) of $\mathcal{A}_1 || \mathcal{A}_2$ with joint locations (l_2, l_1) of $\mathcal{A}_2 || \mathcal{A}_1$. It can directly be seen that the elements L, V, v, Inv and G cause no problems for commutativity and associativity. That the active/passive operator $||$ generates the same transitions for $\mathcal{A}_1 || \mathcal{A}_2$ as for $\mathcal{A}_2 || \mathcal{A}_1$ and generates the same transitions for $(\mathcal{A}_1 || \mathcal{A}_2) || \mathcal{A}_3$ as for $\mathcal{A}_1 || (\mathcal{A}_2 || \mathcal{A}_3)$ is proven in the case of labelled transition systems in [14]. This result can easily be generalized to the case of CPDPs.

5 Bisimulation for PDPs

In this section we introduce a notion of bisimulation for weighted PDPs (i.e. PDPs together with a weight-function on the state space). Briefly said, two PDP states x and y (in two different PDPs) are bisimilar if first, their piecewise deterministic paths simulate each other (i.e. produce the same weight value for each time instant). If second, at any time instant the states of the paths are again bisimilar. If third, the jump intensities at states x and y are equal. If fourth, the transition measures $Q(x)$ and $Q(y)$ are equivalent probability measures. (The notion of equivalent measures will be defined below).

The state space of a PDP as defined in [2] is a standard Borel space. A measurable space $(E, \mathcal{E})$, with $\mathcal{E}$ the Borel sets of E, is called a standard Borel space, if E is homeomorphic to a Borel subset of a complete separable metric space. In order to prove stochastic equivalence of two bisimilar PDPs, we will need that the quotient spaces (induced by a bisimulation relation) are also standard Borel spaces.

We define the equivalence relation on X that is induced by a relation $\mathcal{R} \subset X \times Y$ with the property that $\pi_1(\mathcal{R}) = X$ and $\pi_2(\mathcal{R}) = Y$ as the transitive closure of $\{(x, x') | \exists y \text{ s.t. } (x, y) \in \mathcal{R} \text{ and } (x', y) \in \mathcal{R}\}$. We write $X/_\mathcal{R}$ and $Y/_\mathcal{R}$ for the sets of equivalence classes of X and Y induced by $\mathcal{R}$. We denote the equivalence class of $x \in X$ by $[x]$. We will now define the notion of *measurable relations* and of *equivalent measures*, which we need for our notion of bisimulation for PDPs.

Definition 1. *Let $(X, \mathcal{X})$ and $(Y, \mathcal{Y})$ be standard Borel spaces and let $\mathcal{R} \subset X \times Y$ be a relation such that $\pi_1(\mathcal{R}) = X$ and $\pi_2(\mathcal{R}) = Y$. Let $\mathcal{X}^*$ be the collection of all $\mathcal{R}$-saturated Borel sets of X, i.e. all $B \in \mathcal{X}$ such that any equivalence class of X is either totally contained or totally not contained in B. It can be checked that $\mathcal{X}^*$ is a σ-algebra. Let*

$$\mathcal{X}^*/_\mathcal{R} = \{[A] | A \in \mathcal{X}^*\},$$

where $[A] := \{[a] | a \in A\}$. Then $(X/_\mathcal{R}, \mathcal{X}^*/_\mathcal{R})$, which is a measurable space, is called the quotient space *of X with respect to $\mathcal{R}$. A unique bijective mapping $f : X/_\mathcal{R} \to Y/_\mathcal{R}$ exists, such that $f([x]) = [y]$ if $(x, y) \in \mathcal{R}$. We say that the relation $\mathcal{R}$ is* measurable *if for all $A \in \mathcal{X}^*/_\mathcal{R}$ we have $f(A) \in \mathcal{Y}^*/_\mathcal{R}$ and vice versa.*

If a relation on $X \times Y$ is measurable, then the quotient spaces of X and Y are homeomorphic (under bijection f from Definition 1). We could say therefore that under a measurable relation X and Y have a shared quotient space. In the field of descriptive set theory, a relation $\mathcal{R} \subset X \times Y$ is called measurable if $\mathcal{R} \in \mathcal{B}(X \times Y)$ (i.e. $\mathcal{R}$ is a Borel set of the space $X \times Y$). This definition does not coincide with our definition of measurable relation. In fact, many interesting measurable relations are not Borel sets of the product space $X \times Y$.

Definition 2. *Suppose we have measures P_X and P_Y on standard Borel spaces $(X, \mathcal{X})$ and $(Y, \mathcal{Y})$ respectively. Suppose that we have a measurable relation $\mathcal{R} \subset X \times Y$. The measures P_X and P_Y are called* equivalent with respect to $\mathcal{R}$ *if we have $P_X(f_X^{-1}(A)) = P_Y(f_Y^{-1}(f(A)))$ for all $A \in \mathcal{X}^*/_\mathcal{R}$ (with f as in Definition 1 and with f_X and f_Y the mappings that map X and Y to $X/_\mathcal{R}$ and $Y/_\mathcal{R}$ respectively).*

Suppose we have a PDP with state-space X and $weight_X$ is a real-valued measurable function on X. Then we call the PDP together with $weight_X$ a *weighted PDP*. The function $weight_X$ can be seen as a weight function on the state-space. It can also be seen as an output at the state or as the observable component. We call $weight_X$ the weight-function or the output-function. We will now define a bisimulation notion for weighted PDPs. In this definition we write $Q(x)$ (or $Q(y)$) for the reset map of the PDP with state space X (or Y) at state x (or y). We write $\phi(t, x)$ for the value of the state at time t when the PDP with state space X starts at x at $t = 0$, etc.

Definition 3. *Suppose we have two weighted PDPs with state-spaces X and Y and weight-functions $weight_X$ and $weight_Y$. A measurable relation $\mathcal{R} \subset X \times Y$ is a* bisimulation *iff $(x, y) \in \mathcal{R}$ implies that*

- $weight_X(x) = weight_Y(y)$, $t_*(x) = t_*(y)$ and $\lambda(x) = \lambda(y)$.
- $(\phi(t,x), \phi(t,y)) \in \mathcal{R}$ for all $t \in [0, t_*(x)[$.
- $Q(x)$ and $Q(y)$ are equivalent probability measures with respect to $\mathcal{R}$. Also $Q(\phi(t_*(x), x))$ and $Q(\phi(t_*(y), y))$ are equivalent probability measures with respect to $\mathcal{R}$.

Two states x and y are bisimilar if they are contained in some bisimulation.

The following theorem shows that bisimilar PDPs exhibit equivalent stochastic behavior. We make use of the *Hilbert cube* probability space, which has as sample space $\Omega = \prod_{i=1}^{\infty} Y_i$, where each $Y_i = [0,1]$, and has the product Borel sigma-algebra and product Lebesgue measure.

Theorem 3. *If initial states x and y of two weighted PDPs $(X, weight_X)$ and $(Y, weight_Y)$ are contained in bisimulation $\mathcal{R}$, then, assumed that the quotient spaces are standard Borel spaces, we can construct the stochastic processes x_t and y_t on the Hilbert cube $(\Omega, \mathcal{A}, P)$ in such a way that for each $\omega \in \Omega$ we have $weight_X(x_t(\omega)) = weight_Y(y_t(\omega))$.*

Proof. Let $\mathcal{R} \subset X \times Y$ be a bisimulation such that $(x,y) \in \mathcal{R}$. Let $(\Omega, \mathcal{A}, P)$ be the Hilbert cube and $U_i(\omega) = \omega_i$ be the $U[0,1]$ distributed random variables. We define for any z that has a corresponding survivor function $F(t,z)$

$$\psi_1(u,z) = \begin{cases} \inf\{t|F(t,z) \leq u\} \\ +\infty \text{ if the above set is empty} \end{cases}$$

We define the random variables $S_{1,x}$, $T_{1,x}$, $S_{1,y}$ and $T_{1,y}$ as $S_{1,x}(\omega) = T_{1,x}(\omega) = \psi_1(U_1(\omega), x)$ and $S_{1,y}(\omega) = T_{1,y}(\omega) = \psi_1(U_1(\omega), y)$. Now we can define the sample-functions up to the first jump. For $z \in \{x, y\}$ we define: if $T_{1,z}(\omega) = \infty$ then $z_t(\omega) = \phi(t,z)$ for $t \geq 0$, if $T_{1,z}(\omega) < \infty$ then $z_t(\omega) = \phi(t,z)$ for $0 \leq t < T_{1,z}(\omega)$.

Because $(x,y) \in \mathcal{R}$, we have $t_*(x) = t_*(y)$ and $(\phi(t,x), \phi(t,y)) \in \mathcal{R}$ for $t \in [0, t_*(x)[$. We also have $\lambda(\phi(t,x)) = \lambda(\phi(t,y))$ for $t \in [0, t_*(x)[$. Now it can be easily checked that $F(t,x) = F(t,y)$ for all $t \in \mathbb{R}$ and therefore $\psi(u,x) = \psi(u,y)$ and we have $S_{1,x}(\omega) = S_{1,y}(\omega)$ and $T_{1,x}(\omega) = T_{1,y}(\omega)$. Because $(\phi(t,x), \phi(t,y)) \in \mathcal{R}$ we have $weight_X(x_t(\omega)) = weight_Y(y_t(\omega))$ up to $T_{1,x}(\omega)$.

Now $x_{T_1}(\omega)$ and $y_{T_1}(\omega)$, where $T_1 := T_{1,x}(\omega) = T_{1,y}(\omega)$, need to be chosen in accordance to $Q(\phi(T_1, x))$ and $Q(\phi(T_1, y))$ respectively. Because $(x,y) \in \mathcal{R}$, we have that $Q' := Q(\phi(T_1, x))$ and $Q'' := Q(\phi(T_1, y))$ are equivalent probability measures with respect to $\mathcal{R}$. Therefore, Q' and Q'' define the same probability measure P_Z on the quotient space $(Z, \mathcal{Z})$. Let $P_{X|z}$ and $P_{Y|z}$ be the conditional probability measures of Q' and Q'' given the outcome z in Z. Because X, Y and Z are all separable standard Borel spaces, these conditional probability measures exist uniquely according to Th.8.1 in [15] and according to the same theorem we have that for fixed $A \in \mathcal{B}(X)$ and $B \in \mathcal{B}(Y)$ the maps $z \to P_{X|z}(A)$ and $z \to P_{Y|z}(B)$ are measurable.

Let $\psi_2 : [0,1] \times X \cup \partial X \to Z$ be a measurable mapping such that $l\psi_2^{-1}(A, x) = P_Z(A, x)$ for all $x \in X \cup \partial X$. The existence of this mapping follows from Corollary 23.4 in [2] and from the fact that the mapping $x \to P_Z(A, x)$ is measurable for fixed $A \in \mathcal{Z}$. Let $\psi_{3,x} : [0,1] \times Z \to X$ and $\psi_{3,y} : [0,1] \times Z \to Y$ be measurable mappings such that $l\psi_{3,x}^{-1}(A, z) = P_{X|z}(A)$ for $A \in \mathcal{B}(X)$ and $l\psi_{3,y}^{-1}(A, z) = P_{Y|z}(A)$ for $A \in \mathcal{B}(Y)$. The existence of these mappings follows from Corollary 23.4 in [2] and from the fact that for fixed $A \in \mathcal{B}(X)$ and $B \in \mathcal{B}(Y)$ the mappings $z \to P_{X|z}(A)$ and $z \to P_{Y|z}(B)$ are measurable. Now the processes x_t and y_t restart at time $T_1(\omega)$ from the states $x_{T_1}(\omega) = \psi_{3,x}(U_3(\omega), \psi_2(U_2(\omega), \phi(T_1(\omega), x)))$ and $y_{T_1}(\omega) = \psi_{3,y}(U_3(\omega), \psi_2(U_2(\omega), \phi(T_1(\omega), x)))$ and we have $(x_{T_1}(\omega), y_{T_1}(\omega)) \in \bar{\mathcal{R}}$, where $\bar{\mathcal{R}}$ is defined as $\{(x, y)| f([x]) = [y]\}$ (see Definition 1). To continue the sample function from time $T_1(\omega)$, we define $S_{2,x} = \psi_1(U_4(\omega), x_{T_1}(\omega))$, $S_{2,y} = \psi_1(U_4(\omega), y_{T_1}(\omega))$, $T_{2,x} = T_{1,x}(\omega) + S_{2,x}(\omega)$, $T_{2,y} = T_{1,y}(\omega) + S_{2,y}(\omega)$, and we repeat the procedure above.

It can be seen that the stochastic processes above are well defined and that for all $t \geq 0$ and all $\omega \in \Omega$ we have $(x_t(\omega), y_t(\omega)) \in \bar{\mathcal{R}}$. This means that $weight_X(x_t(\omega)) = weight_Y(y_t(\omega))$. This ends the proof.

Corollary 2. *Because $weight_X$ and $weight_Y$ in Proposition 3 are measurable mappings, we have that $z_t = weight_X(x_t)$ and $z'_t = weight_Y(y_t)$ are well-defined stochastic processes. Because $weight_X(x_t(\omega)) = weight_Y(y_t(\omega))$, the stochastic processes z_t and z'_t are indistinguishable. Thus, if two weighted PDPs have bisimilar initial states (and the quotient spaces are standard Borel spaces) then there is a realization of the stochastic processes of their outputs (on the Hilbert cube) such that the stochastic processes are indistinguishable .*

Remark 3. For sake of simplicity we assumed that weight-functions take value in $\mathbb{R}$. However, all results still hold if we take any other euclidean space than $\mathbb{R}$ as codomain of the weight functions.

6   Bisimulation for CPDPs

We will now generalize the notion of bisimulation for PDPs to CPDPs. To do that, we need to introduce the concept of weighted CPDPs.

Definition 4. *A weighted CPDP is a CPDP together with a set of output variables $W = \{w_1, w_2, \cdots, w_n\}$, where each w_i takes value in $\mathbb{R}^{d(w_i)}$, with $d(w_i)$ the dimension of w_i, and an output function weight which assigns to each $w \in W$ and each CPDP state x a value $weight(w, x) \in \mathbb{R}^{d(w)}$. weight is such that for fixed w the functions $weight(w, x)$ are measurable.*

For composition of two CPDPs with state spaces X_1 and X_2, with disjoint sets of output variables W_1 and W_2 and with output functions $weight_1$ and $weight_2$, the composed output function $weight$ assigns to $(w, (x_1, x_2))$ the value $weight_1(w, x_1)$ if $w \in W_1$ and $weight_2(w, x_2)$ if $w \in W_2$. In order to define bisimulation for CPDPs we also need to introduce the notions of *combined reset map* and *combined jump rate function*:

For CPDP $\mathcal{A} = (L, V, v, Inv, G, \Sigma, B, P, S, C)$ with hybrid state space E, We define R, which we call the combined reset map, as follows. R assigns to each triplet (l, ζ, a) with $(l, \zeta) \in \partial E$ and with $a \in \Sigma$ such that $l \overset{a}{\longrightarrow}$ (i.e. there exists a boundary hit transition labelled a leaving l), a measure on E. This measure $R(l, \zeta, a)$ is for any l' and any Borel set $A \subset Inv_{l'}$ defined as:

$$R(l, \zeta, a)(A) = \sum_{\alpha \in B_{l,a,l'}} C(l, \zeta)(\alpha) R_\alpha(A),$$

where $B_{l,a,l'}$ denotes the set of boundary hit transitions from l to l' with label a. (This measure is uniquely extended to all Borel sets of E). Now, for $A \in \mathcal{B}(E)$, $R(l, \zeta, a)(A)$ equals the probability of jumping into A via a boundary hit transition with label a given that the jump takes place at (l, ζ). Furthermore, R assigns to each triplet $(l, \zeta, \bar{a})$ with $(l, \zeta) \in E$ and with $a \in \bar{\Sigma}$ such that $l \overset{\bar{a}}{\longrightarrow}$, a measure on E, which for any l' and any Borel set $A \subset Inv_{l'}$ is defined as:

$$R(l, \zeta, \bar{a})(A) = \sum_{\alpha \in P_{l,\bar{a},l'}} C(l, \zeta, \bar{a})(\alpha) R_\alpha(A).$$

(This measure is uniquely extended to all Borel sets of E). Now, $R(l, \zeta, \bar{a})(A)$, with $A \in \mathcal{B}(E)$, equals the probability of jumping into A if a passive transition with label $\bar{a}$ takes place at (l, ζ). We define the combined jump rate function λ for CPDP $\mathcal{A}$ as

$$\lambda(l, \zeta) = \sum_{\alpha \in S_{l \to}} \lambda_\alpha,$$

with $(l, \zeta) \in E$. Finally, for spontaneous jumps, R assigns to each $(l, \zeta) \in E$ such that $\lambda(l, \zeta) \neq 0$, a probability measure on E, which for any l' and any Borel set $A \subset Inv_{l'}$ is defined as:

$$R(l, \zeta)(A) = \sum_{\alpha \in S_{l \to l'}} \frac{\lambda_\alpha(l, \zeta)}{\lambda(l, \zeta)} R_\alpha(A).$$

Now we are ready to give the definition of bisimulation for CPDPs.

Definition 5. *Suppose we have two weighted CPDPs with state-spaces X and Y and weight-functions $weight_X$ and $weight_Y$ on a shared set of output variables W. A measurable relation $\mathcal{R} \subset X \times Y$ is a bisimulation iff $(x, y) \in \mathcal{R}$, with $x = (l_1, \zeta_1)$ and $y = (l_2, \zeta_2)$, implies that*

- *$weight_X(w, x) = weight_Y(w, y)$ for all $w \in W$, $t_*(x) = t_*(y)$ and $\lambda(x) = \lambda(y)$.*
- *$(\phi(t, x), \phi(t, y)) \in \mathcal{R}$ for all $t \in [0, t_*(x)[$.*
- *If $\lambda(x) = \lambda(y) \neq 0$, then $R(x)$ and $R(y)$ are equivalent probability measures with respect to $\mathcal{R}$. For any $\bar{a} \in \bar{\Sigma}$ we have that either both $l_1 \overset{\bar{a}}{\nrightarrow}$ and $l_2 \overset{\bar{a}}{\nrightarrow}$*

or else $R(x, \bar{a})$ and $R(y, \bar{a})$ are equivalent probability measures. Also, if we define $(l_1, \zeta_1^*) := t_*(x)$ and $(l_2, \zeta_2^*) := t_*(y)$, then we have for any $a \in \Sigma$ that either both $l_1 \not\xrightarrow{a}$ and $l_2 \not\xrightarrow{a}$ or else $R(l_1, \zeta_1^*, a)$ and $R(l_2, \zeta_2^*, a)$ are equivalent measures.

Two states x and y are bisimilar if they are contained in some bisimulation.

Theorem 4. *The stochastic processes of the outputs of two bisimilar closed CPDPs, whose quotient spaces are standard Borel spaces, can be realized such that they are indistinguishable.*

Proof. The stochastic process of a closed CPDP $\mathcal{A}$ with combined reset map R and combined jump rate function λ is equivalent (i.e. indistinguishable) with the stochastic process of the PDP $\tilde{\mathcal{A}}$ that has the same state space and vectorfields as the CPDP and that has λ as its jump rate function and has transition measure $Q(l, \zeta)$ that equals $R(l, \zeta)$ for interior points and that equals $\sum_{a \in \Sigma} R(l, \zeta, a)$ for boundary points (see [4] for the proof of this stochastic equivalence). This PDP $\tilde{\mathcal{A}}$ is called the corresponding PDP of CPDP $\mathcal{A}$. We prove that the corresponding PDPs of two bisimilar closed CPDPs are bisimilar PDPs, then the result follows from Corollary 2:

The first two lines of Definition 3 follow directly from the first two lines of Definition 5. The third line: The fact that $Q(x)$ and $Q(y)$ are equivalent probability measures for bisimilar interior points x and y follows from the fact that $Q(x) = R(x)$ and $Q(y) = R(y)$ and, according to Definition 5, $R(x)$ and $R(y)$ are equivalent probability measures. Finally, $Q(\phi(t_*(x), x))$ and $Q(\phi(t_*(y), y))$ are equivalent probability measures because $Q(\phi(t_*(x), x)) = \sum_{a \in \Sigma} R(\phi(t_*(x), x), a)$ and $Q(\phi(t_*(y), y)) = \sum_{a \in \Sigma} R(\phi(t_*(y), y), a)$ and, according to Definition 5, $R(\phi(t_*(x), x), a)$ and $R(\phi(t_*(x), x), a)$ are equivalent measures for all $a \in \Sigma$. This ends the proof.

In order to prove the main theorem 5 about bisimulation in the context of composition, we need that a measurable relation $\mathcal{R} \subset X_1 \times X_2$ naturally induces a measurable relation $\mathcal{R}'$ on $(X_1 \times Y) \times (X_2 \times Y)$ for any Y. This result is proved in the following lemma. After that, the main theorem is stated.

Lemma 1. *If $\mathcal{R} \subset X_1 \times X_2$ is a measurable relation such that $\pi_1(\mathcal{R}) = X_1$, $\pi_2(\mathcal{R}) = X_2$ and $X_1/_\mathcal{R}$ and $X_2/_\mathcal{R}$ are standard Borel spaces, then*

$$\mathcal{R}' := \{((x_1, y), (x_2, y)) | (x_1, x_2) \in \mathcal{R}, y \in Y\}$$

is a measurable relation on $(X_1 \times Y) \times (X_2 \times Y)$ and $(X_1 \times Y)/_{\mathcal{R}'}$ and $(X_2 \times Y)/_{\mathcal{R}'}$ are standard Borel spaces.

Proof. From the proof of Theorem 3 we know that (because $X_1/_\mathcal{R}$ is a standard Borel space) there exists a measurable $\psi : [0, 1] \times X_1/_\mathcal{R} \to X_1$, such that $\psi([0, 1] \times [x]) = \{\tilde{x} \in X_1 | [\tilde{x}] = [x]\}$. We first proof that $(X_1 \times Y)/_{\mathcal{R}'} = X_1/_\mathcal{R} \times Y$, which is indeed a standard Borel space.

Take $B \in \mathcal{B}^*(X_1 \times Y)$ (i.e. B is Borel in $X_1 \times Y$ and for any y we have: if $(x,y) \in B$ and $[x] = [\tilde{x}]$ then $(\tilde{x}, y) \in B$). Now there exist Borel sets $B_i^{X_1}$ and B_i^Y such that

$$B = \cup_{i=1}^\infty B_i^{X_1} \times B_i^Y.$$

Because ψ is measurable, we have that for all i that $\psi^{-1}(B_i^{X_1}) \in \mathcal{B}([0,1] \times X_1/_{\mathcal{R}})$. This means that there exist Borel sets $B_{i,j}^{X_1/_{\mathcal{R}}}$ and $B_{i,j}^{[0,1]}$, such that

$$\cup_{i=1}^\infty \psi^{-1}(B_i^{X_1}) \times B_i^Y = \cup_{i,j=1}^\infty B_{i,j}^{[0,1]} \times B_{i,j}^{X_1/_{\mathcal{R}}} \times B_i^Y$$

Because we have that if $(x,y) \in B$ and $[x] = [\tilde{x}]$ then $(\tilde{x}, y) \in B)$, we can also write

$$\cup_{i=1}^\infty \psi^{-1}(B_i^{X_1}) \times B_i^Y = \cup_{i,j=1}^\infty [0,1] \times B_{i,j}^{X_1/_{\mathcal{R}}} \times B_i^Y,$$

from which we can see that $\mathcal{R}'$ maps B to $\cup_{i,j=1}^\infty B_{i,j}^{X_1/_{\mathcal{R}}} \times B_i^Y$, which is a Borel set in $X_1/_{\mathcal{R}} \times Y$ and therefore $(X_1 \times Y)/_{\mathcal{R}'}$ is a standard Borel space. Analogously we get that $\mathcal{R}'$ maps $B \in \mathcal{B}^*(X_2 \times Y)$ to Borel sets in $X_2/_{\mathcal{R}} \times Y$. Measurability of $\mathcal{R}'$ can now, with the results above, easily be derived from the measurability of $\mathcal{R}$. This ends the proof.

Theorem 5. *Suppose we have three weighted CPDPs with state spaces X_1, X_2 and Y, and with output functions $weight_{X_1}$ on W_X, $weight_{X_2}$ on W_X and $weight_Y$ on W_Y respectively. Suppose $\mathcal{R} \subset X_1 \times X_2$ is a bisimulation and $X_1/_{\mathcal{R}}$ and $X_2/_{\mathcal{R}}$ are standard Borel spaces. Then,*

$$\mathcal{R}' := \{((x_1, y), (x_2, y)) | (x_1, x_2) \in \mathcal{R}, y \in Y\}$$

is a bisimulation on $(X_1 \times Y) \times (X_2 \times Y)$ and $(X_1 \times Y)/_{\mathcal{R}'}$ and $(X_2 \times Y)/_{\mathcal{R}'}$ are standard Borel spaces.

Proof. Suppose $((x_1, y), (x_2, y)) \in \mathcal{R}'$ with $x_1 = (l_1, \zeta_1)$, $x_2 = (l_2, \zeta_2)$ and $y = (l_y, \zeta_y)$. We have to prove the three lines of Definition 5 to be true.

First line: For $w \in W_X$, $weight_{X_1||Y}(w, x_1, y) = weight_{X_1}(w, x_1) = weight_{X_2}(w, x_1) = weight_{X_2||Y}(w, x_1, y)$ and for $w \in W_Y$, $weight_{X_1||Y}(w, x_1, y) = weight_Y(w, y) = weight_{X_2||Y}(w, x_1, y)$. $t_*(x_1, y) = \min\{t_*(x_1), t_*(y)\} = \min\{t_*(x_2), t_*(y)\} = t_*(x_2, y)$. $\lambda(x_1, y) = \lambda(x_1) + \lambda(y) = \lambda(x_2) + \lambda(y) = \lambda(x_2, y)$.

Second line: The flow ϕ from states (x_1, y) and (x_2, y) consists of two parts, the x-part: $\phi(t, x_1)$ and $\phi(t, x_2)$, and the y-part: $\phi(t, y)$. The x-part and y-part flows are evolving independently. Then it follows from the fact that $(\phi(t, x_1), \phi(t, x_2)) \in \mathcal{R}$ for all $t \in [0, t_*(x_1, y)[$ that $(\phi(t, x_1, y), \phi(t, x_2, y)) \in \mathcal{R}'$ for $t \in [0, t_*(x_1, y)[$.

Third line (part one): Suppose $\lambda(x_1, y) \neq 0$ (and consequently $\lambda(x_2, y) \neq 0$). Take arbitrary $A_1 \in \mathcal{B}^*(X_1)$ and $B \in \mathcal{B}(Y)$. Let A_2 be the element of $\mathcal{B}^*(X_2)$ that corresponds (according to $\mathcal{R}$) to A_1. Then $A_1 \times B \in \mathcal{B}^*(X_1 \times Y)$ and $A_2 \times B \in \mathcal{B}^*(X_2 \times Y)$. Furthermore, $A_1 \times B$ and $A_2 \times B$ correspond with each other (according to $\mathcal{R}'$). It can be seen that $R(x_1, y)(A_1 \times B) = \frac{\lambda(x_1)}{\lambda(x_1) + \lambda(y)} R(x_1)(A_1) +$

$\frac{\lambda(y)}{\lambda(x_1)+\lambda(y)}R(y)(B) = \frac{\lambda(x_2)}{\lambda(x_2)+\lambda(y)}R(x_2)(A_2) + \frac{\lambda(y)}{\lambda(x_2)+\lambda(y)}R(y)(B) = R(x_2,y)(A_2 \times B)$. It can be shown for $i \in \{1,2\}$, that the σ-algebra $\mathcal{B}^*(X_i \times Y)$ is generated by the collection of sets of the form $A_i \times B$ with $A_i \in \mathcal{B}^*(X_i)$ and $B \in \mathcal{B}(Y)$. Then it follows that $R(x_1,y)$ and $R(x_2,y)$ are equivalent measures with respect to $\mathcal{R}'$ (under the assumption that $\lambda(x_1,y) \neq 0$).

Third line (part two): It can be seen that if $(l_1, l_y) \xrightarrow{\bar{a}}$, then also $(l_2, l_y) \xrightarrow{\bar{a}}$ (and vice versa). Suppose $(l_1, l_y) \xrightarrow{\bar{a}}$ and $(l_2, l_y) \xrightarrow{\bar{a}}$. Take $A_1 \in \mathcal{B}^*(X_1)$ and $B \in \mathcal{B}(Y)$. Let A_2 be the saturated Borel set of X_2 corresponding to A_1. We distinct three cases: If $l_1 \xrightarrow{\bar{a}}$ and $l_y \xrightarrow{\bar{a}}$ (case 1), then $R(x_1,y,\bar{a})(A_1 \times B) = R(x_1,\bar{a})(A_1)R(y,\bar{a})(B) = R(x_2,\bar{a})(A_2)R(y,\bar{a})(B) = R(x_2,y,\bar{a})(A_2 \times B)$. If $l_1 \xrightarrow{\bar{a}}$ and $l_y \xnrightarrow{\bar{a}}$ (case 2), then $R(x_1,y,\bar{a})(A_1 \times B) = R(x_1,\bar{a})(A_1)I_y(B) = R(x_2,\bar{a})(A_2)I_y(B) = R(x_2,y,\bar{a})(A_2 \times B)$ (here $I_y(B)$ is the probability measure that equals one if $y \in B$ and zero if $y \notin B$). If $l_1 \xnrightarrow{\bar{a}}$ and $l_y \xrightarrow{\bar{a}}$ (case 3), then $R(x_1,y,\bar{a})(A_1 \times B) = I_{x_1}(A_1)R(y,\bar{a})(B) = I_{x_2}(A_2)R(y,\bar{a})(B) = R(x_2,y,\bar{a})(A_2 \times B)$. We can now conclude that $R(x_1,y,\bar{a})$ and $R(x_2,y,\bar{a})$ are equivalent probability measures.

Third line (part three): It can be seen that if $(l_1, l_y) \xrightarrow{a}$, then also $(l_2, l_y) \xrightarrow{a}$ (and vice versa). Suppose $(l_1, l_y) \xrightarrow{a}$ and $(l_2, l_y) \xrightarrow{a}$. Take $A_1 \in \mathcal{B}^*(X_1)$ and $B \in \mathcal{B}(Y)$. Let A_2 be the saturated Borel set of X_2 corresponding to A_1. We distinct three cases: If $t_*(x_1) < t_*(y)$ (case 1), then, if we define $x_1^* := \phi(t_*(x_1), x_1)$, $x_2^* := \phi(t_*(x_1), x_2)$ and $y^* := \phi(t_*(x_1), y)$, we get $R(x_1^*, y^*, a)(A_1 \times B) = R(x_1^*, a)(A_1)I_{y^*}(B) = R(x_2^*, a)(A_2)I_{y^*}(B) = R(x_2^*, y^*, a)(A_2 \times B)$. If $t_*(x_1) > t_*(y)$ (case 1), then, if we define $x_1^* := \phi(t_*(y), x_1)$, $x_2^* := \phi(t_*(y), x_2)$ and $y^* := \phi(t_*(y), y)$, we get $R(x_1^*, y^*, a)(A_1 \times B) = I_{x_1^*}(A_1) \times R(y^*, a)(B) = I_{x_2^*}(A_2) \times R(y^*, a)(B) = R(x_2^*, y^*, a)(A_2 \times B)$. If $t_*(x_1) = t_*(y)$ (case 3: double boundary point), then both $R(x_1^*, y^*, a)$ and $R(x_2^*, y^*, a)$ are undefined. We can now conclude that $R(x_1^*, y^*, a)$ and $R(x_2^*, y^*, a)$ are equivalent probability measures. This ends the proof.

Corollary 3. *If a component of a complex CPDP (consisting of multiple CPDPs composed with the composition operator $||$) is substituted by a different but bisimilar component, then the stochastic behavior of the complex CPDP will not change.*

We now give two examples of bisimular CPDPs. The examples highlight different aspects of CPDP bisimulation.

Example 1 (State space transformation/reduction). If we have a CPDP which has linear time invariant dynamics $\dot{x} = Ax, weight(x) = Cx$, in (one of) its locations and T is a state space transformation matrix, then the CPDP that is obtained by transforming the dynamics into $\dot{\tilde{x}} = TAT^{-1}\tilde{x}, weight(\tilde{x}) = CT^{-1}\tilde{x}$, is bisimilar to the original CPDP. Classical state space reduction within a CPDP with LTI dynamics also results in a bisimilar CPDP.

Example 2 (Combining Poisson processes). Suppose we have a CPDP which has two spontaneous transitions, with jump rate functions $\lambda_1(x)$ and $\lambda_2(x)$ and reset maps $R_1(x)$ and $R_2(x)$, that have the same label and the same origin and target location. Replacing these two transitions by one spontaneous transition with the same origin and target location and with jump rate function $\lambda_1 + \lambda_2$ and reset map $\frac{\lambda_1}{\lambda_1+\lambda_2}R_1 + \frac{\lambda_2}{\lambda_1+\lambda_2}R_2$, will not change the CPDP up to bisimilarity.

7   Conclusions

We introduced the CPDP model for compositional modelling of PDP systems. We defined a composition operator on CPDPs based on the communication via active and passive events and we defined a notion of bisimulation. We proved that the output processes of closed bisimilar CPDPs are indistinguishable stochastic processes and we also proved that, within a CPDP composition context, substituting a component by another bisimilar component, does not change the system up to bisimilarity. This means that we can use bisimulation as a compositional technique for state reduction. Components that are state-reduced by bisimulation are still of the PDP type and also the composition of these components is still of the PDP type. This means that both the components and the composite system can in principle be analyzed by using PDP analysis techniques (as developed in [2]).

In for example [8] and [10] algorithms are given for finding maximal bisimulations for a given system. Since the class of CPDPs is very broad, general algorithms for bisimulation may be difficult to formulate or may not be very useful. Instead, an interesting direction for future research is to define subclasses of CPDPs (such as CPDPs with linear dynamics) that allow development of automatic bisimulation techniques.

References

1. Davis, M.H.A.: Piecewise Deterministic Markov Processes: a general class of non-diffusion stochastic models. Journal Royal Statistical Soc. (B) **46** (1984) 353–388
2. Davis, M.H.A.: Markov Models and Optimization. Chapman & Hall, London (1993)
3. Strubbe, S.N., Julius, A.A., van der Schaft, A.J.: Communicating Piecewise Deterministic Markov Processes. In: Preprints Conference on Analysis and Design of Hybrid Systems ADHS 03. (2003) 349–354
4. Strubbe, S.N., van der Schaft, A.J.: Stochastic equivalence of CPDP-automata and Piecewise Deterministic Markov Processes. Accepted for the IFAC world congress 2005 (2005)
5. Milner, R.: Communication and Concurrency. Prentice Hall (1989)
6. Larsen, K.G., Skou, A.: Bisimulation through probabilistic testing. Information and Computation **94** (1991) 1–28
7. D'Argenio, P.R.: Algebras and Automata for Timed and Stochastic Systems. PhD thesis, University of Twente (1997)
8. Hermanns, H.: Interactive Markov Chains. Volume 2428 of Lecture Notes in Computer Science. Springer (2002)
9. Pappas, G.: Bisimilar linear systems. Automatica **39** (2003) 2035–2047

10. van der Schaft, A.: Bisimulation of dynamical systems. In: HSCC 2004. Volume 2993 of Lecture Notes in Computer Science., Springer (2004) 555–569
11. Lafferriere, G., Pappas, G., Sastry, S.: Hybrid systems with finite bisimulations. Lecture Notes in Computer Science **1567** (1999) 186–203
12. van der Schaft, A.: Equivalence of hybrid dynamical systems. In: Proceedings of the 16th international symposium on Mathematical Theory of Networks and Systems. (2004)
13. Strubbe, S.: Public Deliverable 17 of the Hybridge project. Technical report, Twente University (2004)
14. Strubbe, S.: PD16 of Hybridge, Semantics and interaction-structures for the CPDP-model. Technical report, Twente University (2004)
15. Parthasarathy, K.: Probability Measures on Metric Spaces. Academic Press (1967)

Sensor/Actuator Abstractions for Symbolic Embedded Control Design

Paulo Tabuada

Department of Electrical Engineering,
University of Notre Dame,
Notre Dame, IN 46556
ptabuada@nd.edu
www.nd.edu/~ptabuada

Abstract. In this paper we consider the problem of developing sensor/actuator abstractions for embedded control design. These abstractions take the form of inequalities relating sensor/actuator characteristics with the continuous dynamics' output. When satisfied, they allow to decouple control design from the choice of sensor/actuators, thus simplifying control design while ensuring implementability.

1 Introduction

The development of control theory has traditionally ignored hardware implementation to focus on the development of a large and important body of theoretical results. Nevertheless, the existing theory is responsible for the wide success of nowadays highly sophisticated and complex controlled systems. The fundamental reason behind this success has been the availability of dedicated computational hardware and sensor/actuators enabling faithful implementations of theoretically developed control laws. However, with the advent of networked embedded control systems we can no longer rely on such assumption. Instead, control algorithms are needed for tiny embedded devices with reduced computational capabilities, low resolution sensors and actuators and strong power limitations. We have thus reached a turning point where we need to rethink the foundations of systems and control theory in order to incorporate the impact of hardware limitations into the behavior achievable by control.

In this paper we take initial steps along this research direction by developing sensor/actuator abstractions for embedded control design. If, on one hand, one would like to have a design theory incorporating implementation details into feedback design, on the other hand, one would also like to restrict such details to the essential minimum. These apparently contradictory objectives can be met by summarizing implementation platform information in a reduced number of parameters. The approach described in this paper captures such platform abstractions in the form of inequalities relating sensor/actuator parameters and the observations of the continuous dynamics, over which specifications are defined. By satisfying these inequalities, it is guaranteed that *any* control design

M. Morari and L. Thiele (Eds.): HSCC 2005, LNCS 3414, pp. 640–654, 2005.

regulating the output behavior of the continuous dynamics can be implemented in a given platform. Alternatively, these inequalities can also be used to define platform requirements sufficient to run such embedded control software. Finally, the introduced inequalities also emphasize several possible tradeoffs between sensor/actuator quantization and saturation characteristics. In particular, we are able to provide answers to the following questions:

Can we determine if a given control design is implementable with certain sensor/actuator quantization characteristics?

Can we compensate poor sensor quantization by good actuator quantization, or vice-versa, in order to implement a given control design?

Can we determine if a given control design is implementable with certain sensor/actuator saturation characteristics?

Can we compensate sensor/actuator quantization with sensor/actuator saturation, or vice-versa?

The sensor/actuator abstractions presented in this paper are developed in the framework of symbolic control that was introduced by the author and coworkers in the sequence of papers [1, 2, 3, 4]. This symbolic approach is based on the existence of finite abstractions (bisimulations) of continuous control systems in several cases of interest including controllable linear systems and flat systems in discrete time. Once these symbolic models are available, it is possible to automatically synthesize (hybrid) controllers enforcing specifications given by regular languages, finite-state machines or temporal logics. Such finite controllers manipulate continuous states and inputs symbolically and allow for simple software implementations.

Recently, there has been an increase in the attention devoted to problems of control with limited resources. Several authors have addressed the problem of control in the presence of limited communication [5, 6, 7, 8] as well as stabilization in the presence of quantization [9, 10]. Closer to the work presented in this paper is the control of systems with quantized inputs. In [11] the effect of input quantization on reachability is analyzed and in [12] input quantization is used as a tool providing a fresh computational perspective of optimal control problems. The presented work differs from quantized control in that the finite symbolic models (bisimulations) used to derive controllers are not obtained by quantizing the inputs. In fact, the objective of this work is precisely to analyze the validity of our symbolic models across a different range of platforms having different quantization but also saturation characteristics. A clear advantage of the proposed approach is the independence of the symbolic model from the implementation platform. Different symbolic approaches to embedded control include maneuver-automata [13] and motion description languages [14, 15] as well as control under limited computational resources [16, 17].

This paper is organized as follows. In Section 2 we describe the models of control systems used throughout the paper and in Section 3 we recall the symbolic approach to embedded control developed by the author and coworkers. Models of sensor/actuator quantization and saturation are introduced in Section 4. We then present abstraction results for sensor quantization in Section 5, actuator

quantization in Section 6, sensor saturation in Section 7 and actuator saturation in Section 8. The main contribution summarizing the abstraction results is
presented in Section 9 and the paper ends with some discussion of the presented
results in Section 10.

2 The Models

2.1 Notation

We introduce some notation required for the remaining paper. When working
with vectors $x \in \mathbb{R}^n$ or matrices $A \in \mathbb{R}^{n \times m}$ we shall denote by x^T and A^T the
transposed vector and matrix, respectively. The absolute value of a real number
α is denoted by $|\alpha|$ while the infinity norm of a vector $x = (x_1, x_2, \ldots, x_n) \in \mathbb{R}^n$
is denoted by $||x||$ and defined as:

$$||x|| = \max_i |x_i| \tag{1}$$

This vector norm induces a norm on matrices when regarded as the representation of linear transformations between normed vector spaces. We shall denote
by $||A||$ the matrix norm induced by (1) for any matrix $A \in \mathbb{R}^{n \times m}$. This matrix
norm can be computed as:

$$||A|| = \max_i \left(\sum_j |a_{ij}| \right) \tag{2}$$

We will also need some notation to discuss the "size" of sets. Given a set $S \subseteq \mathbb{R}^n$, we denote by $diam(S)$ the diameter of S which is the supremum over the
Euclidean distances between every two pairs of points in S. When dealing with a
finite collection of sets $S = \{S_i\}_{i \in I}$, we shall use the notation $diam(S)$ to denote
$\min_{i \in I} diam(S_i)$.

2.2 Control Systems

In this paper we consider a class of systems which are know to admit finite
bisimulations: discrete time linear controllable systems [1, 2]. Even though many
of these results carry over to nonlinear flat systems we will restrict our attention
to linear systems to make the results more concrete.

Definition 1. *A discrete time linear control system Σ is defined by the following
difference equation:*

$$x(t+1) = Ax(t) + Bu(t), \qquad x \in \mathbb{R}^n, \qquad u \in \mathbb{R}^m, \qquad t \in \mathbb{N}$$

where A and B are matrices of appropriate dimensions.

Throughout the remaining paper we will assume that the columns of B are
linearly independent. This results in no loss of generality since we can always

achieve linear independence by eliminating the inputs associated with linearly dependent columns of B. The Pre operator associated with a linear control system defines the set of all points that can reach in one step a given point $x \in \mathbb{R}^n$:

$$\text{Pre}(x) = \{x' \in \mathbb{R}^n \mid \exists u \in \mathbb{R}^m, \, Ax + Bu = x'\}$$

This operator admits the usual extension to sets $S \subseteq \mathbb{R}^n$:

$$\text{Pre}(S) = \bigcup_{x \in S} \text{Pre}(x)$$

For linear systems controllability admits the following simple characterization:

Definition 2. *A discrete time linear control system Σ is said to be controllable when the following matrix has full row rank:*

$$[B|AB|A^2B|\ldots|A^{n-1}B] \tag{3}$$

In this case, there are m numbers $k_1, k_2, \ldots, k_m$ satisfying $k_i \geq k_{i+1}$, $k_1 + k_2 + \ldots + k_m = n$ and the vector space generated by the columns of (3) is also generated by the following basis:

$$\begin{aligned}
\mathcal{B} = \{\, &b_1, Ab_1, A^2b_1, \ldots, A^{k_1-1}b_1, \\
&b_2, Ab_2, A^2b_2, \ldots, A^{k_2-1}b_2, \\
&\vdots \\
&b_m, Ab_m, A^2b_m, \ldots, A^{k_m-1}b_m\}
\end{aligned}$$

where $b_1, b_2, \ldots, b_m$ are the columns of B up to re-ordering. Basis $\mathcal{B}$ induces a natural observation function $H = [H_1^T|H_2^T|\ldots|H_m^T]^T : \mathbb{R}^n \to \mathbb{R}^m$ for Σ defined by:

$$H_i x = \begin{cases} 0 & \text{if } x \in \mathcal{B} \backslash \{A^{k_i-1}b_i\} \\ \gamma_i & \text{if } x = A^{k_i-1}b_i \end{cases} \tag{4}$$

for $\gamma_i \in \mathbb{R}^+$ and $i = 1, 2, \ldots, m$. The image of the linear map H is then the natural output space of Σ.

The above definition of output map is natural in the sense that it guarantees that the pair (A, H) is observable, that is, the observability matrix:

$$\overline{\mathcal{O}} = \begin{bmatrix} H \\ HA \\ HA^2 \\ \vdots \\ HA^{n-1} \end{bmatrix}$$

has full rank. Full rank of $\overline{\mathcal{O}}$ also implies full rank of the extended observability matrix $\mathcal{O} = [\overline{\mathcal{O}}^T \ (HA^n)^T]^T$. In particular, this implies that $\mathcal{O}$ has a left inverse, simply denoted by $\mathcal{O}^{-1}$. In addition to the extended observability matrix we will also use repeatedly $\gamma_{\max}, \gamma_{\min}$ to denote, respectively, $\max_{i \in \{1,2,\ldots,m\}} \gamma_i$ and $\min_{i \in \{1,2,\ldots,m\}} \gamma_i$.

Specifications for the desired behavior of a controllable linear system Σ are given in terms of a finite number of predicates on the output space $\mathbb{R}^m$ of Σ. These predicates $p \in \mathcal{P}$ are defined by a surjective map $\pi : \mathbb{R}^m \to \mathcal{P}$. Each $p \in \mathcal{P}$ thus defines a set of points in the observation space of Σ by $\{x \in \mathbb{R}^m \mid \pi(x) = p\} = [p]$. We shall say that a point x satisfies predicate p when $\pi(x) = p$, or equivalently $x \in [p]$. In addition, we will abuse language and use the same letter $\mathcal{P}$ to denote the partition of $\mathbb{R}^m$ induced by π and defined by the sets $\{[p]\}_{p \in \mathcal{P}}$.

3   Symbolic Control of Continuous Systems

The sensor/actuator abstractions introduced in this paper are developed in the context of symbolic control of continuous systems based on finite bisimulations. This symbolic control methodology has been developed by the author and co-workers in the series of papers [1, 2, 3, 4]. The essence of the approach is the possibility of constructing a finite abstraction (bisimulation) of the continuous dynamics allowing to translate the initial control problem from the continuous to the purely discrete domain. This process was shown to be possible for a reasonable class of control systems including controllable linear systems and discrete time flat systems. The symbolic model is a finite state representation of all the symbolic output behaviors that can be generated by a given system Σ through a map $\pi : \mathbb{R}^m \to \mathcal{P}$ from the output space of Σ to a finite set of symbols $\mathcal{P}$. Standard supervisory control or temporal logic synthesis techniques can then used to obtain a finite supervisor enforcing any regular or ω-regular language specification on the symbolic output of the finite bisimulation. The resulting finite supervisor is then refined to a hybrid controller combining discrete switching logic with continuous state/input information in order to enforce the desired specification on the continuous plant. Throughout the paper we shall use the expression *symbolic controller* to refer to this type of controller. The architecture of the resulting closed loop is displayed in Figure 1 and can be intuitively described as follows. At any time $t \in \mathbb{N}$, the symbolic controller T_c sends a list of possible symbols $\{\sigma_1(t), \sigma_2(t), \ldots, \sigma_k(t)\}$ to the controlled system. Each symbol σ represents a region $[\sigma] \subseteq \mathbb{R}^n$ in the state space of Σ that can/should be reached in the next time step in order to enforce the specification. Since there are several possible symbols, a choice is made by the white box which represents a discrete decision mechanism. We are thus regarding the white box as a discrete control input capturing the nondeterminism inherent to the specification. Once a symbol has been chosen, it is communicated to T_c (in order to update its internal state) and it is enforced by feedback on Σ. Enforcing symbol σ requires selecting an input u such that the pair (x, u) satisfies $(x, u) \in \text{Pre}([\sigma])$. Continuous input u forces the continuous system Σ to jump from the current state x to a new state contained in the set defined by $[\sigma]$, that is $Ax + Bu \in [\sigma]$. Depending on the sensor/actuator characteristics it may or may not be possible to implement a given

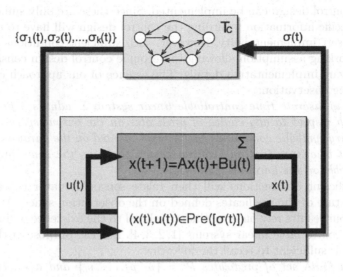

Fig. 1. Feedback interconnection between a symbolic supervisor T_c and a discrete time linear system Σ

symbolic command σ by a pair $(x, u) \in \mathrm{Pre}([\sigma])$. Sensor/actuator characteristics thus limit the behaviors that can be achieved by symbolic control.

To illustrate such limitations consider a control system with output space $\mathbb{R}$ and three predicates neg, zer, pos defined by:

$$\pi(x) = \begin{cases} pos & \text{if } x > 0 \\ zer & \text{if } x = 0 \\ neg & \text{if } x < 0 \end{cases}$$

Consider now the following specifications defined by regular expressions on the labels $\{neg, zer, pos\}$:

$$zer \cdot neg \cdot (neg + pos) \cdot pos^* \qquad zer \cdot neg \cdot pos \cdot pos^*$$

Even though both specifications use the same predicates it may not be possible to implement them on the same hardware platform. At the third time step, the first specification requires the implementation of a transition to the set associated with $(neg + pos)$ while the second specification requires a transition to the set associated with pos. Actuator saturation may now prevent point $x = -10$ to be controlled to a positive value, while it may still be possible to control it to a negative value such that in a subsequent step it can reach a positive value. In this case the hardware characteristics would allow to implement the first specification but not the second.

Two different approaches can be taken towards the study of symbolic control implementability. Specific results for a particular control design can be given or sufficient, but conservative, results applying to *any* control design can be developed. In this paper we consider sufficient implementability conditions ensuring that *any* control design can be implemented. Since these are only sufficient conditions, specific information regarding the control design will have to be used in order to assert implementability. However, such sufficient conditions provide a valuable working assumption allowing to decouple control design considerations from hardware implementation details. The essence of our approach consists in the following observation:

Since any discrete time controllable linear system Σ admits a finite bisimulation with respect to any choice of predicates on the output space[1], ensuring that arbitrary symbolic commands can be implemented on the hardware platform is sufficient to ensure that any control design based on the same predicates is implementable on the hardware platform.

Our sufficient abstractions will then relate sensor/actuator characteristics with the nature of the predicates defined on the observation space. At the technical level our results rely on several facts related to the existence of finite bisimulations of controllable linear systems [1, 2, 3, 4]. For the purpose of this paper, however, it is sufficient to recall the following:

Given a finite set of predicates $\mathcal{P} = \{p_1, p_2, \ldots, p_l\}$ and a surjective map $\pi : \mathbb{R}^m \to \mathcal{P}$ defined on the output space of controllable discrete time linear system Σ, the symbolic commands σ issued by discrete supervisor T_c correspond to subsets of $\mathbb{R}^n$ defined by the following equalities:

$$p_1 = \pi \circ Hx \tag{5}$$

$$p_2 = \pi \circ H(Ax + Bu_1) \tag{6}$$

$$p_3 = \pi \circ H(A^2x + ABu_1 + Bu_2) \tag{7}$$

$$\vdots$$

$$p_{k_1} = \pi \circ H(A^{k_1-1}x + A^{k_1-2}Bu_1 + \ldots + Bu_{k_1-1}) \tag{8}$$

for some $u_1, u_2, \ldots, u_{k_1-1} \in \mathbb{R}^m$ and $p_1, p_2, \ldots, p_{k_1} \in \mathcal{P}$.

In other words, each symbolic command represents a set defined by the existence of a sequence of predicates $p_1, p_2, \ldots, p_{k_1} \in \mathcal{P}$ and a sequence of inputs $u_1, u_2, \ldots, u_{k_1-1} \in \mathbb{R}^m$ such that the current state satisfies predicate p_1, the next state satisfies predicate p_2, the following state satisfies p_3 and so on.

4   Sensor/Actuator Models

In this paper we are mainly interested in two characteristics of sensors/actuators: quantization and saturation. We model a sensor as a map S from $\mathbb{R}$ to some space (finite or infinite) of measurements M. For simplicity of presentation we will assume the existence of a sensor S_i for each state x_i. The complete state measurement is therefore given by the vector $[S_1(x_1) \ S_2(x_2) \ \ldots \ S_n(x_n)]^T$. We will also assume that $M \subseteq \mathbb{R}$ as this allows to model an ideal sensor by the indentity map on $\mathbb{R}$. Quantization is described by the number Δ_S defining how state values are transformed into measurements:

---

[1] See Definition 2 for output space.

$$S(x) = \begin{cases} \Gamma_S & \text{if } x \geq \Gamma_S + \frac{1}{2}\Delta_S \\ \Gamma_S - 1 & \text{if } x \in [\Gamma_S - \frac{1}{2}\Delta_S, \Gamma_S + \frac{1}{2}\Delta_S[\\ \quad \vdots & \\ 2\Delta_S & \text{if } x \in [\frac{3}{2}\Delta_S, \frac{5}{2}\Delta_S[\\ \Delta_S & \text{if } x \in [\frac{1}{2}\Delta_S, \frac{3}{2}\Delta_S[\\ 0 & \text{if } x \in [-\frac{1}{2}\Delta_S, \frac{1}{2}\Delta_S[\\ -\Delta_S & \text{if } x \in [-\frac{3}{2}\Delta_S, -\frac{1}{2}\Delta_S[\\ -2\Delta_S & \text{if } x \in [-\frac{5}{2}\Delta_S, -\frac{3}{2}\Delta_S[\\ \quad \vdots & \\ -\Gamma_S + 1 & \text{if } x \in [-\Gamma_S - \frac{1}{2}\Delta_S, -\Gamma_S + \frac{1}{2}\Delta_S[\\ -\Gamma_S & \text{if } x < -\Gamma_S - \frac{1}{2}\Delta_S \end{cases} \tag{9}$$

A sensor S thus maps sets of length Δ_S into its mid-point and saturates with the value Γ_S or $-\Gamma_S$ when the threshold $\Gamma_S + \frac{1}{2}\Delta_S$ or $-\Gamma_S - \frac{1}{2}\Delta_S$ is reached, respectively. The number Γ_S characterizes the saturation of the sensor. A sensor with quantization Δ_S and saturation Γ_S will be called a (Δ_S, Γ_S)-sensor. Given a set of sensors $S_1, S_2, \ldots, S_n$ used to measure the state we will simply refer to the quantization of such set by $\Delta_S = \max_{i \in \{1,2,\ldots,n\}} \Delta_{S_i}$ and we will refer to the saturation of the set by $\Gamma_S = \min_{i \in \{1,2,\ldots,n\}} \Gamma_{S_i}$.

Actuators are similarly described. They are modeled by a map A from an output space $O \subseteq \mathbb{R}$ to $\mathbb{R}$. Actuators are also described by quantization Δ_A and saturation Γ_A. The map A has the same form as (9) but Δ_S and Γ_S are now Δ_A and Γ_A, respectively.

5 Sensor Quantization

In this section we address the effects of sensor quantization on implementability of control designs. In particular, we answer the following question:

How should sensor quantization be related to the predicates $p \in \mathcal{P}$ in order to implement a given design?

Proposition 1. *Let Σ be a discrete time controllable linear system and $\mathcal{P}$ a finite set of predicates on the output space of Σ. If the following inequality is satisfied:*

$$diam(\mathcal{P}) > ||\mathcal{O}||\Delta_S \tag{10}$$

then every symbolic controller enforcing a specification defined over the symbolic output $\mathcal{P}$ is implementable with (Δ_S, ∞)-sensors and $(0, \infty)$-actuators.

Before proving this result we make some remarks regarding inequality (10). As it was intuitively expected, increasing sensor quantization has the unpleasant effect of increasing also the diameter of the observation predicates. Therefore if a certain minimum diameter for the predicates is required to express certain properties, an upper bound on sensor quantization is also being enforced. Furthermore, the linear relation between $diam(\mathcal{P})$ and Δ_S is characterized by the observability properties of Σ as defined by $||\mathcal{O}||$. In fact, a less conservative estimate for the bound on the diameter of $\mathcal{P}$ is given by $diam(\mathcal{P}) > ||HA^n||\Delta_S$ as can be seen from (18) in the proof of Proposition 1. However, the extended observation matrix captures, in a single object, all the continuous dynamics information required for all the abstractions presented in this paper.

Proof. We first consider the case where $m = 1$, that is, Σ only has one input. In this case, the set represented by a predicate $p_i \in \mathcal{P}$ is of the form $[\alpha_i, \beta_i]$, $[\alpha_i, \beta_i[$, $]\alpha_i, \beta_i]$ or $]\alpha_i, \beta_i[$ for $\alpha_i, \beta_i \in \mathbb{R} \cup \{\infty\}$. For simplicity we will only consider the case $[\alpha_i, \beta_i]$ since the same argument applies to the remaining cases. Let σ be a symbolic command issued by T_c. As discussed in Section 3, each such command is associated with a subset of $\mathbb{R}^n$ defined by points $y \in \mathbb{R}^n$ satisfying:

$$p_1 = \pi \circ Hy \tag{11}$$

$$p_2 = \pi \circ HAy = \pi \circ H(Ay + Bu_1) \tag{12}$$

$$p_3 = \pi \circ HA^2 y = \pi \circ H(A^2 y + ABu_1 + Bu_2) \tag{13}$$

$$\vdots$$

$$p_{k_1} = \pi \circ HA^{n-1} y = \pi \circ H(A^{k_1-1} y + A^{k_1-2}Bu_1 + \ldots + Bu_{k_1-1}) \tag{14}$$

for some $u_1, u_2, \ldots, u_{k_1-1} \in \mathbb{R}$ and $p_1, p_2, \ldots, p_{k_1} \in \mathcal{P}$. If a point x will move to $Ax + Bu = y \in [\sigma]$, then by replacing y with $Ax + Bu$ in equations (11) through (14) and using (4), we see that the only constraint involving u is given by:

$$\pi \circ H(A^{k_1} x + A^{k_1-1}Bu) = p_{k_1} \tag{15}$$

Denoting by $\widehat{x}$ the quantized value of x, we have $x = \widehat{x} + d$ with $||d|| \leq \frac{\Delta_S}{2}$. We can therefore rewrite (15) in terms of $\widehat{x}$ which leads to the following equation that has to be satisfied for all $||d|| \leq \frac{\Delta_S}{2}$:

$$HA^{k_1}\widehat{x} + HA^{k_1}d + HA^{k_1-1}Bu \in [\alpha_{k_1}, \beta_{k_1}] \tag{16}$$

A sufficient condition for solvability of the above equation is:

$$HA^{k_1}\widehat{x} + HA^{k_1-1}Bu \in [\alpha_{k_1} + |HA^{k_1}d|, \beta_{k_1} - |HA^{k_1}d|]$$

Since this equation can always be solved for u, provided that the right hand side is a nonempty set, we must have:

$$\beta_{k_1} - |HA^{k_1}d| > \alpha_{k_1} + |HA^{k_1}d| \Leftrightarrow diam(p_{k_1}) = \beta_{k_1} - \alpha_{k_1} > 2|HA^{k_1}d| \tag{17}$$

Furthermore, as:

$$2|HA^{k_1}d| \leq 2||HA^{k_1}||||d|| \tag{18}$$

$$= 2||\mathbf{n}^T \mathcal{O}||||d||$$

$$\leq 2||\mathbf{n}||||\mathcal{O}||||d||$$

$$\leq ||\mathcal{O}||\Delta_S$$

where $\mathbf{n}$ denotes the vector $(0, 0, \ldots, 0, 1) \in \mathbb{R}^n$, we conclude that if:

$$diam(\mathcal{P}) > ||\mathcal{O}||\Delta_S$$

holds, then (17) also holds and a transition from any $x \in X$ to some $Ax + Bu = y \in Y$ can be implemented.

We now consider the general case. Since we can always under-approximate a set associated with $p \in \mathcal{P}$ by the Cartesian product of m sets of the form $[\alpha, \beta]$, that is $\Pi_{j=1}^n [\alpha_j, \beta_j]$, and since by (4) the observation function decouples the influence of each input channel, we can apply the previous argument to each of the m input channels obtaining m conditions of the form $diam(\mathcal{P}) > ||\mathcal{O}||\Delta_S$. $\square$

6   Actuator Quantization

We now turn to the effects of actuator quantization and the following related question:

How should sensor and actuator quantization be related to the predicates $p \in \mathcal{P}$ in order to implement a given design?

Proposition 2. *Let Σ be a discrete time controllable linear system and $\mathcal{P}$ a finite set of predicates on the output space of Σ. If the following inequality is satisfied:*

$$diam(\mathcal{P}) > ||\mathcal{O}||\Delta_S + \gamma_{\max}\Delta_A \qquad (19)$$

then every symbolic controller enforcing a specification defined on the symbolic output $\mathcal{P}$ is implementable with (Δ_S, ∞)-sensors and (Δ_A, ∞)-actuators.

Equation (19) shows that actuation quantization further contributes to limit the diameter of the predicates. However, we also see that when $diam(\mathcal{P})$ has been fixed by some particular design, several different combinations of sensor/actuator quantization can be used in the implementation.

Proof. We use the notation of the proof of Proposition 1 and start by considering the single input case, that is $m = 1$. To implement a symbolic command σ, the following equation must have a solution in u for every d satisfying $||d|| \leq \frac{\Delta_S}{2}$ (see (16)):

$$HA^{k_1}\widehat{x} + HA^{k_1-1}Bu \in [\alpha_n, \beta_n] - HA^{k_1}d \qquad (20)$$

To solve (20) for u it is sufficient to have:

$$\gamma u \in [\alpha_{k_1} + ||\mathcal{O}||\frac{\Delta_S}{2} - HA^{k_1}\widehat{x}, \beta_{k_1} - ||\mathcal{O}||\frac{\Delta_S}{2} - HA^{k_1}\widehat{x}] \qquad (21)$$

since $|HA^{k_1}d| \leq ||\mathcal{O}||\frac{\Delta_S}{2}$, as shown in the proof of Proposition 1. Using now $u = z\Delta_A$ with $z \in \mathbb{Z}$ and solving for z we obtain:

$$z \in \frac{1}{\gamma\Delta_A}[\alpha_{k_1} + ||\mathcal{O}||\frac{\Delta_S}{2} - HA^{k_1}\widehat{x}, \beta_{k_1} - ||\mathcal{O}||\frac{\Delta_S}{2} - HA^{k_1}\widehat{x}]$$

Since z is an integer, the previous equation is satisfied only when the right-hand side interval has length greater than 1, that is:

$$\frac{1}{\gamma\Delta_A}\left(\beta_{k_1} - ||\mathcal{O}||\frac{\Delta_S}{2} - \alpha_{k_1} - ||\mathcal{O}||\frac{\Delta_S}{2}\right) > 1$$

which can be rewritten as:

$$diam(p_{k_1}) - ||\mathcal{O}||\Delta_S > \gamma\Delta_A$$

and as it must be satisfied for every $p \in \mathcal{P}$, leads to (19).

We now consider now the multi input case. As in the proof of Proposition 1 we under-approximate a set associated with a predicate $p \in \mathcal{P}$ by a Cartesian product of sets of the form $[\alpha_i, \beta_i]$ and use the previous argument for each of the m input channels. We thus obtain a set of sufficient inequalities of the form

$$diam(p_{k_i}) - ||\mathcal{O}||\Delta_S > \gamma_i\Delta_A$$

which are satisfied by taking γ_i to be $\gamma_{\max}$.   □

7   Sensor Saturation

Having discussed quantization effect in the previous sections we now turn to the effects of saturation. The motivation for the results to be presented comes from the following question:

How should sensor saturation be related to the predicates $p \in \mathcal{P}$ in order to implement a given design?

Proposition 3. *Let Σ be a discrete time controllable linear system and $\mathcal{P}$ a finite set of predicates on the output space of Σ. If for every predicate $p \in \mathcal{P}$ the following inclusion holds:*

$$[p] \subseteq \left\{z \in \mathbb{R}^m \mid ||z|| \leq \Gamma_S/||\mathcal{O}^{-1}||\right\} \qquad (22)$$

then every symbolic controller enforcing a specification defined on the symbolic output $\mathcal{P}$ is implementable with (α, Γ_S)-sensors and (β, ∞)-actuators for any $\alpha, \beta \in \mathbb{R}_0^+$.

The previous result shows that by properly restricting the output predicates we can achieve implementability, with respect to sensor saturation, independently of the symbolic controller design. A less conservative approach would require inclusion (3) to hold, not for every $p \in \mathcal{P}$, but only for the predicates appearing in the behavior enforced by a particular choice for discrete supervisor T_c. This option, even though less conservative, would no longer be independent of symbolic controller design as it requires knowledge of T_c.

In any case, the effect of sensor actuation is decoupled from the effect of sensor or actuator quantization. This implies that we cannot trade quantization by saturation or vice-versa.

Proof. Given the sensor saturation characteristics, only the states belonging to $\Pi_{i=1}^n[-\Gamma_{S_i}, \Gamma_{S_i}]$ can be measured. Conservatively, we further restrict the set of observable states to $[-\Gamma_S, \Gamma_S]^n \subseteq \Pi_{i=1}^n[-\Gamma_{S_i}, \Gamma_{S_i}]$. In order to implement symbolic commands issued by T_c, it is sufficient to guarantee that every state trajectory of the controlled behavior remains within the set $[-\Gamma_S, \Gamma_S]^n$. Consider now a symbolic command σ issued by T_c. Such command is associated with a set $[\sigma] \subseteq \mathbb{R}^n$ defined by equations (5) through (8). If the current state x, satisfying

$$Hx = \mathbf{z} \tag{23}$$

will jump to a state $x \in [\sigma]$, then we can compactly write (23) and (5) through (8) as:

$$\mathcal{O}x = Z$$

with:

$$Z = \begin{bmatrix} \mathbf{z} \\ \mathbf{z}_1 \\ \mathbf{z}_2 \\ \vdots \\ \mathbf{z}_{k_1} \end{bmatrix}$$

for $\mathbf{z}_i \in [p_i]$, $i = 1, 2, \ldots, k_1$. Since $\mathcal{O}$ admits a left inverse by construction, $x = \mathcal{O}^{-1}Z$ and:

$$||x|| = ||\mathcal{O}^{-1}Z|| \leq ||\mathcal{O}^{-1}|| \, ||Z||$$

Furthermore, $\mathbf{z}_i \in [p]$ and the assumption $[p] \subseteq \{z \in \mathbb{R}^m \mid ||z|| \leq \Gamma_S/||\mathcal{O}^{-1}||\}$ implies $||Z|| \leq \Gamma_S/||\mathcal{O}^{-1}||$ from which we conclude $||x|| \leq \Gamma_S$, thus ensuring that controlled trajectories remain in the set $[-\Gamma_S, \Gamma_S]^n$, as desired.   □

8   Actuator Saturation

The last considered effect is actuator saturation motivated by the following question:

How should sensor and actuator saturation be related to the predicates $p \in \mathcal{P}$ in order to implement a given design?

Proposition 4. *Let Σ be a discrete time controllable linear system and $\mathcal{P}$ a finite set of predicates on the output space of Σ. If for every predicate $p \in \mathcal{P}$ inclusion (22) holds and:*

$$\Gamma_A > \frac{\Gamma_S}{\gamma_{\min}}(1 + ||\mathcal{O}||) \tag{24}$$

then every symbolic controller enforcing a specification defined on the symbolic output $\mathcal{P}$ is implementable with (α, Γ_S)-sensors and (β, Γ_A)-actuators for any $\alpha, \beta \in \mathbb{R}_0^+$.

As expected, actuator saturation scales linearly with observation saturation. This is natural since an input making the continuous system jump in one step between two maximally distant points inside the sensor range may be required. This lower bound on input saturation can be reduced by requiring, as part of the specification, that only δ length jumps can be taken. In this case we can replace Γ_S by δ in above expression (24) to reduce the lower bound on Γ_A. Once again we see that saturation effects can be decoupled from quantization effects.

Proof. As usual we treat the single input case first. From the proof of Proposition 2 we know that solvability of (21) for u is a sufficient condition for implementability. It then suffices to ensure that γu can reach the following lower bound:

$$\gamma u > \alpha_{k_1} - ||\mathcal{O}||\frac{\Delta_S}{2} - HA^{k_1}\widehat{x}$$

for all possible values of α_{k_1} and $\widehat{x}$. Since both α_{k_1} and $\widehat{x}$ are bounded by Γ_S, it follows that if $\Gamma_A > \frac{\Gamma_S}{\gamma_{\min}}(1 + ||\mathcal{O}||)$ we can choose $u \in [-\Gamma_A, \Gamma_A]$ such that:

$$\gamma u > \Gamma_S + ||\mathcal{O}||\Gamma_S$$
$$\geq \alpha_{k_1} - HA^{k_1}\widehat{x}$$
$$\geq \alpha_{k_1} - ||\mathcal{O}||\frac{\Delta_S}{2} - HA^{k_1}\widehat{x}$$

thus obtaining the desired sufficient condition.

Following the same argument we obtain for the multi-input case m inequalities of the form $\Gamma_A > \frac{\Gamma_S}{\gamma_i}(1 + ||\mathcal{O}||)$ which are enforced by taking γ_i to be $\gamma_{\min}$. □

9   Main Result

For convenience we summarize Propositions 1,2,3 and 4 in the following theorem:

Theorem 1. *Let Σ be a discrete time controllable linear system and $\mathcal{P}$ a finite set of predicates on the output space of Σ. If the following inequalities hold:*

$$diam(\mathcal{P}) > ||\mathcal{O}||\Delta_S + \gamma_{\max}\Delta_A \tag{25}$$

$$\Gamma_A > \frac{\Gamma_S}{\gamma_{\min}}(1 + ||\mathcal{O}||) \tag{26}$$

and for every predicate $p \in \mathcal{P}$ the following inclusion also holds:

$$[p] \subseteq \left\{ z \in \mathbb{R}^m \mid ||z|| \leq \Gamma_S/||\mathcal{O}^{-1}|| \right\} \tag{27}$$

then every symbolic controller enforcing a specification defined on the symbolic output $\mathcal{P}$ is implementable with (Δ_S, Γ_S)-sensors and (Δ_A, Γ_A)-actuators.

Theorem 1 collects, in the form of inequalities, the abstractions developed in this paper. These inequalities represent simple and intuitive conditions for implementability: the sets $[p]$ have to be large enough to accommodate the errors introduced by sensor and actuator quantization as described by (25); sensor saturation limits the range of states that can be measured and the symbolic outputs $p \in \mathcal{P}$ must represent sets $[p]$ reflecting such state limitations as described by (27); and actuator saturation has to permit arbitrary jumps between states that can be measured as described by (26). In all these equalities the system dynamics plays a fundamental role defined by the presence of the extended observation matrix in all the inequalities. A large value for $\|\mathcal{O}\|$ poses additional limitations on the relation between sensing, actuation and output predicates since it implies an increase of the "size" of the sets $[p]$, an increase on actuator saturation and a reduction on the "size" of the output space that can be used to define predicates.

10   Discussion

The sensor/actuator abstractions presented in this paper are clearly conservative and can be improved in several different ways. However, improving the equalities in Theorem 1 would require embedding quantization and saturation information into control design. As with any design problem, the right level of abstraction depends on the particular problem being solved. When the presented abstractions fail to hold, determining implementability of a given design requires a deeper analysis of the effects of the implementation platform in the given design. However, the presented results are still useful as a working assumption for the early design phases decoupling control requirements from hardware requirements.

There several other hardware requirements that should also be addressed and have not been discussed in this paper. These include (real-time) computational capabilities and power consumption among others. Developing similar abstractions to capture the influence of these properties on embedded control design in currently being addressed by the author.

References

1. Tabuada, P., Pappas, G.J.: Finite bisimulations of controllable linear systems. In: Proceedings of the 42nd IEEE Conference on Decision and Control, Hawaii (2003)
2. Tabuada, P.: Flatness and finite bisimulations in discrete time. In: Proceedings of the Sixteenth International Symposium on Mathematical Theory of Networks and Systems, Leuven, Belgium (2004)
3. Tabuada, P., Pappas, G.J.: From discrete specifications to hybrid control. In: Proceedings of the 42nd IEEE Conference on Decision and Control, Hawaii (2003)
4. Tabuada, P., Pappas, G.J.: Linear Time Logic control of linear systems. IEEE Transaction on Automatic Control (2004) Under review, available at www.nd.edu/~ptabuada.
5. Hristu, D., Morgansen, K.: Limited communication control. Systems and Control Letters **37** (1999) 193 – 205
6. Wong, W.S., Brockett, R.: Systems with finite communication bandwidth constraints II: Stabilization with limited information feedback. IEEE Transactions on Automatic Control **44** (1999) 1049–1053

7. Hespanha, J., Ortega, A., Vasudevan, L.: Towards the control of linear systems with minimum bit-rate. In: Proceedings of the Int. Symp. on the Mathematical Theory of Networks and Systems, Notre Dame, Indiana (2002)
8. Tatikonda, S., Mitter, S.: Control under communication constraints. IEEE Transactions on Automatic Control **49** (2004) 1056–1068
9. Elia, N., Mitter, S.: Stabilization of linear systems with limited information. IEEE Transactions on Automatic Control **46** (2001) 1384–1400
10. Liberzon, D.: Hybrid feedback stabilization of systems with quantized signals. Automatica **39** (2003) 1543–1554
11. Bicchi, A., Marigo, A., Piccoli, B.: On the rechability of quantized control systems. IEEE Transaction on Automatic Control (2002)
12. Pancanti, S., Leonardi, L., Pallottino, L., Bicchi, A.: Optimal control of quantized linear systems. In Tomlin, C., Greenstreet, M.R., eds.: Hybrid Systems: Computation and Control. Lecture Notes in Computer Sience. Springer-Verlag (2002) 351–363
13. Frazzoli, E.: Explicit solutions for optimal maneuver-based motion planning. In: Proceedings of the 42nd IEEE Conference on Decision and Control, Maui, Hawaii (2003)
14. Hristu-Varsakelis, D., Egerstedt, M., Krishnaprasad, P.: On the structural complexity of the motion description language mdle. In: Proceedings of the 42nd IEEE Conference on Decision and Control, Maui, Hawaii (2003)
15. Austin, A., Egerstedt, M.: Mode reconstruction for source coding and multi-modal control. In Alur, R., Pappas, G.J., eds.: Hybrid Systems: Computation and Control. Volume 2993 of Lecture Notes in Computer Science. Springer-Verlag (2004) 36–49
16. Krogh, B., Maler, O., Mahfoudh, M.: On control with bounded computational resources. In Damm, W., Olderog, E.R., eds.: Formal Techniques in Real-Time and Fault-Tolerant Systems, 7th International Symposium, FTRTFT 2002. Volume 2469 of Lecture Notes in Computer Science. Springer-Verlag (2002) 147–164
17. Palopoli, L., Pinello, C., Vincentelli, A.S., Elghaoui, L., Bicchi, A.: Synthesis of robust control systems under resource constraints. In Tomlin, C., Greenstreet, M.R., eds.: Hybrid Systems: Computation and Control. Lecture Notes in Computer Sience. Springer-Verlag (2002) 337–350

Modeling and Control of Networked Control Systems with Random Delays*

Yan Wang, Zeng Qi Sun, and Fu Chun Sun

State Key Lab of Intelligent Technology and Systems,
Department of Computer Science, Tsinghua University,
Beijing 100084, P. R. China

Abstract. This paper discusses the problems of control design and stability analysis of the networked control systems(NCSs) with random delays. The network-induced delays of the NCS are considered as interval variables governed by a Markov chain. Using the upper and lower bounds of the delays, a discrete-time Markovian jump system with norm-bounded uncertainties is presented to model the NCS. Based on this model, a state feedback controller can be constructed via a set of linear matrix inequalities. Simulations are given to illustrate the proposed results.

1 Introduction

The research of the networked control systems has a large interest in distributed control applications. In an NCS, the communication network is used as a medium to interconnect the different components of an industrial control system. The networked control architecture reduces cost of installation and reconfiguration, and offers ease of maintenance, and great flexibility (see [11]). Inevitably, the communication network which connects sensors, actuators and controllers introduces different forms of time delay (see [5]). The delays could potentially deteriorate the stability and control performance of the system. Since the network-induced delays are usually time-varying and nondeterministic, the traditional modeling and control methodologies for delay systems may not gain satisfying performance for the control of NCSs.

Based on past output measurement, predictor-based delay compensation method for NCSs with random delays using queues was developed by Luck and Ray in [8]. Liou and Ray proposed the synthesis of a stochastic regulator in the

---

* The work was supported by the National Key Project for Basic Research of China (Grant No: G2002cb312205), the National Science Foundation for Key Technical Research of China (Grant No: 90205008, 60334020), the National Science Foundation of China (Grant No: 60174018 and 60084002), China Postdoctoral Science Foundation (Grant No: 2003034150), and the National Excellent Doctoral Dissertation Foundation (Grant No: 200041). Corresponding author: Yan Wang, E-Mail: w-yan@mail.tsinghua.edu.cn

M. Morari and L. Thiele (Eds.): HSCC 2005, LNCS 3414, pp. 655–666, 2005.

presence of randomly varying delays from the controller to actuator in [7]. The stochastic optimal controller and the optimal state estimator of an NCS on random delay networks were presented by Nilsson in [9]. In [9], a Markov chain was applied to model the delays and the LQG optimal controller was derived for the NCS. Walsh *et al.* analyzed the stability of nonlinear networked control systems using the perturbation method in [11]. The hybrid systems stability analysis technique was used to discuss the stability of NCSs in [13]. Lian analyzed and modeled a MIMO networked control system with multiple time delays in [6]. In the stochastic approaches of [4], [7], [8] and [9] etc., the stochastic Riccati-iteration equation is difficult to solve since the iteration involves expectation calculation of stochastic variables. The linear matrix inequality(LMI) approach offers efficient numerical schemes for the analysis and design of control systems (see [2]). The motivations of this paper are to present a new model for the NCSs with random delays and to design the control law in terms of LMIs.

In this paper, we will first describe the NCS as a discrete-time Markovian jump system. Effects of network queues, varying network loads can be described by the states of a Markov chain. In each different mode $r_k = i$ of the Markov chain, the delay is a variable in an interval instead of the random delay with probability distribution function proposed by Nillson (see [9]). Based on the delay intervals which are related to different modes of the Markov chain, the corresponding NCS is described by a discrete-time Markovian jump system with norm-bounded uncertainties. Using this NCS model, LMI technique can be applied to design the controller.

This paper is organized as follows. The discrete-time Markovian jump system with norm-bounded uncertainties is derived to describe the NCS in Sect. 2. Section 3 studies the stability problem of the networked control system. Section 4 presents the design of the controller based on LMI. A numerical example is provided in Sect. 5. Finally, concluding remarks are offered in Sect. 6.

Notation: If $\breve{A} = [\breve{a}_{ij}]$ and $\hat{A} = [\hat{a}_{ij}]$ are two matrices with property that $\breve{a}_{ij} < \hat{a}_{ij}$ for all i, j, the interval matrix $[\breve{A} \ \hat{A}]$ is defined as

$$[\breve{A} \ \hat{A}] = \{C = [c_{ij}] : \breve{a}_{ij} \le c_{ij} \le \hat{a}_{ij}, \text{for all } i,j\}. \tag{1}$$

Throughout the paper, the superscript T stands for matrix transposition. $\lambda_{\min}(\cdot)$, $\lambda_{\max}(\cdot)$, respectively, mean the minimum and the maximum eigenvalue of the corresponding matrix. R^n denotes n dimensional Euclidean space. $\mathbf{E}\{\cdot\}$ and $\mathbf{E}\{\cdot|y\}$, respectively, denote the expectation operator and the conditional expectation operator on y.

2   System Modeling and Assumptions

Consider the networked control system in Fig. 1. The assumptions about the control system are described as follows:

1. The sensor is time-driven, the controller and actuator are event-driven.
2. For analysis purpose, the sensor-controller delay τ_k^{sc} and controller-actuator delay τ_k^{ca} are lumped together as $\tau_k = \tau_k^{sc} + \tau_k^{ca}$.

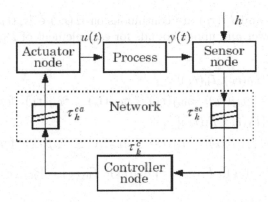

Fig. 1. Networked control system

3. The network induced delay is bounded. The total delay is shorter than one sampling period h.

4. The network clock is synchronized.

5. The probability of data loss, due to noise in the communication medium and protocol malfunctions, is zero.

In this paper, effects of network queues, varying network loads can be described by the states of a Markov chain. The transitions between different states in the network are modeled with a discrete state Markov chain $\{r_k\}$ with transition probabilities:

$$\wp\{r_{k+1} = j | r_k = i\} = \wp_{ij}, \forall i, j \in S. \tag{2}$$

$S = \{1, 2, ..., N\}$ is a finite state space about the network loads. Together with every state in the Markov chain, we provide an interval variable to model the delay for the corresponding network loads. The network delay of the NCS is denoted as $\tau_k(r_k)$, and $\tau_k(r_k) \in [\check{\tau}_k(r_k), \hat{\tau}_k(r_k)]$, $\check{\tau}_k(r_k)$ and $\hat{\tau}_k(r_k)$ are lower and upper bounds of the interval variable at state r_k.

Consider a continuous-time linear plant model:

$$\dot{x}(t) = Ax(t) + Bu(t), \tag{3}$$

where $x(t) \in R^n$, $u(t) \in R^m$. Matrices A, B are real matrices with appropriate dimensions. We assume that the plant state $x(t)$ can be measured directly.

When the control loop is closed over the network, in order to analyze the closed-loop system in discrete-time, we will discretize the continuous-time plant at the sampling instants as:

$$x_{k+1} = \Phi x_k + \Gamma_0(\tau_k)u_k + \Gamma_1(\tau_k)u_{k-1}, \tag{4}$$

where

$$\Phi = e^{Ah}, \; \Gamma_0(\tau_k) = \int_0^{h-\tau_k} e^{As}ds B, \; \Gamma_1(\tau_k) = \int_{h-\tau_k}^h e^{As}ds B. \tag{5}$$

Clearly, $\Gamma_0(\tau_k)$ and $\Gamma_1(\tau_k)$ are continuous on $\tau_k(r_k) \in [\check{\tau}_k(r_k), \hat{\tau}_k(r_k)]$. From (5), we can find lower and upper bounds for each element of $\Gamma_0(\tau_k)$ and $\Gamma_1(\tau_k)$, i.e.,

$$\Gamma_0(\tau_k) \in [\check{\Gamma}_0(r_k), \hat{\Gamma}_0(r_k)]$$
$$= \{\Gamma_0(\tau_k) = [\gamma_{0ij}(\tau_k)] : \check{\gamma}_{0ij}(r_k) \leq \gamma_{0ij}(\tau_k) \leq \hat{\gamma}_{0ij}(r_k), \text{ for all } i, j\}, \quad (6)$$
$$\Gamma_1(\tau_k) \in [\check{\Gamma}_1(r_k), \hat{\Gamma}_1(r_k)]$$
$$= \{\Gamma_1(\tau_k) = [\gamma_{1ij}(\tau_k)] : \check{\gamma}_{1ij}(r_k) \leq \gamma_{1ij}(\tau_k) \leq \hat{\gamma}_{1ij}(r_k), \text{ for all } i, j\}, \quad (7)$$

where, $\check{\Gamma}_0(r_k) = [\check{\gamma}_{0ij}(r_k)]$, $\check{\Gamma}_1(r_k) = [\check{\gamma}_{1ij}(r_k)]$, $\hat{\Gamma}_0(r_k) = [\hat{\gamma}_{0ij}(r_k)]$ and $\hat{\Gamma}_1(r_k) = [\hat{\gamma}_{1ij}(r_k)]$.

Introduce

$$\bar{\Gamma}_0(r_k) = \frac{1}{2}(\check{\Gamma}_0(r_k) + \hat{\Gamma}_0(r_k)), \quad \tilde{\Gamma}_0(r_k) = \frac{1}{2}(\hat{\Gamma}_0(r_k) - \check{\Gamma}_0(r_k)), \quad (8)$$

then the elements $\tilde{\gamma}_{0ij}(r_k)$ of $\tilde{\Gamma}_0(r_k)$ are nonnegative. The interval matrix is given by

$$\Gamma_0(\tau_k) = \bar{\Gamma}_0(r_k) + \Delta\Gamma_0(\tau_k) = \bar{\Gamma}_0(r_k) + \delta \cdot \tilde{\Gamma}_0(r_k), \quad -1 \leq \delta \leq 1. \quad (9)$$

From the interval system theory, $\Delta\Gamma_0(\tau_k) = \delta \cdot \tilde{\Gamma}_0(r_k)$ can be decomposed as

$$\Delta\Gamma_0(\tau_k) = E_0(r_k)\Delta_0(\tau_k)D_0(r_k), \quad \Delta_0^T(\tau_k)\Delta_0(\tau_k) \leq I, \quad (10)$$

where

$$E_0(r_k) = \left[\sqrt{\tilde{\gamma}_{011}(r_k)}e_1 \cdots \sqrt{\tilde{\gamma}_{01m}(r_k)}e_1 \cdots \sqrt{\tilde{\gamma}_{0nm}(r_k)}e_n \right], \quad (11)$$
$$D_0(r_k) = \left[\sqrt{\tilde{\gamma}_{011}(r_k)}f_1 \cdots \sqrt{\tilde{\gamma}_{01m}(r_k)}f_m \cdots \sqrt{\tilde{\gamma}_{0nm}(r_k)}f_m \right]^T, \quad (12)$$

where $e_i (i = 1, 2, ..., n)$ and $f_i (i = 1, 2, ..., m)$ are identity vectors. Thus,

$$\Gamma_0(\tau_k) = \bar{\Gamma}_0(r_k) + E_0(r_k)\Delta_0(\tau_k)D_0(r_k). \quad (13)$$

Similarly, $\Gamma_1(\tau_k)$ can be denoted by

$$\Gamma_1(\tau_k) = \bar{\Gamma}_1(r_k) + \Delta\Gamma_1(\tau_k) = \bar{\Gamma}_1(r_k) + E_1(r_k)\Delta_1(\tau_k)D_1(r_k), \quad \Delta_1^T(\tau_k)\Delta_1(\tau_k) \leq I. \quad (14)$$

Let

$$E(r_k) = [E_0(r_k) \ E_1(r_k)], \quad H_0(r_k) = \begin{bmatrix} D_0(r_k) \\ 0 \end{bmatrix},$$
$$H_1(r_k) = \begin{bmatrix} 0 \\ D_1(r_k) \end{bmatrix}, \quad \Delta(\tau_k) = \begin{bmatrix} \Delta_0(\tau_k) & 0 \\ 0 & \Delta_1(\tau_k) \end{bmatrix}, \quad (15)$$

then

$$[\Delta\Gamma_0(\tau_k) \ \Delta\Gamma_1(\tau_k)] = E(r_k)\Delta(\tau_k)[H_0(r_k) \ H_1(r_k)], \quad \Delta^T(\tau_k)\Delta(\tau_k) \leq I. \quad (16)$$

From the above analysis, when the network-induced delay is varying in an interval defined by a Markov chain, the discretized plant can be denoted by

$$x_{k+1} = \Phi x_k + [\bar{\Gamma}_0(r_k) + \Delta\Gamma_0(\tau_k)]u_k + [\bar{\Gamma}_1(r_k) + \Delta\Gamma_1(\tau_k)]u_{k-1}, \text{ when } r_k = i, \quad (17)$$

where $\Delta\Gamma_0(\tau_k)$ and $\Delta\Gamma_1(\tau_k)$ are given by (16).

Equation (17) can be regarded as a discrete-time Markovian jump system with norm-bounded uncertainties (see [12]). The state feedback controller for system (17) can be written as

$$u_k = F_i x_k, \text{ when } r_k = i. \quad (18)$$

Introduce a new state variable $z_k = \begin{bmatrix} x_k \\ u_{k-1} \end{bmatrix}$. From (17) and (18), we can describe the closed loop system as

$$z_{k+1} = (G_i + \Delta G_i)z_k, \text{ when } r_k = i, \quad (19)$$

where

$$G_i = \begin{bmatrix} \Phi + \bar{\Gamma}_{0i}F_i & \bar{\Gamma}_{1i} \\ F_i & 0 \end{bmatrix},$$

$$\Delta G_i = \begin{bmatrix} \Delta\Gamma_0(\tau_k)F_i & \Delta\Gamma_1(\tau_k) \\ 0 & 0 \end{bmatrix} = \begin{bmatrix} E_i \\ 0 \end{bmatrix} \Delta(\tau_k) \begin{bmatrix} H_{0i}F_i & H_{1i} \end{bmatrix}. \quad (20)$$

Let $M_i = \begin{bmatrix} E_i \\ 0 \end{bmatrix}$, $N_i = \begin{bmatrix} H_{0i}F_i & H_{1i} \end{bmatrix}$, then

$$\Delta G_i = M_i \Delta(\tau_k) N_i. \quad (21)$$

The goals of this paper are to establish the stochastic stability of the closed loop system (19) and to design a controller for the NCS using LMI technique.

3   Stochastic Stability of the NCS with Random Delays

In this section, we will present a sufficient condition for the stochastic stability of system (19). For this purpose, we will introduce the following definition (see [3]) and lemma (see [10]).

Definition 1. *For system (19), the equilibrium point 0 is stochastically stable if for every initial state (z_0, r_0)*

$$\mathbf{E}\{\sum_{k=0}^{\infty} |z_k(z_0, r_0)|^2 \mid z_0, r_0\} < \infty. \quad (22)$$

Lemma 1. *Let* A, E, F *and* H *be real matrices of appropriate dimensions with* $\|F\|_2 \leq 1$. *Then for* $P > 0$ *and scalar* $\varepsilon > 0$ *satisfying* $\varepsilon I - E^T P E > 0$, *we have*

$$(A + EFH)^T P(A + EFH)$$
$$\leq A^T PA + A^T PE(\varepsilon I - E^T PE)^{-1} E^T PA + \varepsilon H^T H. \qquad (23)$$

Theorem 1. *Let the state of the plant (4) and the delay history be available when the control command (18) is calculated. The closed loop system (19) is stochastically stable if there exist matrices* $P_i > 0$ *and constants* $\varepsilon_i > 0$ *satisfying the following LMIs*

$$\begin{bmatrix} G_i^T \tilde{P}_i G_i - P_i + \varepsilon_i N_i^T N_i & G_i^T \tilde{P}_i M_i \\ M_i^T \tilde{P}_i G_i & -(\varepsilon_i I - M_i^T \tilde{P}_i M_i) \end{bmatrix} < 0, \ i = 1, ..., N, \qquad (24)$$

where

$$\tilde{P}_i = \sum_{j=1}^{N} \wp_{ij} P_j, \ i = 1, ..., N. \qquad (25)$$

Proof. Define the Lyapunov function $V_k(z_k, r_k)$ as follows:

$$V_k(z_k, r_k) = z_k^T P(r_k) z_k, \qquad (26)$$

when $r_k = i$, $P(r_k) = P_i > 0$. Then we have

$$\mathbf{E}\{V_{k+1}(z_{k+1}, r_{k+1})|z_k, r_k = i\} - V_k(z_k, r_k = i)$$
$$= \sum_{j=1}^{N} \wp(r_{k+1} = j|i) z_{k+1}^T P_j z_{k+1} - z_k^T P_i z_k$$
$$= \sum_{j=1}^{N} \wp_{ij} z_k^T (G_i + \Delta G_i)^T P_j (G_i + \Delta G_i) z_k - z_k^T P_i z_k$$
$$= z_k^T \{(G_i + \Delta G_i)^T \tilde{P}_i (G_i + \Delta G_i) - P_i\} z_k$$
$$= z_k^T \{(G_i + M_i \Delta(\tau_k) N_i)^T \tilde{P}_i (G_i + M_i \Delta(\tau_k) N_i) - P_i\} z_k. \qquad (27)$$

From Lemma 1 and (24), it follows that

$$\mathbf{E}\{V_{k+1}(z_{k+1}, r_{k+1})|z_k, r_k = i\} - V_k(z_k, r_k = i)$$
$$\leq z_k^T \{G_i^T \tilde{P}_i G_i - P_i + G_i^T \tilde{P}_i M_i (\varepsilon_i I - M_i^T \tilde{P}_i M_i)^{-1} M_i^T \tilde{P}_i G_i + \varepsilon_i N_i^T N_i\} z_k$$
$$= z_k^T Q_i z_k < 0. \qquad (28)$$

For $x_k \neq 0$, $P_i > 0$ and $Q_i < 0$ imply

$$\frac{\mathbf{E}\{V_{k+1}(z_{k+1}, r_{k+1})|z_k, r_k\} - V_k(z_k, r_k)}{V_k(z_k, r_k)} < \frac{z_k^T Q_i z_k}{z_k^T P_i z_k} \leq \alpha - 1, \qquad (29)$$

where

$$\alpha = 1 - \min_{i \in S} \{\frac{\lambda_{\min}(Q_i)}{\lambda_{\max}(P_i)}\} < 1. \qquad (30)$$

Similar to the proof in [1], with $P_i > 0$ and $Q_i < 0$, we have

$$\lim_{N \to \infty} \mathbf{E}\{\sum_{k=0}^{N} |z_k(z_0, r_0)|^2 \mid z_0, r_0\} \leq \tilde{M}, \tag{31}$$

where $\tilde{M}$ is a positive number. Thus the closed loop system (19) is stochastically stable. $\square$

In Theorem 1, we assume the controller has been given. Hence, the sampling period could be designed based on (5), (8), (11), (12), (14) and (24).

4   Controller Design of the NCS with Random Delays

In this section, the state feedback controller in the form of (18) will be designed to stabilize the system (17). Using the new variable z_k, we obtain

$$u_k = [\, F_i \; 0 \,] \, z_k, \text{ when } r_k = i. \tag{32}$$

Let $\bar{F}_i = [\, F_i \, 0 \,]$, $\bar{F}_i \in R^{m \times (n+m)}$, then, the parameters G_i and ΔG_i can be rewritten as:

$$
\begin{aligned}
G_i &= \begin{bmatrix} \varPhi & \bar{\varGamma}_{1i} \\ 0 & 0 \end{bmatrix} + \begin{bmatrix} \bar{\varGamma}_{0i} \\ I \end{bmatrix} \bar{F}_i = L_i + R_i \bar{F}_i, \\
\Delta G_i &= M_i \Delta(\tau_k)\{[\, 0 \; H_{1i} \,] + H_{0i} \bar{F}_i\} \\
&= M_i \Delta(\tau_k)(S_i + H_{0i} \bar{F}_i).
\end{aligned}
\tag{33}
$$

From Theorem 1, the closed loop system is stochastically stable if

$$
\begin{bmatrix}
\begin{array}{cc}
(L_i + R_i \bar{F}_i)^T \tilde{P}_i (L_i + R_i \bar{F}_i) - P_i & \\
+\varepsilon_i (S_i + H_{0i} \bar{F}_i)^T (S_i + H_{0i} \bar{F}_i) & * \\
M_i^T \tilde{P}_i (L_i + R_i \bar{F}_i) & -(\varepsilon_i I - M_i^T \tilde{P}_i M_i)
\end{array}
\end{bmatrix} < 0, \tag{34}
$$

where $*$ is used as an ellipse for terms induced by symmetry.

Define $X_i = P_i^{-1}$. Partition X_i into four blocks corresponding to the structure of $\bar{F}_i$, then

$$\bar{F}_i X_i = [\, F_i \, 0 \,] \begin{bmatrix} X_{11i} & X_{12i} \\ X_{12i}^T & X_{22i} \end{bmatrix} = F_i [X_{11i} \; X_{12i}] = Y_i. \tag{35}$$

Pre- and post-multiplying (34) by $\text{diag}(X_i, I)$ yields

$$
\begin{bmatrix}
\begin{array}{cc}
(L_i X_i + R_i Y_i)^T \tilde{P}_i (L_i X_i + R_i Y_i) - X_i & \\
+\varepsilon_i (S_i X_i + H_{0i} Y_i)^T (S_i X_i + H_{0i} Y_i) & * \\
M_i^T \tilde{P}_i (L_i X_i + R_i Y_i) & -(\varepsilon_i I - M_i^T \tilde{P}_i M_i)
\end{array}
\end{bmatrix} < 0. \tag{36}
$$

Let $\lambda_i = \frac{1}{\varepsilon_i} > 0$ and

$$
\begin{aligned}
U_i &= \left[\sqrt{\wp_{i1}}(L_i X_i + R_i Y_i)^T \cdots \sqrt{\wp_{iN}}(L_i X_i + R_i Y_i)^T \right], \\
V_i &= \left[\sqrt{\wp_{i1}} M_i^T \cdots \sqrt{\wp_{iN}} M_i^T \right], \\
Q &= \operatorname{diag}(X_1 \cdots X_N).
\end{aligned}
\tag{37}
$$

It follows that the inequalities (36) are equivalent to the following LMIs:

$$
\begin{bmatrix}
-X_i & (S_i X_i + H_{0i} Y_i)^T & U_i & 0 \\
S_i X_i + H_{0i} Y_i & -\lambda_i I & 0 & 0 \\
U_i^T & 0 & -Q \; \lambda_i V_i^T & \\
0 & 0 & \lambda_i V_i & -\lambda_i I
\end{bmatrix} < 0, \; i = 1, \ldots, N.
\tag{38}
$$

The following stabilization theorem follows directly.

Theorem 2. *If there exist matrices $X_i > 0$, Y_i and constants $\lambda_i > 0$, $i = 1, \ldots, N$, satisfying the inequalities (38), then the state feedback controller (18) stochastically stabilizes system (17). The feedback gains can be obtained by:*

$$
F_i = Y_i \begin{bmatrix} X_{11i}^T \\ X_{12i}^T \end{bmatrix} (X_{11i} X_{11i}^T + X_{12i} X_{12i}^T)^{-1}.
\tag{39}
$$

In Theorem 2, $X_i > 0$ guarantees $X_{11i} > 0$, hence, the matrices $X_{11i} X_{11i}^T + X_{12i} X_{12i}^T$ are nonsingular.

5   Numerical Example

To illustrate the proposed theoretical results, a numerical example is considered in this section. The system setup is given by Fig. 1. The sampling period is chosen as $h = 0.05s$. The network loads: low network load, medium network load and high network load, respectively, are denoted by the state $r_k = 1, 2, 3$ of a Markov chain $\{r_k\}$ with the following transition probability matrix:

$$
\wp = \begin{bmatrix} 0.5 & 0.5 & 0 \\ 0.3 & 0.6 & 0.1 \\ 0.3 & 0.6 & 0.1 \end{bmatrix}.
\tag{40}
$$

The delays corresponding to the three states are:

$$
\begin{aligned}
\tau_k &\in [0, \, 0.2h] && \text{if } r_k = 1, \\
\tau_k &\in [0.2h, \, 0.6h] && \text{if } r_k = 2, \\
\tau_k &\in [0.5h, \, h] && \text{if } r_k = 3.
\end{aligned}
$$

The remote controlled plant is:

$$
\dot{x}(t) = \begin{bmatrix} 0 & 1 \\ -3 & -4 \end{bmatrix} x(t) + \begin{bmatrix} 0 \\ 1 \end{bmatrix} u(t).
\tag{41}
$$

Discretizing the plant at the sampling instants yields:

$$x_{k+1} = \Phi x_k + \Gamma_0(\tau_k)u_k + \Gamma_1(\tau_k)u_{k-1}. \tag{42}$$

Note that the delay is varying in known intervals governed by the Markov chain. Using (8), (11), (12) and (14), (42) can be described in the form of discrete-time Markovian jump system with uncertainties. The parameters are calculated as follows:

$$\Phi = e^{Ah} = \begin{bmatrix} 0.9965 & 0.0453 \\ -0.1358 & 0.8154 \end{bmatrix}. \tag{43}$$

For $r_k = 1$,

$$\bar{\Gamma}_{01} = \begin{bmatrix} 0.0069 \\ -0.079 \end{bmatrix}, \bar{\Gamma}_{11} = \begin{bmatrix} -0.0057 \\ 0.1242 \end{bmatrix},$$

$$E_1 = \begin{bmatrix} 0.0831 & 0 \\ 0 & 0.3524 \end{bmatrix}, H_{01} = H_{11} = \begin{bmatrix} 0.0831 \\ 0.3524 \end{bmatrix}.$$

For $r_k = 2$,

$$\bar{\Gamma}_{02} = \begin{bmatrix} 0.0007 \\ 0.0322 \end{bmatrix}, \bar{\Gamma}_{12} = \begin{bmatrix} 0.0005 \\ 0.0130 \end{bmatrix},$$

$$E_2 = \begin{bmatrix} 0.0221 & 0 \\ 0 & 0.1141 \end{bmatrix}, H_{02} = H_{12} = \begin{bmatrix} 0.0221 \\ 0.1141 \end{bmatrix}.$$

For $r_k = 3$,

$$\bar{\Gamma}_{03} = \begin{bmatrix} 0.0002 \\ 0.0119 \end{bmatrix}, \bar{\Gamma}_{13} = \begin{bmatrix} 0.0010 \\ 0.0334 \end{bmatrix},$$

$$E_3 = \begin{bmatrix} 0.0123 & 0 \\ 0 & 0.109 \end{bmatrix}, H_{03} = H_{13} = \begin{bmatrix} 0.0123 \\ 0.109 \end{bmatrix}.$$

Introducing the new variable z_k, using Theorem 2, the matrices X_i and Y_i satisfying (38) can be obtained:

$$X_1 = \begin{bmatrix} 303.4385 & -110.5042 & 6.6678 \\ -110.5042 & 428.5714 & -21.9731 \\ 6.6678 & -21.9731 & 345.4269 \end{bmatrix},$$

$$X_2 = \begin{bmatrix} 305.0778 & -109.8815 & 3.9862 \\ -109.8815 & 473.9414 & -7.4259 \\ 3.9862 & -7.4259 & 358.9820 \end{bmatrix},$$

$$X_3 = \begin{bmatrix} 268.5643 & -81.3332 & 2.3294 \\ -81.3332 & 342.7914 & -5.8254 \\ 2.3294 & -5.8254 & 357.9405 \end{bmatrix}.$$

$$Y_1 = \begin{bmatrix} 1.0497 & 12.7165 & -43.1885 \end{bmatrix},$$
$$Y_2 = \begin{bmatrix} 5.4711 & -20.9985 & -4.7462 \end{bmatrix},$$
$$Y_3 = \begin{bmatrix} 4.2948 & -10.3812 & -4.4617 \end{bmatrix}.$$

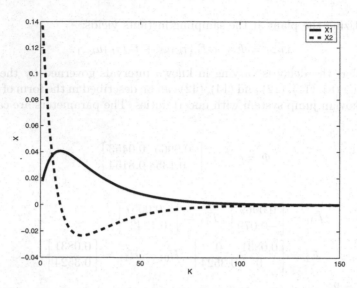

Fig. 2. The control performance of the NCS with initial condition $[0.01 \ 0.17]^T$

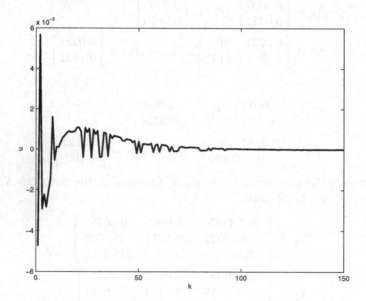

Fig. 3. The control law obtained from Theorem 2

Then the controller is calculated,

$$F_1 = \begin{bmatrix} 0.0172 \ 0.0391 \end{bmatrix},$$
$$F_2 = \begin{bmatrix} 0.0021 \ -0.0437 \end{bmatrix},$$
$$F_3 = \begin{bmatrix} 0.0073 \ -0.0283 \end{bmatrix}. \tag{44}$$

Figure 2 shows the control performance of the system with the initial condition $[0.01\ 0.17]^T$ when the control loop is closed over the network. The controller (44) stochastically stabilizes the original system. The control law is depicted in Fig. 3.

Comparison with earlier results: Based on LQG optimal design technique, the stochastic optimal controller of an NCS on random delay networks was presented by Nilsson. However, in his approach, the stochastic Riccati-iteration equation is extremely difficult to solve and computationally demanding since the iteration involves expectation calculation of stochastic variables. By contrast, the present controller design is in the form of LMI, which offers efficient numerical schemes for the analysis and design of control systems.

6   Conclusion

In this paper, the upper and lower bounds of the network-induced delays of the NCS are defined by the states of an underlying Markov chain. Based on the intervals, the NCS is described by a discrete-time Markovian jump system with norm-bounded uncertainties. The state feedback controller is presented in terms of LMI using the stochastic Lyapunov function approach. The results of stability analysis for the NCS could be used as a criterion to verify the system sampling period.

References

1. Boukas, E. K., Shi, P.: Stochastic stability and guaranteed cost control of discrete-time uncertain systems with Markovian jump parameters. International Journal of Robust and Nonlinear Control. 8 (1998) 1155–1167
2. Boyd, S., Ghaoui, L. E., Feron, E., Balakrishnan, V.: Linear matrix inequalities in system and control theory. (1994) SIAM, Philadephia.
3. Ji, Y., Chizeck, H. J., Feng, X., Loparo, K. A.: Stability and control of discrete-time jump linear systems. Control Theory and Advanced Applications. 7 (1991) 247–270
4. Hu, S. S., Zhu, Q. X.: Stochastic optimal control and analysis of stability of networked control systems with long delay. Automatica 39 (2003) 1877–1884
5. Lian, F. L., Moyne, J., Tilbury, D.: Performance evaluation of control networks: Ethernet, controlNet, and deviceNet. IEEE Control Systems Magzine. 21 (2001) 66–83
6. Lian, F. L., Moyne, J., Tilbury, D.: Analysis and modeling of networked control systems: MIMO case with multiple time delays. Proceeding of American Control Conference. (2001) 4306–4312
7. Liou, L.-W., Ray, A.: A stochastic regulator for integrated communicaiton and control systems: Part I-Formulation of control law. Journal of Dynamic Systems, Measurement and Control. 113 (1991) 604–611
8. Luck, R., Ray, A.: An observer-based compensator for distributed delays. Automatica. 26 (1990) 903–908

9. Nisson, J.: Real-time control systems with delays. 1998 Ph.D. thesis, Department of Automatic Control. Lund Institute of Technology, Lund, Sweden
10. Souza, C., Xie, L.: Delay-dependent robust H_∞ control of uncertain linear state-delayed systems. Automatica. **35** (1999) 1313–1321.
11. Walsh, G., Beldiman, O., Bushnell, L. G.: Asymptotic behavior of nonlinear networked control systems. IEEE Transaction on Automatic Control. **40** (2001) 1093–1097
12. Yuan, C., Mao, X.: Robust stability and controllability of stochastic differential delay equations with Markovian switching. Automatica. **40** (2004) 343–354
13. Zhang, W., Branicky, M. S., Phillips, S. M.: Stability of networked control systems. IEEE Control Systems Magzine. **21** (2001) 84–99

Controllability Implies Stabilizability for Discrete-Time Switched Linear Systems

Guangming Xie and Long Wang

Center for Systems & Control,
LTCS and Department of Mechanics and Engineering Science,
Peking University, Beijing, 100871, China
{xiegming, longwang}@mech.pku.edu.cn

Abstract. A switched linear system is said to be controllable, if for any given initial state and terminal state, one can find a switching sequence and corresponding input such that the system can be driven from the initial state to the terminal state. Necessary and sufficient condition on the controllability of switched linear systems has been established, and a single switching sequence can be constructed to realize the controllability. In this paper, the stabilizability problem for switched linear systems is formulated and we show that controllability implies stabilizability for switched linear systems. In our framework, we using periodically switching sequence and piecewise constant feedback controller. Two stabilization design methods, the pole assignment method and the linear matrix inequality method are proposed. Furthermore, if a switched linear system is both controllable and observable, then an observer-based output feedback controller can be constructed when the system state is not available. In this case, the well-known Separation Principle is shown to still hold. All these results are built upon our previously established fundamental geometric properties of controllability realization as well as the important fact that both controllability and observability can be realized through a single switching sequence.

1 Introduction

Switched systems, an important class of hybrid systems, have received much attention in recent years. In the control of complex and highly uncertain systems, traditional methodologies based on a single controller do not always provide satisfactory performance. The key idea in switched control is to build a bank of alternative controllers and switch among them online based on measurements and prescribed switching strategies. Stability of switched control systems has been studied extensively and some valuable results have been established in the literature. On the other hand, controllability and observability are two fundamental concepts in modern control theory, and have close and essential connections with feedback stabilization, observer design, system decomposition, model reduction, linear quadratic optimal control, etc [1]. Controllability and observability of switched linear systems have been studied by a number of papers

M. Morari and L. Thiele (Eds.): HSCC 2005, LNCS 3414, pp. 667–682, 2005.
© Springer-Verlag Berlin Heidelberg 2005

[2-10]. [2] first studied one-period controllability and one-period observability for periodically switched systems, and some sufficient and necessary conditions were established. Then [3] introduced the concepts of multiple-period controllability and multiple-period observability which are natural extension of the one-period ones, and necessary and sufficient criteria were derived as well. It was also proved that the controllability can be realized in n periods at most, where n is the state dimension.

Aside from [2, 3], [4] first investigated controllability for general switched linear systems, where not only control input but also switching signal were taken as control means. The concept of controllability for switched linear systems is a natural extension of that for ordinary linear systems. Namely, a switched linear system is said to be controllable, if for any given initial state and terminal state, one can find a switching sequence and corresponding input such that the system can be driven from the initial state to the terminal state. A sufficient condition and a necessary condition for controllability of switched linear systems were presented, respectively [4]. It was proved that the necessary condition was also sufficient for 3-dimensional systems with only two subsystems. Subsequently, [5] proved the sufficiency for 3-dimensional systems with arbitrary number of subsystems. Then, necessary and sufficient geometric type criteria for controllability and observability were derived in [6, 7] and [9]. The discrete-time counterparts were addressed in [8]. Furthermore, it was proved that the controllability can be realized by a single switching sequence [6, 9, 10], a direct consequence is the criterion given in [7, 8]. There are many other results on controllability and observability of general hybrid systems[11-16].

As is well known in modern control theory, for a controllable (ordinary) linear system, there exists a (static) state feedback controller such that the closed-loop system is asymptotically stable, i.e., controllability implies stabilizability. Since the concept of controllability has been formulated and well investigated for switched linear systems, it is natural to formulate the stabilization problem for switched linear systems and ask the following fundamental question:

Does controllability still imply stabilizability for switched linear systems?

In this paper, we will try to answer this question in discrete-time domain. We will show that if the system is controllable, then we can adopt periodically switching sequence and piecewise constant feedback controller to stabilized the system. Consider a discrete-time switched linear system given by

$$
\begin{aligned}
x(t+1) &= A_{r(t)}x(t) + B_{r(t)}u(t) \\
y(t) &= C_{r(t)}x(t)
\end{aligned}
\tag{1}
$$

where $x(t) \in \mathbb{R}^n$ is the state, $u(t) \in \mathbb{R}^p$ is the input, and $y(t) \in \mathbb{R}^q$ is the output. The scalar function $r(k) : \{0, 1, \cdots\} \to \mathcal{I} = \{1, 2, \cdots, N\}$ is the switching signal to be designed. Moreover, $r(t) = i$ means that the subsystem (A_i, B_i, C_i) is activated.

The system (1) is said *reversible*, if all the matrices A_i are nonsingular, $i \in \mathcal{I}$. In this paper, we only consider reversible switched systems.

Notations: We use standard notations throughout this paper. Given a matrix $B \in \mathbb{R}^{n \times p}$, denote $\mathcal{I}m(B)$ as the *range* of B, i.e., $\mathcal{I}m(B) = \{y | y = Bx, x \in \mathbb{R}^p\}$. Given a matrix $A \in \mathbb{R}^{n \times n}$ and a linear subspace $\mathcal{W} \subseteq \mathbb{R}^n$, let $\langle A | \mathcal{W} \rangle$ be the *minimal invariant subspace containing* $\mathcal{W}$, i.e., $\langle A | \mathcal{W} \rangle = \sum_{i=1}^{n} A^{i-1} \mathcal{W}$. For notational simplicity, denote $\langle A | B \rangle = \langle A | \mathcal{I}m(B) \rangle$. The notation $\prod_{i=1}^{n} A_i$ stands for the matrix product $A_1 \cdots A_n$, and $\prod_{i=n}^{1} A_i$ stands for the matrix product $A_n \cdots A_1$, respectively. For any integer $M > 0$, set $\underline{M} = \{0, 1, \cdots, M-1\}$. X^T is the transpose of the matrix X and $\mathsf{Sym}\{X\}$ is used for the symmetric expression $X + X^T$. $X > 0$ (resp. < 0) means that X is positive definite (resp. negative definite). I and 0 denote the identity and zero matrices of appropriate size, respectively. In a symmetric matrix, the symbol $(\bullet)^T$ denotes the corresponding symmetric block. A matrix $A \in \mathbb{R}^{n \times n}$ is said to be Schur-stable if all its eigenvalues lie within the unit circle.

In what follows, the stabilizability problem will be first formulated for switched linear systems. In our formulation, we will adopt periodical switching signals and piecewise constant state feedback controllers. We will show that our formulation is a natural extension of that for ordinary linear systems.

For system (1), a switching sequence is to specify when and to which subsystem one should switch at each instant of time.

Definition 1. *A switching sequence π is a set of finite scalars*

$$\pi \overset{def}{=} \{i_0, \cdots, i_{M-1}\} \tag{2}$$

where $M \leq \infty$ is the length of π, $i_m \in \mathcal{I}$ is the index of the mth subsystem (A_{i_m}, B_{i_m}), for $m \in \underline{M}$. Denote

$$A_\pi = \prod_{m=M-1}^{0} A_{i_m} \tag{3}$$

We call A_π the transfer matrix *of the switching sequence π.*

Given a switching sequence $\pi = \{i_0, \cdots, i_{M-1}\}$, an associated periodical switching signal $r(\cdot)$ can be determined as

$$r(kM + m) = i_m, \ m \in \underline{M}, k = 0, 1, 2, \cdots. \tag{4}$$

Definition 2. *System (1) is said to be* stabilizable (via state feedback) *if there exist a switching sequence $\pi = \{i_0, \cdots, i_{M-1}\}$ and a series of state feedback gains $K_1, \cdots, K_M$ such that the system is asymptotically stable under the periodical switching signal (4) and the piecewise constant state feedback controller*

$$u(t) = K_{\delta(t)} x(t) \tag{5}$$

where

$$\delta(kM + m) = m + 1, \ m \in \underline{M}, k = 0, 1, 2, \cdots. \tag{6}$$

Remark 1. If $N = 1$, then system (1) reduces to an ordinary linear system. In this case, it is easy to see that the concept of stabilizability in Definition 2 reduces to the traditional one for ordinary linear systems as well.

Remark 2. The definition is stronger than that given in [9] for continuous case, where stabilizability is defined in open-loop form. The equivalence of them for switched systems is still an open problem.

In the rest of this paper, we will first give a brief review of controllability and observability, and the related realization problem for switched systems in Section 2. The review and discussions will help us to understand the characteristics of controllability and observability of switched systems. Next, we prove that controllability implies stabilizability for switched linear systems in Section 3. Moreover, two stabilization design methods are presented. Subsequently, in Section 4, we will show that observability guarantees the existence of a stable state observer for switched systems. Hence, observer-based state feedback stabilization can be constructed. Then, an illustrative example is presented in Section 5. Finally, we conclude the whole paper in Section 6.

2   Controllability and Observability

In this section, some basic results on controllability and observability of switched linear systems will be given, including definitions, criteria and realizations.

Definition 3. *[8] For system (1), state x is reachable (controllable), if there exist a positive integer M, a switching signal $r(m) : \underline{M} \to \mathcal{I}$, and input sequence $u(0), \cdots, u(M)$, such that $x(0) = 0$ and $x(M) = x$ ($x(0) = x$ and $x(M) = 0$). System (1) is said to be completely reachable (controllable) if any state x is reachable(controllable).*

For system (1), [8] defined a subspace sequence as follows

$$W_1 = \sum_{i=1}^{N} \langle A_i | B_i \rangle, W_m = \sum_{i=1}^{N} \langle A_i | W_{m-1} \rangle, m = 2, \cdots, n \qquad (7)$$

Let $\mathcal{R}, \mathcal{C}$ denote the set of all reachable states and the set of all controllable states of system (1), respectively. Then [8] gave the following result.

Proposition 1. *[8] For system (1), $\mathcal{R} \equiv \mathcal{C} \equiv W_n$.*

By Proposition 1, we know that for system (1), controllability is equivalent to reachability, and the system is controllable if and only if $W_n = \mathbb{R}^n$.

On the other hand, from Definition 3, we know that the controllability of switched systems relies not only on inputs but also on switching signals. Namely, given any two states x_0, x_f, one needs to find not only a suitable switching signal but also a series of appropriate inputs such that the system can be driven from x_0 to x_f. Thus, it is important not only to give mathematical conditions to check controllability, but also to provide a concrete effective method of finding the suitable switching signal and the corresponding inputs to realize it.

[10] discussed this problem and formulated it as the controllability realization problem. In the sequel, we will briefly review the main results in [10]. Furthermore, the simultaneous controllability/observability realization problem will also be discussed.

Given a switching sequence $\pi = \{i_0, \cdots, i_{M-1}\}$, the *reachable state set* of π is defined as

$$\mathcal{R}(\pi) \stackrel{def}{=} \{x | \exists \text{ inputs } u(m), m \in \underline{M} \text{ such that } x(0) = 0 \text{ and } x(M) = x.\} \quad (8)$$

It is easy to verify that the reachable state set is a linear subspace given by

$$\mathcal{R}(\pi) = \mathcal{I}m \left(\left[(\prod_{m=M-1}^{1} A_{i_m}) B_{i_0} \ (\prod_{m=M-1}^{2} A_{i_m}) B_{i_1} \ \cdots \ B_{i_{M-1}} \right] \right) \quad (9)$$

Similarly, the *controllable state set* of π is defined as

$$\mathcal{C}(\pi) \stackrel{def}{=} \{x | \exists \text{ inputs } u(m), m \in \underline{M} \text{ such that } x(0) = x \text{ and } x(M) = 0.\} \quad (10)$$

The controllable state set is also a linear space given by

$$\mathcal{C}(\pi) = \mathcal{I}m \left(\left[B_{i_0}, A_{i_0}^{-1} B_{i_1}, \cdots, \prod_{m=0}^{M-2} A_{i_m}^{-1} B_{i_{M-1}} \right] \right) \quad (11)$$

It is easy to see that $\mathcal{R}(\pi), \mathcal{C}(\pi) \subseteq \mathcal{W}_n, \forall \pi$, and $\mathcal{C} = \bigcup_{\forall \pi} \mathcal{C}(\pi)$, $\mathcal{R} = \bigcup_{\forall \pi} \mathcal{R}(\pi)$.

Given two switching sequences $\pi_1 = \{i_0, \cdots, i_{M-1}\}$ and $\pi_2 = \{j_0, \cdots, j_{L-1}\}$, the product of π_1 and π_2 is defined as

$$\pi_1 \wedge \pi_2 \stackrel{def}{=} \{i_0, \cdots, i_{M-1}, j_0, \cdots, j_{L-1}\} \quad (12)$$

Since it is easy to verify that $(\pi_1 \wedge \pi_2) \wedge \pi_3 = \pi_1 \wedge (\pi_2 \wedge \pi_3)$, we just denote it by $\pi_1 \wedge \pi_2 \wedge \pi_3$. Given a switching sequence π, the kth power of π is defined as

$$\pi^{\wedge k} \stackrel{def}{=} \overbrace{\pi \wedge \cdots \wedge \pi}^{k \text{ times}} \quad (13)$$

Proposition 2. *[10] Given any switching sequences π_1, π_2 and π, we have*

$$\mathcal{R}(\pi_1 \wedge \pi_2) = A_{\pi_2} \mathcal{R}(\pi_1) + \mathcal{R}(\pi_2) \quad (14)$$

$$\mathcal{R}(\pi^{\wedge n}) = \langle A_\pi | \mathcal{R}(\pi) \rangle \quad (15)$$

$$A_{\pi^{\wedge n}} \mathcal{R}(\pi^{\wedge n}) = \mathcal{R}(\pi^{\wedge n}) \quad (16)$$

$$\mathcal{R}(\pi) = A_\pi \mathcal{C}(\pi), \ \ \mathcal{C}(\pi) = A_\pi^{-1} \mathcal{R}(\pi) \quad (17)$$

Theorem 1. *[10] For system (1), there exists a basic switching sequence π_b, such that $\mathcal{R}(\pi_b) = \mathcal{W}_n$.*

Proof. We will provide a brief proof here since the main ideas will be used later. Suppose $\dim(\mathcal{W}_n) = d$. By (7), there must exist subspaces $\mathcal{V}_1, \cdots, \mathcal{V}_d$ such that

$$\mathcal{W}_n = \sum_{l=1}^{d} \mathcal{V}_l \tag{18}$$

and each $\mathcal{V}_l$ has the following form

$$\prod_{m=1}^{M-1} A_{i_m} \langle A_j | B_j \rangle \tag{19}$$

where $i_1, \cdots, i_{M-1}, j \in \mathcal{I}, 0 \leq M < \infty$. Consider the subspace which has the form (19), we can choose a switching sequence as

$$\pi_\alpha = \{\overbrace{j, \cdots, j}^{n \text{ times}}\} \tag{20}$$

such that $\mathcal{R}(\pi_\alpha) = \langle A_j | B_j \rangle$. Furthermore, we can select another switching sequence as $\pi_\beta = \{i_1, \cdots, i_{M-1}\}$ such that $\prod_{m=1}^{M-1} A_{i_m} \langle A_j | B_j \rangle = A_{\pi_\beta} \mathcal{R}(\pi_\alpha) \subseteq \mathcal{R}(\pi_\alpha \wedge \pi_\beta)$. Thus, for the subspaces $\mathcal{V}_1, \cdots, \mathcal{V}_d$, we can select appropriate switching sequences $\pi_1, \cdots, \pi_d$ such that $\mathcal{V}_l \subseteq \mathcal{R}(\pi_l)$, for $l = 1, \cdots, d$. By (18), we have $\mathcal{W}_n = \sum_{l=1}^{d} \mathcal{V}_l \subseteq \sum_{l=1}^{d} \mathcal{R}(\pi_l)$. Since it is obvious that $\sum_{l=1}^{d} \mathcal{R}(\pi_l) \subseteq \mathcal{W}_n$, we have $\mathcal{W}_n = \sum_{l=1}^{d} \mathcal{R}(\pi_l)$.

Now, we can construct the switching sequence π_b as follows. First, if $\mathcal{R}(\pi_1^{\wedge n}) = \mathcal{W}_n$, we can take $\pi_b = \pi_1^{\wedge n}$. If not, there must exist $k \in \{2, \cdots, d\}$ such that (without loss of generality, suppose $k = 2$)

$$\mathcal{R}(\pi_2) \not\subseteq \mathcal{R}(\pi_1^{\wedge n}) \tag{21}$$

By Proposition 2, we have $\mathcal{R}(\pi_2 \wedge \pi_1^{\wedge n}) = A_{\pi_1^{\wedge n}} \mathcal{R}(\pi_2) + \mathcal{R}(\pi_1^{\wedge n})$. By (16), we have $\mathcal{R}(\pi_2 \wedge \pi_1^{\wedge n}) = A_{\pi_1^{\wedge n}} (\mathcal{R}(\pi_2) + \mathcal{R}(\pi_1^{\wedge n}))$. It follows that

$$\dim(\mathcal{R}(\pi_2 \wedge \pi_1^{\wedge n})) = \dim(A_{\pi_1^{\wedge n}}(\mathcal{R}(\pi_2) + \mathcal{R}(\pi_1^{\wedge n}))) = \dim(\mathcal{R}(\pi_2) + \mathcal{R}(\pi_1^{\wedge n}))$$

By (21), we have $\mathcal{R}(\pi_2) + \mathcal{R}(\pi_1^{\wedge n}) \supsetneq \mathcal{R}(\pi_1^{\wedge n})$. Thus, we know that $\dim(\mathcal{R}(\pi_2 \wedge \pi_1^{\wedge n})) > \mathcal{R}(\pi_1^{\wedge n})) \geq 2$. Similarly, we can construct switching sequences $\overline{\pi}_1 = \pi_1, \overline{\pi}_i = \pi_i \wedge (\overline{\pi}_{i-1})^{\wedge n}, i = 2, \cdots, d$ and $\pi_b = \overline{\pi}_d$. By analogous analysis, we have $\dim(\mathcal{R}(\pi_l)) \geq l$, for $l = 1, \cdots, d$. On the other hand, since $\mathcal{R}(\pi_b) \subseteq \mathcal{W}_n$, we have $\dim(\mathcal{R}(\pi_b)) \leq d$. Thus, we have $\dim(\mathcal{R}(\pi_b)) = d$. Hence, $\mathcal{R}(\pi_b) = \mathcal{W}_n$. This completes the proof of Theorem 1.

Remark 3. Reversibility of system (1) is necessary for (15-17). If the system is not reversible, we can not find a single switching sequence in a constructive way to realize the controllability.

Remark 4. Since $\mathcal{R} \subseteq \mathcal{W}_n$ and $\mathcal{R}(\pi_b) \subseteq \mathcal{R}$, by Proposition 2, we have that $\mathcal{C}(\pi_b) = \mathcal{R}(\pi_b) = \mathcal{R} = \mathcal{W}_n$. This proves Proposition 1.

Remark 5. Theorem 1 reveals an essential feature of controllability of switched systems, i.e., one particular switching sequence is enough to realize controllability and reachability, namely, the system can be driven from any initial state to any terminal state through the switching sequence π_b by only choosing appropriate control inputs.

Remark 6. The proof of Theorem 1 presents a constructive procedure to build up the switching sequence π_b.

Remark 7. Since π_b is not unique, which is the "optimal" one, how to define optimality for switching sequences and how to find the optimal one are problems of interest which will be discussed in a separate paper.

As for observability, we can establish similar results as follows.

Definition 4. *[8] System (1) is (completely) observable, if there exist a positive integer M and a switching signal $r(t) : \underline{M} \rightarrow \mathcal{I}$, such that the output sequence $\{y(0), \cdots, y(M)\}$ and the input sequence $\{u(0), \cdots, u(M)\}$ are sufficient to determine $x(0)$.*

Definition 5. *[8] The system (1) is (completely) constructible, if there exist a positive integer M and a switching signal $r(t) : \underline{M} \rightarrow \mathcal{I}$, such that the output sequence $\{y(0), \cdots, y(M)\}$ and the input sequence $\{u(0), \cdots, u(M)\}$ are sufficient to determine $x(M)$.*

We define a subspace sequence as follows

$$\mathcal{Y}_1 = \sum_{i=1}^{N} \langle A_i^T | C_i^T \rangle, \mathcal{Y}_m = \sum_{i=1}^{N} \langle A_i^T | \mathcal{Y}_{m-1} \rangle, m = 2, \cdots, n. \tag{22}$$

By the Duality Principle, we have

Proposition 3. *For system (1), the following statements are equivalent:*
 (i) the system is observable;
 (ii) the system is constructible;
 (iii) $\mathcal{Y}_n = \mathbb{R}^n$.

Furthermore, by analogous analysis and duality, we have

Proposition 4. *For system (1), there exists a basic switching sequence π_o such that the observability can be realized through π_o.*

Remark 8. Consider the switching sequence $\pi_b \wedge \pi_o$, where π_b is given in Theorem 1 and π_o is given in Proposition 4, it is easy to see that *both controllability and observability can be realized by $\pi_b \wedge \pi_o$.* The proof of this fact is omitted due to space limitation. This important property of controllability and observability is the starting point for observer-based state feedback controller design.

3   Controllability Implies Stabilizability

In this section, we will show that controllable switched linear system is stabilizable. Two different approaches, the classical pole assignment method and the more popular linear matrix inequality (LMI)-based formulation are presented, respectively.

Lemma 1. *Given a switching sequence $\pi = \{i_0, \cdots, i_{M-1}\}$, if $\mathcal{R}(\pi) = \mathbb{R}^n$, then there exist state feedback gains $K_1, \cdots, K_M$ such that the matrix*

$$A_c = \prod_{m=M-1}^{0} (A_{i_m} + B_{i_m} K_{m+1}) \tag{23}$$

is nonsingular and Schur-stable.

Proof. Since $\mathcal{R}(\pi) = \mathbb{R}^n$, the matrix

$$Q = \left[(\prod_{m=M-1}^{1} A_{i_m}) B_{i_0}, \ (\prod_{m=M-1}^{2} A_{i_m}) B_{i_1}, \ \cdots, \ B_{i_{M-1}} \right] \tag{24}$$

is of full rank. Moreover

$$
\begin{aligned}
A_c &= A_{i_{M-1}} \prod_{m=M-2}^{0} (A_{i_m} + B_{i_m} K_{m+1}) \\
&\quad + B_{i_{M-1}} K_{i_{M-1}} \prod_{m=M-2}^{0} (A_{i_m} + B_{i_m} K_{m+1}) \\
&= A_{i_{M-1}} A_{i_{M-2}} \prod_{m=M-3}^{0} (A_{i_m} + B_{i_m} K_{m+1}) \\
&\quad + A_{i_{M-1}} B_{i_{M-2}} K_{i_{M-2}} \prod_{m=M-3}^{0} (A_{i_m} + B_{i_m} K_{m+1}) \\
&\quad + B_{i_{M-1}} K_{i_{M-1}} \prod_{m=M-2}^{0} (A_{i_m} + B_{i_m} K_{m+1}) \\
&= \cdots \\
&= A_\pi + \prod_{m=M-1}^{1} A_{i_{i_m}} B_{i_0} K_1 \\
&\quad + \prod_{m=M-1}^{2} A_{i_{i_m}} B_{i_1} K_{i_1} (A_{i_0} + B_{i_0} K_1) \\
&\quad + \cdots \\
&\quad + A_{i_{M-1}} B_{i_{M-2}} K_{i_{M-2}} \prod_{m=M-3}^{0} (A_{i_m} + B_{i_m} K_{m+1}) \\
&\quad + B_{i_{M-1}} K_{i_{M-1}} \prod_{m=M-2}^{0} (A_{i_m} + B_{i_m} K_{m+1})
\end{aligned}
$$

Thus, we can rewrite A_c as

$$A_c = A_\pi + Q \left[\widehat{K}_1^T, \ \widehat{K}_2^T, \cdots, \ \widehat{K}_{M-1}^T, \ \widehat{K}_M^T \right]^T \tag{25}$$

where $\widehat{K}_1 = K_1$, $\widehat{K}_m = K_m \prod_{l=m-1}^{0} (A_{i_l} + B_{i_l} K_{l+1})$, $m = 2, \cdots, M$.

Given a nonsingular and Schur-stable matrix A_c, on the one hand, since Q is of full rank, there exist appropriate $\widehat{K}_1, \cdots, \widehat{K}_M$ satisfying the algebraic equation above. On the other hand, since A_c is nonsingular, we know that each $(A_{i_l} + B_{i_l} K_{l+1})$ is nonsingular. Thus, we can get

$$K_1 = \widehat{K}_1, K_m = \widehat{K}_m \left(\prod_{l=m-1}^{0} (A_{i_l} + B_{i_l} K_{l+1}) \right)^{-1}, m = 2, \cdots, M. \tag{26}$$

This completes the proof of Lemma 1.

Theorem 2. *For system (1), controllability implies stabilizability.*

Proof. Since the system is controllable, by Theorem 1, there exists a switching sequence such that its reachable set equals the full space. Thus, by Lemma 1, we can take the periodical switching signal generated by π and the feedback gains $K_1, \cdots, K_M$ given in (26) such that A_c is Schur-stable. This implies that the closed-loop system is stable as well.

Remark 9. In fact, the proof of Lemma 1 provides a pole assignment algorithm for stabilization design of switched systems, i.e., we can first select any Schur-stable and nonsingular matrix A_s, then calculate appropriate state feedback gains K_m, $m = 1, \cdots, M$ such that $A_c = A_s$. Moreover, it should be pointed out the controllability of a switched linear system does not mean that each of its subsystems (viewed as an ordinary linear system) is controllable (in the sense of Kalman). As a matter of fact, the former is a much weaker condition than the latter [6, 9, 10]. Hence, Theorem 2 reveals a fundamental property of switched linear systems.

In what follows, we will present another design method: the LMI-based method. In our discussion to follow, we will often invoke the following lemma.

Lemma 2. *[17] Let the matrices $U \in \mathbb{C}^{n \times m}, W \in \mathbb{C}^{k \times n}$, and $\Phi = \Phi^T \in \mathbb{C}^{n \times n}$ be given. Then the following statements are equivalent:*
i) There exists a matrix $V \in \mathbb{C}^{m \times k}$ satisfying $UVW + (UVW)^T + \Phi < 0$;
ii) The following two conditions hold

$$\mathcal{N}_U \Phi \mathcal{N}_U^T < 0 \quad or \quad UU^T > 0$$

$$\mathcal{N}_W^T \Phi \mathcal{N}_W < 0 \quad or \quad W^T W > 0$$

where $\mathcal{N}_U$ and $\mathcal{N}_W^T$ are the orthogonal complements of U and W^T, respectively. It follows that

$$\mathcal{N}_U U = 0,$$

$$\mathcal{N}_W^T W^T = 0.$$

By Lemma 1, we know that there exists a positive definite matrix P such that

$$A_c^T P A_c - P < 0 \tag{27}$$

is feasible if $\mathcal{R}(\pi) = \mathbb{R}^n$. Based on this fact, we obtain the following LMI type stabilization result.

Theorem 3. *Suppose system (1) controllable, and hence without loss of generality, suppose there exists a switching sequence $\pi = \{i_0, i_1, \cdots, i_M\}$ such that $\mathcal{R}(\pi) = \mathbb{R}^n$, then there exist a positive definite matrix S, nonsingular matrices V_m, $m = 2, \cdots, M$ and matrices $F_m, m = 1, \cdots, M$ such that the following LMI*

$$\begin{bmatrix} S & A_{i_{M-1}}V_M + B_{i_{M-1}}F_M & 0 & \cdots & 0 & 0 \\ (\bullet)^T & V_M + V_M^T & A_{i_{M-2}}V_{M-1}+B_{i_{M-2}}F_{M-1} & \cdots & 0 & 0 \\ 0 & (\bullet)^T & V_{M-1}+V_{M-1}^T & \cdots & 0 & 0 \\ \vdots & \vdots & \vdots & \ddots & \ddots & \vdots \\ 0 & 0 & 0 & \cdots & V_2+V_2^T & A_{i_0}S+B_{i_0}F_1 \\ 0 & 0 & 0 & \cdots & (\bullet)^T & S \end{bmatrix} > 0$$

(28)

is feasible. Furthermore, the system can be stabilized with the periodical switching signal generated by π and the state feedback gains given by

$$K_1 = F_1 S^{-1}, \quad K_m = F_m V_m^{-1}, \ m = 2, \cdots, M.$$

(29)

Proof. Setting $S = P^{-1}$, (27) is equivalent to

$$A_c S A_c^T - S < 0$$

(30)

Denote

$$\bar{A}_{m+1} = A_{i_m} + B_{i_m} K_{m+1}, \quad m \in \underline{M}$$
$$H_1 = \bar{A}_1, \quad H_m = \bar{A}_m H_{m-1}, \quad m = 2, \cdots, M.$$

Condition (30) can be written as

$$[\, I_n \quad -\bar{A}_M \,] \begin{bmatrix} -S & 0 \\ 0 & H_{M-1}SH_{M-1}^T \end{bmatrix} \begin{bmatrix} I \\ -\bar{A}_M^T \end{bmatrix} < 0$$

Define $\mathcal{N}_U = [\, I \quad -\bar{A}_M \,]$ and $W = [\, 0 \quad I \,]$, then (30) is equivalent, by Lemma 2, to

$$\begin{bmatrix} -S & 0 \\ 0 & H_{M-1}SH_{M-1}^T \end{bmatrix} + \mathrm{Sym}\left\{ \begin{bmatrix} -\bar{A}_M \\ -I \end{bmatrix} V_M[\, 0 \quad I \,] \right\} < 0$$

that is

$$\begin{bmatrix} -S & -\bar{A}_M V_M \\ (\bullet)^T & -V_M - V_M^T + H_{M-1}SH_{M-1}^T \end{bmatrix} < 0$$

(31)

Denote $\Psi_2 = \begin{bmatrix} -S & -\bar{A}_M V_M \\ (\bullet)^T & -V_M - V_M^T \end{bmatrix}$. Since $S > 0$, we get from (31) that Ψ_2 must be negative definite. Moreover, (31) can be written as

$$\begin{bmatrix} I & 0 & 0 \\ 0 & I & -\bar{A}_{M-1} \end{bmatrix} \begin{bmatrix} -S & -\bar{A}_M V_M & 0 \\ (\bullet)^T & -V_M - V_M^T & 0 \\ 0 & 0 & H_{M-2}SH_{M-2}^T \end{bmatrix} \begin{bmatrix} I & 0 \\ 0 & I \\ 0 & -\bar{A}_{M-1}^T \end{bmatrix} < 0$$

By Lemma 2, we get the equivalent inequality

$$\begin{bmatrix} -S & -\bar{A}_M V_M & 0 \\ (\bullet)^T & -V_M - V_M^T & 0 \\ 0 & 0 & H_{M-2}SH_{M-2}^T \end{bmatrix} + \mathrm{Sym}\left\{ \begin{bmatrix} 0 \\ -\bar{A}_{M-1} \\ -I \end{bmatrix} V_{M-1}[\, 0 \quad 0 \quad I \,] \right\} < 0$$

that is

$$
\begin{bmatrix}
-S & -\bar{A}_M V_M & 0 \\
(\bullet)^T & -V_M - V_M^T & -\bar{A}_{M-1} V_{M-1} \\
0 & (\bullet)^T & -V_{M-1} - V_{M-1}^T + H_{M-2} S H_{M-2}^T
\end{bmatrix} < 0 \qquad (32)
$$

Denote

$$
\Psi_3 = \begin{bmatrix}
-S & -\bar{A}_M V_M & 0 \\
(\bullet)^T & -V_M - V_M^T & -\bar{A}_{M-1} V_{M-1} \\
0 & (\bullet)^T & -V_{M-1} - V_{M-1}^T
\end{bmatrix},
$$

Ψ_3 must also be negative definite since $S > 0$. Repeating the similar procedure $(M-1)$ times, we get the equivalent inequality of Mn-dimension as follows:

$$
\begin{bmatrix}
-S & -\bar{A}_M V_M & 0 & \cdots & 0 & 0 \\
(\bullet)^T & -V_M - V_M^T & -\bar{A}_{M-1} V_{M-1} & \cdots & 0 & 0 \\
0 & (\bullet)^T & -V_{M-1} - V_{M-1}^T & \cdots & 0 & 0 \\
\vdots & \vdots & & \ddots & \ddots & \vdots \\
0 & 0 & 0 & \cdots & -V_3 - V_3^T & -\bar{A}_2 V_2 \\
0 & 0 & 0 & \cdots & (\bullet)^T & -V_2 - V_2^T + H_1 S H_1^T
\end{bmatrix} < 0
$$

$$(33)$$

which is equivalent, by Schur complement, to

$$
\begin{bmatrix}
-S & -\bar{A}_M V_M & 0 & \cdots & 0 & 0 & 0 \\
(\bullet)^T & -V_M - V_M^T & -\bar{A}_{M-1} V_{M-1} & \cdots & 0 & 0 & 0 \\
0 & (\bullet)^T & -V_{M-1} - V_{M-1}^T & \cdots & 0 & 0 & 0 \\
\vdots & \vdots & & \ddots & \ddots & \vdots & \vdots \\
0 & 0 & 0 & \cdots & -V_3 - V_3^T & -\bar{A}_2 V_2 & 0 \\
0 & 0 & 0 & \cdots & (\bullet)^T & -V_2 - V_2^T & -H_1 S \\
0 & 0 & 0 & \cdots & 0 & (\bullet)^T & -S
\end{bmatrix} < 0
$$

$$(34)$$

By change of variables

$$
F_1 = K_1 S, \quad F_m = K_m V_m, \quad m = 2, \cdots, M. \qquad (35)
$$

we get (28). This completes the proof.

Remark 10. It can be seen from (28) that $V_m + V_m^T > 0$, $m = 2, \cdots, M$. This means that V_m is of full rank.

Remark 11. Theorem 3 claims two things: first, the matrix inequality (27) can be equivalently transformed into the linear matrix inequality (28); second, controllability is a sufficient condition for the feasibility of that linear matrix inequality.

4   Observer-Based Output Feedback Stabilization

In case the system state is not easy to measure directly, one may design an observer to reconstruct the system state by using input and output information. For system (1), we can construct a full-dimension state observer as follows:

$$\hat{x}(t+1) = A_{r(t)}\hat{x}(t) + B_{r(t)}u(t) + L_{\delta(t)}(\, y(t) - C_{r(t)}\hat{x}(t)\,) \qquad (36)$$

where $\hat{x}(t) \in \mathbb{R}^n$ is the reconstructed state, $r(t)$ is a periodical switching signal generated by some switching sequence $\pi = \{i_0, \cdots, i_{M-1}\}$ (to be designed), $\delta(t)$ is given in (6). Furthermore, we adopt the observer-based output feedback controller as follows:

$$u(t) = K_{\delta(t)}\hat{x}(t) \qquad (37)$$

Denote $z^T(t) = [x^T(t) \quad \hat{x}^T(t) - x^T(t)]$, then the augmented observer-based output feedback (closed-loop) system can be described as

$$z(t+1) = \begin{bmatrix} A_{r(t)} + B_{r(t)}K_{\delta(t)} & B_{r(t)}K_{\delta(t)} \\ 0 & A_{r(t)} - L_{\delta(t)}C_{r(t)} \end{bmatrix} z(t) \qquad (38)$$

By similar analysis, asymptotical stability of system (38) is equivalent to the Schur-stability of

$$\tilde{A} = \begin{bmatrix} A_c & * \\ 0 & A_o \end{bmatrix}$$

where A_c is given in (23) and

$$A_o = \prod_{m=M}^{1} (A_{i_{m-1}} - L_m C_{i_{m-1}}). \qquad (39)$$

It is easy to see that $\tilde{A}$ is Schur-stable if and only if both A_c and A_o are Schur-stable. Hence, the observer-based output feedback stabilization problem for system (1) boils down to finding feedback matrices $K_1, \cdots, K_M$ and gain matrices $L_1, \cdots, L_M$ such that A_c and A_o are both Schur-stable.

Notice that the Schur-stability of A_o is equivalent to the existence of a positive definite matrix P_o satisfying

$$- P_o + A_o^T P_o A_o < 0 \qquad (40)$$

Combining (40) with (30), Theorem 3 can be extended to the case of observer-based output feedback control. Its proof is similar to that of the direct state feedback case, due to space limitation, we present the result without proof.

Theorem 4. *Suppose system (1) is controllable and observable, and hence without loss of generality, suppose there exists a switching sequence $\pi = \{i_0, i_1, \cdots, i_M\}$ such that controllability and observability can both be realized by π, then there exist a positive definite matrix S, nonsingular matrices V_m, $m = 2, \cdots, M$ and matrices $F_1, \cdots, F_M$ such that (28) is feasible, meanwhile, there exist a positive definite* *matrix P_o, nonsingular matrices $G_1, \cdots, G_{M-1}$, and matrices $X_1, \cdots, X_M$ such that the following LMI*

$$
\begin{bmatrix}
P_o & (\bullet)^T & 0 & \cdots & 0 & 0 \\
G_1 A_{i_0} - X_1 C_{i_0} & G_1 + G_1^T & (\bullet)^T & \cdots & 0 & 0 \\
\vdots & \vdots & \ddots & \ddots & & \vdots \\
0 & 0 & 0 & \cdots & G_{M-1} + G_{M-1}^T & (\bullet)^T \\
0 & 0 & 0 & \cdots & P_o A_{i_{M-1}} - X_M C_{i_{M-1}} & P_o
\end{bmatrix} > 0 \quad (41)
$$

is feasible. Furthermore, the system can be stabilized with the periodical switching signal generated by π and the observer-based output feedback controller given in (36), (37) with feedback matrices given in (29) and gain matrices given by

$$
L_m = G_m^{-1} X_m, \; m = 1, \cdots, M-1, \quad L_M = P_o^{-1} X_M. \tag{42}
$$

Remark 12. Theorem 4 shows that the design of state feedback gains is independent of that of observer gains. This means that the Separation Principle holds for switched linear systems as well.

5   Illustrative Example

In this section, we give a numerical example to illustrate the usefulness and effectiveness of our methods.

Example 1. Consider the periodical switched system (1) with $\mathcal{I} = \{1, 2, 3\}$ and

$$
A_1 = \begin{bmatrix} 0 & 0 & 0 \\ 0 & 2 & 0 \\ 0 & 0 & 2 \end{bmatrix}, \; B_1 = \begin{bmatrix} 1 \\ 1 \\ 0 \end{bmatrix}, \; C_1 = [\, 1 \;\; 0 \;\; 1 \,];
$$

$$
A_2 = \begin{bmatrix} 2 & 0 & 0 \\ 0 & 0 & 0 \\ 0 & 0 & 2 \end{bmatrix}, \; B_2 = \begin{bmatrix} 0 \\ 1 \\ 1 \end{bmatrix}, \; C_2 = [\, 1 \;\; 1 \;\; 0 \,]; \tag{43}
$$

$$
A_3 = \begin{bmatrix} 2 & 0 & 0 \\ 0 & 2 & 0 \\ 0 & 0 & 0 \end{bmatrix}, \; B_3 = \begin{bmatrix} 1 \\ 0 \\ 1 \end{bmatrix}, \; C_3 = [\, 0 \;\; 1 \;\; 1 \,];
$$

First, it is easy to verify that the system is both controllable and observable. Next, we construct a switching sequence to realize them. Since

$$
Span\{B_1, B_2, B_3\} = \mathbb{R}^3,
$$

We take $\pi_i = \{i\}$ such that $Span\{B_i\} \subset \mathcal{R}(\pi_i)$, $i = 1, 2, 3$. Let $\pi = \pi_1 \wedge \pi_2 \wedge \pi_1$, it is easy to verify that

$$
\mathcal{R}(\pi) = \mathbb{R}^3.
$$

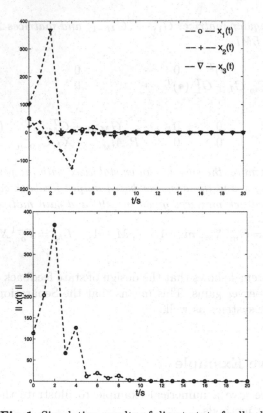

Fig. 1. Simulation results of direct state feedback

Thus, the controllability can be realized by π. Furtermore, it is easy to verify that observability can be realized by π as well.

As a result, by Theorem 2, the system should be stabilizable. In fact, by solving the LMI (28), we can take the direct state feedback control law (5), (6) with

$$K_1 = \begin{bmatrix} 0 & -0.0549 & 0 \end{bmatrix}, K_2 = \begin{bmatrix} 0 & 0 & -0.1519 \end{bmatrix}, K_3 = \begin{bmatrix} -0.1694 & 0 & 0 \end{bmatrix}$$

to stabilize the system asymptotically (see Fig. 1 for simulation results).

Furthermore, by solving the LMI (41), we can construct a full-dimension state observer (36) with

$$L_1 = \begin{bmatrix} 0 & 0 & 0.3 \end{bmatrix}^T, \ L_2 = \begin{bmatrix} 0.1765 & 0 & 0 \end{bmatrix}^T, \ L_3 = \begin{bmatrix} 0 & 0.1279 & 0 \end{bmatrix}^T$$

and take the observer-based output feedback control law (37) with

$$K_1 = \begin{bmatrix} 0 & -0.0549 & 0 \end{bmatrix}, K_2 = \begin{bmatrix} 0 & 0 & -0.1519 \end{bmatrix}, K_3 = \begin{bmatrix} -0.1694 & 0 & 0 \end{bmatrix}$$

to stabilize the system asymptotically (see Fig. 2 for simulation results).

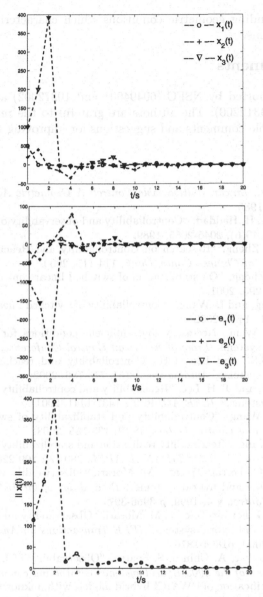

Fig. 2. Simulation results of observer-based state feedback

6   Conclusions

Based upon our previously established geometric properties of controllability realization, we prove that controllability implies stabilizability for switched linear systems. The result is a natural extension of the corresponding feedback stabilization theorem for linear systems in modern control theory. The future work includes finding algorithm to acquire optimal switching sequence to realize controllability and finding geometric conditions which characterize stabilizability for switched systems.

Acknowledgements

This work is supported by NSFC (60404001 and 10372002) and National 973 Program (2002CB312200). The authors are grateful to the reviewers for their helpful and valuable comments and suggestions for improving this paper.

References

1. W. M. Wonham, *Linear Multivariable Control: A Geometric Approach*, Springer-Verlag, Berlin, 1985.
2. J. Ezzine and A. H. Haddad, "Controllability and observability of hybrid systems," *Int. J. Control*, 49(6), 2045-2055, 1989.
3. G. Xie and D. Zheng, "Research on Controllability and Reachability of Hybrid Systems," *Proc. of Chinese Contr. Conf.*, 114-117, 2000.
4. Z. Sun and D. Zheng, "On stabilization of switched linear control systems," *IEEE AC*, 46(2), 291-295, 2001.
5. G. Xie, D. Zheng, and L. Wang, "Controllability of switched linear systems," *IEEE AC*, 47(8), 1401 -1405, 2002.
6. G. Xie and L. Wang, Necessary and sufficient conditions for controllability of switched linear systems, *Proc. of American Control Conference*. 1897-1902, 2002.
7. Sun, Z., Ge, S.S., and Lee, T.H., Controllability and reachability criteria for switched linear systems, *Automatica*, 38(5), 775-786, 2002.
8. S. S. Ge, Z. Sun, and T. H. Lee, "Reachability and controllability of switched linear discrete-time systems," *IEEE AC*, 46(9), 1437-1441, 2001.
9. G. Xie and L. Wang, "Controllability and stabilizability of switched linear systems," *Systems and Control Letters*, 48(2), 135-155, 2003.
10. G. Xie and L. Wang, "Reachability realization and stabilizability of switched linear discrete-time systems", *J MATH ANAL APPL*, 280 (2): 209-220, 2003.
11. A. Bemporad, G. Ferrari-Trecate, M. Morari, "Observability and controllability of piecewise affine and hybrid systems", *Proceedings of the IEEE Conference on Decision and Control*, v 4, 1999, p 3966-3971
12. A. Bemporad, G. Ferrari-Trecate, M. Morari, "Observability and controllability of piecewise affine and hybrid systems",*IEEE Transactions on Automatic Control*, v 45, n 10, Oct, 2000, p1864-1876.
13. R. vidal, S. Shankar, A. Chiuso, S. Soatto, "Observability of Linear Hybrid Systems", *Proceeding of the 2003 Hybrid systems: cotnrol and computation*, p526-539.
14. R. Vidal, "Identification of PWARX hybrid models with unknown and possibly different orders", *Proceedings of the 2004 American Control Conference*, 2004, p547-552.
15. A. Balluchi, L. Benvenuti, M. D. Di Benedetto, A. L. SangiovanniCVincentelli, "Design of Observers for Hybrid Systems", *Proceeding of the 2002 Hybrid systems: cotnrol and computation*, p76-89.
16. A. Balluchi, M. D. Di Benedetto, L. Benvenuti, A. L. Sangiovanni-Vincentelli, "Observability for Hybrid Systems", *Proceedings of the IEEE Conference on Decision and Control*, v 2, 2003, p1159-1164.
17. R. E. Skelton, T. Iwasaki and K. Grigoriadis, "A unified approach to linear control design", Taylor and Francis series in Systems and Control, 1997.

Author Index

Lecture Notes in Computer Science

For information about Vols. 1–3313

please contact your bookseller or Springer

Vol. 3360: S. Spaccapietra, E. Bertino, S. Jajodia, R. King, D. McLeod, M.E. Orlowska, L. Strous (Eds.), Journal on Data Semantics II. XI, 223 pages. 2005.

Vol. 3359: G. Grieser, Y. Tanaka (Eds.), Intuitive Human Interfaces for Organizing and Accessing Intellectual Assets. XIV, 257 pages. 2005. (Subseries LNAI).

Vol. 3358: J. Cao, L.T. Yang, M. Guo, F. Lau (Eds.), Parallel and Distributed Processing and Applications. XXIV, 1058 pages. 2004.

Vol. 3357: H. Handschuh, M.A. Hasan (Eds.), Selected Areas in Cryptography. XI, 354 pages. 2004.

Vol. 3356: G. Das, V.P. Gulati (Eds.), Intelligent Information Technology. XII, 428 pages. 2004.

Vol. 3355: R. Murray-Smith, R. Shorten (Eds.), Switching and Learning in Feedback Systems. X, 343 pages. 2005.

Vol. 3353: J. Hromkovič, M. Nagl, B. Westfechtel (Eds.), Graph-Theoretic Concepts in Computer Science. XI, 404 pages. 2004.

Vol. 3352: C. Blundo, S. Cimato (Eds.), Security in Communication Networks. XI, 381 pages. 2005.

Vol. 3351: G. Persiano, R. Solis-Oba (Eds.), Approximation and Online Algorithms. VIII, 295 pages. 2005.

Vol. 3350: M. Hermenegildo, D. Cabeza (Eds.), Practical Aspects of Declarative Languages. VIII, 269 pages. 2005.

Vol. 3349: B.M. Chapman (Ed.), Shared Memory Parallel Programming with Open MP. X, 149 pages. 2005.

Vol. 3348: A. Canteaut, K. Viswanathan (Eds.), Progress in Cryptology - INDOCRYPT 2004. XIV, 431 pages. 2004.

Vol. 3347: R.K. Ghosh, H. Mohanty (Eds.), Distributed Computing and Internet Technology. XX, 472 pages. 2004.

Vol. 3346: R.H. Bordini, M. Dastani, J. Dix, A.E.F. Seghrouchni (Eds.), Programming Multi-Agent Systems. XIV, 249 pages. 2005. (Subseries LNAI).

Vol. 3345: Y. Cai (Ed.), Ambient Intelligence for Scientific Discovery. XII, 311 pages. 2005. (Subseries LNAI).

Vol. 3344: J. Malenfant, B.M. Østvold (Eds.), Object-Oriented Technology. ECOOP 2004 Workshop Reader. VIII, 215 pages. 2005.

Vol. 3343: C. Freksa, C. Knauff, B. Krieg-Brückner, B. Nebel, T. Barkowsky (Eds.), Spatial Cognition IV. Reasoning, Action, and Interaction. XIII, 519 pages. 2005. (Subseries LNAI).

Vol. 3342: E. Şahin, W.M. Spears (Eds.), Swarm Robotics. IX, 175 pages. 2005.

Vol. 3341: R. Fleischer, G. Trippen (Eds.), Algorithms and Computation. XVII, 935 pages. 2004.

Vol. 3340: C.S. Calude, E. Calude, M.J. Dinneen (Eds.), Developments in Language Theory. XI, 431 pages. 2004.

Vol. 3339: G.I. Webb, X. Yu (Eds.), AI 2004: Advances in Artificial Intelligence. XXII, 1272 pages. 2004. (Subseries LNAI).

Vol. 3338: S.Z. Li, J. Lai, T. Tan, G. Feng, Y. Wang (Eds.), Advances in Biometric Person Authentication. XVIII, 699 pages. 2004.

Vol. 3337: J.M. Barreiro, F. Martin-Sanchez, V. Maojo, F. Sanz (Eds.), Biological and Medical Data Analysis. XI, 508 pages. 2004.

Vol. 3336: D. Karagiannis, U. Reimer (Eds.), Practical Aspects of Knowledge Management. X, 523 pages. 2004. (Subseries LNAI).

Vol. 3335: M. Malek, M. Reitenspieß, J. Kaiser (Eds.), Service Availability. X, 213 pages. 2005.

Vol. 3334: Z. Chen, H. Chen, Q. Miao, Y. Fu, E. Fox, E.-p. Lim (Eds.), Digital Libraries: International Collaboration and Cross-Fertilization. XX, 690 pages. 2004.

Vol. 3333: K. Aizawa, Y. Nakamura, S. Satoh (Eds.), Advances in Multimedia Information Processing - PCM 2004, Part III. XXXV, 785 pages. 2004.

Vol. 3332: K. Aizawa, Y. Nakamura, S. Satoh (Eds.), Advances in Multimedia Information Processing - PCM 2004, Part II. XXXVI, 1051 pages. 2004.

Vol. 3331: K. Aizawa, Y. Nakamura, S. Satoh (Eds.), Advances in Multimedia Information Processing - PCM 2004, Part I. XXXVI, 667 pages. 2004.

Vol. 3330: J. Akiyama, E.T. Baskoro, M. Kano (Eds.), Combinatorial Geometry and Graph Theory. VIII, 227 pages. 2005.

Vol. 3329: P.J. Lee (Ed.), Advances in Cryptology - ASIACRYPT 2004. XVI, 546 pages. 2004.

Vol. 3328: K. Lodaya, M. Mahajan (Eds.), FSTTCS 2004: Foundations of Software Technology and Theoretical Computer Science. XVI, 532 pages. 2004.

Vol. 3327: Y. Shi, W. Xu, Z. Chen (Eds.), Data Mining and Knowledge Management. XIII, 263 pages. 2005. (Subseries LNAI).

Vol. 3326: A. Sen, N. Das, S.K. Das, B.P. Sinha (Eds.), Distributed Computing - IWDC 2004. XIX, 546 pages. 2004.

Vol. 3325: C.H. Lim, M. Yung (Eds.), Information Security Applications. XI, 472 pages. 2005.

Vol. 3323: G. Antoniou, H. Boley (Eds.), Rules and Rule Markup Languages for the Semantic Web. X, 215 pages. 2004.

Vol. 3322: R. Klette, J. Žunić (Eds.), Combinatorial Image Analysis. XII, 760 pages. 2004.

Vol. 3321: M.J. Maher (Ed.), Advances in Computer Science - ASIAN 2004. Higher-Level Decision Making. XII, 510 pages. 2004.

Vol. 3320: K.-M. Liew, H. Shen, S. See, W. Cai (Eds.), Parallel and Distributed Computing: Applications and Technologies. XXIV, 891 pages. 2004.

Vol. 3319: D. Amyot, A.W. Williams (Eds.), System Analysis and Modeling. XII, 301 pages. 2005.

Vol. 3318: E. Eskin, C. Workman (Eds.), Regulatory Genomics. VII, 115 pages. 2005. (Subseries LNBI).

Vol. 3317: M. Domaratzki, A. Okhotin, K. Salomaa, S. Yu (Eds.), Implementation and Application of Automata. XII, 336 pages. 2005.

Vol. 3316: N.R. Pal, N.K. Kasabov, R.K. Mudi, S. Pal, S.K. Parui (Eds.), Neural Information Processing. XXX, 1368 pages. 2004.

Vol. 3315: C. Lemaître, C.A. Reyes, J.A. González (Eds.), Advances in Artificial Intelligence – IBERAMIA 2004. XX, 987 pages. 2004. (Subseries LNAI).

Vol. 3314: J. Zhang, J.-H. He, Y. Fu (Eds.), Computational and Information Science. XXIV, 1259 pages. 2004.